# The Columbia History
# of the American Novel

# The Columbia History of the American Novel

Emory Elliott, *General Editor*

*Associate Editors*
Cathy N. Davidson
Patrick O'Donnell
Valerie Smith
Christopher P. Wilson

Columbia University Press
*New York*

Columbia University Press
New York    Oxford

Library of Congress Cataloging-in-Publication Data

The Columbia history of the American novel / Emory
Elliott, general editor ; associate editors, Cathy N.
Davidson . . . [et al.].
   p.    cm.
   Includes bibliographical references and index.
   ISBN 0-231-07360-7 (alk. paper)
   1. American fiction—History and criticism. I. Elliott,
Emory, 1942–    II. Davidson, Cathy N., 1949–
PS371.C7   1991
813.009—dc20                91-21598
                               CIP

∞

Casebound editions of Columbia University Press books are
Smyth-sewn and printed on permanent and durable acid-free
paper.

Printed in the United States of America

c  10  9  8  7  6  5  4  3  2  1

# Contents

Introduction     ix
     *Emory Elliott*

## Beginnings to the Mid-Nineteenth Century

Introduction     3
     *Cathy N. Davidson*

The Early American Novel     6
     *Jeffrey Rubin-Dorsky*

Autobiography and the Early Novel     26
     *Nellie McKay*

The Book Marketplace I     46
     *Michael T. Gilmore*

The Romance     72
     *Terence Martin*

Romance and Race     89
     *Joan Dayan*

Domesticity and Fiction     110
     *Lora Romero*

Fiction and Reform I                                                          130
    *Robert S. Levine*

# The Late Nineteenth Century

Introduction                                                                 157
    *Christopher P. Wilson*

Realism                                                                      160
    *Robert Shulman*

Fiction and the Science of Society                                           189
    *Susan Mizruchi*

Fiction and Reform II                                                        216
    *Phillip Brian Harper*

Nation, Region, and Empire                                                   240
    *Amy Kaplan*

Gender and Fiction                                                           267
    *Elizabeth Ammons*

Popular Forms I                                                              285
    *Christine Bold*

# The Early Twentieth Century

Introduction                                                                 309
    *Valerie Smith*

Modernist Eruptions                                                          311
    *Margot Norris*

American Proletarianism                                                      331
    *Paul Lauter*

Popular Forms II                                357
*Bill Brown*

Ethnicity and the Marketplace    380
*Thomas J. Ferraro*

Race and Region    407
*Thadious M. Davis*

Fiction of the West    437
*James H. Maguire*

Technology and the Novel    465
*Cecelia Tichi*

Society and Identity    485
*David Van Leer*

## The Late Twentieth Century

Introduction    513 ✓
*Patrick O'Donnell*

Postmodern Culture    515
*Cornel West*

Postmodern Realism    521
*José David Saldívar*

Constructing Gender    542
*Ed Cohen*

Canada in Fiction    558
*Arnold E. Davidson*

Caribbean Fiction    586 ✓
*Sandra Pouchet Paquet*

Latin American Fiction                                    607
    *Debra A. Castillo*

Colonialism, Imperialism, and Imagined Homes             649
    *Ketu H. Katrak*

The Book Marketplace II                                  679
    *John M. Unsworth*

Postmodern Fiction                                       697
    *Molly Hite*

The Avant-Garde                                          726
    *Robert Boyers*


Biographies of American Authors                          753

Selected Bibliography of Critical Works                  821

Notes on Contributors                                    847

Index                                                    853

# Introduction

"The Novel"; "The American Novel": there was a time not long ago when most literary critics and scholars were confident that they had a solid understanding of these terms and had a fair idea of what a book devoted to the "American Novel" would contain. After an introduction that would acknowledge the debt American novelists owe to European predecessors such as Cervantes, Defoe, Swift, Richardson, and Fielding (some might include Homer, Chaucer, Spenser, and Milton), the chapters would follow a chronology beginning with some late eighteenth-century fictions by fledgling American imitators of the English prose giants.

In a chapter entitled "At the Beginning," Alexander Cowie opened his *The Rise of the American Novel* (1951) in this way: "For the dearth of good American literature during the first 150 or 200 years of the white history of the country, apology is needed less than explanation. A new nation, like a new-born baby, requires time before its special characteristics become discernible." Without even bothering to define the "novel" since he assumed everyone knew what that meant, Cowie quotes Julian Hawthorne's definition of "an American novel": "a novel treating of persons, places, and ideas from an American point of view." Presumably everyone then knew what "American" meant as well.

In our own time, scholars, critics, and teachers of the literature of the United States have come to recognize that narrative — storytelling — which forms an essential element of the "novel," began in every corner of the world at a very early point in the development of civilizations. On every continent, including the two to be named "the Americas," stories that began as oral narratives in families and tribes became folk tales, songs, chants, and eventually complex national and regional oral epics. Before the invention of alphabets, stories about the adventures of hunting and war were inscribed as drawings on walls and inside caves and may still be viewed today in the Southwestern United States, Central China, and elsewhere. As a reminder of this long literary history, the contemporary Native American novelist N. Scott Momaday includes in his novella *The Way to Rainy Mountain* (1969) a sketch of a hunter in action drawn by his father.

With the coming of writing, the problem of defining the genres of narratives became even more complex. Are the sacred scriptures of ancient people, such as the Bible and the Koran, histories exactly? Did human imagination play a role in their creations? If so, are they to some degree or in part fictional narratives? By the time Cervantes composed *Don Quixote,* often considered to be the first true novel, people had been writing fictional or semifictional stories with plots, characters, settings, suspense, humor, irony, narrative twists, and surprise endings for centuries. The point at which we can say "there is the first novel in English" is no longer a simple matter.

Defining the novel as a genre even in the eighteenth or nineteenth centuries is difficult because, from the first, experimentation and innovation prevailed: the epistolary form of Richardson, the journal narrative of Defoe, the fantastical tales of Swift, the picaresques of Fielding, the tales of seduction of Susanna Rowson, the domestic intrigues of Austen, the gothics of Mary Shelley and the Brontës. Then, what are we to make of texts of the twentieth century called novels by their authors but that often consist of many elements of writing that would have baffled earlier novel readers, such as fragments of poems, mixed with letters, song lyrics, and pieces of prose narrative that do not appear to connect in any sequential or logical way with other prose in the text? Is a work a novel if the author intentionally refuses to provide a plot or an ending? Who decides these things? The authors, critics, readers, the National Book Awards Committee, English professors?

Certainly, when writers themselves attempt to "advance the form," in John Barth's words, of the novel through experimentation, they have a good idea of what the form of the novel is that they have inherited; it must be for them, at least, a known entity in order for them to change it. But change has always been inherent to the novel, and the literary record is littered with critics who have roasted certain novelists for breaking the rules only to be burned themselves with the discovery that a literary genius was revising the conventions.

For the sake of this literary history, we might define the novel as a text usually of substantial length that is normally written in prose and presents a narrative of events involving experiences of characters who are representative of human agents. It may present events in a fairly linear manner as though cause leads to effect, or it may interrupt time sequences, demanding of readers careful attention to fragmented episodes. The events of the narrative may lead to a conclusion or may be left suspended in seeming inconclusiveness. Most novels depict situations that represent human experiences that readers find believable, but some others may present absurd, tangled situations that bear little apparent resemblance to recognizable human experiences. While some novels allow readers to focus upon action and characters, others require the reader's close attention to nuances of language in order to formulate an interpretation. This definition probably does not account for every text now accepted as a novel—and will account for fewer with the appearance of every new experimental work—but it is broad enough to include most texts called "novels" at the moment.

Some would demand that we not only try to define the novel but that we also provide criteria for distinguishing "good" or even "great" novels from "poor" ones. Which are works of art and which are artistic failures or make no pretense at art? Not long ago, the editor of a book like ours would proclaim that we might recognize a great novel by comparing it to the late works of Henry James or those of Faulkner's great phase in the 1930s or *Moby-Dick*. The criteria for the greatness would have been the intricate but orderly structure, the details of characterization, the profundity of themes, the complexity of the imagery, symbolism, and allusions, and perhaps the power of the setting to evoke particular places, eras, or subtleties of human speech. The persistence of such prescriptive judgments accounts for why great innovators such as Melville or Hurston were initially misjudged.

In casting other novels into the dustbin of "poor" or "trash" novels, critics could simply point to their lack of these refinements and/or their blatant use of sentimentality or gothic horror or to their representations of human situations and conditions of life deemed unfitting for the dominant reading public. Such outcasts were rejected under several labels, such as "popular fiction," "dime novels," "pulp fiction," "agitprop," "muckraking," "women's stories," and "sentimental romances." In short, they were condemned for being "not serious" and "too simple." Most critics felt that men wrote the best fiction because they had the richest experiences to draw upon and because they possessed the complexity of mind to create challenging works of philosophical and psychological complexity. Regretfully, too, many works written by members of racial and ethnic minority groups, especially about experiences within those groups, were slighted and ignored because the subject matter was viewed as marginal and/or the literary techniques, often incorporating elements from non-Anglo cultural traditions, were misunderstood.

Without diminishing any of the acclaim deserved by such writers as Melville, James, Twain, Faulkner, and Wharton for their many extraordinary works, contemporary critics are finding that many works previously rejected under the labels listed above need rereading and reevaluation upon their own terms. To cite one example, Kate Chopin's *The Awakening* (1899) nearly slipped out of literary history in the twentieth century because it was condemned as immoral in its day and damned with faint praise some years later as a competent work of local color and women's fiction. Rediscovery and reevaluation have put this highly structured, imagistic study of psychic torment and sexual passion on the reading lists of hundreds of college courses and have generated many serious studies of Chopin's work.

The process of research and rediscovery is continuing, thus enabling those books that were previously undervalued because they were misread and judged by unsuitable standards or were rejected because of blind prejudice to take their rightful place in our literary history. If literary historians might seem to some to be leaning rather far in the direction of tolerance and inclusion, it is because for much of this century the extreme opposite conditions prevailed, and much of the rich literary heritage of the nation was excluded from public appreciation by the decisions of a few.

The subject of history is change, and literary histories are part of history. Thus, it stands to reason that literary histories both examine change and change themselves with the passing of time. Every literary genre is dynamic, and literary history is no exception. A literary history of the novel in America published in 1991 will be and should be markedly different in many ways from such a work published ten or twenty years earlier. Indeed, this present work differs in many aspects of its approaches from the 1988 *Columbia Literary History of the United States* for which I was General Editor. Planning for that volume began in 1982, and the nine intervening years have brought substantial developments in the theories and methods of criticism and literary history. In fact, the nature and purpose of literary history and the literary canon it surveys have been subjects of much scholarly debate.

For example, consider the titles of the two histories. Because the scope of the *Columbia Literary History of the United States* was so broad, the literature examined was limited to that which had been produced in the part of the world that has become the United States. Since the United States does not constitute all of "America"—in spite of the common usage of the terms as synonymous—we did not use the term "American" in the title. With the present work focusing upon only one genre, there was room to broaden the geographic scope and include chapters on Canadian, Caribbean, and Latin American fiction.

The desire to make the space for these chapters, however, has come from the growing internationalization of literature and the study of it during the past decade. Scholars throughout the world have come to appreciate more fully the extent to which the literature of our various American nations are intertwined. The texts of South America and North America are in dialogue with each other. Novelists of Africa and the Caribbean have a profound effect upon writers in the United States and are affected by them in return. The rapid maturation of the fairly new field of comparative literary study and increasing scholarly interactions and exchanges among those who study these various literatures have deepened our understandings of these cultural connections and made it compelling to the editors of this book to be more internationally inclusive. As evidence of how writing done all over the world has become part of our own culture, a chapter on "Colonialism, Imperialism, and Imagined Homes" rightly includes discussion of some figures who were neither born in nor lived in the Americas but whose works and experiences as novelists and public figures are a vital part of our larger literary culture.

Several other dimensions of this book spring from current critical attitudes. There are no chapters that are restricted to the fiction of women writers or of a particular racial or ethnic minority group. The works of women writers and of African American, Asian American, Chicano/a, and Jewish writers are taken up within chapters that address larger themes that are not limited by such categories. In 1982, the editors of the *Columbia Literary History of the United States* concluded, after extensive consultation with colleagues sensitive to the issues, that it was necessary to have specialists on women writers and on particular minority literatures write essays on those literatures because the large numbers of newly recognized writers of those groups were still not known to most critics who were nonspecialists. We wanted to be certain that the first collaborative literary history of the United States in forty years made the names and works of writers previously excluded from the canon better known so that other scholars and students could study their works. In this literary history we decided not to "ghettoize" the novels of minority writers in order to underscore the impact of minority cultures upon American culture as a whole and to problematize the boundary between "major" and "minor" literatures.

Another way in which this book differs from its Columbia University Press predecessor is that it was not driven by a desire to be comprehensive or to have chapters on single authors that would signal our assertions of who is "major" and who is "minor." There is clearly a chronological progression in the book with four historically organized sections introduced by a specialist in each period, but we did not make an attempt to "cover" every novelist in every decade nor did we assign a certain number of pages to be given to each author according to our sense of an author's relative importance in the canon. We asked each contributor to write an informative chapter about the topic we assigned. We welcomed them to focus closely upon authors whose work most engaged them as critics and to demonstrate for our readers how historical information and critical contexts of the various periods can inform readings of the fictional texts. Some critics chose to be quite inclusive and to provide brief treatments of many authors, while others use a few representative texts to examine complex literary phenomena more deeply, such as the conventions of late nineteenth-century realism. The number of times an author's name appears in the index or the number of pages of the entire volume given to an author's work is not an indication of an editorial decision to pay special attention to particular writers over others but instead to reflect the degree to which a highly diverse group of critics turned to particular works as examples of the development of the novel as a genre and as a reflection of changes in American society.

Because we have chosen a thematic rather than a biographical approach, the reader will not find a consistent presentation of what was once called the "shape of the artist's career" unless one of our contributors happened to find a particular career illustrative of some larger cultural issues. To take the pressure of biography off our contributors and to provide the reader with a convenient summary of the lives and careers of the authors, we have provided an appendix of author biographies where such information is provided for a great many of the authors discussed in the text. For similar reasons, the chapters do not present references to other critical works about the literature through footnotes or parenthetical intrusions. However, those critics who are mentioned in the chapters can be found, along with many others, in the selected bibliography.

The major aim of this "literary history" — a term that has as many definitions these days as there are definers — is to provide readers with lively and engaging discussions of the development of the novel in the Americas. Our emphasis, however, is upon the ways that current critical perspectives provide fresh insights into the texts and into the history of which the novels were and remain a part. For example, after an opening chapter that presents an overview of the emergence of the novel as an art form in the late eighteenth and the early nineteenth century, there is a chapter that examines how the emergence of autobiography in early America, especially those written by slaves and by women, can be seen in relation to the narrative techniques of the novel. There are autobiographical fictions and fictional autobiographies, and this chapter examines the points of contact and divergence between these genres. Our next chapter surveys the book marketplace of the early nineteenth century and the impact of publishers and readers upon the development of the novel. Then, following a general chapter on the Romance form of the novel that explores the works of Hawthorne and Melville, there is a chapter entitled "Romance and Race" that uses the example of Poe in particular to show how mythmaking in the Romance is subtly connected to the public rhetoric that attempted to present slavery as a benevolent institution.

Such a variation of approaches—standard survey treatments interwoven with probing studies of special subthemes—is designed to allow readers to see the multifaceted nature of the novel as a form and the highly complex circumstances that enable, impede, inspire, and restrict the artistic powers of novelists.

In order to alert readers to some of the thematic issues examined across the centuries, we have used roman numerals, as with "Fiction and Reform I" and "II," "Popular Forms I" and "II," and "The Book Marketplace I" and "II." The titles of other chapters indicate subjects for which there is continuity of treatment, such as in the case of race, region, and gender. In much literary theory and criticism of the 1980s, there has been more attention to and more sophisticated discussion of the work of lesbian and gay authors, and our chapters on "Society and Identity" and "Constructing Gender" especially reflect these recent trends.

Yet for all of our innovations in method and in the examination of new areas of fiction, this volume still tells an old story. That story is one that now begins with ancient oral narratives in the Middle East, in Africa, in Central Eurasia, in the Mediterranean, in Central China, in the forests and deserts of South America, and on the plains, along the rivers, and in the hills and mountains of North America. Some of these stories became powerful myths that became the cornerstones of great religions, that helped shape the destinies of peoples and civilizations, and that survived centuries to be echoed in poems and novels of today.

Once people of imagination began to write stories in that part of

North America that became the United States, they drew upon all of these heritages. African slaves told their ancestors' tales and heard those that descended through the families of Welsh, Scottish, Irish, and English settlers. French traders and Spanish explorers swapped stories with Native Americans who may have even memorized some from the Norse explorers centuries before. By the time the first "American novel" was written, a long and complicated cultural history provided a rich resource for the imagination of the novelist.

Thus, it was only a matter of a few decades before novels began pouring off the American presses, and American writers from Irving and Cooper to Stowe, Alcott, Child, Hawthorne, and Melville were achieving success and receiving acclaim. By the latter decades of the nineteenth century, Henry James could challenge Balzac for the honor of being major novelist in the Western hemisphere, while James's contemporaries and those soon following after, such as Twain, Howells, Wharton, Crane, Dreiser, Norris, Chopin, Chesnutt, and Cather, were producing works of international recognition.

With the emergence of Anderson, Hemingway, Fitzgerald, and Stein in the 1920s, the world acknowledged that most of the consequential novelists and writers of the time were from the United States, even if many of them chose to live abroad. Others who wrote in that period would wait decades to attain proper recognition; among them were Hurston, Toomer, and Hughes. When the achievement of Faulkner came to be understood in the late 1940s and 1950s, the world again hailed the United States for having literary genius in its midst.

And so, too, since the mid-century, renowned artists of the novel have appeared: Wright, O'Connor, Ellison, Bellow, Mailer, Baldwin, Malamud, Roth, Barth, Pynchon, Updike, Morrison, Kingston, Oates, and DeLillo, to name just a few. This list of American accomplishments in the novel does not begin to survey the remarkable artists of Canadian, Caribbean, and Latin American literature presented in the latter chapters of this history.

The inevitable limitation of any literary history is that there is never enough space for the inclusion of everyone or for the fullest treatment of those who are included. We regret that we could not provide chapters on every dimension of the novel or more analysis of those we have included. We believe that what we do present will give our readers fresh, contemporary perspectives on the literary history of the "American Novel."

I would like to thank the associate editors and the contributors for the fine work they did for this volume. All of us involved in this book appreciate the important contributions of the excellent people at Columbia University Press. Once again, the President and Director of the Press, John D. Moore, provided the leadership and wisdom that enabled us to see it to completion. The Editorial Director of the Reference Division of the Press, James Raimes, initiated the idea for this book and oversaw the day-to-day progress of the work, and we benefited greatly from his insights, experience, patience, and understanding. James's fine assistant Frances Kim cheerfully and intelligently handled the myriad of details that crossed her desk. As always, William F. Bernhardt expertly edited the manuscripts with intelligence and tact. From the English Department of the University of California at Riverside, Stephanie Erickson and Deborah Hatheway composed the entries for the appendix of biographies of authors, and Deborah and Carlton Smith provided editorial assistance and suggestions for a number of the chapters. I am also grateful to the Faculty Senate of the University of California, Riverside, for general support and to my colleagues and the staff members of the English Department whose good will—and patience while waiting to use the copier—I genuinely appreciate. As always, my wife and university colleague, Georgia, contributed sound suggestions and warm encouragement, and my daughters Constance and Laura were indulgent of my frequent preoccupation.

Emory Elliott

# Beginnings to the
# Mid-Nineteenth Century

# Introduction

Critics, preachers, and other self-appointed moralists hated it; young men and women loved it. The novel was the subject of heated popular debate in the late eighteenth century and, in many ways, was to the early national period what television was to the 1950s or MTV and video games to the 1980s. It was condemned as escapist, anti-intellectual, violent, pornographic; since it was a "fiction" it was a lie and therefore evil. Since it often portrayed characters of low social station and even lower morals—foreigners, orphans, fallen women, beggar girls, women cross-dressing as soldiers, soldiers acting as seducers—it fomented social unrest by making the lower classes dissatisfied with their lot. The novel ostensibly contributed to the demise of community values, the rise in licentiousness and illegitimacy, the failure of education, the disintegration of the family; in short, the ubiquity of the novel—augmented in the early nineteenth century by new printing, papermaking, and transportation technologies—most assuredly meant the decline of Western civilization as it had previously been known.

Predictably, running side by side with the sermons and newspaper editorials condemning the genre was a countering polemic in its favor. Other social commentators on the early novel claimed it was educational, nationalistic, populist, precisely what was required to bring together a nation recently fragmented by a Revolutionary War and further divided by the influx of immigrants in the post-Revolutionary period, European immigrants who did not speak the same language, practice the same religion, or share the same values as those earlier arrived on these native shores. By its linguistic simplicity, the novel was uniquely accessible to working-class readers and would introduce them to middle-class (and, presumably, WASP) values and manners. By its typical focus on women characters and its frequent addresses to women readers, it would help to erase the gender inequities built into the early American educational system. By its preoccupation with seduction as a theme, it would warn women that they had to be smart to survive. And even the early genre's suspect attachment to local scandal as a major source for its materials served a worthy end, for it warned men that their infamies could be broadcast to the community at large and that they could thus be held accountable for private sin in the court of public opinion.

What was the *real* function of the novel in early America? Again one might make the analogy to modern cultural forms such as television: the verdict is still out. But what is obvious is that, in a market sense, the new form triumphed decisively over its detractors. On the most basic, mercantile level, this is evident from late eighteenth-century publishers' catalogs and book advertisements. Prior to around 1790, books that we would now call novels (for example, Henry Fielding's *Joseph Andrews*) were frequently hawked as "narratives," or "personal histories," or simply left unlabeled. After around 1790, virtually any text that could conceivably be connected to the term "novel" (as noun or adjective) wore that designation, and autobiographical and biographical accounts, crime reports, conversion stories, captivity narratives, religious tracts, collections of sermons, even poetic sequences were all peddled as novels. As an established and valued commodity, novels sold.

The early contentious history of the novel in America anticipated in subtle and profound ways the debates, anxieties, and controversies about the genre during the nineteenth century, issues taken up in the chapters in the first section of this volume. Where, for example, is the boundary between the autobiography and the novel? The blurring of one into the other has a long history. That blurring also raises crucial theoretical and even political issues. As-told-to narratives, for example, contest the interrelated notions of "authenticity," "authority," and "authorship." An autobiography must be shaped and controlled and plotted in ways that resemble fiction, but the very concept of fictionality jeopardizes an authoritative "I." Which has more status, novel or autobiography? Which has more cultural power? Questions of genre—especially when we address slave or Native American narratives—turn (as did discussions of the early novel) on questions of social truth and social power.

Authority and authorship also turn on questions of economic power. By the mid-nineteenth century, the "novel" did not exist as any single entity. Popularity produces diversity, and soon there were many kinds of novels designed for a vaguely differentiated and overlapping audience—sensation novels, pulp romances, adventure stories, newspaper serials, reform novels. Some writers, such as Nathaniel Hawthorne, even wanted to distinguish their "romances" from the more prevalent but still partly suspect varieties of the novel.

Hawthorne's trepidation lest he be called a "novelist" seems rooted in virtually all of the early American anxieties about the morality, factitiousness, accountability, moral purpose, and political function of the novel in society, anxieties arising (like Hawthorne's own) from a Puritan preoccupation with the practical social value of products of the imagination. Even Hawthorne's well-known uneasiness about fiction and gender, articulated throughout his life and his fiction in a variety of ways, seems to be a vestigial manifestation of the very first anxieties about the novel in America. The first two American best-sellers, *Charlotte Temple* and *The Coquette,* were both penned, after all, by "scribbling women."

Did the novel forever alter America? Can a literary work really reform/re-form society? Can any cultural form effect social change? Or do cultural forms reflect those changes in progress? Agency, at one theoretical level or another, remains an issue in all discussions of the novel to date, just as it was in the first debates on the morality of fiction. So what else is new? Our fears and our hopes about the social potentialities of any new cultural phenomenon continue to inspire much the same debate (with the attendant tropes of apocalypse or redemption) that surrounded the emergence of the novel in late eighteenth- and nineteenth-century America.

Cathy N. Davidson

# The Early American Novel

The hallmark of the early American novel is its instability, an uncertainty and confusion in almost every area related to fiction making; in order to highlight the most significant result of this instability, I would like to pretend at the outset of this chapter that I am a critic wedded to contemporary critical fashion. With this guise in place, I begin by declaring that, in fact, there is no such thing as the "early American novel." To prove my point, I carefully examine each term in the phrase to show that its intended meaning necessarily evaporates under critical scrutiny. First, take the word "early," which in this context is supposed to signify an event or events (the production of novels) occurring in the first part of some division of time, or of some series. In what sense, then, are the works that I intend to discuss—books by William Hill Brown, Hannah Foster, Susanna Rowson, Hugh Henry Brackenridge, Charles Brockden Brown, and James Fenimore Cooper—early products of American history or culture?

By consensus the first "American novel" is William Hill Brown's *The Power of Sympathy*, which appeared initially in 1789. But the land mass known as America had been called by that name since 1507, when the German geographer Martin Waldseemüller named it after its founder, Amerigo Vespucci; in that regard, "America"—its history and surely its culture—had existed for 282 years before Brown published his novel. If we follow the editors of one older anthology of American writing (1978), who declare that by American literature they mean "literature written in English by people who came to settle in the territory that eventually became the United States of America," then American writing begins in 1630 with William Bradford's history, *Of Plimmouth Plantation;* Brown's book, still 159 years away, is hardly an early American production. (Newer anthologies, if they begin with voyages of discovery, assign dates like 1492 to the first American writings; if they commence with Native American "myths," the dates are earlier still, though mostly unknown.) Perhaps by "early" we intend something like the "beginning" of the American novel, but you do not have to read very far in Brown's book to realize that, as a "novelist," he is totally dependent on Samuel Richardson, and in particular Richardson's *Pamela* (1741–42), where the story, as is Brown's, is told through a series of letters; moreover, Brown's plot centers on the theme of seduction, another Richardsonian gift to the world of fiction. One might plausibly argue that the American novel truly begins with Richardson; without him there would be no Brown. *Pamela*, in fact, was the first English novel printed in America, in 1844. (Another English antecedent would be Laurence Sterne, whose *A Sentimental Journey* is actually mentioned in *The Power of Sympathy*.) Finally, suppose that "early" means, from our perspective, belonging to a period far back in time. This makes the most sense, relatively speaking, if you consider 200 years ago "far back in time"—though our country is still proclaiming its newness, still championing its innocence, still denying that it is drenched in time.

"American" is far more problematic. The word is absolutely meaningless as a descriptive term if all it indicates is that a book—Brown's, Rowson's, Cooper's, anyone's—was published in the United States. In the days before international copyright, the works of many English writers were pirated, printed, and sold by American booksellers under their own imprints; they were, in effect, published in America, and most Americans first read the great eighteenth-century novelists in these editions. Moreover, some nineteenth-century American writers—Washington Irving and Herman Melville are good examples—in order to secure both English and American copyrights, published several of their books in England before they appeared in America. Does the writer have to be born in America? Have written his or her novel in America? Susanna Rowson was born in England, and *Charlotte Temple,* her most interesting novel, was written while

she was living in England. Yet literary historians have always proclaimed it an "American" novel. Anthony Trollope's *North America,*
and some of Frances Trollope's novels, were written wholly while
mother and son (independently) were traveling in America. Are they
American books? Must America then be the setting of the novel for
it to be American? William Hill Brown's book *is* set in America—the
America of the early Republic (New York, Rhode Island, and Boston), but then so is Aphra Behn's *Oroonoko* if, as William Spengemann has argued, you consider that when she wrote it in 1688 Suri-
nam was considered part of America. In *Martin Chuzzlewit,* Charles
Dickens has his title character travel to America and spend about a
fourth of the book there; is the novel then one-fourth American?
Perhaps more to the point: only about one-seventh of *Moby-Dick*
takes place on American soil; is Melville's masterpiece not an American novel?

Scholars have spent an inordinate amount of time arguing that
"American" really refers to "Americanness": national characteristics
shape and mirror the form of a literary work. Some idea of America
animates the narrative, controls and orders the very pattern of words
upon the page. A variant on this idea of "Americanness" would be
that recognizable issues, concerns, preoccupations appear again and
again in books that are supposedly representative of American experience. Thus, Cooper, Hawthorne, Melville, and Twain are the
most American of nineteenth-century novelists, and Whitman is our
true American poet, since something like an American identity can be
discerned from reading their works. Ultimately, Spengemann has
said, "America must make a difference in the way literature is written."

I have in the past believed this to be so (the force of Spengemann's
arguments to the contrary notwithstanding), and to some extent still
do, though I am deeply troubled by the implications of extracting
some notion of identity, some sense of representativeness, from a
canonized literature written almost exclusively by white men. The
newest anthologies of our national literature have attempted to correct for this imbalance, and we now have access to the voices and
visions of so many previously excluded "others." Perhaps, generally
speaking, our literature will finally deserve to be called American, but
can we say the same in particular for the novel, especially the so-

called early novel, where the practitioners are exclusively white, though some indeed are female?

To be sure, the America in the term "the American novel" is a place, with hard outlines and a traceable landscape, but it is also, as it has been from the outset, an idea—often an ideal—imagined first in the minds of enlightened European thinkers, reimagined, and then shaped and configured, in the consciousness of Thomas Jefferson and the other founders of the Republic. *That* America may indeed never have existed in fact, but it always exists in mythic memory, and it is first and foremost a vision of inclusiveness: it deplores restriction and derogation. Can it not be said that to the extent that the nation embodies this vision it is that much closer to becoming America? How, then, can the "early American novel" possibly be American when it lacks any kind of minority and ethnic representation? Without there being a free assemblage of different peoples and an open forum for their genuinely differing points of view, there is no America; without a confluence of voices, expressing a myriad range of experience, there is no American novel. The *American* novel is, in the best sense of the term, multicultural; it may only recently have come into being.

This brings us to the third of our slippery terms: the literary designation "novel." If a novel is, in the simplest possible definition, a "sustained fictional narrative in prose," as the modern editor of *The Power of Sympathy* contends, then it appears as if Brown's, as well as every other book to be discussed here, qualifies as a novel. In fact, almost any form of fiction does, for what does "sustained" mean but that a plan or design has been executed or upheld? Even some autobiographies might fit under this rubric, which is how some contemporary critics view them anyway. A more problematic term, however, is "fiction," which had low status in eighteenth-century America and was often shunned by those who wrote it. Often, too, readers believed they were devouring "true" stories, that is, narratives based on fact—incidents that were historically verifiable (which is the case not only with Brown's *Sympathy* but also with Foster's *Coquette* and Rowson's *Charlotte*). Cathy N. Davidson points out that Rowson promised her readers "A Tale of Truth," and that is exactly how her story was read and appreciated. Some writers, like Washington Irving, went to elaborate steps to deny the fictionality of their work; his assuming the mask of Diedrich Knickerbocker is only one of the ways by which he tried to convince the public he was offering it either history or "true" story.

If today's readers were asked to decide what element of a novel most mattered to them, they would probably emphasize either character or plot development. In other words, for most consumers of fiction, the novel signifies "realism," and this is indeed the distinction M. H. Abrams draws between the novel proper and the "romance": "The novel," Abrams writes, "is characterized as the fictional attempt to give the effect of *realism,* by representing complex characters with mixed motives who are rooted in a social class, operate in a highly developed social structure, interact with many other characters, and undergo plausible and everyday modes of experience." The niceties of generic distinction are not the point; rather, the works usually labeled as early American novels do not look anything like the conception most people have of the novel. Their characters are abstractions, hardly ever realized in any complex psychological way; their plots are mechanical, often clumsy and ill contrived; their "modes of experience" are anything but "everyday." In the modern sense of the term, the one we live with experientially, none of these books are novels at all but perhaps more like sermons or fables.

I must add a note here about what I personally look for in American novels, that is, what makes novel reading a vital experience for me. In each new book I am interested in discovering what I call "cultural voice," the process or the means by which an author with a social conscience and a rich and liberating language, though usually speaking through a persona, presents us with a unified moral vision of American society. "Voice" in this sense is the sound that results when fear is overcome so that truth can be asserted. It is the refusal to internalize, and thus be tamed by, the forces and agents of cultural repression. It is the cry of unsuppressed rage, the explosion of unchecked anxiety, the release of unmitigated anger, the expression of (as much as possible) unmediated passion or desire. A genuine voice can never be truly imitated, duplicated, or reproduced.

The primary function of the "cultural voice" I am describing is to demythologize, to unravel the web of false pieties that would masquerade as virtue, thus exposing sham, duplicity, and pretension cloaked under the guise of authenticity, honesty, and integrity. Directed at those who have assumed positions of authority, power, and privilege, it often reveals claims of superior citizenship to be little more than hypocrisy, a cover for selfish, rapacious deeds. (A prototypical example of my ideal American novel would be E. L. Doctorow's *The Book of Daniel* [1971].) This quality of voice is fundamentally moral: in the novels that really matter, those fictions that change the way readers see or experience their world, expressive language and visionary commitment are aligned so that characters reach moral awareness *through* acts of speech; that is, the utterance of personal truths, values, and beliefs culminates in the long and often painful process of discovery. The "voice" with which a character or a narrator speaks, the language he or she chooses for that expression, are themselves agents of revelation of inner being and moral selfhood.

There are no cultural voices in the "early American novel," and there are four primary reasons for this absence. First, no authentic American language was available for literary purposes. The writers who constitute the canon here, from Foster and Rowson through Irving and Cooper, were thoroughly dependent on the modes, styles, rhythms, and structures of the English language that they found in the books of their favorite seventeenth- and eighteenth-century authors. While America may have proclaimed its political independence from Britain, it nevertheless remained culturally subservient well into the nineteenth century. One reason Irving was hailed as America's first significant author by the British literary establishment, for example, was that his elegant prose sounded as if it had been written by an Englishman. Twenty-five years ago, in *The Colloquial Style in America*, Richard Bridgman showed that not until the nineteenth century did American prose first incorporate a colloquial or spoken speech into its style; American writers, as Bridgman put it, began to "evolve a new means of expression out of the casual discourse of the nation," which included, among other things, an emphasis on "greater concreteness of diction" and "simplicity in syntax." The importance of this development must be underscored: if language creates consciousness, then "means of expression" creates literary forms of resistance; without an originality in either area there could be no genuine American voices.

Second, while the formality, propriety, and correctness of the written English language constrained early American authors, what may have been equally limiting was the lack of cultural support of their creative efforts. America was simply too new and too raw a society to be overly concerned about the development of arts and letters; labor and resources were better expended on building towns and cities, roads and transportation systems, than on constructing an authentic American literature. Why should any healthy, able-bodied American citizen devote time and energy to products of the imagination, which were, after all, only of secondary or tertiary importance? Furthermore, when there was leisure available for literary pursuits, the lack of an international copyright made cheap reprints of British authors readily available. Why pay more for a book written by an American, which in any case was likely to be inferior? No aspiring American author could therefore afford to write full time— there was no profession of authorship in America as there was in England; the American Dr. Johnson did not exist—and without concentrated attention a bold indigenous literature was unlikely to appear. It is worth remembering that when Washington Irving became the nation's first successful professional author, he did so by going to England and winning recognition among the mother country's literati; having been approved abroad he could be sanctioned at home, which meant not only recognition but also, and perhaps even more important, dollars. But it did *not* mean the beginning of an *American* writer.

Third, where American culture did exist it tended to be parochial, thus generally distrustful of any form of written expression that was not expressly didactic. Literature, above all, was supposed to be edifying; its purpose was clearly that of moral improvement. Richardson's significant American following was a good illustration of this belief; as a Christian moralist (though Henry Fielding may have thought otherwise) he satisfied the public's overt need to see virtue rewarded, vice punished, and, whenever possible, raffishness reformed. But the novelist who sought to move beyond these boundaries, to, say, entertain through a tale of terror or adventure (seduction was too charged a subject to be considered entertaining), became highly suspect; such a book, being neither moral, educational, nor "truthful" (then as now, the vaguest of terms), served no socially redeeming purpose, and was condemned by clerical and secular leaders alike. Although the church may have been slowly losing its hegemonic sway in American society, it still held enough authority to have its point of view taken seriously, and time and again the clergy (including such a luminary as Jonathan Edwards) warned that novel reading was an indulgence likely to lead to moral and spiritual decline. In the public sphere, prominent leaders (numbering among them figures no less revered than John Adams and Thomas Jefferson) decried the loss of a civic-minded feeling among the populace, a development they blamed in part on the withdrawal into a private and personal realm of being, emblematized perfectly by the isolated and self-absorbing experience of reading fiction. Such criticism encouraged neither experimentation nor forthrightness among American writers.

Attitudes eventually changed, of course, though the censure of the novel did not fully abate until well into the nineteenth century; what is truly noteworthy, however, was the continued, and in fact widespread, reading of novels in the eighteenth century, in spite of—and here one almost wants to say in opposition to—the criticism emanating from "high" places. By the turn of the century libraries were stocking, in addition to the standard sermons and funeral orations, novels and romances, travel narratives and adventure stories. And these were being consumed, as observers of the social scene noted, not only among middle-class families in seaport towns and cities along the East Coast but also by farmers and other dwellers in what was then the heartland of the country. It is difficult to know exactly what to make of this shift in reading habits, though as a form of popular resistance to the tedious sermonizing against fiction it may very well be part of a more general questioning of authority that occurred in the decades following the Revolution.

Fourth, if you have an unsettled society, there is no stable "American" genre of the novel—or, for that matter, anything else. The challenge to an established hierarchy of political leadership (composed, in the eighteenth century, of men who had wealth, talent, and social status), which is supported by such historical evidence as the worry over increased factionalism (addressed so cogently in *The Federalist*), the fear that the rise of the popular press would lead to a decline in religious and civil authority, and the passing of repressive laws like the Alien and Sedition Acts (1798)—all these point toward the unsettled nature of society in the years during which the novel was (supposedly) rising in America. In a society that was still being formed, and at a time when debates about the nature and shape of the government, and about such vital issues as the inclusivity or exclusivity of the voting populace, were taking place, the novel might very well have played a significant role in redirecting or restructuring power relations. Indeed, Cathy N. Davidson and others have argued that some novels tried to assume an ideological position—as, in Davidson's phrase from *Revolution and the Word* (1986), a "covert or even overt critique of the existing social order"—and that the more popular the genre became the more those vested with cultural authority worried over their loss of dominance. This was true because, unlike sermons, the novel required no intermediaries for interpretation or guidance; addressed to all readers, it presumed no special erudition on their part. In effect, it eliminated the need for mediation; the individual himself or herself assumed the role of authority. Novelists were then in an excellent position to shape public opinion, to become agents of the liberation of the democratic mind.

I contend, however, that such a glorious scenario never really took place: while this may have been an era in which the unprivileged were beginning to demand a place in the political culture of the nation, and while the novel may have validated the legitimacy of the individual reader's responses, the novelists themselves were too conservative in their relation to the state, too ambivalent about the location of legitimate authority, and too uncertain about where their loyalties ultimately lay to have become genuine "cultural voices" and to have written powerful social critiques. Although they located the inequalities and incongruences in an American society that claimed to be egalitarian, and although they occasionally undermined cherished beliefs about reason and liberty as the girders of that society, these writers remained wedded to the rhetoric of the Revolution, and thus were still intent upon educating an American readership to be good citizens of the Republic. An unsettled and turbulent nation did not lead to bold products of the imagination, but rather to didactic textbooklike texts that tried to freeze values that were even then in flux. Unlike our own era, which has witnessed a revolution in Latin American and Eastern European fiction, corresponding to an upheaval in the political life in these parts of the world, late eighteenth- and early nineteenth-century America produced no new forms and configurations of the novel. Rather, we get not the novel as reflection of its society (one standard definition of the term) but a sham sermon to hold change at bay, mere imitations of older British forms. Indeed, the contradictions in the very term "early American novel" that I previously categorized mirror the contradictions in the works of the imagination to which that term applies.

If we examine some of the canonized novels of this period, drawing examples from four subgenres—the sentimental, the picaresque, the gothic, and what might be called the novel of nostalgia or reclamation—we can see the dislocations in the very form, shape, and language of these works. Beginning with the sentimental, and taking the "first" American novel first, we notice immediately that, like Foster's *Coquette* and Rowson's *Charlotte Temple*, Brown's *The Power of Sympathy* defends itself as a novel by claiming "to represent the specious Causes, and to Expose the fatal Consequences of Seduction"; further, it will "set forth and recommend" the "Advantages of Female Education"; but the truth is, as its publisher well knew, and highlighted as part of his advertising campaign, that the book was based on—was in fact an exposé of—the story of Perez Morton's seduction of his wife's sister, Fanny Apthorp, an act at once both adulterous and incestuous according to eighteenth-century law. Politician, statesman, patriot, and Harvard-educated, Morton was a member of the privileged class, a friend to John Adams and other New England elites, who actually defended his honor and reputation after his sister-in-law committed suicide. Clearly, it was this underlying scandal that fueled public interest in Brown's novel, especially since many of his readers believed he would provide them with previously unknown details. Clumsily written, with little attention to the nuances of character, and told through a series of letters that do not even bother to respond to each other, America's first "novel" lacks any memorable novelistic features; furthermore, it owes its enthusiastic reception and recognition not to any realized imaginative conception but rather to the historically verifiable events it purports to illuminate.

Brown certainly leaves no doubt that Morton (changed to Martin in the novel) deserves punishment as well as censure for violating both private vows and civic duty, and in this respect he indirectly challenges men like Adams who blamed the entire episode on Fanny's (called Ophelia in the novel) supposed insanity. Moreover, as it promised, the novel does insist on the importance of education for women; its moralizing, didactic letters are just as often (if not more so) directed toward the audience as to the wayward characters. But as much as Brown may have wanted to defend the victimized, helpless woman, virtually powerless in a society where she was viewed as another form of property, he leaves too many unanswered questions about her possible complicity in the unsavory event of seduction. Ophelia may be innocent, even virtuous, yet she is seduced by her *sister's* husband and in her *sister's* house. There are no psychological clues to this puzzle. Furthermore, as for the other pair of male and female protagonists, Harrington and Harriot (who turn out to be brother and sister), they are unable to break free of their desire for each other. Their story is an enticing, sexually charged one, and cannot be canceled out by the author's moral intentions, no matter how often these are sounded. Seduction may well be a subject that points toward the gross abuse of social power by men of privilege and position, but it is also a titillating one, and Brown has not found a way to negotiate this dangerous issue satisfactorily.

Hannah Foster is more successful in *The Coquette* (1797), though once again we have a work of fiction based on factual incident, one familiar to every reader of the novel since it was a scandal widely publicized in the newspapers of the day. In 1788 Elizabeth Whitman (thinly disguised as Eliza Wharton in the novel), thirty-seven years old, pregnant, and nearly penniless, though from a respected family and well educated for the time, arrived at an inn in Massachusetts and, while supposedly waiting for her husband to arrive, gave birth to a stillborn child and then died shortly after of infection. As it turned out, there was no husband: Whitman was an abandoned woman, a victim of seduction, and in the popular lore of the day she became an example not only of compromised virtue but even more so of unjustified arrogance, since she had rejected what appeared to be two excellent opportunities for marriage in the hope of finding a husband with whom she could share both an intellectual and an emotional life. In other words, she desired compatibility, not merely protection, and for this she was vilified in the press. Foster attempts to retell her story from the victim's point of view, showing how limited were her choices and as a consequence how narrowly circumscribed was her life, a life that, given her talents and abilities, should have been fruitful. It is Foster's point, however, that "should have" itself is an impossibility in a society that accords a woman status only as a male appendage.

Like Brown, Foster relies on the epistolary technique, and while she handles it more fluidly than he—the letters are more individuated, the style of each somewhat more appropriate to the particular correspondent—the narrative still remains leaden, often tedious. Looking forward some years to 1813, when *Pride and Prejudice* was first published, we can see how a master like Jane Austen handles similar material: the wooing of a bright, interesting woman by a dull, self-important cleric, her recognition that such a marriage would be spiritual death, and yet the consequences of refusing what looks like, socially speaking, the best offer the woman is likely to receive. Where Eliza Wharton's story drags, Elizabeth Bennett's sparkles, but then the Reverend J. Boyer, surely as pompous as Mr. Collins, is far less amusing and far more self-serving in his vanity and righteousness; moreover, Mr. Wharton can provide no ironic observations on his daughter's situation as does Mr. Bennett on his. And of course, there's no rescuer like Mr. Darcy to save the heroine and her family from ruin, only a destroyer like Peter Sanford to cause it. While the differences are, to a large extent, generically necessary (the comic as opposed to the sentimental), they are also motivated by the radically distinct social visions of Foster and Austen; for all its proclamations of openness and opportunity, American society is far more limiting and restrictive for women. It strips them of choice, just as it denies them a meaningful voice in their country's affairs, and even in their own.

Indeed, no difference here is finally more instructive than the major one between Elizabeth and Eliza: Austen's heroine combats her situation through brilliant and witty language, a play of sensibility that enables her to triumph over unfortunate, occasionally menacing circumstance, whereas all that Foster can imagine for her protagonist is silence. Her letters ironically demonstrate a lack of creative choice. Eliza Wharton loses her voice or, perhaps more to the point, relinquishes it, but in either case circumstance and event triumph over her. Silence, as critics of the novel have argued, is an appropriate metaphor for a woman's lack of independent legal status in American society; since she has no agency, why pretend that her words mean anything? But to yield the struggle, to accept powerlessness, is to permit the dominant culture not only to go unchallenged but also to take refuge once again in its supercilious moral standards. Eliza passively giving herself to her seducer, falling into sin and, inevitably, death, only reinforces the codes that Foster has in other ways tried to subvert. The novel itself sacrifices the cultural ground it might otherwise have claimed.

If Susanna Rowson was more successful in her social commentary—a point of some debate—it may very well have been because in *Charlotte Temple* (published in America in 1794) she abandoned the Richardsonian form (mercifully, only a few letters appear in the text) in favor of a third-person narrative, though one that she occasionally interrupts to speak in her own voice. It is that voice, however constrained it may be by her culture's suspicion of novel writing (she indicates in the preface her awareness of the novel's suspect nature), and bound though it still is to conventional morality (she advises her young readers to implore "heaven" to "keep [them] free from temptation"), that gives the novel its real interest, for we can hear, underneath the rather formal and even stilted language, her desire to break the bonds of women's cultural subservience, an inherited sphere of expectation that makes Charlotte Temple a prey to male predators like her seducer Montraville and his adviser Belcour. Addressing young women explicitly (perhaps the first time an American novel does so), Rowson warns against listening to the "voice of love"—the very voice women were culturally conditioned to await eagerly—since men, too, are products of their culture. Occasionally tempered by sympathy during the act, perhaps mitigated by remorse afterward, seduction is nevertheless a scenario of the empowered versus the marginalized, the sanctioned versus the disenfranchised, and women will inevitably suffer victimization until the social structure is reformed.

Rowson counsels resistance: men are "vile betrayer[s]," "monsters of seduction," and if they know the meaning of the word "honour" are undoubtedly too swayed by modern fashion and "refinement" to practice it. Forget "romance," she tells her readers (almost as if they were her charges), "no woman can be run away with contrary to her own inclination." But even though she expresses these feminist sentiments and aligns herself with her audience, as if to say we must nurture each other rather than look toward a man for support, Rowson still cannot produce a text that itself resists the pieties and homilies of the culture it has been vilifying (the book actually concludes with the utterly banal biblical platitude that vice eventually leads to "misery and shame"). In the end it winds up promoting the values that cloak forms of (male) oppression; it authorizes the very authorities it has previously sought to displace. The "precepts of religion and virtue" vanish from the novel (if they were present in the first place) as quickly as Montraville when he has the opportunity to make an advantageous match, yet these become the tired ideals to which young women should aspire. If, after everything Montraville has done to disgrace and humiliate Charlotte, she can still declare her love for him, what kind of model has Rowson provided those readers whom she had previously roused to anger and indignation? Moreover, what kind of stability does the sentimental novel offer, when it itself is marked by such prevarication?

If the sentimental novel often failed because it could not sustain a coherent critique of American society, the picaresque often succeeded for the very same reason. This loose, baggy, disjointed narrative form, usually containing several different kinds of discourse, including philosophical reflection, travel essay, and political disquisition, was also perfectly suited for commentary on the politics of republicanism, which in the years following the Revolution, and especially in the time of Constitutional debates, could be highly factious. Cathy N. Davidson has convincingly argued this point, showing how the various and divergent voices of the American polis were sounded out by characters who traveled through cities, towns, and villages, engaging those whom they encountered in argument and debate. What often emerged was a tension—sometimes outright hostility—between Federalist and Anti-Federalist, privileged and common, those who supported the entrenched power and those who demanded its redistribution. The vociferous, highly charged (but implicit) arguments centered, above all, on the meaning of America and who were its rightful inheritors.

But the picaresque also had inherent weaknesses, the most glaring being an inconsistency in its point of view. It was often difficult, sometimes impossible, to tell where its author stood on the vital political issues he (and it almost always was "he") was discussing. It was not until Mark Twain transformed the picaresque with the publication of *Adventures of Huckleberry Finn* in 1884–85 that any kind of stability in tone and vision entered the form. If the journey down the Mississippi seemed random and unplotted, Twain's purposes were nevertheless highly focused. Moreover, with the dual portrait of Huck and Jim, Twain achieved a clarity and depth in character that no other picaresque novel had previously managed. Earlier versions of the genre may also have highlighted socially marginal figures, pitting them against representatives of mainstream society, yet none could maintain the satiric perspective while at the same time realizing the emotional depths of, and eliciting compassion for, their wandering protagonists. The potential for greatness had always been there; it took a great writer, of course, to realize it.

The most successful of the early picaresque novels, Hugh Henry Brackenridge's *Modern Chivalry* (published in irregular installments from 1792 to 1815) combines the best and the worst aspects of the genre. Concerning the latter, the narrative rambles incessantly, digresses willfully, pontificates frequently; moreover, the author interrupts, directly or in postscripts, to discuss both his career and his book (the very one we are reading), even quoting critical reviews of the first two volumes at the outset of the third (the advantage, perhaps, of publishing parts of a work at widely separate intervals). While these practices may seem like contemporary self-reflexiveness by our postmodern standards, they are merely distracting, since they apparently partake of no larger metafictional strategy; nothing, that is, holds the book together as a coherent whole. Concerning the best, however, Brackenridge creates two characters with charged comic energy, the educated and sophisticated Captain Farrago and his ignorant and coarse servant Teague O'Regan. The two have been compared to the classic fictional travelers Don Quixote and Sancho Panza (the novel itself suggests the likeness), but a more illuminating analogy would be the stage and television performers Abbott and Costello; like Abbott, Farrago relies on his superior reasoning ability, constantly offers advice and guidance, and is invariably ignored or, worse, foiled in his attempts to impose order on a chaotic scene. Like Costello, O'Regan depends on Farrago for assistance in difficult situations, always disregards his plea for moderation, and, though he is the butt of the humor, winds up triumphing over the man of reason by becoming the choice of the common people. Had Brackenridge been a greater novelist (had he been Twain), he could have written a comic masterpiece.

What he has produced, however, is a book as contradictory and as confusing in its pronouncements and outlook as the early American Republic itself. Brackenridge cannot seem to decide between the aristocratic assumptions of Farrago and the populist impulses of O'Regan; while he shares Farrago's fear of the mob, for example, he apparently admires O'Regan's determination to rise in American society, even if he is unqualified for every position or office he seeks. If he seems dubious about the leveling tendencies of democracy, he also tends to reject the reactionary declarations and prejudiced views of an (often self-proclaimed) elite citizenry. Not surprisingly, Brackenridge shifts political allegiances in his book just as he did in his life, championing Federalism during the time of the Constitutional debates, then subsequently becoming an Anti-Federalist when government policies began to privilege land speculation at the expense of impoverished farmers. But, finally, the novelist seems unsure as to which version of the democratic system he supports, either total participatory democracy, or some limited form of democratic government where an enlightened leadership rules on behalf of a populace not quite intelligent and therefore trustworthy enough to govern itself. The equivocation may very well mirror the endless uncertainties of political life in the new nation, but it also weakens the already shaky foundations of the fledgling novel.

Perhaps Americans had the most success adapting the form of the novel that would seem to be the least suited to the open, expansive American landscape, the gothic, which depended for its effects on such feudal artifacts as intricately constructed castles and ruined abbeys, and such Old World types as evil barons and mad monks. But the gothic also specialized in such human foibles as superstition and delusion, as well as human anxieties over hidden corruption and uncertain, if not outrightly malign, motivation. The claustrophobic structures and mazelike pathways that tend to recur in these stories become metaphors for the distorted, haunted minds of the protagonists of these novels, characters whose respectable, seemingly normal outer lives mask savage, abnormal inner ones. The gothic thus became the perfect form for expressing the fears that American society, with its concomitant ideologies of liberalism and individualism, not only had continued the abuses of a hierarchical social structure but also had actually opened the way to even greater treacheries: self-made, self-improved, self-confident, and self-determined men abusing power, subverting authority, undermining order.

No practitioner of the gothic was more attuned to these potential problems in American society than Charles Brockden Brown, and no American novelist exploited them more successfully than he did in several books from the late 1790s, including *Wieland* (1798), *Ormond* (1799), *Arthur Mervyn* (Part I, 1799; Part II, 1800), and *Edgar Huntly* (1799). In these experimental and daring, though flawed novels, Brown tested the limits of reason in a country willing to believe in its limitlessness, examined the darker and perhaps evil impulses of unchecked imagination, and explored the consequences of personality unloosed from its moorings in some form of stable, traditional community. Not surprisingly, given his interests, all four novels become fixated on violent disruption of a previously harmonious group of people, sometimes caused by an outside agent (Carwin in *Wieland*), sometimes by an internal one (Edgar Huntly himself). In each case, there is no refuge from the turbulence and confusion that results, no return to the fixed relations of things as they used to be. Drawing on the radical creeds, speculative philosophy, and psychological experimentation of his own time for the plots and metaphors of his novels, Brown introduced such ideas as ventriloquism, somnambulism, and spontaneous combustion into American fiction, suggesting the end of the once stable relationship between appearance and reality, and between the individual and society. Moreover, long before it became a fashionable critical notion, Brown posited the belief that the self was basically unknowable, indeterminate; the more we look for an inviolate order within, the more we discover the basic rule of fragmentation.

These ideas are most prevalent—especially the discovery of disorder within and the consequent inability to reconstruct an ordered self—in Brown's best novel, *Wieland,* which dramatizes, as Jay Fliegelman has argued, one of the most perplexing issues in the early republican period, the "conflicting claims of authority and liberty." The tension within Brown's narrator, Clara Wieland, is precisely between these two mutually exclusive demands, represented by Henry Pleyel, the rationalist who eschews all other forms of knowledge, and Carwin, the man of passionate will who tests and manipulates Clara in order to destroy her faith in the rational side of her being, and by implication in Pleyel as well. (He also manages to ruin her reputation, by inference rather than act, in the mind of Pleyel, who essentially abandons her.) Thus, the authority of supreme reason wars with the license of unchecked liberty, the one constrained and controlled, the other raw and raging. Clara's crazed brother, Theodore, who in his pursuit of religious certainty kills his entire family (and would have added Clara to the list of victims were he not prevented by Carwin), illustrates not only the dangers of enthusiasm but also those of submitting too readily, too pleasurably, to the demands of a higher, more potent will. In other words, Theodore combines the excesses of both authority and liberty, and he must be eliminated. But his death brings no resolution to the essential conflict, and Clara, though she regains health at the end, never achieves self-knowledge. Brown's novel, compelling and powerful in its psychological undercurrents and social implications, ends irresolutely, thus weakly. Novelistically, Brown could not resolve the tensions; culturally, he could not solve the contradictions.

At the close of this period of the "early American novel," James Fenimore Cooper, in all probability America's first significant novelist, if not quite a genuine "cultural voice," produced a novel that indeed sought to reunify the spirit of a discordant nation. In *The Spy* (1821), Cooper concentrates on the issue of virtuous behavior in the Republic, and though his story is set in the Revolutionary era, he means the lesson to pertain to his own, which he saw threatened by the powerful forces of discord, emanating for the most part from a populace that had turned toward the pursuit of material satisfaction at the expense of national loyalty. Cooper illustrates his meaning through the symbolic structure of the novel, which centers on the Wharton family and the patriarch's attempt to preserve the sanctuary of his home in a time of crisis. The attempt is a futile one, for the elder Wharton, like Cooper's America, has conceived the task purely in material terms. As with the businessmen whom Cooper despised, money is Wharton's bottom line, dictating relationships as well as physical movement. The complicated plot turns on the fact that

Wharton has placed his family in a dangerous situation because he has refused to accept the moral responsibilities of citizenship.

Dispossessed as he thought he was from America, Cooper nevertheless writes from within a comfortable position in the cultural hierarchy, and his novel is, not surprisingly, a conservative one about preserving a sense of original virtue, located in the social structure as Cooper perceives it. That structure is in tatters, an idea suggested both by the "divided house" motif and the "neutral ground," the territory that, as it becomes the novel's dominant setting, represents post-Revolutionary America, with its bifurcated loyalties and shifting values. In its essence, it is a wilderness; it is fraught with conflicting passions and points of view, violence and disorder. "The law," Cooper writes, "was momentarily extinct in that particular district, and justice was administered subject to the bias of personal interests and the passions of the strongest." In addition to lawlessness, moral indifference defines the terrain. Thus, the land can only be set in order through the restoration of moral authority.

The problem with the novel—perhaps a mirror of the problem in American society as Cooper saw it—was to find a locus of that authority, and the best that Cooper can do is to invoke the archetypal father—the father of Founding Fathers—George Washington. Possessing both virtue *and* authority, Washington accomplishes the greater task of setting his lands in order by healing the divisions that have threatened their internal security. As the only legitimate paternal figure in the novel, he projects a sense of control that the other characters find reassuring. And when he is unable to act owing to military circumstance, he does not retreat from his sense of public duty but entrusts the task to his spy, Harvey Birch, who, by his disinterested deeds, extends the Father's virtue to the neutral ground. If Washington is Virtue incarnate, Birch is Selfless Action come to life, since his motives are clear: patriotism, not profit, has led him to sacrifice comfort, reputation, and future prospects of happiness for his country. In short, he is a saint, and when Washington smiles upon him he is beatified.

For Cooper, in a time of growing materialism, which would soon run rampant with the coming of industrialization, Harvey's selfless devotion was the single most important virtue Americans needed to practice if the Republic was to survive. But of course that was an impossibility, since it had already vanished into myth and legend, signaled, though Cooper hardly means it that way, by Washington's very presence in the book. Cooper tells a great story, but unfortunately it is an irrelevant one. Whether America had ever enjoyed the golden moment of Revolutionary self-sacrifice and transcendent devotion to the ideals of the Fathers has been long debated by historians, and there will probably never be a definitive view on the subject. But again, it matters little in terms of Cooper's nostalgic vision, since in any case it would never come again. Ironically, Cooper moves the American novel forward by looking backward, for if he had one thing that all the others lacked, it was a consistent, fully realized, forcefully articulated vision of a reconstituted American society. If only all its citizens could be gods like George Washington, or even just angels like Harvey Birch.

To conclude, then, by returning to the beginning: as it turns out, an argument can be made for the existence of an "early American novel," though unless it accounts for the contradictions, inconsistencies, and instabilities in the genre as American writers adapted it, it is falsifying the achievement. Originality of design and form would only arrive with great romantic writers of the nineteenth century; an authentic American idiom and a genuine "cultural voice" would have to await Mark Twain's arrival on the novelistic scene. And the American novel would not truly become "American" until the politically disenfranchised and culturally dispossessed of American society were finally heard in the pages of our literature.

Jeffrey Rubin-Dorsky

# Autobiography and the Early Novel

Concepts of social value in autobiography existed for many centuries before the word was coined. In the Western tradition, the earliest known text in this genre, *The Confessions of St. Augustine,* written at the turn of the fourth to the fifth century, is only one of many that were accommodated under a variety of other names. These include Plato's seventh epistle in the fourth century B.C., the *Essays* of Michel de Montaigne in the latter half of the sixteenth century, and the *Confessions* of Jean-Jacques Rousseau in the 1760s. As legend has it, credit for the initial appearance of "autobiography" in the English language goes to Robert Southey, under whose name it made its debut in *The Quarterly Review* in 1809. In America, *The Autobiography of Thomas Sheperd, the Celebrated Minister of Cambridge, New England* (1830) was the first book to use the term in its title.

In contemporary studies of characterizations of autobiographical narrative, scholars like G. Thomas Couser (*Altered Egos: Authority in American Autobiography* [1989]) have noted the singular aspects of the word used to describe the self: its number, capitalization, and position as the only single-letter pronoun in the language. Moreover, there is its typographical likeness to the Roman numeral I, its phonemic identity with "eye," and its punning on the idea of a single point of view. Although its implied dominance, usually claimed by privileged racial and cultural groups, is now widely challenged by people outside of those groups, these singular qualities of the "I" suggest its elevated status—an acknowledgment of the uniqueness and independent social standing of the first person.

In addition, many Americanists have observed a particular relationship between the nature of autobiographical discourse and texts like *The Autobiography of Benjamin Franklin* that traditionally define the dominant American identity. Almost all such critics (including voices from the margins) agree that while autobiography is not unique to this country, the form embodies peculiar American characteristics. This idea finds reinforcement in the fact that, subsuming boundaries of race and sex, the genre has become the country's preeminent form of writing. Nor is this a recent phenomenon. As early as the October 1909 issue of *Harper's Monthly Magazine,* William Dean Howells, an autobiographer himself, and one of America's foremost novelists and literary critics of that age, spoke of autobiography as a "new form of literature," calling it the most "democratic province in the republic of letters." Of course, literary theories of democratic equality do not mitigate the disadvantages and sufferings of the daily lives of large numbers of Americans, but judging from the quantity of documents identified as autobiographies, it is not difficult to conclude that Howells's judgment was correct. For autobiography, in its valorization of individualism and its focus on the success story, has always been eminently suited to the dominant American temperament.

One of the attractions of autobiography for readers of popular literature is that, generally, Americans presume the absolute truth-value of these texts and an authentic and direct contact with the authors through the written word. Such beliefs grant the form what Elizabeth Bruss described as "empirical first-person" authority, and set the genre of autobiography hierarchically apart from other forms of narrative discourse.

Perhaps for this reason as well as for our innate curiosity about the lives of the famous and the successful, from its beginnings narrative autobiography flourished in America. Euro-Americans began recording their experiences in the new land in the early seventeenth century, and in the closing years of the twentieth century they continue to do so in unprecedented numbers, as ethnic and other minority groups, formerly excluded from recognition in letters, make their voices heard through this medium. But even excluding these aggressive newcomers, by 1961, Louis Kaplan's *A Bibliography of American Autobiographies* listed more than 6000 titles recorded prior to 1945, and Mary Briscoe's *American Autobiography, 1945–1980,* adds 5000 titles to that list. In addition to the sheer numbers of individual self-written lives, these bibliographies demonstrate that the American autobiographical narrative accommodates itself to wide varieties of self-representations—the conversion, captivity, criminal, slave, and travel narratives, ethnic, immigrant, colonial, and transcendental autobiographies, to name a small number of easily recognizable categories.

Interestingly, while writing-the-self began early in the country's history, the study of American narrative autobiography was slow in developing. In 1948, a book almost unnoticed by the literary establishment, *Witnesses for Freedom: Negro Americans in Autobiography,* by Rebecca Chalmers Barton, became the first full-length study of the genre. Barton's text, consisting of twenty-three textual portraits, with a foreword by Harlem Renaissance philosopher Alain Locke, included such figures as Frederick Douglass, Booker T. Washington, Mary Church Terrell, W. E. B. Du Bois, Zora Neale Hurston, Claude McKay, Langston Hughes, and Richard Wright. Sixteen years later, in 1964, *The Examined Self: Benjamin Franklin, Henry Adams, Henry James,* by Robert F. Sayre, appeared, and set the stage for what was soon to become a new and almost instantaneously flourishing field of intellectual inquiry. Today, a multiplicity of critical texts, as wide-ranging in methodologies and interpretive intent as the varying content of the narratives they explore, makes up this burgeoning body of knowledge. These studies constitute a revolutionary reassessment of the relationship between self-representation and other branches of narrative literature.

This revolution has been immensely aided during the second half of the twentieth century by the explosions in literary theory and cultural criticism that, among other things, have led academic critics of American autobiography to define the "I" and to call indiscriminate presumptions of truth-value in the genre into question. Even before this, scholars had discussed the position of autobiography as a hybrid of history and literature, and had come to interesting conclusions about the art of its narrative techniques. But in the new wave of criticism, scholars like Albert E. Stone, in *Autobiographical Occasions and Original Acts* (1982), advanced the idea of the autobiographical act as occupying "the frontiers of 'fact' and 'fiction,' " a viewpoint that helped to open up new avenues for destabilizing the once dominant "I." As Stone describes it, in straddling this frontier autobiography comprises a "literary as well as a historical activity which recreates psychic as well as social experience," simultaneously resisting complete appropriation by the disciplines to which it is connected. The richness of the autobiographical enterprise, he points out, rests in its blending of, and the tensions between, memory, reflection, and imagination. More recent studies in the genre have gone even further, as such works as Couser's *Altered Egos,* Paul John Eakin's *Fictions in Autobiography: Studies in the Art of Self-Invention* (1985), and Herbert Liebowitz's *Fabricating Lives: Explorations in American Autobiography* (1989) take advantage of poststructuralist discourse to further problematize the boundaries of the "I."

In his disputation of a fixed truth-value in autobiography, Couser takes issue with notions that the "I" is first (prior), personal (private), or singular (unique), a position earlier and more conventional critics (primarily white males on white male autobiography) claimed. Couser's view, buttressed by the scholarship of social psychologists, is that the self is not constructed in isolation but continually engages in complicity, negotiation, and collusion in its relationships with others. This point of view inscribes difference in *identity* and acknowledges a contextually variable self that, although integrated, need not embody harmonic unity. Furthermore, memory, which is unstable, plays such an important role in the construction of autobiography that it unsettles the ground on which the truth of a narrative rests. Assuming the validity of this theory, how do we assess the relationship between American autobiography and the American novel in their development? A brief survey of seventeenth- and eighteenth-century American autobiography through the end of the Revolutionary War, followed by a look at the slave narrative and Native American autobiography in the nineteenth century, provides an outline of early patterns in the development of fictional elements in autobiography in this country.

The earliest Euro-Americans to face themselves in writing were explorers in search of New World adventure. Psychologically, these men were attuned to the idea of psychic transformations as a result of their contacts with the Americas. The literature of the period, partly intended to attract additional settlers to the new exotic country, while descriptive of the physical characteristics of the new land and giving accounts of its inhabitants, speaks also to the effects that the environment had on these men. Among these early impulses to create an American self distinct from the one that came out of the old country are the accounts left us by Captain John Smith, which include *A True Relation of Such Occurrences and Accidents of Noate as Hath Hapned in Virginia* (1608), *A Description of New England* (1616), *The Generall Historie of Virginia, New England, and the Summer Isles* (1624), and *The True Travels, Adventures, and Observations of Captaine John Smith* (1630). One of the most well known events in this last-named text recounts Smith's capture by the Indians and his escape from death through the intervention of the princess Pocahontas. The singular importance of the story, in the context of the new "self," is the metaphorical rebirth of Smith who becomes, through Pocahontas's willingness to sacrifice her life to save him from the barbarousness of her people, the son of the Indian chief.

There is little doubt that John Smith met Pocahontas and her chieftain-father Powhatan. Among English settlers, however, the story of Smith's escape from death at the hands of the Indians was built on assumptions that as a white man he was superior to the natives, a superiority that Pocahontas and her father recognized. This belief was further reinforced by Pocahontas's subsequent marriage to another English settler. On the contrary, besides the fact that whites were killed by Indians previously—as well as subsequently—to Smith, therefore negating the idea that Indians believed in a theory of white superiority, recent anthropological evidence indicates that when Powhatan permitted Smith, through a ritual ceremony, to become a young "white" chief, he used him to help him (Powhatan) in his trade for European goods and to strengthen his power base. Smith's was clearly a romanticized version of the events intended to capture the imagination of others with interests similar to his own, to lure them to the American colonies. The intent might have accomplished its goal, but this fictionalized appropriation of the Pocahontas story, the first legend of Euro-American colonialization, set the stage for the subsequent denigration of Native American intelligence and humanity.

The secular stories of explorers like Smith find counterparts in the conversion narratives and Puritan histories, such as those of William Bradford (*History of Plimmoth Plantation* [1650]) and Edward Johnson (*Wonder-Working Providence of Sions Saviour in New England* [1654]). Although accorded the status of autobiographies, these texts more accurately represent collective community biographies that give all credit for the European settlement of the country to Divine guidance and providence, and set the ground rules for individual participation in the community. The best-known Puritan autobiographies are the *Diary* of Samuel Sewall (1673–1729) and the *Diary* of Cotton Mather (1681–1724). Mather also authored *Paterna* (1688–1727), an instructional document intended for his son, and *Magnalia Christi Americana* (1702), a history of the Puritan New England experiment. Other well-known spiritual autobiographies of the eighteenth century include Jonathan Edwards's *Personal Narrative* (ca. 1739), the Quaker writings of Elizabeth Ashbridge and John Wolman, and *A True History of the Captivity and Restoration of Mrs. Mary Rowlandson* (1682), the text that launched America's first unique autobiographical account: the Indian captivity narrative.

As documents that defined the boundaries of life and behavior in the Puritan community, American seventeenth- and eighteenth-century spiritual narratives were mechanical in pattern and restricted in subject matter, and promoted the idea that their writers had the presence of grace in their experiences. Since conversion was not an issue, it was never questioned. Each text was a testimony to the effect that the experiences of its subject conformed to the patterns of feelings and conduct permitted within the confines of the Puritan ethic. It bears mentioning that Puritan spiritual autobiography was not exclusively confined to prose narrative. Anne Bradstreet and Edward Taylor, who also wrote short first-person prose statements, are among those who wrote poetry that falls within the boundaries of this genre.

In their historical and cultural contexts, from the late seventeenth through the middle of the eighteenth century, Indian captivity narratives occupied religious, propagandistic, and sentimental spaces in early American autobiography. The first ones tended to focus on the religious dimensions of captive experience, while later ones became a vehicle for promulgating white hatred of Native Americans and made an argument for Indian removal. The Puritans, believing themselves God's chosen people on a mission to establish the New Zion on this continent, equated Native Americans with the devil, creatures for them to exterminate from the land in a righteous cause. Infusions of melodrama into captivity narratives in the late eighteenth and early nineteenth centuries made them factually exaggerated sensational horror fictions. In *The Indian Captivity Narrative: An American Genre* (1984), Richard VanDerBeets notes that the compelling pattern in the Indian captivity narrative, regardless of emphasis, is of the Archetypal Hero on an initiation journey from Death to Rebirth. The narratives follow a pattern of the subject's Separation from his/her culture (symbolic death), Transformation (through ordeals that ensure the movement from ignorance to knowledge and maturity), and Return (symbolic rebirth). The focus in Mrs. Mary Rowlandson's narrative is on the religious dimensions of the genre, but the pattern held for all captivity narratives.

On February 10, 1676, Narragansett Indians raided the English settlement of Lancaster, Massachusetts, destroying the town, killing seventeen of her family members and friends, and taking Mary Rowlandson, wife of Lancaster's minister, Joseph Rowlandson (away in Boston at the time), and her three children captives. She was immediately separated from her two older children, ages ten and fourteen, while the youngest, six years old, having been wounded in the raid, died a week after the capture. For eleven weeks Mary Rowlandson lived and traveled with her captors, before she and her two children were released in exchange for £20.

In 1677 the Rowlandsons moved to Wethersfield, Connecticut. A year later Joseph Rowlandson died, and in another year Mary, having remarried, dropped out of public view. *A True History of the Captivity and Restoration of Mrs. Mary Rowlandson* appears to have been written in 1677, but was not published until 1682. Under the title *The Sovereignty and Goodness of God*, the narrative was an instant success. *A True History* established the pattern for the early texts in this tradition: a confirmation of the election of God's people, the piety of the captives, and the justification for Indian removal. Mary Rowlandson's narrative went through four editions in its first year, and twenty-three by 1828. To date, at least forty editions have appeared.

*A True History,* a story intended to instruct rather than exploit the stereotype of the savage Indian, focuses on Christian affliction. On the superficial level, Rowlandson tells the story of her 150-mile journey with the Narragansetts, but it is the interior journey that holds our attention; the symbolic landscape more than the literal one; and the darkness of the forest that represents that of the soul when God turns his face away. For Rowlandson, her capture was a rupture in the pattern of the daily life of the Puritan mother and marked the loss of everything that gave meaning to her life. Although her Indians are "murtherous" captors, "merciless Heathen," and "a company of hell-hounds," because she is a faithful Puritan she transcends that symbolic death by finding meaning in her afflictions. In this way she recreates herself, and in the process of transformation seeks to discover what failings led to her punishment. Her duty in captivity is to concentrate on submitting to God's will. Among other things she learns how to provide for herself. During this period, her voice in the text is that of a Christian in the wilderness crying out to God. Her release from captivity assures her of having gained redemption and the promise of salvation. The return is fully accomplished in the writing of her story.

Although admirable for the dignity that its author displays in the face of a terrible ordeal, this text does not inform readers of the author's personal reactions to her trials. Like all spiritual autobiography of its time, *A True Story* reveals more about the strength of Puritan culture than about the true characteristics of Mary Rowlandson. In a time when women led socially restricted lives, she told her story publicly because it was the end of a process, and those who were able to draw the prescribed lessons from such ordeals were obliged to pass them on to others for their moral instruction. In her words, "one principall ground of my setting forth these lines is to declare the Works of the Lord, and his wonderful power in carrying us along, preserving us in the Wilderness, while under the Enemies hand, and in returning us in safety again." Clearly, the narrative was not *her* story. Her place in the flow of events in eighteenth-century Puritanism was to stand still and wait on her Lord.

Another interesting autobiography of that time was *The Journal of Madam Knight,* by Sarah Kemble Knight, the only text of its kind in the American genre. Although written in 1704–5, it was not published until 1825. Acting in her own business interests, Knight describes with humor and bravado her arduous and even dangerous journey from Boston to New Haven at a time when women seldom traveled alone. Her story is one of self-confidence and nonconformity to conventions of her day. At the end of each day she made entries in her diary. These reveal inner resources that enabled her to cope with the obstacles she encountered. The trip took her exactly five months, including a winter spent with relatives in Connecticut. Knight was not the typical woman of her time, but she was also not alone in her independence from conventions that restricted women's lives.

Knight's journal is especially important because of how openly she expresses her fears, misgivings, and loneliness on the road. She was not always alone, however, for she hired guides and met other travelers in the places where she stayed. Although little is known about her outside of her journal, some critics believe that she wrote, not for publication, but for the amusement of close friends. Not unaware of the religious beliefs of her day, she appears to have had little concern about them, and her journal did not follow the pattern of the spiritual quest found in most diaries of her time. Only at the end of the journal, in her expression of gladness over returning home safely and finding warm welcomes from friends and loved ones, does she express gratitude to the "Great Benefactor" for giving his "unworthy handmaid" safe passage during her months abroad.

But if Knight was more secular than religious, she also took class distinctions seriously. A small-businesswoman, she was mindful of treating those of higher social standing than herself with deference while she was condescending in her treatment of country people, African Americans, Native Americans, and others of lower status. Her journal reveals a robustness of taste and a love of good stories. She records several of these. She was also a satirist who wrote in many voices, using the language of colloquial modes of expression, neoclassical diction, and contrasting genres, mixing poetry, dialogue, and fiction into her personal prose. Because of this journal, Knight has a prominent place in travel literature, and it establishes her as a satirist representing significant themes and character types in the tradition of American humor.

The single most well known and often-written-about eighteenth-century American autobiography (frequently characterized as the bridge text between the eighteenth and the nineteenth century) is that of Benjamin Franklin (written between 1771 and 1790). For Franklin the man is the model American hero and patriot. Born in Boston in 1706 of humble Puritan parentage, he lived a life that was the stuff of national legend. In his teens, Franklin rejected the religion of his parents for Deism, then popular among eighteenth-century intellectuals. At age seventeen he ran away from Boston to Philadelphia, and soon went off to England. Back in Philadelphia in 1726, he did well as a printer, bought and reformed a newspapers, *The Pennsylvania Gazette,* opened his own stationer's shop, and became the public printer for the colony. Financial prosperity led him to involvement in local politics. He established a fire company, a lending library, the American Philosophical Society, and proposed an academy that later became the University of Pennsylvania. In 1748 he retired from business to spend his time in politics and science. In the latter field, his discoveries in electricity brought him international fame.

In the world of politics, Benjamin Franklin became a leading member of the Pennsylvania Assembly, and in 1757 he went to England to represent the Assembly in its complaints against the British. He returned to America in 1775 when the country was at war. His greatest fame came to him as a member of the Second Continental Congress and as America's minister to France. He was involved in working out the peace this country made with England after the war, and he signed the Treaty of Paris in 1782. Returning to America in 1785, as an elder statesman, he was a representative to the Constitutional Convention. By the time of his death in 1790, having transcended poverty, low birth, and limited education, he had become to many the embodiment of the dream that in America hard work, virtue, and respect for conventions were the keys to prosperity, independence, and happiness.

*The Autobiography* is Benjamin Franklin's most important written work. Notably, it was the first major text in American autobiography to break with the (Puritan) tradition of the spiritual narrative, and many claim it as the first truly American self-in-writing. Franklin wrote the first part (which, in his treatment of his Boston, early Philadelphia, and London life, resembles a picaresque novel) while in England in 1771; the second part (accounts of his library project and his efforts at moral perfection) in France in 1784, after the Revolution; the third (a record of the 1730s through the 1750s) in America in 1788. The brief and incomplete fourth section (a memoir of London) was also written in America shortly before his death in 1790. This text was Franklin's interpretation of his life as the self-made man, the Franklin he constructed for the world to see. The writing of it was the making of that self in which the "I" took full control of its own destiny. Primarily, Franklin uses his autobiography to promote the classic tale of the poor but talented boy who, through hard work, ability, and learning from his mistakes, makes a success of his life. Addressing his son in the first section, in a voice wise, humorous, and tolerant, the older man juxtaposes age and youth, and provides advice for the younger.

But Franklin's autobiography, the exemplary American text, is not the *true* life story of Benjamin Franklin. As G. Thomas Couser notes, from the beginning Franklin describes his text as the second corrected "edition" of his life, suggesting that the "life" itself was the first edition, and a text at that. Under these circumstances, his writing of his life was equivalent to editing a book, and the "relation between narative and life, or history, is not between 'language' and the 'reality' to which it refers, but between one text and another that it revises." As such, Couser points out that it is impossible to look through the autobiography for the life and the self behind the text. All the reader has for certain is the character with which he begins the narrative: a literal man of letters invented by the autobiographer. For, as Robert F. Sayre concludes, Franklin was writing to and about himself, developing a correspondence between his past and his present. Through his rich imagination he was able to create roles for himself (such as the waif who arrives in Philadelphia) that turned the narrative into an adventure permitting him to live out a variety of identities.

Ironically, within the decade following his death, several inaccurate partial versions of *The Autobiography* appeared. The first full edition, edited by his grandson Temple Franklin, was published in 1818, but critics remain divided on its accuracy of representation. As some experts conclude, even now Franklin's narrative resists publication in a "truly authoritative text." Still, few would deny its achievement: the art of its autobiographical impulse and Franklin's historical place as a master craftsman in the writing of public prose.

While seventeenth- and eighteenth-century European settlers in America created autobiographical narratives by way of the explorer, Indian captivity, travel, and spiritual narratives, and finally through Benjamin Franklin's secular model American life, little or nothing was made of the presence and conditions of Africans or African slaves in their roles in the nation's beginnings. Slave status was equivalent to nonpersonhood and placed its victims outside the boundaries of the rights and privileges expected and enjoyed by the white population. By 1760, however, black autobiography was born, launching the slave narrative as America's second unique form of self-writing. White collaborations with Native Americans in the as-told-to life stories were preempted by more than seventy years when, in 1762, the first black document in this genre appeared, the product of a white amanuensis and a black subject. Between 1760 and 1798, the Revolutionary era, the partial experiences of fifteen African Americans appeared in print, five of them (of which four were self-written) by former slaves seeking to establish identities separate from their earlier slave status, while the remainder were criminal confessions written down by interested whites shortly before the execution of these men. In many cases, editions of the stories of those attempting to create "other" than slave selves appeared in Ireland, England, and on the European continent, sometimes before their American publications. In *To Tell a Free Story: The First Century of Afro-American Autobiography, 1760–1865* (1986), William L. Andrews establishes the relationship between early slave narratives and American autobiography of that time.

In surveying this relationship, scholarship shows that at the beginning of the nineteenth century the former American colonies were settling into new nationhood as the Republic of the United States. The democratic state was grounded on the Declaration of Independence, which reinforced a national sense of individual rights: life, liberty, and the pursuit of happiness. Here was the ideal impetus toward autobiography. Few, if any, among those who found themselves leading the destiny of the new nation, or those enabled by its

new Constitution to participate in its progress, questioned the legitimacy of who automatically shared those rights and privileges, and
who were excluded from that largesse and why. But if the country
ignored the human dimensions of African American life, individually
and collectively, African Americans, including slaves, did not internalize concepts of inferior human status to whites. From its
eighteenth-century beginnings, the first one hundred years of African
American autobiography is the story of women and men struggling to
claim, in writing, for white readers, that they were human beings
capable of telling the "truth" of their experiences. In this context, the
black "I" and the white reader, with separate racial identities within
the same culture, were forced toward a common reading of experience.

Slave narratives, the predominant genre in early African American
writing, were the personal accounts of former slaves telling their own
stories, first, in search of the psychological freedom that the bonds of
physical slavery denied them prior to their escape from its shackles;
and second, as propaganda weapons in the struggle for the abolition
of that slavery. Information and reformation were the root motives
driving their production. African Americans felt that moral and just
whites, especially those in the North, needed to know, firsthand, the
conditions of slavery, and to rise up to purge the country of its
scourge. What the nation needed most, they would have said, was a
mighty contingent of John Browns—white men and women willing to
give their all for the honor of the democratic promises of the Constitution. While the most complex and personally interesting narratives in this tradition were written by their subjects, dozens of narratives were as-told-to life stories, generally mediated through the
offices of white male amanuenses. Much scholarly debate on slave
narratives focuses on the authenticity or lack of it of these latter,
primarily on the editorial authority of the transcriber to compose,
shape, and interpret the textual lives of the former slaves.

In addition to the slave narratives, spiritual autobiographies
emerged in the late eighteenth and early nineteenth centuries. While
escaped slaves condemned the "peculiar" institution by indicting its
atrocities, spiritual narrators claimed selfhood by way of equal access
to the love and forgiveness of a black-appropriated Christian God,
which therefore negated any notions that they were nonpersons as

whites would have them believe. Like the slave narratives, the spiritual narratives compelled a revisionary reading of the collective American experience. Thus, the slave and spiritual narratives, secular and religious self-stories intended largely for white audiences, offered profound second readings of the American and African American experiences against prevailing white American racial perspectives. These personal accounts, dozens in number, recount, expose, appeal, and remember the ordeals of blackness in white America.

The most well known slave stories are *Narrative of the Life of Frederick Douglass, an American Slave, Written by Himself* (1845), and *Incidents in the Life of a Slave Girl. Written by Herself* (1861), by Harriet Jacobs, and published originally under the name of Linda Brent. Both Douglass and Jacobs determined at an early age that the most important goal of their lives was to gain their freedom. To this end, both, overt rebels against the system, devoted their best efforts and eventually succeeded in liberating themselves from their much hated shackles.

Born Frederick Augustus Washington Bailey on a Maryland plantation in 1818, as a slave, Douglass experienced both the harshness of the system and its most benevolent face. However, under all circumstances he refused to compromise his belief that the only acceptable condition of life was in securing his right as an autonomous human being. In 1838, while living in Baltimore, he escaped the South and changed his name. A few days later, in New York City, Douglass married Anna Murray, the free African American woman who had helped him to engineer his escape. The Douglasses lived together for almost four decades. They had two sons and two daughters. Anna was vital to his career but remained in his shadow for all their years together. She died in Washington, D.C., in 1882.

Although as an abolitionist speaker Douglass traveled extensively in the northern United States and Europe for more than twenty years, New Bedford, Massachusetts, was home to him for most of the time until the abolition of slavery. With the encouragement of William Lloyd Garrison, a leading white abolitionist whom he impressed with his articulateness on slavery, Douglass took to the abolitionist stump in 1841. In the years following, he dazzled audiences with his oratorical expertise. In 1845, Douglass, who learned to read and write surreptitiously while in slavery, published his first-person account of slavery, *Narrative*, and in 1855 he brought out a second, *My Bond-age and My Freedom*. He published a third autobiography, *The Life and Times of Frederick Douglass*, in 1881. Douglass held several government appointments after the abolition of slavery, including that of Assistant Secretary of the Commission of Inquiry to Santo Domingo (1871) and United States Marshal for the District of Columbia (1877). He died of a heart attack in Washington in 1895.

*Narrative* was an instant success. More than 30,000 copies were sold in Europe and the United States in the first year after its publication (4500 in the first five months). The story delineates Douglass's firsthand knowledge of his parentage and early life, his struggles toward selfhood within the slave system, the consequences of his overt rebelliousness, one failed attempt at escape, and, finally, his success in achieving his life's goal. While the book is now a classic of African American literature, Andrews observes that, among its other qualities, readers and critics laud this narrative for its declaration of independence in the author's interpretation of his life, Douglass's claims to freedom through his text, and his literary and rhetorical sophistication. Although the second narrative is longer and more detailed, and is written by a more accomplished man of letters—a successful journalist and orator—in this text, as Andrews notes, Douglass turned to exploring his complex relationship with his environment in his search for a new group identity. Douglass biographer Dickson J. Preston (*Young Frederick Douglass: The Maryland Years* [1986]) estimates that for every person who has read either *My Bondage and My Freedom* or *Life and Times,* 300 have read *Narrative*. Both Andrews and Preston subscribe to Douglass's manipulation of the "facts" of his story to achieve greater advantage in audience interest. To this end, Andrews emphasizes Douglass's use of artifice—especially he credits the inventiveness of Douglass's rhetorical style. So successful are these strategies, Andrews concludes, that the imagined, fabricated, or deliberately exaggerated events in Douglass's story are of little significance in comparison to the literary and political effectiveness of the text, even if they remain matters for historians to continue to probe.

Harriet Ann Jacobs was a contemporary of Frederick Douglass's, and like Douglass's narrative, her *Incidents* challenged the institution of slavery. Born in Edenton, North Carolina, in 1813, she enjoyed a reasonably carefree early childhood, unlike Douglass, living with both of her parents and her brother, and having a loving grandmother nearby. This tranquillity was irreparably ruptured at age six when her mother died. But even then the conditions of her life changed only minimally. When she was twelve, however, the mistress who had treated her with kindness also died, and left her as a human legacy to her five-year-old niece. At that point Jacobs learned, to her great distress, that the bane of all slave women was their vulnerability to the sexual abuse of their masters. Soon after she moved into his household, her young mistress's father, a local doctor, began his sexual pursuit of her. The struggle between the two, what Jacobs describes as the "war of her life"—his determination to win her submission and her resolve never to become his victim—went on for many years, even after she escaped from the South in 1842.

In addition to depicting events in her childhood and the unwanted sexual attentions of her master, Jacobs's narrative details events of slave life in Edenton and surrounding communities; strategies she adopted to thwart the master's desire to conquer her; her deliberate decision to become the mother of two children by another white plantation owner and her escape from her master by hiding for seven years in a crawl space under the roof of her grandmother's house; her struggle to free her children; the existence of an antipatriarchal interracial community of women; her flight to freedom; and the events of her life in the North. While the whole narrative is an interesting and moving document, its most memorable passages focus on the sexual victimization of the slave woman and Jacobs's culminating analysis of the meaning of freedom.

Unlike Douglass, in her time Jacobs gained no fame for her story, perhaps because of the combination of its publication during the Civil War and the lesser attention women's narratives enjoyed than men's. *Incidents* rose to prominence in the late 1970s, in the wake of the rise of white and black feminism, and is now universally recognized as a text that is as important as Douglass's *Narrative*.

Straddling the slave narrative and nineteenth-century sentimental novel traditions, and mindful of the power of the "cult of True Womanhood," especially since the implied readers of her story were Northern white middle-class women, Jacobs scores a major achievement in her textual handling of the incidents surrounding her vulnerability to the sexual tyranny of her former master and her willing participation in a miscegenational relationship. A black woman slave and a fallen woman, she presumes to speak to the white women of the North, the upholders of "piety, purity, submissiveness and domesticity," through a rhetoric that invites them to join her in the struggle against the patriarchal domination of all women. *Incidents* was the first book by an African American woman in which the victim made her own plea against the sexual tyranny of her slave master, and as woman and slave Jacobs ably addresses the parallels between race and sex. Finally, in the culmination of her story, when, against her will, a white female friend purchases her freedom, Jacobs does an elegant feminist analysis of the meaning of freedom for women of color. She had insisted that, as a human being, she could not be bought or sold. Although she recognized the impulse of her friend to free her from further harassment by her then dead master's kin, she was offended and disappointed by the act of money changing hands for her.

Unlike Douglass's *Narrative,* the authenticity of *Incidents* was a subject of critical debate for a number of years. At least one historian initially claimed that while the central character may have been a fugitive from slavery, the narrative was probably false because the work was not credible. Much of the debate centered on the extent of the editorial role of white feminist Lydia Maria Child in its production (was this a fiction by Child?), the narrative's use of novelistic conventions like dialogue, and its literary sophistication. Years of research have now gone into locating the "facts" that prove that Harriet Jacobs was indeed a former slave from Edenton, that she was owned by a well-known physician of that town, and that she authored her own narrative.

However, two aspects of the narrative persist to make this a problematic text. One is Jacobs's use of the conventions of sentimental fiction, and the other, her pseudonym. While it is arguable that she used the first to create bridges with her white female readers—bridges that, for cultural reasons, it would have been impossible to build with traditional slave narrative conventions, the pseudonym, a purely literary device, is more difficult to explain. Even more confusing, I suggest, are the contradictions in the narrative's opening statement:

"Reader, be assured this narrative is no fiction . . . my adventures . . . are . . . strictly true. . . . [But] my descriptions fall short of the truth." Yet, like the pseudonym that protects the identity of the author by raising doubts regarding her authenticity, the statement is a camouflage that permits her more control over her narrative. With its novelistic techniques, its pseudonym, and the ambiguity in its declaration of contingent truth, *Incidents in the Life of a Slave Girl,* as effective a text as Douglass's *Narrative,* sits squarely on the frontier of fact and fiction.

The first Native American to publish anything in America was Samson Occom, a Methodist missionary to the Indians, whose *Sermon Preached at the Execution of Moses Paul* (1772) was also the first Indian best-seller. Before that, Occom went to England to raise money for the Indian Charity School in Hanover, New Hampshire, which later became Dartmouth College. Native American authors in the late eighteenth and nineteenth centuries wrote sermons, protest literature, and tribal histories based on oral traditions for similar reasons that former African slaves wrote their autobiographies.

Egocentric individualism was not an aspect of Native American cultures before Europeans arrived on these shores, and autobiography took a long time to develop among the native peoples. Although Native Americans valued personal freedom, self-worth, and personal responsibility, personal autonomy was secondary to the welfare of the group. Even in autobiography, Indian first-person narratives do not probe the nature of the self in the text. Also, since no Indian culture, prior to the European coming, developed a phonetic alphabet, writing did not exist for them as we know it in Western culture. Experts like Arnold Krupat note that tribal writings took the form of "patterns worked in wampum belts, tatoos, [and] pictographs painted on animal skins." Within their cultures, Native Americans constructed their identities not as individuals but as persons in relationship to collective social units of which each person was only a part.

The early Indian forms with the closest resemblances to Western autobiographical narratives were stories and accounts of dreams or mystic experiences. Communicated orally, these included the exploits of war and stories of family events told to assembled audiences of the tribes, among whom were some individuals other than the tellers likely to have been present during the events actually being told. Honors were won, not for the individual, but for the tribe.

In the Western tradition, written Native American autobiography was a nineteenth-century phenomenon and exists in two separate forms: Indian autobiographies that are collaborative efforts produced like the as-told-to slave narratives, with the Indian as the subject; and autobiographies by Indians, texts composed without the mediation of an editor or transcriber. The latter, of course, depended on the Indian's mastery of literacy. However, critics see both groups as bicultural texts that developed as a result of contact with a culture outside of the native one. Krupat tells us that each represents the subject's having sufficiently distanced her/himself from the native culture to be influenced by the "other," and in the case of autobiography written by Indians, to have gained the "other's" expertise to compose one's own story in a nonnative form.

Thus, written Indian autobiography comes out of the oral tradition in contact with Europeans. In Indian autobiography, oral narratives are committed to writing through separate processes: the ethnographic and the as-told-to stories. Both share oral origins and presume a non-Indian mediator, but the ethnographer, usually an anthropologist, collects materials for a different purpose than the editor of the as-told-to story. The first collects for the record—for information on customs, mores, practices, and rituals of special groups of people. The as-told-to editor, on the other hand, not only takes information for the record but also works with the subject to produce a full autobiographical narrative. The product of the collaboration is determined by the narrative skill of the subject and the editorial skills of the editor, especially those of literary techniques. Unlike the ethnographic record, in the as-told-to story it is expected that incidents are reordered especially for their telling and do not represent a mirror image of actual experience. Since imagination plays a vastly important role in the final story, the outcome resembles Western autobiography.

Within the constraints of the transformation of oral narratives to written autobiography, governing patterns within Indian narratives fall into three main categories: the captivity narrative of the early white settlers, the memoirs of Franklin, and the African American slave narrative. Indians converted to Christianity were strongly influenced by the captivity narratives with their penchant for a public declaration of faith, spiritual development, and endurance. The memoirs of Franklin, with their emphasis on historic content and public event, were attractive to Indian males but almost unobservable in female narratives. Women tend to turn to day-to-day activities in their life stories, recording family and personal life along with their roles in preserving the traditions of their people. From the slave narrative tradition, another branch of the Indian personal narrative focuses on those experiences in which the subject develops from within a group identity and tells stories otherwise unknown to white readers, but to whom they are directed. From such stories this audience gains insight into the individual as well as into the society of that individual. Indian autobiography, the product of direct bicultural interaction, and autobiographies by Indians, the product of socialization and influence by several streams of American cultures outside of the Indian experience, may very well represent the most profound example of the complexity of narrative at the junction of history and literature, fiction and autobiography.

Clearly, autobiographers of all groups—seventeenth- and eighteenth-century British settlers in the new colonies, black slaves in the nineteenth-century South, Native Americans forced to give up their cultures and to adopt the ways of white men, as well as the twentieth-century American heterogeneous migrants from across the globe—use techniques of fiction to place discernible patterns on their lives in writing. In autobiography, there is always a necessary relationship between the life of the subject and the life in the text, but the separations between fact and fiction are not always clear. Literature is less chaotic and infinitely more manageable than life and so imagination more than absolute historical truth grounds the autobiographical text. Undeniably, autobiography is a fictional form—a realization that need not diminish its social, historical, or literary value. For autobiography and fiction together provide complementary strategies for the art of writing the self.

Nellie McKay

# The Book Marketplace I

Between 1815 and 1860, Americans lived through a market revolution and saw the novel establish itself as the lucrative art form of middle-class civilization. Lines of force bound these two occurrences together, but the rates of change on both sides were uneven, and writers often had unstable and conflicting relations to the new social universe. Literary patterns, in works and in careers, did not materialize simply as an homologous reinscription of the cultural dominant, in this case the solidifying of market capitalism. Such resemblances certainly existed, and they illuminate the common contours of literature and society. But the novel's flowering represented a multivalent negotiation, involving dissent as well as agreement, with an ideological ascendancy that was itself far from monolithic. Gender complicated integration into historical change and set male and female authors on dissimilar trajectories of development. Women novelists, culturally identified with domesticity, produced functional narratives that evoked an older understanding of the literary, but they far outsold their more experimental male rivals and were paradoxically freed by their prescribed gender roles to accept commercial popularity. The men conceived of themselves as professionals and bequeathed a definition of the aesthetic as the antithesis both of exchange value and of the best-selling women. Male novelists ultimately found acceptance in a space that was neither the market nor the not-market, in the regulated economy of the academy.

A famous quotation and an obscure location: two coordinates

from which to map an economics of the antebellum novel. The quotation comes from Adam Smith's *Wealth of Nations,* a book published in the same year as the Declaration of Independence, and occurs in the midst of remarks about the legal and medical professions. Lawyers and physicians, says Smith, enjoy a respectability and decency of recompense altogether foreign to "that unprosperous race of men commonly called men of letters."

The site, an imaginary one, appears in George Lippard's *The Quaker City; or, The Monks of Monk Hall,* a Gothic thriller issued in ten pamphletlike installments in 1845, almost exactly seventy years after Smith's bible of free-market capitalism. Lippard is describing the setting of Monk Hall, a mansion originally erected on the outskirts of Philadelphia by "a wealthy foreigner, sometime previous to the Revolution," and long since overtaken in its isolation by the expanding metropolis. The ancient building now stands on a narrow street, "with a printing shop on one side and a stereotype foundry on the other," while rows of stores, offices, factories, and tenements stretch brokenly into the distance.

A cultural upheaval separates Smith's "unprosperous race of men" from Lippard's paperbound best-seller, with its image of a sensationalized house of fiction surrounded by the indices of technological and social change. Smith's phrasing accurately defines the state of authorship and literature in the early Republic. Indeed, his inclusion of writers in the same passage with lawyers and doctors indicates the extent to which the literary culture of Great Britain, however unremunerative, was in advance of that of the United States. The American novelist may have followed a profession, but it wasn't composing fiction: earning a livelihood from literature was an impossibility in this country until the 1820s. Only two novelists in the half-century before Irving and Cooper even aspired to professional status. The rest were men and women for whom novel writing remained, by choice and by necessity, a diversion, an amateur activity carried out in moments stolen from regular duties as jurists, clergymen, or educators. The two exceptions, Susanna Rowson and Charles Brockden Brown, labored valiantly to make letters self-supporting but could not overcome the economic and cultural obstacles. Brown, who was eventually forced by poverty to join his family's import business, found novels so unprofitable that he not only stopped writing them but sought to repudiate his efforts in the genre, while Rowson had to turn to schoolteaching and textbooks to supplement the meager rewards of fiction.

Numerous reasons can be and have been adduced to account for these failures. Lippard, who dedicated *The Quaker City* to Brown as his great forerunner in fiction of the metropolis, identifies one impediment when he suggests that culture was the property of "wealthy foreigners." Inhabitants of the new nation, accustomed to associate art with Europe and with aristocratic patronage, looked abroad for their reading matter: over three-quarters of the books published in the United States before the 1820s were of English origin. The copyright law adopted by Congress in 1790 denied protection to these works in an ill-conceived attempt to aid native letters. The paradoxical result of the law was that American printers naturally preferred to pirate foreign novels than to gamble on American ones, whose authors would have to be compensated. The few American works of fiction that made it into print—barely ninety between 1789 and 1820, or an average of just three a year—stood little chance of posting a profit. Books were costly to produce and often priced beyond the means of ordinary readers. Publishing was localized and distribution hampered by the lack of adequate transportation. And Americans, according to contemporaries, faced too many pressing tasks to turn their attention to literature. Building a nation, settling the wilderness, and acquiring a competence all took priority over cultivating the arts. Nor was republican ideology, the dominant creed of the Revolutionary era, nurturant of fiction. Its subordination of personal interest to the community placed it at odds with the novel's focus on the appetitive subject. Brown's titles point to the dissonance: his six novels are named for individuals. He summed up the plight of the early fiction writer: "Book-making . . . is the dullest of all trades, and the utmost that any American can look for, in his native country, is to be re-imbursed for his unavoidable expenses."

Brown's words were prophetic in one respect: he spoke of literature not as a pastime but as a trade. Over the next fifty years, as the United States transformed itself into a market society, writing and publishing assumed the character of a business. The parallel development was anything but fortuitous: Adam Smith's economics harbored the corrective to his own, and Brown's, negative assessment of the writer's plight. An agricultural people lacking a cultivated class of aristocrats could not have a thriving literary culture, nor the prospect of professional authorship, without an exponential increase in the "wealth of the nation." The War of 1812 set in motion an economic "takeoff" that shifted into high gear in the 1840s and 1850s, the decades not just of Nathaniel Hawthorne and Herman Melville but of Lippard, Harriet Beecher Stowe, and Susan Warner. Some changes—for example, the modernizing of production and distribution—were primarily material, but deeper structural affinities tied together the growth of commerce and industry and the maturation of the literary calling. Not only did the marketplace create the requisite conditions for art, it shaped the capacity for reception and determined, or rather produced, the novel's dominance of American literature. But the commercial order's power, though immense, was never total. The narrative of how the American novel became a commodity, of how we get from Brown's *Wieland* (1797) to *The Quaker City*, is a story both of the artist's implication in the marketplace and of his or her resistance to its values.

Technological advances and unprecedented population growth laid the foundations for a national market for printed material. The mechanization of printing and improvements in papermaking and binding meant that books could be manufactured in greater volume and more cheaply than ever before. (Lippard, in his description of Monk Hall, singles out the recent technology of the stereotype, an inexpensive duplicate plate, introduced in 1813, that permitted multiple copies of a work to be printed simultaneously.) Canals, turnpikes, and railroads facilitated interchange between distant geographic regions and diminished the obstacles to distribution. The flood of immigrants and the high native birthrate combined to double population every twenty-five years and to ensure a huge potential audience for books. Thanks to the common school system, the United States at mid-century claimed the largest literate public in history, with about 90 percent of the adult whites able to read and write (the figure was slightly higher for males than for females).

Economic arrangements had an instrumental role in turning these once abstemious men and women into devourers of fiction. As the subsistence orientation of the past yielded to commercial and then industrial production, Americans as a people grew more affluent and had more disposable income to spend on entertainment. The divorce between home and work brought about by the rise of offices and factories particularly favored the consumption of light literature (that is, novels as opposed to history, politics, or theology). Middle-class women, who had traditionally gravitated to fiction because of its attention to female concerns (as in the seduction and courtship novels of the eighteenth century), were no longer involved in household manufacture and enjoyed more free time in which to read. The domestic sphere became identified with relaxation and culture; libraries entered middle-class residences; and men of all classes began to bring home newspapers and periodicals, which regularly serialized works of fiction or published entire novels as low-priced supplements.

Changes in ideology and the organization of social life further contributed to the triumph of the novel. The entrenchment of market capitalism was accompanied by an altered perception of the relationship between the self and the community. Republicanism, with its privileging of the common good, yielded to liberalism, which elevates the particular person and maintains, in the version developed by Adam Smith, that the general welfare is enhanced by the pursuit of private interest. This inversion of priorities meshes with the novel's historic emphasis on the individual. The clarifying of boundaries between residence and outer world also lessened the sway of communalism. The public realm—magistrates, clergy, and the like—had once exercised authority over family matters. (Hawthorne fictionalizes this older habit of public supervision in *The Scarlet Letter* [1850], where the Puritan magistrates regard it as their duty to oversee Hester's upbringing of Pearl.) As the family and the larger social order drew apart, the home emerged as the enclave of privacy and interiority. The public sphere appeared increasingly remote from personal life and hence from the concerns of art. The American novel largely ceased to take interest in public affairs, or rather took interest in them, as in the case of *Uncle Tom's Cabin* (1852), by personalizing political issues and seeking to read them under the sign of the home. There is no antebellum *Modern Chivalry* (1792–1815), Hugh Henry Brackenridge's multivolume satire of civic foibles. Nor is there anything comparable to *A History of New York* (1809), Washington Irving's comic masterpiece that deflates the public realm in laughter.

There are, however, many fictions that replicate the split between household and labor—or, to phrase it somewhat differently, that sort themselves along the gender lines beginning to prevail in the society as a whole. Antebellum literary culture bifurcates into the novel of female domesticity and the novel of masculine adventure and camaraderie. As long ago as 1923, in his *Studies in Classic American Literature,* D. H. Lawrence noticed the pattern of male bonding on the margins that has since been taken as constitutive of the romance genre. The convention should be seen not so much as a flight from social existence as the refraction of an experience that growing numbers of American men were undergoing by mid-century, as they left their families on a daily basis to work alongside other men in banks, commercial enterprises, and factories. The male novel is noteworthy not merely for its distancing from the domestic zone but also for its immersion in the details and lexicon of work. Melville's fictions are among the most memorable on this score, from the early *Redburn* (1849) and *White-Jacket* (1850), through *Moby-Dick* (1851), to the ironic reversal of "Bartleby, the Scrivener" (1853), where the eponymous protagonist's singularity consists precisely in his refusal to do his job.

Masculine novels help to create the work patterns of modern society. As James Fenimore Cooper among others understood, printed literature erodes traditional economic structures (such as the apprenticeship system) by preserving and circulating information that was once hoarded by craftsmen and passed on selectively from older men, often fathers, to younger ones. In *The Last of the Mohicans* (1826), the legendary woodsman Natty Bumppo harangues against the "black marks" on the page for their power to undermine respect for the wisdom of age. Like mechanized production, male fictions render the father/master obsolete in that they teem with technological information and can double as how-to manuals. They construct the unconnected individuals they depict. Popular books of the era offer instruction in the secret of surviving the wilderness (Cooper, William Gilmore Simms, Robert Montgomery Bird's *Nick of the Woods* [1837]); the mysterious metropolis (Lippard, Poe's detective stories featuring C. Auguste Dupin, George Thompson's *New-York Life* [1849]); or at sea (Melville, Cooper's nautical novels, Poe's *Narrative of A. Gordon Pym* [1837–38]).

Nineteenth-century sentimental novels eschew the depiction of male labor but expatiate lovingly on the work carried out in the home. This emphasis divides sentimental fiction from the seduction tales popular a generation earlier, before the separation of spheres gave domestic life its feminized coloring. Neither Rowson's *Charlotte Temple* (1794), the early Republic's best-selling novel, nor Hannah Foster's *The Coquette* (1797), which did nearly as well, shows the heroine doing chores around the house. These were not activities eighteenth-century women saw as defining their nature. The best-sellers of the pre–Civil War era tell a different story, and the chapters in *Uncle Tom's Cabin* that memorialize Rachel Halliday's homemaking skills are exemplary of the change. In Warner's *The Wide, Wide World* (1850), the heroine Ellen Montgomery has to master her aversion to housework to prove her mastery over herself. But mostly what Ellen does is to read books and write. The activity of authorship is one commercial enterprise that, being performed in the middle-class home, turns up time and again in novels both by women and by men. Melville's Pierre Glendinning and Fanny Fern's Ruth Hall meet on this terrain if nowhere else.

Of course the gendering of fictional subgenres always admitted of exceptions, just as the barrier between the home and the economic arena was never impermeable. Domestic fictions were composed by men and adventure narratives by women. Ann Stephens wrote the first volume published in the Beadle series of "dime novels," lurid tales of bloodshed that actually sold for as little as a nickel. And Hawthorne's books incorporate elements from both genres. The pages in *The House of the Seven Gables* (1851) describing Phoebe's facility at cooking, cleaning, and gardening rival anything in women's literature for sentimental effusion.

Rationalization of the book trade was fundamental to the novel's discursive preeminence. Publishers moved swiftly to take advantage of the changed environment—or rather, the category of the "publisher" in the modern sense came into existence as venturesome persons seized the opportunity for profits. In the eighteenth century, the writer had arranged the manufacturing of his or her works and paid the printer or bookseller a commission to distribute them. Over half the country's fiction had originated in relatively small communities like Poughkeepsie, New York, or Windsor, Vermont, and had come from local printers who published notices and newspapers as well as books. By the 1850s, the proportion of local imprints had declined to under 10 percent. Centralization replaced dispersal as large and well-capitalized firms arose in the rapidly growing northeastern cities of New York, Philadelphia, and Boston. Harper Bros., Putnam's, and other publisher-entrepreneurs specializing in books now monopolized the production of fiction. These concerns relieved authors of the risks of publication (while also reducing the author's share of the possible profits) and asserted total control over the business end of literature. They took charge of all commercial responsibilities, from buying paper and overseeing printing to merchandizing the finished product.

The new houses, backed by the financial resources to promote and disseminate their wares, inaugurated the mass marketing of written culture. They made literary works generally available and affordable and dispelled the aristocratic aura of books by turning out inexpensive series under the title of "libraries." Two classics of the American Renaissance appeared in Wiley and Putnam's Library of American Books: Poe's *Tales* (1845), which sold for 50 cents, and a two-volume, paper-covered edition of Hawthorne's *Mosses from an Old Manse* (1846), priced at $1.00 the set. Fifty years earlier, when wages were far lower, American novels had sold for about twice as much. Advertising emerged as an integral part of the literary scene, an essential tool for informing far-flung consumers about the latest publication and stimulating interest in buying. Promotional campaigns included announcements in newspapers, excerpts and blurbs in magazines, posters in bookstores, lecture tours, and inflated reports of sales figures (on the reasonable assumption that people will want to read a book liked by other people). Brown had tried to generate publicity by sending a copy of *Wieland* to Thomas Jefferson with a covering letter asking the third President for a plug. (Jefferson ignored him.) Antebellum publishers eliminated the element of chance and routinized the practice of "puffing," or planting favorable reviews and notices by writers who were often in the publisher's employ.

Under the market regime, works by Americans shed their reputation as money losers. Publishers welcomed home-grown manuscripts because they knew that a successful book could sell more than enough copies to recoup the cost of royalties. The output of native novels surged accordingly, as writers, publishers, and booksellers scrambled to keep pace with demand. One hundred twenty-eight fictions by Americans appeared in the 1820s, or forty more than in the first three decades of the nation's existence. The number tripled in the 1830s, and then jumped again in the 1840s to eight hundred—almost thirty times the yearly average of the early Republic. Buyers snapped up the most popular of these works in quantities that kept rising until the figures peaked in the forties and fifties. *The Last of the Mohicans* qualified as a best-seller in 1826 with 5750 copies in circulation. *The Quaker City,* in contrast, sold 60,000 copies in 1845 and 30,000 in each of the next five years; the total of over 200,000 made Lippard's exposé the best-selling American novel before *Uncle Tom's Cabin.* Stowe's antislavery saga outdid that aggregate in the single year of 1852, and thereafter sales escalated; estimates of total copies purchased before the Civil War range as high as five million. While Stowe's figures were exceptional, other domestic novelists conquered the reading public too, with Fanny Fern's *Ruth Hall* (1855) logging sales of 55,000 and Maria Cummins's *The Lamplighter* (1854) exceeding 40,000 within eight weeks.

The South did not participate in these statistical marvels. The fate of literature below the Mason-Dixon line inverted the experience of the North, as if to underline the close connection between free-market capitalism and the flourishing of native fiction. Thomas Jefferson, the country's leading eighteenth-century man of letters, was a Virginian who practiced authorship as a gentlemanly avocation. In the nineteenth century, as the rest of the nation modernized, an anachronistic understanding of the arts as nonprofessional persisted in the South to the detriment of the area's culture. The South lost its literary luster and didn't regain comparable distinction until the novels of William Faulkner. The problem, of course, was slavery: its expansion committed the region to an agrarian economy, retarded the growth of industry and cities, and had the inevitable consequence of devaluing all forms of labor. The South failed to nourish literature, said the North Carolinian abolitionist Hinton Helper, because it lacked a modern system of production. Its authors "have their books printed on Northern paper, with Northern types, by Northern artizans, stitched, bound, and made ready for the market by Northern industry" — and, added Helper, the books found the vast majority of their readers in the North.

Literary supremacy decamped for the bustling commercial centers the South never had. The area's major fiction writer, Edgar Allan Poe, served a stint in Richmond as a magazine editor before fleeing for the more congenial cultural climes of Philadelphia and New York. The most prolific novelist, William Gilmore Simms, was dubbed the "Southern Cooper" but never attracted a large enough Southern readership to approach Cooper's financial independence. Although he chronicled regional history and mores, Simms remained dependent on Northern royalties and lecture tours. The principal outlet for the Southwestern humorists was a periodical edited and published in New York by William T. Porter, *The Spirit of the Times*. And the major Southern novel written before the Civil War, *Uncle Tom's Cabin,* was the work of a Northern woman and bore the imprint of a Boston publisher.

The African American novelist struggled under far greater disadvantages than the Southerner. Nearly all African Americans were in bondage, and those who gained or were born into freedom had little access to education. A minute pool of possible authors faced an audience problem unknown to whites. Free African Americans numbered barely a quarter million, or about 2 percent of the North's population in 1860, and few among these despised and impoverished people had sufficient leisure time or money to expend on novels. A readership of sympathetic whites failed to materialize. So formidable were the hindrances that just four novels by African Americans reached print before the Civil War. Only Harriet E. Wilson's *Our Nig; or, Sketches from the Life of a Free Black* (1859) was published in book form in the antebellum United States. Martin Delany's *Blake; or, The Huts of America* (1859–62) appeared serially in two African American periodicals but had to wait until the 1960s to achieve publication on its own. The other novels, William Wells Brown's *Clotel; or, The President's Daughter* (1853) and Frank J. Webb's *The Garies and Their Friends* (1857), were issued in London with British imprints.

Unlike the typical slave narrative, which appeared under white (abolitionist) sponsorship and was introduced by white testimony to its authenticity, these novels make few concessions to the sensibilities of white readers. *The Garies and Their Friends* details the racial hypocrisy of Northerners; *Blake* advocates African American separatism and refers to whites as "devils"; and *Clotel* broaches the scandal of Thomas Jefferson, author of the Declaration of Independence and rumored father of two mulatto daughters who are sold into slavery during the narrative. *Our Nig,* easily the strongest of the novels, refuses to honor the conventions of African American publication. Wilson consigns white testimonials to the back of the book and excoriates abolitionists "who didn't want slaves at the South, nor niggers in their own houses, North." Her novel received not a single American review and didn't sell enough copies to keep its author from the almshouse.

Such works make abundantly clear how stifling the antebellum marketplace could be to unwelcome ideas and unpopular voices. White buyers needed to be conciliated before they would agree to patronize African American artists. In *Our Nig* Wilson thematizes the prohibition against African American self-advocacy: the efforts of her protagonist Frado to make herself heard are repeatedly frustrated by whites, who find her words too discomforting to listen to and try to muzzle her. Frado has her mouth stuffed with a towel and a block of wood; her mistress, Mrs. Bellmont, threatens to cut out her tongue to prevent her from "tale-bearing." Written from the perspective of a mulatto servant, *Our Nig* paints a relentlessly bleak picture of race and class relations in the North. The book flaunts its unsalability by debunking the middle-class domestic scene that Stowe and other female abolitionists mobilized against slavery. The family for Wilson is not a stronghold of emancipatory affect; it is a plantation or factory where Nig suffers brutal mistreatment from other women. No other antebellum novel by a woman, white or African American, places itself so far outside the expectations of the feminine reading public.

Although white authors had a much easier time of it, not all of them, even in the North, fared well now that literature was a trade. In general, one can divide the novelists of the 1840s and 1850s into three groupings: the small circle of men who over the course of the next hundred years came to constitute the canon of national literature; the domestic or sentimental women; and the quasi journalists like Lippard, most of them male, whose narratives of urban violence and sexual titillation shaped a sensationalized popular culture. These three groupings constituted the first generation of Americans able to view storytelling realistically as a career, a vocation that promised a decent livelihood and held out the prospect, for the lucky few, of real wealth. Least is known about the purveyors of sensationalism. Their paper-covered pamphlet novels, hawked on street corners or sold through the mails (until the U.S. Post Office withdrew their permits to ship at inexpensive newspaper rates), proved both popular and highly ephemeral.

Our concern here lies with the canonical and domestic writers, the major artists of the period and figures who often seemed to occupy antipodal cultural spheres. Rivals for the respectable, middle-class audience, they differed in subject matter, popular appeal, and understanding of the literary calling. Yet a series of paradoxes and inversions joined them and pointed to a broader area of agreement. In varying degrees, each school internalized but also set itself against the social and economic universe identified with Adam Smith. Although the women enjoyed immense commercial success and frankly viewed their writing as a lucrative form of employment, American culture— and they themselves—defined womanhood as the antithesis of acquisitiveness. They retained traditional ideas of the novel as committed to service; for most of them, the self-expressive dimension of art was subsidiary to the doing of good. The men, on the other hand, sold modestly or poorly in their lifetimes and felt estranged from the market, yet they forged an individualized conception of literature as "high" art, as a separate realm analogous to the newly theorized category of the economic.

Washington Irving and James Fenimore Cooper, fiction writers who came of age in the 1820s, prefigured the allegiances and contradictions of their canonical successors. Of the important male artists active in the mid-nineteenth century, only these two were born in the previous century and attained adulthood before the War of 1812. Performing a complex dance of equivocation, they advanced into the commercialized future while preserving essential characteristics from the preprofessional, foreign-dominated past. The two men were regarded in their own time as imitators of British models: Cooper as the American Scott, Irving as the American Lamb. Irving's international hit, *The Sketch Book of Geoffrey Crayon, Gent.* (1819–20), is suffused with Anglophilia and announces its superiority to the market in its title. Throughout his career, Irving maintained a public image of himself as a gentleman of letters, not a professional; he was forever seeking sinecures in government and cultivating the patronage of great men. Cooper's more abrasive personality ruled out supplication, but he too had an air of being above commercial considerations. His maiden foray into literature, *Precaution* (1820), apes English courtship novels and exudes a reverence for the aristocracy that persists throughout his American works, eventually to reach a pinnacle of shrillness in his last fiction, *The Ways of the Hour* (1850). Cooper's quarrels with publishers and reviewers, and his growing disdain for American democracy, hurt his sales and amounted to a declaration of independence from the reading public.

In spite of their reluctance, these two pioneers gave American fiction respectability and put it on a profitable footing. Irving and Cooper exemplified the man of letters as a man of business, their very aloofness from materialism endowing their works with an aura of highly marketable exclusivity. Gentlemanly aversion to exchange underwrote their appeal to a readership eager to acquire literary culture. Both men turned to writing careers after their families suffered financial embarrassment in the Depression of 1819. Both capitalized on the improved conditions of the 1820s to convert literature into an instrument of economic mobility. Cooper's Americanization of the historical romance in *The Spy* (1821) and *The Pioneers* (1822) took the country by storm, and his keen grasp of his audience's desires made him the Republic's first true professional author, popular enough, at least for a time, to live comfortably on his literary earnings. Irving excelled at recycling his successes: *Bracebridge Hall* (1822) was dubbed his "English *Sketch Book*," *The Alhambra* (1832) his "Spanish *Sketch Book*." But it was the retailing of the original *Sketch Book* that first demonstrated his formidable commercial sense. The collection was issued serially in seven pamphlets and sold for the astronomical figure of $5.37½ the set. Five thousand Americans, according to William Charvat, paid the price, and Irving netted close to $10,000 before the sketches appeared as a separate book.

Irving and Cooper made vital if fitful contributions to the reconfiguring of literature as "a world elsewhere." Irving's *History of New*

*York* struck a blow against the cultural prestige of history writing, a genre esteemed by Americans for its pedagogic authority. In *The Sketch Book,* he portrays the artist as a dreamy idler, someone whose power to entertain has nothing to do with usefulness. Cooper, after making obeisances to patriotism in *The Spy,* claimed to have written *The Pioneers* "exclusively to please myself." The book's exquisite descriptions of natural scenery suggest an ambition to craft a self-sufficient "art" novel, although this aspiration has to contend against Cooper's usual wish to lecture his readers. Neither author proved consistent in absolving his work from "some definite moral purpose" (a phrase Hawthorne uses ironically in the preface to *The House of the Seven Gables*). Irving reverted to writing the kinds of histories he once mocked, while Cooper's didactic impulses, except in the Leatherstocking tales (and sometimes there too), almost invariably got the better of his artistic judgment.

The sporadic suspension of extrinsic purpose in Irving and Cooper not only marked them off from contemporaneous women novelists like Catharine Maria Sedgwick and Lydia Maria Child; it also declared their difference from an earlier cultural formation. In the eighteenth century, American novels had marched under the banner of social utility. They had not fully differentiated themselves from functional discourses such as sermons and patriotic histories. Something like a "moral economy," in which the corporate welfare took precedence over personal interests, had prevailed in cultural life much as it had in material affairs. The nineteenth century saw the gradual eclipsing of this definition of the aesthetic. Relative indifference to the moral or instructional obligation of fiction, an attitude appearing in embryo in the post-Revolutionary period, became a hallmark—perhaps even the distinguishing quality—of the imaginative writing that was subsequently judged canonical.

Literature's ostensible autonomy—its relatively recent status, that is, as a discrete discourse, governed by its own rules and values and emancipated from extraliterary functions—may appear to distance the artwork from a money-oriented social order; and, as I shall argue later, such an ideal did express genuine disaffection from the commercial spirit. But the disembedding of the literary was also part of a larger social trend toward specialization and individuation. The adherents of free-market thought interpreted the economic as a zone apart from morality, theology, and government. Although autonomous art was in advance of mid-century economic practice, fiction's casting free from didacticism reproduced as cultural agenda the same structural imperative that informed liberal individualism. Art now presented itself as a circumscribed terrain analogous to the scene of commerce and no less secure from intrusions by church and state (or piety and politics). The new aesthetic ideology's privileging of disinterestedness bespoke not transhistorical "purity" but rather rootedness in a modernizing capitalist society and affiliation with Adam Smith's increasingly influential defense of the market as a self-regulating sphere that should be "let alone."

Domestic fiction, on the other hand, affirmed connectedness over autonomy. Sentimental discourse retained a pedagogic responsibility that harmonized with the nineteenth-century perception of women as moral guardians. The "cult of true womanhood" venerated selfless, nurturant beings who found fulfillment in serving others. Confined to the home, spared the compromises and pressures of the public world, women were thought to possess a purity and spirituality that ideally suited them for their tasks as wives and mothers. Fiction writing, like nursing or teaching the very young, was an acceptable activity so long as it conformed to the conventional female role. Woman's charge was to edify and improve her audience, only secondarily to strive for the perfection of art. This didactic strain linked literary domesticity to the republican past. Sentimental novels, though avidly consumed by antebellum readers, were residual in their entanglement with moral purpose and their loyalty to the communitarian emphases of the early Republic.

Although they too oscillated in their adjustments to the marketplace, Poe, Hawthorne, and Melville broke far more decisively than Irving and Cooper with the previous cultural configuration. The three major fiction writers of the antebellum canon raised native letters to a par with foreign models. No one seriously thought of Melville as the American Marryat, and Hawthorne and Poe reversed the transatlantic flow of influence, Hawthorne impressing George Eliot among others, and Poe inspiring a long line of French poets beginning with Charles Baudelaire. Poe considered himself a consummate professional: he devoted all his energies to literature and never held a job other than as a writer, editor, lecturer, or free-lance journalist.

Melville, who came from a patrician family fallen on hard times (as did Poe and Hawthorne), looked to the novel as a way of regaining affluence and social position. He could be extremely calculating in his dealings with the reading public, deleting anticlerical passages from *Typee,* for example, in order to avoid offending popular taste. At times Melville spoke of the commodity status of his books with a candor and absence of illusion more often found among the domestic and sensational writers. He described *Redburn* and *White-Jacket* as "two *jobs,* which I have done for money—being forced to it, as other men are to sawing wood."

Hawthorne, more than any other author of the period, came to personify American literature's maturation. He was a direct benefi- ciary of the commercializing of publishing: the shrewd Boston editor- publisher, James T. Fields, persuaded him to expand a long manu- script tale of adultery among the Puritans into a full-length novel. Hawthorne had endured years of obscure and ill-paid story writing, and Fields signed up *The Scarlet Letter* with a promise of an initial printing of 2500 copies and a royalty of 15 percent. The publisher's network of friendly reviewers acclaimed the book, a second edition was needed within days, and Hawthorne had his first (modest) com- mercial success. Prodded by Fields, who urged him to capitalize on his sudden popularity, Hawthorne embarked on a flurry of activity such as he never again approached. He revised and reissued several collections of tales, wrote two books of mythology for children, and completed two more full-length novels, all in the space of three years. He never quite duplicated his earlier success, but Fields's tireless ad- vocacy of his canonization eventually elevated the novelist to the rank of "classic" author, the leading exhibit in the newly erected national pantheon.

But sales during one's lifetime matter to a writer too, as much or more than posthumous recognition, and in this area Poe, Hawthorne, and Melville all suffered repeated disappointments. Poe's literary pro- fessionalism vied with his aristocratic disdain for the common reader, and his occasional dream of suiting "at once the popular and the critical taste" fell dismally short of realization. For the metaphysical treatise *Eureka* (1848), the book he regarded as the culmination of his life's work, he predicted that a first printing of 50,000 would be necessary; an indifferent public slowly purchased 750 copies. A year after this fiasco, Poe died impoverished in a Baltimore hospital, as if driven to actualize the (partial) self-portrait he cultivated—in tales, poems, and poses for daguerreotypes—as haunted, antibourgeois artist. Hawthorne, less histrionic in his patrician reserve, was more ill-at-ease with the exactions of the market. Having begun his career by publishing anonymously, he remained tormented by the violations of privacy demanded by fame. He simply could not sustain his commercial viability and kept trying to flee dependence on the reading public for the greater security of government patronage. (In this, he resembled Washington Irving.) Though he was dismissed from the Salem Custom House, the strategy ultimately paid off: his appointment as consul at Liverpool—a reward for writing the campaign biography of his friend Franklin Pierce—brought Hawthorne more money than all his works of fiction combined.

Melville engaged in a lengthy quarrel with the marketplace that he finally resolved, much like Hawthorne, only by removing himself from its domain. In 1866, while still in his forties, he took a position in the New York Custom House (ironic refuge from trade!) and never again wrote fiction for a living. This was a fate Melville provoked as well as had thrust upon him. In a famous series of letters to Hawthorne, he declared his unwillingness to accommodate his talent to the popular taste. "What I feel most moved to write," he told the older novelist, "that is banned—it will not sell. Yet, altogether, write the *other* way I cannot." Melville's books, early and late, bristle with mistrust of, not to say belligerence toward, the middle-class reader; resentment breaks out into rage in the semiautobiographical *Pierre* (1852), where the narrator rails against the public, and the protagonist, a writer, commits murder and incest. In his disaffection, Melville echoed his frustrated predecessor, Charles Brockden Brown. He complained in 1851:

This country . . . [is] governed by sturdy backswoodsmen—noble fellows enough, but not at all literary, and who care not a fig for any authors except those who write those most saleable of all books nowadays—i.e.—the newspapers, and magazines.

Other male novelists blamed their misfortunes on their female competitors. In a now notorious outburst, Hawthorne vented his spleen at the "scribbling women" whose books sold by the hundred thousand and drove more deserving literature (he meant his own) from the market. Canonical writers regularly depict intellectual women as unnatural and textualize the wish to vanquish them, either by silencing or verbal usurpation. A conspicuous case of fantasy fulfillment occurs at the outset of *The Scarlet Letter,* when Hester Prynne, plainly a type of the female artist, stands in the Boston marketplace and vows never to speak in public. In *The Blithedale Romance* (1852) Hawthorne stills Zenobia's voice more ruthlessly by drowning her; Priscilla's utterances require no such violence because her public performances are orchestrated by a man. Poe's Ligeia, a woman so erudite that the male narrator abases himself before her "infinite supremacy," expires mysteriously and then returns from the dead with a bandage wound about her mouth. One woman who repaid these hostile gestures with disparagements of male narcissism was Fanny Fern, sister of the critic N. P. Willis and an author whose pugnacious spirit won over even Hawthorne. In her *roman à clef, Ruth Hall,* Fern caricatures her brother as a self-regarding poseur whose own works are ghostwritten. Willis is said to resent his sister's success because he "wants to be the only genius in the family."

Fern's novel tells the story of a woman writer who unabashedly regards literature as a trade and sets out, with single-minded determination, to win its financial prizes. The contrast to Melville's portrayal of the artist in *Pierre* could not be more pronounced. Melville's hero, who has been dispossessed of his inheritance, embarks on a literary career ostensibly to support his "family," but, more important, he writes in order to express profound truths about society and man. He loathes commercialism, composes a work far too radical for his publishers, and, thoroughly alienated from his dreams of literary greatness, ends up as a suicide. Fern's text reorders Melville's priorities. After Ruth Hall's husband dies, leaving her penniless, and she has to send a daughter to live with relatives, she decides to try her hand at authorship. She writes to make money so that she can restore her family, and she exults in the "market-value" of her sketches because the demand for them enables her to enter the "port of Independence." Ruth wants her pieces to affect and inspire others, but she thinks of herself above all as "a regular business woman" whose writings secure the wherewithal to cover "shoeless feet" and buy "a little medicine, or a warmer shawl."

Pierre of course was atypical in his extremism, but Fern's version of the female author was representative: most sentimental novelists turned to literature for quite practical reasons and adopted a businesslike attitude toward writing. As Nina Baym puts it in her study of the women, they "conceptualized authorship as a profession rather than a calling, as work and not art." This overstates the case in that it elides the ambivalence many literary domestics felt about appearing in public or even signing their names to their books. Fern's heroine hides behind the androgynous pseudonym of "Floy," and she says that no woman can publicly defend herself from unfair reviews without doing "violence to her womanly nature." But the women seem to have experienced little of the alienation from their audience that beset the men. They saw their role as satisfying their readers' expectations and were largely untroubled by the contradiction, so bitter to Melville, between artistic urges and popular acceptance. Need to provide for one's family justified commercialism. "I am compelled to turn my brains to gold and to sell them to the highest bidder," said Caroline Lee Hentz, author of several best-sellers including *Linda* (1850). Hentz had no hesitation about carrying out such alchemy after her husband was incapacitated by illness. Stowe and Warner became entrepreneurs of the pen because of similar circumstances: the real or imaginary invalidism of Stowe's husband, and the worsening economic situation of Warner's father, who had a history of bad investments. Authorship, it should be remembered, was one of the few professions open to middle-class women in the antebellum period. Little wonder that so many embraced the literary marketplace: it offered prestige, good money, and unmatched range of influence, rewards far beyond those afforded by needlework and schoolteaching.

But aiming for, and achieving, material success did not produce liberal individualists. Commercial groundbreakers, the women remained troubled by conflicts over commercialism peculiar to their gender. Women were supposed to preserve their purity by refraining from the struggles of the marketplace, and Ruth Hall, for all her business acumen, turns over the management of her affairs to the editor John Walter, a gentleman-protector who addresses her fraternally as "Sister Ruth." What Hall did in fiction, Catharine Maria Sedgwick did in fact: she let her brothers handle all negotiations with her publishers. "Our men are sufficiently moneymaking," asserted Sarah Hale, novelist and influential editor of *Godey's Lady's Book*. "Let us keep our women and children from the contagion as long as possible." Legal statute seconded popular thought in quarantining women, especially married women, from financial matters. Harriet Beecher Stowe's husband Calvin signed the royalty agreement for *Uncle Tom's Cabin* because married women couldn't sign contracts and didn't possess control over their earnings. Stowe was one of several female novelists who felt uneasy about the time and energy demanded by authorship. That composing fiction took place in the home merely exacerbated the distress such activity could cause. Wasn't the home the place where one cared for one's husband and children, and didn't the work in progress steal time from more urgent duties?

Carrying the requirement to be useful into the novel, women writers rejected the commercial age's tendency toward categorical differentiation and affirmation of the self. Stowe, who had no peer in either sales or profits, disavowed the authorship of *Uncle Tom's Cabin*, protesting on numerous occasions, "I did not write that book," and "the story made itself." Other women took more credit for their accomplishments, but the instinct to repress personal goals and deny unique capabilities was widely shared. All appealed to higher purposes, whether responsibility to humanity or service to God. The pleasure of exercising one's talent and basking in applause had to be coupled with the duty of instruction; the novel shared this trust with nonliterary utterances. Even Fern voiced the wish, in a didactic note to the reader, that her book would "fan into a flame, in some tired heart, the fading embers of hope." Sedgwick, like Irving and Cooper born in the eighteenth century, voiced traditional fastidiousness about the self-exposure of print. What emboldened her to write, she told a correspondent, was "the consciousness of a moral purpose." In Warner's case, the religious motive was so strong that she alternated works of fiction with homiletic tales and glosses on the Scriptures.

The background to Stowe's great book dramatizes some of the paradoxes common to domestic fiction. Her motives were at once familial, economic, and selfless. The financially straitened Stowes badly needed income from literature, and the royalties from *Uncle Tom's Cabin* exceeded $10,000 in the first nine months of sales alone. But the catalyst for writing was moral outrage at the Fugitive Slave Act; Stowe conceived of her novel as a pulpit from which to rouse readers and convert them to antislavery. She deplored the evil of trafficking in human beings, but about the benefits of selling a book "favorable to the development . . . of Christian brotherhood" she had no qualms. The goal of succeeding for monetary reasons intersected with the desire to better the lives of others: the more books in circulation, the more people influenced for good.

Against this notion of literature as socially constructive, Poe, Hawthorne, and Melville turned the novel into a proto-modernist art form, self-contained and increasingly self-referential. Undoubtedly pushed in this direction by lack of sales, the men were already moving toward aesthetic disentanglement, encoding in their narratives and theoretical pronouncements the impulse to specialize ascendant elsewhere in market culture. Hawthorne, perhaps the best-known spokesman for the canonical viewpoint, termed his fictions "romances" and defined them, in contradistinction to the novel, as taking place in "a Neutral Territory" removed from the actual world. His preface to *The House of the Seven Gables* problematizes the injunction that the work of literature should inculcate a moral. Questioning whether romances teach anything, Hawthorne says that the truth of fiction "is never any truer, and seldom any more evident, at the last page than at the first." Renunciation of advocacy pervades *The Blithedale Romance.* Published in the same year as *Uncle Tom's Cabin,* the book, in its prefatory disclaimer, underscores the divergence between the canon and a sentimental literature resolved to better society. The utopian community at Brook Farm, Hawthorne insists, is "altogether incidental" — a mere backdrop — to the action, and the story has not "the slightest pretensions to . . . elicit a conclusion, favorable or otherwise, in respect to socialism."

Poe and Melville were evolving toward the same position of disinterestedness. In "The Fall of the House of Usher" (1839), Poe imagines the artist as a hypersensitive being isolated from everyday reality, a creator of imageless pictures and self-reflexive songs. Poe's critical ruminations champion autonomous literature, and his appeal to Baudelaire was as a precocious proponent of *art pour l'art.* His essay on "The Poetic Principle" inveighs against "the heresy of *The Didactic*" and extols the "poem written solely for the poem's sake."

Melville's work engages more directly with the issues of his time—among other topics, he wrote on slavery, class, imperialism, and the destruction of the Native American—but the ever-present ironies and ambiguities dissipate external purpose. Melville's fictions awaken awareness of social injustice but leave the reader with no thought of changing things. (In this regard, he is Stowe's opposite, more so even than Hawthorne.) For Melville, the writer was a teller of Truth (invariably capitalized) who had privileged access to perceptions too terrible for common consumption; he had to smuggle his meaning to the select few while concealing it from the multitude.

If the movement toward literary autonomy shared a structure of thought with free-market economics, that movement also generated values opposed to the regimen of capitalism. The canonical writers' modernist orientation espoused a version of professionalism that located itself outside the commercial world. Poe, Hawthorne, and Melville developed occupational ideals different in significant ways from the practical vocational outlook of the domestic novelists, for whom the confirmation of the common reader in sales was a relatively unambiguous gauge of success. The canonical ethic took the form it did as a deliberate act of self-definition against the contrary example of the women. The three male writers simultaneously wanted to demarcate themselves from their female rivals and to associate their practice of authorship with other professions that were emerging or undergoing rationalization during this era. Medicine, law, and teaching, occupations from which women were usually barred (except at the lower levels of teaching), were establishing more stringent requirements to enter the field and stricter standards of practice within it.

These changing fields, as they proceeded to specialize over the course of the century, stressed their dissimilarity from entrepreneurial pursuits governed by profit and loss. The new professionals came to place special emphasis on expertise in one's endeavor. They were comparatively insulated from the market—many collected a fee set by custom or the profession rather than a salary—and skillfulness assumed a value for them distinguishable from the income they received. Of course they wanted to be well paid, but what made them professionals was their sense of integrity and ability in performing a technical service, and what confirmed their professional identity was the recognition of their merit by others in the field. In the egalitarian Jacksonian years, licensing laws and other attempts to restrict entry encountered popular resistance; nevertheless, the trend toward disciplinary rigor was irreversible. The professional ideal may have derived some of its prestige from the older, slowly disappearing tradition of artisanal handicrafts, which mandated a long period of apprenticeship before mastering a trade. The ideal can also be seen as a prefigurement of Thorstein Veblen's principle of workmanship, the devotion to excellence that Veblen attributed to the twentieth-century engineer and that he hoped would topple a system of production in which quality was sacrificed to profit.

But whatever its provenance and filiations—and Veblen clearly overestimated its potential to subvert—there is no doubt that for the canonical authors the professional ethic represented an alternative to the reign of commerce. An element of mystification entered into this, since the novelist, unlike the physician or lawyer, depended directly on sales for his income. But professionalism valorized extramonetary goals and conferred some of the aristocratic prestige, though little of the immediate market appeal, that "gentleman" supplied for Irving and Cooper. Melville was explicit on the disjunction between popularity and professional standards. "Try to get a living by the Truth—and go to the Soup Societies," he exclaimed, and he interpreted audience acceptance as a sign of artistic ineptitude. "Hawthorne and His Mosses," the impassioned essay Melville wrote to celebrate his fellow craftsman, spurns the public's plaudits as "strong presumptive evidence of mediocrity." For the meritorious writer, Melville argues, what counts is not the market but the appreciation of other literary professionals, including trained readers, who can grasp the complex messages encrypted within the multilayered text. A call for "close reading" informs this tribute, one hundred years before the New Criticism revolutionized the study of literature in university English departments. Melville's correspondence with Hawthorne is similarly dominated by his sense of their being practitioners of an exacting discipline, bound together by dedication to the highest standards of art. In this spirit of appreciative collegiality, he inscribed *Moby-Dick* to his brother novelist "In Token of My Admiration for His Genius."

Hawthorne was made uncomfortable by the degree of Melville's

adulation, but he too thought of himself as a professional in an esoteric specialty demanding training and skill. For a dozen years after
his graduation from college, he lived in his mother's house in Salem
and applied himself to mastering the art of fiction. Reclusiveness was
at work here, but so was a commitment to the kind of rigorous
apprenticeship becoming less common in manual crafts and more
frequent in mental occupations. Few writers from the antebellum period brooded so obsessively on the character and mechanics of their
calling. Like the masculine tales of his contemporaries, Hawthorne's
works abound in detailed information about an arduous task. They
are primers imparting instruction on the materials, "laws," and composition of the romance. While *Ruth Hall* is also a how-to manual for
aspiring women authors, in Fern's case the advice deals not with the
process of composition but rather with the best strategies for placing
one's manuscript and coping with editors and publishers.

Poe shared Hawthorne's preoccupation with technique and agreed
that the making of literature was a profession as distinct as medicine
or law. Finding favor with the mass public, he stated in a review of
Sedgwick, "has nothing to do with literature proper." And by "literature proper," Poe meant a self-conscious art pruned of everything
that was not literature, an art obedient to its own regulations and
explainable on its own terms. Like Hawthorne, he invited readers
into his laboratory and allowed them to glimpse the creative process.
"The Philosophy of Composition" describes how he selected the
topic, determined the length, and achieved the effect of his poem
"The Raven"—a palpably fraudulent account that says more about
the pressure to professionalize than about the text's actual preparation.

For Poe, Hawthorne, and Melville, the writer's vocation crystal-
lized as a counterpoise to the articulation of literary domesticity. The
three men defined their callings as artists in opposition to the sentimental novelists. Hawthorne endlessly denominated the romance as a
species of storytelling liberated from the close notation of domestic
manners, thereby proclaiming the form's distance from the fictions of
his female compatriots. In his censure of the scribbling women, he
grumbled that he had no prospect of success while "their trash" monopolized the public taste, and added that he "should be ashamed of
[himself] if [he] did succeed." Melville's Pierre, resolved to astound

the world with a tale of truth, shows his seriousness by repudiating the feminized sentimentality of his juvenilia. And Poe, in his account of "How to Write a Blackwood Article," ridicules as mindless the female authors whose contributions fill the journals of the day. To the canonical figures, the domestic novelists may have stood for the unaesthetic past, a time when native culture had not yet found its voice, or they may have symbolized the materialistic, utilitarian present; but the fact remains that the men could not have formulated their professional identity *without* the alternative model represented by the women. Literary professionalism as a distancing from the market, as an elevation of calling and competence over profitability, was the creation of white male fiction writers reacting against the commercial triumphs of the feminine novel.

Adam Smith had believed that men of letters were less well compensated than physicians and lawyers because the field of literature was overstocked: the more restrictive a profession, the more highly rewarded its members. Despite their efforts to distinguish themselves from their contemporaries, Poe, Hawthorne, and Melville failed to attain financial parity with elite practitioners of medicine and law; in fact, their forbidding standards of professionalism impaired their marketability. But in the long run, membership in a select club did reap economic benefits. Canonization transformed Hawthorne into a belated best-seller, available to the nineteenth-century reader in inexpensive school texts and imposing, clothbound editions of his collected works. Poe and Melville had a longer wait, but they too gained the ultimate in literary exclusivity: the status, and commercial longevity, of national classics.

A series of concluding ironies arises from this peculiarity of cultural history, final complications in the three men's shifting relation to the economics of authorship. Outsold by the more popular women while they were alive, the canonical novelists turned out to have greater staying power in the marketplace after their deaths. They owed their posthumous success not to the triumph of laissez faire but rather to the support of the emergent literary establishment. Whether or not their works possess greater artistic value, what raised Poe, Hawthorne, and Melville above their compatriots was the intervention on their behalf of fellow male professionals—the publishers, critics, and teachers who overruled the market by reprinting their books, promoting their reputations, and assigning them in courses. The novelists who created the aesthetic as a discrete entity, a literary realm parallel to Smith's self-righting economy, achieved immortality through a form of cultural subvention or "welfare." The visible hand of professional authority was needed to rescue the self-sufficient novel from popular disfavor and to convert antebellum remainders into the enduring best-sellers of American literature.

Michael T. Gilmore

# The Romance

Perhaps no literary term has been more descried, analyzed, and debated during recent decades than the term "Romance." Such eminent critics of American literature as Lionel Trilling and Richard Chase have identified its characteristics, contrasted them with those of the novel, and offered a beguiling paradigm focusing our attention on the achievement of Charles Brockden Brown, Washington Irving, James Fenimore Cooper, and (especially) Nathaniel Hawthorne, Edgar Allan Poe, and Herman Melville. But consensus has not rested easy: although such studies as those of Joel Porte and Richard Brodhead refined our sense of romance elements in specific texts, David H. Hirsch and Nicolaus Mills—among others—have balked at the idea of an autonomous genre called the romance and at what seemed to them fuzzy distinctions between narrative forms. Aware of the confusion wrought by evolving perspectives and critical fashions, Michael Davitt Bell has surveyed "the development of American Romance" with perceptive authority as a way of coming to see what happens in narrative when the romance sacrifices (as it does) relation to the quotidian world. And such recent assessments of American fiction as those of Edgar A. Dryden, Robert Levine, and Steven C. Sheer have inquired into the provenance and function of the romance with a fresh sense of purpose. On one thing most parties would agree: the persistent dialogue over the nature of the romance suggests its vital, albeit elusive and ambiguous, importance.

By common consent, the crucial text for discussing the nature of the romance in American fiction comes from the preface to Hawthorne's *The House of the Seven Gables* (1851). "When a writer calls his work a Romance," Hawthorne writes, "it need hardly be observed that he wishes to claim a certain latitude, both as to its fashion and material, which he would not have felt himself entitled to assume, had he professed to be writing a Novel." The novel, he goes on to say, "is presumed to aim at a very minute fidelity, not merely to the possible, but to the probable and ordinary course" of human experience; the romance, while it must adhere to the truth of the human heart, offers a greater freedom of presentation: the writer may manage the "atmospherical medium" so as to "bring out or mellow the lights and deepen and enrich the shadows of the picture." The writer of romance, that is, has the latitude to adjust or refract reality, to fashion what we might call a subjunctive world of fiction different in kind from the socially structured world in which we live but implicated, I would add, in its desires and fears.

Hawthorne was not alone in making such a distinction between the romance and the novel. Nor was the distinction invented by American writers. Both William Congreve and the gothic storyteller Clara Reeve characterized the romance as dealing with the wondrous and unusual and the novel as depicting events of a familiar nature, Congreve in the preface to his otherwise-forgotten *Incognita* (1692), Reeve in *The Progress of Romance* (1795). In a preface to the revised edition of *The Yemassee* (1853), Hawthorne's Southern contemporary William Gilmore Simms made an elaborate case for the romance as the modern substitute for the epic. Important for Simms, as for Hawthorne, is the fact that the romance allows an extravagance of presentation: rather than subjecting "itself to what is known, or even what is probable, it grasps at the possible."

Despite the tendency of some nineteenth-century reviewers to use the terms romance and novel interchangeably (as Nina Baym demonstrates in her study of reviews and readers), Hawthorne could and did assume an established distinction between the two kinds of fiction in his preface to *Seven Gables*. Later descriptions of the romance as an identifiable kind of narrative support the idea of breaking away from the commonplace as a fundamental characteristic. Having already declared his affinity for the romance in *Mardi* (1849), Melville came to think of fiction itself as expansive, replete with wonder: "It is with fiction as with religion," he wrote in *The Confidence-Man* (1857); "it should present another world, and yet one to which we feel the tie." The metaphor of a "tie" brings to mind Henry James's well-known analogy of "the balloon of experience" in his preface to the New York edition of *The American* (1909). The balloon, according to James, carries us into a world of imagination; but it is tethered to the earth by "a rope of remarkable length" that locates us and assures us where we are. If the rope is cut, "we are at large and unrelated." Ever concerned with technique, James concludes that "the art of the romancer" is to cut the cable undetected, with "insidious" craft. James's balloon analogy has long been a favorite among students of the romance. But his preface to *The American* offers an equally provocative and even more precise description of the form. James explicitly disavows the popular idea of the strange and the far as crucial aspects of the romance; they simply represent the unknown, which the increasing range of our experience may convert to the known. Nor is a romantic temperament in a character basic to this kind of narrative (while Emma Bovary is a romantic, "nothing less resembles a romance" than Flaubert's *Madame Bovary*). The romance, he goes on to say, explores a reality that "we never *can* directly know," no matter our resolve. It "deals" with a special kind of experience—and here we come to the essence of James's definition—"experience liberated, so to speak; experience disengaged, disembroiled, disencumbered, exempt from the conditions that we usually know to attach to it" by way of social context.

What emerges from this assemblage of definitions is a sense of the romance as an enabling theory of narrative equipped with memorable and facilitating metaphors. What comes from the theory is a mode of fiction that presents extravagance and courts the "disengaged" (in James's term), a fiction of intensity that feeds on caricature and seeks to confront the absolute. The consequence is a diverse set of narratives, gothic, magical, and psychological (frequently tending toward the allegorical and symbolic), unparalleled as expressive vehicles of revenge. In the work of Hawthorne, Poe, and Melville, one finds achievement of high and diverse order but none more eloquent than in studies of revenge empowered by the narrative energies of romance.

Throughout his twenty years of writing tales before the publication of *The Scarlet Letter* (1850), Hawthorne worked tentatively and at times clumsily to release the imagination for the purposes of his art. He spent a career finding ways to enter what he once called "the kingdom of possibilities." In the context of a society suspicious of imaginative indulgence, his commitment to the imagination was cautious, even intermittent: what he called "the hot, hard practical life of America" never ceased to threaten his creative efforts. Out of his difficulties he wrote a number of tales dramatizing the plight of the imagination in a hostile environment—among them, "The Artist of the Beautiful" (1844), and "The Snow-Image" (1850)—and developed strategies of shaping and presentation that did much to define the nature of the romance as he saw it. (It may be well to note that although the tale is not simply a short form of the romance, any more than the short story is an abbreviated form of the novel, it does deal with the kind of expansive reality typically found in the romance. In his tales as in his romances, Hawthorne worked to set the reader apart from what he continually called the "actual" world.)

Each of Hawthorne's major romances contains a preface explaining that his kind of fiction requires a domain of its own if it is to flourish. In "The Custom-House" sketch, which serves as an introduction to *The Scarlet Letter,* Hawthorne formulates the metaphor of "a neutral territory, somewhere between the real world and fairyland, where the Actual and the Imaginary may meet, and each imbue itself with the nature of the other." In the preface to *The House of the Seven Gables,* as we have seen, he explains that the latitude of fashion and material afforded by the romance is congenial to his imagination. His concern in *The Blithedale Romance* (1852) is "to establish a theatre, a little removed from the highway of ordinary travel," where his characters will not be exposed to direct comparison "with the actual events of real lives." The difficulty of creating fiction without access to a "Faery Land," he admits, "has always pressed heavily" upon him. The same perspective evokes his statement concerning the romance and America in the preface to *The Marble Faun* (1860). Italy, he explains, afforded him "a sort of poetic or fairy precinct, where actualities would not be so terribly insisted upon, as they are, and must needs be, in America."

As much as any of his prefatory statements, Hawthorne's sketch "The Haunted Mind" (1835) suggests the nature of the "neutral ground" and its relation to disencumbered experience. In this sketch Hawthorne writes of an hour of the night when one wakes suddenly into a world of scattered dreams. It is a time out of time when yesterday has vanished and tomorrow has not yet emerged, "an intermediate space where the business of life does not intrude." The sketch epitomizes such familiar features of Hawthorne's fiction as inner guilt and the comforting associations of the hearth. Its larger significance, however, lies in its brooding dramatization of the conditions of his fiction. Hawthorne's subject is the haunted mind, but the setting of the sketch is a kind of neutral ground—out of time, between yesterday and tomorrow. Somewhere behind or below is the haunted mind (Hawthorne's metaphor for the free-floating imagination), which yields up vivid and uncontrolled images never yet encumbered or engaged by social institutions. As they emerge onto the neutral ground (here, the "intermediate space"), they confront actually existing things (furniture in the room, embers on the hearth) that swim into cognition: and the meeting of the two provides the potential for art.

To juxtapose the mental drama of "The Haunted Mind" with a different set of instructions for confronting the terrors of the night gives us a surer view of the context in which Hawthorne lived and wrote. James Beattie was a Scottish moral philosopher, one of the Common Sense school that had widespread significance on American educators, clerics, and writers during the first half of the nineteenth century. In his *Dissertations Moral and Critical* (1783), Beattie describes what he considers the most preferable way of dealing with "imaginary terrors" of the night. "By the glimmering of the moon," he writes, "I have once and again beheld at midnight, the exact form of a man or woman, sitting silent and motionless by my bedside. Had I hid my head, without daring to look the apparition in the face, I should have passed the night in horror, and risen in the morning with the persuasion of having seen a ghost." But determined to discover "the truth, I discovered that it was nothing more than the accidental disposition of my clothes upon a chair." On another occasion Beattie was alarmed to see "by the faint light of the dawn, a coffin laid out between my bed and the window. . . . I set myself to examine it, and found it was only a stream of yellowish light, falling in a particular manner upon the floor, from between the window-curtains."

Here we have two ways of treating the imagination at its most exacerbated. James Beattie has no place for the haunted mind: he moves rationally to discover the facts of perception so that the actual world—what he would call the world of truth—is reestablished around him. In "The Haunted Mind," however, Hawthorne's narrator sustains a series of images within the mind. Retreating (head under the covers) from the wintry world outside, he speculates on the luxury of living forever like an oyster in a shell, then envisions the dead lying in their "narrow coffins." After entertaining such "hideous" fantasies, the narrator finally welcomes the sight of embers on the hearth because it balances the terrors of the haunted mind. What Beattie would banish as a matter of course (in the name of common sense), Hawthorne nourishes "on the borders of sleep and wakefulness" (in the name of imaginative life).

In the terms established by Hawthorne in "The Haunted Mind," failure to achieve the necessary balance of the imaginary and the actual may come about in one of two ways. In an overpowering wakefulness, in the midst of the insistence on empirical fact that James Beattie espouses, the products of the haunted mind are subjected to skeptical attack, rationalized, as it were, out of existence, rendered powerless. Conversely, blocked away from actually existing things and left to itself, the haunted mind could only contemplate its own nightmare visions in an empty and narcissistic exercise. The lurking danger—in this sketch, in Hawthorne's tales and romances, and in his meditations on art and life—is that the imaginative and the actual worlds might somehow be cut off from each other, leaving each in an impoverished and untenable position. When, in the final year of his life, he lamented that "The Present, the Immediate, the Actual, has proved too potent for me," Hawthorne signaled in the coded language he had long employed his awareness of the death of his imagination.

Poe's attitude toward the imagination and thus toward his fiction contrasts sharply with that of Hawthorne. Whereas Hawthorne labors toward the latitude he sees necessary for the romance, Poe leaps boldly into what the narrator of "Berenice" (1835) calls "palace[s] of imagination" and thumbs his nose at the hot, hard practical life of America. Whereas Hawthorne focuses on the consequences of human action with painstaking emphasis, Poe (as we shall see) ignores consequences, at times with sportive insistence. He champions the imagination, proclaims its range as unlimited, and sets it free to play in a realm of its own where it is lord of all it surveys. In his "Marginalia" (1846) Poe describes certain fancies that come to one on the "border-ground" between sleep and wakefulness. His version of a middle ground, unlike Hawthorne's, is not a place where the actual and the imaginary may meet in productive combination; the fancies of which he speaks inspire ecstasy beyond the range of human experience; they reveal "a glimpse of the spirit's outer world." Poe's "border-ground," in other words, is a point from which the imagination, unbounded and free from constraint, may journey into the "supernal."

Poe's fiction enacts the system of priorities suggested by this passage from the "Marginalia." His tales present the spectacle of the imagination playing games of its own according to rules of its own making. And where the imagination is at its purest and most triumphant, we may expect to find it transcending consequences. The narrator of "Loss of Breath" (1832), for example, undergoes startling mutilations that have no "real" effect on him. After cutting off his ears, a surgeon cuts him open and removes part of his viscera. Later, one ear is somehow back on his head. And, although the cats that eat on his nose do cause pain, no more is heard of wounds or their effects. He tells his story in the manner of someone having a bad day.

The most thoroughgoing example of a situation without consequences comes in "A Predicament" (1845), the companion-piece to "How to Write a Blackwood Article." Both "How to Write" and "A Predicament" abound with parody: Poe satirizes the formulas of contemporary magazine fiction, mocks his own style, and presents in burlesque his most fundamental ideas about the imagination. In a context of verbal frolic, the Signora Psyche Zenobia receives her instructions about how to write a story from the editor of *Blackwood's Magazine*. One point predominates: the writer, says Mr. Blackwood, must get into a situation no one was ever in before and then record his (or in this case, her) sensations. Sensations, he says, are the great thing: "Should you ever be drowned or hung, be sure and make a note of your sensations. If you wish to write forcibly, Miss Zenobia, pay minute attention to your sensations."

Readers of "A Predicament" will recall the bizarre manner in which Zenobia chances to follow Mr. Blackwood's advice. As she gazes out the clock-face of a church tower, the minute hand comes around and, to her horror, pins her head in the opening. Then, as the minute hand slowly cuts into her neck, she proceeds to give "minute attention" to her sensations. "It had already buried its sharp edge a full inch in my flesh, and my sensations grew indistinct and confused." "The bar had buried itself two inches in my neck. I was aroused to a sense of exquisite pain." "The bar was now four inches and a half deep in my neck, and there was only a little bit of skin to cut through. My sensations were those of entire happiness." One eye pops out and stares insolently up at her from a gutter. Finally her head comes off and tumbles down into the street. Zenobia concludes the story of her predicament by recalling her singular feelings on the occasion.

"A Predicament" takes us past the ideas of destruction and death. From the moment it becomes clear that Zenobia will continue narrating after her head comes off, we are set apart, fully and finally, from reality as we know it. Though exaggeration and banter have sustained the uneasy tension of the tale up to this point, the decapitation of the narrator is the masterstroke. Poe has liberated *his* imagination from *our* assumptions and given us Zenobia, his only woman narrator and in a way the most Poesque of all, not the unreliable narrator we have come to know and mistrust but the indestructible narrator, whose disencumbered voice transcends all, whose narrative has no relation to the conditions of human existence. She is Ligeia in burlesque, a caricature of a caricature; her name Psyche means "the soul," she tells us. Then she adds: "that's me, I'm *all* soul."

In "The Power of Words" (1845), one of Poe's fables featuring a dialogue between angels after the destruction of the earth, Agathos recalls speaking a star into existence "with a few passionate sentences," something possible because of "the *physical power of words*" to create. Again, in the "Marginalia" entry cited above, Poe writes of his complete "faith in the *power of words*." Such a faith underlies Poe's commitment to the imagination and his empowerment of narrators who speak "supernal" worlds into being. Equally bold but radically different is the position of Melville's philosopher Babbalanja in *Mardi*, who holds that "Truth is in things, and not in words," that "truth is voiceless," that fictions are as real as shovels and trenches—and equally liable to deceive. Melville would never agree with Poe about the power of words (though he used them effulgently); his primary metaphor for romance is a chartless voyage such as he undertook imaginatively in *Mardi*, sustained by the conviction that "those who boldly launch, cast off all cables; and turning from the common breeze, that's fair for all, with their own breath, fill their own sails." If the mention of casting off cables recalls James's balloon-of-experience analogy, the idea of a self-directed quest over "untracked" seas promises (even more severely) discoveries at once disencumbered and disconcerting—the story in brief of Melville's career as a writer of romance.

As *Typee* (1846) and *Omoo* (1847) demonstrate, Melville levied on personal experience for the substance of his early narratives. Both of these narratives deal with his adventure in the South Pacific, where he lived and loitered after deserting an Australian whaling vessel in the early 1840s. By the time he began *Mardi* in 1848, however, Melville was beginning to feel the constraints of writing picaresque travel narratives; because some critics had doubted the factual basis of *Typee* and *Omoo*, he proposed to write "a romance of Polynesian adventure." He would, as he announced, "out with the Romance." Despite these intentions, *Mardi* opens as a straightforward narrative, picking up literally where *Omoo* left off; but it quickly moves to uncharted dimensions. At work on his "narrative of facts," as Melville announced to his publisher John Murray, he "began to feel an incurable distaste for the same; & a longing to plume my pinions for a flight, & felt irked, cramped & fettered by plodding with dull common places." So, "suddenly," he began "to work heart & soul at a romance," something new and original. "It opens like a true narrative—like Omoo for example, on ship board—& the romance & poetry of the thing thence grow continually, till it becomes a story wild enough I assure you & with a meaning too." Replete with elements of allegory, satire, and philosophical speculation, *Mardi* reflects Melville's readings in Dante, Rabelais, Edmund Spenser, and

Thomas Browne, as well as his developing concern for what he called "the great art of telling the truth."

Melville thus came to the romance by way of personal odyssey. Energized by a desire to "plume his pinions" for flight, he felt exhilaration as he cast aside the fetters of convention and moved toward the expansive world of "romance & poetry." The tone of his letter to Murray is typically his own. But his sense of imaginative release is something that all practitioners of the romance envision. To Hawthorne it appeared as a "Faery Land" shielded from actuality; to Poe it was a glimpse of the "supernal"; to Melville it arrived as a "story wild" and unpredicted.

In the work of Poe, Hawthorne, and Melville revenge thrives on an atmosphere of intensity that brings the *self* to stand apart from communal and institutional concerns, to confront what is perceived as a target with the full force of mind and volition. Various strategies of caricature serve each writer well; for by means of caricature the portrayal of self is perforce distorted, at once limited and magnified, invested with incipient violence.

Virtually all of Poe's tales display the human form in distorted and extravagant postures, versions of what Poe called the grotesque. In "King Pest" (1835), for example, the method is that of portrait caricature, which E. H. Gombrich (almost as if he had been reading Poe) defines as "the playful distortion of a victim's face." Poe characterizes each of his strange company by describing one highly exaggerated facial feature—a "terrific chasm" of a mouth, "a pair of prodigious ears," "huge goggle eyes" amazed at "their own enormity." In "The Facts in the Case of M. Valdemar" (1845), caricature accelerates to metamorphosis when the long-dead Valdemar suddenly rots away on his bed—"a nearly liquid mass of loathsome—of detestable putridity."

The distorting violence of Poe's imagination can take caricature an additional step to cruelty and revenge. Hop-Frog, court jester to a brutal king, is both a dwarf and a cripple, who can move along the floor "only with great pain and difficulty." The extreme anguish and abasement of his life (synopsized, as it were, by his deformities) bring him to hoist the king and seven counselors on a chandelier during a masquerade party and burn them alive. And thus a narrative that begins, "I never knew anyone so keenly alive to a joke as the king was. He seemed to live only for joking," ends with "The eight corpses swung in their chains, a fetid, blackened, hideous, and indistinguishable mass." An ominous idea of joking encompasses "Hop-Frog" (1849): Poe twists it through stages of cruelty, uses a masquerade party to reverse its direction, and finally has it consummated by an act of revenge—for which Hop-Frog, incidentally, pays no penalty.

Edward Davidson has suggested that the camouflaged crudeness in Poe's early work—his coarse pun on the name Abel-Shittim in the first version of "A Tale of Jerusalem" (1832), the Shandean play on noses in "Lionizing" (1835)—may have come from an almost compulsive tendency to get even with his society, to ridicule an audience that could be at once amused and fooled. A compulsive aggression against his audience seems indeed to pervade Poe's work, both early and late. And one of its manifestations is the prevailing invitation of Poe's narrators to witness an act of vengeance. In a society that prized the domestic and valued the didactic for its moral utility, Poe became militantly antididactic, mischievously antidomestic. The narrator of "The Black Cat" (1843) presents the garish revenge of his tale as "a series of mere household events." The narrator of "The Cask of Amontillado" (1846) exults in the memory of revenge taken fifty years before—although some readers, uneasy at the amoral calisthenics of this tale and unwilling to accept Poe in undiluted form, see the narrative as confessional rather than celebratory.

In some of his best-known work Poe explores the intricate and baffling nature of the perverse. Characteristically, he uses narrators who seek to destroy the "I"—the *self* driven by an "unfathomable longing" to offer violence to "its own nature" (as we read in "The Black Cat"). Obsessed by the "eye" of his victim, the narrator of "The Tell-Tale Heart" (1843) decides "to take the life of the old man, and thus rid myself of the eye forever." Given Poe's fondness for puns (and his disdain for the transcendentalists' emphasis on *self*), it is tempting to substitute an "I" for an "eye" in this context.

Poe's longest fiction, *The Narrative of Arthur Gordon Pym* (1838), is sustained by the spirit of self-destruction and recurrent strategies of revenge on the reader. We are at the mercy of Poe's imagination in *Pym*—the power of his words is paramount: hot and cold, black and white, are what Poe says they are. Against all odds, Pym battles through to the final dream vision; as it progresses, his narrative casts off and subverts experience. And Poe is not above playing a trick to speed the voyage. He stages his scene of cannibalism brilliantly, in a way that maximizes its horror. The proof of Poe's power as a writer is that he makes us believe him in this scene; he engages us as members of a civilization that regards cannibalism as fearful and regressive, the ultimate sickening gesture to sustain life. And then he sandbags us. After the sailor Parker has been murdered, eaten, and his blood drunk, Poe has Pym remember the whereabouts of an ax with which he can chop through the deck and obtain food. After leading us to credit the terrible extremity of the situation, Poe subverts our reactions by quickly setting things back to "normal." But after this scene we are a good deal less sure where we are. In retrospect, we can see that we are taking a journey into a vengeful imagination.

Hawthorne's use of caricature differs from that of Poe when it depends for its validity on the perceptions of characters. What Giovanni sees in Rappaccini's garden (evidence of Beatrice's poisonous nature) may be the product of his skepticism and inability to love. What Young Goodman Brown sees in the forest (evidence of evil in those he reveres) may be the result of specter evidence. What various people see, and don't see, on Arthur Dimmesdale's breast at the end of *The Scarlet Letter* tells us something about the spectators, something about ourselves, and a lot about Hawthorne—inventor of the first multiple-choice test in the romance.

But Hawthorne, like Poe, can use caricature for his own purposes. And since the distorting effects of monomania produce psychological and spiritual caricature, Hawthorne's work contains what may be a peerless array of figures such as Richard Digby in "The Man of Adamant" (1837), Aylmer in "The Birth-mark" (1843), Ethan Brand in "Ethan Brand: A Chapter from an Abortive Romance" (1850), and of course Roger Chillingworth in *The Scarlet Letter*. Out of a belief that only he can be saved, Richard Digby forswears society, disdains the young woman who (for some reason) loves him, and lives his self-intent life in a cave. Obsessed with his desire for perfection, Aylmer kills his loving wife (who for some reason married him) in the course of a great experiment and thus rejects the best the earth can offer. Ethan Brand confronts the absolute even more starkly than these two destructive protagonists. The sole issue in this tale is whether a human being can commit an unpardonable sin, a sin so grievous that it exceeds God's capacity for mercy. Can Ethan Brand triumph over God? On such an absolute question does Hawthorne construct his "Chapter from an Abortive Romance," a story bleak, intense, formed out of the protagonist's monomania, his presumption, and his final despair and suicide.

Whereas Melville came to *Moby-Dick* (1851) after a burst of activity that included *Mardi, Redburn* (1849), and *White-Jacket* (1850), Hawthorne turned to *The Scarlet Letter* after being fired from the Salem Custom House. Whereas Melville would later present such sportive caricatures as Turkey and Nippers in "Bartleby, the Scrivener" (1856), one temperamentally unable to work in the morning, the other in the afternoon, Hawthorne had long before examined the hallucinatory and even cruel aspect of revolutionary fervor in "My Kinsman, Major Molineux" (1832) and presented as "A Parable" the resolute mystification of the Reverend Mr. Hooper in "The Minister's Black Veil" (1836). But the two writers saw their consummate stories of revenge published only a year apart. *The Scarlet Letter*, of course, came first; and so impressed was Melville with that romance and Hawthorne's earlier work that he inscribed *Moby-Dick* to Hawthorne "in Token of my admiration for his genius."

Vengeance in *The Scarlet Letter* reaches out to affect the entire fabric of the fictive world. The Puritan community, as we know, metes out public punishment to Hester Prynne the sinner. But Chillingworth undertakes a private search for Hester's partner in adultery, and Hawthorne handles the development of his obsession by giving us a virtual anatomy of revenge. Chillingworth begins his search with a sense of objectivity, as if the matter were a problem in geometry rather than one "of human passions, and wrongs inflicted on himself." Gradually, however, what Hawthorne calls "a terrible fascination, a kind of fierce, though still calm, necessity" comes over him. Ultimately, his revenge becomes more intense, more involved, more personal, an obsession that feeds upon itself. When Hester asks if he has not tortured Dimmesdale enough, Chillingworth replies, "No!—no!—He has but increased the debt." Part of Hawthorne's achievement in *The Scarlet Letter* lies in his ability to demonstrate the reflexive nature of revenge, to show convincingly that Chillingworth has caught himself on a vicious blade of vengeance that cuts two ways. Though there can be no getting even, the avenger must intensify his torture; yet the more he does so, the more he destroys himself.

Dimmesdale and Chillingworth, of course, make each other possible in *The Scarlet Letter*. Just as Chillingworth lives to torture, Dimmesdale lives to be tortured. Yet the fundamental falseness of the minister's position yields an idiom of anguish that stands him very well in his professional life. His sermons, for example, are models of efficacy: the more he reviles himself as a sinner (in general terms, from the security of the pulpit), the more his congregation elevates him to new heights of spirituality (as he knows it will) and thinks comparatively of its own unworthiness. His anguish is convincing, compelling, and genuine, although it springs from and compounds his hypocrisy—even because of his awareness that it springs from and compounds his hypocrisy.

Dimmesdale clearly suffers from an excess of self. His weakness and suffering throughout most of the romance have tended to blur for some readers the fact of his pride, which, like his scarlet letter, lies beneath and gives special form to his mask of saintliness. Self-condemnation, self-abnegation, and self-loathing are the stimulants of his psychic life; they constitute as well the price he must pay if he would not strip away the self reverenced by the public. And that self—formed out of a communal wish to admire a young, pious, and learned minister—he cannot bring himself to renounce. That his private suffering contributes to the public mask of spirituality is a kind of masochistic dividend for him.

It is Hester Prynne who breaks the cycle of vengeance and self-loathing in *The Scarlet Letter*. For Hester, who stands in haughty agony on the scaffold at the outset of the romance, neither seeks vengeance nor loathes herself. Proud, unable to hate her sin, she ornaments the letter and thereby (as Nina Baym points out) subverts "the intention of the magistrates who condemn her to wear it." The iron grace of her life for seven years, a discipline bred on suppressed emotion, leads directly to the forest interview with Dimmesdale and the unraveling of the story Hawthorne has set in circular motion. Without Hester, there is nothing in the logic of *The Scarlet Letter* to make it end, so tightly has Hawthorne woven his narrative of revenge and self-absorption. The ending, as it must be, is grim. But the survival of Hester Prynne shows that there is life after the distortions of caricature and obsession.

Chillingworth's revenge is personal, Ahab's cosmic. And while Chillingworth masks his motives during the course of *The Scarlet Letter,* Ahab announces the vengeful purpose of the *Pequod*'s voyage when he first faces his crew from the quarterdeck. Yet Ahab on the quarterdeck does not divulge the full dimensions of his rage. That responsibility falls to Ishmael, Melville's narrator, who is at pains to account for the growth of Ahab's monomania; Ishmael's language registers the intensity, the pitch, of the Captain's burning idea. Since his first and near-fatal encounter with Moby Dick, Ishmael tells us,

Ahab had cherished a wild vindictiveness against the whale, all the more fell for that in his frantic morbidness he at last came to identify with him, not only all his bodily woes, but all his intellectual and spiritual exasperations. The White Whale swam before him as the monomaniac incarnation of all those malignant agencies which some deep men feel eating in them, till they are left living on with half a heart and half a lung. That intangible malignity which has been from the beginning . . . ; which the ancient Ophites of the east reverenced in their statue devil;—Ahab did not fall down and worship it like them; but deliriously transferring its idea to the abhorred white whale, he pitted himself, all mutilated, against it. All that most maddens and torments; all that stirs up the lees of things; all truth with malice in it; all that cracks the sinews and cakes the brain; all the subtle demonisms of life and thought; all evil, to crazy Ahab, were visibly personified and made practically assailable in Moby Dick. He piled upon the whale's white hump the sum of all the general rage and hate felt by his whole race from Adam down; and then, as if his chest had been a mortar, he burst his hot heart's shell upon it.

Strong language, this, an absolute rhetoric with its repetitive all, all, all. It posits the existence of an "intangible malignity . . . from the beginning"; it invokes the "rage and hate" of the human race, "from Adam down." Ishmael notes that Ahab bears a scar, "a slender rod-like mark, lividly whitish," as if he were a tree struck by lightning. According to the Manxman, should Ahab ever be "tranquilly laid out" and made ready for the grave—an unlikely supposition—it would turn out to be "a birth-mark from crown to sole." Maddened, desperate, and scarred (perhaps by birth), Ahab seeks to confront not experience but evil. There are voices of reason in *Moby-Dick,* voices that speak of whaling as a business and of ties to families in Nantucket. Chief among them is Starbuck, who says he has come to hunt whales and not his commander's vengeance. But Ahab, who would confront the absolute, is absolute aboard the *Pequod*. The crew, he says, are his arms and legs; to him, the three symbols on the doubloon are all Ahab. Tied to him alone, the crew share the destructive fate of a captain questing for absolute revenge.

After the publication of *The Scarlet Letter* and *Moby-Dick,* Hawthorne and Melville continued to use the latitude of the romance to fashion narratives of revenge. Both Hawthorne's *The House of the Seven Gables* and *The Marble Faun* extend the revenge story to include gothic elements, the first a family curse that shapes the issues of the narrative, the second an oppressive and haunting figure of malevolence who is murdered by the faunlike Donatello— precipitating a new fall from innocence. Likewise gothic in atmosphere is Melville's provocative "Benito Cereno" (1856), in which revenge comes from slaves who revolt on board a ship carrying them to South America. Finally, in the posthumously published *Billy Budd* (1925), Melville converts the romance to fable with a story of "natural depravity," as seen in Claggart, causing the fall of the pre-Adamic Billy Budd.

Perhaps to demonstrate that the myth of the American Adam was indeed a myth, American writers have shown a fascination for revenge as a motif for the romance. Motives for vengeance cut across race and gender, involving such characters as Magua in Cooper's *The Last of the Mohicans* (1826), Nathan Slaughter in Robert Montgomery Bird's *Nick of the Woods* (1837), Ruth Hall at the end of Fanny Fern's novel of that name (1855)—as well as the plots of powerful twentieth-century texts such as Richard Wright's *Native Son* (1940), Toni Morrison's *Beloved* (1987), and Stephen King's garish *Misery* (1987), in which a reader turns vengefully on a writer. *Native Son,* of course, has never been called a romance; it is a hard-driving novel, unrelenting in its realism. Yet Bigger Thomas takes revenge for his life, for the fact of living, in that novel; and when he says, "What I killed for, I am," in the final chapter, realism falls away before an existential moment akin to the free-floating ventures of the romance. The urge to get even with someone or something or everything may be an essential part of the American sense of story, something articulated out of a deep sense of loss or disappointment. If so, it continues to seek new forms of expression. As Melville said at the end of the broken promises and surfaces of *The Confidence-Man* (1857), "Something further may follow of this Masquerade."

Terence Martin

# Romance and Race

Who ain't a slave? Tell me that.
                                    —Ishmael, *Moby-Dick*

Henry Whistler, writing during the English expedition of
1654–55 against Spanish Jamaica, described Barbados
as "the dunghill whereon England doth cast forth its rub-
bish." In this hub of excrement he lamented how a rogue could so
easily become a gentleman, a whore a lady. Both Edward Long, in his
*History of Jamaica* (1774), and Lady Maria Nugent, in her Jamaica
journal, observing the behavior and appearance of white ladies on
their plantations, complained about these surprising hybrids of the
New World. Long writes: "We see . . . a very fine young woman
awkwardly dangling her arms with the air of a Negroe-servant."
Lady Nugent focuses on the shock of hearing the English language
corroded by the drawling, dissonant gibberish of negro domestics:
"Many of the ladies, who have not been educated in England, speak
a sort of broken English, with an indolent drawling out of their
words, that is very tiresome if not disgusting." Nugent and Long
speak from the position of a dominant culture: threatened by the fact
of *creolization,* a contamination, as they see it, of the pure civilities
of Mother England. A latter-day Rochester in Jean Rhys's *Wide Sargasso Sea* (1966) looks at his white creole wife Antoinette and momentarily confounds her with the negro servant. "She raised her eyebrows and the corners of her mouth turned down in a questioning,
mocking way. For a moment she looked very much like Amélie. Perhaps they are related, I thought. It's possible, it's even probable in this
damned place."
   What happens to romance when we turn to those places where

everything was allowed because thousands were enslaved, where the fact of slavery—the conversion of person into thing for the ends of capital—turned all previous orders upside down? If "masters" claimed civilization on the backs of those they called polluted or bestial—claims ever threatened by evidences of a terrible brutality and abandon—they had to clarify their identity against a background of hybridization, forced intimacies, and pollution. Perhaps we can no longer understand what we mean by romance in the Americas without turning to the issue of slavery. The forced intimacy of what Pierre de Vassière, writing about creole life in Saint-Domingue from 1629 to 1789, called "a very strange familiarity" between those who called themselves masters and those who found themselves slaves made the old practices of idealization unworkable. In plantation isolation, the extremes of differences were blurred in an odd promiscuity, where those who were supposedly inferior became absolutely necessary to those who imagined themselves superior.

If being master or mistress was so addictive a pleasure that the slave as ultimate possession (what Edgar Allan Poe in his review of James Kirke Paulding's 1836 *Slavery in the United States* praised as dependent upon, indeed goaded by, the use of the word "my," that "language of affectionate appropriation") became a necessary part of the master's or mistress's identity, then we are up against a situation where the terms of exclusivity or control, proclaimed and repeated, are somehow confounded by the facts of slavery. What happens to such words as "power," "purity," "love," or "filth" when, as an anonymous planter from Saint-Domingue put it, you have "tasted the pleasures of a nearly absolute domination"?

The development of romance in the United States was linked in unsettling ways to the business of race. Out of the ground of bondage, the curse of slavery, and the fear of "servile war" came a twisted sentimentality, a cruel analytic of "love" in the New World: a conceit of counterfeit of intimacy. So Herman Melville in *Moby-Dick* (1851) presented Ishmael and the cannibal Queequeg locked in a marital embrace. In *Pierre* (1852) the dark, mysterious Isabel and Pierre perform the spectacle of husband and wife, finally to be reciprocally neutered in a stony apocalypse. In "Benito Cereno" (1856) Don Benito and Babo act out a masquerade of servitude and attachment that

Melville will take to its most alarming extreme in the negative romance "Bartleby, the Scrivener" (1856). Poe's *Eureka* (1848) ends with an apocalypse startling in its eroticism: "a novel Universe swelling into existence and then subsiding into nothingness, at every throb of the Heart divine." The atoms in the intensity of their "spiritual passion," in their "appetite for oneness," will at last "flash . . . into a common embrace." This essay on the "Material and Spiritual Universe" Poe called a "Romance."

Speaking about the epic adventures of fugitive slaves in his lecture "The American Scholar" (delivered 1849), Theodore Parker declared that "all the original romance of Americans is in them, not in the white man's novel." The facts of slave life, once turned into heroic and sentimental romances, turned negroes into matter for idealization. Critics as diverse as Winthrop Jordan, William Andrews, Eric Sundquist, and Gillian Brown have noted how the cult of sentiment with its emphasis on self-denial, piety, and pathos signaled a turn away from the ethical problems of slavery. Further, like the idealization of women, which narrowed their realm to the domestic haven of home—a pristine place of comfort and compensation—the conversion of the negro into a figure for romance or a call to formal lament turned the oppressed, whether slave or ex-slave, man or woman, into an object in someone else's story, deprived of the possibility of significant action. The very question of love, as Ann Douglas argued in *The Feminization of American Culture* (1977), had to be de-natured when both ministers and ladies found themselves marginalized and awash in a language of spirit that allowed another reality to perpetuate itself. While Sarah Hale of *Godey's Lady's Book* celebrated the powers of feminizing and angelic "influence" on the brute, money-making men, the divide between those who wielded the terms of mastery and power and those who were busy sanctifying, serving, and suffering increased.

"What then is the American, this new man?" To answer St. John de Crèvecoeur's question in *Letters from an American Farmer* (1782) demands that we recognize that the Declaration of Independence always meant independence for white men only: an exclusion implied in the title of Lydia Maria Child's essay, *An Appeal in Favor of That Class of Americans Called Africans* (1833). A Calvinist fear of pollution and dread of the flesh would find ready objects and necessary victims in those marginalized by the curse of color: the blackness that marked for the racist imagination depravity and corruption.

In the first half of the nineteenth century more Africans than Europeans arrived in the Americas. William Bird wrote to Lord Eymons as early as 1732: "They import so many Negros hither, that I fear this Colony will some time or other be confirmed by the Name of New Guinea." It is therefore not surprising when reading Nathaniel Hawthorne's "The Custom-House" (the preface to *The Scarlet Letter* [1850]) to note that he describes the street running through the old town of Salem as having "Gallows Hill and New Guinea at one end, and a view of the almshouse at the other." In "Free and Coerced Transatlantic Migration: Some Comparisons," *The American Historical Review* (April 1983), David Eltis writes: "In every year from about the mid-sixteenth century to 1831, more Africans than Europeans quite likely came to the Americas, and not until the second wave of mass migration began in the 1880s did the sum of that European immigration start to match and then exceed the cumulative influx from Africa. . . . In terms of immigration alone, then, America was an extension of Africa rather than Europe until late in the nineteenth century."

The revolution in Saint-Domingue (1791–1804)—the only successful slave revolt in the New World—forced the call for "Liberty, Equality, Fraternity" to crash hard upon the facts of Property, Labor, and Race. For Edmund Burke in *Reflections on the Revolution in France* (1790), as for other apologists of Empire, the emancipating year of 1789 turned the French into "a nation of low-born servile wretches." The colonists of Saint-Domingue had been proved right. That one could speak freedom for *all* humans, no matter the color of the skin, did mean "the end of Saint-Domingue." What might have remained vague ("The rights of men," Burke claimed, "are in a sort of *middle*"), once on the soil of Saint-Domingue became quite clear. When mulatto *and* black began to compete for pieces of "republican" entitlement, race, what Aimé Césaire has called "the terrifying negro problem," would explode what might have remained abstract, safe, or static.

In the United States the first successful *slave* revolution in the New

World qualified the "democracy" of the "Founding Fathers" and gave substance to the specter of the racial Armageddon prophesied by Thomas Jefferson in his 1781 *Notes on the State of Virginia*. "Deep-rooted prejudices entertained by the whites; ten thousand recollections by the blacks, of the injuries they have sustained; new provocations; the real distinctions which nature has made; and many other circumstances, will . . . produce convulsions which will probably never end but in the extinction of one or the other race." Thomas Carlyle's "African Haiti" — "black without remedy. . . . a monition to the world" — and reported scenes of vengeance would haunt those proslavery writers who sought to prove the deep bonds of affection between masters and their slaves: a compelling empathy and disciplined love that no "crude" or "fanatic" abolitionist could understand.

The duplicity in such spectacles of feeling, the hitch in the business of sentiment would be enacted in the writings of Edgar Allan Poe. Critics, myself included, have ignored the way the romance of the South and the realities of race were fundamental to his literary production. Poe was not an exotic, a writer displaced "out of Space, out of Time." He knew the South, and for the most part remained ambiguous and cautious about the practice of chattel slavery. Yet the terrors of barbarism, and his own alternating unease with and attraction to the language of the heart, mark his tales of revelation and revenge. In the course of his life, something strange happened to what might have remained mere regionalist sentiment. But that gradual transformation should not blind us to the way Poe perpetually returns to his sense of the South, while attempting to screen his increasingly subversive concerns: the perils of mastery and nightmares about the decay of all fictions of status, the rot at the heart of the Great House.

Nowhere does Poe reveal his comprehension of the power extended over another in love, the terrible knot of complicity, as in his treatment of *bondage:* that unerring reciprocity between one who calls him or herself master and one who responds as slave. It is quite possible that Poe's most parodic exaggerations, his most sentimental posturings, have their source in what remained for Poe the ground of "civilized" society: human bondage. For Poe, as for Burke, Carlyle, or Jefferson, also severe (and enlightened) constructors of English prose, the fact of the negro made possible the empirical elevation of something they call "human," with its finest image in tow, the Marie Antoinettes of this world. And yet, in Poe's writings how slippery, how easily reversed is the divide between human and brute, lady and slave.

Let us try to give a history to the dark side of Poe's romance. On June 22, 1815, according to *The Poe Log: A Documentary Life of Edgar Allan Poe* (1987): "John Allan writes Charles Ellis to sell Scipio, a slave, for $600 and to hire out others at $50 a year." On December 10, 1829, two years after Poe left the Allan household, Poe acted as agent for Maria Clemm of Baltimore in the sale of a slave named Edwin to Henry Ridgway for a term of nine years. In the *Baltimore Sun* (April 6, 1940), May Garrettson Evans begins her article by explaining that "a Baltimore man who wishes his name withheld quite by chance came across an old document relating to Edgar Allan Poe, which seems thus far to have entirely escaped the poet's biographers." It is easy to understand why a Baltimore gentleman might want to remain unnamed as he provides information that those who prefer to monumentalize a rarefied Poe would prefer to ignore.

I Edgar A. Poe agent for Maria Clemm of Baltimore City and County and State of Maryland, for and in consideration of the sum of forty dollars in hand paid by Henry Ridgway of Baltimore City at or before the sealing and delivery of these presents the receipt whereof is hereby acknowledged have granted, bargained and sold by these presents do grant bargain and sell unto the said Henry Ridgway his executors administrators and assigns a negro man named Edwin age twenty one years on the first day of March next to serve until he shall arrive to the age of thirty years no longer.

Poe was then awaiting the time for his entrance to West Point and had already written his early "romantic" poems, including "Al Aaraaf," "Tamerlane," "To the River—," "A Dream," and "Fairyland."

What happens if we add the despotism of slavery to the cult of sentiment: to Poe's "fair sex" and the "romance" she appears to demand? Race remains crucial to Poe's treatment of women and "womanliness." For Poe understood the matter of idealization better than most of his contemporaries. He knew how praise, or the sanctifying of women, can become easy handmaid to a deadly, conservative ideology. For mystification is always a matter of power: a decreeing subject ordains the terms for a silenced object to attain the status, or stasis, of myth. The master makes the myth through which the other must seek his or her identity.

If to sentimentalize is to colonize the image, then Poe will ironize fantasies of love and domesticity. More important, as becomes evident in Poe's letters recycled to his various beloveds, there is nothing more compelling than *possession:* you love most what you own. And yet that love, as Virginia Woolf realized when she reviewed Caroline Ticknor's *Poe's Helen* in the *Times Literary Supplement* in 1916, can be "tedious" and "discreditable," languishing in an "atmosphere . . . of withered roses and moonshine." Poe understood the terrible burden of feeling, the tyranny of the "law of the heart," as the late "love poems" — "To Marie Louise Shew," "To Helen," and "For Annie" — demonstrate.

Poe knew that the language of romanticism allowed the covert continuation of inequality. What does man love in woman? Her transformation into superlatives, or as Poe repeats and overdoes it, her reduction into generality. Recall the exaggerations of his landscape sketch "Landor's Cottage" (1849), when the narrator introduces "Annie," *the angel of the house:* "So intense an expression of *romance* . . . had never sunk into my heart of hearts before. . . . 'Romance,' provided my readers fully comprehend what I would hear implied by the word — 'romance' and 'womanliness' seem to me convertible terms: and, after all, what man truly *loves* in woman, is simply her *womanhood.*"

If Poe's women become shadowy, losing substance in attributes repeated and recycled no matter for whom or when he wrote, the writer himself seems to be most "heartfelt" when most vague. If Poe's narrators in the tales about women, in "Ligeia" (1838), "Berenice" (1835), or "Morella" (1835), for example, become as vain, abstract, and diseased as the objects of their desire (the women the madmen had idolized), Poe's letters and his love poems also trade on a sexual exchange. If women in nineteenth-century America must bear the trappings of style, must inhabit most fully the external as essence, Poe shows how such a spectacle both exploits and consumes its participants, both men and women.

What happened to the tough, sometimes delirious skepticism of the critic of a society "sunk in feeling," when he turned to an institution that sustained itself by the most incredible mystifications? What were the effects of Poe's characterization of Jupiter in "The Gold Bug" (1843) or the fiendish "brute" whose shrill "jabberings" are unidentifiable—the terribly marked deeds of the "Ourang-Outang" driven wild by "the dreaded whip" in "The Murders in the Rue Morgue" (1841)—on readers for and against human ownership?

When Poe was an editor of the *Southern Literary Messenger* in Richmond, Virginia (1835–38), he corresponded with Thomas R. Dew, professor of history at William and Mary College, author of the *Vindication of Perpetual Slavery* (1836), and he published an introductory note to Thomas R. Dew's "Address" delivered at the College on October 10, 1836. In the April 1836 issue of the magazine a review of two books on slavery appeared, known as the "Paulding-Drayton Review." As Bernard Rosenthal writes in "Poe, Slavery, and the *Southern Literary Messenger:* A Reexamination," in *Poe Studies* (December 1974), his excellent argument for Poe's authorship of this contested document, the review was traditionally assumed to have been written by Poe. The essay was included in James Harrison's Virginia edition, but in 1941 and subsequently, some scholars claimed that the review had been "misattributed" to Poe and identified Nathaniel Beverley Tucker as author. The review is excluded from *Essays and Reviews* in the Library of America edition of Poe's work.

If we place Poe in his historical and social context, reread his comments on Longfellow's *Poems on Slavery* (with his jibe that the collection is especially suited for "the use of those negrophilic old ladies of the north"), reconsider his scattered attacks on the fanatic coterie of abolitionists and transcendentalists, and recall his deep faith in human imperfection, we can see how much Poe's politics concerning slavery, social status, and property rights owed to the conservative tradition of the Virginia planter aristocracy.

Though Poe tried to subvert his society's idealizing rhetoric about women, he could not apply the same irony and skepticism to the institution of slavery. I now turn to what could be called Poe's most disturbing, because most authentic, "love poem," his review of James Kirke Paulding's *Slavery in the United States* and an anonymous work, *The South Vindicated from the Treason and Fanaticism of the Northern Abolitionists.* The review appeared the same year as Lydia Maria Child's *Anti-Slavery Catechism* (1836). What I have argued about Poe's defiance of masculine disempowering of women is confounded by the question of slavery. Here, Poe produces straight the language of affection and subservience he seems to hyperbolize and mock when imaging women. The bond between master and slave that Poe portrays reads like a case of pietism gone wild.

Poe begins his review with a discussion of the French Revolution. Like Edmund Burke before him, he argues that since "property" is what everyone most wants, it is the secret law of any upheaval: "the many who want, band themselves together against the few that possess; and the lawless appetite of the multitude for the property of others calls itself the spirit of liberty." After condemning the Revolution, which he calls "this eccentric comet," he uncovers its real object. And he is far more honest than many historians of revolutionary France: "the first object of attack was property in slaves; that in that war on behalf of the alleged right of man to be discharged from all control of law, the first triumph achieved was in the emancipation of slaves." Poe, ever rigorous in his analysis, suggests how deeply dependent was the progress of the French Revolution on slave revolts in the Caribbean. For Poe, private property and the possession of slaves remained at the center of events in France and put such abstractions as "the rights of Man" to the test. Before turning to "Domestic Slavery," however, Poe turns to what he refers to as "recent events in the West Indies," treating them as foreboding what he deems "the parallel movement here."

Writing in 1836, Poe no doubt refers to the slave revolt of 1831–32 in Jamaica, also known as the Christmas Rebellion of 1831–32, the Baptist "War," or the Sam Sharpe Insurrection, involving between 18,000 and 50,000 slaves and their sympathizers over five parishes in North and North-Central Jamaica. The revolt lasted only ten days—December 28, 1831, to January 5, 1832. At the end, fourteen whites were dead and 312 slaves executed, with over 1000 shot in battle or while fleeing. What Poe leaves unsaid is significant. He says nothing about the Nat Turner rebellion of 1831, too unspeakable to mention, perhaps because it took place too close to home in Southampton, Virginia.

Poe wants his readers to recognize that abolitionists who "come to us in the name of our common Redeemer and common country" seek "our destruction under the mask of Christian Charity and Brotherly Love." Ever alert to the way totalizing rhetoric screens more devious concerns, Poe now substitutes a few unalienable facts for what he sees as the dangerous masquerade of liberation. What follows are five of the most disturbing pages Poe ever wrote. Here, all the language of sentiment—the cunning use of the claims of the heart to remove or deny real human claims—what Poe recognized in his writings about women, is used, with no irony intended, as he turns to blacks.

What he introduces as "a few words of [his] own" is far more vehement than Paulding's discussion of slave devotion and the master's "kindly feeling and condescending familiarity." Here, Poe takes his own romantic postures, the supine poet dead or dying in "For Annie," or the varying deathbed scenes in his tales about women, and gives what was literary parody or philosophical crux a ground in reality. And the reality is ugly, and perhaps made more so by Poe's moralizing idealism, his attempt *to turn a thing into a man,* to paraphrase Philip Fisher's words in *Hard Facts* (1985). "We speak of the moral influences flowing from the relation of master and slave, and the moral feelings engendered and cultivated by it." Poe depends for his lesson about this *relation* on what he calls the "patriarchal character." This character is both sustained and necessitated by what he calls "the peculiar character (I may say the peculiar nature) of the negro." No less a suggestion than that the enslaved want to be mastered, for they *love*—and this is the crucial word for Poe—to serve, to be subservient. What follows is an *excess of devotion* that becomes the focus, as Poe sees it, of the master-slave relationship. In "The Black Cat" (1843) Poe will reveal the consequences of such an inextricable bond through the horrific reversals possible in a formally benevolent attachment: "the unselfish and self-sacrificing love of a brute" and the "docility and humanity" of the master.

But before Poe gets to his theory of servitude, cast as devotional sermon, he presents the *essential* negro. Poe never has problems with invention, and yet his inventiveness, his masterly design, is confounded in his attempt to "develop the causes which might and should have blackened the negro's skin and crisped his hair into wool." Since Poe admits it might be a while before anyone can answer the why of the curse of pigment and frizz, he gives us his theory of the institution of slavery. This theory is based on the reciprocity between what he describes as "loyal devotion on the part of the slave" and "the master's reciprocal feeling of parental attachment to his humble dependent." These "sentiments in the breast of the negro and his master," Poe explains, "are stronger than they would be under like circumstances between individuals of the white race." So, slavery becomes something akin to divine devotion, a lock of love that no mere mortal white man can sunder. As Melville reiterates in "Benito Cereno" when Captain Delano thinks about the "negro":

When to this [the good humor and cheerfulness of the negro] is added the docility arising from the unaspiring contentment of a limited mind, and that susceptibility of blind attachment sometimes inhering in indisputable inferiors, one readily perceives why those hypochondriacs, Johnson and Byron . . . took to their hearts, almost to the exclusion of the entire white race, their serving men, the negroes, Barber and Fletcher.

If there is any doubt that Poe is raising the "childlike" devotion of the slave and the "fatherly" concern of the master to the status of something akin to courtly love (where, however, the heart is made noble by *not* possessing), note what follows.

That they [these sentiments] belong to the class of feelings "by which the heart is made better," we know. How come they? They have their rise in the relation between the infant and the nurse. They are cultivated between him and his foster brother. They are cherished by the parents of both. They are fostered by the habit of affording protection and favors to the younger offspring of the same nurse. They grow by the habitual use of the word "my," used in the language of affectionate appropriation, long before any idea of value mixes with it. It is a term of endearment. That is an easy transition by which he who is taught to call the little negro "his," in this sense and *because he loves him,* shall love him *because he is his.* The idea is not new, that our habits and affections are reciprocally cause and effect of each other.

Applying the same analytic skill to this nearly incomprehensible (and incommensurate) relation as he will apply to the cosmic attractions of *Eureka,* Poe bases the cause of reciprocity in what is *cultivated, cherished,* and *fostered.* In this diagnosis, he goes far beyond the discourse of James Kirke Paulding in *Slavery in the United States.* Paulding argues that "the domestic relations of the master and slave are of a more familiar, confidential, and even respectful character, than those of the employer and hireling elsewhere." He praises the reciprocal and natural attachment, "this state of feeling, which a Southern life and education can only give," and concludes: "It is often the case, that the children of the domestic servants become pets in the house, and the playmates of the white children of the family." But Poe is less interested in what Southerners claimed as a type of familial proprietorship—feelings that could elevate or mask what was merely the best use of valuable property—than in elucidating a gothic tale of excessive obedience, reminiscent of Caleb Williams's confession to Falkland: "Sir, I could die to serve you!"

No cause for attachment is more powerful than a linguistic practice, the use of "the possessive 'my' . . . the language of affectionate appropriation." This recognition that you love what is *your own*, or "propre" in French ("ce que quel qu'un, quelque chose a, possède a l'exclusion de tout autre"), returns us to Poe's romance. For the remainder of the review gets its force from two proofs for "this school of feeling": in the sickroom and on the deathbed. As Poe says, "In this school we have witnessed scenes at which even the hard heart of a thorough bred philanthropist would melt."

Love and piety flow from both sides, from both the proprietor and the property. "But it is not by the bedside of the sick negro that the feeling we speak of is chiefly engendered. They who would view it in its causes and effects must see him by the sick bed of his master— must see *her* by the sick bed of her *mistress*. We have seen these things." Poe takes what he calls "the study of human nature" out of the closet, as he reports intimate scenes of a black nanny shedding tears over her white "foster babe," of a black servant, "advanced in pregnancy, and in bad health," who kept returning at night to the door of her "good lady" mistress. Poe repeats the words of the faithful, "crouched down at the door, listening for the groans of the sufferer." Ordered home, she cries, "Master it ain't no use for me to go to bed, Sir. It don't do me no good, I cannot sleep, Sir."

In this world of noble sentiments, nothing less than love "prompts" the master, not "interest" or "value." Since the black was for Poe savage, childlike, and brute, a near mystical reliance on a cult of feeling becomes most fit for any discussion of race relations. Appropriative language is appropriate for a piece of property. For Poe, biological traits would accomplish the full metaphysical right of exclusion. Except for this one review, and a brief discussion of Longfellow's *Poems on Slavery* (1845), Poe omits the discussion of race from his critical reviews and essays.

For Poe the analogy between women and slaves was unthinkable. Poe could never, in spite of his awareness of women's subordination, entertain the conjunction of race and gender. For example, his review of Elizabeth Barrett's *The Drama of Exile, and Other Poems* in the *Broadway Journal* in 1845 expresses his concern about how women writers are treated when "the race of critics," as he put it, "are masculine—men." The greatest evil resulting from the absence of women critics, he explained, is that "the critical *man*" finds it "an unpleasant task . . . 'to speak ill of a woman.' " Yet though here Poe refused to condescend to women, taking both their persons and their writings seriously, he blots out the activism of women writers who also happen to be abolitionists.

"Gracious heaven! What a prostitution!" James Kirke Paulding ends his *Slavery in the United States* with a warning to those women members of the abolition societies: "with all that respectful deference to the sex," he reminds them "that the appropriate sphere of women is their home, and their appropriate duties at the cradle or the fireside." For women must never forget that they are "the guardian angel of the happiness of man; his protector and mentor in childhood; his divinity in youth; his companion and solace in manhood; his benign and gentle nurse in old age."

In spite of Poe's subversion of the romantic idea of woman—his interrogation of women's coercion into image—he could never make the connection between slavery and the condition of white women in his society. No woman will ever be named by Poe as part of "the small coterie of abolitionists, transcendentalists and fanatics in general," who are a "knot of rogues and madmen." Recall Margaret Fuller's *Woman in the Nineteenth Century* (1845), which Poe will review in "The Literati of New York City" in 1846: "There exists in the minds of men a tone of feeling toward women as toward slaves, such as is expressed in the common phrase, 'Tell that to women and children.' " When Poe reviews *Woman in the Nineteenth Century*, he ignores Fuller's conjunction of woman and slave but praises the essay as "nervous, forcible, thoughtful, suggestive, brilliant . . . for all that Miss Fuller produces is entitled to those epithets—but I must say that the conclusions reached are only in part my own. Not that they are too bold, by any means—too novel, too startling, or too dangerous in their consequences." That Poe did not, or would not, make overtly the connection between women and slaves is also evident in his review of Lydia Maria Child, also in "The Literati of New York City." Throughout his praise of her poetry, there is never a reference to her well-known *Anti-Slavery Catechism* (1836), *The Evils of Slavery and the Cure of Slavery* (1836), or *An Appeal in Favor of That Class of Americans Called Africans* (1833), even though he begins by noting—without naming—those compositions by which she has "acquired a just celebrity." He concludes by merely saying: I need scarcely add that she has always been distinguished for her energetic and active philanthropy."

Poe remained haunted, as did Jefferson, by the terrible disjunction between the ideology of slavery (the abstract and rather benign parental ideology grounded in the equally abstract assumption of negro inferiority) and the concrete realities of mutilation, torture, and violation. Jefferson's inability to deal with the issue of slavery leads directly to the apocalyptic terminology at the end of Query XVIII in *Notes on the State of Virginia:* "Indeed I tremble for my country when I reflect that God is just; that his justice cannot sleep forever; that considering numbers, nature and natural means only, a revolution of the wheel of fortune, an exchange of situation, is among possible events: that it may become possible by supernatural interference!" The gospel of apocalypse, the blood, fire, and overturning of Poe's tales of terror, gain their force from Poe's problematic relation to notions of mastery and subordination. More important, he understood how the idealization of women in his society depended for its force on the dehumanization of blacks. When he writes *Eureka* at the end of his life, his version of "the realm of Ends," he demonstrates the "convertibility" of matter and spirit, destroying the divisions that were at the heart of racialist discourse.

In the South's official mythology, the negro was forever non-Adamic: he/she had no task of naming and no gift of language. In

"The Murders in the Rue Morgue," Poe uses Dupin's acuteness in detection to reveal his own fantasy of barbarism. Poe had no doubt read that most severe of colonial historians, Edward Long, who in his *History of Jamaica* wrote: "That the oran-outang and some races of black men are very nearly allied, is, I think, more than probable." As Long admitted with Buffon: "the oran-outang's brain is a senseless *icon* of the human; . . . it is meer matter, unanimated with a thinking principle, in any, or at least in a very minute and imperfect degree . . . an oran-outang . . . is a human being . . . but of an inferior species . . . he has in form a much nearer resemblance to the Negroe race, than the latter bear to white men."

The most difficult problem in knowing what manner of brute is the murderer in the Rue Morgue is the "very strange voice," the unrecognizable language of the criminal. Dupin explains: "How strangely unusual must that voice have really been . . . —in whose *tones,* even, denizens of the five great divisions of Europe could recognize nothing familiar! You will say that it might have been the voice of an Asiatic—of an African." Poe concludes the story by describing a scene of wrath and revenge that suddenly, whether intentionally or not, moves us from Paris to the South, from Madame L'Espanaye to the brute's master:

Gnashing its teeth, and flashing fire from its eyes, it flew upon the body of the girl, and imbedded its fearful talons in her throat, retaining its grasp until she expired. Its wandering and wild glances fell at this moment upon the head of the bed, over which the face of its master, rigid with horror, was just discernible. The fury of the beast, who no doubt bore still in mind the dreaded whip, was suddenly converted into fear.

What Poe calls the "catastrophe of the drama" in the supposedly "humorous" story "The System of Doctor Tarr and Professor Fether" (1844), we should now recall: "But I shall never forget the emotions of wonder and horror with which I gazed, when, leaping through these windows, and down among us *pele-mele,* fighting, stamping, scratching, and howling, there rushed a perfect army of what I took to be Chimpanzees, Ourang-Outangs, or big black baboons of the Cape of Good Hope."

Poe's "Hop-Frog; or, The Eight Chained Ourang-Outangs" (1849), one of his last tales, written some seven months before his death, after the end of his engagement to Sarah Helen Whitman, while he fought illness and despair, remains Poe's most horrible tale of retribution. What Thomas O. Mabbott regards as merely "a terrible exposition of the darkness of a human soul" is Poe's final revelation of the national sin of slavery. Did Poe know Hegel's analysis of convertibility? The master, dependent on the labor of the slave, would end by depending on the slave, and the terms of domination would be reversed. As Hegel wrote in his *Phenomenology of Mind:* "Just as lordship showed its essential nature to be the reverse of what it wants to be, so, too, bondage will, when completed, pass into the opposite of what it immediately is." In any case, Poe would have been familiar with Jefferson's description of the effect of slavery "as a perpetual exercise of the most boisterous passions, the most unremitting despotism," which turned the master into brute.

The eight masters of "Hop-Frog" get turned into orang-outangs, tarred and flaxed (not feathered), by an enslaved dwarf "from some barbarous province that no person ever heard of." Then, chained in a circle, facing each other in a stupor of coincidence, they are burned to "a fetid, blackened, hideous, and indistinguishable mass." The shocking blind spot of most critics to the practice of slavery as fundamental to the horrors of "Hop-Frog" is exemplified by Mabbot's reflection in introducing the story in his *Collected Works of Edgar Allan Poe:* "The manner of chaining apes described is not mentioned by any authorities consulted, and since it is integral to the plot, may well be invented on the basis of the captive wild men described by Froissart." In the final incendiary climax of "Hop-Frog" Poe gives "the power of blackness" its obvious, though repressed cause. Poe recalls, in a bloodcurdling way, his own earlier preoccupation in the "Paulding-Drayton Review" with *what,* in God's name, might "have blackened the negro's skin and crisped his hair into wool." But the tables have turned. The epidermic curse—the fatality of being black, or blackened—has been visited on the master race.

Writing his 1855 "Preface" to *Leaves of Grass,* Walt Whitman declared: "Great genius and the people of these states must never be demeaned to romances. As soon as histories are properly told there is no more need of romances." By the 1850s the apparent division between fact and fiction was breaking down. The "romance" of the fugitive slave depended for its force on being a "true history." These "verifiable" romances were janus-faced, pointing to both truth and fable. Hawthorne precedes *The House of the Seven Gables* (1851) with a discourse on "Romance" that grants the writer the use of the "Marvelous" in writing a tale that attempts "to connect a bygone time with the very present that is flitting away from us." And as Poe had argued against Hawthorne's heavy-handed use of allegory in his 1847 review of *Twice-Told Tales,* now Hawthorne emphasizes the importance of keeping any moral "undercurrent" to the tale unobtrusive. Unsubtle didacticism can kill the effect proper to revealing "the truth of the human heart."

Whereas Hawthorne can choose to err on the side of fiction, no African American writer who had recovered his freedom only to work for the abolitionist cause could afford such flights of fancy. On the one hand, the conversion of brute to man depended on a language so extraordinary that it could make the horrible facts of slavery into romance. On the other hand, these titillating narratives had to be based on true experiences. Harriet A. Jacobs, writing her "Preface" to *Incidents in the Life of a Slave Girl,* published in 1861, begins: "Reader, be assured this narrative is no fiction. I am aware that some of my adventures may seem incredible; but they are, nevertheless, strictly true." And her editor, Lydia Maria Child, authenticated the document in the introduction to Jacobs's drama of what happens when romance—or more precisely, sexuality—is locked into race. She assures readers that she knows the writer and adds: "I believe those who know her will not be disposed to doubt her veracity, though some incidents in her story are more romantic than fiction."

Toni Morrison writes in *Beloved* (1987): "Definitions belong to the definers—not the defined." The black fugitive turned hero or heroine found not only that there had to be limits to invention—imagination had to be accountable to a reality often invented by someone else—but also that these facts could then be embellished or made to serve the often demeaning romantic fantasies about the "African character." So, terms like *romance* and *history* (like liberty and bondage) underwent some strange but instructive metamorphoses. In the history of the United States, where a slave, a piece of property, could become an object of "love," linguistic distinctions were undone, humanitarian definitions derailed and dismantled.

The oft-repeated "power of blackness" thus could be argued to be absolutely necessary to the continued construction of whiteness. As Frantz Fanon argued in *Black Skin, White Masks* (1952, tr. 1967): "The black soul is a white man's artifact." Who holds the claims on the business of racial identity? Melville knew that the claims of color are nothing more than a sometime masquerade, depending on who wields power when. *The Confidence-Man* (1857) remains the most astonishing narrative of convertibility. But as early as *Pierre; or, The Ambiguities* (1852), Melville attempted to "gospelize the world anew" by reveling in a wild blurring of opposites, what Poe had called "Infernal Twoness." Reviewers were quick to condemn *Pierre* when it appeared, recognizing how dangerous were the excesses of his language (not only his subject) to morals and to the very myths of purity and domestic love on which Americans of "good taste and good sense" depended.

Like Poe in *Eureka*, Melville dealt with impossible inversions, unspeakable mergings. But Melville humanized or gave flesh to Poe's Newtonian mechanics and cosmic attractions. He attempted nothing less than to give a moral to what might have remained an abstract story. "This history goes forward and goes backward, as occasion calls." The convertibility between matter and spirit that Poe cast as atoms moving to and fro in the throes of attraction and repulsion, Melville articulated as the inevitable reciprocity between "Lucy or God," "Virtue or Vice," light and dark, "wife or sister, saint or fiend!" In Pierre's remarkable dream of Enceladus, the burden of whiteness—parasitical, destructive, and sterile—is embodied in the white amaranthine flower. These flowers multiply, contribute nothing to the agricultural value of the hillside pastures, and force the tenants to beg their "lady" to abate their rent: "The small white flower it is our bane! . . . The aspiring amaranth, every year it climbs and adds new terraces to its sway! The immortal amaranth, it will not die, but last year's flowers survive to this!"

The dark world, the trope of aggression and excess, Melville reassigns to an overpowering whiteness. After all, if natural philosophers had argued about the cause of human blackness, the pollution of color, the barbaric stain, Melville put inscrutable *whiteness,* the "colorless, all-color," the "shrouded phantom of the whitened waters" at the heart of the terror and the fascination of *Moby-Dick,* his other quest romance. In 1837–38 Poe wrote a story that no doubt influenced Melville. *The Narrative of Arthur Gordon Pym of Nantucket* was his own "narrative" of whiteness, a romantic voyage to the "*white* curtain of the South." If the Southern slave made his perilous journey from bondage to the North—a place that, as Frederick Douglass and other African American autobiographers would find, was no salvation from degradation—Poe takes his reader from the North to a terribly iterated South. Ostensibly a trip to the South Seas, the narrative at times seems to mime and invert the narratives of American slavery. The title page reads as a burlesque of captivity, catastrophe, and incredibility: ". . . the massacre of her crew among/ A group of islands in the / EIGHTY-FOURTH PARALLEL OF SOUTHERN LATITUDE; / Together with the incredible adventures and discoveries / STILL FURTHER SOUTH / To which that distressing calamity gave rise."

In the "Preface" to his narrative, "A. G. Pym" places a "Mr. Poe, lately editor of the Southern Literary Messenger," quite firmly in the role of Southern gentleman, one of those "several gentlemen in Richmond, Va., who felt deep interest in all matters relating to the regions I had visited." Although Pym fears his story will lack "the *appearance* of that truth it would really possess," that only family and friends would "put faith in [his] veracity," and that the public would judge his writing "an impudent and ingenious fiction," he agrees to a "*ruse*" suggested by Mr. Poe. The adventures will be published in the *Southern Literary Messenger* "*under the garb of fiction.*" Yet the public refuses to receive the "pretended fiction" as a "fable," and Pym decides "to undertake a regular compilation and publication of the adventures in question."

Poe will later claim *Eureka* to be his "Book of Truths" as well as a "Romance." Convertibility is essential to both his style and his metaphysics. Fact becomes fancy and fancy fact in the mutual adaptation that remains for his earthbound readers the sure sign of God's perfection. But what is being made convertible in Pym's strange narrative? Pym's narrative is based on other chronicles of polar exploration and travel, most notably Benjamin Morrell's *Narrative of Four Voyages* (1832). This story, however, is less a romance of voyages to distant seas than a spectacular and violent staging of "civilization" defining itself through the conquest of savagery. Yet there is no possibility of definition or conquest in this world of shifting appearances. Before Pym and Peters reach the black island of Tsalal (meaning "to be shaded, dark" in Hebrew and "to be shade" in its ancient Ethiopian root), the reader has already endured scenes of butchery, drunkenness, treachery, and cannibalism. So, although Pym's story leads us to the islands of the South Seas where we encounter "barbarians" and "savages," when the explorers finally visit the island village, the common racist divisions between "civilization" and "barbarism," good and evil, black and white, are no longer operative.

The "savages" are described with their "complexion a jet black, with thick and woolly hair." The natives dread the complexion of "the white race" and, most of all, the strange white thing "lying on the ground," earlier described by Pym as "a singular-looking land-animal," with a "body . . . covered with a straight silky hair, perfectly white." The complex working out of the narrative depends upon a duplicity or *doubling* of color. As the explorers journey farther into the interior to that "country differing essentially from any hitherto visited by civilized men," any simple splitting of color into black and white—with the metaphysical truths normally attached to such biological facts—becomes more vexed and shifting than any racialist polarity allows.

Color becomes Poe's subject, as in the celebrated description of the water of Tsalal: not black, not white, but "*not* colourless: nor was it of any one uniform colour—presenting to the eye, as it flowed, every possible shade of purple, like the hues of a changeable silk." If the justification of slavery depended on the curse of color as sign of inferiority—what Jefferson stressed as the "real distinction which nature has made"—this story depends upon a crisis of color. Even though the waters manifest an uncommon variability of color, upon closer examination Pym discovers that "the whole mass of liquid was made up of a number of distinct veins, each of a distinct hue . . . these veins did not commingle."

Without pushing too far the problematic symbolic construction of a totalizing category called *race* in this *romance,* I turn to the final entries in Pym's narrative, before his fall into the vacancy of whiteness. Moving quickly southward, Pym, Peters, and the black-teethed Nu-Nu are absorbed by an inexplicable whitening: the warm water has a "milky hue"; a "fine white powder, resembling ashes" falls over the canoe; another white animal floats by. In the apocalyptic end, they are in between a "sullen darkness" and "milky depths." Then the darkness spreads except for the "veil" or "curtain" of whiteness. Pym's final vision—the mysterious "shrouded human figure" with a complexion "of the perfect whiteness of snow"—has been described as God, Lord of Death, or the "Deity of *Eureka*," ushering all things into the final Unity. However we choose to interpret the figure, the ultimate revelation of light becomes deadly, absorbing the previous nuances of shadow or darkness.

In the "Note" that follows Pym's death and the abrupt end of his story, the unnamed writer refers to "the most faintly-detailed incidents of the narrative." Attempting an interpretation of the figures of the chasms on the island of Tsalal, he moves his reader toward "The region of the south." The arm of the " 'most northwardly' of the figures" is "outstretched towards the south," and the displaced Virginian Poe concludes with a litany on *white:* "the carcass of the *white* animal picked up at sea. . . . the shuddering exclamation of the captive Tsalalian upon encountering the *white* materials in possession of Mr. Pym. . . . the shriek of the swift-flying, *white,* and gigantic birds which had issued from the vapoury *white* curtain of the South. Nothing *white* was to be found at Tsalal." And in the region beyond, Poe suggests we can know nothing. Yet, perhaps his Southern readers, especially those Virginians who had followed closely the debates about slavery in the Virginia Legislature in 1831–32, would not be immune to the final effect of this strange commentary on the vicissitudes of white power. The unaccountable and prophetic final sentence of the "Note" reads: "*I have graven it within the hills, and my vengeance upon the dust within the rock.*" What G. R. Thompson in *Poe's Fiction: Romantic Irony in the Gothic Tales* (1973) calls a divine and "perverse vengeance for some unknown offense," no doubt recalled for some readers the *known* offense of slavery, and the fears of some Southerners, like Jefferson and Poe, that God's judgment would not be stayed, that the inevitable catastrophe is at hand.

Joan Dayan

# Domesticity and Fiction

Literary histories have employed a variety of terms to describe the novels written by women in the United States during the middle decades of the nineteenth century: the sentimental novel, the female *Bildungsroman*, the domestic novel. This proliferation of terms is useful, if for no other reason, because it suggests that women novelists of the period were hardly the undifferentiated mass that Nathaniel Hawthorne represented them as being when (rankled by the success of the women novelists with whom he competed for the public's attention) he complained to his publisher that "America is now wholly given over to a damned mob of scribbling women."

Although rakish characters like Charles Morgeson in Elizabeth Stoddard's *The Morgesons* (1862) and St. Elmo in Augusta Evans Wilson's *St. Elmo* (1867) owe more than a little to Samuel Richardson, the seduction plot so prominent in the early sentimental fiction intrudes only occasionally in women's novels published after 1820. Female *Bildungsroman* more adequately describes much of this fiction. Yet, while Susan Warner's *The Wide, Wide World* (1850) and Martha Finley's *Elsie Dinsmore* (1867) are exemplary instances of the novel of female development, Caroline Lee Hentz's *Linda* (1850) and E. D. E. N. Southworth's *The Hidden Hand* (1859) flaunt the realist conventions of the *Bildungsroman* and might be more accurately classified as female picaresque or sensation fiction. Finally, to call women's popular fiction "domestic novels" *is* also somewhat misleading. Catharine Maria Sedgwick's *Home* (1835) *is* little more than a fictionalized treatise on housekeeping and child-rearing, but

Fanny Fern's semiautobiographical *Ruth Hall* (1855) records the adventures of a woman whose domestic ties have been severed and Caroline Chesebro's *Isa: A Pilgrimage* (1852) tells the story of a radical feminist who lives with a man to whom she is not married.

"Women's novels" might be the only rubric elastic enough to encompass the diversity within this literature. But since historically the gender distinction has worked at the expense of women writers (as Hawthorne's comment suggests), we now must wield it very carefully. Arguably, the only way to avoid inadvertent replication of the invidious nineteenth-century gender distinction would be to dispense with the category of "women writers" altogether. And yet, entirely abandoning this category of analysis seems unwise at this particular historic juncture. Literary historians, accepting Hawthorne's comments about scribbling women at face value, have assumed that women novelists of the period do not merit serious study, and hence these writers languish in undeserved obscurity. Given that women novelists have been excluded *as a class,* feminist literary histories must include them *as a class*—albeit with the understanding that the category of "women novelists" intervenes rather than describes, which is to say that it is used provisionally to redress strategic omissions in the scholarship rather than used to suggest either that women's novels are all the same or that they are necessarily different from men's novels.

One could argue that the ill-repute of mid-century novels by women owes less to their individual literary infelicities than to the rhetorical uses toward which scholars attempting to define the classic tradition of the novel have deployed them. Acts of definition are necessarily acts of differentiation. The highly contingent process of defining a classic tradition in part involved distinguishing it from what is *not* the classic tradition. By aligning the distinction they produced between canonical and noncanonical with gender difference, scholars could give that distinction the look of a difference found in nature (as it were) rather than in the opinions of mere human beings. Literary historians evolved a complex history of nineteenth-century culture in which they associated femininity with the passive reproduction of the status quo and masculinity with the willful transgression of norms. In defining the classic tradition they excluded not just women but also male novelists whom they perceived as capitulating to the conventional, and they exalted those male novelists who most visibly thematized their own defiance of cultural expectations.

The crucial role of gender difference in defining the classic tradition of the novel helps explain some counterintuitive representations of the male classics that have been taken as truisms—for example, that James Fenimore Cooper's historical romances and what are called his "Indian novels" are a reaction against the feminization of the vocation of novel writing and an attempt to articulate a "masculine" novelistic countertradition. This claim is made despite the fact that Lydia Maria Child's "Indian novel" *Hobomok* (1824) exercised a profound influence on *The Last of the Mohicans* (which appeared two years *after* Child's book) and despite the fact that the historical romance was a preferred mode amongst women writers. Further evidence of the role played by the rhetoric of gender in the construction of the American Renaissance is the fact that, rather than describing *The Scarlet Letter* (1850) and *The House of the Seven Gables* (1851) with the "feminine" term of "domestic novels," literary historians generally refer to them as "romances," and they do this despite the fact that Hawthorne's relentless and gendered opposition of public and private spheres, his hostility toward the Puritan patriarch, and his representation of imperiled womanhood are precisely the materials of the domestic novel. Similarly, the need to manufacture the difference that would separate canonical from noncanonical, one could argue, dictates that Herman Melville's *Pierre* (1852) be generally regarded as a *parody* of the domestic novel rather than an *instance* of it.

Traditional concepts of the American Renaissance do not ignore women novelists so much as use them as the demonic double of the classic novelists of the period. Taking their cue from Melville's "Hawthorne and His Mosses" (a review of a collection of Hawthorne's tales that Melville published anonymously in 1850), literary historians have argued that classic writers used the conventions of best-sellers in order to communicate their own original and profound meanings. Popular women novelists, they have claimed, merely reproduced a standardized product that appealed to a mass audience composed primarily of undereducated and underemployed middle-class women desperate for something to fill their empty days.

Yet, even if women writers (like male writers) had to fulfill certain conventions in order to sell their novels, what prevented them from manipulating those conventions toward their own ends, as Melville describes Hawthorne doing or as he himself perhaps does in *Pierre?* In *Little Women* (1869) Louisa May Alcott's satiric transposition of E. D. E. N. Southworth into S. L. A. N. G. Northbury, her humorous treatment of Jo March's conflicting commitments to economic success and truth-telling when she launches her career as a writer, and Jo's disparaging references to notions she finds too "sentimental" — these suggest that the classic male novelists were not the only ones who felt that writing for the literary marketplace imposed some limits on what they could say. Only if one assumes that women writers were incapable of manipulating popular conventions can one read *Little Women* (as it so often is read) as an uncomplicated and unselfconscious capitulation to the demands of the marketplace.

Revisionary feminist scholarship has suggested that women like Alcott encoded "subversive" feminist messages in texts that merely *appear* conventional. Women novelists may also have been in the business of "hoodwinking" a public composed primarily of "superficial skimmers" (to borrow Melville's language). A more radical feminist critique, however, would note that the images of passivity and addiction characteristic of descriptions of the rise of mass culture are themselves gendered. The belief that by mid-century the reading audience was increasingly (if not overwhelmingly) female may itself account for scholarly consensus that antebellum Americans were hostile to any novel that manifestly challenged the literary, moral, or political conventions that permitted the masses to proceed through their lives with as little reflection as possible.

Literary historians' use of a rhetoric of gender in the construction of the American Renaissance has antecedents in the work of the canonical male writers of the period. For example, in *The Spy* (1821) Cooper (who published his first novel, *Precaution,* under a female pseudonym) satirizes the literary predilections of "our countrywomen, by whose opinions it is that we expect to stand or fall." Taking statements by male writers at face value, scholars have gone so far as to claim that the antebellum United States was "a society controlled by women." One dubbed the middle decade of the nineteenth century "the feminine fifties" and exclaimed: "And to think of the masculine Melville and Hawthorne and Thoreau condemned to work through their literary lives in an atmosphere like that."

Increasingly, the "feminization of American culture" (that is to say, the alleged determining influence exercised by women over mid-century culture at the level both of consumption and of production) appears to be largely a fiction created by the nineteenth century and perpetuated by literary historians in the twentieth. No direct evidence corroborates Cooper's assertion that the success or failure of a novel depended on women's tastes; contemporary historians of reading have little firsthand data on the gender composition of the early nineteenth-century reading audience. The belief in the femininity of the audience for novels rests primarily upon indirect evidence like *The Spy*'s introduction and upon the patently chauvinist assumption that because most middle-class women were "only housewives" they had enormous quantities of free time on their hands that they squandered reading trash. (Harriet Beecher Stowe's letters suggest that some middle-class women were in fact driven to states of nervous exhaustion by the amount of work required to run a household prior to our age of "modern conveniences." Her descriptions of trying to dry sheets in the humid summer air while a cholera epidemic that would eventually take the life of one of her children raged through Cincinnati seems particularly to the point.)

Nor is it clear that women dominated culture at the level of production. To the contrary, there is evidence that at mid-century men produced more than twice the number of novels as women. Mid-century women writers like Warner, Harriet Beecher Stowe, and Maria Cummins (who wrote the first "best-sellers" in the modern sense of the term) far outsold the "classic" male novelists with whom they are usually compared. But Hawthorne, Melville, and Cooper were not the only male novelists of the period. William Ware, T. S. Arthur, and Donald Mitchell are just a few of the male novelists whose popularity rivaled that of their female competitors. Finally, even if (as it indeed appears) the best-selling novels of the period written by women outsold the best-sellers written by men, the book-publishing industry was entirely in the hands of men, a fact that greatly complicates the issue of who "controlled" the literary marketplace. In the face of such facts about production—and in the absence of direct evidence about consumption—perhaps the time has come to ask not whether the "feminization of American culture" was a bad thing (the traditional view) or whether it was a good thing (the feminist revisionary view) but *whether it even happened in the first place.*

How is it, we might ask, that writers in this period came to believe that America (to paraphrase Hawthorne) had been wholly given over to women?

The belief that society had been feminized grows out of exaggerated claims for the influence of women generated by the rise of domestic ideology. By 1830 the nature of woman's contribution to society had become a regional obsession amongst intellectuals of the Northeastern United States, and by virtue of the dominance this region exercised over cultural production it necessarily became a national obsession as well.

The Revolutionary-era idea of republican motherhood is in some sense the precursor of domestic ideology. The Enlightenment concept that youth was particularly susceptible to both good and bad influences led late eighteenth-century American educators like Judith Sargent Murray and Benjamin Rush to argue that in their capacity as mothers women exercised a tremendous power over the fate of the Republic in the values they taught boys who would grow up to lead the nation. It was therefore necessary, argued these writers, to pay more attention to women's education than had previously been given, lest mothers communicate undemocratic tendencies to their male offspring.

Whereas Murray and Rush attempted to incorporate women into the ongoing Revolutionary project by representing men and women as *equally* capable of contributing to the moral well-being of the Republic, early nineteenth-century writers increasingly represented women as the *sole* repository of virtue in society. At the same time that they began characterizing men as naturally aggressive, sensual, and godless, authors of countless sermons, newspaper articles, and treatises began to argue that if through their relations with fathers, husbands, and sons in the home women did not exercise a civilizing influence on men, society would collapse into complete anarchy. In one of the scores of sermons bearing the title "Female Influence" written in the period, the Reverend J. F. Stearns proclaimed to his women parishioners in 1837: "Yours it is to decide . . . whether we shall be a nation of refined and high minded Christians, or wheth-er . . . we shall become a fierce race of semi-barbarians."

While such theories of female influence claimed that women ulti-mately controlled society, they also stressed that women exercised that power through indirect *influence* rather than through direct *force*. If a woman attempted to influence society directly—through, for example, winning the right to vote—she would lose her control over men, since brute force rather than moral suasion governed the political realm. Woman's physical delicacy would prevent her from battling with men on their own terrain, it was argued, and hence it was in her own best interest to remain within her "proper sphere."

For some writers, however, even moral suasion within her proper sphere was too direct a manifestation of woman's power. Child's 1831 treatise *The Mother's Book* (a somewhat more philosophical statement than *The American Frugal Housewife,* which Child pub-lished one year earlier) asserts that it is better for mothers to instruct through the example of their own virtuous behavior rather than through precept. Its dialogic form made narrative a particularly ap-propriate vehicle for what the age defined as women's proper exercise of power. Child (herself a novelist) recommended the reading of up-lifting fiction, but she took care to distinguish uplifting fiction from fiction with a "good moral": "The morality should be *in* the book," she wrote, "not tacked upon the *end* of it." No doubt Cummins was thinking of the educational uses to which her own work might be put when, in *The Lamplighter* (1854), she describes Emily Graham ju-diciously selecting uplifting narratives of the "triumph of truth, obe-dience and patience" for Gerty Flint to read. This method of incul-cating moral principles in her willful ward conforms with Emily's more general commitment to exerting her authority only covertly—a method contrasted with her father's disastrously manifest exertions of his authority. Emily, writes Cummins, "preached no sermons, nor did she weary [Gerty] with exhortations and precepts. Indeed, it did not occur to Gerty that she [was being] *taught* anything; but simply and gradually [Emily] imparted light to the child's dark soul." Be-cause narrative was not considered rhetorical (rhetoric being associ-ated with the "masculine" political sphere), novel writing was seen as a particularly appropriate way for women to exert their indirect influence for the good of society.

The cult of domesticity and its appropriation of the genre of the novel provide a cultural context in which to understand Hawthorne's comment that America had been taken over by a mob of scribbling women (a comment that, by the way, was prompted specifically by the success of *The Lamplighter*). Hawthorne's overstatement of the case was informed as much by his culture's belief in the feminization of American society as it was by his own professional jealousy. In fact, in *The Scarlet Letter*, five years before writing the letter to his publisher, Hawthorne suggested that in American society the masculine-identified characteristics of Puritan times (the physical vigor and moral callousness of the Puritan elders) had given way to feminine-identified qualities of antebellum times (the exquisite delicacy and sensitivity of the narrator of "The Custom-House," which is presaged by the nervous behavior of the Puritan male hysteric Arthur Dimmesdale).

The theory that society had grown more feminine was by no means limited to male novelists of the period. One could argue that male writers manifested more hostility toward the changes they perceived than did most women writers, a hostility that they evidenced in their fondness for narrating the flight of male characters into the wilderness or out to sea (and thus away from the rule of women); however, a novel like Harriet Beecher Stowe's *Pearl of Orr's Island* (1862) suggests that it is more complicated than this. Like *The Scarlet Letter*, Stowe's local color tale is set in Puritan times (its titular "pearl" Mara Lincoln in fact recalls Hawthorne's character Pearl). Stowe's narrator, coyly prophesying the situation that nineteenth-century Americans felt increasingly characteristic of their own century, associates seventeenth-century New England with the haughty masculinity of the young Moses Pennel and suggests: "There may, perhaps, come a time when the saucy boy, who steps so superbly, and predominates so proudly in virtue of his physical strength and daring, will learn to tremble at the golden measuring-rod, held in the hand of a woman." As an adolescent, Moses begins to chafe at the virtuous Mara's "apron strings" and goes to sea to sow his wild oats—an act of rebellion that anticipates Huck Finn's decision at the end of Mark

Twain's *Adventures of Huckleberry Finn* (1885) "to light out for the Territory" in order to evade Aunt Sally's "sivilizing" designs on him. One might argue that women's novels already contain the narratives of male rebellion against the rule of women that are generally associated with male writers. In other words, far from challenging the principles of domestic ideology, male narratives of rebellion against women's rule merely reinforce domesticity's association of men with "semi-barbarism" and women with "high minded" Christianity. Similarly, one could argue that theories of the American Renaissance that represent the classic male novelists as rebels against the acceptable conventions of a literary marketplace controlled by women merely perpetuate the belief in the moral inequality of the sexes fundamental to domestic ideology.

The cult of domesticity may have become culturally dominant by the mid-nineteenth century, but it is important to bear in mind that, at least in its origins, it was an oppositional ideology. Domesticity's origins are explicitly antipatriarchal, and while to argue this is not the same thing as arguing that domesticity was feminist, it does explain why so many women took up the pen in behalf of a philosophy that seems, from a contemporary perspective, so at odds with women's political, economic, and personal independence.

Domesticity proceeds from a critique of the commodification of womanhood in the aristocratic patriarchal family. Jean-Jacques Rousseau captures the spirit of the patriarchal view of womanhood when he, in his cursory treatment of female education in *Emile* (1762), explains the difference between male education and female education as the difference between "the development of strength" and "the development of attractiveness." Responding in part to Rousseau in her *Strictures on the Modern System of Female Education* (1799), British educator Hannah More (who is generally credited with the founding of domestic ideology) criticized her contemporaries for educating their daughters "for the world, and not for themselves." Patriarchal interests dictated the shape of the system of female education More wanted to reform. Consisting almost exclusively in ornamental graces requisite for obtaining an advantageous familial alliance through the marriage contract, this education, More felt, treated women as little more than commodities bought and sold on the marriage market. Rousseau expressed the degree to which women were raised "for the world" rather than for themselves when he argued that a woman's knowledge and powers of reasoning should be developed only enough so as to prevent her from being tedious in conversation with her husband. Using the home as a metaphor for interiority (in the sense of "selfhood"), More was attempting to re-define woman's value in terms of internal qualities: sound judgment, knowledge of how to run a household, moral tendencies— qualifications that suited a woman to be a good wife and mother rather than merely making her satisfying to the male gaze.

Historical romances written by women clearly express domestici-ty's antipatriarchal content. We see this in Child's romance of ancient Greece, *Philothea* (1836). Aspasia, who herself relentlessly cultivates the gaze of the crowd, holds entertainments at her home in which women dance and sing before a male audience. Child's retiring her-oine Philothea, seemingly voicing the author's view, explains to Aspa-sia that the renown women gain from performing before men is a sign of their thralldom rather than a measure of their freedom. The pres-ence in the narrative of a woman who is literally enslaved (Philothea's friend Eudora) only strengthens the force of an analogy that later antislavery novels like Stowe's *Uncle Tom's Cabin* (1852) and Child's *A Romance of the Republic* (1867) would pursue in a native and more contemporary setting.

Like *Philothea,* Eliza Buckminster Lee's *Parthenia* (1858) con-structs the domestic woman in order to criticize patriarchy. Set in the fourth century, the novel describes the youth of Emperor Julian, who dedicated himself to reviving the worship of the pagan gods just as Christianity seemed on the verge of establishing its ascendancy. Lee transforms the struggle between paganism and Christianity into a struggle between men and women. The warrior Julian (reputed to be a woman-hater) believes that Christianity is a religion suited only to women. In its story of the crucifixion he sees none of the male her-oism he so admires in Homeric literature. In meeting the beautiful and wise pagan priestess Parthenia, however, Julian learns firsthand that there are forms of power other than physical force. He proposes that she become his empress and use her feminine charms to promote the cause of paganism. But because in her gradual conversion to Christianity she learns that the only way to make woman a "purifying and refining influence infused through society" is to "elevate [her] to her true place in the *family*," Parthenia declines the honor. Lee, it seems, detects in Julian's offer the patriarchal tendency to reduce women to mere objects for public display.

More was concerned that the patriarchal display of woman robbed her of any authentic identity. Hence she associated the fashionable life with a lack of authenticity. The life of the young lady, More had lamented, "too much resembles that of an actress: the morning is all rehearsal and the evening is all performance." The association of wealth and fashion with the loss of female authenticity is particularly apparent in some of the more didactic novels of the period, including Sedgwick's *Clarence* (1830) and *The Poor Rich Man and the Rich Poor Man* (1836), Elizabeth Oakes Smith's *Riches Without Wings* (1838), and Ann Stephens's *Fashion and Famine* (1854). The association, however, also seems to inform Alcott's compelling and not in the least bit didactic novella *Behind a Mask* (1866). Subtitled "A Woman's Power," Alcott's gothic romance is set in an aristocratic English household. The young and lovely governess Jean Muir ingratiates herself with the members of the Coventry household—particularly its male members—until she has all of them at *her* beck and call. At the end of the first chapter the reader sees what the Coventry family does not. Alone in her room after a first impressive day on the job, Jean declares aloud, "[T]he curtain is down, so I may be myself for a few hours, if actresses ever are themselves." She then proceeds to remove her makeup, wig, and several false teeth. The narrator remarks that the "metamorphosis was wonderful, but the disguise was more in the expression she assumed than in any art of costume or false adornment." The setting of the tale suggests that Alcott, like More, saw loss of authenticity as the inevitable fate of women in the patriarchal household. Like Lee and Child, Alcott selects a foreign setting for her novel in order to suggest that such a household has no place in the modern United States.

More's American protégé Catharine Beecher used images of physical confinement to express patriarchal culture's violence against the integrity of female selfhood. Beecher authored what is probably the single most influential statement of American domesticity, *A Treatise on Domestic Economy* (1841), which she later (with the aid of her sister Harriet Beecher Stowe) revised and published under the title

*The American Woman's Home* (1869). Throughout her work, Beecher expresses concern that young girls spend too much time indoors in overheated rooms and that when they are permitted outdoors are instructed not to run around and "romp" like boys. Women are further restrained by corsets and other "monstrous female fashions," which, by impeding the natural growth and development of the body, "bring distortion and disease"—literally to the female body, but metaphorically to the female self. The tomboy Jo March in *Little Women* expresses the domestic critique of monstrous patriarchal fashions when she complains, "I hate to think I've got to grow up and be Miss March, and wear long gowns, and look as prim as a China-aster." In *Little Women* Alcott uses the backdrop of the Civil War to create a value system that gives priority not just to women but to women as the representatives of the interior life.

The figure of domestic woman then cannot be separated from the modern reconstruction not just of the female self but of selfhood in general. In *Little Women* the March sisters remain at home, while the Northern men have gone off to fight. Jo rails against the destiny of her sex: "I'm dying to go and fight with papa, and I can only stay at home and knit like a poky old woman." Through her representation of the March sisters' attempts to overcome their "bosom enemies," Alcott relocates within the home the heroism traditionally identified with the battlefield. Alcott suggests that, in part because heroics attract the attention of the world, it is far easier to be a hero than it is to purify one's own heart; temporary hardship and even death in the name of a virtuous cause are more easily endured than a quiet, lifetime struggle for virtue. The same logic that led Alcott to valorize the (feminine) quotidian over the (masculine) heroic led minister Horace Bushnell to propose a new "domestic" form of worship. Referring in part to the histrionic conversion experiences that accompanied the religious revivals that punctuated the entire antebellum period, Bushnell complained in *Christian Nurture* (1860): "We hold a piety of conquest rather than of love, a kind of public piety, that is strenuous and fiery on great occasions, but wants . . . constancy." In Bushnell's opinion all Christians, not just women, should cultivate domesticity of character.

During the Civil War years the influential women's magazine *Godey's Lady's Book* never once alluded to the conflict that so engrossed the attention of the nation. Along with the novels *Northwood* (1827) and *The Lecturess* (1839), *Godey's* was an important vehicle for its editor Sarah Hale's rather conservative domestic philosophy, and Hale's critics have taken the magazine's failure even to acknowledge *the* major conflict of the day as evidence that women intellectuals retreated to the home to escape harsh realities. "Reality," however, was not something these women were attempting to escape so much as something the particular form of their antipatriarchal critique encouraged them to redefine. According to Child's *The Mother's Book,* "Nothing can be real that does not have its home *within* us." If under the editorship of Hale *Godey's* manifested little interest in the war, this is in part because domestic ideologues were skeptical about the importance of the merely external. Hence in addressing the question of discipline, *The Mother's Book* stresses that behavior matters far less than the motives that impel it. The modern concept of the self and the modern experience of the self would be inconceivable without the transvaluation that domesticity helped effect.

Domesticity's valorization of character over conduct gave novelists license to produce some of the era's more reverent representations of non-Western cultures. In *Hobomok* (1824) the prolific Child (whose 1868 *An Appeal for the Indians* refers to the belief in white superiority as a "curse") protests the undue harshness of Calvinist doctrine that would damn the unconverted but noble savage to everlasting punishment in the afterlife. Like Stephens's later *Malaeska* (1860), *Hobomok* is a tale of interracial marriage. At one point Mary Corbitant, who marries Hobomok and bears his child, has a vision of the Christian God smiling "on distant mosques and temples" and "shedding the same light on the sacrifice heap of the Indian, and the rude dwellings of the Calvinist." The narrator lays the groundwork for an early theory of cultural relativism when she asserts that "spiritual light" shines equally on all people but is refracted in many different ways.

Women novelists' willingness to entertain notions of cultural relativism was not entirely disinterested, of course. Like her earlier *A New-England Tale* (1822), Sedgwick's *Hope Leslie* (1827) employs relativism to buttress its own antipatriarchal critique as much as to ennoble aboriginals. Through the generous actions of her native heroine Magawisca, Sedgwick legitimates the alien culture rejected by Puritan "fanatics" because it does not conform to their ethnocentric standards. At the same time, and through a similar logic, Sedgwick legitimates the acts of defiance against the Puritan elders committed by her white heroine Hope Leslie. In an age of what Sedgwick calls "undisputed masculine supremacy," Hope fails to demonstrate the "passiveness" that the Puritans define as woman's chief virtue. Sedgwick describes Hope as someone whom the Puritans perceive as, like the natives, in need of "civilizing" restraints. But Hope's conduct only *appears* immoral; steadfast principles in fact guide her actions throughout the novel.

The domestic emphasis on cultivating principle in order to preserve the authenticity of the self may also account for the frequency with which orphans appear in women's novels. In three of the most popular novels of the time, Warner's *The Wide, Wide World*, Cummins's *The Lamplighter*, and Finley's *Elsie Dinsmore*, the death of one or both parents or the abandonment of children is a compelling *donnée* for women novelists because it provides an opportunity for distinguishing between character and conduct. Only with the parent absent can the child's internalization of principle be gauged. In women's novels, as in Ralph Waldo Emerson's essay on the subject, "self-reliance" is not freedom from duty but rather subjection to an internalized standard of duty. This is not to say that by internalizing duty domesticity merely introjected patriarchal rule but rather to suggest that even oppositional ideologies can have normalizing as well as liberating aspects.

While one could read assertions of women's moral superiority to men as empowering to women, historical romances written by women suggest that because theirs is the power of influence rather than of force, domesticity is always on the verge of reproducing patriarchal culture's male gaze. Harriet Vaughan Cheney's historical romance *A Peep at the Pilgrims* (1850) suggests that even in her private relations the domestic woman is necessarily a spectacle (as suggested by the titular "peep"). Even more so than Lee, Cheney

makes clear the erotic nature of the influence that domesticity assigned to women. Mr. Grey, voicing the wisdom of the Puritan patriarch, warns his daughter Miriam that she must accept male authority without question because women are more prone to err than
men. "Women are born to submit," he claims, "and as the weaker
vessel, it is meet they should be guided by those who have rule over
them." Miriam argues in response that to the contrary women appear
better suited to dispense the gospel rather than to receive it—since
their erotic power makes their "influence" over men well-nigh irresistible: "If the entreaties of Delilah could subdue Samson, how much
more powerful must be the arguments of religion from the lips of a
virtuous woman," she asserts. Even though Miriam works toward
Christian ends, Cheney cannot rid her "virtuous woman" of all the
erotic power represented by the biblical Delilah.

Similarly, Stowe's representation of the virtuous Tina Percival in
*Oldtown Folks* (1869) participates in the logic of the male gaze. Like
Cheney, Stowe suggests that women's power over men depends upon
their ability to please them. Tina's spectacular beauty, far from being
a source of temptation for Stowe's male characters, is instead presented as, potentially, an agent of their regeneration. The narrator
speaks of romantic "LOVE" as "greatest and holiest of all the natural
sacraments and means of grace." Stowe contrasts this perspective
with that of the Calvinist minister Dr. Stern, who believes that "the
minister who does not excite the opposition of the natural heart fails
to do his work." Significantly, the minister's sermons excite only
"revulsion" among the townsfolk. Stowe had previously relocated
gospel authority from the clergy to the eroticized domestic woman in
*The Minister's Wooing* (another local color tale set in Puritan New
England that Stowe published in 1859). There her character James
Marvyn asserts that he does not understand a word of the minister
Dr. Hopkins's tedious sermons but that the lovely Mary Scudder is
his "living gospel"—the same phrase that the skeptic George Harris
uses to describe his pious wife Eliza in *Uncle Tom's Cabin*.

Although thinking of women as the living gospel for men gives
women a certain authority, it also defines them strictly in terms of
men's needs. Because domestic ideology posits a moral difference between men and women, it always threatens to reduce women to little
more than vessels for male salvation. One could argue that Stowe's

representation of the virtuous heroine not long for this world (the archetypal expression of which is, of course, Eva St. Clare in *Uncle Tom's Cabin*) results from the moral difference between the sexes posited by domestic ideology. Referring to Mara Lincoln's little Eva-like demise at the end of *Pearl of Orr's Island,* the narrator notes that some people die young in order to aid in the spiritual development of those whom they leave behind. Mara's death has this effect on her skeptical fiancé Moses Pennel, whose salvation seems much more assured after her death than before it. In fact, on her deathbed Mara asserts that her Christian influence on him will be greater when she is dead than it would have been had she lived to marry him. For Stowe, then, a woman's *dying* gospel is perhaps even more potent than her *living* one.

Yet Mara Lincoln's martyrdom for the sake of her fiancé's spiritual well-being is just one logical extreme to which domestic ideology's claims for the moral superiority of women could lead. It is important to stress that domesticity was not an ideology in the impoverished sense of the term. Domesticity did not become a dominant discourse because it provided people with a finite and orderly set of beliefs relieving them from the burden of thinking; to the contrary, domesticity was compelling precisely because it gave people an expansive logic and a series of rich cultural symbols through which to *think* about their world. As a result, domestic ideology, while it certainly manipulated antebellum intellectuals, could also be manipulated by them. Hence Alcott could take it to what is perhaps its feminist extreme in her novel *Work* (1873). *Work* opens with the orphan Christie Devon (invoking the "Declaration of Sentiments" revealed by women's rights supporters at their convention in Seneca Falls in 1848) announcing to her guardians that "there's going to be a new Declaration of Independence," namely, her declaration of economic independence from them. Alcott uses domestic ideology in order to identify not just work but *meaningful* work for women. Christie ultimately becomes a mediator in an organization composed of both middle- and working-class women. There she helps to heal the class conflicts that arise. Alcott's fictional character Christie, one could argue, anticipates historical figures like Jane Addams, who at the turn of the century established social work as a legitimate profession for women. Because domesticity placed the welfare of society in women's able hands, women could claim that certain social professions outside of the home were the logical extension of their work inside the home.

Alcott perceived that the particular skills and knowledge women developed in managing households had extra-domestic applications, and this perception no doubt influenced her own decision to become a nurse during the Civil War. After the war other women intellectuals like Dr. Elizabeth Blackwell (who in 1849 received the first medical degree granted to a woman in the United States) also tried to expand the terrain of women's civilizing mission to include all of society and not just her own household. Declarations of women's moral superiority and civilizing influence, as well as claims for the managerial and practical skills they acquired through labor in the home, buttressed women's entrance into careers in medicine, education, and social welfare. Ironically, in the second half of the century domesticity itself enabled women's forays out of what the antebellum period identified as women's proper sphere. To add to the irony, postwar suffragists like Elizabeth Cady Stanton even used the logic of domestic ideology in their fight for women's political empowerment. Amongst these suffragists, antipatriarchal domesticity seems at last to have developed a recognizably feminist character.

The influence of domestic ideology on the suffragists, however, guaranteed that early feminism would not be without its political ambiguities. As early as 1838 in her *Letters to Mothers* Lydia Sigourney attempted to expand the terrain of domesticity into the world at large. Appalled that "the influx of untutored foreigners" had made the United States "a repository for the waste and refuse of other nations," Sigourney maintained that it was the responsibility of women "to neutralize this mass" through an internal missionary movement that would spread the good word of the Anglo-American middle-class home. Unfortunately, postwar suffragists, retaining domesticity's vision of the custodial role of women, used an argument reminiscent of Sigourney's to press for the vote. If white women were enfranchised, they argued, it would help offset the deleterious influence of lower-class immigrants and recently emancipated slaves (who during Reconstruction were allowed to vote). The same millennial zeal that gives domesticity its custodial mission, then, also makes it both classist and ethnocentric.

A reading of Harriet E. Wilson's novel *Our Nig; or, Sketches from the Life of a Free Black* (1859) suggests that some African American women were acutely aware of domesticity's normative contents; however, because most of the other important mid-century African American women intellectuals (including Sojourner Truth, Harriet Jacobs, and Elizabeth Keckley) expressed their suspicions about domestic ideology in nontraditional literary forms, any history devoted to a genre like the novel will necessarily underrepresent the contributions of African American women to the discourse on domesticity. Wilson's autobiographical tale (believed to be the first novel published by an African American in the United States) is yet another story of an orphaned girl in search of what Wilson calls "self-dependence." This orphan, however, is an African American woman living in the North who is taken in as a servant by a white family when her mother abandons her.

The willfulness of the orphan Frado recalls that of Cummins's character Gerty in *The Lamplighter*, but unlike Gerty's guardian Emily Graham, Frado's mistress Mrs. Bellmont is hardly a domestic woman. Intent upon "breaking" Frado's will, she rules over not just Frado but the entire Bellmont household with an iron hand. Wilson opposes Mrs. Bellmont's method of governing to Aunt Abby's more gentle methods. Befriending the abused child, the Bellmont family's maiden aunt manifests their concern for her spiritual welfare by attempting to convert her. But Wilson establishes this opposition between Mrs. Bellmont and the domestic woman Aunt Abby only to render visible what they have in common. The author orchestrates the death of Frado's defender James Bellmont in such a way as to provide an opportunity for Frado to provide evidence of her conversion to Aunt Abby's god. As the opening of Elizabeth Stuart Phelps the younger's novel *The Gates Ajar* (1869) suggests, in the nineteenth century the death of a loved one was often seen as an occasion for manifesting one's submission to a divine wisdom that passes human understanding. But just when she appears on the verge of submitting to the higher authority that Aunt Abby attempts to impose on her, Frado suddenly rebels against Mrs. Bellmont, threatening henceforth to return any blows that her mistress inflicts on her. At the same time the narrator abruptly drops the question of Frado's conversion. Because race gave Wilson a marginal status within the dominant culture, perhaps she was in a better position to see the way in which the advocates of what Bushnell called a new "domestic" religion had not entirely erased "conquest" from Christianity.

Introducing the women's novel into the canon of the American Renaissance, some object, will involve discarding aesthetic criteria and instituting political considerations as the determinants of literary merit. We must not forget that even the acknowledged male "classics" of the American Renaissance were themselves at one point non-canonical and that their cultural ascendency in fact owes a good deal to politics in the form of American nationalism. Few critics have found even the handful of acknowledged male classics (including *Moby-Dick, The Scarlet Letter, The Last of the Mohicans*) entirely satisfying from a strictly aesthetic standpoint, particularly in comparison to the British and European "masterpieces" of the same period. Indeed, a comment by Melville in "Hawthorne and His Mosses" suggests that if nineteenth-century critics had applied aesthetic rather than political standards to literature, most of the classic male novelists we now read might languish in the same literary obscurity to which their female contemporaries have been relegated. Concerned over the ill-repute of American writers and wondering where the American Shakespeare was, Melville enjoins, "[L]et America first praise mediocrity even, in her own children, before she praises . . . the best excellence in the children of any other land. Let her own authors, I say, have the priority of appreciation."

Neither were strictly aesthetic criteria F. O. Matthiessen's principle for selection when he introduced the concept of the American Renaissance in 1941—the same year in which the United States entered World War II and democracy both at home and abroad seemed so imperiled. In his *American Renaissance* (which for almost half a century helped determine which mid-nineteenth-century writers were read), Matthiessen asserts that the best authors "all wrote literature for democracy," and he notes excluding Edgar Allan Poe from his study because Poe "was bitterly hostile to democracy."

Both Melville's and Matthiesen's comments suggest that political considerations have for a long time and quite explicitly informed our sense of literary value. Introducing novels by women into the canon may not entail a drastic change in our concept of literary merit, after all. Instead it may require something far more radical—a change in our politics.

Lora Romero

# Fiction and Reform I

"In the history of the world," Emerson proclaimed in "Man the Reformer" (1841), "the doctrine of Reform had never such scope as at the present hour." Indeed, as he surveyed the cultural scene, he sensed a "new spirit" and "new ideas" pervading Northeast reform activity. But whereas many of his acquaintances became involved in group efforts at social reformation, such as the communitarian experiment at Brook Farm, or abolitionism, Emerson insisted on the primacy of individual reformation. All desires for reform, he argued, emerged from "the conviction that there is an infinite worthiness in man" and an "impediment" standing between individuals and their essentially divine nature. As he insisted even more strenuously in "New England Reformers" (1844): "society gains nothing whilst a man, not himself renovated, attempts to renovate things around him." That same year, however, Emerson began to read widely in the history of slavery, and in a pivotal lecture, "Emancipation in the British West Indies" (1844), he called on the "great masses of men" to take a larger role in changing laws and affecting social policy. Seven years later, in a lecture on the Fugitive Slave Law, he advised his auditors that civil disobedience would be an appropriate response to the government's efforts to enforce "the most detestable law that was ever enacted by a civilized state." Abolitionism, the most pressing social reform movement of his time, had taken hold of Emerson, and during the 1850s the champion of self-culture addressed numerous abolitionist meetings and even campaigned for Gorham Palfrey on the Free Soil Ticket. Slavery was by no means the only reform movement to capture his attention; in addition to offering occasional remarks on temperance, in 1855 he spoke to a women's rights convention in favor of women's suffrage, arguing that "if in your city [Boston] the uneducated emigrant vote numbers thousands, representing a brutal ignorance and mere animal wants, it is to be corrected by an educated and religious vote, representing the wants and desires of honest and refined persons." Nevertheless, despite his various reform commitments of the 1840s and 1850s, in his journals of the period he continued to muse skeptically on the value of group efforts at social renovation.

Emerson's ambivalent but increasingly engaged response to social reform suggests that he wrestled with some of the large questions his more individualistic philosophy of the 1830s and early 1840s tended to avoid: Can self-reformation proceed in a social vacuum somehow apart from the debates, institutions, and laws of antebellum culture? To what extent is group reformation dependent on individual reformation, and vice versa? Fearing that the "civilized state" was falling into barbarism, he also began to address different sorts of questions, as his unattractive remarks on the "brutal ignorance" of the emigrants suggest, about the state of the union: Who should lead the nation, and to what end? What constitutes legitimate authority? How achieve civilized harmony and progress during a time of heightening sectional, ethnic, and class conflict?

As the literary genre most responsive to social debates and discourses, and, at least traditionally, the genre most attentive to situating the individual in society, the novel is naturally suited to address all of these large (and representative) questions from a variety of perspectives. Given the enormous social impact of reform movements during the 1825–60 period, both in England and in America, and given not only the increasingly dominant place of the slavery debate in antebellum culture but also the increasingly tense ethnic, class, and gender relations of the period, it should not be surprising, then, that a conflict between individual and social action, a questioning of authority, a fear of social breakdown, and a utopian desire for social regeneration are some of the key issues and concerns informing and energizing the antebellum novel.

Of course the starting point of American reform is problematic. Historians have argued for the primacy of evangelicalism to the rise of reform, pointing to the mid-1790s—the beginnings of the "Second Great Awakening"—as the point of origin for subsequent reforms. However, because of the centrality of secular Enlightenment thought to some of the great reformist crusaders, we might argue for the primacy of Jefferson's authoring of the Declaration of Independence. Or, taking an even longer view, the Protestant Reformation itself— with its affirming of the individual over the traditional and institutional—could be viewed as the beginning of "American" reform. For the reform movements of the antebellum period, however, which drew on all of these sources, the revivals and religious debates of the 1820s and 1830s had the greatest immediate impact, channeling energies toward antislavery, feminism, temperance, hydropathy, penology, spiritualism, phrenology, peace crusades, and numerous other related causes. Dubbed "the Sisterhood of Reforms" by Thomas Wentworth Higginson, these various movements sometimes contradicted or were at odds with one another, but they shared in a set of fundamental beliefs: a rejection of Calvinist determinism; an insistence on the individual's ability to shape his or her own fate (even though, paradoxically, many reformers would endorse the use of institutions to achieve this end); a millennialist conviction of the nation's potentially glorious destiny.

The social and religious dimensions of these beliefs were developed in the perfectionist theology of the itinerant minister Charles Grandison Finney, who began his career in the West but had a major impact on the Protestant revivals of upstate New York's "burned-over district" during the late 1820s and early 1830s. Preaching that "God has made man a moral free agent," Finney insisted that, in tandem with God's love and grace, individuals could achieve an immediate and saving conversion. The regeneration and perfection of individuals, he argued, would ultimately serve to regenerate and perfect the nation. In more complex ways, Emerson, influenced by his former teacher William Ellery Channing and various Continental Romantics, argued for the importance of intuition and self-culture, rather than Unitarian institutional and historical authority, in encouraging individuals to discover their own miraculous divinity. A wave of such self-discoveries of the "Divine Soul" within, the utopian conclusion of "The American Scholar" (1837) implied, would ensure the renovation and reformation of American society.

Despite the providential calm and ease of such large-scale transformations, as envisioned in the optimistic writings of both Finney and Emerson, many of the reform movements of the period were actively directed by Protestant elites concerned with maintaining their social hegemony during a time of increasing class and ethnic diversity. For many other reformers, however, the impulse toward reform emerged from a more genuine desire to bring about change in a nation whose idealistic values were believed to be compromised by rampant materialism, class and gender inequities, various abuses of authority, and the intransigent presence of slavery. To be sure, even these reformers sometimes betrayed a meanspirited hostility toward those perceived as marginal or different, but overall the religious revivals, along with the romantic theorizing of Emerson and his circle, played an enormously productive role in the emergence of a number of progressive reforms, such as the temperance, communitarian, antislavery, and women's rights movements. Although Finney and Emerson were themselves somewhat suspicious of group efforts at social reform, many of their auditors and readers, newly convinced of the regenerative potential of the individual and the nation, thought concerted social action the best possible approach to purging America of its accumulated evils and renewing consensual ideals.

Convinced that American society was in need of complete renovation, communitarian reformers, for example, established familial subcommunities based on noncompetitive principles of group association that were intended to serve as models for national reform. Over one hundred such groups, mostly short-lived, came into existence between the Revolution and the Civil War. Notable early groups, whose religious beliefs provided their chief inspiration and *modus operandi,* included Ann Lee's Shakers, the German pietistic Harmony Society, and the Mormons. Other groups, such as Robert Owen's New Harmony Society in Indiana and Frances Wright's group at Nashoba, Tennessee, were more secularly inclined. Both the socialist ideals of Charles Fourier, as popularized by Albert Brisbane's *Social Destiny of Man* (1840), and the millennialist ideals of the revivalists and the transcendentalists informed the 1840s communitarian experiment at Brook Farm. During the same period Adam Ballou established the nearby Hopedale Community, with the evangelical aim of promoting world peace. Many of these reform associations attempted to implement nonsexist modes of social organization, though none was more committed to this end than John Humphrey Noyes's upstate New York Oneida community. During its relatively long life from 1848 to 1880, the community practiced "complex marriage"—shared marriage partners—and male continence, an arrangement intended both to protect women from the bonds of repeated pregnancies and to protect men from what was believed to be the debilitating expenditure of semen.

Surprisingly, Nathaniel Hawthorne, who in an 1835 notebook entry compared the "modern reformer" to an escaped lunatic, joined the Brook Farm community for seven months of 1841. His retrospective *The Blithedale Romance* (1852), set at a reform association similar to Brook Farm, reveals his conflicted attitudes toward the reform impulses that he himself briefly embraced. Conceiving of themselves as disinterested reformers in the spirit of the Pilgrims, the participants at Blithedale appear to be self-important and just plain selfish: Hollingsworth secretly pursues his prison-reform project; Coverdale apparently seeks a private refuge and literary material; the feminist reformer Zenobia, modeled partly on Margaret Fuller, seems in search of the limelight and a man. Though the community embraces gender reforms, women continue to do the cooking and men the physical labor, and there is a strong suggestion that Zenobia commits suicide out of her frustrated love for Hollingsworth (whereas Fuller in *Woman in the Nineteenth Century* [1845] had mocked the idea that women exist only for the love of a man).

Hawthorne's treatment of spiritualism further contributes to his apparently skeptical portrayal of the group's character and intentions. Whereas the Fox sisters' 1848 "spirit-rapping" communications with the dead helped to give rise to spiritualism as a reform movement of sorts, promising to provide access to the invisible and divine, in *Blithedale* Hawthorne analogizes Westervelt's decadent spiritualistic practices, which link mediums in "one great, mutually conscious brotherhood," to the associative practices at Blithedale, which link reformers in a "general brain"—with the large intention of underscoring both groups' propensities toward revolutionism. This is never so clear as when the novel shifts from Westervelt's lyceum display to the festive masquerade at Blithedale, where the associationists, as Coverdale describes them from his hiding place in the hermitage, whirled "round so swiftly, so madly, and so merrily, in time and tune with the Satanic music, that their separate incongruities were blended all together." In his imaging of associationism and spiritualism as forms of demonic revolutionism, Hawthorne would seem to be in the same reactionary camp as the Roman Catholic convert Orestes Brownson, whose novel *The Spirit-Rapper* (1854) portrayed spiritualism as Satan's invisible tool for bringing forth the French Revolution, the European revolutions of the 1840s, and the emerging women's rights movement.

Yet *Blithedale* is more complicated than that, in large part because of Hawthorne's use of the first-person narrator Coverdale to enact both the suspicion of and the desire for reform. As presented in the novel, Coverdale is simultaneously an insider and outsider, a character who, leading an aimlessly drifting life in the anomic city, deeply desires the structure and community offered by Blithedale. He is a character, too, whose sexual anxieties and insecurities, and chronic cynicism, make him an unreliable critic of reform. The novel, to a large extent, is a study in power, desire, and impotence, as the voyeuristic Coverdale, simultaneously attracted to and frightened by Zenobia's sexuality, Hollingsworth's "masculine" fixedness of purpose, and, indeed, the carnivalesque energies of the festive Blithedalers, weaves melodramatic tales of flight and entrapment suggestive of his own wavering desires. Though the satirical elements of the novel would appear to suggest, in the manner of early Emerson, that individuals must first achieve their own private reforms in order for communitarian reforms to succeed, the larger thematic thrust of Hawthorne's skillful creation of the ironic and at times loathsome Coverdale is to suggest the importance of the self having some sort of ground, some sort of context, against which that self-reformation can be initiated. Unwilling to make any social commitment, whether at Blithedale or in the city, and fearful of losing control over his self-regulated imagination and body, Coverdale simply drifts on, unattached, unengaged, unhappy. In this sense he is quite different from the erstwhile reformer Holgrave (Maule) of *The House of the Seven Gables* (1851), whose ability both to locate himself in history and to honor the integrity of individuals—most dramatically when he resists taking mesmeric control over Phoebe's body—allows him to forge redemptive and potentially transformative bonds with others.

In his use of mesmerism, in *House* and *Blithedale,* Hawthorne dramatically brings to focus a large impulse of social reform: the desire to take control of the body—individual and social. Whereas some Americans of the 1840s and 1850s regarded mesmerism—a species of hypnotism—as a reformatory science potentially bringing individuals and nature into perfect harmony, Hawthorne presents it, in his accounts of Matthew Maule's cruel domination of Alice Pyncheon, and of Westervelt's and Hollingsworth's manipulations of Priscilla and Zenobia, as merely the selfish enactment of hyperintrusive patriarchal power. Despite the demonizations of mesmeric control, however, an underlying anxiety of both books is a fear of losing control, an anxiety that in *Blithedale* finds its most haunting expression in the figure of the decaying inebriate Moodie. Devastated by the ravages of the marketplace, Moodie, like the sherry-loving Coverdale and the Blithedale masqueraders "with portentously red noses," remains in search of "a boozy kind of pleasure in the customary life" even as he wastes away. Coverdale, who does everything he can to deny his likeness to Moodie, remains haunted by a fear that their characters, fates, and resting places—the tavern—might not be so very different after all.

Coverdale's fears of decline, dissipation, and loss of control parallel the fears giving life and urgency to the temperance movement, the largest reform movement of the antebellum period. In part, the popularity of temperance reform can be attributed to the fact that Americans had a real drinking problem: the national per capita consumption of distilled spirits jumped from under two gallons in 1800 to just over five gallons in 1830. But temperance also melded well with a variety of ideological orientations. In the tradition of Protestant admonitions, ranging from Increase Mather's *Wo to Drunkards* (1673) to Lyman Beecher's *Six Sermons on Intemperance* (1826), Finney warned that temperance was of crucial importance because alcohol wreaked havoc on the spiritual and rational resources necessary for conversion. Emerson similarly believed that "unnatural" intoxication crippled the individual's spiritual resources and, like the Enlightenment temperance reformer Benjamin Rush, he also remained concerned about the effects of drinking on bodily health. The institutional sources of temperance activity in America were set in place by Federalist and Protestant directed societies—such as the

Massachusetts Society for the Suppression of Intemperance, founded in 1813, and the American Temperance Society, founded in 1826 — which concerned themselves with reforming the drinking habits of the working classes. Proclaiming the virtues of self-denial and thrift, temperance tracts from these organizations promulgated a capitalist ethic conducive to the demands of the newly expanding factories. Many of the male workers who took the temperance pledge, however, were influenced less by these elitist groups than by the working-class Washingtonian Societies of the 1840s, which championed temperance in the Ben Franklin tradition of self-help and upward mobility.

Women, too, participated in great numbers in the temperance movement, as they saw drinking as a male activity threatening to violate the purity and harmony of the home. During the 1820s and 1830s, middle-class women organized female moral reform societies, which regularly conducted home visits of urban working-class tenements in an effort to purge those dwellings of the alcoholic beverages believed to transform honest laborers into shiftless, wife-beating beasts. (Concerns about violation and purity contributed as well to the rise of Magdalene Societies — groups of evangelical women offering refuge and the possibility of reformative conversions to urban prostitutes.) Women were also particularly responsive to a variety of health reforms championed by writers who took temperance as their starting point. Sylvester Graham's high-fiber cracker, William Alcott's vegetarianism, Orson Fowler's nondeterministic phrenology (according to Fowler, the defects of character detected in the skull could be remedied through diet and exercise), Amelia Bloomer's dress reforms, and the spiritualist Mary Gove Nichols's hydropathic water cure — all of these reforms were embraced by a number of women as ways of regaining control of their bodies from an increasingly professionalized male medicine and, more generally, the impinging male body.

An issue that spoke to a wide range of constituencies, temperance became a central motif of the writings of the period. Between 1829 and 1834 the New York State Temperance Society circulated over four million copies of its publications, while the American Tract Society distributed over five million of its temperance pamphlets by 1851. Significantly, in 1836 the American Temperance Union, challenging Finney's assertion that novel reading was a corrupting waste of time, endorsed temperance fiction as an efficacious method of gaining converts to the cause. For temperance crusaders, the novel itself was of special importance, as book-length fiction, in the narrative tradition of William Hogarth's print cycle *The Rake's Progress* (1734), could trace the degeneration over time of the individual tempted to drink, and could trace as well the impact of drinking on the individual's family. An important forerunner of antebellum temperance fiction was Mason Weems's *The Drunkard's Looking Glass* (1813). During the 1830s, Mary Fox's *The Ruined Deacon* (1834) and George B. Cheever's *Deacon Giles' Distillery* (1835) achieved a considerable readership. In 1842 Walt Whitman wrote a temperance novel, *Franklin Evans,* for the Washingtonians, and three years later George Lippard published his enormously popular and sensationalistic *The Quaker City; or, The Monks of Monk Hall,* which presented numerous scenes of depraved group drinking among Philadelphia's degenerate aristocrats.

Temperance themes had an important, though often satirical, place in Herman Melville's sea fiction (recall Aunt Charity's failed temperance work in *Moby-Dick*), as he tended to romanticize the fraternal bonds forged among his drinking sailors. Redburn's short-lived allegiance to the Juvenile Abstinence Association, White-Jacket's perception of the *Neversink* as "the asylum for all the drunkards," and Ishmael's initial shock at the unrestrained drinking at the Spouter Inn are meant to signify the greenhorn status of characters soon to become fraternal salts. That said, Melville's extended account in *Redburn* (1849) of dissipation in Liverpool's sailor bars, his portrait of despotic, hard-drinking Captain Claret in *White-Jacket* (1850), his demystifying picture of fraternal drinking in "The Paradise of Bachelors and the Tartarus of Maids" (1855) as dependent on the exploitation of women and the working class, and his wonderfully perverse rendering of the cunning con games masked as fraternal drinking between Charlie Noble and the Cosmopolitan in *The Confidence-Man* (1857)—all suggest that he, like the conventional temperance writers of the day, viewed alcohol as a considerable social problem.

Temperance themes and images also found their way into many of the popular women's novels of the period. Concerned with addressing the problem of patriarchal power, women writers tended to image the drunken husband or father as a brute who, under the influence of ardent spirits, gave unconstrained sway to his predatory passions. In Caroline Chesebro's *Isa: A Pilgrimage* (1852), for example, the heroine's adoptive father is an abusive drunkard who, fortunately, dies early on in the novel. Devoting her novelistic energies principally to the temperance cause, Metta Victoria Victor wrote two temperance novels, *The Senator's Son; or, The Maine Law: A Last Refuge* (1853) and *Fashionable Dissipation* (1854). In *The Senator's Son* in particular, Victor underscores the ravages wrought over time by paternal drinking. Opening with the protagonist accepting a glass of wine from his father at the age of four, the novel shows how this seemingly innocent act leads to the death of the boy's mother and, eventually, assorted ills to his sister, wife, and daughter before he kills himself while suffering delirium tremens. A more complex account of the ravages of drinking appeared in Elizabeth Stoddard's *The Morgesons* (1862), which, in the larger service of exploring the themes of free will and companionate marriage, counterpoints an alcoholic, who fathers a retarded child and dies of the d.t.'s, to a reformed drinker who participates in the shaping of a potentially happier marriage.

By far the most influential temperance novelist of the antebellum period, and the most successful in linking themes of individual and social dissipation, was Timothy Shay Arthur, who produced nearly 200 books, edited several popular journals, and published numerous sketches and tales. His best-selling collection of temperance sketches, *Six Nights with the Washingtonians* (1842), sold 175,000 copies by 1850; even more popular was his novel *Ten Nights in a Bar-Room, and What I Saw There* (1854), which, like Stowe's *Uncle Tom's Cabin*, achieved enormous sales and spawned numerous stage productions. An advocate of socialism, Swedenborgianism, women's suffrage and right to divorce, and various other reforms, Arthur in *Ten Nights* devoted his considerable narrative talents (and penchant for melodrama and sensationalism) to demonstrating the need for legislation prohibiting the sale of alcoholic beverages at a time when the nation was beginning to react against just such legislation—the Maine law of 1851. Set at the Sickle and Sheaf, Cedarville's new tavern run by the former miller Simon Slade, the novel traces from the point of view of an unnamed traveler the downward course of town and tavern during a ten-year period. As the tavern becomes increasingly degenerate—the inevitable result, Arthur suggests, of the miller's abandoning the life of productive labor for the speculative hope of quick and easy profit—so too, in a suggestively organic relationship, does everything else in Cedarville. Slade's son Frank, twelve years old at the novel's outset, succumbs to the temptation to drink while serving customers, and by the end of the novel is an impoverished patricide. The town's fathers and sons suffer similarly dire fates, while the town's women, acutely aware of what the narrator calls "moral consequences," can only watch helplessly as the town falls apart: one mother dies grief-stricken over the body of her murdered son, and Mrs. Slade herself ends up in an asylum. Among the female characters, only Mary Morgan, the eleven-year-old daughter of Slade's former mill worker Joe Morgan, possesses the power to influence events. Mortally wounded by an empty glass Slade had thrown at the drunken Morgan, Mary on her deathbed, in the manner of little Eva, extracts a promise from her father to free himself from the enslaving clutches of alcoholic beverages. By the end of the novel the still-abstinent Morgan has the one neat and clean house in the neighborhood.

Concerns about social decay, the ill effects of materialism, the tyranny of the patriarch, and, especially, apocalyptic violence—central to much temperance activity—were also central to the antislavery movement. For abolitionists, as for other reformers of the period, America had betrayed its founding ideals and millennial promise, and was drifting toward barbarism. Like the temperance and communitarian movements, antislavery grew in large measure out of the "ultraist" perfectionism of the 1820s and 1830s revivals, while owing a considerable debt to Enlightenment ideals of self-control and natural rights. As a reform movement, antislavery had important eighteenth-century sources in the work and writings of the Quaker humanitarian Anthony Benezet, who enlisted Benjamin Franklin to the cause, though antislavery took a somewhat conservative turn in 1816 with the formation of the American Colonization Society. Galvanized by the evangelical movements of the 1820s and 1830s, however, William Lloyd Garrison and many others came to view slavery as a national sin that, as long as it persisted, compromised the nation's hopes of achieving its millennial potential. Unlike Finney, who counseled his parishioners to avoid "angry controversy on the subject," Garrison adopted a bold and confrontational rhetoric intended to develop in his readers a conviction of slavery's evil and an immediate need to abolish it. Writing in the inaugural issue of *The Liberator* (January 1, 1831), which appeared less than a year before Nat Turner's bloody slave rebellion in Southampton, Virginia, Garrison drew on the injunctions of the Bible and the Declaration of Independence to assert the moral imperatives of antislavery, warning that "till every chain be broken, and every bondman set free. . . . let all the enemies of the persecuted blacks tremble." Garrison's mobilization of antislavery forces contributed to an upsurge in antislavery publications, most notably Richard Hildreth's *The Slave; or, Memoirs of Archy Moore* (1836)—one of approximately twelve antislavery novels published before *Uncle Tom's Cabin*—and Theodore Weld's *Slavery As It Is* (1839), an important documentary source for Stowe's antislavery fiction.

Although most antebellum Northerners opposed to slavery were far more moderate than Garrison in their opposition, by the mid-1840s there was shared common ground among a range of groups and individuals opposed to slavery. It was viewed as an affront to republican ideals of free labor, as an act of great hypocrisy on the part of a supposedly Christian and democratic nation, and as an indication of an apparent quest by a small group of states, or plantation owners, for national power—hence the currency of a "slave power" conspiratorial fear during the late 1840s and 1850s, especially after Congress passed the Compromise of 1850. Perhaps the dominant rhetorical concern of antislavery texts, however, was with the unchecked mastery of the slaveowner over the slave. Endowed with godlike power, but hardly gods, enslavers, according to antislavery writers, found it nearly impossible to keep their passion for mastery under control. "Intoxicated" by their power, "enslaved" by slavery, they brutally inflicted cruelties on their slaves, who, for good reason, became increasingly vengeful. Inevitably, then, slavery undermined civilized restraint and promised to bring forth the most catastrophic breakdown of all: an apocalyptic war of extermination between the races.

Given the centrality of concerns among abolitionists about the ways in which slavery undermined self-control, it is not surprising that many of the leading antislavery writers were also involved in temperance reform — Garrison, Theodore Weld, Gerrit Smith, and the African American writers Frederick Douglass, Sojourner Truth, William Wells Brown, and Frances Harper, among numerous others, saw the temperance movement and antislavery as intimately related. And given that slavery was viewed as a manifestation of unchecked, brute patriarchal power, it is not surprising that antislavery, like temperance, drew heavily on women participants.

Women's involvement in antislavery activity became a significant phenomenon in the early 1830s, as 1832 saw the formation of the Boston Female Anti-Slavery Society and 1833 the publication of Lydia Maria Child's seminal *An Appeal on Behalf of That Class of Americans Called Africans*. Angelina and Sarah Grimké, South Carolina Quaker sisters of a slaveholding family, presented their antislavery views during an 1837 public speaking tour of New England, thereby prompting the critical condemnation of the Congregationalist churches and of Catharine Beecher, who argued that women should exercise their moral influence within the privacy of the domestic sphere. As the hostile response to the Grimké sisters might suggest, women in antislavery remained in subordinate roles within the institutional structures of the movement. The refusal by the 1840 World's Anti-Slavery Convention in London to seat or give voice to women delegates from America intensified feminist thinking among Elizabeth Cady Stanton, Lucretia Mott, and others (as the refusal by an 1851 New York temperance convention to allow Susan B. Anthony the right to speak would help to raise her feminist consciousness). Abolitionism, as an ideology and social practice, therefore taught many of the "feminist-abolitionists" about their own subordinate status, and, arguably, together with temperance, helped to fuel the emerging women's movement of the period.

Because marriage and property laws, along with the lack of suffrage, denied women rights thought to accompany republican citizenship, in feminist writings the analogy of woman to slave was seen as particularly apt, despite the fact that it was, after all, metaphorical. As Angelina Grimké remarked in *Letters to Catharine E. Beecher* (1838), "The investigation of the rights of the slave has led me to a better understanding of my own." Margaret Fuller, in her impassioned and poetical celebration of woman's potential, *Woman in the Nineteenth Century* (1845), published the same year as Frederick

Douglass's *Narrative*, likened woman to a slave and man to a slave trader. In *Letters on the Equality of the Sexes* (1838), Sarah Grimké pictured the situation of the typical wife in this way: "man has exercised the most unlimited and brutal power over woman, in the peculiar character of husband,—a word in most countries synonymous with tyrant." At the epochal Seneca Falls women's rights convention of 1848, the early culmination of organized feminist activity, Stanton, in her resounding "Declaration of Sentiments," therefore revised Jefferson's Declaration, substituting male for British tyrannical authority, in order to call attention to the ways in which the nation's social institutions and legal codes mainly served the interests of America's white male citizenry. That same year, the New York State Legislature, in response to thoughtful women critics like Stanton, passed the nation's most liberalized married women's property act, which made it legal for women to maintain control over property they brought to their marriages.

The Married Women's Property Act of 1848 followed in the wake of the land reforms modifying the near feudal control New York's upstate landholding families held over their tenants. The antirent agitation leading up to these reforms prompted James Fenimore Cooper's Littlepage trilogy—*Satanstoe* (1845), *The Chainbearer* (1845), and *The Redskins* (1846)—which forecast a reign of demagoguery should the landed gentry lose its leaseholds—and the land reforms, along with the married women's property act, lay behind his *The Ways of the Hour* (1850). In portraying in this late novel a woman who deserts her husband, is falsely accused by a mob of murder, and is eventually revealed to be insane, Cooper suggests that allowing women too much liberty could lead to the breakdown of civilization itself. (A similar argument informed the pseudonymous Fred Folio's *Lucy Boston; or, Women's Rights and Spiritualism* [1855].) During the 1850s, divorce was addressed from a very different perspective by women writers, who remained convinced of the need for liberalized divorce laws. Fanny Fern (Sarah Payson Willis Parton), whose first novel, *Ruth Hall* (1855), touched on the wretched marriage and eventual death in a mental hospital of Ruth's friend Mrs. Leon, focused in *Rose Clark* (1856) on a divorced woman who, hardly debilitated by her condition, develops her self-possession and self-reliant virtue to the point where she remarries her former husband on egalitarian terms. More boldly, Mary Sargeant Nichols, in her autobiographical novel *Mary Lyndon* (1855), presented the eponymous protagonist divorcing her tyrannous and cloddish husband, and eventually attaining a happier second marriage with a man who shares her ideals of the primacy to marriage of free, unconstrained love.

Of all the novels published before the Civil War, Harriet Beecher Stowe's million-copy best-seller, *Uncle Tom's Cabin* (1852), the novel Lincoln credited with making "this big war," most compellingly interwove the major strands of antebellum reform: feminism, temperance, and antislavery. Temperance, for example, is central to the novel's representation of power relationships—between masters and slaves and, analogously, between men and women. The novel begins with Shelby signing over the slaves Tom and Harry to the obnoxious slave trader Haley, as the men sit together drinking wine and brandy. By the end of the novel we descend from this relatively restrained scene of intemperance to the unrestrained hell of the hard-drinking brute Simon Legree's plantation. Along the way Stowe depicts a typical Kentucky tavern, wherein a crowd of slave hunters, "free-and-easy dogs," spit gobs of tobacco juice, drink tumblers "half full of raw spirits," and, significantly, wear hats, what Stowe terms "the characteristic emblem of man's sovereignty." White male sovereignty, rather than a prohibitionary politics, is the central issue here, with temperance blending into feminism, as Stowe presents male enslavers rendered intoxicated (and dangerous) less by alcoholic beverages than by their seemingly unlimited power over slaves and women. Representing "home-loving and affectionate" slaves, male and female, as admirably domestic and womanly, Stowe not only places the slaves at the center of her culturally revisionary idealization of matriarchy but also, in the tradition of the Grimkés, Fuller, and Stanton, points to the "enslaved" status of women in patriarchal society. The tragic destiny of the slave Prue, therefore, who was raised as a "breeder," speaks in part, Stowe implies, to the situation of all women in America. In this respect, the slave warehouse, where "stubbed-looking, commonplace men" physically examine the slaves Susan and Emmeline, provides a metonymic picture of race and gender relationships in America, with the suggestion that Simon Legree should be taken as the representative American man *in extremis* (just as the antipatriarchal Simeon Halliday of the Quaker settlement represents the bright reverse image that Stowe hoped would accompany America's regenerative transformation). Violating women and slaves alike in the secluded space of his unregulated plantation, insisting in blasphemous ways on his mastery—"*I'm* your church now," he proclaims to Tom—Legree, having rejected the spiritual guidance of his mother (and thus of God), revels in his mastery until Cassy resourcefully debilitates the enfeebled, guilt-ridden drunkard.

As suggested by Cassy's rage, and also by Stowe's analogizing of George Harris's armed battle against fugitive slave hunters to the American and Hungarian Revolutions, natural rights theory figures prominently in the feminist politics of *Uncle Tom's Cabin*. Moreover, in addressing the evils of the Fugitive Slave Law, the novel offers critiques of Northern capitalism's implication in slavery, and of the implication of Northern and Southern organized religion as well. Reform must be national and wide-ranging, according to Stowe, or dreadful consequences will follow. For one, as St. Clare prophesies, America under slavery risks falling into a bloody, apocalyptic race war. For another, as Stowe's sermonic final pages portend, America under slavery, as a nation of sinners, risks God's apocalyptic wrath. In this sense evangelical reform—as embodied by Eva and Tom—is of special urgency. As Stowe explains, if readers can "*feel right,*" as Eva makes Miss Ophelia and St. Clare (and the reader) feel right, or as Tom makes the slave overseers Quimbo and Sambo (and the reader) feel right, conversion of self and society would proceed naturally, thereby fending off the various cataclysms—racial and eschatological—informing the dark imagination of the novel. In important ways, then, the emphasis on evangelicalism, with its millennial promise, serves to contain the novel's more troubling insurrectionary dimension, particularly as embodied by the rebels George Harris and Cassy. The novel concludes with a series of Christian conversions on the part of the rebels, and with Stowe, through Harris, endorsing African colonization as a possible solution to America's racial problems—as a safety outlet, as it were, provided less by moderate racialists, such as her father Lyman Beecher, with whose politics Harriet disagreed, than by God, who has a larger design.

A fear of uncontained racial violence informed a number of the novelistic "responses" to *Uncle Tom's Cabin*, such as Caroline Lee Hentz's *The Planter's Northern Bride* (1854) and William Gilmore

Simms's *Woodcraft* (1854), though, unlike Stowe, slavery apologists insisted that the well-ordered plantation could control such violence. In her subsequent novel, *Dred: A Tale of the Great Dismal Swamp* (1856), Stowe countered this notion, and in doing so revealed even more clearly than in *Uncle Tom's Cabin* the social fears and desires underlying her antislavery position, and the underlying elitism as well. In *A Key to Uncle Tom's Cabin* (1853), Stowe worried over the debilitating effects of slavery on Southern whites, and remarked on the pervasiveness in the South of what she termed "Poor White Trash": "This miserable class of whites form, in all the Southern States, a material for the most horrible and ferocious of mobs. Utterly ignorant, and inconceivably brutal, they are like some blind, savage monster, which, when aroused, tramples heedlessly over everything in its way." In *Dred,* while sympathetically addressing the revolutionary perspective of the escaped slave Dred—presented as the son of the historical slave conspirator Denmark Vesey and modeled, as millennialist revenger, on Nat Turner—Stowe's principal focus is on the increasingly intemperate mobs of "poor white trash" under the control of demagogues. For, after the death of the newly converted plantation mistress Nina Gordon, who, under the guidance of her beloved Edward Clayton, had begun to adopt antislavery beliefs, her plantation and slaves fall into the hands of her brother Tom Gordon, a Legree-like enslaver intoxicated by alcohol and power. The novel concludes with the picture of an utterly degenerate mob under the control of Gordon, and a despairing sense of the nation falling apart under the pressure of the insurrectionary energies of the proslavery rabble. Clayton, who had wanted to reform slavery from within by educating and freeing his slaves, flees to Canada where he sets up a model township; Dred is shot and killed when he attempts to rescue an escaped slave from the drunken Tom's drunken mob.

Anxieties similar to Stowe's about the poor and working classes arguably lie behind much of the middle-class reforms of the period. In this respect, reform could sometimes serve the interests both of change and of the status quo—that is, preserving the hegemony of white Protestant elites. Desires to preserve and control can be viewed at an unattractive extreme in the period's pervasive nativism, itself a kind of Protestant reformism. For it was the opinion of a considerable number of Protestants that the increasing Catholic immigration of the period was the greatest cause for alarm about social decay, signaling America's need for a "Protestant reformation": 54,000 Catholics arrived in the 1820s, 200,000 in the 1830s, 700,000 in the 1840s, and 200,000 in the year 1850 alone. To meet the challenge posed by these immigrants, the evangelical community developed the vast publishing network of the American Tract Society (founded in 1825) and related organizations to disseminate and perpetuate Protestant-republican values. Lyman Beecher, in his widely read nativist tract *Plea for the West* (1835), emphasized the role of the word in this "reformatory" campaign: "Whatever European nations do, our nation must read and think from length and breadth, from top to bottom." And read Americans did, as they made best-sellers of numerous convent captivity novels dramatizing putative Catholic plots to undermine the values and institutions of the Republic. In their popular first-person narrative accounts, Rebecca Theresa Reed's *Six Months in a Convent* (1835) and Maria Monk's notorious *Awful Disclosures of the Hotel Dieu Nunnery* (1836) presented sadistic nuns and priests, violations in the confessional, evidence of Roman Catholic conspiracies, and, ultimately, a summons to Protestant reform (and to spend money on this kind of fiction) by remaining vigilant to Catholic subversives. Monk's sensational book of horrors sold upwards of three hundred thousand copies through 1860, spawned numerous other convent captivity novels, such as Charles Frothingham's *The Convent's Doom* (1854) and Josephine Bunkley's *Miss Bunkley's Book: The Testimony of an Escaped Novice from the Sisterhood of Charity* (1855), and helped to legitimize nativist discourse, which played an important role in the founding of the Republican Party, as a discourse of social reform.

Nativism and fears of insurrectionary disorder from the poor and working classes also played an important role in the urban reform movement of the period. Like Southerners concerned about the possibility of slave revolts and abolitionist conspiracies, Northerners remained concerned about the dangers lurking beneath the surface of what came to be regarded as the mysterious and wicked city—a trope central to a number of antebellum urban novels, such as Ned Buntline's *Mysteries and Miseries of New York* (1848) and Ann Stephens's *Fashion and Famine* (1854). Especially worrying to cultural elites was the marked upsurge in riots in Northeast cities between 1830 and

1860, and the upsurge during the same period of labor organizing and discontent—or, we might say, urban reform from below. Frances Wright and leaders of the New York Workingman's Party, for example, spoke out against "wage slavery," and writers as diverse as Orestes Brownson, in "The Laboring Classes" (1840), Theodore Parker, in "A Sermon on Merchants" (1846), and George Lippard, in such urban reform novels as *The Quaker City* and *New York: Its Upper Ten and Lower Million* (1853), excoriated the rich for exploiting the working poor. In "The Laboring Classes" Brownson went so far as to predict a violent uprising from the workers similar to a slave revolt, "the like of which the world as yet has never witnessed, and from which . . . the heart of Humanity recoils with horror"; and in *The Quaker City* Lippard presented a dream vision of God wreaking vengeance on "the factory Prince" for his crimes against "the slaves of the city."

Fearful of confronting rebellious "slaves" in their own region, urban reformers of the middle and upper classes invoked the putative republican ideals of hierarchy and order and sought to perpetuate these ideals through the creation of reformatory institutions— prisons, mental asylums, almshouses, juvenile delinquent homes, and, relatedly, schools and factories. These new institutions of social reform, so argued their promoters, for the most part Whigs convinced of the malleability of human nature (and concerned about the Democrats' mobilization of Catholics and other "undesirables"), would make model republicans of the dangerous working classes. At the very least, these institutions would keep in check, as reformer Horace Mann put it, the "mutinous" tendencies of those down below.

Indeed, with their emphases on discipline, hierarchy, and custodial isolation, the new asylums, prisons, and other self-contained reform institutions resembled not only the slave plantation but also the institution afloat of the period's popular nautical romances—the well-ordered ship at sea. A tension between the claims of the "organic" state and the claims of the aggrieved and exploited individual—the tension, as it were, between urban reform from above and urban reform from below—is therefore central to much of the "escapist" sea fiction of the period. In many of these nautical narratives the hierarchical ship, like the idealized Northern reform institution, endows impoverished young men with a sense of place and purpose. In

Charles Briggs's popular *The Adventures of Harry Franco: A Tale of the Great Panic* (1839), Franco recuperatively takes to sea to escape bankruptcy. Similar financial situations motivate Melville's narrators in *Redburn* and *White-Jacket,* who bear some resemblance to the greenhorn of Richard Henry Dana's best-selling *Two Years Before the Mast* (1840). Like the ship in Dana's *Two Years* and the reform institutions of America's urban centers, the ship in *White-Jacket,* compared to "a city afloat," "a sort of state prison afloat," and an "asylum," adopts the order of the factory and the prison, not only because it houses sailors in search of purposive order, but also because it houses the disorderly poor—a rough lot of sailors—that urban reformers wanted isolated and enclosed.

Central to this institutional order, however, was the disciplinary prerogative of flogging, and for naval reformers William McNally and John Lockwood, whose *Evils and Abuses in the Naval Merchant Service* (1839) and *An Essay on Flogging* (1849), respectively, galvanized support among Northerners for the eventual abolition of flogging in 1850, ships commanded by authoritarian "lords of the lash" resembled slave plantations. For others, however, flogging, whether at ship or social institution, remained a necessity; even prison reformer Dorothea Dix believed it "sometimes *the only* mode . . . by which an insurrectionary spirit can be conquered." Dana, though highly critical of flogging, as he sympathetically imaged the flogged seaman as a type of slave, nonetheless argued for the right of captains to flog or even execute sailors in extreme situations. Increasingly suspicious of unchecked democratic energies among the masses, Fenimore Cooper, in his nautical romances of the 1840s, most notably *Afloat and Ashore* (1844), idealized captains as benevolent republican gentlemen for whom flogging or execution at sea were regrettable but ultimately necessary last resorts.

Melville's early sea fiction typically demystified the institutional ideals of the well-ordered ship—and, by implication, the well-ordered urban reform institution—by developing the analogy of the ship not only to the reform institution but also to the slave plantation. In *White-Jacket,* for example, Captain Claret, like the captain of Dana's *Two Years,* sadistically flogs an apparently innocent sailor while blasphemously asserting his shipboard supremacy: "I would not forgive God almighty!" Whereas the greenhorn of *Two Years* somewhat genteelly resists mutiny when faced with a similar situation, White-Jacket's emergent belief that the captain's authority rests on "arbitrary law" leads him to develop a rationale for resistance that appeals, as many abolitionists appealed, to the higher law of God and Nature. Thus, when the captain subsequently orders him flogged following an unfair charge of not being in his proper place, White-Jacket, on "plantation" *Neversink,* where "you see a human being, stripped like a slave," in effect entertains the possibility of a slave revolt. Through Melville's presentation of White-Jacket's "wild thoughts"—his meditation on resistance—the reader is taken inside to experience what it means to be subjected to the institutional authority of ship, reform institution, and plantation. Yet White-Jacket, thanks to the intervention of corroborating sailors, does not have to risk becoming a "murderer and suicide," a rebellious slave. Perhaps because Melville shares with elites some of the anxieties about the consequences of unleashed insurrectionary energies, he keeps White-Jacket's anger under constraints. Though other abuses of authority are represented in the novel, an informing fear of revolutionary social disorder, nowhere more apparent than in the account of the riotous "head-beaking" of the skylark, suggests that even in this reformist text Melville adopts a politics of "nautical" order not so radically different from the more aggressively institutionalist politics of a Dana or a Cooper.

That said, Melville's abhorrence for chattel slavery is evident in all of his novels, and it is precisely his ability to provide an "inside" perspective on what it means to be victimized by arbitrary authority—a perspective lacking in much antislavery and reform writing—that makes his antislavery thematics so powerful and challenging. Yet in his novella "Benito Cereno" (1855), his greatest treatment of slavery, Melville denies readers the inside perspective of the rebellious slave Babo while tempting them inside the perspective of the racist Delano. Melville, it would appear, had come to see reform as a balm for the middle class, and thus, in situating the reader in "Benito Cereno" outside the slave revolt—thereby making the reader a victim of the plot—he implicates even self-proclaimed "good" whites in the perpetuation of slavery. In a novella published two years before "Benito Cereno," Frederick Douglass, in "The Heroic Slave" (1853), similarly keeps the white reader at a distance from a rebellious slave. Although a sympathizing white aids Madison Washington in his early prison escape, by the end of the novella, which culminates in Washington's successful engineering of an uprising on the slave ship *Creole* (the novella is based on the actual 1841 rebellion), the slave acts on his own. As in "Benito Cereno," the mutinous events are conveyed from the outside: the rebellion is narrated after the fact by an eyewitness, the *Creole*'s mate, who remains impressed yet terrified by the slaves' intelligence and heroic rebellious energies. Like Melville, then, Douglass points to the limits of reform by situating blacks in a world marked by pervasive racism and slavery's institutional hegemony.

In such a world, "The Heroic Slave" and "Benito Cereno" both suggest, revolutionary action on the part of the slaves is perhaps the only sensible course of action. The African American activist Martin Robison Delany came to a similar conclusion. In his novel, *Blake; or, The Huts of America* (1859–62), serialized in the *Anglo-African Magazine* and *The Weekly Anglo-African,* he depicted white racism in America culminating in a proslavery plot to set up Cuba as a locale for reestablishing the African slave trade in the Americas. Rather than leaving matters for white antislavery reformers to address, Delany has his hero Blake—"a black—a pure Negro—handsome, manly and intelligent"—organize violent countersubversive actions: a black rebellion in Cuba, an attack on an African king who continues to sell his people to slave traders, and slave revolts in the American South. Slave revolt also has an important place in William Wells Brown's *Clotel; or, The President's Daughter,* first published in London in 1853, as Brown, in his account of the New Orleans cholera epidemic of 1831, metaphorically links the fever to the feverish insurrectionism of the rebel Picquilo lurking in the swamps. Modeled after Nat Turner and a possible prototype of Stowe's Dred, he "was a bold, turbulent spirit; and from revenge imbued his hands in the blood of all the whites he could meet." Yet Brown, who worked as a temperance reformer among Buffalo's free African Americans, can seem more moderate than Delany, as he presents the noble reformer Georgiana advising her newly freed slaves thus: "If you are temperate, industrious, peaceable, and pious, you will show to the world that slaves can be emancipated without danger." But while the freedmen pose no danger to the whites, whites continue to pose danger to them.

In a conclusion that both ratifies and undercuts Georgiana's counsels, Brown portrays a happy marriage between Clotel's daughter Mary (a granddaughter of Thomas Jefferson and his slave mistress) and the former slave George, who, after escaping from slavery, educates himself and becomes a partner in a merchant house. Significantly, however, this success story occurs abroad: Mary and George are reunited and married in France and they choose to remain in London.

Similar pessimism about racial and class oppression informs Harriet E. Wilson's *Our Nig; or, Sketches from the Life of a Free Black* (1859), the first African American novel published in America, which, like *Clotel,* takes on the related issue of gender oppression as well. The poor white and African American women of Wilson's novel find it next to impossible to find decent work; though not actually enslaved, they suffer from the ravages of "wage slavery." In this respect, Wilson addresses the exploitation of women in ways that parallel and develop the treatment of the same issue in the fiction of white women writers—Fern's *Ruth Hall* and Ann Sophia Stephens's *The Old Homestead* (1855) depicted the desperate plight of New York's working women, and Rebecca Harding Davis, in her short novel *Life in the Iron Mills* (1860) and her first novel, *Margret Howth* (1862), explored the spiritual impoverishment and exploitation of women working in Northern factories. Frado, the "Nig" of *Our Nig,* is the daughter of a poor white working woman who, as she falls deeper into poverty, marries "a kind-hearted African," by whom she has two children. Unable to support them, she abandons one, Frado, with the rich and respected Bellmonts. Emphasizing the intersecting issues of class and race, Wilson presents as the most brutal character of the novel the "haughty, undisciplined, arbitrary, and severe" Mrs. Bellmont, whose privilege and cruelty link her to Stowe's Marie St. Clare of *Uncle Tom's Cabin.* Intent on exploiting and humiliating Frado, whom she raises as a servant, Mrs. Bellmont beats, chokes, and otherwise degrades and brutalizes her. When she leaves the Bellmonts at age eighteen, Frado, impoverished and the mother of a sickly son in Massachusetts, eventually has no one to turn to for help. The narrator refers scornfully to "professed abolitionists, who didn't want slaves at the South, nor niggers in their own houses, North," and, as fictional and real worlds collapse—Wilson herself was the mother of a sick child who eventually died—

the author offers the novel to "my colored brethren" with the hope that their willingness to purchase it would provide her with funds to help her ailing son.

Harriet A. Jacobs casts an equally jaundiced eye on the problems of race, class, and gender in antebellum America in her novelized autobiographical narrative, *Incidents in the Life of a Slave Girl* (1861). An account of Linda Brent's amazingly resourceful escape from slavery by hiding for seven years in her grandmother's attic space, the book exposes from an African American woman's point of view the sexual brutality inherent in slavery. As Jacobs remarks about the situation of the typical slave woman: "Women are considered of no value, unless they continually increase their owner's stock. They are put on a par with animals." The most "animalistic" character of the narrative, however, is Brent's slave master Dr. Flint, consumed by his desire to possess Linda sexually: "No animal ever watched its prey more narrowly than he watched me." As in Stowe and other antislavery and feminist writers, in Jacobs the patriarchal will to sexual mastery is presented as a form of intoxication. And like the scourge of alcohol in T. S. Arthur's fiction, slavery, in Jacobs's narrative, "makes the white fathers cruel and sensual; the sons violent and licentious; it contaminates the daughters, and makes the wives wretched." Indeed, because the plantation mistress and the slave mistress are portrayed as victims of the male enslaver's lust for power, sexual and otherwise, there are intimations that Jacobs, like Stowe in *Uncle Tom's Cabin,* is invoking a sisterhood of white and African American women, especially mothers, as the best possible reformatory solution to the problem of slavery. Yet Jacobs is clear-sighted about the gulf between the races and the classes, as Dr. Flint's wife, Brent's fellow "victim," absolutely fails to see any analogy in their respective situations. Though the privileged New Yorker Mrs. Bruce, following Brent's escape to the North, helps Linda to escape from her pursuers and eventually purchases her freedom, she stands as a rare exception to the racism rampant in the North, where segregated boats, trains, and hotels, and wandering fugitive slave hunters, remain the order of the day. As is true for George and Mary in *Clotel,* or the African American sailor in Melville's *Redburn* unselfconsciously walking the streets of Liverpool, Linda experiences her greatest sense of freedom when she visits England.

By emphasizing the intractability of racism in America, particularly as it "invisibly" undergirded the nation's social, religious, and economic institutions, African American writers made clear what Emerson only occasionally faced up to: just how difficult it would have been for any American to achieve "transcendental" individual reform within a social system countenancing slavery. In this respect, African American writers presented a fundamental challenge to white reformers who, in advocating various specific programs, could lose sight of the need for larger structural and ideological reorientations. Reading African American novelists therefore presses us to reread white middle-class novels of social reform with a skeptical eye, alert to the ways in which, despite their authors' reformist intentions, they participated in the reproduction of dominant ideologies. Yet to engage in a thoroughgoing demonization (or deconstruction) of these novels as complicitous in, rather than subversive of, the reigning order—the interpretive thrust of recent New Historicist approaches to the Anglo-American novel of reform—may be anachronistic. Such a critical perspective, in affiliating white reform novelists in particular with the disciplinary and institutional practices of the state, and thus with the persistence of racial, gender, and class inequities in America, may even be self-righteous. More productively, we could regard novelists of reform, African American and white, as dialogical writers, alternately pragmatic and visionary, who, even as they were inevitably inscribed by their culture, found much in it to critique as they sought to imagine and hopefully thus to create a better America.

Robert S. Levine

# The Late Nineteenth Century

# Introduction

As the single most severe disruption in America's political economy, the Civil War has often come to mark an important watershed in the nation's literary history as well. If, as Walt Whitman predicted in *Specimen Days* (1875–76), the "hell and the black infernal background" of the war would remain relatively "unwritten" for decades, its social repercussions naturally made their way into fictional representation: into the new forms of wage slavery dramatized in Rebecca Harding Davis's *Life in the Iron Mills* (1861); into Henry Adams's *Democracy* (1880), where postbellum Mugwump reform was satirized as washing a "donkey's head"; into William Dean Howells's *The Rise of Silas Lapham* (1885), which bore witness to the pain and guilt of newly integrated market economies; into the bitter pages of Mark Twain's *Pudd'nhead Wilson* (1894), which burlesqued the invidiousness of Jim Crow and the color line. American commoners, often the symbol and occasionally the brunt of these social conditions, were given central "title" over national fiction: names like Lapham, Carrie, Jekl, or Maggie now appeared before the eyes of American readers. But these experiments in social "realism," and after it "naturalism"—the labels with which literary historians have usually marked the dominant conventions of this period—only loosely describe the narrative modes of the late nineteenth-century novel. At a deeper level, postbellum History pushed these traditionally individuating moral economies of the novel to new limits—evincing what Georg Lukács once called a struggle of an essentially biographical form to master the "bad infinity" of heterogeneous social events. If the Gilded Age institutionalized the novel as never before in American culture, the form also became a locus of unease and dissent—simultaneously an expression of unstable centers *and* new challenges at the boundaries of American literary life.

At such centers of institutionalized literary culture in the North—in cities like Boston, among gentlemanly publishing houses, and at family magazines like the *Atlantic Monthly, Scribner's,* or *The Century*—the Reconstruction-era project of shoring up antebellum genteel culture initially meant disdaining both novelistic versimilitude and the "sensational" melodrama of cheap fiction in favor of more sedate, idealized, and usually historical romance. Fiction continued to be guarded against what Victorian critics called unhealthy "tendencies." Meanwhile, throughout the period genteel magazines would underwrite a variety of regional recovery projects—picturesque renditions of ostensibly disappearing local cultures—thus exhibiting a nostalgia that often subtly underwrote a growing political reconciliation of North and South (with disastrous consequences for African Americans). Even Howells's editorial challenge to romantic fiction from his post at the *Atlantic* assumed that the conventional realism customarily associated with the novel—initially modeled upon the knowable community of Jane Austen—would sustain "sanity" and balance in the American republic, provide a consensual middle-class culture by portraying "men and women as they are, actuated by the motives and passions in the measure we all know."

Yet the hegemony of such guardianship was always incomplete. Even Howells's "measure" could only be a nostalgic standard, an attempt to hold a moderate republican American center against the signs of the times: against European and Asian immigration (nearly nine million new arrivals between 1880 and 1900); against growingly bellicose expansionism, so evident in the Spanish-American War of 1898; against spasmodic class warfare and violence in the railroad strikes of 1877, the Haymarket Riot (1886), the Homestead strike (1892). In Howells's adopted home of Massachusetts, there were hundreds of strikes in the 1880s alone. Much of late Victorian literary culture dramatized whether the Howellsian center would (or should) hold. In other hands, the novel would be both formally more varied and ideologically more radical than the "Dean" envisioned: in the sociopolitical comedies of immigrant life by the Russian American

Abraham Cahan; in the openly discursive, spiritualized gender myths of Sarah Orne Jewett (who readapted the conventions of local color); in the political refashioning of historical romance by African American magazinist Pauline Hopkins; in the Cinderella class fables of Laura Jean Libbey.

Of course, the quarrel and the reciprocity between boundary and center, affirmation and dissent, never quite disappeared even as realism fragmented—and as the marketplace expanded. Even among the writers above, dependent as they were upon an audience created by their own professionalization, the challenge was often to work *through* popular forms that had received Victorian sanction. Among the seemingly naturalistic writers Howells greeted so uneasily as his logical successors—Stephen Crane, Theodore Dreiser, or muckrakers like Jack London, Frank Norris, and Upton Sinclair—the sway of popular romance had hardly been forsaken. True, some measure of change can be felt in the new literary explorations of the slum, the factory, the "mysteries of the city"—subjects at which Howells had once only shuddered. The new material bounties of industrial society, however, were hardly disdained altogether. Despite the dark ruminations of a Twain or a Henry Adams, the industrial dynamo's own energy undercut many attempts at resistance. Indeed, the power and technical ingenuity of machine culture, and the mass spectacles of consumption it often created—in the hands of a Crane, a Dreiser, a Wharton, or a Henry James—became the substance of fictions that mixed their doubts with celebratory awe. In these ways, the turn-of-the-century novel registered the war's final, yet mixed victory: a new North and a New South, a populace "unified" and allured by mass consumption—the nation's productive reach enhanced within its territories and without—yet a society still internally divided over the spoils.

Christopher P. Wilson

# Realism

> Money is the most general element of Balzac's novels;
> other things come and go, but money is always there.
> —Henry James, "Honoré de Balzac" (1875)

"At the Station" opens with a passage that sounds familiar, perhaps because it is from a Howells or Twain story we can't
quite place. "Nothing could well be more commonplace or
ignoble than the corner of the world in which Miss Dilly now spent
her life," the story begins. "A wayside inn, near a station on the
railway which runs from Salisbury, in North Carolina, up into the
great Appalachian range of mountains; two or three unpainted boxes
of houses scattered along the track by the inn; not a tree nor blade
of grass in the 'clarin'; a few gaunt, long-legged pigs and chickens
grunting and cackling in the muddy clay yards; beyond, swampy
tobacco fields stretching to the encircling pine woods." The emphasis
on the commonplace, on the ignored or despised; the attention to the
unpainted houses, the muddy clay yards, and the gaunt pigs and
chickens—or their human equivalents; the possibility of sympathy
and satire; the awareness of regions and regional differences; the
sensitivity to American dialects and their class and racial implications; the conversational middle—and middle-class—style, vocabulary, and syntax; the focus on Miss Dilly, not on Captain Ahab or
Leatherstocking—here is a preliminary list of the traits of American
realism. Because Rebecca Harding Davis is not working at the height
of her powers in "At the Station" (1892), the story, unlike her pioneering *Life in the Iron Mills* (1861), does not take us deep into the
unexplored territory of America's emerging industrial capitalism or
make us see the complex realities of money and power that were
affecting women and men in the new America. The first generation

of American realists, however, writers who began publishing during or soon after the Civil War, authors as different as Davis and James, Twain and Howells, each gave distinctive individual accounts of these vital, disruptive forces. By the end of the century they and successors like Charles Chesnutt had also probed the complexities of race in post–Civil War America.

They did so as professional authors who were personally engaged in writing for the market in the new entertainment industry. Their insights, conflicts, compromises, and triumphs are inseparable from their experience in the new world of mass markets, advertising, and big money. These developments had begun before the Civil War but accelerated as the scale of production expanded, the railroad system was completed, and the need to create consumer demand intensified. The corrosive, vital power of an expanding market society under-mined moral, religious, and social stabilities. No wonder that a ques-tioning of conventions and the conventional is perhaps the central unifying convention of American realism.

In their literary criticism the writers explicitly questioned conven-tions and the conventional. In his Declaration of Independence, "The Art of Fiction" (1884), Henry James affirmed the creator's freedom to choose both subject and approach, even as James defied the "keep off the grass signs" of the guardians of official taste. Even a writer as moderate as William Dean Howells, America's minister of culture, argued against the demand for a conventional love plot and all it signified, particularly a focus on marriage as the goal of life and an avoidance of the full range of contemporary concerns. After the Hay-market Riot in 1886 Howells attempted to explore the energies that were transforming American cities and threatening the moral and religious ideals he believed American writers should celebrate. The conflict between his desire to affirm his Emersonian values as the prevailing American reality and his commitment to render honestly what was happening in the new America goes to the heart of How-ells's dilemma as an American realist. Mark Twain, for his part, ridiculed James Fenimore Cooper's conventions, which in "Fenimore Cooper's Literary Offenses" (1895) emerge as the improbabilities, exaggerations, and stilted language of the Leatherstocking tales. Twain is in effect arguing for a new set of conventions privileging the spoken language and fidelity to ordinary experience.

Although we can create a composite portrait of American realism, differences and diversity are crucial. James, for example, had serious reservations about what he saw as Rebecca Harding Davis's sentimentality and the value she attributed to ordinary characters. Twain's colloquial immediacy is far removed from James's language and upper-class social world. Unlike the Europeans centering on Balzac and later on Flaubert and later still on Zola, we did not really have a school of American realism. Both in critical theory and in literary practice, moreover, the questioning of convention and the other formal and substantive traits all have antecedents in the work of earlier American writers, in the colloquial dialogue of Melville's *Redburn* (1849), for example, the sensitivity to the details of place in Hawthorne, or the practical, Yankee side of Emerson. It is a matter of degree, of emphasis. Similarly, younger authors like Dreiser, Crane, and Cather built on and reacted against what often seemed to them the timidity and limitations of the first-generation realists. In nineteenth-century America "realism" is a relational term defined partly by what people in a particular generation were accustomed to accept as plausible and lifelike, partly by what they responded to as pushing toward and beyond the boundaries of middle-class acceptability.

The first-generation realists and their successors did justice to the surfaces of American life through the conventions of presentational realism—plausibly rendered speech, recognizable settings and recognizable characters facing everyday problems, all open to the interpretation of a middle-class, predominantly feminine audience. American realists also penetrated beneath the surface to engage with the underlying energies of men, women, and society in the Gilded Age. I will be examining some of the ways significant writers during and in the decades immediately after the Civil War rendered their sense of the surfaces and depths of American social and psychological life. "Conventions" has a ring of traditionalism at odds with what they were committed to. But the term usefully highlights the constructed nature of the enterprise both for the writers and for us.

For James's contemporaries, his *The Portrait of a Lady* (1881) was—and remains for us—an exemplary representative of American realism. Early in the book James describes the Archers' old double house in Albany and the full family life connected with it. James then carries Isabel Archer into the recesses of her childhood past and into the recesses of her favorite room, "a mysterious apartment" filled with old furniture with which "she had established relations almost human." The double house, the humanized room, and the sense of an inner life establish an intimate connection between house and self. Like the house, Isabel's self is divided or at least pulled in opposing directions. The door to the mysterious room is bolted, the door's sidelights are covered with green paper, and though as a little girl Isabel knew the door opened out onto the street "she had no wish to look out, for this would have interfered with her theory that there was a strange, unseen place on the other side—a place which became to the child's imagination, according to its different moods, a region of delight or of terror." Like the Emerson who celebrates the inner life of the self-sufficient individual, in this version Isabel looks inward into the depths of the imagination, creates a drama of delight or terror, and on principle avoids testing her theories against what she will find on "the vulgar street." As an adult in this same room she blithely tells her aunt, "I don't know anything about money." It is not really fair to equate Emerson, inwardness, and the imagination with the romantic and the street and money with realism. Emerson, after all, spoke for the meal in the firkin, the milk in the pan, and Isabel has an immense appetite for experience. In part James conceives Isabel so that he can explore a conflict between two sides of his American cultural heritage. As an American writer and realist, he is especially sensitive to the issue of the reliability of the imagination under the pressure of money and the vulgar street.

For James, the imagination and the inner self are not isolated or reified. In Isabel's case they are intimately related to her sexuality. James has Isabel encounter a series of suitors. "Deep in her soul—it was the deepest thing there—lay a belief that if a certain light should dawn she could give herself completely; but this image, on the whole, was too formidable to be attractive." The thought causes "alarms" that become increasingly intense. She is cold toward Lord Warburton because of "a certain fear." The drama builds because James keeps the sources of the fear unspecified and the entire issue in suspension.

As a representative American, Isabel often fuses the language of American political culture with the language of Emersonian self-reliance. "I like my liberty too much," Isabel says to justify turning down Lord Warburton. She continues in the accents of a Fourth of July address or of the Declaration of Independence, "it's my personal independence. . . . my love of liberty." Or in a recognizably Emersonian mode, "I only want to see for myself." Isabel's pursuit of happiness is a central concern, as is her fear that in marrying Lord Warburton she will be escaping unhappiness, "what most people know and suffer." In rejecting Lord Warburton, Isabel is affirming the American values of independence and love of liberty as over against the security of established English wealth, landed property, and aristocratic position.

Inseparable from this drama of conflicting political cultures is the depth of Isabel's feelings, expressed in a characteristically Jamesian metaphor. Isabel resists like "some wild, caught creature in a vast cage." Although Isabel often sees Lord Warburton as kind, he can also emerge "with his hands behind him giving short nervous shakes to his hunting-crop." As a potent male keeper, "booted and spurred," Lord Warburton thus plays a part in a submerged drama of sexual politics, a drama that is much more open with her American suitor, Caspar Goodwood. Isabel's feelings about sexual power, her own and her suitors', animate the overt drama of mind and values. "Who was she, what was she, that she should hold herself superior?" Isabel thinks. "What view of life, what design upon fate, what conception of happiness, had she that she pretended to be larger than these large, these fabulous occasions? If she wouldn't do such a thing as that then she must do great things, she must do something greater." She worries that she is "a cold, hard, priggish person, and, on her at last getting up and going rather quickly back to the house, felt, as she had said to her friend, really frightened at herself."

James throws further light on the self Isabel fears after the dilettante Gilbert Osmond declares his love. "What made her dread great," James reiterates, "was precisely the force which, as it would seem, ought to have banished all dread—the sense of something within herself, deep down, that she supposed to be inspired and trustful passion. It was there," James stresses, "like a large sum stored in a bank—which there was a terror in having to begin to spend. If she touched it, it would all come out." On this view the self is not a wellspring of infinitely renewable energy but a bank, a repository of a finite sum of money. James reveals that the market society has infiltrated the deepest recesses of the self, even of Isabel Archer, who knows nothing about money. Her fear of "giving herself completely" is a complex fusion of her fastidiousness, her desire for independence, her unwillingness to subordinate and cage herself, her deep feelings about sexual power and powerlessness, and her mixed feelings about money and all it stands for.

Caspar Goodwood inspires the deepest fear of any of the suitors because he directly expresses his sexual passion. Throughout her last meeting with Goodwood, Isabel is "frightened" at his "violence." She feels "she had never been loved before. She had believed it, but this was different; this was the hot wind of the desert, at the approach of which others dropped dead. . . . the very taste of it, as of something potent, acrid and strange, forced open her set teeth." Death and sexual love merge as James's imagery enacts the physical emotions connected with a fierce seduction or rape. Isabel "floated in fathomless waters. . . . in a rushing torrent." Sounds come to her "harsh and terrible. . . . in her own swimming head." "She panted" when she pleads with Goodwood "to go away." Instead, "he glared at her a moment through the dusk, and the next instant she felt his arms about her and his lips on her own lips. His kiss was like white lightning, a flash that spread, and spread again, and stayed." In the conventions of the period a kiss, reinforced by James's imagery, has the force of sexual intercourse. For Isabel, Goodwood's "hard manhood," his "aggressive" physical presence, culminates in an "act of possession." The possession is sexual but also involves the issues of freedom, independence, and money. Osmond sees Isabel as a commodity, as his prize possession. In returning to Osmond, a choice open to multiple interpretations, Isabel is in part fleeing from the intensities of Goodwood's passion, from the possession he threatens, although overtly he argues for their complete freedom to do what they please. Isabel, however, is also affirming her independence and rejecting her status as a possession as both Goodwood and Osmond define possession.

In a possessive market society, money is the ultimate commodity, the ultimate possession. Isabel wants to see for herself, to judge for herself, but she does not know anything about money. She is also torn between her impulse to know the world, to throw herself into it, and her impulse to trust herself, to devalue worldly possessions, and to ignore the vulgar street. After she inherits a fortune, she is afraid. "A large fortune means freedom," she tells Ralph Touchett, "and I'm afraid of that." If she failed to make good use of it, she goes on, she "would be ashamed." The stakes are high because shame is intimately connected to a sense of personal identity and self-worth.

Isabel argues for a sense of self that excludes possessions. "Nothing that belongs to me," she tells Madame Merle, "is any measure of me; everything's on the contrary a limit, a barrier, and a perfectly arbitrary one." Isabel is particularly indifferent to houses and dress. Madame Merle disagrees. "What shall we call our 'self?' " she asks. "Where does it begin? where does it end? It overflows into everything that belongs to us—and then it flows back again. I know a large part of myself is the clothes I choose to wear. I've a great respect for *things!* One's self—for other people—is one's expression of one's self; and one's house, one's furniture, one's garments, the books one reads, the company one keeps—these things are all expressive." James has Madame Merle give a working definition of the self appropriate to an expanding consumer and possessive market society. On this view, the self expands or contracts in relation to possessions. "There's no such thing as an isolated man or woman," Madame Merle argues; "we're each of us made up of some cluster of appurtenances."

Until well after her marriage Isabel does not realize the extent to which Madame Merle and Osmond, two artists, two dramatists, have manipulated her. They present Osmond as a refined man indifferent to the opinion of the world, indifferent to money, indifferent to the "cluster of appurtenances." His relative poverty allows Isabel to feel generous. She is bestowing something on a worthy recipient. The power relations are the reverse of a marriage to either Lord Warburton or Caspar Goodwood. Osmond is also much less of a masculine sexual presence than either of his rivals. Isabel imagines a Gilbert Osmond and falls in love with her own creation. In the destabilizing crosscurrents of a changing market society, the imagination is both necessary and problematic. Isabel, committed to seeing for herself, is unable to see that Osmond worships money and the opinion of the vulgar society he professes to despise.

James tests and qualifies Isabel's view of the self and imagination.

He probes the web of sexual and market society pressures that affect the way she sees. In a patrician green world apparently far removed from the vulgar street, James reveals that even for Isabel Archer, profit, money, and gain are at the center of her marriage, just as they have penetrated to the center of her self.

In James's version of psychological realism, he uses metaphoric language to take us deep into a character's consciousness. James repeatedly recognizes the intimate connection between houses and selves in a possessive market society, a relation that for him has moral, psychological, and sociopolitical implications. Isabel, for example, gradually becomes aware that in marrying Osmond she is being confined in a house of darkness, that she is being imprisoned in a mind that lets in no air or light, that is a dungeon. Osmond's hatred, contempt, and egotism are overwhelming. Isabel's terror builds. The imagery is dense and deep, as are Isabel's painful moral and psychological realizations. Rooted in American political culture, her concern with freedom and independence is as alive as her eventual sense that she has been turned into a commodity, another *objet d'art* for Osmond to add to his collection, like the antique Roman coin he meticulously copies. James does justice both to the gradual, oblique way the mind works and to Isabel's sudden flash of awareness as she watches the intimacy between the standing Madame Merle and the seated Gilbert Osmond. But for all his sensitivity to the inner workings of the mind, James's psychological probing is not privatized. James shows the relation between the inner self and the environing world of the vulgar street.

Ironically, under Osmond's fastidious surface, under the aspect of taste, he and Madame Merle come to embody money and the vulgar street. Through Madame Merle, James exposes not metaphysical evil but the socially constructed evil of a society that places money above everything. For profit Madame Merle, gifted, aware, and sensitive, nonetheless lies to and betrays her closest friends. " 'I don't pretend to know what people are meant for,' said Madame Merle. 'I only know what I can do with them.' "

In a world where Osmond and Madame Merle are dominant forces, where their imagination, art, and dramatic skill are important, the world becomes a social text that may not be incomprehensible but that is also not easy to read. Osmond and Madame Merle embody the deception, manipulation of appearances, and obsession with profit that many social observers regard as basic to consumer capitalism. In his way Ralph is also manipulative but, as opposed to Osmond, Ralph is generous and loving. Ralph sees clearly that Osmond is a sterile dilettante who will grind Isabel in the mill of the conventional. Although he accurately reads the social text, Ralph is unable to prevent the marriage. Isabel comes to understand but the inner and outer obstacles are formidable.

These forces are even more pronounced in the great works of James's final phase. His concerns remained remarkably consistent—the house of the mind, the role of the imagination, and the impact of money and power on the divided self in "The Jolly Corner" (1908), for example, or the central role of commodities, of money, and of love and betrayal in *The Golden Bowl* (1905) and *The Wings of the Dove* (1902). James's style, however, became denser and more impenetrable, the moral and social discriminations became subtler, the ambiguities more difficult to understand. In his later works James created a style adequate to render his sense of the emerging twentieth century. For James, the impact on the mind of the dominant forces of modernity impelled him beyond what we would ordinarily see as "realism."

Even William Dean Howells found the realism he himself practiced and advocated inadequate to deal with his most principled social concerns. After *A Hazard of New Fortunes* (1890), Howells engaged with the large forces of the new America not in realistic fiction but in the utopian novels *A Traveler from Altruria* (1894) and *Through the Eye of the Needle* (1907).

Responding to the energies of the new post–Civil War America, Mark Twain gave the period its name in a novel of the present, *The Gilded Age* (1873). In successive works, however, Twain moved farther into the past. He drew on his own boyhood and his years as a cub pilot in "Old Times on the Mississippi" (1875), *The Adventures of Tom Sawyer* (1876), *Life on the Mississippi* (1883), and *The Adventures of Huckleberry Finn* (1885), his masterpiece of vernacular realism. In these works he deals with contemporary concerns suggestively but indirectly, a tendency that intensifies in *A Connecticut Yankee in King Arthur's Court* (1889), set not in the America of Twain's lifetime but in the England of a mythical past. His sense of the American present seemed to make it difficult for Twain to deal with it imaginatively in anything like the mode of realism he had perfected in *Huckleberry Finn.* Except for *Pudd'nhead Wilson* (1894) and his essays and travel books, Twain turned increasingly to fable, as in the searing "The Man That Corrupted Hadleyburg" (1899), or dream tales, as in "The Mysterious Stranger" (published posthumously).

Early in his career, however, in "Old Times on the Mississippi," Twain began to develop his characteristic version of American realism as a way of knowing, seeing, and saying. For all the differences in class, cultivation, and milieu, Isabel Archer and her epistemological situation are similar to those of Mark Twain's cub as he tries to learn the constantly changing shapes of the river. In "Old Times on the Mississippi" the river in nightmare fog and darkness, the river with its energy and shifting banks and channels, becomes a metaphor for the fluid, shifting American social world Mark Twain experienced in the years after he served his own apprenticeship as a cub. The cub must learn all 2000 miles of the river. But the banks cave, the river at night looks different from the river in daylight, and the mind itself plays tricks and turns a ripple on the surface of the water into a dangerous reef. Knowledge is based on empirical experience, on the hard work of memorizing soundings and landmarks, on courage and an artist's intuition. The epistemological dilemma is that the cub must "learn *the* shape of the river, and you learn it with such absolute certainty that you can always steer by the shape that's *in your head,* and never mind the one that's before your eyes." No wonder the cub is often terrified and demoralized. He comes to the river with romantic ideas of glory and finds out about the cruel hard work and danger involved. Part of the reader's fun is watching the cub's pretensions get their comeuppance as the greenhorn repeatedly underestimates the challenge of the river and the capacity of the veteran pilots, particularly the exemplary Mr. B.

As the jokes accumulate, they elevate the pilot to the status of a demigod who can see in the dark, steer a boat through a deadly channel while he is fast asleep, and who, like the steamboat that brings the dead town to life, "if he can do such gold-leaf, kid-glove, diamond-breastpin piloting when he is sound asleep, what *couldn't* he do if he was dead." The language combines the tall-tale hyperbole of frontier humor with the racy, precise language of piloting as an American occupation. As a realist, Twain taps into the energy of both traditions. American realists like Mark Twain may use such conventions to render a lifelike quality but they are rarely literal or one-dimensional. Twain, for example, does justice to the world of the river in the 1850s and endows it with a suggestive charge that engages with his concerns as an American writer in the Gilded Age of moneymaking and accelerating technology. As a writer in such a destabilizing period, how does he know for sure? What can he rely on? What value does his work have? How trustworthy is the imagination?

For the cub, as for the writer, the pilot is a demigod, a death-defying, life-giving savior figure. He thrives on the changing American world of the river. "That's the very main virtue of the thing," Mr. B. explains. "If the shapes didn't change every three seconds they wouldn't be of any use." It takes a special sensibility to see the virtue in these rapid changes and an equally special person to turn them to use. "As long as that hill over yonder is only one hill, I can boom right along the way I'm going; but the moment it splits at the top and forms a V, I know I've got to scratch to starboard in a hurry, or I'll bang this boat's brains out against a rock. . . . If that hill didn't change its shape on bad nights," Mr. B. concludes, "there would be an awful steamboat grave-yard around here inside a year." The cub amplifies the mythic implications when he says, "When I get so that I can do that, I'll be able to raise the dead, and then I won't have to pilot a steamboat in order to make a living."

"The true pilot," Twain affirms, "cares nothing about anything on earth but the river, and his pride in his occupation surpasses the pride of kings." Encoded in this view is a revealing contradiction. The courage, intuition, and hard work of the pilot who "cares nothing about anything on earth but the river" are at odds with that same pilot who glories in his princely salary, who looks down on and runs over lowly raftsmen, and whose pride "surpasses the pride of kings." The pilot was "the only unfettered and entirely independent human being that lived on earth. . . . His movements were entirely free; he consulted no one, he received commands from nobody." This supreme American individualist, however, is also enmeshed in a system of supply and demand that keeps his wages high, that supports the luxury of the pilothouse and apprentices to do the menial work, and that contributes to the "exalted respect" he commands. Against odds the pilots form a union, systematize the distribution of information, and regulate wages and entry into the profession. Insurance companies and government regulations reinforce the union. The Civil War and a new technology, the railroad, also affect piloting. A union treasurer, like his Gilded Age successors, steals the retirement fund. The contradictions within the true pilot and his rapidly changing situation deconstruct this exemplary figure.

Just before the union surfaces in Twain's narrative, he brings to life how "you are tortured with the exquisite misery of uncertainty" as you grope through "an impenetrable gloom of smoke from a hundred miles of burning bagesse [sugar cane] piles. . . . You find yourself away out in the midst of a vague dim sea that is shoreless, that fades out and loses itself in the murky distances; for you cannot discern the thin rib of embankment, and you are always imagining you see a straggling tree when you don't. . . . You hope you are keeping the river, but you do not know. All that you are sure about is that you are likely to be within six feet of the bank and destruction." When Huck Finn is lost in the fog, his moral bearings are disoriented. In "Old Times" the issue is epistemological. Twain repeatedly comes back to the torment of uncertainty in a threatening, shifting, murky world. He leaves the issue unresolved, or rather he tells one more story about the demigod pilot, the savior figure who can steer a boat in his sleep and triumph over death and destruction.

After he deals with the union, the Civil War, and the railroad, however, Twain is unable to imagine the pilot as demigod. The epistemological dilemma nonetheless remains. But in place of Mr. B. and his like, who resolve the torment of uncertainty and who preside over parts I-IV of "Old Times," Twain now invokes another figure, the pilot Stephen W. Appropriately enough for a Gilded Age narrative, Stephen's identifying trait is his involvement with debt and money. The suppressed element in the figure of the true pilot is now overt. Money and debt were urgent concerns for Twain and many others in the Gilded Age. Unlike the demigod pilot, however, Stephen W. does not even temporarily resolve the issues he embodies. The jokes are funny, but because money totally dominates, the tensions that impel the narrative are no longer in active play; the narrative loses force, and Twain brings "Old Times" to a close.

In "Old Times" another unresolved tension involves the lively colloquial language of the pilot as opposed to the genteel language of the landscape tradition. The narrator consciously favors "the red hue brightened into gold," the "tumbling rings, that were as many-tinted as an opal," the "leafy bough," "the unobstructed splendor," the "graceful curves, reflected images, woody heights, soft distances" — all the stock language and conventional way of seeing of the nineteenth-century landscape tradition. As the cub learns the river, the stock beauty and glory fade. Instead of a charming ripple the cub who has learned his trade now sees a deadly reef, "the very best place he could have found to fish for steamboats." He has also found a vital language rooted in ordinary American experience, a colloquial language Twain perfected in *The Adventures of Huckleberry Finn*.

This language has a beauty appropriate to a developing realism. But Twain and other realists experienced a dilemma as they attempted to render observed American life, since they associated beauty with a set of conventions they were in the process of subverting. For Twain the new language of realism is in part connected with the masculine realm of work and with an evolving professionalism that involved a use of precise measurements at odds with the hyperbole of frontier humor and the irreverent colloquialism of ordinary speech. It was also at odds with his conscious conception of beauty. Using the gendered image of the woman's body, Twain associates beauty with femininity and deceptive surfaces, with the flush of fever hiding "some deadly disease." For the professional and the realist, "are not all her visible charms sown thick with what are to him the signs and symbols of hidden decay?" On this view the realist sees through the surface deceptions to the underlying disease, as Isabel Archer does in her way or as the narrator of *Life in the Iron Mills* grapples with in hers. Especially for the early Twain and the early Rebecca Harding Davis, realists in process, no wonder if they sometimes asked whether they had "gained most or lost most by learning [their] trade."

As a pioneer realist, in *Life in the Iron Mills* (1861) Rebecca Harding Davis probed a crucial area of American life a generation in advance of successors who by the end of the century had forgotten her achievement. More pervasively than in "Old Times," the smoke that dominates the prologue to *Life in the Iron Mills* embodies both the material conditions of the mills and the difficulty of penetrating through "the fog and mud and foul effluvia" to a resolution of the questions this new way of life poses for all those affected by it. Partly because of the narrator's point of view, partly because of the dislocating impact of the mill world, the revelations in *Life in the Iron Mills* are not fixed and absolute but problematic.

Deb, malnourished and deformed, recognizes that the Welsh mill worker Hugh Wolfe has "a groping passion for whatever was beautiful and pure—that his soul sickened with disgust at her deformity." On this view, Wolfe accepts an etherialized, middle-class aesthetics that equates "the beautiful" and "the pure," an aesthetics at odds with the powerful art Wolfe in fact creates. Even more than the narrator of "Old Times," Wolfe is divided. The narrator of "Old Times" consciously values a language of beauty quite different from the art he actually creates out of the processes of piloting. Similarly, Wolfe's achievement is to create strong, moving art from the material conditions of the industrial process. His basic material, the korl, is "the refuse from the ore after the pig-metal is run." His Korl Woman statue expresses the spiritual hunger, the oppression, and, depending on the observer, the protest, the warning, or the supplication of the men and women who work in the mills. Wolfe's creativity is inseparable from the working-class reality that permeates his life. Part of his tragedy is that Wolfe does not have a verbal, conceptual language that allows him to value what he has created.

Instead, his consciousness is penetrated by middle-class ideas of beauty that denigrate his own class and fit in with the narrator's view "of the disease of their class. . . . a reality of soul-starvation, of living death, that meets you every day under the besotted faces on the street." The statue, however, embodies strength as well as soul-starvation; a rugged, muscular beauty, not disease. The statue embodies a more complex and nuanced view of working-class men and women than either Wolfe or the narrator is able to articulate or the upper-class observers are able to comprehend. The Korl Woman statue also speaks to the unacknowledged situation of middle-class women like Rebecca Harding Davis and the narrator, who find in the overt oppression of the workers an analogue of their own position.

For Wolfe the central "mystery of his life" is the question not of class conflict but of class difference. "He seized eagerly every chance that brought him into contact with this mysterious class that shone down on him perpetually with the glamour of another order of being. What made the difference between them? That was the mystery of his life." In his art, Wolfe does not explore the difference but instead goes deep into the complex realities of his own class. "With his artist's sense," however, Wolfe "did obeisance to . . . the thorough-bred gentleman, Mitchell, . . . unconscious that he did so." In light of his obeisance to the glamour of the upper class at the expense of his own class, the wonder is that Wolfe is able to produce "figures—hideous, fantastic enough, but sometimes strangely beautiful"—but not beautiful by the standards of the class he worships, standards he himself partly accepts.

Through what the narrator sees as his God-given "artist's sense," Wolfe responds not only to the sensuous glamour of the other, the genteel class, but also to the middle-class emblems of popular romanticism: "There are moments when a passing cloud, the sun glinting on the purple thistles, a kindly smile, a child's face, will rouse him to a passion of pain." Wolfe may judge himself on these genteel standards but in his actual creative work he probes rather than avoids "this vile, slimy life" that has been forced on him. He then produces powerful masterpieces like the Korl Woman instead of images of sun-touched thistles and kindly smiles.

For all his longing, Wolfe is excluded from the life, art, and religion of the refined upper classes. In the fullest sense he does not speak or understand their language. When Mitchell, the intellectual, and Kirby, the owner's son, discuss a newspaper article, "at every sentence, Wolfe listened more and more like a dumb, hopeless animal"—a Wolfe, indeed. In church he is unable to understand the language of the supposedly universal religion the minister expounds. Does Christianity apply to a Wolfe who cannot understand the language of Christianity? "There was nothing of which he was certain," the narrator observes, "except the mill and things there. Of God and heaven he had heard so little that they were to him what fairy-land is to a child: something real but not here; far off." The matter is crucial, since Wolfe concludes "in all the sharpness of the bitter certainty, that between [him and Mitchell and Kirby] there was a great

gulf never to be passed. Never!" For Wolfe the class barrier is absolute. On grounds quite different from Kirby's belief in the American system as a ladder of opportunity, the narrator, however, is
unwilling to accept Wolfe's view. The narrator believes that "veiled
in the solemn music ushering the risen saviour was a key-note to solve
the darkest secrets of a world gone wrong—even the social riddle
which the brain of the grimy puddler grappled with madly tonight."

Searing, lurid hellfire lights the mill world, the world Wolfe knows
and turns into art. Can another light penetrate the mills or have
validity for Wolfe? He longs to be "other than he is." At the turning
point of the story, the narrator places Wolfe in a natural setting
outside the mills. "Overhead, the sun-drenched smoke-clouds opened
like a cleft ocean,—shifting, rolling seas of crimson mist, waves of
billowy silver veined with blood-scarlet, inner depths unfathomable
of glancing light." The assumption underlying this conventional language of the picturesque and sublime is that, in the midst of the
beauties of nature, we gain access to the divine. In "Old Times" as
this language and its ideology lose their hold, the narrator experiences an understandable sense of loss. For Hugh Wolfe, even more
than in his attraction to the glamour of the refined upper class, to
Janie, and to sun-drenched purple thistles, "Wolfe's artist-eye grew
drunk with color. The gates of that other world! Fading, flashing
before him now! What, in that world of Beauty, Content, and Right
were the petty laws, the mine and thine of mill-owners and mill
hands?" Wolfe experiences a momentary "consciousness of power"
but the narrator indicates that the entire experience is a delusion.
"His soul took in the mean temptation [to keep the stolen money],
lapped it in fancied rights, in dreams of improved existences, drifting
and endless as the cloud-seas of color."

Wolfe understandably wants to be free of the misery of the mills.
But under the corrosive pressures of industrial capitalism, how reliable is "the artist's sense" as the narrator conceives of it? Does it give
Wolfe access to "that other world" of gentility and the risen savior
or does it delude Wolfe into ignoring his own insights into the American realities of oppression and class barriers? Wolfe convinces himself that "God made this money" but the narrator implies a separation between the realm of God and the realm of Caesar, between true
Christianity and Mammon. The issues are tangled and commendably

contradictory. As disturbing as they are to her, the narrator faces up to the central role of money and class in America. As an underpaid mill worker, Wolfe can never fully realize his talent. Money would help but accepting stolen money reinforces rather than changes the system. The narrator knows that change is necessary. In showing the way Kirby's father manipulates his foreign-born workers through appeals to spectacle and patriotism, the narrator, however, has ruled out change through the electoral process. Mitchell has raised the prospect of revolutionary change led by a Cromwell or Jean-Paul of the oppressed. Wolfe has imagined himself in this role but nothing comes of it, partly because Wolfe is too thwarted, partly because the workers are too fragmented and too easily coopted. The narrator herself believes the solution is the risen savior and the redemptive power of the other world beyond, but she recognizes that nothing in Wolfe's experience justifies the belief for him. Just as she believes in the risen savior, the narrator believes that Beauty resides in kindly smiles and sun-drenched thistles but she is honest enough to present Wolfe as drunk and deluded in his response to the crimson light from the sunlit heavens.

The narrator believes that "the artist's sense" comes from God. If so, it is a God suspiciously aligned with her own class. If "the artist's sense" does not come from God, could the phrase be a sign that the middle class, the dominant class, has penetrated and warped Wolfe's consciousness? The narrator does not say so explicitly but her usage is open to that interpretation. When Wolfe functions as a creator he shapes grotesque, powerful, working-class figures. The narrator is honest enough never to connect these figures with "the artist's sense," a term she reserves for the kind of art, beauty, and religion she herself values. But when Wolfe acts on the perceptions of what the narrator calls "his artist's sense" or his "artist's eye," he steals money, denies his own best perceptions, reinforces the prevailing system, and ends up committing suicide in prison. As in works like Melville's "Bartleby, the Scrivener," Kate Chopin's *The Awakening,* and Charlotte Perkins Gilman's "The Yellow Wallpaper," the prison and suicide are signs of impasse, of a dead end, of a situation the writer wants to expose but can imagine no way out of. In *Life in the Iron Mills* an emerging realism, the power of class, and the hellfire energies of industrial capitalism undercut established canons of beauty and religion. The dilemma is even more extreme than in "Old Times on the Mississippi." Like Isabel Archer and the cub, moreover, Hugh Wolfe's imagination both creates and falsifies under the pressures of the new American world the realist artist struggles to explore.

At the end of *Life in the Iron Mills* the narrator cannot forget Hugh Wolfe and the statue of the Korl Woman, which call into question all of her affirmations. No wonder she keeps the statue behind a veil. On her interpretation, the arm of the statue is stretched out "imploringly," whereas for Mitchell the arm is a "wild gesture of warning." What she sees as the statue's "thwarted life, its mighty hunger, its unfinished work" is deeply threatening to the narrator, partly because they challenge her religious and artistic commitments, partly because they express the situation of many middle-class white women like the narrator and Rebecca Harding Davis. "Molly" Wolfe has created "the white figure of a woman" that faces both Mitchell and the narrator "in the darkness,—a woman white, of giant proportions, crouching on the ground, her arms flung out" in a gesture Mitchell interprets in his way and the narrator in hers. The powerful image of the white woman is open to interpretation like any image that emerges from and speaks to the deepest recesses of the self and society. The narrator's concluding hope is that her redemptive solution is universal but she knows that even behind the veil Wolfe's statue continues to express its recalcitrant and subversive realities.

We must be grateful to a narrator who gives us compelling insights into class barriers, into the hegemonic infiltration of working-class consciousness, and into the thwarting and spiritual hunger of middle-class women as well as of foreign-born workers. Part of what is missing from the narrator's story, however, is any sense of the kind of working-class consciousness and cohesion Herbert Gutman finds among actual nineteenth-century American workers. The story also negates the prospect of radical change. In these respects Rebecca Harding Davis and her narrator are at one with almost every other writer in the American canon. A decade ago *Life in the Iron Mills* was practically unknown. We now recognize that, in the words of the *Norton Anthology of American Literature,* "the story affords one of the most overwhelming reading experiences in all American literature." Now that works like *Life in the Iron Mills* are at last receiving the attention they deserve, however, we must ask why some works are and other works are not entering the canon. In the early 1990s is it a condition for entry into the canon that a work should be open to subversive interpretation and at the same time reinforce the sense both of the need for and the near impossibility of fundamental change?

The statue of the Korl Woman prefigures the turn-of-the-century work of the German artist Käthe Kollwitz—the same muscular intensity, sensitivity to darkness, and insight into working-class and feminine oppression—but in Kollwitz the raised arm is never imploring. She gives us instead figures of angry, cohesive protest. Even as we value the statue of the Korl Woman and all it embodies, perhaps we also need to keep our eyes open for American literary equivalents of Käthe Kollwitz. This is one question for readers to pose as they examine Rebecca Harding Davis's still-neglected novels, *Margret Howth* (1862) and *Waiting for the Verdict* (1867).

Charles Chesnutt is another talented but relatively unknown realist. As a black writer white enough to pass, Chesnutt was a fluent speaker of America's main social dialects. From the frame tales in the collection *The Conjure Woman* (1899) through the facades of his subtly ironic novel of passing, *The House Behind the Cedars* (1900), to *The Marrow of Tradition* (1901), Chesnutt presents a surface as impeccable as any in the *Atlantic Monthly* of his period. Playing off against the genteel prose, however, are underlying revelations, sometimes in black vernacular, sometimes the result of conflicting voices that expose the racial contradictions of the era of "separate but equal."

In *The Marrow of Tradition* Chesnutt unpolemically uses a series of double relations to test basic American views and practices about blacks and whites and the power relations between the races. Tom Delamere and Sandy look like "twin brothers." The degenerate son of a distinguished North Carolina family, Tom applies blackface and puts on the clothes of the family servant, Sandy, takes over Sandy's identity, and wins the cakewalk contest. He borrows money from Sandy and frames him after robbing and murdering his aunt. Chesnutt perceptively connects the white theft of black identity with the white theft of property. Elsewhere in nineteenth-century American literature divided selves are intimately connected with the underlying dynamics of the market society, as in Melville's "Bartleby, the Scrivener." In *The Marrow of Tradition,* the formal device of the double has the added force of encoding and judging America's racial divisions.

Chesnutt is equally good at revealing a range of white racial views and the way they are used to further another theft, of the government. In the language of his patrician class, Major Carteret argues that the entire black race "was morally undeveloped, and only held within bounds by the restraining influence of the white people." Sandy's "murder" and "assault . . . upon our race in the person of its womanhood, its crown and flower," is, according to the Major, "the logical and inevitable result of the conditions which have prevailed in this town for the last year." As in the Wilmington, North Carolina, Riot of 1898, the historical basis for *The Marrow of Tradition,* the Major, General Belmont, and Captain McBane are committed to a revolutionary ouster of the elected Fusion Party, which includes blacks. Chesnutt acutely unmasks the contrast between the Major's language of the "logical" and "reasonable" and his race- and class-biased views and practices. Chesnutt also consistently uses the plebian Captain McBane to expose the underlying realities Major Carteret's genteel language obscures. " 'Burn the nigger,' reiterated McBane. 'We seem to have the right nigger, but whether we have or not, burn *a* nigger.' "

According to the prevailing white view of blacks, "no one could tell at what moment the thin veneer of civilization might peel off and reveal the underlying savage." Through characters like Tom Delamere and Captain McBane, Chesnutt effectively turns this argument around. At the end the whites turn the town into a hell-on-earth in the name of "civilization." Chesnutt realizes that, in white eyes, the blacks who are defending themselves are not heroes; instead, "a negro's courage would be mere desperation; his love of liberty, a mere animal dislike of restraint. Every finer human instinct would be interpreted in terms of savagery."

Deepening these concerns are the contrasts between Josh and McBane and Josh and Doctor Miller, two other double relations. McBane, the son of an overseer, has made his money exploiting convict labor. He is driven by a sense of social exclusion that intensifies his racial hatred. Chesnutt illuminates the class antagonisms within the ruling group as well as its use of the press to manipulate the opinion of ordinary white people. The implications for American democracy are sobering. McBane is blunt, violent, forceful. He has lost an eye in a fight with a convict and "his single eye glowed ominously." Before the end of slavery he has also killed a slave, Josh's father. Josh's desire for retribution motivates him as powerfully as race hatred drives his antagonist.

The spectacle of Josh, a looming "great black figure," also plays off against the moderation of the light-skinned Doctor Miller. Miller believes "the meek shall inherit the earth" and that armed "resistance will only make the matter worse—the odds against you are too strong." Josh, in contrast, affirms, "I don' call no man 'marster.' . . . I'd ruther be a dead nigger any day dan a live dog!" When Miller refuses to assume leadership, Josh takes over. "A gun is mo' dange'ous ter de man in front of it dan ter de man behin' it. . . . We'd ruther die fightin' dan be stuck like pigs in a pen!" Although he is killed at the end, he takes McBane with him. "A pistol-flame flashed in his face, but he went on, and raising his powerful right arm, buried the knife to the hilt in the heart of his enemy." In imagining and doing justice to Josh, Chesnutt had to overcome his own personal preference for the beliefs of Doctor Miller. In creating Josh he also taps into imagery and energies deeply threatening to the white readers of his period. The symbols of the gun, the knife, and the defiant refusal to accept injustice contribute to make Josh the most sustained instance of black militancy between Frederick Douglass and Richard Wright's Bigger Thomas.

The final double relation involves the two half-sisters, Olivia Carteret and Janet Miller, on opposite sides of the color line. Their father, Mr. Merkell, had secretly married, freed, and willed his property to Julia, his black mistress. In a story that gradually unfolds as the novel progresses, we learn that Polly Ochiltree has destroyed the will and marriage license that would have established Julia and Janet's claims to legitimacy and half the estate, the money that is now financing Major Carteret's newspaper. "I saved the property for you and your son!" Polly tells Olivia. "You've got the land, the houses, and the money." Mrs. Ochiltree charges Julia with pollution but the pollution the novel dramatizes is the moral blight of whites whose entire material edifice is built on what they have stolen from blacks.

No wonder Olivia Carteret's son is sickly and nearly dies in the presence of Janet Miller.

Chesnutt further complicates the material of domestic fiction by probing the deepest sources of Olivia Carteret's "nervous condition," which dates from the time of Aunt Polly's revelations. As the custodian of conscience, white women like Olivia were basic to the moral structure of the South. Olivia comes to "dimly perceive" that the crime Aunt Polly has revealed epitomizes the larger crime of slavery, "which, if the law of compensation be a law of nature, must some time, somewhere, in some way, be atoned for." Her troubled conscience is her share of the larger dilemma.

Mrs. Carteret "could, of course, remain silent," but what then of her "cultivated conscience, . . . her mentor and infallible guide?" In a quiet, deadly exposure of the moral confusion of an entire people, under the influence of her conscience Mrs. Carteret finally decides that to tell is to bring on bankruptcy and ruin, that she cannot even acknowledge Janet as her sister, but that "sometime in the future" she would contribute to Doctor Miller's hospital. In examining Olivia's conscience, her ability—or inability—to deal with the basic moral issue of her family, region, and race, Chesnutt has undermined the inner sanctum of white legitimacy.

Between Josh at one extreme and Mrs. Carteret at the other, William Dean Howells understandably felt that for all its power of "justice without mercy," finally *The Marrow of Tradition* was "bitter, bitter, bitter." The judgment, however, says more about the sensitivity of Howells and his audience than it does about Chesnutt's novel. As Robert M. Farnsworth observes, in *The Marrow of Tradition* Chesnutt "stepped over the bounds of racial decency and . . . shook his white audience's faith in him." Chestnutt published one more book and then gave up professional authorship for a successful career as the head of a firm of legal stenographers. For reasons quite different from those of James, Twain, and Howells, Chesnutt, too, finally found that the pressures of the period were inimical to the practice of realism.

Howells had earlier written an encouraging review of Chesnutt's *The House Behind the Cedars,* a ratification that counted, since Howells was the most influential middleman of culture in the post–

Civil War period. As a critic and editor he introduced advanced European realists like Zola, Turgenev, Tolstoy, and George Eliot to an American audience. He similarly made the case for contemporary American realists as diverse as John De Forrest and Mary E. Wilkins Freeman. He supported both Henry James and Mark Twain, "supported" as a friend, as a critic, and as an editor who published and paid for stories and novels. He also mediated between the American West and East, between Twain's vernacular world and the Boston of Emerson and the *Atlantic Monthly*. Deeply encoded in his career and fiction is Howells's complex involvement in the worlds of literary art and the publishing business. This is a particular instance of the larger tension facing all of those realists who were compelled to render both the surfaces and the underlying energies of the new America.

In *The Rise of Silas Lapham* (1885) Howells deals explicitly with the issues of realism and the morally threatening power of big money. He intertwines a series of stories centering on the ideal of self-sacrifice as this value emerges in the fictional sentimental novel *Tears, Idle Tears*, as it emerges in a love story within the novel *The Rise of Silas Lapham*, as it emerges in the story of the self-made millionaire, Silas Lapham, and as it emerges in the theory of realism of the minister, Mr. Sewall. Self-sacrifice is the cornerstone virtue of the nineteenth-century true woman. Howells exposes a false version of this ideal through *Tears, Idle Tears*, or *Slop, Silly Slop*. In this book the heroine sacrifices herself by giving up the man she loves because someone else has cared for him first. The details are realistic but the feelings and characters are "colossal" and of flattering "supernatural proportions." In contrast, the realistic novel championed by Howells and Mr. Sewall paints "life as it is, and human feelings in their true proportions and relation." One test, then, is empirical, so that Howells looks at the world of experience, which in his practice is the world of middle-class America. Another test is metaphysical, since Howells assumes that finally ordinary American life will confirm ideals of beauty, decency, and truth. In *The Rise of Silas Lapham*, Howells tests and illustrates his theory partly through the love plot, which sets up precisely the situation of *Tears, Idle Tears*.

Irene Lapham, beautiful but culturally limited, falls in love with the patrician Tom Corey. Everyone assumes Corey is interested in Irene, whereas he has fallen in love with the older sister, Penelope.

Penelope has a lively wit, a gift for mimicry, and an independent way of seeing and storytelling. She is described as "dark," not because she is sultry but because in contrast to her sister's lovely color she is not beautiful. At first Penelope epitomizes the realistic novelist, sensible, acute at social observation, and intelligent about character and values. But the sentimental ethos of self-sacrifice retains considerable power; it infiltrates the consciousness of a character as sensible as the appropriately named Penelope. She succumbs, decides it would be wrong to accept Corey, but finally comes to her senses, marries him, and vindicates Howells's version of realism. Irene does, too. She suffers, matures, and, instead of either pining away or marrying, remains single, with the author's full approval.

But however much Howells seems assured in his view that finally everyone agrees on what is true and lifelike, in practice he recognizes important strains and qualifications. It is significant that the women in the novel collaborate in constructing the conventional love story of the beautiful but limited Irene and the handsome patrician, Tom Corey, as if Corey could not be interested in the lively realist, Penelope, the "dark," unglamorous one. By exposing their susceptibility to a false, sentimental way of seeing, Howells is illuminating an important crack in the edifice of the middle-class true woman, since in this ideology women are the guardians of moral value and conscience. Mrs. Lapham plays a central role in misperceiving and constructing the love story. Howells is particularly astute in showing that Mrs. Lapham has suffered a serious decline. In the early days of her marriage she was actively involved in Lapham's affairs, but as they become more prosperous she loses touch. She simultaneously sees less clearly than she did in the early, hard working years.

Displaced from the world of affairs, Mrs. Lapham at one point becomes insanely jealous of the attractive "typewriter" or secretary who is at home in Lapham's office. Mrs. Lapham's hysteria is driven by her sense that she no longer has a useful economic function. Instead, her main function in life is to be a moral guide and her confidence in her judgment has been seriously weakened. For Howells the situation of prosperous middle-class women is both enviable and precarious. In *A Hazard of New Fortunes* (1890), it becomes even more extreme. Mrs. Dryfoos, Mrs. Lapham's successor, is separated by her husband's wealth from her original rural home and religious tradition. She is an invalid with no connection to the confusing urban world her children must negotiate. Howells shows that the old republican virtues of simplicity, hard work, and suspicion of luxury are not easy to sustain in the new America of stock gambling, capital expansion, and the self-made millionaire. Howells is particularly sensitive to the dilemmas of prosperity for women caught in the crosscurrents of republicanism and capitalism or in the conflicts internal to the republican tradition.

In *The Rise of Silas Lapham,* Mrs. Lapham contributes to the dilemmas centering on money, business, and success. At the outset of Lapham's career, Mrs. Lapham is the one who realizes that to convert Lapham's paint mine into a gold mine, capital is required. She persuades him to take a partner, Rogers, to supply the capital necessary for full development and expansion. Partly because Rogers is not competent, partly because Lapham wants sole control of what he worships, the paint, Lapham forces Rogers out of the business. He does it legally, fairly, and precisely as any reaonable capitalist would but Mrs. Lapham's conscience is troubled because Lapham has taken advantage of Rogers in favor of his own self-interest. A kind of original sin is involved, since Lapham's prosperity is inseparable from his use of Rogers's capital. Rogers and his capital plus Lapham's hard work and good judgment lead to growth, wealth, and the ambiguous morality connected with ambition and big money.

The ambiguity is grounded in the agrarian, republican values that animate Mrs. Lapham's conscience. The paint in its original condition is associated with the old rural, republican world: it is rooted in the land itself, vividly symbolized by the ore clinging to the exposed roots of a great tree. The paint comes from the old farm, associated with Lapham's father and the graves of the family. Once Mrs. Lapham introduces Rogers and his capital, financial success follows but the earlier virtues are tainted. Mrs. Lapham cannot accept that to succeed as a capitalist, Lapham must behave impersonally. Her conscience keeps alive what she sees as the wrong Lapham committed. In this paradigm of the move from the old republican, agrarian America to the new America of large fortunes and capital expansion, Howells taps into conflicts deeply encoded in the republican's relation to capitalism. For Howells, Mrs. Lapham's conscience is both a strength and a nagging, punitive weakness.

As for Lapham, his wife accuses him of making the paint his God and worshiping it. Under the pressure of Rogers's capital and the dynamics of capitalistic growth, the worship of paint begins to merge with the worship of money as God. Howells handles this change circumspectly, not overtly, in that Lapham continues to value primarily the tangible, earth-grounded product. But Lapham knows that "you wouldn't want my life without my money," and when he is with the patrician Coreys he brags incessantly about his money as well as his paint. Under his no-nonsense surface, Lapham has also been infected with the virus of social ambition, not so much for himself as for his daughters. He has bought a prize piece of property on the Back Bay and he decides to build an impressive house so that his family can be in society.

All of Lapham's underlying social longings and feelings about money and class difference come to a focus in the house. At the outset Mrs. Lapham also connects the house and all it stands for with Rogers and with Lapham's success. "You can sell it for all me," Mrs. Lapham says. "I shan't live in it. There's blood on it."

Lapham may not worship money but he does worship the house. The house is the beautiful embodiment of the new self as distinct from the old Jeffersonian, republican self of Lapham's origins. The republicans had a deep suspicion of luxury and of wealth gained through financial speculation. Lapham is infatuated with the lovely, luxurious improvements his architect suggests. Lapham also finances the house partly from money he has recently made as a stock gambler. Republicans, moreover, valued a general equality of conditions, not the economic, social, and class differences the house symbolizes. In Howells's recognizable version, republicans stress restraint, self-control, discipline, moderation, and a life lived close to the land, symbolically in the old house on the patriarchal farm.

To satisfy his wife and perhaps his own sense of right and wrong, Lapham lends Rogers money and accepts stock in return. To save his original investment, Lapham becomes more deeply entangled with Rogers, he gambles on the market, and he suffers serious losses. The market for paint is glutted and a competitor has a product that undersells Lapham's. At a key moment in this gradually developing scenario, Lapham realizes that to save his business he must sell the unfinished house. Although his pride is deeply wounded, he decides to go ahead. But instead he accidentally burns the house to the ground. The usually careful Lapham, moreover, has neglected to renew the insurance, so that the house is a total loss.

The result is that Lapham begins to purge or expiate the wrongs of a violated republicanism through what amounts to a valued act of self-sacrifice, a sacrifice of the possession that embodies the new self Lapham has achieved as a self-made man. Lapham's self-sacrifice contrasts and develops in counterpoint with Penelope's *Tears, Idle Tears* version. Also in contrast to *Tears, Idle Tears* and in accord with his own views about realism, Howells does not have Lapham make a conscious decision to behave virtuously and heroically. Instead, Howells has a sure sense of unconscious motivation rooted in the morally charged conflicts of a possessive market society and the American republican tradition.

In the sequel, Lapham, a secular Job or Christ, faces up to a series of temptations Rogers poses. Lapham consciously chooses to sacrifice his own self-interest—his business and fortune—rather than to take advantage of a legal but morally shady scheme to defraud a group of idealistic English investors. As the Satan-figure in this drama, Rogers is a plausibly rendered businessman who manipulates his appearance of "bland and beneficent caution," just as he turns to his own advantage his republican surface as "a man of just, sober, and prudent views, fixed purposes, and the good citizenship that avoids debt and hazard of every kind." His arguments are as specious and plausible as his appearance. Lapham and the reader, however, easily see through the mask. In this important respect Howells contrasts with those contemporaries, predecessors, and successors for whom the deceptions and acquisitive impulses make for irreducible epistemological uncertainty.

At the end Howells arranges it so that Lapham returns to his origins on the patriarchal, republican farm. He moves back into the old home and runs a scaled-down version of his business. He regains both the good sense and the moral virtue he lost under Rogers's influence. His fall in fortune corresponds with a rise in virtue. In illustrating the success of failure, Lapham thus validates Howells's belief in the agrarian, republican tradition. Lapham also exposes a weakness in Howells's theory of realism, since the pastoral ending highlights the contrast between Howells's deepest values and the un-

derlying realities of an increasingly urban, industrialized market society. The metaphysical and empirical sides of Howells's theory do
not really coincide in the emerging America of the 1880s and 1890s.

Far from being literal and artless, Howells's practice of realism is
full of revealing contradictions, nuances, and a suggestive interplay
between surface and depth. The same holds for the other realists of
the post–Civil War era, although the precise content and intensity
vary from writer to writer and novel to novel. Art and imagination,
moreover, are central concerns of the American realists. Cumula-
tively, they give us a complex sense of the fate of the imagination and
its creations in the context of a vital, changing America. They often
represent the epistemological consequences of the new America
through images of impenetrable fog and darkness, from Twain's river
through the house of darkness at the highest reaches of the class
system in *Portrait of a Lady* to the dark cellar and fog in *Life in the
Iron Mills*. Sometimes sensitive to the moral and ideological conflicts,
as in Howells, sometimes to the moral, epistemological, and sociopolitical implications, as in James, American realists explored the
intimate connection between houses and selves, between possessions
and character in the new America. They were also unusually alert to
the situation of women, as in the suggestive ambiguities of Davis's
Korl Woman, Howells's insights into the consequences of prosperity,
and James's awareness of Isabel's fear and freedom.

Of all the American realists, Charles Chesnutt in a series of novels
gave the subtlest, most probing treatment of the relation between
whites and blacks. In *Waiting for the Verdict*, Rebecca Harding Davis
anticipated Chesnutt's *The House Behind the Cedars* in exploring the
dilemmas of passing and of interracial love relations. Mark Twain
opened up these and other dimensions of American racial practices
and their impact on identity in *The Tragedy of Pudd'nhead Wilson*.
In *Huckleberry Finn* Twain had earlier imagined the escaping slave,
Jim, as humane and knowledgeable, in touch with the mysteries of
the natural world and close to his family even as he is separated from
them. But at the end Twain also allowed Tom Sawyer to turn Jim
into an object, a stage figure in Tom's romantic fantasy world. These
contrasting views of Jim have implications within and beyond the
novel. At the turn of the century Twain wrote "The United States of
Lyncherdom" (1901). The concluding image of a mile of torches—

kerosene-lighted bodies—throws a terrible light on the grimmest side of American racism. The fact that Twain was compelled to write "The United States of Lyncherdom" but decided not to publish it during his lifetime—he feared loss of sales in the South—highlights the situation of the realistic writer engaging with market pressures and with perhaps the deepest fault line in American culture.

To shift to another highly charged concern, from the vantage point of later generations, say of Dreiser or later Hemingway or, later still, Updike, the first-generation American realists are circumspect or relatively indirect in their treatment of sexuality, one of the touchstone interests of the realistic novel from Balzac to the present. Money in all its implications is the other major preoccupation of nineteenth- and twentieth-century realism. On this count the post–Civil War American writers are as full and perceptive as we can ask for. Their sense of reality is open and varied, responsive to the surfaces and recesses of American selves and society. Stimulated and sometimes thwarted by the energies of the Gilded Age, James, Twain, Davis, Chesnutt, and Howells, representative post–Civil War realists, help us map the emerging new America whose construction is no more certain than the shifting shores of Mark Twain's fog-shrouded Mississippi.

Robert Shulman

# Fiction and the Science of Society

In *The Incorporation of America* (1982), Alan Trachtenberg describes the significance of the White City as symbol, its ability to transform the diverse and conflicted America of 1893 into an image of national unity. White City was a study in managed pluralism: organized into twenty departments and two hundred twenty-five divisions, contained within one overarching "symmetrical order . . . each building and each vista serving as an image of the whole." The choice of White City as the main design for the Chicago World's Columbian Exposition of 1893 was suggestive at the most fundamental level. As Herman Melville knew, the color white is a negation of the various rays of the color spectrum. It reflects but it does not absorb. One indication of White City's strategy for managing diversity was its presentation of certain cultures. Instead of being invited (like other constituencies) to portray their experiences in the nation's history, African Americans and Native Americans were presumed to be represented by an exhibit on primitive populations throughout the world. This ambition—unity without absorption, harmony through denial—is no doubt one reason why Frederick Douglass renamed the fair "white sepulchre."

It seems appropriate in retrospect that just one year earlier the city's foremost educational facility, the University of Chicago, had instituted one of the country's first sociology departments. Of all the social science disciplines developing at this time, sociology was most driven by the vision of social interdependence and unity that inspired the architects of White City. For the early sociologists, knowing so-

ciety meant knowing the social whole. Other social scientists—
economists, psychologists, political scientists, anthropologists—saw
social reality piecemeal, through the narrow lens of their specialization. Sociology was unique in its aim to combine these disparate
specialties into one integral discipline. This methodological imperative was matched by a theory that saw an unprecedented affinity of
human consciousness and interests throughout modern life. In the
landmark essay in which he declares "the scope of sociology" to be
the organization of the "human sciences into a system of reciprocally
reinforcing reports," Albion Small characterizes society as a "realm
of circuits of reciprocal influence between individuals and groups." In
keeping with the strategies of White City, Small's image is achieved
at the cost of an evolutionary sleight of hand. What Small calls at one
point, for example, that "serious scientific problem, the status of the
coloured race in the United States," is subsumed in the image of "the
last native of Central Africa . . . whom we inoculate with a desire for
whiskey add[ing] an increment to the demand for our distillery products and effect[ing] the internal revenue of the United States."

Small's vision of human reciprocity, his description of alien populations that can be "innoculated" into a worldwide web of social
and economic interest, was framed in a society fragmented by a be-
wildering heterogeneity of interests. This late nineteenth-century
landscape of social change included: unprecedented immigration
rates, especially from Southern and Eastern Europe; escalating
capital-labor conflict; challenges to traditional women's roles that
brought increasing numbers of women into an embattled labor force;
rapid urbanization and industrialization; the rise of trusts; and the
ever-intensifying problem of race relations. Like any discursive field,
sociology was an attempt to tell a certain kind of story about a
particular historical reality. The burden of American sociology at its
moment of origin was to reinscribe a conflicted and potentially explosive social reality as a terrain of consensus and integration.

The dedication to knowing the social whole that gripped an
emerging sociological discipline is readily seen as consistent with the
ambitions of contemporaneous American novelists. What is less often
recognized are their various involvements (direct and indirect) with
the anxieties, premises, and methods of this new science of society.
The response of writers such as Herman Melville, Henry James, Ger-

trude Stein, Theodore Dreiser, to the formulation of a science that professionalized the main business of novelists—social observation, description of human types and types of interaction, the classification of these types—is an untold story whose narration provides a critical index to the social engagement of American novels. At the same time, to explore the rise of sociology in terms of contemporary novels is to enhance our understanding of the imaginative aspects of this new science.

The most vivid link between sociological and novelistic writings of the period is their shared interest in a language of social types. From Max Weber's "Protestant Ethic" (1905) to Theodore Dreiser's "An American Tragedy" (1925), from W. E. B. Du Bois's "Philadelphia Negro" (1899) to Henry James's "American Heiress" (1903), sociologists and novelists sought uniform types for mediating a vast and heterogeneous modern society. While literary authors have always been drawn to type categories, the typological methods employed by American novelists of this period have a particular historical resonance. They were formulated in response to the same pressing social landscape that gave rise to a modern discipline based on typological method. Type categories invested individuals and social phenomena with the semblance of predictability and control. They were key tools in turn-of-the-century efforts to circumscribe an ever-expanding society—to clarify, order, and label the social world. Types also served to promote and exclude different forms of social being. As Ian Hacking suggests in the essay "Making Up People," "numerous kinds of human beings and human acts came into being hand in hand with our invention of the categories labelling them." This interest in the varieties and limits of human action points to another central concern of the era: the question of individualism. American sociologists and novelists were at the forefront of changing conceptions of the individual. Their use of type categories was part of their struggle to mediate the divide between social determination and individuality in support of an ideal that was basic to American values, as well as essential to capitalist development.

What did it mean to *know* society for the first formulators of social science? For Adam Ferguson, whose *Essay on the History of Civil Society* (1767) is generally recognized as a key forerunner of sociological analysis, knowing society involved viewing it as a total-ity: describing its interrelated institutions, classifying its various parts, identifying its stages of development. Ferguson stressed empir-ical method; social study must be based on scientific observation, rather than on speculation. If sociological beginnings are detectible in the work of Ferguson, it was late eighteenth-century France that gave the emerging field a sense of urgency and purpose. Vitalized and christened in an era of revolution, sociology pointed toward a per-manent condition of post-revolution. The Enlightenment values that had inspired revolution were now rechanneled into the shaping of a stabilizing social science.

The institutional origins of American sociology lie in the 1850 founding of a Board of Aliens Commission by the State of Massa-chusetts, whose charge was "to superintend the execution of all laws in relation to the introduction of aliens in the Commonwealth." From the ranks of this organization, the American Social Science Associa-tion was founded in 1865. The motto of the association, "Ne Quid Nimis" (Everything in Moderation), and a representative sample of papers from the association's journal ("Pauperism in New York City"; "The Emmigration of Colored Citizens from the Southern States"; "Immigration and Nervous Diseases"; "Immigration and Crime") suggest its anxiety about immigrants and internal marginals.

American sociology was shaped by specific social and political pressures, as well as by strong international influences. At the point of its emergence it was also substantially supported by Christian re-form organizations, as evidenced by the abundance of articles on Christian sociology in the early years of *The American Journal of Sociology*. The links between sociology and Christianity are consist-ent with the fact that many of the first American sociologists had close ties to the ministry.

American sociology in this period was often broken down into three interrelated clusters of inquiry: (1) attention to society's *static* dimensions, which addressed the question of social stability: how does society manage to preserve the status quo? (2) attention to so-ciety's *evolutionary* dimensions, which addressed the question of change: how did society come to be as it is and what might we predict about its future? (3) attention to society's *technologic* dimensions, which addressed the question of control: what actions can be taken to improve society and ensure a better future? Running through each of these lines of exploration was the ongoing struggle with the subject of individualism. As Albion Small observed, "Today's sociology is still struggling with the preposterous initial fact of the individual. He is the only possible social unit, and he is no longer a thinkable possibility. He is the only real presence, and he is never present." Sociology's emphasis on social determination, its insistence that human consciousness was formed and existed in interaction alone, seemed to undermine an American tradition of individualism. But in fact the task of "reconstructing individualism" was a continuing preoccupation. Thus, for static analyses the question was: how could individuals be fit into the existing social system? For evolutionary analyses the question was: how do individual differences come about; are they products of inheritance or environment? For technologic analyses the question was: can education and scientific knowledge equip certain individuals with special powers for social betterment? In what follows I will discuss these three clusters of sociological analysis by way of specific American novels. I consider in turn Herman Melville and realism, Henry James and naturalism, and W. E. B. Du Bois, Gertrude Stein, and experimentalism. This genealogy moves from writers whose major concerns coincided with those of social science, to writers who absorbed social science into their very techniques. The works of Stein and Du Bois, I argue, were overburdened with social scientific methods, which compromised their aesthetic power but made them ideal registers of the ties between sociology and literature in this period.

The overriding concern of Herman Melville's novella *Billy Budd, Sailor* (written from 1886 to 1891) is social transformation: how to channel the revolutionary energies of the late eighteenth century into the industrial work of the nineteenth century. As a work written in the turbulent closing decades of nineteenth-century America, and set in a climactic moment of revolution and consolidation at the beginning of the "modern" era, *Billy Budd* parallels the situation of late nineteenth-century sociology, a discipline that draws upon founding principles framed in the same revolutionary Europe.

Riding the nervous British seas of 1797, haunted by British Jacobinism, Revolutionary France, and mutinies that year at Nore and Spithead, authorities aboard the *Bellipotent* are consumed with the problem of social order. Like the early European sociologists who were fresh from the experience of social revolt, Captain Vere and his officers fear lower-class uprising. Described as one whose "settled convictions were as a dike against those invading waters of novel opinion social, political and otherwise, which carried away as in a torrent no few minds in those days," Captain Vere knows the reparative powers of a careful and consistent empiricism. The *Bellipotent* operates through an elaborate network of watching and cataloging: methods of social description and typecasting that keep everyone on board, especially potentially disruptive elements of the sea commonalty, identified and ordered. The power to label and interpret the world around him is critical to Captain Vere's rule.

A key instance of typecasting is the parable of the black sailor at Liverpool that opens the novella. Transformed kaleidoscopically from an ideal to a sacrificial type, the black sailor foreshadows the experiences of Billy Budd. As a handsome cynosure, the black sailor elicits the "spontaneous homage" of his fellow sailors, a moment of collective tribute that is threatening in its ability to "arrest" the normal affairs of the Liverpool wharf. In keeping with this threat, another type, which casts the sailor as the sculptured bull of the Assyrian priests, emerges with a kind of grim necessity at the close of the passage. Now an object of sacrifice within an order of nature and ritual, the black sailor is neutralized. This double echo from the past (a mid-eighteenth-century moment that recalls an ancient rite) points to a simpler era when societies cohered by means of a common conscience reinforced by violence. It also registers the traces of primitivism still lurking in modern forms of social control.

Like the black sailor, Billy Budd is marked early on as an outstanding specimen, capable of inspiring his fellow sailors in unpredictable ways. Had Billy not killed Claggart, Captain Vere would have had to find some other reason for his demise. The necessity of his sacrifice, in other words, seems built into the situation from the beginning: a nervous ship in a time of mutiny and revolution, a handsome sailor who inspires collective pride, his execution. Typing Billy as the "Angel of God" who "must hang," Vere transforms Billy into a visual emblem of his power. Billy's execution is a spectacle that confirms Vere's ability to contain collective sentiments.

The link between typecasting and social control brings us to contemporary sociological theories on social types. In *Social Control* (1901), E. A. Ross argued that a heterogeneous mass society like modern America required deliberate strategies for ensuring social obedience. He advocated the promotion of social models, ideal types, which society "induces its members to adopt as their guide." Based on the principle of self-regulation, what Ross called "bind[ing] from within," Ross's types left the individual "with the illusion of self-direction even at the moment he martyrizes himself for the ideal we have sedulously impressed upon him." "The fact of control," Ross continues, "is in good sooth, no gospel to be preached abroad . . . the wise sociologist . . . will not tell the street Arab, or the Elmira inmate how he is managed." Ross's use of types for the purposes of social control had its analogue in various disciplines of this era. According to philosopher Josiah Royce, the value of an ideal type lay in its ability to instill a feeling of subordination to a unified whole. The loyal individual, he suggested in *The Philosophy of Loyalty* (1908), embodied the ideal union of individual identity and social commitment. "You can be loyal," he wrote, "only to a tie that binds you and others into some sort of unity . . . the cause to which loyalty devotes itself has always this union of the personal and the seemingly super-individual about it." For the William James of *The Varieties of Religious Experience* (1902) as well, the sign of the healthy religious type is his or her "sense of integration" in a benevolent social whole.

Like these social philosophers, Captain Vere seeks more than Billy's compliance; he needs Billy to believe in his sacrifice, as socially necessary and beneficial. After typing him "fated boy," Vere takes various measures (their "closeted interview," for example) to ensure that Billy embrace his fate. Billy's declaration at the point of execution, "God bless Captain Vere," signals the success of Vere's methods.

Perhaps an even deeper threat to Captain Vere's methods of social control is his master-at-arms, John Claggart. As one who eludes classification, described at one point as an "uncatalogued creature of the deep," Claggart seems uniquely resistant to Vere's authority. Yet Claggart is ultimately as tied to Vere's system as Billy through his burning desire to rise in the ship's hierarchy. Both Billy and Claggart represent to authorities like Captain Vere the hope that the dream of vertical mobility, through success in Claggart's case or martyrdom in Billy's, can be counted on to offset lateral threats of collective identification. It is this hope that underlies sociological reconceptions of individuality. In an exemplary formulation, Albion Small moves from the observation that "individuals are different," to the claim that "the associated state [Small's phrase for society] is a process of making them different." As he explains further in adopting what he calls "the genetic view," the social process is "a progressive production of more and more dissimilar men." Though he intends another meaning of "genetic," Small's use of the term here foregrounds the sense that the modern liberal state has become an active producer of human types. For Small, social processes conspire to produce uniformly related selves, whose functional attributes can be neatly fit into the social system. Unsolicited differences—of race, ethnicity, political or religious belief—that threaten the status quo are subsumed by produced differences that support it. In the creation of type categories that provided model individuals capable of succeeding in modern society, sociologists were responding to contemporary anxieties about the erosion of individual initiative. At the same time they were controlling perceptions of human possibility.

An assumption governing the sociological use of types, which Captain Vere shares, is that the maker of these classifying terms is himself a neutral analyst. For Captain Vere, neutrality is part of being a professional. Off duty, Vere "never garnished unprofessional talk with nautical terms," a sign of the strict division in his mind between public office and private life. Vere's personal discretion is matched by a professional objectivity that brings him to substitute an "imperial code" for the claims of "private conscience." Vere's call for the suppression of instinct confirms a late nineteenth-century ethic of professionalism. Like its other key tropes, this professional ethic aligns the novella with a literary realist movement that coincided with Melville's final decade: the years when he was working in the New York Custom House and writing *Billy Budd*.

The novels of William Dean Howells, Stephen Crane, Henry James, Mark Twain, the paintings of Thomas Eakins, picture the frozen status quo worlds dreamed of by the rulers of the *Bellipotent*.

In realism, social conflict is shifted to the borders of scenes or swiftly quelled. The worlds of realism are controlled by vigilance: the vulnerable visibility of the poor, the empowered visibility of professional elites, the invisibility of the rich. In an analysis of publicity in this period, Philip Fisher considers Thomas Eakins's *The Gross Clinic* as an instance of professional transcendence: the modern expert as God. Eakins's representation of the master surgeon at work presupposes the surgeon's power to select the moments when he is publicly seen. This moment is balanced by access to a privileged invisibility, which Fisher locates in the self-enclosed homes designed by Frank Lloyd Wright, homes that ensure the absolute immunity of their inhabitants from outward detection. While the public images of professional elites were carefully circumscribed, society's *most* powerful were invisible altogether. Eric Hobsbawm describes the increasing obscurity of governing elites in the late nineteenth-century era of mass democratization: "When the men who governed really wanted to say what they meant, they had henceforth to do so in the obscurity of the corridors of power." This is corroborated by Henry James's analysis of that pivotal political figure, "the boss," who operates in a shell of oblivion, his "political role" at once "so effaced, but so universal."

In the case of the lower classes, this situation was inverted: their lives, at work and at home, were increasingly exposed to public scrutiny in this period. The introduction of production methods systematizing industrial work led to greater vigilance in the factories. The activity of social reformers, increasingly devoted to the domestic lives of the poor and the immigrant, led to greater surveillance at home. The impact of these reformers was mixed: while their obvious goal was improvement, they also participated in a more ominous campaign to know and manage a potentially dangerous underclass. Social scientists adopted a more remote attitude, but their relationships to the impoverished lives they cataloged from a greater remove were equally ambiguous. Liberal sociology mainly identified with the sober middle class, and kept the poor and the wealthy (whose interests they nevertheless implicitly supported) at a distance. The main concern of realist literature as well was the conventional and the middle class. A notable example of realism's occasional forays into the world of the poor is Henry James's *In the Cage,* his only work narrated from the perspective of a lower-class character.

The protagonist of this 1895 novella is a featureless telegraph operator, whose one distinctive trait is a classically overactive Jamesian imagination. The telegraph operator spends her days serving the wealthy who have grown addicted to a new technology that facilitates the rapid conduct of their (usually extramarital) affairs. To her customers, she is no more significant than the machine that relays their messages. Indeed, the novella ingeniously inverts its titular metaphor that casts the telegraph operator as a caged zoo animal. While she does work in a cage, it is her customers rather than she who are exposed to view. "It had occurred to her early," the novella begins, "that in her position—that of a young person spending, in framed and wired confinement, the life of a guinea-pig or a magpie—she should know a great many persons without their recognizing the acquaintance." The story's plot centers on her effort to exploit this circumstance of being hidden but ever vigilant. Scrutinizing their faces like a detective, she assumes a fantastic intimacy with her customers, a knowledge of their every desire and scheme. Thus the predictable lower classes become the predictors of the upper class. By investing his telegraph operator with the story's main imaginative value, James identifies her as an artist of sorts. And through this character, James presents the Jamesian artist as a predatory dissector of the wealthy. Ultimately, however, James foils the visual powers of the telegraph operator, restoring realism's usual hierarchy of vigilance. The telegraph operator is foiled because she attempts to enter into the lives of her subjects. By trying to realize her visual intimacy, she violates the boundary of vigilance. Empirical control over others requires distance.

As one of the gentile poor, James's telegraph operator fulfills Emile Durkheim's theory of anomie. Defined in his classic study *Suicide,* anomie (literally, "without norms") is a condition of rootlessness bordering on self-annihilation that occurs when human desires are raised beyond their realistic life expectations. According to this theory, hopeless poverty is a protection against suicide. But unqualified desire leads to disorientation and worse. It is appropriate, therefore, that the novella's final scene pictures the telegraph operator standing before a bridge while a policeman eyes her suspiciously. The policeman is an externalization of the control the telegraph operator no longer exercises over herself.

The telegraph operator is an anomaly in James's realist canon, not only because she is poor, but also because she doesn't police herself. Rather than an internal plane for the individual's struggle and eventual reconciliation with social law (as in the case of a typical Jamesian heroine like Isabel Archer), the imagination of the telegraph operator is a plane of transgression. The task of regulating one's imagination, of internalizing external forms of vigilance, is a key activity of realist fiction. Realism emphasizes selective incorporation, its primary reflex is establishing borders. This is reflected in the claustrophobic atmospheres of realist works, which feel uniformly cramped whether depicting the interior spaces of Henry James or the battlefields of Stephen Crane. The scene of Stephen Crane's "The Open Boat" (1897) can be taken as paradigmatic. The challenge for the story's characters is maintaining the integrity of their craft ("no bigger than a bathtub," the narrator snaps with characteristic cruelty) against an encroaching ocean. The homely similes, which seem to crowd the characters as much as the ocean (the captain is like a father "soothing his children," the seaweed is like "carpets"), are there not only to taunt the characters by reminding them of the habitual protections they lack but to represent their inevitable restitution. Moreover, these similes are products of the characters' imaginations; the narrator is merely miming their familiarization of the threatening landscape. Like the wobbling boat that serves as its controlling metaphor, the story is concerned with what can be taken in, and what must be kept out, in order to ensure sanity and social stability. No matter how vast and wild its territory, realism concentrates on the most local mechanisms for stabilizing the social world—human perceptions and categories.

The central features of realism—the trope of vigilance, the emphasis on internalization, and the focus on individual over collective experience—come together in the most distinctive aspect of realist fiction—its view of character as type. The type supplies an immediately identifiable public persona, a boundary around the self. But it also acknowledges some residual aspects of personality that are inexpressible to others and perhaps even unknown to the individual. In the essay "How Is Society Possible?" Georg Simmel refers to the "non-social imponderables"—temperament, fate, etc.—those features that lend "a certain nuance" to an individual but do not fundamentally change his "relevant social category." This makes the self potentially limitless in idiosyncratic terms, but poses a limit on what individuals can be in social terms. In keeping with this, Stephen Crane's "Oiler," "Westerner," "Cook," and "Gambler," as well as Henry James's "Heiress" and "Dilettante," are individuals limited by function. But the idiosyncratic freedoms allotted James's more central characters are finally inconsequential in terms of plot. They are not allowed to stand in the way of their social function. Thus, Isabel Archer, the "intelligent but presumptuous girl . . . affronting [her] destiny," for all her expansiveness, is fundamentally a type, and is so conceived by her fellow characters.

The typing of realist characters counters a threat that continually pressures the realist text: the threat of collective identification. The concept of type provides a view of self-sufficient, uniformly related individuals, whose collective existence is a matter not of choice or identity but of interdependence. Society promotes differences among its members so that they may be profitably related. This ideology of interdependence was set against the forms of spontaneous association that from the late eighteenth-century era of revolution to the late nineteenth-century era of expansion social observers most feared.

The novels of Henry James may appear to have little in common with naturalism. But in fact the issue of social evolution is a dominant concern of James's fiction, especially the fiction of the major phase. Poised on the edge of a new century, imposing its titular category of adolescence on society as well as on women, *The Awkward Age* (1899) is an exemplary case of this deepening concern. What are the differences among cultural rites for socializing women? how do those of modern society compare to those of primitive society? are there elements of barbarism in modern culture?—these are the questions the novel addresses. Like Thorstein Veblen's *The Theory of the Leisure Class* (published the same year), which ruthlessly cataloged the primitive offenses of modern elites, James's satire on the British ruling class focuses on their treatment of women. The marriage market of James's modern London looks suprisingly like the barter systems of primitive societies described by contemporary social theorists such as Herbert Spencer and J. F. McLennan (whose *Primitive Marriage* James owned and almost certainly read).

In her essay "The Traffic in Women," Gayle Rubin discusses the ominous constancy of women's treatment from primitive to modern times. "Women are given in marriage, taken in battle, exchanged for favors, sent as tribute, traded, bought, and sold. Far from being confined to the 'primitive' world, these practices seem only to become more pronounced and commercialized in more 'civilized' societies." From its opening pages, *The Awkward Age* is explicit about the commodification of women in the modern era. It seems to go out of its way to press the similarities between primitive and modern societies. For the novel's upper class shares a critical affinity with the primitive populations described by the era's sociologists: their demise is at hand. The novel's elite offers little hope for generational continuity. Its female protagonist, Nanda Brookenham, is described at one point as just the kind to preside over "a fine old English family" of "half-a-dozen." The projected size of Nanda's family is statistically precise: four was the minimum number of offspring specified by population experts of this era for a stock to maintain itself. The novel's end, however, pictures Nanda's retreat to the country as the ward of a man three times her age, her prospects for marriage and family ruined. James's portrait of an upper class in decline, stripped of its reproductive powers, is consistent with the perceptions of other social observers of his day.

James's seedy upper class helps to shed light on social taxonomies of the era, where elites appeared in catalogs of "special classes" requiring scientific scrutiny. In a 1900 essay on social types published simultaneously in Durkheim's *L'Année Sociologique* and excerpted in *The American Journal of Sociology*, S. R. Steinmetz cites the variety of social characters about whom too little is known. "There are great entomological studies for the study of insects," he observes, "but we do not give ourselves any trouble to know the people around us." Among these unknowns, he cites the "primitive populations" "rapidly disappearing." He includes as well what he calls "special classes of the population": "prostitutes, the criminal and dangerous classes . . . wandering artists, nobles, millionaires." The obvious mystery on this list is social elites ("nobles, millionaires"). Why would its members require scientific attention? What does it share with these other groups? Each of these groups is marginal to the interdependent community of socialized selves described by Albion Small. At the same time, each helps to define the boundaries of that functional society by its very marginal relationship to it. As our observations so far have suggested, James's social circle has most in common with the "disappearing" "primitive peoples."

Yet why would primitives and nobles require scientific scrutiny? Primitives and nobles need to be managed intellectually because they contradict the narrative of evolutionary progress favored by social analysts of the era. Primitives threaten the thesis of evolutionary uniformity that ascribes a fundamental similarity to the development of all peoples. Primitives are defined as vestiges of a previous evolutionary stage, with little promise of meeting the demands of evolutionary progress, and their rapid decline is predicted. As a supposedly superior class that is regressing, nobles are living contradictions of the evolutionary thesis. Degenerate rather than vital, incapable of transmitting their valuable traits, they are defined as a social excrescence, a class that has been living off the fruits of others' labor for too long.

James's attentions to the place of his bourgeois and aristocratic characters on the evolutionary scale goes to the heart of a fictional enterprise usually considered alien to his fiction, naturalism. By exposing the barbaric propensities of civilized society, James revises the dominant nineteenth-century narrative of evolutionary progress. If James pictures a reservoir of social superiority that cannot sustain itself, Frank Norris and Theodore Dreiser explore a self-destructive sphere of social difference, the world of the lower class and the immigrant.

Naturalist literature provided an analytical yet voyeuristic view into the low life. Both senses of this perspective—the detached and the compulsive—are important. Even when naturalist narrators betray overt hostility (a naturalist trademark) toward their precivilized characters, there is still room for identification with them. For turn-of-the-century readers, immersed in ideas of progress, naturalism provided the experience of looking into an evolutionary mirror. Readers could see themselves at an earlier historical moment: barbaric, unconscious, twisted. Thus naturalist characters incited an antagonism that might easily be internalized, illuminating one's own carefully hidden savagery. The difference of naturalist characters, then, was a difference that had to be reckoned with. As Michel Foucault has observed, prior to the seventeenth century every species was identified in and of itself, by a certain mark that it bore *independent* of all other species. But from the seventeenth century onward, identity was established in relation to all other possible identities. By the nineteenth century, difference was understood in terms of a larger conviction about the cohesiveness and unity of the social organism. Naturalist literature solved the problem of how to accommodate the alien and brutal with a normative reading of human progress in accordance with that of Herbert Spencer. At its most extreme, naturalist characters threw into relief the progress of "normal" Americans.

The worlds of Frank Norris, in *Vandover and the Brute* (1914) and *McTeague* (1899) in particular, are worlds of extreme naturalism. *McTeague* features inbred, sterile, and insane characters—the wasted undesirables who are better left to die out. Immobilized oddities (Old Grannis and Miss Baker), distorted gold worshipers (Maria Macapa, Zerkow, and Trina McTeague), brutes (McTeague and Marcus Schouler), these are human types who fail at everything: love, business, mere survival. Nor is it accidental that these characters have strange-sounding names. *McTeague*'s abnormals were the immigrant and worker populations, whose features when seen up close justified their domination. Norris's fundamental contempt for his characters is exemplified by the novel's ending, where McTeague survives a monumental desert struggle against Marcus Schouler only to find himself handcuffed to the dead body. What the perverse underworld of *McTeague* shares with the hypercivilized community of *The Awkward Age* is the incapacity for self-generation.

The works of Theodore Dreiser offer a different perspective on naturalism by highlighting a modern capitalist social order that has subsumed the natural. In contrast to Norris's degenerate (and eminently expendable) social types, Dreiser's fiction features functional types who become dysfunctional. A register of the differences between Norris's and Dreiser's naturalism is their metaphorical use of newspapers. Norris's characters don't read newspapers (it's not clear that they can even read); rather they are the stuff of newspapers. Dreiser's characters, in contrast, are guided by them. Far from Norris's sites of extremity, newspapers in Dreiser are repositories of human possibility to be imitated. In Dreiser newspapers are a paradoxical medium both craved and feared. To be an object of publicity is an ideal state. Yet publicity can also mean that one is a victim or a casualty. Dreiser's fictions are themselves like newspapers, representing the unlikely but accessible circumstances that elude the majority. Consider, for example, Clyde Griffiths, the everyman who becomes the dastardly object of awed crowds as he enters prison, or Hurst-wood, who begins *Sister Carrie* (1900) as a generic businessman and ends as a pathetic object of urban voyeurs in a panhandler's line. Publicity is also the lot of Sister Carrie in her acting stardom, but it is the nature of a "star" to fall as well as rise. As they fall, Dreiser's characters become spectacles, illustrating the potential decline of any-one in the risk-driven society of capitalism. The vicissitudes of mod-ern capitalism as portrayed in Dreiser's works put barbarism always within our reach.

Thus, where Norris's naturalism tends to corroborate a social ev-olutionary scheme, Dreiser's naturalism, by showing how such a scheme justifies and entrenches a man-made social system, tends to challenge it. Dreiser is interested in social science and capitalism as interpenetrating ideologies. He is at once more committed to and reflective about social scientific analysis. Like contemporary social scientists, he is drawn to the situations and individuals that repeat in modern life: the social fall or rise, the sexual conquest, the double-dealing, the "American Tragedy," the ambitious youth, the coquette, the female innocent, the fast-talking city slicker. This cataloging im-pulse, however, defines the limit of Dreiser's fascination with Amer-ican capitalism. Likewise, Dreiser parts ways with the passive vision of Social Darwinism, including its instrumental version. In shadow types like the Captain of *Sister Carrie,* who opposes the sentimental idealism of the supposed hero, Ames, in portraits of immobile worlds dominated by rhetorics of social mobility (*An American Tragedy* [1925]), Dreiser reveals the prevailing social theory of his era to be the ideological handmaid to a basically unjust capitalist system. Drei-ser's resistance to the naturalist assumptions embedded in liberal so-cial theory brings us to the final set of literary examples to be con-sidered: two writers who first embraced the practical potential of social science, and ended up more critical of its assumptions than any of the authors so far discussed. Yet however critical they became, W. E. B. Du Bois and Gertrude Stein remained attached to social science in ways that informed the works that are of concern to the history of the novel—*The Souls of Black Folk* (1903) and *The Mak-ing of Americans* (1906–8).

W. E. B. Du Bois and Gertrude Stein share the position of social marginals, as well as the experience of social scientific training. Both were also self-exiles from American society: Du Bois settled in Ghana at the end of his life, Stein moved to Paris before she was thirty. Perhaps the most significant similarity is that both studied with William James and were heavily influenced by his pragmatist social science.

For Du Bois and Stein, typecasting was not an inevitable process but a political activity. Both saw the damaging effects of typecasting on their respective social groups and believed that greater control over their group's representation would extend its social possibility. They sought out the role of the expert cataloger of modern social life as a means of remedy and instruction.

As two writers who were personally implicated in questions of social difference and drawn to the promise of liberal social science, Du Bois and Stein represent powerful confrontations with the central intellectual concerns of their era: the seductive potential of categories and types, the social scientific conflation of knowledge and uniformity, individualism versus collectivism as competing ideals, the role of literature in relation to social science. They are distinctive, and crucial to our exploration, in having recognized the pivotal role that social science played in the modern era. While they were critical of this role, they also pursued it. This ambivalence toward the posture of social scientific expertise is built into the narrative personae of their two major novelistic works.

Of all the literary authors discussed so far, Du Bois is unique in actively combining sociological and literary methods. As a student of history and sociology at Harvard in the 1890s (with two years of study in Germany), Du Bois was drawn to the potential of this new discipline for arbitrating the problem of race in America. He more often found, however, that sociology was a symptom of the problem rather than a solution to it. Even the most enlightened of sociologists, W. I. Thomas, in a 1904 article, "The Psychology of Race-Prejudice" (*American Journal of Sociology*), came perilously close to calling racial prejudice inherent. And F. H. Giddings's concept of "the consciousness of kind," which held that the sense of community inevitably diminished with the increase of racial and ethnic differences, was used to justify turn-of-the century schemes for the deportation of African Americans.

Du Bois's earliest training was in history and economics, culminating in his dissertation *The Suppression of the African Slave-Trade 1638–1870* (1896). The book's bias is historicist, that is, Du Bois focuses on the historical genesis of slavery in order to redress the condition of African Americans in his contemporary society. Like *Billy Budd, Suppression* is most drawn to the closing decades of the eighteenth century: Melville's post-Revolutionary era of consolidation matches Du Bois's post-Revolutionary America, the moment of enlightenment that managed to entrench the most oppressive of slave systems. "There never was a time in the history of America," wrote Du Bois, "when the system had a slighter economic, political, and moral justification than in 1787, and yet with this real, existent, growing evil before their eyes, a bargain largely of dollars and cents was allowed to open the highway that led straight to the Civil War." By delineating the economic considerations that consistently overshadowed the moral question of slavery, *Suppression* embodies the weight of historical memory that tempered Du Bois's faith in social instrumentalism. Any program of social action had to contend with the historical process that had created and still informed African American possibility.

Given Du Bois's career-long interest in the theoretical problem of racial difference and its relationship to conceptions of social evolution, it seems appropriate that his entry into social science was through history. Du Bois's historical approach is consistent with the methods of the era's classic sociological theorists, for whom sociological analysis required a broad command of different cultures as well as historical periods. Like Spencer, Durkheim, and Weber, Du Bois is interested in the transformation of societies, as well as in the persistence of certain ideas and habits over time. Du Bois differs from these analysts in attending to the ways in which social evolution occurs and also fails to occur as a consequence of deliberate social policy. Du Bois likewise departs from an essentially static evolutionary script (favored by Spencer and Durkheim) that projects a normative pattern of development and evaluates all populations according to that pattern. The culmination of Du Bois's training as a social scientist was his classic anatomy of African American society in Philadelphia.

The central drama of *The Philadelphia Negro* (1899) lies in Du Bois's effort to strike a balance between assessing the collective condition of Philadelphia's African Americans and distinguishing the various strata of that community, with their different relationships to American norms and values. His study contains the seeds of his growing dissatisfaction with social science while it lays the groundwork for the problem that would plague his career: how could a commitment to a collective African American destiny be accommodated to the promise of individual assimilation and progress dividing that collectivity? Sociological theories of stratification together with his continuing absorption in Spencerian ideas formed the unsettling core of Du Bois's method. His turn away from sociology following *The Philadelphia Negro* may have had as much to do with the ways in which it magnified an emerging contradiction in his own thought as with the limitations he saw in the discipline itself. In practicing sociology, he adopted the dominant sociological trajectory of his era: the supplanting of basically conservative, essentialist notions about human potential with a liberal ideal that emphasized assimilation and training. This new ideal, however, retained a fundamental tie to the essentialist view, in upholding a belief in "the survival of the fittest." The superior elements of any social group, went the argument, would inevitably rise and prosper. Given this sociological climate, it is not surprising that an outgrowth of Du Bois's Philadelphia study was his first conceptualization of "the talented tenth," an attempt to distinguish the best "strata" of the African American race.

Du Bois's adaptation of these sociological principles for African American Philadelphia was timely, given a prevailing racial ideology of two nations, one white, one black, that relentlessly homogenized African Americans. Against this biological fiat of racial homogeneity, Du Bois set another biological fiat implicitly condoned by social science, which emphasized inherent differences of talent within each group. Du Bois thus used Social Darwinist ideas to challenge a prevailing racial ideology.

The irony is that his struggle against a white conspiracy that intentionally muffles African American achievements was mirrored by the response to his book. Through the reception (or more accurately, nonreception) of *The Philadelphia Negro* by the sociological profession—which took over half a century to confer its "classic" status—Du Bois experienced firsthand the limits upon all African Americans. Du Bois's failure to gain a hearing as a sociologist signaled the failed promise of the discipline's liberal assumptions. In declaring his next major study, *The Souls of Black Folk* (1903), a work of "faith and passion," he seemed to be deliberately distancing himself from the rational agenda of *The Philadelphia Negro*.

In *The Souls of Black Folk*, Du Bois undertakes the imaginative reconstruction of the territory he covered in his sociological classic. His desire to gain control over the representation of African Americans will not be accomplished through the straitjacket of sociological method, he implies, but requires a more literary technique. If *Philadelphia* undertakes the work of social description, *Souls* undertakes the work of social change. *Philadelphia* selects among preexisting African American types assigned by the dominant society, while *Souls* surveys all the available African American types and, finding them wanting, begins to recover the powers of self-identification for African Americans themselves.

The two books are best seen as companion pieces, which need to be read together in order to understand their deepest implications. The striving Philadelphian bent on self-improvement joins the collectivity of African American souls. The insistence of *Souls* on plurality suggests Du Bois's new attitude toward the liberal individualism of sociology—it has never represented a true possibility for African Americans. *Souls* dismisses the claim that African Americans are individuals, the "fittest" capable of assimilating and rising like any "immigrant" group. What was deplored in *Philadelphia*, the "tendency on the part of the community to consider the Negroes as comprising one practically homogeneous mass," is embraced in *Souls*. The homogenizing of African Americans is transformed into an enabling device; African Americans become a self-identified and therefore empowered collectivity. *Souls* explodes some other powerful sociological myths as well. The trajectory of *Philadelphia* is from South to North, as the book charts the making of a modern African American populace, a narrative of liberal progress that pictures the race's "fittest" rising to the top. *Souls*, however, moves from North to South, thus implying that African Americans must come to terms with the roots of their experience in America, by returning to "the scene of the crime," as it were. The static evolutionary reading of African American history in *Philadelphia*—history in the sociological vein as a grand narrative that explains the present via the past—is replaced by history as *bricolage*. *Souls* is *annales* history: an amalgam of tales, songs, mythologies, critiques, autobiography, elegy. Its concern is not progress measured in terms of the dominant society but the shaping of collective identity.

*Souls* seems in every way opposed to its social scientific predecessor, yet in fact Du Bois never strays very far from an implicitly sociological agenda. His achievement is that he manages at once to criticize and to revitalize the new science of society. *Souls* is filled with critical references to "the cold statistician," the "sociologists who gleefully count" African American "bastards" and "prostitutes," "the car window sociologist . . . who seeks to understand and know the South by devoting the few leisure hours of a holiday trip to unravelling the snarl of centuries."

Du Bois's answer to these limitations is the aestheticizing of sociology. The sociological method of typecasting becomes exploratory, experimental. Far from merely typologizing, *Souls* elaborates a theory of types. For what is the color line but the penultimate type or boundary demarcating the limit of African American possibility? The book is a sustained effort to extend the boundary around the African American self. Du Bois devotes each chapter to elaborating a different unrealized potential: the African American as failed transmitter of a generational legacy (chapter 11, on the death of his son); the African American as failed educator (chapter 4, on his teaching career in Tennessee); the African American as failed spiritual leader (chapter 12, on Alexander Crummel). These promising but unfulfilled types are played off against the degraded types of the dominant society. The book is thus a dialectic of typological categories, and Du Bois's major insight is that the African American self internalizes them all. Thus the "warring" within that derives from this "double-consciousness": "looking at one's self through the eyes of others . . . measuring one's soul by the tape of a world that looks on in amused contempt and pity." The African American self is alienated from both versions of self: the type of the white society, and the inner soul with which it conflicts.

But as Du Bois suggests, this condition of double-consciousness is also basic to the practice of sociology. As a discipline that enacts the dilemma of being subject and object simultaneously, whose practitioners are inevitably the objects of their own investigations, sociology epitomizes the circumstances of the African American soul. Because contemporary sociology failed to come to terms with this paradox, it could not realize the promise it held out to Du Bois.

By conceptualizing a different kind of social science founded upon a critique of capitalism, as well as an awareness of its own perilous objectivity, Du Bois pointed the way toward a critical social theory that would not be fully articulated until the rise of the Frankfurt School thirty years later. This perspective, formulated by Theodor Adorno and Max Horkheimer, among others, rejected orthodox social science, the American version in particular, as an apology for capitalism. They adopted in its place a theory based on the method of negative dialectics, critical of all reigning forms of analysis, and directed toward fundamental social change. For W. E. B. Du Bois, as well as for Adorno and Horkheimer, a social theory without this commitment was unworthy of the name.

Du Bois's ventures in literature after *Souls* had limited results. His first full-fledged novel, *The Quest of the Silver Fleece* (1911), has all the trappings of socialist realism, with its cast of dark and light characters: the idealized African American hero and heroine, Bles and Zora; the weak and selfish whites, most of them monstrous vessels of capitalist greed; the weak African Americans who succumb to the evil temptations of capitalism. It is telling that however ambivalent Du Bois was toward the sociology of his day, he never equaled the powerful blend of literary and sociological imaginings he achieved in *Souls.*

"Mostly no one knowing me can like it that I love it that everyone is a kind of men and women, that always I am looking and comparing and classifying them, always I am seeing their repeating." So writes Gertrude Stein in *The Making of Americans,* expressing her era's simultaneous attraction and resistance to social categorization. Her own most obvious response is parody. The lists of human types that pervade Stein's "great American novel" are often absurd. One such list runs to: "being one liking swimming, being one tired of ocean bathing before they have really been in more than twice in a season." But despite such parodic attitudes, she was deeply committed to the enterprise of knowing human kinds. How did Stein come to be a maker of lists? What brought her to desire a unified knowledge of America? A clue to these questions lies in her pursuit of social science.

Stein's advanced education began at Harvard in the 1890s, where she studied mainly psychology, and ended at Johns Hopkins at the turn of the century, where she studied brain anatomy. Both of these educational experiences suggest provocative sources for *The Making of Americans*. Stein's Harvard research (which was published as "Cultivated Motor Automatism: A Study of Character in Its Relation to Attention," in *The Psychological Review,* 1898) was based on experiments with Harvard and Radcliffe students. It addressed the question of how automatic behavior can be cultivated in human subjects; how can subjects be made to internalize suggested actions as their own habits? Among the issues that Stein's experiment takes up is the question of gender difference: is there a consistent opposition between male and female responses to suggested action? Another is the problem of change: once learned, how can subjects be induced to abandon old actions and adopt new ones? Stein's research produced its own catalog of human types. Type I, "girls . . . found naturally in literature courses" and men bound for law, is "nervous, high-strung, very imaginative." Type II, "blond and pale," is "distinctly phlegmatic," a general "New England" type that is repressed and self-conscious. The parallels between Stein's research and the ideas of William James are revealing. James describes habit, in the famous essay of that name, as "the enormous fly-wheel of society, its most precious conservative agent. . . . It also prevents the hardest and most repulsive walks of life from being deserted by those brought up to tread therein." With this observation, James links the intricate psychology of habit to larger mechanisms of organization and control. And this points to the larger arena Stein will create for her psychological studies in *The Making of Americans*.

At Johns Hopkins Medical School, where she went on the advice of James, Stein sought even more objective knowledge of human minds. Garland Allen, a historian of biology, has characterized the dominant tradition at Hopkins during this period as "descriptive naturalist." This involved an emphasis on morphology—the study and classification of form—which assumed the underlying unity of diverse organisms. Among the techniques taught was the construction of family trees and phylogenies, which identified a single common ancestor as the progenitor of modern lines.

Stein's developing interest in typology culminated in her preoccupation with the work of Otto Weininger, the German psychologist, whose book *Sex and Character* (1906) inspired her during her writing of *The Making of Americans*. A precursor to Nazi ideology, Weininger's book offered a system of characterology, whose main purpose seemed to be the identification of human types that threatened the deterioration of nations. However rigidly schematic Weininger's ideas, he was willing to accept ambiguity, by admitting that some despised characteristics were present to varying degrees in all human types. Significantly, in light of Stein's Jewish-lesbian identity, the two main sources of degeneracy in Weininger's system were Jews and women. The extent of feminine possibility for Weininger was prostitute, mother, servant, saint, and masculine woman. Jews occupied a unique position in Weininger's typology since Jewish traits were confined to the race alone. They therefore provide an opportunity for the in-depth study of degeneracy.

What is so obviously startling about Stein's adoption of Weininger's ideas, which she claimed expressed "her own thoughts exactly," was that it required the complete suppression of her own identity. Indeed, she seems to have identified so fully with Weininger that she sometimes referred to his system as her own. As she wrote in her notebook, "That thing of mine of sex and mind and character all coming together seems to work absolutely." Stein's engagement with Weininger points to an important feature of *The Making of Americans*. Stein's representation of her own subjective processes, her use of herself as an object of study, was a means of self-distancing. Stein's spectacular detachment fulfills Georg Simmel's sociological prescription for aesthetics, from *The Philosophy of Money*: "The basic principle of art was to bring us closer to things by placing them at a distance from us." It also reveals what is perhaps the most elitist aspect of Stein's vision: that other human beings are to her objects, with readily identifiable "bottom beings," while Stein's own identity is endlessly elusive and revisable.

*The Making of Americans* is an effort to bring us closer to the various mythologies of American culture, by analytically detaching ourselves from them. American minds, the book's narrative suggests, are thickets of repetition: filled with a finite set of stories, plans, opinions. Stay with one for a certain length of time and you begin to hear the repetitions, to note patterns, which hold the clue to that individual's "bottom being." This white noise exists in our minds apart from the practical thoughts that impel our action. When we sit back to reflect on ourselves, or to present ourselves to others, we become aware of the fog of repetition in which we are always enveloped. If this is true on an individual level, it is also true of nations. Perhaps more than any other American writer, Stein is devoted to the idea of a national mind. For Stein this national mind, like the repetitions that reveal individual being, comes alive through cliché, parable, all the little stories that form the mental tissue of American life. Another name for this mental tissue is ideology, and Stein aims to crack the enormous web of images and ideals that go into the making of Americans.

The central creation of Stein's novel is the great American writer. Stein claims supreme authority for writers. Stories are powerful. They exploit, indeed they create, the appetite for fantasy that is essential to any successful nation.

Yet how are we to take Stein's emphasis, starting with the title, on the production side of American culture? As a catalog of the seemingly infinite number of American types, Stein's book can be understood as celebrating the sheer activity of production. This is consistent with the spirit of her gargantuan 925-page book. It seems to contradict, however, her continual undermining of human reproduction and hereditary transmission. What Stein is suggesting is that this patriarchal model is becoming obsolete, the concept of fathering is losing ground to another kind of manufacture. Progress, as Stein defines it, involves the displacement of traditional forms of production by a modern capitalist ideal of production, with which the monumentally productive writer implicitly identifies. At the same time, Stein's American writer has become an active producer of selves, in the sociological vein. To this end, the novel begins with a sputtering, fantastically abbreviated patriarchal plea for the maintenance of tradition. And the remainder of the book can be read as a rebuttal of this two-line dictum.

The patriarchal figure who threatens to dominate the book is David Hersland, who closely resembles Stein's own father Daniel. In contrast to the other fathers, this immigrant who made good fulfills a very liberal, very modern American pattern. He had "gone west to make his fortune . . . he was big and abundant and full of new ways of thinking." An Emersonian type, "he was as big as all the world about him . . . the world was all him, and there was no difference in it in him . . . there were no separations of him or from him, and the whole world he lived in always lived inside him." David Hersland is the representative of the misguided dream of human transparency and uniformity. And in a sense Stein's whole book is an assault on this dream. The world, Stein argues, does not conform to the domineering unities of this patriarch. And yet the real action of her book involves not so much his discrediting as his rebirth in the form of the great American novelist. Stein's own penchant for knowing the social world, for cataloging its various parts, derives from this figure. Every restriction of this desire, every assertion that society resists knowledge and codification, is balanced by a reaffirmation of the desire to know. Though Stein readily admits that any such effort is bound to be a process of self-codification, she also recognizes this as a truth too dark to accept.

In one of the book's most brilliant passages, Stein records our stubborn inability to accept this darkness. She describes "being with someone who has always been walking with you, and you always have been feeling that one was seeing everything with you and you feel then that they are seeing that thing the way you are seeing it and then you go sometime with that one to a doctor to have that one have their eyes examined and then you find that things you are seeing, you are writing completely only for one and that is yourself then and to every other one it is a different thing. . . . You know it then yes but you do not really know it as a continuous knowing in you for then in living always you are feeling that someone else is understanding, feeling seeing something the way you are feeling, seeing, understanding that thing."

This passage is paradigmatic of Stein's vision. It reflects her preoccupation with the very processes by which human beings process knowledge, a subject as visceral as the function of the retina. Harking back to her interest in anatomy and automatic action, the passage reveals her conviction that predispositions, ideas, myths, once absorbed, are as stubborn as biology. This does not make Stein a biological determinist. Rather she imaged ideology in physical terms as a reminder of its power. The passage is most striking in its awareness of the limits of awareness. You can know this "truth," about the limits of knowing, she says, you can look it square in the face, but it won't change your fundamental need to know. It won't alter the presumptuous habits that form the basis of American liberalism—that society and its members are transparent, that they are just like us.

*The Making of Americans* brings us full circle in our analysis, back to Ian Hacking's sense of "Making Up People." For Stein, as for Hacking, to classify is to invent; describing is a creative activity. Typological description involves not only the invention of human beings but the invention of language. "So I found myself getting deeper and deeper into the idea of describing really describing every individual that could exist," Stein writes in "The Gradual Making of The Making of Americans" (1934–35), "while I was doing all this all unconsciously at the same time a matter of tenses and sentences came to fascinate me." Stein's experimental language, this passage suggests, comes directly out of her addiction to social scientific methods of description. Her understanding of social scientific method reveals its fundamentally aesthetic aspects. While it locks others into typological schemes, it frees the typologist for acts of invention.

Stein's America, a turn-of-the-century scene of immigration, scientific discovery, economic expansion, looming sexual liberation, offers an open field for the making of Americans. The typological thinking of this era reveals a moment when the concerns of American novelists were vividly aligned with those of more scientific social analysts. In keeping with the other novelists we have discussed, Stein's sustained meditations on typological thinking remind us that literature tends to absorb contemporary ideologies. But they also remind us that literature can give us insight into social categories—the historical pressures that shape them, the human beings they affect—and, in so doing, may provide a source of resistance as well as a source of understanding and critique.

Susan Mizruchi

# Fiction and Reform II

The second half of the nineteenth century in the United States was characterized by an enormous number of social reform movements. Indeed, roughly the last twenty years of the century have been designated by some historians as the Age of Protest and Reform. This period began around 1878, when the nation was racked by postwar financial panic and depression, and ended in 1898 with a return to "prosperity" occasioned by the discovery of gold and by inflation related to the Spanish-American War. But even before the onset of this officially recognized period of social protest, authors were using the novel form to lodge criticisms about social injustices they felt marred American life. Among the issues that were foremost in national debate during the period are abolitionism, feminism, agrarian protest, and industrial labor conditions. Each of these issues is treated directly and explicitly in at least one of the novels under consideration in this chapter. At the same time, as will become clear, it is possible to trace relations between these works and other less obviously "political" works of the era, and in doing so we will be able to identify the interest in social reform as not merely the discrete characteristic of a few writers and activists but rather as constitutive of an entire culture in which these persons performed their work.

If we are to understand that work fully, we must first understand what sort of undertaking is designated by "reform." The term is commonly used to refer to an improvement in social and political conditions that is brought about without a radical change in existent social and political structures. Of course, the question of what constitutes "radical change" is a very difficult one to answer. We may be aided here by recourse to what are currently taken as the three dominant modes of social categorization—gender, race, and class. Contemporary social theory and cultural criticism are developing an ever-increasing sense of the fundamental interrelation of these categories in the constitution of our society. Thus, to the extent that any given movement fails to recognize that interrelation, it then falls short of envisioning a really *revolutionary* social transformation—it is properly *reformist*. The movements characteristic of the late nineteenth century (like most of those current today) were constituted in precisely this way. Moreover, even when activists proposed social changes that would no doubt have brought about developments that most people would have *experienced* as radically new—the socialization of the economy, for instance, or the admission of women into all spheres of public life—the means by which they sought to incorporate these changes were by and large characterized by moderation, gradualism, and/or work through established social and political mechanisms, as opposed to sudden revolutionary transformation. Having posited this definition of reform culture during the latter half of the nineteenth century, we are now well prepared to be confronted with the many exceptions to it that any survey of the period will undoubtedly uncover. And yet, any modifications we must make in our understanding of the reform impulse should be seen not as invalidating this initial conception but rather as indicating the great difficulty of painting with broad strokes a national history whose import will lie largely in the fine, specific details of the individual experiences that constitute it.

Any history of the reform novel in the latter half of the nineteenth century would have to begin with a consideration of *Uncle Tom's Cabin*, by Harriet Beecher Stowe. This novel—an abolitionist narrative that advocated the ultimate repatriation of African Americans from the United States to colonies in West Africa—crystallizes the effect of a major political development that occurred right at the midpoint of the nineteenth century. The year 1850 saw the passage of the Fugitive Slave Act, which mandated the return of fugitive slaves even from the nonslaveholding Northern states into which they might have escaped. By legislating the North's complicity in slavery, the law merely exposed the fact that the entire nation had been implicated in the horrors of the system from the beginning, and indicated that the ramifications of the institution were not peculiar to the South. The act was an element in the Compromise of 1850, the other major aspect of which allowed for the admission of Western territories into the Union as nonslave states. Its passage marked a moral watershed for many Northerners, who were finally brought face to face with the full significance of the slave system; and the fact that the law was signed in 1850 provides us with a means of neatly bifurcating the century so that we can consider the reform culture of the latter half as a relatively contained phenomenon. Stowe, like many other citizens who harbored antislavery sentiments, was indignant with President Millard Fillmore and, especially, with New Hampshire Senator Daniel Webster—the bulwark of New England liberalism—for supporting the bill. She turned that indignation to the writing of her abolitionist novel, which was published in 1852, and which launched her on a long public career. As *Uncle Tom's Cabin* provides us with a means by which to understand the strategies incorporated in all of the rest of the works we will consider, it will be necessary to give it substantial attention here.

As numerous commentators have suggested, *Uncle Tom's Cabin* stands not only as a testament to Stowe's strong antislavery sentiment but also as an indication of the degree to which abolitionist rhetoric was forged in the crucible of feminine—and feminist—sensibility. Organized American feminism itself had strong roots in the antislavery movement, emerging from the women's auxiliaries to male-dominated abolitionist groups of the 1830s and 1840s. In fact, it was in response to the barring of women delegates from the floor of the 1840 World's Antislavery Convention in London that Elizabeth Cady Stanton began the organizing for the first women's rights convention, held at Seneca Falls, New York, in 1848. Thus the two movements—for women's rights, including, but not limited to, suffrage, and for equality between African Americans and whites, beginning with the abolition of slavery—have long been intertwined. They have also frequently been set at odds with each other in a political context that plays different disenfranchised groups against one another. Despite the historically vexed relationship between feminism and abolitionism, however, *Uncle Tom's Cabin*, in its particular stylistic treatment of its peculiar subject matter, actually synthesizes the two social movements in one triumphant political work.

Since at least the mid-1970s, scholars have been engaged in a reassessment of the function of the sentimental novel in the nineteenth-century United States. This reassessment has led to an understanding of the form's potential for effecting progressive social change through its adaptation of narrative conventions that actually seem to reflect women's passivity and subservience to men. The stereotypically feminine traits that are associated with the Victorian-era "cult of true womanhood"—piety, purity, submissiveness, domesticity—combine to make women the guardians of society's moral standards. This has provided for two primary types of plot in the sentimental novel: the plot of romantic seduction, whereby a woman's virtue is tested by the insistent overtures made to her by a relatively less scrupulous man; and the plot of moral improvement, whereby the superior virtue that is considered to characterize women actually empowers them to sway the actions of the men who come under their domestic care. It has been argued that *Uncle Tom's Cabin* suppresses the former sentimental structure and emphasizes the latter, depicting women as the primary agents of the antislavery activity in the novel. Stowe's work thus actually loosens the sentimental novel from its associations with the apparently profoundly private concerns of the domestic sphere and transforms it into a forum for public agitation for social reform. This mode of politicizing the domestic sphere by introducing into it the consideration of public events will be central to much reform fiction through the 1880s—and it will also provide the context within which we can understand the development of the reform novel in the final decade of the century—so it is worth emphasizing here the role Stowe's novel plays in originating the strategy.

To understand this strategy fully requires that we examine exactly how *Uncle Tom's Cabin* makes its argument. Obviously, there are any number of aspects of Stowe's presentation on which we might focus. It will be instructive, though, to take a cue from the author herself, whose novel, when originally published in two volumes in 1852, was subtitled "The Man That Was a Thing." For Stowe's purpose, evident in much of her rhetoric in the novel, was to impress upon her readers the dehumanizing effects of slavery upon African Americans held in its thrall. This was not a new undertaking; abolitionist orators and writers had been broadcasting a very similar message throughout the 1830s and 1840s. To be sure, that most influential abolitionist tract, *The Narrative of the Life of Frederick Douglass, an American Slave, Written by Himself,* which was published in 1845, based its polemical effect on precisely the fact that the institution of slavery rendered its victims (both African American slave and white master) less than human. The difference between Douglass's treatment and Stowe's, however, lies in the specific type of dehumanization that each sees at work in slavery. Douglass repeatedly emphasizes slavery's effect of imbuing human beings with an array of animalistic traits—"behold," he says, as he describes his own downward trajectory, just before the climactic turn of the narrative, "a man transformed into a brute!" Stowe, on the other hand, specifies again and again the intended effect of slavery to transform humans not into some lower order of animal but rather into inanimate objects, traded and held as property. In the very first chapter of her novel, Stowe, having presented the slaveowner, Arthur Shelby, reflecting on his need to sell his faithful hand, Tom, and the young son of his wife's maid, makes the following pronouncement:

So long as the law considers all these human beings, with beating hearts and living affections, only as so many *things* belonging to a master,—so long as the failure, or misfortune, or imprudence, or death of the kindest owner, may cause them any day to exchange a life of kind protection and indulgence for one of hopeless misery and toil,—so long it is impossible to make anything beautiful or desirable in the best regulated administration of slavery.

This statement is only a prelude to numerous other references to the status of slaves as things throughout the first eight chapters of the book.

We might well ask what is accomplished by Stowe's positing of the matter as she does. It is possible to argue that, by emphasizing a desired *inanimate* status for African American slaves, Stowe actually allows for the question of slavery itself to be brought within the compass of domestic, feminine concerns, and thus to be commented on through the mechanism of sentimental fiction. In order to understand how this works, we need first to recognize the complicated relation between the realms, mentioned earlier, of the public and the private. Let us remember that, even if Uncle Tom—and the other slaves, too, for that matter—is legally a *thing*, a piece of property, he is a particular *kind* of property: specifically, as a plantation laborer, he is a form of capital—a fund of wealth managed specifically with the aim of producing more wealth. To the extent that capital presupposes a marketplace in which different persons' wealth can be exchanged in the form of various commodities, then its function is calculated as a relatively "public" one. On the other hand, distinguished from the category of capital, there exists that set of commodities whose implication in the larger system of exchange is relatively veiled, or mystified, through their fairly infrequent circulation in it. I am thinking of property that is not only "private" but emphatically "personal," and I have in mind one particular example of such personal property from *Uncle Tom's Cabin* itself.

In chapter 5 of the novel, when Mr. Shelby informs his wife, Emily, of the necessity of selling Tom and the young boy, Harry, she is first horrified, and then attempts to rally to the call of economic necessity by offering a substitute bargain for the sale of the two slaves. When Mr. Shelby hopes aloud that he has convinced his wife of the necessity for his action, she responds emphatically:

"O yes, yes!" said Mrs. Shelby, hurriedly and abstractedly fingering her gold watch,—"I haven't any jewelry of any amount," she added, thoughtfully; "but would not this watch do something?—it was an expensive one, when it was bought. If I could only at least save Eliza's child, I would sacrifice anything I have."

Mrs. Shelby's insight into the nature of her family's economic straits allows her to effect the transmutation of her watch—the private possession that, for all its practical use, is still primarily a personal adornment—into an item for exchange in the public marketplace. Simultaneously, and conversely, as the personal item is being offered as a substitute for the slave in the proposed exchange, an equivalency is established whereby the status of the slave must be recognized as related to the personal, private life of, in this case, the slave mistress. Once slave status is clearly demonstrated to fall within the realm of the private, the personal, the *domestic,* then the questions pertaining to slavery may logically be considered by women, whose stereotypical realm, after all, is the actual and metaphorical private, domestic space of the nation. In short, *Uncle Tom's Cabin* depends for its power on a demonstration of the fundamental interrelatedness of the private and public spheres—on showing that the private *is* the public or, to put it in the terms of second-wave feminism, that the personal is political.

The confusion between private and public in the matter of slavery is explicitly manifested in the novel in a scene between Senator and Mrs. Bird, who assist the runaway slave, Eliza, as she makes her way toward the North. Just before Eliza's arrival at the Birds' home, Mrs. Bird remonstrates with her husband for his support, in the Ohio state legislature, of a fugitive slave act: "Things have got to a pretty pass, if a woman can't give a warm supper and a bed to poor, starving creatures, just because they are slaves, and have been abused and oppressed all their lives, poor things!" Her husband responds with what he considers to be typically masculine rationality:

"But, Mary, just listen to me. Your feelings are all quite right, dear, and interesting, and I love you for them; but, then, dear, we mustn't suffer our feelings to run away with our judgment; you must consider it's a matter of private feeling,—there are great public interests involved,—there is such a state of public agitation rising, that we must put aside our private feelings."

On the contrary, however, it is precisely by filtering public events through private feelings that the reform impulse is developed in the historical context under consideration, and this strategy certainly accounts for Stowe's ability to mount an abolitionist protest through the feminized form of sentimental fiction.

In its narrative treatment of the public/private relationship, *Uncle Tom's Cabin* prefigures much other reform fiction from the latter half of the nineteenth century. Nine years after the publication of Stowe's novel, just at the outbreak of the Civil War, Rebecca Harding Davis published her remarkable *Life in the Iron Mills* in the April 1861 issue of the *Atlantic Monthly.* This piece of fiction, which has been seen as representing the first step in American literature's transition from romanticism to realism, depicts the fate of two immigrant workers in the mills of a Midwestern industrial town. Hugh Wolfe rolls iron in the vast works that, by the time of Harding's writing, are operating around the clock; his cousin, Deborah, is a "picker" in a cotton mill. The structure of Harding's narrative is such that it demonstrates the oppressive conditions of life in the factories both as they are experienced by Hugh and Deb themselves *and* as they are viewed from the vantage of a middle-class observer, represented in the narrator.

The opening of Harding's tale has become famous since its reprinting by the Feminist Press in 1972:

A cloudy day: do you know what that is in a town of iron-works? The sky sank down before dawn, muddy, flat, immovable. The air is thick, clammy with the breath of crowded human beings. It stifles me. I open the window, and, looking out, can scarcely see through the rain the grocer's shop opposite, where a crowd of drunken Irishmen are puffing Lynchburg tobacco in their pipes. I can detect the scent through all the foul smells ranging loose in the air.

And, three paragraphs later:

Can you see how foggy the day is? As I stand here, idly tapping the window-pane, and looking out through the rain at the dirty back-yard and the coal-boats below, fragments of an old story float up before me,—a story of this old house into which I happened to come to-day.

From this point, the tale is related of the Welsh-born industrial workers who are the focus of Harding's story. But these opening lines are crucial, for they posit the grim reality of the mill workers' lives as an irruption into the narrator's apparently comfortable middle-class existence. After all, we do learn, at the end of the narrative, that the storyteller is ensconced in her domestic library, which is scattered with a number of objects of distinction: "A half-moulded child's head; Aphrodite; a bough of forest-leaves; music; work; homely fragments, in which lie the secrets of all eternal truth and beauty." It is striking then that, as she meditates in her insulation, the narrator should remark about the air of the mill town, "It stifles me." The personal effect that the stifling atmosphere of the mills has on the narrator indicates the degree to which the private, middle-class domestic space is penetrated by the machinery of industrial capital. The inevitable implication of the industrial world in the domestic realm is underscored, as well, by the fact that the story of Hugh and Deb

Wolfe, which the narrator relates, is the story, too, "of this old house," which the narrator presently occupies, and which is also "the one where the Wolfes lived."

The plot of *Life in the Iron Mills* is relatively simple. Hugh Wolfe, oddly independent and standoffish from the other millhands, is visited by two parties one evening as he labors overtime at the ironworks. One is his cousin Deb, a young, hunchbacked woman who ardently loves Hugh, and who this night, as on other evenings when he works the night shift, brings him a dinner pail; the other is a group of men from the upper classes come to take a tour of the mill while Deb is there. They include a Mr. Kirby, son of one of the millowners, the factory overseer, a town physician, a newspaper reporter, and a relative of Kirby's from out of town, named Mitchell. While at the mill, they marvel not only at the roar and bustle of the works themselves but also at a strange female figure that Hugh has carved out of korl, the refuse from the iron ore (the subtitle of *Life in the Iron Mills* is "The Korl Woman"). She has a strained and anguished-looking countenance, but is so muscular—in clear contrast to the Victorian "true woman"—that the gentlemen cannot understand when Hugh explains her pained expression by saying "She be hungry." Obviously, her hunger is a spiritual one, born of the stifling existence that her class endures as laborers in the industrial machine, which is evidently Davis's point; and this fact is clarified when Hugh specifies to his inquisitors that she is hungry for "Summat to make her live, I think,—like you." This statement provokes a debate amongst the visitors about exactly who is responsible for the social welfare of the factory workers.

While this exchange is going on, though, Deb makes her own grab at "summat to make her live" by stealing from Mitchell's pocket a wallet that contains a little cash and a check for a substantial amount of money. Following some persuasion on her part after she and Hugh leave the mill, he decides to keep the wallet, and is arrested the next day for theft. He is quickly tried, convicted, and sentenced to nineteen years in prison (literally half his life, as is pointed out in the Feminist Press notes to the book: the life expectancy at the time for men in his position was thirty-seven years; Hugh is nineteen when he is incarcerated). Deb gets a three-year jail sentence for acting as his accomplice. Rather than waste away in prison, Hugh kills himself by slicing his veins with a piece of sharpened tin. Deb is befriended by a helpful Quaker woman, and lives a pious life among the community of Friends after her release.

What remains, however, is the figure of the korl woman itself, which stands, hidden behind a curtain, in the narrator's library. Its position there suggests the status of the story of Hugh and Deb, which, it has been proposed, is a realist narrative set in the romantic frame of the narrator's rhetoric. The korl figure represents unsettling questions about social inequities within the newly developing system of industrial capitalism, and its position in the narrator's library represents the introduction of those questions into the private realm of the domestic space, in which context they become fodder for a reform movement that is both represented in and occasioned by such works as *Life in the Iron Mills*.

In terms of literary history, *Life in the Iron Mills* is a remarkably prescient indicator of the characteristics of later works of United States literature. Observers have drawn links between its motifs and those of such disparate naturalist novels as Stephen Crane's *The Red Badge of Courage* (1894), Frank Norris's *McTeague* (1899), Kate Chopin's *The Awakening* (1899), and Theodore Dreiser's *Sister Carrie* (1900). Davis's exposure of the millhands' lives has been likened to the exploration of turn-of-the-century urban ghettos represented in Jacob Riis's text-cum-photo essay, *How the Other Half Lives* (1890). The dramatic theatricality that characterizes the behaviors of her fictional personages has been seen as prefiguring a similar strain in Crane's *Maggie: A Girl of the Streets* (1893), Norris's *The Pit* (1902), and Edith Wharton's *The House of Mirth* (1905). These associations are all traceable through the narrative techniques that Davis utilizes, many of which appear repeatedly in the later works. But *Life in the Iron Mills* is not merely a precursor of American literary realism and naturalism; it is also a powerful instance of reform fiction—a status to which most later naturalism was prevented from acceding, however graphic its depiction of social inequality and the squalor of the poor, owing to its equally strong sense of the immutably determined and deterministic nature of those very conditions. Davis's work *is* deterministic, without a doubt—suggesting that Hugh and Deborah have inherited the conditions of their parents before them, just as does the wealthy Kirby; and that the future may be beyond their ability to control—but it also suggests the possibility of transcendence of these conditions through Deb's association with the Quaker community, well known during the period for its interest and activity in effecting social reform through individual action. Consequently, Davis's work can illuminatingly be aligned with later realist works of social criticism, such as Hamlin Garland's *A Spoil of Office* (1892) and Upton Sinclair's *The Jungle* (1906), both of which will be taken up here. Critics have also considered it to be centrally positioned amongst a trio of social reform works that establish the conventions for the later material: Stowe's *Uncle Tom's Cabin,* the Davis work, and *The Silent Partner* (1871), by Elizabeth Stuart Phelps.

Phelps's novel incorporates a number of aspects of literary naturalism, including grimly realistic depictions of the life of Sip Garth and other workers in the cotton mills of Five Falls, Massachusetts. Moreover, Phelps utilizes what critics have identified as a key symbolic structure of naturalism, whereby one particular entity is early on associated with the main character of the story and its significance evolves along with the fate of that character. In Norris's *McTeague,* gold is such an emblem; in Dreiser's *Sister Carrie,* it is the rocking chair; in Crane's *The Red Badge of Courage,* it is Henry's wound; in *Life in the Iron Mills,* it is the iron itself. In *The Silent Partner,* this naturalistic emblem is the hand of Perley Kelso, the daughter of one of the owners of the factory where Sip works. At the beginning of the novel that hand is beautiful and beringed, for Perley is to be married to Maverick Hayle, her father's junior partner. After she meets Sip in the street one evening, though, subsequent to which news of her father's sudden death is rapidly conveyed to her, Perley decides to test the limits of her new status as a silent partner in the firm (the only status that her fiancé and his father will allow the young woman with respect to the business) by trying to reform the condition of the mill-hands. Her insistence on this course of action—along with her growing realization that it is through the agency of the firm's partners and other members of her own class that the workers are kept down—alienates her from Maverick, and she terminates her engagement to him. By this point in the story her ring has already been broken, as she has forcefully brought down her hand on a table in a fit of passionate frustration over the plight of Sip and the other mill workers, and the resultant bruise on her finger is a constant portent throughout the rest of the novel.

We mustn't forget, however, what the ring has signified: betrothal, marriage, domesticity—in short, precisely the type of insulated existence characteristic of high-bred ladies such as Perley, who would normally be ignorant of the goings-on at the factories their husbands and fathers control. Perley's mission, however, becomes precisely to incorporate the world of the mills into her own private sphere; or, rather, she comes to recognize that the factory has always been implicated in her own life of luxury and opulence. For, while it is true that, after her father's death, Perley leaves her comfortable home in Boston to live permanently in the family house at Five Falls and, thus, in closer proximity to the activity at the mills, the interrelation of her life and that of the mill workers is actually pointed out to her through a much less dramatic incident.

Having become acquainted with the squalor that characterizes the lives of the mill workers, Perley insists to Maverick that a number of improvements must be made at the factories, including the establishment of a library, reading rooms, lectures, schools, relief societies, and tenement housing, all for the benefit of the laborers. Maverick protests that Hayle and Kelso cannot afford to provide such amenities, but Perley makes a cogent rejoinder based on her own knowledge not just of the resources of the company but of the manner in which they are distributed, with the employees continually stinted in their share: "I think, if I may judge from my own income, that a library and a reading-room would not bankrupt us, at least this year." Thus, Perley's impulse to reform is developed through her growing sense of the relation between the condition of the mill workers and her own rather more comfortable existence, which she actually comes to use as an index of the wrongs suffered by the workers. The consciousness that she thus develops (though it seems to slip in a way that betrays the entrenchedness of her class conditioning during her effort to mollify the workers when they consider striking over a cut in wages) influences her to eschew marriage altogether and devote her life to personal efforts at reform within the mills, which she undertakes as a means to realize her rather naive utopian vision of social equality among the classes.

But *The Silent Partner* is not merely a utopian vision; it is also a political tract, an attempt to convince its readers, through the example of Perley Kelso, of the necessity of bettering the lot of factory workers. Consequently, it is characterized by a fair amount of didacticism in its presentation. Indeed, throughout the novel Phelps cites extensively from the *Reports of the Massachusetts Bureau of Statistics of Labor* in order to support her claims about the laborers' existence. In this respect she shares much with other reform novelists of the era, particularly those writing about slavery, such as the African American writers William Wells Brown (*Clotel* [1853]) and, especially, Frances Ellen Watkins Harper (*Iola Leroy* [1892]), whose characters themselves give direct voice to Harper's appeals for social justice. The combination of utopian vision and the moral exhortation that characterizes *The Silent Partner* is seen, as well, in the central utopian fiction of the late nineteenth century, Edward Bellamy's *Looking Backward* (1888).

Bellamy's novel is the first one treated here to fall squarely within the era that has been termed the age of protest and reform. While the period lasted, it spawned numerous movements of dissent within the United States, and saw the publication of nearly 500 social gospel and utopian novels, among which Bellamy's is the foremost. But if *Looking Backward* gives us the most fully developed depiction of a utopian community, it nevertheless does not suggest that this ideal social order is a "nowhere" land the attainment of which is impossible. On the contrary, Bellamy suggests that a full socialist "Nationalism," as he called it, is not only possible but inevitable, and that, to paraphrase from the contemporary artist Laurie Anderson, "paradise is exactly like where you are right now—only much better." For, indeed, Bellamy's hero, Julian West, never leaves his Boston home. He merely goes to sleep in it—or, rather, in a soundproof chamber beneath it, which he has built as a haven from the bustle of the city that prevents him from sleeping—with the aid of a mesmerist who helps him treat his insomnia. The profound power of hypnotism keeps him in a sort of state of suspended animation until he awakes, Rip Van Winkle-like, 113 years later, in the year 2000, not a day older than when he first dozed. He soon learns that Boston, and, indeed, the entire society, has been fully socialized, and he is familiarized with this brave new world under the aegis of a Dr. Leete, who discovers him, and Dr. Leete's daughter, Edith. Julian spends some time becoming oriented to the fact that his new life in the future is not really a dream, and even once he assimilates this fact he actually does dream that he is back in the year 1887, bemoaning the myriad social ills attendant to the full-scale industrial capitalism of the era. He is awakened from this nightmare by Edith Leete, learns that she is actually the great-granddaughter of Edith Bartlett, who had been his fiancée in 1887, becomes engaged to her, and is installed in a university position as a lecturer in history so that they might live happily ever after into the twenty-first century.

It is the nightmare of Julian's reentrance into the nineteenth century that actually provides for the novel's transcendence of the standard representation of utopian bliss as a social impossibility, and transforms it into a novel of reform. By the time that Julian has this horrific vision, he—and the reader—has been thoroughly convinced of the superiority of twentieth-century society, so much so that, given the choice, he—and, again, the nineteenth-century reader—would clearly opt for the socialist state. It is this presentation of *choice* that characterizes Bellamy's novel as a reformist work, in that it implies that United States citizens must take the initiative if they hope to bring about the Edenic society *Looking Backward* depicts. This choice is made clear in an excerpt from a speech Bellamy gave on "Nationalism—Principles and Purposes," in Boston in 1889. As Caroline Ticknor, daughter of Bellamy's publisher remembered it, Bellamy addressed the issues of " 'Plutocracy and Nationalism,' expressing his belief that one, or the other, must be the choice of the American people at the end of ten years' time." As commentators have noted, however, *Looking Backward* is prevented from being a call for *revolution* through an aspect of Bellamy's philosophy that actually runs counter to this notion of choice—that is, his sense that his brand of socialism will be an *inevitable* evolutionary outcome of the capitalist development characteristic of the late nineteenth century. There is a contradiction here, then, but the two elements that constitute the paradox might alternately be seen as the means by which Bellamy's novel is made to fit the bounds of reform fiction.

It is worth noting, however, what happens to the conventions of the reform novel as identified thus far once Bellamy takes up the genre. Structurally, Bellamy's framing of his tale within the conventional plot of romantic marriage seems to recapitulate the strategy already identified as operative in the other works under discussion, whereby reform is constituted through the introduction of the consideration of the public good into the context of the private, domestic sphere. *Thematically*, however, this public/private dynamic is not played out nearly so forcefully as it is in the earlier works. Indeed, if it is true that Julian comes to a realization of the correctness of socialist principles right in his own home, it is equally true that his never stepping out of that home indicates a striking passivity in his relation to social reform—he, personally, never has to *do* anything, inside his home or out of it, in order to bring about social transformation. Thus *Looking Backward*, while using the domestic locale as a structural device in the narrative, actually evacuates that locale of any real political significance, and, consequently, reduces the significance of the feminist impulse that is implicit in the works by Stowe, Davis, and Phelps. *Looking Backward* actually effectively contains its feminism by dislocating it from a domestic space that is the primary stage for the novel's action, and in which concrete reformist activity takes place, and resituating it in the relatively more limited scope of a particular character in the story: the federal government of Bellamy's twentieth-century United States provides for one female elected official who works in the federal government—an official who has the authority to veto any legislation that concerns the well-being of women.

This dislocation of feminist politics within Bellamy's novel signals a parallel reconception of the reform fiction genre during the time of Bellamy's writing. Specifically, the domestic setting itself—which in the earlier fiction had been the locus within which any number of social concerns might be considered and acted upon, and thus implicitly linked with feminist politics—is by the 1880s reconceived as the locus specifically for the treatment of particular issues pertaining to women's social status. Thus feminism, rather than continuing to function as a fundamental guiding principle with respect to the reform activities depicted in social protest fiction, became instead merely one more issue among others, to be treated in individual works that focused on women's status in the domestic sphere. Works such as Kate Chopin's *The Awakening* (1899) and, especially, Charlotte Perkins Gilman's story "The Yellow Wallpaper" (1892)—which were not necessarily even considered as reform fiction at all, but rather as stories of personal complaint, until their resurrection in the late twentieth century—exemplify this emergent genre beautifully.

*The Awakening* provides what commentators have identified as a Whitmanesque portrayal of the evolution of a woman's sensual life and her concomitant rebellion against the restrictions of marriage through her abandonment of her husband and children and her attachment to a charming but licentious rogue. "The Yellow Wallpaper" depicts the plight of another young married woman whose physician husband has diagnosed her as suffering from hysterical nervousness and has prescribed a cure of complete inactivity and bedrest that frustrates her energetic character. Both Chopin's Edna Pontellier and Gilman's unnamed protagonist come to tragic ends: the former, overcome by the constraints of social convention, finally opts for release from her stifling situation by walking into the sea, which act represents both her death and her giving herself over to the sensuality for which she has developed such a passionate craving; the latter, baffled by the patriarchal rule that keeps her confined to her chamber and suppresses her creative impulses, becomes obsessed with decoding the pattern on the wallpaper that covers her room. She begins to see that pattern as representing a hunched, deformed, "creeping" woman struggling to escape from behind a series of bars that entraps her. As time goes on, she determines to get the woman free, and the story ends in a frenzied climax in which she maniacally strips large portions of the paper from the wall with her bare hands while her alarmed husband and sister-in-law try to reach her through the bedroom door, which she has locked. When they finally enter the room, the woman has gone completely mad, envisioning *herself* as the one who had been trapped in the yellow wallpaper, and who now "creeps" freely around the room, refusing ever to be put back into her prison.

These works are reformist insofar as they imply the need for change in the social conditions that constrain women to the detriment of their psychic well-being. Indeed, Gilman's work is a very specific indictment of the practices of Dr. S. Weir Mitchell, a Philadelphia physician (and novelist) of the time who became famous for developing the cure of enforced rest for "neurotic females," and under whose care Gilman herself was once placed by her well-meaning but paternalistic husband. At the same time, while the works by Gilman and Chopin graphically illustrate the difficulties women faced within the society about which they wrote, they do not explicitly outline programs for change that might be taken up by social reformers. This omission undoubtedly prevented these works from being perceived as serious reform fiction for decades, and facilitated their rejection by readers as the private idiosyncratic (and shocking) visions of their authors. But if the florescence of a vital feminist scholarship during the 1970s provoked readers to reassess the genre of sentimental fiction as a primary means by which the most pressing social and political issues of the day were taken under consideration, so too has it provided for a new conception of these two works as classics of political fiction, crucial to a full understanding of the turn-of-the-century literary depiction of United States social life.

In the meantime, female protagonists continued to represent the moral center of much reform fiction "proper" through the turn of the century. Just as Perley Kelso seeks a way, in *The Silent Partner*, to ameliorate the lives of the millhands of Five Falls, so too does Annie Kilburn, in the novel of that title by William Dean Howells (1889), seek the most effective way to uplift the masses from their degraded social level. Annie is the daughter of the late Judge Kilburn, with whom she had lived for eleven years in Rome, far from her home in the Massachusetts manufacturing town of Hatboro'. When she returns to New England, she is faced with a newly ascendant merchant class whose social agenda conflicts with the old aristocracy of which she is a member. This new bourgeoisie is represented by the shopkeeper, Mr. Gerrish, who clashes with the Reverend Mr. Peck about the latter's refusal to espouse a Christianity that conforms to capitalist ideology. When Peck's plan to leave Hatboro' for a ministry among the working classes in Fall River is thwarted by his sudden death in a train accident, Annie takes up his moral standard and works to establish the Peck Social Union. Even in this context, however, Annie's contributions amount to little, as she occupies herself with keeping the books for the organization rather than actually ministering directly to the needs of the working classes, a point that the narrative makes clear in a bitingly satirical reference to Annie's dwelling "in a vicious circle" in which she "mostly forgets, and is mostly happy."

The cul-de-sac in which Annie finds herself at novel's end typifies the irresolvable moral questions that Howells raises about the privileged individual's responsibility for the general social welfare. The reformist nature of Howells's work lies not in its clear depiction of what is to be done to remedy social inequalities but rather in its guiding assumption that such inequities are indeed the central moral problem of the era. This is clear in the majority of Howells's vast body of work, and certainly in the seven or so works of economic fiction he produced from 1885 through 1894, of which *Annie Kilburn* and *A Hazard of New Fortunes* (1890) are the most striking examples.

While Howells's fictions might themselves demur at providing specific prescriptions for the social ills they depict, they nonetheless emerge from very specific social and political contexts that shape their general themes. Just before beginning *Annie Kilburn*, Howells had announced his intention of bringing attention to the injustice of the hanging of four anarchist laborers after the Haymarket bombing in Chicago in 1886. While the novel has little to do with the actual historical occurrence or the specific issues related to it, in depicting Annie's haplessness at finding the proper means of exercising her conscience it does nonetheless underscore Howells's belief that what is at stake in the struggle of the workers is not charity, but justice. This conviction is laid out much more elaborately in the more complex *A Hazard of New Fortunes*, written right after *Annie Kilburn*.

Simply stated, *Hazard* expands on the ideological conflict represented in *Annie Kilburn* in the tension between Mr. Gerrish and the Reverend Mr. Peck. That conflict is centered, in the later novel, on the characters of Mr. Dryfoos, an Indiana farmer who has become a millionaire when natural gas is discovered on his land, and his son, Conrad, who wants to minister on behalf of industrial workers. Their conflict is played out through Mr. Dryfoos's founding of a new magazine, *Every Other Week,* for which he wants Conrad to become the publisher; at the same time, his two daughters desire to become situated within New York society after Dryfoos, his wife, and his children move there upon the founding of the journal. The actual day-to-day management of the magazine is undertaken by Basil March (who, with his wife Isabel, is actually the central character in the story)—who serves as its editor after having left an unsuccessful career in insurance in Boston—and the promoter, Fulkerson. The catalyst for the explicit eruption of the social tensions that underlie the relations among these characters is provided by the elderly Henry Lindau, a German socialist who is an old friend of Basil March's and who handles foreign correspondence for the magazine. At a dinner party Dryfoos holds to celebrate the success of the new journalistic venture, he and Lindau clash over politics with the result that Lindau is disassociated from the magazine. This scene prefigures the explicit break between the elder Dryfoos and his son, who forsakes the business of the magazine to work on behalf of the striking streetcar workers. During a riot between the strikers and the police, Conrad sees Mr. Lindau being beaten by an officer, and is killed by a stray bullet as he runs to the old man's aid. Lindau himself dies as a result of his injuries, unable to appreciate the elder Dryfoos's change of heart after his son's death. Broken by his loss, Dryfoos sells the magazine to March and Fulkerson, who foresee a prosperous future, and moves his family to France, where they settle in fairly well among Parisian society. This removal of the upwardly mobile family from the American context—and the accession of apparently more moderate parties to the position that they vacate—indicates the degree to which, by this time in the history of the reform novel, the domestic locus has ceased to serve as the prime site in which the transformation of social consciousness can occur, and has become, rather, the source of new converts to bourgeois ideology in the capitalist context.

This transition in the novelistic function of the family may well be linked to the rather less obviously didactic strategy that characterizes the work of Howells as opposed to that of, say, Stowe or Phelps. Howells's treatment of social division amongst the urban classes in *A Hazard of New Fortunes* was admired by the younger writer Hamlin Garland, who noted that "the author nowhere speaks in his own person, nowhere preaches, and yet the lesson is there for all who will read." In a novel that followed on the heels of Howells's *Hazard*, Garland attempted to do for the Midwestern farmer and the cause of agrarian reform what Howells had done for the rights of industrial workers.

From 1870 until the end of the century, United States farmers of the West and South were caught in a struggle with the industrial and financial centers of the East as the country's economic base shifted from agriculture to manufacture: the mechanization of farming produced glutted markets and low crop prices; the development of railroad monopolies provided for high transportation costs that farmers were hard pressed to meet; high interest rates and an inflated money market added to the farmers' financial burden; a series of natural disasters made the welfare of rural families uncertain from one moment to the next; immigration and the opening of public lands in the West to homesteading increased the size and diversity of the rural population to such an extent that it was difficult for them to meet on common social territory to address their concerns. These problems that United States farmers faced were taken up through a number of burgeoning mechanisms for protest, including the National Grange, the Greenback movement, and the Populist Revolt. It was the complicated interrelation of these various developments that Garland attempted to treat in *A Spoil of Office* (1892), which illustrates the intense interest in social reform that characterized his early career.

The plot of the novel is bifurcated into an early section (developed from an unfinished novel on the Grange movement) that traces the development of Bradley Talcott's career first as an Iowa farmhand, then as a farmers' advocate and state legislator; and a later section that portrays his life as a politician in Des Moines and Washington. The central moral issue in the story involves Bradley's temptation, once elected to political office, to surrender the populist ideals on which his career had been based and succumb to the relative comfort of his position, a fate from which he is saved by the energetic Ida Wilbur, a Grange lecturer whose commitment to and understanding of the reform movement are much deeper than his own. Their union in the story results in the symbolic birth of a newly energized populist movement that will continue its vital work at the end of the novel.

What is notable about *A Spoil of Office*, beyond what most critics agree is a flawed structure and a nonetheless extremely accurate historical depiction of agrarian revolt, is its explicit treatment of women's subjection as a primarily economic problem. In a church lecture that Ida gives on "The Real Woman-question," she emphasizes that feminism "is not a question of suffrage merely—suffrage is the smaller part of the woman-question—it is a question of equal rights. It is a question of whether the law of liberty applies to humanity or to men only. . . . The woman question is not a political one merely, it is an economic one. The real problem is the wage problem, the industrial problem. The real question is woman's dependence upon man as the bread-winner. As long as that dependence exists there will be weakness."

This position, which resembles orthodox Marxism's subsumption of all social inequality under the problem of class division within capitalism, characterized Garland's treatment of women's status in much of his early work, and the importance of his recognition of economics as a major factor in women's oppressed condition cannot be overlooked. At the same time, in works from 1894 and 1895, such as "The Land of the Straddle-Bug" and *Rose of Dutcher's Coolly,* Garland focused specifically on women's rights as a social as well as economic issue, thus broadening his treatment of that social movement—feminism—which had largely laid the framework for the development of reform fiction as we have come to know it since the turn of the century.

Throughout the period under consideration, much of the work of social reform continued to be performed by women of the likes of Ida Wilbur. During the 1860s and early 1870s, Anna Dickinson was extremely popular on the Lyceum lecture circuit, speaking on numerous topics, including feminism, the rights of immigrants, and union organizing. Carry Nation and Frances Willard led the temperance movement through the 1870s. During the 1890s, Ida B. Wells produced explicitly detailed articles and addresses outlining the atrocities of lynch law in the South. And Ida Tarbell raised before the reading public questions about the integrity of the leading capitalist institutions of the day; her "History of the Standard Oil Company," published in *McClure's Magazine* in 1902, exposed the corrupt practices of the Rockefeller empire, and launched "muckraking" journalism. The great specificity of Tarbell's piece was duplicated in Upton Sinclair's 1906 novel, *The Jungle,* which detailed the degraded life of immigrant workers in the Chicago stockyards and meatpacking houses. Influenced largely by Jack London's 1903 attack on capitalism and the class system, *People of the Abyss* (London would go on to write a further indictment of this system in his 1906 novel, *The*

*Iron Heel*), and by the techniques of Tarbell and fellow muckraker Lincoln Steffens, *The Jungle* represents the culmination of the social protest novel before its impulses became dispersed in the global developments leading to World War I and in the various strains of American literary modernism.

The central figure in *The Jungle* is Jurgis Rudkus, a Chicago stockyard worker originally from Lithuania. Along with his wife, Ona, whom he marries after they both arrive in Chicago, his father, and several members of Ona's family, Jurgis ekes out a living in the meatpacking industry. Their lives are a continual struggle to make ends meet, as they all have only the most tenuous hold on their jobs—which are themselves extremely dangerous—owing to their age or youth, their uncertain health, personal injury, and the vicissitudes of industrial management. Jurgis's father, Antanas, dies of consumption, which he develops in the cold dampness of the meatpacking plant. Ona's cousin, Marija, loses her stockyard job and the family income significantly diminishes. At this point, Jurgis, who is taking night-school classes in English, becomes an active member of the workers' union. The constant strain on the family resources takes a toll on Jurgis, however, and, with Ona having given birth to one child and pregnant with another, he takes to drink. Ona hopes to make money by prostituting herself to her plant supervisor, whom Jurgis assaults upon learning of the arrangement. The narrative moves rapidly through Jurgis's month in jail, the family's loss of their house, Ona's death in childbirth, and the death by drowning of their first son, culminating in Jurgis's stint as a migrant farmworker in the agricultural fields of the West. Upon returning to Chicago, he progresses through another succession of misfortunes, losing a job as a tunnel digger owing to an injury, begging for money on the street, returning to jail for attacking a saloonkeeper who tries to swindle him, working as a holdup man in Chicago's underworld, and, finally, returning to work as a scab in the meatpacking plant during a general strike. While there, he once again attacks Ona's former boss and, while subsequently fleeing the law, he comes upon Marija who is herself working as a prostitute. They are both thoroughly degraded now, until Jurgis hears a speech by a socialist organizer, after which he finds work in a hotel with a socialist manager, and begins a new and, finally, hopeful life.

This expectant ending, coming as it does at the end of a long string of personal calamities for Jurgis, suggests Sinclair's primary intention in writing *The Jungle:* he wanted to call public attention to the conditions in which Midwestern industrial workers lived, and to urge social activism as a means of ameliorating those conditions. Indeed, the graphic manner in which he depicts the meatpackers' experiences leaves no doubt as to the unjust conditions under which they labored. At the same time, though, what caught public attention about Sinclair's book was not so much the degraded condition of the workers' lives but rather the appalling practices of the meatpacking industry in its preparation of foods for market. Concern about sanitation in the industry led to the passage of the Pure Food Bill of 1907, which President Theodore Roosevelt signed into law; but *The Jungle* had little effect in raising public outcry about the treatment of the *workers* in the meatpacking industry.

There is an irony here, in addition to the obvious one about the unintended effect that Sinclair's effort had in the public arena. The age of the protest novel began with an effort by Harriet Beecher Stowe to introduce issues of public concern into the realm of private, domestic life so that the push for reform might be born at home. By and large, that strategy worked in the case of *Uncle Tom's Cabin,* and it was further developed by writers such as Rebecca Harding Davis and Elizabeth Stuart Phelps through the 1870s. When the domestic setting itself became displaced as the site in which novels depicted social transformation as originating, however, and when it became reconceived as the realm in which only certain issues pertaining to women were to be negotiated, the connection between private life and public concern became reformulated as well. Consequently, by the time that Upton Sinclair published *The Jungle,* in 1906, its effect was bound to be not that readers would come to understand the treatment of others in the realm of labor as a public disgrace that ought to become their private concern, but rather that they would become aware that the sanctity of their private domains, their very families, homes, kitchens, and dinner tables, ought to be protected through the mechanisms of public policy. The development of such regulation is, of course, itself a type of reform; and the logic of the reform novel over the course of the historical period under consideration demonstrates that the primary site of reform, like charity, is the home. The question that the age raises and leaves unanswered, however, is whether the home marks the beginning of any real social reform, or merely its end, and what is at stake in the difference.

Phillip Brian Harper

# Nation, Region, and Empire

The Civil War, noted Henry James in his 1879 study of Nathaniel Hawthorne, represented to many Americans a collective national fall into reality. No wonder a novel about that war, *Miss Ravenel's Conversion from Secession to Loyalty* (1867) by John William De Forest, has long been considered one of the first works of American realism. Praised for its starkly accurate battle scenes, the novel, however, has been damned for its excessively romantic frame. Yet both plots—of war and of love—work to the same end of national reunification, the cultural project that would inform a diversity of American fiction for the following three decades.

The novel rejects the romance of the Old South in the Louisianan heroine's misguided marriage to an older Virginian "gentleman," who though he fights for the Union, also drinks, spends, and loves too hard and too much. At his death, however, and with the heroine's final marriage to a young New Englander who has been toughened by battle, the novel reinscribes a new romance of national restoration. In the conversion of the title, the heroine does more than simply change sides and husbands; she weans herself from a fiercely local attachment to home—a quality identified as female—to a broader national allegiance. Finally, her Southern Loyalist father characterizes his home, with condescension and fondness, as barbaric, primitive, and childlike, and compares its inhabitants to Ashantees, Hottentots, Seminoles, Pawnees, Chinese, and cannibals. As a mineralogist, he maps the South as a peripheral undeveloped "region" or colony and views reunion as a matter of natural evolution.

De Forest also initiated the search for the "Great American Novel" in 1868, for which he nominated Harriet Beecher Stowe's *Uncle Tom's Cabin* (1852) as the only work with sufficient "national breadth" to link a wide spectrum of characters from different regions, races, and classes. (Not surprisingly, many post–Civil War novels, including his own, aspired to correct, negate, or expand upon Stowe, including works by Charles Chesnutt, Helen Hunt Jackson, Sutton Griggs, and Thomas Dixon.) Less sanguine about a post–Civil War novel achieving such broad dimensions, he saw two factors working against it: the sectional divisiveness that made the United States a "nation of provinces," and the rapid rate of social change. "Can a society which is changing so rapidly," he asked, "be painted except in the daily newspapers?" From a different angle, De Forest's obstacles to a national imagination have been viewed recently by Benedict Anderson as its building blocks. Anderson's useful understanding of nations as "imagined communities" posits their foundations on print culture, on the circulation of both newspapers and novels that unite diverse members, otherwise unknown to one another, through a shared sense of a present and of simultaneous participation in historical change. (It is well known that many authors of the late nineteenth century served their apprenticeship in journalism and continued to write in both modes.) De Forest and his contemporaries, however, found the shared present of their imagined community radically challenged by the immediate past that had nearly destroyed the nation, and that set the agenda for novelists of reimagining a community and rebuilding a nation.

To do so meant reimagining the past. "Forgetting," claimed the French philologist Ernest Renan in 1882, "is a crucial factor in the creation of a nation." He went on to state that "the essence of a nation is that all individuals have many things in common, and also that they have forgotten many things," largely the foundation of the nation in violent conflicts, invasions, or massacres. Yet Renan does not imply that nations therefore have no past and inhabit an eternal present, a misconception often applied to the United States, but that present collectivity depends on "possession in common of a rich legacy of memories," particularly of noble deeds and shared sacrifice. His reflections are particularly relevant to the pervasive memory of the Civil War, which writers and politicians actively "forgot" as mutual slaughter and rewrote as a shared sacrifice for reunion. Also forgotten and reinvented was the legacy of slavery and the questions it posed of a contested relation between national and racial identity.

In a period known for discovering contemporary social reality, writers were equally obsessed with the past, or with multiple pasts, largely of their own invention, whether the pre–Civil War South of Twain, Cable, Chesnutt, and others; the romanticized Revolutionary past; a mythologized medieval past of popular historical romances; island communities of regionalists, such as Jewett, Freeman, and Garland, that seemed to elude historical change; or the primitive past of the race imagined by naturalists, such as London and Norris. Much of this fiction expresses a Janus-faced nostalgia in which desire generated by a modern industrial society longingly projects alternatives onto the screen of the past, which refracts multiple images of the present back to itself. Novels traditionally identified with such different genres all enact a willed amnesia about founding conflicts, while they reinvent multiple and contested pasts to claim as the shared origin of national identity.

Another axis for late nineteenth-century novels lay in reimagining the shifting spatial contours of the nation, for the Civil War not only restored a familiar map but also opened new territory for expansion. History was inseparable from geography as well in Frederick Jackson Turner's famous address "The Significance of the Frontier in American History" at the World's Columbian Exposition of 1893 in Chicago, an icon of nationalization. In a period in which the United States was in the process of securing the continental borders that now define it, through a series of "forgotten" Indian wars, his speech voiced nostalgia for a past as well as anxiety about the bounded space of the future, and his argument was deployed on behalf of further United States expansion abroad. Turner defined the center of American "civilization" through its edges, its confrontations with the "primitive," at a time when new "Indians" were sought, at home and abroad, as "others" against which to imagine American nationhood. Many novels of the period explore past and present borders and frontiers to imagine a community through exclusion as much as inclusion.

What De Forest called "conversion," implying only one tenable resolution to the conflict, writers of the post-Reconstruction period called reconciliation or reunion, implying the transcendence of conflict. (Even in De Forest's novel, Southerner and Northerner fight on the same side.) This erasure of conflict from the legacy of the Civil War was performed by fraternal meetings of Union and Confederate veterans to commemorate former battle sites, and by publications such as *The Century*'s series, "Battles and Leaders of the Civil War," recounting the same battles from both sides to foster mutual respect. In addition to the war itself, the past of slavery needed reinterpretation as a shared legacy of North and South, rather than a history of violent contention spilling over into race relations in the present. To this end, in the 1880s and 1890s, the region De Forest called barbaric (which means foreign tongue) prolifically spoke for itself to the North in its major publications. Curiosity about Southern "local color" was inseparable from understanding its past, which often recast "the peculiar institution" of slavery in a romantic light. Yet this nostalgia that invented a palatable past for North and South was often double-edged and could turn against the present, exploring racism as a major legacy of the Civil War.

George Washington Cable's *The Grandissimes* (1880) directly addresses the issues of national and racial identity in the past and indirectly in the present in its epic story of an extended Creole family, whose white hero, Honoré, has a free mulatto half-brother of the same name. Set at the time of the Louisiana Purchase (1803), at the frontier of shifting national boundaries, the novel represents "America" as a foreign power speaking a foreign tongue. The native-born son of German immigrants, Frowenfeld, plays an interesting central role as outsider to the local community but representative of the nation. The Grandissimes undergo a conversion of sorts, by splitting into old and new. The die-hard slaveholding, dueling *citoyen* dies off (along with his part-Indian blood), and the white Honoré defies his aristocratic past by going into business with his mulatto half-brother, adopting English and allegiance to the nation, and marrying the victim of a former family feud. The novel rejects the explicit statement of an old era that "we the people" always means white, but makes that concept implicit in the new era. While business unites white and black, the love triangles of the novel demarcate the limits of imagining an interracial community: the mulatto Honoré is hopelessly in love with the beautiful and powerful ex-slave Palmyre, who loves his white brother; she was once married to an enslaved African king, Bras-Coupé, who she had hoped would lead an insurrection but who died imagining his return to Africa rather than be broken by slavery. The novel ends with the double marriages of two generations of white Creoles (the younger to Frowenfeld), and the exile of Honoré and Palmyre to Bordeaux, France (an echo of the exile of free African Americans in Stowe's novel). This end to the story of slavery mirrors the post-Reconstruction imagined community, where Cable, among others, argued for political equity for freed African Americans and social separateness. Palmyre remains outside the boundaries, however, unassimilated and threatening as the repository of "forgotten" memory and desire, tying the 1880s to 1803, in a palimpsest of earlier histories of massacres, Indian origins, and slave ships.

Reviewers tried to limit Cable to "local color" writing in order to separate geography from history and its resonance in the present, and they linked him unfairly with Thomas Nelson Page's invention of the "plantation tradition," which overtly romanticized slavery in *In Ole Virginia* (1887), a collection of dialect stories narrated by a faithful ex-slave who reminisces nostalgically about "dem good ole times." With Page, critics also joined Joel Chandler Harris's famous collections of Uncle Remus stories, which have a more double-edged effect. They participate in the nostalgic recuperation by framing slave stories in the voice of an elderly black "uncle" entertaining a white boy, but the stories themselves often speak in the subversive voice of a popular oral tradition that provided a cultural source of resistance to slavery and racism in the past and the present.

Charles Chesnutt's *The Conjure Woman* (1899) most fully exploits the multivocal potential of the dialect tale to turn the plantation tradition against itself. He frames stories told by ex-slave Uncle Julius with two conventions: the white Northern narrator and his wife who have bought an old plantation for both economic development and a bucolic retreat, and a marriage at the end between a

Northern and Southern young couple, whose reconciliation Julius's story facilitates. His stories, however, subtly subvert the plantation tradition to reinscribe its willfully "forgotten" history of slavery's brutal violence and slave resistance. As conjuring becomes a rich metaphor for storytelling as historical memory, Julius links the de-romanticized past with the present reenslavement of blacks. The first tale, "The Goophered Grapevine" (which launched Chesnutt's career in the *Atlantic Monthly*), undoes the Northern romance of the Southern garden by exposing natural cycles under the institution of slavery as inseparable from economic exploitation and dehumanization. In the second story, "Po' Sandy," the history of severed slave bodies is inscribed in the haunted houses of the present, in the very wood that the Northern family wishes to use for a new kitchen. Chesnutt re-charts the projection of an exotic and romantic Southern landscape as a palimpsest of destruction linking the past to the present. The final story reconciles the white lovers through the narration of sla-very's destruction of a black couple, which exposes the broader na-tional allegory of reconciliation through marriage that is founded on the expulsion of blacks from the national family in the Jim Crow laws of the New South.

Like Cable and Chesnutt, Mark Twain reinvents the prewar South in *The Adventures of Huckleberry Finn* (1885) and *Pudd'nhead Wilson* (1894) to interrogate the present. By shifting Huck Finn's nar-rative journey from Northbound to Southbound, from freedom to further enslavement, from Jim's agency as an escaped slave to Tom's antics to set a free man free, Twain is doubling past and present, North and South, to question the meaning of freedom for African Americans and the nation at large in the aftermath of Reconstruction. Twain's devastating satire of all levels of Southern society "debunks" the romantic fictions the South tells about itself (though even his famous attack on the Sir Walter Scott disease as a cause of war here and in *Life on the Mississippi* [1883] tends to externalize an internal conflict as one between real Americans and pseudo-Europeans, thus contributing to the drama of reunion).

*Huckleberry Finn* is best remembered by readers for imagining an interracial community between Huck and Jim on the raft in the mid-dle of the Mississippi—a subject of multiple interpretations and crit-icisms. The powerful appeal of this vision far outstrips its fragile and fleeting appearance in the text, for the raft is continually threatened, run over, and invaded by the world of the shore it aims to escape. The problematic ending of the novel has a nightmarish logic in culminating the journey toward reenslavement. Jim, the legally free man, is enslaved in Tom's romantic novels and the town's racist fears, and Huck, after choosing to "go to hell" against his community and help Jim escape, is reborn as Tom Sawyer. The ending could be seen as a macabre parody of Reconstruction with Jim happily accepting forty dollars from Tom for his "trouble" (instead of forty acres and a mule?), and Huck lighting out for the territory ahead of the rest, to the "forgotten" history of white settlement and Native American displacement.

The dependence of racism and slavery on the power of social fictions at the end of *Huckleberry Finn* sets the starting point for the nightmarish playacting of *Pudd'nhead Wilson,* which interestingly echoes Cable's novel. Cable's doubling of the Honorés as the visible genealogy of slavery turns into Twain's switch of the white and black babies who are visibly indistinguishable. The imperial figure of Palmyre turns into the devilish mother-trickster, Roxana, who threatens the social hierarchy with her switching of babies, but who obeys her own son as her master and endorses the "fact and fiction of law" that declares one baby black and the other white according to an invisible "drop of blood." While in Cable the immigrant represents "America," he is split in Twain into the real American, Wilson, and the more alien Italian twins, reflecting the nativist fear of immigrants in this period. A ridiculed outsider at first, Wilson becomes an insider at the end, when he uses fingerprints—which he compares revealingly to a map—to uncover the "facts" of racial identity and to right the hierarchy that Roxana threatened. Wilson's legal and professional authority has been likened to the role of the Supreme Court in endorsing the imposition by states of the "separate but equal" doctrine in *Plessy* v. *Ferguson.* Although set in the prewar South, Twain's plot of national restoration imagines Wilson's incorporation into the community as a reunion between North and South at the expense of selling African American rights down the river, back into slavery. Even the problematic invisibility of race resonates with post–Civil War—rather than antebellum—anxiety about the threat of an interracial community as American nationality.

Registering the same hysteria about racial intermixing, Thomas Dixon resolves Twain's unsettling ambivalence about race as a "fiction of law or custom" in his unabashedly racist and popular novels, *The Leopard's Spots* (1902) and *The Clansman* (1905), the basis for D. W. Griffith's landmark movie, *The Birth of a Nation* (1915). Dixon's historical romances reinvent the Civil War and the downfall of Reconstruction as the story of the reunification of a white nation. His first novel plots the end of Reconstruction as a second Revolutionary war (in the town Independence) of whites against black dominance. The novel is punctuated by the repeated anxious refrain: "Shall the future American be an Anglo-Saxon or a Mulatto." The obvious answer is offered by the eruption of two events: the threatened rape of a white girl by a black man and the Spanish-American War. The war does for the nation what the rape does for the small town, fusing former secessionists and unionists, rich and poor, Protestant and Catholic, into one "homogeneous white mass." The connection between domestic racial conflict and international imperialism is made clear by the subtitle, "A Romance of the White Man's Burden."

Dixon's next novel carries this burden back in time to the Civil War and widens its national scope to imagine the birth of a nation from the rape of a white woman by a black man that spawns the rise of the Ku Klux Klan. Dixon's racist caricatures rescue the romance of the white South by a kind of splitting that projects the negative stereotypes of Southern shiftlessness, barbarism, superstition, childishness, and violence (seen in De Forest) onto African Americans. This splitting allows for the national reunion in a double marriage of white couples from the North and the South. As in the *The Grandissimes* and *Pudd'nhead Wilson*, the fate of the most threatening character, Lydia, the politically and sexually domineering mulatto mistress of the evil Reconstructionist (who himself is reconstructed as white at the end), remains unresolved. These mulatto figures exiled to the border of the imagined community—but not killed off—represent the "forgotten" history of slavery founded in the white rape of the black woman that cannot be totally erased from the national plot of reunion.

While the Spanish-American War sews up Dixon's plot of national restoration by bringing together the Gray and the Blue on distant shores, the war has the opposite effect in the plot of black national unification in Sutton Griggs's less well known *Imperium in Imperio* (1899). Here the presence of the mulatto as the visible history of slavery is as threatening to the romance of black nationalism as it is to Dixon's white supremacism. The novel depicts the organization of an underground black nation, founded to fill the constitutional gaps and to protect and enfranchise African Americans. When the war breaks out, concurrent with heinous cases of lynching, the Imperium is destroyed by discord between those who wish to join the United States in supporting Cuba's "largely Negro" revolution and those who wish to bring the revolution home. The radical voice of the founder (the son of a white senator) prevails and convinces the Imperium to launch a new Civil War by siding with America's foreign enemies and then claiming Texas as a separate state. The more moderate President of the Imperium, of humble black roots, urges that they remain in the Union to fight for full citizenship with the pen rather than the sword. Overruled, he willingly submits to execution, pledging his double allegiance to the laws of the Imperium and those of the United States and is buried with an American flag. The marriage plots as vehicle to national unity are also thwarted in the novel, as the lover of the radical founder commits suicide rather than marry a mulatto and contribute to the degeneration of the race, while the moderate President leaves his wife when his newborn baby appears to be white, only to discover just before his execution that the baby darkened as he grew. Narrated by a traitor to the Imperium in the interest of averting the violence of a race war, Griggs's novel leaves African Americans in a no-man's-land of national identity between patriotism and treason.

Though both Griggs and Dixon create extreme political fantasies, they highlight an important intersection in the 1890s between domestic racial strife and the acquisition of an overseas empire in Cuba and the Philippines. Dixon voiced a common welcome of the Spanish-American War as a final destination on the road to reunion between North and South at the expense of African Americans. In the new frontier of the empire, the nation could be reimagined as Anglo-Saxon in contrast to the inferior races of Cubans and Filipinos, who were identified with African Americans at home and considered equally incapable of self-government. This identification supported contradictory positions: the imperialist acceptance of Rudyard Kipling's position in his poem "A White Man's Burden" (which was written to urge the United States annexation of the Philippines); the Southern opposition to imperialism in order to keep nonwhites out of the republic; and African American identification of revolutionary anticolonial struggles abroad. W. E. B. Du Bois linked domestic and colonial racial oppression in his prescient declaration in *The Souls of Black Folk* (1903), originally written for the first Pan-African Congress: "the problem of the twentieth century is the problem of the color-line." Theodore Roosevelt, whose *The Strenuous Life* (1900) bequeathed a title for the decade, subordinated race to manliness as the common bond of national restoration. Proven on the battlefield and tried in the assumption of colonial rule, American manhood forges the bond that transcends social conflict and turns a former divided nation into a reunited global power.

Stephen Crane's *The Red Badge of Courage* (1895) links the cultural interpretation of the Civil War and the Spanish-American War as two stages in the plot of national reunion. This might seem strange to say of a novel by a twenty-three-year-old written thirty years after the first war and three years before the next war, which he would report at first hand. Crane's novel is also considered less ideological than iconoclastic, one of "enormous repudiations," as H. G. Wells said, which would lead many to agree with Ernest Hemingway that it was "the only real literature of our Civil War." Yet Crane is a master of forgetting: the novel radically divorces the Civil War from its historical context by parodying the conventional reinterpretations of the war through the frameworks of reunion, slavery, or romance. Yet this parody of convention does not merely open up the reality of the battlefield but revises the Civil War through the framework of the heightened militarization of the 1890s. The novel looks back at the Civil War to map a new arena in which modern forms of international warfare can be imaginatively projected. Divorced from a prior political context, the novel focuses on the construction of manhood in war, and while it parodies the romance *Bildungsroman* in which the private, Henry Fleming, reads himself, it reconstitutes manhood on the battlefield as a theatrical performance separate from confrontation with a largely invisible enemy but dependent on the eyes of the spectator. Crane's representation of war as a spectacle both adopts and subverts Roosevelt's interpretation of the battlefield as a crucible for redeeming primal virility; Fleming's constant need for an audience destabilizes the identity of the "real man" by exposing it as a social construction. The transformation of the representation of war from the narration of conflict into an exotic spectacle was to provide Crane with a lens for reporting real battles in Cuba. It is not surprising that a headline in Joseph Pulitzer's *New York World* reporting the first major battle of the Spanish-American War read: THE RED BADGE OF COURAGE WAS HIS WIG-WAG. The mass circulation journalism of the 1890s not only created a shared domestic present chronicling the sensations of everyday life (as De Forest and Benedict Anderson would have it) but also made possible the projection of larger-than-life images of a renewed American manhood fighting "Indian" wars on remote frontiers of what Brooks Adams dubbed the "New Empire."

At the end of an annual picnic for the extended family around Dunnet's Landing, in Sarah Orne Jewett's *The Country of the Pointed Firs* (1896), the narrator comments: "Perhaps it is the great national anniversaries which our country has lately kept, and the soldiers' meetings that take place everywhere, which have made reunions of every sort the fashion." Jewett here links two public arenas often considered separate or even antagonistic, the national and the local. Indeed, it might be difficult to imagine a fictional space more distant from the national drama of men on the battlefield than the isolated, largely female-dominated rural communities of Jewett, Mary E. Wilkins Freeman, and Hamlin Garland. Just as these communities appear prenational, they take fictional forms that seem prenovelistic, consisting mostly of collections of short stories often incorporating vernacular storytelling and lacking overarching linear narratives. Yet the provincialism De Forest lamented as blocking a national novel, William Dean Howells celebrated thirty years later as "our decentralized literature." Paradoxically, this profusion of literature known as regionalism or local color contributed to the process of centralization or nationalization, as Jewett recognized by linking family and national reunions in the same passage as forms of "Clanishness," which she calls "an instinct, or a custom; and lesser rights were forgotten in the claim to a common inheritance." The decentralization of literature contributes to solidifying national centrality by reimagining a distended industrial nation as an extended clan sharing a "common inheritance" in its imagined rural origins.

The celebration of regional difference has several contradictory functions in the national agenda of reunion. On the one hand, regionalist fiction expands the boundaries of the imagined community and democratizes access to literary representation, which can be heard in the multivocal introduction of the vernacular through the dialect of different regions. On the other hand, regionalism contained the threatening conflicts of social difference, just as dialect itself bracketed the speaker as uneducated and inferior to the urban narrator with his standard English. This hierarchy structured the conditions of literary production for regionalist writers as well, who were published by a highly centralized industry located in Boston and New York that appealed to an urban middle-class readership; this readership was solidified as an imagined community by consuming images of rural "others" as both a nostalgic point of origin and a measure of cosmopolitan development. By rendering social difference in terms of region, anchored and bound by separate spaces, more explosive social conflicts of class, race, and gender made contiguous by urban life could be effaced. The native inhabitants of regional fiction could be rendered, on the one hand, as "the folk," the common heritage from which urban dwellers had simply moved, always available for return. Even regionalists like Garland, known for depicting the punishing conditions of a squalid Midwestern farm life, still excavated this folkish figure from the social rubble when, for example, he identifies a veteran returning to his farm as Walt Whitman's "common American soldier." Ironically, the commonality of the folk here is mediated through literature. In contrast to this rooted national identity, regional inhabitants could also be rendered as exotically other, with the quaint and strange customs and speech of New Orleans Creoles, for example, painted with the luster of empire. Their exoticism makes them more familiar and less threatening than the feared flood of immigrants whose foreignness lay too close for comfort in an urban context.

At the World's Columbian Exposition where Turner identified the frontier as the fundamental Americanizing influence, Garland, in his lecture "Local Color in Fiction," propounded regionalism as an indigenous movement, undefiled by artificial foreign influence, as though Turner's receding frontier could be dispersed and frozen in timeless island communities. Although Garland claimed that "the tourist could not write the local novel," tourists did and could read local color fiction, which, after all, could not be read by the people it depicted. Like the subjects of anthropological fieldwork (developing as a scientific discipline in this period), native inhabitants possessed primitive qualities that made them worthy of study also and left them in need of interpretation by outsiders. Regionalism performs a kind of literary tourism in a period that saw the tourist abroad and at home as a growing middle-class phenomenon; tourism was no longer limited to the grand tours of the upper class. Regionalists share with tourists and anthropologists the perspective of the modern urban outsider who projects onto the native a pristine authentic space immune to historical changes shaping their own lives. If historical novels invent pasts, regionalists invent places as allegories of desire generated by urban centers. Yet the reader of regionalism often finds less the nostalgic escape desired than a contested terrain with a complex history that ties it inseparably to the urban center.

America's best-known regionalist, Mark Twain, started his career with an immensely popular parody of the American tourist in Europe and the Middle East, *The Innocents Abroad* (1869). One of the multiple meanings of "innocence" is the tendency of tourists to sever a place from its historical context by literally ripping off specimens and souvenirs as fetishes. Yet their violent innocence makes them vulnerable to the social context they efface. This double "innocence" of the tourist is dramatized within regional fiction by the figure of the outsider: in Jewett's unnamed urban narrator in search of a quiet retreat where she can meet her publishing deadline; in Mary Murfree's amateur archaeologist of *In the "Stranger People's" Country* (1891); in Hamlin Garland's young men returning home from the city or the war in *Main-Travelled Roads* (1891); and most often in the narrator who comments on, interprets, and translates the life of the natives to an urban audience.

In many cases the "region" first appears as the projection of a desire for a space outside of history, untouched by change, but this projection is always challenged by a counter story and a prior history. Jewett's narrator is disappointed to find her hoped-for retreat at Mrs.

Todd's too noisy, too cluttered with a complex society and social intercourse, so she retreats farther to the isolated schoolhouse to write. But she ends up abandoning her writing in order to adopt the role of listener and participant, which cedes to the local the authority to define itself through its vernacular history, conversation, natural rhythms. Yet this movement from outsider to insider oversimplifies Jewett's complex narrative, which charts a struggle between the inhabitants, who have a highly particularized cosmopolitan view of their own history based on international trade, and the narrator, whose desire it is to turn Dunnet's Landing into a place both outside history and at the origin of human history. She sees eternal childhood in the aging inhabitants, in whose lives she finds vestiges of ancient Greek myths and Norman conquerors. In these premodern analogies she can posit a common inheritance, more ennobling than the alternative view of the countryside she momentarily grasps as "a narrow set of circumstances [that] had caged a fine able character and held it captive." Yet to view the rural life as entrapping, as do Garland and Freeman, is not simply more realistic than idealizing it; such a response could also be seen as the projection of the outsider's desire to view his or her life as less confining, more sophisticated and "adult." Tourists, after all, do go home.

Most regional fiction that posits a still timeless island community is characterized paradoxically by restlessness and motion, by the repeated acts of escape and return that frame many of Garland's stories and that produce the sense of a settled space. In "God's Ravens," an overworked and underpaid city newspaperman moves to the country in search of regeneration, only to find an oppressively narrow small town. When he falls sick, the community rallies to his side, and he comes to appreciate its truly human generosity beyond his own caricature. Only his illness and delirium, however, can conjure this idealized image.

In response to the complexity of place, which never remains outside historical time, the regionalist often projects a more distant remote retreat. Twain dramatizes this dynamic in *Roughing It* (1872), which starts with an escape to the West, to the "new and strange," and repeats this movement again from the West to the farther West of Hawaii, which appears at first as a kind of Eden, defined simply in terms of the absence of San Francisco's complexity. But very soon the Edenic landscape of the most remote islands is shown to be inscribed by the history of colonial conquest, a history itself subject to prior political struggle over interpretation, as the monument to Captain Cook demonstrates.

Other texts in less extreme ways enact this movement of receding retreat to the more remote primitive spaces. Jewett's narrator not only looks farther back in time for analogies in which to cast the native inhabitants but also restlessly seeks more remote islands to explore, as though Dunnet's Landing has become a stifling center with its own periphery, whether in the folksy domestic Green Island, or the more exotic island of Joanna, who is compared to a medieval nun. Lafcadio Hearn also depicts this infinite regression in *Chita* (1889), where he moves from Grand Isle to more isolated islands, only to show that none could escape either the devastating storm or the historical devastation of the Civil War, and that the reunion with the past, in the father's longing for his missing daughter, is tantalizingly close but never achieved. Hearn's career enacted this restless motion structuring regionalism, as he moved from writing of the Gulf of Mexico coast to the French Caribbean of colonial times, and finally to Japan, where he could imagine time and space meeting in his discovery of "fairy-folk" of childlike charm and simplicity, the subject that made his career as the best-known popularizer of Japanese culture. Domestic regions are often doubled with more remote colonial spaces.

Kate Chopin has rightfully been removed by feminist critics from the confines of local color in which she made her career. Yet even *The Awakening* (1899) uses local color tradition against itself. Edna Pontellier, as the outsider to Creole culture, projects onto this highly hierarchical confining culture her own desire for sensuality and freedom, and she seeks more remote exotic retreats from Grand Isle to the fairy-tale-like acadian island, and ultimately to the sea. Yet her novel was so scandalous to reviewers because of its sexual frankness and also, as with later work of Chesnutt and Cable, because it deployed the local periphery to cast a critical eye on the national center in a critique of the social oppression that linked region and nation.

Mary E. Wilkins Freeman, in her stories and in her novel *Pembroke* (1894), stayed within domestic regional boundaries while subverting them as centers of social protest. Deromanticizing small-town

New England, she exposes its oppressive denial of mobility and independence to women in its class stratification that controls even the remote village through its elders, its church, and collective gossip. Women protest their confining conditions and assert their independence, often paradoxically by denying desire and transforming their denial into creative power, as in "A New England Nun," or by turning traditionally confining spaces into centers of power, as in "The Revolt of 'Mother' " and "A Church Mouse." In *Pembroke,* a young man and woman defy their parents and their oppressive community by denying and deferring their desire for one another; while their final reunion seems to attest to the redemptive power of love, it is unleashed, ironically, by their capitulation to communal disapproval.

Eliding the inescapable social tensions that structure the growth from childhood to adulthood in Freeman's communities, Jewett's narrator recovers in Dunnet's Landing the common "instincts of a far forgotten childhood," thus linking the New England family picnic to the rites of ancient Greeks. This sense of the region as a space where a collective childhood can be recovered pervades literature of the West as well. Forerunners of Garland, such as Edward Eggleston in *The Hoosier Schoolmaster* (1871), Edgar Watson Howe in *The Story of a Country Town* (1884), and Joseph Kirkland in *Zury* (1887), are known for contrasting the idealized vision of the West, as a site that develops rugged individual virtues, with the more squalid reality of violence, economic oppression, and narrow provincialism. Most of them, including Garland in his *Boy Life on the Prairie* (1899), seek another more romantic retreat from this West in their depiction of the life of boys. In contrast to the exploitation of child labor that Garland calls attention to in "The Lion's Paw," novels and autobiographies were popular that represented the West as an arena of perpetual boyhood, where gangs of boys do little but play cowboys and Indians. Nostalgia for pre–Civil War innocence comes together with a scientific view of childhood as an earlier stage of evolutionary development; as G. Stanley Hall put it, "the child revels in savagery."

In this formulation, the boyhood of white settlers comes to displace the history of Indian settlement, a story that underlies Twain's *Adventures of Tom Sawyer* (1876). There Tom's famous stunt where he turns the work of whitewashing into boy's play might symbolize this dynamic of rendering the whitewashing of a community founded on racial conflict as child's play. For Twain's complex vision of children makes them both innocent of social ideology and repositories of it. Like the island communities outside urban centers, childhood is colonized by adult desire for a pristine past prior to social indoctrination, which is exposed as impossible. Tom's childish desire for heroism takes concrete social form in a court of law where he exposes Injun Joe as the real murderer of the doctor (much like Pudd'nhead's final revelation of racial identity). Escaping the courts, Joe meets a natural punishment, suffocated by the same cave where Tom finds money and flirts with his male sexuality. The earth that swallows the Indian turns the white boy into a man, while allowing him to remain perpetually a youth by rendering his entry into the economic system as the discovery of buried treasure.

Thus regionalism in its many forms both fosters and thwarts the desire for a retreat from modern urban society to a timeless rural origin, the "common inheritance" of the clan. The regions painted with "local color" are traversed by the forgotten history of racial conflict with prior regional inhabitants, and are ultimately produced and engulfed by the centralized capitalist economy that generates the desire for retreat.

Both the desire for and the impossibility of escaping the changes wrought by modern industrial capitalism propel the narrative of Twain's *A Connecticut Yankee in King Arthur's Court* (1889). The richness and the contradictions of the novel open the text to a multivalent allegory of almost every aspect of late nineteenth-century American society. The novel can be read as an allegory of reconstruction and colonialism, as it conflates the genres of regionalism and the historical novel (which Twain contributes to without irony in *Personal Recollections of Joan of Arc* [1896]). *Connecticut Yankee* plays out its double meaning in the drama of national reunion: in relation to internal regions, it refers to Hank Morgan's Northern background and makes him a kind of carpetbagger, eradicating the last vestiges of slavery and modernizing King Arthur's "southernized" England. But *Connecticut Yankee* also represented a collective national identity to those outside America's borders and subject to its power. An island at once outside of time and at the origins of history, King Arthur's England appears as the ultimate primitive col-

ony, or region, with inhabitants who are compared to children, Indians, barbarians, bound by superstition, violence, and laziness.
Knocked over the head as a foreman in an industrial dispute at home,
Morgan, by becoming "Boss" of Camelot, gains the power he lacked
at home. Like other colonists, he imagines the island as a backward
blank slate on which he can create a utopian image of nineteenth-
century capitalism, freed of its threatening conflicts. Like other imagined timeless islands, this one, however, clings tenaciously to its own
history and culture in order to resist or assimilate his projections of
development. The tension informing Morgan's project of reform, between modernization as social change and modernization as social
control, leads to the violent confrontation of cultures, both the source
of humor in this diabolically funny book and the source of the final
massacre. Whether resonant of the Civil War, Indian wars, or class
conflict, or prescient of mass twentieth-century destruction (all seen
by critics), the final massacre of the knights, paradoxically both
Hank's victory and his defeat, represents the foundational violence
that must be "forgotten" in order to imagine a nation, sixth-century
England's natural evolution into America. Hank's destruction of
Camelot tellingly spawns his nostalgia for the "lost land" he has
destroyed. *Connecticut Yankee* sounds Twain's death knell for expanding United States frontiers abroad, which end up reproducing or
magnifying the social conflicts at home they sought to alleviate.

Yankees abroad conquering lands remote both in time and in
space were not unusual in fiction of the 1880s and 1890s; in fact,
these heroes were the staple of the popular historical romance, from
*Ben-Hur* (1880) to *The Virginian* (1902). Dismissed by literary historians as escapist, these narratives of escape echo the political argument for overseas expansion in this period. Leaving his overcivilized surroundings for adventure in a primitive arena, the hero (an
overt or thinly disguised American) fights theatrical swashbuckling
battles to liberate a backward realm from its threatening barbaric
enemies, subdues and wins the love of an aristocratic heroine, rejuvenates his own masculinity, and finally returns home to the corporate commercial world he escaped. This formula is strikingly pliable
to vastly different settings, from imperial Rome, to Latin American
republics, to European history, to mythological medieval kingdoms,
to colonial America, and finally to the West. In the national project

of reinventing origins, these works colonize the past as allegories that turn national reunification into empire building.

Vying with *Uncle Tom's Cabin* as the all-time best-seller of the nineteenth century was Lew Wallace's *Ben-Hur,* which reached the height of its popularity on stage and in print in the 1890s (a text in need of the kind of critical attention recently paid to Stowe's novel in its cultural context). The novel appealed to the fascination with origins, and it reinvented a most important originary moment, the birth of Christian civilization out of the ruins of the Roman Empire. Yet rather than focus on the saintly life of Christ, the novel spends most of its time on a hero who is confused about whether he is fighting a material battle for a new earthly kingdom of the Jews or a spiritual one for an unknown messiah. Fortunately, he does not have to decide until the end of the novel after he wins the climactic chariot race (as well known in the 1890s from its repeated staging in lavish outdoor spectacles as it is today from the film versions). What does this have to do with American culture in the period? The New Kingdom of Christ—anti-imperial in its origins—might allegorize and spiritualize the imagined New American Empire, which was propounded by ideologues such as A. T. Mahan and the Reverend Josiah Strong at least a decade before the Spanish-American War. They imagined American global power as anti-imperial in nature and not territorially based, but depending instead on international commerce and the spread of United States cultural institutions. Popular at a time of heightened militarism and the movement of "muscular Christianity," *Ben-Hur* highlights virile body-building in the service of a spiritual global empire. The book also would have appealed to interest in the origins of slavery, as well as to curiosity about the exotic distant ancestors of more recent Italian and Jewish immigrants, ancestors who were superseded by the Christian civilization to which Ben-Hur finally converts as an apostle. Lew Wallace, a veteran of the Mexican War, a Union general in the Civil War, and governor of the territory of New Mexico, lived a career that followed the Westward Course of Empire. His first popular historical novel, *The Fair God* (1873), treated the Spanish conquest of Mexico (à la Prescott), a lens through which he would view the Christian conquest of Rome. No wonder President James Garfield appointed him minister to Turkey as an expert on "the East."

In the courts of Constantinople, Lew Wallace lived the life a younger writer, Richard Harding Davis, was famous for writing about in his novels of high society and colonial adventures. While Ben-Hur conquered Rome, Davis's hero of *Soldiers of Fortune* (1897), a dashing American mercenary and civil engineer, triumphed over the decaying British and Spanish Empires to save a fictional Latin American republic from dictatorship and revolution, and to marry an athletic "New Woman" whose father owns the mines there. In the abundance of best-selling romances around the time of the Spanish-American War, Davis's backward but alluring republic of Olancho was easily interchangeable with Tudor England, in Charles Majors's *When Knighthood Was in Flower* (1898), or with the mythical medieval principality of George Barr McCutcheon's *Graustark* (1901), all sites where playful physical virility represents aggressive national muscle-flexing abroad. In all of these fantasies, the hero can rejuvenate an authentic American self only outside United States borders in the new frontiers abroad.

The revival of the historical romance culminated in the proliferation of best-sellers about the colonial period and the American Revolution, such as Winston Churchill's *Richard Carvel* (1899), S. Weir Mitchell's *Hugh Wynne, Free Quaker* (1897), Paul Leicester Ford's *Janice Meredith* (1899), Mary Johnston's *To Have and to Hold* (1900). These novels participate in the mass cultural invention of national traditions along with the writing of the pledge of allegiance, the establishment of flag ceremonies in schools, and the rise of genealogical societies such as the Daughters of the American Revolution. These novels rewrite the American Revolution to underplay political conflict with Britain and to unite the two countries in a uniquely Anglo-Saxon heritage of manliness. The novels whitewash the Revolution as an exclusive inheritance against both the influx of immigrants aspiring to national identity and the claims of colonial subjects, such as the Cubans and Filipinos, to revolution and self-government.

Owen Wister's popular novel *The Virginian* takes its immediate genealogy from the popular historical novel of the 1890s and its romance of empire. Wister sees the cowpuncher as the direct linear descendant of the Anglo-Saxon knight, and by imagining contemporary American imperialism as the return to an original virile past the historical romance reopens the closed frontier and reinvents the West as a space for fictional representation. The West, furthermore, becomes the site for uniting South and North, in the courtship and marriage of the unnamed Virginian to the Vermont schoolteacher (herself with a Revolutionary genealogy). Wister's West expunges traces of Native Americans, while the Virginian takes on characteristics of the noble savage without tinting his essential Anglo-Saxon identity. The West also rejuvenates the overcivilized East, as one of the most erotically charged relationships in the novel is the narrator's attraction to the Virginian's natural virility. Like a regionalist narrator, he escapes from the overheated clubs of New York City and projects his desire onto the "handsome ungrammatical son of the soil." Yet the Virginian does grow up, a fact lamented by many readers, including Henry James. He combines not only natural aristocratic civility with democratic violence but also rugged individualism with obedience to his employer, a large landowner. The Virginian protects his property by controlling his unruly workers with a tall tale, leading a vigilante lynching of his friend (a figure for his younger self), and shooting the villain Trampas. The romance of lawless frontier violence is ironically a means of forgetting the history of the West as a political conflict over the land among Indians, homesteaders, and large ranchers, and of reinventing it as a place for the righteous punishment of criminals. The Virginian grows up at the end to become a prosperous landowner and a domesticated husband, but the novel projects for readers the counter-homoerotic plot of reunion, where the West remains as a perpetual melting pot of boys from farms and cities of all regions: "the romance of American adventure had drawn them all alike to this great playground of young men," where they never grow up.

Wister's romance renders Native Americans invisible except for their traces in the white bodies they leave wounded. Fifteen years earlier Helen Hunt Jackson's *Ramona* (1884) employed the plot of romance to make visible the forgotten plight of Indians in the American Southwest. Set right after the Mexican War, the novel presents the American nation, as it is in Cable's book, as a foreign occupier in California, where Spanish landowners and native Indians are equally dispossessed by aggressive American settlement. Indians, represented by the hero Alessandro, occupy either a natural primitive innocence outside of history or a culture completely absorbed by the exotic Spanish mission. Alessandro marries Ramona, who is half-Indian and half-Scot, and who was raised by a Spanish family whose imperious mother detested her and whose timid son ineffectually adored her. When she elopes with Alessandro, she returns to the roots she never knew and follows Alessandro's inevitable decline and banishment from the town of his father and every subsequent home, until in a state of insanity he accidentally takes the wrong horse of a white man and is shot as a horse thief. Like Stowe, to whom she was positively compared, Jackson effectively chronicles the abuse of Indians at the hands of the Spanish, the American settlers, and government bureaucracy, but she cannot imagine Native American agency except as insanity. Ramona is redeemed by the motherly love of Aunt Ri, a folksy dialect figure from the passages of local color, a real American, and by her final marriage to her adopted brother, Felippe, who takes her and Alessandro's daughter to Mexico City. As in Cable's novel, the love triangle sets the limits of the imagined community, whose interracial contours—Spanish, Anglo, and Indian—can only be projected over the border, where the woman of mixed race preserves the forgotten history of the nation's westward expansion.

In his historical novel about California, *The Octopus* (1901), Frank Norris deromanticizes the West of Jackson and Wister. In place of freewheeling cowpunchers, we find sophisticated wheat ranchers (most of them college men) out to exploit, not merge with, the land. In place of Jackson's victimized exotic Spanish past, we find the Spanish mission as a site of violence from within, where a young girl is raped by a mysterious "Other." The novel opens with a familiar Eastern outsider, Presley, who has come West to recuperate his health and who desires to write a romantic "Epic of the West." The first chapter exposes this desire as fantasy, through his disgust at the presence of German immigrants (not "The People" he expected), and more violently through the slaughter of sheep by the railroad, foreshadowing the climactic slaughter of the ranchers. In his depiction of the violent confrontation between the ranchers and the corporate railroad, Norris makes visible the capitalist economic structure that undergirds the mythical space of the West. Yet like the urban narrators of Wister, Jewett, and Garland, Presley (and the novel) do not simply travel from naive romance to more trenchant realism. Instead, they continually try to recuperate in the West a desire for prehistorical origins or a utopian vision of national unity.

What better symbol of national unity and what better subject for a national novel than the railroad, a complex economic and industrial phenomenon that physically transformed part of a continent into a nation by linking commerce and communication among widely dispersed local communities? The novel exposes the contradictions of this nation building as the railroad destroys the settlements and livelihoods of the same communities it brings into being. Against the overarching force of the railroad, which controls the means of representation in the press, as well as the government through the militia, the novel explores alternative definitions and symbols of the national public sphere. At an assembly of the farmers' league after the massacre, Presley proposes the model of a nation unified by conflict, by the struggle of people against trusts. But the novel diffuses this threat of class conflict, in part by making the original confrontation one within the family (the Derricks) and within the capitalist class, and in part by having Presley—the intellectual—engage in a desperate act of anarchism by ineffectually throwing a bomb, without political or narrative consequence. Countering the threat of class conflict is a nostalgic view of the folk as an Anglo-Saxon clan, represented by the marriage of Annixter and Hilma—ultimately doomed—and embodied in a barbecue, where we see "pure Americans at the starting point of civilization, coarse, vital, real sane." Another symbol of unity that appears to transcend social conflict is the natural cycle of the wheat, which recurs as a powerful symbol of the earth's female-identified fecundity. Yet the wheat is never "natural" to start with, as the mechanical planting and reaping appear throughout in images of military conquest or sexual violation echoing the rape by "The Other." Furthermore, the capitalist, Shelgrim, merges nature and the machine as an ahistorical apotheosis of "force." If, as he claims, the railroads make themselves as the wheat grows itself, neither is subject to contest by human agency.

The conclusion of *The Octopus* abandons the depiction of class contrast between an elite dinner party and a starving immigrant mother for a ship about to carry wheat to India with Presley on board. Not yet cured of his overcivilized consumption by his sojourn out West, he plans to light out for a more distant territory. His spiritual passage to India complements the manifest destiny voiced by the owner of the ship, who has given up domestic industry and the class conflicts it spawns to fulfill America's global mission of feeding the world while opening it up to commerce. His overt imperialism rounding the globe finds echo in Presley's Nirvana, the "full round of a circle whose segment only he beheld." On board the same ship and buried under tons of wheat is Behrman, the agent of the railroad. The wheat, which takes its natural revenge on Behrman, represents a revitalization of the American economy, as a spiritual and natural course of empire. Despite his ironic critique of America feeding the world while immigrants starve on the streets of San Francisco, Norris can turn imperial expansion from a history of violent conquest to one of global and spiritual nourishment.

The ending of *The Octopus* suggests an important but overlooked historical context for American literary naturalism: America's shift from continental expansion to an overseas empire at the turn of the century. Frank Norris and Jack London were deeply influenced by Rudyard Kipling, and themselves spent time in contested colonial arenas of Europe and the United States (Norris in the Transvaal and Cuba, London in the Pacific, the Klondike, Japan, and Korea). More important, they took up Kipling's "white man's burden," not simply in overt racism against Asians, Mexicans, and all nonwhites, but by reconstructing American identity as a biological category of Anglo-Saxon masculinity. They also projected imperial adventures onto imaginary open frontiers of the "Wilds," the open seas, arctic exploration, and the primordial beast within modern man. Norris hardly endorsed American imperialism as he equated the Anglo-Saxon inclination to dominate the world (in his essay "The Frontier Gone at Last" [1902]) with the definition of masculinity: in *McTeague* (1899), as the desire to dominate women. If regionalists seek primal origins of American nationality in prenational communities and clans, naturalists invent more distant yet immanent origins in biological conceptions of race and gender. Yet their fiction not only celebrates the ascendancy of the Anglo-Saxon male hero but also permits us to view him less as a biological fact than as a social construction built out of anxieties about the claims of women and immigrants at home and colonized people abroad, who threaten this primacy and against whom he is defined. Anglo-Saxon becomes synonymous with American as both the height of civilized development and a form of primitive regeneration that "forgets" history and social conflict as the basis of nation building.

Norris's and London's fascination with the primordial power within civilized man must be understood in relation to the imposition of civilizing power over people defined as primitive by the developing social sciences. Obsession with the primitive takes two opposing narrative trajectories of degeneration and regeneration. The same process of shedding the veneer of modern civilization can reveal the debased criminal within (McTeague, Vandover, Wolf Larsen), or can reawaken the ennobling heroic Anglo-Saxon warrior (Ross Wilbur, Van Weyden, Scott Weedon). This doubleness in primitive identity turns social difference into inherited biological fact. Yet the atavistic primitive within is also exposed as a projection of the violence of modern society onto an internalized "other." The ambiguity of the "primitive" as a site of either regeneration or degeneration can reflect critically upon the meaning of the civilized, which its boundary is meant to protect.

London's *The Call of the Wild* (1903) may seem as far away from a national novel, as De Forest imagined it, as the Yukon is from United States borders, and as dogs are from men. But the novel and its companion piece, *White Fang* (1906), enact an allegory of national development that unites the double trajectory of the primitive as degeneration and regeneration. The debasing bestiality in *Vandover and the Brute* (1914), where the hero literally acts like a wolf in his insanity, can be celebrated in real animals, who enact a primal violence that regenerates virility. The romance of dogs and men allows the exclusion of women, so intrusive in the narrative of *The Sea-Wolf* (1904) where the castaway woman mediates and deflects the powerful homoerotic desire between men as a symbol of national unity.

Buck in the primordial wilderness is homesick not for California but for a deeper memory of a hairy wild man, which posits a Social Darwinian origin of the race. In this primal world of violence and the hunt, the dog can nobly cross the boundary between civilization and the wilderness to become a wolf (so debasing to Vandover). Here is a version of Turner's frontier, an originary space producing real

Americans. Projected onto nature is a nationalist fantasy. The first dog Buck kills to assume the position of leader of the pack is the German Spitz, from a nation increasingly threatening to America at the time. As the Yukon becomes crowded and domesticated, Buck is tortured by the incursion of a bourgeois family, dominated by a hysterical woman, who receive their natural justice by falling through the ice, "the inexorable elimination of the superfluous." Buck is then rescued by the ideal frontiersman, Thornton, with whom he reconstitutes the perfect American family along with an Irish terrier who mothers him and a huge black dog named "Nig," of boundless good nature. Thornton embodies the feminine virtue of tenderness along with his unquestioned virility. After Buck proves his love for Thornton by turning work into play in a sled-pulling contest, they light out for the territory before the rest—this time eastward, in search of a fabled gold mine (the dream of wealth as natural rather than social). While Thornton lives like an Indian, Buck lives a similar frontier idyll by running and hunting with a pack of wolves while returning for perfect civility to the man he loves. The end of the novel reinvents the conquest of America—this time as the invasion of Indians who destroy the primal unity between man and beast in the wilderness. Thornton and Buck are not seen as intruding into the Yeehats' prior history, marked only by an arrow in the body of a moose hunted by Buck. When Buck attacks the Indians for revenge, they shoot one another in confusion. Yet their presence serves the purpose of both cutting Buck's ties to civilization and preserving his memory in their myths, while he represents a "younger world," prior to civilization.

*White Fang* is a more overt allegory of evolutionary origins as the wolf-dog moves up the human developmental scale from brutal Indians only bent on survival who domesticate him through terror, to lower-class whites who exploit him for gratuitous violent entertainment, to the upper-class Scott Weedon, who tames and civilizes White Fang with love, and who, like Thornton, incorporates the civilizing qualities shunned in women. Brought back to California, the wolf reaches the height of his civilized career when he recognizes a criminal intruder about to kill a judge, and when he unleashes his primitive killer instinct to tear out the throat of this lower-class criminal, a degenerate beast. The lower-class degenerate threatens the national class structure, which the primordial beast from the wilderness has been trained to protect. More laborious and less compelling than the immensely popular *Call of the Wild, White Fang*, through its frame that starts with a search party to recover the body of an aristocrat and ends by leashing primordial violence to protect a judge, exposes the deeply seductive call of "the wild" as the projection of "civilized" desire.

Amy Kaplan

# Gender and Fiction

In *The Responsibilities of the Novelist* (1902) Frank Norris explains in "Why Women Should Write the Best Novels" that women are much better suited to writing great novels than men. First, "writing is a feminine—not accomplishment merely—but gift." Moreover, women have the leisure, the right kind of education, and the temperament for novel writing. So they should surpass men at the task.

That they did not surpass men was an obvious source of relief to Norris. Women may have been writing more novels than men, he conjectured, but they were not writing better, or even equally accomplished, ones. Their lives were too sheltered to allow them the kind of engagement with experience—with "life itself, the crude, the raw, the vulgar"—that Norris considered essential to the production of great novels. Further, Norris believed that women lacked the physical and psychological strength necessary for the creation of great art. The mental strain of writing quickly debilitated them, resulting in "fatigue, harassing doubts, more nerves, a touch of hysteria occasionally, exhaustion, and in the end complete discouragement and a final abandonment of the enterprise."

Norris's wishful thinking about women not being able to write great novels and his construction of literary creativity as a virile activity illustrate how entangled the subjects of gender and novel writing had become by the end of the nineteenth century. In fact, even as Norris argued that women could not write great, or even good, novels, Edith Wharton, Ellen Glasgow, Pauline Hopkins, and Kate

Chopin were doing just that; and they would be followed by writers such as Willa Cather and Zora Neale Hurston. But in 1902 Frank Norris needed to claim that women could not be great novelists. He, along with many of his white male colleagues, felt extremely nervous about two things. First, the accomplishments of women novelists as artists were becoming increasingly difficult to deny. Second and related, the long-standing anxiety among many white men in the United States about novel writing as an effeminate occupation was, if anything, intensifying rather than abating.

For both men and women in nineteenth-century America, gendered ideas about novel writing grew out of and reflected larger political realities. Even before the Civil War, white women and people of color had embarked irreversibly on asserting their right to define themselves for themselves; and in the decades following the war, they continued, despite setbacks, to make dramatic inroads into social, intellectual, economic, and political territory previously staked out by white men as theirs alone. Change and upheaval were ubiquitous by the turn of the century. Immigrants arrived in large numbers from Italy, Ireland, Eastern Europe, and, before quotas, China. African Americans began moving North in significant numbers, as did Mexicans in the West. Native Americans waged desperate, defiant battles against United States imperialism.

The struggles of women to achieve change took many forms. By the end of the nineteenth century, many middle-class young white women, rebelling against the unwritten rule that they must not support themselves, sought to enter the ranks of paid employment, while growing numbers of African American women, most of them expecting to work throughout adulthood, fought to enter occupations from which they had been barred by discrimination. Across the nation, women's clubs devoted to self-improvement and civic involvement sprang up; African American clubs actively campaigned against lynching, the convict lease system, and institutionalized racial segregation, while all of the clubs lobbied for such social reforms as kindergartens, women matrons in women's prisons, and an end to child labor. Marking a major change in childbearing for many women, the average number of children for a woman of forty dropped from seven or eight in 1800 to three or four in 1900. Individuals such as Mary Cassatt, Emily Putnam, Maggie Walker, and Emma Goldman achieved fame as artists, scholars, entrepreneurs, and activists, while others such as Ida B. Wells and Jane Addams became well known as advocates for specific political and social reforms. Female enrollment in colleges and universities increased during the first two decades of the twentieth century by 1000 percent in public institutions and 482 percent in private ones. The campaign for women's suffrage intensified and ended successfully in 1920 in the passage of the Nineteenth Amendment.

It is important not to overstate women's gains during the Progressive Era—nor should divisions and inequalities be ignored. Most women who worked for pay held low-paying, unprestigious jobs. Those who worked in the home for no pay typically faced unending cycles of hard physical labor combined, frequently, with killing monotony. Birth control and divorce did not exist for huge numbers of women, who continued to have to bear more children than they wished and to endure oppressive, often violent, marriages. Most important, the life-situations of immigrant women and of women of color often differed radically from those of native-born white women, who in many cases were their exploiters and oppressors every bit as much as white men were. As a result, deep divisions existed. Often displaying itself in magnanimous attempts to "lift up" one's inferiors, the social reformist activities of privileged women frequently provoked resentment in poor and working-class women, even as circumstances forced them to accept the aid rendered. And racism more often than not made talk of "sisterhood" ludicrous. As Charlotte Hawkins Brown, one of four African American women invited to speak at an interracial conference in Memphis, Tennessee, in 1920, bluntly told the white women listening to her: "We have begun to feel that you are not, after all, interested in us and I am going still further. The negro women of the South lay everything that happens to the members of her race at the door of the Southern white woman. . . . We feel that so far as lynching is concerned, that, if the white women would take hold of the situation, lynching would be stopped."

However, important as the differences and conflicts among women were they should not obscure the fact that from the white, male, dominant-culture point of view at the turn of the century—as well as from the point of view of many women at the time—major, fundamental change in the status and position of women was taking place.

In fact, by the turn of the century feminist ideas and activities, referred to at the time simply as the Woman Movement, had become so widespread and powerful that a strong reactionary counterattack had settled in. No less a spokesman than Theodore Roosevelt, President of the United States from 1901 to 1909, denounced the fight for suffrage, for example, as "a thousandth or a millionth part as important as the question of keeping, and where necessary reviving, among the women of this country, the realization that their great work must be done in the home."

All of this determination of women to change their economic, social, and political situations found clear expression in their relationship to the novel, the most popular but also, it was becoming more and more evident, the most prestigious literary form in the United States. During the second half of the nineteenth century and then early in the twentieth, women writers increasingly set out to write their way into the national literature not simply as money-making professionals but as artists—as the equals of great international figures such as Flaubert, Tolstoy, or Balzac, or their rare female counterpart such as George Eliot or George Sand. Alice Dunbar-Nelson declared at the turn of the century that she wished to write the best novel ever written. Edith Wharton (for a while) enjoyed being compared to Henry James. Kate Chopin named as her favorite author and primary model Guy de Maupassant. Willa Cather began her career by denouncing feminine writing and aligning herself instead with men. By the turn of the century the battle over white male ownership of the high-art novel in the United States had come to a head. Even more important, it was a battle that took place within a context of more women from various backgrounds being able to become authors than ever before in the nation's history. African American women published more novels between 1892 and 1902 than in all previous decades of United States history combined. White women, in the opinion of many turn-of-the-century readers and reviewers, virtually owned the form. Women previously unrepresented among American writers launched careers. The sisters Edith and Winnifred Eaton, whose mother was Chinese and who wrote under the names Sui Sin Far and Onoto Watanna, respectively, began publishing at the end of the nineteenth century. The Native American authors Zitkala-Ša (sometimes known as Gertrude Bonnin) and Hum-ishu-ma (also known as Mourning Dove) began writing for publication. Similarly, the short-story writer María Cristina Mena, thought to be the first woman of Mexican descent to publish in English in the United States, began her career at the turn of the century.

Debate about gender and novel writing was not new in the United States at the end of the nineteenth century. Fierce rivalry had emerged as early as the 1850s. Inspiring Hawthorne's much-quoted complaint about that "damned mob of scribbling women" supposedly stealing his audience, popular white novelists such as E. D. E. N. Southworth, Maria Susanna Cummins, and Susan Warner dominated the mid-century novel market. Indeed, their best-sellers about and for women shaped the domestic novel to such an extent that their work affected not only the next generation of white male novelists such as Henry James and William Dean Howells but even their successors such as Frank Norris, Theodore Dreiser, and Sinclair Lewis, all of whom had to deal (comfortably or not) with the predominance of women among their readership. To be sure, most popular mid-nineteenth-century women novelists did not define themselves as artists. Typically, they protested that they were writing merely to make a living; they emphasized that they were not attempting to lay claim to the traditionally male province of high art. Nevertheless, their extraordinary popularity forced subsequent generations of novelists, male and female, to take into account the audience served by them—and for women novelists, the public image of the woman novelist that they created as well.

A case in point is the influence of popular mid-nineteenth-century novels by and for women on the two best-known male authors of realistic fiction in the second half of the nineteenth century, William Dean Howells and Henry James. As Alfred Habegger explains, the two men came of age during a period when women wrote almost all of the major novels in the United States. It is therefore not surprising that pleasing an overwhelmingly female readership accustomed to narratives about women and women's concerns created a basic—if not the basic—challenge for both men. Howells himself theorized in "Mr. James's Later Work" that his colleague's male readers were "of a more feminine fineness, probably, in their perceptions and intuitions, than those other men who do not read him." Raising the issue many decades later in *Henry James* (1951), F. W. Dupee summarized critical opinion by calling his subject "the great feminine novelist of a feminine age of letters." Similarly, Howells was routinely identified with women. As Habegger relates, the author Charles Dudley Warner wrote to his friend at one point: "You must have been a woman yourself in some previous state, to so know how it is yourself. You are a dangerous person. Heaven grant you no such insight into us men folk." Less charmed, one irritated male reviewer said: "Mr. Howells is never exciting; the most nervous old lady can read him without fear."

If the label "feminine" was complicated for male novelists such as Howells and James (it could be either a compliment or an insult, depending on who used it, why, and when), the issue of gender and novel writing was even more tangled for women writers. For those who wished to continue in the popular-novel tradition of their mid-century, white, domestic-novel predecessors, identification as a woman writer posed little problem. Traditional Victorian codes of femininity emphasizing modesty, intellectual conformity, and primary commitment to home and family dovetailed with the occupation of producing ostensibly formulaic novels that did not claim to be "art" — by which in the modern West is meant work that is original and idiosyncratic, individualistic, and frequently challenging or even upsetting. However, for many women late in the nineteenth and then early in the twentieth century, the mid-nineteenth-century mainstream American image of the domestic novelist no longer applied, if it ever had in the first place. Increasingly, women writers as a group were determined to assert their right to write not simply to make a living but for the same reasons that ambitious men (and a few women) had always turned to novel writing: to create original works of art.

Perfectly reflecting the period is Charlotte Perkins Gilman's argument in her essay "Men and Art" in *The Man-Made World* (1911). She points to a major difference between "art" and "Art," the former being what women had been allowed to do according to Gilman, the latter what men had reserved for themselves. Consequently Gilman declares of the "primitive arts" of women such as "pottery, basketry, leatherwork, needlework, weaving," and the like: "Much of this is strong and beautiful, but its time is long past." Such creations are "not Art with a large A, the Art which requires Artists, among whom are so few women of note." What women in the modern world need to do, Gilman argues, is invade and then redefine and adapt for themselves the territory of high art traditionally denied them, including and especially literature.

By the time Gilman's book saw print, there were many women in the United States already asserting their right to be, in her shorthand, Artists. For a number of native-born white women such as Sarah Orne Jewett, Edith Wharton, Kate Chopin, Mary Austin, Ellen Glasgow, Gilman herself, or Willa Cather, it is probably accurate to say that the most pressing issue was finding a way to reconcile the conflict embodied for them in the terms "woman" and "artist." For other equally ambitious women who were women of color or immigrants (or both), authors such as Frances Ellen Harper, Pauline Hopkins, Alice Dunbar-Nelson, Winnifred Eaton, Sui Sin Far, Hum-ishuma, and Anzia Yezierska, the challenge was even more complex. It involved combating racist, cultural, and entrenched class biases as well as gender issues.

One way of understanding the range and complexity of the issues dealt with by women novelists in the United States in the late nineteenth and early twentieth centuries is through brief consideration of a few representative careers. Useful for the purpose here, although many different choices could be made, are the following five writers: Pauline Hopkins (1859–1930), Edith Wharton (1862–1937), Winnifred Eaton (1875–1954), Willa Cather (1873–1947), and Hum-ishu-ma (1888–1936).

A biographical sketch published in *The Colored American Magazine* in 1901 (and no doubt written by the author herself) outlines Pauline Hopkins's ambition as a novelist. The piece announces that she aims to write fiction about racism that will reach all classes of readers and explains that "*Contending Forces* [1900] is her first published work." It was also her last separately published novel. As the sketch bluntly observes: "Pauline Hopkins has struggled to the position which she now holds in the same fashion that *all* Northern colored women have to struggle—through hardships, disappointments, and with very little encouragement. What she has accomplished has been done by a grim determination to 'stick at it,' even though failure might await her in the end." After *Contending Forces*, Hopkins was able to bring out three more novels serially in *The*

*Colored American Magazine,* where she served as literary editor from 1900 to 1904: *Hagar's Daughter* (1901), *Winona* (1902), and *Of One Blood* (1902). But she was not able to publish those novels as individual volumes nor to follow *Contending Forces* with any other separately issued novel. The difficulties announced in the 1901 sketch proved all too real.

Hopkins's resolve as an African American woman writer to create her own kind of art and to speak her mind pitted her against tremendous obstacles of racial, sexual, and therefore economic discrimination. Like that of any writer, her life as a publishing artist depended on having a publisher. But as an African American woman committed to writing honestly about race issues and needing to support herself financially, finding an outlet for her work was extremely difficult. During the few years that she worked at the *Colored American* while it was published in Boston, she was indefatigable and prolific. However, when the magazine changed direction and moved to New York following its secret purchase by Booker T. Washington, whose accommodationist policies Hopkins opposed, she lost her outlet. She tried to place work elsewhere and even created her own publishing company. But her efforts failed. Though she lived until 1930, she was not able to continue to publish novels after the four that appeared in the unbelievably short span of 1900 to 1902.

All four of Hopkins's novels focus on African American people's battles with racism in the United States, three of them giving preeminence to women's stories; and each shows her testing and expanding the form of the novel to make it serve her purposes. Interweaving stories of familial rupture and reunion, violation and restoration, *Contending Forces* links past and present to expose late nineteenth-century, white, rape-lynch mythology as the modern reincarnation of the ethos underlying slavery. Similarly, *Hagar's Daughter* and *Winona* deal with the institution of slavery and connect it to the modern African American woman's struggle to define herself against powerful forces of erasure. Most experimental formally is Hopkins's last novel, *Of One Blood,* which mixes realism, melodrama, journalism, dime novel techniques, and dream prophecy to create a parable about racism, healing, the African American woman artist, and pan-African wholeness.

Hopkins's images of the African American woman artist in *Contending Forces* and *Of One Blood* clearly signal her anger about her own situation as an African American woman writer. The woman artist in her first novel is shadowy. Significantly named Sappho, she reveals her creative potential only in hints: her name, the beauty she creates around herself, the passion she feels for her child, the occupation of stenography (Hopkins's own occupation) by which she supports herself. This character is important yet vague—purposefully hard to see and know. In *Contending Forces,* the African American woman artist's fate in the United States is to have been raped by her white uncle, and her story is one of painful reclamation of identity.

Much less optimistic in its conclusion is Hopkins's account of the woman artist in her last novel. In *Of One Blood,* the soprano Dianthe Lusk is deceived, sexually violated, silenced, and finally murdered by the book's principal white male character. In this book Hopkins openly celebrates the African American woman artist, connecting her to a long, ancient line of foremothers in Africa. She then shows her violent silencing in the modern United States. Rendered doubly vulnerable by race and gender, Hopkins's woman artist has a rich, glorious past. What she does not have, in this story, is a future. Violent racism kills her.

Born to privilege in a wealthy, white, Old New York family, Edith Wharton enjoyed a career that contrasts sharply with Hopkins's. Inherited income, leisure, freedom from domestic labor, and the security of an excellent private education positioned Wharton for success. Her impressive production of close to twenty novels, eleven volumes of short stories, and numerous essays and articles from the late 1890s to the early 1930s cannot be separated from the advantages of her race and class.

Edith Wharton did have to struggle to turn herself into an artist. Totally leisure-class in their expectation that she would devote herself to nothing but marriage, motherhood, and a life of constant hostessing and visiting, her parents were drawn neither to the arts nor to the life of the mind; and the marriage that she made in 1885 turned out to be deadly. Acutely depressed, she involved herself, on her doctor's advice, in fiction writing in earnest; but as she grew stronger, her husband grew severely depressed. Finally Edith Wharton sued for divorce—against the Wharton family's wishes—in 1913. Although she had an affair early in the twentieth century, she never remarried; and she lived most of her life after the turn of the century in France.

Wharton's rebellion against her class's, her family's, and her husband's expectations reflected the historical moment. Although highly conservative and elitist in many ways, she was nevertheless part of a new generation of women at the end of the nineteenth century who believed in their right to realize their own creativity and ambitions much as privileged men, at least in theory, always had. Indeed, a central issue for Wharton, many scholars argue, was the intensity of her male identification as an artist. If the production of high art, historically, was reserved for men, then how was one as a woman to pursue that goal? Was it possible to be both an artist and a woman? Wharton's most direct answer appears in her first novel, *The Touchstone* (1900), which has at its center the novelist Margaret Aubyn. She is brilliant, critically acclaimed, and prolific. She is also ugly, unrequited in love, and, by the time the novel opens, dead. The fears embodied in this early representation of the woman artist are clear; desexualization, rejection, and an early death are her fate.

After *The Touchstone* Wharton's novels return only covertly to the subject of the woman artist. She included the figure obliquely in *The Age of Innocence* (1920) in the character of Ellen Olenska, but frequently Wharton made her artists and artist-figures male. Looked at one way, this disappearance of the woman artist after *The Touchstone* suggests resolution. The author acknowledged her fears in her first novel and exorcised them. Looked at another way, however, Wharton's fiction suggests lifelong, unresolved conflict about her own identity as a woman writer. Critics have commented on the almost too-perfect precision and distancing of narrative technique in her work—her fear of admitting feeling and emotion—and Wharton has been charged with hostility toward her women characters. Both practices can be interpreted as manifestations of conflict. They can be read as the author's self-defensive attempt to secure her status as an artist in a male-dominated world by separating herself from "feminine" fiction—that is, allegedly soft, second-rate work—and from other women.

Edith Wharton succeeded brilliantly at writing her way into the tradition of the high-art novel in the United States. Her work enjoyed critical acclaim and a popular readership; given her presence, it was difficult to doubt women's abilities as literary artists. Indeed, one reason that the next generation of young white male authors such as Hemingway, Fitzgerald, and Faulkner needed so desperately to assert the masculinity of novel writing was that their youth had been dominated not by great male novelists but by great female ones. Attacking writers such as Edith Wharton, Ellen Glasgow, and Willa Cather as old-fashioned, prudish, and boring was one way of making room for themselves.

In contrast to Edith Wharton and her ambition to create elite art, Winnifred Eaton aimed directly for popular commercial success. Born in Canada the daughter of an English father and a Chinese mother, she was one of fourteen children and the family was poor. As an adult, she wrote most often under the Japanese-sounding pseudonym Onoto Watanna, supporting herself and her four children, particularly after her divorce, by writing popular romances, most of them set in Japan and almost all of them love stories. That is, she capitalized upon rather than rejected the well-established tradition of popular women's fiction in the United States; and she was extremely successful. The first woman of Chinese ancestry to publish novels in the United States, Winnifred Eaton brought out fourteen novels between the late 1890s and the mid-1920s.

Unlike her sister who published short fiction under the name Sui Sin Far and thereby openly acknowledged her Chinese ancestry, Winnifred Eaton responded to virulent anti-Chinese sentiment in the United States at the turn of the century by suppressing her own heritage and assuming, instead, a Japanese identity. Her strategy, as Amy Ling argues, was one of adaptation, subterfuge, and subversion rather than open confrontation. By reinventing her background, she could cater to the reading public's fascination with Japan and thus exploit Asian subject matter in a positive, albeit stereotypic, way without churning up the racism—or at least the same kind or the amount of racism—that Chinese subject matter would produce.

The full meaning and the cost of Eaton's successful disguise are not easy to measure. She brilliantly participated in a strategy of deliberately assumed false identity and infiltration that women artists, defined as outsiders, have made use of from George Eliot (and earlier) on. At the same time, as Onoto Watanna she centered her creative life in an act of denial that clearly seems to have created pain as well as a degree of freedom. Her autobiography, *Me* (1915), in which she calls herself "Nora Ascough" and identifies her mother simply as "foreign," reflects bitterly at one point: "My success was founded upon a cheap and popular device. . . . Oh, I had sold my birthright for a mess of potage [*sic*]." In alluding here to the biblical story of Esau and, even more immediately and tellingly, to the famous reference to it at the end of James Weldon Johnson's *The Autobiography of an Ex-Coloured Man* (1912), Eaton suggests how hard it was for her, at least at times, to pretend to be someone she was not. The rampant anti-Chinese bigotry of her era placed her in an untenable position. As she saw it, and certainly she was not imagining things, to survive and thrive as a novelist she had to deny a basic part of herself.

This confusion and guilt about hiding one's identity appears clearly in Onoto Watanna's early novel about a woman artist, *A Japanese Nightingale* (1901). In order to secure enough money to help her brother come home to Japan, the heroine, a teahouse dancer who is half Japanese and half Caucasian, sells herself in marriage to a white American. In keeping her economic motive a secret, she keeps from her husband her full story as a human being and her pain and isolation at having to live a lie. As a "real" story about a woman artist in Japan, the book is frequently thin and farfetched. As a disguised story about its author's own disguise as an artist, however, it is revealing. It says that economic necessity, secrecy and isolation, and flattery of whites consume the major part of a Eurasian woman artist's life.

Willa Cather's ambition as a novelist, like Wharton's, was to distinguish herself as an artist. As Sharon O'Brien has argued, Cather's long apprenticeship as a novelist was dominated by the conflict she felt as a middle-class white woman between the identities of "woman" and "artist," the former associated for her with domesticity, nurture, and relationality; the latter with public accomplishment, daring intellect, and rule-breaking. Publishing her first short story in 1892, she did not write her first novel until 1912; and during that twenty-year period, as well as occasionally thereafter, Cather outspokenly denigrated women writers. It was a way of separating herself from public accomplishment that was "feminine." By attacking women writers she could identify herself with real artists—that is, men. Then in large part through the friendship and example of Sarah Orne Jewett, as O'Brien explains, Cather gradually arrived at a way of integrating her identity as a woman and her ambitions as an artist. Although that integration was always shaky, she was nevertheless able to produce nine novels in about twenty years, as well as many short stories, essays, articles, and autobiographical writings.

Where Cather's story differed radically from Wharton's was in her struggle against homophobia. Profoundly complicating Cather's public career as an artist was her primary, private identification with women, romantically and emotionally, at precisely the time historically that such same-sex relationships were being defined as pathological. Because Victorian ideology assumed that respectable women were asexual, a woman of the previous generation such as Jewett might write with considerable freedom about love between women. But with the breakdown of Victorian ideology toward the end of the nineteenth century came a redefinition of all women (not just "bad" women) as sexual. Consequently, deep intimate bonds between women no longer qualified as "innocent." They became, instead, potentially and even inherently sexual—*and,* given their rejection of men, clearly "deviant." This invention of lesbianism as deviance by the mainstream culture occurred at the same time that Cather was trying to find her voice as an artist. As might be expected, these changes in cultural attitudes toward same-sex emotional and romantic identification among women generated tremendous creative tension for Cather—both inhibiting and fruitful.

Cather wrote most openly about the woman artist in her third novel, *The Song of the Lark* (1915), and it is significant that the singer Thea Kronborg has her most complete and transforming creative experience in a moment of solitary, magical communion with the earth itself, which Cather clearly depicts as female and simultaneously erotic and maternal. Deep in Panther Canyon, which is described as "a gentler cañon within a wilder one," a secret protected place "hollow (like a great fold in the rock)," Cather's artist, standing naked in a still pool in the sunlight, experiences an epiphany. Embraced by the earth, Thea understands in a flash the utter interconnectedness of earth, flesh, womb, female sexuality, and artistic form. As a consequence of this powerful, symbolic, same-sex experience deep in the earth she finds herself reborn and renewed as an artist.

Similar covert exploration of same-sex love and of its relationship to artistic creativity exists throughout Cather's fiction. Most obvious probably are the loving relationships between men in *The Professor's House* (1925) and *Death Comes for the Archbishop* (1927). But even in *My Ántonia* (1918), many critics argue, the central love relationship between Jim and "Tony" (Ántonia) makes most sense if it is read not simply as a heterosexual attraction but also as a camouflaged same-sex one.

Existing in tension with such subversive energies in Cather's novels, however, is her racism. Writing during a period of mounting homophobia, Willa Cather struggled against powerful biases, which she could circumvent only surreptitiously. It is therefore an irony of her work, as must also be said of many other white women's writing at the time, that it is deeply racist and ethnocentric. Even as Cather wrote about white women's struggles against discrimination, including those of immigrants, she ignored living Native Americans in favor of celebrating dead ones, rendered Mexican women invisible, and caricatured African Americans. Like most privileged white women at the time, she did not use her own situation to understand the situations of people of color in the United States.

In sharp contrast to a career such as Cather's, Hum-ishu-ma, also known as Mourning Dove, published one novel, *Cogewea, the Half-Blood*. Written around 1912, it did not come out until 1927; and the story of its revision and publication forms a critical chapter in United States literary history.

A member of the Okanogan people of the American Northwest, Hum-ishu-ma is usually cited as the first Native American woman novelist. She grew up in what is now Washington state and then on the Flathead Reservation. Although she had little formal schooling, she had impressive talent and determination and around 1912 wrote the first draft of *Cogewea*. In 1914 she shared her manuscript with Lucullus Virgil McWhorter, a white man actively involved in championing Native American rights. McWhorter added some notes and quotations, did some editing, and tried to place the book for Hum-ishu-ma. He did not succeed, perhaps because of World War I; and then after the war he continued to make changes in the manuscript—but this time without telling Hum-ishu-ma. The book, as Alanna Kathleen Brown explains, now became the work of two people with two separate objectives. When the novel finally came out in 1927 McWhorter had so altered it that Hum-ishu-ma wrote to him: "I feel like it was someone elses book and not mine at all. In fact the finishing touches are put there by you, and I have never seen it."

Hum-ishu-ma wrote *Cogewea* at night after exhausting labor all day as a migrant farmworker; she trusted McWhorter with her manuscript; and her reward was a book she could barely recognize as her own. As Dexter Fisher points out, McWhorter no doubt meant well. He wanted to revise *Cogewea* to make it more timely, impressive, and therefore marketable. Nevertheless what he did was to appropriate and rewrite Hum-ishu-ma—transform her work into his image of what it should be. He repeated on the personal level precisely the process of colonization and erasure that he claimed as an advocate of Native American issues to be fighting against in white culture.

Despite the manuscript's violation, it seems possible to identify the basic plot and design of *Cogewea* as Hum-ishu-ma's. The book has in its foreground a simple if tangled love-plot. Rejecting a young man who, like herself, comes from a mixed Okanogan and Anglo background and is therefore at home in both the Native American and the white world, Cogewea runs away with a white man who turns out to be a racist liar. When he abandons her, it is actually a good thing. Cogewea returns to her people and, most important, to new respect for her grandmother, her Stemteema, who had warned her against the white man. Quite overtly, *Cogewea* is a cautionary tale about the dangers of trusting white men and leaving the world of one's grandmother. It is, ironically, almost uncannily prophetic about Hum-ishu-ma's experience as a writer.

It may be that Hum-ishu-ma's struggle as a writer against colonial domination and particularly white sexism shows up most powerfully in *Cogewea*'s form. Three times she inserts the Stemteema's traditional, cautionary tales into her conventional Western plot design. These tales, either remembered by Hum-ishu-ma or gathered by her for the novel, thus interject into the book a traditional, oral narrative that both opposes and interacts with the love-plot. Consequently the form of Hum-ishu-ma's book, probably even more than its content, articulates what was obviously a fundamental issue for her as a woman writer, at least in this work. How does one fuse the modern Western novel—whether popular or high-art—and the traditional art of generations of Native American foremothers? Is it possible, or even desirable? Can the two meet, interact, coexist, or connect in the same text?

After *Cogewea* Hum-ishu-ma published *Coyote Stories* (1933), a collection of traditional Okanogan tales. Also, it is reported that she was determined to write another novel, this time without anyone's "help." Whether she did so is uncertain, however, as no manuscript has been found.

Certainly the careers of Pauline Hopkins, Edith Wharton, Onoto Watanna, Willa Cather, and Hum-ishu-ma suggest no unitary story or pattern. Rather, what a sketch of representative women novelists' ambitions and fates at the turn of the century indicates is both how feasible and how very difficult it was for different women to become novelists in the United States at the beginning of the twentieth century.

They all had behind them a strong tradition. By the end of the nineteenth century American women had been publishing novels for well over fifty years. Led by writers such as E. D. E. N. Southworth and Susan Warner, a number of them had succeeded so phenomenally that the popular novel in the 1850s was dominated by white women. Following the Civil War, other white women such as Elizabeth Stuart Phelps, Constance Fenimore Woolson, and Sarah Orne Jewett published novels that significantly altered the earlier pattern. They wrote books that simultaneously sold well and attracted praise as "art," thus preparing the way, it can be said, for the explosion of talent and achievement among women novelists at the end of the century. Earlier there had been isolated women such as Elizabeth Stoddard or Harriet E. Wilson who had attempted novels substantially or even completely different from those produced by the popular white domestic novelists. But it was not until the third quarter of the nineteenth century that such experimentation and individuality became the norm rather than the exception.

Empowered by various, vigorous women's movements, as well as by various literary traditions that included autobiographies, poetry, slave narratives, travel literature, and a number of oral forms in addition to the novel, women writers from many backgrounds turned with increasing ambition and confidence at the end of the nineteenth century to the novel, whether as high art or as popular fiction. African American women such as Frances Ellen Harper, Emma Dunham Kelley, Amelia Johnson, and Pauline Hopkins brought out novels in the 1890s and the first years of the new century. Onoto Watanna and Hum-ishu-ma likewise began novel-writing careers at the turn of the century. Many white women such as Edith Wharton, Kate Chopin, Willa Cather, Mary Austin, Gertrude Atherton, Ellen Glasgow, Zona Gale, and Mary Roberts Rinehart began their careers as novelists at the end of the nineteenth century.

Indeed, as a group white women novelists were so successful that their work clearly threatened white men at the time. Theodore Dreiser's beginning his own career with two novels about women, *Sister Carrie* (1900) and *Jennie Gerhardt* (1912), or Sinclair Lewis's debut with *Main Street* (1919) suggests how aware they were of the feminine market. Even more telling, the exaggeratedly muscular novels of men such as Richard Harding Davis, Frank Norris, Winston Churchill, and Harold Bell Wright point at least in part to their anxiety not simply about virility in general but specifically about gender and the novel—who should be shaping it and what it should look like.

A second and equally if not more important conclusion to draw from any overview of women novelists at the turn into the twentieth century is that gender cannot be separated out from race, ethnicity, and class when thinking about the struggles and accomplishments of women writers in the United States. As women, all of the writers I have mentioned shared the challenge of having to combat sexism and misogyny in order to write and publish. Also all, in one way or another, benefited from changing attitudes toward women in the broader social and political context. However, the differences among and for women created by racism, colonialism, cultural bigotry, and class discrimination often reduced to insignificance the similarities produced by gender. Edith Wharton's publication of seventeen novels and Hum-ishu-ma's publication of one—which she could barely recognize as her own by the time her benevolent white "friend" got through with it—indicate how inextricable the issues of gender, race, class, ethnicity, and culture are in United States literary history. The subject of gender empowerment and the American novel does not exist independent of questions of race, class, and culture.

Elizabeth Ammons

# Popular Forms I

The only men, as a class, in America today, who are able to live by pure literary labor, are the writers of what you call "dime novels," that is to say, of books written for the largest possible market in this country. . . . Had Poe lived in these days he would have been a writer of dime novels; for his prose stories have all the qualities which are required in a good "dime." Had he done so, he might have ended his days in comfort, instead of dying in misery, for good dime work pays well.        —Frederick Whittaker, *Dime Novels: A Defense by a Writer of Them* (1884)

When Frederick Whittaker mounted his defense of cheap fiction in the late nineteenth century, he was reacting against criticism of it as a degenerate, corrupt, and corrupting form. His tactic was to legitimize the processes of authorship and reception (or literary production and consumption) within the marketplace. The argument and counterargument nicely gesture to the warring definitions, theories, and assumptions that inform discourse of the "popular" in the industrial age. Disentangling the terms of that discourse is crucial, because each leads to a different construction of the literature. I will argue in this chapter that popular or mass literature of the nineteenth century made available to authors and readers a negotiated response to historical, ideological, and commercial developments of the period.

Critics of popular culture in the industrialized era have theorized alternative models of the relationship between popular forms and society, or specifically the effect of the commodification of culture on literary production. At one end of the spectrum, the Frankfurt School condemned the "culture industry" as a capitalist operation manipulating and deceiving a passive public. That reading of mass culture is one that echoes through many avowedly untheorized attitudes: Ralph Ellison is not unusual in perceiving the debasement of African American culture in its appropriation by mass forms of entertainment. The opposite response is epitomized by some of Leslie Fiedler's work, which celebrates mass literature as the spontaneous expression of modern folk culture. These diverse connotations are represented in the multiple definitions of the term "popular," itemized by Raymond Williams in *Keywords* (1983):

Popular was originally a legal and political term, from *popularis*, L—belonging to the people. . . . The transition to the predominant modern meaning of "widely favoured" or "well-liked" is interesting in that it contains . . . a sense of calculation. . . . Popular culture was not identified by *the people* but by others, and it still carries two older senses: inferior kinds of work . . . ; and work deliberately setting out to win favour . . . ; as well as the more modern sense of well-liked by many people, with which of course, in many cases, the earlier senses overlap. The sense of popular culture as the culture actually made by people for themselves is different from all these.

In more recent years an intermediate position has developed, one that is compelling in its recognition of both the trivializing and the empowering potential of popular forms, and that acknowledges the manipulations of the mass media while arguing that the needs and desires of the reading public can act as a counterforce in the collective production of meaning. This perspective is partly a response to the perceived disjunction between critics' and audiences' explanations of the stories that popular forms tell. Privileging the critics' readings assumes and perhaps encourages the passivity of "untrained" readers, implicitly characterizing them as gulls to the ruses of the manifest content of popular works. The theory of "negotiation" answers this assumption by ascribing agency to the material institutions of production, distribution, and consumption, to the publishers, authors, and readers of mass literature, all of them being understood to invest the text with their own agendas, vocabularies, ideologies. Michael Denning provides one of the most succinct articulations of the dynamic of negotiation when he says of cheap books that

they are best seen as a contested terrain, a field of cultural conflict where signs with wide appeal and resonance take on contradictory disguises and are spoken in contrary accents. Just as the signs of a dominant culture can be articulated in the accents of the people, so the signs of the culture of the working classes can be dispossessed in varieties of ventriloquism.

The later nineteenth-century explosion of American cheap fiction grew out of major innovations in antebellum popular publishing. This chapter sketches in the early period by tracing the rise of story papers, dime novels, and nickel series, all of which flourished in the latter half of the century. It pays attention to the material circumstances of these works' production and consumption, their textual inscriptions, their authors, and their readers, as the collective coordinates of the "contested terrain" of popular literature. Such grounding facilitates our understanding of how these popular works spoke to their age—as well as how they speak to our age about the imaginative life of the past—and how they offered to authors and readers models of accommodation, qualified resistance, and negotiation.

In the antebellum period key moments facilitated the onset of cheap fiction: the explosion in America's market economy, the huge increase in its population, the spread of literacy, and the rapid advances in transportation, industrialization, and print technology made possible the production and continental distribution of low-priced literature to a mass audience for the first time. The first entrepreneurs to take advantage of these material conditions were the publishers of story papers: cheap, weekly compilations of serialized melodramas, didactic sketches, and news digests. The composition and contents of story papers were a direct result of marketing calculations. The large folio sheets with their cramped columns of diminutive typeface, the paucity of illustrations, and the very low price—3 cents to 6 cents per issue—were the result of a narrow calculation about how to attract the largest audience as cheaply as possible. Snippets of commentary and international gossip were added to make the story papers look like newspapers, since only newspapers were eligible for the cheapest, third-class postage. The first story papers were *Brother Jonathan* and *New World,* both founded by Park Benjamin and Rufus Griswold in 1839; the most popular and long-lasting were Robert Bonner's *New York Ledger* (1855–98) and Street and Smith's *New York Weekly* (1855–89), each claiming at different times to sell 350,000–400,000 copies a week. These titles and others appeared up to the end of the century, but the form was distinctively forged in its early years: as enthusiasm for the dime novel escalated after the Civil War, later story papers could claim only one-half to one-quarter of the earlier versions' circulation; in 1877, *Publishers Weekly* said of weekly story papers: "These have not been pushed of late years as they used to be, and their readers perhaps are ready for something new."

The political climate also had a palpable effect on story papers. The rhetoric of Manifest Destiny provided a nationalistic discourse within which publisher-editors could legitimize merchandising calculations of scale and popularity, translating commercial practices into patriotic principles in the apparatus that surrounded and spoke to the fictional contents. In the years when America was battling with Mexico and Britain in its efforts to expand its Western territories, nationalist sentiment was stirred by iconic story-paper titles such as *The Flag of Our Union, The True Flag, The Flag of the Free, Uncle Sam, The Yankee Nation, The Star-Spangled Banner,* all accompanied by flamboyant heads of eagles, flags, and cameos of the founding fathers. The democratic ethos was invoked in editorial columns and publicity announcements that accommodated readers to the upheavals of industrializing America, by explaining the technology of story-paper production as a process entirely at the service of the public, making "a paper that shall please the million."

Story-paper authors also functioned as icons of emergent nationalism. The first story-paper publishers pirated European material, but once that source ran dry, they stimulated American production, first with cash prizes for published stories, then with fees—anywhere from $100 for a novelette to $1600 for a novel. The need to fill pages, then, turned American writing into a paying profession for the first time. Mining that commercial calculation for all its nationalistic potential, publishers vied to boast about the Americanness of their authors and the size of fees paid to certain stellar names (stressing output and price more than genius of production), again emphasizing that these measures were adopted for the public's delectation.

The array of fictional formulas perpetrated by the story papers included some residual forms unchanged from the European tradition: for example, aristocratic costume romances. The most distinctive narratives, however, adapted inherited patterns of sensational action, multiple plot-lines, and stereotyped figures to American settings and the current political climate. The genre "mysteries of the city," for example, adapted by George Lippard and, later, Ned Buntline from Eugène Sue, was marked by the peculiarities of the American city in the 1840s as well as by the displacement of rural dwellers after the Panic of 1837.

Melodramas of two types predominated. Stories of masculine adventure on the sea, in the wilderness, or in historical and contemporary wars with Britain, Mexico, and Native American tribes justified the nationalist cause in specifically democratic terms. Typically, Charles Averill's *The Secret Service Ship; or, The Fall of San Juan D'Ulloa*, first published in *The Flag of Our Union* in 1849, focuses its sensationalized propaganda about the contemporaneous Mexican War on the heroic spy, Midshipman Rogers. In his complicated tangle of plot lines, character disguises, false deaths, and indigestible coincidences, Averill entirely sacrificed the convention of secrecy to the allegorical imperative. Far from camouflaging himself in the dress of his Mexican surroundings, Midshipman Rogers accouters himself as follows:

> his right arm rear[ed] proudly aloft to the breezes of the Gulf, a superb dark blue banner, on which was embroidered in bright golden characters, the inscription "UNITED STATES SECRET SERVICE," surrounded by a circle of thirty glittering stars, such as ever gem the Flag of our Union; while the azure sash which encircled his manly waist . . . was itself a star-spangled standard, folded into a semblance of a scarf.

At a climactic moment in the plot, Rogers unfurls the United States flag and drapes himself in it. Simultaneously boosting both the nationalistic cause and the paper's title, Averill insists that what has infiltrated and vanquished Mexico is the type of America, the democracy where the common man (the midshipman) is hero.

The other prominent formula was a sensationalized version of the domestic, sentimental novel, which sold so successfully at midcentury and which Jane Tompkins has read as an expression of the revival movement. Women's narratives in the story papers also told of female trials and fortitude in the face of sudden poverty, orphanhood, abusive guardians, and evil suitors, but their florid, feverish action was more "high wrought," in Nina Baym's term, than that of Susan B. Warner and Maria Cummins. The most lavishly touted author of this melodramatic genre was Mrs. E. D. E. N. Southworth, who was published in the *New York Ledger* from 1855 and whose writings still attracted a large audience in the 1880s and 1890s, when they appeared alongside the dime novels. Southworth's successful formula involved mistaken identities, vicious love triangles, and horrific bouts of insanity, all of which are represented as distortions of the domestic propriety at which the heroine aims. The heroines typically earn their happiness by being chaste and Christian, but that virtue does not inhibit them from undertaking some sensational cross-dressing adventures. While clearly speaking to the religious enthusiasm and women's topics of the age, these melodramas also offered illicit thrills.

Some of these melodramas were delivered, textually, by strong authorial voices that translated the commodity status of the literature into a highly metaphorical process of commodity exchange between authors and implied audiences. These authorial gestures seem a more characteristic dimension of male than female narratives; this difference may well be historically specific, in that the first identifiable voice was a male one that emerged from the patriarchal system of the publishing industry. Maturin Murray Ballou was one of the first entrepreneurs to take advantage of the new print technology, most successfully with *The Flag of Our Union* (1846–70). He also seems to have been the first story-paper author to incorporate the businessman's perspective into his authorial voice, when he turned author himself in the face of dwindling indigenous materials to fill his pages. In adopting his new role, Ballou never renounced his old one; in the midst of his melodramatic storytelling, he pauses to inform the reader how much time and money the process of writing has cost; and he extends the public accountability of the author from the editorial rhetoric to the fiction itself, by explaining and justifying his decisions about the composition of his tale, in, for example, *Fanny Campbell, the Female Pirate Captain* and *Red Rupert, the American Bucanier* [*sic*], both published in *The Flag of Our Union* in 1845. The most prolific author to follow Ballou's practice was E. Z. C. Judson, best known under one of his many pseudonyms, "Ned Buntline."

Buntline's voice was more politicized than Ballou's, because he carried into his fiction the perspectives of both publisher-editor (Judson produced his own story papers intermittently) and tribune of the people (at one time heading the Know-Nothing Party, he was a prominent participant in the Astor Place Riot of 1849). He also used the serialized format more aggressively, to respond to his critics and comment on his political and legal adventures beyond the pages of his fiction. Peter Buckley has elucidated the strategies by which Buntline carried the rhetoric of mass meetings from the streets of New York City into the story papers and back again, breaking the bounds of novelistic form to argue political, legal, commercial, and personal cases to his audience. This whole ongoing commentary was intertwined within stirring tales of the American Revolution—such as *Saul Sabberday, the Idiot Spy; or, Luliona, the Seminole* (1858)—or of urban vice—for example, *The Mysteries and Miseries of New York City* (issued in parts between December 1847 and April 1848). In Buckley's words: "Practicing the serial form . . . appears to have brought writers into new relations with the audiences assembled, so to speak, by the texts themselves"; in Buntline's: "I hope you feel as if you had got your money's worth."

The sum of these authorial, narrative, and publishing strategies is that story papers did much more than flood American society with cheap, sensational adventure stories. Their editorial and authorial rhetoric acknowledged the operation of the market on the contract between author and reader, and inscribed that contract into the nationalist history of America, implicating commercial practice just as much as martial pursuits into the democratic ethos of the new Republic. At the same time, their fictional narratives positioned American women and men in heroic roles. While the editorial apparatus communicated reassuring messages about the technology and scale of industrialization, it also mediated the sensational fiction in such a way that the adventures read not simply as dissociated escapism but as displaced allegories of American life. The effect was that story papers offered readers accommodation to the speed, change, and growth of modern America.

The popular form central to the post–Civil War period was the dime novel, which flourished from 1860 to about 1900. Dime novels were introduced by Beadle and Adams, who were soon joined by a host of imitators, the most successful being Frank Tousey, George Munro, Norman Munro, and Street and Smith (the last transferring from the story paper to the dime novel late, in 1889, but immediately becoming Beadle and Adams's main rival and surviving as pulp magazine publishers until 1950). Beadle shifted the emphasis in cheap publishing away from serials to uniformly packaged series: each consisted of complete, predominantly American novels presented as compact pamphlets priced at 10 cents or 5 cents, with illustrated covers, which became increasingly lurid and vividly colored through time.

Pamphlet novels had been issued, irregularly, in the antebellum period, but usually in installments for 25 cents each. Beadle and Adams's major innovation was the marketing of their line: the portable format was an important selling point in an age of escalating rail travel; the recognizable, appealing format took effect with the onset of the newsstand as a major outlet for cheap fiction; and the very low price ("A DOLLAR BOOK FOR A DIME!!" as the publicity blared) opened up the market to readers of all income levels. The dime novel publishers also pared away most of the editorial paraphernalia characteristic of story papers; in time, they tapped the audience loyalty bred by serialization in the earlier format by organizing titles into "libraries," a device that also facilitated the frequent reprinting of novels. The results were massively successful; Beadle and Adams published 3158 separate titles and sold copies in the millions. In the words of W. H. Bishop, in 1879, dime novel literature was "the greatest literary movement, in bulk, of the age, and worthy of very serious consideration for its character, the phenomenon of its existence cannot be overlooked."

The authors of dime novels were implicated in the industrial processes more directly than their story-paper predecessors, primarily because dime novel publishers attempted to rationalize (and thereby deskill) writing as well as production, advertising, and distribution. At first, with Beadle and Adams, editors regimented authors' production mainly in terms of quantity, speed, length, and fixed payment rates, supplying only general instructions on content. With the advent of Street and Smith, however, the principle of systematization penetrated much more deeply into relationships among publisher, editor, author, and audience. They supervised their writers closely, taking over more and more authorial decisions, until, by 1896, Ormond Smith dictated character, plots, and scenes to the author who was ostensibly "inventing" Frank Merriwell. Increasingly, too, all dime publishers shunted authors around from one house pseudonym to another; in the case of Street and Smith, multiply authored series under one trademark name came to be the rule.

Fitting writing to production-line techniques inevitably shaped both the public's and the writers' conception of authorship. From the statements that have survived, it is clear that many authors came to absorb the values of commercial publishing, willingly subscribing to the conditions of labor in the fiction factories. William Wallace Cook, for example, who wrote for Street and Smith between 1893 and 1928, off and on, described authorship:

A writer is neither better nor worse than any other man who happens to be in trade. He is a manufacturer. After gathering his raw product, he puts it through the mill of his imagination, retorts from the mass the personal equation, refines it with a sufficient amount of common sense and runs it into bars—of bullion, let us say. If the product is good it passes at face value and becomes a medium of exchange.

Laura Jean Libbey, who won a massive readership through the Munroes' story papers, wrote plays in later life according to the method she had learned as a dime novelist. Eschewing outline or notes, she dictated two or three plays a week, 120 in eighteen months, then produced a list of 120 titles, to which she matched the plays as they came to hand. The more complex inscriptions of authorial accents in the fiction itself are part of the textual story told below.

Sizes and types of audience are notoriously difficult to establish, the more so in the case of historical publishers of ephemeral literature. Nevertheless, informed hypotheses are important, because we read this literature now partly through our construction of how it was received contemporaneously. Certain clues point to a large and diverse audience for dime novels, but with a majority of this readership belonging to the working class toward the end of the nineteenth century. Beadle and Adams themselves explicitly announced in 1860: "it is hoped to reach all classes, old and young, male and female"; they advertised books in the nationally influential *New York Tribune;* and some of their publications were reviewed (favorably) in the highbrow *North American Review.* The Civil War produced a captive audience of soldiers, who were highly responsive to the sensational adventure that some publishers became adept at producing. Later, industrialization, urbanization, and economic calculations seem to have delivered the working classes as the main audience for cheap fiction. Frederick Whittaker specifically enumerated: "The readers of the dimes are farmers, mechanics, workwomen, drummers, boys in shops and factories"; extrapolating from this and other evidence, Michael Denning has averred that "the bulk of the audience of dime novels were workers—craftworkers, factory operatives, domestic servants and domestic workers." At least once formulaic fantasies were adapted to quasi-realist urban settings, Street and Smith appeared to believe that they had a proletarian audience (and potential, unpaid sales force) reflecting their proletarian protagonists. The editorial apparatus of an 1871 *New York Weekly* reads, in part:

> Every sewing machine girl in the United States should not only read *Bertha Bascomb, the Sewing Machine Girl,* but should make it her especial business to see that everybody else reads it. The story is designed to benefit the working girl, and therefore every working girl in our broad land should constitute herself an agent for its distribution.

Given that it was Francis Smith, coeditor, who had written *Bertha Bascomb,* this rhetoric can be read as not just addressing but actively constituting a working-class following. Retrospectively, commentators tended to style dime novels "part of the youth of many of us" (this from an editorial in the *New York Sun* in 1900). In fact, however, it was only toward the end of Beadle and Adams's life and throughout Street and Smith's dime career that a specifically juvenile audience was targeted.

The characteristic dime novel narratives aimed at this shifting audience were action-packed melodramas that told, again, stories of nationalism and commerce. Several formulas are familiar from the story papers—tales of heroic, patriotic wars and of the frontier—but others developed in response to historical circumstances: the fictionalizing of outlaws, detectives, male factory operatives, and working girls, for example, was particular to the newer form, as it developed in the 1880s and 1890s. All of these fictions were quick to exploit the topical, from scientific and technological inventions to industrial strife to Teddy Roosevelt's triumphs in the Spanish-American War.

The formula most actively promoted by Beadle and Adams and their imitators in the early years was the Western. While there had been individual best-selling frontier romances—each of Cooper's Leatherstocking tales (1823–41) was a best-seller, as was Robert Montgomery Bird's *Nick of the Woods; or, The Jibbenainosay* (1837)—the genre as a mass phenomenon took off with the advent of the dime novel. The historical context was clearly a factor: accompanying the human migrations from East to West before the Civil War and the cattle trails from West to East after was a vibrant, optimistic political rhetoric that characterized the Far West as site of national, economic, and personal regeneration. Also bearing upon the response to the dime Western was the general shift in popular trends, as women's fiction waned and men's gained ascendancy, as Nina Baym and others have shown. Finally, the specific story of Beadle's first Westerns suggests that commercial calculations also had a bearing.

Beadle and Adams opened their publishing venture with a tale set on the early frontier: *Malaeska: The Indian Wife of the White Hunter,* by Ann S. Stephens, which was Number One of *Beadle's Dime Novels* in June 1860. It sold at least half a million copies, yet turned out to be an unusual dime novel. Its structure was untypical: though its melodrama was vivid, its plot entanglements and subplots and coincidences were considerably more restrained than in later dimes, and it ended tragically. The subject matter was handled equally unusually: *Malaeska* traces the fate of a Native American woman, who is left widowed by her white soldier-husband, robbed of their son by her aristocratic in-laws in New York City, forced to witness his suicide when his Indian heritage is revealed to him years later, and finally killed by her own grief on her boy's grave. That this is a distinctively female, as well as native, experience is suggested by the narrator's comment on Malaeska's self-sacrifice: "It was her woman's destiny, not the more certain because of her savage origin. Civilization does not always reverse this mournful picture of womanly self-abnegation." When Irwin Beadle chose this story, reprinting it from serialization in *The Ladies' Companion* of 1839, he seems to have made an astute commercial calculation, grafting an example of the provenly popular sentimental fiction onto a new format and new publicity that emphasized the frontier adventure more than the prominent religiosity.

*Malaeska*'s failure to articulate the West in topically optimistic, patriarchal terms may well have doomed it in the long run as the forerunner of a genre of women's Westerns. More immediately, happenstance worked against its institution as a formulaic model. Later in 1860, Edward S. Ellis, a young schoolmaster, brought to Beadle and Adams a wilderness adventure with clear sales potential. *Seth Jones; or, The Captives of the Frontier* took plot, character, and setting from Fenimore Cooper. But Ellis transformed Cooper's Natty Bumppo—the backwoodsman isolated between two races—and

Bird's Nick—the schizophrenic Indian killer—into a backwoodsman who harmonizes savagery and civilization. Seth Jones is the avuncular, Indian-slaying hunter who, after saving various captives from the Mohawks, turns out, beneath his disguise, to be a young, aristocratic Easterner suited to marry the white heroine. Ellis produced a sunny, optimistic ending that erased the tension between East and West evident in Cooper's and Bird's divided endings: an important symbolic function in a time of national strife. Beadle mounted a massive advertising campaign for *Seth Jones* for several days before the novel's publication, running newspaper advertisements, billboards, and handbills with their tantalizing question "Who is Seth Jones?" followed by lithographs of a coonskin-capped hunter declaring "I am Seth Jones." The response was even more massive than to *Malaeska*. Ellis was a new, twenty-year-old author willing to join the Beadle stable and turn out endless imitations of his model for the next thirty years, whereas by 1860 Ann Stephens was almost fifty years old, an established author and editor whose production was more wedded to middle-class magazines than to Beadle and Adams's dime novels (though she continued to write for them intermittently). For various reasons, from the historical to the commercial to the personal, Ellis's version of the frontier adventure, a version that appropriated the wilderness for the glorification of white men rescuing white women and killing Indians, held sway in the Beadle production line.

This model was also perpetrated by the dime authors who brought the Western into the modern era. Ned Buntline introduced Buffalo Bill as a Western hero—both in dime fiction and on the New York stage. Then Prentiss Ingraham hammered home the point that this violent plainsman could fill the romantic role because his gentlemanly demeanor and exotic appearance brought together the savage and the civilized. Edward Wheeler created the Western outlaw when he introduced Deadwood Dick, another Easterner, disguised this time in a black costume and mask, in *Beadle's Half-Dime Library* of 1877. In the twentieth century, partly in response to the strictures of the Postmaster General, dime publishers turned to moralistic adventure stories about clean-cut boys; the most popular Western version of this formula was *Wild West Weekly,* a series about a gang of boys in the West led again by a displaced Easterner, which Frank Tousey began in 1902. In 1904 Street and Smith produced a close imitation, *Young*

*Rough Rider Weekly*, which played on associations with Teddy Roosevelt and carried Western adventure into the modern age, with battles revolving around commerce, property, and sport, not the killing of Native Americans. The characteristic line that survived through these decades of ritualized adventure was the imperative to marry frontiersman and gentleman, or West and East.

In terms of publishers, writers, and fictional formulas, dime novels were a male-dominated genre. However, from the beginning, publishers were interested in catching women readers, too, and made efforts to develop a distinct women's formula. As well as beginning the dime novel with Ann Stephens, Beadle published a number of women authors. One steady contributor was Metta V. Victor: her work is interesting not only because she was married to Beadle's chief editor but also because her *Maum Guinea and Her Plantation "Children"; or, Holiday-week on a Louisiana Estate, a Slave Romance* (1861) is an imitation of Stowe's *Uncle Tom's Cabin* that can stand alongside *Seth Jones* in literary historical significance; and her detective novel *The Dead Letter* (which appeared in *Beadle's Monthly* in 1866) is the first known detective story by a woman. Street and Smith also worked to produce an identifiably female genre with their "Bertha M. Clay" stories, first in the late 1870s, when *New York Weekly* pirated stories of Charlotte M. Braeme, a European author, under that name, and then in their dime series as a house pseudonym. In fact, Street and Smith used their regular stable of male authors—including William Wallace Cook—to produce these stories. There was no doubt, however, that they were designed to appropriate female ideology: Cook understood that he had been directed to write "a bit of sentimental fiction for young women."

This attempt to imitate the success of domestic women's fiction of the 1850s reaped massive rewards only once the formula was fitted to the changing social patterns of urbanizing America, toward the end of the century. Laura Jean Libbey became the stellar author of sensationalized stories set in the city, revolving around the trials, temptations, and romances of young working women. These novels were serialized in the Munroes' *Fireside Companion* and *Family Story Paper* in the 1880s and 1890s before being reprinted innumerable times by cheap publishers up to the 1920s. Accumulatively, they garnered such a huge audience that they won trademark status: in 1910,

*The Bookman* labeled the genre of working-girl romances "Laura Jean Libbeys." Libbey's formulaic plot revolved around a poor factory operative, shopgirl, or mill worker who manages to resist the unwelcome advances of the wealthy, upper-class villain, yet is often forced—unwittingly—into an illegal marriage with him, and finally ends the novel marrying an upper-class hero who admires her for her personal virtues that transcend her humble background. Although this formula privileges sentimentalism and romanticism, it is distinctly different from the mid-century domestic novel and from the post–Civil War novel of female religious zeal (for example, Augusta Jane Evans's *St. Elmo* [1868], the *sine qua non* of the type). Libbey sloughs off religiosity and focuses away from the middle-class domestic sphere, to follow the romantic dramas of the proletarian heroine in paid employment. (Her tales are also different from those by Horatio Alger, the other prolific formulist of the city in that period, partly because sexual passion rather than juvenile adventure is central to her treatment.)

In many ways, these novels are celebrations of working women, though that impression is complicated by the heroine's removal at the end of the novel to a wealthy domestic sphere and by the frequent revelation that the working girl was, unbeknownst to herself, a lost heiress. Critics have read these plots to different allegorical effect, some arguing that they told working-class readers that they could be both workers and heroines, others arguing that the endings betray and trivialize workers. In general, however, these plots clearly speak to the changes in women's status between about 1870 and 1920. More and more women were joining the work force, often with low-paying factory jobs, and considerable concern was being voiced about the effect of public employment on young women's virtue; in such a climate, the very figuring of the working girl as democratic heroine, her entry into a popular pantheon that included such nationalistically approved types as the hunter, the detective, and the honest mechanic, signaled some level of legitimacy. Fiction that heroized women outside the domestic sphere offered working-class women some kind of accommodation and justification, some means of negotiating the transition from private to public.

The messages of all these dime narratives are complicated not only by the relationship between formula and social agency but by the inscriptions of authorial voices in the texts. The Beadle and Adams authors forged a facsimile of a storyteller's relationship with their audience by talking to their readers about the commercial paraphernalia of the dime novel. In their earliest form, these tactics are familiar though exaggerated versions of inscriptions in the antebellum story papers. Buntline, for example, mounted a running commentary on his place in the production line, within his repetitive dime tales of captivity, chase, and rescue on the frontier, acknowledging the competitive commercialism of his task as author. Prentiss Ingraham and Edward Ellis implicated authors, characters, and readers in codes, conventions, and sign-systems, thus moving the fiction closer to an acknowledgment of its status in the publishing field. Edward Wheeler's characters completed the last refinement, by becoming independent of their author to the extent that they wrote their own plots, devised their own identities, and fought their own publishing battles. For example, just at the time that Street and Smith marketed an imitation of the Deadwood Dick series, Wheeler had his hero declare: "I see that counterfeits are being shoved on the market—that is, sham Deadwood Dicks. We have one here in Eureka.... I wish to meet this chap and learn where he obtained the right to use my copyrighted handle?" The voice that recognizes the rules of the marketplace and the systematic interchange between producer and the consumer now belonged to the characters. The shift in rhetorical power is a textual illustration of the diminution of authorial power, just around the time when authors were losing more of their autonomy in the publishing hierarchy. Libbey's tactic was rather different: she too recognized her readers, partly by representing them and constructing their responses in her fiction. In *Leonie Locke; or, The Romance of a Beautiful New York Working-Girl* (1884), for example, she wrote:

Many a working-girl read the story of Leonie Locke, and their honest hearts thrilled as they read the story of her struggle against adverse fate. She had been a working-girl like themselves; she had known all their privations, the early rising, hurried toilet and hurrying steps to the work-shop. She had known what it was to toil late and early for the sweet bread of life, and she had known all their sorrows and the pitiful desolation and fear of being discharged from work.

Libbey also maintained a strong authorial voice, but one reserved to the prefaces and advice columns that accompanied her fiction. Speaking in her own voice, she tempered her fantasies with comments on the harsh realities of urban life and contemporary gender relations, warning her young female readers about advances by men above them in social status. In different ways, these male and female narratives sustain a double vision, constructing formulaic fantasies accompanied by a demonstration of the realities, commercial and otherwise, supporting and implicitly critiquing these fictions.

Under the heavy hand of Street and Smith, these authorial gestures disappear, usurped by the publishers, who talk directly to the audience themselves. In juvenile nickel series, an editorial voice at the end of the story comments on the construction of the fiction, encourages readers to distribute it for financial rewards, and, in time, invites the audience to participate in its composition. The most emphatic example of this process occurred in the letters pages of *Rough Rider Weekly;* in response to conflicting advice from readers about whether Ted Strong, the hero, should or should not marry Stella, the heroine, the editor threw open the author's study and invited all the readers in: "So you think Ted and Stella should marry? What do the rest of our readers think about it? . . . There are two sides to this question, and we should like to have it decided by our readers." The fiction has become an overt bargaining tool between publisher and public; the only role left to the author was to carry out the audience's demands. It is the logical conclusion of the rhetoric initiated by the early story papers.

Reconstructing readers' responses to these authorial and narrative signs is even more problematic than classifying audience demographics. Some hypotheses have been constructed about the extent to which authorial resistance to the production line was matched by readers' responses, by scholars piecing together evidence from a patchwork of autobiographies, diaries, and reports by social reformers. The evidence suggests that male and female workers, at least, read dime fictions in ideologically charged ways. Denning argues that workers read cheap novels allegorically or typologically, interpreting a range of scenarios as microcosms of their social world. Thus, especially at times of industrial agitation and strikes in the late nineteenth century, workers could read the triumph of labor in stories of

Western outlaws—such as Edward Wheeler's *Deadwood Dick, the Prince of the Road; or, The Black Rider of the Black Hills* (1877)—as much as in those of honest mechanics exposing corrupt capitalists— in, for example, Frederick Whittaker's *Larry Locke, the Man of Iron; or, A Fight for Fortune. A Story of Labor and Capital* (1883–84). Similarly, working girls seem to have fashioned their fantasies toward self-empowerment. Dorothy Richardson's 1905 autobiography, *The Long Day: The Story of a New York Working Girl,* along with Joyce Shaw Peterson's analysis of it, suggests that women workers read Libbey as encoding their public situations, by dignifying labor and acknowledging the harshness of their city lives, yet also offering them visions of survival and transcendence that gave them private suste- nance. It can also be argued that the ways in which these women shared and constructed community around their reading signal their appropriation of these commercial productions into their own cul- ture. (The potentially empowering effects of such a communal re- sponse have been charted for our contemporary period by Janice Radway's account of women revisioning Harlequin romances.) Even beyond the consciously political environment of the adult world, in young audiences' responses, there is evidence that popular reading involves an active shaping of narrative, an expression of choice. Re- flecting on his son's response to 1950s comics, Robert Warshow speculated that the boy's fascination with the publishing house, the staff, and the drafting processes indicated a specific strategy on the part of the juvenile reader:

I think that Paul's desire to put himself directly in touch with the processes by which the comic books are produced may be the expression of a funda- mental detachment which helps to protect him from them; the comic books are not a "universe" to him, but simply objects produced for his entertain- ment.

One could object that the post–World War II boy was a more so- phisticated reader than his turn-of-the-century counterpart; the ex- tensive and ingenious editorial gestures of that era suggest, however, that publishers envisioned their audience as both potentially mallea- ble and ever resistant.

In the dime novels and nickel series of the later nineteenth cen- tury, publishers, authors, and readers staked their claims to self-empowerment and prominence. Reading these opposing moves—which are both productive of and expressed by the formulaic narratives—as "negotiation" is not to ignore the dangers of social control. After all, the culture industry ultimately circumscribed authors and readers by implicating them in the mass production process. Nor is the intent to represent these melodramas as seriously argued discourses on the political situation. However, fantasizing, as much as reading and writing, is a socially constructed activity with ideological implications; and collective fantasies accent the meanings of popular literature quite as much as individual authorial gestures do.

Some of that delicate balance may have been lost, at least at the textual level, in the imitators of dime novels spawned later in the twentieth century. Partly because of the postal restrictions on series of complete novels, pulp magazines took over from dime novels after World War I, bringing with them a new format and different editorial methods. These weekly and monthly magazines were miscellanies of short and long fiction with various features like quizzes, letters pages, and factual articles, printed on cheap pulp paper and selling for 10 cents or 15 cents. Pulps were invented in 1896, but they reached the height of their popularity only once they began to specialize after 1919: Street and Smith were first with this innovation, with their all-Western *Western Story Magazine*. The pulps died as a popular form around 1950.

By and large, pulp magazines offered the same formulaic narratives as the dime and nickel novels, dispensing with the juvenile emphasis and adding some violence and sex to the action. Perhaps because these formulas were so entrenched, pulp editors did not direct their authors very closely. Instead, they switched their most intense surveillance to the audience, trying to gauge and manipulate audience response through letters pages and editorial columns. Readers' contributions became formularized in departments—such as the "Wranglers' Corner" in *Wild West*—where characters respond to readers' letters in a facsimile of direct contact between readers and fictional figures, orchestrated by the editor. By this point, the authors often disappeared as personalities. In a final sign of mechanization, when the latter-day pulp *Far West* was launched in 1978, the readers' responses were limited to a multiple-choice questionnaire. Even the most commercial individuation was ultimately denied, in what reads as a logical process in the rationalization of labor.

By design, I have concentrated on the distinctive forms of popular production from the mid-nineteenth to the early twentieth century, in an effort to understand the central machinery driving the cheap fiction of the age. Complicating the narrative, however, are best-sellers that were not produced within mechanisms described above, yet clearly signaled significant ideologies. Running parallel to story-paper and dime-novel production, for example, were the monthly middle-class, middlebrow magazines aimed at a female audience. Periodicals such as *Godey's Lady's Book* (1830–98) and *Peterson's Magazine* (1842–98) made a significant impact on women's popular culture, though their sales were much smaller than those of the story papers and the dime novels: *Godey's,* the most popular magazine of this class, claimed to sell 150,000 copies a month. These publications encoded more genteel formulas and constructed a more middle-class audience: they carried sentimental, moralistic miscellanies of verse, sketches, and domestic stories, abundantly illustrated with engravings and full-color fashion plates; and they cost around $3 per year. Significantly, however, their editorial gestures are marked by the same commercialism as the cheaper publications. Although the intimate address developed by the first publisher-editor stressed gallantry and advice to the "fair Ladies," it also paid considerable attention to the annual expenditures and authorial fees involved in production.

Also significant among periodicals was the fiction serialized and reviewed in *Harper's Monthly* (1850–), *Harper's Weekly* (1857–1916), and *The Century* (formerly *Scribner's Monthly;* 1870–1930). Frank Luther Mott has styled the nineteenth-century *Harper's Monthly* as "the great successful middle-class magazine"; *Harper's Weekly* was subtitled "A Journal of Civilization": essentially, these periodicals sought to address "the plain people" in uplifting accents. To that end, they promoted lavish illustration, a predominance of British fiction, and a miscellany of essays of topical and educational interest. At the times of its very greatest popularity, *Harper's Monthly* sold around 200,000 copies (for $3, later $4 per annum). Where these magazines dovetail significantly with dime novels of

Western adventure, however, is in their publishing of Owen Wister's, Frederic Remington's, and Theodore Roosevelt's Western tales and illustrations in the late nineteenth century. The gentrification of the Western at the hands of these Ivy League authors, particularly as directed at a middle-class audience, brought the popular genre into the "mainstream" culture of the East and helped to deliver both the massive sales and the favorable reviews of Wister's *The Virginian* in 1902. This success also fed back into dime production in its influence on juvenile dime series of the early twentieth century.

Finally, another category of novels proved popular by consumption, and they appear in the standard bibliographies as "best-sellers" of the period. Such works are Mark Twain's *The Adventures of Tom Sawyer* (1876) and *The Adventures of Huckleberry Finn* (1884) and Stephen Crane's *The Red Badge of Courage* (1895), clearly works of a different order from the sensational narratives of dime novels and story papers. While these works lie beyond the scope of this chapter, even here it should be recognized that mass techniques left their imprint on novelistic rhetoric and reception. Twain, for example, borrowed the strategies of popular literature to parodic effect in his handling of dime novel blood-and-thunder stories voraciously devoured by Tom Sawyer and piously sentimental, female narratives hilariously misread by Huck Finn.

Story papers and dime novels were the most visible fictional forms of nineteenth-century America; explicitly conjoining the market economy with literary production, they set an agenda that could not be ignored. In literary historical terms, the cheap publications affected the larger climate of conventions and expectations governing literary production and consumption. Culturally, their mixture of commercial rhetoric, fictionalized history, and democratized sensationalism created stories that could be appropriated and accented by quite opposite groups. By this point, it is clear that Raymond Williams's definition of "popular" describes not discrete possibilities but the force field of conflicting interest groups, classes, individuals, and discourses activated by and in popular fiction. These stories were spoken by the people, inasmuch as story papers and dime novels fostered a massive new reading public, especially from the working classes, and those readers collectively and individually "authored" meanings in their own interests. At the same time, some authorial voices attempted to speak to the people, to fashion a direct address that sustained an impression of intimacy and individual relationship within the homogenizing effects of mass production. And the publishers sought to speak for the people. Developing marketing strategies to demarcate their audience by gender and generation, they produced several distinct formats for cheap fiction, each with its own ideology, agenda, and vocabulary. Fastening on historically and politically charged moments, the formulaic narratives and editorial mediations worked to incorporate both audience and authors into the economically driven "juggernaut" of the culture industry. Understanding both the "cultural work" and the rhetorical presence of popular literature in America involves reading this contest of resistant, assumed, and dominant voices.

Christine Bold

# The Early Twentieth Century

# Introduction

The chapters in this section remind us that culture and cultural production in the United States and around the world in the first half of the twentieth century were shaped by momentous political, technological, economic, and social developments. Large numbers of immigrants from Eastern Europe, Asia, Latin America, and other parts of the world; the unimaginable devastation of two world wars and the Korean War; the economic catastrophe known as the Great Depression; the migration of large numbers of African Americans from the deep South to population centers in the Northeastern, Midwestern, and Western states; the enactment of increasingly repressive laws and practices to monitor, control, and segregate members of disenfranchised racial and ethnic groups; changing constructions of gender and sexuality; the rise of new technologies and industries, among them motion pictures and television; the reforms associated with the New Deal; the scourge of McCarthyism—these developments, as well as others, altered inexorably the meanings that attach to the idea of "the American."

It is therefore not surprising that fiction produced in such an apparently turbulent period would respond in a variety of ways to these changes. Indeed, even a quick glance at the titles of the chapters in this section indicates that the authors all consider American novels in relation to circumstances under which they are produced, circulated, and read. Readers of this section will, no doubt, be struck by the various challenges that writers of the period offer to the meaning of a national identity and to the practice and work of fiction in the wake of the globalization of the United States economy, the internationalization of American culture, and the evolution of new media.

In this period, writers from groups historically underrepresented in the canon of American letters explored ways of representing the specific cultural practices of their communities that were accessible to a wider readership. Drawn, perhaps inevitably, to received literary forms such as realism, naturalism, regionalism, the romance, the Western, the detective novel, and so on, they challenge the boundaries of these genres by writing from fresh perspectives. In addition, the emergence of expatriate movements helped to situate American writing in an international scene and heightened the relationship between American narrative experimentation and innovations in other art forms.

Readers of this section should notice as well the prescience of American novelists in the first half of the twentieth century. In their search for narrative strategies that speak to the fabric of American experience; in their explorations of the space between fiction and history; in their quest for a language to address the power of visual media upon life in the United States; and in their simultaneous gestures toward universality and particularity, they anticipate movements and developments we have come to associate with postmodern and contemporary culture.

Valerie Smith

# Modernist Eruptions

An earthquake, the great San Francisco earthquake of 1906, becomes in Gertrude Stein's *The Autobiography of Alice B. Toklas* (1933) the massive disruption that loosened Alice B. Toklas from her American moorings and launched her on her journey to Europe and into modern literary history. Like many of Stein's narratives, the anecdote makes only tenuous sense: apparently the earthquake forced Stein's brother and his wife to return abruptly from Europe, and Alice B. Toklas, her placid life already shaken by earthquake and fire, became even more unsettled when she saw what the Steins brought with them. "Mrs. Stein brought with her three little Matisse paintings, the first modern things to cross the Atlantic." Thus Stein's narration slyly links the natural earthquake in America to the first tiny rumblings of the European modern art movement that would become a cultural cataclysm in the early twentieth century. This traffic of modern art between Europe and America turned sensational in 1913, when over 1500 international works of highly experimental art were exhibited at the 69th Regiment Armory in New York City, and a shocked American audience found Marcel Duchamp's *Nude Descending a Staircase* insane and depraved.

American artists, generally committed to a national literature as free as possible of British influence, responded in a variety of ways to the lure of modern European culture. Some, like Robert Frost and Carl Sandburg, stayed home and continued to work "in the American grain," to borrow William Carlos Williams's phrase. Some were drawn to Chicago, which became a hub of American literary activity and the home of such important modernist publications as *Poetry*, edited by Harriet Monroe, and the early *Little Review,* edited by Margaret Anderson and Jane Heap. As Hugh Kenner argued in *A Homemade World* (1974), the Continental influence eventually found its way back to America, where it produced a "homemade" variety of modernism. Meanwhile, other young artists, equipped with that spirit of experimentation they considered quintessentially American, went off to Europe. T. S. Eliot, Ezra Pound, and Hilda Doolittle ("H. D.") first stopped in London, and the rather conservative Eliot, his temperament responding to the tradition, order, and Anglicanism of England, stayed on. Some, like Ernest Hemingway and F. Scott Fitzgerald, were swept across the Atlantic with the tides of war or its aftermath, and were caught up in the excited cultural tumult they encountered there. France, especially, offered Americans a place where they suffered none of the anxieties that threatened their postcolonial psyches in England, and Paris became a Mecca for young American "expatriates," who revolved around a series of literary salons and centers usually dominated by brilliant and enterprising American women—Gertrude Stein's salon at 27 rue de Fleurus, Sylvia Beach's bookstore Shakespeare and Company, Natalie Barney's *pavillon* with its leafy garden and Doric temple in the rue Jacob.

Gertrude Stein was the first of the American expatriates to cross the Atlantic and settle in Europe—arriving in Paris in 1903, after having acquired a fine education at Radcliffe that included instruction from the psychologist William James, brother of the novelist. Within a year of her arrival she was studying a painting by Cezanne of his wife, in order to appropriate his techniques for her own experimental verbal portraits, which she eventually published at her own expense in 1909 as *Three Lives*. In these three portraits of American women, two German-American servants and a young African American woman, Stein dismantled the mythology of the American dream by using her newly discovered Continental techniques to forge a writing capable of illuminating its hypocrisies and ironies. At the same time, her technique, like postimpressionist painting, drew attention to its own procedures. Inspired by Gustave Flaubert, whose story "Un Coeur Simple" she had translated to improve her French, Stein told the stories of these exploited women in a severely unadorned and stripped prose that would make Flaubert's style the enduring standard of the language of modernist fiction. Ezra Pound would, ten years later, promote James Joyce's *Dubliners* and *A Portrait of the Artist as a Young Man* on precisely this ground: the verbal economy that Joyce called "a scrupulous meanness" reflected the clean, clear, disciplined, impersonal expression inaugurated by Flaubert's quest for *le mot juste* as an antidote to Romanticism both in expressive language and in sentiment.

But in *Three Lives* Stein was not only looking backward to the French novel tradition, she was also looking toward "the new" with a canny combination of insights from the American pragmatism that she had learned in college, applied to understanding the European postimpressionism that was confounding art lovers with the exorbitant demands it made on them for an active, fragmented, and creative perception. William James's theories taught Stein to think of cognition as an active, selective, purposive process aimed not at finding transcendent truths but at creative exercise of its own powers. She toyed with automatic writing in the wake of his classes (as the Surrealists and other moderns, notably the wife of W. B. Yeats, did also) to demonstrate to herself the creative and alert potential of cognition and its language even when removed from intention—like Sigmund Freud, whose *Interpretation of Dreams* (1900) showed the intense poetic activity of the sleeping mind. As a result, her first encounter with postimpressionist painting in France did not discomfit her as it did the many Europeans who felt disoriented by the abandonment of a focalized perspective and by the fragmentation of the viewer's position that would become even further radicalized by Cubism during the next decade.

The abstraction of formal elements that she found in Cezanne's still lifes, the attention to the geometries of shapes that made his canvases a composition of spheres and cones, Stein adapted in a prose that foregrounded the geometries of language, the nouns and verbs and adjectives, the pauses and punctuations that she would love all of her life. In the careful construction and repetitions of her sentences in *Three Lives*—"It was a very happy family there all together in the kitchen, the good Anna and Sally and old Baby and young Peter and jolly little Rags"—Stein created a stylistic primer of the symmetry and formality of the common sentence while simultaneously rendering its fatuous logic ironic. In later years she would write this sentence again, only this time about the sentence itself: "It makes everybody happy to have words together. It makes everybody happy to have words apart."

These experiments culminated in the collection of prose pieces she called *Tender Buttons* (1914), where Stein moved from the postimpressionism of *Three Lives* to the extreme abstraction of a verbal Cubism with only vestigial references to represented things. In *Tender Buttons* Stein abandons even the already abstracted mimesis of the still life hinted at in her subtitle—"objects food rooms"—to concentrate on the concrete qualities and compositional possibilities of words themselves. It is not objects, food, and rooms that she represents but the playful disposition, in juxtapositions we now recognize as collage, of the sounds and look of words associated with objects, food, and rooms. "A sight a whole sight and a little groan grinding makes a trimming such a sweet singing trimming and a red thing not a round thing but a white thing, a red thing and a white thing." With this writing, the reader becomes a viewer who must forgo communication with a work of art that does not ask to be "understood" but obtrudes its medium—words as concrete as though they were laid on with a knife, like the thick paint Stein reports the outraged public tried to scratch off Matisse's *La Femme au Chapeau* at the autumn salon—and as full of harmonic gradations as a musical composition by Stein's friend Erik Satie, who himself playfully invoked painting in such titles as "Three Pieces in the Shape of a Pear."

But Stein's grand opus, a thousand-page American genealogy called *The Making of Americans,* represents an astonishingly early text of modernistic maturity: well underway while T. S. Eliot was still a Harvard undergraduate, the work was completed in 1911 (but not published until 1925), several years before Ezra Pound published his Imagist manifesto in the March 1913 issue of *Poetry* magazine or Ernest Hemingway saw his first Red Cross ambulance in 1917. Written far ahead of its time, this big book should have established itself as Stein's revolutionary masterwork, her *Finnegans Wake,* as it were: the most avant-garde of the modern family epics that include John Galsworthy's post-Victorian *Forsyte Saga,* Thomas Mann's neobaroque *Buddenbrooks,* and D. H. Lawrence's scandalous *The Rainbow.* From its startling opening narration—"Once an angry man dragged his father along the ground through his own orchard. 'Stop!' cried the groaning old man at last, 'Stop!' I did not drag my father beyond this tree" — Stein makes her own writing a violent remembering of violent rememberings, an allegory of the verbal and stylistic manhandling of one's literary forebears and traditions. Her remarkable grammatical effects in this text reflect her progress in elaborating the metaphysical implications for the collapse of traditional notions of space and time that were inaugurated with Albert Einstein's publication of his work on the special theory of relativity in 1905, and that Stein, like many other American writers including William Faulkner, attended more closely in the works of the French philosopher Henri Bergson's notion of a *durée,* a subjective quality of time as a present duration observable in memory. Stein, who was also friendly with Alfred North Whitehead and therefore familiar with his work on the relations of time, space, and matter, made the syntactical handling of tense in her writing a performance of the way the times of life in individuals and families felt during their present duration:

Repeating is always in every one, it settles in them in the beginning of their middle living to be a steady repetition with very little changing. There may be in them then much beginning and much ending, but it is steady repeating in them and the children with them have in them the pounding of steady march of repeating the parents of them have in them.

Stein's prose too has in it the steady pounding of the repeating, thereby rendering its own voice or speech, its own speaking ego or narrating subject, itself as intuitively atremble as the living being of the Herslands, whose story it tells. Before "stream of consciousness" was even properly implemented by Virginia Woolf and James Joyce as a salient technique of novelistic modernism, Gertrude Stein was already problematizing it and dismantling it in her texts.

Stein insisted throughout her life that she had invented modern writing, yet both in her own time, and during the decades after World War II when critical opinion was shaping the literary history of the modern period, her significance as an innovator was eclipsed by that of the "lost generation" novelists (to borrow her own term), Ernest Hemingway, Sherwood Anderson, and F. Scott Fitzgerald, whom she befriended, encouraged, and instructed. Until a recent critical tendency began to elevate and foreground avant-garde texts over more traditional modernist productions, Stein's reputation survived mainly on the basis of her salon, her art collection, her patronage of Picasso, Matisse, and Gris, and her dominant personality that evoked both subtle and crude ambivalences in people made uncomfortable by the unconventional way she deployed her own gender identity. Her intellectual and artistic ambitions and her social power tended to be construed as egotistical and patriarchal in this gifted woman, who had been writing and experimenting for nearly twenty years before the Nineteenth Amendment gave women the vote in the United States in August 1920. The feminist impulses that led her to make her first sustained text a coded lesbian novel (*Q.E.D.; or, Things as They Are* [1903]), and to treat in *Three Lives* the conditions of lower-class ethnic women who are, in fiction, the most invisible Americans, flowered in her most popular and famous book, the 1933 *Autobiography of Alice B. Toklas*. Turning conventional perspectives upside down, like a Cubist painting, this revisionary history restores to the success of the modern art movement the labors and contributions of the wives, mistresses, sisters, and servants who invisibly cooked, kept house, posed, inspired, typed, managed, published, and loved the artists and made their work possible. Matisse may have been master to his disciples (Stein playfully called him the C. M. or *cher maître*), but it was Madame Matisse who posed until she was exhausted, took care of his diphtheritic daughter, accepted his abuse, and taught him how to haggle with buyers. She more than deserved to season her soup with the laurel wreath her husband eventually had bestowed on him. With the cunning inversion that lets Alice's voice and interest tell the story of modern art, Stein offers her own companion a silver anniversary gift in the form of a textual embrace, a text that problematizes the notion of authorship with a principle of female collectivity that makes it ambiguous and undecidable whether it was Gertrude or Alice who "created" the books, having become two in one mind and one life as well as in one flesh.

The issue of gender was just one of many complex factors informing the extremely heterogeneous and complex ideology of modernism. Much of the conservatism of "high modernism," the classical poetics of T. S. Eliot and Ezra Pound, was produced by the fusion of an antiromantic intellectual bias, formally articulated by the young

English critic T. E. Hulme (who fell in World War I), and wedded to an elitist reaction against what was perceived, in the tradition of Matthew Arnold, as the greedy materialism, cultural philistinism, and spiritual bankruptcy of modern society. In his *Culture and Anarchy* (1869), Arnold wrote, "Our society distributes itself into Barbarians, Philistines, and Populace; and America is just ourselves, with the Barbarians quite left out, and the Populace nearly. This leaves the Philistines for the bulk of the nation." Art, by imposing a geometry, discipline, and order on itself, served the modernists as a formal bulwark against what Eliot in his essay on Joyce's *Ulysses* was to call "the immense panorama of futility and anarchy which is contemporary history." Pound, in his essay "Why Books?," was to write of "the damned and despised *litterati*" — "when their very medium, the very essence of their work, the application of word to thing goes rotten, i.e. becomes slushy and inexact, or excessive and bloated, the whole machinery of social and individual thought and order goes to pot." In the principles of Imagism, which Pound articulated for poetry during the years 1912 to 1915, he promoted a poetic language "austere, direct, free of emotional slither." This technique of verbal economy and precision was supplemented with a psychology of impersonality, encouraging the poet to adopt many voices, masks, or personae in place of poetic subjectivity or personal commentary.

During this same period, Pound along with the artist, critic, and writer Wyndham Lewis and the sculptor Henri Gaudier-Brzeska began to augment the formalism of Imagism with an emphasis on the creation of energy and the celebration of violence that they shaped into a short-lived movement called Vorticism, and whose chief product was a highly avant-garde journal that began publication in June 1914 called *Blast: The Review of the Great English Vortex*. This movement included among its inspirations the 1909 manifesto by the Italian Futurist Filippo Marinetti with its glorification of war, violence, virility, and speed: "We wish to glorify War—the only health giver of the world—militarism, patriotism, the destructive arm of the Anarchist, the beautiful ideas that kill, the contempt for women." These values anticipate those of the fascist ideology that would engulf Italy and Germany in the thirties, and that swept not only Marinetti but also Pound and Lewis into its destructive philosophical vision. Pound and Lewis's *Blast* was first published in June 1914; within three months war was declared, and the conflict that we call World War I began: the first fully mechanized modern war fought for four years, 1914–18, with machine guns, mortars, bombers, aerial dogfights, tanks, and poison gas—much of it in seemingly endless and stalemated trenches. The unprecedented slaughter and horror of this war created a virtually indeterminable number of casualties. The conservative estimate is 10 million dead and 20 million wounded, and the dead included a generation of European poets and writers, claiming T. E. Hulme, Wilfred Owen, Isaac Rosenberg, Alan Seeger, Julian Grenfell, and Rupert Brooke among the English, the Germans Georg Trakl, August Stramm, and Ernst Stadler, the French poet Guillaume Apollinaire, and Pound's friend, the sculptor Gaudier-Brzeska. The war poetry produced by these writers before their deaths reflects the state of art in their countries at the time of the war. The English poets struggled with mixed success to free themselves from the Georgian pastoralism that was the established and accepted form of English poetry at the same time that Pound and his American cohorts were turning it upside down with their modernist manifestos. The Germans and the French, in contrast, were using the avant-gardism already flourishing in their countries to produce a far more experimental, ironic, and nihilistic poetry, like that of August Stramm, for example, who uses destroyed syntactic forms to express the destroyed worlds and consciousnesses of dying soldiers. Because America did not enter the war until 1917, American soldiers largely escaped the "troglodyte war" (as Paul Fussell calls it in *The Great War and Modern Memory* [1975]) of the claustrophobic, nightmarish trenches, and the American literary treatment of World War I is consequently different as well. The American "high modernists," Pound and Eliot, treat World War I chiefly as a metaphor, a sign or symptom of a spiritually rotten modern world. "There died a myriad/ And the best,/ among them,/ For an old bitch gone in the teeth,/ For a botched civilization," Pound wrote in *Hugh Selwyn Mauberley* in 1919.

In the work of Ernest Hemingway, the young American novelist whom Pound praised as a prose "imagist," the high modernist remedy of using a disciplined, muscular, classical style to redeem the fragmentation, loss of value, and chaos both symptomatized and produced by the war, without wasting the energy of its violence, achieved its most successful fictional realization. Even before Pound gave Hemingway a moral theory of style, Hemingway learned to think of writing as a rigorous craft of producing clarity, simplicity, and strength of statement and expression while working as a young reporter for the *Kansas City Star*. This early journalistic training was interrupted by his decision to volunteer for Red Cross service as an ambulance driver and canteen operator for Italian soldiers in the summer of 1917—an experience itself disrupted when he was wounded in the leg by machine gun fire and shrapnel. Over ten years later, his fictionalized version of this early adventure was published as *A Farewell to Arms* (1929), the story of a young American serving as ambulance driver for the Italian army, who deserts and escapes the horror of the war with a young English nurse, only to have his idyllic sanctuary destroyed by her death in childbirth. Compared with Erich Maria Remarque's horrific and despairing tale of trench warfare published nearly at the same time (*All Quiet on the Western Front*), Hemingway's novel could be construed as romanticizing the war by displacing it onto a tragic love story. But the clean, hard prose keeps any sentimentality or idealism at bay: "He said there was so much dirt blown into the wound that there had not been much hemorrhage. They would take me as soon as possible. He went back inside. Gordini could not drive, Manera said. His shoulder was smashed and his head was hurt. He had not felt bad but now the shoulder had stiffened." The simple declarative sentences built on a strong scaffolding of substantives have been stripped of adverbial or descriptive excess and poetic adornment to the point where Ihab Hassan refers to Hemingway's style as an "anti-style."

But its modernistic impersonality, the way Hemingway replaces direct emotional expression with what T. S. Eliot called an "objective correlative," that is, the displacement of mood and feeling onto an impersonal and objective image, scene, or description that evokes, rather than names or speaks the emotion, allows him to transform style—in writing, gesture, and living—into an ethical act. He does this quite strikingly with a daring rhetorical maneuver in his first, and perhaps major novel, *The Sun Also Rises*, published in 1926, in which the protagonist narrator, Jake Barnes, is a man literally castrated by the war, whose language must emblematize a mode of coping with the sterility, nihilism, and corruption of the postwar modernity without self-indulgence or self-delusion. The jaded coterie of the opening Paris episodes of the novel was based on a circle of Hemingway friends that gives *The Sun Also Rises* the status of a *roman à clef*—Brett Ashley derived from Duff Twysden, Robert Cohn from Harold Loeb, Pedro Romero from the bullfighter Cayetano Ordonez. The plot describes the quest of this group (a quest often read by critics as a mythic variant of the same Grail legend whose themes of impotence and regeneration served T. S. Eliot as poetic paradigm for *The Waste Land*) for an alternative to the forced gaiety and shallow pleasures of the Paris café scene by way of a bucolic fishing trip to Burguete ("Before I could finish baiting, another trout jumped at the falls, making the same lovely arc and disappearing into the water that was thundering down") and a fiesta visit to the Dionysian running of the bulls in Pamplona in Spain.

In the figure of the perfect bullfight Hemingway offers his emblem of modernist art as redemption of modern sterility and futility by interpreting its ritual as the transformation of violence, by discipline and control, into art and beauty. Hemingway's description of Romero's technique might double as a description of his own craft as a writer:

Romero never made any contortions, always it was straight and pure and natural in line. The others twisted themselves like corkscrews, their elbows raised, and leaned against the flanks of the bull after his horns had passed, to give a faked look of danger. Afterward, all that was faked turned bad and gave an unpleasant feeling. Romero's bull-fighting gave real emotion, because he kept the absolute purity of line in his movements and always quietly and calmly let the horns pass him close each time.

Hemingway's own straightness and purity of line, that is, his refusal to contrive inflated emotional effects or extravagant plots and ornamental prose, become the stylistic equivalent of the proto-existentialist stoicism that makes Jake Barnes able to accept and face existence as it is—without the crutch of romanticism, idealism, or illusion. The novel ends in a famous line announcing Jake Barnes's naming and resisting of romantic delusion. To Brett's mourning the loss of their love—"Oh, Jake . . . we could have had such a damned good time together"—he responds, "Yes. . . . Isn't it pretty to think so?"

One of the few moderns without a college education, Hemingway tended to be regarded as the least intellectual of the modernists, called the "dumb ox" by the critics for his promotion of unreflective brawn in his fiction. But Hemingway read widely during the twenties, borrowing books assiduously from Sylvia Beach's lending library at Shakespeare and Company, and he read under the productive tutelage of Stein and Pound. From both he learned to value Flaubert; from Pound he learned the importance of the stylistic inventions of T. S. Eliot and James Joyce. Hemingway seems not to have read philosophy widely or deeply, but he may have acquired the vision we now recognize as his proto-existentialist code of courage and fatalism in the face of *nada,* nothingness, from reading the Russians, particularly Dostoevsky ("Dostoevsky was made by being sent to Siberia"), Tolstoy ("I thought about Tolstoi and what a great advantage an experience of war was to a writer"), and Turgenev. This code generates the figure of the solitary individual coming to terms with an existence of meaningless violence and extremity, the soldier, the hunter, the bullfighter, the fisherman, the writer, obliged to prove not only physical valor but also the moral courage implicit in honest, undeluded judgment and precise, undistorting language, that continues to dominate such later fiction as *For Whom the Bell Tolls* (1940), Hemingway's novel about the Spanish Civil War, and the haunting *The Old Man and the Sea* (1952) about an old fisherman's solitary struggle to bring in his greatest fish. But when Hemingway ventures into the realm of philosophical writing, as he does in his nonfiction works on bullfighting (*Death in the Afternoon* [1932]) and safari hunting (*Green Hills of Africa* [1935]), the hidden hypocrisies and perversities of his project are betrayed by his writing, as in life they were betrayed in the growing personality cult that made him a media celebrity and masculinist icon until his death by suicide in 1962. His Nietzschean individualism (although Hemingway seems to have read little Nietzsche beyond *Thus Spake Zarathustra*) can be seen to mask an egotism that escapes social responsibility in forms of adventurism such as war, bullfighting, and safari hunting. Its amoral anti-altruism further licenses a blatant array of oppressive discursive practices in Hemingway's writing: homophobia ("the nasty, sentimental pawing of humanity of a Whitman and all the mincing gentry," he writes in indictment also of Gide, Wilde, and other "fairies"); anti-Semitism ("it certainly improved his nose," Jake Barnes says of Robert Cohn, the Jewish boxer in *The Sun Also Rises*); racism ("I had had no chance to train them; no power to discipline," of his black African guides. "If there had been no law I would have shot Garrick"); his misogynistic portraits of women as "bitches"; and a penchant for sadism found in his culturally rationalized love of cruelty, aggression, and violence that, in spite of his Loyalist sympathies during the Spanish Civil War, revealed some affinities shared with the violent futurist ideology. In pointed contrast to Stein's relatively benign memoir of Paris in the twenties, Hemingway's 1956 reminiscence, *A Moveable Feast,* seems an unworthy surrender to ingratitude and self-indulgent malice.

Against the background of the changing social and political developments of America in the twenties and the thirties, the exoticism of Hemingway's settings and the solipsism of his concerns gradually made his fiction seem escapist and relevant only on the level of a specific American mythology, his modern and cosmopolitan updating of the figure of the American Western hero, the pioneer, the gunslinger, the cowboy. The broader, extremely vital and complex, historical panorama of American life during these decades was left to other American novelists to express: William Faulkner, inventing highly experimental forms to articulate the moral conundrums of the emerging modern South; John Dos Passos, who expressed the urban American immigrant experience as a montage of vernacular speech and a collage panorama of struggling lives and historical events in *Manhattan Transfer* (1925) and his *U.S.A.* trilogy (collected 1938); the writers of the Harlem Renaissance, like Langston Hughes and Zora Neale Hurston, who incorporated the rich voices of African American dialect, old folkloric storytelling rhythms, and new blues sounds into poetry and prose; and F. Scott Fitzgerald, the simultaneous lyricist and demystifier of the modern American dream. Dos Passos and Fitzgerald could well be paired to emblematize the fractured and schizophrenic nature of the American reality for the different American populations of the early decades of the twentieth century.

Rapid technological advances and the increasing urbanization of American labor by immigrants and Southern African Americans brought in their wake an era of great union and populist political activity, ideologically vitalized by the Russian Revolution of 1917 but increasingly resisted by a government alarmed by "the Red scare" into enacting such controversial paranoid gestures as the Sedition Act of 1918, the deportation of the anarchist Emma Goldman to Russia in 1919, and the 1920 trial and 1927 execution of the anarchists Sacco and Vanzetti. Dos Passos's novels allude to these events and fictionally elaborate both the emotional texture and the ideological grain of the historical milieu in which they were engendered. But the work of F. Scott Fitzgerald, one of the most popular and financially successful of the American novelists of the modernist period, gazed over these churning classes and masses populating the American landscape, much as his own character Daisy Buchanan is described, as enjoying "the mystery that wealth imprisons and preserves, of the freshness of many clothes . . . gleaming like silver, safe and proud above the hot struggles of the poor." Fitzgerald captures less the reality than the fantasy of another America that occupied the cultural horizon during the twenties: the "Jazz Age" (he called two collections of short stories *Flappers and Philosophers* [1921] and *Tales of the Jazz Age* [1922]), the era of Prohibition and wild financial speculation, the jostling of Jamesian "old money" with vulgar American *arrivistes,* the aesthetics of glamour produced by material and social extravagance—simulated and stimulated by the celluloid images of the burgeoning movie industry for which Fitzgerald intermittently wrote. Some would say he prostituted his talent writing for the screen, but he would also have demystified the film industry had he lived to complete his final novel, *The Last Tycoon,* a book edited by his friend Edmund Wilson and published in 1941.

Fitzgerald's more privileged milieu—his attendance at Princeton, which lent him the material for his first novel, *This Side of Paradise* (1920), which in turn brought him the fame and money to court successfully a beautiful, highstrung woman from Alabama, Zelda Sayre—generated more specifically social and ideological concerns voiced in a more symbolistic style than that of the other modernists. Fitzgerald arrived in Europe later than Hemingway, in 1924, and it was during this Continental sojourn, when, like Hemingway, he too fell under the tutelage of Pound and Stein, that he published *The Great Gatsby* (1925), a work still frequently nominated as "the great American novel." But although *Gatsby* bears the modernistic hallmark of a clean, hard prose, its craft is less foregrounded and self-displaying, less the logopoetic focus of its own fiction than is the work of Hemingway and Stein. Hemingway and Fitzgerald seem also to have been influenced differently by their literary traditions, with Hemingway choosing *Huckleberry Finn* as his American gospel, while Fitzgerald grounded himself in the late nineteenth-century architects of the American moral imagination, Henry James and Theodore Dreiser. From the Continental tradition, too, Fitzgerald seemed to derive a larger share of irony, not just *le mot juste* of Flaubertian fiction, but Flaubert's curious logocentric modernization of the Continental adultery novel that allows him to determine the function of romances, books, and magazines in shaping the dreams and desires of, say, an Emma Bovary. Jay Gatsby outlines his Horatio Alger program on the flyleaf of *Hopalong Cassidy,* and Jordan Baker's beauty reminds Nick Carraway that "she looked like a good illustration." This stylistic and philosophical divergence in the strategies of Hemingway and Fitzgerald was already etched in their different secular "occupations" before coming to Europe: Hemingway's stints as a reporter and journalist against Fitzgerald's work for an advertisement agency and as a contributor to H. L. Mencken and George Jean Nathan's *Smart Set.* In a *Gatsby* vignette that updates the adultery novel, Fitzgerald represents Myrtle Wilson, the lower-class mistress of wealthy Tom Buchanan's slumming, reclining with her nose broken by her lover "on the couch, bleeding fluently, and trying to spread a copy of *Town Tattle* over the tapestry scenes of Versailles." Versailles, the emblem of monarchical glamour whose nineteenth-century dregs Emma Bovary tries to recapture in her "aristocratic" adulteries (as well as site of the disastrous treaty that marked the closure of World War I), has become commodified as pretentious home and hotel decor of the American rich, while the society gossip rag is used to mop up the blood that will be spilled far more copiously by the socialite Buchanans before the ends of their double affairs.

Fitzgerald also read and admired the work of Joseph Conrad, and although he is known to have read Conrad's preface to *The Nigger of the Narcissus* just before writing *Gatsby,* it is Conrad's *Heart of Darkness* that leaves the clearest imprint on that text. They would seem to have little in common—*Heart of Darkness,* Conrad's dark tale of the European rape of Africa, and *The Great Gatsby,* Fitzgerald's tale of a single, hot Long Island summer in 1922, when Jay Gatsby, the fabulously wealthy and glamorous tycoon is unmasked and destroyed in his attempts to realize the American dream by recapturing his lost and now married sweetheart, Daisy Buchanan. But Fitzgerald keeps his focus on the same issue as Conrad—the disastrous moral cost in hypocrisy and destructiveness that civilization at its most opulent and attractive entails: "They were careless people, Tom and Daisy—they smashed up things and creatures and then retreated back into their money or their vast carelessness, or whatever it was that kept them together, and let other people clean up the mess they had made." The novel's polemical task is the seduction and disillusionment of the reader, and to this end Fitzgerald borrows Conrad's narrative device of adopting the impressionable and corruptible vision of an implicated *naif*, Nick Carraway, the nice Midwestern boy who, like Conrad's Marlow, must disentangle the moral enigma of a charismatic man whose immense idealism—"he found that he had committed himself to the following of a grail"—becomes too large, and, passing beyond good and evil, betrays itself. Instead of the suborning of justice in the Sacco-Vanzetti case that so obsessed Dos Passos and the American writers of the Left, Nick Carraway's great moral shock comes from Gatsby's implication in the betrayal of an institution invested with the mythology of the American dream: the "Black Sox" scandal over the fixing of the 1919 World Series. Nick Carraway's negotiation of the attractions and repulsions by the glamorous world of Gatsby and the Buchanans is conducted through a poetic language charged with moral complexity. Of Daisy Buchanan's seductive voice, Nick Carraway tells Gatsby:

"She's got an indiscreet voice," I remarked. "It's full of—" I hesitated.
    "Her voice is full of money," he said suddenly.
    That was it. I'd never understood it before. It was full of money—that was the inexhaustible charm that rose and fell in it, the jingle of it, the cymbals' song of it. . . . High in a white palace the king's daughter, the golden girl . . .

Like Conrad's Marlow, Nick Carraway too is ultimately confronted with a choice of nightmares, and like Marlow, who sides with the demonic idealism of Kurtz against the hard greed of the Company, Carraway sides with the doomed and self-corrupting questing of the impostor Gatsby against the hard amorality of the rich Buchanans: "I found myself on Gatsby's side and alone."

Fitzgerald achieves both Nick's and the reader's troubled repulsions in the world of Gatsby by producing spiritually resonating distortions and symbols that defamiliarize the world and make it strange, and that we associate with the techniques of Expressionism that James Joyce had already incorporated into the brilliant and shocking Nighttown section of his modernistic 1922 novel *Ulysses.* The valley of the ashes that separates West Egg and New York—"a fantastic farm where ashes grow like wheat into ridges and hills and grotesque gardens"—is such an expressionistic device, as is the ghostly giant oculist's billboard of "the eyes of Doctor T. J. Eckleburg," whose function as a blind panopticon inserts an image of an ineffectual conscience (ironically created by advertisement) into the amoral spiritual landscape of America. Fitzgerald's brilliant early promise was not sustained, even though his long-anticipated *Tender Is the Night,* with its more opulent and richly poetic prose, was considered by many a second masterpiece. This tragic story of the dissolution of the doomed marriage of a beautiful, wealthy, glamorous couple, in which many readers saw a reflection of the Fitzgeralds' own struggles with alcoholism, infidelity, madness, and institutionalization, failed in 1934 to make its panorama of the private angst of an American moneyed elite, disporting itself on the Riviera, relevant to an America in the grip of the brutal Great Depression. When Fitzgerald died prematurely in 1940 of a heart attack hastened by alcoholism and depression, none of his books were in print.

Modernism, then, changed during the thirties, with the Depression, the New Deal reforms, the Federal Writers' Project, and other WPA projects that followed in the wake of the stock market crash of 1929. Although that year saw the publication of William Faulkner's *The Sound and the Fury,* a book that overtakes *The Great Gatsby* as a great modern American novel, the politicalization of American fiction by such writers as Dos Passos, James T. Farrell, Richard Wright, Meridel Le Sueur, and John Steinbeck marked the end of American high modernism, as stylistic experimentation was put increasingly in the service of revolutionary and protest literature. During this period the critical voice of *Partisan Review,* especially, promoted an engaged literature organized around a new "proletarian" fiction that would make art socially responsible to the economically and racially oppressive times reflected in such events as the coal miners' strikes of Harlan County, Kentucky, and the 1931 trial for rape of a white woman by eight African American men, the "Scottsboro boys," sentenced to death by an Alabama court and eventually pardoned. The remains of a more purely logopoetic American fiction of the kind associated with high modernism took an avant-garde form inspired by the German expressionism and French and Spanish surrealism of the early twentieth century, and issued in the thirties in an American version strongly marked by gothic elements. The high modernistic prototype of this neogothic mode of fiction was created by Sherwood Anderson, who wrote his "Book of the Grotesque," a collection of tales of hidden, anguished, small-town lives published as *Winesburg, Ohio* (1919), under the influence of the pure syntax and language he had first encountered in the writing of Gertrude Stein's *Three Lives* and *Tender Buttons*. Anderson, who in 1932 joined fifty-one other writers in signing a "manifesto" backing a Communist presidential ticket, in turn influenced William Faulkner and Nathanael West (*Miss Lonelyhearts* [1933] and *The Day of the Locust* [1939]), two other American novelists in whose fiction the lives of simple, poor, and alienated people are dilated, by sometimes fantastic narrative and stylistic distortions, into subjectivities invaded by nightmare, criminality, and madness.

It was James Joyce, whose *A Portrait of the Artist as a Young Man* had served in the teens as model of the verbal purity of high modernistic prose, who led the way into the stylistics of verbal excess and derangement with the neologistic, densely allusive, hallucinogenic nightlanguage of his avant-garde 1939 dream text, *Finnegans Wake.* Published throughout the thirties in installments in Eugene Jolas's magazine *transition,* an avant-garde publication committed to "the revolution of the word," Joyce's new work revitalized the surrealistic tendencies that were to mark the avant-garde maturity of modernism at the same time that they inaugurated the self-consuming, self-exhausting, self-conscious fictionality of postmodernism. Samuel Beckett, who served as Joyce's amanuensis and friend during the writing of *Finnegans Wake,* became the first of the *Wake*'s postmodern heirs, which later included Vladimir Nabokov and Jorge Luis Borges. Of American novelists, it was Djuna Barnes who brought this strange subversive amalgam of nightmare and unreality, of verbal illogicality and brilliant discursive excess, of philosophical destruction and nihilism saved only by pure, nonsensical language itself, to fruition in her own 1936 night-novel, *Nightwood*. Trained as an artist in New York—she would later illustrate some of her texts with fine woodcuts—Barnes, like Hemingway, worked as a journalist (albeit a very different sort of journalist) in the United States before going to Paris on assignment for *McCall's* magazine in 1919. Her feature writing covered circus and vaudeville, and prompted her occasionally to participate in both sensationalistic and serious "stunts"—jumping from a skyscraper into a fireman's net or allowing herself to be forcefed in order to articulate the plight of imprisoned, hunger-striking suffragists. Before coming to Paris, she had several one-act plays produced by the Provincetown Players, and during her two decades in Paris she was a lively member of Natalie Barney's lesbian salon, whose coterie she celebrated and lampooned in the hilarious eighteenth-century pastiche of lesbian eroticism she had privately printed and circulated as *Ladies Almanack* in 1929. Barnes enjoyed as well the patronage of two powerful modernist giants, James Joyce, who granted her a rare interview for *Vanity Fair* in 1922, and T. S. Eliot, who wrote an admiring introduction to *Nightwood*: "What I would leave the reader prepared to find is the great achievement of a style, the beauty of phrasing, the brilliance of wit and characterisation, and a quality of horror and doom very nearly related to that of Elizabethan tragedy."

*Nightwood* (1937), whose biographical core is thought to have been Djuna Barnes's disastrous affair with the American sculptor Thelma Wood, uses the setting of the lesbian demimonde of Paris in the twenties as the venue for the decline and fall of Western civilization. The aimless plot, as unfocused as Robin Vote's nocturnal prowling, presents the collapse of the heritage of the House of Hapsburg through miscegenation and imposture, culminating in the sterile issue of the celibate child of Felix Volkbein's marriage to the mad and mysterious Robin Vote. Robin Vote, who leaves Felix for a series of women whom she in turn abandons and betrays, emerges as an emblem of human "otherness" in the text, as the concentration of everything dark and strange, unintelligible and alien, in a suffering nature reduced by novel's end to that of a crawling beast: "Then she began to bark also, crawling after him—barking in a fit of laughter, obscene and touching." Barnes's philosophical subversiveness resides in her comprehensive dismantling of the symbolic order, the system of everything that signifies in a culture and a society. In *Nightwood* every aristocrat is a phony, every doctor a quack, every priest defrocked, every story a lie, every vow a betrayal, every caress a blow, Europe is a circus and America a zoo, and *Nightwood* itself a novel that destroys its own coherence in the telling. The figure who embodies all these self-negations is the magnificent creation of "Dr. Matthew-Mighty-grain-of-salt-Dante-O'Connor," whose medical books are dusty and unread, his forceps rusty, his room a degraded den of filth ("A swill-pail stood at the head of the bed brimming with abominations"), as he lies in bed in woman's wig, rouge, and flannel nightgown, spewing a torrential logorrhea at Nora Flood on the subject of the night: "Though some go into the night as a spoon breaks easy water, others go head foremost against a new connivance; their horns make a dry crying, like the wings of the locust, late come to their shedding." Nora Flood thinks, as she looks at him and listens to him, "God, children know something they can't tell; they like Red Riding Hood and the wolf in bed." The residue that remains from all the negations in the text is language, like Dr. O'Connor himself making an unforgettable and unintelligible spectacle of itself: a poetic sound and fury, signifying nothing—or, as Matthew O'Connor would put it, "I'm a fart in a gale of wind, an humble violet under a cow pad."

Modernism, like any other historical literary period or movement, is a critical construct—both of its own time and its own actors, and of the ensuing critical tradition. In their own day, the modernists—especially the Americans expatriated to Europe—self-consciously responded to what they perceived as a spiritually bankrupt modernity by inventing new poetic and novelistic forms to express, critique, and redeem their age. "The age demanded an image/ Of its accelerated grimace" Ezra Pound wrote in *Hugh Selwyn Mauberley,* and thereafter put "The Age Demanded" in quotation marks to indicate the instant peril of becoming a pious cliché or a self-parody to which modernism's mission of poetic virtuosity made it vulnerable. But true to the motto Pound is said to have worn stitched on his scarf in London, "Make It New," they did indeed make it new. How their newness, their innovations, have been valued and judged has changed with the critical evolution of the later twentieth century. The greater admiration for the "lost generation" novelists, Hemingway and Fitzgerald—which was inspired by New Criticism's formalistic emphasis from the forties to the sixties when the canons and values of modernism were being codified—has shifted during the seventies and eighties to the avant-garde productions of Gertrude Stein and Djuna Barnes, who respond far more interestingly to the metaphysical inquiries of poststructuralist theory. During the nineties, increasing concern from Marxist and Frankfurt School critics over the ideological implications of literary experimentation may yet shift attention once more, toward the critically occluded writers of political engagement from the American thirties. Modernism will thus itself continue to be remade anew.

Margot Norris

# American Proletarianism

The title of this chapter may strike some readers as quaint, if not altogether contradictory. The extent to which it does measures how the language of criticism embodies the dominance of certain political narratives. "Proletarianism" (or "proletarian") has, in the cultural discourse of the United States, come to be associated with a "foreign" way of speaking, historically that of Soviet or Soviet-identified leftists, specifically that of Marxist political rhetoricians, more particularly yet, that of Stalinist cultural critics of the 1930s. In its more barbarous manifestations, this set of connections has led to the view that "proletarian" and "American" are mutually contradictory terms, and thus that their deployment in a title must represent a reprehensible effort to resurrect some (at best) outdated ways of thinking about literature from the dustbin of history into which the upheavals in Eastern Europe have swept them.

I am, of course, stating a somewhat extreme version of this argument, but until recently virtually every essay or book on the subject of proletarian culture (with a very few honorable exceptions like Walter Rideout's *The Radical Novel in the United States, 1900–1954* [1956]) has in some degree given expression to much the same narrative. Indeed, few if any of the cultural narratives of this country have been rehearsed with such unanimity of voice—a fact that, in itself, might make one suspicious. The story told is that "proletarian art" was a failed venture of an admittedly troubled time, the years of the Great Depression of the 1930s, doomed from its very beginnings because it attempted to place the individualism of creation in service to the social goals of a collectivist ideology. To the extent that such art succeeded, the story continues, it did so only because its creators by accident or design moved outside this ideological orbit and thus from under the stifling, humorless power of Communist Party functionaries.

But sustaining this narrative has, in fact, required the obliteration of much of the terrain it is ostensibly designed to map. White women and writers of color, for example, virtually disappear from these histories, as does any serious discussion of efforts to create art by people from working-class origins. The exclusion of women writers and intellectuals from these accounts and the marginalizing of writers of color have been necessary to the process of producing the dubious master narrative I described above. In short, to shift metaphors, "proletarian art" has over the last half-century taken on the qualities of an archaeological mound: one knows that something lies deeply buried under the debris, excrement, and ash of decades of Cold War propaganda, but the shape of what has been so entombed, much less its story, is only now, and slowly, beginning to be discerned.

We are better able, now, to tell a more complete story. In the first place, important texts, like Meridel Le Sueur's *The Girl* and *I Hear Men Talking* and Tillie Olsen's *Yonnondio*, are for the first time fully in print, as they were not in the thirties. And other works, like those of William Attaway, Josephine Herbst, Claude McKay, and Clara Weatherwax, are again widely available, as they were not when critics were both constructing and responding to the earlier Cold War narrative. Second, important recent works of criticism and biography have begun to redraw the pictures of twenties and thirties writers and the world they inhabited. This criticism engages the relationship of art and proletarianism in general, and the character of thirties fiction in particular, not as static subjects for antiquarian study or as occasions for inspirational panegyrics; rather, it sees the period and the cultural issues raised in it as important for contemporary debates over the relationship of art and politics and about the very nature of what a socialist transformation of society might mean. Such criticism has, I think, been more attentive to what previously repressed and marginalized voices reveal about that earlier cultural discourse. Finally, the evaporation of the Cold War has, in itself, weakened the political urgency of the old dominant narrative. For those interested in proletarian art, the decline of what has been designated as the Left has, perhaps ironically, thus been liberating.

Given the advantages of these changes, a number of newly "rearticulated" (Cary Nelson's word) narratives of the literary history of proletarianism and the American novel can be constructed. All will differ from earlier accounts in a number of ways. In addition to new evidence, they will bring the fresh perspectives of feminist and Third World criticism to important issues that were overtly contested in the thirties. First, the debate over the social functions of art, especially the notion of "art as a weapon," will demand a new look at the often discounted impact of Soviet—and other European—models on American practice. I think it will become clearer that Soviet examples, illustrated by translations of Russian fiction, reports on Soviet critical debates, showings of Soviet films, and the like, significantly influenced American writers. The problems of form, particularly of the relevance of modernist stylistic departures, will be illuminated by considering together the practices of writers and visual artists. The autobiographical character of so much of proletarian fiction offers a distinctive entrance to the debate over the value of art created *by,* as well as on behalf of, the proletariat. A revisionist view will, as I illustrate below, conclude that far from being the crude products of Stalinist *aparatchniks,* theories of proletarian culture were—and remain—coherent and challenging expressions of a frankly engaged criticism.

Rearticulated narratives must also emphasize concerns that were less clear in the 1930s, but that came into focus with the emergence of the 1960s movements for social change. First, of course, historical omissions of white women and minority writers need correction. More important, perhaps, the analytic categories of gender and race help reattach the politics of proletarianism to the work of earlier writers like Charlotte Perkins Gilman and W. E. B. Du Bois, who had insisted that radical change involves transforming not only economic but social relations. Further, the ideal of collectivity, cooperation, socialism, or "solidarity" has historically distinguished the working class from the individualism that defines bourgeois social relations and cultural production. Recent criticism argues that women's proletarian fictions dramatize, differently from men's, that putting into practice a collective ethos is central to fundamental social transformation. Most basically, perhaps, a rearticulated narrative would maintain that the discourse represented by the term "proletarianism," which came into and then faded from critical prominence in the 1930s, marks simply one manifestation in the long history of efforts by working-class people to express, communicate, and alter the nature of their lives. All these issues cannot be explored in depth here; in summarizing them I am suggesting the outlines of the significantly revised map of proletarian art now being drawn.

Two autobiographical novels, published within a few months before and after the 1929 stock market crash that precipitated the Great Depression, provide symbolically useful starting places for this discussion. In their working-class subject matter, their autobiographical origins, their fundamentally revolutionary politics, and perhaps most of all in their class-conscious viewpoint on the world, Agnes Smedley's *Daughter of Earth* (1929) and Mike Gold's *Jews Without Money* (1930) represent a new, "proletarian" literary departure. Jack Conroy, an active writer and editor during and after the thirties, has suggested that "the rebellion of the 20s was directed principally against the fetters of form and language taboos"; whereas, after the crash, "editors and publishers began to realize that people *would* read about such unpleasant things as unemployment and hunger." Conroy's is a simplistic but still useful paradigm of the movement from formalism to the idea of art as a means for shaping social values. Driving this transformation was a profound, widespread emotional response to the sudden crash: to most ordinary Americans it represented the devastating, unthought-of collapse of an earlier, hopeful dream that their work was destined to fulfill. By 1933 at least 12 million workers were unemployed. While many stood on soup lines waiting for handouts, the government, in an effort to bolster prices, was paying farmers millions of dollars to plough under wheat, kill off hogs, and dump milk into ditches. Such experiences of hunger, Hoovervilles, and hopelessness brought people to question the economic and social values they had been taught to revere. Yet to some, the calamity seemed to open a new opportunity: to build out of the wreckage of capitalism an economic system of cooperation and equality. In this effort, those on the Left developed special prestige: not only had the Soviet Union avoided the horrors of the Depression, but the Communist Party and its allies took the lead at home in organizing the unemployed, fighting for aid to the dispossessed, turning despair into militance. For many writers, painters, and dramatists, also, the grim downward spiral offered a chance to turn art from a marginal commodity into an instrument for inspiring and shaping change. I would symbolize this leap into a new, "proletarian" art of hunger and fear, of protest and search, of old anger and fresh hope by the publication of Smedley's and Gold's books.

It is not that stories about working-class life nor fictions devoted to social protest or even revolutionary activity were recent developments in American, much less in European, culture. Herman Melville, Rebecca Harding Davis, Elizabeth Stuart Phelps, Jack London, Upton Sinclair, and Sinclair Lewis, among others, had written powerfully in such modes. It would be untrue to picture the 1920s wholly as a period in which artists were devoted to creating experimental works directed to sophisticated upper-class audiences. Yet, relatively little of the fiction of the 1920s was concerned with working-class life, much less with revolutionary politics. Thus, the publication of *Daughter of Earth* and *Jews Without Money* represents something more than an arbitrary divide.

Both books are fictionalized accounts of coming-of-age in working-class communities. Both dramatize the tensions between working-class families and bourgeois institutions of acculturation and social control, like schools, landlords, and employers. Both, like many proletarian fictions, chronicle the painful efforts of their young, often abrasive working-class protagonists to gain, through education, work, or politics, a sense of agency, a meaningful vocation in a fundamentally hostile world. And both, perhaps most significantly, express a deep yearning not just to gain a "place" in that world but to help transform the predatory society they picture into a true community; neither book, also characteristically, dramatizes real success in that critical project. Taken together, both in what they accomplish and in how they fail, they offered for their time a basic definition of proletarian fiction: it is focused, generally in realistic forms, on the experiential details of working-class life; energized by an often angry, sometimes bitter, insistence on forcing American culture to recognize the particular qualities of working-class experience and to respond to the distinctive imperatives of working-class values; and committed to the act of writing in order to critique the dying old society, to validate the beauty often buried in working-class life, and thus to help inspire the movement to create a new, just, and therefore socialist future. Both these novels are also products of writers who devoted almost all their literary energies to the causes they supported: in fact, while both Smedley and Gold continued to write extensively, mainly as chroniclers and propagandists of revolutionary movements, neither again completed a substantial piece of fiction.

For all these parallels, it would be hard to find two books more different either in tone or in their subsequent receptions. The differences were functions not simply of subject matter or style. Gold's book, written in short, punchy, journalistic sentences, and in a voice that combines outrage, sentiment, and bitter humor, offers a series of loosely related sketches of early twentieth-century life in the ghettos of New York's Lower East Side. The tone and mid-American origins of *Daughter of Earth* are established in the opening pages: "To die would have been beautiful. But I belong to those who do not die for the sake of beauty. I belong to those who die from other causes— exhausted by poverty, victims of wealth and power, fighters in a great cause. . . . For we are of the earth and our struggle is the struggle of earth." *Jews Without Money* went through eleven printings within the eight months after its publication in February 1930; was translated into at least sixteen languages, including German, Yiddish, Bohemian, and Tartar, by the time Gold himself prepared an "Introduction" for a new edition in 1935; and, with his more polemical writings, rapidly helped project Gold as one of the leading figures of the cultural Left in the United States. Further, the book became something of a model for proletarian fiction, which Gold had been making efforts to define since the early twenties. It helped generate a group of semiautobiographical novels that constitutes one major form in which *men* of working-class origins expressed their lives in fiction during the 1930s.

*Daughter of Earth,* while it was also reprinted in 1935 with an appreciative introduction by Malcolm Cowley, never gained anything remotely resembling the currency of Gold's book, and Smedley remained, at best, a marginal figure on the Left cultural scene. To be sure, that was partly because she lived in China for much of the thirties and worked at the fringes of the Communist movement rather than, like Gold, at the very center of the American Communist Party. Still the differences in the books, and in their receptions, express more fundamental tensions.

About a year before the publication of *Jews Without Money* Gold pictured his idea of a proletarian writer in a frequently quoted *New Masses* editorial, "Go Left, Young Writers" (January 1929):

A new writer has been appearing; a wild youth of about twenty-two, the son of working-class parents, who himself works in the lumber camps, coal mines, harvest fields and mountain camps of America. He is sensitive and impatient. He writes in jets of exasperated feeling and has no time to polish his work. He is violent and sentimental by turns. He lacks self confidence but writes because he must—and because he has real talent.

The style is perfect Gold—as is, one suspects, the image of the proletarian writer he projects, complete with impatience, loud feelings, and masculine assertiveness, as well as the sense of swallowing life whole, like Walt Whitman and Jack London, to whom Gold refers in a succeeding paragraph. But the image, for all its individual resonance, is not simply a projection of Mike Gold; rather, it represents a widely held conception on the Left not only of the proletarian writer but of the idealized proletariat. It insists that mines, mills, and lumber camps are the only true sites of proletarian action. And it reveals the extent to which even those ideologically committed to a collectivist ethos bought into quite individualistic conceptions of agency—in art and in society as well.

Smedley's Marie Rogers confronts many of the same problems encountered by Gold's hero. But for Marie, there is nothing like the easy solution almost accidentally provided by the discovery of socialism on the last page of *Jews Without Money*. When she moves to New York from the West seeking an active political community, Marie finds herself altogether ill-at-ease among the middle-class intellectuals whose Bohemian lifestyle seems to dominate the socialist movement early in the second decade of the century. The talky, sexually experimental Greenwich Village Bohemia of Floyd Dell and Max and Crystal Eastman, of *The Masses* magazine, of the Provincetown Playhouse, of John Reed and Louise Bryant, paralyzes

Marie, and Smedley herself. The culture of her class becomes, ironically, a barrier to her participation in a movement ostensibly designed to liberate her class. Subsequently, she becomes deeply engaged in the movement to free India from British rule, spending some
months in jail as an "enemy" collaborator during World War I. But
her involvement in this movement, too, is cut short by sexual blackmail and by the inability of male members of the movement, including her husband, to accept real equality for a woman comrade. Thus
*Daughter of Earth* concludes on the edge of despair, rather than with
the "proletarian optimism" Gold prescribed for proletarian fiction
and expressed in the familiar concluding peroration of *Jews Without
Money:* "O workers' Revolution. . . . You are the true Messiah."

Like a number of other thirties novels by women—for example,
Myra Page's *Gathering Storm: A Story of the Black Belt* (1932),
Fielding Burke's (Olive Tilford Dargan's) *Call Home the Heart*
(1932), and Tillie Olsen's *Yonnondio: From the Thirties* (1974)—
*Daughter of Earth* dramatizes class struggle differently, as Barbara
Foley points out, from comparable men's books: as a phenomenon
not just of "making history" but of making daily life (in Richard
Flacks's terms). Smedley's book insists that the kitchen and the bedroom are, as much as the mill, the union hall, and the strike, places
where the struggle for a new socialist society must be joined. Fewer
than a quarter of all women and less than 15 percent of married
women worked outside the home through most of the thirties. If the
industrial "workplace" only was to be the focus for art, as it mainly
was for organizing efforts by the Left, then relatively little of wom-
en's lives would be discovered in art. Further, if the working class was
defined and portrayed entirely in terms of its relation to the means of
production, then the significance of other distinctive group
experiences—of gender, race, ethnicity—would be diminished.

It would not be accurate to claim that Smedley's book offers a
paradigm for the experience of women on the Left. To the contrary,
as has frequently been pointed out, the Left broadly and the Communist Party specifically, for all its patriarchal practice, provided encouragement and support for women artists unusual in American
society. The "Woman Question" was taken seriously on the Left: the
Party press published substantial analyses that, with older classics like
those of Engels and Bebel, provided the basis for political discussions.

Moreover, in significant ways the Left carried on the heritage of feminism that spoke for radical change (Smedley, for example, was deeply involved in the movement to provide birth control to working-class women), and it provided opportunities for many women to be active on behalf of themselves and others in the working class. In fact, some women, like Meridel Le Sueur and Josephine Herbst, played significant public roles in Left cultural circles during the Depression. The Book Union, a leftist book club, selected three novels by women — *A Stone Came Rolling* by Fielding Burke (Olive Tilford Dargan), *Marching! Marching!* by Clara Weatherwax, and *A Time to Remember* by Leane Zugsmith — as its primary selections of "proletarian novels." Still, the "pessimism" of *Daughter of Earth,* like the long-delayed completion and publication of important works by Le Sueur and Olsen, suggests that the thirties Left, including its women writers, had no secure answers for vital questions about the relationship of social and cultural transformations (especially those having to do with gender roles) to a political and economic revolution.

The books that most resonate with *Jews Without Money* include some focused on the blighted worlds of the "bottom dogs" of society, as well as others that detail the efforts of plain working-class Americans to live through the multiplying disasters of Depression, Dust Bowl, and dispossession, to find jobs, and perhaps to organize. It became the object of a number of writers of the late 1920s as well as the 1930s to extend a "downward" view to the bottoms of American society generally unseen by the middle-class reading public. Edward Dahlberg's novels *Bottom Dogs* (1929), *From Flushing to Calvary* (1932), and *Those Who Perish* (1934) gave a name and one definition to such fictions. His first book follows Lorry Lewis as he grows up around his mother's barber shops, especially in Kansas City, in a Cleveland Jewish orphanage, hobo camps, the YMCA and Solomon's Dancepalace in Los Angeles. The second book finds Lorry and Lizzie Lewis in and around New York, as Lizzie, rapidly aging, tries to establish herself as a lady eligible for marriage and Lorry tries to discover himself along the waterfront, in the cemetery, at a Coney Island festival, and finally through a pilgrimage back to the orphanage. One can observe how, as the first two books progress, the style changes from what Dahlberg himself later derogated as "the rude American vernacular," conveyed with a kind of ironic gusto, to the increasingly erudite and allusive technique that marks his later works. In 1929 he had written with a Whitmanesque sense of the expressiveness of everyday details: "The barber shop, with its odor of soap and hair tonics, the Paramount Building on Times Square with its tawdry lighting effects at night, the offices and hotels along Broadway, a cheap yellow and red symphonic surge in brick are just as artistically suggestive as the Chartres Cathedral or the cafes along the walk of the Montmartre." In *Bottom Dogs* and *Calvary* Dahlberg carries out the artistic program implicit in this comment, capturing and, as Jules Chametzky has suggested, legitimizing, even celebrating that seamy, loathsome landscape just at the edges of destitution—the deluded lower middle-class America of Lizzie Lewis that at once repels and consumes Lorry. *Those Who Perish,* one of the first American fictions to dramatize the Nazi threat and also to attack Jewish collaborationism and self-interest, is written in a much more self-consciously literary style; and the wandering, rootless young hero of the earlier books, who anticipates Jack Kerouac's road-drawn hipsters and, perhaps, Saul Bellow's tamer Augie March, emerges as the suicidal Eli Malamed. Dahlberg's work finally constitutes an increasingly elaborate (self)portrait of the artist transformed from hobo to guru. Politics is not his occupation, nor does revolutionary optimism characterize his people: *Bottom Dogs* ends with Lorrie wondering whether he has caught the clap from a dance-hall girl. And all the central characters of *Those Who Perish* do, indeed, die needlessly or by their own hands.

Dahlberg's people skirt the bottom, in fact; Tom Kromer's live there. *Waiting for Nothing* (1935), Kromer's essentially autobiographical narrative, captures from the inside the experiences of men on the fritz. The book begins—and ends—nowhere, or anywhere: a dark, nameless urban street where the hungry narrator backs off from clubbing a passing man, to an anonymous flophouse, where he lies caught between aching weariness and the fierce biting of lice. Dahlberg's wanderer hitches rides on the rails; Kromer's nails a fast drag at night, smashing against the side of the boxcar, hanging on for life, knowing that, like others he has seen, he will end in a ditch or be cut to ribbons under the wheels if his grip fails. Lorry Lewis always seems to find a friend; Kromer's narrator can, at best, fall in with a smart stiff who teaches him to earn his daily keep by diving "down on a doughnut in front of a bunch of women."

Kromer's is probably the least romanticized of the books portraying the lower depths of America. His title echoes ironically one of the era's best-known works, Clifford Odets's agitational drama *Waiting for Lefty*. Kromer's narrator, waiting for no future, cut off from any past, isolated from any movement, is confined at the end to thinking only about "three hots and a flop." Even Nelson Algren's gloomy *Somebody in Boots* (1935) provides glimpses, if transient, of real companionship and of a movement for a better society, though his central figure, Cass McKay, seems utterly unable to turn himself toward them. Like Lorry Lewis, Cass takes to the road partly from aimlessness, partly from hunger, though partly to escape the meaningless brutality and ugliness of his Texas home. But he finds, finally, that there is no place much better to go in Depression America, only a jungle where "the strong beat the weak" and all "strike out at something" when they can, if only to pass on to others their own pain. In Chicago, he is beaten for befriending an African American Communist, loses his job, is left by Norah, a young working woman with whom he has struck up a relationship, and drifts back onto the bum. Cass can briefly perceive that his condition is a result of the corruption and greed of capitalism, and briefly understand, too, how racism keeps working people separated. But to the extent that he comes to have a class identification, it seems to be that of the lumpen-proletariat, the breeding ground for Fascist recruits. Indeed, Richard Pells has suggested that "Algren suspected that the 'people' were not incipient socialists but potential brownshirts who might come together solely for an orgy of looting and arson," like the people of Chicago's depths in Jack London's *The Iron Heel*. That judgment may be unfair to Algren's effort to symbolize in the nightmare jungles traversed by his homeless men and women the American dream that vanished with the Depression. Like his later and better-known postwar work, *The Man with the Golden Arm* (1949) and *A Walk on the Wild Side* (1956), *Somebody in Boots* may best be read not as a realistic coming-of-age novel but, like most of the books I am discussing, as "a gloomy parable" (Pells) of disconnection from that older, pastoral American society now "gone with the wind."

In many ways, the book that most fulfilled the promise of *Jews Without Money* is Jack Conroy's *The Disinherited* (1933). Like Gold working class in origin, Conroy came from a very different tradition of American radicalism: Midwestern, small-town, populist, native, anarchic—represented by Moberly, Missouri, where Conroy was born and grew up. *The Disinherited* originated as a series of auto-biographical sketches published by H. L. Mencken in the conservative *American Mercury* and was then adapted into the form of a novel in order to get a commercial press to publish it. An expert storyteller and an important editor, Conroy had always been interested in the folk dimensions of working-class culture: the tales, ballads, jokes of a rich oral tradition. In fact, *The Disinherited* is a treasure-chest of such materials, and it may best be understood as the search of its first-person protagonist, Larry Donovan, to find a meaningful cultural and communal center to his life after the traditional miners' world of Monkey Nest Camp has been destroyed by lost strikes, the mining deaths of his father and brothers, the fragmentation of modern society, and plain poverty. Initially, Larry believes that he can "rise" to a white-collar job if he gains sufficient education. Later, he works in a steel mill and in the burgeoning auto industry, spending his wages on the pleasures of the moment. Left broke and jobless by the crash, he returns to Monkey Nest Camp, works in construction, and ultimately discovers his solidarity with all other workers:

I could no longer withdraw into my fantastic inner world and despise these men. I did not aspire to be a doctor or a lawyer any more. I was only as high or as low as the other workers in the paving gang.

In the book's climactic scene, farmers organized by Larry's German World War I veteran friend Hans force a foreclosed farm and its contents to be sold back to the farmer for pennies. And Larry, having led a group of town men to support the farmers, makes a speech in cadences recognized by an old-timer as those of Larry's union-leader father. Having thus reclaimed or reconstructed the cultural heritage of his class, Larry goes off with Hans into the unromantic world of union organizing.

The most popular novel to capture Depression America on the road was, of course, John Steinbeck's *The Grapes of Wrath* (1939).

Steinbeck's novel, while it points toward a more humane future, is in many ways also an exercise in nostalgia. For its center of value remains a kind of "agrarian utopia" (Warren Susman's term), maintained in the limbo of an idealized encampment by New Deal social policy. And its concept of breaking out of selfish individualism, dramatized in the famous scene of Rose of Sharon sharing her breast milk, involves incorporating outsiders into the more or less traditional family. But in many novels like those I have been discussing, and in 1930s America, it is precisely the disintegration of the family under the stresses of exploitation and the Depression that forces marginalized men and women onto the road.

Books like *The Disinherited* and the poems, stories, and "reportage" published in *The Anvil* and in other magazines (*Left Front, Leftward, New Force, Dynamo, The Cauldron, Partisan Review*) mainly begun in the early 1930s in connection with the Communist Party's John Reed Clubs represent an important part of the American response to the idea that a revolutionary working class should produce its own writers and artists. In the context of the postrevolutionary Soviet Union, there were those who saw little point in burdening a newly self-conscious proletariat with the decayed culture of Russia's aristocratic and bourgeois past. Rather, they believed, workers should be organized into what amounted to literary study groups within which, through practice and criticism, they would learn to develop an art true to their own experiences and needs and integral to their everyday lives. The resulting "Proletcult" had, by 1920, become a mass movement, with a membership (between 300,000 and 450,000) perhaps as large as that of the Soviet Communist Party itself. The subsequent heeling of the movement under Party control, the later debates over the validity of the idea of a proletarian culture (notably if problematically engaged in Trotsky's *Literature and Revolution*), the intricacies of organizational infighting in the Soviet Union and elsewhere throughout the twenties and thirties, and the emergence of the idea that literary content and ideas should be directed by the policies of a proletarian "vanguard party" do not concern us here, except to the extent that these developments help to explain the growing disrepute of the idea itself.

In the United States, however, Mike Gold in particular continued throughout the twenties to push this idea of proletarian culture; ultimately in 1928 he succeeded in turning *The New Masses* into what Eric Homberger has accurately described as "a Proletcult magazine." In this phase the magazine received numerous submissions from working people like Jack Conroy, H. H. Lewis, Herman Spector, and Edwin Rolfe. And while, in 1930, *The New Masses* was turned back to better-known—and, perhaps, less gritty and more middle-class—contributors, it had helped lay the groundwork for the success of the John Reed Clubs and of their magazines. These were the fertile grounds from which sprang important novelists like Richard Wright and Tillie Olsen, and which encouraged many other young working-class writers like Conroy. Such institutional supports are critical to the development of a culture rooted in working-class experience.

Many of the men and women who joined the John Reed Clubs were working on novels, but ultimately few were published. In part, the shorter forms of poetry and story were obviously easier to complete for people with full-time work and family commitments. In part, too, the Communist Party's 1934 decision (as part of its movement toward "popular front" politics) to eliminate the John Reed Clubs in favor of a League of American Writers constituted by more traditional, better-known, and largely middle-class authors short-circuited the slow development of a militantly working-class literary culture, and helped condemn at least some of the emerging writers to what Tillie Olsen has eloquently termed "silences."

It may be, however, that the central problem was the novel itself. For how could the novel, which emerged with the development of capitalism and which, as a form, privileges "the position that individual destiny occupies in capitalist culture" (Christian Suggs's words), be reshaped to envision the emergence of a collective future implicit in proletarian politics? Suggs goes on to point out that "the novel's unique ability to focus for considerable numbers of pages on the most internalized processes of the mind and soul could have the collateral effect of isolating private sensibility from public identity" and consequently undermining the political purposes of proletarian fiction. The essentially autobiographical fictions I have been describing found it difficult to evade this dilemma. On the other hand, experimental efforts to decenter the narrative from one single hero, like Robert Cantwell's *The Land of Plenty* (1934), William Rollins's *The*

*Shadow Before* (1934), and Clara Weatherwax's *Marching! Marching!* (1935), ran the risk of losing a mass audience more accustomed to straightforward stories.

In fact, the variety of technical experiments would be surprising if one took too seriously critical strictures enforcing realism. Many efforts were influenced by John Dos Passos's techniques, especially multiple narrative centers, in his trilogy *U.S.A.* (1930, 1932, 1936), and behind him very likely the "unanimist" fictional tactics of Jules Romains. In *Union Square* (1933), Albert Halper provides a kind of sociological cross section of the variety of human beings who work, live, engage in politics, and hang out in and around the Square. In *A Time to Remember* (1936), Leane Zugsmith interweaves a series of stories about the lives of department store workers who become caught up in a strike. Robert Cantwell begins *The Land of Plenty* "Suddenly the lights went out." We are in the head of Carl, the foreman; subsequent chapters pick up that same moment from the perspectives of Hagen, Marie, and others in the factory, and then in the town. Weatherwax uses a wider, if generally less well-controlled, set of devices: one chapter of *Marching! Marching!* consists of what are presented as clippings, ads, and strike bulletins; the text moves without signal from narration to internal monologue and from the head of one character to another; the narrative of a strike meeting is suspended for six pages to describe the lumber operations in which one man works. In her trilogy of the Trexler family, Josephine Herbst places brief vignettes, out of chronological sequence, between the chapters of her main narratives. Like Dos Passos's "Newsreels," though different in form, these are mainly efforts to capture a sense of American public life as it converges with the "private" experience of the autobiographical Victoria Wendel. It is true that an insistent, and sometimes one-dimensional, naturalism constituted the mainstream of proletarian fictional technique through the 1930s. It is also true that some of the anti-Stalinist writers gathered around *Partisan Review* were more committed than others to sustaining the legacies of 1920s modernism. But as these examples suggest, the interest in modernist techniques was widespread; indeed, Marcus Klein presents proletarian literature as "a literary rebellion within [the] literary revolution" called modernism. However that might be, it is essential, I think, to understand how such sophisticated later works as those of Tillie Olsen are grounded in these efforts to use modernist experimental tactics to reconfigure the novel to proletarian social purposes.

Proletarianism takes yet a different shape when it intersects with race. While Conroy's protagonist sought community within the framework of Midwestern radical traditions, Claude McKay's central figures looked toward the values of the African diaspora to counteract the disintegration and anomie of Western culture. McKay, a black Jamaican by birth and a published poet of dialect verse before he immigrated to the United States in 1912, became well known in Left and Bohemian circles in post–World War I New York as an editor of *The Liberator* (successor to *The Masses*) and writer of both lyric and militant verse in generally traditional forms like the sonnet. In London during 1920 he worked as a journalist on Sylvia Pankhurst's working-class feminist newspaper, *Worker's Dreadnaught,* and in 1922 he visited the Soviet Union. There he published an account of race relations in the United States (*The Negroes in America* [1923]) and a collection of fiction whose nature is expressed in its title, *Trial by Lynching* (1925). In France, beginning in 1923, McKay set out to establish himself as a novelist by sketching the "semi-underworld" of urban African American workers that he had inhabited between 1914 and 1919. The draft of one novel, "Color Scheme," McKay evidently destroyed after its rejection. Later, however, he was encouraged to expand a short story into his first published novel, *Home to Harlem* (1928).

In *Home to Harlem* McKay tries to maintain in tension the three elements that interest him about the lives of rootless, urban African American working men in America; they are represented by the three central male characters, Jake, Zeddy, and Ray. Jake is drawn back to Harlem from abroad by its night life, its Baltimore, Goldgraben's, and Congo bars. But while Harlem's dark-eyed women, its "couples-... dancing, thick as maggots in a vat of sweet liquor, and as wriggling," dominate his desires, he rejects the role of "sweetman": "Never lived off no womens and never will. I always works." By contrast, Zeddy is always out for the main chance, arguing against Jake's refusal to scab:

"Youse talking death, tha's what you sure is. One thing I know is niggers am made foh life. And I want to live, boh, and feel plenty o' the juice o' life in mah blood. I wanta live and I wanta love. . . . I loves life and I got to live and I'll scab through hell to live."

On the other side, the educated Ray envies Jake's natural spontaneity and his capacity for happiness: "I don't know what I'll do with my little education. I wonder sometimes if I could get rid of it and go and lose myself in some savage culture in the jungles of Africa." The underlying ambivalence of Ray's views suggests that McKay (who slightly differentiates himself from Ray when the latter reappears in *Banjo*) has not altogether worked through the political dimensions of his deep attraction to the "primitive" and presumably exotic qualities of black life. McKay clearly differentiates Jake's natural decency and sense of proletarian solidarity from Zeddy's comic and sometimes ugly blundering, but the roots of that difference, personalities aside, remain unclear. Nor does there seem to be any real way of reconciling Jake's desire for some of Ray's Western "edjucation" and Ray's need for the resources of Jake's earthy happiness. Robert M. Greenberg has suggested that Jake's virtues are "essentially preindustrial ones, qualities that can only foster a marginal life for an individual in the urban North." The characters of *Home to Harlem* are marginal in another sense, too: they are able to pick up jobs, gigs, money because, though the novel seldom touches on it, times are still flush in the white world.

In *Banjo* (1929) the ideological drift of *Home to Harlem* is more fully worked out. Ray meets Banjo—Jake without traces of working-class ideology—comes to reject the Western civilization that has been taking "the love of color, joy, beauty, vitality, and nobility out of *his* life," and decides to throw in with Banjo's marginal and dangerous but joyful style of living. What distinguishes black life on the Marseilles waterfront in *Banjo* is its specifically *African* quality, defined by the variety of African and diaspora characters who populate the Ditch. Marginality emerges here not as a crushing burden or, at best, a temporary declivity from which people will eventually climb but as a soulful, rhythmic space within which an alternative life to that of white culture can be enacted. It is, perhaps, a differently romanticized, and equally problematic, version of the "muck" in Zora Neale Hurston's *Their Eyes Were Watching God* (1937).

One may read in the changes from McKay's earlier stories to *Banjo* and his later Jamaican novel, *Banana Bottom* (1933), a movement from a fundamentally class to a largely racial basis of solidarity, a movement opposite to that dramatized in Richard Wright's powerful novella "Bright and Morning Star." Jake's commitment to worker solidarity is limited: while he will not scab, neither will he join a union—like most "bottom dogs," though he is "no lonesome wolf," he is suspicious of all forms of entanglement—especially if they come in white. In "Bright and Morning Star" Sue, who is suspicious of virtually all whites, ultimately sacrifices her own life to protect her Communist son's comrades, white as well as black, and also to exact some vengeance for his lynching. The stories of *Uncle Tom's Children* (1938), of which "Bright and Morning Star" is the last, move from African American protagonists who are victims toward those who increasingly embrace radical struggle. In the process, they also seem to move away from the black folk culture (especially religion) associated with the rural South, as well as with the Caribbean or ultimately Africa, that sustains McKay's central characters. In *Native Son* (1940) that has disappeared; indeed, James Baldwin complained of the book that it lacked "any sense of Negro life as a continuing and complex group reality." There is, of course, a good deal of truth in that criticism. But it misses precisely the sense in which Wright's title links Bigger Thomas to the long line of utterly marginal men who populate proletarian novels of the thirties—especially those written in Chicago by men from mid-America. Bigger is the most thoroughly dispossessed victim of the social processes also dramatized by Algren, Kromer, and Conroy, among others, the processes by which Depression Americans were finally, wrenchingly cut off from earlier, mostly rural sources of traditional value and set adrift in the urban jungles of capitalism. In *Native Son* the American dream of freedom and flight passes overhead as an advertising gimmick while Bigger and Gus play out the distance in harsh laughter.

At the same time, the ending of the novel focuses Wright's doubts about the ability even of a developed class analysis to account for such thoroughgoing alienation. What emerges in Bigger's final encounter with Max is much the same problem that William Attaway confronts in *Blood on the Forge* (1941). Like hundreds of thousands of African American people in the decade after 1914, Attaway's three Moss brothers, Mat, Chinatown, and Melody, flee from the exploitation and violence of rural Kentucky to the steel mills near Pittsburgh. As Richard Yarborough has pointed out, Attaway portrays the men's movement into the promised Northern land as, in fact, a *descent* into an industrial wasteland. All three are destroyed in that process: China is blinded in a mill explosion; Melody injures the hand that enables him to root himself in music; and Big Mat is killed leading strikebreakers.

From one point of view, the experience of Wright's and Attaway's characters represents at its extreme the experience of all working-class men caught between a dying rural world and an industrial system whose humane potential is waiting to be born. But reading *Blood on the Forge* against Thomas Bell's novel of three generations of immigrant Slovak steel workers, *Out of This Furnace*, published the same year, suggests that the differences are, finally, critical. For Bell's book ends triumphantly, with an impending birth and with the victory of the Steel Workers Organizing Committee in Braddock presented as the expression of the American values embodied in the Declaration of Independence and the Bill of Rights. Moreover, in *Out of This Furnace* African American workers like the Moss brothers are altogether invisible—except, perhaps, in the name of a particularly violent trooper called "Blackjack." Attaway wrote no novels after *Blood on the Forge*. What seems to me played out in these novels of African American life are a series of unresolved conflicts: between the values embodied in forms of cultural nationalism and forms of class-based solidarity; between the construction of the South as "home" and value-center and the North as "promised land"; between versions of pastoral and versions of proletarianism. Arna Bontemps perhaps tried to avoid such conflicts by setting his groundbreaking novel of African American self-assertion and rebellion, *Black Thunder* (1936), in the antebellum South. Still, by modeling black militance even in a historical slave revolt like that of Gabriel, Bontemps encountered the demand from the Alabama school in which he was teaching that he renounce his radical associations—mainly his friends engaged in the struggle to save the Scottsboro Boys and in support of Gandhi's nonviolent demonstrations in India. How to show his renunciation? Why, burn all the "race-conscious" and therefore pro-vocative books in his library. African American intellectual life in the United States simply provided no refuge from the politics of race.

In a formal sense, other working-class women writers of the thir-ties did not follow Agnes Smedley's autobiographical lead. More fun-damentally, however, *Daughter of Earth* was paradigmatic, for nar-ratives of coming to consciousness and fathoming the painful contradictions of gender and class were at the heart of books by writers like Meridel Le Sueur, Olive Tilford Dargan, Myra Page, and Tillie Olsen. In *The Girl*—only parts of which were published in the 1930s—Le Sueur succeeds perhaps better than in any of her other work in holding together the contradictory imperatives that have marked her long, complex career as writer and Communist Party activist. These involve the tensions between sexual awakening and "political" consciousness, between modernism of style and the effort to reach a working-class audience, between the writer as seller of words or as peoples' oracle, and above all between the logic of in-dividual advancement and the power of collective action. In her work, these are all linked. In certain ways, *The Girl* duplicates the pattern of other books that trace the coming to consciousness of a working-class protagonist. We meet the nameless girl as she begins waitressing in a St. Paul speakeasy and follow her developing affair with Butch, a young, marginal worker. We watch with horror as she becomes the driver for a botched bank robbery plotted by the pred-atory Ganz and as she and the fatally wounded Butch flee into the countryside. Pregnant, out of work, and separated from all the men who had tried to control her life, the girl returns to the city to become part of a community of "bottom dog" women, surviving through the bitter winter in an abandoned warehouse, where in the book's climax she gives birth. What the girl discovers can be seen as a version of class solidarity, especially when she communicates with a deaf girl in a scabrous relief maternity home about the Workers Alliance. But the content of that solidarity is markedly different from what Larry Donovan comes to in *The Disinherited* or Mickey stumbles upon in *Jews Without Money*. For its emotional basis is the commonality of *female* experience.

Le Sueur tells us that reading D. H. Lawrence first enabled her to think positively about women's sexuality. She had early been taught that sex meant danger, and, as in many women's novels before and after the 1930s, it continued to be threatening: an illusion fostered by Hollywood, the trapdoor to impoverishment through repeated cycles of pregnancy and childbearing, or a commodity demanded by men as token of their power. Indeed, Le Sueur's young male characters, like Bac in *I Hear Men Talking* (1984) and Butch in *The Girl*, are often predatory individualists, strikebreakers, violent to women, intent above all on "beating." Nevertheless, heterosexuality opens a way for Le Sueur's young women to discover what "nobody can tell you," to step out of the constrictions of selfhood, finding, like the girl, not only unity among women but also a relationship to the earth itself that Le Sueur often symbolized by the Demeter and Persephone myth. Many of Le Sueur's early stories (for example, "Annunciation," "Spring Story") illustrate the intensity of her concern with women's bodies and sexuality—a concern that brought her into conflict with some Left critics and editors and, indeed, with at least some of the audiences for most Left-wing magazines of the thirties.

Ishma Waycaster, the central figure of Olive Tilford Dargan's (Fielding Burke's) *Call Home the Heart*, is caught in a similar set of conflicts: between her mountain home and the industrial lowland; between her passion for her husband, Britt, and her attraction to the scientific and politicized doctor, Derry; between her desire for the personal satisfactions of her own farm and hilltops and her commitment to the revolutionary struggle of the National Textile Workers' Union to organize the Winbury (Gastonia) mill workers; between irrational desire and the life of reason. These remain ideologically unresolved though humanly convincing in *Call Home the Heart* as Ishma, after an irrational outburst of racism, retreats from the union struggle back to mountains, husband, home. Dargan's dramatization of the persistence of racism even among enlightened white Southern workers has been praised as an honest effort to confront realistically a main barrier to worker solidarity. But, in fact, the dilemmas of racism are not central to the novel, any more than they were fundamental to the Gastonia strike. What is much more critical in the book, and what seems to me displaced onto the issue of race, are questions about gender and the relation of personal to social transformation. Gender is much more marginal in the Left discourse upon which Dargan is drawing and appears at once less critical and much more intractable than racism, the solution to which is, at least theoretically, clear. As Deborah Rosenfelt comments about another novel on the Gastonia strike, Myra Page's *Gathering Storm: A Story of the Black Belt* (1932), "the author [is unable] to acknowledge fully the very subversiveness of the women's issues raised. They are subversive not only of the dominant culture's sex-role ideology but also of the Left's insistence on the seamlessness and unity of the working class." But more fundamentally, perhaps, the novel is struggling with the question of what Ishma, who is so much an image of American possibility, will finally become. There is nothing fixed and predetermined about that in Dargan's book: Ishma is created and recreated in relation to the material circumstances of her life. The problem, then, is to imagine circumstances capable of energizing both her passions and her intellect—a task neither novelist nor movement accomplished. Indeed, when she tries to resolve such dilemmas in the sequel *A Stone Came Rolling* (1935), Dargan is much less convincing.

Le Sueur's style also seems pulled in contrary directions: a lyric, repetitive, incantatory modernist technique (influenced, perhaps, by Gertrude Stein as well as by Lawrence) sometimes jostles against the reportorial voice (influenced, perhaps, by Sherwood Anderson and Ernest Hemingway) she honed in articles like "Women on the Breadlines" and "What Happens in a Strike" (collected in *Harvest Song* [1990]). The lyrical, Le Sueur writes in *I Hear Men Talking,* could be "used as reaction to the deathly action of the economics and history of the town." But it poses a problem to the audience she seeks: "A farmer in North Dakota said to me once, 'You write too beautiful.'" So, like some critics, she came to "question the lyricism of my early stories." For if the writer's role was to become an "oracle of the people" (Linda Ray Pratt's term), like Whitman, hearing, gathering, expressing, returning to the people their own stories, she could not distance herself from them by language, as modernist writers often did. Further, to serve a political function in a communist movement, a writer could not simply reproduce the relationships of bourgeois culture, appropriating people's lives into narratives and selling them back as commodities. One can see in Penelope, the developing central consciousness of *I Hear Men Talking,* Le Sueur's effort to create an alternative to the portrait of the artist as young appropriator that one finds, for example, in Anderson's "Death in the Woods" or *Winesburg, Ohio.*

The tensions about the relationship of artists and intellectuals to a social movement were not easily resolved, especially for authors of middle-class origins in the aggressively working-class movement of the thirties. Commenting on Horace Gregory's angst over his conflict between artistic individualism and Communist discipline, Le Sueur wrote in *The New Masses* (February 26, 1935):

For myself I do not feel any subtle equivocation between the individual and the new disciplined groups of the Communist party. I do not care for the bourgeois "individual" that I am. I never have cared for it. . . . I can no longer live without communal sensibility. I can no longer breathe in this maggoty individualism of a merchant society.

But "maggoty individualism" is never so easily exterminated; indeed, it reappears here as a kind of self-hatred, which can lead to artistic paralysis or to shrill assertion of one's correct politics. Le Sueur dramatizes the effort to cast off bourgeois separateness and step into working-class solidarity in a piece like "I Was Marching" (1934), but a certain insecurity persists. Indeed, the question comes to be central to a significant number of novels of the time.

The work of Tess Slesinger and Josephine Herbst is not, on the whole, focused on the life of industrial workers. Slesinger's only completed novel, *The Unpossessed* (1934), and her collection of stories, *Time: The Present* (1935), concern the personal and political lives of people best characterized as middle-class intellectuals. And while she was later active in Hollywood in the long battle to establish the Screen Writers Guild, her movie scripts are not very involved with working-class struggles. *The Unpossessed* provides an unusually frank view of the tensions between ideological commitment and personal desires among the class of leftist intellectuals to which most writers of proletarian novels in fact belonged. Loosely based on the group around Elliot Cohen, editor of *The Menorah Journal* and later, having moved to the far Right, founding editor of *Commentary,* the novel tells about the efforts of the men in the group, and the student acolytes of one of them, Bruno Leonard, to set up a magazine that will at once express their political aspirations and satisfy their quite varied personal desires. By alternating scenes of public activities—

meetings, fund-raising efforts, and the like—and private interactions, Slesinger suggests how the personal and the political remain in tension, how, indeed, unresolved personal conflicts come to abort expressed political commitments.

Most particularly, the men in the group seem unable to relate honestly to the women closest to them, much less to the rather callow students who help drive the magazine enterprise or to the variety of ordinary people with whom they interact daily and on whose behalf they would write. The contradictory impulses of the group are most devastatingly satirized in Slesinger's account of the lavish fund-raising party thrown for the magazine, the public climax of the novel. The parallel "private" climax is provided by the final chapter, in which Margaret Flinders, one of the book's central characters, returns from an abortion, pushed on her by her bitter, withheld husband, Miles. Probably the first widely circulated American fiction to deal in detail with an abortion, the chapter was first published in 1932 as a separate short story, "Missis Flinders." The book does mock all the protagonists at one level, playing their withdrawals from commitment against the fanaticism of Dostoevsky's characters evoked by Slesinger's ironic title. But it also presents them with a certain sympathy born of Slesinger's recognition that decent political values can, and usually do, live side by side in human beings with rather less noble motives of personal aggrandizement or sexual conquest.

Herbst's trilogy (*Pity Is Not Enough* [1933], *The Executioner Waits* [1934], and *Rope of Gold* [1939]) is one of three—the others are John Dos Passos's *U.S.A.* and James T. Farrell's *Studs Lonigan*—published by Left-leaning writers during the thirties. They are strikingly different: Dos Passos tries to achieve in his choice of characters, his use of "Newsreels," his capsule biographies of notable Americans, a panoramic view of the country in the decades before and after World War I. Farrell focuses narrowly on the decline of a lower-middle-class urban family as representative of the fate of millions of other Americans, lost in ideological confusion and economic dislocation. Herbst centers her narrative on a few members of the Trexler family, a fictionalized version of her own, but tries to achieve scope by tracing them over most of a century and across much of America. Her primary protagonists, especially as the trilogy goes on, are female, which some critics have suggested may account for the trilogy's lack of wide readership. But it may also be a function of its very inconclusiveness. *Rope of Gold* in particular suggests that the trajectory of Victoria Wendel's and Jonathan Chance's private lives as writers and political activists and that of world-changing economic and political forces are somehow converging. But a novel cannot leap out of history, especially if it is committed to historical representation, like Herbst's. And none of the novel's concerns—the rise of fascism, duplicity and male chauvinism on the Left, the distant promise of a classless society—are resolvable within it. The recent revival of interest in Herbst—partly stimulated by Elinor Langer's important biography—may suggest that the very ambivalence that kept her slightly apart from total commitments in the period's politics is appealing, in a way that forced conclusions are not, to a postmodern generation of readers.

But the proletarian writer who has most appealed to contemporary readers is, ironically, one who published hardly anything during the thirties. Nevertheless, Tillie Olsen's fiction does, in certain respects, epitomize the best of the time. *Yonnondio*, as it has been published, was mostly written by 1938 or 1939, and a portion of it printed as "The Iron Throat." But then the novel's manuscript was set aside for other work, child-rearing, earning a living, surviving the repressions of the Cold War, and lay in a trunk until 1972 when its bits and scraps were resurrected, painstakingly copied, reassembled into the narrative that exists. Like many of the books I have discussed, *Yonnondio* is a story of growing up, particularly of Mazie, daughter of Anna and Jim Holbrook. The narrative follows the family in the early 1920s from mining community to farm to packingtown in their search for decent jobs and room for children to grow. It was planned to follow Mazie's continued development beyond her early teens, perhaps into a writer who could, like her creator, "limn" the "hands" of America. For what this Mazie knows are the endless frets of too many children in too little space, the violence engendered by a father's inability to get at what is consuming him, the desperation of toil gone to waste. The last scene portrays the stifling of life in the packinghouse and at home by 106-degree heat, shifting from consciousness to consciousness to create a mosaic of pain.

What Olsen accomplishes in *Yonnondio*, I think, is drawing together technical strategies and thematic materials seldom unified in proletarian fiction. Her methods of varying narrative voices and presenting scenes from very different points of view—now Mazie's innocent eyes, now Anna's weary glance, now a narrator's knowledgeable vision—represent one of the most successful adaptations of experimental techniques to subject matter characteristic of the consciousness of the thirties. But she also joins the work and household worlds. Thus she brings to imaginative life the intersections of these domains, which ideology and the habits of patriarchal society have largely kept separate.

What the foregoing seems to me to illustrate is the variety of the texts one can usefully think about under the rubric "proletarian." For the term does not represent merely a political prescription for cultural work—though there were undoubtedly those who preferred that it should—but an angle of vision on the art of another time. That angle of vision is, as I have illustrated, different in the 1990s from what it might have been in the 1930s. It will continue to change as our understandings of class, and particularly its intersections with other categories of social structure and of cultural analysis, develop. This work, therefore, is presented not as the definitive account of "proletarianism and the American novel" but as one among the many differing narratives that might, and undoubtedly will over time, be constructed from the variety of texts now open before us.

Paul Lauter

# Popular Forms II

W hen Horatio Alger died in 1899, his rags-to-riches formula had already been contested by a different kind of adolescent achievement: the heroics of the athlete Frank Merriwell. First appearing in 1896—at the hand of "Burt L. Standish" (Gilbert Patten) and at the behest of publisher Ormond Smith—Frank and his brother pitched the winning pitch in over 200 novels, which sold an estimated 126,000,000 volumes by the end of the 1920s. Alger's novels gained in popularity during the first decade of the twentieth century, and his name soon became synonymous with the American myth of self-improvement. But it was Patten's fiction in Street and Smith's "Tip Top Weekly" series that commanded the juvenile field, marking an abrupt shift in the site and the style of American success. The hero of *Ragged Dick; or, Street Life in New York* (1867) must *rise* to respectability and to a job as counting room clerk. In contrast, Frank Merriwell enjoys perpetual triumph outside the confines of the city and the economic order.

In its relocation of success, the sports novel escapes the specific contradiction of ideology and plot that characterizes the Alger formula: the wealthy Mr. Whitney explains to Ragged Dick that "in this free country poverty in early life is no bar to a man's advancement," that "your future position depends mainly on yourself"; but Whitney's very presence in the novel, his role as Dick's benefactor, refutes the platitude. In *Frank Merriwell at Yale* (1903), the platitude changes, the hero himself explains that "in athletics" (rather than in this country) "strength and skill win, regardless of money or family," and he himself, all by himself, triumphs from the beginning to the end of each novel, requiring no assistance from a surrogate father. We might say, then, that in fiction, as in the American society of the era, sports established an arena of success that the economy could no longer provide. But a novel like *Frank Merriwell in Wall Street* (1908) actually transforms the economy into one more playing field where Frank invariably triumphs. While Alger's Luke Larkin, the "son of a carpenter's widow," must "exercise the strictest economy" in *Struggling Upward* (1890), Frank Merriwell, whose financial reserves appear no less vast than his strength, can exercise an economy of wild speculation in which "need" has given way to "desire." All told, the Merriwell series does not so much suppress the economic as it rewrites the economy in accordance with *The New Basis of Civilization,* as the economist Simon Patten understood it in 1905, where an "economy of pain" has been supplanted by an "economy of pleasure," and the primary task of education becomes to "arouse" the worker to participate in American "amusements."

Still, a simpler way to understand the disjunction between the Alger novel and the Merriwell novel is to recognize that, just as Alger's fiction once served as an alternative to the sensationalist dime novels of the 1860s and 1870s, so the baseball novel serves as a means of reestablishing the adventure paradigm that postulates "directly the inborn and statically inert nobility of its heroes," as Bakhtin says, rather than portraying any "*gradual* formation" of character: Ragged Dick, despite his inborn "pluck," must learn the behavior that will enable him to succeed; but Frank Merriwell's success springs from an absolute "stability of character." Describing the relation between formula fiction and American ideology can begin with this point, for the narrative in which America represents itself to itself insists on precisely such a stability. Within the dominant ideology, "America" never appears as a product of economic or social forces, but as a permanent and autonomous character, the adventure hero, as it were, confronting a series of tests. Theodore Roosevelt's imperialist rhetoric voices this heroism with especial clarity—waging war in the Philippines appears as a test of the individual's and the country's "manly and adventurous qualities"—but throughout the twentieth century both liberal and conservative rhetoric insistently portrays "America" on trial, the resolution to both domestic and international crises residing in the character of "America." Not change, but permanence, will solve the crisis at hand; not a process of becoming, but a more exact fulfillment of being, will guarantee success. The ideology of formula fiction, this is to argue, should be thought in relation to the narrative form of ideology, for if Frank Merriwell embodies the ideal of American "individualism," then "America," likewise, fleshes out the narrative grammar of adventure.

Above all, it was "adventure" and "action" that the pulp magazines promised their readers, beginning with Frank Munsey's *Argosy* (1896). And it was the pulps that produced the typology through which formula fiction has been displayed and consumed. In the 1920s and the 1930s, the expansion of the pulps—numbering over 200 during the Great Depression—particularized "adventure" to the point where, for instance, one could read not just *War Stories* or even *Navy Stories,* but, more exactly, *Submarine Stories* and *Zeppelin Stories*. Street and Smith published the first truly popular specialized pulp, *Detective Story Magazine,* in 1915, and it was detective fiction, science fiction, and the Western that claimed the most attention from both editors and readers. The serialized novels from these magazines established generic formulas; the pulp industry produced, as Marx would say, "not just an object for the subject, but a subject for the object"; and the subject produced was a new male readership. To oversimplify, we can claim that while the most popular fiction of the 1850s was written and read by women (under the auspices of male publishers), by the 1950s much of the most popular fiction, such as Mickey Spillane's hard-boiled detective novels and Max Brand's Westerns, was written and read by men. The modern emphasis on fiction's mass distribution—marked by publishing's involvement with Marshall Field and with Sears, by Robert de Graff's invention of Pocket Books (1939), by the emergence of mail-order book clubs— includes an attempt to masculinize the reading process. As Charles Madison explains in his history of publishing, the distribution of paperbacks to the armed forces during World War II developed "millions of readers who previously had seldom looked into a book." Thus, the masculine/feminine opposition that had long encoded the distinction between high and mass culture began to blur, and the hypermasculinity of the adventure hero looks not least like a compensatory reaction to this shift in literary consumption.

Just as the character of the adventure hero, always on trial, resists all change, so too the adventure formula resists modernity, providing an alternative experience to what Thorstein Veblen described, in 1904, as "the cultural incidence of the machine process" — "the disciplinary effect" of the "movement for standardization and mechanical equivalence" and the insistence on "matter-of-fact habits of thought." At the same time, that alternative, to the degree that it repeats a standardized formula, perpetuates this "disciplinary effect"; like any commodity, it creates only illusory difference; and it invites the reader to submit, like the author, to the prescriptions of (the very rhythm of) the productive apparatus. Nonetheless, formula fiction is not reducible to its formula, and reading science fiction, detective fiction, and the Western amounts to encountering a perpetual renegotiation of "adventure" and "modernization" (which is to say: "adventure" and its own mode of production).

In modern science fiction, the confrontation between "adventure" and "modernization," heroic stasis and modern progress, appears as a bifurcation within the industry itself: one strain of the genre emphasizes "adventure," most simply represented by the Flash Gordon film serials (1936, 1938, 1939), based on the popular comic strip; the other emphasizes invention or "hard science," initially represented by Hugo Gernsback's *Ralph 124C 41+* (1911), a novel serialized in his own publication, *Modern Electrics,* the country's first radio magazine. Gernsback's hero displays his technological genius in the act of saving a village girl from multiple crises, finally bringing her home to New York and the 650-foot, round glass tower that is his home. The novel takes as its task the presentation of a future metropolis and the careful description of future inventions, but this "Romance of the Year 2660" remains an adventure. The hero's genius — symbolized by the tower, technology's own phallus rising above New York — is inspired by the vulnerability of woman, the given, without which the narrative could neither begin nor end. And this point complicates the typical charge against science fiction, the claim that it promotes an unexamined and untenable myth of technological progress, as Lewis Mumford has argued. For that myth of progress inhabits a structural stasis: the stereotypical gender code makes science make sense, providing it with its very reason to be. Indeed, a second glance at the genre's modern history suggests that science fiction just as assiduously perpetuates a *myth of no progress*; it guarantees the stability of certain social relations despite technological advance; and in this sense it typically naturalizes the technologies of gender, sexuality, and race, by casting these human constructions outside the realm of the properly technological and historical.

Tracing the nineteenth-century foundations of science fiction means looking away from America, to the work of Mary Shelley, Jules Verne, and H. G. Wells, and yet a few American texts also opened up some basic avenues of enquiry. Edward Ellis's *Steam-Man of the Plains* (1868), a dime novel, initiates a fascination with the technological elimination of human labor that attains its most complete expression in Isaac Asimov's *I, Robot* (1950) and his three "laws of robotics," which adjudicate relations between the human and the technological. Edgar Allan Poe's "Balloon Hoax" (1844) and "Hans Pfaal" (1835) inaugurate an emphasis on travel that, in E. E. Smith's Skylark series, beginning with *The Skylark of Space* (1928), becomes intergallactic, providing writers with a new realm of exploration, made limitless with Asimov's invention of "hyper-spatial" travel in the 1940s. And Mark Twain's *A Connecticut Yankee in King Arthur's Court* (1889) introduces time travel as a means of highlighting the effects of technology. In L. Sprague de Camp's *Lest Darkness Fall* (1941), Twain's dystopian vision becomes utopian: the American hero finds himself transported from Mussolini's Rome to Justinian's Rome, where, with the reinvention of the semaphore telegraph and the printing press, he both prevents the Western Interregnum and establishes social justice. De Camp never addresses the absence of such technological resolution to the modern Western crisis, his hero remains in the safety of the past, but his novel exemplifies science fiction's increasing tendency, in the 1930s and 1940s, to address contemporary crisis explicitly before displacing it, spatially or chronologically, and providing its readers with the pleasure of scientific resolution. The splitting of the atom in 1938 realized many of the achievements and anxieties science fiction had been predicting for years, and it made the earth itself the most obvious new stage for adventure. By the 1950s, science fiction films take the 1950s as their very point of departure, developing a variety of monsters released or created by atomic explosion, notably *The Beast from 20,000 Fathoms* and *Them!,* where ants appear as the first of Hollywood's giant insects.

In contrast, the first chapter of Edgar Rice Burroughs's *The Princess of Mars* (1912), serialized the same year as his *Tarzan of the Apes,* tries to compensate for American history: John Carter, a Virginian who fought in the Civil War and then found himself a captain "in the cavalry arm of an army which no longer existed," has ventured West and become a wildly successful prospector in Arizona, where his partner is attacked by Apaches, from whom Carter himself takes refuge in a cave. By means of psychic projection, he ends up on Mars, this planet of war becoming, as it were, the new locus of American "adventure" — American adventures, both military and economic, having all but played themselves out within the continental United States. His strength and prowess enable him to resolve the conflict between the red and green races of Mars, to liberate the greenmen from their despotic ruler, and to defend the princess he loves from repeated assault; he thus reclaims, beyond the closing Western frontier, the chivalry of the Southerner. The logic of empire that underlies Burroughs's Martian novels (eleven in all, concluding in 1942) more obviously informs his Pellucidar series, beginning with *At the Earth's Core* (1914) and *Pellucidar* (1915), in which David Innes brings both American technology and the American political system to the primitive peoples residing in the Earth's hollow center. If H. G. Wells, during Africa's partition, tried to give his readers some sense of the horror of being colonized in *The War of the Worlds* (1898), then Burroughs, in contrast, insisted on the heroics of colonial subjection.

It is, of course, a racist axiom that makes this heroism possible, rendering global conflict as a Social Darwinist battle of races, and insisting on the priority of the body to the point where, despite any technological marvel, the first and final sign of superiority is always physical. The warlord John Carter is 6 feet, 2 inches tall, "broad of shoulder and narrow of hip," and David Innes, American emperor of Pellucidar, is a comparable physical specimen (as is, of course, Tarzan, that noble savage whose nobility derives from his aristocratic parentage). More obviously, it is the ethnographic and biological attention to the creatures of Mars and Pellucidar that grounds Burroughs's fiction in the body, and in racial history: the red and green races of Mars can be traced back to one "very dark, almost black" race, and one "reddish yellow race." And in all Burroughs's work, it is the threat of interracial abduction that emerges as the most heinous crime that his heroes must prevent: Carter must save the red, almost humanoid Martian princess from the sexual assault of a bestial green jeddack. That the popularity of Burroughs's first novels occurred between the extraordinary success of Thomas Dixon's *The Clansman* (1905) and D. W. Griffith's filmic version of the novel, *The Birth of a Nation* (1915), makes obvious sense, for the Martian novels also depict a white Southern male reestablishing racial order.

Simplistic as his adventure formula may seem, the simplicity still characterizes far more substantial works. George Allen England's *Darkness at Dawn* (1912), the first novel of a trilogy, provides a very different type of plot, but one that manifests the same ideology. In England's first science fiction story, "The Lunar Advertising Co." (1906), technological advancement takes place within the modern economy: the moon, as a giant projection screen, becomes America's premier billboard. But in the trilogy, the economy disappears along with human civilization: an engineer and a stenographer wake up in a New York skyscraper to find themselves the last two humans alive in a world that has been destroyed by an "Epic of Death." They are soon attacked by "demoniac hordes" of black, apelike creatures with a "trace of the Mongol," and Allan Stern, "the only white man living in the twenty-eighth century," must defend himself and the woman he grows to love against racial extinction. Facing a world "gone to pieces the way Liberia and Haiti and Santo Domingo once did, when white rule ceased," Stern nurtures his "deep-seated love for the memory of the race of men and women as they had once been." Finally, in the last of the novels, *The Afterglow,* he establishes a new social system among the other survivors they encounter, a system in which man is free at last because of the elimination of money, the proliferation of scientific thought, and the introduction of the English language, that "magnificent language, so rich and pure," its purity mimicking the racial purity achieved once the "horde" has been "wiped out." More precisely than Burroughs's work, then, England's trilogy occupies the ideology of its era, most familiar in Theodore Roosevelt's claim, from *The Winning of the West* (1899), that "the spread of the English-speaking peoples over the world's waste spaces has been . . . the most striking feature in the world's history." And England's novels exhibit the same contradictions as does Roosevelt's ideal of the "strenuous life," a call away from "overcivilization" that is still a call to "civilize" the world. For only in the face of civilization's demise does Allan Stern retrieve the ideals of "labor and exploration" and transform himself from the "man of science and cold fact" into a man who can feel the "atavistic passions"; only in defending the woman he loves does the "engineer" become an "American." The triumph of civilization simply leaves "man civilized" with no "other" against which to define himself; it leaves the hero and his world in a nonnarratable state.

This nonnarratable state is the very topic of John W. Campbell's prologue to *Islands of Space* (1930). In the typical history of science fiction, Campbell's editorial work at *Astounding,* begun in 1938, appears as the moment when science proper became the subject of science fiction. But just as this history itself writes that moment as an adventure—the hero Campbell rescuing science fiction and inaugurating the so-called Golden Age—so too his own fiction foregrounds the problem of adventure despite its greater scientific realism and its location of technology within an American corporate economy. *Islands of Space* begins by summarizing the previous endeavors of Transcontinental Airways: having initiated interplanetary travel and landed on Venus, the corporation found that, though "similar to Earthmen," the "Venusians" had blue blood and double thumbs, making them "enough different to have caused distrust and racial friction, had not both planets been drawn together in a common bond of defense" against the Black Star, Nigra. The Nigrans, functioning as the absolute other that cements comradeship, have been defeated, making the world of science uninteresting: "The War was over. And things had become dull. And the taste of adventure still remained." While there is some possibility that "commerce over quintillions of miles of space" will satisfy this taste, the band of scientists soon find themselves involved in an interplanetary confrontation far from earth. They settle the dispute, adjudicate interplanetary relations, offer their technology to the winning side as a means of ensuring further peace, and thus establish American technocratic, neocolonialist hegemony. The corporate adventure remains a fantasy of domination.

As science fiction begins to address the historical moment of its own production, the politics of such fantasies—politics per se—become more explicit and more explicitly resisted, as in *When Worlds Collide* (1933), a novel by Edwin Balmer and Philip Wylie that rewrites the Depression as a *natural* disaster. News of a planet's trajectory toward earth is first encountered in the papers as "something novel, exciting," but the ensuing panic requires careful governmental management: the unemployed are "corralled *en masse*" to build shelters in the heart of the country, away from the coasts, which will disappear in the first tidal waves. A great migration from the coasts to the plains (reversing the historical migration from the Dust Bowl) transforms even millionaires into "Oakies," driving "with their treasures heaped around them." The president shows "the good sense to kick politics in the face and take full authority upon himself," and his radio reports ("we stand now on the brink of a situation from which we cannot hide") suggest a commitment to reason abandoned elsewhere, such as Germany, where fascists have begun to execute both communists and Jews. But even such "non-political" acumen, of course, cannot forestall humanity's devastation. Outside any governmental auspices, a scientific "League of the Last Days," the focus of the novel, has secretly developed two rocket ships to take five hundred of the world's best minds to another planet, leaving "the hordes" (science fiction's ubiquitous "hordes") behind. Thus, the heroes of the novel accomplish their own eugenicist ends, but with a rational means that appears to stand fully outside politics (what the novel assesses as good and bad politics) and to stand outside economics—to stand *for* science itself. This account of the scientists' escape can be read as an allegory of science fiction's escapism—an effort to erase such earthly matters as fascism and depression while ultimately rewriting them.

The complications of technological resolution, which is to say technocratic domination, eventually become the object of science fiction's own scrutiny. In Fritz Leiber's *Gather Darkness* (1943), a "Hierarchy" rules Megatheopolis by duping "the masses" with scientific "miracles"; in Jack Williamson's *The Humanoids* (1947), "the virus of science" appears in the form of robots who protect human beings to the point of denying them all pleasure. But these explicit challenges to science and its myth of progress may tell us less than the adventure formula's inability to understand that narrative of progress outside other narratives—of racial, economic, and national conquest. While Jean-François Lyotard, for one, has suggested that the postmodern moment is a time when the metanarrative of science (the grand narratives of speculation and emancipation) faces a legitimation crisis, that crisis already inheres in science fiction, which can find no grounds for science outside its ability to serve as an instrument and sign of power.

Unlike science fiction, which, with its focus on technology, necessarily confronts the idea of "modernization," the Western at its most formulaic simply preserves an unspecified American space and time within which gunslinging heroes can conquer villains and win hearts. Max Brand's first Western novel, *The Untamed* (1918), further delocalizes its action with references to mythology, which continued to provide him with metaphors, themes, and plots that universalize the protagonist's heroism rather than restricting it to any historical West. Proclaimed by *Publishers Weekly* as "the king of the pulps," so prolific as to need twenty pseudonyms, Frederick Faust, most famous as "Max Brand," accomplished such feats of productivity—writing over a hundred Western novels, working in all the popular genres (and inventing Dr. Kildare), inspiring as many as five movies in a single year (1921)—that it is little wonder his Westerns, purged of complication, have paradigmatic value. In *Hired Guns* (1923), for instance, Billy Buel, a gunman who loves to fight and hates to work, is hired to fight in Gloster Valley's nine-year family feud over the identity and possession of Nell (a Western Helen of Troy). His courage, gunmanship, and personal code of ethics resolve that feud and win the heart of the beautiful girl, with whom he leaves the valley. Just as the novel's isolated community stands outside time, so the hero stands outside the community, resolving its conflicts only to flee. The narrative syntax—the outsider establishes social justice, then returns to the outside—remains the staple of the adventure formula, which depicts a need for social change, but a change that must come from without, and from an individual's changeless heroism.

This syntax underlies far more complex renditions of the Western, such as John Ford's *Stagecoach* (1939), which reestablished the popularity of the Hollywood Western in the sound era. Based on a story by Ernest Haycox, Ford's film, displaying the desert crossing of a stage from Tonto to Lordsburg, isolates the passengers, consisting of social outcasts, into a society of their own (a microcosm that has been read allegorically as "America," the country struggling against the natural world). The most socially disreputable of the characters (a prostitute, an alcoholic doctor, a gambler), threatened by Apache attack and faced with the birth of a child, reveal a humanity and a morality that far surpass the Victorian principles of the town, represented by the Ladies' Law and Order League. The opening scenes of the movie allow us to glimpse their lives within society, but the outlaw hero of the story, Ringo Kid (John Wayne), appears only once the coach is well on its way: he looms up, as if from nowhere, isolated by the camera with Monument Valley as a backdrop; he appears as if from nature itself, more completely beyond the confines of the town. And once he secures the passage of the stagecoach, and, in a shoot-out, avenges his brother's death, he leaves the social order again, riding off to the Mexican border with the woman he has come to love (the prostitute), both of them "saved the blessings of civilization," as the doctor says, watching them take off. (At the same time, the doctor, who has sobered up to deliver the baby, accepts the offer of a drink, reestablishing his own exteriority.) Thus, while defending civilization against the uncivilized Native Americans, Ringo defends himself against civilization by (as Huck Finn would have it) lighting out for the territories.

Nonetheless, in *Stagecoach,* as in *Hired Guns,* the hero's union with a woman provides the sense of closure denied by this escape; and as Laura Mulvey has said of Western films, "marriage" functions to sublimate "the erotic into a final, closing, social ritual." But the Western's resistance to society—most vociferous in its attack on business interests and Eastern decadence—is exemplified not least by the formula's tendency to exclude this "social ritual" from the plot itself, to project the possibility of "marriage" into an unknown future (the possible basis of an Edenic society elsewhere), or to idealize love outside this social institution. *Points West* (1928), written by "B. M. Bower" (Bertha Muzzy Sinclair, the one woman who consistently worked in the genre), portrays as its heroine a "fighting cowgirl" who is very much the fighting cowboy's equal; their relationship is based on a type of filial rivalry that negates the typical asymmetry of the gender code and thus the threat of domestication; nonetheless, as the novel closes, Billy simply has his "eye on the girl," and marriage as such (that social mark of change) remains excluded from the pages of the novel. More simply, in Zane Grey's *Riders of the Purple Sage* (1912), which defines the "love of man for woman" (noticeably not *between* man and woman) as "the nature, the meaning, the best of life itself," the hero and heroine disappear together into the uninhabited Surprise Valley, the "nature of life" dissolving into nature. And if this marginalization of marriage suggests the thoroughness with which the Western resists society, with which it resists the idea of its hero's socialization, then the status of law, explicitly addressed in one novel after another, more clearly confirms the idea that existing social institutions stand in the way of happiness and success. The hero of Eugene Manlove Rhodes's *Barnsford in Arcadia* (1913) puts the matter simply: law "rouses no enthusiasm in my manly bosom," he claims; "I am endowed by nature with certain inalienable rights, among which are the high justice, the middle, and the low." It is only this endowment that enables every Western hero to establish a justice that transcends law. In Owen Wister's *The Virginian* (1902), it is the very voice of the law, the voice of Judge Henry, who legitimizes extralegal activity, the vigilante justice of the West: "far from being a *defiance* of the law," the judge argues, "it is an *assertion* of it."

This extrainstitutional status of true law and true love converges with the extrasocietal status of the adventure hero, and the atemporal and atopian action, to make the adventure formula not just escapist but a lesson in escapism: a study in the need for the individual to get beyond society. But this is true only of the Western at its most formulaic. In fact, Wister's novel, which marks the advent of the modern Western, finally suggests an altogether different emphasis—not on the separation of the hero from society, but on his integration. *The Virginian*, indebted less to the dime novel and more to Cooper's Leatherstocking tales and the American historical romance (as Wister suggests in his preface), provides the modern formula with its basic semantic elements (above all the cowboy, a loner, a "handsome ungrammatical son of the soil") and the ideology of Anglo-Saxonism and individualism. But its plot concludes by locating the hero within society, the family, and the economy. Furthermore, Wister locates the story in a specific time and place, Wyoming, between 1874 and 1890, and implicitly addresses a moment in recent history: the Johnson County War (1892) between cattlemen and homesteaders. The love story between the cowpuncher and the Eastern schoolmarm resolves the antinomies that structure every Western (East/West, civilization/nature, society/individual), and just as she learns the necessity of the West's code of violence ("how it must be about a man"), so too he learns the beauty of Shakespeare and Scott. Both characters change before their marriage, and the Virginian himself rises within the cattle industry: he begins as a hand on Judge Henry's ranch, advances to manager, becomes the judge's partner, and, with the coming of the railroad in the 1890s, ultimately establishes himself as "an important man, with a strong grip on many various enterprises and able to give his wife all and more than she asked or desired," the sort of "important man" who will later serve as the formula's embodiment of evil. Wister reports these last two stages of success hastily, in the closing pages, but they serve to foreground the fact that *The Virginian* is an economic novel: its central dispute, between the Virginian and Trampas, is a dispute between management and labor; by serving Trampas "an intellectual crushing," the Virginian suppresses the organization of men against the judge's interests. Thus, the outsider (who, as a Virginian, is actually an outsider to the West) serves to stabilize an economic "civilization" within which he occupies a central place.

The point, then, is that *The Virginian* finally insists not on the exteriority of the West and the Western hero but on their centrality, their pertinence to modernization's advance. In a Wyoming "as wild as was Virginia one hundred years earlier," Wister's hero, as a latter-day Thomas Jefferson, exemplifies for the Eastern narrator the central point of American democracy: "It was through the Declaration of Independence that we Americans acknowledged the *eternal inequality* of man"; "true democracy and true aristocracy are one and the same thing." The fact that true aristocracy finds itself confirmed by economic hierarchy makes the origin of America coincide with its turn-of-the-century corporate end. In contrast to Brand, who ignores the "modern world," Wister implicitly confirms it, and Zane Grey, who did more than anyone to establish the popularity of the genre, confronts the problem of modernization explicitly, and most compellingly in those novels where the West serves to rejuvenate an individual from the misery of modern warfare. In *The Call of the Canyon* (1924), *The Shepherd of Guadaloupe* (1930), and *30,000 on the Hoof* (1940), shell-shocked soldiers return to America physically and emotionally depleted, ignored by their government, misunderstood by their friends. But despite grim prognoses from their doctors, a trip West initiates a slow recovery, one in which men learn above all the pleasures of physical work and the superficiality of Eastern life.

The very sight of the Western landscape can inspire change, but the fact that such sights had become a part of Eastern culture turns visualization itself into a point of contest. By 1900, William Henry Jackson was mass-marketing his photographs of Yellowstone; in 1910, D. W. Griffith shot *Ramona* in Ventura, the very locale of Helen Hunt Jackson's novel (as the film reminds us); in 1917, John Ford included a dramatic mountain pass in *Straight Shooting* and closed the film with his signature shot of the sunset. But while modern technology had brought the West to the East with an "authenticity" that surpassed the paintings of Thomas Moran and Albert Bierstadt, for Grey such representations would not do. In *The Call of the Canyon,* Carley Burch, having ventured to Arizona to see her fiancé, but returning East without him, finds that she hates "the motion pictures with their salacious and absurd misrepresentations." In *The Vanishing American* (1925), Marian Warner finds that motion pictures have little to do with the truth of the West. The dichotomous imagination of the Western novel here incorporates the Western film into its schemata—East vs. West can be read, likewise, as Western film vs. Western reality—and literature's Sisyphean task of debunking the literary (hardly a task confined to realism) is now compounded by the job of having to debunk the cinematic. And yet, by 1922, when the novel was first serialized, Grey had written sixteen Westerns, and already twelve of these had been made into movies, beginning in 1918 with Samuel Goldwyn's six-reel version of *The Border of the Legion.* Which is to say: Marian Warner's "impressions of the West" are, in the plot's historical moment, impressions most likely derived from Grey. This irony extends somewhat further: while the cinema, like jazz, can typify the "speed-mad, excitement-mad, fad-mad, dress-mad" decadence of the East in *The Call of the Canyon,* Grey himself was introduced to the far West, in New York in 1907, when he saw the films of Yellowstone produced by "Buffalo" Jones. He then accompanied Jones on a trip to Arizona, recounted in *The Last of the Plainsmen* (1908), during which he himself served as cameraman.

*The Call of the Canyon,* for all its romantic antimodernism, situates itself within this modern visual culture, trying to share in what Griffith called the "universal language" of moving pictures. Appearing serially in the *Ladies' Home Journal* (1921–22), in the midst of full-page ads for Paramount Studios and articles on Griffith's latest success (*Way Down East*), the novel tries to teach "modern woman" the Western lesson of antimodernity through the image alone, restricting the meaning of the West to the "visual." It is "mere heights and depths, mere rock walls and pine trees, and rushing water"—these mere sights—that transform the "modern young woman of materialistic mind" into an "American woman," dedicated to a life in the home. Grey's "purple prose," in competition with cinematic culture, might be understood foremost as a way of arresting the image, keeping it within the reader's "view" in order to effect a transformation such as Carley's. While science fiction adheres to the logic of adventure despite its espousal of modernization, the Western's most explicit antimodernism all but abandons that logic: only the land itself, an enduring frontier, stands as the unchanging hero.

While the objective in and of *The Call of the Canyon* is to redeem modern woman, in the hard-boiled detective novel she appears unredeemable, threatening the very life of the hero. Only the rejection of women, as opposed to any union with them, provides the sense of an ending. Even in more classical versions of the genre, a "really good detective never gets married," as Raymond Chandler said, with characteristic bluntness. In part, this results from the seriality of the form, the need to maintain the static character of the hero from one adventure to the next: Erle Stanley Gardner, who wrote voluminously for the pulps in the 1920s, created Perry Mason in 1933, with *The Case of the Velvet Claws,* and the extraordinary popularity of the novel prompted eighty-one further cases (more than fifteen bestsellers in the 1930s), most of which portray the lawyer defending a young and naive woman. They thus present a paternal figure who can protect female innocence against crime, the idiosyncrasies of the legal system, and the general chaos of the Depression. Obviously, being married would complicate Mason's physical attraction to his clients, just as any romantic involvement beyond that attraction would compromise his role as the good father who rescues his clients from the wiles of bad men. To survive, the Perry Mason formula mandates its hero's celibacy.

The hard-boiled detective novel brought "adventure" to the heart of the modern city in the 1920s, and it transformed the cerebral art of classical detection into physical action. In a world of gambling and drinking, political corruption and organized crime, it is female sexuality, "woman" as signifier of sex, that functions to generate peripeteia, distracting the hero and thus retarding the process of detection, conflating the pleasures of reading with the hero's sexual pleasure. Only the renunciation of this sexuality can prompt a satisfactory denouement, the end of desire, most severely represented by Mickey Spillane's late contributions to the hard-boiled formula. In *I, the Jury* (1947), the title of which proclaims its hero's monomania, Mike Hammer finds himself the irresistible object of women's lust; he falls in love with, and he hopes to marry, Charlotte Manning, the woman who turns out to have murdered his partner. The novel's famous closing pages syncopate his sequential revelation of the crime to her, on the one hand, and, on the other, an account of her "self-revelation" to him, a striptease performed before the .45 he points at her, that performance, the relationship, and the novel itself reaching their consummation as she reaches out to him and he shoots her in the stomach. The scopic regime of the detective formula has become violently scopophilic. Pathological as *I, the Jury* may seem, it has remained one of the most popular American detective novels, a fact that may stem from its very celebration of an erotics of reading, or its simple, pornographic equation of knowledge and power. But this is only the most extreme version of a misogynist gender code that pervades both the hard-boiled detective novel and Hollywood's *film noir*, where the crisis of the city is ultimately locatable in the chaos that is "woman."

Before discussing the emergence of this code in the 1920s, I want to point out that "hard-boiled" detective fiction—admired by Sartre and Camus, associated stylistically with Hemingway, and championed for its urban realism—has virtually become synonymous with "American" detective fiction and has thus obscured important variants. Mary Roberts Rinehart, for instance, one of the century's most prolific and popular writers, produced the first American best-selling detective novel, *The Circular Staircase* (1908), quickly followed by *The Man in Lower Ten* (1909) and *The Window at the White Cat* (1910). The spinster who assumes the role of amateur detective in the first of these foreshadows Agatha Christie's Miss Marple (English, of course, and considerably older), but she herself harks back to Amelia Butterworth, the heroine of Anna Katherine Green's *That Affair Next Door* (1897), a "lonely and single" woman, living in Gramercy Park, who "discovers herself" by joining the murder investigation headed by Detective Ebenezer Gryce. While solving the mystery, Rinehart's heroine rescues her sister's orphaned children from suspicion, enables them to marry the individuals they love, and secures their (matrilinear) inheritance. As a vicarious mother, she preserves the components of the familial institution while asserting an ego that does not depend on that institution but on her public rivalry with male professionals. Not only does *The Circular Staircase* provide an alternative to such celebrations of motherhood as Kathleen Norris's *Mother* (1911), indebted to Louisa May Alcott and Susan Warner; it also foregrounds its heroine's status as an independent and rational woman by intertextually embracing other genres of "women's fiction," providing, for instance, a miniature sentimental plot in one woman's "sad and tragic" story of being abandoned, pregnant, by her worthless husband. The single woman's independence from men, which is an independence from that story, grounds her ultimate power over them.

Despite the proliferation of detective pulps in the 1920s (*Flynn's, Clues, Dragnet Magazine, Detective Tales*), the original venue for hard-boiled detection, *Black Mask* (1920), began eclectically, not specializing until the end of the decade, at which point it emerged not only with a generic focus but also with a recognizably spare style, cynical hero, and sordid urban scene. The stories of Carroll John Daly and Dashiell Hammett inaugurated these features in 1923, and their private investigators, Race Williams and the unnamed Continental Op, eventually appeared in serialized novels that took book form in Daly's *The Snarl of the Beast* (1927) and Hammett's *Red Harvest* (1929). Unlike the aristocratic amateur—who remained a best-selling favorite in the 1920s, in the form of S. S. Van Dine's scholarly Philo Vance, "sedulously schooled in the repression of his emotions" and "aloof from the transient concerns of life"—the hard-boiled private-eye works for a living, talks tough, carries a .45, and typically tells his own story. In *The Simple Act of Murder* (1950) Raymond Chandler locates this new hero, who "talks the way the man of his age talks," within a democratic vision: "He is a common man or he would not go among common people." And in *The Big Sleep* (1939), Chandler's detective, Philip Marlowe, must explain this new, pedestrian heroism to a client: "I'm not Sherlock Holmes or Philo Vance. . . . If you think there's anybody in the detective business making a living doing that sort of thing, you don't know much about cops." Likewise, in Hammett's *The Maltese Falcon* (1930), Sam Spade must explain that *his* "way of learning is to heave a wild and unpredictable monkey-wrench into the machinery." The detective formula's faith in the powers of reason finds itself abandoned for an urban existentialism. "It's what you do," Race Williams concludes.

The lack of narratological distance (of the sort provided by mediating commentators like Holmes's Dr. Watson) combines with an effacement of cultural, psychological, and class distance to the point where the hero's very distinction from the criminal world he inhabits becomes suspect—this, despite his fidelity to individualism. In *Red Harvest*, the Op enters "Poisonville" (Personville) in the aftermath of labor hostilities that the city czar (owner of the mills) has resolved only with the help of organized crime, and this class conflict (the novel's "past") gets transposed into the detective's refusal to obey both his client's commands and the detective agency's regulations. But this violation of the rules readily becomes absorbed into a world without rule: rather than trying to "swing the play legally," the Op finds it both "easier" and "more satisfying" to provoke the gangsters to kill one another until the city erupts into a "slaughterhouse." Foremost, the transcription of "Personville" into "Poisonville" signifies this disappearance of "the person," the hero's inability to establish his own autonomy.

His opening description of Poisonville—"an ugly city of forty thousand people, set in an ugly notch between two ugly mountains," with "a grimy sky that looked as if it had come out of the smelter's stacks"—is generally taken to crystallize the distinction between hard-boiled and classical detective fiction. But, more exactly, it is the difference between this opening panorama and the rest of the novel that makes those distinctions clear, for once the Op enters the city, the very possibility of vision, of a perspective that depends on exteriority, disappears: the hotel lobbies, hospital rooms, and abandoned warehouses produce a claustrophobic interiority from which there is no relief. The pursuit of crime continues to take place according to a logic of the gaze, but a logic where intense perception prompts no totalizing vision. The "iron-legged, tile-topped tables outside under the striped awning," the "quilted gray chenille" of a Packard interior—these remain part of the accumulation of detail without gestalt. Chandler triumphantly described the new American style as "emotional and sensational rather than intellectual," expressing "things experienced rather than ideas." But the style triumphs only at the traditional formula's expense: while Poe's Dupin explained, in the 1840s, that "the necessary knowledge is that of *what* to observe," no such discretion controls the proliferation of detail in the hard-boiled novel. And the most salient feature of Chandler's prose, its obsession with the simile—a cigarette tastes "like a plumber's handkerchief," a handrail is "as cold and wet as a toad's belly," Marlowe feels "like an amputated leg"—rhetorically marks the same dilemma. For synecdoche and metonymy are the figures "proper" to the art of detection, which understands the whole from the part, the cause from the effects; instead, Marlowe's figure (Chandler kept a separate notebook of similes) registers an incessant, flickering likeness of parts that fit no whole, a world of mere effects.

The absence of totalizing knowledge extends more fully to the hard-boiled novel's account of the human body. Classical detective fiction, even such precursors as *Oedipus Rex* and Poe's "The Man of the Crowd," attends to the idiosyncrasies of physique; like Poe's narrator, it regards "with minute interest the innumerable varieties of figure, dress, air, gait, visage, and expression of countenance"; and it peoples the fictional world with cripples, invalids, grotesques. But this attention serves foremost to render the body legible, to incorporate physiognomical explication within the art of detection. In contrast, *Red Harvest*, resisting the sort of typology provided by Poe, creates a world of resemblances: the corrupt chief of police "is gray, flabby, damp, like fresh putty," the Op's fellow agent is "a big slob with sagging shoulders," and the Op himself is described by Dinah Brand as "fat" and "middle-aged." In this morass of likeness, the body disappears as a site for psychological or moral symptomatology. Similarly, physical gestures in *The Maltese Falcon* seem to resonate with significance and erotic overtones—he "rearranged his hands on his lap so that, intentionally or not, a blunt forefinger pointed at Spade"—but they remain opaque. And this inability to regulate somatic semiosis has its correlative in the detective's apparent alienation from his own body: it is not "Sam Spade," but "Spade's thick fingers" that make "a cigarette with deliberate care," as though the body operates on its own. In *Farewell, My Lovely* (1940), Philip Marlowe's self-representation reflects a comparable disjuncture: "The hand jumped at the inside pocket of the overcoat." We might expect moments of instinctual action to resolve this alienation of the self from itself, but the descriptive hyperspecificity permits no such resolution: "Spade's elbow went on past the astonished dark face and straightened when Spade's hand struck down at the pistol." Man remains a mere sum of body parts.

The resolution comes instead under the sign of "woman." It is in relation to the desired but deceitful *femme fatale* that the detective exerts a self-control that produces a coherent self, displayed most clearly in the closing pages of *The Maltese Falcon*. Sam Spade, though he has slept with Brigid O'Shaughnessy and though he admits to loving her, refuses to protect her from the police. While he reveals to her his knowledge of her crime—the murder of his partner—he is able to reveal himself to himself, to articulate a personal code of ethics, to enumerate seven reasons why, despite her pleas, he can neither escape with her nor let her escape on her own. The very process of numbering these reasons reflects the sudden triumph of reason in the midst of this irrational world. But just as the need of "woman" to define the "hero" tarnishes any ideal of self-reliance, so Spade expresses the most pedestrian anxieties: above all, he's afraid of being "played the sap."

More women appear in Chandler's novels, and their perpetual interest in the tall and handsome Philip Marlowe ("Hold me close, you beast") more completely infiltrates the detection of crime with desire. His client in *The Big Sleep* (1939), General Sternwood, an old man confined to a wheelchair, centralizes the figure of the body in the novel by describing the business of detection as the "delicate operation" of "removing morbid growths from people's backs." While Marlowe finds one woman after another almost unbearably attractive, he is able to transcend their sensuality, though "it's hard for women—even nice women—to realize their bodies are not irresistible." And this ability to control himself stands in obvious contrast to the uncontrollable excesses of the novel's rich and liberated women, not just drinkers and smokers but exhibitionists and nymphomaniacs. It is the younger Sternwood daughter who has committed the initial murder that prompts the novel's escalating crime. In the midst of an epileptic fit, she shot the brother-in-law who would not sleep with her. Only the physical reenactment of the crime with Marlowe (her gun now loaded with blanks) provides the solution to the mystery, one where woman's body exposes itself as monstrous: "Her mouth began to shake. Her whole face went to pieces. Then her head screwed up towards her left ear and froth showed on her lips. Her breath made a whinnying sound." While Marlowe solves the mystery, he can hardly resolve the problem; he simply insists that the girl be taken "where they will keep guns and knives and fancy drinks away from her." Unable to put a stop to the pornography and blackmail rings that have involved the Sternwood daughter, he can only perform the medicalized task of detection as her father initially defined it, removing a morbid growth, the girl's body, from social circulation.

In *Farewell, My Lovely,* the figure of the seductress, in contrast to this almost innocent girl, appears as a rich and ruthless woman. And in James M. Cain's hard-boiled mysteries, *The Postman Always Rings Twice* (1934) and *Double Indemnity* (1936), beautiful, predatory women seduce men into a world of crime. Even outside the hard-boiled version of the genre, desire now appears as a complication to be reckoned with. Rex Stout's obese detective, Nero Wolfe, remains aloof from the world and from women—"I carry this fat to insulate my feelings," he explains in *Over My Dead Body* (1939)— but his assistant, Archie, remains immersed in a world that includes beautiful women, the division of labor in Stout's novels reflecting the division between classical and hard-boiled detection. In turn, the *film noir* of the 1940s and 1950s, indebted thematically to the *Black Mask* school, stylistically to German Expressionist cinema, portrays a shadowy and claustrophobic world of the city, a world of perpetual night, in which the ruthless female predator embodies the modern world's threat to modern man. The long opening shot of Billy Wilder's version of *Double Indemnity* (1944) provides a memorable image of this man: an obscure figure in the fog . . . a coat and a hat . . . a man alone, hobbling along on crutches. But it is Mickey Spillane's *Vengeance Is Mine* (1950) that, for all its simplistic hyper-masculinity, finally complicates the threat of "woman." Mike Hammer finds himself desperately attracted to Juno ("the best-looking thing I ever saw"), the powerful manager of an advertising agency, the heart of modern culture's manipulation of appearance and desire. Revealing her, too, as a murderer, he must shoot this woman he longs for, only to discover that—she is in fact a man. Not "woman," then, but a man and the very opposition between "woman" and "man," along with the tough guy's own sexuality, now constitute the center of uncertainty.

In the trajectory of modern "adventure" as I've drawn it (not chronologically but generically), the most visible transformation occurs—while the locus of adventure moves from Mars, to the West, to the modern city, back to Alger's urban scene—in the shift from "woman" as a figure to be saved (from dark men) to "woman" as the dark figure to be fought off. At the same time, the hero shifts from being wholly self-sufficient to someone struggling to construct a coherent self. Of course, this look at formula fiction has looked away from many popular novels—notably, Margaret Mitchell's *Gone With the Wind* (1936)—novels that bear a less recognizable relation to the narrative paradigms stabilized by modern shifts in the mode of literary production and distribution. And investigating this fiction as a site of negotiation between "adventure" and "modernization" has meant isolating only a dominant thematics—the relation of male heroism to social change. But that negotiation provides an exemplary instance of the "transformational work" of the popular text, as Fredric Jameson understands it, the text's ability to express but neutralize social anxiety, providing symbolic satisfaction for genuine emotional needs. In this light, Tania Modleski, writing about such forms as the Harlequin Romance (invented in 1958, and quickly stabilizing a very different formula), has argued against simply denigrating the work as delusive, and for appreciating its ability to satisfy "*real* needs and desires." For his part, Max Brand, that king of the pulps, simply reminds us that "the sadness of life" does not "appeal to the horny-handed sons of toil," but only to "those who eat strawberries and cream." The fiction that attained mass appeal still registers that sadness, helping to make the desires of that sadness explicit. It also constrains those desires by configuring heroism within a cultural code that relies foremost on race and gender to generate meaning, no matter *where* or *when* the adventure occurs. The adventure, even as it strives to project a hero unchanged by the world, protects that world from change.

Bill Brown

# Ethnicity and the Marketplace

Immigration to the United States occurred in two waves: the "old migration" of 1820 to 1860, which numbered about 3.5 million persons, and consisted mainly of Northwestern Europeans including the British, the Irish, and the Germans, who settled primarily in rural areas, building the railroads (along with Chinese working from the West), manning the mines, supplying domestic labor, and opening up the homesteading regions of the far Midwest; and the "new" or "great" migration, from 1870 to 1913, which entailed close to 25 million immigrants, including many of British and German descent, homesteaders from Scandinavia and Bohemia, and increasingly large percentages from Eastern and Southern Europe-Russian-Polish Jews, Austrian and Rumanian Jews, Catholic Poles, Southern Italians, Slovaks, Serbs, and Croatians—who came as wage laborers to build and work the industrial Northeast and Midwest and who settled in urban enclaves that were called, pointedly, "colonies" of the Old World. Of marked cultural distinction but far less conspicuous in number were 23,000 Japanese and 85,000 Chinese immigrants as well as those of Spanish-Mexican, French-Canadian, or French-Creole descent who had been incorporated by annexation and territorial expansion. By the onset of World War I, the United States had been transformed, in Werner Sollors's phrase, from "a British-dominated, triracial country" into a "modern, polyethnic, and also increasingly urban nation."

Compared to the antebellum immigrants, the newcomers of the great second wave were far more numerous, more concentrated in the cities, and—above all—more distanced from the English Puritanism out of which had been woven much of the country's cultural fabric. Their arrival provoked national fascination, at first curious, but increasingly resentful and obsessive. Why had they come and what did they want? What were their folkways, their habits, their concerns— their religions, especially? Didn't they want to become "like us"? Were they going to be able to succeed, and if so, what then? What would be the future of the "American way of life" if it was to be rewoven by hands not of Anglo-Saxon extraction?

From the onset of the great migration through at least the early 1920s, the debate over the ethnic transformation of America was carried out more saliently by writers from established Anglo-Saxon families and their cultural allies of Northwestern European descent. The dominant genre was sociological journalism, running the gamut from xenophobia to pluralist philosophy and from tenement reformism to cross-cultural interpretation: from Charles Loring Brace's *The Dangerous Classes of New York* (1872), Jacob Riis's *How the Other Half Lives* (1890), and Henry Pratt Fairchild's *The Melting-Pot Mistake* (1926) to Hutchins Hapgood's *The Spirit of the Ghetto* (1902), Jane Addams's *Twenty Years at Hull House* (1910), and the essays of Josiah Royce and Randolph Bourne. But the most resounding assessment of the new ethnic presence came by deed, not word. In 1924, the United States Congress completed passage of a series of laws that drastically reduced immigration, favoring Northwestern Europeans, restricting Southern and Eastern Europeans, and excluding the Chinese entirely as well as all but the tiniest numbers of other Asians.

Well after the golden door of immigration had been closed to a bare crack, the door of ethnic literary mediation remained open to anyone with a claim to the authority of an "insider." The marketplace beckoned to immigrant intellectuals, some of whom had been educated in Europe and most of whom had already established themselves in the foreign-language presses; and it beckoned to the offspring of immigrants raised in the United States, many of whom had risen from poverty and even illiteracy to achieve some form of American higher education and most of whom had already been guided toward letters by an old-stock literary mentor, often of national repute. Whatever their institutional credentials, writers from immigrant backgrounds schooled themselves in the national "ethnicity" debate, with particular attention to prevailing formulas that denigrated their peoples or equated the pursuit of economic self-determination with assimilation and Anglo conformism. It was natural that they were provoked by the stereotypes and the typifying conventions; natural that they would be interested in righting the portraits of the communities left behind and in exploring for themselves developing ethnic agendas.

For those seeking to depict immigrant experience for a mainstream audience, three major genres were available—autobiography, the social science treatise, and fiction in the realist tradition—each requiring varying credentials and offering varying kinds of cultural impact. The classic ethnic novel was an effort, roughly speaking, to split the difference between populist autobiography and hard-core sociology: to exercise the authority of personal experience, yet to make the story speak to a group history; to reach a considerable public, but to reveal to them unexpected, often unhappy, truths. Told at a more or less autobiographical proximity, the classic ethnic novel ranged from reconstructing the earlier years of settlement ("the ghetto" narrative and its rural equivalents) to depicting more recent dramas of passage out of the colony into the middle classes (the "up-from-the-ghetto" narrative and equivalents), drawing upon the writer's memories of those left behind and the writer's continuing struggle for cultural rapprochement. It was created by reworking the established nineteenth-century genres of realism, naturalism, and regionalism—the literary conventions with which, in decades past, the quest for upward mobility had been depicted. Of the many dozens of books of ethnic fiction that were produced by mid-century, almost all had as their primary motive setting the record straight: to tell representative narratives that either countermanded or contextualized stereotypes, to acknowledge the opportunities but protest the obstacles facing newcomers, and to introduce the public to the debate within ethnic homes and communities over alternative American dreams.

If not best-sellers, most of these narratives circulated conspicuously enough; they were published by respected houses, previewed and promoted in popular magazines and highbrow journals, favorably reviewed by important critics, given literary prizes, purchased for use as screenplays, reprinted by the Book-of-the-Month Club or the Modern Library, and (then as now) anthologized alongside the canonical high modernists. With singular exceptions, the best of these novels have either remained in print steadily since publication or been granted republication as part of renewed academic interest: a process of recovery that began as soon as the mid-century drew to a close (with the earliest efforts of Isaac Rosenfeld, Harold Ribalow, Leslie Fiedler, and others concerned with Russian Jews) and became a central business after the mid-1970s with the opening up of the canon and the growing effort to recover works depicting the social margins.

From the beginning, immigrants of Anglo-Saxon origin, no matter the desperateness of their working or living conditions, were thought to be too much of a piece with the mainstream culture to warrant special concern except as a kind of picturesque footnote, exemplified in such long-buried narratives as Helen Reimensnyder Martin's *Tillie, a Mennonite Maid* (1904) and Arnold Muller's *Bram of the Five Corners* (1915). Immigrants from certain little-known places of Eastern Europe were occasionally depicted in autobiographical and biographical narratives—Czech Simon Pollack's *The Autobiography of Simon Pollack* (1904), Croatian Victor Vecki's *Threatening Shadows* (1931), Slovakian Thomas Bell's *Out of This Furnace* (1941), and Edith May Dowe Minister's *Our Natupski Neighbors* (1916), about Polish Catholic immigrants. Yet these books did not attract much attention because the groups they depict remained amorphous in the national imagination and did not seem to pose too much of a cultural threat (for various reasons having mainly to do with patterns of settlement and interaction). The first accounts of immigration from outside of Europe appeared by the end of the 1930s—most notably, by Jamaican-born Claude McKay, Korean-born Younghill Kang, and Armenian-born William Saroyan—but the novelistic portrayal of these peoples and those of the incorporated Hispanic Southwest remained largely the work of outsiders until after World War II.

Commentators ranging from Malcolm Cowley to Daniel Aaron have noted that writers with immigrant backgrounds began to appear in mainstream letters—journalism, poetry, drama, criticism, sociopolitical commentary—a short time after settlement had begun in earnest and that they did so in numbers reflecting each group's rate of upward mobility, its pursuit of higher education, and its embrace of secular letters. What seems not to have been observed is that ethnic fiction—particularly the novel of cultural mediation (the phrase is Jules Chametzky's)—developed at an alternative pace. The major novels between the wars came from the Jews (especially those from the Russian-Polish Pale), the Scandinavians (especially the Norwegians), the Irish, and the Southern Italians (including the Sicilians), roughly in that chronology, which is not the order of settlement and is accountable only in part by the demographics of mobility. Between the wars the classic ethnic novel was written by and about these four immigrant populations, who were taken to present the most serious cultural and social challenges to the nation at large.

During the years of the migration itself, the national appetite was for testimonials from inside working-class precincts, reflecting the increasing assumption, in the words of a Chicago clergyman in 1887, "that every workingman is a foreigner." The market for insider tales of ethnic labor inspired New England-descended and Yale-educated Hamilton Holt, the managing editor of *The Independent* of New York City, to solicit and publish some seventy-five autobiographical sketches, sixteen of which later appeared in a single volume, *The Life Stories of Undistinguished Americans as Told by Themselves* (1906; reprinted 1990). Tellingly, the reviewers focused on the contributors who were representative of the four central populations of the great migration, all in stereotypical occupations—a Jewish garment worker from Poland, a Swedish farmer, an Irish maid, and an Italian bootblack—even though Hamilton included alongside the classic types oral histories of such non-European immigrants as a Syrian who clerked in an "oriental goods" store, a Chinese laundryman, and a Japanese servant, as well as that of an Igorrote Chief (representing the 237,000 surviving Indians).

The first popular series of immigrant novels—*The Yoke of the Thorah, Mrs. Prexiada,* and several others—treated German Jewish merchants and were published with much fanfare in the 1880s; they appeared to be experientially based and were signed by "Sidney Luska," a writer whom almost everyone (including the Jewish American press) took to be a German Jew. In a pattern that would reappear, Luska was unmasked as an Anglo American, Henry Harland. Ernest Poole released his novel about Italian immigrants, *The Voice of the Street* (1906), under his own name, having hired Joseph Stella, an American-trained artist born in Italy, to provide illustrations; in his preface, Poole admitted to his status as an interested outsider yet wielded the figure of Stella to imply an Italian American seal of approval. The earliest novels written by ethnic insiders, little remembered now, were often investigations focused on the workplace. The title character of the first Italian American fiction, Luigi Donato Ventura's *Peppino* (1886), was a bootblack befriended by an aspiring writer. Elias Tobenkin presented East Side street peddlers in the first of the Russian Jewish best-sellers, *Witte Arrives* (1916).

In the teens and twenties, national concern began to shift from life among the foreign workers to whether or not they could or would "assimilate," an idea that (like the melting pot itself) vibrated between an enforced Anglo conformism and a more generous sense of achieving sufficient economic and educational mobility to participate in national public life. By this time, many immigrants had in fact climbed from obscurity to prosperity and thus could supply success stories that were reassuring on the question of whether immigrants could "make it" or not; indeed, they often sang the praises of the United States and of "100 percent Americanism" to loud public applause. The prevailing ethnic genre in terms of sheer numbers was the undisguised and unimaginative ethnic autobiography. These life stories of more "distinguished" Americans fused Benjamin Franklin's autobiography with the Horatio Alger tales and were given titles indicative of how little open to reinterpretation was "genuine Americanness": Edward Bok's *The Americanization of Edward Bok* (1920), Riis's *The Making of an American* (1901), Angelo Patri's *The Spirit of America* (1924), Mary Antin's *The Promised Land* (1912), M. E. Ravage's *An American in the Making* (1917), Edward Steiner's *From Alien to Citizen* (1914), and Michael Pupin's *From Immigrant to Inventor* (1923).

In 1894 William Dean Howells caught sight of an early story by Abraham Cahan—a labor organizer and co-founding editor of the *Jewish Daily Forward*—and encouraged him to produce a fuller narrative. Two years later Cahan published *Yekl: A Tale of the New York Ghetto*, which Howells reviewed alongside another novella, Stephen Crane's *Maggie: A Girl of the Streets* (1893), as allied portrayals of the customs and domestic tragedies of the migratory proletariat. Cahan's principal achievement was to delineate the growth and evolution of difference within what was too easily taken to be a homogeneous Yiddish-based subculture. Cahan used the device of an immigrant couple growing apart (the novel ends with a divorce) to dramatize divergent philosophies of advancement and cultural accommodation: Jake's assimilation to American consumerism, admirably energetic yet neglectful of the past, versus Gitl's preferences for cautious accumulation and a homelife more respectful of Orthodox Judaism and Yiddish folk culture. Today *Yekl* is respected as an innovative rendering of the immigrant's perspective (much as it was originally), though it may be better known by the film version of 1974, *Hester Street*.

Cahan's masterpiece, *The Rise of David Levinsky* (1917), began as a four-part series commissioned in 1913 by an editor at *McClure's*, who was looking for a muckraking exposé of Russian Jewish success in American business. Cahan agreed to take on the assignment, in part because he was aware of the potential anti-Semitism that could be unleashed if *McClure's* was to put the assignment in less conscientious hands. With realistic detail reminiscent of Howells, Dreiser, and the European Russian tradition, Cahan tells how Levinsky, a former student of the Talmud, becomes a major garment-manufacturer worth millions: not only through hard work and ingenuity but also through cynical manipulation of his workers and their faith. Yet Levinsky becomes more sympathetic than his actions warrant as he comes to recognize that he has betrayed Judaism and isolated himself from his people. Undermining the Shylock stereotype, Cahan attributes Levinsky's entrepreneurial energy not to blood but to the internalization of mainstream American values, his success not to inheritance but to innovative applications of modern business skills.

In 1922, Carl Van Doren proclaimed *The Rise of David Levinsky* "the most important of all immigrant novels"; a decade later, Albert Halper concurred that it was "the first and only skyscraper among the early work of Jewish-American writers." Through the mid-1930s, mainstream critics such as Van Doren and Carter Davidson often praised more popular East Side novelists—including Elias Tobenkin, Konrad Bercovici, and Fannie Hurst—for working in Cahan's shadow. In contrast, critics of Jewish extraction such as Halper and Lionel Trilling favored the more aesthetically ambitious works that began to appear in the late 1920s, including two by German Jewish men of letters—Ludwig Lewisohn's *The Island Within* (1928) and Paul Rosenfeld's *A Boy in the Sun* (1928)—as well as Charles Reznikoff's *By the Waters of Manhattan* (1930).

The most important of the Jewish American headliners of the 1920s was Anzia Yezierska, a sometime schoolteacher and housewife turned creative writer, who between 1920 and 1932 published two collections of short stories and four novels about the trials of Russian Jewish immigrants fighting the economic and social circumscriptions of the East Side. In 1919, her second published story, "Fat of the Land," which revisited Cahan's theme of the loneliness of the successful immigrant from the perspective of a Riverside Drive housewife, was nominated Best Story of the Year by Edward J. O'Brien. The story typified Yezierska's most general agenda, which was to challenge what she regarded as the marketplace's sentimentalization of her "own people." Throughout her work, she demonstrated that in the United States there had been and still were Jews without money, that the struggle against poverty was always enervating and often futile, and that ties of family and community were being destroyed as self-determination was achieved: "It's black tragedy that boils there, not the pretty sentiments that you imagine!" one of her protagonists tells an East Side sociologist, who seems to be a compendium of the scholars, social reformers, and literati with whom Yezierska had worked—including John Dewey, Amy Lowell, and William Lyon Phelps (Yale professor and popularizer of Yeats). Yezierska's first novel, *Salome of the Tenements* (1923), while ostensibly a fictionalized account of Rose Pastor's seduction of philanthropist James Phelps Graham Stokes, can also be read as an allegorization of the dangers of ethnic self-marketing.

"Fat of the Land" took up the particular perspective of female immigrants, following in Mary Antin's footsteps (Houghton Mifflin published both Antin's *The Promised Land* and Yezierska's first short-story collection, *Hungry Hearts* [1920]), but with a feminism honed on the issues of the "new womanhood" of the 1920s. A committed student of Emerson, Yezierska demonstrated how the quest for self-determination drove women beyond the "uptown" compromises between Old World patriarchy and New World domesticity that most of the men she knew took for granted and to which most of the women she knew—daughters as well as mothers—were unhappily resigned. Yezierska's best novel, *Bread Givers* (1925), looked back at East Side mobility through a feminism that may have been self-referential—in the mid-1910s she left her husband and daughter for rooms of her own—but was tutored as well: it was no coincidence that *Bread Givers* was published almost simultaneously with *The Home-Maker* (1924), a brilliantly didactic role-reversal novel scripted by Yezierska's close friend and mentor, Dorothy Canfield.

*Bread Givers* narrates in the first person the bitter rebellion of young Sara Smolinsky from her tyrannical father, a failed Hebrew teacher and sometime grocer who greedily and disastrously intervenes in the marriages of Sara's three older sisters. After flirting with making an upscale marriage of her own that would reconcile her to the family, Sara accepts being ostracized and works her way through night school and college to become a schoolteacher. Unfulfilled and lonely, Sara agrees at the novel's end to marry the principal of her East Side grammar school, who is a "new man" of nearly identical origin as Sara and who inspires her to ask her father, now widowed, into their future home. A Freudian figure of incest, articulating Sara's sense of obligation to return to the paternal fold, governs the conclusion. This conclusion has proved troubling, for it seems to dismiss Sara's hard-won, and in many ways elegant, rapprochement between culture and opportunity as a pyrrhic victory. Although the nascent Russian Jewish critical establishment was originally supportive of Yezierska, Alter Brody, Yosef Gaer, and Johan Smertenko expressed dismay at *Bread Givers*, questioning its unflattering stereotypes (of men especially) and its seeming commitment to a radically Emersonian "freedom" beyond community.

Public interest attached itself less to Yezierska's books than to the figure of the author. To counteract the disappointing sales of *Hungry Hearts*, Yezierska recruited innovative publisher Horace Liveright, who staged a publicity banquet at the Waldorf-Astoria where, it was claimed, she had once been denied work as a chambermaid: by excising her education and twenty-year sojourn among the middle classes from the public record, Liveright was able to market Yezierska as "Cinderella of the Tenements," an overnight success story, fairy-godmothered into professional authorship. On an even more popularizing front, Samuel Goldwyn purchased *Hungry Hearts* and *Salome* for filming, and in the first instance brought Yezierska to Los

Angeles, ostensibly to collaborate with dialect humorist Montague Glass on the screenplay but also for the purpose of parading her before the Hollywood gossip columnists. The double publicity for the book and the films turned Yezierska into a Sunday Supplement celebrity through the mid-1920s. Although her sketches were occasionally anthologized in the 1930s, and Charles Scribner's Sons published her autobiography in 1950 (*Red Ribbon on a White Horse*) with an introduction by W. H. Auden, her books were invisible from mid-century until the mid-1970s when Alice Kessler-Harris edited four volumes for republication, including *Bread Givers,* arguing for their importance as documents of the immigration of working women.

With something of the fervor if not the cosmopolitanism of the Jews, Scandinavians who had settled in the states and territories of the Northwest Plains built for themselves, language-group by language-group, strong periodical presses, sectarian schools and universities as well as churches, and organizations for the promotion of their Old World literatures and cultures. Despite the institutional commitment to their native tongues, writers were soon using English to treat Old World themes, and those that won national attention were, time and again, of Norwegian background: from the early novelist Hjalmar Hjorth Boyesen to the historian Marcus Hansen, who set forth the principle of "third generation return." The first Norwegian American novel, Boyesen's *Gunnar* (1874), was written in English, though its material was, in the words of one critic, "all Norwegian," meaning not only that it was set in Norway among goatherds but also that it featured a mermaid and several trolls. Boyesen's subsequent books were realist novels in the progressivist tradition, without Norwegian themes; so that the depiction of the Scandinavian migration and settlement actually was not achieved until the mid-1920s—with the translation into English of a novel written by a Norwegian, Johan Bojer, for the Norwegian market and with the release of competing works by two Norwegians, O. E. Rölvaag and Martha Ostenso, who had been immigrants themselves and who had been educated in the Norwegian North American community.

Born in 1876, and having settled in the United States at age twenty, Ole Edvart Rölvaag had dedicated the better part of his life to Norwegian American affairs, as a prized student at St. Olaf College, a cofounder in 1910 of the Society for Norwegian Language and

Culture, and the author in 1912 of the semiautobiographical *Amerika-Breve* (Letters from America). Rölvaag's *I de Dage* (In Those Days) was published in Oslo in two parts in 1924 and 1925; the translation, which Rölvaag did with Lincoln Colcord, was published by Harper and Brothers in 1927 as *Giants in the Earth,* then rereleased two years later with a special introduction by Vernon L. Parrington, a major scholar and promoter of early twentieth-century realism.

*Giants in the Earth* narrates the settling of the South Dakota frontier by a small community of Norwegian pioneers. In Book One of the novel, we see the work of clearing the land, of coming to terms (not always honestly) with the native inhabitants and with Irish settlers who had laid prior claim, and of fending off the fierce Dakota winters; in Book Two, we see how, despite such scourges as locusts and disease (including the mental disease of great isolation), the pioneers moved steadily from bare sustenance to lucrative cash farming, established a school, "civilized" their living conditions, and, perhaps most difficult of all, reached a genuinely productive balance between competition and community among themselves. For Rölvaag, however, and in marked distinction to Cahan, the drive for "kingdom building" is as much "Norwegian" as it is "American" — Scandinavian Lutheran in its origin, and American to the extent that it contributes to and participates in the general Protestant spirit of United States capitalism. Yet the force of resistance to this spirit on the Dakota frontier is also Norwegian in origin: a countervailing energy of self-vigilance within Scandinavian Lutheranism itself. It is a spiritualism among the pioneers (especially the women) that comprehends as ungodly the mania with which they (especially the men) have pursued personal kingdoms beyond established society. The fear of having radically individualized and hence subverted God's mission drives the novel's central female protagonist — Beret Holm — to the edge of insanity as it drives her husband, Per Hansa, into a suicidal act of contrition.

Buoyed in part by the novel's critical acclaim both in Norway and in the United States, as well as by his own missionary zeal to depict more recent developments, Rölvaag completed two sequels focused on the maturation and adulthood of Beret and Per Hansa's son:

*Peder Victorious* (1929) and *Their Fathers' God* (1931). In *Peder Victorious*, he narrated the boy's break from Lutheranism to a less vigilant modern secularism and from the Norwegian farm community to a "melting pot" of varied Northern European origins. In *Their Fathers' God*, Peder marries an Irish Catholic woman and together, as entrepreneurial farmers in their fathers' tradition, they face the boom-or-bust cycles of both nature and the increasingly nationalized farm economy, which threatens not only to bankrupt individuals but also to destroy the forward-looking alliance between his Norwegians and her Irish. Although both these books put in short appearances on best-seller lists, and are worth reading as continuing chapters in the settling of the frontier, they are in the final analysis unhappily schematic.

Martha Ostenso was born in Norway and raised from the age of two in various small towns in Minnesota and South Dakota. When she was fifteen, her family moved north to the farmlands of Manitoba, Canada—conditions there approximating those of Minnesota and South Dakota thirty or so years earlier, in the immediate post-pioneer period—where she went to high school and began college. From 1921 to 1922, she studied fiction writing at Columbia University, not three years after Anzia Yezierska's studies there, and became interested for a time in the Lower East Side. From 1925 to 1958, Ostenso published sixteen novels, three of them set in the Canadian frontier, the rest of them in Minnesota, the Dakotas, and Wisconsin. Her first novel, *Wild Geese*, won a 1925 competition—against 1300 entries for a prize of $13,500—sponsored by the *Pictorial Review*, Famous Players–Lasky Corporation, and Dodd, Mead and Company, who immediately published it. Though also published by McClelland & Stewart of Toronto, the novel was scarcely noticed in Canada. In the first year alone it went through twelve printings in the United States, where she resettled permanently.

In "The Immigrant Strain in American Literature" (1936), Carter Davidson of Carleton College cited Ostenso, after Rölvaag, as the most notable of Scandinavian American writers. In recent years scholars have suggested that Ostenso's novels were in significant measure ghostwritten by her Anglo-Saxon Canadian husband, Douglas Leader Dirkin. If one then wonders why they were released under her name only, consideration must go to the marketing of her maiden name, which authenticated the authorship of her books as doubly "other": Norwegian and female.

*Wild Geese,* set in Manitoba, is Ostenso's best-known and most respected work. It narrates the rebellion of willful and forward-looking Judith Gare against her brutal father, who blackmails Judith's mother into submission and whose continuing success as a multicrop farmer continues at the expense of the labor and life-choices of his three children. With the help of a young female school-teacher, Judith learns to take herself and her desires seriously, ultimately defying her father and jettisoning his bloodless Protestantism to run away with her lover (with whom she has conceived a child) to the city. As Mary Dearborn has pointed out, Ostenso's plot is remarkably close to that of Yezierska's *Bread Givers.* The engagement that concludes *Wild Geese* is also haunted, but it is understood as a flight rather than a partial return, and therein lies a difference that Western readers (especially Canadian readers) have found significant: for the doom that hangs over Judith Gare is not that of an imperfect Emersonian autonomy (as it is with Sara Smolinsky) but that of being torn from the farm and displaced to an urban modernity, civilization at the cost of primal woman-earth ties to the land.

Like the popular autobiographies of the teens and twenties, the major novels of Cahan, Yezierska, Rölvaag, and Ostenso all examined "making it" in America. With the onset of the Great Depression, the Levinskys and Per Hansas as well as the Gatsbys and Buchanans receded from sight, and the nation at large renewed its interest in economic and social marginality: the naturalist novel came back in ethnic and proletarian form as an interrogation into the forces behind mass poverty, and the local color novel came back in ethnic and urban form as a testament to the power of folkways in America's economic backwaters. For ethnic writers—who had made their own personal journeys out of wage labor and the poverty of the uneducated—the marketplace premium shifted from the middle-class dilemmas immediately bearing down upon them to the ghetto environs of those they had left behind. The shift of emphasis energized writers whose imaginations, for all their social and cultural dislocation, remained steeped in circumscribed childhoods, be they haunting or nostalgic; and it placed in especially high demand the depiction of those groups that had, in fact and in the popular imagination, come to represent either the near-hopeless underclasses or the honest laboring classes now tragically frustrated.

During the 1930s, Jewish Americans published a number of novels offering insightful, good-humored reconstructions of immigrant experience in an anthropological vein: among them, Daniel Fuchs's Williamsburg trilogy (1934-37), which has a mélange of characters; Vera Caspary's *Thicker Than Water* (1932), portraying a Portuguese Jewish family in Chicago; Meyer Levin's *The Old Bunch* (1937), about a cohort of Chicagoans coming of age; and Sidney Meller's portrait of a saintly California rabbi, *Roots in the Sky* (1939). Yet even these novels, for all their remembrance of transplanted folkways, placed Jews squarely on the rise, assimilating. Marcus Klein, Morris Dickstein, and other recent critics have shown that the more representative of the Jewish writers of the 1930s were those identified with the proletarian literature movement: Tillie Olsen, whose *Yonnondio: From the Thirties* was not published (except for one chapter) until 1974 and, more to the point, does not focus on Jews; and Michael Gold and Henry Roth, whose novels, despite the proletarian tag, spoke more strongly, then as now, as novels of ethnic cultural mediation.

The leading spokesman for Communist aesthetics in the United States, Mike Gold (né Itzok Granich), began his call for a proletarian art in the February 1921 *Liberator,* but the novel that embodied his praxis, *Jews Without Money,* did not appear until 1930. With great expectations, Horace Liveright published the novel in a handsome first edition, with woodcut illustrations, and its sales met those expectations, earning Liveright and Gold fair sums. Carroll and Graf republished it in 1984. Less a novel than a set of dark vignettes, *Jews Without Money* revealed poverty and lives of desperation among East Side Jews, foregrounding the social types once favored by the yellow journalists and the naturalists: pimps and prostitutes, boy gangs and thieves, bloodsucking landlords and bereft tenants predominating. Given the stereotype of the rich Americanized Jew that had been generated throughout the preceding decade, the novel set forth even more starkly than had Yezierska the underside of the Jewish American success story. Yet Gold's hyperrealism was undercut by an equally hyperbolic romanticism—part Socialist, part Russian-Polish, and part Gold—in which the goodly innocent of the *shtetl*-based Old World are understood to have fallen into the clutches of urban modernity, vague in detail but Satanic and fatal.

Under the tutelage of N.Y.U. professor Eda Lou Walton, Henry Roth found in the work of the three giants of Anglo-American modernism—Joyce, Eliot, and O'Neill—courage to return to the scene of his troubled East Side boyhood and techniques of narrative inquiry to exorcise its ghosts. Within the framework of immigrant naturalism, Roth produced a lyrical stream-of-consciousness novel—*Call It Sleep* (1934)—focused on the Oedipal struggles between David Schearl, from age six to nine, and his father, Albert, an immigrant from rural Austria earning a precarious living as a sometime printer's helper and sometime milkman. Insecure and, for most of the novel, impotent, Albert Schearl stirs in David shockingly precocious fantasies of patricide and sexual displacement. David pushes these fantasies to near fruition by provoking his father to violence (giving his mother little alternative but to alienate her husband and embrace her son), a recurrent cycle that climaxes with David brandishing a crucifix and declaring his real father to have been a Gentile.

When the novel was originally published, Roth's supporters fended off the charge of his sacrificing social realism to sexual prurience by underscoring the stunningly sensual rendering of the East Side (which the novel makes the reader see, hear, and smell in all its fiercesomeness and occasional glory) and by insisting that the political agenda of literature is better served when the truth, whatever its makeup, is told without ideology's prepackaging (an implied criticism of Gold et al.). Since the 1960s, what has most interested critics is Roth's 60-page penultimate chapter, in which David strives for a symbolic cessation of his Oedipal battles against the backdrop of a cacophony of lower-class voices, who are at once down-'n'-dirty and rhapsodically spiritual. Prose poetry modeled after Eliot and reminiscent of Hart Crane's *The Bridge,* chapter 21 of *Call It Sleep* yields an orgy of ethnic multivocality partly for its own sake, a lyrical envisioning of intergroup toleration and solidarity, and partly for the sake of the novel's protagonist, realizing in high modernist artistry David's yearning for mercy and redemption.

The vicissitudes of *Call It Sleep*'s reception reflect the novel's unusual combination of high modernist structure (it is arguably the most Joycean of any novel written by an American) and ethnic themes, a combination that continues to embarrass our terms of critical inquiry. In its Ballou edition of 1934, *Call It Sleep* did not find an enthusiastic readership beyond the coterie of New York intellectuals then coalescing around the *Partisan Review,* whose reviewer praised it as the best first novel since James Joyce's *A Portrait of the Artist as a Young Man.* In 1956, long out of print, it was proclaimed "the most neglected book of the past 25 years" by Alfred Kazin and Leslie Fiedler. In 1964, Avon released a paperback edition that was heralded in a front-page review by Irving Howe in the *New York Times Book Review* (the first ever for a paperback), which initiated a resuscitation of the novel: over a million in sales, translation into several languages, and some salience in modern American fiction courses. By 1973, its reputation seemed to have been secured— R. W. B. Lewis proclaiming it "incomparably the best of those novels which, from the perspective of the thirties, looked back on the ghetto life and the immigrant Jewish community." Yet the half-dozen state-of-the-art anthologies released in the late 1980s and early 1990s have passed over *Call It Sleep* and chosen instead selections from Cahan, Yezierska, and Gold.

From the 1870s through the 1920s, Irish materials were a stock-in-trade for important creative journalists such as Finley Peter Dunne and Fitz-James O'Brien as well as for major figures of the American stage including Edward Harrigan and, of course, Eugene O'Neill himself. Yet the country's most notable novelist with an Irish surname, F. Scott Fitzgerald—half "black Irishman" and "half old stock American," scion to an alliance of wealthy, educated families—had chosen to depict neither the Irish settlement nor the American Catholic Church that set the Irish apart. Similarly, in the mid-1930s, John O'Hara began a well-received series of novels in the tradition of Fitzgerald and Sinclair Lewis that also avoided foregrounding Irish themes. In 1928, an Ohio-born writer of Irish background, Jim Tully, published a semiautobiographical novel, *Shanty Irish,* that by its focus on a poor Irish family set the theme and by its title's ugly epithet set the tone for the breakthrough of Irish Americans into the fiction of cultural mediation.

From 1932 to 1978, James T. Farrell published forty-seven books of fiction. In 1941, he was elected to the National Institute of Arts and Letters; and in 1979, the year of his death, he received the Emerson-Thoreau Award of the American Academy of Arts and Letters for his lifetime achievement. Despite his prolificness, Farrell's reputation stands on a trilogy of novels that recalled the South Side of his Chicago boyhood and that focused on "a normal American boy of Irish-Catholic extraction"; not on Farrell, who had made the long cultural journey to the University of Chicago, but on the young men he had left behind, trapped by and among themselves. Farrell's famous 800-page saga, written proudly in the tradition of Theodore Dreiser, began with his very first book, *Young Lonigan* (1932), and was completed with two sequels, *The Young Manhood of Studs Lonigan* (1934) and *Judgment Day* (1935). Critical acclaim from the beginning was high. A Guggenheim fellowship and selection in the Book-of-the-Month Club followed immediately; and the Modern Library canonized the trilogy only three years after the publication of the third volume. Of the work that followed, a second trilogy and some of the short stories, focusing on Farrell's alter ego Danny O'Neill, are occasionally read by scholars for their insight both into the adolescent preoccupations fueling Farrell's writing and into the origins of those preoccupations in the Irish American community itself.

In 1929, while a student at the University of Chicago, Farrell wrote a short story, "Studs," in which a South Side Chicago street gang gathers at the wake of their buddy, the title character, who has died of double pneumonia at the age of twenty-five. Two of Farrell's teachers, James Weber Linn and Robert Morss Lovett, waxed enthusiastic and urged him to expand the narrative, concentrating on Studs's "social milieu." The resulting trilogy opened with Studs graduating from grammar school at age fifteen in 1916 and closed with his death (later than the original story) at age twenty-nine in 1931. Not quite progressivist in the manner Professors Linn and Lovett probably expected, the novel told how an intelligent and decent boy, born to industrious petit-bourgeois parents, talked himself out of high school into the poolhalls and onto the street corners—where he participated in interethnic gang warfare, alcohol abuse, and a gang rape for which he is nearly imprisoned.

Farrell found his account of Studs's typicality in the immaturity of men who sought womenfolk to save them from themselves, and in the immaturity of women who wished to see their men (even Studs!) only as priests; in a Northern European Catholic Church marked less by the transubstantiation of the flesh than by a repressive Victorianism (a sex-denial that may have been of some use in the food-scarce Irish countryside but that was grotesquely inadequate to desire and its opportunities in the modern polyethnic city); and in an ethos of male Irish camaraderie that, for all its occasional attractiveness, was melancholic to the point of individual paralysis and bigoted to the point of communal immolation. However stereotypical the characterizations, Farrell revealed the social forces that produced them, attributing the unhappily familiar to neither an Irish legacy nor consumer capitalism per se but to a disastrous evolutionary intercourse between them. Although the first volume of the trilogy is most often taught and analyzed and the third volume probably comes in second, *The Young Manhood of Studs Lonigan* is the most acute and speaks to issues not just of the Irish in the early twentieth century. In this second volume, Farrell focused on the formation of violent urban gangs out of lower-class youth, whose energy of self-determination is admirable but whose strategies are self-defeating; presciently, the novel concludes in a replay of a crucial earlier scene, replacing its Irish American protagonists with incidental characters whose names sound Southern and whose skins are black.

Mary Doyle Curran was the first strong voice of Irish American women. The youngest child of an Irish-born woolsorter and his American-born wife, she worked her way through the Massachusetts State College and then took a Master's degree at the State University of Iowa, where she studied with Norman Foerster, René Wellek, and Austin Warren. Her one book, *The Parish and the Hill* (1949), is a memoir of familial vignettes, elegiac, loosely structured, and narrated by an authorial surrogate, young Mary O'Connor. It covers the settlement, long struggle, and qualified successes of O'Connor's kinfolk, who migrated in fits and starts from County Kerry, Ireland, to an unspecified central New England mill town. *The Parish and the Hill* tells a representative tale of intergenerational mobility—slow, painful, costly, but ultimately fruitful—and thus serves as an important historical corrective to Farrell's far more familiar portrayal of a big-city Irish American underclass. Crucial to Curran's account are the

O'Connor women, who envision gaining security and comfort without assimilating to the "lace curtain" materialism and individualism of the "Hill" and who take the lead in bringing that vision to reality (while several O'Connor men fall prey to alcohol, violence, crime, or suicide). Little noticed in its own time, *The Parish and the Hill* did help to win its author positions at Queens College, where she founded an Irish Studies program, and at the University of Massachusetts at Amherst.

One of the better kept literary secrets of this century is the literature of Italians and their descendants in America. From the late teens through the early thirties, novels treating the immigrant colonies and Italian memory, twenty or so in number, were published by Bernardino Ciambelli (in Italian), Silvio Villa, Giuseppe Cautela, Garibaldi Marto Lapolla, John Antonio Moroso, Louis Forgione, and Frances Winwar (Francesca Vinciguerra, the first Italian American woman novelist). These novels by writers most of whom were educated in Italy did not stir the imagination of the American reading public (many were published by small presses) and provide little of nonhistorical interest to us today—with the exception perhaps of Forgione's *Men of Silence* (1928), a forerunner of both the mafia novel and hard-boiled detective fiction (predating Dashiell Hammett's *Red Harvest* by two years). Of greater import in the earlier decades were several immigrant autobiographies by men of humble background who rose to some prominence after migrating: Antonio A. Arrighi's *The Story of Antonio, the Galley Slave* (1911), Constantine Panunzio's *The Soul of an Immigrant* (1920), and Pascal D'Angelo's *Son of Italy* (1924). Yet, for all the contributions to the archive before the mid-1930s, it was not until the maturation of the children of immigrants that Italian Americans produced a *risorgimento* of fiction about immigration. Around 1940, as if on cue, there arose a coterie of second-generation writers: John Fante, Pietro DiDonato, Jo Pagano, Guido D'Agostino, Jerre Mangione, Michael DeCapite, George Panetta, and Mari Tomasi. They produced two dozen novels and collections of shorter fiction, a majority of them works of considerable historical insight and emotional force.

Fante's *Wait Until Spring, Bandini* (1937) depicts adultery among Abruzzi immigrants in Boulder, Colorado, when a despondent stonemason compounds the humiliation of poverty with the shame of transgressing family and faith. The title character of DeCapite's *Maria* (1940) is a Cleveland-born woman who accepts a marriage arranged by her immigrant parents and suffers the consequences with an inarticulate sensitivity that comes, by novel's end, to speak for itself. Mari Tomasi, the first significant Italian American woman novelist, published in 1940 a novel looking back to her ancestral town in the Piedmont Hills, then wrote a second treating her own childhood. A local color tapestry of Piedmontese granite workers and their families in Vermont, *Like Lesser Gods* (1949) examines the interaction of three forces: the impassioned artistry of the men, the market-driven callousness of the business in which they are employed, and the quest for security and a sense of cultural belonging by the women they love. Of these minor classics, only *Bandini* has ever been reprinted (by the arts press Black Sparrow), and it is better known in Europe than in North America (as is often the case with United States immigrant literature). In contrast, two of the writers from this period—Pietro DiDonato and Jerre Mangione—won national attention right from the start and retained some measure of salience as spokesmen for Italo-America.

In 1937, DiDonato, the son of an Italian bricklayer and one himself for fourteen years, published a short story in *Esquire* telling of an Italian bricklayer who is buried alive on Good Friday when a wall he is building collapses. Proclaimed the Best Story of 1938 by Edward J. O'Brien, "Christ in Concrete" was greeted with a level of enthusiasm unrivaled for the short form. In the image of brick and mortar crushing the life out of a man who knows what is happening to him (and thus to his loved ones), the story tallied the horrendous toll enacted on those who had little choice but to earn their wages with their backs; in illuminating the fact of unnecessary suffering it lays blame not on capitalism but on shameless profiteering and on corruption within the political and legal systems. What made the story most effective, however, was the rendering of the consciousness of its protagonist, Geremio. In a way unprecedented, at least for Italian Americans, DiDonato made manifest how intelligent and sensitive was this man, whatever his lack of literacy and formal education. "Christ in Concrete" also challenged popular Marxist romanticisms of the centrality of the workplace. Although the business of laying brick and pouring concrete left an impression on Geremio, especially on his tactility, the work did not determine his being: Geremio's soul was of a piece with humanity in general (as his faith dictated), and his particular sensibility—a consciousness rendered in Joycean Italianate English—was interwoven from Latin Marianist Catholicism, the peasant earthiness of the Italian South, and the pleasures and burdens of the large extended family.

At a time when proletarian fiction seemed by its formulas to have worn out its welcome, the public clamored that DiDonato give them more, and what emerged two years later was a novel, as it were, by popular demand. DiDonato let the original story serve as a first chapter, then focused on Geremio's son Paul, who must fill his father's shoes though only twelve years of age. Although distended in places, *Christ in Concrete* (1939) expands upon what made the story successful: its rendering of the impact of the job upon those immersed in peasant Italian culture. DiDonato was praised for rendering real Italians rather than, as Louis Adamic put it, working-class "puppets" manufactured according to "intellectuals' notions of synthetic Marxians." On the one hand, we see Paul's uncle lose his leg in another accident, the court back the construction company in welching on Geremio's death benefits, and Paul be underpaid, forced into kickbacks, and refused a rightful bonus. On the other hand, we are reminded of what motivates Paul: we are treated to his mastering of the bricklaying craft, to his prideful support of the family, to his passionate participation in the family rites of the Catholic calendar, and to his sexual initiation. The Book-of-the-Month Club—by 1939 the most influential institution in the middlebrow press—chose *Christ in Concrete* as its main selection over what was then judged to be a more predictable, more ideologically tainted protest novel, John Steinbeck's *The Grapes of Wrath*.

DiDonato's reviewer in *The New Republic* was Jerre Mangione. Mangione had made his way out of working-class surroundings to Syracuse University, was currently serving as national editor of the Federal Writers' Project, and would later join the faculty at the University of Pennsylvania. In 1942, he released *Mount Allegro*, subtitled "A Memoir of Italian American Life." *Mount Allegro* was set among a network of extended Sicilian families in Rochester, New York, where the construction market was more hospitable to the skilled than in DiDonato's New Jersey. It was narrated by a boy about the

age of Paul, Gerlando Amoroso, who unlike Paul enjoyed moderate
security, including the luxury of school. Mangione jettisoned most of
the darker sides of the immigrant experience to explicate the communal life that centered on the Amorosos' dining room table: storytelling, operatic quarrels carried over from the Old World, the sexual
intrigues of two generations, innovative shortcuts to serviceable English, and the expression of a Catholic sensibility tempered by superstition and a disdain for Church authority.

By giving us a young narrator, Mangione produced the effect of a
"native informant" who is happy to explain the perceived significance of phenomena within his culture but is loath to pronounce
broad generalizations. Folklore sans sociology exposed the narrative
to criticism, including a charge by Isaac Rosenfeld that Mangione
was encouraging a condescending readership marked by "the tourist's mentality" and a comparison by Diana Trilling to *Life with
Father*. Rosenfeld and Trilling were right that the book lacked a
certain ambition; Mangione hadn't even conceived of his memoirs as
a novel, but his publishers, Houghton Mifflin, had insisted on a fic-
tionalization for marketing purposes. Yet the book does have a critical edge. "In Sicily," Gerlando is recurrently reminded, "people are
so poor they will follow a donkey, hoping he will move his bowels,
and will squabble over the manure the moment it hits the earth"—
which is, as Gerlando later sees for himself, scarcely exaggerated. In
the hill towns and seaports outside of Palermo, where Gerlando's
relatives still live, the institution of the family is the primary weapon
of survival. The historical lesson haunting the otherwise playful
*Mount Allegro* was that the attractive communality of these immigrants had not been transported from the Old World but was fashioned here through the relative largesse of wage labor.

World War II was a watershed in ethnic literature because it was
a watershed in the national social imagination. The campaign to
unify the country, discredit the Nazi race theory, and celebrate democracy led to a redrawing of the boundary between desirable and
suspect ancestries: the circle of cultural anxiety that had once designated the descendants of Northwestern Europeans as "American"
but Southern and Eastern Europeans as "other" shifted outward to
embrace a melting pot of Europeans—"Protestant-Catholic-Jew" in

the title of Will Herberg's central book—at the expense of those whose ancestors were not European and/or not "Judeo-Christian." On Columbus Day, 1942, President Franklin Delano Roosevelt lifted the "enemy-alien" designation from Italian Americans to national applause—barely six months after the government had begun the war-long process of interning guiltless Japanese Americans. Symbolic of European ethnics generally, the Italians had through the twenties if not the thirties been understood to be of a different "race" (that is the word that was used) than that of Anglo-Saxon Americans, but were now incorporated under the general designation of the white mainstream. This redefinition authorized European Americans to suspend much of their ethnic consciousness and Americans at large to regard the depiction of European Americans—especially middle-class ethnics—as reflections, more or less, of themselves.

As early as 1940, a celebrated symposium on "American Literature and the Younger Generation of American Jews" (held by the forerunner of the magazine *Commentary*) pronounced an end to Jewish self-consciousness in American writing: "they are spectators no longer but full participants in the life of this country." The symposium was prophesying a major shift in the identities and writing agendas of American Jews, a shift to be facilitated by wartime and postwar prosperity and that was to apply as well to other European-descended ethnic groups. Even if assimilation was often pursued less vigorously than economic security, and even if some institutions (the boardrooms of many *Fortune*-500 firms, much of the Ivy League, and so forth) remained closed to them, still for the public at large the long-standing association of urban poverty with foreign accents had been laid to rest, and the invitation was open to writers from such backgrounds to forgo emphasizing difference in favor of developing more central voices.

Jewish American novelists led the way in developing middle-class and upper-middle-class scenarios, with or without an ethnic cast. Budd Schulberg's Hollywood novel, *What Makes Sammy Run?*, was published in 1941, and its expression of suburban Jewish alienation as a North American malady was soon echoed in major novels by Saul Bellow, Philip Roth, and a small host of darkly comic writers (Stanley Elkin, Bruce Jay Friedman, Canadian Mordecai Richler). Immediately upon their heels came portraits of other ethnic middle classes, including the excellent novels of Edwin O'Connor focusing on Irish American politics and of J. F. Powers focusing on the clergy and laity of comfortable American Catholic communities. Into the 1970s arose writers who had been raised in first- or second-generation homes—Norman Mailer, J. P. Donleavy, Don DeLillo—and who occasionally created protagonists with one or another ethnic awareness, yet who managed to create the overreaching effect of having transcended ethnic consciousness themselves.

For all their acuity about the long-term direction of ethnic European writing, contributors to the 1940 *Commentary* symposium could not but have underestimated how large the need would soon be to put the question of Jewish identity (which seemed from the perspective of the United States comfortably on the wane) in global perspective. The postwar novel of the Holocaust constituted a special flooding of the mainstream, some of it in Leslie Fiedler's words "profoundly sentimental" (especially when written by Gentiles). Yet other novels were devastating in examining the aftermath of surviving the death camps, for instance Edward Lewis Wallant's *The Pawnbroker* (1961) and Bernard Malamud's "Fidelman" stories, or provocative in rebalancing the equilibrium between Jewish particularity and the sufferings of humankind, such as Bellow's *The Victim* (1947) and Malamud's *The Assistant* (1957).

Post-Holocaust novels were by no means the only sign of renewed ethnicity in American writing after the war. Already by mid-century, and increasingly through the next quarter-century, the prewar experience of immigration reasserted its hold over the imaginations of certain writers: this time because European ethnics no longer felt the stigma of otherness and could revisit their recent origins on their own terms, without having to be, first and foremost, cultural mediators. While too late to intrigue mass audiences, yet written with the advantages of historical, political, and psychological distance, these later works often outstripped their better-known prewar forerunners in accuracy and evocativeness. Yet the primary business of these narratives was far less a matter of intergroup representation and far more a matter of intergenerational tribute and reconciliation. In rehearsing the settlement experience, postwar novelists bore witness to the generation of immigrants who had dared to initiate cultural revolution, who had suffered not only the physical burden of overcoming poverty but also the deeper damages of self-recrimination for rupturing inherited traditions and of double estrangement from their homelands and from their Americanized offspring.

Mangione's *Mount Allegro* and Curran's *The Parish and the Hill* typified the local-color family narratives of the 1940s, which in effect bridged the generic shift from mediation to memory. Children of Russian Jews produced similar memoirs, including two by symposium participants that seemed in direct defiance of its recent mandate: Isaac Rosenfeld's *Passage from Home* (1946) and Alfred Kazin's *A Walker in the City* (1951), the first in a trilogy. In subsequent years would come many minor texts by members of almost all European ethnic groups, verging upon an industry around 1970 as part of "white ethnic" pride (which imitated and responded to the rise of African American self-consciousness). A few major treatments of the great migration and settlement brought smaller European groups to the fore for the first time—Elia Kazan's *America! America!* (1962) on the Greeks, David Plante's *The Family* (1978) on French Canadians in New England, Chaim Potok's *The Chosen* (1967) on the Hassidim. A few others revealed wonders within material thought too familiar: including Tillie Olsen's *Tell Me a Riddle* (1961) on Russian Jewish women, Mary Gordon's several novels on the Irish Catholics, and Mario Puzo's *The Fortunate Pilgrim* (1964), which is the consummate narrative of the postwar period and possibly the most powerful immigrant novel of them all.

Focused on a fictional version of Puzo's mother, *The Fortunate Pilgrim* narrates the struggles of Lucia Santa, an illiterate peasant woman from the south of Italy burdened with six children in Hell's Kitchen, Manhattan. As an heir to *la miseria*, Lucia Santa cannot understand her children's clamoring for something they call "happiness" when the family's centuries-long search for "bread and shelter" has not yet been achieved. Mesmerized by Hollywood films and library books, the children do not understand that their American-wrought dreams—of romantic love and intimate friendship, of work that is ethical and engaging, and of life lived in general according to dictates of the imagination—may threaten the very process of obtaining the wherewithal to begin to countenance such dreams. As a young man coming of age, Gino, the eldest of the three younger children and Puzo's alter ego, has the greatest case of wanderlust and the largest insensitivity to the reasoning of his mother: he comes to hate Lucia Santa for consigning his father to the asylum, for approving his sister's abandonment of school and his brother's transformation into a petty gangster, and for driving yet another brother (harnessed to a railroad clerk's desk) to suicide. The novel ends in separate, bitter victories: Lucia Santa and the rest of the family move to the Long Island suburbs while Gino enlists in the army vowing never to return home.

In composing *The Fortunate Pilgrim*, Puzo made manifest in 1964 what Gino could not have seen twenty years earlier. He credited his magnificent protagonist, Lucia Santa, with the vision and courage to conquer poverty, with indirectly legitimating the pursuit by her younger children of dreams not her own, and with comprehending in almost insupportable pain the "crimes" she has committed against her family along the way. What made *The Fortunate Pilgrim* a representative postwar narrative was this hidden agenda—to enact in writing a reconciliation between the generations that was not possible in fact. Its cutting edge came not from the politics of ethnic representation, as mediated by a marketplace skeptical of Southern Italian otherness, but from the repercussions of intergenerational cultural transformation, in which an ethnic son felt the need to wage battle against his own suspicions of the past. Although noted as a "small classic" by the *New York Times Book Review*, *The Fortunate Pilgrim* in its first edition did not sell beyond its first printing and netted Puzo, after nine years of work, $3000. Since then, the unrivaled success of *The Godfather* (1969) and its film versions has prompted three different publishing houses to rerelease *The Fortunate Pilgrim* in mass paperback and NBC-TV to produce a mini-series with Sophia Loren in the title role.

As writers of European background like Puzo began the work of second- and third-generation recovery, the business of cultural mediation fell upon writers associated with "the new ethnics"—those with ancestries in the Caribbean, the Spanish Americas, and the Far East. Soon after the war a diversity of Asian American writers— Carlos Bulosan, Monica Stone, John Okada, Diana Chang, and Louis Chu among them—followed in the steps of Younghill Kang, the Korean-born writer whose *East Goes West* (1937) is credited with rising above conventions of Asian and Asian American exoticism. At the same time there appeared the first works by immigrants from the Caribbean Rim including Mexico—by Paule Marshall, José Antonio Villarreal, John Rechy, and Piri Thomas. These two coteries of early writers were pioneers in the second era of the literature of cultural mediation.

The year 1964 marked the beginning of a new period in United States immigration and racial politics that completed this transfer of the ethnic literary mantle. In that year, Congress democratized the immigration laws, repealing after almost fifty years the Chinese exclusion and related acts and thus inviting migration from East Asia, Mexico, and the Caribbean as well as, increasingly, from the Middle East and the Indian subcontinent. The recent influx may or may not reach as large a percentage of the total United States population as the great migration once did, but the new ethnic groups are of course as distanced from the still-dominant European heritage of the United States as the immigrants of the great migration Southern were from Anglo-Saxon Protestantism. To answer the need for cultural mediation, there have arisen formidable writers and coteries of writers, who have produced narratives of the new "new migration" while at the same time (many of them activists and/or scholars) working to defend civil rights, to promote cultural pluralism, and to reclaim non-European contributions to the history of the Continent. Among those of Asian descent, the more prominent have included several Chinese Americans—Frank Chin, Maxine Hong Kingston, Shawn Wong, Amy Tan, and others—as well as Japanese Canadian Joy Kogawa. Among those to the south, the prominent have ranged from Chicanos, including Luís Valdez, Rudolfo Anaya, Richard Rodriguez, and an impressive array of poets, to émigrés from the islands such as Paule Marshall of Barbados, Edward Rivera of Puerto Rico, and Oscar Hijuelos of Cuba. Over the past fifteen years or so, these writers have achieved national and sometimes international acclaim as individuals—garnering literary prizes, support for continued work, and honor for their respective communities. Taken together, they are just now receiving widespread identification and praise for penning a new chapter in the history of the American novel: the literature of immigrant "peoples of color."

Thomas J. Ferraro

# Race and Region

During the first two decades of the twentieth century, the range and experience of writers in the United States broadened. No one literary center predominated, but urbanization and industrialization contributed to large cities remaining the focal points of writerly activity. In the East, New York, long a major center for book and magazine publishing, grew rapidly as a cultural capital attracting men and women of literary ambition from across the nation. A transforming second city, Chicago functioned as a magnet for talented writers from throughout the Midwest, so much so that by 1912 the converging of artists coalesced in the Chicago Renaissance. In the West, San Francisco continued its rise of literary prominence begun after the Civil War. The South, from upper to lower, began to generate coteries of writers with publishing outlets in its old centers of culture—Richmond, Charleston, Atlanta, Nashville, and New Orleans. By the period of World War I, not only was an expansive literary culture anchored in separate regions apparent but also a general movement toward redefining American experience within literary production.

A proliferation of little magazines and literary groups in the Midwest, the South, and the Northeast during the postwar years gave greater visibility to an increasing number of aspiring authors, who emerged from diverse socioeconomic levels and who were intent upon writing from their own experiential perspectives. Their perspectives, however, had been substantially altered by a world at war and by an awareness of America in international contexts. Their larger referential context was a social and political modernity propelling the nation and its regions away from isolation and simplicity and into interdependence and complexity.

No small part of the emergent modern experience and its complexity was the issue of identity—individual, regional, national, the same triumvirate that had in various guises characterized much of the country's history. However, the issue assumed a renewed urgency with the contemporary resituation of the United States, viewed from abroad as an international political power and a world leader in industry and technology, and with a concomitant transformation at home, particularly in population shifts, foreign immigration, and racial distribution. Industrial and technological advances fueled economic growth and opened additional marketplaces, but also propelled the movement from rural to urban areas, the influx of people from other nations, and the migration of African Americans from the South to the North and West. Conventions and habits gave way under the pressures of mobility and motion to new modes of behavior, language, and dress. Dislocations and disruptions were inevitable. Old relationships to communal values, to moral codes, to hierarchical social positions, and to familiar patterns came under stress and were decentered.

In literature, different sets of external identifications and more varied markers of identity were not only more visible but more viable as well. Racial heritage, regional affiliation, ethnic background, class position, political inclination, gender identity, and sexual orientation appeared more frequently within texts by authors who understood that a writer in the United States no longer had to subsume personal identification into a vision of the artist as male, white, Anglo-Saxon, native-born, upper middle class, and Protestant. For some writers the result was exhilarating, because they were free to explore the new and the modern within themselves and society. A Gertrude Stein decoding the psychology of language, a Sherwood Anderson examining sexual repression, an F. Scott Fitzgerald heralding the "Jazz Age," a Djuna Barnes exploring gender boundaries, an Ernest Hemingway testing the limits of masculinity, all were stimulated by societal rearrangements. For others, like the Fugitives and later Agrarians in Nashville, the transformations were troubling, because they could neither easily nor quickly replace their sense of past, of tradition, of stability. For still others, like the "New Negroes" in Harlem, the fluidity meant that they could assume for the first time an authoritative space in the literary landscape.

One aspect of identity that reconfigured differently during this period was that of race. Not only was race construed as a marker of individual identity, but it was also a way of representing transformations in the larger society. For some writers, authentic and meaningful American experience could best be approached through an understanding of the "other," and more typically a racialized other. Though the United States was becoming more multiracial and multiethnic with increased immigration from Asia, Central and South America, two racial groups, and the two most oppressed in American society, became the center of these representations. Native Americans and African Americans, both largely marginalized in literature as in the political and social economies, functioned as racialized embodiments of the modern, of the traditional, or of the primitive, and of the contradictions and tensions among them. In the face of dramatic changes and mechanization, the existence of Native Americans was conflated to represent an unchanging simplicity, an untroubled communication with nature and the spirit. Oliver La Farge, born in the Northeast and a Harvard graduate who studied and taught anthropology and ethnography, received a Pulitzer Prize for his novel of Navajo life, *Laughing Boy* (1929). Mabel Dodge Luhan encouraged attention to Native American subjects in her New York salon and later at Taos, New Mexico. Racialized others represented one way of countering the perceived failure of the dominant group to sustain a fixed center of existence.

Even more than Native Americans, African Americans became symbolic of otherness. Their increased visibility outside of the closed South, their continuance of folk customs, practices, and beliefs, and their contribution to the rhythmic "new music" of jazz and its accompanying dances attracted some writers to their potential as literary subject. The early modern writer Gertrude Stein in "Melanctha" (*Three Lives* [1909]) had rendered the subjectivity of an African American female in a text devoted to the psychology of three working-class women. Following Stein's groundbreaking, but brief, attention to the African American, Sherwood Anderson considered the race one of the richest sources of subject matter for the American literary artist, as he put it in "Notes Out of a Man's Life": "If some white artist could go among the negroes [*sic*] and live with them much beautiful stuff might be got. The trouble is that no American white man could do it without self-consciousness. The best thing is to stand aside, listen and wait. If I can be impersonal in the presence of black laborers, watch the dance of bodies, hear the song, I may learn something."

Anderson, like others of his generation who had attained adulthood before World War I, perceived that motion, the fast pace of contemporary life, mobility, and the increased ease of traveling far from home combined with the knowledge of mechanical power and impersonal destruction to produce individual fragmentation and spiritual malaise. From the perspective of an Anglo-American from the Midwest, Anderson observed in the novel *Dark Laughter* (1925) a "consciousness of brown men, brown women coming more and more into American life." With this consciousness of "the dark, earthy," America in Anderson's formulation could return to an elemental connection with the earth, nature, human feelings and emotions, and thereby stave off the debilitating emotional complexity of the postwar modern world or what he perceived as "the neuroticism, the hurry and self-consciousness of modern life." Anderson was seeking a means to represent continuity and essence in the face of enormous changes in the conception of a "good Life." Anderson attempted, as did others, to distill an essential difference between peoples on the basis of racial characteristics. Though not suggesting a racial hierarchy on the basis of right, power, or intellect, he relied upon a perceived and inescapable difference attenuating emotional complexity in whites and blacks. African Americans for him were the extreme other yet unsoiled by modern complex civilization. Though he figured the other as positive, he did not examine the stereotypical assumptions beneath the surface: the African as primitive, simple, sexual.

Carl Van Vechten, who like Anderson was a Midwesterner and a novelist during the 1920s, also appropriated the experience of the African American other to symbolize not merely the perceived failures of modernity but the contradictions and contradictory impulses of emergent areas of expressive culture. While Anderson sought a black folk essence in rural settings, Van Vechten explored the newly urbanized African American's assimilation into a blandly homogenized society with the complicating difference of an African heritage that he construed as rhythmic, sexual power. In New York, Van Vechten observed the growth of the black population from 152,467 in 1920 to 327,709 in 1930, and as a music and drama critic he witnessed the development of a "Negro Vogue" in Manhattan, particularly after the arrival of the musical revue *Shuffle Along* on Broadway in 1922. From that point on, Van Vechten promoted and cultivated the talent and the difference within black New York. He helped launch the careers of novelists Walter White, Jessie Fauset, and Nella Larsen. In his own novel *Nigger Heaven* (1926), he ventured into the cabarets of black New York, where music and dance marked freedom and abandon from everyday constraints. Basically, he delved into the "primitive" underside of an emerging black middle class concerned with propriety, morality, and upward mobility. The ground for his representation of a larger societal problem, however, functioned not only to stratify and offend the vulnerable African American community but also to codify and extend the negative implications of an uncivilized racial other lurking beneath the veneer of finery, education, and manners. Van Vechten, who was a supporter of African Americans, did not fully appreciate the dangers of attributing racial characteristics to one side of the warring impulses of modernity.

Despite the well meaning of sympathetic observers, such as Van Vechten or Anderson, the exploration of the racial other was not necessarily contingent upon concern for the subordinate position of minorities in society or upon a belief in the desirability of increased racial understanding or harmony. C. Vann Woodward has remarked that the post–World War I years witnessed the "greatest stratification of the races and widespread enactment of 'Jim Crow' laws." Segregationist practices hardened into fresh restrictive codes and laws designed to delimit the position of African Americans within the society, and with the tacit approval of the presidential administration of Woodrow Wilson these modern segregation laws became widespread throughout the nation, not merely in the South where old grievances against African Americans as responsible for the region's economic woes surfaced in overt efforts to keep African Americans in their "place" (which meant keeping them subordinate to whites in the social and economic structures). As Lillian Smith, one observer of the rigidity and intent of segregation in the South, recalled an African American woman saying to her: "We cannot ride together on the bus, you know. It is not legal to be human down here." In the aftermath of World War I, returning African American veterans, by and large, refused to accept racist practices restricting their humanity and their participation in a world they had fought to keep safe for democracy. Much of white America, however, was not yet willing to concede a new era in race relations. During the summer of 1919, twenty-five race riots occurred across the nation, in urban and rural areas, such as Washington, D.C., Chicago, Omaha, Longview, Texas, and Elaine, Arkansas. By the end of the summer, eighty-three African Americans had been lynched and scores of others injured. Race relations deteriorated, and conditions generally worsened for all people of color.

Race, in both its positive and negative implications, was posited as a way of focusing cultural issues in literary, social scientific, popular, and scholarly discourses. It was more persistently visible in writings about the American South, perhaps because implicit in the burgeoning of racial matter in literature is a focus on region, on understanding and representing the land, the people, the customs and manners, the history that together distinguish one part of the nation from another. In the South, though clusters of Native Americans still lived in Tennessee, North Carolina, and Virginia and though smaller tribal groups were dispersed from Mississippi to Florida, the primary race-defined peoples were Caucasians and African Americans. These two, interconnected in history and culture because of the existence of chattel slavery until after the middle of the nineteenth century, were long familiars in the region and antagonists on the issue of race. Thus, it is not surprising that during the first fifty years of the twentieth century, according to Howard Odum's study of Southern culture and writing, 800 nonfiction works on African American life, 400 on nature and the folk, and 100 on socioeconomic studies appeared. Simultaneous to being prominent in writings about the South, race has been an insistent, though not always audible or explicit, presence in texts emanating from other regions, in multiple forms of expressive culture, and, most often, in reference to African Americans. Increasingly throughout the twentieth century, African Americans were positioned as referential structures for whites, and within the dominant cultural constructs they became more visibly operatives, if limited, as opposed to being merely respondents. By mid-century, Richard Wright would reflect that "the Negro is America's metaphor," by which he intended to conflate the African American's moral and political struggle for parity and recognition with the nation's grasp of its ideals of equality and freedom. Whether or not Wright formulated an exaggerated claim for the position of the African American within a reading of the American condition, he nonetheless identified race as a major point for accessing meanings about twentieth-century America.

Race is in part a metaphorical construction, as Wright may have implied in his statement. The dominant group usually does not construct its own identity by delineating its specific racialism. Race as a classification is more typically used against others—those who are different from the majority, different from those in control of language and tradition. As Henry Louis Gates, Jr. has observed: "Race has become a trope of ultimate, irreducible difference between cultures, linguistic groups, or adherents of specific belief systems which—more often than not—also have fundamentally opposed economic interests. Race is the ultimate trope of difference because it is so very arbitrary in its application."

Whether arbitrary or not, the apprehension of race and racial ideologies marks much of the writing of the early twentieth century. W. E. B. Du Bois exposed the problem of the twentieth century as the problem of the color line in *The Souls of Black Folk* (1903). He suggested that race as a sociocultural construct was the battleground for the delineation of a modern self within society. Debilitating views of racial inferiority not only constricted the potential of people of color, those within the veil, but also limited the development of people who, by reason of their Caucasian ancestry, could only view the world in hierarchical terms, with themselves at the higher end of intellectual, moral, and cultural achievement. Undergirding Du Bois's notion of the color line is his conception of the centrality of race: "The history of the world is the history, not of individuals, but of groups, not of nations, but of races, and he who ignores or seeks to override the race idea in human history ignores and overrides the central thought of all history."

For writers in the American South, racial identity was one of the givens of their literary and cultural perspectives. Owing to a shared regional heritage with slavery as a major component and a present existence with segregation as a legal practice replete with "For Colored Only" and "For Whites Only" signs in public places, few Southern authors of any race could ignore the idea of race in social history, though not all chose overtly racial matter for their writings. Flannery O'Connor, who recognized that one source of tension in human existence had very much to do with belonging and not-belonging, was nevertheless uncomfortable with representing the other, the African American, in her rural world. In a letter she observed her discomfort with African American subjects, making her perhaps one of the few Southern writers of her generation to acknowledge the difficulty of entering into the consciousness of characters of a different race: "The two colored people in 'The Displaced Person' are on this place now. . . . I can only see them from the outside. I wouldn't have the courage of Miss Shirley Ann Grau to go inside their heads." O'Connor was responding to Grau's collection of short stories, *The Black Prince and Other Stories* (1954), that announced her entry into the field of Southern fiction linking race and region (New Orleans and Louisiana for Grau), and that anticipated her Pulitzer Prize novel *The Keepers of the House* (1964), which treated a dynamic family saga against a Louisiana backdrop of interracial marriage, miscegenation, and racial prejudice. Interestingly enough, unlike Grau, O'Connor was not at all comfortable with her native region though she depicted it almost exclusively as setting, background, and force in fiction.

Neither of O'Connor's novels, *Wise Blood* (1952) and *The Violent Bear It Away* (1960), treats race as a significant aspect of region; however, in several of her short stories published in the posthumous volume *Everything That Rises Must Converge* (1965), she turned to an exploration of racial interaction just as the Civil Rights movement began to change the face of the South. In altering her perspective, O'Connor was much like Robert Penn Warren, one of the Nashville Fugitives during the 1920s and one of the Southern Agrarians in the 1930s.

In 1923, Robert Penn Warren began publishing poetry in *The Fugitive*, the little magazine founded by a group of Vanderbilt University professors and Nashville intellectuals who showed little interest in race as configured in the South. After graduation from Vanderbilt in 1925, Warren studied at the University of California (M.A., 1927), at Yale University (1927-28), and, as a Rhodes Scholar, at New College, Oxford University (B. Litt., 1930), where he completed a biography, *John Brown: The Making of a Martyr* (1929), and wrote "The Briar Patch," an essay defending segregation on economic grounds for *I'll Take My Stand: The South and the Agrarian Tradition by Twelve Southerners* (1930). His earliest writings suggested that he had wider areas of interest than the majority of his Fugitive or his Agrarian cohorts.

Although known as a poet and scholar throughout his long career, Warren was also one of the major novelists to emerge from the modern South. His first novel, *Night Rider* (1939), evolved out of his long story "Prime Leaf" (1931), a treatment of the early twentieth-century tobacco wars in Kentucky's Cumberland Valley, and established his concerns with issues of class and conscience. *At Heaven's Gate* (1943), *World Enough and Time* (1950), *The Cave* (1959), and *A Place to Come To* (1977), all reflect a characteristic tendency in his fiction to combine philosophical meditation, individual idealism, and deterministic naturalism. Jed Tewkesbury, the poor white in search of happiness along with material success, discovers in *A Place to Come To*, "It is not that I cannot stand solitude. Perhaps I stand it too easily, and have been, far beyond my own knowing, solitary all my life." Jed's conclusion in Warren's last novel is comparable to Jack Burden's in Warren's best-known novel, the Pulitzer Prize-winning *All the King's Men* (1946), which traces the rise and fall of a New South self-made politician, Willie Stark, whose story is based on Louisiana governor Huey P. Long. Jack Burden, Warren's prototypical protagonist, proceeds from an ironic vision of an alienated self in a mechanized world to a compassionate, yet terrifying understanding of human and cosmic interdependence: ". . . and soon now we shall go out of the house and go into the convulsion of the world, out of history into history and the awful responsibility of Time."

Warren's meditations on history and the individual's relationship to historical process invariably brought him to a consideration of slavery and its impact on the individual, particularly the white Southerner. The historical novel *Band of Angels* (1955), with its focus on the Civil War and the consequences of miscegenation, and the experimental *Brother to Dragons* (1953; rev. 1979), with its imaginative exploration of Thomas Jefferson's response to his kinsmen's ax murder of a slave, demonstrate Warren's commitment to untangling the complicated racial heritage and conflicted moral agency of individuals functioning within a closed social and political system. Both texts revealed his increasing interest in race relations in Southern history, which he attended to explicitly in an analysis of the region's "separate but equal" educational system, *Segregation: The Inner Conflict in the South* (1956), in a discourse on the 1960s Civil Rights movement, *Who Speaks for the Negro?* (1965), and in a final book of poetry, *Chief Joseph of the Nez Percé* (1983). Warren's associates from the Nashville groups of his youth, Allen Tate, Donald Davidson, John Crowe Ransom, and Andrew Lytle among others, would not have anticipated his empathetic turn to race-specific materials and issues.

Yet, as James Weldon Johnson observed in the novel *The Autobiography of an Ex-Coloured Man* (1912; 1927) of the omnipresent race question: "It would be safe to wager that no group of Southern white men could get together and talk for sixty minutes without bringing up 'the race question.' If a Northern white man happened to be in the group, the time could be safely cut to thirty minutes." Johnson collapsed the debates about race into a dialogue between representatives of the different possible positions. Removing the discussion from a fixed landscape in either the North or the South, he utilized as setting for the dialogue the neutral territory of a train, yet in his portrait even the mobile, contained site could not foster a conciliation of the multiple, antagonistic threads of racial discourse. Johnson suggested that the problem of race is grounded in individual and group perspectives and within specific historical moments, by which he attempted to show that the problem is static and, thus, subject to change.

For white and black Southerners writing in the first half of the century, communal perspectives and historical contexts were not so easily disengaged from the individual's position within the society and at a fixed point in time. W. J. Cash in *The Mind of the South* (1941) attempted to chart the psychological history of the upper South. In unraveling the threads of racial dependency and domination, Cash stated:

And in this society in which the infant son . . . was commonly suckled by a
black mammy, in which gray old men were his most loved story-tellers, in
which black stalwarts were among the chiefest heroes and mentors of his
boyhood, and in which his usual, often practically his only companions until
he was past the age of puberty were the black boys (and girls) of the
plantation—in this society in which by far the greater number of white boys
of whatever degree were more or less shaped by such companionship, and in
which nearly the whole body of whites, young and old, had constantly before
their eyes the example, had constantly in their ears the accent, of the Negro,
the relationship was by the second generation . . . nothing less than organic.
Negro entered into white man as profoundly as white man entered into
Negro—subtly influencing every gesture, every word, every emotion and
idea, every attitude.

Cash's delineation is both personal and relative, but he attempted to
account for one result of racial interaction in the South as he perceived it.

White Southern writers, such as T. S. Stribling, Julia Peterkin, and
DuBose Heyward, depicted African Americans in a central space in
their novels, perhaps out of recognitions comparable to those Cash
identified. They may also have written racial portraiture out of an
awareness of cultural shifts and of H. L. Mencken's attack on the
South as a literary wasteland in "The Sahara of the Bozarts," published in the *New York Evening Mail* (November 13, 1917) and
collected in *Prejudices, Second Series* (1920). Editor of *The Smart Set*
(1908–24) and of *The American Mercury* (1924–33), Mencken saw
a vacuum in literary production in the South and issued a challenge
to Southerners to explore the realities of their region and to create a
viable art. While his influence cannot be linked directly to all Southern creative literature treating race after the appearance of "The Sahara of the Bozarts," his prominence in the literary world and his
strident call for new voices from the South surely impacted upon the
nature of subsequent novels issuing from the South. Mencken specifically aided the developing careers of both Julia Peterkin and Du-
Bose Heyward by praising their work for its more complex treatment
of Southern blacks.

Peterkin drew upon her observations of Gullahs from coastal
South Carolina to create the stories and sketches of *Green Thursday*
(1924) and the novels *Black April* (1927), *Scarlet Sister Mary* (1928),

and *Bright Skin* (1932). Peterkin's attention to the beliefs and practices of the Gullahs helped to legitimize folk portraiture and to identify a viable market for unsentimental fiction treating Southern
blacks. Her portrayal of an African American female, who struggles
to sustain herself in a debilitating world and who triumphs by using
her wit, sexuality, and strength, earned Peterkin a Pulitzer Prize for
*Scarlet Sister Mary,* but her study of a mulatto in the novel *Bright
Skin* was not well received.

DuBose Heyward attended to another aspect of race in South
Carolina, the urban African American community struggling against
poverty and marginalization. In his best-received novel, *Porgy*
(1925), he explored the interactions among the black residents of
Charleston's Catfish Row. Following the success of *Porgy* and its
adaptation for the Broadway stage, Heyward wrote *Mamba's Daughter's* (1929), which, though continuing the focus of his first novel,
was less well received, in part because by the end of the 1920s African Americans were producing more complex portraits of their own
people and culture.

Significantly, Mencken's identification of the South as a field for
fiction awaiting discovery can be linked to the turning to racial material in writers outside the South. Waldo Frank and Jean Toomer are
two of the writers who turned for the matter of their fiction to the
richness of the South and to race as a complication in realistic explorations of the region. Frank and Toomer traveled together through
the South with the intention of gathering materials for their writing.
Frank's novel *Holiday* (1922), tracing the interracial attraction and
the psychological dimensions of Southern life that culminate in lynching, appeared first, but its mild success could not have predicted the
impact that Toomer's *Cane* (1923) would have. While not a financial
success, Toomer's avant-garde novel combining prose, poetry, and
song in three large sections was a major breakthrough in the conception and representation of Southern blacks, particularly in their
relationship to the soil and their heritage. Toomer captured in *Cane*
the emotions he had recognized during a three-month sojourn in
Sparta, Georgia: "Georgia opened me," he remembered of his "initial
impulse to an individual art" based in the soil. In pointing to "the soil
every art and literature that is to live must be embedded in," Toomer
also identified a folk spirit that he thought was "walking in to die on

the modern desert." He responded to the folk songs and to the land-scape itself, so much so that he believed "a deep part of my nature, a part that I had repressed, sprang suddenly to life." *Cane* recovered both the beauty and the pain of African American life in the South, and as a celebration of racial self-discovery it recuperated an identity that had been undermined and distorted by racial oppression and economic victimization.

In three interconnected sections, Toomer traced the social, moral, and psychological limitations of Southern folk life along with its cre-ative power and spiritual essence. The first section concentrates the dual edge of black Southern existence imaged in pine needles, cane fields, and cotton flowers and in the stories of women who are vic-tims of religious hypocrisy, social rigidity, and sexual oppression. The women, ripened too soon, like the men destroyed by bigotry, feel their way through racist economic and cultural forces that would mute and crush them. Brief, imagistic poems and lyrics function to underscore the thematic idea of a people who have the strength and determination to change their own lives, but who have little chance of transforming themselves or their environment; for example, in "Cotton Song," men at work sing: "We aint agwine t wait until th Judgment Day! . . . Cant blame God if we dont roll,/ Come on, brother, roll, roll." The second section utilizes the urban environment of the North to underscore the dilemma of Southern blacks alienated from their roots in the soil. Conspicuous materialism, bourgeois con-sumerism, class snobbery, and color consciousness all function to impede interaction and communication. In the third section, entitled "Kabnis," a return to the South is a harbinger of transformation. The ritualized search for identity and meaning evident in the first two sections has its greatest opportunity for completion in the survival strategies of religion and education characterizing the Southern folk. In the text as a whole, however, Toomer insisted that the Southern folk existence and oral heritage were essential for representing the complex truth of African American life. In doing so, he foreshadowed the Harlem or New Negro Renaissance and illustrated how the past, including the African cultural homeland and Southern chattel slavery, might be envisioned so that modern African Americans could reclaim their history and heritage yet maintain personal dignity and racial pride.

*Cane* appeared a year after the watershed of 1922 in which the publication of fiction positioned at the intersection of region (the South) and race (the "Negro") proliferated. For example, Hubert Shand's *White and Black,* T. S. Stribling's *Birthright,* Clement Woods's *Nigger,* and Ambrose Gonzales's *Black Border* are only a sampling of the texts appearing in 1922. From that point to the end of the decade, the thematic intersection of race and region, along with writerly interconnections, would become a major part of the flowering of modern American fiction.

Interconnections were perhaps inevitable at a time when both Southerners, situated as a regional minority in cultural achievement, and African Americans, marginalized as a racial minority in literary achievement, were rewriting the dominant views of their insignificance. Stribling's novel *Birthright,* for example, provoked a discussion among Mencken, Walter White, and Jessie Fauset regarding who could best portray the reality of African American life in fiction. In asking White to review Stribling's novel, Mencken had not anticipated objections to its sympathetic treatment of race and Southern race relations. As African Americans, White and Fauset, along with Nella Larsen, pointed to the shortcomings of a white outsider's perspective on African Americans, and accepted Mencken's challenge of writing their own novels. Of the three, only Walter White was a Southerner, and only his *The Fire in the Flint* (1924) of those novels initially produced by the three was confined to the South as setting. In responding to Stribling's novel, White, Fauset, and Larsen were not only confronting the issue of authenticity regarding African American materials in fiction but were also seizing authority and agency by shifting the dominant perspective inside the racial group and by acquiring control of the representations and the stories told. Each, of course, assumed a different subject position in the resulting novels. White's *The Fire in the Flint* traces the idealism of an African American physician, Dr. Kenneth Harper, who returns to practice medicine in the South and learns that an educated person of color and conscience cannot exist impervious to racism or outside a coalition of African Americans from all social classes. Jessie Fauset's *There Is Confusion* (1924) centers on the experiences of a middle-class African American female in New York who also comes to a recognition of racism but within gender discrimination. Fauset's Joanna Marshall, the daughter of a Virginia slave who rises to economic prosperity and social prominence, however, insists on the exemplary individual's ability to overcome the structural barriers and personal attitudes that restrict the development and achievement of African Americans. Nella Larsen's *Quicksand* (1928), the last of the three racial novels responding to Stribling and encouraged by Mencken, assumes a more complex stance toward both race and gender identification and the limitations of both. Larsen's Helga Cane, similar to Kenneth Harper and Joanna Marshall, is positioned within the African American middle class, but her situation is more tenuous, because Larsen attends to the matter of Helga's heightened consciousness of gender and sexuality, along with race.

White, Fauset, and Larsen functioned as part of the New Negro or Harlem Renaissance, in which African Americans, acting out of race consciousness and self-determination called a "transformed and transforming psychology" by Alain Locke in *The New Negro* (1925), initiated a literary and cultural movement based upon taking artistic control of their own images and representations. The novels of White, Fauset, and Larsen, appearing during the high point of literary activity in Harlem, combined with Toomer's groundbreaking *Cane* to chart the course for the modern African American novel in its struggle to emerge from the margins of literary enterprise and to assume the centrality of its vision of self, race, and society. Langston Hughes in *Not Without Laughter* (1930) and Arna Bontemps in *God Sends Sunday* (1931) and *Black Thunder* (1936) were part of the development of the African American novel inspired by the revisioning of a racial self and an assumption of authorial control articulated by the first novels to issue from a New Negro consciousness.

One of the major voices first heard during the Harlem Renaissance in short stories and plays was that of Zora Neale Hurston, who like Toomer had an affinity for the folk. Hurston had come of age in Eatonville, Florida, where she had listened to the stories and talk of her relatives, friends, and neighbors. When she left the South, she was already grounded in the language and the nuances of folk existence. After having worked and studied in Baltimore and Washington, she settled in New York where she began to study anthropology with Dr. Franz Boas. "I was glad," Hurston recalled in *Mules and Men* (1935), "when somebody told me, 'You may go and collect Negro folklore.' " She was already familiar with folklore, having listened to and absorbed the stories and customs of her all-black hometown:

> Eatonville . . . was full of material. . . . As early as I could remember it was the habit of the men folk particularly to gather on the store porch of evenings and swap stories. Even the women folks would stop and break a breath with them at times. As a child when I was sent to Joe Clark's store, I'd drag out my leaving as long as possible in order to hear more.

The talk and the folk of Eatonville made their way into "The Eatonville Anthology" (1926), a series of short sketches in which she recognized the value of folk such as Mrs. Tony Roberts (the Pleading Woman), Joe Clark, Mrs. Joe Clark (the prototype of Janie Crawford in *Their Eyes Were Watching God*), Coon Taylor, and Sister Cal'line Potts. These Eatonville characters were preparation for the people of her first novel, *Jonah's Gourd Vine* (1934), and her most accomplished novel, *Their Eyes Were Watching God* (1937).

Novelist, anthropologist, folklorist, and storyteller, Hurston remained both an insider and an outsider throughout her rich life. When she arrived in New York in January 1925, she had exactly $1.50, but "a lot of hope," and the advice of her dead mother Lucy, who had urged her to "jump at de sun" and "to have spirit," so that she would never become "a mealy mouthed rag doll." Fun-loving, free-spirited, and sassy, Hurston was an audacious "natural," a down-home Southerner whose bold antics embarrassed her more high-toned African American associates in her Harlem. Her storytelling, or "lies" as she termed it, made the uncultured, primitive black folk of the South all too vivid for the cultured New Negroes who, with the exception of Rudolph Fisher, Langston Hughes, Claude McKay, and Jean Toomer, preferred to intellectualize and idealize life in the South and the Southern folk. Hurston was too ethnocentric even for the new racial awareness marking the literary movement in Harlem. Wallace Thurman satirized her antics in his novel about the Harlem Renaissance, *Infants of the Spring* (1932); the Hurston character, "Sweetie May Carr," is an opportunistic young artist frequenting Niggeratti Manor who is not embarrassed to manipulate white patrons with dialect tales of down South.

Precisely because she had "spirit" and was not "a mealy mouthed rag doll," Hurston could take full advantage of her insider-outsider position. She accepted not only the difference of her cultural heritage but also its validity. Through the folk she found a means of expressing a culturally grounded self and racial identity. She could therefore create images of African American life that are among the most powerful expressions of the strength and promise of African American culture in the United States. *Jonah's Gourd Vine* is an exploration of that culture based upon the position of Hurston's parents within it. The Reverend John Pearson and his wife Lucy are the central characters, who shape a marriage and a life out of different social backgrounds and values. Pearson is a mulatto whose sharecropping family function on a subsistence level; Lucy Potts is the daughter of landowners who object to her marrying beneath her. The difference in their socioeconomic status contributes to Pearson's feelings of inadequacy, manifested in his adultery, and to Lucy's attempts to conceal her husband's weaknesses. In telling their story, Hurston revises the picture of the African American minister and, though leveling his exalted position in the communal hierarchy, humanizes him. The concern with folk religion in the text anticipates the novel *Moses, Man of the Mountain* (1939), in which Hurston employed humor and satire to render the legend of Moses and the Hebrews in the folk tradition and dialect of Southern African Americans, who connected their plight in slavery to that of the Hebrews.

While *Jonah's Gourd Vine* is a skillful treatment of the conflict between social classes and between religious and secular impulses contextualized by a vibrant folk culture, *Their Eyes Were Watching God* is a masterpiece of that culture. Janie Crawford Killicks Stark Woods is Hurston's testimony to the proud unselfconscious black folk, especially black womenfolk, who achieve a meaningful synthesis of self. Written in seven weeks in late 1926 when she was in Port-au-Prince, Haiti, collecting folklore, the novel is a result partly of what she discovered, "a peace I have never known anywhere else on earth." This peace enabled her to see even more clearly the meaning of African American life as it was lived in Eatonville. The novel is a culmination of her knowledge of the folk, of her faith in folklore and folklife, and of her consciousness of a woman's right to selfhood and self-definition, so that it is an expression of freedom from the constrictions of black folklife even while it celebrates that life.

Because in Haiti Hurston also confronted the end of a love affair that meant personal liberation and reconciliation of her artistic career and her personal emotions, she could represent through Janie's development and maturation the unpacking of multiple layers of domination and oppression operating upon the woman of color: "the colored woman is de mule of the world." Janie Crawford realizes that male domination exists in a world where only men sit on the porch and swap tales, where men view wives as property. She goes through three marriages—to Logan Killicks, to Joe Stark, and to Teacake Woods—but in the process she earns her freedom to speak, to express her own female self, her independence from subjugation, and her acceptance of her own life. Janie affirms herself because she has the courage and the verbal techniques to position herself in something other than a dependent relationship. Janie's strength lies in her recognition of power in language and the ability to speak for oneself. In telling Janie's story of learning to love self, Hurston reckons the value and the costs of being fully female in a society that would oppress on the basis of race and gender, and she introduces a discourse on female autonomy, agency, and power.

Hurston's novels, published after the concentrated activity of the Harlem Renaissance and during the Great Depression, generated limited audiences for her inscriptions of self and folk. In recent years, however, her novels—*Their Eyes Were Watching God*, in particular—have been reevaluated not in the context of race and the folk but rather in the contexts of gender identifications and feminist readings of her strategies for female liberation and autonomy.

In a sense, Hurston addressed in fiction the concerns with gender oppression in a regional society that Lillian Smith would explore in *Killers of the Dream* (1946). Smith, best known for the novel treating interracial love, *Strange Fruit* (1944), attacked the sexual basis of racial discrimination in the South. Smith also transfigured the commonly held assumptions about a white girlhood and womanhood in the region to include racial indoctrination and oppression as part of the cultural constraints upon women, "pushed away on that lonely pedestal called Southern Womanhood," as she observed: "We cannot forget that their culture had stripped these white mothers of profound biological rights, had ripped off their inherent dignity and made them silly statues and psychic children, stunting their capacity for understanding and enjoyment.... In many ways there was a profound subservience; they dared not question what had injured them so much. It was all wrapped up in one package: sex taboos, race segregation,... the duty to go to church, the fear of new knowledge that would shake old beliefs, the splitting of ideals from actions—and you accepted it all uncritically."

Although white Southern women authors did not write prose fiction as explicitly confrontational as Smith about the debilitating racial customs and gender conventions of the region, they did engage in the discourses on race and gender within their fictional texts. Katherine Anne Porter drew small portraits of evolving awareness of how one fits into spaces and families, into history and region, and into categories such as race and gender, while attempting to grasp the meaning of memory and imagination. In "The Old Order," a sequence of stories in *The Leaning Tower and Other Stories* (1944), Porter depicts two old women, one black and the other white, who emerge from the period of slavery to survive husbands and children. The portrait of the elderly black woman Nannie in "The Last Leaf," a subsection of "The Old Order," is significant because in it Porter subverts sentimental views of the black mammy in the South: "The children, brought up in an out-of-date sentimental way of thinking, had always complacently believed that Nannie was a real member of the family, perfectly happy with them." While Nannie and Sophia Jane, the children's grandmother and Nannie's former owner, are both victims of patriarchal power and hegemony, Nannie is also delimited by her racial identity. Married to another slave for the purpose of producing marketable children, she performs her duties, but as soon as she is beyond childbearing years she dismisses her husband, Uncle Jimbilly, from her life. Similarly, once she is too old to perform the duties of mammy to the children of the white family, she severs her ties with them and moves to her own house without explanation or regret: "she was no more the faithful old servant Nannie, a freed slave: she was an aged Bantu woman of independent means, sitting on the steps, breathing free air." Porter, however, did not develop her awareness of the links between race and gender oppression in a full-length novel.

In "The Old Order" and several of her other stories appearing in

*The Leaning Tower,* as in *Old Mortality,* from *Pale Horse, Pale Rider: Three Short Novels* (1949), Porter took on issues comparable to those Lillian Smith outlined as her subject:

In this South I lived as a child and now live. And it is of it that my story is made. I shall not tell, here, of experiences that were different and special and belonged only to me, but those most white southerners both at the turn of the century share with each other. Out of the intricate weaving of unnumbered threads, I shall pick out a few strands, a few designs that have to do with what we call color and race . . . and politics . . . and money . . . and how it is made . . . and religion . . . and sex and the body image . . . and love . . . and dreams of the Good and the killers of the dream.

In presenting the "dissonant strands" in "a terrifying mess," Smith paused to consider how she had learned "the bitterest thing a child can learn: that the human relations I valued most were held cheap by the world I lived in," and "that in trying to shut the Negro race away from us, we have shut ourselves away from so many good, creative, honest, deeply human things in life."

While white authors such as Stribling, Peterkin, and Heyward garnered contemporary recognition for their efforts on racialized subjects, they did not achieve the lasting significance of the major novelist to emerge from the American South during this period, William Faulkner, of Oxford, Mississippi, who won the Nobel Prize for literature in 1950 and who did not follow the pattern of shutting himself "away from so many good, creative, deeply human things in life" that Smith had observed. In assuming a racial heritage based on dominance and difference, Faulkner understood himself and his work in both racial and regional perspectives. The situating of race in his thinking was complicated by his position within a closed and traditional regional society. As a Southerner, he tapped the richness of his region for creative writing, but he also functioned under the dominant ideology of a biracial hierarchy in the South. "We were taught," Smith recalled, "to love God, to love our white skins, and to believe in the sanctity of both." For Faulkner, the hierarchy was a way of life, one that he had not instituted and one that he could not comfortably challenge from his position within the majority and dominant culture. While he struggled with the implications of a biracial society for the creative writer throughout his career, he could not satisfactorily resolve the issue. At the beginning of his career, however, he acknowledged how Southern African Americans had helped to shape his fiction:

So I began to write, without much purpose, until I realized (that to make it . . . truely [*sic*] evocative it must be personal. . . . ) . . . So I got some people, some I invented, others I created out of tales that I learned of nigger cooks and stable boys (of all ages between one-armed Joby, . . . 18, who taught me to write my name in red ink on the linen duster he wore for some reason we both have forgotten, to . . . old Louvinia who remarked when the stars "fell" and who called my grandfather and my father by their Christian names until she died) in the long drowsy afternoons. Created I say, because they are partly composed from what they were in actual life and partly from what they should have been and were not.

In fiction published between 1926 and 1962, Faulkner found the incorporation of race into his vision of subject a necessary aspect of his creation of "people" invented or reimaged from the oral tales of the African Americans figuring in his youth. Beginning with *Soldiers' Pay* (1926), a first novel centering on returning World War I veterans, he utilized African Americans as part of the landscape, physical, imaginative, and moral, of his fiction. Though initially given to stereotypical representations in *Soldiers' Pay*, Faulkner moved farther than almost any other white Southern fiction writer of his generation in portraying people of color, African Americans and Native Americans, with a measure of sympathy and dignity. In fact, he moved away from the existing discourses on race in the South by extracting an alternative vision of life offered by Southern African Americans, in particular, as a major part of the tensions about being, existence, and place that characterized the dialectic of much of his work as a modernist and fictionist.

In both *Sartoris* (1929) and the uncut version of it, *Flags in the Dust* (1927; published 1973), and in *The Sound and the Fury* (1929) he portrayed African Americans as contrapuntal to white Southerners and the moral and social malaise of their lives. His portrait of Dilsey Gibson, the enduring and sustaining force for a deteriorating white family, is representative of his view of the moral superiority of African Americans who retain hope and faith in a world collapsing under the strain of moral degeneracy and cultural despair. In *Light in*

*August* (1932) and *Absalom, Absalom!* (1936), Faulkner treated race as the unacknowledged social construction undermining the lives of white Southerners and constricting the lives of black Southerners. Joe Christmas of *Light in August*, who never knows his racial identity in a society built upon racial certainty, moves outside of race until he can no longer sustain his own isolation. His literal castration and symbolic lynching culminates his acceptance of an identity as a black man. Quentin Compson of *Absalom, Absalom!* combines a search for himself with a reconstruction of a myth of the Southern past, and in the process confronts the racial hierarchy and abuse that shapes both the actual and the imagined historical South. In *Go Down, Moses* (1942), Faulkner explored the ways in which attitudes of racial superiority and enslavement functioned to destroy a family and confound its efforts to perpetuate itself. Ike McCaslin, who operates as the conscience of his family and society, ultimately discovers in old age that he can neither atone for the racial sins of his fathers nor free himself from their prejudices. Despite his initiation into the world of nature and the wilderness by the part Indian, part black Sam Fathers, Ike cannot transpose the values of the natural, primitive world to the divided racist world of civilized Mississippi. Lucas Beauchamp, who figures in *Go Down, Moses* as the black male descendant of the founder of the McCaslin dynasty, reappears in *Intruder in the Dust* (1948) as a mentor to Chick Mallison, a white youth who, like Ike McCaslin, confronts the bigotry of his society and the racism within himself. Lucas enables Chick to transcend artificial boundaries separating the races and to restore a measure of justice in the interactions between blacks and whites. In all of these novels, Faulkner, though unconcerned with rendering African Americans outside of their relationships to white Southerners, nonetheless created a large number and a fairly diverse range of people of color, not all of them sympathetic representations.

Unlike F. Scott Fitzgerald, his contemporary from the Midwest who married a Southerner, Zelda Sayre of Alabama, Faulkner did not fear the rising up of people of color. Faulkner sought to explain and perhaps expiate the white South's destructive racial positions. Whereas Fitzgerald, heralded as the writer of the Jazz Age, removed his interest in the rhythms of jazz from that of the African Americans who first created it, Faulkner did not. While black characters are noticeably absent from Fitzgerald's novels and negative racial views presented go unexamined, his notions about race were clear: "The negroid streak creeps northward to defile the Nordic race. . . . My reactions [to Europe] were all philistine, antisocial, provincial, and racially snobbish. I believe at last in the white man's burden. We [Americans] are as far above the modern Frenchman as he is above the Negro." Faulkner, on the other hand, while sharing his culture's traditional views of race, did not dismiss the centrality of race and the legacy of African Americans in that culture. Whatever his failings in representing race in his novels, Faulkner did not set out a simplistic assertion of the racial superiority of whites or a conflated representation of "the Negro" as scapegoat for the vicissitudes of regional identity in a modernizing South. He attended to the problems and dynamics of race relations, caste privilege, and agrarian reform within the contexts of industrialization and urbanization in a region reluctant and resistant to change. Race, then, was one of the facets of regional continuity and regional transformation that he could not deny and would not ignore.

Faulkner's attention to African Americans in the maturation of white Southerners is one of his legacies to writers who followed him. In *The Member of the Wedding* (1946), Carson McCullers brought to bear her insights as a modern female within the culture who, in the process of revisioning the maturation of a young white female, Frankie Addams, considered as well the relationship of the African American surrogate mother, Berenice Sadie Brown, to that process. McCullers outlined the maturation of a young Southern girl in her season of budding awareness of self and difference. In portraying Frankie Addams, who grew too tall too quickly and who faced the puzzling problem of relating to her home and community when she longed for other worlds, McCullers valorized the role of the African American woman charged with Frankie's care by showing how Berenice represented difference and experience useful to maintaining a selfhood within a society expecting conformity. In the popular play adapted from the novel and also entitled *The Member of the Wedding* (1951), however, McCullers draws weaker, less racially positive African American characters in a manner duplicating the myths and stereotypes of their lives; for example, the men are weak, dishonest, sexually aggressive, and drug- or alcohol-addicted, while the women are superstitious, servile, and promiscuous. More recently, Kaye Gibbons in *Ellen Foster* (1987) concentrates not on the older nursemaid or housekeeper in the development of the white girl character but on the peer, the African American of the same age whose friendship functions to foster and to complicate the maturation process for the white friend. These novels suggest that though the cultural, racial, and gender dynamics have changed since Faulkner created Dilsey, Lucas, and Sam Fathers, his vision in rendering one of the major points of interaction in the black and white South has not gone unnoticed by subsequent writers seeking to portray in human terms the complexities of their region.

Though Faulkner remained in the South for most of his career, the exception being a few brief stints in Hollywood as a scriptwriter for motion pictures, white Southern writers like Katherine Anne Porter, Tennessee Williams, Carson McCullers, and, for a time, Flannery O'Connor more often fled their region because of its inadequacies for the development of their careers as professional writers. African American Southern writers fled out of another set of imperatives. Restricted to second-class citizenship, when their citizenship was acknowledged at all, blacks lived on the edge in their native region. Legally constricted by the resurgence of Jim Crow laws after World War I when black soldiers returning from Europe sought full access to the democracy they had fought to preserve on foreign soils, modern blacks found themselves no better off than their forebears at the end of the nineteenth century. Segregated in housing, education, employment, transportation, and every other social aspect of their lives, they found themselves marginalized and, if at all visibly resentful of their unequal treatment, endangered. The external codes and customs of a separated society deposited internally led to a dual vision of self within two sets of limitations; the one, that of the oppressive white society, and the other, that of the repressive black society. Richard Wright, Ralph Ellison, and their contemporaries writing of the South from the perspective of the race traditionally seen as other struggled against the projected negative self-representations embedded in the ideology of race and racial difference used by whites to uphold their legal policies, moral beliefs, and literary practices. Simultaneously, they struggled with the social fragmentation and psychical fractures emanating from the accommodations made by African Americans to retain their humanity and dignity. Separated from their white cultural and literary counterparts by what Richard Wright labeled "a million of psychological miles" in "The Man Who Killed a Shadow," black writers in order to exist as creative beings felt compelled to leave the South in the early decades of the twentieth century.

Richard Wright's experience is perhaps paradigmatic. Born into a sharecropping family in Mississippi, Wright came to prominence as a writer during the 1930s when he both assumed and rejected a racial heritage based on subordination and difference. For Wright, the inescapable necessity was to distance himself from a humiliating, inferior position in a biracial hierarchy. Rage in his response to the South exacerbated fragmentation and division, emphasized it to a maximum and almost unbearable degree; nonetheless, rage, righteous and focused, was also the source of integrated action. Wright prevented his own disintegration by the process of remembering, despite the pain and shame of reenvisioning himself within the racist structures of his native region. He states in *Black Boy: A Record of Childhood and Youth* (1945):

I was not leaving the South to forget the South, but so that some day I might understand it, might come to know what its rigors had done to me, its children. I fled so that the numbness of my defensive living might thaw out and let me feel the pain—years later and far away—of what living in the South had meant.

Yet, deep down, I knew that I could never really leave the South, for my feelings had already been formed by the South, . . . instilled into my personality and consciousness. . . . So, in leaving, I was taking a part of the South to transplant in alien soil, to see if it could grow differently. . . . And if that miracle ever happened, then I would know that there was yet hope in that southern swamp of despair and violence, that light could emerge even out of the blackest of the southern night. I would know that the South too could overcome its fear, its hate, its cowardice, its heritage of guilt and blood, its burden of anxiety and compulsive cruelty.

As a result of this recognition, in his fictional texts Wright was able to ward off personal disintegration by creating powerful protagonists who are "stripped of the past and free for the future," as he asserted in *White Man, Listen!* (1957). Rather than transcendence, his aim was to control the rage so that it became creative energy, directed toward exposing the sources of his rage and toward expunging his individual sense of guilt for not having been able to do more in the literal rather than the literary world to change his condition.

At the same time, Wright transformed his shame at having been the victim of humiliations, perpetrated both by the external society of whites and by his immediate family of blacks attempting to survive. Survival has its costs, as he recognized in distancing himself from his family, his parental relatives and their heritage and folk culture, as well as from his maternal relatives with their dependency upon religion and their emphasis upon upward mobility within the land of the oppressors and in terms acceptable to their oppressors. None of his novels affirms folk culture and the African American family for their capacity to sustain the individual. In his fiction, Wright was the explosive in attacking all institutions (family, political parties, Southern segregation, economic systems, and racial hierarchies) that would deny his individual manhood. He refused to celebrate racial survival at all costs, as white writers such as Faulkner did with representations of exemplary black servants (Dilsey Gibson in *The Sound and the Fury* or Lucas Beauchamp in *Go Down, Moses* and *Intruder in the Dust*). Like the contemporary writers Alice Walker in *The Third Life of Grange Copeland* (1970) and Ernest Gaines in *A Gathering of Old Men* (1983), Wright insisted that survival is not enough. Walker's Grange, for instance, lives the life of a black Southerner emasculated by his environment but eventually struggles to regain his manhood through the next generation, specifically that of his granddaughter Ruth. Grange Copeland expresses his hard-won knowledge in the end when he says that it is not survival, but survival *whole*, that is the key to being and meaning. Gaines's old men rise from a lifetime of survival by means of subjugation and passivity to a stance for personal wholeness; in a concerted front of resistance and autonomy, they seize control of what is left of their lives and, with guns in hand, confront not only the white power structure but also their own past acquiescence to it.

Unlike these later configurations of the possibilities of black Southern existence, Wright emphasized neither survival nor wholeness within the lifetime of his characters. Like Bigger Thomas, the "scared colored boy from Mississippi" in Wright's Chicago novel *Native Son* (1940), they more often die without the recognition that their actions are integrally connected to that of their people and progeny, which is

Grange's final achievement. Yet it is clear that even a Grange or the old men are similar to Wright's characters in that they suffer from the malformations that the environmental factors of the South create as pressures and restrictions on the lives of African Americans and that their own consequentially dehumanized and demoralized acts partly account for the shame and the humiliation of their lives.

Wright's parables in the novels *Native Son, The Outsider* (1953), *The Long Dream* (1958), and *Lawd Today* (1963) ultimately strike out at the white world, by taking revenge for the ills suffered through generations, and breaking the boundaries of codes and laws that would legally and practically circumvent the ambitions and the dreams of blacks. Bigger Thomas kills for what he ultimately believes is a valuable but inexpressible part of himself. The intellectual Cross Damon exists outside the parameters of societal law, and from that alienated position he explores a murderous, raceless freedom, but acknowledges "it was . . . horrible." Jake Thomas, the protagonist of Wright's posthumously published first novel, *Lawd Today*, reacts in a naturalistic manner to his entrapment in the urban environment. These men all become indifferent to violence in the process of rejecting external authority over their lives. In representing their attempt to alter the power relationships that determined them impotent, Wright circumvents the dominant discourses on African American subserviency and creates a different reading of power, its manifestations and its limits.

Wright identifies women with codifying the behavior of blacks according to the dictates of whites. He understands the strategies and concessions devised to exist within the oppressive and restrictive world of the South, as indicated by his essay "The Ethics of Living Jim Crow," his fictionalized autobiography, *Black Boy: A Record of Childhood and Youth,* the short stories collected in *Uncle Tom's Children* (1938; 1940) and *Eight Men* (1961), and particularly his novel *The Long Dream*. More pronounced, however, is his understanding of the legacy of paralyzing wounds to the psyche of succeeding generations that functions in his texts as a gap between generations that can neither be removed nor bridged. Divisions between fathers and sons might be expected, given the integral relationship of Wright's biography as a son of the segregated South to his fictional vision. The absence of the father in *Native Son* is not surprising, and the deceptive, obsequious father feigning power in *The Long Dream* is equally predictable; however, the division between mothers and their sons is also present, and, unexpectedly, the mother is often more of a liability than the father, because she cannot be protected by the male son and her motives and her methods of protecting her offspring are even more detrimental than those of the father.

In this aspect Wright is similar to Faulkner in *Light in August*, in which the character Joe Christmas comes to expect the cruelty and the strict discipline of male father figures, but cannot fathom or tolerate the seeming weakness of the female mother figures, who seem impenetrable, incomprehensible, and, above all, unpredictable, which is the main key to the mothers in Wright. Paradoxically, though the mothers stand by the sons to the best of their ability, they are often held more responsible than the fathers for the conditions under which the sons exist and come to manhood. The situation is the same in *Savage Holiday* (1954), Wright's "white" novel in which Erskine Fowler's damaged psychological state is attributed to the mother, whose promiscuity and neglect of the son in favor of lovers is the memory that the adult Erskine must confront and that he must unravel in order to understand his rage against a young woman and his identification with her son Toby; he kills the son accidentally, but predictably so in the context of his having to call up the memories of his own childhood and youth in order to exorcise the ghost of his mother and his literal and symbolic childhood illness.

A comparable childhood illness figures prominently in both *Black Boy* and *The Long Dream*. In *Black Boy*, it is brought on by a beating inflicted by the mother on her son for fighting with white youths instead of deferring to the codes of survival that she and her kind insist upon in order to "save" the lives of black youths, but in the process she and they severely damage the internal life and psyche of their male children. As maternal figures, they resultingly do not emerge as loving individuals who teach the sons to be strong and to be men, as does the mother in Ernest Gaines's short story "The Sky Is Gray" (from *Bloodline* [1968]). In Gaines's representation, the mother acknowledges her son's manhood and teaches him by her example, rather than with her words, what it means to be a black man in a hostile environment. Similarly, in *The Long Dream*, the illness, brought on by Fishbelly's brief imprisonment for a transgression that is not unlike that of Big Boy and his cohorts in "Big Boy Leaves Home," but brought on also by the father's response, marks the indelible strain between the mother and the son, who is no longer able to respect his mother or to submit to her authority. His manhood means that she becomes irrelevant to his existence and that she can teach him nothing that he feels he needs to know. Mothers who leave sick children for whatever reason, whether the rationalization is positive, that is, to visit the sick or to attend church or to go to work, are somehow guilty of abandoning their sons to nightmares, literally and symbolically. Their waking reality will thereafter have the marks of the dream, dark and threatening, frightful and debilitating. The break in the relationships between mothers and sons is crucial for understanding the generational conflict underscoring Wright's subtexts and permeating his thinking about the maturation processes of his Southern black youths. The break is long remembered and little understood, but it is paradigmatic of the alienation from family and heritage, from comfort and kin, from childhood innocence and adult awareness, all of which combine to mark the unhinged maturity of the Southern black male child.

Wright's novels pointed the direction for Ralph Ellison in his major work, *Invisible Man* (1952). Ellison re-visioned the ground of Wright's fiction and, concomitantly, the history of modern African Americans. He charted a fresh course for making race a viable metaphor for the condition of the human being entrapped in circumstances beyond individual comprehension and yet moving toward a full realization of self and significance. In the background of *Invisible Man* is Booker T. Washington, whose Tuskegee Institute figured prominently in discourses on racial uplift and progress in the early twentieth century and whose autobiography, *Up From Slavery* (1901), set an agenda for individual success to overcome racial barriers. Ellison's oratorical novel responds to the notion of the separation of the races and to the ideology of racial cooperation popularized by Washington. In speaking for and to the problematics of race, Ellison envisioned that, despite Washington or perhaps because of him, in the early decades of the twentieth century, resolutions to raciality as a basis of individual identity were not yet apparent. Economic self-sufficiency was no guarantee of racial acceptance or cultural assimilation for African Americans. He also foresaw, as Wright had, no immediate reconciliation of the private and the public in matters of racial identity or of the relationship between race and region.

Race and region, once considered inseparable in the case of the South, are now two distinct and discrete areas of inquiry. Yet the association of the two in novels during the early modern period gave rise to much of America's major writing.

Thadious M. Davis

# Fiction of the West

The richly varied novel of the West has a long and complex history. Its formulaic version—the popular Western—maintains such a strong hold on the national imagination that all other cultural expression in the West falls under its shadow. Yet the West has always had a literature that does not follow any popular formulas; and the "literary Western novels," those that go beyond popular formulas, have offered readers a distinctive ontology and point of view, particularly since the 1930s. Although this chapter begins with the novel of the frontier and traces the history of both popular and literary Westerns through the nineteenth and early twentieth centuries, its main focus is on the literary Western from 1955 to 1990. During the last thirty-five years, most Western novelists have articulated in their art the conviction that we must stop exploiting not only other human beings but also the natural world that sustains all life.

The novel of the West developed from narratives of exploration and settlement and from the novel of the frontier, a subgenre initiated by Charles Brockden Brown's *Wieland* (1798) and made internationally famous by James Fenimore Cooper's Leatherstocking tales (1823–41). Among other early frontier novelists, James Kirke Paulding wrote *The Dutchman's Fireside* (1831) about upper New York during the French and Indian Wars; Timothy Flint, author of *The Shoshonee Valley* (1830), depicted a Far West he had never seen; and Robert Montgomery Bird created a fictional Indian-hater in *Nick of the Woods; or, The Jibbenainosay* (1837).

Frontier novels sometimes include such detailed descriptions of the landscape that the land assumes an importance as great as the characters, who are drawn from the European and Native American cultures that clashed on the frontier. Since such violent clashes generally attended the process of settlement, the novel of the frontier offered tales filled with action and adventure. Women played limited roles in these tales, but their gentle presence drove farther west frontiersmen such as Cooper's Natty Bumppo, a white who had been raised by Native Americans and who thereafter tried to live by the best of his "red gifts" and "white gifts." Most frontier novels and many novels of the West exhibit these features developed by Cooper and his contemporaries: (1) an emphasis on the land; (2) action and adventure; (3) cultural clashes; (4) a hero who champions good, fights evil, and deplores the passing of the wilderness; and (5) a world either without women or with women in only minor roles.

In 1860, a little less than a decade after Cooper's death, the House of Beadle and Adams published the first dime novel, *Malaeska: The Indian Wife of the White Hunter,* by Ann S. Stephens. A flood of pulp fiction soon followed, and for the next seventy years, dime novels (most of them Westerns) reached an audience of millions and portrayed the famous types of the westward expansion: the plainsman, the outlaw, and the cowboy. Even more adventure-packed than the frontier novels of Cooper, dime novels glorified the exploits of frontier heroes such as Daniel Boone and Kit Carson and reduced the elements of frontier narrative to a simple formula. Prentiss Ingraham, Edward L. Wheeler, E. Z. C. Judson (pen name "Ned Buntline"), and other dime novelists also wrote works that created popular heroes such as Buffalo Bill Cody.

While dime novelists busily created the West that won the popular imagination, other post–Civil War authors recorded a different sort of West in novels of local color, realism, and naturalism. Bret Harte, Mary Hallock Foote, E. W. Howe, and Helen Hunt Jackson gained a national audience with novels that looked at the West not only as a wild frontier but also as a place of settlement. Yet in spite of Foote's honesty, Howe's pioneering psychological portraits, and Jackson's feminism and defense of Native Americans, *The Led-Horse Claim* (1883), *The Story of a Country Town* (1883), and *Ramona* (1884) seem freighted with much Victorian melodrama and exhibit many of the flaws of apprentice efforts. Less melodramatic and more polished are Frank Norris's *McTeague* (1899), and *The Octopus* (1901); Jack London's *The Sea-Wolf* (1904) and *Martin Eden* (1909); and Andy Adams's *The Log of a Cowboy* (1903). Although no school of Western fiction yet existed, and Wallace Stegner may be right in saying that no such school has ever existed, writers such as London and Adams probably shared Norris's view that "the Westerner thinks along different lines from the Easterner and arrives at different conclusions. What is true of California is false of New York."

Despite the truth of Norris's observation, it was an Easterner who wrote what came to be regarded as the model for the novel of the West. Owen Wister's *The Virginian* (1902) "presents Wyoming between 1874 and 1890" and laments the passing of that "vanished world," brought to an end by the closing of the frontier with the last of the free land. Although Wister extols the cowboy as "a hero without wings" and "the last romantic figure upon our soil," *The Virginian* subtly promotes elitism. The Virginian is no common cowboy; he is, rather, one of nature's aristocracy, a born leader that Wister portrays as having the right to circumvent the law in order to obtain justice. Wister's novel enjoyed considerable popularity, but not so much because of its elitism as because the Virginian courageously fights the evil Trampas and because the Virginian's marriage to Molly Wood, a transplanted New England schoolmarm, symbolized national reconciliation and union. What works against Wister's better purposes is his effectism—that is, the attempt to awaken vivid and violent emotions in the reader without respect for the truth. As Edwin H. Cady has written, *The Virginian* and its progeny teach "the fatally false lesson that violence does not really matter; that it has no real consequences because the good guy is invulnerable and the bad guy is 'a creature.' In the 'effectist' world, violence is not real."

Among the many writers whose works follow the pattern of *The Virginian*, Zane Grey became the most famous. In dozens of Grey's novels, the good guy invariably defeats the bad guy, simultaneously saving the beautiful heroine and winning her hand. Dozens of Grey's imitators, some more prolific than Grey, copied his formula and flooded pulp and slick magazines and paperback racks with adventurous tales of the Old West, some of them actually based upon real-life incidents. Generalizations about popular Westerns should be suspect, partly because it is unlikely that any critic could read them all, but mainly because all sorts of popular writers have varied the pattern, and some have occasionally broken out of the formula. Consider the variety apparent in a random selection from the hundreds of novels by some of the most popular Western writers: Will Henry's *From Where the Sun Now Stands* (1960) recounts the history of the Nez Percé War from the Native Americans' point of view; Louis L'Amour sometimes gives mini lectures on events such as Custer's Last Stand; Matt Braun's *Mattie Silks* (1972) depicts a notorious Denver whore; Max Brand shows sympathy for Mexican peons in his Montana Kid series (1933–36); and Luke Short's *Rimrock* (1955) is set during the uranium boom in Colorado and Utah.

Moreover, many popular authors let their publishers market their novels as Westerns, although their works have been shaped less by the formula than by the results of historical research. Judy Alter's *Mattie* (1988) is full of authentic details about the life of a woman doctor. The real-life experience of Cynthia Ann Parker, captured by Comanches in 1836, forms the basis of Benjamin Capps's novel *A Woman of the People* (1966). Max Evans's *The Rounders* (1960) takes a typical Western subject, a New Mexican cowboy, but creates a tragicomedy from his experiences. Of her several dozen Western novels, Jeanne Williams says: "I like to take little known events and dramatize them so that readers will get a picture of the many influences that shaped the West . . . and [of] man's responsibilities to other creatures and the earth that supports us all." Like many popular Western writers, Williams visits the places she writes about and then conducts research in libraries with information about Western life and lore.

Library shelves constitute the only West that some popular Western writers ever see, for since the nineteenth century, Westerns have been written in such faraway lands as Germany, England, Norway, Italy, Turkey, Japan, and Czechoslovakia. Since the 1960s, many popular Western writers, including some in foreign countries, have doubled their novels' effectism by adding gratuitous sex to the formula of violence. Moreover, the violence and sex often seem twice as stimulating—and appalling—when conveyed by other media. Even before Edwin S. Porter's one-reeler movie *The Great Train Robbery* (1903), movies capitalized on the Westerns' popularity, and Hollywood has continued to milk profit from the genre. Radio Westerns filled the airwaves during the 1930s and 1940s; and since the 1950s, television series such as "Gunsmoke," "Wagon Train," "Bonanza," and "The Young Riders" have brought "the West that wasn't" to millions of living rooms.

The widespread and long-lasting influence of the popular Western has overshadowed the artistic achievements of those who have written about the West that was and is. Although she was a Westerner and a contemporary of Zane Grey, Willa Cather avoided the formula of the popular Westerns. And although she wrote about the frontier West and its passing, she looked to the ancient classics and to the masterpieces of English and American literature for models and inspiration. Her subject matter, however, was usually Western.

In *O Pioneers!* (1913), Cather wrote: "The great fact was the land itself, which seemed to overwhelm the little beginnings of human society that struggled in its sombre wastes." In *The Song of the Lark* (1915) the land inspires Thea Kronborg to be a great artist. In *My Ántonia* (1918), a drama of memory, the land helps sustain and in some measure compensates the title character. In *A Lost Lady* (1923), *The Professor's House* (1925), and *Death Comes for the Archbishop* (1927), Cather lamented the loss of the frontier's early potential. She gave her novels an apparent simplicity that masks an underlying complexity of style, structure, and material.

Many of the West's immigrants wrote novels about their experiences, often in their native languages. The best-known works of this immigrant fiction (much of it still untranslated) include Ole Rölvaag's *Giants in the Earth* (1927), Sophus K. Winther's *Take All to Nebraska* (1936), and Herbert Krause's *Wind Without Rain* (1939). By mid-century, these works, as well as other pioneer-prairie novels such as Herbert Quick's *Vandemark's Folly* (1922), had created a literary West more akin to Greek tragedy than to the melodrama of Hollywood's silver screen.

The only Western novelist awarded the Nobel Prize for literature, John Steinbeck drew inspiration primarily from the Bible and Arthurian legend, rather than from Greek tragedy. As its title (taken from a line in Milton's *Paradise Lost*) suggests, Steinbeck's *In Dubious Battle* (1936) depicts the hell of self-hatred, a parable ironically set in Edenic California, where Communist organizers battle rich farmers and where both the Party and the farmers exploit migratory fruit pickers. *Of Mice and Men* (1937) focuses on two itinerant workers whose dream of having their own Western ranch falls victim to uncontrollable instinct and passion. *The Grapes of Wrath* (1939) follows the Depression wanderings of the Joad family, who are "tractored off" their farm in Oklahoma and have to travel across the Southwest to seek work in California—a westering saga with parallels to the Book of Exodus.

Often labeled "protest novels," Steinbeck's works do protest against injustice, but like Cather's novels they also lament the lost potential of the frontier. Long after Steinbeck had received the Pulitzer and Nobel prizes, some critics continued to fault him for his optimism and his "apple-pie radicalism." In expressing these sentiments, they seem to have forgotten his *East of Eden* (1952) and his evident commitment to Jeffersonian democracy.

How could a writer as competent as Steinbeck be so misread? Because the view of ontology held by Western novelists of the 1930s and 1940s is often not understood by people from other regions. In his landmark study of Walter Van Tilburg Clark, Max Westbrook explains the Western ontology:

The essential connections of man and his universe are not subject to the verbal abstractions of the intellect. If we insist on confining knowing to rational knowledge, then we can know nothing beyond our own powers to create; and man has created neither himself nor his universe, neither his reason nor his "little man inside" ["the voice of intuition in the service of the unconscious"]. Western artists do not propose a formula—they would not be worth study if they did—but they do offer a direction, a possibility. If we reason about our place in linear time and learn to intuit with the unconscious our more fundamental place in primordial time, we have the possibility of maintaining an individual ego while feeling the generative power of our archetypal selves.

Unfortunately, Western artists have to express their view of ontology within the context of a regional tradition that includes the stereotypes of the standard "horse opry."

In a letter written in 1959, Clark said the stereotypes had blocked his way, "So, in part, I set about writing *The Ox-Bow Incident* [1940] as a kind of deliberate technical exercise. It was an effort to set myself free in that western past by taking all the ingredients of the standard western (which were real enough after all) and seeing if, with a theme that concerned me, and that had more than dated and local implications, and a realistic treatment, I could bring both the people and the situations alive again." All that and more comes to life in *The Ox-Bow Incident*, the psychological tale of a lynching, and in Clark's other two novels: *The City of Trembling Leaves* (1945), a *Künstlerroman* set in twentieth-century Reno; and *The Track of the Cat* (1949), the story of a hunt as richly symbolic as the one in *Moby-Dick*. Clark's novels and those of like-minded Western artists show, says Westbrook, that "both a capacity for naked purity and a capacity for brute murder are within each one of us."

What did some reviewers on the Hudson see in *The Ox-Bow Incident?* Just "another cowboy story." So, too, well into the 1970s did otherwise good critics misread and mislabel H. L. Davis's *Honey in the Horn* (1935, Pulitzer Prize) and *Winds of Morning* (1952); Harvey Fergusson's *Grant of Kingdom* (1950) and *The Conquest of Don Pedro* (1954); Vardis Fisher's *Dark Bridwell* (1931) and *In Tragic Life* (1932); A. B. Guthrie's *The Big Sky* (1947) and *The Way West* (1949, Pulitzer Prize); Paul Horgan's *Far from Cibola* (1938) and *Whitewater* (1970); Frederick Manfred's *The Golden Bowl* (1944) and *Riders of Judgment* (1957); Conrad Richter's *The Sea of Grass* (1937); and Frank Waters's *The Man Who Killed the Deer* (1942) and *The Woman at Otowi Crossing* (1966). Writing sometimes of mountain men and pioneers, cowboys and Indians, these authors, like Clark, often found themselves ranked with Zane Grey and B. M. Bower, which is a good deal like placing William Faulkner in the same artistic category as Margaret Mitchell on the ground that they both wrote about the South.

Wallace Stegner and Wright Morris, two other Western artists whose novels began to appear before 1950, have earned national acclaim partly because Western ontology is not the dominant force in their work, but also because they are among the most skillful literary artists of our time.

Three of Stegner's novels had been published before *The Big Rock Candy Mountain* (1943), an autobiographical novel about his family's moves throughout the Northwest to Saskatchewan in search of the American dream. In that novel, feeling he should "have lived a hundred years earlier," Bo Mason (Stegner's fictional portrait of his father) eventually moves his wife and two sons to Salt Lake City, where he supports his family on what he can make selling bootleg whiskey. Stegner says that a dozen years after he wrote the novel, "I began to realize my Bo Mason was a character with relatives throughout western fiction. I could see in him resemblance to Ole Rölvaag's Per Hansa, to Mari Sandoz's Old Jules, to A. B. Guthrie's Boone Caudill, even to the hard-jawed and invulnerable heroes of the myth. But I had not been copying other writers. I had been trying to paint a portrait of my father, and it happened that my father, an observed and particular individual, was also a type—a very western type."

Trying to understand his father, Bruce Mason writes: "A man is movement, motion, a continuum. There is no beginning to him. He runs through his ancestors, and the only beginning is the primal beginning of the single cell in the slime. The proper study of mankind is man, but man is an endless curve on the eternal graph paper, and who can see the whole curve?" In all of his work Stegner traces as much of the curve as will reveal a connection between past and present. Yet it is not mere historical facts or ideas that Stegner seeks to convey. Rather, as he puts it, "The work of art is not a gem, as some schools of criticism would insist, but truly a lens. We look through it for the purified and honestly offered spirit of the artist."

One of Stegner's kindred spirits is surely Wright Morris, seven of whose novels had been published before *The Field of Vision* appeared in 1956 and won the National Book Award. Like Stegner, Morris writes mostly about the middle class, revealing the wonder of what is uncommon in the commonplace. Like Cather's, his narratives have an apparent simplicity that masks complexity. Like Hemingway and Faulkner, Morris makes his readers piece together a story from fragments that come from different points of view. *The Field of Vision* ostensibly centers on a Mexican bullfight, but the memories of five of the characters range far back into the past, dredging up bits of narrative that, taken together, tell the story of much of their lives. As in Faulkner's *As I Lay Dying*, the characters' thoughts reflect their temperament, education, and intelligence; and they show, too, that, as the novel's epigraph from *Paradise Lost* puts it, "The mind is its own place, and in itself/ Can make a Heav'n of Hell, a Hell of Heav'n." Morris also shares Faulkner's ability to create a mythic territory corresponding to the actual home country of his memories. *The Field of Vision, Ceremony in Lone Tree* (1960), and other Morris novels include characters who have lived in or had some connection with Lone Tree, Nebraska.

Critics have noted that Morris's view of life darkens in his later novels, particularly *Plains Song* (1980). Throughout many of his nineteen novels runs an irony sometimes so subtle that even so astute a reader as Wayne C. Booth admits to difficulty in understanding it. Referring specifically to *Love Among the Cannibals* (1957), Booth says: "I can be certain that I sometimes judge when judgment is not intended, sometimes fail to judge when Morris expects me to, and sometimes judge on the wrong axis: Morris may intend undercuttings that many readers will overlook, yet many a reader may make moral and aesthetic judgments against Morris that he in fact intends to be made against the narrator." But Booth also points out that reading more than one of Morris's works helps readers correctly identify and gauge the ironies.

Complex irony also pervades the novels of William Eastlake, a native New Yorker who as a young man moved to a New Mexico ranch. In a series of three novels set in Indian Country—*Go in Beauty* (1956), *The Bronc People* (1958), and *Portrait of an Artist with Twenty-Six Horses* (1963)—Eastlake undercuts virtually every stereotype of the popular Western. For example, instead of being blood-thirsty fiends or taciturn Noble Savages, the Native Americans often function almost as a sophisticated Greek chorus, wittily commenting on the other characters. However, Eastlake's novels offer much more than ironic undercuttings. He probes the psychological and emotional sources of conflict between brothers, between races, between cultures. His persistent irony strips away the stereotypes people use to conceal their real motives. And like Faulkner and Wright Morris, Eastlake presents many of his novels as a series of seemingly separate stories or sketches, thereby making the reader piece together the narrative fragments.

Eastlake's symbolism shows the dualities that split the American mind and divide American society. Yet the chorus of Indian comments reminds us that from the Native American perspective those dualities matter very little, since they constitute the yin and yang of a world view that continues to "civilize" the continent. Because of its tonal complexity and its penetrating critique of American civilization, critics Delbert Wylder and Gerald Haslam have rightly called *The Bronc People* a classic in the literature of the West.

Another novel of the 1950s, Jack Kerouac's *On the Road* (1957), drew national attention because it seemed a paean to the controversial Beat movement. Consisting of Sal Paradise's account of his transcontinental journeys with or in search of his buddy Dean Moriarity, *On the Road* seemed to some of its first readers only a picaresque travelogue. Initially denounced by many critics as non-art and an irresponsible glorification of Bohemian irresponsibility, *On the Road* nevertheless was heralded by a *New York Times* reviewer as a "major novel," and it hit the best-seller lists. A decade later, another wave of critics saw Kerouac's work not as random ramblings in his notorious "spontaneous prose" but as a carefully structured love story. Although Kerouac's characters only crisscross the West, seldom staying in one place for long, *On the Road* deserves classification as a novel of the West not because it recounts Bohemian antics in the region but because it depicts at least one undying notion about the West: that it is a land of possibility.

Westerners live "out where the sense of place is a sense of motion," as Stegner puts it; and *On the Road* shows mid-century Americans pulled by this aspect of the westering impulse as the pioneers in Emerson Hough's *The Covered Wagon* (1922) and the Okies in *The Grapes of Wrath* are pulled by it. Yet Stegner and other Westerners disapprove of Bohemianism like Kerouac's. Was this Beat a martyr to the truth, savagely attacked for trying to reveal the hollowness and decadence of the American Wasteland? Or was he a latter-day Pied Piper who led thousands to forsake responsibility in exchange for lives eventually ruined by promiscuity and the drug culture? Some Westerners answer "yes" to the first question, some "yes" to the second. Their differing responses show that the Beat movement and *On the Road* helped create a counterculture within the West, further fragmenting an already complex society.

Whatever their differences, contemporary Western novelists stand united in their opposition to the rape of the land. They know that the frenzied rush toward ecocide will not abate until we gain a new consciousness of our relationship to the earth and its creatures. Most contemporary Western authors try to fashion the beginnings of the necessary new consciousness. Westerner Gary Snyder, the subject of Kerouac's novel *The Dharma Bums* (1958), writes poetry infused with Native American and Far Eastern thought that sees wilderness as a source of spiritual sustenance, not as a source of maximum profits. Don Berry, who once roomed with Snyder around the time when they were students at Reed College, shares Snyder's outlook. In a remarkable trilogy—*Trask* (1960), *Moontrap* (1962), and *To Build a Ship* (1963)—Berry probes the psychological forces that impelled whites to settle the Oregon Coast in the years from 1848 to 1854.

*Trask* takes for its title character a mountain man who has married and settled near Astoria. Stirred by a restless desire to possess new lands, he sets out with two Native American guides to chart a route to Murderer's Harbor, where he hopes to establish a new settlement. As Glen A. Love has noted, a brief plot summary makes *Trask* sound similar to formula Westerns. But like other Western authors (most notably Fergusson, Fisher, Guthrie, Manfred, and, most recently, Bill Hotchkiss) who have written novels about the mountain men, Berry sees the natural world as sacred and he deplores the forces within us that have driven us to attack and destroy so much of that world. Trask's journey goes beyond the pioneering of a Natty Bumppo, because Trask's experiences force him to explore his own psyche. Indeed, the novel's ambiguous ending starts with Trask's vision quest, or Searching—terms for the Native American rites of passage to spiritual awareness. Because *Trask* captures so vividly the process of enlightenment, it belongs, as Love says, "among the small group of works by which Northwest literature will be enduringly defined."

That small group of works also includes Ken Kesey's *One Flew Over the Cuckoo's Nest* (1962). Set in an Oregon insane asylum and narrated by an escaped inmate (an Indian named Chief "Broom" Bromden), Kesey's novel exposes the repressive institutions of modern industrial societies that demand sterile conformity. Into a ward of "loonies" comes Randall Patrick McMurphy, a convict who has opted for a stretch in the asylum rather than a term of hard labor at the state prison farm. When McMurphy notices how cowed and hopeless his fellow inmates are, he tries to revivify them. Frustrated when his efforts are opposed by Big Nurse Ratched, who represents and defends the "Combine" (the Establishment), McMurphy tries to strangle and rape her. His violent attack gives her an excuse to have him lobotomized. Although she successfully destroys his mind, his free spirit lives on in Chief Bromden, who in mercy kills what is left of McMurphy and then escapes from the asylum.

In the first half of *Cuckoo's Nest,* McMurphy swaggers onto the scene like a hero from a Hollywood Western and spins yarns like a frontier rip-tail-roarer. His weapon against Big Nurse and the Combine initially is nothing more nor less than a laughter that seems to burst forth inexhaustively from his boundless energy. His initials, R.P.M., which in machinery stand for "revolutions per minute," reveal his quintessential Westernness, for his free spirit comes from the sense of place that in the West is a sense of motion. But by novel's end McMurphy has been transformed from a confidence man into a cowboy Christ who willingly sacrifices himself for the good of others. He is, as Jerome Klinkowitz has observed, "the first fictional hero to practice that key strategy of sixties leadership: *raising the consciousness of the people,*" and he also invents "a new way of perceiving reality, which is nothing less than a new reality itself." And who is the Ishmael of Kesey's modern *Moby-Dick?* Significantly, a Native American who has learned from McMurphy that the Combine will never capture his spirit if he tries McMurphy's new way of perceiving reality.

During the 1960s, novelists outside the American West also used the Western *donnée* to show the power of language to shape reality. A native New Yorker, E. L. Doctorow wrote *Welcome to Hard Times* (1960) after reading screenplays of Westerns for CBS Television and Columbia Pictures. The novel consists of a chronicle written by a dying man who has witnessed the destruction and then the rebuilding of a settlement, only to see it destroyed again. Doctorow undercuts or inverts elements of the traditional Western in order to create a novelistic version of the Theater of Cruelty, twentieth-century plays intended to exorcise erotic cruelty by depicting it in virtually religious rites.

Another Easterner, Thomas Berger, composed a novel of the West after reading some seventy books of Western autobiography, history, and anthropology. But *Little Big Man* (1964) has a narrative structure more complex than that of Doctorow's novel, for Berger uses the framing device characteristic of the humorous tall tales of the Old

Southwest. The main narrator, Jack Crabb, tells us that after Native Americans had killed his pioneer father, they raised Jack. Crabb says he reentered white society and then returned to the Indians, a cultural seesawing repeated throughout the novel. Most amazingly, Crabb says he rode with Custer at the Little Big Horn and survived to the overripe age of 111 to tell his tale.

Clearly, Crabb's literary lineage starts with Natty Bumppo, but with a twist explained by Brooks Landon: "Jack's *achievements* are Cheyenne, his *aspirations* are white, and therein lies a kind of captivity against which his shiftiness has no power." However trapped by a language that will not release him from his white cultural bias, "Jack Crabb," according to French critic Daniel Royot, "is no radical dropout keeping *Without Marx or Jesus* in his pocket, but an American picaro teasing his reader out of conformity and confirming once more America's saving grace which is to laugh at herself."

Yet no one laughs at two of the "nonfiction novels" set in the West: Truman Capote's *In Cold Blood* (1966) and Norman Mailer's *The Executioner's Song* (1979, Pulitzer Prize). One of the murderers in Capote's book has a Native American mother, and parts of *In Cold Blood* remind one of a bloodcurdling Indian captivity narrative. Likewise, Mailer's "true-life novel" overflows with authentic details of contemporary Mormon life, but the structure of *The Executioner's Song* resembles that of a Bret Harte story in which a bloody killer eventually reveals a heart of gold. Just as romanticized but more concise, Mailer's earlier novel *Why Are We in Vietnam?* (1967) takes us bear-hunting in Alaska.

Other Eastern novelists have also used the West as a setting for one or two of their novels. Bernard Malamud based *A New Life* (1961) on his experiences as a professor at Oregon State University, and place plays a role in that novel, though mostly as a target for Malamud's satire. John Updike sets *A Month of Sundays* (1975) and *S.* (1988) in the West, mainly to shock his protagonists into serious reflection on their Eastern lives.

Former Easterners who have moved west have had greater success in writing novels of the West. The Western works of Thomas McGuane, Richard Ford, and John Nichols have generally improved as these writers have come to a deeper understanding of their adopted region. See especially McGuane's *Keep the Change* (1989), Ford's *Wildfire* (1990), and Nichols's *American Blood* (1989), a powerful example of a novelistic Theater of Cruelty.

Before his apparent suicide, Richard Brautigan had lived near McGuane in Montana, although Brautigan had also taken to spending part of each year in Japan. Born and raised in the Northwest, Brautigan moved to San Francisco in the mid-1950s when the Beat movement was under way. He first found print as a poet, and some critics argue that his masterpiece, *Trout Fishing in America* (1967), should be read not as a novel but as a serial poem like those of Jack Spicer, Brautigan's friend and mentor. Although knowing Spicer's work can help a reader to understand Brautigan, *Trout Fishing* should be classified as a novel, for its author intended it to be one, as he indicated when he published "The Lost Chapters of *Trout Fishing in America*" in *Esquire* (October 1970).

Allusions abound in *Trout Fishing*, providing necessary clues to the novel's meaning. The first chapter, for example, alludes to Benjamin Franklin's *Autobiography*, to Tom and Jerry cartoons, to Dante's *Paradiso*, and to Franz Kafka's *Amerika*. This hodgepodge of allusions alerts the reader to the book's mixture of wit, humor, irony, idealism, and angst.

Other novels by Brautigan fall short of his achievement in *Trout Fishing*, although *The Hawkline Monster* (1974), *The Tokyo-Montana Express* (1980), and *So the Wind Won't Blow It All Away* (1982) also provide an interesting mix of postmodernism with a Western sensibility. No one has yet equaled *Trout Fishing*, although Ishmael Reed's *Yellow Back Radio Broke-Down* (1969), Tom Robbins's *Even Cowgirls Get the Blues* (1976), Gino Sky's *Appaloosa Rising* (1980), and Gerald Locklin's *The Case of the Missing Blue Volkswagen* (1984) join Brautigan's best to form what half a century ago would have seemed an unlikely tradition: Menippean satire of the West.

Fifty years ago the West did have the novels of Dashiell Hammett. His *The Maltese Falcon* (1930), James M. Cain's *The Postman Always Rings Twice* (1934), Horace McCoy's *They Shoot Horses, Don't They?* (1935), and Raymond Chandler's *The Big Sleep* (1939) explored the seamy side of urban life. Yet such tough guy writers omitted truly shocking details of crime, sex, drugs, and violence.

Now such details can be found in John Rechy's *City of Night* (1963) and Charles Bukowski's *Ham on Rye* (1982). In the late twentieth century, parts of some Western cities have become more violent and dangerous than the old frontier.

The novel of Los Angeles already constituted a subgenre of American fiction when Joan Didion's *Play It as It Lays* appeared in 1970. The novelists who created that subgenre rank among the most important of the early twentieth century. Besides the tough guy and detective writers, they include F. Scott Fitzgerald, John O'Hara, Nathanael West, and Budd Schulberg. To that list must be added British exiles Aldous Huxley, Christopher Isherwood, and Evelyn Waugh. As these names indicate, "any discussion of the Los Angeles novel must begin with the observation that it is chiefly the work of the outsider—if not the tourist, then the newcomer." David Fine, who makes that observation in his introduction to a collection of critical essays titled *Los Angeles in Fiction* (1984), also notes that "the displacement experienced by the writers fostered a way of writing about the region that differed qualitatively from the way other regions have been written about."

Most Los Angeles novels satirize Hollywood and southern California, pointing to the wasteland that lies behind the Disneyland facade. On one level, *Play It as It Lays* tells a story of the real heartbreak and despair in such a wasteland; but "at another level," as Mark Royden Winchell says, "Didion seems to be writing a parody of the novel of despair." Didion's husband, John Gregory Dunne, is a transplanted Easterner whose *True Confessions* (1977) and *Dutch Shea, Jr.* (1982) match Didion's satirization of California life. Many of Didion and Dunne's contemporaries—Alison Lurie, Thomas Pynchon, and Robert Stone, to name a few—have also written Los Angeles novels.

Wallace Stegner's *Angle of Repose* (1971, Pulitzer Prize) not only debunks Hollywood's myth of the West but also links past to present and explores universal themes such as integrity and love. The first-person narrator, Lyman Ward, has suffered both the loss of a leg from a crippling bone disease and the desertion of his wife, who has run off with the bone surgeon. A retired history professor, Lyman retreats to his grandparents' old home in Grass Valley, California. There, to keep his son from moving him to a nursing home, Lyman proves his mental fitness by researching his grandparents' papers and writing a book about them. Stegner created the portrait of Lyman's grandparents by using as models an actual nineteenth-century Western novelist, Mary Hallock Foote, and her husband Arthur. In fact, up until the last third of the novel, so closely does Stegner recreate the details of the Footes' lives that he quotes and paraphrases passages from Mary's letters and novels. Between chapters of Lyman's biography of his grandparents, Stegner dramatizes Lyman's inner struggle to overcome bitterness and loneliness, along with his caustic reaction to the counterculture of the 1960s.

Appearing predisposed to side with his grandmother, Lyman eventually assumes the worst about her and imagines his grandfather to have been a kind of demigod like the hero of *The Virginian*. Under his professorial demeanor, Lyman tries to conceal from himself his view of women as ultimately weak and faithless. He also tries to hold on to his self-image as blameless victim, but a shocking nightmare forces him to consider a reconciliation with his ex-wife.

Stegner's use of the nightmare is a brilliant and significant tour de force. He initially presents the nightmare as if it were an actual event. Such a dream sequence with its Freudian implications seems similar to a passage from a modernist novel, but Stegner has argued that "the kind of western writer who writes modern[ist] literature immediately abdicates as a Westerner." In appropriating a modernist technique, however, Stegner should be seen not as abdicating his regional identity but as taking a necessary step toward the recognition of a conflict concealed in the Western psyche.

In that conflict, which is both personal and social, desire clashes with responsibility. Lyman's nightmare reveals the conflict and parallels the scene of infidelity that he imagines must have happened if his grandmother was guilty of adultery. He admits there is no proof of her guilt, but he imagines the infidelity as taking place during the summer of 1890. A watershed date in Western history, 1890 marked not only the official closing of the frontier but also what Stegner has said, in his "Wilderness Letter," was the beginning of a decline in American optimism and idealism. In short, the forces at war within Lyman Ward's psyche are the same ones battling within the minds of most other Americans, especially those in the West.

Like Western American literature in general, as Forrest Robinson has described it, *Angle of Repose* is "characteristically American in its often complex, if frequently indirect, negotiations of difficult questions of value." Recognized as a classic novel of the West and a masterpiece of American fiction, *Angle of Repose* appeared during the height of the Vietnam War. Many Westerners saw in that war parallels with our westering experience, marked as it was by our nearly genocidal treatment of Native Americans and by our oppression and exploitation of minorities and women, all of which are directly or indirectly present in Stegner's benchmark novel.

By the early 1970s, women and minorities increasingly spoke for themselves. Although Mexican Americans have a literary tradition that goes back to the colonial era, the first Chicano novel to gain much attention from Anglos—José Antonio Villarreal's *Pocho*—did not appear until 1959. Over the next two decades other writers helped to create a new subgenre: the Chicano novel. Portraits of migrant farmworkers or of barrio residents appear in Floyd Salas's *Tattoo the Wicked Cross* (1967), Richard Vasquez's *Chicano* (1969), Raymond Barrio's *The Plum Plum Pickers* (1969), and Tomás Rivera's *"... y no se lo tragó la tierra"* (1971).

Sometimes militant in espousing the cause of *la Raza* ("the people"), the Chicano novel helped inform Anglos about Mexican American culture at the same time that it instilled pride in and raised the consciousness of Chicanos. Rudolfo A. Anaya's *Bless Me, Ultima* (1972) does all that and more, and its use of some Spanish words and of narrative passages derived from Chicano *cuentos* and *corridos* shows readers the need for cultural relativism. Arturo Islas's *The Rain God* (1984) also uses the techniques employed by Anaya; and both novelists probe the tensions and divisions within the Mexican American family. Narrated from a woman's point of view, Lucha Corpi's *Delia's Song* (1989) tells the story of a Chicana who has to struggle against both her male-dominated family and the dominant Anglo culture in order to create her own identity.

Like Chicanos, Native Americans have had to struggle against an Anglo culture that tried to deny them a separate sense of identity. They have long been among those most alienated by modern urban life; nevertheless, extreme poverty and anomie have given members of many tribes no choice but to leave reservations for the cities. Parts of N. Scott Momaday's *House Made of Dawn* (1968, Pulitzer Prize) take place in a Los Angeles that is representative of most urban centers. Not only Native Americans suffer from isolation in such an environment: one of Momaday's Euro-American characters "had been in Los Angeles four years, and in all that time she had not talked to anyone. . . . No one knew what she thought or felt or who she was." Although she meets Abel, the Indian protagonist, and their friendship seems to promise an end to their isolation, a brutal beating by a policeman sends Abel back to the Indian society from which he was outcast.

In his summary of *House Made of Dawn,* Momaday identifies its sociological and psychological levels of meaning:

The novel is about an Indian who returns from World War II and finds that he cannot recover his tribal identity; nor can he escape the cultural context in which he grew up. He is torn, as they say, between two worlds, neither of which he can enter and be a whole man. The story is that of his struggle to survive on the horns of a real and tragic dilemma in contemporary society.

The Indian world of Abel's childhood provides some of the other levels of meaning. A circular structure, reflective of the Native American's sense of time as cyclical, encloses the narrative units arranged in Euro-American linear chronology; and Indian mythology and ceremony influence Abel and other characters. Like other literary Western novels, *House Made of Dawn* uses irony to shape a new perception of reality. Momaday's irony, however, surpasses that of his contemporaries, for he creates a character who preaches an ironic sermon that includes verbatim passages from *The Way to Rainy Mountain* (1969), Momaday's moving account of the beliefs of his Kiowa ancestors.

Added to that complex self-reference is an even more provocative passage on language:

In the white man's world, language, too—and the way in which the white man thinks of it—has undergone a process of change. The white man takes such things as words and literatures for granted, as indeed he must, for nothing in his world is so commonplace. On every side of him there are words by the millions. . . . He has diluted and multiplied the Word, and words have begun to close in upon him. He is sated and insensitive; his regard for language—for the Word itself—as an instrument of creation has diminished nearly to the point of no return. It may be that he will perish by the Word.

Can we recapture the sacred power of language? Momaday offers no simple solution, offers instead in a variety of genres an oeuvre that weaves strands from the oral tradition of his ancestors into the fabric of contemporary literature. Although Momaday is not the first Native American novelist—precursors include Mourning Dove (Humishu-ma), John Joseph Mathews, and D'Arcy McNickle—*House Made of Dawn* certainly inspired the Native American Renaissance.

In 1970s novels about Native Americans, alternatives to the miseries of reservation life and urban alienation seem possible, if at all, only after great suffering. Of Anglos who wrote about Native Americans after *House Made of Dawn,* historical novelists Oakley Hall and Douglas C. Jones treated them sympathetically. Dee Brown had used the Native Americans' own words in *Bury My Heart at Wounded Knee* (1970), his nonfiction account of the Old West's Indian wars; but his novel *Creek Mary's Blood* (1980) is not as successful at presenting the Native American point of view. Thomas Sanchez's *Rabbit Boss* (1973) shows the weaknesses of the Washo Indians and thereby, according to Sanford E. Marovitz, "implies that with similar myopia America on the whole has abandoned its heritage and promise." Frederick Manfred delighted readers with *The Manly-Hearted Woman* (1975), a hilarious mock epic that is, in Robert C. Wright's words, "essentially religious in tone," providing "a kind of bible explaining the community life and mystical religion of the Indians."

Foremost among contemporary Anglo interpreters of Native American life is Tony Hillerman, whose detective novels offer more than popular conventions. Born in Oklahoma, Hillerman moved to New Mexico in 1952 and wrote his first Navajo police procedural novel, *The Blessing Way,* in 1970. He has since written almost a dozen more detective novels, all with Navajos as protagonists. Hillerman's early reading of Arthur W. Upfield's Australian detective stories undoubtedly heightened his sensitivity to cultural differences, a sensitivity reflected in his fictional treatment of Native American cultures. In his latest novels—*A Thief of Time* (1988), *Talking God* (1989), and *Coyote Waits* (1990)—Hillerman has focused increasingly on the influence of the past. Of the rich texture of his recent novels, Fred Erisman says: "Weaving myths of the past and problems of the present into police procedural novels, he dramatizes the intricate intermingling of cultures that shapes the region's life." In enriching the mystery novel beyond the popular formula, many other contemporary Western novelists have joined Hillerman. Eminent among these are James Crumley, Ridley Pearson, and M. K. Wren (Martha Kay Renfroe).

Among 1970s novels by Native Americans, James Welch's masterpiece, *Winter in the Blood* (1973), has comic elements but it also depicts Montana's reservation life with its drinking, fighting, death, pain of loss, and solitude. Although it deals with experiences so bleak and painful, "*Winter in the Blood* challenges us," Stephen Tatum says, "to recognize how experience is defined, like language, as a system of relations of difference, and to recognize that the ambiguities, paradoxes, and contradictions inherent in both desire and language undo the promise of closure and the potential solace of transparent, self-evident, and final meanings."

When Leslie Marmon Silko's *Ceremony* (1977) appeared four years after *Winter in the Blood,* those two novels along with Momaday's *House Made of Dawn* soon came to be viewed as the trio that established the renaissance of Native American literature, one of the most notable developments in the recent history of the American novel. Like Welch, Silko shows the poverty, drinking, violence, and heartache endemic on many reservations. Like Momaday, she creates a mixed-blood protagonist psychologically and emotionally wounded by his combat experience in World War II. Restored to sanity by native stories and ceremonies, Tayo, the combat veteran, realizes that "he was not crazy; he had never been crazy. He had only seen and heard the world as it always was: no boundaries, only transitions through all distances and time."

Referring to Silko's use of native tradition to restore Tayo to harmony, Italian critic Laura Coltelli says: "Myth and reality have a skillfully constructed interdependence and they interact in Silko's narrative very much in the same way as the oral transmission and the written act of storytelling: they form complementary, dynamic, dialogical connections which are a meeting ground for past and present, oral performance and fiction strategies, Western [European] aesthetics and Native mythopoesis, engaging the reader and the critic in a new way of reading and listening."

Starting in the late 1970s, many new authors contributed to the

Native American Renaissance inaugurated by Momaday and sustained by Welch and Silko. Gerald Vizenor's *Darkness in Saint Louis Bearheart* (1978) employs irony in a self-reflexive novel that Paula Gunn Allen has said is "one of the more adventurous excursions of modern Indian fiction writers into bicultural prose," an assessment that applies as well to her own novel, *The Woman Who Owned the Shadows* (1983). The new writers also include a pair whose novels have been highly praised by reviewers and critics and who happen to be husband and wife: Michael Dorris and Louise Erdrich. Both create portraits of twentieth-century Native Americans, Dorris in *A Yellow Raft in Blue Water* (1987), Erdrich in *Love Medicine* (1984), *The Beet Queen* (1986), and *Tracks* (1988). To these achievements have been added more works by the initiators of the renaissance. Silko has published a collection of stories and poems titled *Storyteller* (1981), and Momaday a second novel, *The Ancient Child* (1989). But the most remarkable of the first-rate Native American novels of the 1980s is James Welch's *Fools Crow* (1986).

The story of a band of Blackfeet Indians in 1870, *Fools Crow* recounts the exploits of eighteen-year-old White Man's Dog as he joins a war party, receives his new name (Fools Crow), marries, and tries to help his people when they encounter the whites and are decimated by a smallpox epidemic. Welch's historical novel gives us a rich portrait of Native American life on the eve of its devastation by the encroaching Euro-American civilization. Moreover, Fools Crow has visions in which animals speak to him, and so skillfully does Welch weave these episodes into the narrative that the effect surpasses the achievement of Latin American "magic realism," a novelistic form of surrealism. Welch's "magic realism" brings us so much closer to understanding Native American culture that his characters seem neither wild nor noble savages but believable human beings. In its fusion of the novel and Native American myth, *Fools Crow* satisfies the desire for a full, entertaining, and substantial narrative.

Like Native Americans and Chicanos in the late 1960s, women began expressing their concerns in the novel. In the process, they found many precursors. Feminists rediscovered Western women novelists such as California's Gertrude Atherton, Texas's Dorothy Scarborough, Idaho's Carol Ryrie Brink, Montana's Dorothy Johnson, Minnesota's Meridel Le Sueur, Nebraska's Mari Sandoz, Utah's Virginia Sorensen, Colorado's Jean Stafford, and Iowa's Ruth Suckow. Long ignored or marginalized, these authors faced formidable obstacles in their efforts to create a women's fiction, obstacles that are movingly described in Tillie Olsen's *Silences* (1978), a collection of essays and lectures. Olsen's own novel, *Yonnondio* (1974), stands as a classic example of the tradition she describes.

Begun in 1932, the novel could not be completed because Olsen lacked the necessary time and support. In the 1970s she chose to publish the unfinished manuscript from the thirties "to tell what might have been, and never will be now." Told from a woman's point of view, *Yonnondio* depicts Western life during the Great Depression; and along with Steinbeck's *The Grapes of Wrath* and Frederick Manfred's *The Golden Bowl,* it helps convey the raw emotion of that era's human misery. Olsen's critique of capitalism in the American West also bears some resemblance to the earlier social protest novels of Upton Sinclair, Robert Cantwell, and James Stevens.

Marilynne Robinson's *Housekeeping* (1981) is not a protest novel, but it ranks among the best works of contemporary women's fiction. The novel requires a new way of reading and listening, for it reshapes American literary tradition by presenting a female protagonist, Ruth, who lights out for the territory with the same autonomy and self-reliance usually reserved for male characters such as Cooper's Natty Bumppo, Twain's Huck Finn, and the eponymous hero of Jack Schaefer's *Shane* (1949). Not only does *Housekeeping* give to a woman the heroic role, but it also sustains a poetic lyricism within the novel's prose format, as though Emily Dickinson had been reborn a north Idaho novelist. With the kind of self-reliant spirit advocated by Dickinson and Emerson, Robinson's Ruth achieves an authentic selfhood but at the same time binds herself, in love, to her aunt Sylvie.

After the two women attempt to burn their family's home, they begin a life of riding the rails as transients. "The frontier in this contemporary novel is not," Martha Ravits says, "a geographic or historic construct but the urge to move beyond conventional social patterns, beyond the dichotomy of urban and rural experience, beyond domestic concerns and physical boundaries into metaphysics." Viewed from the metaphysics to which *Housekeeping* transports us, buildings and social conventions seem less important than relationships forged from love.

Of great importance to many Westerners is wilderness, and efforts to save the remaining wilderness gave rise to a new form of protest in the West of the 1970s: environmental activism. Environmentalists found a spokesman in Edward Abbey. He had written several Western novels at the start of his career—*Jonathan Troy* (1954) and *The Brave Cowboy* (1956)—but by the early 1970s he was best known for *Desert Solitaire* (1968), usually classified as nature writing. Abbey scholar Ann Ronald has argued, however, that "in many ways *Desert Solitaire* is more a work of fiction than of nonfiction"; and she maintains that Abbey designed each of his major books "not like a romantic Western but like a formal romance."

However classified, Abbey's *The Monkey Wrench Gang* (1975) changed the course of Western American history. A "mock-heroic" late twentieth-century picaresque tale that borrows some elements from the popular Western, *The Monkey Wrench Gang* recounts the exploits of four characters: Doc Sarvis, an Albuquerque surgeon; Bonnie Abbzug, his receptionist; Seldom Seen Smith, a jack Mormon river-runner; and George Washington Hayduke, an ex-Green Beret. Uniting to stop the destruction of the Western environment, this unlikely quartet uses *ecotage,* the sabotage of any machine that damages ecology. The four ecological anarchists do nothing that would endanger human life, but they use any other form of outlawry that will help them save the natural world. Often hilarious, sometimes ironic, occasionally philosophic, *The Monkey Wrench Gang* divided opinion among those in the West's environmental groups and inspired a new movement that calls itself Earth First!

Abbey and other nature writers would continue to warn about imminent ecocide, and Abbey gave *The Monkey Wrench Gang* a sequel: *Hayduke Lives* (1989). Despite its flaws, which are "those of exuberance," *The Monkey Wrench Gang* remains the classic environmental protection novel—in Ronald's words, "a rollicking testimony to non-violent violence." Most other Western novelists have also been outspoken in opposing the destruction of the environment, and some of them have been especially ingenious in imagining alternatives to our present ecocidal course, most notably Ernest Callenbach with *Ecotopia* (1976) and Ursula Le Guin with *Always Coming Home* (1984).

While Abbey and other novelists imagined alternatives to our ruinous lifestyle, Larry McMurtry focused on the Western myth's destructive effects on personal relationships. Acclaimed for his early novels—*Horseman, Pass By* (1961), *Leaving Cheyenne* (1963), and *The Last Picture Show* (1966)—McMurtry expressed his ambivalence about rural and small-town Texas, hating its crudity, violence, and bigotry, wistfully eulogizing the free spirit and self-reliance of the cowboys who had been crude, violent, and bigoted. With *Moving On* (1970), *All My Friends Are Going to Be Strangers* (1972), and *Terms of Endearment* (1978), McMurtry created the "urban Western," a novel that reveals the hollowness at the core of the late twentieth-century urban West.

As if seeking the very heart of urban darkness, McMurtry picked Hollywood, Washington, D.C., and Las Vegas as the respective locations for his next three novels—*Somebody's Darling* (1978), *Cadillac Jack* (1982), and *The Desert Rose* (1983). Although his novels of the 1970s and early 1980s show McMurtry experimenting with different points of view and with varying levels of realism, his next work established him as one of the masters of American fiction.

*Lonesome Dove* (1985, Pulitzer Prize) not only dominated the best-seller lists for months but was also recognized as "a masterpiece in the genre of trail-driving novels," as Jane Nelson put it. As long and sprawling as a real trail drive, *Lonesome Dove* keeps us interested by making us care about the two principal characters: Woodrow Call and Augustus McCrae. Former Texas Rangers, Call and McCrae decide to drive a herd of cattle to Montana, where they plan to claim land and start ranching. They reach their goal, but not without encountering dozens of life-threatening dangers along the way.

McMurtry's description of a nest of snakes attacking a hapless cowboy is one of the most bone-chilling scenes in contemporary fiction. Indeed, so much violence fills the novel that it seems as if McMurtry was trying to drive a stake through the heart of the Hollywood myth that the good guys always rode off unharmed into the sunset. Paradoxically, *Lonesome Dove* resuscitates interest in the Old West by making it more believable. McMurtry's trail drive includes passages of metaphysical questioning and angst as well as scenes of sex and violence—all of which make the novel palatable to late twentieth-century taste. More important, *Lonesome Dove* satisfies the desire for a sustained narrative that creates the illusion of "the real thing."

A complete history of the novel of the West will have to include dozens of other authors who have not achieved fame as great as McMurtry's but who have nevertheless influenced the development of the West's fiction, usually with one or two "small masterpieces." Such a reputation attaches to William Goyen, William Humphrey, and Tom Lea, Texas writers from the generation preceding Mc-Murtry's. Of novels written by McMurtry's contemporaries, Diane Johnson's *The Shadow Knows* (1972) depicts the terror of a victim-ized California woman; Larry Woiwode's *Beyond the Bedroom Wall* (1975) portrays several generations of a North Dakota family; Rob-ert Flynn's *North to Yesterday* (1967) beautifully describes the hu-man comedy of a trail drive; and Charles Portis's *True Grit* (1968) tells with comic genius the story of a frontier lawman and an ado-lescent girl who join forces in their pursuit of justice. Although Mc-Murtry overshadows many of his contemporaries, recent novels by Clay Reynolds, Tom Spanbauer, Douglas Unger, and Norman Zollinger have shown that these writers might eventually match Mc-Murtry's achievement.

In its scrupulous authenticity, *Lonesome Dove* reflects extensive authorial research. By itself, authenticity does not, of course, make a novel first-rate. But when serious novelists make authenticity one of the primary qualities of their art, the basis of fact can help to create the illusion of reality, and the best of such authentic fiction serves not only as satisfying literature but also as a form of history. Many con-temporary Western novelists might be classified as "neorealists," but some of them place an especially high value on authenticity. In John Keeble's *Yellowfish* (1980), the characters reflect on the history of the Chinese in the Old West. Pete Dexter's *Deadwood* (1986) follows Wild Bill Hickock and Calamity Jane in the South Dakota of 1876-78, and Frank Bergon's *Shoshone Mike* (1987) is based on an actual Indian-white conflict in early twentieth-century Nevada. Research into later twentieth-century Western history enriches Craig Lesley's *Winterkill* (1984), about a Northwest Indian rodeo contestant, and also Levi Peterson's *The Backslider* (1986), about a Mormon cowboy's struggles with desires of the flesh. Women have also enhanced their novels by a similar dedication to authenticity. Gretel Ehrlich's *Heart Mountain* (1988) depicts a Wyoming-Montana relocation camp that held Japanese Americans during World War II; and Molly Gloss's *The Jump-Off Creek* (1989) portrays a single woman homesteader in the Oregon mountains during the 1890s.

Of all the Western neorealists, Ivan Doig has seemed the most likely to become heir-apparent to Wallace Stegner. *This House of Sky* (1978), Doig's memoir about growing up in Montana, was nominated for a National Book Award and is reminiscent of Stegner's *Big Rock Candy Mountain* and *Wolf Willow*. Doig's Montana trilogy— *English Creek* (1984), *Dancing at the Rascal Fair* (1987), and *Ride with Me, Mariah Montana* (1990)—recasts in fiction his memories of his family, his childhood, and his home place. If the late Richard Hugo was right when he said that "the place triggers the mind to create the place," then what sort of place emerges from the work of Ivan Doig? No Eden, Doig's Montana can almost match the violence of McMurtry's Texas. But Doig's characters, although no angels, seem generally less hopeless or hollow than McMurtry's. Strong sentimentality marks Doig's characters and passages of his prose, but the sentiment is genuine and balanced by his account of over a century of unremitting losses. *Ride with Me* not only celebrates Montana's centennial and the West's first post-frontier century, it also articulates the view of most contemporary Western authors that we must change our minds and our lifestyle in order to save the planet.

Most recently, the novel of the West has been significantly enriched by the outstanding first novels of Asian Americans Amy Tan and Maxine Hong Kingston. Asian Americans have lived in the West since the California gold rush of 1849, and their experiences have been those of a minority excluded for decades from landownership and confined to Chinatowns. Their literary tradition has developed in stages similar to those marking the traditions of the region's other minorities. At first, like other minorities, Asians appeared in Anglo literature as stereotypes. Eventually, authors arose from among each ethnic group.

After World War II, Carlos Bulosan's *America Is in the Heart* (1946) depicted Filipino immigrant workers, Toshio Mori's *The Woman from Hiroshima* (1980) told about Japanese American life before World War II, and John Okada's *No-No Boy* (1957) portrayed a Japanese American who refused to be drafted. Tan and Kingston are the first Asian American novelists to achieve great popular and critical acclaim. Tan's *The Joy Luck Club* (1989) consists of related stories and anecdotes told by different female characters who are all united by their Chinese background and by their membership in the same social club.

Usually classified as nonfiction but including many fictional elements, Kingston's *Woman Warrior* (1976) and *China Men* (1980) had earned for her recognition as "America's first major writer of Chinese ancestry." With *Tripmaster Monkey* (1989), Kingston established herself as one of the American West's leading novelists. Naming her 1960s protagonist Wittman Ah Sing (in a witty allusion to that most American of poets, Walt Whitman), Kingston tells the story of a young Chinese American college graduate who refuses to conform. Like Kesey's McMurphy, Wittman first clashes with authority, loses his job, then tries to set up a community within an advanced industrial system that splinters communities. Unlike McMurphy, Wittman has more than his natural intelligence upon which to rely. He also draws upon all he learned as an English major at UC Berkeley and all he knows about China's centuries-old cultural tradition.

During one of the novel's first scenes, Wittman reads out loud to fellow bus passengers, and he then imagines himself starting a tradition of such readings on all public transportation, leading "to a job as a reader riding the railroads throughout the West," regaling passengers with works by John Steinbeck, William Saroyan, Jack Kerouac, Mark Twain, John Muir, Jack London, Wallace Stegner, and John Fante. The world of *Tripmaster Monkey* consists not only of character and place but also of all that the main character reads and thinks. Kingston has said she will write a sequel depicting an older and more mature Wittman, so we may eventually see how the contemporary West looks to an Asian American who has learned from the past, his own as well as humanity's.

A century after the official closing of the frontier in 1890, the novel of the West needs that more mature vision promised by Kingston. Notwithstanding that need, the western part of the United States now has a rich and varied tradition of regional fiction. But because of its great variety, few generalizations can be made about that tradition. For example, Thomas Pynchon's long-awaited fourth novel, *Vineland* (1990), is set in the West, but the characters' minds seem more an amalgam of mass popular myths and stereotypes than individual perspectives shaped by a particular place. But if Lewis Thomas is right in saying that one of the ways by which we rapidly "transform ourselves" is by exchanging "codes disguised as art," it is worth noting that since the 1920s the West's best novelists have encouraged not only cultural relativism, tolerance, and magnanimity but also a deep respect for the earth and other living creatures. Encoded in the art of these Westerners is the message that if we are ever to live in harmony—if we are indeed to survive, if we are to avoid ecocide and nuclear annihilation—we must begin to respond to the novel of the West by transforming ourselves. And we must do so not only as individuals but as a society, whole and complete and with unyielding purpose.

James H. Maguire

# Technology and the Novel

> It is the novelist's business to set down exactly manners and appearances: he must render the show, he must, if the metaphor be permitted, describe precisely the nature of the engine, the position and relation of its wheels. —Ezra Pound, *Patria Mia* (1913)

Engines and wheels were everywhere in Ezra Pound's 1910s, with the automobile ascendant, rail lines ubiquitous, and large-scale images of machinery available even to the most rural of Americans who subscribed to a monthly magazine like *Harper's* or got the Sears, Roebuck catalog. Yet Ezra Pound radically redefined the novel when he invoked the analogy of the machine. In effect, he removed the novel from its lineage in print texts. From the 1700s, as is well known, American writers had allied novels with established genres, including history (for example, James Fenimore Cooper's "Indian history"), moral philosophy (Charles Brockden Brown), romance (Nathaniel Hawthorne), biography (Herman Melville's *Israel Potter* [1855])—all rubrics embedded in the tradition of print.

Invoking the machine, however, Pound disrupted that formulation in ways that invite inquiry. Shuttling the novel to a new rubric, one intended to seize the twentieth-century industrial moment and instate the prose fiction narrative in it, Pound assigned the novel a defamiliarizing relation to culture. He asserted that the novel could perform its traditional function—social disclosure—insofar as it met engineering standards.

Pound's statement, particular to the high modernism of the 1910s, additionally serves to focus the relation of the novel to technology throughout the history of the United States. In fact, his analogy assumes the "long foreground" of machine technology dating from the eighteenth and nineteenth centuries, when industrialism brought into visibility the machines and structures identifiable from their gear wheels, pulleys, belts, pistons, ball bearings, etc., which were displayed to the public on railroad passenger platforms and at expositions and amusement parks, not to mention the numerous woodcuts and etchings of machinery appearing weekly and monthly in the periodical press. But Pound's statement, bonding the novel to contemporary technology per se, also implies the extension of the technological relationship into futurity. It suggests a time line through modernism into the postmodern age of telecommunications, during which the novel has continued to evolve according to technological developments. In this sense, over some three centuries, fictional narrative carries forward—and is carried forward by—a dynamic range of technologies from the American hand ax of Daniel Boone to the computer simulation of the cybernetic age.

Technology, at least since the 1960s, has attracted the attention of students of the American novel, who have recognized opportunities for explication in its very artifactual state, its presence as part of the material culture. In the literary text, technology thus can be seen to function at a base level for verisimilitude, say, when late nineteenth-century New York is materialized by the representation of elevated transit lines (in William Dean Howells's *A Hazard of New Fortunes* [1890]), or when the United States of the 1970s is evoked in the presence of portable TVs (in Mona Simpson's *Anywhere but Here* [1987]). In this way, technology assists in furnishing the fictional world or in establishing shared assumptions between text and reader.

One step up, interpretively speaking, technology has been approached as a sign or symbol representationally revelatory of the culture, for instance, the ax in James Fenimore Cooper's *The Chainbearer* (1845), which exalts "the American axe [which] has made more real and lasting conquests than the sword of any warlike people," or Mark Twain's utilitarian machinery of the contemporary late nineteenth century, say, the armaments and bicycles in *A Connecticut Yankee in King Arthur's Court* (1889). In fiction published one century after *Connecticut Yankee,* it is the electronic technology of television that can be recognized as a central subject matter, for instance, in Meg Wolitzer's *This Is Your Life* (1988), with television in limousine backseats, with wristwatch design like a TV screen, with a picture window-sized television. The dominant figure in Wolitzer is a

TV comedian, just as Twain's protagonist is a factory foreman. For purposes of social criticism, Twain's text exploits the arms factory as a comment on violence, just as Wolitzer's text exploits the TV sitcom to consider familial dysfunction.

Explicating technological signs and symbols in the American novel, scholar-critics have often proceeded to what seems the reasonable next step, namely, discerning the subject position taken toward the particular technology at hand, then generalizing about which attitudes toward technology prevail in the novel and constitute the presumptive views of the author. It might seem possible to say, for instance, that because John Dos Passos portrayed fatigued industrial assembly line workers as "gray shaking husks" and scorned popular, that is, hack, writers as daydream artists "feeding the machine like a girl in a sausage factory shoving hunks of meat into the hopper," then his novels *The Big Money* (1936) and *Three Soldiers* (1921) are antitechnological. Similarly, Melville can apparently be judged as hostile to industrial technology because his narrator, Ishmael, in the "Try-Works" chapter in *Moby-Dick* (1851), comments on the process of rendering whale oil: "the smoke is horrible to inhale," having "an unspeakable, wild Hindoo odor about it, such as may lurk in the vicinity of funereal pyres," then adds that "it smells like the left wing of the day of judgment; it is an argument for the pit." These kinds of local passages can appear to be emblems of the whole, and readers, self-identified as humanists in an adversarial relation to technological values, have understandably inferred an intratextual hostility to technology in the American novel over the past two centuries.

From this late twentieth-century vantage point, however, with cultural studies revealing ways in which technology is but one part of a larger cultural process, it is possible to reconsider the relation of technology to the novel, in part by surveying the ideological role of technology in national narratives dating from the seventeenth century, and in addition by taking Pound's statement as a factual, not a metaphoric, one when considering the relation of fiction to technology of the twentieth century.

Not surprisingly, technology was integral with representations of the New World before it found expression in the American novel. Colonial New England writers had particular millennial motives to privilege technological power in their writings, since they thought it a means of expediting the Christian Millennium. While the Puritan minister Increase Mather was denouncing "vain romances," meaning novels imported into the colonies, his Puritan cohort Edward Johnson, a Massachusetts town clerk and engineer, wrote *The Wonder-Working Providence of Sions Saviour in New-England* (1653), a historical narrative in which the Christian army, called to the New World, prepares for the Second Coming of Christ by carving farms and villages from the North American wilds. Technology — of carpentry, smithing, masonry, oenology, and every branch of artisanry — becomes the means for the development of the millennial New Earth prophesied in the New Testament Book of Revelation.

Narrative in the form of the epic poem continued in the Revolutionary and Early National periods to be invested with technological themes. Joel Barlow's *Vision of Columbus* (1787) and his subsequent revised version, *The Columbiad* (1806), both advanced the idea of an imminent secular millennium achievable via technology. Barlow's envisioned American empire encompasses the North and South American continents united in a vast transportation and communications network of engineers' flood-proofed rivers and canals, and to that end the poet formed a friendship with the inventor Robert Fulton, with whom he planned a collaborative poem, "The Canal: A Poem on the Application of Physical Science to Political Economy." The extant fragment of the uncompleted verse shows the heroic couplet pressed into the service of technological vision ("Canals careering climb your sunburnt hills,/ Vein the green slopes and strow their nurturing rills"). Barlow's narrative of American development is one in which "new engines" will enable limitless moral and material progress.

Texts like Johnson's and Barlow's augured the deployment of technology in prose fiction of the United States because they reveal the presumption that there is a national American story to narrate, and that the national narrative is largely enabled by technological impetus for environmental and sociocultural change.

And the work of Ralph Waldo Emerson so sustained that position that he, too, must be a part of any discussion of technology and the American novel. "Let every man then know his worth, and keep things under his feet. Let him not peep or steal, or skulk up and down with the air of a charity-boy, a bastard, or an interloper, in the world which exists for him"—this in Emerson's "Self-Reliance" (1841).

Emerson's position ramifies directly into the human relation to technology. For of course the relation of the individual to place is of paramount importance when one considers the prerogatives to shape and reshape the world, and to exercise the authority to assign meaning to the acts of formation and reformation of the material environment. The authority to act and to interpret is predicated on possession of self and of place. Emerson identifies the "man in the street [who] finding no worth in himself which corresponds to the force which built a tower . . . feels poor when he looks on [it]," and enjoins that man to "take possession."

In Emerson's view, the imagination in America is already fully participant in these very historical processes. In "The Young American" (1844), Emerson talks about "improvements" in America, waxing warm about the new America of internal improvements (surveying, planting, building the railroad, farming, etc.). Emerson's America is asserting itself "to the imagination of her children." Some of the statements in this essay are most familiar in Emerson, for example, "Railroad iron is a magician's rod" and "The land is the appointed remedy for whatever is false and fantastic in our culture." He writes, "This rage of road building is beneficent for America . . . not only is distance annihilated, but when, as now, the locomotive and the steamboat, like enormous shuttles, shoot every day across the thousand various threads of national descent and employment, and bind them fast in one web, an hourly assimilation goes forward."

Emerson, it is true, dismissed the Etzlers, as he called them, meaning the technocratic utopians like the German-born Johann A. Etzler, who in 1842 had published the first part of his *The Paradise within the Reach of All Men, without Labour, by the Powers of Nature and Machinery*, a text Henry David Thoreau criticized for its materialism and neglect of metaphysics. And yet, from the late twentieth-century vantage point, Emerson's position can be seen as that of the white imperialist, and self-evidently dangerous with its dual assurances of power and innocence. Technological modernization is open solely to white men as a birthright, virtually as a mandate insulated against error or any kind of transgressive act. "Every line of history inspires a confidence that we shall not go far wrong," said Emerson, "that things mend." In affirming the progressive "hourly assimilation," Emerson does give credence to the intrinsic importance of the technological development of the North American continent in ways that ramify into the novel. He goes on, "I hasten to speak of the utility of these improvements for creating an American sentiment. . . . railroad iron is a magician's rod, in its power to evoke the sleeping energies of land and water," and he praises engineering, architecture, and scientific agriculture.

Emerson thus continues and reaffirms American technology in the tradition established in the Colonial and Early Republican eras. Assuming the white American male to be the center of the universe, he celebrates the forces that would, in the twentieth century, become those of modernism. Emerson, in whom transcendentalism means the transcendence of history, nonetheless marks and legitimates the very civilizing processes that would appear in the two American novels most closely associated with technology, Mark Twain's *A Connecticut Yankee in King Arthur's Court* and Edward Bellamy's *Looking Backward, 2000–1887* (1888). The railways and telegraph, telephone, bicycles, efficient factories, together with the versatility and resourcefulness and centrality of the engineer (whether Twain's Hank Morgan or Bellamy's unnamed research-and-development group)— these are put into place by Emerson precisely because he presumed that the young American possessed the continent. "Nature is the noblest engineer," he wrote, but the young American participates in nature, embodies it—and we remember Emerson's bitter lamentation about Henry David Thoreau, that he led a berry-picking party when he could have undertaken engineering for all America.

As for historical process, "America is the country of the future," proclaims Emerson, and the young (male) American participates in that destined future via democratizing trade, innovative governmental forms, and utilitarian reformation of the continental environment. The utilitarian reform is subsumed under the reassuring rubric of destiny. It is true that Emerson, as scholarship has shown, favors the pastoral ideal for American life. He complains that cities "drain the country of the best part of its population," and urges the formation of gardens over the entire North American continent. But the pastoralizing process is to be accomplished by ingenuity and the technology it manifests. In Emerson, there is no fundamental antagonism between machine and garden. On the contrary, the machine is requisite to the garden. And the machine, which would become central to modernism, is privileged as an integral part of the vivified imagination.

This brief survey argues the need to reevaluate the ways in which technology has been understood in the literary tradition. The interpretation of the representation of machinery cannot confine itself to binary divisions *for* or *against* technology. Ideologically, it is the case that until the turn of the twentieth century, roughly the point at which Pound called the novel a machine, technology was deployed as a means by which to measure national aspirations and anxieties. Through the nineteenth century, machinery was present in the novel to test and measure sociocultural national status, especially in the realm of the ineffable, including such abstract ideals as liberty, justice, equality. Within the text, technology was the heuristic means by which to investigate the degree to which the nation was moving toward these ideals or regressing into such retrograde states as greed, violence, anarchy. Thus the Cooper who celebrated the hand ax as the tool of civilization also loathed the gun that was fired skyward, in *Home as Found* (1838), to decimate the pigeon flocks for a townspeople's momentary novelty. And the railroad in the corporate-capitalist era of Frank Norris's *The Octopus* (1901) becomes, not a transit system, but a plutocratic-oligarchic "ironhearted monster ... its entrails gorged with the lifeblood of an entire commonwealth," while the mechanized meatpacking plant of Upton Sinclair's *The Jungle* (1906) proves so dangerous to its immigrant workers that it is represented as an industrial-age inferno. These pejorative representations of technology really indict the nation for heedlessness, squandering of resources, greed, indifference, and cruelty. They become quotidian symbols indicating sociocommunal failure.

It is the polar possibilities of technological utopianism and dystopianism, accordingly, that would recur virtually obsessively in nineteenth-century American novels. The social anxiety about human shortcomings haunts the novel of dystopia, while the potential for the attainment of social and national ideals proves irresistible to the utopian. At the former extreme lie such titles as P. W. Dooner's *Last Days of the Republic* (1880), *The Fall of the Great Republic* (1885),

by Sir Henry Standish Coverdale (a pseudonym), and Ignatius Donnelly's *Caesar's Column* (1889), a fascist technological nightmare of
advanced weaponry turned against the American populace as a small
band struggle for survival.

In this sense, *A Connecticut Yankee in King Arthur's Court* is also
a dystopian text, and one worth review here precisely because it is the
American novel most prominently associated with technology. Readers initially encounter the humor of anachronism as Mark Twain
thrusts Hank Morgan, his practical, technologically sophisticated late
nineteenth-century Yankee, into a twelfth-century Arthurian England
mired in superstition (including that of the Church) and frozen in
aristocratic hierarchy. We cheer as the Yankee engineers a new society based on technological efficiency and democratic values—then
experience the anguish of the Church-State vendetta against Hank
just at the point at which he is distracted, preoccupied, along with his
wife, by the grave illness of his baby, Hello-Central (named, technologically, for a telephone exchange), whom, on doctors' advice, Hank
and wife Sandy have taken to France, hoping that the better climate
will "coax her back to health and strength again." But from the
sickbed watch, the Morgans reenter the world only to find Hank's
technocracy in shambles: the entire nation under a papal interdict, an
ecclesiastical death sentence on his head. King Arthur is dead, the
queen in a convent after a horrible internecine war. "Our navy had
suddenly and mysteriously disappeared! Also just as suddenly and as
mysteriously, the railway and telegraph and telephone service ceased,
the men all deserted, poles were cut down, the Church laid a ban
upon the electric light!" Hank's protégé, Clarence, has recruited fifty-
two loyalist boys, and thereupon Hank and Clarence make their
plans for the war of modern technology against the benighted, this
the horrific, climactic Battle of the Sand-Belt.

It seems altogether inevitable, this rush to technological armageddon. In a few strokes, Mark Twain has demolished the Yankee's
England and, as if by predetermination, moved him into the rationalized madness and obsession with mechanized warfare and mega-
deaths. The passages of text that move us from Hank's departure
from wife and baby into war plans with Gatling guns and mass electrocution seem, in fact, so seamless and inevitable, so much predes-
tined (especially as readers begin to graph Hank's hankerings for

power and his violent impulses), so much a *given* in the story that one scarcely thinks to ask, Why not go back to France? Why not return, that is, to Sandy and the baby?—and therefore, on Twain's part, reclaim and reaffirm the most deeply felt and recurrently reinscribed values in the novel. For scenes of separated lovers and sundered families recur throughout *A Connecticut Yankee* and form its emotional center. The injustice of Arthurian England is personalized as injustice to human beings in their bonds of kinship and domesticity. The model of and the ideal for human relationships in the novel are family bonds of love and enduring devotion, emphatically affirmed whenever threatened by mortal illness and the vagaries of politics and economics.

This ideal of familial love, moreover, has come to Hank Morgan in his marriage and fatherhood, as he tells us in recounting the very sequence of events that separates him from his wife and baby. Sandy is "a flawless wife and mother. . . . a prize." Hank says, "I became her worshipper; and ours was the dearest and perfectest comradeship that ever was. People talk about beautiful friendships between two persons of the same sex. What is the best of that sort, as compared with the friendship of man and wife, where the best impulses and highest ideals of both are the same?"

Why not, then, return to France, seeing the shambles in England? (For Hank has realized that the "church was going to *keep* the upper hand and snuff out all my beautiful civilization . . . my dream of a republic to *be* a dream, and so remain.") Yet for him, as we have learned, another dream, that of familial bliss, has become a reality. And so—why not return?

Implicitly, of course, Twain has attempted to foreclose that possibility. The doctors who prescribed the journey for the baby's health, we learn—the very captain and crew in whose care the Morgans sailed—were agents of the church in service to the scheme for interdiction. Hereafter no site in Christendom is safe for the Yankee.

Yet what is significant here is the absence of the posed alternative, the posed consideration of domesticity affirmed in a return to Sandy and the baby. From his command post inside the magician's, Merlin's, cave, Hank tells us he could sit by the hour evoking a surrogate family scenario by writing the unmailable letters that enable him to pretend to be in the midst of his loved ones. "It was almost like having us all together again. . . . it was almost like talking; it was almost as if I was saying, 'Sandy, if you and Hello-Central were here in the cave, instead of your photographs.' " The husband-father summons them in self-referential narratives and in photographic signs but does not once consider slipping away (with or without Clarence and the fifty-two boys) to rejoin them. The Yankee does not pose the possibility of this alternative. Much less reject it, he does not bring it to conscious consideration.

In fact, Mark Twain's omission of this alternative—even of consideration of it—is deeply rooted in the technological eschatological tradition extending from Colonial texts through Emerson. For Mark Twain's decision in this novel to enter into the world of contemporary technology virtually precluded the domestic-familial alternative that, by the late nineteenth century, was identified with the women's sphere. In trying to claim both technological and domestic American culture within one realm, Twain inevitably discovered that he could not have both but must choose between them. The ostensible choice, however, had really been made for him, predetermined as a millennial-technological legacy extending from Puritan colonialism through Emerson. For Mark Twain's Yankee was Emerson's young American, a white man in and of the New World, in full possession of it. And that world is constituted on masculine terms of precise calibration in the survey, and of engineering, of construction, of design. When Twain's predetermined adherence to the masculine technological world leads him to take leave of domesticity, Hank Morgan becomes himself the incarnation of positivist, rationalist technological values gone mad. He becomes a deformed figure, monomaniacal and monstrous. Readers are caught in the Emersonian realm inverted into madness by this agent of holocaust. The national technological narrative thus takes dystopian form.

Contrarily, however, American utopian technological novels also have abounded, undergirded by belief in inevitable progress. Their advocates have believed in societal perfection attainable by changes in material conditions and focused on the heightening of the general welfare, which is to say that they rely on the expertise increasingly attributed to the engineer. These novels include King Camp Gillette's *The Human Drift* (1894), Henry Olerich's *A Cityless and Countryless*

*World: An Outline of Practical Co-operative Individualism* (1893), Herman Brinsmade's *Utopia Achieved: A Novel of the Future* (1912).

Though the gendering of technology as a mainly male sphere has militated against its exploitation by women in the American novel, one prominent women's technological utopia is feminist reformer Charlotte Perkins Gilman's *Herland* (1915), which presents a women's civilization in a mountainous, remote region so difficult to reach that it has evaded discovery even in the great Victorian era of exploration. Herland, begun two thousand years ago with a slave revolt, is a civilization of "clean, well-built roads, attractive architecture, ordered beauty" hidden beyond "a desperate tangle of wood and water" over craggy mountains. Sustained by single-sex reproduction, Herland locates its ideological basis in maternal love ("Maternal Pantheism") and sisterhood extended for "Beauty, Health, Strength, Intellect, Goodness." Knowledge and expertise are shared and disseminated. Gilman's narrators, a group of male explorers, come technologically equipped with machinery from a "big steam yacht" to an airplane, to discover a world solely inhabited by women: "old women and young women and a great majority who seemed neither young nor old, but just women." Herland becomes Gilman's vehicle for criticism of contemporary industrial America, its barbaric exploitation of women workers, cruelty to animals, economic inequities, military aggression, separation of home from work. Herland's industrial attainments (including eugenics) are presupposed, though its readers encounter a discourse that is mainly pastoral, for example, of the babies growing "just as young fawns might grow up in dewy forest glades and brook-fed meadows." *Herland* propounds the values of a rationalized, egalitarian society asserted to be technologically advanced but pastoral in practice. Its geographic remoteness suggests Gilman's anxiety about masculine appropriation of women's sphere.

Sharing Gilman's outrage at the human misery concomitant with capitalist economics, Edward Bellamy wrote the best known of all American technological utopian novels, *Looking Backward, 2000–1887*. Bellamy, a newspaper journalist, determined to combine popular romance with a vision of the engineered, utopian American future. His protagonist, a Bostonian named Julian West, falls into a trance-sleep and awakens in the year 2000 to find that his late nineteenth-century Boston, a synecdoche for the United States, no longer suffers from the socioeconomic instability that precipitates human tragedy—orphanage, destitution, crime, insanity, suicide. These he terms "prodigious wastes" that are susceptible to correction in the rationalized system of human planning and design. In short, Bellamy's protagonist awakes to learn that social amelioration has been accomplished by the engineering of society and its means of production. Certain inventions, such as radio, pneumatic transfer, central heat and ventilation, and electric lighting, increase human comfort and health and remind one that technology is a part of the discourse of this novel. But the ethos of the engineer is uppermost, with the valuation of efficiency and the means for its achievement. *Looking Backward* is a celebration of efficient America and of the engineers entrusted to plan and sustain it. It is a reprise of the millennialist technological visions extending back to the seventeenth century.

The reliance upon engineering enters into Ezra Pound's identification of the novel as an engine with precisely positioned wheels. His definition of the novel as machine shifts emphasis from story to functional design, from narration to construction. The values of modernism, as he and others knew, claimed kinship with those of engineering—functionalism, efficiency, stability, utilitarianism, design, and construction.

Nor was the linkage to engineering a recondite or high-culture relation, for early twentieth-century America saw the engineer become a popular culture hero for the industrial age, just as the cowboy had symbolized the era of westward expansion. Engineers, as one writer said, were now "true poets, makers whose creations touch the imagination and move the world." One manifestation of this socially broad-based engagement in engineering was the so-called efficiency movement of the 1910s, when one engineer, Frederick Winslow Taylor, disgusted by the wasteful inefficiency of industrial work practices rife with superfluous movements, analyzed workers' motions down to the smallest components and, working with a stopwatch, reconstituted work motions into the most efficient patterns. He developed a "science" of efficient management and, as a result of a widely publicized court case, became a kind of media celebrity and initiated a Progressive Era national fad for efficiency, one that extended from high school curricula to home economics. Throughout American culture, all the while, engineering was increasingly evident in bridges, tunnels, aquaducts, skyscrapers, and the figure of the engineer became the hero of boys' books, such as the Tom Swift series, of such toys as the Erector set, of best-selling novels like Richard Harding Davis's *Soldiers of Fortune* (1897), Rex Beach's *The Iron Trail: An Alaskan Romance* (1913), and Harold Bell Wright's *The Winning of Barbara Worth* (1911), which became a motion picture starring Ronald Colman. As Richard Harding Davis wrote, "The civil engineer . . . is the chief civilizer of our century."

Under the aegis of engineering, the American novel of the early twentieth century conceptually changed. The lineage of the narration yielded to one of construction, as such avant-garde novelists as Ernest Hemingway and John Dos Passos reformulated the basis of the novel in accordance with the new paradigm of the engineered machine. Of course, readers, then as now, recognized certain traditional elements of the novel. Readers of Dos Passos's trilogy *U.S.A.* (*The 42nd Parallel* [1930], *1919* [1932], *The Big Money* [1936]; collected 1937) encounter fictional characters whose lives can be followed throughout, just as Hemingway's *In Our Time* (1925) and *The Sun Also Rises* (1926) present the kinds of scenes and characterizations customary in fiction.

Yet the basis for novelistic design changes conceptually in the work of these two novelists, as the notion of fictional story yields to the engineering values of design and construction. The engineering value of efficiency, for instance, directly influenced Hemingway's much-discussed style. As a cub reporter on the *Kansas City Star*, he was tutored from a style sheet prepared at the height of the efficiency movement, its directives focused on short sentences and opening paragraphs, and on the elimination of adjectives. And one confronts that value in the opening pages of *The Sun Also Rises*, in which the narrator, Jake Barnes, repeatedly describes Robert Cohn in the adjective "nice." In college Cohn was "a thoroughly nice boy . . . a nice boy, a friendly boy . . . who married the first girl who was nice to him." Later, with the publication of Cohn's successful novel, says Jake, "several women were nice to him. . . . and he was not so simple, and he was not so nice." One sees Hemingway wring multiple meanings from that one-syllable word, which ramifies to include purity, geniality, good manners, sexual favor, consideration for others — as if

Hemingway had moved resolutely through each dictionary definition for the one word. Like a fuel, the term "nice" is utilized and reutilized until it is exhausted, and this becomes Hemingway's efficiency of diction.

Far from being a mere word game, this kind of verbal economy meant power, and Hemingway's characteristic declarative sentences became the equivalent of the engineer's steel beams. The Hemingway style is essentially the twentieth-century, machine-age diction and syntax advocated in *The Elements of Style* (1959), the rhetoric book for college students coauthored by William Strunk, Jr., and E. B. White. White attributed the following statement from the year 1919 to his coauthor: "Vigorous writing is concise. A sentence should contain no unnecessary words, a paragraph no unnecessary sentences, for the same reason that a drawing should have no unnecessary lines and a machine no unnecessary parts." Vigor was the goal, achieved by the work or functioning of every word, with each to be considered a working component of an overall design. Hemingway's fiction is the exemplum of industrial-age writing.

In Dos Passos, too, the novel itself becomes a designed construction. Committed to the representation of twentieth-century American life in its sociocultural entirety, resolved to incorporate the diverse elements of popular culture from music to diners to train travel and movies, insistent upon a vertical cutaway view of caste and class, and determined to work on a continental scale, Dos Passos needed an innovative model for fiction. Lacking belief in an omniscient deity and inhabiting a modern world he believed to be loosed from traditional bonds of kinship and community, Dos Passos nonetheless felt committed to the all-encompassing fictional purview, the very one traditionally in accordance with the omniscient viewpoint. Had he proceeded to cast his novels from techniques of narrative omniscience, however, he would have found himself in an untenable state of artistic hypocrisy.

It was in machine technology that Dos Passos discovered the path out of his representational quandary. He found the structural paradigm for fiction in the complex machine. Dos Passos's genius lay in grasping the paradigmatic possibilities for fiction as these were displayed in machine parts. Seeing that he, like the engineer, could combine these component parts into an overall complex design, Dos Passos realized the opportunities for a new kind of fiction. It could be likened, say, to the structure of the automobile, with its electrical system, cooling system, braking system, engine, etc. Dos Passos organized his materials accordingly, systematizing them in subsystems within his panoramic design. The subjective consciousness would be presented in sections entitled "The Camera Eye," while biographies of representative, prominent Americans constituted another system (the efficiency expert Frederick Taylor was one biographical subject, along with Henry Ford, the Wright brothers, the silent-film star Rudolph Valentino, the dancer Isadora Duncan, and numerous others). Dos Passos's fictional characters constituted yet another subsystem, all of them American social types, as if prefabricated parts in an off-the-shelf inventory of the national population. A fourth system, the "Newsreels," included popular songs and slogans, together with newspaper headlines Dos Passos clipped (again, with the precedent of the prefabricated part assembled on site) and formed into a montage intended to capture the temper of the time. All these were coordinated within the novel as a whole, the text in its entirety a complex machine.

Readers of Dos Passos learn virtually immediately that this writer found corporate capitalism and its vast industries anathema to human interests. He detested powerful organizations of the corporate state with a vehemence matched, say, by that revealed in Frank Norris's *The Octopus*. Dos Passos's hostility, for instance, toward the corporate titan Henry Ford is palpable and, together with the kinds of antitechnological imagery noted earlier in this discussion, would seem to locate the author of *U.S.A.* as a novelist locked in firm opposition to technology.

It is, however, in the structure of his texts that Dos Passos reveals his inadvertent compliance with the machine age, just as Hemingway's novel about American expatriates of the "lost generation" proves in its very sentence structure to be consonant with its industrial moment although it shows no more overt technology in the fictional scenes than a bus and a fly rod.

From these examples, in fact, it seems possible to hearken back to the mid-nineteenth century to ask whether *Moby-Dick*, whose author served a short stint in an engineering course, may have augured the industrial-age novel in ways we have failed to appreciate. Recent work on the insurgence of an industrial economy in the mid-nineteenth-century United States has opened literary study to questions about the ways in which the canonical writers of the American Renaissance were participants in the newer means of production rapidly supplanting agriculture. It is possible now to notice that Melville's roll call of production workers on the whaleship compares them to "the engineering forces employed in the construction of the American Canals and Railroads," and to speculate that *Moby-Dick* not only shows the factory ship processing whales into oil but also discloses the ways in which the literary raw material is processed into a finished product, a symbol. The cetological chapters, "Extracts," "Cetology," the chapters on representations of whales, become, in this light, the writer's raw material that he converts, in full view of the reader, into the literary symbol. Viewed in this way, it becomes clear once again that technology bears a very complicated relation to the novel and the novelist, that antitechnological discursive remarks and negative images cannot, by themselves, suffice to answer hard critical questions about the part technology plays in the American novel.

To discuss the relation of technology to the novel is to understand that in any given era there exists a dominant technology that defines or redefines the human role in relation to the environment, that within the span of some three centuries technological orientation has shifted from a technology of visible moving parts, which is to say the technology Pound understood as one of gears and girders, to an electrical technology of broadcast radio (which Stanley Elkin exploits in *The Dick Gibson Show* [1973]) and thence to the micro-circuitry in which the cathode-ray screen has instigated fictional innovation. Bearing in mind that the history of American fiction is correlative with the history of technological development, it is necessary to indicate the ways in which broadcast television is currently affecting the American novel.

The novel itself has taken up arms against television, notably in Ray Bradbury's *Fahrenheit 451* (1950), which pits a totalitarian television culture against one of books and learning, and more recently in John Gardner's *October Light* (1976), which again positions the book against TV. Still, a generation of younger writers have grown up with television and the cognitive processes characteristic of it.

They reject the binary oppositional division between the worlds of television and literature. The narrator of a William Warner story remarks, without embarrassment, on "some writers *first* trained by reading Dickens or Fitzgerald . . . others by watching TV." Warner and others reject the position that television is alien, even inimical, to the literary imagination. They simply refuse those terms of engagement and the hierarchy explicit in the terms. One recent novel, Jill McCorkle's *The Cheer Leader* (1984), presents at length the holistic relation of television and literary texts. It mixes the two freely, even promiscuously, to represent the contemporary consciousness of the writer, who reads Proust and Emily Dickinson but also watches sitcoms and reruns ("I Love Lucy," "Then Came Bronson") and plans to continue doing so in adult life.

The ways in which television affects the form of the novel in the 1980s and 1990s may be approached through theorists of the video medium, especially Raymond Williams, who in *Television: Technology and Cultural Form* (1974) cautioned that television reviewers were misguidedly, anachronistically operating like drama or film critics or book reviewers, approaching individual programs as "a discrete event or a succession of discrete events." Williams, the British Marxist social analyst with particular interests in the cultural institutions of print, had been a BBC television reviewer between 1968 and 1972, and he became convinced that forms of broadcasting in the TV age were altering perceptual processes. Prior to broadcasting, Williams observes, "the essential items were discrete. . . . people took a book or a pamphlet or a newspaper, went out to a play or a concert or a meeting or a match, with a single predominant expectation or attitude." The fundamental expectation was of a discrete program or entity.

But increasingly, Williams finds, in the era of television broadcasting the discrete program has yielded to a structure far more fluid. "There has been a significant shift from the concept of sequence as *programming* to the concept of sequence as *flow*." He goes on: "there is a quality of flow which our received vocabulary of discrete response and description cannot easily acknowledge."

Williams's identification of "flow" has proved a benchmark in differentiating the experience of broadcast television from other narrative forms. Conceding that vestigial elements of discrete programs remain intact in the timed units of a "show," he argues nonetheless that the intervals between these units have disappeared. In American broadcast television the advertisements are incorporated into the whole, so that "what is being offered is not, in older terms, a programme of discrete units with particular insertions, but a planned flow, in which the true series is not the published sequence of programme items but this sequence transformed by the inclusion of another kind of sequence, so that these sequences together compose the real flow, the real 'broadcasting.' "

Turning to a group of writers cognitively informed by this kind of flow, writers who from childhood belonged to a world that has spent untold hours watching television, the analyst of televisual form can prove heuristically helpful. The concept of flow, applied to the TV-age novel, can help us understand the new fictional structures that otherwise draw censure for their apparent defection from form itself. By implication, Williams and others enable readers to understand that the experience of flow, enacted cognitively in fiction, makes certain formal traits become virtually inevitable.

These will not be narratives of the beginning-middle-end structure. Flow enables entry at any point. The narrative of flow is continuous, open, apparently without end. Thus it is unsurprising that a school of novelists, including Ann Beattie and Bobbie Ann Mason, begin to "violate" a onetime cardinal rule of fiction writing, namely, that the principal fictional tense be the simple past. Instead, in the 1970s and 1980s, they began to cast narrative in the present tense, the tense that best enacts the experience of flow and the primacy of the present moment within it. The television-age novels, one is made to feel, could start anywhere. They are not a version of *in medias res,* a concept that presupposes the Aristotelian structure of beginning-middle-end. They do not work to show symmetry and proportion. Ideas of the bounded text change in the television era, when the primacy of flow takes precedence. Fluidity supersedes boundary. Indeed, these texts do not begin, they simply start, as if turned on or come upon. And they can now exploit the accelerated flow of the channel-changing remote, as the African American novelist Trey Ellis does in his satirical *Platitudes* (1988), in which an entire chapter is structured according to a ten-second-interval change of channels through all cable stations.

One TV characteristic dominates all others—the screen itself, by now so naturalized in the culture that it has become an environment susceptible to incorporation in the novel. And the contemporary fiction writer has been quick to exploit the potential of the TV screen for his or her own work. An onscreen moment represented in a novel can take the place of the excursion into characters' minds usually signaled by the speech tags "he thought," "she felt." It can supplant the often awkwardly triggered flashback into past events. The televised scene can reveal new dimensions of the fictional characters' lives directly in the moment, as Richard Ford shows in one scene in his novel *The Sportswriter* (1986), in which the protagonist and his girlfriend watch championship ice skating on TV, an occasion that ramifies to include the sportswriter's musings about his own life by interpreting the onscreen event. Ford's novel shows how the televised scene can reveal new dimensions of the fictional characters' lives directly in the moment. The screen becomes the locus of the bared psyche. If the onscreen images seem at first unrelated to the fictional scene in progress, readers must understand that the writer positions the two—the images onscreen and off—in a kind of fictional haiku, in which two seemingly unrelated sets of images are juxtaposed, the reader challenged to discover their apposition.

One additional TV-era trend is insurgent in recent fiction, that of the hyperreal or virtual reality. At this point we necessarily revert to Umberto Eco's paradox that says the "completely real" becomes identified with the "completely fake." This is the realm also addressed by the French anthropologist Jean Baudrillard, who argues that categories like real/unreal, authenticity/imitation, firsthand/vicarious, and actual/illusory are now superannuated, persisting in our discourse because we invoke them from unexamined convictions inherited from a previous age. These categories, Baudrillard says, no longer pertain to the condition of things in a media age. Even such terms as imitation or reduplication are now beside the point, he says, are in fact invalid. Baudrillard writes: "It is rather a question of substituting signs of the real for the real itself. . . . simulation is. . . . the generation of models of a real without origin or territory: a hyperreal." And the contemporary American novel participates in that hyperreal, one case in point being Mark Leyner's *My Cousin, My*

*Gastroenterologist* (1990), a blatantly hyperreal fiction self-evidently indebted to TV:

I am on every channel and that infuriates you
that I have the ability to jump out of the television screen,
     burrow into your uterus, and emerge nine months later tan and rested
     bugs you very much
you're using the violent vocabulary of the u.s.a., you're violently chewing
     your cheez doodles and flicking the remote control.

Disjunctive, flaunting discontinuity and simulation, this kind of writing evidently finds an audience who welcome the print text that can ratify their TV-age cognitive reality. This is the simulation of the hologram, the 3-D instead of the fully dimensional. This kind of technological trend will probably continue in the American novel as the computer screen merges with the TV screen and the simulated space of cyberpunk fiction, formerly engaging principally to a coterie of computer amateurs, becomes more culturally widespread. In due course, finally, a generation growing up with the video game will doubtless take its turn in the innovation of the American novel.

Cecelia Tichi

# Society and Identity

Between the violence of World War II and Vietnam lay the relative calm called the American 1950s. The period is not popular with modern critics. From our current vantage, the postwar generation seems most notable for its isolationism, consumerism, conformity, and apathy. The rise of competitive individualism may have been a natural reaction against the compulsory cooperation of the New Deal and war years. It may have been a response to the evolving socioeconomic structure of a postindustrial culture, as detailed in such contemporary classics of sociology as David Riesman's *The Lonely Crowd* (1950), William H. Whyte's *The Organization Man* (1956), and C. Wright Mills's *The Power Elite* (1956). Or it may have been psychological fallout from advances in technology, as argued in such popular accounts as Paul Goodman's *Growing Up Absurd* (1960) and Marshall McLuhan's *The Gutenberg Galaxy* (1962). Yet whatever the sources of fifties alienation, we tend today to remember the age of Eisenhower as repressive and anaesthetized— the generation of the Mouseketeers and "Leave It to Beaver."

Most representative of the new conservatism of the postwar period were the collapse of radical politics and the reentrenchment of gender stereotypes. Throughout the first half of the century there had been strong support for various forms of socialism in America, and intellectualism and Marxism often went hand in hand. During the war, the intellectual support for Marxism and for Russian Communism was reinforced by the United States military alliance with the

Soviet Union against fascism. But in the late 1940s and early 1950s, a political disaffection with the Communist Party that had been growing since the late 1930s reached a head. In *The God That Failed* (1949) a number of influential intellectuals and literary figures announced their rejection of the socialist principles they had earlier espoused. This early disaffection turned into a wholesale exodus from the Party when in the mid-1950s the excesses of Stalinist persecution were publicly revealed. Contemporaneous with the defection of Party members was the rise in national influence of the anti-Communist movement, climaxing with the ascendancy of Senator Joseph McCarthy and the investigations of the House Un-American Activities Committee (HUAC) in the first half of the decade. The climate of betrayal and recrimination that characterized the HUAC hearings, and more covertly discriminatory practices like blacklisting, reinforced the general paranoia of the Cold War and the age's retreat into a politics of naive pro-Americanism.

Equally distressing were the losses in the movement toward women's rights. The first quarter of the century saw a slow but steady growth in equality between the sexes, largely focused on the issue of the vote. The war accelerated these advances by opening job opportunities for women. With the men called overseas, women were actively recruited to take their places on the job market, especially in munitions factories. At the war's end, however, women were forced out of their jobs to free positions for returning veterans. With this shift in economics came a shift in gender propaganda. During the war "Rosie the Riveter" was a widely touted model for women's role in the defense effort. In the postwar period, however, the model reverted to the more traditional one of the housewife. Manual labor in particular was deemed unfeminine, a threat to women's supposedly delicate physiologies and to their domestic duties as mothers. Even those women not literally ousted from their wartime positions found the sudden redefinition of female excellence disorienting. This attempt to reinstitute the discarded cult of domesticity resulted in the creation of what Betty Friedan in 1963 called "the feminine mystique," a sociopsychological theory constructed to protect male access to power by restricting women's place to the home.

The conservative tone in politics and gender stereotyping was reinforced by the individualistic bias of the age's dominant intellectual trends. Existentialism defined the generation's conception of self and society. Rebelling against traditional notions of authority, dogma, and political ideology, the existentialists spoke instead of an individual's "being" in or "engagement" with the world, in such European works of philosophy as Martin Heidegger's *Being and Time* (1927) and Jean-Paul Sartre's *Being and Nothingness* (1943). As a philosophical movement, existentialism critiqued the falsely scientific tone of certain analytic schools of thought and rejected metaphysicians' pursuit of foundational truths. When translated into a popular idiom, however, the philosophy tended to encourage individual self-absorption over social involvement. What began as an attempt to explain and overcome the absurdity of modern life at times seemed to support and celebrate it. Alienation became not a symptom of the general malaise but a mark of one's superiority to the conformist mentality of the masses.

A similar devaluation attended the popularization of the age's other great school of thought—the psychoanalytic movement, most closely associated with Sigmund Freud. Freud's insights into the unconscious and the anxieties attending creativity and sexual maturation were among the central enabling insights of modern culture. Yet the general conclusions drawn from his theories (frequently without close examination of the actual texts) often moved in directions antithetical to Freud's own. Slavish adherence to the specifics of any theory tends of course to distort its underlying truths. In the case of psychoanalysis, such distortions were intensified by its therapeutic dimension. In treating psychological abnormality, postwar therapists unintentionally supported the age's "idolatry of the normal"—its fanatical pursuit of uniformity. Psychoanalytic practitioners were not always sensitized to problems of economic or social inequity. As a medical treatment available primarily to the wealthy, analysis tended to reinforce class distinctions. The psychiatric characterizations of certain group-specific problems—like "housewife syndrome" or "homosexual panic"—did not overcome the culture's discriminatory practices; they internalized them. Even apart from the excesses of specific postwar formulations, the preoccupation of psychoanalysis with the individual and the internal may have reinforced the age's more general tendency to divorce questions of personality from those of history and politics.

The conservative character of society and thought was echoed in the academic community, especially in its conception of literary value. Truth was thought to be universal, the essential core that remained after the layers of cultural particularity were peeled away. Historians like Richard Hofstadter and Clinton Rossiter saw this universality in terms of "consensus," an optimistic vision of nationally shared goals. Literary scholars tended to speak more generally about "reality," "culture," or "tradition." Such accounts as *The Great Tradition* (1948) of British scholar F. R. Leavis or *The Liberal Imagination* (1950) of American Lionel Trilling located excellence in moral realism, a neo-Arnoldian concern with stylistic and psychological richness that implicitly rejected the ideological criticism of the 1940s.

This general turn from politics was institutionalized in America in the school of New Criticism. Combining political conservatism with nostalgic agrarianism, the New Critics emphasized the separation between the social and the literary. Developing ideas implicit in earlier theories of T. S. Eliot, I. A. Richards, and E. M. Forster, such critics as John Crowe Ransom, Robert Penn Warren, and Cleanth Brooks saw literature as different in kind from scientific writing. Literary language was a multilayered one of paradox and ambiguity, more concerned with connotation than denotation. Literature, the New Critics argued, was eternal, to be studied apart from the social conditions and even authorial sensibilities that created it. Although the main focus of such criticism was on poetry and the English literary tradition, the influence of the New Critics on all scholarship of the postwar period cannot be overestimated. New critical values informed literary history, in René Wellek's famous distinction between the "intrinsic" and "extrinsic" characteristics of a text. In Americanist scholarship, New Criticism surfaced in the repeated claim that American literature was more romantic and less socially engaged than its European counterpart. American authors effected, in Richard Poirier's seminal phrase, a stylistic escape to "a world elsewhere."

The explicit ahistoricism and apoliticism of the New Critics was matched less obviously in the development of a new interdisciplinary study of Americanness. American literature had begun to be an object of scholarly work as early as the 1920s. Departments and programs in American literature were widely instituted in the academy in the 1930s and 1940s. After the war, however, the study of Americanness began to cross departmental boundaries, especially those between literature and history—in such works as Henry Nash Smith's *Virgin Land* (1950), R. W. B. Lewis's *The American Adam* (1955), and Leo Marx's *The Machine in the Garden* (1964). The purpose of these and other works in the developing field of "American Studies" was to overturn (New Critical) standards of literary excellence, which judged American works linguistically unsophisticated. Such scholars argued instead for the historical importance and imaginative power of the myths that organized supposedly "unliterary" texts. In their willingness to mix history and literary analysis, and to break down the artificial barriers departmentalizing thought in the university, the proponents of American Studies were clearly involved in politicizing postwar aesthetic paradigms, and even in restructuring the academy. Yet in its concern with overarching symbols and its preoccupation with a uniquely "American" experience—which, as always in the 1950s, took the United States to represent all the Americas— American Studies itself reflected as well the homogenizing and isolationist tendencies of culture in the 1950s.

Novelists reaching their intellectual maturity in the postwar period, then, faced a culture (and literary establishment) not predisposed to consider the novel as a product of social conditions, let alone as an instrument for social change. The tradition of socialist literature that had flourished during the previous two decades—and acclaimed the writing of Richard Wright, John Steinbeck, and John Dos Passos, among others—did not survive the anti-Communism of the 1950s. Freudianism and existentialism recognized the importance of human agency, but conceptualized that agency as individual activity, being more skeptical about the possibility of large-scale social reform. And the prevailing standards of literary excellence reinforced this individualism by emphasizing the stylistic and psychological subtlety of texts over their narrative scope, thematic significance, or variety of characterization.

As a result, much literature of the postwar period intentionally minimized its social situation, aspiring instead to the kind of timeless universality applauded by the New Critics. Even those authors who saw themselves as social critics had to confront an essential paradox of postwar individualism—the conflict between the private demands of self-realization and the public ones of group activity. One species of "problem" novel tended to isolate a social issue and solve it through the efforts of enlightened individuals. The role of institutions in maintaining and even aggravating the problem remained largely unexamined; their potential for alleviating it, wholly unexplored. Laura Z. Hobson's *Gentleman's Agreement* (1947), for example, exposed the conspiracy of silence surrounding anti-Semitism, but trusted that right-minded liberals would be able to teach the masses to abandon their discriminatory practices. In *The Ugly American* (1958), authors William J. Lederer and Eugene Burdick criticized the failure of American foreign policy in Southeast Asia to consider the character and needs of the cultures it addressed. Yet even this fierce attack on American ethnocentrism conceived the solution in terms of isolated achievements by empathetic field workers, much along the lines later implemented in John F. Kennedy's Peace Corps.

Often this paradoxical faith in the individual was epitomized by the representation of the judicial system, whose practices were depicted as inadequate, even corrupt, while its practitioners were celebrated as moral exemplars. Herman Wouk's *The Caine Mutiny* (1951) and Robert Traver's (John D. Voelker's) *Anatomy of a Murder* (1958) both recounted the trials of morally suspect defendants, whose acquittals were in some respects legal miscarriages; yet both applauded the verdicts as indications of the defense attorneys' moral superiority. Similarly the upbeat ending to Allen Drury's *Advise and Consent* (1959) contradicted the novel's more generally negative assessment of legislative amorality: the seediness of the backroom politics surrounding the Congressional ratification of a mediocre Cabinet nomination was transcended in the miraculous last-minute appointment of a qualified candidate. Harper Lee's prize-winning *To Kill a Mockingbird* (1960) dissected Southern racism in a richly textured variation on the traditional coming-of-age novel. Yet here too the narrative subordinated the inequities of the legal system and the malignity of community prejudice to the moral integrity of the heroine's father, the courageous (though unsuccessful) defense attorney, and to his belief that most people are "real nice" when viewed on their own terms.

Tensions between radical individualism and group morality were occasionally played out in an explicitly religious context. Both J. F.

Powers and Flannery O'Connor were best known for their short fiction. Like their stories, however, their novels—his *Morte d'Urban* (1962) and *Wheat That Springeth Green* (1988) and her *Wise Blood* (1952)—set individual idiosyncrasies against an unironic background of Catholic orthodoxy: Powers's worldly priests and O'Connor's gothic grotesques found meaning in a potential for grace and moral depth that caught them unawares. And in Walker Percy's string of comic novels—most notably *The Moviegoer* (1961), *The Last Gentleman* (1966), *Love in the Ruins* (1972), and *The Second Coming* (1980)—his heroes confronted existential dread and entertained annihilation only to pull back from the abyss to reaffirm the traditional values of Christian community as epitomized by marriage and the nuclear family. Whatever the nature of their specific social criticisms, such religious works tended to an otherworldliness that unintentionally reinforced the status quo.

For those dissatisfied with religious consolations, existentialism offered a popular secular model for engagement with and revolt against social convention. One common form of such rebellion grew out of novelists' attempts to deal with the experience of World War II. In the traditional neorealist war novel, like James Jones's *From Here to Eternity* (1951), the conflict between personal authenticity and the army's need for conformity was reinforced by the contrast between the everyday tedium of military life and extraordinary events, like the attack on Pearl Harbor, from which an official history of war is constructed. In a more experimental text, like Joseph Heller's *Catch-22* (1961), the struggle between individualism and authoritarianism was depicted through hyperbolic black comedy, which used military incompetence as a symbol for the absurdity of all modern existence. Despite differing literary techniques, however, at the heart of such narratives lay a fundamental contradiction: the war whose very existence was explicitly criticized as a failure of political community was implicitly valorized as a proving ground for individual integrity, usually conceived in narrowly masculine terms.

The anxiety fostered under fire continued into the postwar period as a more general uncertainty in the face of shifting moral values. Removed from his military battleground, the existential hero in the 1950s warred against society in general. Paul Bowles's *The Sheltering Sky* (1949) combined a Hemingwayesque narrative of expatriates in

Africa with a New Critical awareness of the poetic qualities of prose to characterize crises of self-identity resulting from the confrontation with an alien culture. In Bernard Malamud's early novel *The Natural* (1952) and Mark Harris's chronicles of pitcher Henry Wiggen— especially *The Southpaw* (1953) and *Bang the Drum Slowly* (1956)— the national pastime of baseball became a metaphor for American society and for the difficulty with which an individual accommodates his own moral standards to the needs of the team.

Most representative of the virtues and limitations of such popularized existentialism, however, were the works of J. D. Salinger— *Franny and Zooey* (1961), *Raise High the Roof Beam, Carpenters* (1963), *Seymour: An Introduction* (1963), and the extraordinarily successful *The Catcher in the Rye* (1951). Through the Glass children and especially Holden Caulfield, Salinger captured the voice of adolescent anxiety; and Holden, along with film characters portrayed by James Dean and Marlon Brando, came to symbolize the disorientation of a generation searching for authenticity in a culture deemed (by Holden's dismissive reckoning) "phony." Yet Salinger's own solutions to alienation were incomplete. Holden's youth might excuse the sentimentality of the novel's depiction of him as a twentieth-century Huck Finn. Yet the suicide of the more mature Seymour Glass, and perhaps even Salinger's own refusal to publish after the mid-1960s, suggested that the elevation of the individual over society did not lead to a constructive program for growth or change.

A more influential model for rebellion was seen in the work of the "Beats," antiestablishment poets and novelists of the late 1950s and early 1960s. These countercultural figures were revolutionary not only in their personal philosophy and politics but as well in their prose style and means of publication. Eschewing the rule-bound traditionalism represented by Lionel Trilling or *The New Yorker,* the Beats sought to convey the transcendental experience of grace in an unrestrained prose that seemed unpolished, even automatic. Such underground classics as John Clellon Holmes's *Go* (1952), John Rechy's *City of Night* (1963), and Hubert Selby's *Last Exit to Brooklyn* (1964) celebrated bohemian culture—jazz music, recreational drugs, and unconventional sexuality—as an alternative to the institutionalized mediocrity of middle-class experience. The greatest of these novels—like William Burroughs's *Naked Lunch* (1959) and especially Jack Kerouac's *On the Road* (1957)—combined unusual subject matter with an incantatory use of language that recalled the prophetic cadences of Walt Whitman and the Puritan jeremiads. Yet for all their revolutionary fervor, the Beats were unable to overcome fully their white middle-class roots, which surfaced in an implicit classism, racism, and sexism that weakened even the strongest of these narratives.

The stylistic innovations and political rebelliousness of the Beats were reincorporated into establishment fiction in novels like Ken Kesey's *One Flew Over the Cuckoo's Nest* (1962) or Robert Stone's *Dog Soldiers* (1974). But perhaps the best summary of the whole tradition of postwar individualism was the career of Norman Mailer. Like Jones, Mailer began in a neorealist mode, with his war novel *The Naked and the Dead* (1948). He soon, however, forsook the literary mainstream to become a spokesperson for the counterculture. In his essay "The White Negro" (1957; reprinted in 1959 in *Advertisements for Myself*), he celebrated the beatniks as "hipsters," whose life on the existential edge approached the degree of authenticity that Mailer (with little racial sensitivity) thought "natural" to African Americans. Mailer compounded the error of his racial primitivism in *An American Dream* (1965), where a white male's search for personal integrity seemed to depend on his sexual violence against women. Mailer finally acknowledged the limitations of radical individualism in his masterpiece, *The Armies of the Night* (1968). Here, combining the techniques of nonfiction and the novel, he satirized his own persona as existential hero to suggest that although true political activism might arise in conjunction with individual rebellion, it could never result from it.

In voicing reservations about postwar conformity and the attendant loss in moral intensity, the literature of individual rebellion stood as one of the few audible protests from a generation otherwise preoccupied with maintaining the status quo. Its fervor carried over into the more radical decades that followed, and figures like Kerouac, Kesey, and Mailer were hailed as precursors and mentors by the youthful rebels of the late 1960s. Yet the very individualism of this critique worked against its ability to translate intellectual rebellion into practical reform. The existential hero confronted his fate alone, and discontent was expressed not through revolution but through transcendence and acceptance.

A more wide-ranging social change was effected, ironically, in narratives superficially more traditional. Throughout the postwar years appeared what might be called "novels of identity," works that explored the new conditions of modern life. These novels were not always politically self-conscious or even technically sophisticated. By shaping its audience, this literature functioned as an agent of social control, reconciling its readers to the oppressive stereotypes of the age's political and sexual conservatism. Yet for all their traditional character, these works played as well an important transitional role in the literature of social change. In speaking to an audience already established but as yet unrepresented, even the most conventional of these accounts were liberating. Through their concern with the particularity of cultural experience they introduced into the novel facts and scenes that had not before been deemed sufficiently important for literary treatment. The interests of specific minority groups became acceptable subject matter for fiction, and the environments of the home and the workplace received more attention than they had since the mid-nineteenth century. But most simply, in writing on such special concerns, this literature fostered a sense of group identity, a spirit of community lacking in the more individualistic novels of rebellion. And the rebirth of group identity begun in these novels paved the way for the possibility of group activity that characterized later decades.

The most sophisticated novels of identity were the works dealing with problems specific to a particular race or ethnicity. All minority writers confront the debate between particularity and universality. Postwar critics, however, tended to judge work focused on a single cultural group as too narrow to embody general human truths or values. This conservative aesthetic evaluation had its practical side as well. Minority writers addressing the widest audience often had to compromise the very subcultural specificity they sought to portray, while those attending closely to the details of community existence confused (even lost) many readers unfamiliar with these cultural traditions. Political considerations as well governed the narratives. Within minorities, it was hotly debated how much the general readership should be told about the community, and particularly how much of their people's flaws should be paraded before an audience not predisposed to admiration. Those fearing that accurate representation would reinforce stereotypes urged writers not to wash the community's dirty linen in public. Even so apparently sympathetic a literary device as the imitation of speech patterns through dialect could be read by insensitive readers as a mark of a group's ignorance and inferiority.

Such debates were less pronounced in those works, like the African American and the Jewish American novels, that built on long-established literary traditions. Yet here too authors made their peace with the universalizing literary standards of the time. African Americans had to confront the powerful but problematic influence of their immediate predecessor Richard Wright, whose best-selling *Native Son* (1940) was both the most celebrated black novel of the age and the one least likely to appeal to New Critical sensibilities. Ralph Ellison met the challenge with his prize-winning *Invisible Man* (1952), a novel as ambiguous and verbally inventive as Wright's is direct and visceral. Arguably the finest American novel of the postwar period, and certainly one of the most technically accomplished, *Invisible Man* followed an unnamed protagonist's picaresque search for identity in a racist culture with a symbolic intensity recalling the best work of Melville, Hawthorne, Twain, Conrad, Dostoevsky, and Dante. Even as he annexed the techniques of modernism to the African American literary tradition, Ellison never lost sight of the political underpinnings of his racial protest. Yet the very range of his literary references allowed readers to distance themselves from that critique and to admire the poetic qualities of the narrative apart from the political project that underwrote it. Unlike Wright's polemic, Ellison's multifaceted representation of the African American experience inspired in its white audience admiration and even guilt, but never fear.

Other writers responded differently to the conflicting demands of their white readership and of the post-Wright literary tradition. Chester Himes began very much in imitation of Wright, with his protest novel *If He Hollers Let Him Go* (1945). Yet in such later works as *The Real Cool Killers* (1959), *Cotton Comes to Harlem* (1965), and *The Heat's On* (1966), Himes adapted accurate and brutal depictions of the Harlem community to the generic conventions of the hard-boiled detective novel of Dashiell Hammett and Raymond Chandler. Such African American "mysteries" allowed him to portray negative aspects of uptown culture without charges of racism; the detective story had since Poe been preoccupied with the lurid. Moreover, the popularity of detective fiction afforded Himes an audience that might not otherwise have been attracted to so un-universal a depiction of a minority subculture.

James Baldwin, like Himes, wrote primarily in a neorealist mode. Yet Baldwin's identification of an audience was complicated by his doubly disenfranchised status as a black homosexual. Early in his career he addressed these issues separately. His first novel, *Go Tell It on the Mountain* (1953), dealt exclusively with familial strife within the context of black pentecostal preaching. His second novel, *Giovanni's Room* (1956), examined white expatriates in the gay subculture of Paris, in imitation of the "lost generation" motif of Hemingway and, to a lesser extent, of Wright and Himes. Later works— especially *Another Country* (1962) and his final novel, *Just Above My Head* (1979)—treated more ecumenically the pressures that generated both racism and homophobia. Adopting the prose rhythms of the Beats to characterize the variety of bohemian experience, Baldwin presented differences of race and sexual preference as forms of a more general cultural alienation that he sought to overcome. The assimilationist urge that in Ellison occasionally resulted in a tension between style and content surfaced at times in Baldwin as a contradictory advocacy for racial separatism and universalizing love.

The postwar novels of African American women seemed not so informed by the conflicting demands of black politics and white readers. Although favorably reviewed, their work was less well marketed and, after a first flurry of sales, frequently passed out of print, only to be republished in the feminist revival of the late 1970s and 1980s. This relatively slim chance of commercial success may ironically have afforded female writers greater freedom of expression; denied a wide audience, they escaped the concomitant fears of inaccessibility and overparticularity. Ann Petry's *The Street* (1946) depicted ghetto experience in terms of a naturalist determinism recalling *Native Son*. Yet despite the novel's apparently neorealist account of the environmental factors leading inevitably to murder, Petry did not reproduce in her heroine the individualist search for identity characteristic of male authors like Wright, Ellison, and Baldwin. Instead she presented, in chapters largely constructed out of interior monologues, fully realized members of a community, seeking for the practical means to achieve their already well-defined goals.

Although lacking the sociological detail of Petry's novels, *Maud Martha* (1953), the sole novel of poet Gwendolyn Brooks, developed further the interior life of its protagonist. As critic Mary Helen Washington has remarked, the novel's very structural innovations—its brief chapters, discontinuous narrative, and elliptical prose—imitated structurally the silencing that Maud Martha experienced sociologically, and that previous authors had represented thematically. Responding explicitly to the richness of Maud Martha's consciousness, Paule Marshall in her *Brown Girl, Brownstones* (1959) combined Brooks's psychological subtlety with Petry's sense of place to depict the coming-of-age of a Barbadian woman in Brooklyn. Her characterization of the West Indians' aspirations to middle-class status, epitomized in the ownership of house and land, distinguished her work from the customary focus on ghetto experience. Yet the very particularity of her interests permitted Marshall to introduce into that tradition a cultural specificity and density less evident in the more universalizing work of the males.

The same conflicts between the universal and the particular informed postwar Jewish American fiction. Many writers, like Heller, Mailer, and Salinger, worked within this tradition only implicitly, borrowing elements of Jewish intellectual life (especially its sardonic humor) without attention to their cultural origins. Those writers self-consciously examining Jewish life in America faced specific problems of audience and accommodation. Among Jewish American writers Saul Bellow stood, like Ellison among African Americans, as the novelist most interested in representing his cultural tradition through the literary conventions of modernism and the American faith in liberal humanism. In a large body of work from the early picaresque *The Adventures of Augie March* (1953) through the valedictory *Humboldt's Gift* (1975), Bellow explored the tensions between individual self-expression and social responsibility, often focusing on a hyperbolic Emersonian individualist at odds with his environment. Yet Bellow was not always able to balance ethnic themes with a more universalizing humanism. In his most powerful novels—like *Seize the*

*Day* (1956), *Herzog* (1964), and *Mr. Sammler's Planet* (1970) — philosophical debate took place within the carefully delineated context of Jewish culture in America. In others, like *Henderson the Rain King* (1959), the range of address became so broad and the issues so cosmic that the narrative fell victim to the very cultural imperialism and tourism it critiqued.

If Bellow rehearsed humanist issues for the widest possible audience, other writers limited their focus (and readership) to allow for greater cultural particularity. Isaac Bashevis Singer's decision to publish both his stories and novels in Yiddish made unlikely any widescale commercial success. Yet by narrowing his audience, Singer was able — in such novels as *The Family Moskat* (1945–48) and *Enemies: A Love Story* (1966) — to draw extensively on the historical, religious, and folk traditions of East European Jewry, material alien to a general readership in postwar America. The position of Bernard Malamud was more vexing; he was pronounced both the least "Jewish" writer of the postwar period and the most. Not all his work had Jewish themes or even characters, although the mature novels — especially *The Fixer* (1966) and *The Tenants* (1971) — located the narrative within specific sociological and historical situations. Some readers regretted his tendency to reduce Jewishness to passivity and victimization. Yet in its flirtations with the supernatural, its dark vision of the redemptive dimensions of suffering, and perhaps even its late preference for the actual over the mythic, his work embedded characteristics of Jewish American culture deep in narratives whose focus was superficially universal.

In the controversial work of Philip Roth the Jewish American novel reached a turning point, both for its pursuit of universalizing truths and for its representation of the subculture. A generation younger than Bellow or Malamud and less aligned with modernism than with the experimental techniques of postmodernism, Roth rejected the older writers' attempts to filter general issues of high moral seriousness through the lens of Jewish culture. He focused instead on phenomena specific to the culture, especially its particular problems with familial strife and upward mobility. In early works like *Goodbye, Columbus* (1959) and the notorious *Portnoy's Complaint* (1969), his negative evaluations were read as a form of Jewish anti-Semitism. As reformulated in the later, self-reflexive Zuckerman saga—*The Ghost Writer* (1979), *Zuckerman Unbound* (1981), *The Anatomy Lesson* (1983); collected with the epilogue *The Prague Orgy* as *Zuckerman Bound* (1985)—these criticisms juxtaposed the limitations of middle-class Jewish American experience against the thorniest characteristics of Freud, Kafka, and the Holocaust writers to offer a broader (and finally more positive) account of his cultural inheritance.

The debates within the traditions of African American and Jewish American literature were comparatively sophisticated. For less established ethnic literatures, the problems were the more preliminary ones of finding publishers and an audience. The autobiographical character of previous Asian American literature reflected its readers' need to imagine Asians as isolated individuals within American culture. In the postwar years fictional representations of a more complex communal experience began to appear, perhaps in response to soldiers' growing interest in these cultures encountered during the war. As a result of Chinese war efforts against Japan, Chinese American authors were given greater freedom of expression. Yet what these novelists could say was limited by the preconceptions of their audience. The most popular novels, like Lin Yutang's *Chinatown Family* (1948), viewed Chinese society with anthropological remoteness and condescension. Names were Anglicized and cultural traditions stigmatized as "charming" and "exotic." Anti-Communist and assimilationist, such accounts celebrated America as a land of economic opportunity and minimized problems of employment, racial discrimination, and social readjustment. Not until Louis Chu's *Eat a Bowl of Tea* (1961) did a book address the psychological and sociological implications of ghettoization and immigration quotas. The first accurate account of the Chinese American community, Chu's exploration of marital problems resulting from the "bachelor" society in New York's predominantly male Chinatown received poor reviews and passed silently from sight until its reprinting in 1979.

Although before the war Japanese American writers were more prolific than Chinese Americans, anti-Japanese feeling severely limited their audience throughout the 1950s. Familiar problems of assimilation—often represented through the generational conflict between foreign-born *issei* and their American-born *nisei* children—

were intensified during the war by the internment of Japanese Americans, a policy that disrupted community structures and made ethnic identification a public issue rather than a personal one. Scheduled for publication in 1941, Toshio Mori's *Yokohama, California* did not appear until well after the war in 1949. Despite good reviews this collection of interconnected stories depicting a Bay Area community was even then commercially unsuccessful, and some of Mori's novels still remain unpublished. John Okada powerfully portrayed the aftermath of internment, imprisonment, and ambiguous wartime patriotism in *No-No Boy* (1957). Yet his grippingly honest account of strife within the postwar community was treated harshly by critics and his remaining unpublished manuscripts were destroyed after his death in 1971. Only since the novel's republication in 1976 has he begun to receive the critical attention he deserved.

In such a climate of surveillance and implicit censorship, Asian American writers in the postwar period still managed to offer significant critiques of American cultural imperialism. Even the most accommodating accounts asserted the literary value of ethnic materials, educating Anglo audiences and reinforcing in Asians a sense of group identity and pride. C. Y. (Chin Yang) Lee's popular *The Flower Drum Song* (1957) exoticized San Francisco's Chinatown in a way that modern readers find offensive. Yet the novel's apparent pro-Americanism was subtly undermined by its oblique references to the problems of bachelor society and its use of generational conflict to characterize the cultural sacrifices attending assimilation. Similarly, despite its tone of passive acceptance, Monica Sone's autobiography *Nisei Daughter* (1953) actually inverted the traditional themes and structure of the second-generation narrative of assimilation, established in Jade Snow Wong's more conventional *Fifth Chinese Daughter* (1950). By detailing her discovery of a racial identity in the very process of repressing it, Sone turned an apparently upbeat account of Americanization into a mournful record of the destruction of the Japanese American community, symbolized by the narrative's progression from the opening hospitality of her parents' hotel to the final isolation of the camps.

Like other minority writers, Mexican American authors experienced problems with publication and audience. Not until the formation of the Quinto Sol publishing house in 1967 did authors have a means of addressing directly readers knowledgeable about and sympathetic to their culture. During the postwar period, most found it easier to place short stories than novels. Focused on the Mexican experience, Josephina Niggli's *Mexican Village* (1945) intertwined ten stories about a small community to depict her American-born hero's attempt to integrate himself into this culture without losing his American qualities, especially his individualism and skepticism. The strengths of the work lay in its combination of a romantic depiction of the folk traditions with a realist recognition of the sociological limitations of the community, especially its racism and sexism. Mario Suarez examined with power and dignity the "Chicano" experience in a series of short stories. The sole Chicano novel of the period, José Antonio Villarreal's *Pocho* (1959), sympathetically portrayed the sacrifices necessary for cultural assimilation. Yet, to win an Anglo audience, Villarreal felt the need for extensive explication and a final rejection of Chicano culture. As a result *Pocho*, like the more assimilationist of Asian American novels, seems today a necessary but preliminary stage in the delineation of Chicano experience.

In the postwar period, gay men and women did not experience social and economic discrimination so directly as other persecuted groups. Those gay men willing to mask their sexuality, in fact, were afforded relatively complete access to traditional forms of male power. At the same time, however, homosexual behavior was officially deemed pathological by the religious, legal, and medical establishments. In the popular imagination sexual preference was lumped with other forms of social and political deviance as threats to the national security. Literary treatments of sexuality, like all public expressions on the topic, were carefully regulated. Lesbian fiction had enjoyed a renaissance in the first half of the century, in such high modernist classics as Gertrude Stein's *Three Lives* (1909) and Djuna Barnes's *Nightwood* (1937). In the decades after the war, however, lesbian novels were more discreet. Bantam Press published a highly successful line of mass-market lesbian paperbacks, of which the most notable was the interconnected series of conscious-raising works by Ann Bannon. In more prestigious publications, like the sexually ambiguous thrillers of Patricia Highsmith and her pseudonymous *The Price of Salt* (1952), however, the sexual references tended to be coded and indirect. Only after the rebirth of feminism in the early

1960s did fiction regularly represent lesbians as other than deviants or martyrs, most notably in Jane Rule's *Desert of the Heart* (1964).

Gay male fiction was more mainstream. Gay writers like Burroughs and Rechy held positions of authority in the counterculture. Large commercial houses published such gay love stories as Baldwin's *Giovanni's Room,* Gore Vidal's *The City and the Pillar* (1948), and Fritz Peters's (Arthur Anderson Peters's) *Finistere* (1951). The price of such publicity was capitulation to heterosexual stereotypes. These novels depicted gay love as pathological, gay life as criminal, gay culture as nonexistent. The plots were deterministic and most ended in violence, often with the death of the protagonist. Although the self-loathing of such narratives cannot be denied, gay readers probably did not take seriously their melodrama and sentimentality. The value of these novels in forging a gay identity resided instead in those neutral moments when they reassured isolated homosexuals of the existence of others like themselves, even hinting subtly how such others might be met and identified in the straight world.

A more indirect strain in gay male writing avoided homosexual themes or situations altogether. Instead it presented straight plots in a gay style of parodic writing usually called "camp." Patrick Dennis (Edward Everett Tanner) wrote a string of wildly successful comic novels, most notably *Auntie Mame* (1955), that used extravagant female characters as mouthpieces for a gay critique of heterosexual behavior. Dennis's domestication of camp entered into the establishment tradition in the work of Truman Capote. His novella *Breakfast at Tiffany's* (1958) obscured the sexual dynamics between its male narrator and female protagonist to afford to both a gay sensibility only slightly less flamboyant than Dennis's Mame. Similar sexual undertones informed all his subsequent work. In his uncompleted final novel *Answered Prayers* (1987), Capote acknowledged the explicitly sexual character of his more discreet narratives through controversial stories about a gay hustler and the straight rich women he entertained.

As a sophisticated form of the literature of identity, minority novels tended to face directly questions of assimilation and cooptation. Yet in the problematic work of such popularizers as C. Y. Lee and Patrick Dennis we can begin to sense a more covert attempt to define group identity. For while some commercial works did not treat seriously the moral and political dilemmas facing a subculture, they nevertheless studied community dynamics with sociological precision. Though not significant additions to the literature of ethnic sensibility, these novels might be said to have contributed to a related subgenre—the literature of environment—which defined cultural identity less in terms of who or what one was than in terms of where one lived and worked.

Novels of environment rarely experimented with the technical innovations of the age. The fractured time scheme and unreliable narrators favored by modernist authors in the first half of the century were largely rejected. Nor was it a literature of high sensibility and fine moral distinctions. The narrative voices were matter-of-fact rather than ruminative. Characters were stereotypes, and their moral dilemmas relatively straightforward. The authors avoided ambiguity and frequently displayed an explicit hostility to psychological explanations of human motivation. While not, like the Beats, in conscious revolt against academic criticism, they ignored traditional aesthetic criteria and valued as antecedents works little admired by the New Critics.

In some respects, the novels of environment looked back to the proletariat fictions of the 1940s; their prose was simple and declarative, crafted to reach the widest audience possible. They recalled as well the work of the turn-of-the-century naturalists, especially Norris and Dreiser, in their precise attention to the minutiae of everyday experience. Yet they possessed none of the reforming tendencies of these earlier traditions: neither the socialist underpinnings of proletariat novelists nor the philosophical pessimism, sexual candor, and social outrage of the naturalists. These works tended instead to be politically conservative, celebrating middle-class mores. In this conservatism, their truest antecedents were perhaps the English Victorian novel, especially the chronicles of Anthony Trollope, and its American counterpart, the sentimental novel of domesticity. Like their three-volume ancestors, these postwar popular fictions were often leisurely works, rich in descriptive detail, and overflowing with characters and plot. And like them, they coddled rather than challenged the bourgeois expectations of their readers.

The success of these commercial novels can be understood sociologically. There had long been popular fiction—indeed, the novel as a genre was sometimes understood as a middle-class alternative to more elite literary forms like poetry. During the 1930s, however, technical advances in printing and binding made possible the publication of large printings of inexpensive texts. These advances culminated in the rise of the paperback edition in the final years of the decade and the shifts in production and marketing policy associated with that development. Drugstores and bus stations replaced bookstores as the primary sites for these new paperbacks. To maximize sales potential, editors sought work that was familiar, even formulaic, in nature. Such traditionalism was probably augmented by Broadway's and Hollywood's interest in optioning popular novels whose characters and plot lent themselves most readily to dramatic treatment. In postwar authors' response to these developments, the modern best-seller was born.

Such commercialized accounts had only a rudimentary interest in the political and psychological realities of ethnic identity. Leonard Q. Ross's (Leo Rosten's) *The Education of H\*Y\*M\*A\*N K\*A\*P\*L\*A\*N* (1937) reduced problems of acculturation to the low comedy of the dialect tradition. Herman Wouk's *Marjorie Morningstar* (1955) and Chaim Potok's *The Chosen* (1967) and *My Name Is Asher Lev* (1972) simplified the problems of Reform and Orthodox Judaism examined more fully by Bellow and Roth. Wouk's Marjorie Morgenstern, for example, fought off threats to her virtue and career goals for four hundred pages only to capitulate on both counts in her final retreat into middle-class domesticity. And Potok's Asher Lev was merely Roth's Portnoy recast as a "nice Jewish boy." Similarly stereotypic and inspirational were Betty Smith's account of Irish Americans in *A Tree Grows in Brooklyn* (1943) and Kathryn Forbes's (Kathryn Anderson McLean's) reminiscences about Scandinavian San Francisco in *Mama's Bank Account* (1943). Yet even as they pandered to the sentimentality and self-satisfaction of their readers, they did get on the record some of the sociological details essential to the process of identity construction. Although Hyman Kaplan was a baggy-pants comic, he had a better feel for living language than the smug WASP teacher who narrated the novel. If Wouk's understanding of Marjorie's libido was weak, his depiction of Jewish teenagers on the Upper West Side was precise. And while it left unexamined a whole set of family stereotypes, Forbes's sentimental portrait of a community of urban-dwelling Norwegians at least overturned the clichéd representation of Scandinavian Americans as stoic Midwestern farmers.

The function of such a popular "literature of environment" as a necessary preliminary to social change could be best seen in postwar women's fiction. Even after the reinstatement of oppressive models of female domesticity, some women writers continued to work valiantly against gender stereotyping. Carson McCullers examined the alienation of African Americans, children, the handicapped, and especially women in such works as *The Heart Is a Lonely Hunter* (1940), *The Ballad of the Sad Café* (1943), and *The Member of the Wedding* (1946). Her lyrical prose and her interest in the isolating aspects of love strongly resembled those of males writing in the same tradition of Southern gothic. Yet her sexual candor, eye for domestic detail, and focus on the female viewpoint made her narratives proto-feminist (and implicitly lesbian).

Late in the postwar period the generalized sense of female unrest received a name and a focus from the publication of Betty Friedan's *Feminine Mystique* in 1963. Even such universalizing writers as Mary McCarthy began to admit the existence of experiences uniquely female. In her best-selling *The Group* (1963), McCarthy directed at a circle of Vassar graduates the same jaundiced eye with which she analyzed all her characters. While hardly a feminist reading, the novel's very willingness to single out women's experiences as qualitatively different from men's suggested a growing public awareness of women as a group. This awareness received its most sympathetic public statement with the publication the same year of poet Sylvia Plath's only novel, *The Bell Jar*. Not published in America until 1971, Plath's moving account of her attempt to conform to traditional models, as taught by the woman's magazine where she was a teenage editor, and her ensuing mental breakdown was the decade's most detailed indictment of the psychological inadequacy of the age's assessment of women—and its most tragic.

Such preliminary statements of defiance stood as immediate antecedents to more explicitly feminist (in some cases lesbian) novels by such contemporary writers as Joyce Carol Oates, Alison Lurie, Joanna Russ, and Toni Morrison. Despite these courageous exceptions, however, much postwar women's literature accepted uncritically the generation's gender stereotypes. This acquiescence need not be judged too severely. In her study of domesticity in the nineteenth century, Nancy Cott argued that conservative ideologies can have liberating social consequences. According to her famous play on words, the "bonds of womanhood" that bound women to a repressive ideology of hearth and home also bound them together as women. It is in a similar light that we should read the domestic fiction of the postwar period. From its opening characterization of women as "ripe, hotly passionate, but fickle," Grace Metalious's *Peyton Place* (1956), the period's best-selling novel, seemed calculated to reaffirm every sexist stereotype of the generation. Yet its willingness to treat clinically such topics as abortion and menstruation marked its interest in naturalizing the then sensational topic of female sexuality. More subtly, its depiction of successful women at work belied its own tendency to represent women as ruled by emotions. Whatever its debts to the male-dominated traditions of regional literature and the revolt against the village, *Peyton Place* situated women at the economic foundation of the community as fully as at its emotional center.

Similar undercurrents of rebelliousness were seen in the period's workplace novels. Rona Jaffe's best-selling *The Best of Everything* (1958) characterized the career girl as someone merely marking time while waiting for the right man, without considering the role that employment discrimination and sexual double standards played in women's choice of marriage over career. Yet despite the book's conventional morality, its workplace setting implicitly returned to its characters some of the autonomy that their love lives denied them. However passive Jaffe made these women in their relations to men, she showed them savvy and assertive in handling their workload (and their bosses). In her heroine Caroline Bender, Jaffe offered a proto-feminist revision of Theodore Dreiser's "Sister" Caroline Meeber. Unlike her literary namesake, Jaffe's Caroline did not recite male writing, she edited it. And rather than succumbing to general transcendental longing as did Sister Carrie, Bender focused her dissatisfaction on the specifically female conflict between career and domesticity.

Even highly conventional literary treatments of the housewife functioned unintentionally to increase female awareness. Shirley Jackson was best known for her gothic accounts of dysfunctional families in *We Have Always Lived in the Castle* (1962) and matricide in the short story "The Lottery" (1949). It was not surprising, then, that her comic account of her own family, *Life Among the Savages* (1953), should view skeptically the joys of suburban existence with four "savage" children. But less well crafted works—like Jean Kerr's wisecracking *Please Don't Eat the Daisies* (1957) and *The Snake Has All the Lines* (1960)—played as well a role in identity formation. All suburban novels reinforced clichés about the importance of the family and of the mother's role as nurturer and moral exemplar. Yet their comic tone established a conspiratorial relation to their audience. The author wrote not to indoctrinate readers but to dramatize experiences she assumed they shared with her as homemakers. Such narratives implied that commonplace domestic events—like measles, the car pool, or the selection of wallpaper—were worth an individual's attention. In so defining "housewife" as a job (and subject of literature), these novels set the stage for Friedan's subsequent critique of society's evaluation of that job. Only after readers recognized they were housewives could they decide whether or not "housewife" was something they wanted to be.

A comparable liberalizing function was served by male novels of environment that examined the morality of the marketplace and of suburbia. Max Shulman's *Rally Round the Flag, Boys!* (1957) and John McPartland's *No Down Payment* (1957) offered respectively parodic and earnest accounts of the sexual tensions resulting from the claustrophobia of modern suburban housing. Cameron Hawley's *Executive Suite* (1952) focused on the immorality of big business, while Sloan Wilson's more ambitious *The Man in the Gray Flannel Suit* (1955) represented the two worlds of Connecticut domesticity and Manhattan business as complementary threats to individual authenticity. None of these novels seriously challenged middle-class assumptions about the work ethic or the sexual division of labor. Even the most sensitive—Wilson's critique of the flannel business suit as "the uniform of the day"—embodied the self-satisfaction of 1950s morality, complete with a crusading liberal judge. Yet like their female counterparts, these novels at least attended to the details of business and community life. Today Wilson's account seems less striking for its final rejection of the organization man than for the implicitly loving precision with which it recorded the process of his depersonalization.

It is in the context of this popular tradition of the male novel of environment that one must view the work of two of the most honored authors of the period—John Cheever and John Updike. These writers have been attacked for their stylistic traditionalism and lack of interest in social issues, characteristics associated with *The New Yorker,* where both men first published much of their work. Yet the error lay less with the authors' material than with readers' tendency to read their WASP suburban characters as representative of some generalized American ideal. Cheever's Wapshot novels examined skeptically the very WASP privileges presupposed by the genre of the family saga. In *The Wapshot Chronicle* (1957), the frequent shifts in story line and the mythologizing tendency of the narrative voice called into question the reliability of any such unifying account. Its sequel *The Wapshot Scandal* (1964), less mythological and more focused on social issues and characters only indirectly related to the Wapshots, used global settings to reveal the provinciality of its characters. Cheever addressed explicitly the cultural specificity of his customary material in his revisionist *Falconer* (1977), where he presented sexual fulfillment through an idealized homosexual experience; evidently even his previous focus on straight love had been merely conventional, without meaning to affirm the normative quality of heterosexuality.

The same self-consciousness about his WASP identity increasingly informed the work of the highly prolific John Updike. Concerned like Cheever with the shallowness of modern life as evidenced in the commercialization of culture and the difficulty of marital relations, Updike differed from the older man in his sexual explicitness and his extended use of unifying symbolic patterns. After experimenting with mythological metaphors in *The Centaur* (1963), Updike constructed in *Couples* (1968) both an apotheosis of the suburban sex novel and its reductio ad absurdum. This intricate burlesque of novels like *Peyton Place* or *No Down Payment* not only used a more imaginative sensual language than its models but also hinted at the historical underpinnings of middle-class promiscuity in the Kennedy years. The social setting implicit in *Couples* became central in Updike's masterpiece—the four books treating Harry "Rabbit" Angstrom. The earliest, *Rabbit Run* (1960), seemed to present its protagonist's sexual crisis in the broadest existential terms. Yet with each subsequent reencounter—*Rabbit Redux* (1971), *Rabbit Is Rich* (1981), and *Rabbit at Rest* (1990)—Rabbit's anxiety was more fully related to its temporal setting, and especially the conflict between middle-class Protestant mores and a society whose values lay elsewhere. Although occasionally the novels allowed Rabbit to pontificate on the general failure of America, at their best they used the peculiarity of Rabbit's cultural position to doubt the very existence of a single, homogeneous "America."

The issue of social change in the novel is a complex one, involving questions about the desirability and effectiveness of the novel as an agent of change, and even about the nature of change as such. The position of postwar literature in this debate is uncertain. It is nevertheless necessary to challenge the traditional view of such novels as apolitical and elitist. Most of these works did not have social reform as their primary goal. And in embracing the universalizing aesthetic criteria of the generation, postwar authors often left unexamined some of the discriminatory implications of middle-class liberalism. Yet the literatures of identity, especially minority literatures and the literature of environment, fostered a sense of group solidarity at odds with the pronounced individualism of the times. And if such identities at times themselves reinforced the age's cultural stereotypes, they were at least the necessary precursor to what would become in subsequent generations a more truly oppositional literature.

David Van Leer

# The Late Twentieth Century

# Introduction

Readers who glance at the titles of the chapters in this section cannot help noticing that, for the authors of these chapters, the idea of "American" literature has undergone significant change in the latter part of this century. The crucial questions surrounding the canon, national and class boundaries, race, personal identity, genre, gender, the scene and nature of writing, and history are reflected in the proliferations of the "American" novel over the last forty years. One could only call the development of the novel in this period "rhizomic," in the sense of French philosophers Giles Deleuze and Félix Guattari's conception of the "rhizome" as a weedy growth, like crabgrass, with multiple crossings and branchings, growing everywhere.

To write an impossibly comprehensive or total history of the American novel in this (or any) period would be a contradiction in terms, for not only is the period itself open-ended and dynamic, but also many of the intellectual currents that have risen out of the novels written during this time are at odds with each other as they render problematic, for example, the relation between fiction and history, the relation of "major" to "minor" literature, the constitution of the author and the constituencies of the readership, the nature of representation, or the nature of writing itself. How, then, to write a representative history—as literary histories have been traditionally conceived—of the major authors and works of a determined place and period? Rather than chase after that illusory and highly questionable goal, the writers in this section (indeed, throughout this *His-*

*tory*) have chosen to take local and specific points of departure that might be seen as incursions or interventions into the inconceivable totality of the American novel in the late twentieth century. Together, the chapters in this section might be seen as a mosaic in process, unfinished, with indefinite frame and border, yet conveying a colorful impression of the liveliness and utter heterogeneity of the literature of this period. In fact, it is this very openness, this sense of "presentness," that forms one of the most attractive features of the contemporary American novel that challenges the "the," the "contemporary," the "American," and the "novel" as the defining limits of its exfoliations.

The reader of these incursionary chapters, then, may or may not find her or his favorite author mentioned in these pages; scholars of contemporary American fiction may or may not find discussed in detail those authors they deem most important or "major." We have not attempted, here, to be either exhaustive or canonical since, as I have suggested, exhaustiveness and canonicity are two of the many issues the contemporary American novel puts into question. But the writers of these chapters *have* attempted to be historical in their collective sense of history—including literary history—as a collage of proliferating movements and subjects interacting in ways seen and unseen, neither wholly determined by some larger plan or system, nor wholly indeterminate within the intertwined matrices of event and inscription. It is this sense of "history" that pervades the discussion of authors and works in these chapters. With this in mind, the reader is invited to roam across the capacious, worldly, bordering yet borderless country of the contemporary American novel, therein to discover the vitality and power of this writing, along with its faults and its fragility, its resistances and complicities, its indelible *being there*.

Patrick O'Donnell

# Postmodern Culture

What do we mean by "postmodern culture?" Does this vague phrase refer to crucial features of contemporary life? Or is it a categorical device deployed by critics and artists to further their own projects? Has the term "postmodern" become such a buzz word that it means anything, refers to everything—hence signifies nothing?

These questions exemplify the degree to which the debate about what does or does not constitute "postmodern culture" is not a mere disagreement about the use or misuse of a phrase but rather a raging battle over how we define and conceive of the role of culture in American society (as well as those abroad). More pointedly, it highlights how we interpret the current crisis in our society and best muster resources from the past and present to alleviate this crisis. Any interpretation of this crisis that alludes to "postmodern culture" presupposes some notions of the modern, modernity, modernization, and modernism—when they began, when they peaked, when they declined, when they ended, what was good and bad about them, and why the advent of "postmodern culture" has emerged. And any use of these notions bears directly and indirectly on how one conceives of what is worth preserving and changing in the present. In this regard the way in which one characterizes "postmodern culture" reflects one's anxieties, frustrations, allegiances, and visions as a critic. In short, one's very intellectual vocation is at stake in one's conception of "postmodern culture."

Because of the promiscuous uses of the adjective "postmodern" in conjunction with philosophy, literature, et al.—and the various reductions of "postmodern culture" to a variety of "postmodernisms"—we must be clear as to the level on which our inquiry proceeds. We are not proceeding at the level of the *popular* mind that usually associates "postmodern culture" with a set of styles, forms, and figures—be it the historical eclecticism of building-making as in the decorative and ornamental references to older styles in the architecture of Michael Graves, Robert Venturi, Philip Johnson, and Robert A. M. Stern, the desequentializing music of John Cage, Laurie Anderson, and Philip Glass, the denarrativizing literature of Donald Barthelme, Ishmael Reed, and John Barth, or the defamiliarizing photography of Barbara Kruger and the early Martha Rosler.

Nor are we proceeding at the level of the *academic* mind that often views "postmodern culture" as a product of the recent French occupation of the American intellectual landscape—be it Jean-François Lyotard's claim about the increasing incredulity toward master narratives (for example, Marxism, Enlightenment rationalism, or Whiggish liberalism), Jean Baudrillard's reflections about the saturation of simulacra and simulations in consumer-driven America, or poststructuralists' (Jacques Derrida or Michel Foucault) pronouncements about decentered, fragmented subjects caught in a labyrinthine world of no escape.

The popular and academic minds tend to be fixated on symptomatic emblems of "postmodern culture," yet we must probe deeper if we are to grapple seriously with our present moment—the moment of postmodern culture. On the one hand, the popular mind is right to see that discourses about postmodernism—especially in architecture, literature, and the arts—were initiated in the United States as a kind of revolt against domesticated modernisms of the academy, museum, and galleries during the Cold War period (1945–89). Since European artists and critics tended to link modernisms with transgression and revolt against authority, their critiques of domesticated modernisms were usually put forward in the name of more radical modernisms. On the other hand, the academic mind is right to note that French post-Marxist issues of difference, otherness, alterity, and marginality are central to "postmodern culture." Ironically, the waning of Marxist influence on the Left Bank of Paris, along with transgressive revolts against homogenizing Communist parties and expanding French bureaucracies, seized the imagination of world-weary ex-New Left academics in the United States caught offguard by feminist, black, brown, red, gay, and lesbian challenges in the name of identity and community. Yet neither the popular nor the academic mind—given the relative lack of a historical sense of both—fully grasp the major determinants of postmodern culture: the unprecedented impact of market forces on everyday life, including the academy and the art world, the displacement of Europe by America in regard to global *cultural* influence (and imitation), and the increase of political polarization in cultural affairs by national, racial, gender, and sexual orientation, especially within the highly bureaucratized world of ideas and opinions.

These determinants of postmodern culture are inseparable, interdependent, yet not identical. If there is a common denominator, it is the inability of a market-driven American civilization—*the* world power after 1945—to constitute a culture appropriate for its new international (and imperial) status given its vast mass culture, its heterogeneous population, and its frustrated (often alienated) cultural elites of the right and left. Hence, contradictions, paradoxes, and ironies abound. The leading Marxist critic, Fredric Jameson, and an exemplary conservative critic, Hilton Kramer, both view the commodification of culture and the commercialization of the arts as major culprits of our moment, while both are suspicious of liberal cultural administrators who promote these market processes in the name of diversity, pluralism, or multiculturalism. On this matter, the left postmodern journal *October* joins the revivified spirit of T. S. Eliot echoed in the right, modernist periodical *The New Criterion*. Similarly, the uncritical patriotism from above—or, more pointedly, the atavistic and jingoistic mutterings of the cultural right—is paralleled by the uncritical tribalism from below of many of the proponents of multiculturalism, even as both accuse the other of their lack of cosmopolitanism or internationalism. And cultural wars of the canon erupt over bureaucratic turf—managerial positions, tenure jobs, and curriculum offerings—alongside an already multicultural mass culture (especially in popular music), with little public opposition to hi-tech military cannons of mass destruction targeted at tens of thousands of Iraqi civilians in the most massive air attack in human history. In this crude sense, postmodern culture is what we get when a unique capitalist civilization—still grappling with a recent memory of cultural inferiority anxieties toward a decimated and divided Europe—with an unwieldy mass culture of hybridity and heterogeneity and a careerist professional class of museum managers and academic professors tries to create consensus and sustain some semblance of a common culture as a new political and military imperium. These efforts—on behalf of the left, right, and middle—are bold in intent yet often pathetic in consequence. They are bold in that they are unashamedly utopian. Conservative Eurocentrists, liberal pluralists, moderate multiculturalists, and radical feminists or leftists all assume that their grand designs for cultural citizenship in American civilization can be implemented in the face of market forces, bureaucratic demands, and political expediencies in American society. Yet, for the most part, this assumption proves to be false. Instead their efforts tend to be pathetic, that is, they frustrate both themselves and their foes by not only reinforcing dissensus but also undermining the very conditions to debate the nature of the dissensus and the points of radical disagreement. This occurs principally owing to the larger *de facto* segregation by political persuasion, race, and subculture in a balkanized society; it is sustained by suspicion of common vocabularies or bridge-building nomenclatures that facilitate such debate. The collapse of a civic culture, once undergirded by left subgroupings (now gone) and liberal enclaves (now in disarray), contributes greatly to this tribal state of cultural affairs. Conservative ideologies promote a patriotic fervor to replace this collapse—as witnessed in William Buckley's recent call for national service or the melodramatic flag-waving to unify the nation. Yet market forces promote the proliferation of differentiated consumers, with distinct identities, desires, and pleasures to be sold and satisfied, especially in peacetime periods.

But what are these mysterious, seemingly omnipotent "market forces"? Are they not a kind of *deus ex machina* in my formulations? Are they not under human control? If so, whose control? My basic claim is that Hilton Kramer and Fredric Jameson are right: commodification of culture and commercialization of the arts are the major factors in postmodern culture. These powerful social processes can be characterized roughly by a complex interplay between profit-driven corporations and pleasure-hungry consumers in cultural affairs. T. S. Eliot rightly noted decades ago that American society is a deritualized one, with deracinated and denuded individuals "distracted from distraction by distraction"—that is, addicted to stimulation, in part, to evade the boredom and horror Baudelaire saw as the distinctive features of modern life. And in a society and culture that evolves more and more around the buying and selling of commodities for stimulatory pleasures—be it bodily, psychic, or intellectual—people find counsel, consolation, and captivity in mobs, be that mob well-fed or ill-fed, well-housed or homeless, well-clad or ill-clad. And such mobs are easily seduced by fashionable ideas, fashionable clothes, or fashionable xenophobias. This Eliotic insight turns Lyotard's conception of postmodern culture on its head. There is not an increasing incredulity toward master narratives. Instead, the fashionable narratives— not just in the United States but around the world—are nationalist ones, usually xenophobic with strong religious, racial, patriarchal, and homophobic overtones. And Eliot's major followers in postmodern culture chime in quite loudly with this chauvinistic chorus. Yet, many multiculturalists who oppose this chorus simply dance a jingoistic jig to a slightly different tune. In this sense, postmodern culture looks more and more like a rehash of old-style American pluralism with fancy French theories that legitimate racial, gender, and sexual orientational entrée into the new marketplace of power, privilege, and pleasure.

But is this entrée so bad? Is it not the American way now played out in new circumstances and new conditions? Does it not democratize and pluralize the academy, museums, and galleries in a desirable manner? This entrée is not simply desirable, it is imperative. The past exclusion of nonwhite and nonmale intellectual and artistic talent from validation and recognition is a moral abomination. And it is the American way—at its best—to correct exclusion with inclusion, to democratize the falsely meritocratic, and to pluralize the rigidly monolithic. Yet it is easy to fall prey to two illusions: first, the notion that inclusion guarantees higher quality and the idea that entrée signifies a significant redistribution of cultural benefits. Inclusion indeed yields new perspectives, critical orientations, and questions. It makes possible new dialogues, frameworks, and outworks. Yet only discipline, energy, and talent can produce quality. And market forces mitigate against intellectual and artistic quality—for the reasons put forward by Thomas Carlyle and John Ruskin, Matthew Arnold and W. E. B. Du Bois, William Morris and Virginia Woolf. Second, entrée of new talent is salutary yet it benefits principally those included. Despite the hoopla about group consciousness and role models, *class* structures—across racial and gender lines—are reinforced and legitimated, not broken down or loosened, by inclusion. And this indeed is the American way—to promote and encourage the myth of classlessness, especially among those guilt-ridden about their upward social mobility or ashamed of their class origins. The relative absence of substantive reflections—not just ritualistic gestures—about class in postmodern culture is continuous with silences and blindnesses in the American past.

These silences and blindnesses hide and conceal an undeniable feature of postmodern culture: the pervasive violence (psychic and physical) and fear of it among all sectors of the population. Critics and theorists usually say little of this matter. Yet in the literary works of contemporary masters like Toni Morrison, Russell Banks, Joyce Carol Oates, or Thomas Pynchon, violence of various sorts looms large in a sophisticated and subtle manner. And most of this violence—with the exception of police treatment of African American males—is citizen against citizen. The hidden injuries of class, intraracial hostilities, the machismo identity taken out on women, and the intolerance of gay and lesbian orientations generate deep anxieties and frustrations that often take violent forms. These violent acts— random, unpredictable, sometimes quite brutal—make fear and fright daily companions with life in postmodern culture. The marvels of the technological breakthroughs in communications and information stand side by side with the primitive sense of being haunted by anonymous criminals who have yet to strike. In fact, the dominant element in the imagination of dwellers in postmodern culture may well be this ironic sense of being anesthetized by victims of violence, given its frequent occurrence, and of being perennially aware that you may be next. In this way, postmodern culture is continuous with Eliot's modernist wasteland of futility and anarchy and Poe's modern chamber of horrors.

Cornel West

# Postmodern Realism

While we do not need yet another definition of what the postmodern really is, it seems clear to me that the pan-American narratives by Alejo Carpentier, Gabriel García Márquez, Toni Morrison, Arturo Islas, Maxine Hong Kingston, Raymond Carver, Helena María Viramontes, Joyce Carol Oates, Robert Stone, E. L. Doctorow, and others are emphatically implicated in any attempt to map out the specificity of postcontemporary culture and literature in the Americas and thus to gauge this transnational culture's distance from what might be called "high modernism." Whether or not one uses the term postmodernism, there can be no doubt about the fact that the position of women and men of color, Jews, gays and lesbians, and so on in postcontemporary society and their effect on our hemisphere is fundamentally different from what it used to be in the period of high modernism and the historical avant-garde. Put differently, postmodern theory ought never to be viewed as a homogeneous phenomenon (Ihab Hassan, Jean-François Lyotard, Jürgen Habermas) but rather as one in which political contestation is central. As Cornel West suggests, postmodernism illuminates "the ragged edges of the Real, of Necessity, not being able to eat, not having health care, all this is something that one cannot not know."

Seen in this light, postmodernism is an attempt to negotiate "the ragged edges of the Real," and to think historically; it either expresses what Fredric Jameson calls "some deeper irrepressible historical impulse" (in however "derealized" a fashion as writers from the

Americas might have it) or unsuccessfully represses or avoids history, like a bad dream, full of displacements, representations, condensations, and secondary revisions. Linda Hutcheon, moreover, suggests that postmodernist narratives are closely related to "historiographic metafiction," and includes texts that are "intensely self-reflexive and yet paradoxically also lay claim to historical events and personages." Hutcheon's position in effect links postmodernism with Louis Althusser's late Marxism and its rejection of the postulates of realism and Judith Butler's feminist deconstruction of the real.

Like many postmodern realists, Althusser reminds us that "realism" is not a style that gives us an undistorted reflection of the world. Realism, in his formulation, represents the ideologically hegemonic way of conceiving and expressing our relationship to the natural and social worlds around us. In other words, as Althusser suggested in his classic essay "Ideology and Ideological State Apparatuses" (1969), realism functions ideologically: it offers itself as a neutral reflection of the world when it is but one way of imagining a world. More recently, Judith Butler in her essay "Feminism, Mapplethorpe, and Discursive Excess" (1990) argues that fantasy is not to be equated with what is not real but rather "with what is not *yet* real, or what belongs to a different version of the real." In any case, this chapter is not a survey of the postmodern realist writers from the Americas, for the postmodern condition cannot account without strain for all the literary productions that follow. Rather, I have merely tried to explore postmodern realism as a space of affinities and alliances among diverse histories.

It is generally accepted that the (postmodernist) magic realist movement in the Americas led by Alejo Carpentier, Carlos Fuentes, Gabriel García Márquez, Manuel Puig, and, more recently, Isabel Allende has had a powerful influence on a diverse group of postcontemporary United States writers of color: Toni Morrison's *Sula* and *Song of Solomon;* Arturo Islas's *The Rain God* and *Migrant Souls;* Maxine Hong Kingston's *The Woman Warrior, China Men,* and *Tripmaster Monkey;* Helena María Viramontes's *The Moths and Other Stories;* and Alberto Ríos's *The Iguana Killer.* While the works of these United States writers of color have been widely praised for their oppositional, feminist, gay, and minority discourse poetics, and for their powerful supernatural lyricism, their use of (postmodern) magic realism has received little attention in our largely Anglophonic Departments of Literature, owing to an inadequate understanding of a vast and rich literary and cultural movement in the Americas that began over forty years ago.

To be sure, the concept of (postmodern) magic realism raises many problems, both theoretical and historical. I will not retrace the rich polemical debate among Latin American and United States scholars over the concept "magic realism," for Fernando Alegría, Roberto González Echevarría, and Amaryll Beatrice Chanady have written the most cogent and useful critical surveys of the debate. Instead, my task is to make the very demanding argument about (postmodern) magic realism available to readers in the United States who have heard about its importance but so far have been baffled by it. To simplify matters and to save some space, I will focus only on Alejo Carpentier's "Prologue" to his revolutionary novel *The Kingdom of This World* (1949) — arguably, the first magic realist text in the Americas — and on Gabriel García Marquez's *The General in His Labyrinth* (1990) — perhaps the latest exemplary postmodern realist novel.

For many scholars, magic realism as a concept appears in three different moments in the twentieth century. The first appears during the avant-garde years in Europe when the term was used by Franz Roh in his *Nach-Expressionismus: Magischer Realismus* (1925), and when André Breton proclaimed the marvelous an aesthetic concept and as part of everyday life. The second moment was in the late 1940s when the related concepts *el realismo mágico* (magic realism) and *lo real maravilloso* (marvelous realism) traveled, as they say, from Europe to the Americas and were appropriated by Arturo Uslar Pietri and Alejo Carpentier as a yardstick to measure, compare, and evaluate indigenous cultural art forms in the American grain. Whereas Pietri adopted Roh's term "magic realism," Carpentier, the more influential novelist and theorist, used Breton's version of *le merveilleux* and theorized in the "Prologue" to *The Kingdom of This World* his famous concept of "marvelous American reality."

A third period of (postmodern) magic realism can be said to have begun in 1955 when Angel Flores published his influential essay "Magic Realism in Spanish American Fiction." This third phase, as Roberto González Echevarría suggests, continues through the 1960s "when criticism searches for the Latin roots of some of the novels produced during the 'boom' and attempts to justify their experimental nature." As we shall see, there is a fourth phase or "crack" as Toni Morrison, Arturo Islas, Maxine Hong Kingston, among others, expand the magic realist tradition in postmodernist and often "signifyin[g]" ways.

Flores had argued that what distinguishes magic realism from other realisms is that it attempts to transform "the common and the everyday into the awesome and the unreal." Moreover, Flores emphasized the connections between magic realism and examples of European modernist aesthetics practiced by Franz Kafka in his novels and Giorgio de Chirico in his paintings. In 1967 Luis Leal joined the growing debates by refuting Flores's essay. In "El realismo mágico en la literatura hispanoamericana," he argued that magic realism was an exclusively New World literary movement. Included in his school of magic realist writers were Arturo Uslar Pietri, Miguel Angel Asturias, Felix Pita Rodríguez, Alejo Carpentier, Juan Rulfo, and Nicolás Guillén. According to Leal, the basic difference among the competing schools of "magic realism," "realism," and "surrealism" is the following: "The magic realist does not attempt to copy (like the realists) or make the real vulnerable (like the surrealists), but attempts to capture the mystery which palpitates in things." But Leal's essay ignores the profound impact European surrealism, modernism, and ethnography had on the generation of writers he analyzed, especially Alejo Carpentier.

Born and raised in Cuba, Alejo Carpentier made these connections in his "Prologue" to his African Caribbean novel *The Kingdom of This World*. In the rhetorical question "What is the history of the Americas but the chronicle of *lo real maravilloso?*" Carpentier suggests the ideology that lies at the center of his magic realist narrative: how to write in a European language—with its Western systems of thought—about realities and thought-structures never before seen in Europe. Carpentier asks for the first time in 1949 the following questions, which would influence generations of writers from the Americas: What is the African, Amerindian, and *mestizo/a* heritage of the Americas, and how can it function as a stylistics, an ideology, and a point of view? Years later, Robert Coover would note that the *nueva narrativa* from Latin America "was for a moment the region's headiest and most dangerous export."

While Carpentier learned much from the Surrealists' experiments to explore a kind of second reality hidden within the world of dreams, the unconscious, political tensions that arose among the Surrealists themselves caused him to break away from them. Carpentier probably also went his own way because, as González Echevarría emphasized, European surrealism clashed with the Cuban's "Spenglerian conception of man and history he had absorbed through avant-garde journals like the *Revista de Occidente*."

Thus, in spite of his early fascination with surrealism, Carpentier never became a committed disciple of Breton. Unlike Breton and his followers, Carpentier argued in *The Kingdom of This World, The Lost Years* (1953), and *Explosion in a Cathedral* (1962) that the "second reality" the Surrealists explored in automatic writing is merely part of everyday life in America. Furthermore, as a follower of Oswald Spengler's *Decline of the West* (in Spengler's universal history there is no fixed "center"), Carpentier eschewed the Surrealists' Eurocentric doctrine of the marvelous and argued that all things of a truly magical nature are, in fact, found within the reality of the Americas—not the "boring" cities of Europe. According to Carpentier, the "discovery," conquest, and colonization of the New World are magical events in themselves: "Open Bernal Díaz del Castillo's great chronicle [*True History of the Conquest of New Spain* (1552)] and one will encounter the only real and authentic book of chivalry ever written: a book of dust and grime chivalry where the genies who cast evil spells were the visible and palpable *teules,* where the unknown beasts were real, where one actually gazed on unimagined cities and saw dragons in their native rivers and strange mountains swirling with snow and smoke." For Carpentier, then, Bernal Díaz del Castillo's chronicle of the Spanish conquest of Mexico is an exemplary magic realist narrative because Díaz (unwittingly) had written about the clash of cultures—Old World and New World—and had described in thick detail the superposition of one layer of reality upon another.

Forming a background for Carpentier's theory and thematized in *The Kingdom of This World* is what he sees as the "fecundity" of the

New World landscape. Carpentier's concept of *lo real maravilloso* can, therefore, be summarized in the author's own words: "due to the untouched nature of its landscape, its ontology, the Faustian presence of the Indian and the Black, the revelation inherent in the continent's recent discovery and the fruitful cross-breeding this discovery engendered, America is still very far from exhausting its wealth of mythologies. Indeed, what is the history of America if not the chronicle of the marvelous of the real?"

In short, Carpentier set up an antithesis between surrealism, on the one hand, and *lo real maravilloso,* on the other. As is clear from the "Prologue" to *The Kingdom of This World,* Carpentier unfavorably compares Surrealism with a privileged New World aesthetic grounded in a reality that is inherently magical (voodoo, *santería,* and so on). To be sure, Carpentier's thesis rests on the claims that New World artists and people experience the marvelous in their everyday lives—what Raymond Williams called in a different context "structures of feeling"—and therefore have no need to invent a domain of fantasy. Thus on the basis of local New World privilege, Carpentier rejects surrealism as sterile, and legitimizes, in near postmodern realist fashion, the mode of writing he elects: a "chronicle of the marvelous of the real." Carpentier's *The Kingdom of This World* is, therefore, emblematic of the kind of narrative experimentation we now take for granted in postmodernist American fiction: historical events move in reverse; characters die before they are born; and "green" tropical winds blow away the New World landscape.

Although Gabriel García Márquez's use of magic realism includes Carpentier's familiar tropes of the supernatural—one of the foundation concepts of magic realism—his version differs from Carpentier's and inaugurates the rise of (postmodern) magic realism globally. As is well known, García Márquez's concept of postmodern (magic) realism in *Leafstorm* (1955), "Big Mama's Funeral" (1962), *One Hundred Years of Solitude* (1967), and *The Autumn of the Patriarch* (1976) presupposes an identification by the narrator with the oral expression of popular cultures in the Latin American pueblo. In other words, as I argued in *The Dialectics of Our America* (1991), García Márquez's thematization of (postmodern) magic realism and the politics of the possible are usually expressed in his early stories about the rise and fall of Macondo through a collective voice, inverting, in a jesting manner, the values of the official Latin American culture. More recently, García Márquez has written a postmodern realist novel, *The General in His Labyrinth,* that reverses his past attempts as a novelist to transform the ordinary into the mythical and magical, for in this controversial text he takes on the saintly image of Simón Bolívar, the Great Liberator of the Americas, by rendering this national hero as a man of ordinary, even crude, attributes.

In *The General in His Labyrinth* the postmodern real is at the center: it focuses on a real historical personage, Simón Bolívar, and is based, according to the author, on two years of "sinking into the quicksand of voluminous, contradictory, and often uncertain documentation." In other words, if Bolívar went out at night prowling the mean streets of Bogotá when the moon was full, then we can be assured that García Márquez, along with the assistance of the Cuban geographer Gladstone Oliva and the astronomer Jorge Doval, had made an inventory of nights when there was "a full moon during the first 30 years of the last century."

Of course, García Márquez avoids, like the plague, a conventional chronological narrative of Bolívar's life. Rather, in postmodernist fashion, he begins his narrative *in medias res* when Bolívar is forty-six years old, shrunken by an unnamed illness that will surely kill him. Rejected as president by the elite and the lumpen of Colombia—the new country he helped liberate—Bolívar leaves Bogotá for a wild, whirling journey by boat down the Magdalena River, eventually hoping to sail to London.

But the General never gets "out of this labyrinth." In the fierce light of death's shadows, Bolívar is defeated by the backwater elements, by the chicanery of his enemies (especially General Santander), by the rancor of his ambitious colleagues, by his "persistent constipation" or by his "farting stony, foul-smelling gas," and by his own solitary nostalgia for his former revolutionary self. Embarking with his noisy retinue from port to port, city to city, safe house to safe house, the General endures either celebrations and fiestas in his honor or is hounded by an army of widows who follow him everywhere, hoping to hear his "proclamations of consolation."

While Simón Bolívar had "wrested" from the Spanish colonists an empire five times more vast than all of Europe, and while he had led twenty years of war "to keep it free and united," he is at the end of his life a solitary man, praying for the right moment when he might make a political comeback.

Like the labyrinthine journey down the Magdalena River, the structure of the novel is postmodernist and serpentine. Deconstructing its own "return to storytelling," *The General in His Labyrinth* twists and disrupts historical time and space until not only Bolívar but the reader cannot tell where he is. Like the postmodern arts of memory themselves, full of traumas and resistances of all sorts, are scenes from the General's earlier triumphant life: his utopian proposal to turn the huge continent "into the most immense, or most extraordinary, or most invincible league of nations the world had ever seen"; his eternal temptations "by the enigma" of beautiful women; his latent homoerotic desires for the Baron Alexander von Humboldt who had "astonished" him in Paris by the "splendor of his beauty the likes of which he had never seen in any woman."

Just before he dies in December 1830, Bolívar proclaims that America is "ungovernable," for "this nation will fall inevitably into the hands of the unruly mob and then will pass into the hands of almost indistinguishable petty tyrants." He prophesies, moreover, the postcontemporary perils of what Andre Gunder Frank called "the development of underdevelopment": "I warned Santander that whatever good we had done for the nation would be worthless if we took on debt because we would go on paying interest till the end of time." In any case, the United States, in Bolívar's eyes, is "omnipotent and terrible, and its tale of liberty will end in a plague of miseries for us all."

Arguably the most important of American writers, Gabriel García Márquez takes up the slack of Carpentier's *lo real maravilloso* and the traditional historical novel in his postmodern realism, and combines them into a genuine postcontemporary dialectical aesthetic. In *The General in His Labyrinth*, García Márquez presents the reader with a semblance of historical verisimilitude and shatters it into alternative, dizzying patterns, as though the form of historiography was retained (at least in its traditional versions) but now for some reason seems to offer him a remarkable movement of invention.

If it makes sense to evoke a certain "return to storytelling" in the postmodern period, the return can be found in the wild genealogies and speculative texts of Toni Morrison, Arturo Islas, and Maxine

Hong Kingston. In their novels and experimental memoirs, they shuffle, like Petra Cotes in *One Hundred Years of Solitude,* historical figures and names like so many cards from a finite deck. Recovering alternative American histories in the unwritten texts of history (songs, *cuentos,* and talk story), these postmodernist realists' texts resemble the dynastic annals of "small-power kingdoms," as Jameson puts it, and realms very far removed from the traditional whitemale American novel.

Toni Morrison's *Sula* (1974), *Song of Solomon* (1977), *Tar Baby* (1981), and *Beloved* (1987), like most of the postmodern narratives under discussion, are embedded in the historical. For example, no mild apocalypse is the total destruction of the black neighborhood at the beginning of *Sula:* "In that place, where they tore the neighborhood and blackberry patches from their roots to make room for the Medallion City Golf course, there was once a neighborhood." The Bottom's segregated history in Ohio—cut across, contested, and obliterated—is written in a single sentence whose content extends from the dialectics of underdevelopment to the glossy, postmodern projects of urban renewal. Thus the "blackberry patches"— Morrison's imagery of nature—have to be "uprooted" to make way for what Marx referred to as capitalism's modernization.

After describing the leveling of the Bottom, Morrison focuses on the other hurts wrought by capitalism's (late) modernizations: Shadrack's unforgettable imagined bodily deformation as a part of the posttraumatic stress disorder resulting from his World War I experience and Eva Peace's radical act of self-mutilation. Abandoned by her husband Boy Boy around 1921, Eva sets out to keep her family together and financially sound: "Eighteen months later, she swept down from a wagon with two crutches, a new black pocketbook, and one leg." Eva's self-mutilation allows her then to build a new life and an African American feminist architecture on 7 Carpenter Road.

As in the case of García Márquez's *One Hundred Years of Solitude,* Morrison's *Sula* is a signifyin[g] chronicle of *lo real maravilloso* with a difference, but is entirely accessible to the reader since there are no real boundaries created by difficult narrative techniques. Moreover, like the chronicles of Carpentier and García Márquez, *Sula* covers the Bottom's history (which seems to move in reverse), from its apocalyptic endings to its rich beginnings. The sense of de-reality in *Sula* has nothing to do with language games; it is created by events, by what Morrison says happens. We may have doubts about the probability of what happens (Eva's self-mutilations, Plum's attempt to return to his mother's womb, the plague of robins announcing Sula's return to the Bottom, and Ajax's command of yellow butterflies) but there is never any doubt about what the narrator says.

*Song of Solomon*—a magical travel story about returning to one's local and global roots—won a National Book Critics Circle Award and was the first African American novel since Richard Wright's *Native Son* (1940) to be included for selection by the Book-of-the-Month Club. As Morrison suggests, Milkman Dead has "to pay attention to signs and landmarks" in order to discover "the real names" and with these the author allows her black middle-class protagonist to piece together his fantastic genealogical history all the way back to Africa. "How many dead lives and fading memories," Morrison writes, "were buried in and beneath the names of the places."

Arturo Islas is fascinated in his work by the liminal United States–Mexico borderlands, a postcontemporary "laboratory" where we can see culture of the First World imploding its postmodernist strategies into the Third World. Planned as a trilogy about the Angel family, *The Rain God* (1984) and *Migrant Souls* (1990), read collectively, are sprawling narratives, with genealogical trees as convoluted as Faulkner's and García Márquez's. Islas's last installment, however, was never completed, for the author died from complications of AIDS in February 1991.

The first novel, *The Rain God,* was published by Alexandrian, a small, Silicon Valley press of Palo Alto, California. Although rejected and censored by over twenty mainstream presses and editors in New York (who decide what counts as culture for the rest of the United States), *The Rain God* was named one of the three best novels of 1984 by the California Bay Area Reviewers' Association. Telling his story from the point of view of a Faulknerian Quentin-like narrator with a radical difference—"I don't hate Mexicans! I don't hate Anglos! I don't hate Gays! I don't hate the Third World!"—Miguel Chico is a bookish English professor living the epistemologies of the closet in San Francisco. A two-toned narrative, written at times in the pan-American styles of James, Faulkner, Rulfo, and García Márquez, *The Rain God* covers three generations of Angels—from just before the Mexican Revolution (1910–17) to the 1980s—who migrated north from Mexico.

Despite this large chronotope, imaginative geography, and complex genealogy, *The Rain God* is a high minimalist novel of subtlety and psychological nuance: "He, Miguel Chico, was the family analyst, interested in the past for psychological, not historical, reasons. Like Mama Chona, he preferred to ignore facts in favor of motives, which were always and endlessly open to question and interpretation." Islas's postmodern "open text" thus offers the reader a poetic landscape that, like the borderlands themselves, is both overdetermined and profound. The narrative, too, moves in electric *telenovela* chapters from one family crisis to another: Miguel Chico visits the cemetery on the Day of the Dead; Mama Chona, the family matriarch, puritanically controls her family's values; Miguel Grande cannot resist the soap opera passions of Lola, his wife's best friend; Miguel Chico's uncle, Felix Angel (the Rain Dancer), is murdered in the desert by a white, homophobic soldier.

If one of the most significant features of postmodern narratives is their attempt to negotiate forms of high art with certain forms and genres of mass culture and the cultural practices of everyday life, Islas's second installment, *Migrant Souls,* exploits this postcontemporary impulse by bringing together the impact of the classic Puritan rhetoric upon our culture, what Clifford Geertz, among others, calls the shaping influence of religious or quasi-religious symbols of society (Book 1 is appropriately entitled "Flight from Egypt"), with references to the 1950s through the mambo, doo-wop, Elvis, and mass cultural magazines such as *Popular Romance.*

More significantly, Islas reconceives in *Migrant Souls* literary and cultural practices. What happens, Islas asks, when American culture and literature are understood in terms of "migration," not immigration? How is the imagined community of the nation—to use Benedict Anderson's term—disrupted by hybrid, mestizo/a borderland subjectivities? Caught between the postcolonial border zones of past and present, Spanish and Indian cultures (Doña Marina's tamales and Miguel Chico's "Tlaloc"), Josie Salazar and her cousin Miguel Chico attempt to cross over the borderland contradictions of their everyday lives in Del Sapo, Texas. Like Ernesto Galarza in *Barrio Boy* (1972), Islas in Book 1 of *Migrant Souls* allows us to witness the Angel family's migration, north from Mexico. This change from one culture to another corresponds to the actual course of travel the founding Angel clan undertakes: "The Rio Grande—shallow, muddy, ugly in those places where the bridges spanned it—was a constant disappointment and hardly a symbol of the promised land to families like Mama Chona's. They had not sailed across an ocean or ridden in wagons and trains across half a continent in search of a new life. They were migrant, not immigrant, souls."

Within this simple form, however, are subsumed the postmodern themes of transformation, hybridity, and multiple subject positions— what feminist Gloria Anzaldúa in her border-defying writing *Borderlands/La Frontera* (1987) called the "new mestiza/o consciousness." If Islas's narrative had focused exclusively on this literal border-crossing story, he would have written, perhaps, a fairly conventional ethnic tale about acculturation and immigration. But he did not. Instead, Islas also examines the border zones of sexuality, gender, ethnicity, nationality, and so on. In fact, Islas's only other border-crossing tale in Book 1 is the hilarious scene of Josie's father smuggling an illegal turkey across the United States–Mexico border (after he had made it clear that he prefers enchiladas for Thanksgiving dinner). After a humiliating border check at the International Del Sapo bridge, he treats his family to menudo and homemade tortillas.

Just as the founding Angels crossed the "bloody river" in search of their city upon a hill, the younger Angel generation migrates to Chicago, Washington, D.C., and California. Book 2, entitled "Feliz Navidad," thus looks ahead to Vietnam and the Chicano Student Movement, where Miguel Chico's cousin Rudy appropriates and recodifies the term Chicano from borderland oral culture and unsettles all of the conservative Hispanic identities conferred on the Angel family by Mama Chona. More important, "Feliz Navidad" looks ahead to the publication of Miguel Chico's first novel, *Tlaloc* [*The Rain God*]: "Miguel Chico's novel had been written during a sabbatical leave when he decided to make fiction instead of criticize it. A modest semi-autobiographical work, it was published by a small California press that quickly went out of business. *Tlaloc* was an academic, if not commercial success and its author became known as an ethnic writer." For Islas, the point is not to declare that *The Rain God* and *Migrant Souls* are postmodern ethnic texts and stop there, but to show in hybrid perspectives how it was that ethnicity was invented and with what consequences.

Such nontraditional and critical views of acculturation and the polyethnic United States are readily apparent in the blurred genre works of Maxine Hong Kingston. In *The Woman Warrior* (1976) and *China Men* (1980), Kingston's texts are developed as postmodern fragments of traditional "talk story," myths, and the draconian rules imposed by Chinese parents. "No Name Woman," a talk story about the father's sister who is forced to have an illegitimate child in the pigsty, and who then commits suicide, is used by MaMa to caution the author from transgressing the family's rigid sexual codes. "Shaman," another talk story written by the author, exemplifies MaMa's attempts to tell her children "chilling" ghost stories to cool off the unbearable heat in the family's Stockton laundry. In both cases these oral tales are powerful stories of survival migrant cultures used by the Chinese Americans to fight the discriminatory United States government policies against Asians.

When Kingston declares that *China Men* is a book about "claiming America," her declaration characterizes the mood of a new generation of United States postmodern realist writers of color. Like Carpentier's and García Márquez's speculative chronicles, *China Men* (at times, also written in the oppositional poetic style of William Carlos Williams's *In the American Grain*) is a highly inventive history of Gold Mountain (U.S.A.). Kingston's earliest episodes begin in fact where Williams's leave off—around 1850—and the book ends with visions of American violence and the Vietnam war. At the same time, Kingston documents in fragmentary pieces the California Gold Rush and describes in excruciating detail the various racist Exclusion Acts the United States government passed against Asians.

Against the American grain, Kingston's *China Men* not only challenges whitemale constructions of American history but also aligns itself with the discovery by the professional historians that "all is fiction" and that there can never be a correct version of history. Because the narrator's father does not talk story—only the women do ("You say with few words and the silences")—Kingston invents different versions of the father's migration from China to America. In one of her most speculative and magical versions, the author describes how, perhaps, he sailed first to Cuba, where the sky drops rain the size of long squash, or to Hawaii, where papayas grow to the size of jack-o'-lanterns. Another version imagines how a smuggler brought him to New York by ship, locked in a crate, and how he rocked and dozed in the dark, feeling "the ocean's variety—the peaked waves that must have looked like pines; the rolling waves, round like shrubs, the occasional icy mountains; and for stretches, lulling grasslands." Still another version has BaBa coming to America, not illegally, but "legally"—he arrives in San Francisco to endure incarceration at the Immigration and Naturalization Service prison on Angel Island.

The ultimate goal of Kingston's *China Men* is thus to elaborate a logic of postmodern possibility, divergence, and the politics of the possible through a rhetoric of speculative historiography. Like Islas, Kingston explores the dialectics of the differential in order to emphasize cross-cultural interpenetration and transculturation rather than assimilation. In other words, Kingston offers alternatives to mythologies predicated on the lingering white supremacist "master narratives" of Anglocentric cultural centrality.

In sum, all the precursors fall into place in our new postmodern realist genealogy: the writers of the "Boom," like Carpentier and García Márquez, and their heirs, the United States writers of color, recover alternative histories in the unrecorded texts of history (songs, *cuentos,* and talk story) at the very moment when historical alternatives are in the process of being systemically expunged—CIA and FBI archives notwithstanding. Unlike the historical fantasies of other epochs, the postmodern narratives by these writers do not seek to diminish the historical event by celebrating the so-called death of the referent or of the subject, nor do they wish to lighten the burden of historical fact and necessity by transforming it into what Jameson calls "a costumed charade and misty revels without consequences and without irrevocability."

Their postmodern narratives, however, can be seen as entertaining a more active relationship to resistance and the politics of the possible, for they construct a speculative history that is simply their substitute for the making of the real kind. Postmodern *cuento,* fabulation, or talk story is no doubt the reaction to social and historical bankruptcy, to the blocking of possibilities that leaves—as Jameson stresses—"little option but the imaginary." Their very invention and contagious inventiveness, however, privileges a creative politics by the sheer act of multiplying events they cannot control. Postmodern realist invention thus by way of its very speculation becomes the figure of a larger politics of the possible and of resistance.

Another form of postmodern realism in the United States is in some ways more quotidian than the previous ones. Here a new K Mart/mass cultural realism, minimalized and self-examining, has grown up in the various writings of Raymond Carver, Helena María Viramontes, Joyce Carol Oates, Robert Stone, and others. If, as Malcolm Bradbury noted, there has been for our postcontemporary generation "warfare in the Empire of Signs, there is also every sign . . . that the Empire can indeed strike back." While these writers hardly share a homogeneous ideological sensibility, they do share a common sense that a crisis in representation is clearly at hand. Our old-fashioned and socially constructed American realism (Howells, Dreiser, and Norris) is now increasingly combined with a minimalism that deals with the new underclass of silenced peoples in our cities of quartz (workers, women, and so-called ethnic minorities) who typically feel adrift, or who feel that their histories have been systematically erased by urban planners and Immigration and Naturalization Service death squads, or who feel "controlled" by their access to controlled substances.

Raymond Carver, for example, in *What We Talk About When We Talk About Love* (1981) addresses the local, urban vernaculars and blends them by focusing on slight plots and elliptically structured dramatic conflicts. Minimalist in form, perhaps symptomatic of the reading public's dwindling attention span, Carver's texts, as John Barth suggests in "A Few Words About Minimalism" (1986), dramatize "the most impressive phenomenon of the current (North American, especially the United States) literary scene (the *gringo* equivalent of *el boom* in the Latin American novel): the new flowering of the (North American) short story." While Barth's comments on the "flowering" of the postcontemporary short-story scene are on target, I am distressed by his Anglophonic mapping of the hemisphere. Like that of many United States mainstream writers, Barth's criticism remains largely confined to well-established and long-standing disciplinary and geopolitical borders, with the result that our American (using the adjective in its genuine, hemispheric sense) literary history

remains largely provincial. For Barth, there is no real dialogue be-
tween Latin American writers and "gringo" postmodern minimalists.
In any case, America, for him, becomes a synonym for the United
States.

In a more pertinent and global essay entitled "The Short Story:
The Long and Short of It" (1981), Mary Louise Pratt suggests that
the formal marginality of short story cycles enables them to become
arenas for the development of alternative visions and resistances, and
often introduces women and children as protagonists. Marginal
genres such as the short story thus are often the site of political,
geographical, and cultural contestation. Likewise, Renato Rosaldo in
his postmodernist essay, "Fables of the Fallen Guy" (1991), on the
minimalist short story cycles of Alberto Ríos's *The Iguana Killer*
(1984), Sandra Cisneros's *The House on Mango Street* (1985), and
Denise Chavez's *The Last of the Menu Girls* (1986), argues that these
writers' worlds are "fraught with unpredictability and dangers, and
yet their central figures have enormous capacities for responding to
the unexpected." Deconstructing disciplinary and generic borders of
all sorts (unlike Barth and the INS), these Chicana/o writers collectively move toward liminal terrains and border zones that readily
include newly arrived migrant workers from south of the border,
Anglos, African Americans, and heterogeneous neighborhoods.

Similarly, Helena María Viramontes's short-story cycle *The Moths
and Other Stories* (1985) focuses on the internal and external urban
borders that often disrupt the neighborhoods of East Los Angeles.
These borders, Viramontes suggests, are reproduced in our ethnic
neighborhoods by urban planners who provide us with the maps for
the hegemonic discourse of boundaries. Such glossy, postmodern designs, from Portman's Westin Bonaventure hotel to the sprawling
freeways, thus serve to erase and displace the old, ethnic neighborhoods. In "Neighbors," for example, postmodern urban planners destroy the Chicano barrios in East Los Angeles: "the neighborhood
had slowly metamorphosed into a graveyard. . . . As a result, the
children gathered near in small groups to drink, to lose themselves in
the abyss of defeat, to find temporary solace among each other."

Although a prolific novelist, poet, and essayist, Joyce Carol Oates
may be best known for her "neorealist" short stories, which are frequently exercises in postmodernist experimentation. Like Carver and

Viramontes, she focuses on ordinary characters whose lives are vulnerable to powerful threats from a (patriarchal) society. Influenced by the mass cultural songs of the 1960s, Oates in "Where Are You Going, Where Have You Been?" transforms the traditional, young adult "coming-of-age" story. Written in 1967 and dedicated, as the title suggests, to Bob Dylan, the story poses crucial questions about female sexuality and gender inequalities in the relatively "safe" suburbs of upper-state New York, and, at the same time, gives us a powerful critique of our electronically mass-mediated cultural songs.

The story begins by describing Connie, a young woman dreamily at ease in the world of adolescent romance culture: fan magazines, platonic high school crushes, and so on. Her sense of sexual desire, however, has been shaped by whitemale "light" rock music and the movies. Connie, indeed, has learned everything from "the way it was in the movies and promised in songs." Like the rest of her white, middle-class peers, she is destined, or so it seems, to a solid bourgeois existence. But Oates radically undermines Connie's security by showing us how many women are seduced by the romantic "promises" in our pop songs: her young protagonist in fact becomes a victim of Arnold Friend, who, in the end, is not very friendly at all. Oates's short story is, therefore, fascinated with male violence (both psychological and physical) against women, for, as she says about her prodigious work in general, "I sense it around me, both the fear and the desire, and perhaps I simply have appropriated it from other people."

Like Islas's and Viramontes's narratives, Robert Stone's work, which we may call postmodernist *meditative* realism, concentrates on stories that are already embedded in an inter-American, hemispheric, and global dimension. *Dog Soldiers* (1975), a novel about heroin and drug dealers, for instance, travels globally between Saigon, San Francisco, and a middle-class retreat near the United States–Mexico borderlands. Stone's hard-nosed language and lurid scenes of sexual violence bring him clearly within the orbits of K Mart realism. *A Flag for Sunrise* (1981), however, places itself at the intersection between North and Central America. Stone's archaeology of the Americas allegorizes for us the persistence of an antithetical geographical space in the New World landscape. His novel, indeed, uncovers many layers of American identity by demonstrating how the United States government tries constantly to project its structures outward, creating and recreating its North-South dichotomy in order to render the South as "primitive" and victim.

Frank Holliwell, a burned-out anthropologist, at the request of his Vietnam army friends who are now running the C.I.A., travels to the mythical Central American country Tenecan to spy on a Catholic liberation theologian, Justin Feeney, who is suspected of Marxist revolutionary activities. Our postmodern ethnographer soon becomes a double-agent who falls madly in love with a nun, and who is caught in Stone's postcontemporary dialectics of romance: Marxist revolutionaries are depicted as "children of light" and the Central American death squads are described as being farted out of the devil's ass. At worst, Stone's postmodern romance appropriates Central America by turning it into a sexual and religious playground for the hip *norte-americanos;* at best, he can be seen, through the wondrous dialectical transformation of romance, to be breaking hold of a "Real" that seems unshakably set in place.

In contrast, E. L. Doctorow's narratives—from his award-winning *Book of Daniel* (1971) to his most recent novel, *Billy Bathgate* (1989)—in some ways do the inverse of what I have been arguing above. More precisely, the "ragged edges of Real" have entirely disappeared. Doctorow's work thus reveals a new spatial historiography that has unique things to tell us about what has happened to the postmodern sense of history.

Read collectively, Doctorow's major novels map out generational "moments" in the epic of American history: *Ragtime* (1975), in its collagelike production of real-life characters and events among whom appear imaginary WASP and ethnic characters (Morgan, Ford, Younger Brother, Coalhouse Walker, and so on), sets itself, like *World's Fair* (1985), in the first three decades of the twentieth century. *Billy Bathgate,* like *Loon Lake* (1980), reconstructs the Great Depression, while *The Book of Daniel* juxtaposes, without apologies, the Old and New Left Marxisms in America—thirties communism and sixties student radicalism.

In a blistering review of Doctorow's American "epic," in his influential essay "Postmodernism; or, The Cultural Logic of Late Capitalism" (1984), Fredric Jameson argues that the author's novels not only resist our political interpretations but also are precisely organized to "short-circuit an older type of social and historical interpretation which [they] perpetually hold out and withdraw." Jameson is, of course, absolutely right in his reading of Doctorow's simple, declarative sentences (especially in *Ragtime*), for unlike, say, the dialectical sentences of Gabriel García Márquez or Maxine Hong Kingston, he only allows himself to write in the digestible, best-seller style. While Doctorow's novels are splendid in their own right, and, perhaps, the author has merely decided to convey his great theme—the disappearance of our homemade radical past—formally, through the glossy surface style of the postmodern itself, the sharp edges of the Real have entirely disappeared, substituted by pop images and the simulacra of that history.

One of the most hybrid interventions in our postcontemporary narrative traditions comes from Jaime and Gilbert Hernández, whose *fotonovela* realist Chicano writings are a postmodern blend of comic books, science fiction, southern California *cholola* (Chicano youth culture), signifyin[g] magic realist storytelling, and subaltern theorizing. In the late 1970s the Hernández brothers became deeply involved in the musical signifiers of punk, and this postmodern phenomenon opened their eyes to the possibilities of expressing themselves in the *fotonovela* realist novel. Their literary productions are in many ways aligned with the incorporation of habits of "futurology" into our everyday life and the magic realism of García Márquez's Macondo, but they also repeat the deterritorializing gestures of borderland theorists such as Renato Rosaldo, Gloria Anzaldúa, and Néstor García Canclini, who see in their postmodern ethnographies and feminist theories of the United States–Mexico border a laboratory for the postmodern condition, where migrant workers smuggle into their new baroque homelands regional art and medicinal herbs from the South and send back from the North contraband VCRs and CD players.

In their *Love and Rockets* (1982—present) *fotonovela*, Jaime and Gilbert Hernández extend the borderlands to Los Angeles by interspersing in their work tongue-in-cheek science fiction stories (the "Mechanics" series) with postmodern realist tales set in a barrio they call "Hoppers 13." More recently, Gilbert Hernández, like Robert Stone, has moved his texts in utopian directions by creating a series of stories based in the mythical Central American town of Palomar.

*Love and Rockets* was the first United States *fotonovela* to adopt the European method of "album collection" after magazine serialization. Despite representation in a West Coast bimonthly magazine of relatively modest circulation (it sells between 18,000 and 19,000 copies), the Hernández brothers are arguably the most widely read Chicano writers in America today. Since 1982, the Hernández brothers have produced thirty issues of the regular magazine and several album collections of their work: *Music for Mechanics* (Book 1); *Chelo's Burden* (Book 2); *Las Mujeres Perdidas* (Book 3); *House of Raging Women* (Book 4); *Heartbreak Soup* (Book 5); *The Reticent Heart* (Book 6); and *Locas* (Book 7). Their texts, read collectively, are a dizzying mix of polyglot love comics and super-hero, reckless adventure; their virtuoso drawings, moreover, represent derealized characters of intelligence, wit, and human frailty.

For Jaime and Gilbert Hernández, whitemale superiority has had its chance, and they now see their postmodern narratives as engaged with the dynamics of the articulate ascendance of others. These new dynamics may be what many commentators mean when they speak about a "crisis" in the humanities, but as Houston Baker notes, "one man's crisis can always be an-Other's fields of dream, ladder of ascent, or moment of ethical recognition and ethnic identification."

To conclude on a personal note, when I recently asked my literature students at the University of California, Santa Cruz what the phrase "narrative for the next society" meant, many of them said that the *fotonovelas* of Jaime and Gilbert Hernández are the narratives for the next society. My students' thinking about these postmodern *fotonovela* historiographies seems characteristic of the turn-of-the-century human moments when we seek new definitions and utopian designs to resist the despair of things on many of our contested college campuses.

What their answer suggests to me is that many students in California (the Baudrillardean site of the postmodern) believe the function of narrative belongs to a *fotonovela,* popular space in which an extended global borderland audience interacts with visual and performative artists. If Rap, as Houston Baker says, is "the form of auditions in our present era that utterly refuses to sing anthems of, say, whitemale hegemony," the borderland *fotonovelas* of Jaime and Gilbert Hernández may be the new heterogeneous and heteroglot form articulating the hurts wrought by and before the emergence of the "State Line," which always constructs and preserves homogeneity.

José David Saldívar

# Constructing Gender

> The sage's science . . . of life requires thorough investigation of principles as the first step.
>
> —#11 "Treading," *The Taoist I Ching*

> Oh! It is absurd to have a hard and fast rule about what one should read and what one shouldn't. More than half of modern culture depends on what one shouldn't read.        —Algy to Jack in
> *The Importance of Being Earnest*

## (T)Reading for My Life

Today, when literary types talk about "constructing gender," more often than not what we're really talking about is "deconstructing gender." That is, we're attempting to call attention to the social and historical contingency of the ways people make sense out of the embodied experiences we come to "know" as "sexual." Now, as the troubled syntax of this last sentence suggests, the effort involved in making this attempt is anything but "natural." Indeed, to many of its critics, this counterintuitive and somewhat abstract undertaking seems a silly ("academic") endeavor at best, unnecessarily complicating what should certainly be the most natural thing in the world. As Cole Porter put it, "birds do it, bees do it, even educated fleas do it," so why can't we do "it," without all the fuss? Part of the problem, which the "fuss" of deconstructing gender seeks to explore, lies in what we mean by "it" and who we mean by "we" here. For some of us, like lesbians and gay men, whose experiences of sexuality have been historically castigated as "unnatural," or women, whose supposed "sexual nature" has been used to legitimate their social, economic, and political subjugation, or the many others whose "eccentric" forms of pleasure have subjected them to religious, legal, medical, and moral censure, "sexuality" has never been such a "natural" phenomenon. Indeed, the attempt to "deconstruct gender" is an attempt both to destabilize the systems of meaning that establish certain forms of ("sexual") desire and behavior as "natural" or "normal" and simultaneously to create a context of affirmation in which new forms of relationship and pleasure can emerge. Thus, when we speak about "constructing gender," part of the project is precisely to call into question something—perhaps the very thing—that many people take most for granted about their lives in order to see if it is possible to begin to live our lives otherwise.

But of course this is only part of the project. For after the calling into question of the taken for granted has begun, there is the larger problem of how we start to imagine, let alone create, such "otherwise" ways to live our lives. In order to understand what this kind of creativity might mean or how it might happen, it is important to consider the powerful effects of imagining generally and, for the purposes of this chapter, imagining-as-reading or reading-as-imagining specifically. I'm choosing to focus on reading here, not because I believe that it is unique among imaginative practices, but rather because, on the contrary, it is so common. For, although in our century reading has been eclipsed as a cultural activity by television watching, it still popularly functions as a (per)formative experience that shapes the ways we learn to make sense of our everyday lives. Ironically, we might argue that precisely because reading has been displaced from the cultural centrality it commanded in the nineteenth and early twentieth centuries—where in its ubiquity it performed much of what Mary Poovey calls the "work of ideology"—reading now takes on a more highly charged valence as "purely imaginative" work. And the contemporary significance of such *work* should not be underestimated. For despite our years of TV viewing, many of us have still had the experience of reading a book that we "knew" to be fictional, and yet that seemed so "real" to us it opened up new possibilities for how we see the world. Indeed, for some of us, the reality of such possibilities was so critical that at times it—and it alone—has kept us alive. The existence of those imaginary worlds in which we could "live" unfettered by the constraints that imprisoned us emotionally, physically, intellectually, politically, or spiritually, even if such worlds existed only in those moments when our eyes traced across pages bound between the covers of a few books, provided enough inspiration to continue to struggle with and through the painful difficulties of our daily experience.

In writing these sentences I am struck by how much they recall to me my own experiences of growing up. For as a sensitive, intellectual, myopic child born to displaced second-generation, urban Jews, residing in the emphatically non-Jewish, emphatically nonintellectual, suburbanizing countryside of northern Maryland, books were the only place I felt at home. Spending hours of each day curled up on the couch in my parents' living room reading indiscriminately through classics, mysteries, romances, sci-fi, historical adventures, and lots of just plain schlock, I repeatedly fled the unarticulable pain of my own life to "live" in the imaginary realms of literature. Yet more than my own cultural, religious, or temperamental alienation, there was an even more profound experience of aloneness—one for which I had at the time no name or concept—that drove me to seek my companions in the leaves of those tomes I pulled from the library's shelves. Retrospectively I would describe this isolation as the experience of a male child who has since become a gay man but who was then growing up in a world in which such a possibility was not only unspeakable but quite literally unimaginable. At the time, however, I could neither say nor imagine any of this and so I simply checked out more books.

It is one of the truisms of gay and lesbian self-help literature—which does not make it any less "true"—that we often experience a kind of emotional dissociation that results from never having some of our most poignant feelings mirrored back to us by the worlds in which we live. Indeed, it often seems as if the very feelings that make us feel most alive are the same feelings that make us feel most alone: an unbearable paradox at best, a mutilating reality at worst. Unlike most other children in our culture who grow up with others who are in socially recognizable ways "like" them (though of course not without excruciating differences), children who emerge later in life as "gay" or "lesbian" grow up in contexts where almost everyone—and most emphatically their parents—is not "like" them. While in the twenty years since I was a child there has (thankfully) been some significant change in this regard, by and large it is still the case that most people who denominate themselves as gay or lesbian come to maturity in a social and historical context in which there are few affirmations of their emotional or affectional experiences. And if this is true in "reality," it is more true in the "imaginary"—if we can differentiate between these realms. Thus, it is of both material *and* psychological significance that the structuring stories we commonly use in order to make sense of our daily lives provide us with very few plots that do not emplot us in normative versions of gender and sexuality. Whether we think of television, movies, magazines, books, radio, video, records, or newspapers, the narratives that most of us regularly draw upon in order to give telling shape to our lives do so by privileging certain limited sets of acts, behaviors, feelings, relationships, styles, and appearances as "acceptable," "proper," "normal," or "desirable." These limitations have important consequences for all of us in the sense that they mark out a range of possibilities within which we are largely constrained to represent—both to ourselves and to each other—the parameters of our movements. However, they have special consequences for those of us whose movements appear to transgress the possibilities of such acceptable representations, effectively rendering us "unrepresentable." As Adrienne Rich has remarked:

> . . . invisibility is a dangerous and painful condition and lesbians are not the only people to know it. When those who have the power to name and socially construct reality choose not to see you or hear you, whether you are dark-skinned, old, disabled, female, or speak with a different accent or dialect than theirs, when someone with the authority of a teacher, say, describes the world and you are not in it, there is a moment of psychic disequilibrium, as if you looked into a mirror and saw nothing. Yet you know you exist and others like you, that this is a game with mirrors. It takes some strength of soul—and not just individual strength, but collective understanding—to resist this void, this nonbeing, into which you are thrust, and to stand up demanding to be seen and heard.

Here Rich suggests that the condition of "invisibility" must be understood as at once a collective and a personal one. As such it has devolved in "our" American culture onto the many individuals and groups whose presence is perceived and represented primarily as an absence—an absence of those particular qualities that are asserted as necessary, normal, or natural for all human beings. Yet, as the challenges posed by the Civil Rights, Women's, and Gay and Lesbian Liberation Movements, among others, have taught us, such normative descriptions are in fact contingent and conventional, fabricated by some human beings in order to legitimate the valuing of particular forms of experience and expression over others. It is in the slippage between the desire to fix certain qualities as eternal, unalterable, or pregiven (by God, by Law, by Custom) and the complex movements that mark out our everyday lives that many of us seem to "disappear."

Living through the profound pain of such an absent presence as a sexually confused adolescent, my disappearance seemed almost complete to me. Not only in the suburbanizing small-town culture in which I was reared but also in my regular circuits of the public library's shelves, where I found few texts that would act as my mirror. The two to which I was repeatedly drawn, Dr. Rubin's (homophobic) pop-psychology best-seller *Everything You Ever Wanted to Know About Sex* (*But Were Afraid to Ask)* and Kinsey's soberly scientific *Sexual Behavior in the Human Male* did provide some comfort inasmuch as they informed me that there existed other males like me— though a statistical minority to be sure—who had had fantasies about, or perhaps had even engaged in, sexual acts with other men. Yet, while these texts provoked something like a flash of self-recognition, they were hardly untarnished mirrors since they failed to provide me with any of the stories for which I longed: stories that would have helped me give shape to the confusing jumble of feelings, thoughts, beliefs, and sensations that characterized my life. So, instead, I read novels—or more accurately, devoured them—in the vain hope of fitting my feelings into their plots. From the time I was nine until I was in my mid-twenties, there was rarely a moment when I was not in the middle of some novel or another. And as soon as one was completed there was always another waiting to be begun. Today when I reflect on this period in my life, I am astounded by the range and compulsiveness of my reading. I indiscriminately wended my way through most of Dostoevsky, Tolstoy, Dickens, Flaubert, Stendhal, Austen, the Brontës, George Eliot, Hawthorne, Melville, Faulkner, Woolf, Fitzgerald, Hemingway, Ellery Queen, Agatha Christie, and Isaac Asimov, among many, many others, and except for a few books by Ursula LeGuin and Rex Stout, Wilde's *The Picture of Dorian Gray,* and a passionate episode with Willa Cather, all of the hundreds of thousands of pages I turned seemed inevitably to return me to the same basic plot: boy meets girl, boy wants girl (albeit with frustrating complications), boy gets—or alternatively, but rarely, does not get— girl. Now in saying this I am not trying to claim that there is only one story that Anglo-American and European literatures tell over and over. Rather I'd simply like to recognize that, whether or not that basic plot initiates the unfolding/enfolding action of the text, the dynamics of gender difference very frequently provide the "knot" that the novel's denouement unravels, thereby explicitly or implicitly organizing the novelistic narrative as a temporal resolution of a structural opposition between "male" and "female." A limited and limiting structure in any event and especially so for those of us whose knot is not tied in this way.

It wasn't until I got to college that I began to find both the books and the people who could begin to help me unravel the feelings that had knotted themselves in my intestines and not in my stories. (I mean this quite literally, since from the age of thirteen on I had been plagued by a serious inflammatory bowel disease that kept me moving between toilets and hospitals in an unconscious attempt to give material form to the emotional pain that flowed through me. Thus, what Adrienne Rich calls the "psychic disequilibrium" of being unmirrored took on for me the somatic force of an earthquake zone where the movements of unseen tectonic plates repeatedly shook me to the edge between life and death. Now, admittedly, I'm what some might call a drama queen, so I tend to take things to their extremes and perhaps this case is no different from many others in my life, but I'm including this anecdote here in order to help you understand why the effects engendered by certain books affect me as they do.) The first "gay" book I remember reading was James Baldwin's *Giovanni's Room* (1956), which I discovered when I was about eighteen. In reflecting back on this seminal reading experience, I am struck by what I remember distinctly about it: it wasn't the mirroring of the desire for another man that was so moving for me, nor the possibility of giving aesthetic form to my sexual desires, but rather it was the searing emotional pain that pervaded the book's imaginary world that deeply touched my sense of self. The claustrophobia induced by Giovanni's eponymous room metonymically evoked for me the cramped subcultural space in which circuits of male desire were routed around the male/female divide, circling back onto and into men who desire each other. In Baldwin's text, this space of male same-sex eroticism marks out the edge of imprisonment where pleasure and pain elide into an experience from which there is no escape.

Baldwin's narrator crystallizes this dilemma when he describes his first visit to Giovanni's room: "He locked the door behind us, and then for a moment, in the gloom, we simply stared at each other—with dismay, with relief, and breathing hard. I was trembling. I thought, if I do not open the door at once I am lost. But I knew I could not open the door, I knew it was too late; soon it was too late to do anything but moan." The ambiguity of the narrator's sound—the moan of pleasure, the moan of pain—articulates the tension that the narrative resolves only in the book's final pages when Giovanni has exchanged his room for a prison cell and the narrator, anticipating Giovanni's execution, looks into the mirror in his own room in order to "see" Giovanni's last moments. In this final instance of mirroring the two men become one (at least for the narrator) in the face of pain and death:

> *It's getting late.*
> The body in the mirror forces me to turn and face it. And I look at my body, which is under the sentence of death. It is lean, hard, and cold, the incarnation of a mystery. And I do not know what moves in this body, what this body is searching. It is trapped in my mirror as it is trapped in time and it hurries towards revelation.
> *When I was a child, I spake as a child, I understood as a child, I thought as a child: but when I became a man, I put away childish things.*
> I long to make this prophecy come true. I long to crack that mirror and be free. I look at my sex, my troubling sex, and wonder how it can be redeemed, how I can save it from the knife. The journey to the grave is always, already, half over. Yet, the key to my salvation, which cannot save my body, is hidden in my flesh.
> Then the door is before him.

The door to Giovanni's prison cell, like the door to his room, proves to be an impossible threshold between life and death, between pleasure and pain. Here in the liminal zone between worlds, here where bodies melt into death and thereby find the "key to . . . salvation," the two men separate to meet as one. The contradiction of a "troubling" sex that seeks its own seems in Baldwin's text necessarily "always, already" caught between the knife and the grave, a mirror space from which the novel arises (the book opens with the narrator contemplating his reflection) and yet never quite escapes. Needless to say, by giving such exquisite shape to something I could recognize as akin to my own pain, this book both thrilled and depressed me. Yet while Baldwin's book helped me to imagine the complex dynamics of male desire for men in a world that both condemns and mutilates it, the novel did not help me to "construct" a new sense of gender that affirmed the possibility—if not the desirability—of the life and love I hoped to feel.

After *Giovanni's Room,* this bifurcated experience of delight and despair recurred frequently as I dived into the "gay" novels that were available to me. I was fortunate in this regard since the late 1970s, unlike any other earlier historical period, witnessed the appearance in the United States of many popular and sometimes mass-market paperbacks that sought explicitly to depict the lives and loves of (predominantly white, largely middle-class) gay American men. Books that quickly became cult classics like Andrew Holleran's *Dancer from the Dance* (1978) and Larry Kramer's *Faggots* (1978) devoted themselves to chronicling the developments in the urban gay male subcultures that thrived on "the coasts" throughout the seventies. Assuming the sexual ethos of a post-Stonewall "liberation," such books self-consciously set out to mirror the subcultures from which they emerged. Thus, they situated themselves within the complex networks of human relationships organized by a developing sexual community in which human contacts were often mediated by physical experiences whose longevity or intensity could not be defined or depicted solely in terms of the traditional emplotments provided by novelistic conventions. Instead, these novels fragmented their narrative developments between characters who moved in parallel directions so that the texts themselves often became pastiches of anecdotes, vignettes of sexual conquest or defeat. To some extent, then, these novels took as their protagonists a community, or at least an urban network, whose collective sexual practices seemed to position them outside both "straight" culture and the stories it told about men. In this way, they sought to articulate what could be seen as a transformation in male sexual ethics and activities by transforming the very structure of the stories they told about the sexual subculture with which they enthusiastically (if critically) identified.

While I gratefully consumed such books, thankful for the glimpse they gave me onto a world I was still too young and too timid to claim for my own, I was also disturbed by implications they had for how sexuality takes shape in contemporary American society. It seemed to me then and it certainly seems to me now that these late 1970s depictions of gay male sexuality were implicated in the (re)production of a certain kind of male sexuality that was predicated upon the objectification of (male) bodies as the sources of both aesthetic and erotic pleasure. Now don't get me wrong: with the right body a little objectification can go a long way toward pleasing the senses, as well as the soul. Moreover, in the political and historical moment in which they appeared, such texts certainly interrupted the totalizing force of the dominant narratives that sought to emplot sexual behavior within the dynamics of (heterosexual) love and marriage. But what seemed/seems hard for me to comprehend (maybe because I grew up reading too many nineteenth-century novels and watching too many 1940s movies) was how the dynamics of this new expression of male desire created either texts or contexts within which one could explore the ways overdetermined objectifications of (male) bodies engendered different kinds of male subjects, whether "gay" or "straight."

Even as beautiful and erotic a text as Renaud Camus's *Tricks* (1981) provides an excellent example of this dilemma. In the "25 encounters" that Camus narrates in the course of his text we are regaled with the compelling details of sexual adventure as they border on the banality of everyday life. In the italicized commentary that follows the account of each encounter, the narrator reframes the poignancy of sexual passion within the moment of retelling the adventure, so that these retrospective reflections come to foreground the erotics of narration as well as the narratives of the erotic. Indeed, it is precisely this "erotic" dynamic between the telling and the tale that the text would seem to ask us to consider: within the course of the book, the book's own writing becomes part of the narrative and even part of the narrator's sexual experiences, so that the distinction between the stories of sexual activities and "the sexual itself" loses its definition. And perhaps this is the book's "trick." In the twenty-five episodes that structure the text, the same elements of cruising, seduction, sucking, penetration, coming, exhaustion, and relief are reiterated, in almost exactly the same order, over and over again. What makes them appear as different moments seems to depend not upon the sexual acts or actors but upon the effects of narration itself: the details that give the stories their "character," the nuances that produce the frisson of singularity. Yet belying this particularity is the iterability and substitutability of the "tricks" themselves. While it is this lack of distinction that the book seems to celebrate as if in righteous—and joyful—defiance of the traditional novelistic emplotments that "properly" situate sexuality within the narratives of romance and marriage, the recognition of the necessary intercourse between sexuality and narration fails to produce the sense that such an imaginary relation might enable us to reimagine "the sexual" or "the male" per se. Instead, *Tricks* offers a limited (if fairly exhilarating) repertoire of sexual acts as the telling shape that such stories take, thereby eliding the question of how such shapings create the understanding that who gay men "are" derives from what they "do" with and to each other—and just as important, what they say about "it" afterwards.

While such an elision might seem to subsume the representations of a "gay" male gender easily within the representations of gay male sexuality, the prominence with which the relations among sexual acts, sexual identities, and sexual narratives appeared in the gay male novels written during the early 1980s suggests that it took a fair amount of literary work to keep this "imaginary" constellation together. In the first few years of the decade, a spate of gay men's "coming-of-age" stories appeared, inaugurating the development of what we might call a "gay" *Bildungsroman*. Ranging from Edmund White's *A Boy's Own Story* (1982), to Robert Ferro's *The Family of Max Desir* (1983), to John Fox's *The Boys on the Rock* (1984), to David Leavitt's *The Lost Language of Cranes* (1986), to Larry Duplechan's *Blackbird* (1987), these novels constitute an emergent narrative genre whose definition is itself predicated on a narratively produced gender. That is, they are all novels that depict a central character's development through or against the structure of a story we colloquially call "coming out." Since the late 1960s, "coming out" has served as a rubric for the processes of self-affirmation and self-definition through which men and women begin to denominate themselves as "gay men" and "lesbians" in their relations with themselves, their families, friends, loved ones, and communities— processes that have been central to the creation of both gay and lesbian identities and gay and lesbian collectivities. But more than just processes of emergence and identification, "coming out" is also a way of telling a life story. Indeed, to some extent the "coming out story" becomes the basis for the production of an identity to which the narrating individual lays claim precisely by pronouncing this story to be his or her own. Schematically, the coming out tale is often described as depicting a passage from the darkness, ignorance, and repression of the non-self-affirming "closet" to the colorful, illuminated, self-affirming freedom of gay/lesbian "identity." A recent Keith Haring graphic designed to advertise National Coming Out Day makes the implications of this movement clear: in the center of the drawing is a large black rectangle (which symbolically doubles as both the closet and the grave) from which a typically dynamic Haring figure emerges into the boldly colored, vividly alive world of queer identity. Sort of like what happens to Dorothy when she lands in Oz and suddenly the movie goes into Technicolor. The significance of this imaginary movement from darkness into color, however, is not simply one of "enlightenment" or "liberation," for the most profound force of the coming out story is not prospective but *retrospective.* That is, the effective dynamic of the narrative structure gives shape not just to the landscape into which the figure steps but more prominently to the black box from which the figure has emerged, now retroactively defined both as having a (safe) regular shape and as being (safely) confined to the past.

To a large extent, gay coming-of-age novels necessarily partake of such a retrospective perspective: these narratives attempt to give meaning and form to a variety of experiences both sexual and nonsexual that prior to the moments of gender redefinition often seem disparate, unconnected, and confusing, but which after the fact of coming out—either explicitly or implicitly—seem to have been leading inevitably up to such a conclusion all along. The preternaturally aware narrator of Edmund White's *A Boy's Own Story* provides perhaps the most explicit example of this imbrication between identity and narrative when he attempts to describe his decision to enter psychoanalysis:

Just as years before, when I was seven, I had presented myself to a minister and had sought his understanding, in the same way now I was turning to a psychoanalyst for help. I wanted to overcome this thing I was becoming and was in danger soon of being, the homosexual, as though that designation were the mold in which the water was freezing, the first crystals forming a fragile membrane. The confusion and fear and pain that beset me — initiated by my experience with the hustler, intensified by Mr. Pouchet's gentle silence and made eerie by my fascination with the "Age of Bronze" — had translated me into a code no one could read, I least of all, a code perhaps designed to defeat even the best cryptographer. . . .

I see now that what I wanted was to be loved by men and to love them back but not to be a homosexual. For I was possessed with a yearning for the company of men, for their look, touch, and smell, and nothing transfixed me more than the sight of a man shaving and dressing, sumptuous rites. It was men, not women, who struck me as foreign and desirable and I disguised myself as a child or a man or whatever was necessary in order to enter their hushed, hieratic company, my disguise so perfect I never stopped to question my identity. Nor did I want to study the face beneath my mask, lest it turn out to have the pursed lips, the dead pallor and shaped eyebrows by which one can always recognize the Homosexual.

As this slippage between the "now" of the first paragraph and the "now" of the second paragraph suggests, the narrator here is awkwardly positioned in time. Simultaneously evoking the boy who seeks psychoanalytic "understanding" and the adult man who comprehends that "what I wanted was to be loved by men and to love them back but not to be a homosexual," the narrative "I" holds both the "boy's" prospective yearning and the "man's" retrospective awareness in tension. This divided articulation constitutes the character's "identity" neither as disguised man-child who fears being frozen into the death mask of "the Homosexual," nor as the mature consciousness of the man who has moved beyond pathology to self-affirmation, but rather as the discrepancy between these two positions that is reconciled only through the implied transformation of the character's coming out. Although this transitional moment is not "in" the novel itself (appearing as a narrative event only in the sequel *The Beautiful Room Is Empty* [1988]), the logic of this retroactively narrativized identity is so embedded and emplotted in the novel's unfolding that the narrator's professed lack of self-knowledge ("The confusion and fear and pain that beset me . . . had translated me into a code that no one could read, I least of all . . .") makes sense precisely because he *has* become the adept cryptographer who can read meaning backwards into his earlier opacity. It is this opacity, then, that the novel reiterates even as it consistently affirms its interpretability in order to offer the reader a perspective of understanding, a perspective that (if adopted) positions the reader to make sense of the protagonist's struggles through the knowledge that there is meaning to the unknowing character's struggles: the knowledge that he is gay.

While such a perspective might implicitly indicate that gender is "constructed" through acts of knowing, or perhaps even more radically suggest that the reading of such "gay" narratives might be an act of gender construction itself, the fixing of this gender as an effect of knowledge, as a quality that can be "known," undermines the possibilities for imagining gender as a continual process of "constructing." Since it's impossible for me to begin to discuss here the limitations that claims to identity impose upon ec-centric gender/ sexual practices, I will instead offer by way of example a text that makes no such claims to identity, Samuel Delany's brilliant *Stars in My Pocket Like Grains of Sand* (1984). Appearing two years after White's autobiographical novel, Delany's book does not fit any of the rubrics devised to assimilate contemporary fiction into "knowable" gender categories. Instead *Stars in My Pocket Like Grains of Sand* is the first volume in an as yet unfinished science fiction diptych that addresses the political struggle between two rival groups whose competing cosmologies/epistemologies set them at odds for the control of an interstellar network of life worlds. In this extraterrestrial con(text), Delany explores the problematic relations between gender and sexuality as critical elements in the constitution of an imaginary dynamic that organizes both the narrative's unfolding and the development of coherent characters within this unfolding. Narratively, the novel weaves between the dead world of Rat Korga, an industrial slave who was the only survivor of his planet's destruction, and the complex galactic network of Marq Dyeth, an industrial diplomat from a venerable "nurture stream" on the planet Velm, which combines humans and nonhumans. Rescued from his world's holocaust by "The Web," a shadowy organization that controls the flows of information between worlds, Korga is paired by them with Dyeth because, as Japril, a Web operative, explains to Dyeth, "Korga happens to be your perfect erotic object—out to about seven decimal places. . . . More to the point . . . out to about nine decimal places, you happen to be Rat's." The novel's larger depiction of a contest for political control, then, hinges on the statistical perfectibility of this erotic preference between two human males whose coupling in turn threatens to undermine the stability of interworld systems. By the end of the volume the two men have been separated by the Web when Rat's popularity on Dyeth's home planet gives rise to massive demonstrations and cultural chaos and we are left to await their reunion (?) in the sequel.

More than just the centrality of the sexual bonding between the male protagonists, however, the novel's thematization of sexual pleasures across and between sexes and species structures the very possibilities of telling the tale itself. While much of the narrative description is devoted to exploring the permutations of erotic practices on a variety of worlds, *Stars in My Pocket Like Grains of Sand* reads not so much as a chronicle of sexual activities as an inquiry into the ways the movements of and between bodies mark out—or indeed create—the distinctions we come to know as character, identity, and relationship. In part the force of this intricately structured questioning derives from a challenging innovation that Delany employs in order to reorient our habituated patterns of reading. By shifting the expected correspondence between the gender of pronouns and the anatomical sex of their antecedents, Delany's text foregrounds the "unnatural" articulations of gender and sexuality embedded in our "normal" grammatical usages. In other words, the reader of *Stars in My Pocket Like Grains of Sand* finds that rather than "he" designating a biological male of whatever species and "she" designating a biological female of whatever species, with the former serving as a generic indicator of "speciesness," "she" serves here as the universal generic pronoun and "he" refers specifically to individuals of either biological sex of whatever species with whom one has had or with whom one desires to have sexual encounters. The text thus works against the reader to expose the usually ignored "imaginary work" that engenders meaning as gendered: not only the transformation in the expected gender correspondence between pronouns and referents but also the new erotic significance attributed to pronoun usage itself invests the reading process with an unexpected element of decoding that continually causes the reader to resist ingrained patterns of attributing gender to markers of sexuality—a disorienting resistance for even the most astutely "deconstructive" of readers. More than a "gay" science fiction novel, then, Delany's book invites us *as readers* to consider *and to learn to overcome* some of the "imaginary" limitations that circumscribe how we conceptually attempt to encompass the wide-ranging practices and pleasures available to us as embodied beings.

In his autobiographical memoir, *The Motion of Light in Water* (1988), Delany reflects on what he has learned as an African American male writer who lived through the bohemian years of the East Village in the 1960s, who is sexually attracted to other men, and who for many years was married and still remains close to the poet Marilyn Hacker. Commenting upon the significance of his self-reflexive undertaking, Delany remarks:

> What is the reason, anyone might ask, for writing such a book as this half a dozen years into the era of AIDS? Is it simply nostalgia for a medically feasible libertinism? Not at all. If I may indulge in my one piece of science fiction for this memoir, it is my firm suspicion, my conviction, and my hope that once the AIDS crisis is brought under control, the West will see a sexual revolution to make a laughing stock of any social movement that til now has borne the name. That revolution will come precisely because of the infiltration of clear and articulate language into the marginal areas of human sexual exploration, such as this book from time to time describes, and of which it is only the most modest example.

In meditating upon his autobiographical motivation, Delany underscores the significance that "fiction" has for him both as an individual and as a social activity. His utopian impulse leads him to conjecture that in the wake of the current historical conjuncture—in which the epistemological and epidemiological "truth" of AIDS has problematized the elision between sexuality and gender for most gay men, as well as for many others—there will be a revolutionary era in which sexuality will flourish as an aesthetic, ethical, personal, and political expression. Yet the impetus for such a radical transformation, he suggests, will derive not from the spontaneous "liberation" of previously (currently) repressed sexual energies but rather from "the infiltration of clear and articulate language into the marginal areas of human sexual exploration." Here Delany foregrounds the connection between imaginative and embodied experience that I have argued above constitutes a necessary element in creating an affirmative sense of "constructing gender" as the engendering of new possibilities for how we move through, transform, and enjoy our life worlds. Indeed, much of my own autobiographical impulse in this chapter derives, like Delany's, from the belief that in the processes of narrating our experiences for ourselves and for each other, we materially engage in processes of (re)producing realities that both reiterate the past and give new shape to the future.

In these few pages, I have somewhat arbitrarily chosen to focus on recent texts written by American gay male authors because these texts have provided seminal reading experiences for me as well as for many other gay men of my gen(d)eration. Yet these are by no means the only texts that have had this effect: indeed, for me, many contemporary novels written by American women of color—with their relentless questioning of the historical articulations of gender and race—have been equally inspiring. If I focus now on the former rather than the latter, it is because I know that in a volume like this one it is likely that the works of women of many races and ethnicities will have been addressed heretofore, while the works of men who are exploring the possibilities for sexual and emotional intimacies with other men will most probably remain eccentric. Thus, in many ways this chapter, like the texts I describe in it, is a "fiction" that constructs gender, a "fiction" that attempts to fabricate other possibilities for imagining forms of relationship and pleasure both in our writings and in our lives. Yet this is not to say that there is no "truth" in what I say; rather it is to remark that the processes of producing the stories through which we represent our truths to ourselves and to each other are part of the processes through which we (re)produce our "selves." And so we are "constructing gender" even now: I, as I write, and you, as you read. And so we keep (t)reading for our lives.

Ed Cohen

# Canada in Fiction

The North American novel begins, of course, in Canada. Although *The History of Emily Montague* was written by Frances Brooke, a British woman of letters, and was published in London in 1769, this first New World fiction is both record and product of the coming into being of what will be Canada. Brooke had sailed from England in 1763 to join her husband, who was the chaplain of the British garrison recently stationed in Quebec City. On the basis of five years' residence, she vividly contrasted the newly victorious English and the just defeated French, the Christian settlers and the "savage" Indians, the European paradigms whereby her main characters perceive the new (to them) country and the different reality of the land itself. Moreover, the author's marriage plot (another metaphor for "settling") is effectively at odds with her most intriguing character, Arabella, who capably coquettes her way through the work and who, at one point, can even contemplate that she might "marry a savage, and turn squaw" because of the liberty Indians allow their wives but who just as precipitously decides not to because of the liberty they do not allow their daughters. The juxtaposition of such balances and imbalances anticipates more the Canadian national myth of the mosaic than the American myth of the melting pot, even though America too, as the thirteen colonies with their own political and social problems, is also present in the discourse of the novel. Brooke's *History* is, admittedly, more a historically interesting document than a major work of literature. Nevertheless, Canadians can take pride in this first novel and in the novels that followed it, just as they can also take a certain pride in how well the American novel has done despite branching away from its Canadian beginning.

If the foregoing paragraph seems a belated and dubious Canadian attempt to claim credit for the form, I would here stress that Americans have long been claiming just about everything else: texts, titles, readerships, and publication rights. In this context, the case of Major John Richardson's *Wacousta; or, The Prophecy: A Tale of the Canadas* (3 vols., 1832) is particularly relevant. The author, of United Empire Loyalist and perhaps Indian ancestry, was the first novelist to be born in Canada. He had grown up in frontier posts where his father, a British Army medical officer, had been stationed. Richardson himself had served in the War of 1812, had fought with Tecumseh, and had been captured following Tecumseh's defeat to be held for a year as a prisoner-of-war in Ohio and Kentucky. Those experiences provided much of the basis for his best book, *Wacousta,* a high gothic tale of an earlier episode of white/Indian frontier warfare, the 1763 Pontiac uprising, and an account in which the implacably savage leader of the Indians, Wacousta, turns out to be an Englishman in disguise but is still no worse than his former rival in love and present rival in war, Colonel De Haldimar, the ostensible representative and defender of "civilization." Everything in this novel is doubled, undone, inverted, and reversed, including the usual sexual implications of imperial conquest. "Instead of Mother Nature versus a paternalistic military establishment," Gaile McGregor argues, "*Wacousta* seems to pit a feminine garrison against a masculine gothic landscape." McGregor is so struck by the different "theoretical wilderness/civilization dichotomy" set forth in this novel as compared to "the American wilderness romance" (particularly the novels of James Fenimore Cooper) that she titles her massive study of language and landscape in Canadian literature *The Wacousta Syndrome.* Yet even though *Wacousta* is a founding text of Canadian literature, until very recently the novel was available in Canada only in the condensed edition early published in the United States, a version that suppressed almost all the explicitly anti-American passages.

Canada has long contended with what might be termed the Wacousta problem. Throughout the nineteenth century and until well into the twentieth century, a relatively small population spread over the vast expanse of the country made difficult the support of any substantial indigenous publishing industry. Books were commonly obtained from England or the United States, as, indeed, they still mostly are. Canadian authors wrote to be published in those countries as well as at home, and foreign audiences were not always particularly interested in things Canadian. According to an early movie mogul, if a boy meets a girl in New York City you have a story, but—to quote the Hugh MacLennan essay title taken from this American observation—"Boy Meets Girl in Winnipeg: Who Cares?" Care, however, might be generated by sounding New York, and numerous Canadian novels of the nineteenth and the early twentieth century are curiously placeless. Nor has the success of the last few decades completely dispelled old "branch plant" views of Canadian letters. For example, Alice Munro's American publisher objected to her title *Who Do You Think You Are?* (1978). Americans presumably know who they are and are not troubled by questions of identity. The American edition was titled *The Beggar Maid.* Yet that very substitution of a fairy-tale designation for a Canadian one merely gives another reference and relevance to the original title.

Canadian wry, it was early discovered, was one major way to achieve more than local notice. Humor was an effective way of subverting perceived second-class status and was also eminently marketable in England and the United States as well as in Canada. Indeed, Canada's first best-selling author was Thomas C. Haliburton, whose Sam Slick sketches collected into the three series of *The Clockmaker; or, The Sayings and Doings of Samuel Slick of Slickville* (1836, 1838, 1840) went through some one hundred printings in the nineteenth century. Their main appeal was the ambivalently portrayed comic protagonist, Sam Slick, a Yankee peddler in rural Nova Scotia whose verbal facility contributed such expressions as "upper crust," "conniption fit," and "stick-in-the-mud" to North American English. Are the literary Yankee, American humor, and even, perhaps, Uncle Sam all, like the New World novel, Canadian inventions? Stephen Leacock similarly achieved great popularity with *Sunshine Sketches of a Little Town* (1912), his comic exploration of the private and public foibles of life in provincial Ontario.

Admittedly, *The Clockmaker* and *Sunshine Sketches* seem more collections of stories or sketches than novels. But Canadian writers frequently blur the distinction between the two forms. In Clark

Blaise's *A North American Education* (1973), for example, separate stories of loss and dislocation add up to an appropriately disjointed anti-*Bildungsroman*. Or, conversely, in Alden Nowlan's *Various Persons Named Kevin O'Brien* (also published in 1973), what at first seems a novel reconstitutes itself through the refracturing of the protagonist into a series of short stories. Similarly, Canadian women writers have long conjoined stories and novel—as exemplified by Alice Munro's *Lives of Girls and Women* (1971)—in a feminist querying of both artistic and social categories. In view of this tradition and in the spirit of claiming that so far characterizes this chapter, I here claim *The Clockmaker* and *Sunshine Sketches* as Canadian novels and as the beginning of a comic fictional form that will later include such works as Ray Smith's wry, experimental, subtly interconnected *Lord Nelson Tavern* (1974).

Another way to broad appeal for the Canadian writer was through the documentation of place. A naming of parts—and Canada, starting with Upper and Lower Canada, has always seen itself as constituted of parts—could attract a regional, a national, and sometimes even an international readership. For example, Prince Edward Island, surely one of the least exotic islands in the world, becomes one of the best-known island settings thanks to Lucy Maud Montgomery's *Anne of Green Gables* (1908) and its sequels. Of course, the character of Anne has much to do with these novels' huge success but, I would suggest, so does the setting, portrayed as both comfortably distant and comfortably familiar, whether the reader is British, American, or Japanese (and Montgomery's novels well might be the most widely read Western fiction in all Japan).

All regions of Canada have contributed substantially to the country's fiction. But rather than assess in any detail David Adams Richards's stark portrayal of poverty in the rural Miramichi area of New Brunswick in *Blood Ties* (1976) and *Road to the Stilt House* (1985), or Matt Cohen's Southern Gothics—Southern Ontario, that is—such as *The Disinherited* (1974), or numerous other possible writers and works, in the interests of brevity I will consider only two areas, French Quebec and the far West. Each has particularly appealed to English Canadian writers, perhaps because, in each case, regional narratives can also be seen (in a modest Canadian way) as national epics, and in the case of the West often, in fact, they are.

In the case of Quebec, however, the many novels of New France written in English during the nineteenth and early twentieth centuries are too obviously intended primarily for English readers. Thus Rosanna Leprohon's *Antoinette de Mirecourt; or, Secret Marrying and Secret Sorrowing, a Canadian Tale* (1864) sees the secret marriage between the French Canadian protagonist and an English officer whose "royal standard" had recently "replaced the fleurs-de-lys of France" as the hope and pattern for Canada; or William Kirby's *The Golden Dog* (1877), a historical novel in the high romantic fashion, posits Old World villainy in New France to be countered by Providence and the English, who thereby deserve the fidelity of the not conquered but liberated French. Admittedly, Francis Grey's more convincing study of the complicity of church and state in turn-of-the-century Quebec, *The Curé of St. Philippe* (1899), does acknowledge the problem of "two nations — no other word is adequate — separated, not only by race and creed, but by language as well." Most of these novels, however, are much more about English Canadian attitudes and aspirations than French Canadian actualities and, as such, erase difference rather than record it.

Another difference was differently inscribed in the case of the Canadian West, which looms large in the country's literature precisely because it is Canadian (that is, non-American). The standard trappings of American frontier fiction are excluded from the start, as when Ralph Connors, in best-selling missionary Westerns such as *The Sky Pilot: A Tale of the Foothills* (1899), casts the preacher's sermons, not the sheriff's pistols, as the way to civilization. Dick Harrison, in *Unnamed Country: The Struggle for a Prairie Fiction*, argues at length that a different Western history in which the frontier was largely missing precluded in Canada the male-centered dichotomies of good and bad endlessly adumbrated in the American Western — cowboys and rustlers, cavalry and Indians, lawmen and outlaws. Canadians could consequently write different versions of their different West against the pervasive American version that regularly threatened to incorporate Canada into its imaginative space.

Writing the Canadian West foregrounded more the processes of narrative than the product of the West and the Western, which is to say that there is a distinct metafictional element in much of this Canadian fiction. Thus Howard O'Hagan's *Tay John* (1939) begins with the problem of naming the protagonist. The title is the English version of the French version, Tête Jaune, of the blond Indian protagonist's original Shushwap name, which also meant "yellow head." Poised between Indian and white names, Indian and white mythologies, this ambiguously mythic hero only sporadically inhabits his novel and finally walks, apparently, back into the earth from which he was miraculously born to inscribe on that earth and in the text a circle of problematic emptiness. The novel itself is mostly the telling of not telling his story: "Indeed, to tell a story is to leave most of it untold," Jack Denham, the main narrator of *Tay John*, finally admits before he turns the novel over to another who does no better. "You have the feeling you have not reached the story itself, but have merely assaulted the surrounding solitude."

As *Tay John* suggests, a different dialectic between white and Indian characterizes the Canadian Western as compared to the American. The American vision of Manifest Destiny necessarily casts Native American people as the savage "other" who must be defeated, supplanted. In Canada, however, and perhaps as a reflection of Canada's own sense of marginality, the Indian is more often portrayed as an alternative than as an enemy. In W. O. Mitchell's *The Vanishing Point* (1973), for example, a teacher at a reserve school sets out to civilize his prize pupil but she ends up Indianizing him. Or in Robert Kroetsch's *Gone Indian* (1973), the protagonist, a United States graduate student, finally finds—after the pattern of Grey Owl (alias Archibald Bellaney)—his real life as a fake Indian in the Canadian north. Or in a rather different vein Rudy Wiebe can "doubt the *official* given history" of the Canadian West. To tell "another" and "maybe even truer" side of the story, he writes novels such as *The Temptations of Big Bear* (1973) that radically deconstruct the official history and the Western form on which they are based. Much the same deconstructive enterprise also informs Peter Such's *Riverrun* (1973), Canada's most Eastern Western and a powerful account of the extermination of the Beothuk in Newfoundland when the natural cycle of their existence (one of the Joycean references of Such's title) was broken by intruding whites. Or, again in a comic vein, George Bowering in *Burning Water* (1980) and *Caprice* (1987) portrays impossibly contemporary, ironically postmodern Indians (but no more unlikely, it must be stressed, than any other depiction), whereas

Philip Kreiner's *Contact Prints* (1987) emphasizes the imposture implicit in any white rendering of Native life and art.

In other ways, too, novels of the Canadian West contravene the American Western. Margaret Laurence's *The Stone Angel* (1964) portrays an old woman, not a young man, who is searching for a Western escape from the limitations that circumscribe her life. Moreover, this search takes, in part, the odd form of lighting out from the retirement home, not for the frontier. Laurence, in her first Canadian novel, graphically reverses the phallic-thrust teleology of the American Western, the celebration of the conquering of a new land as the simultaneous claiming of a future of boundless possibility. Hagar Shipley, Laurence's protagonist, has most of her life behind her. But she still has to come home to that life, to admit what it has been, to come to terms with it, to reinvent herself as the product of a particular Canadian West (instead of inventing the West as an expression of the id's unbridled desire—male desire, of course).

When the protagonist in *The Stone Angel* came home, so, too, did the author. After living in and writing of Africa, Laurence returned imaginatively to the small town in Manitoba where she grew up, renamed it Manawaka, and began a series of fictions that soon established her as one of Canada's most respected authors. Both the Manawaka novels and the writing of those novels illustrate another distinguishing feature of Canadian fiction. In contradistinction to the Thomas Wolfe claim that "you can't go home again," Canadian writers insist that you can and you must. Or differently put, if the American dream is a dream of the future, a vision of what the country (and/or the representative citizen) might be when it has become all that it should be, the Canadian dream is, in Robert Kroetsch's evocative wording, "a dream of origins." Where you originally come from is more important than where you are finally going, which is, after all, as *The Stone Angel* points out even with its graveyard title, only to death. In her Manawaka novels, Laurence especially asserts claims of place and past, claims that are regularly gendered female instead of male—and this too is typical of much Canadian fiction.

The Canadian West has produced some of the country's best realistic fiction—works such as Frederick Philip Grove's *Settlers of the Marsh* (1925) or Ethel Wilson's *Swamp Angel* (1954). It has also produced some of Canada's best historiographic metafiction (Linda Hutcheon's useful term). Sheila Watson's *The Double Hook* (1959) crosses the story of an isolated and perhaps Indian community with T. S. Eliot's *The Waste Land* and then poises the account between Christianity and Coyote, the Native trickster deity. Or in Robert Harlow's *Scann* (1972) the telling of a self-serving mythopoeic history of a British Columbia town self-destructs (the manuscript is burnt) at the end and yet remains as the novel. Or Jack Hodgin's west-coast magic realism conjoins Vancouver Island and Ireland in a fantastic *Invention of the World* (1977) as both the establishing of a fraudulent religious community and the subsequent attempts to counter and recount that story. Similarly, Bowering, in *Burning Water*, intersperses the history of George Vancouver's heroic mapping of the British Columbia coast with the account of another George (Bowering himself) recounting it and thereby flaunts the problematic narrativity of both "stories," while Daphne Marlatt, in *Ana Historic* (1988), shows that Ana/woman is not without history/story at all, either in the present or in the past.

Another avenue to effective fiction, and one seen in both Canadian Westerns and "Easterns," was to make novels out of the very impediments to their production—a limited audience, a "colonial cringe" mentality that denigrated anything Canadian, traditions (both English and French) of distrusting and/or censoring literature. Moreover, the paradigmatic story of the country well might be its reluctance to sanction any official story. "Canadian literature," Kroetsch has claimed, "is the autobiography of a culture that insists it will not tell its story." Or as Sam Solecki has observed, "No other established literature treats national identity as a *question*." No wonder a number of novels are oblique and paradoxical narratives that tell of not telling, or that "the paralyzed artist"—one of Margaret Atwood's chapter titles in *Survival: A Thematic Guide to Canadian Literature*—is a common Canadian protagonist. In Sinclair Ross's *As For Me and My House* (1949), for example, Philip Bentley's failure to be an artist is so pervasive that even the recounting of it must be turned over to his wife. Or David Canaan in Ernest Buckler's *The Mountain and the Valley* (1952) does not live up to either of his biblical names. Instead of going to the mountain top to write his story and the story of his people, he dies early, and they are left bookless, still in the valley of artlessness, with no redeeming vision of themselves. Yet that story and that vision constitute the novel itself.

Such works represent the novel "written under erasure." They also illustrate Canadian deference and deferral with a vengeance—the great Canadian novel as the novel that best avoids advancing any claims to greatness. In this context, Ross is the premier eraser, and his *As For Me and My House* has been put forward as Canada's "paradigmatic text." Philip Bentley's failings as an artist and then as a minister and a husband are rendered in his wife's highly problematic account of an unhappy year the couple spends in what seems (everything in this novel is questionable) a narrow and restrictive small prairie town aptly misnamed Horizon. That calculated misnomer situates both place and promise elsewhere even as it also denies the difference between center and circumference, situation and defining circumstances. And the novel itself similarly becomes what Kroetsch terms "the missing text," an "unwritten novel" implicit in Mrs. Bentley's diary entries addressed to a fiction that is not there.

After the late sixties, however, and through the seventies and the eighties, fiction, unquestionably, is there. Margaret Atwood has recently observed that, if she were now redoing *Survival,* she would downplay "The Paralyzed Artist" chapter. Canadian authors began, in the sixties, to write in unprecedented number, and they did so for a number of reasons: the stocktaking engendered by the country's centennial, a sense of national pride in opposing United States policy in Vietnam, a desire to be (in Canada as well as in Quebec) "masters in our own house," the fact that the Canada Council had begun to fund substantially writers and publishers, and a growing demand, especially in the schools, for Canadian texts. Canadian writers also began to produce works of unprecedented quality. Indeed, the variety and the scope of the novels written during the last twenty-five years preclude any substantial assessment of types and trends or even of major authors. So I will not try to come up with rubrics that might contain, say, Hugh Hood's ongoing twelve-volume *roman fleuve* documentation of twentieth-century Canada collectively titled *The New Age* (1975–) and Susan Kerslake's brief, lyric, intensely poetic and almost impenetrable *Penumbra* (1984); Timothy Findley's exuberant reimagining of the story of Noah in *Not Wanted on the Voyage*

(1984) and Aritha van Herk's rereading of Tolstoy's *Anna Karenina* in the far north in *Places Far from Ellesmere* (1990). Instead I will merely name a few authors (in addition to those already noted) whom anyone seriously interested in English Canadian fiction should read: Robertson Davies, Mavis Gallant, Janette Turner Hospital, Joy Kogawa, Michael Ondaatje, Leon Rooke, Audrey Thomas. But most of all I would here rename Atwood herself. From *Surfacing* (1972), early hailed as a feminist classic, to the dystopian warning of *The Handmaid's Tale* (1985) and the reprising in *Cat's Eye* (1988) of her major fictional and feminist concerns, Atwood has been a protean novelist, engaged and challenging. She especially exemplifies the accomplishment of recent English Canadian fiction on both the national and an international level. There is even a newsletter and an official society devoted to the study of her work, and a writer can hardly be more established than that.

For French Canada the story of narrative coming into being is, if anything, even more impressive. The Durham Report of 1840 described the French Canadians as a poor people, without history and without literature, and saw them as destined to be soon swallowed up by English Canada. They themselves had other ideas, one of which was the "revenge of the cradle." Huge farm families would ensure that the habitant survived. Literature could also prove Lord Durham wrong. The first French Canadian novel, *L'Influence d'un livre* by Philippe-Ignace-François Aubert de Gaspé, had appeared in 1837, the same year as the rebellions in Upper and Lower Canada that led to the Durham Report. A melodramatic account of an alchemist's adventures, including his search for a *main de gloire,* the dried hand of a hanged murderer, this first novel was followed by other romantic fictions, some of which were soon given a more historic cast. Coincidentally, one of the best of the historical romances is *Les Anciens Canadiens* (1863; *Canadians of Old,* 1974) by Philippe-Joseph Aubert de Gaspé, Philippe-Ignace's father, who published his own first novel when he was well into his seventies.

Novels such as *Les Anciens Canadiens,* set in the Seven Years War and after, grounded French Canadian life in history and in surmounting the setbacks of that history. Another fictional development grounded the continuation of that life in remaining on the land. What has been called *le roman de la terre* made its appearance in 1846 with Patrice Lacombe's *La terre paternelle,* a celebration of French Canadian heritage passed from father to son and centered in the family farm. In these novels, British Canada was not the only force that had to be resisted. In Louis Hémon's *Maria Chapdelaine* (1916; English translation, 1921), one of the best of the novels of the land, the female protagonist must choose between two suitors, one offering her escape to the wealth and ease of industrial New England and the other only the harsh country life that she has always known. Continuing that life of, among other things, female sacrifice in the service of patriarchal order, Maria marries the second of the two, a decision vindicated in the novel by the "voices" of the land. Their directive is to "stay in the province where our fathers have stayed, and live as they have lived, to obey the silent command which formed in their hearts and which passed to ours, and which we must pass on to our numerous children: In the country of Quebec nothing must die and nothing must change."

Change comes nonetheless, and one measure of that change is Felix-Antoine Savard's *Menaud, maître-draveur* (1937; *Master of the River,* 1976), a masterful reprising of *Maria Chapdelaine* in which a logger attempts to heed the warning sounded by the voices in the land in Hémon's novel but succeeds only in driving himself insane to repeat endlessly a tag phrase from the same crucial passage that had earlier inspired him to action. A poetic study of self-sacrifice is transmuted into a psychological study of self-disintegration; the prophetic warning that "strangers have come" to take "almost all the power . . . almost all the money" gives way to the flat assertion that "Strangers came! Strangers came! . . . ," which, in its mad reiteration, suggests mostly that they will go on coming to further the victimization of Menaud and his people. Yet the darker implications of the latter novel are not, it should be noted, entirely missing from the earlier one. Maria makes her crucial decision only because the choice she would have much preferred has already been precluded by the death of her fiancé, François Paradis (Paradise lost?), in the frozen north.

Although Maria's life is movingly portrayed, the contemporary reader, especially if of an anticlerical and/or feminist bent, is apt to question the heavy constraints under which she acquiescently labors.

Other novels more explicitly countered the ethos of *le roman de la terre* and particularly the idea that the twentieth century could be faced on the basis of a nineteenth-century reinscription of eighteenth-century French ideals about country living and landownership. Albert Laberge's *La Scouine* (1918; *Bitter Bread,* 1977), for example, is a sustained indictment of a brutal rural existence represented not so much by the work of the harvester as by the work of the gelder. Or Ringuet's (Philippe Panneton's) *Trente arpents* (1938; *Thirty Acres,* 1960) describes how old Euchariste Moisan is tricked out of his thirty acres by one son and sent to visit another in the United States where he remains in permanent exile and cultural isolation, unable to speak to even his own grandchildren. Euchariste ends up a nightwatchman in an American factory, a total reversal of the day work he earlier did on his Canadian farm and the very fate from which the farm should have saved him. Still more recently, Marie-Claire Blais, in novels such as *Une saison dans la vie d'Emmanuel* (1965; *A Season in the Life of Emmanuel,* 1966) can comically transmogrify the whole pastoral/Catholic tradition of the earlier fiction with such telling details as brutalized children in a large farm family who are regularly identified only by number or the religious daughter who passes from the convent to the brothel barely noticing the change, with, indeed, "tears in her eyes" that there were "so many strangers who needed her."

Laberge's *La Scouine* and Ringuet's *Trente arpents* anticipate the massive social and literary changes that Quebec experienced in the post–World War II era. More and more the province went in exactly the directions earlier works had warned against, and the novel, in documenting those transgressions, changed too. The enduring truths of the family farm gave way to tales of disordered city living such as Roger Lemelin's best-selling novel of urban poverty and crime, *Au pied de la pente douce* (1944; *The Town Below,* 1948), or Gabrielle Roy's landmark novel, *Bonheur d'occasion* (1945; *The Tin Flute,* 1947), which studies the case of the Lacasse family as they try in ways both heroic and tawdry to transcend poverty. Early recognized as one of Quebec's and Canada's major novels, *Bonheur d'occasion* especially situates fiction firmly in the city. Dreams of Arcadia can still persist, but as dreams, not as recipes. When, in Roy's subsequent *Alexandre Chenevert* (1954; *The Cashier,* 1955), Alexandre at one point imagines living in the country, he does so as one measure of the many limitations of his city life, not as the author's career advice to bank clerks.

Urbanization and industrialization led, as feared, to a deem-phasizing of religion. One sign of this change was the precipitous decline of the provincial birthrate, which went, following World War II, from one of the highest to one of the lowest in the world. Another sign was the increasingly anticlerical tone of much of the fiction. In Gerard Bessette's *Le Libraire* (1960; *Not for Every Eye,* 1977), for example, a Bartleby of a book clerk prefers not to sell (discreetly and for a high price, of course) works on the Index. The hypocrisy of both the book and the religion business justifies the clerk's final theft of the texts in question and his selling them cheaply on a more open—and honest—market.

Other changes also followed the move from the family farm to the nation's factories. One does not work in the latter in the same way and to the same end as on the former, especially during a depression. The consideration that the Great Depression was not countered in Canada by any government measures such as the New Deal prompted French Canadians to begin asking just what kind of deal they were getting from their national government and whether a number of contracts did not require negotiation. World War II and Canada's reluctance to come to the aid of France as opposed to how much the country was willing to sacrifice for the sake of England furthered this process that culminated in the "Quiet Revolution," the radical shift in Quebec values witnessed after the war.

The Quiet Revolution was accompanied by a not-so-quiet literary revolution. As in the nineteenth century, literature was deemed a force of paramount social significance. Fiction could both express and create the new identities, individual and collective, that were coming into being. Thus Jacques Ferron advocates and allegorizes Quebec's need for political independence in *La Nuit* (1965; *Quince Jam,* 1977), an account of an ordinary man mysteriously called from slumber to a night of portentous violence. Still more explicitly, Jacques Godbout's *Le Couteau sur la table* (1965; *The Knife on the Table,* 1968) conjoins the violence of World War II with the first bombs of the FLQ (Front de Libération du Québec), and the knife of the title is finally raised against the Québécois narrator's former English Canadian mistress, Patricia, and the rule of her people. Or in another novel from the same year, Hubert Aquin's *Prochain épisode* (1965; English translation, 1972), the author, arrested as a suspected terrorist, creates a narrator similarly arrested who, to pass the time while he is incarcerated and to hold suicide at bay, sets out to write a novel that is itself another doubled and displaced version of the author's/narrator's predicament. The result is an intricately crafted parable of revolution both demanded and deferred as well as an early expression of Aquin's genius for ambivalence and angst. And as Aquin's first novel also illustrates, in much of this fiction of rebellion, form, too, is revolutionized. Linear narratives charting a way to some rural *Bildungsroman* fulfillment are replaced by inventive and experimental fictions (often metafictions) celebrating breaks, bits and pieces, fits and starts. Literary effect is also fractured. For example, in Roch Carrier's *La guerre, Yes Sir!* (1968; English translation, 1970) when a young man cuts off his hand to avoid being drafted into a war that seems to have little to do with him, we have a telling example of how a Québécois must mutilate himself in order to maintain his own identity, but when the dismembered part is subsequently used as a hockey puck, political parable suddenly shifts to total black humor farce.

Another feature of recent Québécois fiction is the use of *joual*, a French dialect that takes its name from its pronunciation of *cheval* (horse). This dialect was spoken in rural Quebec but more and more became in modified form (incorporating Anglicisms and English words) the language of the lower classes in Montreal. It was also long regarded as proof of second-class status and as quite unsuitable for any literary purpose other than marking such status. But starting with Jacques Renaud's *Le cassé* (1964) and Claude Jasmin's *Pleure pas, Germaine* (1965), novelists exploited the literary possibilities of *joual* (its different pronunciation, fractured syntax, graphic obscenities) and made it, appropriately, the main vehicle for explorations of alienated proletarian life. One of the best of these novels is Godbout's *Salut Galarneau!* (1967; *Hail Galarneau!*, 1970), the "memoirs and reflections" of a hot-dog vendor rendered in a *joual* of Rabelaisian verve. Marie-Claire Blais's *Un Joualonais, sa Joualonie* (1973; *St. Lawrence Blues*, 1974) soon parodies the excessive and inauthentic use of *joual* (intellectuals discuss language while workers die), but its literary credentials had already been fully established.

The literary credentials of French Canadian fiction are also, by this time, fully established thanks to the writers already noted (or to be noted) and many others, only some of whom I will here name: Yves Beauchemin, Jacques Benoit, Monique Bosco, Réjean Ducharme, Diane Giquère, Suzanne Paradis, Jacques Poulin, Michel Tremblay. And I use the adjective French Canadian rather than Québécois because two of Canada's major Francophone writers come from outside Quebec. Gabrielle Roy was born and raised in Manitoba and sets some of her fiction there, for example, *La Petite Poule d'eau* (1950; *Where Nests the Water Hen,* 1970), a poetic account of the small heroisms whereby a French family survives in the isolated north of that province. Antonine Maillet is Acadian and writes of the French in or scattered from the Maritime settlements, as with *Pélagie-La-Charrett* (1979; *Pelagie,* 1982), probably her best novel and a mythic account of an indomitable late eighteenth-century Acadian woman gathering together a group of her people in the southern United States and conducting them, "by the back door," to history, story, and home—in short, back to Nova Scotia, which was, we tend to forget, also New France.

That conjunction of Nova Scotia and New France suggests a large question about the novels hitherto discussed. How do the English fictions and the French interrelate? Do we see mostly accidental resemblances (the result of two European traditions being transplanted to and developing in roughly the same broad expanse of northern North America over the same historical period) or the expression of some larger unity (the ways shared geography and shared history have shaped literature)? By and large, English critics (such as Ronald Sutherland in *Second Image*) have argued the latter, and French critics (for example, Jean-Charles Falardeau in *Notre société et son roman*) have assumed the former, thereby replicating the different way Canadians and Americans tend to view one another across the 49th parallel, one asserting essential difference and the other largely denying it.

In *All the Polarities,* an aptly titled comparison of the English Canadian novel and *le roman québécois,* Philip Stratford maintains that differences still outweigh similarities. He sees the English novel as grounded in historical realism and the documentation of both place and protagonist and as inviting moral evaluation more than psychological understanding, whereas *le roman québécois* is little concerned with particulars of time and place or the minutiae of individual lives but instead sets forth a highly symbolic rendering of the protagonist's psyche in both its conscious and subconscious manifestations and invites the reader to share in that experience rather than to judge it. Stratford thereby suggests that the comparison provided over a century ago by Pierre-Joseph-Olivier Chauveau, an early novelist who was also Quebec's first prime minister, still holds true. Chauveau argued that the two literatures resembled the famous double-spiral staircase of the Château de Chambord, a staircase that two people could climb without meeting until they reached the top. Except, of course, that fictional traditions, as opposed to staircases, have no tops, just as they can also twine together in more complicated forms than the double spiral.

As Barbara Godard, in "The Discourse of the Other: Canadian Literature and the Question of Ethnicity," has recently emphasized, "definitions of Canadian literature have developed on a binary model," and that model of an English-French interface "mirroring the official bilingual policy of the country . . . has precluded the discussion of writing by ethnic writers." The hyphen separating French or English from Canada situates each literature as a dislocation, a writing into being of difference. But, Godard continues, "what began as a thematic representation of difference in the nineteenth century, a difference between Quebec and Canadian literatures and those of the mother countries, has become in contemporary Canadian and Quebec literatures, a difference within, linguistically inscribed." In short, it is easy to stay on that double-spiraled staircase, caught in what E. D. Blodgett has termed "the bind of binarism." It is easy, too, not to see how much this metaphor of double defining differences precludes noticing still other differences. Is there, for example, an Icelandic or, say, a West Indian turn anywhere in all that twisting? And do not Native people have anything to say of, to, or in the literary structures that are being erected on what was, after all, originally their land?

Joy Kogawa has observed that "a Canadian is a hyphen and . . . we're diplomats by birth." The hyphen in ethnic-Canadian leaves considerable room for negotiation and might even in the absence of any "codified Canadian-ness to which one could even credibly pretend" (Robert Schwartzwald's formulation) take precedence over the two connected terms and particularly the second one, leaving for the ethnic-Canadian novelist the task of writing the hypen, the conjoining disjunction, the break that is also in part a bridge. No recent writer has done this better than Kogawa herself in *Obasan* (1981). Yet, paradoxically, her novel about Canada's brutal refusal to allow Japanese Canadians to be Canadians during and after World War II is itself essentially Canadian and comes out of a long tradition. "We are all immigrants even if we were born here," Margaret Atwood has Susanna Moodie observe in *The Journals of Susanna Moodie* (1970), and to choose to remain is to choose "a violent duality." As a character in Sky Lee's *Disappearing Moon Cafe* (1990) notes of the killing of a white woman that is part of this intricately structured chronicle of four generations of life in Vancouver's Chinatown: "Under the strain of bigotry, they were outlaws. Chinamen didn't make the law of the land, so they would always live outside of it. In fact, it was a crime just for them to be here."

Immigrant and ethnic novelists such as Naim Kattan, John Marlyn, Alice (Poznanska) Parizeau, Josef Škvorecký, W. D. Valgardson, Adele Wiseman, and others have charted the violence and duality of negotiating the divide between something else and Canada. For example, *Final Decree* (1982) by George Jonas tells of a protagonist who comes in his twenties (as did the author) from Hungary to Canada; who marries a woman of partial Hungarian descent but cannot cope with her New World values, especially as they are shaped by contemporary feminism to be totally at odds with his Old World ways, just as he cannot reconcile memories of his European past with his ongoing Canadian present. Neither can he cope with divorce and the prospect of losing his wife and their two children. During protracted legal proceedings, he shoots her lawyer, and the novel ends with him awaiting a final decree on a charge of murder, a trial in which he is doing no better than he earlier did in divorce court.

Of course not all ethnic protagonists fare as disastrously as does Jonas's Kazmer Harcsa. In Brian Moore's *The Luck of Ginger Coffey* (1977) Canada could not possibly live up to Ginger's Irish dreams. Nevertheless, this character retains his integrity and survives his numerous setbacks by finally saying, graphically, "piss on this." During the course of his subsequent trial for public indecency Ginger even manages to win his wife back. But most of the characters in immigrant and ethnic novels are ambivalently poised between paradigms of defeat and possibilities of victory or at least survival. Thus Mordecai Richler's *The Apprenticeship of Duddy Kravitz* (1959) ends with Duddy well on the way toward the wealth he has so avidly pursued even though he is again temporarily short of funds. To reach this uncertain position, he has trampled over various other characters, particularly Yvette, his French Canadian girlfriend who has shared in his aspirations and efforts but who, by the novel's end, cannot countenance all his means. So it is hard to say which best finally defines Duddy—what he is in the process of gaining or what he has already lost. An ambiguous dialectic of dream and disaster also characterizes Austin Clarke's novels about Caribbean immigrants in Toronto, such as *Storm of Fortune* (1971), while a slightly different reading of that dialectic is seen in Harold Sonny Ladoo's *Yesterdays* (1974) when a Trinidadian Hindu decides that his mission should be to go forth to convert and subjugate the Canadians. Or to run that Canadian/Caribbean connection and journey the other way, both Clarke with *The Prime Minister* (1977) and Neil Bissoondath in *A Casual Brutality* (1988) show that in the hyphenated Canadian context, as opposed to a plain Canadian one, Thomas Wolfe was right in positing you can't go home (to "home" in the old sense) again, for the attempt to do so only demonstrates how much the hyphen has become home. But *Obasan* especially charts the life of dislocation in between, as it positions the protagonist, Naomi Nakane, between her two aunts, Aunt Emily, "a word warrior" who strives for justice and for some acknowledgment of the wrongs done to her and her people, and Obasan (the Japanese word for "aunt"), who tries, just as unsuccessfully, to remain silently Japanese in the face of inflicted disasters. By gradually recovering and remembering her own story, Naomi speaks (Aunt Emily) the silence (Obasan) at the heart of this novel and in the process gives the lie to the country's claim of a mosaic ideal and its view of itself as a kinder, gentler North American nation.

Native writers are also more and more giving the novelistic lie to other (read white) renderings of Native life. Admittedly, much of this other rendering is, as already noted, sympathetic. But there is still a crucial difference between the depiction of harsh arctic survival in

Yves Theriault's *Agaguk* (1958; English translation, 1976) as compared to Markoosie's *Harpoon of the Hunter* (1970). Theriault, although of partly Native ancestry, necessarily writes from outside Inuit experience. Markoosie writes from within that radically changing experience and that makes a difference. *Agaguk* ends with the heroic hunter-protagonist allowing his infant daughter, born in a difficult time, to live (she would have traditionally been put to death). *Harpoon* ends with its heroic hunter refusing to be rescued, drifting on an ice pan out to sea and to death. Each conclusion is presented as a parable of still more change to come. Theriault sees promise in that process; Markoosie, only further desolation.

Numerous other novels, such as Maria Campbell's *Halfbreed* (1973) and Beatrice Cullerton's *In Search of April Raintree* (1983), present firsthand accounts of the fracturing of Native or Métis culture (especially as seen in the partial breakdown of the family and the forced separation of parents and children) and document the contradictions inherent in the ideal of total assimilation (such as the fact that white society refuses to countenance the very assimilation that it demands of Natives), as well as how those contradictions are endured (partly through the survival of the traditional family and particularly the grandmother). As Margery Fee has recently pointed out, *In Search of April Raintree* and Jeannette C. Armstrong's *Slash* (1985) especially "debunk the 'choices' that white acculturation has forced on Native peoples in Canada." Similarly, in Joan Crates's *Breathing Water* (1990), a young Métis wife has to discover her own "voices" from her past, which she cannot do in her marriage to her wealthy white former employer. Or in Thomas King's *Medicine River* (1990) the male protagonist comes back from a successful career in Toronto to Medicine River (obviously based on Lethbridge, Alberta) and partly comes to terms with his own dispossessed childhood by standing in as the father for a child not his own. The novel slyly advocates self-determination (the vacillating protagonist, named Will, does come to merit that name) and self-portrayal (Will as a photographer refutes the convenient white hypothesis about Native apprehensions regarding representation).

Perhaps the best book on the whole difficult question of rendering Native experience in white forms is *The Book of Jessica* (1989), a novel/memoir/script/trial transcript about authoring and acting a play based on Maria Campbell's painful life as a Métis woman and an account that records the additional pain of having that experience appropriated and romanticized by the very people who inflicted it. Written jointly by Maria Campbell and Linda Griffiths, the white author/actress who "represented" her, *The Book of Jessica* powerfully records both sides of an extended case of cross-cultural artistic negotiation/theft. Of course, one solution to this problem of expropriation is to make the whole process of writing and publishing mostly Native, as with Jeannette Armstrong's En'Owkin Writing Center (from an Okanagan word meaning, roughly, "a challenge and incentive given through discussing and thinking together to provide the best possible answer to any question") along with its associated publishing house, Theytus ("preserving for the purpose of handing down") Books in Penticton, British Columbia, or Fifth House Publishing in Saskatoon, Saskatchewan.

The Native novel as one product of the country's most recent literary "explosion" should feel right at home, for one of the most obvious features of Canadian fiction is its recent flourishing. The Canadian Renaissance, so far as the novel is concerned, is right now, the present generation, from, roughly, the sixties forward. There is something exhilarating about the fact that the best writers are not, mostly, safely dead but very much alive and writing. One can study the kaleidoscopic interplay of texts, as a major literature comes into being (and the unique opportunity that the Canadian novel allows in this respect has not yet been adequately apprised). One can also study unfolding careers (and here the opportunity has been seized, especially with respect to Atwood). One can study, too, the ways in which a new literature has been institutionalized and canonized in a partly postfeminist and even postcanonical time.

As late as 1965, Northrop Frye could maintain that any "rigorous" attempt to ascertain the "genuine classics [of] Canadian literature would become only a debunking project leaving it a poor naked *alouette* plucked of every feather of decency and dignity." Fortunately, there are now many texts for the picking, and the Canadian novel has been canonized even as it was coming into its own. *Taking Stock: The Calgary Conference on the Canadian Novel*, for example, sets forth both the top ten Canadian novels and the top one hundred, as voted on by "teachers and critics across the country." The top ten, incidentally, are Laurence's *The Stone Angel,* Robertson Davies's *Fifth Business* (1970), Ross's *As For Me and My House,* Buckler's *The Mountain and the Valley,* Roy's *Bonheur d'occasion,* Richler's *The Apprenticeship of Duddy Kravitz,* Watson's *The Double Hook,* Hugh MacLennan's *The Watch That Ends the Night* (1959), Mitchell's *Who Has Seen the Wind* (1947), and Laurence's *The Diviners* (1974). There is, of course, something dubious in any such listing. The inclusion of only one Francophone text, for example, is particularly suspect, nor do any enunciated criteria justify placing MacLennan and Mitchell ahead of, say, Aquin or Anne Hébert (and it is hard to imagine what such criteria might be). But, as one of the participants in *Taking Stock* pointed out, the first Nobel Prize for literature awarded in 1901 while Tolstoy, Chekhov, Ibsen, Strindberg, and Hardy were all alive was given to the French poet René-François-Armand Sully-Prudhomme—a fact of literary history that anyone assessing the relative merits of different writers would do well to remember. Still, canonization has consolidated the recently achieved status of the novel, as is attested by a whole new industry of publishing, teaching, and writing on Canadian texts. Scholarly editions are available (at last a Canadian *Wacousta* instead of the American one), while series such as McClelland and Stewart's New Canadian Library make literally hundreds of works available for public school and university courses. (I would here parenthetically note that Canadians of my generation typically did not read a single Canadian novel during the course of their public schooling—a situation that has now radically changed.)

Robert Lecker has recently maintained that the Canadian "canon is the conservative product of the conservative [academic] institution that brought it to life." Concerned with nationalism and with naming, "the canonizers" exhibit "a preoccupation with history and historical placement; an interest in topicality, mimesis, verisimilitude, and documentary presentation; a bias in favor of the native over the cosmopolitan; a concern with traditional over innovative forms; a pursuit of the created before the uncreated." All in all, they prefer "texts that are ordered, orderable, safe." Lecker's argument with the canon as so far conceived brings me to another major point, the observation that conservative novels tend to be valued more than experimental ones, and consequently Canadian fiction is generally perceived as being formalistically old-fashioned. The only structurally idiosyncratic novel in *Taking Stock*'s "top ten" is *The Double Hook*, and its textual experiments derive from Eliot and early modernism. Conversely, Robertson Davies, despite his deployment of Jungian archetypes and esoteric learning, has been aptly described as the twentieth century's "oldest living Victorian novelist," yet he writes the second "most important" novel, whereas Ann Rosenberg's wonderfully inventive assessment of "beeing" and humanness, *The Bee Book* (1981), has been little noted and is now out of print.

Experimentation, particularly in English Canadian fiction, tends to be modest and modernist instead of a radical postmodern fracturing of language and form. Language does occasionally play with the breakdown of meaning as when Audrey Thomas "sees the 'other' in 'mother,' " as one critic notes, or Nicole Brossard conjoins both the sea ("la mer") and the bitterness ("l'amer") of the sea with mother ("la mère") in her *L'Amèr, ou le chapitre effrité* (1977; *These Our Mothers; or, The Disintegrating Chapter*, 1983), which is itself a merging of poetry and fiction. And experiments with form do tend to be more the kind of generic blurring seen in *L'Amèr* rather than radical fracturings of the text. Michael Ondaatje, for example, similarly merges poetry and the novel in *The Collected Works of Billy the Kid* (1970) or autobiography and the novel in *Running in the Family* (1982). Or forms can be used to new ends as when Atwood creates her intriguing *Lady Oracle* (1977) out of the formulaic gothic romance, or André Major in his "deserteurs" trilogy uses the detective novel for a sustained symbolic assessment of Quebec during the 1970s.

The preponderance of women's novels in Canadian fiction is also obvious and deserves note. In contrast to the American 7 percent solution (the proportion of women writers in textbooks and anthologies that, according to Joanna Russ and others, a primarily male literary traffic will bear), the Canadian novel can show a 50 percent solution (*Taking Stock*'s top ten) or even a 70 percent solution (the top ten when the readers of a national literary magazine and not mostly male academics do the voting). But for whatever reasons—a "deconstructionist urge to displace traditional authority," the conjunctions of "colonial space" (in Dennis Lee's usage) and feminine space, the absence of the frontier and its attendant male-centered myths, a national case of penis envy ("to be from the Canadas," a character in Susan Swan's 1983 novel, *Biggest Modern Woman of the World,* observes, "is to feel as women feel, cut off from the base of power")—Canadian fiction is strikingly feminine not just in the prevalence of women writers but also in the way in which women's experience and/or writing is regularly validated and sexual polarity is downplayed. Thus the Canadian *Künstlerroman* is typically a portrait of the artist, or the future artist, as a young woman, as in Laurence's *A Bird in the House* (1970), Munro's *Lives of Girls and Women* (1971), or Audrey Thomas's *Munchmeyer and Prospero on the Island* (1971), two novellas published as one novel and contrasting Munchmeyer's and Miranda Archer's different (as even their names suggest) ways toward different careers as writers. I would also here note that male Canadian writers regularly center novels on female characters and affirm female experience. Kroetsch, for example, in *Badlands* undoes a father's search for origins by having it both doubled and reversed by the daughter's subsequent search, which concludes with her renouncing his record and his rules. Or Aquin concludes *Neige noire* (1974; *Hamlet's Twin,* 1979) by affirming a lesbian love affair (lovers here portrayed as doing much better than the heterosexual partners in Aquin's earlier novels who generally managed to drive one or the other to murder or suicide).

But the main consequence of this writing in the feminine is a whole body of major works, only some of which I have previously noted, that give to Canadian fiction much of its force and effect. *Angéline de Montbrun* (1884; English translation, 1974) by Laure Conan (Marie-Louise-Félicité Angers), for example, tells of a young woman who, after the death of her father and a disfiguring facial injury, renounces her fiancé and immures herself in a convent where, in tortured diary entries, she voices her partly self-inflicted loss. It is a problematic fate that has been read differently by succeeding generations—most recently as "the *huis clos* of the patriarchal world"—yet the novel remains as a classic of nineteenth-century Quebec fiction. And my choice for the great twentieth-century Quebec novel would be Anne Hébert's *Kamouraska* (1970; English translation, 1982), a historic tale of nineteenth-century Quebec marriage and murder both gone very much awry, and, like *Angéline,* another example of the Canadian proclivity for the gothic. I would also here note that a number of Quebec women writers have envisioned fiction through the lens of French feminism (Hélène Cixous, Luce Irigaray, and Julia Kristeva) to produce experimental works that radically critique both patriarchal language and linear master narratives based on the epistemologies of the father. Thus Louky Bersianik's *Le Pique-nique sur l'Acropole: Cahiers d'Ancyl* (1979) replaces Plato's *Symposium* with a more physical and feminist one and in the process situates the conscious murder of Iphigenia by her father, not Oedipus's unconscious killing of his father, as "the story at the heart of Western culture," and, on a more contemporary note, makes Lacan subject to "Lacanadienne." Or Jovette Marchessault, a radical lesbian of Native American descent, seeks, in novels such as *La Mère des herbes* (1980; *Mother of the Grass*, 1989), to conjoin "the ecstatic vision of the shaman to the heightened consciousness of the contemporary feminist," thereby to establish a Native and matrilineal language and myth. Or Nicole Brossard's *Le Désert Mauve* (1987; *Mauve Desert*, 1990), as a feminist text incorporating its own intertextuality, is a novel, a reading of that novel, and a translation of the novel. Like the desert in which it is set, the work, too, "is indescribable" (try visualizing a file folder in the middle of the text—the reader simply must see for him/herself). But if this novel shows just how successfully experimental Canadian fiction, especially in its Québécois manifestations, can sometimes be, it also shows those experiments as thoroughly tied to tradition. The author of the first "Mauve Desert" in *Mauve Desert* is Laure Angstelle; the translator of Angstelle's "novel" is Maude Laures; both names obviously evoke Laure Conan whose *Angéline de Montbrun* has here been transposed to a starker and more vivid setting (a mauve desert rather than a brown mountain) and has been thus incorporated into a different text that especially dramatizes differences in the text.

Another feature of the contemporary Canadian novel is its cosmopolitan maturity. It can, as *Mauve Desert* demonstrates, confidently claim a place on the same stage as its American cousin instead of trying to pass off, say, a Winnipeg "Love Story" as a New York one (indeed, with the lesbian love stories of *Mauve Desert* we have come a long way from boy meets girl in Winnipeg or New York). Or Thomas Kinsella's *Shoeless Joe* (1982), to take another example, has even been called "a great [contemporary] American novel" for its idyllic portrayal of the power of dreams and of baseball. If Canadians are finally competing again (for we do have that first entry) in the Great American Novel Sweepstakes, other likely candidates are Atwood's *The Handmaid's Tale* (1985), with its vision of religious America run amok to produce the nightmare that has always haunted the dream of a new and perfect life in the new land, or Victor-Lévy Beaulieu's three-volume novel/biography *Monsieur Melville* (1978; *On the Eve of* Moby-Dick, *When* Moby-Dick *Blows,* and *After* Moby-Dick; *or, The Reign of Poetry,* 1984) in which Beaulieu as Melville pursues Melville as Moby-Dick. Moreover, and as Atwood's updating of *The Scarlet Letter* or Beaulieu's researching for Melville/ *Moby-Dick* each suggests, the Canadian novel also claims the right to rewrite and reread a whole range of other master texts. Findley's *Not Wanted on the Voyage* (1984), for example, reenvisions the biblical flood to counter the patriarchal narratives of Noah and of God, while Bersianik's *L'Euguelionne* (1976; English translation, 1981), as "a French-Canadian feminist anti-Bible," totally subverts God's story of man, and Freud's and Lacan's accounts too. Or in *Famous Last Words* (1981) Findley has Ezra Pound's Hugh Selwyn Mauberley write on a bare wall (a wall is all that is left to him) his account of what his fascist "age demanded"—which is hardly authenticity, biblical (that writing on the wall) or otherwise: "All I have written here," Mauberley can finally claim, "is true; except the lies." Still more intricately, Aquin, in his last great novel *Neige noire,* redoes *Hamlet* as an attempt to make a snuff movie version of a television production of the play. In this *Hamlet* with a difference two Ophelias survive by rescripting their part and falling passionately in love with each other. Or—another recasting of Shakespeare—Leon Rooke's *Shakespeare's Dog* (1983) is a "woof-woof and arf-arf damn you all" directed at Elizabethan England as well as a canine account of the Bard's beginnings. Still different workings of intertextuality are van Herk's *Places Far from Ellesmere* (1990), which conjoins setting and text, the work in hand and the work read in that work (Tolstoy's *Anna Karenina*) as all "geografictions" and ultimately "unpossessible" ("Oh Anna," *Places* ends, freeing Tolstoy's protagonist from his death sentencing), or Kroetsch's *Badlands* (1975), as a search for source turns on an archaeological textual layering of virtually every quest narrative in Western literature, from *Gilgamesh* to

Atwood's *Surfacing* (1972). As all of the novels just noted attest, "parody and irony" have "become major forms of both formal and ideological critique in Canadian fiction"—so much so that Linda Hutcheon's *Study of Contemporary English-Canadian Fiction* (her subtitle) is conducted almost entirely in terms of those tropes of re-textualization.

Claims of prominence, however, sometimes still ring a little hollow, like the earlier political promise that the twentieth century would belong to Canada, and Canadian novels frequently display a certain anxiety of influence especially as they try to write the United States into its place as other, elsewhere, and different. Consider, in this context, Atwood's opening sentence in *Surfacing* noting "the disease . . . spreading up from the south" or, later, the fact that the callous killers of the heron, taken first to be Americans, turn out to be Canadians, but are "still Americans," and "what's in store for us [other Canadians], what we are turning into" (unless, like the narrator, we can turn into something more mythically elemental than the "astronaut finish" of these "Americans"). Similarly, in Susan Swan's *Biggest Modern Woman,* after the protagonist Anna Swan (who is based on an actual nineteenth-century Nova Scotia giantess) joins the circus and marries "the Kentucky Giant," Martin van Buren Bates, she soon finds that she has dwindled from a giantess into a wife and that this transformation especially mirrors Canadian/American contrasts. As she at one point writes to her mother, she must now play the "wifely manipulator whose sole purpose is moderating the behavior of her husband," and in so doing she is "acting out America's relationship to the Canadas. Martin is the imperial ogre while I play the role of the genteel mate who believes that if everyone is well-mannered, we can inhabit a peaceable kingdom. That is the national dream of the Canadas, isn't it? A civilized garden where lions lie down with the doves." The irony cuts both ways, undermining each dream by opposing them (note that the "national dream of the Canadas" is presented as a question), but not erasing their differences. And her husband's different dream of a world of giants (he advocates a eugenics program to that end—the American dream of the world as "me") is a dream of no difference, even though as a giant he is different. The paradoxes of differences proliferate to deny the sameness that would subsume Anna (Canada) into this marriage. Nevertheless, Anna still married Martin even though there was a preferable and authentically Canadian male giant back home. Circuses have their necessities too.

At a time when the United States is flooding the globe and especially Canada with its pop-products, Canadian assertions of distinct difference and achieved postcolonial status are not totally convincing. The chronological implications of the term "postcolonial" serve to place any history of cultural subservience safely in the past, yet rampant American neoimperialism hardly warrants such placing. This combination of postcolonial aspirations and more colonial apprehensions constitutes what I would term the "paracolonial perplex" that characterizes much of the Canadian fiction asserting—and doubting—national identity, as evidenced, for example, by the two novels noted in the previous paragraph. I would also suggest that this same "paracolonial perplex" partly explains a Canadian proclivity to set novels in Africa. There is a whole body of work—what W. H. New has called "Africanadiana"—that both explores and distances colonialism, some of the best examples of which are Dave Godfrey's *The New Ancestors* (1972), Audrey Thomas's *Blown Figures* (1974), or the early works of Margaret Laurence. The West Indies has also provided a setting that serves much the same paracolonial project, as is seen in such novels as Atwood's *Bodily Harm* (1981), Kreiner's *Heartlands* (1984), and Bissoondath's *A Casual Brutality*.

Francophone and Anglophone; Eurocentric and Native American; oldest and newest; conservative and experimental; conservative and feminist; colonial, postcolonial, and paracolonial—this excess of adjectives does not bring the subject into clearer focus, and "The Novel in Canada" necessarily remains itself a fiction, a narration of narrations produced in a place that is as much a narrative entity as a geographical or a historical one. Or perhaps not so much a narrative entity as a discordance of different narratives; as Robert Kroetsch has recently claimed, the "very falling apart of our story is what holds our story—and us—together." Yet the French stories are different enough from the English stories, the western from the eastern, the immigrants' from the Native peoples', that we regularly wonder (as with the recent failure of Canada's Meech Lake accord) if this very excess of stories might not eventually undo the country itself. Moreover, the governing questions of which "Canada" to tell and what novels to select for that telling constitute from the outset a kind of ouroboros trickster conjunction, a snake with its tale in its mouth, that tale being the recounting into existence of this particular snake. "Our fictions make us real," Kroetsch also asserts. One must pick one's fictions carefully, realizing that any picking is both an impossible and an enabling fiction.

Fortunately, Canadian fiction can sustain many pickings, many realities, and so exceeds any summary assessment such as the one here provided. As for all the authors and works I have overlooked, I can only acknowledge that their different stories are as valid as this account that leaves them out, which is to say that the master narrative of the Canadian novel might well be its resistance to master narratives, first to those imposed from Britain and the United States and then, following such training, to ones formulated in Canada as well. There is more to Canadian fiction than *The Bush Garden* or *Butterfly on Rock* or *Patterns of Isolation* or *Sex and Violence* or *Survival* or being *Between Europe and America*. The very divergences of these larger readings (and more could be provided, including *A Due Sense of Differences*) suggest, as Linda Hutcheon has recently observed in another context, that a postmodern "valuing of difference . . . makes particular sense in Canada." In this sense, the Canadian novel is especially Canadian in the very way in which it persistently unwrites and rewrites that problematic adjective, "Canadian."

Arnold E. Davidson

# Caribbean Fiction

Many contemporary writers and critics subscribe to the idea of the Caribbean as a distinct cultural as well as geographical entity with a coherent regional ethos beyond divisive national and linguistic premises. This view recontextualizes the literary history of the English-speaking Caribbean, which was defined historically as West Indian in recognition of the formative nature of its colonial relationship to Great Britain. An all-inclusive Pan-Caribbean approach to the literary history of the region reconceives the literature and culture of the English-speaking Caribbean as a New World phenomenon with a cultural validity that is distinct from the ideological values of Pan-Africanism and Commonwealth literature, which privilege Africa and Britain as ancestral landscapes. This historical inversion is a significant rerooting of literary and cultural history in the English-speaking Caribbean. An all-inclusive Pan-Caribbean approach privileges geographical locality and the affiliative relationships that derive from locality as formative factors in the postcolonial Caribbean.

The use of both West Indian and Caribbean to identify native space, and the interchangeability of these designations by so many writers and critics, attests to the fluidity of historical and cultural perspectives in the now independent nations of the English-speaking Caribbean. The perception of overlap suggests that identity in the region is tied to the historical process of change and development as a process of emergence, and calls attention to the conflation of the political and the literary in the regional novel. This chapter deals with the development of the novel of the English-speaking Caribbean and the shifting hierarchies of identity construction that coexist within the integrative vision of an all-inclusive Caribbean community. Under this rubric, the ideological values of Commonwealth literature and the literatures of the African and Indian diasporas are contextualized as facets of the region's cultural diversity.

The identification of the Caribbean as an all-inclusive native space overarches but does not erase linguistic and national boundaries in the region. One may speak legitimately of the Dutch-, French-, Spanish-, and English-speaking Caribbean, and there are further subdivisions dictated by peculiarities of politics and government, race and ethnicity. Yet, many writers and scholars of the English-speaking Caribbean view the literature of the entire region collectively. Writers as various as Wilson Harris, Sam Selvon, George Lamming, Derek Walcott, Edward Kamau Brathwaite, and V. S. Naipaul speak and write of the Caribbean as a coherent cultural entity. This rubric provides a context for self-definition validated by the writers themselves.

In describing the cultural context out of which he writes, the poet Derek Walcott describes West Indian and Caribbean as interchangeable: "I think you can also trace through the entire archipelago a sort of circle of experience which can be called the 'Caribbean Experience.' . . . the whole historical and, to a degree, racial experience is a totality in the Caribbean. I wouldn't confine West Indian literature to literature written in English." Caribbean interconnectedness is also a recurring theme in the public lectures and novels of George Lamming. In his address to the St. Lucia Labor Party's 37th annual convention in 1987, Lamming urged his audience "to forget all this nonsense about the English-speaking and French-speaking Caribbean. . . . we in the Caribbean have no idea what an enormous capacity we have for the creation of a unique civilisation, when we come to know our region freely, from territory to territory." Barbadian poet and historian Edward Kamau Brathwaite has made the material and spiritual basis for Caribbean interconnectedness a core theme in his work. In "Caribbean Man in Space and Time," he defines Caribbean society as fragmented but rooted in a common sociocultural matrix that is geographically and historically determined:

> The unity is submarine
> breathing air, the societies were successively amerindian,
> european, creole. the amerindian several; the european
> various; the creole plural
> subsistent plantation maroon
> multilingual multi-ethnic many ancestored
> fragments
> the unity is submarine
> breathing air, our problem is how to study the fragments/whole.

However the inner structure of the Caribbean is defined, however it is resolved in time and space, these writers all envision the entire Caribbean as the cultural community in which their works are embedded.

This affiliation across language and national barriers, as opposed to an older, historically imposed filiation to the cultural centers of Europe, and, more recently, to the cultural centers of North America, attests to the development of significant cultural relationships within the "postcolonial" Caribbean. The idea of a culturally distinct Caribbean rests on a perception of organic connectedness in the region that is based on a common historical and racial experience and a common passion to define this experience in terms that distinguish it culturally and ideologically from the metropolitan centers of Europe and North America. The novel in the English-speaking Caribbean is characterized by a distinctive sense of the Caribbean as a cultural entity original to itself, whether the writer's relationship to the developing Caribbean ethos is celebratory, elegiac, or even hostile, as is sometimes the case with V. S. Naipaul. It is preoccupied characteristically with self-discovery and self-definition, with redefining ancestry, community, and kinship through the restoration of an evolving indigenous culture devalued by a Eurocentric view of the world.

Despite the paradox of continuing dependence on the patronage and support of publishing houses and reading audiences in Europe and North America, the novel serves a self-authenticating, self-validating function in a region battered by a Kurtz-like extermination of the islands' original inhabitants, hundreds of years of authoritarian/colonial rule, and the menace of North American hegemony. It confirms the existence of a cultural community in a region of the world where political and economic stability is, more often than not, a vision of the future. Novelists as different as George Lamming, Wilson Harris, Sam Selvon, and V. S. Naipaul write about the Caribbean experience in terms that are geographically and culturally distinct; terms that foster the idea of a regional consciousness and a regional identity. In one of the best-known novels of the region, *In the Castle of My Skin* (1953), George Lamming projects his native island of Barbados as a representative Caribbean island, so that cultural identity is constructed in regional as well as insular terms. Subsequently, he uses the device of a fictive Caribbean island, San Cristobal, which is a composite of many Caribbean territories, to facilitate his vision of a comprehensive Caribbean sharing essential conditions.

The cultural ideology posited by creative writers and intellectuals in the region advances the notion of a cultural community unified by the common experience of slavery, colonialism, and ensuing cultural diversity. Present reality suggests that art may achieve a unity and coherence that is unlikely, perhaps impossible, on a political level. The creativity of the region seems energized to an extraordinary degree by the rapid and profound political changes occurring throughout the region. The disparity that exists between artistic vision and historical climate in many parts of the Caribbean suggests a dramatic struggle to consolidate a sense of regional identity that runs counter to divisive linguistic and national boundaries.

The emergence of the novel in the English-speaking Caribbean is a twentieth-century phenomenon. It begins tentatively and develops independently in Jamaica, Guyana, and Trinidad until the 1940s when unprecedented interterritorial cultural exchange promoted a new awareness of the West Indies as a collective community. The idea of a collective West Indian identity as a national framework for development became entrenched in the press toward democratization and independence following World War II. It gained legitimacy with plans for a British West Indian Federation in 1947 and the establishment of the University College of the West Indies in 1949. The West Indian Federation was established in 1958 and collapsed in 1962, but the sense of collective identity as West Indian endures in the popular imagination and in institutions like the University of the West Indies and West Indian cricket, even as the more inclusive multinational collective Caribbean identity in regional and extraregional discourse gains currency.

Despite the fluidity implicit in the changing values attached to collective identity, the development of the novel in the region is intimately bound up with the rise of national consciousness. The depiction of native space and an indigenous reality, its unavoidable specificity and concreteness, generated expanding levels of self-awareness—geographic, economic, sociopolitical, and quotidian. Over time, the novel generated a sense of native land with its own organizing center for seeing and depicting that was quite distinct from the colonizing values that shaped the ideology of the British West Indies.

Production of the indigenous novel in the British colonies of the Caribbean begins in Jamaica, not as a regional enterprise but as an insular and colonial undertaking. The architects of this enterprise were two white Jamaicans, Thomas MacDermott (1870–1933) and Herbert G. de Lisser (1878–1944), who had no moral or intellectual commitment to an independent Jamaica. MacDermott used his influence as editor of the *Jamaica Times* to establish "The All Jamaica Library" in 1904. He intended to publish and market poetry, fiction, history, and essays that dealt "directly with Jamaica and Jamaicans." Two of MacDermott's novels were published by "The All Jamaica Library" under the pseudonym of Tom Redcam: *Becka's Buckra Baby* (1904) and *One Brown Girl and—: A Jamaican Story* (1909). Despite his intimacy with Jamaican life there is a pronounced sense of otherness in MacDermott's relationship to his African-Jamaican subjects that reflects a colonial Jamaica divided by race, class, and ethnicity.

Herbert G. de Lisser, editor of the *Gleaner,* shared MacDermott's interest in Jamaica's cultural distinctiveness within the constraints of a "Jamaica directly owing allegiance to the mother-country." He published ten novels altogether, three of which were published in Jamaica. "The All Jamaica Library" was not financially viable, but de Lisser was committed to the idea of providing Jamaican literature to a Jamaican audience at an affordable price. Five of de Lisser's novels were historical romances, the most famous of which is *The White Witch of Rosehall* (1929), a sensational account of Jamaica's brutal history. Three of his novels dealt with the Jamaican middle and upper classes, and two with the Jamaican working poor. Given the subsequent preoccupation of West Indian novelists with the region's African and Indian majority, the most interesting of these is his first, *Jane's Career* (1914), or *Jane: A Story of Jamaica,* which was published locally in 1913. The central character is a young black Jamaican who goes to Kingston to work as a domestic and eventually finds the happiness and security she seeks in marriage. However, despite de Lisser's passionate interest in Jamaica and Jamaicans, the sympathy he extends to his heroine is qualified by his condescending and, at times, contemptuous treatment of the poor and black. His other novel about the Jamaican working class, *Susan Proudleigh* (1915), is set in Panama where Jamaican laborers work under terrible conditions. It is interesting as the first West Indian novel of expatriation and is similarly disfigured by a racist stereotyping of the black working class.

Claude McKay is the first of the major novelists of the English-speaking Caribbean to emigrate and achieve international recognition as a writer. McKay immigrated to the United States in 1912 and never returned. He wrote three novels celebrating black life and culture, *Home to Harlem* (1928), *Banjo* (1929), and *Banana Bottom* (1933). The first is set in Harlem and the second in Marseilles. In *Banjo,* black characters from the United States, the Caribbean, and Africa meet to discover and appreciate their cultural difference. The central characters are men on the move, however, expatriates who are either unable or unwilling to commit themselves to family and community.

*Banana Bottom* posits different values. Major tropes of the Caribbean novel are drawn here with an exemplary specificity and concreteness. This is a novel of departure and repatriation, in which the Jamaican heroine, Bita Plant, educated away from her peasant origins by a well-intentioned Jamaican minister and his English wife, is restored to her family and community. The organizing center of value in the novel is the language, belief systems, the ethics and mores of the Jamaican peasantry. Unlike MacDermott and de Lisser, McKay recognizes and affirms the syncretic character of Jamaican culture as fundamentally African. McKay's Jamaican idyll is an expatriate affair; it is shaped by a memory of home, travel in the United States, Europe, Russia, and North Africa. There is no sense of collective

Caribbean identity here, though there is a pan-Africanist evocation of Africa as the cornerstone of Jamaican life and culture that is fundamentally anticolonial and anticapitalist.

Within the British West Indian colonies, a cultural nationalism of a different sort was being forged by communities of writers and intellectuals who chafed under the humiliations of British colonial rule. In Trinidad, two short-lived antiestablishment reviews, *The Beacon* (1931–33, 1939) and *Trinidad* (1929–30), provided a forum for young writers like C. L. R. James, Alfred H. Mendes, and Ralph de Boissiere. These were political as well as literary reviews; they were anticolonial, anti-imperial, anticapitalist, and, reflective of their wide-ranging interests, they published articles on local and world politics, on African and Indian history and culture, as well as short fiction and poetry. They made an explicit connection between aesthetics and national politics. They insisted on specificity and concreteness; they demanded authenticity in West Indian settings, speech, characters, and situations, and inspired fiction rooted in an indigenous reality. Writing out of these values, Mendes and James pioneered the novel of the barrack-yard, described by James in his story "Triumph" as a type of slum dwelling with "a narrow gateway, leading into a fairly big yard, on either side of which run long low buildings, consisting of anything from four to eighteen rooms, each about twelve feet square." The novel of the yard would be taken to new heights by the Jamaican novelists Roger Mais and Orlando Patterson, and the Trinidadian Earl Lovelace. The social realism of James's *Minty Alley* (1936) and Mendes's *Pitch Lake* (1934) and *Black Fauns* (1935) deepened the representation of native space as fundamentally poor and black though they were themselves middle class by birth and education. They depicted the pain and squalor of the everyday life of the urban working poor—domestic servants, carters, porters, prostitutes, and washerwomen—and were obsessed with its vitality and intensity when compared with the predictability and safety of their own lives. They wrote out of an awareness that what they depicted was representative of the larger Caribbean, but what they depicted was characterized in the specifics of their native island.

Both James and Mendes left Trinidad in 1932. James went to England to become a major black intellectual of our time. He wrote extensively on culture and politics, and had a foundational influence on cultural production in the Caribbean. He stated the case for self-government in *The Case for West Indian Self-Government* (1933). In his groundbreaking *The Black Jacobins: Toussaint L'Ouverture and the San Domingo Revolution* (1938), he linked the genesis of the West Indian personality to the economic and cultural complexities of the Haitian revolution. *Minty Alley* was his only novel. Mendes went to the United States. Ralph de Boissiere immigrated to Australia in 1948, where he published two novels about life in Trinidad in the 1930s and 1940s, *Crown Jewel* (1952) and a sequel, *Rum and Coca Cola* (1956). De Boissiere's novels are broader in scope than those of James and Mendes. They deal with class and racial conflict, with social unrest and the growing militancy of the labor movement in Trinidad. His indictment of the middle class is harsh and uncompromising; his sympathies are with a resistant militant working class.

The emigration of these writers with their highly defined insular depictions of native space would become the norm for the West Indian writer in search of an audience and a publisher. There were no publishers in the British West Indies that could support them and a very limited audience for their work. The majority of novelists of the next generation would go to England and, ironically, their sense of exile would strengthen the idea of a collective West Indian community. For all of them, expatriation would be a process of reeducation interwoven with the withdrawal of the British Empire and the restructuring of life in a politically independent Federated West Indies. Interisland cultural exchange prompted new levels of self-awareness at home and in the United Kingdom. Reviews like *The Beacon, Kyk-over-al* (1945–61) in Guyana, *Bim* (1942–) in Barbados, *Focus* (1943, 1948, 1956, 1960) in Jamaica, and the British Broadcasting Service's weekly edition of "Caribbean Voices" had helped to shape and define the literature of the region as both a regional and national as well as a territorial enterprise, as West Indian as well as Jamaican or Trinidadian or Barbadian or Guyanese. Communities of writers congregated around the editing and publication of these reviews. Jamaican novelists like Vic Reid, John Hearne, and Roger Mais all published in *Focus*. Edgar Mittelholzer and Wilson Harris published in *Kyk-over-al,* and *Bim* drew contributions from all over the British West Indies. In *The West Indian Novel and Its Background* (1970), Kenneth Ramchand notes that between 1949 and 1959, fifty-five novels by twenty-five different writers from the British West Indies were published, almost all of them in the United Kingdom.

Some of the novelists to emerge in the decades following World War II are George Lamming, Wilson Harris, Sam Selvon, V. S. Naipaul, Edgar Mittelholzer, Roger Mais, John Hearne, Vic Reid, Orlando Patterson, Jan Carew, Garth St. Omer, and Andrew Salkey. With the exception of Phyllis Shand Allfrey, Sylvia Wynter, and the "repatriated" Jean Rhys, this was a distinctly male enterprise. Even in the works of major novelists such as Lamming, Harris, Selvon, and Naipaul the position of women as subjects of history is marginal to national and racial identification. Their novels reflect a preoccupation with the structure and values of colonial societies, with social and political change and its attendant crises, with race, class, and ethnic conflicts, with identity and the alienation from native space wrought by colonialism, with recovering the obscured cultural roots of the African majority, and with the role of the writer in charting national consciousness. The overlap of thematic concerns did not mean ideological or stylistic uniformity, however. Each of the major writers has a distinctive stylistic approach to the novel, drawing freely both from the literate traditions of Europe and America and from the linguistic and social modes of indigenous oral traditions peculiar to the region.

The novelist who dominates the literary scene at first is George Lamming from Barbados. Between 1953 and 1972, he published six novels: *In the Castle of My Skin* (1953), *The Emigrants* (1954), *Of Age and Innocence* (1958), *Season of Adventure* (1970), *Water with Berries* (1971), and *Natives of My Person* (1972). Lamming writes out of a deep moral and intellectual commitment to the collective Caribbean community, to "the shaping of national consciousness,"and to "giving alternate directions to society." Each of his novels deals with some aspect of the colonial experience, which provides the framework for a fully articulated vision of the Caribbean emerging in national-historical time. Chief among his themes are alienation and exile as facets of the colonial experience and the restructuring of Caribbean societies around the needs of its peasant and working-class majority. Major tropes of the Caribbean novel are drawn here in full self-consciousness of the dynamics of decolonization and the specific cultural constitutions of Caribbean personhood, among them: the dissolution of colonialism, expatriation, repatriation, and national reconstruction.

The most widely read of Lamming's novels are *In the Castle of My Skin* and *Season of Adventure*. *In the Castle* is a foundational auto-biographical novel about childhood in a colonial society. Its seminal value is easily seen when read in conjunction with fictional novels about childhood such as Michael Anthony's *The Year in San Fernando* (1965), Ian McDonald's *The Hummingbird Tree* (1969), Merle Hodge's *Crick Crack Monkey* (1970), Erna Brodber's *Jane and Louisa Will Soon Come Home* (1980), and Jamaica Kincaid's *Annie John* (1985). *Season of Adventure* is a much-celebrated novel of emergence interwoven with the breakdown of postcolonial society and the process of psychic and social reconstruction. Lamming's central character is a strong heroine in the tradition of McKay's Bita Plant, but Lamming's highly refined sense of historical process is quite distinct from McKay's cyclicity. Lamming's heroine is actively engaged in the political process of national reconstruction.

*The Emigrants* and *Water with Berries* are novels of emigration and exile. In *The Emigrants* Lamming delineates the cultural dynamics of the massive West Indian immigration to Great Britain after World War II. In *Water with Berries* he examines the immigration of three West Indian artists to London and the effect this has on their development as men and as artists. Lamming's novels of expatriation stand in sharp contrast to the elegiac tones of V. S. Naipaul's *The Enigma of Arrival* (1987) and the satiric humor of Naipaul's *The Mimic Men* (1967). Lamming views immigration to the "mother country" as fundamentally destructive to the Caribbean psyche, and *Water with Berries* has a distinctly apocalyptic tone. Lamming's last novels are allegorical in design. *Natives of My Person* is a historical novel that characterizes the genesis of colonialism in the New World in an allegorical reconstruction of a sixteenth-century voyage that ends in mutiny. Lamming describes it as "the whole etiology of *In the Castle of My Skin, The Emigrants,* and *Season of Adventure.*"

Lamming's collection of essays, *The Pleasures of Exile* (1960), is one of the first attempts to chart the intellectual and cultural history of the new West Indian literature. He delineates the outlines of national consciousness in contexts as varied as *The Tempest* and *Othello*, C. L. R. James's *The Black Jacobins,* his own experience of

Haitian religious rituals, and his extended visit to Africa. He provides a theoretical framework for reading the syncretic character of the West Indian novel. "The education of all these writers is more or less middle-class Western culture. But the substance of their books, the general motives and directions, are peasant." Lamming now speaks and writes out of a more inclusive collective identity, about the Caribbean novel rather than the West Indian novel, but his observations about the contours of colonial and postcolonial consciousness in *Pleasures* remain an authoritative, insightful approach to the literature and culture of the colonial and postcolonial Caribbean.

Austin Clarke, also from Barbados, creates a different discursive space in his novels of expatriation. In his Toronto trilogy, *The Meeting Point* (1967), *A Storm of Fortune* (1973), *The Bigger Light* (1975), he explores with humor and insight cultural and racial conflict and the psychological stress of life in Toronto among working-class immigrants from the Caribbean. Expatriation has a different level of intensity in Clarke's novels. This is also true of Sam Selvon's novels of expatriation: *The Lonely Londoners* (1956), *Moses Ascending* (1975), and *Moses Migrating* (1983). Selvon's comic vision changes perceptibly from sympathy to vicious satire as his West Indian subject reconstructs a parasitic identity that is superficially Black British.

Wilson Harris brings an entirely new dimension to the novel with his extravagant use of the vast Guyanese landscape as a metaphor for the obscured roots of community in the New World, his fluid characters, his fantastic reality, and his mythological approach to time. His themes are not so different—identity, memory, history, ancestry, community, cultural conflict, violence, greed, and exploitation—but his approach to the novel is far removed from the social realism of Mendes and James, from McKay's agricultural idyll, and from Lamming's increasingly allegorical conception of the past as prehistory. In *Tradition, the Writer and Society: Critical Essays* (1967), Harris rejected outright "the conventional mould" of the West Indian novel of persuasion "in which the author persuades you to ally yourself with situation and character." He invented a form that would project the fluidity of the West Indian personality and situation as a potential for growth and change. Harris was concerned from the outset with the role of the creative imagination in engendering a new civilization and a new literary tradition in the Caribbean.

Harris has published sixteen novels to date, and all but five of them use a Guyanese setting. His first four novels, *Palace of the Peacock* (1960), *Far Journey of Oudin* (1961), *The Whole Armour* (1962), and *The Secret Ladder* (1963), are known as the Guiana Quartet. Harris's obsession with the drama of consciousness as "an infinite movement" and "a ceaseless task of the psyche" is fully articulated in these early novels about the people, the landscape, the history, and the legends of Guyana. In the five novels that follow, *Heartland* (1964), *Eye of the Scarecrow* (1965), *The Waiting Room* (1967), *Tumatumari* (1968), and *Ascent to Omai* (1970), the impact of the Guyanese heartland on the subjective imagination deepens into elaborate explorations of memory and identity. The novels that follow are set in Edinburgh, London, India, and Mexico. *Black Marsden* (1972), *Companions of the Day and Night* (1975), *Da Silva da Silva's Cultivated Wilderness and Genesis of the Clowns* (1977), *The Tree of the Sun* (1978), and *The Angel at the Gate* (1982) share common images and characters, all variations of Harris's exploration of the human capacity for growth and development in different cultural contexts. *Carnival* (1985) and *The Infinite Rehearsal* (1987) are "spiritual biography" and "fictional autobiography" respectively. Set in Guyana and in the United Kingdom, they are an elaborate deconstruction of the ambiguities and deceptions that attend any attempt to apportion fixed value to human consciousness.

Harris's four books of criticism are helpful in sorting out the stylistic and linguistic theories that shape his fiction in such a distinctive way. The first of these, *Tradition, the Writer and Society,* provides an invaluable theoretical frame of reference for Caribbean literature as a whole. *Fossil and Psyche* (1974) and *Explorations* (1981) are collections of his essays and lectures. In *The Womb of Space: The Cross-Cultural Imagination* (1983), Harris examines cultural heterogeneity as a value in the creative imaginations of writers as different as Ralph Ellison, Jean Rhys, and Patrick White.

Three other Guyanese novelists of note are Edgar Mittelholzer, Jan Carew, and Denis Williams. Edgar Mittelholzer was the first of his generation to immigrate to the United Kingdom with the intention of earning his living as a writer. He wanted to become "rich and famous by writing books for the people of Britain to read." He was a prolific novelist and published twenty-two novels altogether. Mittelholzer recognized no particular responsibility to a collective West Indian community, which he felt was doomed by virtue of its heterogeneity. His novels are obsessed with sex and violence as facets of miscegenation. His racially mixed characters suffer from recurring, destructive crises of identity that have their root in a split sensibility. Like those of Harris and Carew, Mittelholzer's vast and primitive landscapes are richly evoked as a source of wonder and terror in his Guyanese settings. Mittelholzer's better novels are the early works set in Guyana, *Corentyne Thunder* (1941), *Shadows Move Among Them* (1951), and his Kaywana trilogy—*Children of Kaywana* (1952), *The Harrowing of Hubertus* (1954), and *Kaywana Blood* (1958). The books in the Kaywana trilogy are sensationally written historical novels about Guyana's brutal history of slavery and colonial settlement to the mid-twentieth century. Mittelholzer makes it seem inevitable that these narratives become mired in sex, violence, and death. *A Morning at the Office* (1950) is an interesting contrast to Mittelholzer's rural settings in Guyana. Set in Port of Spain, Trinidad, this is a well-made novel about the tedium and stasis of colonial society with its elaborate hierarchies of race, color, and ethnicity.

Jan Carew and Denis Williams bring a different sensibility to the Guyanese novel. Jan Carew published two novels of adventure, *Black Midas* (1958) and *The Wild Coast* (1959). Carew's novels are highly conventional adventure stories of frontier life in Guyana. The impact of the vast continental landscape dominates these novels as does the varied racial and ethnic composition of Guyanese society. Carew's undoing, if it can be so described, lies in an uncritical and often indulgent use of racial stereotypes. Denis Williams is a painter and archaeologist as well as a novelist. His *Other Leopards* (1963) is set in the Sudan where Williams lived for five years. This novel is usefully compared with Vic Reid's *The Leopard* (1958), about the Mau Mau rebellion in Kenya. Both novels are essential to any study of the impact of Africa on the modern Caribbean sensibility.

The Jamaican novelists Vic Reid, Roger Mais, John Hearne, Andrew Salkey, and Orlando Patterson bring a distinct sense of their island's geographical, social, and cultural particularity to the Jamaican novel. Vic Reid's best-known work is *New Day* (1949), a historical novel celebrating Jamaica's new constitution in 1944. National and historical consciousness is embodied in the history of one family's participation in resistance against colonial oppression beginning with the 1865 Morant Bay rebellion. The novel is written in a modified dialect and represents an early attempt to shape the language of narration in the novel to the rhythms of a rich oral storytelling tradition.

Roger Mais wrote a different kind of fiction altogether. In *The Hills Were Joyful Together* (1953), he transforms the social realism of the barrack-yard novel of James and Mendes into an unqualified denunciation of "the dreadful conditions of the working classes" in "the real Jamaica." With great effect, he conceptualizes the occupants of the Kingston yard collectively as the center of consciousness in this novel. In his second yard novel, *Brother Man* (1954), Mais takes a sympathetic look at Rastafarianism as a transformative value in the lives of the poor and oppressed. Mais's novels are full of energy and passion in part because he is willing, like Lamming and Harris and Reid and Selvon, to experiment freely with literary forms and language. His third novel, *Black Lightning* (1955), is a moving portrait of the relationship between the artist as blacksmith and sculptor and his community.

Orlando Patterson's *The Children of Sisyphus* (1964) is usefully compared with the yard novels of Mais. Patterson builds his representation of the dreadful conditions of Kingston's poor around the Dungle, a community of misery formed on the site of the city's garbage dump. This is a bleak novel that records the failure of the island community to nurture and sustain its own. Patterson wrote two other novels, *An Absence of Ruins* (1967) and *Die the Long Day* (1972), a well-researched historical novel about slave culture in Jamaica in the late eighteenth century.

The substance of John Hearne's novels is the Jamaican middle class, their ethics and values and their relationship to the vast majority of Jamaicans who are poor, uneducated, and black. The most impressive of these is *Voices under the Window* (1955), which examines the efforts of a middle-class Jamaican politician to provide leadership to a society in the throes of violent social upheaval. Hearne has published five other novels: *Stranger at the Gate* (1956), *The Faces of Love* (1957), *Autumn Equinox* (1959), *Land of the*

*Living* (1961), and *The Sure Salvation* (1981). In all of these Hearne examines the personal choices available to a middle class that is finally unable or unwilling to restructure its relationship to the needs of the society as a whole.

Andrew Salkey also writes about the Jamaican middle class but his best novel is not about this class at all. *A Quality of Violence* (1959) is set in a rural parish in Jamaica during a devastating drought that leaves the community weak and vulnerable to hysteria. Salkey sets peasants who believe in Pocomania, an African-Christian religious cult, against a brown, Bible-fearing minority of small landowners. This is a well-made novel about Jamaica in a state of physical and spiritual crisis. The novel is usefully compared with McKay's *Banana Bottom* and Mais's *Brother Man*.

Trinidadian writers like Sam Selvon, V. S. Naipaul and Shiva Naipaul, Michael Anthony, Earl Lovelace, and Ismith Khan widened the scope of the Caribbean novel even further. Sam Selvon was the first of these to publish. He left Trinidad for the United Kingdom with George Lamming in 1950, and has lived abroad ever since, first in the United Kingdom and then in Canada. Selvon's accomplishments are many; he writes both about an indigenous reality specific to Trinidad and about the West Indian immigrant experience in the United Kingdom. Selvon's Trinidad novels add a new dimension to the Caribbean novel with his sympathetic depiction of a transplanted Indian peasantry in the process of creolization. *A Brighter Sun* (1952) and its sequel *Turn Again Tiger* (1958) are peasant novels that employ different modes of looking at roughly the same world of the Indian peasant emerging from the feudal structure of the sugar-cane estate or plantation. *A Brighter Sun* is a novel of emergence, or *Bildungsroman,* in which a newly married, young Indian couple painfully adjust to the possibilities of life in the creolized space of a suburban village beyond the conservative ethnicity and humiliations of Indian life in a sugar estate village. Selvon represents creolization as a necessary prelude to individual growth and fulfillment in multiracial, multiethnic Trinidad. *Turn Again Tiger* replaces this compositional design with a version of McKay's agricultural idyll. Tiger and his family return to the sugar estate for a year, from planting to harvest time, and, in the process, cyclic time is reestablished as a stable, restorative framework for growth and fulfillment.

Selvon's London novels reveal the same imaginative approach to fictional composition. His Moses trilogy—*The Lonely Londoners, Moses Ascending,* and *Moses Migrating*—displays innovative approaches to the representation of immigrant life in the United Kingdom. The most accomplished of the trio are *The Lonely Londoners* and *Moses Ascending,* where West Indian otherness is savored and emphasized in linguistic experiments and comic representations of the West Indian immigrant as misfit, clown, fool, and clever rogue in an alien landscape.

V. S. Naipaul's relationship to his Indian ancestry and creolization is very different from Selvon's. Selvon continues to affirm the syncretic character of Caribbean life and culture. Living in the Caribbean, he explains, "You become Creolized, you not Indian, you not Black, you not even White, you assimilate all these cultures and you turn out to be a different man who is the Caribbean Man." On the face of it, V. S. Naipaul finds nothing in the prospect of Caribbean Man to celebrate: "History is built around achievement and creation; and nothing was created in the West Indies." This much-quoted statement in *The Middle Passage* (1962) has generated a discourse of its own within the Caribbean on history, on culture and mimicry, and on "nothing," in the works of writers as accomplished as Walcott, Brathwaite, Rhys, and Lamming. However, Naipaul's extravagant success as a novelist and travel writer with British and North American audiences is independent of controversy within the Caribbean, and his contribution to the Caribbean novel stands regardless of the controversy that surrounds his pronouncements about the bankruptcy of Caribbean society. He has published nine novels to date and seven of these are recreations of Caribbean life: *The Mystic Masseur* (1957), *The Suffrage of Elvira* (1958), *Miguel Street* (1959), *A House for Mr. Biswas* (1961), *The Mimic Men, Guerrillas* (1975), and *The Enigma of Arrival.* Naipaul's fiction suggests that the discourse of Naipaul the travel writer and essayist is distinct from that of Naipaul the novelist. There is a great deal of fun and laughter in *The Mystic Masseur, The Suffrage of Elvira, Miguel Street,* and *A House for Mr. Biswas.* The comic element in these early novels is not a rejection of native space so much as a celebration of its otherness. The quality of Naipaul's humor is not that different from Selvon's in the Moses trilogy; it turns on a self-conscious ritualized delight in observed details and incongruities. Naipaul's humor, when it depends most viciously on satire and vulgarity, is not dissimilar to the folk humor of the calypso and ritual forms of insult-trading popular in Trinidad.

The adventures of Pundit Ganesh in *The Mystic Masseur,* Mr. Harbans in *The Suffrage of Elvira,* and Mr. Biswas all describe the identity-altering process of Indian immigrants settling into a new cultural landscape. Of these, *A House for Mr. Biswas* is by far the most accomplished. It is more than an adventure novel of everyday life, it is a novel of Caribbean emergence frozen in epic time by a skillfully engineered prologue and epilogue of endurance and continuance. Mr. Biswas emerges as everyman and as a man of the people; an East Indian becomes a representative West Indian and occupies a "native" space of his own. Second only to *Biswas,* Naipaul's *The Mimic Men* is a brilliantly irreverent study of "the complete colonial," a recurring figure in Caribbean literature. The portrait is rendered with energy and humor as the autobiography of a neurotic, untrustworthy, failed colonial politician. *The Mimic Men* critiques autobiography as a genre and mocks the proliferation of fictive autobiographies in contemporary Caribbean literature. *Guerrillas* and *The Enigma of Arrival* are very different in tone. In *Guerrillas* the journalist in Naipaul takes the upper hand in a fictive account of sensational murders in Trinidad. *The Enigma of Arrival* is a novel of rejection and withdrawal to an ideal English landscape. *A Bend in the River* (1979) reiterates Naipaul's disaffection with the social and political vagaries of postcoloniality and multiculturalism in an African setting.

Other Trinidadians of Indian descent have written authoritatively and well about Indian immigrants settling into the colonial Caribbean. Naipaul's brother, Shiva Naipaul, published two novels, *The Fireflies* (1970) and *The Chip-Chip Gatherers* (1973). In *The Jumbie Bird* (1961) by Ismith Khan, the theme of generations is characterized by a general striving ahead and engagement with multiracial, multiethnic Trinidad. Khan's second novel, *The Obeah Man* (1964), reflects the author's wide-ranging engagement with national consciousness. Like Selvon, Khan embraces all aspects of Trinidad's culture as facets of his creative vision.

The novels of Trinidad's Michael Anthony and Earl Lovelace have a different relationship to Trinidad as native space. The sense of native country in these writers of African descent is well established. Though Michael Anthony has published several histories of Trinidad and Tobago, he shuns national-historical discourse in his best fiction. He has published six novels, among them *The Games Were Coming* (1963), *The Year in San Fernando,* and *Green Days by the River* (1967). The most outstanding of these is *The Year in San Fernando,* which is about one year in the life of a twelve-year-old boy living away from home. Anthony uses the innocence and naiveté of his protagonist to great advantage in this classic Caribbean novel of adventure and everyday life in the limited environment of a small town in Trinidad. Growth and development are limited by a cycle of return marked by the passage of the school year, by seasonal changes, and by the agricultural cycle of planting and harvest.

Earl Lovelace writes about the rural and urban poor in Trinidad, their coping mechanisms, their strategies for survival, their struggle to maintain a sense of identity and community in a rapidly changing environment. National identity is delineated in the competing claims of Trinidad's "multi-ethnic many ancestored" community. His most accomplished novels are *The Dragon Can't Dance* (1979) and *The Wine of Astonishment* (1984). In *The Wine of Astonishment,* enduring conflicts of race, class, and ethnicity are concrete and are localized in the historic struggle of Trinidad's Spiritual Baptists for legitimacy. In *The Dragon Can't Dance,* Carnival and Calypso are stripped of their exoticism as facets of urban poverty and underdevelopment.

The publication of Jean Rhys's *Wide Sargasso Sea* (1966) called attention to the fact that there were few novels written by women from the English-speaking Caribbean. Phyllis Shand Allfrey's *The Orchid House* (1953) anticipated some of the issues raised by Rhys in *Wide Sargasso Sea* about what it means to be a white West Indian woman in the regional press toward democratization and independence. Sylvia Wynter's *The Hills of Hebron* (1962) was conceived in the nationalist mold; her emphasis was on the transformation of Jamaican society as a whole, not on the liberation of women as a distinct social category. Clara Rosa De Lima and Rosa Guy, both born in Trinidad, also published first novels in the mid-1960s though neither is set in the Caribbean. De Lima's *Tomorrow Will Always Come* (1965) is set in Brazil and Guy's *Bird at My Window* (1966)

is set in New York. Rhys's *Voyage in the Dark* appeared in 1934 but
the significance of her West Indian heroine's ethnicity—"I'm a real
West Indian, I'm in the fifth generation on my mother's side"—was
not appreciated at the time. Through the novel's female characters,
*Wide Sargasso Sea* made a dramatic statement about the victimization and silencing of women in the Caribbean. Antoinette's fortune is
stolen, her affections are scorned, and she is imprisoned in an attic in
a strange land. Amelie is seduced by her master and paid off for her
trouble; she leaves to start a new life in Guiana. Politically aware and
resistant Christophene challenges Edward with her insight into his
cultural chauvinism, sexism, and greed, and he silences her with
threats of imprisonment and the confiscation of her property.

Since the publication of Rhys's novel women have been writing
and publishing at an unprecedented pace. The Caribbean novel in
English is no longer a male enterprise. Issues of female difference and
discrimination have altered the terms of national, racial, and cultural
identities in the novel and in critical theory. Certain overarching issues, however, remain the same, among them the postulation of an
all-inclusive Caribbean identity, the migration of the writer, the restoration of indigenous culture, the need to break with a Eurocentric
bias, a preoccupation with the poor and the disadvantaged, education
and alienation, expatriation and return, childhood and adolescence as
paradigms of the national experience, and concrete geographical lo-
calization. With few exceptions feminist consciousness in the new
Caribbean writing does not occupy a discursive space beyond the
ethnicity and nationalism typical of the literature as a whole. The
female subject is embedded in the dynamics of nationally and region-
ally drawn economic and cultural processes. Two critical anthologies
published recently underscore this: *Out of the Kumbla: Caribbean
Women and Literature* (1990), edited by Carole Boyce Davies and
Elaine Savory Fido, and *Caribbean Women Writers: Essays from the
First International Conference* (1990), edited by Selwyn R. Cudjoe.

The women other than Rhys who have received most critical attention in recent years are Erna Brodber and Jamaica Kincaid.
Though both write out of the specific cultural constraints of a Caribbean identity, feminist consciousness has a different value in the
novels of each writer. In both of Brodber's novels, *Jane and Louisa
Will Soon Come Home* and *Myal* (1988), the liberation of women

from attitudes of containment is embedded in issues of national reconstruction. National identity does not have the same value in Kincaid's work. In her *Annie John* (1985), an island nation is a mother from whom one must escape in order to have a life of one's own. The gendered space of Kincaid's *Annie John* redefines the parameters of the Caribbean novel of childhood and adolescence. In Kincaid's *Lucy* (1990), expatriation is a necessary prelude to emergence. Kincaid's novels make a feminist argument beyond ethnicity and nationalism on behalf of the psyche of the New World black woman who would write her own script.

Issues affecting women specifically and Caribbean societies generally are being refashioned by novelists as different as Michelle Cliff, Marion Patrick Jones, Janice Shinebourne, Clara Rosa De Lima, Rosa Guy, Valerie Belgrave, Merle Hodge, Sybil Seaforth, Elizabeth Nunez-Harrell, and Zee Edgell. Rosa Guy and Clara Rosa De Lima are well-established writers now. Guy has published six novels to date and De Lima has published five. In the 1970s Merle Hodge published *Crick Crack Monkey* (1970), and Marion Patrick Jones published *Pan Beat* (1973) and *Jouvert Morning* (1976). To Merle Hodge from Trinidad, fiction is a national enterprise: "Caribbean fiction can help to strengthen our self-image, our resistance to foreign domination, our sense of the oneness of the Caribbean and our willingness to put our energies into the building of the Caribbean nation." To Michelle Cliff from Jamaica, writing fiction is an attempt "to draw together everything I am and have been, both Caliban and Ariel and a liberated synthesized version of each." In the last decade she has published four novels: *Claiming an Identity They Taught Me to Despise* (1980), *Abeng* (1984), *The Land of Look Behind* (1985), and *No Telephone to Heaven* (1987).

Until the emergence of modern Caribbean literature, literate traditions of the English-speaking Caribbean were largely dictated by the interests of European imperialism. The achievement of the Caribbean writer has been to dislodge the tyrannical subordination of indigenous cultural expression without surrendering rights of access to cultural traditions that are rooted in Europe as well as in Africa, Asia, and an Amerindian past. Right now there is a dominant sense of new beginnings among writers who are laying the groundwork for a cultural community that eschews linguistic and national boundaries and celebrates the unity and diversity of Caribbean life. A critical view of the novel of the Caribbean that cuts across the barriers of language, politics, space, and time to comparison with Dutch-, French-, and Spanish-speaking counterparts and contemporaries is a logical extension of the multinational contours of the West Indian novel discussed here. Issues of filiation and affiliation are complex in the multiracial, polyglot societies of the Caribbean, where cultural identity is fluid and tradition has value as preamble rather than as main text. The novel of the Caribbean is enlarged rather than diminished by complementary discursive rubrics that provide a basis for comparison with other New World literatures and with African and Indian diasporan perspectives.

Sandra Pouchet Paquet

# Latin American Fiction

A number of years ago the Mexican historian Edmundo O'Gorman published a slim volume entitled *The Invention of America*. Columbus did not discover America in 1492, he argued; rather, "America," and the idea that it was "discovered," are much later inventions, projected interweavings of desire and imagination that find their typical form in the "chronicles" and histories of writer/explorers like Bernal Díaz de Castillo (*Verdadera historia de los sucesos de la conquista de la nueva España*), Alvar Núñez Cabeza de la Vaca (*Naufragios*), Fray Bartolomé de las Casas (*Historia de las Indias*), or Hernán Cortés (*Cartas de Relación*). In his reevaluation of such records, or such dreams, O'Gorman sounds the call for an ontological understanding of history. It will be necessary, he says, "to reconstruct the history, *not of the discovery of America, but rather of the idea that America was discovered*." This radical reevaluation of history has taken on increasing prominence, and it is, perhaps, time to extend O'Gorman's interrogation to the terrain of literary studies as well, that is, "as a process producing historical entities and no longer, as has been the tradition, as a process that takes as given the existence of such entities."

From the side of Latin America, the necessity for such a questioning seems painfully obvious, as it is painfully obvious that the concept of "Latin America" is itself a slippery one, suggesting a cultural unity among approximately twenty-five countries with different histories, different traditions, different political systems, different geographies, different languages. Paradoxically, for many of these countries' best thinkers, it is the search for this unremediably absent definition that marks the essential unity of "Latin American" cultural identity. As E. Mayz Valenilla puts it, American Latinity constitutes itself around a sense of "forever-not-yet-being," a sense of permanent disequilibrium intensified by an often defensive inferiority complex toward the cultural productions of the United States and Europe, as well as an unbalancing conviction of the Latin American's anachronism not only on the world scene but within the local geographies as well. One result of such questioning is that Latin American literature often addresses the impossibility for Latin Americans of situating themselves in a specific historical moment, and reminds them of the inescapability of living simultaneously and of bridging all historical periods from the Stone Age to the Space Age. One of the most persistent dreams of Latin American literature is a longing to escape this trap and to construct a time corresponding to the Latin American space; one of the most notable effects of Latin American literature is to deconstruct that dream and that longing.

At the same time, Latin America—unproblematically defined—has come in recent years to be "put on the map"—rediscovered or reinvented once again—for United States–European consciousness. It has been reinvented politically as Nicaragua, Colombia, El Salvador, Chile, Mexico take on new reality in our nightly news, and, with a continually renewed, strikingly anachronistic astonishment, reinvented poetically as well. The source of this baroque superabundance of superb creative work can be, for us citizens of the United States used to referring to ourselves simply as "Americans" with a kind of unconscious superiority complex, disconcertingly exotic; the Great American Novels are arriving as an import, in translation, from that other, intermittently forgotten, America, and the names of their authors stumble hesitatingly off our monolingual tongues: Mario Vargas Llosa, Guillermo Cabrera Infante, Gabriel García Márquez, José Lezama Lima, João Guimarães Rosa, Domitila Barrios de Chungara (a first elemental hesitation: which *is* a particular author's last name, after all?), Pablo Neruda, Carlos Fuentes, Isabel Allende, Julio Cortázar, Elena Poniatowska, Jorge Luis Borges, Rigoberta Menchú, Alejo Carpentier, Clarice Lispector, José Donoso, Luisa Valenzuela, Octavio Paz, Manuel Puig . . .

I planted the words "baroque" and "exotic" deliberately in the previous paragraph; they are two of the key terms that echo most insistently in the North American reception of these masterpieces by the other Americans. William Gass, writing in 1980, compares the contemporary reaction to the phenomenon of the Latin American novel with the intellectually overwhelming effect of the Russian novel on the British reading public a century earlier: "They were long, those damn books; they were full of strange unpronounceable names: loving names, childhood names, nicknames, patronyms; there were kinship relations which one can imagine disconcerting Lévi-Strauss; there was a considerable fuss made concerning the life, sorrows, and status of the peasants, the *oblige* of the *noblesse;* and about God, truth, and the meaning of life there was even more; moods came and went like clouds, and characters went mad with dismal regularity. . . . Must we do that again?" The answer, clearly, is "yes." Once again we are asked to deal with strange names, settings as mysterious and exotic as the Russian steppe, a style that, even in translation, suggests the breathtaking grandeur of the original and hints at a use of language so innovative it expands the boundaries of the possible. Notably, however, even in such a knowledgeable critic as Gass, the question is posed in anachronistic terms, a reading of late twentieth-century fiction that reduplicates a nineteenth-century literary experience. The sense of temporal disjunction persists on other levels as well. Borges, whose most significant production is from the 1940s, continues to be read as an author of the 1970s. Alejo Carpentier (1950s) is reinvented as a contemporary, rather than a precursor, of Miguel Barnet (1980s).

The question that exercises me, a Latinamericanist transplanted into a volume on American literature largely oriented toward the United States, is that of which Latin America to invent in these pages. Should I invent a single entity analogous to the United States? Should I follow the now well-established lines of a comparatist practice of putting together García Márquez and Faulkner, Marechal and Joyce, Borges and Hawthorne, Gámbaro and Beckett, Paz and Stevens, Sarmiento and Cooper? Should I reinvent Latin America, that land of poets (three of Latin America's five Nobel Prizes have been given to poets: Gabriela Mistral, Pablo Neruda, and Octavio Paz), as a continent dominated by narrative, with just a footnote given to its most pervasive form of expression—Afro-Hispanic: Nicolás Guillén,

Nancy Morejón; revolutionary: Giaconda Belli, Ernesto Cárdenal; feminist: Rosario Castellanos, Julia de Burgos? Should I outline a traditional literary historical progression: *costumbrismo,* nineteenth-century realism, *modernismo,* telluric novel, avant-garde, "Boom," post-Boom? How do I contextualize the fact that John Douglas edits both Avon's fantasy series and its Latin American translation series?

In 1967 John Barth published an article inspired by his love for the Argentine poet and short-story writer Jorge Luis Borges entitled "The Literature of Exhaustion," in which he set the Argentine master into a more general context that included references to works by James Joyce, Samuel Beckett, and Franz Kafka. It is not necessary at this point to review the history of the readings and rereadings and misreadings of Barth's article, the appreciative reception that turned "literature of exhaustion" into a critical commonplace. I would like to note two rather interesting consequences, however. First of all, while Borges was well known and much appreciated in Latin America in his own right and as a precursor of the Boom writers, for many inhabitants of North America Barth's article was a revelation of a startling new talent on the world literary scene. Borges was, through Barth, reinvented as an American author, becoming, achronologically for Barth's readers, if not for Barth himself, the contemporary of United States fiction writers like John Hawkes, William Gass, Donald Barthelme, Thomas Pynchon, and John Barth himself. Indeed, in a later reflection on his famous exhaustion article entitled "The Literature of Replenishment," John Barth becomes, unconsciously perhaps, seduced by this now-pervasive writing of contemporary literary history, and puts Borges into the group of postmodernists along with such writers as those listed above, including as well Colombian Nobel laureate Gabriel García Márquez (the quintessential Boom author) and Italian Italo Calvino as his contemporaries.

The second point I wish to make is that this curious violation of chronology in the conflation of two or three generations of writers is bizarrely appropriate, and both reflects and respects the implicit aesthetics of much recent Latin American literature. Just so Borges himself often violates temporal schemes in order to have books converse with each other across the shelves of a library; in one instance among many, to bring alive once again Borges's precursor, Leopoldo

Lugones (1874–1938), as a commentator on his miscellaneous volume of short sketches and poetry (*El hacedor* [1960]).

Even for a continent characterized by anachronism, the novelistic production of the early part of this century seems particularly out of step. Roberto González Echevarría's study of Rómulo Gallegos's *Doña Barbara* (1929; English translation, 1931), the best known of the "telluric novels," emphasizes just this point. The *novela de la tierra*, he says, suffers from a "double anachronism" in both its writers and its critics: at the same time that the High Modernists were changing the shape of Euro-American fiction, these novels were praised and promoted for launching realist narrative in Latin America. *Doña Barbara* and its counterparts display a third anachronism as well; in a period of rapid urbanization, all of these novels are relentlessly rural. *Doña Barbara,* as the title indicates, is an allegorical tale of the conflict between civilization and barbarity set in the Venezuelan *llanos* (plains), a conflict worked out not so much between the two main characters, Doña Barbara and Santos Luzardo, as between the forces of Man (used advisedly) and Nature. The other great narrative tendency of the period, the *indigenista* novel (which is not indigenous, but pro-Indian), develops along similar lines, but with a more strongly marked element of concrete political commitment. Thus, Clorinda Matto de Turner's *Aves sin nido* (1889; Birds without a Nest) and later novels of this tendency expose the miserable conditions obtaining in the remote, often non-Spanish-speaking, Indian villages controlled by a creole landowner, and denounce the system that undergirds and sustains such exploitation. As is the case in Gallegos's novel, individual characters revert to position holders for a politically charged description of elemental conflict set against a realist landscape. Nevertheless, despite their anachronism, such works can and should be seen as the foundation of modern Latin American narrative. They draw a specifically Latin American landscape, populate it with characters drawn from local customs, and commit themselves to an identifiable sociopolitical program.

It is in this context of the preoccupation with specifically Latin American landscapes that we can understand the comments of Alejo Carpentier, the Cuban novelist and precursor of the Boom generation. He suggests that the widely perceived baroque quality of Latin

American fiction reflects not a love of fussy ornament but a necessary response to near-universal incomprehension of the most mundane details: "Heinrich Heine speaks to us, suddenly, of a pine and a palm tree. . . . The word 'pine' suffices to show us the pine; the word 'palm' is enough to define, paint, show, the palm. But the word 'ceiba' . . . " And here Carpentier must pause, in a baroque gesture, to define his terms, to paint a picture of a natural phenomenon equally unfamiliar to inhabitants of the lands of palm as to the lands of pine, to discover (or recover) an unacknowledged reality not only for the Eurocentric literary establishment but also for fellow Latin Americans, for fellow Cubans, and, in some essential sense, for himself. "The word 'ceiba,' " says Carpentier, "—the name of an American tree called by Black Cubans 'the mother of all trees'—is insufficient for people of other latitudes to see the aspect of rostrate column of this gigantic, austere, and solitary tree, as if drawn forth from another age, sacred by virtue of its lineage, whose horizontal branches, almost parallel with the earth, offer to the wind a few handfuls of leaves as unreachable to the human being as they are incapable of any movement. There it is, high on a hillside, alone, silent, immobile, with no birds living in its branches, breaking apart the earth with its enormous scaly roots. . . . At a distance of hundreds of meters (because the ceiba is neither a tree of association nor of company) grow some papayos, plants erupted from the first swamps of creation, with their white bodies, covered with grey medallions, their leaves open like beggars' hands, their udder-fruits hanging from their necks." The ceiba is placed by reference to the papayo, which also requires definition, and, potentially, so on in infinite regress. Carpentier concludes, "These trees exist. . . . But they do not have the good fortune of being named 'pine' nor 'palm tree' nor 'oak' nor 'chestnut' nor 'birch.' Saint Louis of France never sat in their shade, nor did Pushkin ever dedicate them a line of verse. . . . We must not fear the baroque, our art, born of our trees, . . . a baroque created out of the need *to name things,* even though with it we distance ourselves from other fashionable techniques."

What Carpentier sees as a culturally necessary neobaroque style distinguishes the Latin American effort from the more aesthetically motivated formal games of the seventeenth-century European tradition. Rather than a superabundance, the baroque style that typifies these novels is reflected in, and derivative of, an order of experience that represents the near opposite of that excess traditionally associated with the baroque, by a need to assign names to each animal and plant, establishing its reality for a translocal audience.

More contemporary authors, writing after Carpentier, have also been deeply concerned with the issues involved in inscribing a Latin American identity for (or against) a supposedly "universal" audience. Mexican writer Carlos Fuentes defines the linguistic challenge succinctly by reference to "la palabra enemiga"—ambiguously, "the word enemy" or "the enemy word"—with all the gravity of that phrase's implicit linguistic, cultural, and political density. Fernández Retamar's *Calibán* eloquently explores the issue of linguistic alienation not only in relation to the Spanish-speaking Latin American's relation to indigenous and other minority peoples but also in terms of a vexed consciousness of the overriding effects of cultural imperialism. In Juan Marinello's famous formulation, "Somos a través de un lenguaje que es nuestro siendo extranjero" [We *are* through (are traversed by) a language that is ours despite its foreignness (is our foreign be-*ing*)], Latin American literature, as an entity, is continually in crisis, continually reinventing itself, continually questioning its very existence. It is, perhaps, unnecessary to belabor the point that Latin America's most exportable literary products can be identified with the narratives of the 1950s and 1960s, where the very label applied to the group—the Boom—is an English word hinting at stock market fluctuations and atomic bomb capabilities, for many critics a marker of cultural imperialism at its worst.

Literary critics like Fernández Retamar with a particular commitment to postcolonial thought find the tracks and scars of cultural imperialism throughout Boom writing. There is no doubt that focusing, as Carpentier does, on the dynamics of narrative exchange value offers critics a justifiable method of analysis, one with premiums of its own on the literary-critical market. But Fernández Retamar would argue that such writers and critics are themselves "commodified" by the resources of their respective choices of literary code, by the analytical traditions they so ably manipulate. He uncovers the extent to which the implied value system recommodifies the native subject into yet another version of the stereotypical object of a Westernized gaze, an unreconstructed Shakespearean Caliban, in this case one in which a non-Western author inserts himself into a system that many other non-Westerners have, with good reason, found to be peripheral, if not totally alien, to their own traditional views. Thus, suspiciously, the adulated Third World writer or critic can be neatly inserted into a (white) critical discourse through the distortional, patronizing mythologies of the quaintly exotic. Furthermore, Fernández Retamar adds, the valued indigenous tradition is itself produced and reified, in very concrete ways, by European thinkers and their postcolonial heirs.

Writing in Latin America is often carried out under dismal conditions either at home or in exile, under the pressure of long days spent in other work, against the instituted situations of subtle or overt censorship, sometimes with the risk of imprisonment, torture, disappearance. Critics and authors of fiction alike have recognized as one of their prime responsibilities the obligation to commit themselves to the "mad" struggle over the history of meanings, not only to reveal the ways in which rhetorical concerns discursively construct reality, but also to intervene into and counter these processes of reality-construction. Fiction politicized is often not enough; the reading public demands more concrete manifestations of commitment. Furthermore, as Trinh Minh-ha reminds us in *Woman, Native, Other,* "It is almost impossible for [writers] (and especially those bound up with the Third World) to engage in writing as an occupation without letting themselves be consumed by a deep and pervasive sense of guilt." And she continues later with the wry observation that while committed writing, on the one hand, helps alleviate this guilt, on the other hand, it involves a simple displacement: "Committed writers are the ones who write both to awaken to the consciousness of their guilt and to give their readers a guilty conscience. Bound to one another by an awareness of their guilt, writer and reader . . . [carry] their weight into the weight of their communities, the weight of the world. Such a definition naturally places the committed writers on the side of Power." A similar statement might be, and often is, made in reference to fictional works in Latin America, where the tangled lines of power and commitment are peculiarly complex, where favored authors are frequently awarded political appointments of some power, and authors in disfavor face exile or death.

Along other lines, feminist literary critics, too, have been reexamining these now-classic texts. The Boom writers who engaged in the deconstruction and resemanticization of so many of the meaning systems of official mythology seem oblivious to the degree to which they reaffirm the hoary myth of the maternal body as equivalent to a state of nature and of maternal "nature" as an unproblematic concept. This institutionalization of the figure of the feminine as a natural, primordial, but containable and manageable, element is evident even in the works of Latin America's most internationally well-known female writer, the openly feminist Chilean novelist, Isabel Allende, who has arrived belatedly on the Boom scene, twenty years after its vogue, but with the same assumptions intact. In her works, as in older Boom novels written a generation earlier, the maternal body may be a utopian site, but the mother's lack of access to subjectivity is a nonnegotiable given.

Correspondingly, the fictional existence of women—and I am thinking particularly of the much-lauded sensitivity to the feminine, indeed, the "feminization" of the prose, of Boom writers like Gabriel García Márquez in *Cien años de soledad* (1967; *One Hundred Years of Solitude*, 1970) or José Donoso in *El obsceno pájaro de la noche* (1970; *The Obscene Bird of Night*, 1979)—though real, is interpolated into the fiction in such a way as to highlight for the sensitive reader the insistent, and unquestioned, assumptions of an unproblematized, masculinist discursive base. Ursula Buendía, the strong mother figure of *One Hundred Years of Solitude,* is frequently cited by approving critics as a particularly fine example of García Márquez's sensitivity to female subjectivity. I would argue, though I do not have the space to do so here, that the case is very nearly exactly the opposite, that in Ursula the figure of the woman is displaced twice over. Masquerading as subject, as the dominant figure within the home and as the figure of sanity, she is taken informally, and more pervasively, if subtly, as object: the metaphorized discourse of woman as, problematically, constitutive of the impersonated, explicitly displaced but implicitly reconstituted, discourse of man. The case is even more obvious in Donoso's novel, where the male narrator is straightforwardly feminized (that is, castrated), turned into a woman, by the strange old hags inhabiting the convent, and reduced to a sightless, deaf—but fortunately not speechless—"imbunche." Donoso's character not only speaks for but *as* a woman, as the outcast

male vision of the virgin-mother-child, feminized in the imperson-
ation of a criminal grotesque, while symbolically on his way to transformation into the ultimate phallic symbol: the "imbunche" as transcendental signifier. In both works, significantly, the language of
women's desire only enters the enclosure of the created fictional space
as monstrous, and productive of monsters. In *One Hundred Years of
Solitude,* the birth of the incestuous infant with the pig's tail precipitates apocalypse; in Donoso, the grotesquely deformed "Boy" anticipates the same function.

Jorge Luis Borges and the Colombian novelist, scriptwriter, and
journalist Gabriel García Márquez represent the two archetypal figures of the Boom. Borges's *Ficciones* (1944; English translation,
1962) and García Márquez's *One Hundred Years of Solitude,* though
from two different generations, remain the Boom's most typical and
most enduring products. Curiously, it would be difficult to imagine
two writers more different in personality, politics, enduring obsessions, or literary style. García Márquez represents the Boom's search
for a "total" novel, those long, long books; Borges is the Boom's
minimalist. García Márquez's narratives derive from oral storytelling
and mass media; Borges's metaphysical fables ignore such influences.
García Márquez rewrites Colombian history, Borges extends the implications of European idealist philosophy; García Márquez is associated with magic realism, Borges with fantasy; García Márquez's
political leanings are strongly leftist, Borges's superficial apoliticism is
paired to a reactionary political commitment. Yet, together they define the parameters of what the Boom has come to mean in classical
literary studies.

Borges is a master of what we might call a desperate comedy of
inaccessibility, marked and defined by an adamant insistence on a
few, intensely imaged symbols: the dreams, the labyrinths, the mirrors, and the tigers so familiar to his readers. Likewise, he relies
heavily on a few insistently reiterated metaphors. In his works we are
drawn into the temptations and unrealities of mathematics, and especially the physical sciences. In Borges, as John Updike notes, "we
move . . . beyond psychology, beyond the human, and confront
. . . the world atomized and vacant. Perhaps not since Lucretius has
a poet so definitely felt men as incidents in space." Thus, Borges's
tenuously imagined librarians, his dreamers within the dream, his

immortals, and his metaphysical *gauchos* are so comically overdetermined, so full of meaning that they are atomized and exploded by their very richness.

Such relativization and negation reach into all levels of these confections. Carefully constructed and firmly established plot lines are demolished at a stroke through infection by impossibly corrupt, or undeniably fictitious, elements. Even at the micro-level of the noun clause the author gives us nothing firm and resistant, without also suggesting the irrational fault lines running through its architecture; he pairs abstract nouns to concrete modifiers and the reverse: "innumerable contrition," "rigorously strange," "the interminable fragrance," "that equivocal and languid past," "the almost infinite Chinese wall," or makes statements like "he retired to a figurative palace," and "our destiny . . . is horrifying because it is irreversible and of iron." In a similar manner, Borges's dreamer who dreams a real man in his story "The Circular Ruins" reminds the reader of the singularly corrupt copy of Borges's 1917 edition of *The Anglo-American Cyclopaedia* testifying to the existence of Tlön in the story "Tlön, Uqbar, Orbis Tertius," and parallels the frustrated searches of any number of Borgesian librarians who hypothesize the existence of a Book of Books in the infinite stacks of the library of Babel, or the philosophers who attempt to discover the name of God written in the stripes of a tiger.

Certainly, Borges's dramas of dazzling combinatorics and differential decay respond to the pre-posthum(or)ous dissection of the postmodern condition, the wary, weary recognition that the search for eternal verities—God, Science, a Center—are inevitably conditioned and contaminated by the seeking mind, that the unrealities of existence militate against the very possibility of the search, much less its successful conclusion. The disturbing and seductive corollary for fiction is clear. No longer is the fictional universe bounded by classical rules of verisimilitude and plausibility; instead, it is conceived, in a fictional parallel to quantum physics, as a self-contained game with the sole responsibility of maintaining consistency to its own implicit rules. For Borges the rules are deceptively simple; in the words that Borges puts in the mouth of his character Herbert Quain in *Ficciones*, "I revindicate for this work the essential elements of every game: symmetry, arbitrary rules, tedium."

Borges is a writer's writer. García Márquez is a cult. He has said
many times that his role is to transcribe ordinary Colombian reality;
the manner of this transcription, however, represents the enduring
enchantment of his confections. Chilean José Zalaquett says of
García Márquez that "his *One Hundred Years of Solitude* hit Latin
American readers much as St. Paul was struck on his way to Damas-
cus." Zalaquett is not far off; García Márquez's variation on marvelous realism ran through Latin America like a conversion experience. What is particularly powerful in García Márquez's
hybridization of folk culture and high art is that it reflects a new,
highly improvisational, cognitive mode that both emerges from Colombian history and engages with it critically, while at the same time
transforming that history and that fiction into a new way of seeing.

The reader's struggle to create a historical narrative against the
grain of García Márquez's texts responds to the appeal of the rhetorical mode of history as a meaningful ordering system in modern
life. Frequently, García Márquez's narrator tantalizes this desire for
order in the readers by providing just a few of the dates and references that Morse Peckham calls "indicators of pastness" in historical
narrative. At the same time, the undermining of such indicators,
which becomes a covert structural imperative in the text, responds to
the narrator's recognition that, in Peckham's words, "such
indicators—historically authentic details—are not only symptoms of
the rhetorical overdetermination of history. They can also become
ends in themselves." García Márquez's indicators are *underdeter-
mined;* no matter how our rage for order compels us to rearrange the
scattered facts, the result is inevitably a recognition of discontinuity.
Clearly, time itself is deformed by irony; the sequence that can be
derived from the story reveals no law, no access to meaning, no
culmination of a teleological historical endeavor. In the retelling of
the episode of the massacre of the banana workers, for example, *One
Hundred Years of Solitude* develops this theme. The omniscient narrator's tacit support for the unofficial versions of the massacre represented in the stories told by José Arcadio Segundo and the unnamed
child makes the question of oral history unproblematic in outline,
though often unreliable in specific detail—for example, in the discrepancy about the number of dead carried by the hallucinatory train.
Curiously, García Márquez's fictional account has historically served

as an impetus to permit the unwritten episode to be recognized and reinserted into the offical history of Colombia.

The inhabitants of Macondo in *One Hundred Years of Solitude,* the lonely old dictator eking out his waning years in *El otoño del patriarca* (1975; *The Autumn of the Patriarch,* 1976), the bitter ex-soldier in *El coronel no tiene quien le escriba* (1974; *No One Writes to the Colonel,* 1968), the half-forgotten hero in *El general en su laberinto* (1989; *The General in His Labryinth,* 1990), all suffer from the same loneliness, from the same plague of forgetfulness. In *Autumn,* the dictator's mother tries to reveal the "true" story of his conception and birth to her inattentive son, a story that diverges radically from the accepted historical version of his immaculate conception and miraculous birth. Significantly, it is the essential that is ignored in this episode: Bendición Alvarado "tried to reveal to her son the family secrets that she did not want to carry to the grave, she told him how they threw her placenta to the pigs, Sir, how she could never determine which of so many fugitives had been your father, she tried to tell him for the historical record that she had conceived him standing up . . . , but he did not pay her any attention."

The contagious plague of forgetfulness spreads throughout the village of Macondo, throughout the entire country, throughout the world, and even reaches past the pages of the text to affect us, its readers. We tend to forget how much of the story we owe to the manipulations of the various narrative agents. The storyteller, who filters the whole of the work through his perception and controls it with his imaginative recreation, is at the same time in García Márquez a curiously reticent figure. Despite his eagerness to define his position in traditional storytelling terms, despite the fact that we are often given the narrator's name—most famously, the Cervantine Melquiades, in the case of *One Hundred Years of Solitude*—the narrator remains unidentifiable. This ruse, for we must see it as such, of choosing a site and then refusing efforts at situation, defines the storyteller's art, which ostensibly chooses one site (even in the most concrete sense: the room in the Buendía house, or the stool set out in front of a store) while mediating (or occupying simultaneously) two places: that of history and that of myth. It is a position the storyteller/narrator cannot maintain easily; in fact, he could not maintain it at all without the readers' forgetfulness, our unconscious complicity in his ostensibly overt placement of the story's center and in his devious usurpation of that place.

Mexican Carlos Fuentes's work includes several of the misshapen masterpieces described by Gass, attesting to his own profound engagement with the problem of a language that does not always do justice to indigenous reality; astonishingly innovative and rewarding works like his *La muerte de Artemio Cruz* (1962; *The Death of Artemio Cruz,* 1964), about the twelve hours of dying, and seventy-odd years of life, of an unsavory post–Mexican Revolutionary opportunist named Artemio Cruz, a spurned illegitimate peon offspring of a mulatto woman and the local landowner. Or *Terra Nostra* (1975; English translation, 1976), a mythic-philosophical-historical recreation of four hundred years of combined Spanish and Spanish American relations, a novel in which the reader may soon come to the conclusion that not only has Fuentes read absolutely everything ever written but that it all, somehow, has found a way into this vast book.

The problem of how language structures reality is also central to his *Cristóbal Nonato* (1987; *Christopher Unborn,* 1989), a post-punk, Laurence Sternian, dystopic projection of a 1992 Mexico City in which inhabitants speak a stylized Spanglish and worship a governmentally created concoction of myth and media hype named "Mamadoc." Sterne, and particularly Balzac, are acknowledged influences on Carlos Fuentes, and the last month of the first trimester of the novel, "It's a Wonderful Life" (the Spanish original calls the same section "Una vida padre"), contains a delicate and specific homage to Fuentes's forerunners in his Shandyian placement of prologue and epigraph at page 132 and his adornment of that passage with a graphic representation of the sperm/serpent, Shandyian in basic shape, that also, with ironic wink, reminds the reader, should she choose to be reminded, of the snakes inherited by Balzac through fortune and typesetters' creativity, allusions that Fuentes complicates with a host of tributes to other texts including, of course, those ever-present masters, Vico and Joyce, who peek in on its "vicogenesis."

At issue is no longer a matter of rational understanding of the truth or of any truth-claims whatsoever, but another enabling/disabling condition: that which forces us to recognize the world as the world of the text, whose only significance lies precisely in its existence as text. And furthermore, to recognize the subterfuge of languages as well: one of the overriding concerns in this stubbornly, playfully polyglot novel. "La lengua," that fleshy, material thing, becomes a word, a multilingual pun, a fragile verbal arabesque delicately framed between figurative quotation marks, an unreadable—if undeniably aesthetic—cipher, a zero-degree artifact of writing. As in Sterne's novel, and even more consistently so, the narration of Fuentes's work is from the point of view of a first-person voice, given overridingly to a narrator who, by traditional standards, should be an eyewitness to the events described, but who, in both books, is clearly in no condition to witness anything at all. The novel begins as Cristóbal's future parents conceive him in an ecstatic union on Acapulco's beaches, and ends, congruently, with his birth.

The shape of Fuentes's tale, however, as befits the man Suzanne Ruta has called "our leading North American political satirist," is more solid, darker, and more socially committed than that of his eighteenth-century precursor, more closely aligned with Fuentes's stated aims to create a Latin American counterpart to Balzac's massive "Comédie humaine" than with the antic satires of Sterne. The arabesque snake curve takes on another signification, as the whipping tail of the sperm-snake becomes the whip—"a black whiplash in his mind": grammatically bi-generic in Spanish, physically transsexual. Its political referents are likewise double and ambiguous: the symbol of the master's authority or the torturer's tool, the whipping curve becomes, at the same time, the liberating arabesque of graffiti on oppression's pristine wall. One reading of Fuentes would align him with the lash of that master's whip, another with the helplessness of the whipped child; one with the potent snake, another with the undigested, indigestible meal, one with the "Elector," brother to Cortázar's "lector complice" (the complicitous reader, from *Rayuela* [1963; *Hopscotch,* 1966]) who freely picks and chooses among the allusive/elusive offerings, one with the unhappily coerced child, sister to Cortázar's despised "lector hembra" (female reader): "the most likely thing is that You are a poor adolescent girl from the Colegio del Sagrado Corazón forced to copy out . . . some classic passage from this novel."

Like *Terra Nostra,* to which it serves as counterpart and counterpoint, *Cristóbal Nonato* is a novel about discovery, and about the continuing drama of the encounter between cultures that began at the

Conquest. Not the least of its peculiarities, however, is that this is a novel set at angles to the more common Hispanic bias in Latin American historiography; in *Cristóbal Nonato* the perceptive filter is, shockingly, dominated by an Anglo-American and Northern European range of metaphors, and despite their revolutionary rejection of things gringo in their terrorist "acapulcolipsis," Angel and Angeles are, as a punning play on their names might suggest, more anglo than angel. "What distinguishes the Spanish conquest from that of other European peoples," says Octavio Paz, "is evangelization," and what distinguishes Fuentes from other quincentenary conquistadores is not evangelization but what might be called his insistent return to the Sternian/Lawrencian metaphor of a dangerous invaginalization.

Like Carlos Fuentes, the Peruvian novelist Mario Vargas Llosa's complete works include a startling variety of styles, ranging from the hilarious send-up of military jargon as applied to a regularly scheduled Amazonian prostitution service for the benefit of soldiers in a distant outpost (*Pantaleón y las visitadores* [1973; *Captain Pantoja and the Special Service,* 1978]), to his politically freighted version of a detective novel in *¿Quién mató a Palomino Molero?* (1986; *Who Killed Palomino Molero?,* 1987). For Vargas Llosa, increasingly over recent years, the space of writing has become his field as well, and in all of his novels since *Conversación en la catedral* (1969; *Conversation in the Cathedral,* 1975), the writer and his writing take central roles in the unfolding narrative. Layers accumulate in the text as the reader observes the writer writing and the writer observing himself writing and reflecting on what has been written. Santiago Zavala in *Conversación* is a journalist, a mediocre one, who has intentionally chosen this mediocrity so as to avoid, by his resounding failure, the more banal mediocrity of conformity.

His masterpiece, *La casa verde* (1965; *The Green House,* 1968), is considered one of the very best from the outpouring of Latin American masterpieces, a worthy candidate for what Vargas Llosa calls "the impossible novel, the total novel," combining fantasy and realism, myth and psychological verisimilitude, simultaneously unfolding all of the potential manifestations of reality and history. A kind of tropical *War and Peace,* this weighty (in both senses of the word) novel carries the reader along with an imaginative force and intensity that is nothing less than mesmerizing. However, it would be a serious mistake to read Vargas Llosa's call for a total fiction in terms of a simplistic or reductionist espousal of continuity, synthesis, or a single, sovereign form. The novel is impossible to summarize; it has no single plot in the conventional sense of the term. The field of action of this palimpsest, however, revolves around a bordello in Piura on the northern coast of Peru, and Santa María de Nieva, an underdeveloped provincial outpost of that underdeveloped country, virtually inaccessible by any but the most tortuous means. Its narrative trajectory involves three generations, thirty-five major characters, and five intricately interrelated major plots. "Literature," said Vargas Llosa in a famous formulation, "is fire; it signifies nonconformism and rebellion." For Vargas Llosa, a deeply moral author with a well-documented concern for the problematics of the total fiction, the twinned issues of history and fiction, of fact and representation, of a past repeated, as Marx reminds us, as tragedy and as farce, signify more than the presence of a leitmotif in the work. Of such entanglements the web of the oeuvre is woven. Nevertheless, his works, as Luis Harss shrewdly writes, "within their more or less tortuous 'realism' are much better than they ought to be." There is a symmetry, Vargas Llosa notes, between literary and political fictions, a suspension of disbelief in the face of a systematic set of ideas. Since both are fundamentally *fictions,* neither can capture or organize reality in a logical, scientific fashion. Logically, then, his "historia/novela" reveals an attempt to use history parodically, as a weapon against itself, against reality, against recognition.

It is a truism of standard Latin American literary histories that Latin American women do not write, and certainly do not write narrative. What little they do write—poetry, mostly—deserves oblivion. What narrative they produce, straightforward neorealist domestic fiction, does not stand up to comparison with the great male writers of the Boom and after, and is mercifully relegated to a mere footnote. The occasional exceptions—Western-trained and European-oriented women like María Luisa Bombal in Chile, Elvira Orphée, Victoria and Silvina Ocampo in Argentina, the Puerto Ricans Rosario Ferré and Ana Lydia Vega, Mexican women like Elena Garro, Margo Glantz, Barbara Jacobs, and Elena Poniatowska (whose non-Hispanic-sounding last names are almost too suggestive)—neatly demonstrate the point, but they represent something of a conundrum

in traditional literary histories. Certainly these women refuse to subscribe to the synthetic, neatly patterned style typical of traditional
nineteenth-century realism, or to the other, recognizably constructed,
pseudo-disconnected narratives of the Boom. Their works, like their
lives, are fragmented, other-directed, marginally fictionalized. Yet these
women are the privileged minority in society and in literary history.
And even among privileged women, few are accorded the accolades of
strength, lucidity, intelligence: the virile virtues begrudgingly handed
out to the occasional and extraordinary Sor Juana Inés de la Cruz.

Brazilian Clarice Lispector is the one contemporary woman writer
always included in a survey of Latin American great writers, although
with puzzlement because, while contemporaneous with the Boom,
she does not fit any of the neat categories. Clarice Lispector was born
in transit to Brazil, in the Ukraine, of parents who had already left
their homeland, and she arrived in Brazil at the age of two months.
This fact, a mere curiosity or accident of birth that Lispector considered meaningless, is generally mentioned by way of explanation
for one facet or another of Lispector's astonishing talent. She is not,
by implication, *really* Brazilian. An otherwise perceptive Rodríguez
Monegal writes, for example, "Clarice was two months old when her
parents settled in Alagoas. Because of this fact, this writer—one of
the most important writers Brazil has produced—had to learn Portuguese as a foreign language"; Brazilian-born two-month-olds, by
implication, would never have arrived at Lispector's markedly original deformations of Portuguese syntax. Neither is she *typically* Brazilian: according to Alceu Amoroso Lima, "No one writes like Clarice Lispector. And she doesn't write like anyone." She is not a
feminist; and while her central concerns are ontological, she writes in
neither an autobiographical nor psychoanalytic mode. She rejoices in
a nonidentity: the Lispector/Specter evoked by Rodríguez Monegal,
dressed up in the conventional, fashion-page terms for the mysteriously (mystery is the definition of the genre) attractive woman of
society: "a beautiful woman, with deep and unfathomable eyes, high
Slavic cheekbones, and a mouth like a painful sensual wound, . . . a
mysterious surface." This is the language typically used to describe
the infinitely interchangeable and languishingly seductive *femme fatale* of B-movie and pulp novel fame.

Clarice Lispector is the representative of a spectral life, the documenter of the way in which her society codes itself for confrontation—or avoidance of confrontation—with the feminine. "I perform incantations during the solstice," says a character in *Água viva* (1974; *The Stream of Life*, 1989), "specter of an exorcised dragon." No mystic ecstasy here; Lispector's writing points to another style of approaching the unnameable, through the difficult, rock-hard process of coming to terms with the recognition of the specter as specter, in expecting little, and receiving that little as the only possible joy. Thus Lispector warns her potential readers of *A paixão segundo G. H.* (1964; *The Passion According to G. H.*, 1988):

> I would be happy if [this book] were read only by people with fully formed characters. People who know that an approach, of whatever sort, must be carried out gradually and laboriously—traversing even the opposite of that which is being approached. They . . . will understand that this book exacts nothing of anyone. To me, for example, the character G. H. little by little began to give a difficult joy; but it is called joy.

This difficult happiness is not unlike that contained in the enigmatic smile on the face of the smallest woman in the world or in the insane self-possession of Laura in the presence of the roses, both from stories in the collection *Laços de família* (1960; *Family Ties*, 1972): the fleeting happiness of transitory possession, of beauty ciphered in the minuscule, the evanescent, the happiness of minimal creature comfort, of not being devoured—yet.

All of these Boom (and post-Boom) narratives represent what González Echevarría calls "archival fictions," sealed into the hegemonic discourse of the masterstory. The time has come, and more than come, to historicize the Boom itself, to set ourselves at a distance from the masterstories that have dominated talk about Latin American narrative for thirty years. In his book *The Voice of the Masters* (1985), González Echevarría intends us to strip away the factitious complicity between language and authoritarianism, to deconstruct their unsalutary propping up and propping upon each other. He intends to achieve this object in two ways: both in the texts he studies and in the way he studies those texts. First, he says, such representatives of modern Latin American literature as Fuentes, Cortázar, and Cabrera Infante dismantle the link between authority and rhetoric through the operations of their critical-literary works. Second, his own critical style, unlike the "authoritarian" criticism he deplores, is intentionally disconnected. Such authoritarian voices, he would argue, falsify what they attempt to explain. Therefore, he proposes, the examination of literary as well as political institutions should begin with a careful critique of the language used to support them. At the end of his 1990 book, *Myth and Archive,* González Echevarría goes one step further in his examination of these institutions. He asks, "Is there a narrative beyond the Archive? . . . [T]here seems to exist a desire to break out of the archive, one that is no longer merely part of the economy of the archive itself. Is a move beyond the Archive the end of narrative, or is it the beginning of another narrative? Could it be seen from within the Archive, or even from the subversions of the Archive?"

González Echevarría's *Myth and Archive* is very much imbued with the current academic identity crisis that has driven scholars in various fields to rethink the implications of the traditional objects of study and the accepted methodologies for studying them. As scholars like González Echevarría reflect on the limits of what he calls "the archive," so too do they come to an awareness of the limitations of a field of knowledge that more and more comes to seem provisionally situated. González Echevarría begins to write beyond the limits of his own text when he suggests, in a final footnote, that writers like Severo Sarduy (Cuba) and Manuel Puig (Argentina) seem to be plotting an escape from the archive in their post-Boom fictions: Sarduy, perhaps, through his commitment to French deconstructive theories; Puig in his obsession with popular art forms.

Manuel Puig is a particularly interesting case in point. Unlike the Boom novelists, his crucial referent is neither elitist high culture nor autochthonous reality. Instead, Puig's characters most commonly define themselves in terms of popular culture—the songs from the top 40, the "in" soap opera, the movies, generally Hollywood imports, that dominate the theater screens. Puig's gently ironic vision of his hapless small-town dwellers is both compassionate and comprehending. While he displays the emptiness of an existence defined by Tinseltown values, his works, including *La traición de Rita Hayworth* (1968; *Betrayed by Rita Hayworth,* 1971), *Boquitas pintadas* (1972; *Heartbreak Tango,* 1973), and *Pubis Angelical* (1979; English translation, 1986), also offer a sincere homage to the films of the 1930s and 1940s that are his particular resource.

Perhaps most well known of his novels in the United States is *El beso de la mujer araña* (1976; *Kiss of the Spider Woman*, 1979), a work released in a film version in 1985. This novel is told almost entirely through dialogue between two cellmates, one a political prisoner, one jailed for overt homosexual behavior (corruption of a minor). The story is essentially one of seduction—of seduction of each of the two apparently incompatible prisoners by the ideas of the other, a mutual seduction mediated by the romantic films the homosexual describes to escape mentally from the confines of prison and the even more stifling confines of a middle-class morality he paradoxically, yearningly espouses, a seduction that also implies that of the reader into the web of the text. The multiply negotiated kiss occupies a central symbolic role: the kiss of affection between friends, the passionate kiss of lovers, the fatal kiss of the panther woman that turns her into the assassin of the one she loves, the betrayer's kiss that sends the confederate to a horrible death. In *Kiss of the Spider Woman,* the stereotypically lush movie settings contrast with the implicit barenness of the cell. Curiously, at the end of the novel the lavish romantic fantasies legitimated by Hollywood merge with the harshly murderous reality of the unnamed Latin American country as the homosexual, Molina, doubly seduced by movies and by politics, suffers either the romantic death of a movie heroine or/and the heroic martyrdom of a political activist. Or perhaps, cognizant of our own seduction by either of the two versions, we readers might glimpse another dimension in which Molina's death would become merely another in a frighteningly long line of meaningless disappearances, becoming in the Latin American context a metaphor for the violence authoritarian governments often exercise against their own citizens. Molina, the homosexual, has always been and still is part of a "disappeared" segment of Latin American society: the homosexual subculture that is alternately ignored and persecuted by revolutionaries and reactionaries alike. In the United States context, Molina's senseless death by fiction can be taken as an allegorical tale of all such disappearances, social and political, including the mysterious disappearance, and equally mysterious reappearance, of the entire continent from our collective memories.

Manuel Puig's works epitomize an ill-defined area of literature that I call, borrowing the term from Mexican "cronista" Jose Joaquín Blanco, "la novela de la transa."* The "transa" (sting or con operation) is, as Blanco notes, also a "trenza" (a weaving together) of disparate elements of society, with the common ground of a "supervivencia ilusionada" (an illusionary survival) based on the con-artist's confidence in his own cleverness. Unlike the United States model of the confidence game, the Mexican "transa" is less focused on the individual doing the manipulating, more on the action as transaction between two individuals, each of whom knows that a "transa" is taking place, each of whom thinks he (it is usually a "he") has the advantage. "Transa" then, eventually involves "autotransa." It is a quintessentially urban phenomenon, powered by young people who derive their models from television and popular culture. These young people may not know English, and their superficial indifference to politics does not mask a deep historical resentment to United States policies, but they can sing along with the latest heavy-metal rock bands from the United States and are attentive to fashions coming out of New York. They are also aware of sexualities ignored/disguised by the bourgeoisie. For simplicity's sake, I will divide the "novela de la transa" into two dominant thematic tendencies, one emphasizing the social transaction, the second focusing on the sexual transaction. Clearly, however, most novels include both tendencies: Puig's works, for example, deal importantly with cultural imperialism, while also addressing areas of ambiguously negotiated sexualities. Likewise, Severo Sarduy's technically complex dramas, like *Cobra* (1972; English translation, 1975), highlight ambiguously *trans*-sexual characters such as Cobra/Cadillac, the one castrated, the other endowed with a penis to cover her/his original lack.

The hormonal charge of a differently gendered discourse is nowise esoteric. It confronts directly an ingrained institutional history of seeing differently gendered literature as inherently limited when held up to a "universal" standard. Ethel Krauze, a young writer and critic from Mexico, responds to those who uncritically adopt variations on

*The term is hard to translate. Roughly, it means the "con novel." "Transa" is a Mexicanism for a con-artist; the word probably derives from "transacción" (transaction) and referred originally to the transactions between hip middle-class urban youths and lower-class drug dealers in the late 1960s.

heterosexist, masculinist assumptions when she sensibly argues that the historical positioning of the gendered self applies to all the products of the imagination:

I felt that the feminine, as it has been interpreted throughout history, approximated me to zoology more than to humanity, inserted me more into a permanent provisionality where I would never stop being a woman, where I would never be able to create true literature: the literature men make. But my stubbornness won out. I started to write, period, with the sole desire of telling things: literature has no sex. And out came these pages where women dominate perhaps more than I might have proposed. And reading them over, I realized, then, that it is the same world, with its swamps and its heat, only that it is seen, or better, felt, from a woman's profile. Masculine literature has made its contribution: to describe men and invent women; probably feminine literature covers the other half, there where woman is really herself, and man begins to look at himself, in his own perplexity, out of her eyes.

What Krauze proposes is not the successive approximation of writing by women to a supposedly sexless, but inherently masculinist, model of "good" writing, but rather the development of that model's complementary other side(s). Krauze, furthermore, signals the impossibility of doing anything else, for she is both a woman and a writer, and not a transvestite man. Her work will of necessity be inflected by this historical, social, and sexual positioning, and it is, moreover, to her advantage to recognize the usefulness of exploring the potentialities in writing from different points of view. In so doing, writers outside the male heterosexist orientation will instigate what Sylvia Molloy calls "a new praxis of writing, subverting the authoritarian language that puts them 'in their place,' displacing themselves." And from this other place, such authors can complete an image of the world that has, inevitably, only been partially drawn.

Overtly homosexual/lesbian writing has a particularly powerful charge in this context. Reina Roffé's *Monte de Venus* (1976) was highly controversial in Argentina for its frankly portrayed lesbianism. The novel, in many ways a rehash of tired romantic clichés drawn from countless sentimental love stories, popular music, and banal cinema, was banned in that country alongside other works with the cast of a more overtly political denunciation. As David William Foster notes, for the authorities, "a novel that gives voice to an aggressive lesbian, whose inverted behavior threatens sacred institutions by parodying them with notable fidelity, is clearly a new threshold in the allegedly mindless corruption of the national moral fiber." The censors are probably right; novels like Roffé's do indeed pose a challenge to the precariously maintained facade of bourgeois gentility.

The aggressive point-by-point homage to/parody of heterosexual mores appears in other works as well, and for clarification I take my example from Mexican Luis Zapata's second novel, *En jirones* (In Shreds), the journal of a much-vexed love affair. At one point in the novel, the (male) narrator explicitly describes his authorial stance in relation to his work. A severely edited version of this authorial positioning reads "like a man," that is, it flows along the traditional pathways of an archetypally conceived, heterosexually oriented male discourse: "Independently of the solicitudes, of the specifications, of the position-taking, and the detailing of desires and preferences, whose author or designated audience could be anyone, I discover a sentence in the Institute's bathroom that seems to address me specifically. . . ." In Zapata's novel, however, this commonplace sentence is interrupted at each point by parenthetical remarks that prevent that kind of active misreading. When the parenthetical remarks are returned to the text, the authorial positioning becomes strikingly, shockingly unconventional, and still, in the Latin American context, largely unacceptable: "Independientemente de las solicitudes (busco verga), de las precisiones (19 años, la tengo grande y cabezona), o de las tomas de posición (soy puto) y la especificación de deseos y preferencias (me gusta mamar, soy pasivo), cuyo autor o destinatario puede ser cualquiera, descubro una frase en el baño del Instituto que parece concernirme directamente: 'Dame tiempo, papacito: llegará el momento en que me la retaques hasta el fondo' " ["Independently of the solicitudes (I'm looking for a prick), of the specifications (19 years old, I have a big one with a large head), of the position-taking (I'm a hustler), and the detailing of desires and preferences (I like to suck, I'm passive), whose author or designated audience could be anyone, I discover a sentence in the Institute's bathroom that seems to address me specifically: 'Just give me a little time, daddy-boy: the time will come when you'll really give it to me' "]. The reader, shaken from the comfortable pathologies of a "neuter" reader-relationship, is insistently gendered and redefined by sexual preference. Resistance too is subsumed in the prophetic phrase on the bathroom wall, a narration still framed, but now out of the closet, the seductive promise of a deferred penetration between men, between a forthright author and a coyly (self) deceptive reader, without the place-holding, face-saving symbolic exchange of women to mediate the act. Zapata's insistently marginalized discourse also intuits the potency of the fragmented fac-simile, the "transa" that is both other-directed and profoundly self-critical, and the charge of his hormonal injection is disruptive of the pathologies of least resistance.

Already during the same period in which literary studies were dominated by references to the Boom novelists, the literature of social "transa" was inventing its place and its form. In Mexico, the literature of disaffected middle-class youth strung out on too much rock, too much sex, and too many drugs was called, at the end of the 1960s, "literatura de onda" (new-wave literature). The work of writers like José Agustín—*De perfil* (1966; Profile), *Se está haciendo tarde* (1973; It's Getting Late), *Ciudades desiertas* (1982; Deserted Cities); Gustavo Sainz—*Gazapo* (1965; Rabbitkin), *Obsesivos días circulares* (1969; Obsessive Circular Days), or the edited volume *Corazón de palabras* (1981; Heart of Words); Salvador Elizondo—*Farabeuf; o, la crónica de un instante* (1965; Farbeuf; or, The Chronicle of an Instant), and others has a hyper real quality that is very conscious of its interconnectedness with modern media and modern means of communication. Cars, telephones, televisions, tape recorders, and stereo systems are very much in evidence. Many of these fictions involve preposterously contorted multilingual plots and dashes of provocative metatelephonic analysis with the reader/auditor, all written to a rhythm falling between the Rolling Stones and Bob Dylan—set to mariachi music, of course. In José Agustín's story "Cuál es la onda" (What's Shaking/What Is the Wave), the group of disaffected youths speak to each other in lines from their favorite rock songs and television shows, and adopt/adapt Americanisms like the exclamations "Oh, Goshito," "buen grief," or "en la móder," call each other "darlita," and suggest meeting "a tu chez." The rebel-without-a-cause quality of the "onda" writers now seems a bit dated, but their lingering influence can be discerned in the vexed bilingualism of other writers who sprinkle their works with street slang that includes Anglicisms and loan blends like "gufeándose jevi" or "friquiao" or "fóquin," as well as in such overwhelmingly popular confections as Guadalupe Loaeza's series of "chronicles" of high life in the capital. Clearly, we are meant to laugh at the foibles of Loaeza's society women, their concern for being *comme il faut,* their penchant for *shopping* (a word Loaeza always uses in English) in New York, their exclusive preoccupation with class (having it, and belonging to the right one), their interpretation of Mexican folklore: *huitlacoche* crepes, *huipiles* over Calvin Kleins. Loaeza represents, as she captures, the smug *chic* of those who find a certain *cachet* in the practice of *épater le bourgeois.*

Argentina's Enrique Medina's eloquent *Strip-Tease* (1976) exemplifies the counterpart and the reverse of such works as those of Agustín and Loaeza. It too enacts a social "transa," but his point of view is not that of the rich kid slumming with lower-class companions out of either boredom or political conviction; rather Medina takes as his charge that of defining those characters most traditionally associated with the underworld side of these negotiations. He is well positioned to do so. Medina, who has since the easing of censorship been Argentina's best-selling writer, is one of the few well-known Latin American writers from a lower-class background. His father was a boxer; Medina's first work, *Las tumbas* (1972; The Tombs) is a "testimonio" of his life in a prison for adolescents; *Strip-Tease* is at least partially based on his own experience as a striptease show director and as a doorman in a house of prostitution. In this work, as in all his later works, Medina insists on what is alternately called "writing without concessions" or "contestatorial writing" as he writes in the violent street slang of his marginalized characters and deliberately refuses to prettify the gratuitous violence of their surroundings.

In *Strip-Tease,* Medina creates a fictional representation of the social pressures obtaining in Buenos Aires's underworld, and the premature adolescence of its youth, their disillusionment and boredom and hatred and impotence that leads them to second-rate striptease shows, dirty massage parlors, and rerun movie parlors. His characters move in a world where violence is the norm; it is his aggressive portrayal of those assaults and rapes, without concessions to dominant morality, that caused his long-term problems with Argentina's censors. This novel, like most of his other books, was banned in Argentina for many years. Like the more privileged characters of

Agustín et al., Medina's throwaway people are deeply imbued with Western mass-culture clichés; in their mouths, however, such clichés take on a frighteningly literal twist:

> Quién más quién menos, todos iríamos al fondo. La muerte es la muerte and dats ol.
> ¿Cómo caí en la trampa? . . . Lo único que sabía era que la inundación seguía subiendo and que no pararía jamás. Nadie se salvaría. Era el fin de todo. Mañana sería un magnífico día.

> One more or less, we'll all go down. Death is death and that's all, folks.
> How did I fall in the trap? All I know was that the flood kept rising and would never stop. No one would be saved. It was the end of everything. Tomorrow would be a wonderful day.

*Strip-Tease* is exceptionally powerful in depicting this world of hoodlums and hookers and minor-league criminals who draw from popular culture but deform/subvert it to their own ends.

Other "transas" with/of literary history have become increasingly common, if understudied: rewriting popular art forms, appropriating high art for alternative contexts, proposing new aesthetics of reading.

Rosario Castellanos, herself the author of two novels generally misread as *indigenista*, *Balún Canán* (1957; *The Nine Guardians*, 1959), and *Oficio de Tinieblas* (1962; Service at Dusk), recognizes and takes into account a tradition that marks women readers as superficial and morally deficient, but she realigns the terms to right the misappropriation of the reading woman as immoral, while reversing the negative charge on the accusation of superficiality:

> When the Latin American woman takes a piece of literature between her hands she does it with the same gesture and the same intention with which she picks up a mirror: to contemplate her image. First the face appears. . . . Then the body. . . . The body is dressed in silk and velvet that are ornamented with precious metals and jewels, which changes her appearance like a snake changes its skin to express . . . What?
> Latin American women novelists seem to have discovered long before Robbe-Grillet and the theoreticians of the *nouveau roman* that the universe is surface. And if it is surface, let us polish it so that it does not present any roughnesses to the touch, no shock to the gaze. So that it shines, so that it sparkles, in order to make us forget that desire, that need, that mania, of looking for what is beyond, on the other side of the veil, behind the curtain.
> Let us remain, therefore, with what has been given us: not the develop-

ment of an intimate structure but the unenveloping of a series of transformations.

Castellanos here confronts directly the rhetorical tradition that defines good prose as clear, straightforward, masculine, and bad taste in prose as a fondness for the excessively ornamented, and therefore effeminate. In her challenge to this ingrained metaphor Castellanos intuits the startling possibilities of a feminine aesthetics as a radically different model for feminist politics. She rejects the meek, tidy housewife and evokes instead the unmistakable image of the bored upperclass woman, filing her nails (sharpening her claws?), slipping, menacingly, out of her Eve-snake skin, creating herself affirmatively in the appropriation of the polished, superficial, adjectival existence allotted her, making the fiction yet more impenetrably fictive until it glows as the revolutionary recognition of an amoral forgotten truth. The mirror is her talisman, a weapon for dispelling, as it creates, illusion: aesthetics and politics brought home, as it were, from their travels, made homey, personal, private, quotidian.

In Castellanos's metaphorical history of language as an instrument for domination, she writes, "La propiedad quizá se entendió, en un principio como corrección lingüística. . . . Hablar era una ocasión para exhibir los tesoros de los que se era propietario. . . . Pero se hablaba ¿a quién? ¿O con quién?" [Propriety/property was perhaps understood, in the beginning, as a linguistic correction. . . . To speak was an occasion to exhibit the treasures of which one was proprietor. . . . But to whom did one speak? Or with whom?]. To speak is to create a surface of propriety, of proprietary relationships that can be exploited in various directions. The works of these Latin American women novelists cited by Castellanos do not provide a model either to imitate or to appropriate nor do they provide a mimetic reflection to contemplate, but rather a polished surface to triangulate desire in which the apices of the triangle are (1) the adorned body of the text, (2) the implicitly male motivator and first recipient of this textual adornment, and (3) the female reader, a free space for self-invention. The cultivation of a polished superficiality suggests a willed, willful transvaluation of values that surpasses mere reversal. While leaving the surface of complacency available for the desiring eyes of those whom Alicia Partnoy, based on her bitter experience as a disappeared poet in the "little houses" of Argentina's prisons, calls "el lector enemigo," the woman writer produces a layered look for the discriminating eye of her "lectora hembra" for whom the constructs of life as a staged aesthetic performance are not unfamiliar.

All of Puerto Rican Rosario Ferré's writings work explicitly with this conflict described by Castellanos, from her early stories and poems in *Papeles de Pandora* (1976; Pandora's Papers) to her more recent novella *Maldito amor* (1986; *Sweet Diamond Dust*, 1988). In the case of Rosario Ferré's short stories "Cuando las mujeres quieren a los hombres" ("When Women Love Men") and "Isolda en el espejo" ("Isolda's Mirror"), the play of unreadability is posed in the text as a problem and as part of the project of the work, in which the issue of making-up for a particular audience becomes part of the message of the text. "When Women Love Men" ostensibly addresses itself to an absent seducer—"you, Ambrosio"—the man who oppresses the two women in his life, his wife and his mistress, in the most traditional and intimate ways. Now dead, Ambrosio in his will leaves his house to both women jointly, perhaps in revenge for unstated discomforts they have caused him, perhaps as a joke. Ultimately, elaborately, Isabel the wife and Isabel the mistress find their liberation from his presence and from his instructions in following his will (both senses) exactly, and thus subverting Ambrosio's intent. Rather than declaring war, the two women coalesce like two surfaces gliding over each other. The objective correlative for this process is, for each of them, a particular shade of violently red nail polish they both prefer, and this unexpected merging "was our most sublime act of love."

These women do resist, and they resist precisely at the textual level. By fixing the reading on the Cherries Jubilee nail polish (in "When Women Love Men") or the "Coty facial powder in the 'Alabaster' shade" (in "Isolda"), Ferré unbalances conventional expectations: the tension is not buried deep within the women but displayed prominently and unexpectedly on the surface. Nail polish and facial powder are not even symbols to be decoded; because their function is decisively literal they are all the more potent. Cosmetics, then, along with race, serve as the fundamental visual clues of social class. It is with cosmetics and—as Castellanos intuited—with language that the process of emancipation must begin, and if the stories represent Ferré's verbal praxis, it is through a revolutionary use of make-up that her characters in "When Women Love Men" and "Isolda" stage their rebellion. Instead of making themselves up for a man, they are making themselves up as a form of emancipation that, along the way, serves as a potent demystification of the myth of everlasting love in its conventional forms. Ostensibly, all the women in Ferré's stories are making themselves up "for" men. Ostensibly, the denunciation would be of a male power base that turns women into dolls and sensual playthings and mute works of art. That is part of it, of course. But the men in Ferré's stories are too defeated, too unmanned by other circumstances to bear the weight of a nuanced cultural critique. Her male characters, while seemingly prepotent, are curiously caricaturesque or easily discounted as forces of civic and political authority. The rum barons are drunken has-beens, Ambrosio is dead, Don Augusto is old and bankrupt. Likewise, while the Yankees loom on the horizon as the new masters of economic power, their power is still only distantly felt, and their impact on social interactions is minimal. We could even say that if the women are surfacing in these stories, the men are drowning. Evidently, too, Ferré's concern is as much with empowerment (of men as well as women) as with denunciation. It is in this respect that the author of these stories asks women to look at themselves, to see themselves making themselves up in the mirror of her text, to see their own complicity in and responsibility for their subjugation. It is here that the slipwise mediation of the male gaze (to use Jacques Lacan's term) allows the female reader to reflect upon the shifting dynamics of male-female relationships; it is in the mediation of the textualized male gaze that she is protected from a self-critique too devastating to be helpful. Rosario Castellanos suggests polishing the surface, making it shine, slipping in a space for an evolving, transformative self; Rosario Ferré offers a buffered (male-coded) space for mediation between the transformative surfaces of the female narrative and the constantly self-displacing, transforming surfaces of the female reader.

The particular form of this appropriative gesture has already been named, in the felicitous coinage of Clarice Lispector, a "fac-simile." "I write you," says the unnamed female artist of *Água viva* to her lover, her interlocutor, her (male) literary audience, and implicitly the gesture of homage is also a weapon of appropriation: I write (of myself) to you, and that which I write is constitutive of you. In writing—by definition "like a man"—she creates a likeness of the man and a self-likeness, consciously manipulating a style sanctioned by tradition and undermining its pathological assumptions (when I say this I have in mind Eve Sedgwick's definition of one of the functions of tradition as "to create a path-of-least-resistance (or at the last resort, a pathology-of-least-resistance)." Tradition can be most effectively subverted just along such well-worn pathways. At first glance Lispector's narrator hints at an incomplete or distorted autobiographical account; at second, a kind of inept role-reversal Pygmalion to her sculpted lover: "I write you this fac-simile of a book, the book of one who does not know how to write." In fact, she is neither incomplete, distorted, nor inept. The appropriative gesture turns the knowledge of the other against the lover; she constitutes him as she deceptively inscribes a so-called constitution of the self. She appropriates, but with an injection of estrogen escapes the confinements of the model in her reconstituting of herself as a false copy, a simulacrum, the split simile, like and not like, that which affirms and negates the model in the same word. In so doing, Lispector—herself the author of a story with the resonant title of "The Fifth Story"—decries both mimesis and genealogy. The crucial question, perhaps, is not that of the origins of the gesture but the uses to which it may be put, and is continually being put: a way of being that is a way of speaking, or not speaking, or writing, but which always involves the informed interaction of the reader.

The novella "Fourth Version," from Argentine Luisa Valenzuela's *Cambio de armas* (1982; *Other Weapons*, 1985), enacts another version of this displacement. The narrator, a frustrated co-author and editor of Bella's scattered papers, organizes the fourth fac-simile of the story of the actress and the ambassador. At each step the attempt at a rational restructuralization of key elements fails. Materials at hand are scarce, key elements are silenced or lost, and what remains seems more appropriate for another genre. The editor, faced with the impossibility of constructing a traditional narrative according to conventional formal properties, eventually breaks down into a fac-simile of a critic: "The papers tell her story of love, not her story of death"—either an indecipherable code or, worse, an incomprehensible reversal of priorities. Later, disgruntled, the editor-critic complains about the difficulty of assigning a genre to the papers: "Verbose Pedro, respecting a certain kind of silence which ended up spreading to Bella too, to the extent that her alleged indirect autobiography, her confessional novel, ended up deflating itself in certain parts," and, finally, acknowledges that her preferred reading of events stumbles against a lack of supporting materials: "I don't understand why the crucial information has been omitted regarding this key encounter." Each version—the internal author's, the fourth; the critic's, the fifth; this one, the sixth—carries its own preassumptions and presuppositions, each writes the text as a variation of self-writing (of the critic, not of either Bella or Pedro), each limns another portion of the appropriative field, works another inversion/subversion of the writing of the fac-simile.

In one such variation, "Fourth Version" reenacts in a fictional setting one of the critical moments of Valenzuela's own political activism during the Videla regime. It has as its counterpart the final story of the collection, the title story "Other Weapons," a story told from the point of view of one of those to whom the protective net did not extend. "Other Weapons," like "Fourth Version," projects the limit case of society's censorship of women through the unexpected metaphor of a traditional middle-class marriage. For "Other Weapons" 's "so-called Laura," all of her past life is an ellipsis. Nouns are particularly elusive: "the so-called anguish," "the so-called love," or "What might the prohibited (repressed) be?"; as are verbs: the meanings of verbs like "to love" and "to hate," "to make love" and "to torture," slip indistinguishably into each other. Her experience is conditional, hypothetical, based on a series of subordinate clauses responding to the main clause, the spoken orders of the man: her lover, her torturer, her one friend, the enemy she must assassinate. Her touchstone is her own wounded body—"una espalda azotada" (a wounded back)—which is continuous with her wounded mind, her aphasia: "la palabra azotada," in which the weight of reference falls not on the noun but on the adjective, "azotada." The nameless protagonist, for convenience "the so-called Laura," tastes the bittersweet of her blood in the slash on her back, the shattered words on her tongue; denied refuge, she has no place to treasure up her scattered bits, no force to bring them together out of their fragmentation. Her story is that of a veiled and unspeakable pornography, rescued through the tentative workings of the subjunctive.

In "Other Weapons" the colonel reminds the so-called Laura, "I've got my weapons, too," and in "Fourth Version" the narrator muses: "And I, who am putting all of this back together now [*Y yo, quien ahora esto arma*], why do I try to find certain keys to the whole affair when those being handed to me are quite different keys?" "Armar" (to put together) is always a model for potential violence, intuitively pointing toward its opposite: the revolutionary blowing apart of a system or a text. Fellow Argentinian Julio Cortázar's novel *62: Modelo para armar* (1971; *62: A Model Kit*, 1972) stands as a precursor text for this double meaning of the verb. To write (rewrite) this story is to give it a particular construction, to appropriate its multiplicity for a single point of view, to aim the weapon in a particular direction: "There is no author [*autor*] and now I am the author [*autora*], appropriating this text that generates the desperation of writing." The too-easy slippage between masculine "autor" and feminine "autora" is in itself reason for despair, one of the reasons, perhaps, that this markedly feminine author insists upon the multiplicity of stories, as if the repeated reminder of the absence of a claim of authority and the admittedly incomplete nature of the editorial enterprise are enough to deflect the critical weapons that may be aimed at it. "Stop talking to me in capital letters," Bella complains to Pedro; the crystallization of role and function—the Ambassador, the Actress, the Messengers, the Great Writer—refracts in the multiple mirrors of the layered text as frivolously parodic emblems: arms perhaps, but either sinisterly distanced or singularly ineffective ones. To identify too closely with them would be to lose the freedom to escape behind the mask, to play with the roles while enacting a subtle "apropriamiento." What the "autora" fears is the danger of falling into the text, one of a chorus of "las mujeres escritoras" (note redundancy) to whom "they have sold the idea of transexuality," in the words of Monserrat Ordóñez. Most critically, she rejects the pompous and self-congratulatory "Great Writer," who arrives all unaware in the midst of an all-too-real revolution, only to find himself weaponless.

There is, we begin to suspect, an element of the theatrical in all of this emphasis on mirrors and masks and bodies that react with the discipline of trained mimes. There is, particularly in Bella's repertoire of practiced gestures, the highly overdetermined artificiality of the woman often dismissed as merely decorative. Women, apparently, demonstrate naturalness through well-defined and highly conventionalized artifices of mock-spontaneity. Even more strikingly, this development is defined, albeit condescendingly, with a military metaphor: "her weapons, her arsenal." This is, of course, precisely the first image we have of Bella. The actress is depicted behind the scenes, "sharpening her weapons, her arsenal of grace," readying herself for the battle, practicing her lines, putting on her makeup for that night's performance on the stage, for the self-representation that is her personal/political weapon in the undeclared war on the streets, declaiming, "My role is to be alive" while "she made herself up carefully to go to the party." For Bella, maintenance of a superficial frivolity is a radical and rigorous form of work. It is, in fact, her life work, preserving her life to protect others. For Bella, the distance professionally enforced between representation and reality constitutes a shadowy revolutionary praxis. She knows all too well that at any moment the stage set could easily give way to the torture chamber, the theatrical gesture of faked beating might seamlessly merge with the drama of questioning and of pain maliciously inflicted, politically compromised roles could become political reality, the almost pain of self-erasing could slip into the unendurable pain of a reality that recreates the body in destroying it:

From performance to truth, from simulation to fact. One step. The one we take when we step from the imagination over to this side—what side?—of so-called reality. . . . If I go back to my country and they torture me, it will hurt. If it hurts I'll know that this is my body (on stage I shake, I squirm under the supposed blows that almost really hurt—is it my body?). It will be my body if I go back. . . . When they pull a piece off, it will be my whole body. . . . And thus I perform it; and performing I am. Torture on stage.

On the one hand, in her imagination, Bella's body will become her own on participating in real terror. Paradoxically, she also knows that she *is* only insofar as she *represents,* that her whole being is absorbed in a scene of torture/a drama about torture, that she is herself an embodiment of "torture on stage." To the degree that she enforces this perception she openly identifies herself as literary rather than corporeal. Thus, the fragmentation of her text enacts the scene of physical dismemberment. On the other hand, like the so-called Laura, Bella knows that reality has at least two sides, that in leaping from imagination to the torture chamber she has only crossed the first of the border lines. Laura would remind her that the second door, the one with the peephole, represents the most ambiguous and dangerous transgression of all, and requires another arsenal of weapons to vanquish.

Still another variety of "transa" is involved in the appropriation of the traditional means of expression for nontraditional purposes. It is perhaps to be expected that much of contemporary Latin American writing specifically constitutes itself as a refusal of traditional restrictions and customary censorship. When Valenzuela in one of her essays speaks specifically of the need for women to engage in "a slow and tireless task of appropriation [*apropriamiento*] of transformation," she speaks of the important task of taking back the use of the language that uses them. She calls for an appropriation of language that not only asserts a woman's rights to an estranged linguistic property as her personal possession but is also involved in a making-one's-own of oneself, of realigning alienating categories, and of creating a new understanding of what is proper in the careful and intentional use of improprieties. "Apropriamiento" is the public assertion of rights to that personal and private space. It is to take that which has been assigned to another for her own, for the first time to take herself and take for herself the woman customarily appropriated by another as his property. "To take" and not "to take back": the original appropriation—of words, of bodies, of power—is credited to human nature. It is an insight that can be extended to other kinds of appropriation as well.

Thus, in Doris Sommer's words, referring to the politically active women of Bolivia's "Housewives' Committee," "These women who take up men's tools also use language in a way that doesn't fall into a 'visceral emptiness' [Elaine Marks's term] but rather adjusts and challenges the very codes they adopted from their admirable men." These are far too busy and far too committed to worry about emptiness other than the emptiness of their children's stomachs. Nevertheless, they provide a concrete instance of the practice taken up at more theoretical or abstract levels: traditionally marginalized writers take up both tools and language, and in so doing forge new instrumentalities. In the Latin American context, as Valenzuela reminds us, a subtle transformation occurs with the appropriation of critical weapons—she calls it an injection of estrogen into dominant ideologies—so that when the sensitized readers—male or female—look again at canonical texts—male or female authored—they too begin to appropriate the texts differently. Texts like those of Luisa Valenzuela, Reina Roffé, or Manuel Puig that subtly employ heterosexist/masculinist assumptions against themselves require attentive gender-conscious readings with special urgency. It is this type of reading that they were prematurely born to elicit, and are in fact eliciting in the interstices of even the most traditional critical discourse, marginally undermined along the double-voiced fault lines of what is said to be, of what is called, of the preemptive "as if" of an incomparable, unexpected appropriation.

For Francine Masiello, Latin American writing at its best displays what she calls, following Bakhtin, a "double discourse," a hybrid language "that recognizes the structures of power at the same time that it offers an alternative." In Julieta Campos's work, the discourse is never solely double, never offers only one alternative. Then, too, her best work links the recognition of social and political structures of power to a forceful recognition of the equally significant rhetorical structures that are among power's essential building blocks. Furthermore, her reader is not complicitous but embattled, engaged in a struggle for control within the universe of the fiction. The novel, says Campos in her *Función de la novela* (1973; Function of the Novel), "is a reality created by the word and the fabula, a constant gestation of . . . an *estar siendo,* a gerundial universe where the author, the characters, and even the reader fight incessantly for life." The point here is precisely the unorthodox and untranslatable play between the two Spanish verbs of being, *ser* and *estar.* English uses the gerund "being" to represent the noun; in Spanish the infinitive is employed: "el ser" (never "el estar"). Campos's proposition of a gerundial form, "un estar siendo," brings together the two modes of being, both the gerundial and the infinitive—responding to cultural as well as linguistic imperatives—and brings together as well two nuances of existing, a peculiarly Spanish shade of meaning, one the shadow-dream-reflection of the other, and does so in a world that slips in and out of conventional fictional illusions, or slides from the illusions of fiction to the illusions of "reality."

Deeply problematized in the rereading of the body's poetic topography is the role of the reader or viewing public. The audience's gaze upon these public/private spectacles is hypothetically voyeuristic, but the issue becomes more complicated because the circuit of exchange involves a recognition of the audience as voyeur looking upon a primal scene of narcissistic self-contemplation that is, nevertheless, a staged scene, meant to be overlooked. In the archetypal economy, the man (lover, writer, critic) reads (seduces/is seduced by, writes, interprets) woman (the mistress, the work of art, the text). But what happens where "you" is a female reader? Is the text unreadable? Does the reader automatically reposition herself as a transvestite? Is the female reader a she posing as a he posing as a she?

One of the most extended and concrete explorations of this problematic can be found in Julieta Campos's novel *Tiene los cabellos rojizos y se llama Sabina* (1974; She Has Red Hair and Her Name Is Sabina). In this novel, written almost entirely in the conditional tense and in the subjunctive mood for verbs (an observation already made by Alicia Rivero Potter), writers, critics, editors, readers, and commentators proliferate around a single character—a woman—and a single action—looking out to sea. One of the voices tells us that the only certainty in the novel is the one given in the title, that is, that the woman has red hair and her name is Sabina. Readers external to the text are inclined to believe this voice, if only because the assertion reappears in both French and Spanish and is reinserted on the cover and the title page of the book. There is, certainly, no other reason for accepting this assertion over any of the other contingent, inconsistent, and contradictory assertions made in the book about the woman, her present circumstances, and her past. My own inclination would be to discount the assertion "she has red hair and her name is Sabina," like all the other parallel assertions made in the text about the woman, her life, attitudes, genealogy, etc., as totally gratuitous. In fact, I would argue that the primary narrative node generating the text is not the title phrase but another also seemingly straightforward statement, also frequently reiterated, this one couched not in the third but in the first person: "I am a character that looks out to sea at four in the afternoon . . . from a scenic overlook in Acapulco." This single assertion is the crucial starting point for the adventure of reading and writing, what Stephen Heath calls the "scriptural" of narrative in this text. From this statement depends, first of all, a nonsystematic sequence of relationships among the various agents of the verb: "I" refracts into "you" (both the informal "tú" and the formal "usted"), as well as into "he" and "she." "I," "you," "he," "she," and intermittent "we" and "they" in turn serve as nodes organizing a proliferation of other characters, or character-positions, some of whom carry on dialogues with each other, some of whom ignore each other's existence, some of whom contradict each other or logically cancel each other out, some of whom occupy the space of the subject in near-simultaneity: "The novel that she, I, you would write begins at last to displace the other, the one that he would be writing." Likewise, the concept of "character" itself serves as another nodal juncture. At one extreme, the reader could suggest that the novel has only one character, the woman who looks out to sea and whose entire fictional existence is consumed in that gaze; at the other, the various novelists, readers, critics, editors, and characters from other novels (by Campos, by other contemporary Latin American and European writers: the novel is to some extent a postmodern literary detective's delightful garden of allusive clues) impinge and infringe upon this space, gazing (voyeuristically) at her, defining and interpreting her look, situating her in a particular fictional construct that says more about the needs and desires of the narrator/reader/critic/literary canon than it does about the simple action of gazing out to sea. In the same manner, the sea becomes, at different moments, the Pacific Ocean, the Atlantic Ocean, the Caribbean, the Mediterranean; four o'clock in the afternoon indistinguishably fades into other times, "It's twenty to ten. . . . It is midnight and/or it is noon"; the overlook may be a dock, a hotel room window, or an imagined/remembered scene; Acapulco is Havana, New York, Venice, a movie backdrop.

For Campos, the operative metaphor for the surface/depth discussion can be found in her obsession with the sea. One could attempt to argue that the sea is both feminine and explicitly maternal in her work. *Sabina*, for example, is dedicated "to Terina de la Torre, my mother," and the dedication page is followed by an epigraph from Chateaubriand: "Je reposerai donc au bord de la mer que j'ai tant aimée" [I will rest beside the sea I loved so much]. The juxtaposition of dedication and epigraph suggests the familiar and much-exploited play on "la mer" (sea) and "la mère" (mother). Such a reading is plausible, but requires nuancing. At this point, let me just say that while the images of the sea, repeated throughout Campos's work, are associated with the female characters, the sea itself, while beautiful and strangely compelling for Campos's female characters, is not itself particularly feminized. It is in no wise a metaphor for an imagined maternal depth, but rather a metaphor of the more generalized *human* need for surfacing from meaningless voids. The sea, simply, is the place where a human being must remain afloat to live, and the depths of the sea bring not enlightenment but death: "And it involves telling something it is because one supposes that things happen that do not explain themselves and that look for words in order to come to the surface [*para salir a flote*] like someone on the point of drowning looks for a piece of wood to grab onto and hold oneself up."

The reader, constantly, is called upon to respond to the experience of reading by the same chorus of contradictory voices that determine the labyrinthine structure of the self-conscious text. Clearly, this novel, like many contemporary "elite" novels with which it might be compared, highlights the process of a novel's creation: how to structure a beginning and an end, how to repress or emphasize stylistic quirks. It includes debates on the use of symbols and concerns itself about whether or not to leave in or take out all punctuation: "Take out the commas, the periods, the semicolons, all the signs of punctuation, of interrogation, of exclamation and allow the interior discourse to flow. Make the reader work a little. Forgive me . . . I think in periods and commas." At the same time, it plays with these postmodern obsessions, these eminently readable confections of a now-established, and highly stylized, tradition of unreadability, the contemporary novelist's verbal equivalent of the Conceptual artist's make-up. By insisting on this saturation of fictional techniques, this dizzying declension of narrative possibilities, Campos underlines the constitutive importance of the process of reading to the creation of the fiction, as well as the unretrievability—or ultimate irrelevance—of any kind of originary or founding statement.

One of the most exciting new developments in Latin American literature today is the attention paid to "testimonios." Partly, such works respond to our recognition of a major lack in traditional literary studies that "indigenista" literature does not even begin to fill. The increasing critical attention to such works has raised a number of methodological and procedural problems, however. Black, mestizo, and Indian peoples tend to be poor and illiterate. To understand their "literature" it is generally necessary to go beyond books; poetry may be sung, rather than written, stories often pass from village to village in oral form. The extraordinary *campesino,* mine worker, or guerrilla fighter may, in extraordinary circumstances, dictate his/her testimonial to a more privileged, politically compromised poet, anthropologist, or novelist, but frequently in such cases the unlettered person is stripped of agency. Rosemary Geisdorfer Feal has made the striking observation that the Spanish edition of Rioberta Menchú's testimony— *Me llamo Rigoberta Menchú y así me nació la conciencia* (1983; *I, Rigoberta Menchú: An Indian Woman in Guatemala,* 1984)—is credited to Elizabeth Burgos, the ethnographer who took the Guatemalan woman's testimony and edited it with her; in contrast, the English edition lists Menchú as author and Burgos as editor, a telling shift. A similar displacement takes place in relation to *Biografía de un cimarrón* (1966; *The Autobiography of a Runaway Slave,* 1968) where in the Spanish original Miguel Barnet is listed as the author, and in the English translation he is cited as the editor of Esteban Montejo's testimony. The shift in the title from "biography" to "autobiography" reflects this transformation, but also disguises Barnet's very real creative function in adapting Montejo's story to his narrative purposes.

Feal comments not only on the loss of agency implied in this co-option of authorship but also on the political significance of such power plays, which in effect counter the testifiers' appeal to immediacy and authenticity by screening their words with a veil of art: "To call the speakers subject or object denies the creative, autonomous act they perform when they recount their lives; to call them characters confines them to a fictive world." It is also significant that in English translation the reference to the revolutionary struggle, for Rigoberta Menchú the sole reason for providing her testimony, is muted in favor of a general ethnographic reference. Rigoberta Menchú's is not the only case of such, often well-meaning, appropriation; other examples include Domitila Barrios de Chungara's *Si me permiten ha-*

*blar . . . Testimonio de Domitila, una mujer de las minas de Bolivia* (1976; *Let Me Speak! Testimony of Domitila, a Woman of the Bolivian Mines*, 1978), dictated to Moema Viezzer; Leonor Cortina's *Lucia* (1988; Mexico); Claribel Alegría's *No me agarran viva: La mujer salvadoreña en la lucha* (1983; *They'll Never Take Me Alive*, 1986) (El Salvador); Patricia Verdugo and Claudio Orrego's *Detenidos-desaparecidos: Una herida abierta* (1983; Detained-Disappeared: An Open Wound) (Chile); or Elena Poniatowska's non-fiction novel, *Hasta no verte Jesús mío* (1969; Until We Meet Again, My Jesus), recreating the life of a Mexico City laundrywoman and ex-*soldadera* pseudonymously named Jesusa Palancares in (more or less) her own words.

Well-meaning ethnographers who appropriate authorship of the "testimonios" in effect reproduce a noxious class-gender system they consciously reject, even while deploying the rhetoric of liberation. Even worse: the use of the rhetoric of liberation sounds like bad faith. It is not surprising, then, that, from the other side of the power axis, the maids and factory workers look on such scholars with suspicion, as yet another imperialist weapon. One of the responses to this oppression is a violent rejection of all that privileged class members are, and all they represent. Thus, for example, Bolivian Domitila Barrios de Chungara, in a famous altercation, confronts the chair of the Mexican delegation to a "Tribuna del Año Internacional de la Mujer" (Steering Committee of the International Year of the Woman). Domitila's rejection of the privileged woman derives from a long history of silencing and oppression; of being spoken about and spoken for, as if her needs were subsumed in the demands of the upper-class women who oppress women like her. Their differences, says the Bolivian mine worker's wife, are so salient as to constitute almost another species; even to say both are "women" is a grave misnomer.

Despite these caveats and concerns, however, it is important to reiterate that all of these testimonios demonstrate a signal lucidity, all represent important contributions to the still nascent emergence of majority voices into the public forum, with all of the revisionary resonances implicit in the unstifling of radically different perspectives. Regardless of the in-fighting and the rejection of similarities between classes, and notwithstanding the real concerns raised, for example, in the problematic attribution of testimonial authorship, the greater attention given to literature of/by the oppressed majorities in Latin America has specific implications that are more than trite ones: (1) literature by Latin Americans involved in the revolutionary struggle (the main group of testimonios) can clearly *not* afford the luxurious autobiographical impulses besetting middle-aged Anglo-European men; the record that needs to be set straight is always a more than personal one; the threat, in countries where intellectuals regularly "disappear," is not existential angst or encroaching senility but government security forces; (2) for the critic, assertions made about these texts have to be accompanied by readings made cumbersome through the need to introduce, even to a knowledgeable audience, a group of works that barely circulate, even (or especially) within their own countries; (3) the critic feels an uneasy suspicion that s/he may be behaving, in her own context, in a way parallel to that Gayatri Spivak uses to describe Kipling in India as the unwitting, and therefore all the more culpable, participant in a questionable cultural translation from a colonial to a metropolitan context that enacts a literary structure of rape. Well-intentioned mistranslation or misapplication of theory, like the equally unintended misrepresentation or oversimplification of primary texts, is a specter that looms large in the minds of dedicated cultural critics.

Debra A. Castillo

# Colonialism, Imperialism, and Imagined Homes

historicized account of the movements of peoples from one geographical area to another as immigrants, expatriates, or exiles reveals that, in our contemporary world, writers' origins and locations are often at variance. The conditions of expatriation and exile carry particular configurations at different historical times. Our contemporary world has seen migrations of peoples on a scale as never before in human history. For colonized peoples, migrations by "choice" and/or by economic necessity are rooted within a colonial and postcolonial history and within continuing imperialist dominations today. Postcoloniality itself overdetermines the "choice" to migrate. In their journeyings as exiles and expatriates, postcolonial peoples embody a hyphenated condition of identity: for example, Indo-American, Jamaican-Canadian, Indo-Pakistani-Britisher—the phenomenon of having too many roots, too many locations, both to belong to and to un-belong in, negotiating indigenous and Western languages. These predicaments necessitate a type of tightrope walking where, even as we travel with relative ease on supersonic jets, we cannot with as much ease step out of our skins and assume identities and kaleidoscopes of colors as we step off the plane into the humid air and tropical smells of Bombay, or into the brisk coolness of jetway corridors and the whitewashed efficiency of Heathrow or Kennedy.

In this chapter I will explore the complex terrain of the politics of representations of contemporary writers of different racial origins living in North America—United States citizens of different ethnicities, exiled and/or expatriated writers whose identities are mediated by a historically necessitated self-consciousness. Autobiography and autobiographical fictions dominate explorations of writers' own histories and those of their peoples. External colonizations, such as invasions by colonizing powers as well as continuing imperialist dominations, and internal, that is, mental colonizations, such as through education, are some of the historical factors that account for migrations. British colonizations and empire building resulting in English-language writers (the empire writing/striking back), as well as contemporary American imperialism and the unnamed American Empire, play crucial roles in the "chosen" language (English) and location (North America) of contemporary writers. I will also explore some metaphoric resonances of colonization—for instance, of women within patriarchal cultures, of "minority" groups who must struggle to make spaces for themselves within hegemonic white academic institutions and literary marketplaces.

In part, colonialism and imperialism historically account for migrations of peoples of color into the industrialized North. A multiethnic and polyglot cosmopolitanism pervades this new diaspora visible in contemporary London, New York, Toronto. Today, alliances between colonialist and imperialist forces ensure a continuing imbalance of power and hegemonic control of "third world" nations by covert colonizations in the guise of international aid agencies, as well as multinational capital, that transcend geographical boundaries and that make it increasingly difficult to hold any single entity accountable for perpetuating poverty in the "third world."

In general, material factors and, in particular, the conditions of cultural production—book production, publishing, audience, critical reception—vastly different in "first" and "third world" areas, often necessitate migrations. New configurations to the novel as a literary form emerge from this history of postcolonial writers who have moved to the United States or to Britain; who straddle continents, taking on half-year academic positions in United States universities and returning "home" to Trinidad, Barbados, or India for the other half. Andrew Gurr's analysis that "the normal role for the modern creative writer is to be an exile" ignores the particular conditions of cultural production that necessitate exile; for instance, neocolonial regimes like the present Kenyan government that threaten lives and practice intellectual repression leave no choice but exile to a writer like Ngugi wa Thiong'o. Gurr also problematically merges the issues of home, identity, and history, as if the finding of "home" will automatically entail the discovery of "identity." These two categories are often in contestation—what one might have to consider "home" for economic reasons does not necessarily provide an unanguished sense of identity.

As with colonialism, external and internal, exile and expatriation may be experienced in metaphoric and in literal ways: metaphoric exile as undergone by marginal, minority communities, or by women within patriarchal cultures; literal exile for political reasons, as is common for writers from South Africa like Dennis Brutus who lives in the United States, Bessie Head who lived in Botswana until her recent death, Caeserina Kona Makhoere who lives in Britain; expatriation for willing or unwilling subjects, as with children of immigrant parents. Postcolonial writers of certain classes and educational levels who write in English [given a colonial(ist) educational system] experience different kinds of marginalization as cultural workers both inside their "home" environments and outside, in the economically privileged spaces of Britain and North America. They face conflictual realities of literal and metaphoric exile—inside "Western" spaces where they and their work are commodified in a marketplace eager, at certain times, to consume "third world" products; and outside that space, that is, within "third world" areas where United States domination is present in everyday realities of satellite communications bombarded into living rooms, of International Monetary Fund stranglehold on local economies forcing constant currency devaluations that foster and perpetuate poverty and economic crises. "Home" assumes a deromanticized and demystified harshness; these are societies deeply under stress where economic crises make daily survival a painful reality.

Postcolonial writers often enter a Western metropolis precisely to make their cultural productions possible. The reasons for migration are various and complex—material and intellectual resources, an audience and critical reception that may not be possible within their "homes" (places of origin) for political or other reasons. Joseph Brodsky, in an essay entitled "The Condition of Exile," remarks that a search for "home" is often a search for a negotiated physical and mental space that brings a writer "closer to the seat of ideals that inspired him all along. . . . Displacement and misplacement are this century's commonplace." Brodsky perceives a contestation between exile as "a metaphysical condition" and the reality of exile wherein a writer is "constantly fighting and conspiring to restore his significance, his poignant role, his authority."

Writers' identities are negotiated along issues of race, gender, class, language, nationality, and, crucially for this group of writers, geography. When racial and ethnic origins differ from those of a majority population in a writer's "chosen" geographical location, and political and economic positions of power determine which ethnic groups are marginal and which are centered at particular times, writers are caught in the fluctuating and fluid borderlands between majority and minority populations in terms of the themes of their work (which often transport them "home"), their audience (often outside "home"), and their sense of belonging and identity.

The uses of the English language, of the novel form, of literary styles and cinematic techniques, demonstrate a blending, at times happy, at other times conflictual, of indigenous cultural memory with Western education and location. Brodsky's generalized remark that "an exiled writer is thrust, or retreats, into his mother tongue" is hardly true for postcolonial writers who come into the West, most of them inculcated in a colonial(ist) educational system and a Western literary tradition, and who write in English. Of course this reality is full of conflicts. Brodsky's exiled writer is "invariably homebound . . . excessively retrospective [and since s/he feels] doomed to a limited audience abroad, he cannot help pining for the multitudes, real or imagined, left behind." For postcolonial writers, the opposite is true—they often move away from "home" in order to find an audience.

Economic and political expediency at different historical times forcibly transported, or "welcomed," peoples of color—African, Chinese, Japanese, Filipino, Chicano, and, more recently, Caribbean, Vietnamese, South Asian—into North America. "Minority" groups range from United States citizens, African Americans, or third-generation Japanese and Chinese Americans, to newer immigrants (noncitizens) of color driven to the United States for professional and economic reasons. In Britain, ex-colonials from Asia and Africa, after fighting on the allied side during World War II, were "invited" into the Mother Country for labor. The struggles that these Black Britishers (as peoples from Asia, Africa, the Caribbean, in solidarity, describe themselves), first-generation migrants or second-generation immigrants, face in creating spaces for themselves in contemporary Britain are explored by writers like Salman Rushdie, Hanif Kureishi (of Indo-Pakistani origin), Joan Riley (Jamaican-British), Joan Cambridge and Beryl Gilroy (Guyana-British), and Merle Collins (Grenada-British), among others. In the United States, writers like the Filipino Bienvenido Santos undertake a personal and literary search for "home"; South Asian Meena Alexander, Padma Perera, and Bharati Mukherjee delve into the complex parameters of expatriate-immigrant-citizen; Japanese-Canadian Joy Kogawa uncovers the racism faced by her family and her people in Canada during World War II; Chinese-American Maxine Hong Kingston writes novels that blend autobiography and fiction in intergenerational explorations of identity between two cultures. Other writers who share this hyphenated identity are Tobagan-Canadian Marlene Nourbese Philip; Jamaica Kincaid (Antigua–United States); Barbadian–African American Paule Marshall; Michelle Cliff (Jamaica–United States); Opal Palmer Adisa (Jamaica–United States); and Trinidadian Earl Lovelace, who divides his time between the United States and Trinidad, as does St. Lucian Derek Walcott.

As these writers negotiate their own and their characters' identities on the borderlands among immigrant, expatriate, and citizen, they bring new dimensions to the contemporary novel in English through a genre that may be called the immigrant novel or the cosmopolitan novel. In speaking of the writer, it is important to note that one is leaving out other types of workers. The writer as cultural worker is more privileged certainly than a working-class population that crosses borders: for instance, Mexicans coming into the United States to work in kitchens and on farms, or Indians and Pakistanis "welcomed" into oil-rich Middle East countries for menial labor, or Indo-Ugandan-Britishers who when expelled from Uganda entered the M/Other Country.

Both in their novelistic explorations and in their personal histories, writers like Salman Rushdie whose racial origin and whose geographical location are at variance exemplify a paradoxical reality of belonging and not-belonging (Rushdie's example, as he remains under British government protection, is particularly ironic and mediated), of a kind of self-colonization in their use of the colonizer's language, of a search for identity, audience, constituency. Their work has given new configurations to a literature of exile that has been a prominent part of twentieth-century English literature, for example, non-English writers like James Joyce and Samuel Beckett. Novels of postcolonial expatriates and exiles represent the conflictual realities of geography, location, and language, the myth and reality of a return "home," the search for intellectual spaces with their "chosen" exile and/or expatriate "homes."

Physical acts of conquest and aggression constitute only one aspect of colonial aspirations; mental colonizations perpetuated in a colonizer's language, education, and cultural values are often more devastating and resilient. One can trace a historical trajectory from the British Empire and its particular imperialist weapons like overt military force and more insidious ideological tools like the English language and British values, to American imperialism at free play in the world right now. In his 1955 text, *Discourse on Colonialism,* Aimé Césaire sounded a warning about the growing aspirations of American imperialist expansionism, amply evident in recent years.

United States imperialism works to its economic advantage through multinational corporations, international aid agencies, exploitation of cheap labor (creating loss of jobs and poverty within the United States). United States imperialism is also manifested in the display of military muscle and overt invasions of Grenada and Panama in recent years, flaunting with bravado both international law and the often merely symbolic U.N. resolutions. It is doubly ironic that in the recent conflict with Iraq, the United States was the loudest proponent of U.N. Security Council measures against Iraq—it suited the United States this time around to wave aloft U.N. Security Council resolutions, notwithstanding its previous record of vetoing such measures, even blocking the will of an entire world against certain types of aggression. Historical amnesia is a widely prevalent disease in the United States and it is effectively propagated by media complicitous with the status quo.

Within the United States itself, forms of internal colonizations—of

"minorities" who may or may not be American citizens, "social exiles," and disenchanted populations on the margins of the "American
dream"—are sustained in part by United States aggressions *externally*
against peoples of color. Terry Eagleton's distinction between "literal
expatriates" and "social exiles" illuminates these marginal minority
conditions faced by peoples of color in the United States. Hence, in
the same breath, one hears of racist attacks on minority students on
a college campus that is also loudly proclaiming "cultural diversity,"
"multiculturism" in the curriculum, "civility" codes, and so on. Just
as covert and insidious as United States cultural imperialism and its
impact on peoples of color outside its borders is this covert alliance
between a continuing racism and a loudly proclaimed need to erad-
icate it.

As with British colonial aggression, which consolidated itself with
the chalk and the blackboard, the tools of American cultural imperialism are often more lasting and more devastating than physical acts
of aggression. Several postcolonial writers testify to the lasting and
devastating psychic fractures rooted in colonial(ist) educational systems. This history is significant in terms of understanding some of the
causes of expatriation and exile. Mental colonizations result in states
of exile—physical displacements and metaphoric exile within one's
own culture, to which, given one's education, one un-belongs.

The English language is a shared legacy of British colonialism.
Language, culture, and power are integrally related, especially within
a colonial history that imposed the English language and British educational systems. The economic and psychological repercussions of
English-language interventions as a language of power among colonized peoples who spoke other languages are part of postcolonial
societies today. The type of English one is equipped to use often
shapes one's position both inside postcolonial society and outside, as
immigrant. English language/s exist in standard, creole, and other
manifestations—what Edward Kamau Brathwaite calls "nation language," an English that can imitate "the sound of the hurricane,
wind, howl, waves"; or, what Honor Ford-Smith renames "patwah"
to be distinguished from "patois." Issues of cultural domination, educational policies, the status of English studies, and the role that
"English Literature" played in a liberal colonial enterprise are of

concern in postcolonial scholarship today. Even as colonies such as India and Kenya absorbed the imposition and institutionalization of English Literature into curricula, there were countermovements—for instance, Ngugi wa Thiong'o's dramatic call for the abolition of the English Department from the University of Nairobi and its replacement by a Department of Literatures and Languages.

In her Introduction to *She Tries Her Tongue: her silence softly breaks* (1989), Marlene Nourbese Philip probes the complex dilemmas surrounding the use/s of the English language by writers like herself from the Caribbean and the difficult task of recovering the African aspects of their history that were often more effectively preserved in nonverbal forms like music rather than language. (Rex Nettleford's influential work is evident here, especially his concept that nonverbal forms like dance could, within the very body of the slave, preserve cultural memory in ways that language could not.) Nourbese Philip proposes that "fundamental to any art form is the image. . . . The process of giving tangible form to this i-mage may be called i-maging, or the i-magination. Use of unconventional orthography, i-mage in this instance, does not only represent the increasingly conventional deconstruction of certain words, but draws on the Rastafarian practice of privileging the 'I' in many words. 'I-mage' rather than 'image' is, in fact, a closer approximation of the concept under discussion in this essay." According to Nourbese Philip, since the English language has served to "den(y) the essential humanity" of African peoples, it needs to be changed fundamentally by those very people now. An enforced English simultaneously gave voice to and silenced the African in terms of expressing his/her own experience during slavery and forced re-locations. "That silence has had a profound effect upon the English-speaking African Caribbean writer working in the medium of words." For the Caribbean writer, the situation is particularized by the fact that there is no language to return to. "In the absence of any other language by which the past may be repossessed, reclaimed and its most painful aspects transcended, English in its broadest spectrum must be made to do the job. . . . It is in the continuum of expression from standard to Caribbean English that the veracity of experience lies." Nourbese Philip argues forcefully for a subversive English transformed from "Queenglish and Kinglish," an English that will "make nouns strangers to verbs," techniques that have, in fact, linguistic roots in different African languages.

During colonization, education became the key to assimilating the "new ex-slave society" to the norms of "a civilized community" acceptable to the colonizers. The Reverend J. Sterling justified the education of negroes in a report to the British government in 1835: the production of "a civilized community will depend entirely on the power over their minds." If they are not educated, "property will perish in the colonies." Education was devised further to create a civil servant class that would aid a colonial administration. This same class would continue to work for the colonizers' benefit even after their physical departure (Frantz Fanon's "black skin, white mask" phenomenon). Colonial educational policies and educational levels are also a part of the history of contemporary expatriate populations that consist of a growing number of the educated-unemployed. This class migrates to new "homes" for employment and economic reasons.

Color, class, and gender divisions often denied educational opportunities to women in the Caribbean region, evoking resonances of British colonial practices in other occupied territories of the so-called Empire. The colonial enterprise of educating the natives was both ideological and gendered. Female colonization carried the burden of patriarchal domination that most often not only predated colonialism but was reinforced by it. English education often contradicts "traditional" cultural expectations of female behavior; women, however "modernized" with an English education, must remain "traditional." For an educated woman to overstep the boundaries as codified within patriarchal control of female sexuality can be disastrous, as explored in Zimbabwean Tsitsi Dangarembga's novel *Nervous Conditions* (1988). Nyasha, intellectually precocious, is uprooted from her home and taken to England at a young age. She returns "home," having "forgotten" her mother tongue, Shona, and generally alienated from both her Shona identity and her English education. She finds herself metaphorically homeless to the fatal extent that she cannot even belong within her female body, which becomes, in her anorexia and bulimia, the sad victim of her mental anguish. Nyasha's authoritarian father, Babamukuru, makes her "a victim of her femaleness," as the narrator, Tambu, notes. Babamukuru, who has been educated by missionaries in their "wizardry," has internalized a colonial mentality of inferiority before whites, but superiority before his own people. Ironically his colonial, patriarchal education reinforces his male privileges in the family.

Even as an English education and a liberal enterprise served by English literature within the colonies fulfilled certain ideological goals in sustaining a colonial administration, the imperialist project within the colonizers' home-spaces was carried forward by a literature of imperialism embodied, for instance, in Rudyard Kipling's "white man's burden." Kipling was only one among several popular writers in nineteenth-century England who dealt with imperialist matters. The very titles of some of these popular novels—like *Love by an Indian River, A Mixed Marriage*—tell the tale. Configurations of Empire in such works enable the sharing of a common consciousness by writers and readers mutually reinforcing stereotypes. The serious impact, conscious and subconscious, in terms of how visual and literary manifestations control the popular imagination of the British reading public (both in India and in Britain) is especially important when we historicize such images and bring them up to date, calcifying into racist manifestations that range from the subtle to the obvious.

Cultural productions in the West continue to sustain and validate such stereotypes—as exemplified by the vastly popular British renditions of the Raj in television extravaganzas like *The Jewel in the Crown* and *The Far Pavilions,* as well as in films like Richard Attenborough's *Gandhi* and David Lean's *A Passage to India.* These projects have serious ideological underpinnings even as one concedes that the British may need to look back upon their often inglorious work in colonies like India, and they may need to absolve their own relentless guilt about their imperialist adventures. However, from the colonized peoples' point of view, these projects once again make us, as Salman Rushdie puts it, "bit-players in [our] own history." If such shows as "the blackface minstrel-show of *The Far Pavilions* . . . and the grotesquely overpraised *Jewel in the Crown*" were anomalous productions, the situation would not be so serious. As such, they are "only the latest," notes Rushdie, "in a very long line of fake portraits inflicted by the West on the East." The situation is much more serious now than in the early part of the century, given the power of electronic media.

Within a predominantly capitalist postcolonial world that remains, after "flag independences," stifled in poverty and dependence, extreme economic conditions often necessitate migrations. Further back, migrations of peoples of color from Africa and Asia into Britain were rooted within a colonial past that spanned nearly three centuries. More recently, colonized peoples, after fighting on the British side in World War II, were "invited" into the "M/Other Country." These migrants became part of a new working class in Britain, and as they struggle to make Britain their "home" they face new forms of racism, such as immigration policies, Paki-bashing, and other forms of harassment.

For writers in particular, such a history of migrations and of new racisms throws into relief issues of location and origin—where one lives and works, and where one may be transported without choice, as a child. This history presents new configurations to the mediated notions of identity and belonging, of audience and constituency. For Salman Rushdie, Indo-Pakistani-Britisher, for instance, one cannot simply assert that his audience is "Western" since there are 1.5 million Muslims who live in Britain itself. Or, for Hanif Kureishi, racially mixed (Pakistani father and English mother), who grew up in Britain culturally British and within a racist society, and who can be identified as a "Paki," the parameters of identity and belonging are extremely complex. What it means in the 1980s and 1990s to be a Black Britisher, living in Britain, and, equally significantly, what it means to be an indigenous, native Britisher are matters fraught with contradictions. Is citizenship one aspect of this troubled notion of identity? Is citizenship sentimental, symbolic, and also somewhat expedient, as Rushdie's continued protection by the British government testifies?

Migration and expatriation have given new meanings to the notion of "identity," which remains important within the field of postcolonial literature. Despite the tyranny of certain aspects of deconstruction and poststructuralism that cannot tolerate "old-fashioned" notions of identity and reality, I think that it is crucial to restore these terms, much in the spirit of recovering our own subjugated and subaltern histories. Of course, one is not asserting any single, monolithic notion of identity; rather, racial and cultural differences are themselves mediated along new parameters of language and geography.

Fearful of an old-fashioned identity issue being replaced by "subject-positions," one does not need to assume new and somewhat fashionable stances of "cosmopolitanism" and "internationalism." Rushdie's novels, for instance, are interpreted as "transnational" since they carry modernist and postmodernist echoes, playing with levels of fantasy and reality, fragmenting history, dis-placing so-called significant events in history by presenting various contesting versions. Does "transnational" somehow remove the disturbing vestiges of an old-fashioned nationalism? The term assumes more than what it can accomplish; moreover, it mystifies the really dangerous elements of nationalism, such as state fundamentalism, by pretending that they have somehow been trans-cended. State and religious fundamentalisms can call for the death of an author like Rushdie because his novel has "offended"; examples of fundamentalism proliferate, almost grotesquely, in so many parts of the world.

The novelistic representations of a mediated personal identity for writers like Rushdie amalgamate various worlds. In his novels, Rushdie returns to the source, so to speak, through memory, through historical re-creation of a time and place, such as India's independence in *Midnight's Children* (1980), Pakistan's military rulers in *Shame* (1983), and through an incorporation of the South Asian and British locales and transformations of identities necessitated by locales and by one's level of comfort and discomfort within a racist society in *The Satanic Verses* (1988). Rushdie's voice as a writer is significantly a part of this historical process in which "third world" peoples struggle for self-determination as Black British citizens. And amid the furor surrounding *The Satanic Verses* we might unfortunately fail to recognize how creatively Rushdie illuminates these shifting lines of allegiance determined along racial, class, gender, and ethnic lines, and how these issues create contradictory, often painful situations for his characters, and for himself as a writer.

As in his other novels, Rushdie explores these threads of identities—what happens to human beings when they are transported, transplanted, by choice or otherwise, into alien environments—even more openly in *The Satanic Verses*. The first line of the novel presents a kind of migration/reincarnation/metamorphosis—the birth of a new self that must necessarily adapt to a new environment, and the death of an old self that belongs to a different world: " 'To be born again,' sang Gibreel Farishta tumbling from the heavens, 'first you have to die.' " And a few pages into the novel, the narrator asks, "Is birth always a fall?"

Connected to the necessity of forming new identities is the need to assume a new voice, a new language. Saladin Chamcha (Chamcha, in Hindi, indicates a fawning attitude) is "The Man of a Thousand Voices and a Voice. If you wanted to know how your ketchup bottle should talk in its television commercial . . . he was your very man. He made carpets speak in warehouse advertisements, he did celebrity impersonations, baked beans, frozen peas. . . . Once in a radio play for thirty-seven voices, he interpreted every single part under a variety of pseudonyms and nobody ever worked it out." When Saladin visits India, Zeenat tells him, "They pay you to imitate them, as long as they don't have to look at you. . . . You goddamn lettuce brain." The visit home disconcerts Saladin; he almost loses his acquired British "voice/identity," slips into distressing Indianisms, and decides to rush back to Britain. As John Leonard, reviewing the novel in *The Nation*, puts it: "History is out of control, and metamorphosis too. We've left home once too often. No more avatars of Vishnu. Instead of rising out of the ashes like a phoenix or resurrecting like a Christ, we are reborn, devolved into parody, bloody farce, false consciousness, bad faith. . . . Like Chamcha, we are on the run."

With the recent publication of *Haroun and the Sea of Stories* (1990), it is heartening to find that Rushdie has not been silenced. Living in hiding, he has created an enchanting tale, veiled as a children's story, but replete with dark echoes of silencing forces that constantly threaten Rashid Khalifa, the storyteller. In the land of "Guppees [storytellers] and Chupwallas [silence-enforcers]," Haroun, the son, tries to keep his father's storytelling talents alive. Although this seems like a thinly veiled allegory of Rushdie's personal life, wider resonances of different types of silence-imposing forces, self- and state-imposed, are evoked.

Hanif Kureishi belongs to the contemporary generation of Black Britishers. In an autobiographical essay, "The Rainbow Sign," he discusses his own origin and chronicles the racism he experienced growing up in London. His personal story is set within a broader context; for instance, he notes that "[he] was afraid to watch TV" because of the portrayal of Pakistanis as comics. Such images sanc-

tioned "the enjoyed reduction of racial hatred to a joke . . . a celebration of contempt in millions of living rooms in England." Kureishi
discusses a phenomenon like Enoch Powell, "a figurehead for racists,
[one who] helped create racism in Britain." Kureishi felt "racially
abused" since he was five, located in a socially enforced self-loathing:
"Pakis . . . these loathed aliens. I found it impossible to answer
questions about where I came from. The word 'Pakistani' had been
made into an insult. It was a word I didn't want to use about myself.
I couldn't tolerate being myself."

From the start I tried to deny my Pakistani self. I was ashamed. It was a curse
and I wanted to be rid of it. I wanted to be like everyone else. I read with
understanding a story in a newspaper about a black boy who, when he
noticed that burnt skin turned white, jumped into a bath of boiling water.

At school, one teacher always spoke to me in a "Peter Sellers" Indian
accent. Another refused to call me by my name, calling me Pakistani Pete
instead. So I refused to call the teacher by his name and used his nickname
instead. This led to trouble; arguments, detentions, escapes from school over
hedges, and eventually suspension.

Kureishi records his feelings of violence embedded in anger and
fear that are documented commonly in racial situations. He discovers
James Baldwin, the Panthers, identifies with race politics, with the
working class, and through the African American parallel, Kureishi
recognizes the futility of the myth of a return to Africa, or wherever
one comes from. As an adolescent, he records rejecting Islam as a
route to identity and he does not visit Pakistan until he is an adult.

In his father's home, Pakistan, he cannot identify with the class of
"English-speaking international bourgeoisie. . . . Strangely, anti-
British remarks made [him] feel patriotic." His identity as a playwright means little in Pakistan—an important loss in terms of his
identity. Kureishi recognizes the economics behind migrations:
"thousands of Pakistani families depended on money sent from England." He also notes the psychological burdens placed on a society
that was losing its people to the West and a further burden when
these people returned, dissatisfied because "they had seen more, they
wanted more. . . . Once more the society was being changed by outside forces, not by its own volition." The two societies, Pakistani and
British, were both closely bound and miles apart; for instance, a

villager tells him that when his grandchildren visit him from Bradford he has to hire an interpreter in order to talk to them.

Kureishi's recent novel, *The Buddha of Suburbia* (1990), explores the layered realities of race, class, gender, and geography in the protagonist Karim's search for identity and belonging. The opening of the novel presents his genealogy, an "Englishman" with a name like Karim Amir:

> My name is Karim Amir, and I am an Englishman born and bred, almost. I am often considered to be a funny kind of Englishman, a new breed as it were, having emerged from two old histories. But I don't care—Englishman I am (though not proud of it), from the South London suburbs and going somewhere. Perhaps it is the odd mixture of continents and blood, of here and there, of belonging and not, that makes me restless and easily bored.

Karim's narrative frames other stories of immigrant lives in contemporary Britain—for example, Anwar and his daughter Jamila, a poignant portrait of a tradition-bound father who insists on his daughter Jamila, who has grown up in Britain, having an arranged marriage. Anwar, in the Gandhian tradition of passive resistance, goes on a hunger fast unto death unless his daughter agrees to abide by his wishes. "I won't eat. I will die. If Gandhi could shove out the English from India by not eating, I can get my family to obey me by exactly the same." Karim reflects on the "similarities between what was happening to Dad, with his discovery of Eastern philosophy [Karim's father is 'the buddha of suburbia'], and Anwar's last stand. Perhaps it was the immigrant condition living itself out through them. For years they were both happy to live like English-men. . . . Now, as they aged and seemed settled here, Anwar and Dad appeared to be returning internally to India, or at least to be resisting the English here. It was puzzling: neither of them expressed any desire actually to see their origins again."

When Anwar's self-destructive tactics are revealed to Karim's father he remarks, "We old Indians come to like this England less and less and we return to an imagined India." The parents' inner conflicts often embroil their children tragically in a collision between a traditionally sanctioned authoritarianism and an independent life that the children have imbibed in their immigrant-citizen identities. For the parents' generation, British citizenship is merely symbolic and convenient—spiritually and in terms of their values they belong more to India and Pakistan; their Britain-born children are citizens who have imbibed the values and lifestyles of a Western locale. The unfairness of the conflict comes down heavily on Jamila—should she risk losing her father, or should she "save" his life by marrying a man whom she has never met? Jamila gives in and then forges her own British-Indian path of resistance by refusing to have any sexual life with her husband, Changez. And even as Karim befriends Changez, Karim continues to be Jamila's lover.

When Karim, as part of his budding acting career, is asked to "create" a portrait of current immigrant life in Britain, he elects to tell the story of Anwar and Jamila, particularly the fact that Anwar's scheme had backfired: Changez, the son-in-law from whom Anwar expected a new "life-transfusion," had been a devastating disappointment. Anwar's life, running "Paradise Stores" in a fascist neighborhood where "racist graffiti appeared on the walls every time you removed it," has deteriorated. The ramifications of presenting a narrow-minded, dogmatic father to a predominantly white audience whose racist stereotypes would be validated by such an image are pointed out to Karim by Tracy, a black member of the group:

Anwar's hunger-strike worries me. What you want to say hurts me. It really pains me! And I'm not sure that we should show it! . . . I'm afraid it shows black people—Black and Asian people—one old Indian man as being irrational, ridiculous, as being hysterical. And as being fanatical. . . . And that arranged marriage. It worries me. . . . Your picture is what white people already think of us. That we're funny, with strange habits and weird customs. To the white man we're already people without humanity. . . . We have to protect our culture at this time.

Karim is attacked as a reactionary. He bristles at this "censorship" and wants to "tell the truth." Although there is a need for genuine criticism of problems within one's own community, positions that are often thwarted by "race relations"—positions like Tracy's in this case—Karim has rather unselfconsciously stepped beyond the bounds of constructive criticism; he wishes to entertain a white audience at the expense of Anwar's humanity. Karim's self-awareness develops and he withdraws that story from a public vision not ready to cope with the interstices of race, class, and gender as they are played out for an expatriate-colored-citizenry that deals with prejudice in its daily life. The issues of reception and audience bring us into the arena of markets, publishing, and financial resources—the means of production necessary for cultural production.

The above discussion on colonialism and educational policies and of continuing imperialist dominations, economic and cultural, in postcolonial societies traces some of the historicized reasons for writers' expatriation and/or exile into Britain and North America. As writers settle into these new "homes," what are the forces that confront them in a literary marketplace? Who publishes their work? Who reads their novels and why is the novel the most highly desired form? Who reviews them? Who is their audience and is it radically different from their constituencies at "home"? And can writers meet the challenge of making their audience into their constituencies?

In the West, the privileging of the novel as a form is problematic, particularly in terms of the market and publishing houses. This is hard to contest, given the prevalence of publishers and distributors of "third world" writers in the West. Recall, for instance, Chinua Achebe's most recent novel, *Anthills of the Savannah* (1987), hailed as Achebe breaking his "silence" of nearly thirty years since the publication in 1966 of *A Man of the People*. Such judgment falsely assumes Achebe's "silence," ignoring his work in his own Igbo language. Only by writing a novel, and writing it in English, can Achebe effectively break "silence." This demonstrates a Western hegemonic response appropriating the rest of the world into its own vocabulary, its literary forms where the novel and its critical evaluation is privileged.

Postcolonial novels that are published by Western houses get better distribution than the struggles of local publishing can woefully accomplish. Since the "West" may not even hear of writers published locally, we must not conclude that they do not exist. Hence, in our discussion of the novel we must bear in mind, very crucially, what we leave out—not only the local publications that may not be available in the West, and why that is so, but also the oral forms that do not get into print. These are particularly important for largely nonliterate societies.

A dialectic relationship between cultural and critical productions both creates and responds to economic and political factors controlling a consumer marketplace. Marginality as a concept is useful in this discussion because "marginal" cultural productions are commodified in today's Western marketplace. The "marginal" is not a given; there is a complex process that leads to marginalization. Imagine, if you will, the literary marketplace as the many-handed god Shiva (who has both creative and destructive potential in Hindu cosmology). When marginality is commodified as a selling tactic, such modes of production have serious implications for expatriate postcolonial writers and critics—the dangers of a commodification that can change the very terms of what is written, and that can dictate what themes will sell. The marketplace is a key conditioning factor in producing and consolidating marginality. The commodification of "blackness" or of "third worldism" as items for sale in the marketplace, which includes affirmative action policies, publishing priorities, and conference topics as well, has serious consequences for the creative artist/worker. Complicitous in this profitable relationship are not only publishing houses but also, closer to our own lives, critics and scholars who enhance or challenge commodification in the types of theoretical production that they engage in.

However, the notion of marginality as a term in critical discourse has served to ghettoize certain literatures and "minority" fields in the academy. The terms "margin" and "center," along with their conceptual baggage, need to be contested, for they fail to account for the layers of cultural hegemony firmly in place despite challenges to a Western literary canon, as well as factors that shape who and what is "centered" in literary studies. The advocacy of one "common Western heritage" in texts like E. D. Hirsch, Jr.'s *Cultural Literacy* (1987) enshrines a literary canon that is increasingly threatened by powerful non-Western cultural products making inroads, however peripherally, into curricula.

I would like to reclaim the term "marginal" in a very different sense from the commodification of "marginal voices" for commercial gain. For postcolonial writers, who may inhabit their "home" spaces, or who may inhabit expatriate and immigrant spaces, it is important to distinguish between "marginality" as a term in academic discourse and the *actual conditions of marginality* that sustain or disdain their very lives and create or destroy the very conditions of their artistic work. Personal and political configurations within postcolonial writers' lives encompass various marginalities—by race and ethnicity; by geography (literal and metaphoric exile, expatriation, migration); by language (English-language interventions); by class and color (for creoles in the Caribbean); by education.

For postcolonial writers, there is a central contradiction between the modes of production available to them that commodify them in the "first" world as "minority," as "female," and their struggles against the actual conditions of marginality in their lives in the "first" or "third worlds." When "marginal" identities—for example, Lorna Goodison, Jamaican woman writer, and Ama Ata Aidoo, Ghanaian woman writer—are commodified, they set up rigid boundaries of what is expected by publishers, readers, and the market. An exotic enthusiasm for women writers blows hot and cold for reasons that have very little to do with their work. Such commodification can hardly be nurturing for a writer or for a literary field.

Our critical practice must recognize that cultural productions—oral, written—are also commodified in response to audience and literacy levels. Such issues as who makes it into print and what themes are profitable are further complicated because postcolonial societies have large nonliterate populations. The use of oral forms—street theater versus published drama—is strategic for nonliterate audiences. Our critical practice must stretch the boundaries of strictly "literary," printed forms (like the novel) and include oral cultural productions, and also put pressure on publishers to recognize and support new literary forms—for example, oral tradition of feminist songs in India, new forms of dance, street theater. This is important since oral forms—for instance, street theater, activist songs organized by women's groups like Saheli, the Lawyers' Collective in India, or the Sistren Collective in Jamaica—are more involved in struggles for social change than, say, the more easily available novels of Buchi Emecheta. A profit-oriented publishing industry capitalizes on the low literacy levels in postcolonial societies so that, ironically enough, even literate people in these societies cannot find or afford books by their own writers who are published in the West. For example, when the Nobel Prize for literature in 1986 was awarded to Wole Soyinka, his books were unavailable in his native Nigeria. In general, African academics speak of a "book famine" in African countries. This scenario raises serious questions about the control and dissemination of knowledge and cultural productions.

If migrations are undertaken for economic reasons in general, there are also more particular reasons in terms of the realities of cultural productions that face writers within postcolonial societies, ranging from inhospitality to downright hostility, silencing, and various forms of censorship and self-censorship. In a recent essay entitled "Twice-Bitten: The Fate of Africa's Culture Producers" (1990), Wole Soyinka discusses a very serious condition faced by writers and intellectuals—what he terms "the internal brain drain," that is, writers who are silenced, imprisoned by their own governments, or who are forced into exile in order to continue their work. South African writers such as Dennis Brutus who are forced to leave because of the brutal apartheid regime may offer some obvious examples; however, a writer like Ngugi wa Thiong'o has had to live outside Kenya for political reasons, as has Nurrudin Farah of Somalia, Mongo Beti of Cameroon, and so on. This type of internal brain drain, actively supported by a hostile state, is very different from simply blaming the "West" for a brain drain of skilled workers lured from "third world" areas into highly paying Western hospitals and academic institutions. Characteristically, Soyinka takes a searing look at the very conditions within African societies, and draws attention to the fact that these regimes have to be accountable and to take responsibility for silencing writers and intellectuals.

For Caribbean writers as well, on the surface, those who struggle to work in extremely difficult conditions of cultural production have a more difficult time than those who leave and migrate to the ever-beckoning North, projected via satellite communication as the desirable reality in which one can be transmogrified literally or in fantasy. The entrance of international aid agencies and at times their patronizing of "the arts" creates a visibility for the artist, ironically supported by neocolonial tendencies that await validation of one's own writers from the outside. As Honor Ford-Smith of the Sistren Collective has noted, there are complicated levels of dependency that have effects on the kinds of cultural work that are allowed with particular types of aid. For example, aid agencies sometimes raise the question of whether the arts, particularly those aimed at education, can be truly "productive." Aid agencies are also totally product-oriented. At the end of a specified time frame, the product has to be delivered and all responsibility toward the group ends. Such commodification of cultural products leads to their value being judged solely on their marketability.

In historicizing the diverse representations of "American minorities" in contemporary times, a chronological view is a useful vantage point from which to examine the experiences of internal colonizations and metaphoric exile of so-called American citizens—Native Americans, Africans involuntarily transported into the New World, Chinese, Japanese, Chicanos. Since the 1950s, the ravages of United States wars have brought in Filipino, Vietnamese, and Central American peoples, and, most recently, "voluntary" migrations for economic and professional reasons have allowed entry to South Asian, Caribbean, and African peoples. First-, second-, and third-generation "minorities" must still struggle on the borderlands of literal and metaphoric exile, of the myth and reality of a return "home," of fluctuating identities as immigrant-expatriate-citizen—from Ellis Island to J. F. Kennedy airport, as well as other ports of entry, not to mention "illegal" border crossings.

Within these ethnically diverse groups, the exclusion in this chapter of non-English-language writers among recent immigrants into the United States and a focus on the novel form with its high profile and public promotion circumscribe this study even as it speaks volumes for the hegemony of academic and publishing institutions. One must acknowledge that the oral transmission of cultural memory through song, dance, festival, that is, through nonprint media, is extremely significant—often these forms are more resonant in preserving ethnicity and in giving participants a sense of belonging. The essential communal nature of activities is distinctly different from the isolated production and consumption of a novel.

Race, ethnicity, and difference, along with broad commonalities of a search for belonging, mark the novelistic production of writers like Jamaica Kincaid, Bharati Mukherjee, Paule Marshall, Maxine Hong Kingston, among others noted earlier. Apart from the significant linguistic and formal contributions to the contemporary novel in English, the work of these writers is instructive in the critical reception accorded to them within the United States marketplace, eager to commodify "third world" bodies and products. In looking at expatriated identities such as Jamaica Kincaid (Antigua–United States), Michelle Cliff (Jamaica–United States), or Marlene Nourbese Philip (Tobago–Canada), and their insider/outsider positionings, one gets an illuminating perspective on, say, American-born writers like Paule Marshall (who grew up in the Barbadian community of New York) or Audre Lorde (Grenada–New York). Lorde, in moving from New York to St. Croix, has made a reverse move geographically from the majority of writers dealt with here.

Paule Marshall recreates a vivid Caribbean world from the vantage point of her New York upbringing. Personal and collective histories unfolding within particular cultural contexts guide her work. Her autobiographical novel, *Brown Girl, Brownstones* (1959), portrays a memorable story of girlhood and adolescence caught in the parameters of American dreams and Caribbean values strongly held by recently immigrated parents. In an essay, "Shaping the World of My Art," Marshall acknowledges the influence of women of her mother's generation on her own linguistic and artistic sensibility—what she learned from "the wordshop of the kitchen." Although the novel was reviewed favorably, it "was a commercial failure," notes Barbara Christian, "a commentary perhaps on the times." The novel was relegated to the juvenile shelf, a fate that also befell Toni Morrison's *The Bluest Eye* (1970)—novels that American society found too uncomfortable. None of Marshall's other novels, such as *Soul Clap Hands and Sing* (1961), *The Chosen Place, the Timeless People* (1969), and *Praisesong for the Widow* (1983), have been commercial successes, partly because she does not write stories about overt racism and violence as expected by a marketplace that commodifies "black women writers." She deals with themes of black community, old age, the struggles to integrate experiences from different cultures into the "home" spaces of the West. As Avey in *Praisesong for the Widow* rediscovers her ancestry and her name, Avatara, she touches the depths of her own history.

The writing of India-born Bharati Mukherjee and Antigua-born Jamaica Kincaid, both first-generation immigrants (Mukherjee passionately embraces her "naturalized" status as American citizen since

1988), is revelatory as much in terms of their explorations of identities as in the critical receptions that they have received. In 1989, Mukherjee's novel *Jasmine* and Kincaid's *Lucy* were critically acclaimed. Both authors' personal trajectories that locate them now in the United States encompass some uncanny connections thematically and formally; both female protagonists (after whom the novels are titled) have served as au pairs, as "caregivers," Asian and Caribbean nannies to white middle-class families in New York City—a twentieth-century version of governessing, of being situated in the heart of mainstream American families, in unique positions to observe, assimilate, and report. "*Lucy* is not a roman à clef of New York literary society," remarks the *Boston Globe*'s Louise Kennedy, who cannot resist the temptation of noting the black-women-race-class issue, "just as it is not the sociopolitical examination of race and class in America that some reviewers seem to think a black woman should be writing."

Kincaid, columnist for *The New Yorker*, author of *Annie John* (1985), her first novel, was puzzling to her American reviewers. The novel explores an intense love-hate relationship between mother and daughter, expressed in a metaphoric, surreal style. The daughter struggles to assert her individuality from the mother's domination; even a final "escape" into England is prefaced by the mother's words, "It doesn't matter what you do or where you go. I'll always be your mother and this will always be your home." Kincaid's works can be described as encompassing different explorations of the history of self-discovery and self-location in various "homes" near and far from the Caribbean.

The bold experimentation of form in her collection of stories, *At the Bottom of the River* (1983), was received as "irritatingly difficult [and] pretentious." As a "Caribbean" writer, she was stepping out of her skin a bit too much, treading uncomfortably to rhythms that Western sensibilities were not used to hearing from a Caribbean writer. Why didn't Kincaid write like a typical Caribbean? A similar reception was given to South African–Botswanan Bessie Head's *A Question of Power* (1973) when it was first published—for example, Arthur Ravenscroft's assertion that "the topography of madness" is familiar to the "West," but that it is unexpected, perhaps too unnerving, to deal with "nervous breakdowns" from "third world" writers. They should stay within the boundaries of what is expected from them—stories about community, colonialism, local tradition.

In her next work, *A Small Place* (1988), Kincaid, with the full talent of her sarcasm, launches a "telling like it is" story of "the ugly tourist" who eagerly and irresponsibly consumes the sun, sea, and sand of the Caribbean, "in harmony with nature and backward in that charming way." Kincaid has a remarkable and disarmingly lucid ability to reveal the most blinding truths, and to force accountability where it belongs, because as the narrator states, one "cannot forget the past, cannot forgive, and cannot forget." By evoking slavery and the painful reality that slaves could not hold their slave traders accountable for their inhuman actions, Kincaid draws lessons from that past for this present, such as the Antiguan neocolonial regime where "all the ministers in government go overseas for medical treatment. All the ministers have 'green cards' [United States Alien Residency]"; in Antigua there is no decent health care for the majority. New colonizations have taken the place of the old ones: "Eventually, the masters left, in a kind of way."

"*Lucy* is about a girl who lives on an island and goes to a continent," remarked Kincaid on one of her book-promotion tours. *Lucy* was serially published in *The New Yorker,* though only its publication in novel form has drawn critical attention. Even as Lucy needs the distance from her home to be able to write about it, her words are suffused in the Caribbean reality. As Kincaid remarks about herself, "I don't know how to live there [in Antigua], but I don't know how to live without there."

Whereas Jamaica Kincaid recognizes this contradiction of being "here" and "there" simultaneously in imaginative space, both for herself as writer and for her characters, South Asian Bharati Mukherjee, in personal statements, embraces the "here" and celebrates her sense of belonging as an American citizen. This sense of unanguished belonging is not always true for Mukherjee's fictional characters, though she asserts this belonging for herself personally. In an essay that prefaces her collection of short stories, *Darkness* (1985), Mukherjee discusses the advantages of moving from a racist Canada (where she lived from 1966 to 1980) into a United States where she feels more culturally integrated. In Canada, as an outsider, she adopted an "expatriate" identity: "In my Canadian experience, 'immigrants' were lost souls, put upon and pathetic. Expatriates, on the other hand, knew all too well who and what they were, and what foul fate had befallen them. Like V. S. Naipaul, in whom I imagined a model, I tried to explore state-of-the-art expatriation." Expatriation was made painfully real in a racist Canada. A change of locale to the United States was transformative in positive aspects for Mukherjee's creativity, "a movement away from the aloofness of expatriation, to the exuberance of immigration." Mukherjee records with some bitterness her personal history in Canada:

I was frequently taken for a prostitute or shoplifter, frequently assumed to be a domestic, praised by astonished auditors that I didn't have a "sing-song" accent. The society itself, or important elements in that society, routinely made crippling assumptions about me, and about my "kind." In the United States, however, I see myself in those same outcasts; I see myself in an article on a Trinidad-Indian hooker; I see myself in the successful executive who slides Hindi film music in his tape deck as he drives into Manhattan; I see myself in the shady accountant who's trying to marry off his loose-living daughter; in professors, domestics, high school students, illegal busboys in ethnic restaurants.

Mukherjee's adoption of an immigrant as opposed to an expatriate identity has been profoundly enabling for her writing. In her own words, she has "joined imaginative forces with an anonymous, driven, underclass of semi-assimilated Indians with sentimental attachments to a distant homeland but no real desire for permanent return."

Indianness is now a metaphor, a particular way of partially comprehending the world. Though the characters in these stories [in *Darkness*] are, or were, "Indian," I see most of these as stories of broken identities and discarded languages, and the will to bond oneself to a new community, against the ever-present fear of failure and betrayal.

Further, Mukherjee does not see her "Indianness" as an isolated configuration that can only be at "home" with other Indian people: "instead of seeing my Indianness as a fragile identity to be preserved against obliteration (or worse, a 'visible' disfigurement to be hidden), I see it now as a set of fluid identities to be celebrated." Mukherjee takes this further, and relates her personal identity to that of her identity as a writer; she "sees [herself] as an American writer in the tradition of other American writers whose parents or grandparents had passed through Ellis Island." *Darkness* is dedicated to Bernard Malamud.

Mukherjee's novels *The Tiger's Daughter* (1971) and *Wife* (1975) trace a trajectory of an upper-class female protagonist, traditional and modern, socialized within Brahmin (the highest caste) religious and social codes, and equipped with an English-language education. In *Jasmine* (1989), her most recent novel, the protagonist is variously named Jyoti at birth, Jasmine by a nontraditional Indian husband, Jase by an American New York suitor, Jane by an American Iowa banker. Her multiple identities embody the physical and mental spaces that she traverses between the village of Hasnapur in India and the United States, fleeing immigration authorities and murderous ghosts from her past, seeking a belonging amidst the anguished thorns of various identities that struggle for integration. The confident tone of this novel reflects the protagonist's boldness, her search to escape the fate of widowhood and exile foretold by an astrologer at the beginning of the text. Mukherjee's previous novels do not present women like Jasmine, who is ready by the end of the novel to "re-position the stars . . . greedy with wants and reckless from hope."

In *The Tiger's Daughter*, Tara, an upper-class Bengali woman, enters the United States for an undergraduate degree at Vassar. A familiar trajectory of the immigrant experience is explored—higher education and research facilities beckon one into the United States. Often, the qualifications acquired may disqualify one from finding a job in India, hence, the straddling of continents. Tara marries an American, and the novel traces her conflicts of belonging as she returns "home," familiar and strange, and gets to know the "David [her husband] of aerogrammes . . . a figure standing in shadows, or a foreigner with an accent on television. 'I miss you very much. But I understand you have to work this out. I just hope you get it over with quickly. . . . Remember the unseen dangers of India. Tell your parents to cable me if you get sick.' " "A foreignness of spirit" takes over Tara's consciousness as she struggles through a sense of exile both in her childhood "home" and in the newly acquired "home" of the United States. Mukherjee's explorations of the personal dimensions of female identity and belonging within marriage, an integral part of traditional Indian socialization for females, now resonates in a new key as Tara's husband belongs "elsewhere," and so her home "should" be with him, even though that space is not yet "home."

In *Wife*, Dimple Dasgupta fantasizes that "marriage would bring her love . . . her father was looking for engineers in the matrimonial ads. . . . She thought of premarital life as a dress rehearsal for actual living." As she fetishizes marriage, Dimple exemplifies the dangerous hold of subconscious socialization patterns of female submissiveness and suffering, enshrined in Hindu legend and myth, and validated by a patriarchal culture: "Sita, the ideal wife of Hindu legends, who had walked through fire at her husband's request. Such pain, such loyalty seemed reserved for married women." Dimple cannot easily shed these notions after she moves geographically into the United States. With the actual marriage, the predictable disillusion sets in. Her husband decides to change her name from Dimple to Nandini. Names are one type of personal markers of identity; when named by others, Mukherjee's female protagonists in *Jasmine* (as noted above) have certain identities thrust upon them. Dimple's socialization has not prepared her for the isolation of a wifely homebound existence in the United States. Her predicament is like that of newly brought over wives, sometimes by husbands who travel home for a couple of weeks, "interview" several prospective brides, and select one. The realities of life here—isolation, winter, loss of community—hit much later. An independent lifestyle here, the fact that one's family does not have a say in one's every decision, also entails a bitterly lonely self-reliance. "Losing" one's family's control also entails losing their warmth and love. Dimple becomes suicidal, thinking about where to die, in Calcutta, or in New York. Mukherjee's narrative does not allow her protagonist much interaction with the "natives" within her immigrant locale. America hardly exists except as a backdrop, a physical location where Dimple finds herself geographically. Her mental space is in turmoil; she is not really at home anywhere, desperately needing help but unable even to articulate her needs.

Mukherjee grows in confidence in presenting Americans and American life. In *Jasmine*, her depictions of Iowa, and of the tragedies of small farmers unable to make their bank payments, ring with truth and poignancy. Ironically, Mukherjee's depictions of India are trapped in exoticism and a self-exoticism of her "foreign" female protagonists. Mukherjee's vision seems at times to be frozen in time. Her depictions of certain regressive customs like *sati* (widow-burning), of child-marriage, and of widowhood are not mediated by changes and challenges to these traditions in contemporary India. The boundaries of what Mukherjee often presents as sacrosanct and fixed traditions are shifting, however slowly.

Mukherjee's success as a short-story writer is noteworthy. Her first collection, *Darkness,* documents the struggles of newly arrived South Asians, their experiences of alienation and racism as they try to find their "place" in American society. Their personal and professional lives within mainstream America often carry severe psychological costs. Mukherjee explores different ways of coping between first- and second-generation immigrants, and the often tragic colliding of values, particularly between father and daughter. For instance, in "The Father," a daughter's decision to do something as "artificial" as to reject marriage and get herself artificially inseminated results in her father's violent physical attack. Not only is the father alienated from a mainstream American culture where he works as a lonely, petty salesman (echoes of Arthur Miller's *Death of a Salesman*), but he is equally distant from his daughter, who has adopted some of the values of her locale. Similar experiences are echoed in personal stories and testimonies of Black Britishers in Amrit Wilson's *Finding a Voice* (1978). Horrendous conflicts between fathers and daughters constitute a sad refrain. Controls over female sexuality and clashes of traditional versus a freer, Western behavior nearly always make the fathers more authoritarian, dogmatic, and destructive. (Recall the discussion of Zimbabwean Tsitsi Dangarembga's *Nervous Conditions* mentioned earlier in this chapter.) In the interest of saving the family *izzat* (honor), fathers will destroy their daughters' lives.

In her latest collection of stories, *The Middleman and Other Stories* (1988), Mukherjee "has vastly enlarged her geographical and social range," remarks Jonathan Raban in the *New York Times Book Review;* "the immigrants in her new book come fresh to America from Vietnam, the Caribbean, the Levant, Afghanistan, the Philippines, Italy and Sri Lanka as well as from India." According to Raban, Mukherjee in this collection hijacks the whole tradition of Jewish-American writing [the immigrant experience being classically recorded in Jewish-American fiction] and flies it off to a destination undreamed of by its original practitioners.

   Her characters . . . see the surfaces of America with the bug-eyed hang-over clarity of the greenhorn afloat in a gaudy new world. Yet they're not tired, huddled or even poor: they own motels, work scams, teach in colleges, breeze through on private funds. Their diaspora is a haphazard, pepperpot dispersal. They have been shaken out, singly, over a huge territory, from Toronto in the North down to a steamy Central American republic. They're in Ann Arbor, Cedar Rocks, Flushing, Manhattan, suburban New Jersey, Atlanta, Florida.

What Raban does not note (typical of *New York Times* reviewers) is Mukherjee's own upper-class background, and the classist and some-what elitist tone in the stories. She overtly endorses the melting-pot concept and regards American society as the most welcoming of any in the world toward the "other." Even when racism is part of her exploration and critique, there is no attempt to place that racism within larger political systems of exploitation and inequality in the United States. Mukherjee gets a lot of mileage out of contrasting her own experiences in Canada, which were more overtly racist than in the United States, and endorses American society as "safer" for peo-ples of color than almost any other in the world. In an interview she remarks:

In the U.S. I feel I am allowed to see myself as an American. It's a self-transformation. Canadians resisted my vigorous attempts to see myself as a Canadian. They exclude, America includes. And everywhere else, in Europe, France, Germany, Switzerland, the newcomer is a guest worker. To a Swede, whatever their egalitarian traditions are, a Burundian becoming a Swede is impossible. To be a Swede, a German, a Frenchman is a quality of soul and mind that takes hundreds of generations.

Mukherjee ignores the fact that, for peoples of color of lower class and educational background than hers, America is not always wel-coming. In Mukherjee's work, the power mechanisms behind system-atic oppressions of particular racial groups remain ultimately mar-ginal. In *Jasmine*, she attempts to engage with the larger systems of domination that sustain racism through her portrayal of Bud and Jane's adopted Vietnamese son, Du. "This country has so many ways of humiliating, of disappointing," notes the narrator as she, in her various selves as Jasmine, Jane, Jase, relates to the outsider/insider status that she shares with Du. Du adopts a hyphenated identity, Vietnamese-American; the narrator wants to shed her past, even use violence if necessary to create a new self: "There are no harmless, compassionate ways to remake oneself. We murder who we were so we can rebirth ourselves in the image of dreams." This denial of a past is as problematic as an exoticizing of the same past that lingers in her memory. In general, Mukherjee stays within a safe "political" space with regard to the politics of race in the United States. This partly accounts for the type of applause that a Western readership and critical establishment gives her.

In conclusion, the realities of expatriation and immigration, of literal and metaphoric exile, of external colonization and imperialism, along with the internal colonization of mental and psychological states, are played out in our contemporary world as never before in history. In a conversation with Günter Grass, Salman Rushdie speaks aptly about the predicament of "the migrant": "This is, after all, the century of the migrant . . . there have never been so many people who ended up elsewhere than where they began, whether by choice or by necessity." This chapter has explored some of the complexities facing postcolonial writers—multiplicities of identities that are necessarily negotiated in terms of "choices" of language or of location, the search for belonging and for an audience. For contemporary writers who have lived through, who almost embody, colonial histories, external and internal colonizations, literal and metaphoric exiles, the politics of representations are mediated partly within market forces, that is, within radically different conditions of cultural production for those who continue to live and work inside their postcolonial societies and for those living outside.

Ketu H. Katrak

# The Book Marketplace II

The literary marketplace has always had three essential elements: authorship, publishing, and audience. Each of these has been shaped by market forces from the very beginning, and each in its own way has mirrored the successive phases of Western capitalism—preindustrial/premodern, industrial/modern, and, in the last fifty years, postindustrial and postmodern. Our immediate concern is with the literary marketplace in the last of these phases, but as we consider how that market has changed since World War II, it will be important to keep in mind that at least some of its features are perennial.

The postmodern period of capitalism has been characterized by rapid technological development, mass production, inflation, and consumerism—factors that, according to Marxist cultural critics from Theodor Adorno onward, have altered the way in which all goods, including cultural goods, are produced, distributed, and consumed. Magalia Larson has suggested that, because postmodern capitalism is a technocracy, it values and rewards expertise, which results in the rise of professionalism in intellectual life. Fredric Jameson argues that in the age of multinational oligopolies, free-market rhetoric is used to discourage the social planning of production, while the "free choice" of consumers is effectively limited to selecting standardized goods on the basis of superficial differences. Per Gedin, a Swedish socialist critic, has concluded that because postmodern capitalism is fundamentally inflationary, it requires growth and therefore inculcates the consumption of quantity rather than quality.

Seen from this point of view, the consequence of postmodern capitalism for the author is that s/he now competes for survival in an environment that is economically demotic but intellectually hieratic. The increasing distance between the popular and the respectable means that although literacy is widespread and many people do still read during their leisure time, the writer who aims for intellectual prestige, formal originality, or artistic merit is likely to have a day job. As for publishing, the foregoing account of the general economy of the postmodern era can easily be adapted to explain those features most frequently cited in discussions of the current state of that industry in America—the emphasis on essentially interchangeable bestsellers, the precarious position of independent bookstores, the declining fortunes of "serious" literature, and the amalgamation of the novel with television and film.

Some in publishing have argued that many of these "changes" are really nothing new: highbrow literature has rarely paid well in its own day because readers have always preferred a more easily digestible fare, and publishers have distributed their resources accordingly. Moreover, the "blockbuster complex," which Thomas Whiteside describes as characteristic of the direction publishing has taken in the last decades of the twentieth century, may in fact have been with us well before the advent of the cause (conglomerate ownership of publishing houses) to which he attributes it. As Gedin himself notes, in 1901 "*Publisher's Weekly* maintained that of the 1,900 titles published during the preceding year, a maximum of 100 had sold more than 10,000 copies. Profits, and in some cases they could be huge, were thus earned on vast printings of a very few books."

A classically trained economist, looking at what Whiteside and others see as new and negative developments in the publishing industry, might see only a demonstration of the well-established capital asset pricing model, which holds that people like to be compensated for risk. The fixed costs for printing a book are relatively high, and the profitability of any one book is extremely uncertain: this generates publishers (since authors cannot afford to print their own books), and it encourages those publishers to diversify their risk across many books. Since any one author needs a publisher more than that publisher needs any one author—unless the author in question is one of the few whose novels always sell well—the author is in a weak bargaining position and will be likely to sign a contract that gives the publisher most of the rights to future profits in exchange for a relatively meager payment up front. If the novel is a success, the conglomerate—which may well own not only the hardcover house that published the book but also the paperback company, the film company, and the television network to which subsidiary rights will have been sold—will reap the reward; if the novel is a failure, the conglomerate will be able to absorb the loss, which is likely to be small in relation to its total assets.

These economic "truths" of publishing may be altered significantly in the near future by desktop publishing and other forms of computer-mediated text dissemination. The fixed costs for these forms of publishing can be very low, which means that authors can afford to become their own publishers: that many have already done so is demonstrated by a look at FactSheet Five, a monthly catalog that lists thousands of limited-circulation alternative and underground magazines, many of them devoted to poetry and fiction. The barriers to alternative publishing have always had as much to do with status as with costs, though, and it remains to be seen whether such desktop literary productions will be regarded as anything but another form of "vanity" publishing. On the other hand, the electronic dissemination of text by academic and scientific publishers (proprietary and nonprofit alike) has already begun, and a number of commercial publishing houses have begun to experiment with using computers to tailor textbooks to the requirements of individual instructors and even to deliver books on-line through commercial database services where one can read part of the book, punch in a credit card number, and download the full text. Assessments of the impact that computers and electronic text will have on authorship, reading, and publishing vary from extreme optimism to extreme pessimism, according to whether the person making the assessment feels that this new technology will necessarily overturn or inevitably reinforce the monopolization of information.

One of the things that has not changed very much over the last two hundred years is the fact that most writers have not been able to subsist on what they earn from writing. In 1986, Paul W. Kingston and Jonathan R. Cole published a book-length study entitled *The Wages of Writing*, based on the results of a 1980 survey of 2241

American authors ("authors" being defined only as those who had published at least one book). According to this survey, in 1979 the median annual income for an author—including book royalties, movie and television work, and payments for newspaper and magazine publication—was $4,775. "Median income" means that 50 percent of all the authors surveyed earned *less* than that amount; fully 25 percent earned less than $1,000 from writing during this year, and only 10 percent had incomes of $45,000 or more. Not surprisingly, almost half of the writers surveyed had other jobs: of these, 36 percent taught at colleges or universities, 20 percent were employed in other professions (as lawyers, doctors, computer programmers, etc.), and 11 percent were editors or publishers. Among those who wrote full time, the median income was only $7,500 (or slightly less than fifty cents per hour). Genre fiction was the most profitable type of writing, with 20 percent of its authors earning more than $50,000 a year—about three times the income enjoyed by authors of adult nonfiction, the next most profitable type of writing.

Kingston and Cole's survey also brings to light some interesting information about race, class, and gender as it correlates with income from writing. According to the data they gathered, race and class were not significant factors in predicting a writer's income, nor was it important where an author lived or even whether the author had a college education. On the other hand, there was a noticeable difference between the income of men and that of women: the median income for male writers was 20 percent higher than that of female writers, and men were almost twice as likely as women to be among the highest-paid authors (that 10 percent who made more than $45,000 a year from writing).

Authors of both genders continue to pursue their craft in spite of the odds against success because they are willing to sacrifice income for the privilege of doing what they enjoy (something economists call "self-exploitation"), and also because unknown authors do sometimes stumble into stardom. Stories of overnight success are common in publishing, even though their significance is more psychological than statistical. One such story is that of Judith Guest, whose novel *Ordinary People* (1976) was submitted to Viking Press, where it was published after a young assistant pulled it out of the "slush pile" of unsolicited manuscripts. Guest's novel became a best-seller and was made into a profitable motion picture by a major studio. At the time that this happened, Viking Press was receiving about fifty unsolicited manuscripts every week, or 2600 a year; *Ordinary People* was the first unsolicited manuscript they had published in ten years—odds of approximately 26,000 to 1. Arthur Kadushin, Lewis A. Coser, and William W. Powell, who tell this story in *Books: The Culture and Commerce of Publishing* (1982), cite a *New York Times Book Review* article that calculated the odds against the publication of unsolicited novels at almost 30,000 to 1. Sixty percent of the trade publishers interviewed by Kadushin, Coser, and Powell said they received over one thousand unsolicited manuscripts every year; the president of one of the larger general trade houses, Doubleday, estimated that his firm receives "an average of ten thousand unsolicited manuscripts a year, out of which three or four may be chosen for publication."

Most literary fiction is not plucked from the slush pile: editors rely on agents, friends, and even other editors to help them find publishable work. But even though an inside connection of some sort may be a necessary condition of publication, it is not a sufficient one. Once a work of fiction finds its way into an editor's hands, what determines its fate? One obvious answer would be, "the editor's taste." Kadushin, Coser, and Powell found that the average editor was white, Protestant, male, and middlebrow in cultural orientation. Although the editors in their sample read a great deal, they also went to the movies often and attended sporting events: the authors' conclusion was that "the needs of the market, not personal preference, seem to rule" where an editor's taste is concerned.

Referring taste to "the needs of the market" only means that one needs to know how editors determine those needs. The answers editors themselves give to this question tend to be somewhat contradictory. Those I have spoken to about the publishing of literary fiction tended to describe themselves as seeking to publish "quality" work, and as being unconcerned with profit: one editor went so far as to express the opinion that no writers of quality go unpublished. According to these editors, literary fiction always loses money, and is routinely subsidized by commercially successful publications. Asked about advertising and market research, an editor I interviewed remarked that "one of the strange things about publishing is that one doesn't have a very good sense for most books of who the audience really is. . . . We don't do any research on it"; another responded by reciting one of the basic credos of publishing, that "the problem with market research in publishing is that every book is a different product: it's not like toothpaste, where once you have a certain brand, every tube is the same as every other tube." In place of planning, editors cite the mysterious exercise of free choice by the audience as the major factor in determining the success or failure of a book.

None of these claims accords very well with the known facts of the publishing industry, though: the profit from best-sellers is at least as likely to be absorbed by the huge advance for the next best-seller as it is to subsidize "serious" but commercially unsuccessful works of fiction, and commercial considerations do enter very directly into all aspects of editorial decision making. According to the survey by Kadushin, Coser, and Powell, decision-making meetings at major publishing houses were attended by the editor in chief (85 percent of the time), publisher (75 percent), sales staff (63 percent), president (58 percent), managing editor (50 percent), marketing staff (46 percent), production staff (27 percent), assistant editors (24 percent), and, last, representatives of the parent corporation (16 percent). Sales and marketing people tend to take a less mystified view of what they do, and there is ample evidence that, in many cases, it is these people who cast the deciding votes.

The pressure to consider sales has always been part of publishing, but there are indications that it now enters into the process much earlier than it once did: Roger Straus III explains that, whereas traditionally the decision to publish came first and questions about how to find the audience for that book came later, now marketing considerations are likely to determine whether the book will be published at all. Editors themselves are not immune from these pressures, especially since in many houses editorial "productivity" is now a condition of employment. As Morton Janklow candidly observed, "For good or ill, the old style of editor and publisher is slowly passing from the scene. Now there's a much more energetic, more driving— and, I must say, more profit-oriented—publisher arising."

It should be added, though, that prestige has its own market value, and the prestigious author may be worth publishing even if his or her books are unlikely to sell many copies or be made into movies. Kadushin, Coser, and Powell found that 70 percent of the editors they interviewed listed the prestige of an author as either "critical" or "very important" in deciding whether to publish. Publishing authors of certified literary merit has both personal and professional value for an editor: personally, it helps to justify the time spent on other, less estimable projects; professionally, it benefits the editor's reputation with authors and other editors. This value may be intangible, but it can be indirectly profitable, since authors who are themselves commercially viable may be more inclined to publish with a house that lists a number of artistically renowned authors among its clientele.

Deciding what to publish is only half the battle: getting that book to the reader is the other half. The major problem facing the novel has always been to identify and reach its audience, and in America this problem has been exacerbated by the historical lack of an adequate distribution system. The size of this country, the dispersion of its population, and the practical difficulties of transporting goods across long distances at reasonable costs have always posed a problem for American publishers. In the nineteenth century, the advent of a railroad system began to solve some of these problems, but even then a nationwide marketing system did not develop.

As James L. W. West points out in his *American Authors and the Literary Marketplace Since 1900* (1988), the absence of such a system was a determining factor in the success of "two of the most important innovations in book distribution during this century—paperbacks and book clubs." Both of these methods of "recycling" the texts originally produced by trade publishing houses took hold during the twenties and thirties "because trade publishers could not exploit the national market through conventional means"; the solution hit upon by paperback publishers was to use the existing magazine distribution network (this is why we have paperbacks in airports, drugstores, and supermarkets), and book clubs solved the problem by using the United States postal service. Book clubs were opposed by trade publishers, often in court, until the 1950s; by that time, clubs like the Book-of-the-Month Club (founded in 1926) and the Literary Guild (founded in 1927) had become ineradicable features of the publishing landscape, in large part because of their success in reaching a targeted group of paying readers through direct mailing. Modern paperback publishing, which began with the establishment of Pocket Books in

1939 and Bantam Books in 1945, received a critical boost in its rise to power in the literary marketplace at about the same time. During World War II, the Council on Books in Wartime (founded by Farrar, Norton, and other leading publishers) issued more than 123.5 million copies of paperback books to servicemen, in the Armed Services and Overseas editions.

The success of both paperbacks and book clubs is part of what many have seen as the commercialization of publishing during the last fifty years. A number of people, notably Ted Solotaroff and Thomas Whiteside, have cited the so-called blockbuster phenomenon as a principal culprit in this process. Beginning in the 1960s, publishers started paying huge amounts for the rights to potential bestsellers: a major part of this sudden inflation in contract prices has been the rise in the importance of subsidiary rights. Kadushin et al. observe:

> In the nineteenth century, a hardcover trade book's profit was determined by the number of copies sold to individual readers. Today, it is usually determined by the sale of subsidiary rights to movie companies, book clubs, foreign publishers, or paperback reprint houses.

Subsidiary rights can also involve television, merchandise (T-shirts, dolls, etc.), and other tie-ins; in fact, the sales of the book itself often depend on the successful promotion and sale of subsidiary items and productions. The result of this is that the direct sale of books to individuals is far less important than it once was—a situation analogous to that in professional sports, where (as West points out) gate receipts have been overshadowed by the sale of television rights. In the words of Richard E. Snyder, chairman of the board of Simon and Schuster, books "are the software of the television and movie media," and, in fact, one-third of the movies produced each year are based on books. Richard Kostelanetz gives the worst-case account of the influence of subsidiary rights on editorial decision making when he says that "suitability to the mass media determines not only whether a novel will be offered to a large audience, but whether it will be published at all."

It is not coincidental that the ascendency of subsidiary rights was established at the same time conglomerates began buying up publishing houses. Charles Newman, in *The Post-Modern Aura* (1985), records that

as of 1982, more than 50 percent of all mass market sales were accounted for by five publishers, and ten publishing firms accounted for more than 85 percent. Nine firms accounted for more than 50 percent of "general interest" book sales. The largest publishers in the country are Time, Inc., Gulf and Western, M.C.A., Times Mirror, Inc., The Hearst Corp., C.B.S. and Newhouse publications, conglomerates which all have heavy stakes in mass-market entertainment media, such as radio, book clubs, cable TV, pay TV, motion pictures, video discs, and paperback books. All of them have become significant factors only in the last ten years.

Gulf and Western, which was originally a manufacturer of auto parts, now owns Paramount Pictures, Simon and Schuster, and Pocket Books; Warner Communications, a major producer of films and records and the part owner of the third-largest cable-TV system in the country, is also the owner of Warner Books and Little, Brown; MCA, the owner of Universal Pictures, is also the owner of the hardcover publishing houses G. P. Putnam's Sons, Richard Marek, and Coward, McCann & Geoghegan, and the paperback houses Berkley Publishing and Jove publications.

Another very important force shaping the literary marketplace in the late twentieth century has been mass-market book retailers like B. Dalton and Waldenbooks (the latter now owned by K Mart). Whereas, in 1958, independents accounted for 72 percent of all bookstore sales, by 1985 the bookstore chains had almost half of the market. In some cases, these chains have an influence on the publishing process that goes well beyond retailing: with every cash register hooked up to a computerized inventory system, B. Dalton has been able to track the "item velocity" of each book it sells, and it provides that information to publishers in the *B. Dalton Merchandise Bulletin*—"one of the most influential publications in the entire book-publishing business," according to Whiteside. Chain stores such as B. Dalton are divided into metropolitan stores and suburban shopping-mall outlets; a work of literary fiction may well be carried in the metropolitan stores, but if it is judged (by the buyers at the chain) unlikely to sell in the shopping malls, this directly affects the size of the printing that book will receive. An informal survey of publishers at the 1987 American Booksellers Association convention showed, among other things, that the mean for book sales was 10,000 copies, with sales of 70,000 or more copies generally considered necessary to place a book on a major best-seller list: unless a book is carried in the suburban outlets, sales beyond 10,000 copies are unlikely. The chain bookstores also have an effect on what books are kept in print: shelf-life is short in these stores, for the simple reason that "item velocity" drops precipitously as books move to the backlist: the same ABA convention survey showed that, on average, 91 percent of a book's total sales were registered in the first year.

In the opinion of some, the influence of the chain bookstores has been more significant than that of conglomerate ownership in publishing. Richard E. Snyder argues that the chains "serve a different community of book readers from any that the book business has ever had before. . . . the elitism of the book market doesn't exist any more." According to Snyder, "the minute you get into the suburbs, where ninety percent of the chain stores are located, you serve the customers, mainly women, the way you would serve them in a drugstore or a supermarket." While some have decried the supermarket approach to selling books as a major contributing factor in the decline of "quality" publishing, Snyder sees the "book supermarket" as an essentially positive development: "Sometimes a publisher will publish a commercial book and that might be sold to Waldenbooks and some people might say that's bad. I say it's good—better that people read a commercial book than read nothing. It's a step up."

However distasteful Snyder's endorsement of the literary supermarket may be to some, his description of that supermarket's customer—nonelite and usually female—matches the historical profile of the audience for the novel itself. Although reading has a long tradition as an activity of the elite, the history of novel reading is linked to the more recent emergence of an educated middle class. Ian Watt, Lewis Coser, and others have pointed out that the rise of the novel in England during the mid-eighteenth century was due, in large part, to the broadening distribution of wealth: as the numbers of the moderately wealthy grew, there was a corresponding increase in leisure time, literacy, and education, all of which were conditions favorable to the novel. The rise of the novel is also attributable to what might be called the rise of domesticity. The literal expansion of the domestic sphere is part of this: reading is by nature a solitary activity, and larger living quarters allowed individuals the privacy in which to pursue it. In our culture, the domestic sphere has traditionally been the domain of women, and middle-class women, although generally excluded from the worlds of business and formal education during the eighteenth and much of the nineteenth century, were increasingly literate and leisured, and made up a majority of novel readers during this period (as they still do, according to Snyder and others in the publishing industry).

The fortunes of the novel are linked not only economically but also ideologically to the fortunes of women. According to William Charvat, American readers of the late eighteenth century consumed quantities of reprinted British novels, many of them written "by women working in anonymous secrecy" for a publisher who paid them a flat fee; this anonymity did not prevent novels from being identified as a form of entertainment by and for women, and American literary critics were nearly unanimous in denouncing the triviality and vulgarity of the genre, effectively depriving the novel of cultural status despite (or perhaps because of) its popularity.

These same considerations obviously made writing novels an unattractive profession in America—especially for male authors concerned with prestige. In explaining how authorship became a viable profession in this country, Charvat concentrates on the economics of the novel: by the 1830s, he says, American authors had begun to write on subjects of broad appeal, American readers had the money to buy their books, and American publishers had the means to deliver them. But he also notes, in passing, that it was the financial success of British authors such as Byron and Scott that finally raised the cultural status of authorship in an "increasingly pecuniary" American society. It would appear, then, that as long as novel writing was regarded as the occupation of women, its cultural status (as well as the remuneration afforded its authors) remained low.

Recent discussions of the literary canon, and particularly of the American canon, have made it clear that the laurels for "serious" literature have been awarded disproportionately to men. This is not because women have not written novels, or have written only bad novels; rather, it is because both the writing and the reading of novels by women has been consigned to the realm of popular (that is, disposable) culture. In the twentieth century, the bifurcation of the novel into "serious" and "popular" literature has been accelerated not only by mass marketing (which has increased the disparity in size between the audiences for these two categories of cultural production, even though it may not actually have diminished the audience for literary fiction), but also by professionalization, which has provided a positive incentive for certain (mostly male) writers to make their fiction less accessible to the amateur reader.

This account of the current state of literature is likely to meet the same objection from liberal humanists that the Marxist cultural critic's and the classical economist's would, namely, that "the mysterious force of all serious art is the extent to which it always exceeds the requirements of the market" (in Charles Newman's words). But even the liberal humanist would have to admit that the struggle of "serious" literature in America has always been in large part a struggle for an audience, and thus has been a struggle with the marketplace and its requirements. The two types of fiction most frequently identified as postmodern conveniently mark the poles of contemporary artistic response to these requirements. One is the response of writing fiction that is deliberately unmarketable: Charles Newman calls this sort of writing

a true future fiction for an audience which not only does not exist, but *cannot* exist unless it progresses with the same utopian technical advancement of expertise, the same accelerating value, which informs the verbal dynamic of the novels written for them. This represents an act of ultimate aggression against the contemporary audience.

The other pole of response is represented by postmodern fiction that incorporates and even celebrates mass-market commodities and mass-culture icons. This adaptation to the market may have survival value from an economic point of view, but it is likely to arouse the contempt of intellectuals:

By becoming kitsch, art panders to the confusion which reigns in the "taste" of the patrons. Artists, gallery owners, critics, and the public wallow together in the "anything goes," and the epoch is one of slackening. But this realism of the "anything goes" is in fact that of money; in the absence of aesthetic criteria, it remains possible and useful to assess the value of works of art according to the profits they yield. Such realism accommodates all tendencies, just as capital accommodates all "needs," providing that the tendencies and needs have purchasing power. As for taste, there is no need to be delicate when one speculates or entertains oneself.

This tirade by Jean-François Lyotard against kitsch eclecticism and commercial realism clearly demonstrates that even those who reject the marketplace still define art in relation to it. The identification of literary merit with opposition to the marketplace derives from the tradition of the historical avant-garde: Flaubert's remark, in 1852, that "between the crowd and ourselves no bond exists" is an early but characteristic rejection of philistinism. This attitude intensified as the marketplace and its cultural influence expanded: Flaubert went on to sigh, "alas for the crowd; alas for us, especially," but sixty years later, Ezra Pound seems to have felt no such regret when he remarked to Harriet Monroe, "So far as I personally am concerned the public can go to the devil."

The artist's claim of autonomy may be one of long standing, but it takes on new significance in an age of professionalism. As Magalia Larson points out, professional autonomy always derives from exclusivity, and "the secrecy and mystery which surround the creative process maximize the self-governance conceded to experts"; Louis Menand, in his study of T. S. Eliot's literary reputation, demonstrates that Eliot was instrumental in teaching both academics and artists that such self-governance depends on establishing "the experts' monopoly of knowledge." Seen in this light, "Art for Art's sake" is a paradigmatically professional credo, since every profession

aggrandizes itself most effectively by identifying with a higher standard than self-interest. This double motive is reflected in the argument all professions offer as their justification, the argument that in order to serve the needs of others properly, professions must be accountable only to themselves.

In the words of Eliot himself, "professionalism in art [is] . . . hard work on style with singleness of purpose" — in short, literary professionalism manifests itself in artistic formalism and New Criticism, both based on the doctrine of aesthetic autonomy. Discussing this same "autonomy aesthetic," Peter Burger points out that it "contains a definition of the function of art: it is conceived as a social realm that is set apart from the means-end rationality of daily bourgeois existence. Precisely for this reason, it can criticize such an existence." And, in fact, the service that both art and criticism have offered the twentieth century has been a constitutively professional one: the analysis of culture from an allegedly disinterested and uninvolved perspective.

The claim to an aloofness from the marketplace is a dubious one at best, not least because the professionalization of "serious" literature has coincided with the movement of the writers of that literature into the academy. As the founding editor of *Perspective* magazine recalls,

> The generation of writers that shaped twentieth century literature (Eliot, Pound, Hemingway, Faulkner, etc.) earned their livings outside of Academia. In the forties, there was a mass migration of writers into the universities as teachers of courses in "creative writing."

This dating of the professionalization of creative writing coincides with a marked growth in academic publication: sociologist Diana Crane's "analysis of the growth of publications in English literature from 1923 to 1967 reveals a linear pattern of growth until 1939, followed by a very slow rate of exponential growth (doubling every seventeen years rather than every ten years as in the basic science literature)." Some would say, as Per Gedin does, that the result of this coincidence has been "the development of a literary activity which in many cases exists only for the critics."

In "The Shaping of a Canon: U.S. Fiction, 1960–1975" (*Politics of Letters* [1987]), Richard Ohmann argues that, in addition to sales and major reviews, attention from intellectuals (who in twentieth-century America tend to be academics) and inclusion on the college syllabus also play a crucial role in establishing literary merit. A book must sell well in order to survive in the short run, regardless of its merit, but a book must also receive the imprimatur of academia if it is to survive in the long run. Ohmann sees inclusion on the college syllabus as the "all but necessary" form of that imprimatur: "the college classroom and its counterpart, the academic journal, have become in our society the final arbiters of literary merit, and even of survival [for literature]."

According to Gerald Graff, there was no such thing as a course in the modern novel until the very end of the nineteenth century, and it was not until the middle of our own century that even "serious" contemporary fiction would have been considered an acceptable subject for academic study. It has only been in the last twenty years that English departments have routinely offered courses in contemporary literature, and only in the last ten that this has established itself as a field in its own right within the discipline. New Direction's James Laughlin corroborates Graff's account when he recalls:

At Harvard in '33, believe it or not, there still were no courses being given in [Eliot, Pound, Yeats, and Joyce]. They were not yet accepted. . . . in those days, the Professor of Rhetoric . . . would get so angry if the name of Eliot or Pound were mentioned in his course that he would ask the student to leave the room.

Laughlin and Graff (and many others) again point to World War II as the turning point: after the war, Graff says, "an institution that had once seen itself as the bulwark of tradition against vulgar and immoral contemporaneity [became] the disseminator and explainer of the most recent trends." Harold Rosenberg, in a 1960 essay entitled "Everyman a Professional" (*The Tradition of the New* [1982]), offers the broadest cultural explanation for this shift when he says that in an age of specialization teaching has become a matter of

popularization, which acts as journalistic or educational intercessor between the isolated mind of the theorist-technician and the fragmented psyche of the public, [and] is the most powerful profession of our time . . . gaining daily in numbers, importance and finesse.

In his essay "After the Book?" from *On Difficulty, and Other Essays* (1978), George Steiner goes so far as to suggest that reading itself is splitting into real and pseudo literacy, the former practiced by a small elite mostly consisting of academics, the latter describing the limits of the practice of reading in the culture at large. In Steiner's view, there is nothing wrong with this, except that the elite today no longer has the power or receives the respect that it deserves. On the substance of Steiner's point, Ted Solotaroff agrees, remarking with regret on "the widening gulf between the publishing culture and the literary or even literate one. For if the former is advancing steadily into the mass culture, the latter is retreating to a significant extent from it into the confines of the university." Solataroff does cite the influx of writers into academia as a solution of sorts to the "age-old" problem of the starving artist, but he sees a danger in the increasingly common career-path of the writer from MFA student to teacher of writing, with little adult experience outside the university.

Indeed, many of the authors discussed by these critics have, like the 36 percent of the writers surveyed by Kingston and Cole, spent all or most of their adult lives in the academy. They are also mostly male: though he doesn't point it out, less than 20 percent of the authors whom Ohmann calculates to have made it into the "intermediate stage in canon formation" are women. Moreover, as the discussion of professionalism in literature might lead us to expect, the authors named are frequently those whose fiction emphasizes formal elements, sometimes at the expense of narrative.

In *Distinction: A Social Critique of the Judgement of Taste* (1984), Pierre Bourdieu argues that "to assert the autonomy of production is to give primacy to that of which the artist is master, i.e., form, manner, style, rather than the 'subject', the external referent, which involves subordination to functions—even if only the most elementary one, that of representing, signifying, saying something"; this attitude of detachment from function is, he suggests, "the paradoxical product of conditioning by negative economic necessities—a life of ease—that tends to induce an active distance from necessity." By contrast, those who cannot afford this distance tend to require representationalism and apply "the schemes of the ethos, which pertain in the ordinary circumstances of life, to legitimate works of art, [resulting in] a systematic reduction of the things of art to the things of life." In short, Bourdieu contends that our hierarchy of taste, which values formalist sublimation and detachment more highly than "vulgar" and unselfconscious realism, serves to reproduce the hierarchy of class.

It also reproduces a hierarchy of gender, and perpetuates the association of the popular (instinctive, unreflective) with the feminine, and the difficult (deliberate, conscious) with the masculine. In his essay "The Publishing Culture and the Literary Culture" (1984) bemoaning the increasing distance between what is commercially viable and what is artistically valuable, Ted Solotaroff finds hope in the fact that

women writers today have a genuine subject and a passionate constituency, and a really gifted writer—an Alice Walker, Alice Munro, or Anne Tyler, a Lynne Schwartz or a Marilynne Robinson—is able to surmount the obstacles that the conglomerates and the bookstore chains and the mass culture itself place between her and her readers.

Solotaroff's remarks, and his examples, suggest that in order to overcome the barrier between literary merit and marketability, even "really gifted writers" must still be realists, and must appeal to "a passionate constituency"—code for "women readers," as they are perceived in publishing. This reading may seem to infer too much about the role of gender stereotypes in the literary marketplace, but a prominent woman editor with whom I spoke suggested that "difficult" fiction is generally written by men and for men, while women writers reach a larger audience (of women) by addressing themselves more directly to spiritual concerns. The flip side of this essentialism is that women who write experimental fiction are likely to be told by editors that their work is not what women want to read—a stricture that may be intensified when the author in question belongs to a "spiritual" race as well as a "spiritual" gender, as bell hooks's experience demonstrates:

[The] creative writing I do which I consider to be most reflective of a postmodern oppositional sensibility—work that is abstract, fragmented, nonlinear narrative—is constantly rejected by editors and publishers who tell me it does not conform to the type of writing they think black women should be doing or the type of writing they believe will sell.

In sum, the literary marketplace is, for better or worse, the most reliable indicator of how we value literature. Literary taste, literary status, and literary production are all determined to a significant extent by the economics of that market and, in turn, by the hierarchy of values that are expressed in those economics. In the postmodern era, publishing has become part of a multinational and multimedia marketplace for narrative, and therefore it competes with movies, television, and even "nonfictional" formats such as TV news, which increasingly adopts the trappings of narrative to attract its viewers. In this environment, the most profitable type of novel is that which can be easily translated into other media, namely, the realist narrative. The best-paid authors of such narrative are disproportionately male, as are those who manage the mass market for narrative, but the product is, especially in the case of the novel, marketed to women— often on the basis of essentialist stereotypes of the proclivities and desires of that gendered market. "Serious" fiction that is nonrealist in its aesthetic orientation is prestigious but unprofitable, and those who write it tend to be men confined to the academy, which is the only place that their professionalism does have a market value. In addition to reflecting our hierarchy of gender, the literary marketplace reflects our presuppositions about race and our predispositions toward class, not so much in who gets published as in what gets published and what gets preserved—and it is the difference between these last two that may tell us most about how literary value is determined.

John M. Unsworth

# Postmodern Fiction

The "post" in "postmodernism" signifies both a temporal condition (postmodernism is a period after modernism and thus in certain respects an evolution from it) and an attitude of resistance (postmodernism is a turn away from modernism and thus in certain respects a radical break with it). Postmodernism is thus both a late modernism and an antimodernism. Although this definition seems peculiarly oxymoronic, literary history offers precedents, one of them being modernism itself. "Modernism," as the word is used to define the major avant-garde movements of the first half of the twentieth century, is both a continuation of and a radical break from the dominant literary modes of the nineteenth century—in the case of prose fiction, the modes of realism and naturalism. Although as a descriptive term "postmodern" seems particularly vulnerable to commonsense cavils (how could anything be after, or more modern than, the modern?), "the postmodern novel" has in critical usage a relatively clear range of reference, denoting a group of works and foregrounding the themes and narrative strategies that these works share.

Like the modernist novel, the postmodern novel can be described as an avant-garde tendency within a literary period, in this case the post-1945, or contemporary, period. It cannot be called simply *the* avant-garde tendency because during this period there have been various kinds of innovative fiction that make even more demands on commensurately more specialized readers (see Robert Boyers's chapter below on the avant-garde novel). To advance an apparent paradox, the postmodern novel is the mainstream avant-garde novel of the contemporary period, with "mainstream" here a function of the material conditions of production—of how a book is published, distributed, and advertised. Of the twelve major novelists discussed in this chapter, only two, Kathy Acker and Joanna Russ, have published a substantial part of their work with small presses. Whatever the claims for the subversiveness or marginality of writers like Thomas Pynchon, Donald Barthelme, and Don DeLillo, their works have always been widely available and widely reviewed. To cite one of the most evident examples of how relatively established this experimental genre is, Pynchon's notoriously long and difficult magnum opus, *Gravity's Rainbow,* was a Book-of-the-Month Club selection.

The "mainstream" character of postmodern fictional innovation has other implications. The American postmodern novel is widely perceived—and criticized—as a white male genre. It is significant that the two writers mentioned above as the only major novelists in the canon to have published a substantial part of their work with small presses are also the only two women novelists. Some feminist critics have gone on to claim that the postmodern novel is essentially masculinist or misogynist, inasmuch as a number of the most famous works, especially those produced in the 1950s and 1960s, are preoccupied with aggressive, often violent male sexual behavior and the denigration of female characters. It seems unlikely, however, that instances of identifiable sexism are necessarily connected with postmodern experimentation per se, especially given the fact that other kinds of novels produced by male writers in the early contemporary period also celebrate aggressive male sexuality and present denigrating images of women. Nor is the relative scarcity of women in the American postmodern canon by itself evidence that American women are not writing postmodern novels—much less that they are "not interested" in stylistic and structural innovation; it is only evidence that such novels are not getting the publication and publicity given to the male postmodernists—and, for that matter, to female writers of realist fiction. Furthermore, postmodernism is to some extent a matter of packaging. When in his 1979 essay "The Literature of Replenishment" John Barth drew up a list of international postmodern fiction writers, he included twenty-three men and only one woman, the

French "new novelist" Nathalie Sarraute. But Barth's tentative catalog primarily reflects his own affinities and range of reading, in that it includes only those works already identified with high culture. It mentions no "genre" novels, for example, although some of the most exciting experimentation of the period was going on within the field of science fiction: Joanna Russ and Samuel R. Delany (one of only two African American writers in the canon—the other is Ishmael Reed) are science fiction writers whose work has "crossed over" into the more reputable category of postmodernism. A number of experimental novels by women are also explicitly aligned with the feminist critique of ideology and published in feminist series, usually by small presses: Russ's *The Female Man*, for example, was initially published as a science fiction novel, then reissued as a feminist novel; only recently has it become established as a postmodern work.

As Cornel West has suggested, postmodern culture is by definition multinational. English-language postmodern fiction, however, is a phenomenon most often associated with the United States, where it appears inevitably engaged with the question of what it might mean to be American in an epoch variously summed up in the paradigms of the global village, the cybernetic revolution, postindustrial capitalism, the triumph of kitsch, the reign of media-ocrity, and the new populism. Such American novels at the center of the postmodern canon as Vonnegut's *Slaughterhouse-Five*, DeLillo's *Libra*, Coover's *The Public Burning*, Reed's *Mumbo Jumbo*, and Pynchon's *Gravity's Rainbow* are fundamentally concerned with the construction of recent American history and ideology. Other key postmodern novels—Nabokov's *Lolita, Pale Fire*, and *Ada*, Barthelme's *Snow White* and *The Dead Father*, Barth's *Giles Goat-Boy* and *Sabbatical*, Acker's *Kathy Goes to Haiti* and *Don Quixote*, and Russ's *The Female Man*—are less overtly concerned with historical data but undertake sustained critiques of social and cultural presuppositions.

The American postmodern novel is thus not in any obvious respects the disengaged, aestheticist, and ultimately narcissistic project denounced by such detractors as Charles Newman and the late John Gardner, nor is it fundamentally ahistorical and superficial, as Fredric Jameson has suggested. The continuing controversy over whether postmodern fiction can have moral or political implications revolves around the question of whether only certain conventions of representation—realist or, on occasion, modernist conventions—are capable of evoking "real world" concerns. The defining condition of postmodernist textual strategies is of course that they disrupt precisely these conventions.

During the 1960s and early 1970s, theorists of the postmodern like Julia Kristeva and Philippe Sollers argued that the undermining of established narrative conventions is not only formally but also politically subversive or even revolutionary. The reason, they maintained, is that conventions of representation are inextricably linked to ideology, so that to disturb accepted and seemingly natural modes of writing is to raise questions about whether accepted and seemingly natural ideas—for instance, about the fundamental sameness of "human" experience and nature—are not similarly arbitrary and culturebound. Although few critics now hold that formally disruptive writing is by definition politically disruptive writing, this analysis helps clarify how formal disruption can be *aligned* with ideological critique and why the consequent "difficulty" of certain politically engaged postmodern novels is not necessarily willful obscurantism.

These observations suggest that postmodern fiction has a certain amount in common with the various poststructuralist theories of the contemporary period. Both postmodern fictional practice and poststructuralist critical theory tend to question a commonsense view of language as simply the vehicle that relays the world to the mind, or as an ideally transparent medium guaranteeing the unequivocal presence of meaning in efficacious discourse. Both postmodernism and poststructuralism treat literary language as inseparable from the discourses of praxis and power and deny that literary language—or any language—can be disinterested and value-neutral. Both assert a fundamental continuity between text and world, not because texts reflect or imitate reality but because reality is inevitably experienced as *textualized*—that is, as already-interpreted within a social and cultural construction of what the world is and how it works. Indeed, one of the great themes of postmodern fiction is the world as text, as a system of codes already constructed by shadowy others for unguessable purposes. In such fiction, the experience of characters trying to interpret the text in which they are enmeshed replicates the experience of the reader, who is trying to interpret the text in which these characters appear.

Such metafictional loops, in which readers enact—and are similarly entrapped within—searches undertaken by characters, are among the most distinctive structural features of the postmodern novel. They indicate how in the postmodern novel structural features are characteristically wound up with thematic features. They also epitomize one of the primary effects of postmodern writing, an effect partly implied by the notion of a convention-breaking genre. This is the effect of textual mastery. To read a postmodern novel is to be surprised and frequently to be overwhelmed; it is to have expectations thwarted and strategies of interpretation anticipated, attacked, parodied, or simply taken on as topics of discussion within the fiction. Although postmodern novels are not invulnerable to critical mastery, they do actively resist those modes of criticism that aim to get the better of a work, to expose its latent and by implication inadvertent presuppositions. In opposition to the premise that a strong reading can master a novel, postmodern novels tend to initiate the agonistic struggle with their implied audiences, inviting tactics that will lead to narrative impasses and cognitive confusion.

Literary categories rarely have essential definitions—that is, definitions identifying the one quality that makes the mode or genre what it is and separates it from every other mode or genre. For example, the judgment that a given work is realist or modernist is largely a matter of degree and emphasis; moreover, it is based on "family resemblances" within the genre, in which, as in the case of biological relatives, each member of a given category possesses some but not all of the family features. There is thus nothing anomalous in the fact that no one structural or stylistic feature is present in all postmodern novels and absent from all novels that are not postmodern. The metafictional loop noted above, in which the activity of the reader interpreting a novel doubles the interpreting activities of characters within the novel, is an example. This kind of effect, in which an aspect of the fiction is represented on some embedded level within the fiction, occurs frequently in postmodern novels but is not limited to them (Patricia Waugh cites Cervantes's *Don Quixote* as an early instance of metafiction), nor do all postmodern novels have conspicuous metafictional components: the works of John Hawkes, Ishmael

Reed, and Joanna Russ, for example, are not in any obvious respects about writing or reading.

But although metafictional strategies do not define the postmodern novel, they are very pronounced in much of the writing usually identified as postmodern. One of the most extreme manifestations of the metafictional tendency is the *mise-en-abîme,* in which a recognizable image of the primary text is embedded within that text. Nabokov's *Pale Fire,* which incorporates within a text-and-commentary format a long poem called *Pale Fire,* and Coover's *The Universal Baseball Association,* in which the main character obsessively develops and documents an imaginary system called the Universal Baseball Association, are particularly interesting examples, which will be discussed at some length in the next section. Such strategies of embedding lead *en abîme,* "into the abyss," both because they are recursive— Nabokov's Kinbote (or Botkin) and Coover's John Henry Waugh are reflecting quasi-parodically the reader's efforts to make sense of the works in which they occur—and because they have the potential for infinite regress—Kinbote indicates at the close of *Pale Fire* that he might well disguise himself as Nabokov and write novels, among them, presumably, this one; in the last chapter of *The Universal Baseball Association* Waugh's imaginary baseball players begin to write competing histories of the Universal Baseball Association.

Postmodern metafictional situations tend to differ from modernist metafictional situations in emphasizing the reading rather than the writing of fiction. The distinction suggests a fundamentally altered view of the artist and of literary creation. In postmodern fiction, even when a protagonist is engaged in producing a text, this writing is represented not as original creation but as a kind of rereading. John Barth maintained in "The Literature of Exhaustion" (1967) that the writer in the contemporary period is confronted with the "used-upness" of all the viable stories, but such "exhaustion" becomes in the terms proposed by this argument an impetus to write self-consciously postmodern fiction; indeed, much of Barth's own fiction dramatizes the process or product of reinscription and raises the mechanics and motivations of narrative to central importance. Moreover, if to write is invariably to replicate what one has read and thus to reread, to read is also to rewrite. A recurring dilemma in Thomas Pynchon's novels is that to read history for its meaning is also to postulate connections among events in order to *make* them mean something. Characters are constantly faced with the question of whether they are reading a historical script that preexists their critical endeavors or whether they have in important respects constructed this script through their desire to read it and their expectation that it will prove readable. In Pynchon's fictional universes, the distinction between reading and writing is both wholly untenable and wholly necessary.

Another metafictional strategy not restricted to postmodern novels but prominent within them is the introduction of a figure who is not only a persona of the author but a persona of the author *of this book:* in John Barth's *Chimera,* "John Barth" time-travels to talk with Scheherazade about the used-upness of all the viable stories; a minor character in Kurt Vonnegut's *Slaughterhouse-Five* is suddenly identified as Vonnegut himself: "That was I. That was me. That was the author of this book." This kind of strategy is in Brian McHale's words "frame-breaking," in that it intrudes a heretofore "factual" being into a "fictional" landscape. Like the postmodernist use of the *mise-en-abîme,* this postmodernist use of the authorial persona disrupts both realist and modernist strategies of reading, in that it resists the reader's desire to assign a textual phenomenon to a particular ontological level, such as the level of real-world fact, fictional "fact," or fictional "fiction."

To break narrative frames by allowing one ontological level of the plot to intrude on another ontological level is to introduce radical instability into a work of fiction. Inasmuch as this kind of frame-breaking is one of the most important features of postmodern writing, it aligns the postmodern novel with a kind of radical undecidability, a suspicion that the question "What's the real story here?" cannot be answered in any satisfying way — satisfying, that is, in terms of the sorts of expectations bred by realist and modernist fiction. The "real story" is unavailable in the face of contradictions or divergent accounts, not simply because it is unknowable (in which case there is a real story, but readers don't have access to it — a familiar situation in such modernist fiction as William Faulkner's *Absalom, Absalom!*), but because there is no single "real" in the story, no sanctioned reality with reference to which other stories can situate themselves as distorted, fictionalized, partial, biased, hallucinated, or simply lying. To put it another way, discrepancies in a postmodern story resist being *naturalized* as functions of a perceiver—"the" world of the fiction itself is irreducibly multiple. The character Stephen Albert, in Jorge Luis Borges's influential *ficcione* "The Garden of Forking Paths" (1945), describes a situation in which multiple possibilities are realized simultaneously: "[The writer] thus *creates* various figures, various times which start others that will in their turn branch out and bifurcate in other times. This is the cause of the contradiction in the novel." The intimation of such parallel realities leads to the impasse at the conclusion of Pynchon's *The Crying of Lot 49,* presents irresolvable counter-stories in Vonnegut's *Slaughterhouse-Five,* explodes the convention of embedding in the last chapter of Coover's *The Universal Baseball Association,* and ultimately dissolves the science fiction convention of time-travel in Russ's *The Female Man.*

Postmodern novels characteristically violate conventions of genre and decorum as well, and violate both inasmuch as they fuzz the border between high and low culture. For example, poetry can invade the narrative prose without explanation, as in the blank-verse reinscriptions of public documents in *The Public Burning,* or the invasion may be explained in ways that seem flagrantly inadequate or inappropriate: Pynchon's characters, for instance, regularly burst into song. Nonfictional texts may be embedded in the fiction with apparent haphazardness, like the extracts from histories and memoirs in Ishmael Reed's *Mumbo Jumbo,* or may take the form of disruptive direct address, as when, in the middle of Donald Barthelme's *Snow White,* the reader encounters a questionnaire that begins, " 1. Do you like the story so far? Yes ( ) No ( )." Ostensible fictions may carry their own commentaries: for example, Delany's novels have long appendixes, which occupy up to a third of the pages in the book and which link elements of the story to issues in anthropological and linguistic theory.

Postmodern novels also tend to violate conventions of decorum in their use of allusion and documentation. Mythic and literary allusions occur in deflating contexts (Slothrop in *Gravity's Rainbow* compares himself with the questing hero Tannhäuser but promptly appends the epithet "the Singing Nincompoop"; John Henry Waugh in *The Universal Baseball Association* initiates a new covenant by vomiting a rainbow of partially digested pizza over his beer-flooded game) or are dragged in with hyperbolic gratuitousness (one of the dwarfs in *Snow White* smokes a cigar "that stretches from Mont St. Michel and Chartres to under the volcano"). The range of allusion embraces the texts of mass culture as well as high culture. Postmodern novels may quote or allude to popular magazines, newspapers, advertising slogans and jingles, brand names, radio and television programs, movies, and computer games. The massing of allusions often occurs as part of a tendency to parade the apparatus of research rather than subordinating documentary evidence as background or setting. One of the most extreme manifestations of this tendency is the catalog, in which data of varying degrees of relevance and importance are simply listed. Less radically, a number of postmodern novels are *encyclopedic,* in the sense of comprehending and schematizing the knowledge that defines the period in which they are written. For instance, Pynchon's *Gravity's Rainbow* and DeLillo's *Ratner's Star* make extensive use of scientific and mathematical information; Delany's Nevèrÿon series puts mathematics together with semiotics; novels by Reed, Vonnegut, DeLillo, Barth, Coover, and Pynchon are explicitly concerned with historiography as well as history. In their amassing of information and theories as to how this information is organized, as well as in other respects, postmodern novels may represent the flowering of the tradition of Menippean satire, which began in late antiquity. According to narrative theorist Mikhail Bakhtin, Menippean satire is a seriocomic genre that mixes modes and comprehends multiple styles and voices. It deals with the "ultimate questions" of philosophy, involves radical structural and stylistic experiment, and incorporates improprieties and contemporary satire. Bakhtin's analysis places the postmodern novel in a long tradition, paradoxically establishing its continuity through literary history precisely because of disruptiveness.

In general, the postmodern novel emphasizes plot rather than character. Postmodern plots tend to be labyrinthine, difficult (even impossible) to follow, contrived, often entrapping. In a number of works this emphasis on plot seems to entail a corresponding diminution or flattening of character. Characters are often stereotypes and can be drawn from other high or low cultural narratives, as is the case with Coover's Cat in the Hat, Barth's Menelaus, Proteus, and

Theseus, Barthelme's Snow White, Acker's Don Quixote, and Reed's Minnie the Moocher. Conversely, they can be taken from the documents of "real" history, as is the case with Coover's Rosenbergs and Richard Nixon, Pynchon's Walther Rathenau and Mickey Rooney, Reed's Warren G. Harding and Abraham Lincoln, and DeLillo's Lee Harvey Oswald. Or they can be allegorical figures, like Pynchon's quester Oedipa or Susan Sontag's Diddy (Did He?) in the novel *Death Kit* (1967). When characters are more developed, the effect of depth or psychological reality tends to be undercut by the satiric or implausible nature of the fictional universes they inhabit—cases in point are John Hawkes's Skipper in *Second Skin,* Nabokov's Humbert, Kinbote, and Van, and DeLillo's John Gladney, the professor of Hitler Studies in *White Noise.*

Characters in postmodern novels are also likely to be fragmented or multiple: Slothrop in *Gravity's Rainbow* is described as disintegrating, and in the fourth section of the novel becomes less a character than a sort of thematic trace; the four main characters of *The Female Man* seem to be possible versions of a single authorial persona; John Henry Waugh dissolves into a hitherto secondary level of the fictional universe in the last chapter of *The Universal Baseball Association.* Rarely agents of their own destinies, postmodern protagonists tend to be passive, manipulated by a plot they perceive as already inscribed in their fictional universes. This passivity is consonant both with the self-referential theme of a world that comes to acculturated subjects already textualized and with the more overtly political exploration of what it means to be American in a period where power is increasingly global in its scope and diffused in its manifestations.

These structural features may have analogues on the level of style. In the fiction of Donald Barthelme, syntax is often wrenched to the point of noncommunication, or into a kind of sublime clunkiness. In the works of Pynchon, DeLillo, Acker, and Coover, narrative voices are permeated by period and class-coded slang or the catchphrases of media cliché, and there can be enormous tonal shifts within a single narrator's account. Perhaps because postmodernists tend not to separate the aesthetic from other kinds of discourse, there is less markedly "fine writing" in postmodern novels than in the corresponding modernist novels. There are exceptions, however: Nabokov and

Hawkes are both acclaimed as superb prose stylists, Pynchon's menu of stylistic techniques in *Gravity's Rainbow* produces some of the most brilliant and moving passages in American literature, and De-Lillo's remarkable ear for arcane vocabularies and the cadences of spoken syntax effectively redefines the whole idea of narrative style.

Born and raised in prerevolutionary Russia, Vladimir Nabokov alludes to his expatriate status throughout his work, making the idea of national and cultural homelessness increasingly the basis for the games that unground and destabilize his narratives. In *Lolita* (1955), he builds on the modernist convention of the unreliable narrator, presenting Humbert Humbert's retrospective account as at once prurient, sentimental, and satiric. The resulting mix is difficult to interpret, especially given the pervasive wordplay, in that the reader is not given unequivocal cues about how to take this story, but there does seem to be a story, albeit an unsettled and unsettling one.

In *Pale Fire* (1962), however, the unreliable narrator goes over the edge, and the novel becomes a wholly unreliable text. As a consequence of this postmodern turn, the question "What's the real story here?" becomes both pressing and inapplicable. *Pale Fire* is metafictionally *about* the question of the "real story," dramatized as a quest for the correct reading. The novel takes the form of a text plus critical commentary. It consists of a long conversational poem by the recently murdered poet John Shade, followed by a purported explication that immediately acquires a life of its own, situating the poem as an allegorically veiled account of the past of the commentator himself, the expatriate professor Charles Kinbote. The question becomes how to read the reading—that is, how to evaluate the reading strategies that reflect on the reader's own reading strategies. Evaluation takes the form of discriminating between ontological levels of the text, that is, deciding what is "real" in terms of the fictional universe of the novel and what, within this universe, is "unreal"—fantasized, fictionalized, hallucinated, mistaken, and so on.

But the activity of reading as a process of discriminating the "real" story from superadded accretions turns out to be impossible. If the details of Shade's poem seem wholly unamenable to the interpretation that makes them an allegory for the history of the deposed King of Zembla, then it seems likely that Kinbote has "read into" his text, turning it into his own story. But the wordplay that gives Kinbote his opposite and equal reflection in the character Botkin, that folds ana- grams of the name of the assassin Gradus through the poem as well as the commentary, and opposes the fictitious New England college town of Arcady to an equally fictitious, if curiously refractive King- dom of Zembla (as in "semblance") suggests that "Kinbote" himself is a fiction within the fictional universe of *Pale Fire*. The problem then becomes where to draw the line. Under this suspicious scrutiny, the entire world of *Pale Fire* begins to collapse into unreality, so completely that it is also impossible to maintain that there is a "real" commentator within the text who is responsible for all this fabula- tion. It becomes impossible, that is, to maintain the concept of "fic- tional reality" as opposed to "fictional fiction."

Yet *Pale Fire* continues to hold up its various unsustainable read- ings as lures, promises of coherence and significance that demand to be followed out even when following them out leads in a circle. In this novel, as in the subsequent *Ada* (1969), Nabokov plays with the expectation of discovery by manipulating ontological levels so that the ground or source of all the fabulation seems continually about to be revealed. *Pale Fire* not only engages this quest but also parodies it, in that the narrator searches industriously but never quite stumbles on the origin of the quotation giving the poem, and thus the book itself, its name. And as in *Ada,* one ontological level being manipu- lated is outside the fictional universe of the novel: *Pale Fire* is to a degree a *roman à clef,* in its advancing and withholding of autobio- graphical information. At the close of the commentary, the narrator surmises that his future will involve "other disguises," and adds, "I may turn up yet, on another campus, as an old, happy, healthy, heterosexual Russian, a writer in exile, sans fame, sans future, sans audience, sans anything but his art." The parallels between the ex- patriate professor Kinbote and the expatriate professor Nabokov move into prominence at this moment, within a novel about the ob- sessive need to inscribe one's own life story in the pages of another text. But the parallels present another metafictional loop, for it is ultimately the reader looking for traces of Nabokov's own personal history in *Pale Fire* who is reenacting the monomaniacal quest of the narrator, and thus the critical activity of locating what the novel is "really" about repeats the reading that is in so many palpable respects a "reading into."

This final implication of the reader in the questionable strategies of the protagonist is an instance of the kind of mastery that the postmodern novel characteristically exercises. Characteristically, too, *Pale Fire* anticipates the gendered nature of the struggle in the way the masterful reader is constructed to be pitted against a narrator who in sexual terms is the dominant culture's embodiment of subordination. The narrator is clearly homosexual; moreover, his homosexuality is presented as one of the mores of an alien nation that has already been overmastered by a superpower. A reading that exposes his commentary on the poem as the pitiful attempt to assert, without the requisite author-ity, superseded and debased values would reinforce the values of the dominant culture. *Pale Fire* invites such a reading, only to betray it. Like the quasi-Soviet agents who search in vain for the crown jewels of Zembla, such a reader quests after the kernel of reality presumed to be behind all the masquerades of art. And like these agents, who tear apart a trompe-l'oeil nut box inset in a painting to find "nothing . . . except the broken bits of a nutshell," such a reader finds this quest forever compromised. In this book of nested embeddings, art and reality are on an equal footing, and the inside *is* the outside.

Like Nabokov, John Hawkes is fascinated by the convention of the unreliable narrator and prone to align narrative unreliability with what the dominant culture identifies as social and especially sexual degradation. Much of his work invites the reader to perceive deficiencies in a narrator and to attempt to ascertain the "real story" from evident contradictions and lacunae, but in *Second Skin* (1963) the narrator is so literally ungrounded that no basis exists for the reader to judge this narrator's account as deluded, deceptive, or otherwise mistaken. This narrator is a widowed ex-Navy officer named Skipper, a character who by his own testimony is a cuckold and a rape victim, someone the people around him regard as gullible, cowardly, and impotent. Yet his story by his accounts is a triumph that shows him to be "a man of love" and "a man of courage as well." The discrepancy between the violence and sordidness of the events of his story and the interpretation he claims for this story invites readers to master Skipper just as he seems continually to be mastered by everyone else. The contradictions and anomalies in the facts he details invite the reader to naturalize the text by finding deficiencies in the narrating subject—to find psychological reasons for aspects of the account that do not fit into the reader's own interpretation.

But the ground from which such a reader can make this judgment has been pulled out: Skipper claims to be telling his tale of betrayal and death in retrospect from the vantage of a floating island, a determinedly irrealistic setting shot through with allusions to Shakespeare's *The Tempest*. Here Skipper is reigning magician, and if he says he has triumphed, his say-so is the only thing the reader can go on. The premise of this romantically untethered scene of narration seriously undermines the apparent contrast between the self-justifying and doggedly optimistic cast of Skipper's interpretation and the sordid details of the events he narrates. The line between fictional "facts" and fictional "fiction" (or false interpretation) is impossible to maintain given the irrealism of the scene of narration, which can be located only through allusion and symbolism. Skipper's island has existence only in a literary universe, with respect to the Shakespearean landscape it evokes and the unnamed New England island it "doubles," to use Hawkes's own term.

Skipper's story thus cannot be identified as being something other than the "real story," because it is impossible to ground Skipper's story in Skipper's own motivation and/or mental condition. While Humbert in *Lolita* narrates from prison—a fact that allows readers to assess his reliability given his evident motives for self-exoneration and confession—Skipper cannot be presumed to narrate, say, from a mental institution and simply *claim* to be on a floating island, because nothing in the novel warrants seeing a mental institution as more intrinsically real than a floating island. The question "What's the real story here?" is a means to mastering an unreliable narration by dividing its elements into various ontological levels and thus putting them in their place in a coherent, hierarchically organized story. But this story—as in *Pale Fire*, a story of emasculation—ultimately resists such mastery and overmasters the attempted reading because it refuses to give readers a stable ground from which to make judgments.

John Barth first wrote about postmodernism in the influential essay "The Literature of Exhaustion," where he argued that postmodern innovation derives from the "used-upness" of all the available plots. His own innovations seem to have arisen, like Nabokov's and Hawkes's, from earlier works that pushed at the boundaries of certain existing narrative conventions. *The Floating Opera* (1956) and *The End of the Road* (1958) are experiments with the genre of the philosophical novel, or novel of ideas, in which characters are fundamentally concerned with the nature of reality and the self. In both books, however, the protagonists find themselves involved in enterprises analogous to the making of fiction. Todd Andrews in *The Floating Opera* erects a series of provisional plots to bring order to an apparently chaotic reality. Jacob Horner in *The End of the Road* is engaged in Mythotherapy, an existential version of psychoanalysis that aims to compensate for the fundamental nonexistence of the subject by helping the analysand invent the self as an arbitrary but consistent character. The metafictional component grows more emphatic in *The Sot-Weed Factor* (1960), which plays with the boundaries separating historical "fact" from fiction and is explicitly concerned with its own status: "*the truth of fiction is that Fact is fantasy; the made-up story is a model of the world.*"

With *Giles Goat-Boy; or, The Revised New Syllabus* (1966), the metafictional turn becomes a characteristic Barthian tendency to expose the artificiality of narrative while at the same time maintaining a certain emotional investment in narrative outcomes. In this encyclopedic novel, Barth explores the structure and functions of myth, manipulating the paradigms of the heroic quest and the founding religious document: he has referred to this work as a "souped-up bible." An inflated allegory, *Giles Goat-Boy* plays out the consequences of seeing the (American) university as the world. Barth's next major work, the collection *Lost in the Funhouse: Fiction for Print, Tape, Live Voice* (1968), is the fictional complement to "The Literature of Exhaustion" in that it self-consciously reveals various kinds of fictional strategy by foregrounding conventions and techniques to the point where these supplant the traditional priorities of character, plot, and setting. The individual fictions include a story in which the story itself is the narrator, a protean first-person account that dramatizes the convention of embedding, and a story that enters into a dialogue with a series of writing-workshop observations about the making of fiction. In *Lost in the Funhouse*, Barth also initiates the process, continued in *Chimera* (1972), of reinscribing existing myths, in illustration of his contention that the apparent exhaustion of new stories can be interpreted as a motive for rewriting those stories by emphasizing their hitherto hidden aspects, in the process "transcending artifice by insisting on it," as he remarked in a 1968 interview.

Barth's next novel, the long and demanding *Letters* (1979), uses the epistolary form to bring together protagonists from the preceding novels with the author, "John Barth," already an ontologically unsettling character in *Chimera*. In this particularly self-referential twist of the literature-of-exhaustion technique, Barth reinscribes his own stories, giving the characters authorial functions and making the authorial persona subject to the logic of his own various plots. Using the university setting less allegorically than in *Giles Goat-Boy*, *Letters* deals on the one hand with the political microcosm of the 1960s campus, on the other hand with the status of language and letters in a world where books are in danger of being supplanted by advanced technologies, especially those of film. The most recent novels, *Sabbatical: A Romance* (1982) and *Tidewater Tales* (1987), are more overtly political than any of Barth's previous works. Both introduce new characters, in each case married couples whose union is a primary instance of the synthesis of apparent antitheses. Both are self-conscious in their preoccupation with the mechanics of narrative, their continuing reinscription of prior Barth stories, and their pervasive wordplay, and both use the scientific notion of indeterminacy to unsettle the implication that narrative closure ever closes anything for good. But both also explore the analogies between aspects of the writing process and techniques of surveillance and control in 1980s America. Barth had been widely regarded as one of the most aestheticist of the postmodern novelists: in 1968 he was quoted as declaiming, "Muse, spare me (at the desk, I mean) from Social-Historical Responsibility, and in the last analysis from every other kind, except Artistic." His most recent novels, however, suggest that his own practice has led him to explore the affinities between the examination of narrative strategies and the critique of ideology.

Like most of the novelists under discussion, Robert Coover has made explicit statements about his reasons for disrupting established forms of representation. In a 1969 interview, he maintained that "the first and primary and essential talent of the artist is to reach the emotions. . . . I mean when something hits us strong enough, it means it's something real." For Coover, "something real" is precisely not what is conveyed through the habitual doctrines of humanism and strategies of realism: "the contact occurs when there is communication across reality links, not across conventional links which is what most second rate writers make, you know, things you'd expect, you know how the endings are going to be." Coover's first published works, among them a number of the short stories collected in the 1969 volume *Pricksongs and Descants,* seem determined to counter "things you'd expect." Like the fictions in *Lost in the Funhouse,* which was published in the preceding year, and like Cervantes's *Don Quixote,* Coover's own paradigm, the *Pricksongs and Descants* stories explicitly attack "exhausted art-forms," forms Coover not only sees as "used-up" but aligns with "adolescent thought-modes." A number of the stories are reinscriptions of folktales and myths; many deliberately violate conventions of decorum in treating playfully an extremely inflammatory subject matter—murder, mutilation, and rape, for instance (the last also symptomatic of the masculinism that infected much experimental writing by men during the 1960s). All of them foreground conventions of fiction-making and reading. Probably the best known, "The Babysitter," seems a North American realization of the radically nonlinear narrative described in Borges's *ficcione* "The Garden of Forking Paths." In "The Babysitter," the question of the "real story" does as much violence to the forking paths of narration as the various versions of the story do to the story's erotic victim, the babysitter.

Coover's first novel, *The Origin of the Brunists* (1966) is in many respects a more traditional work of fiction than the contemporaneous short stories, exploring the evolution of a religious cult in terms insisting on an allegorical relation to the founding and institutionalization of Christianity. The concern with demystifying myth, a constant in Coover's work, here allows the reader a sort of benevolent outside position from which to assess events variously interpreted as mundane or miraculous. Such a reader is invited to conclude that if this is how myths arise, there is a standard of objectivity and accuracy that can be invoked to arrive at some sense of what the real story might be. This privileged vantage point disappears gradually in Coover's second and definitively postmodern novel, *The Universal*

*Baseball Association, Inc., J. Henry Waugh, Prop.* (1968). This work not only synthesizes the major Coover themes and strategies—the origins and developments of religious belief, the affinities between historical and fictional narrative, the reinscription of folklore and myth into convention-disrupting forms—but carefully explores the potentiality of the novel, defining the genre accretively as a game, a ritual, a system evolving its own tendencies and trajectories and ultimately subject to the same entropy as any closed physical system, an analogue of history (particularly history conceived as the sort of totalizing teleological and rule-governed system that postmodern theorist Jean-François Lyotard calls a master-narrative of legitimation), and finally as encompassing and constituting a putatively "outside" or "real" world.

The author and God-figure of this system John Henry Waugh (JHWH—part of an elaborate structure of Judaeo-Christian allusions in a story that manages to bring such providential events as the flood, the Covenant, and the betrayal and death of Christ into a tabletop game modeled on baseball) changes his relation to the embedded Universal Baseball Association, until in the eighth and final chapter he has disappeared entirely into the game/novel/world that was presented as his creation. The embedded fiction becomes all there is and begins to reenact not only the versions of providential history concocted within this same fiction in the preceding chapter but also the kinds of authorial questions that Waugh had raised about his capacities and responsibilities as maker of this fiction. The question about the "real" story is thus displaced into a question about origins and control: Where did this world come from and who or what is responsible for its events and outcomes? In making a fiction *about* how the making of fiction becomes a process comprehending all of experience, Coover has allowed metafiction to insinuate a whole series of questions about the nature and scope of interpretation, power, and design.

These questions take political shape in Coover's great encyclopedic work *The Public Burning* (1977), a novel so disruptive of the borders between history and fiction that legal problems delayed its publication for several years. *The Public Burning* is about the trial and execution of the Rosenbergs, and about the Manichean theology implicit in United States foreign and domestic policy during the Cold War. In this novel, too, history resembles fiction in having a design, author, and purpose, but in this case the confusion of ontological levels is complete from the outset. "Fiction" and "fact" mingle uneasily in the exuberantly xenophobic prologue and become thoroughly entangled with the first sentence of the opening chapter, "I was with the President at his news conference that Wednesday morning when the maverick Supreme Court Justice William Douglas dropped his bombshell in the Rosenberg case." The narrative voice is unmistakably that of Richard Nixon in his mid-career memoir *Six Crises*. The question of the "real story" is immediately irrelevant in a fictional universe where figures like Nixon (who is the principal narrator), John F. Kennedy, Julius and Ethel Rosenberg, and Dwight D. Eisenhower interact with corporate trademarks like Betty Crocker, national symbols like Uncle Sam, and political stereotypes like the Phantom, the fictional embodiment of that 1950s catchphrase "the spectre of world Communism."

Throughout *The Public Burning*, Coover literalizes the symbolism of the dominant ideology, most evidently by having the electrocution of the Rosenbergs take place in Times Square, "the ritual center of the Western world." The ritual murder performed as a national spectacle becomes the central event in a theological construction of history that takes as its revealed text the nineteenth-century American doctrine of Manifest Destiny. According to this Manifest theology, history has a plot—and perhaps this plot is also a conspiracy. It has an origin in the machinations of Uncle Sam and the Phantom. It has a design and perhaps an ultimate purpose, although the dimensions of these are not visible to characters enmeshed in its workings, characters like Coover's disconcertingly sympathetic schlemiel-hero Nixon, who in the closing pages is finally made privy to the central mystery of the politico-providential plot, the secret of Incarnation. In *The Public Burning*, the strategies of narrative fiction are writ large in the world that is represented. But this world is not merely overdetermined and artificial; it is also in unexpected ways an accurate depiction of Cold War reality—and is accurate precisely because of this overdetermination and artificiality. For Coover, as for most other postmodern writers centrally engaged with events in the public sphere, the irrealist strategies of metafiction have mimetic power, revealing the extent to which official history is inevitably structured like a fiction.

Thomas Pynchon, arguably the most important of the postmodern novelists, is similarly preoccupied with the relations between history and fiction and with the entailed issues of author-ity, control, and design. Maintaining a public profile so low that it approaches ano-nymity, Pynchon creates fictional universes shot through with inti-mations of conspiracies vast and pervasive enough to undermine the possibility that there can be anything personal or individual about identity. Pynchon's characters tend to be both allegorical and stereo-typical, embodying mythic functions of the quest hero while acting, dressing, and speaking out of the preoccupations of mass culture, thereby deflating corresponding connotations of high seriousness. Plots are labyrinthine and endlessly self-referential: if narrative design is always incipiently a synonym for global conspiracy, paranoia is the state of mind not only of characters struggling to apprehend their place in the pattern but also of readers struggling to comprehend a text that works actively to implicate and overwhelm them. The re-curring suggestion is that the reader's own world is a text that be-haves in the same way, inscribing ostensibly free agents in preexisting stories that ultimately determine them. Pynchon's novels amass his-torical evidence documenting this extreme vision of control at the same time as they advance other sources for intimations of fatality: paranoia as a predisposition to "read into" reality for connections and meanings that have only psychological necessity.

Pynchon's first two novels develop the distinctively postmodern motif of the "real story" and explore the implications of a formal refusal to authorize one version of fictional reality as definitive. In *V* (1963), the central action of the quest reflects the reader's act of interpretation while the structure of the novel raises questions about the structure of historical knowledge. The title initial refers to a mys-terious woman who seems to turn up at key moments of chaos during the late nineteenth and early twentieth centuries. Allusions to *The Education of Henry Adams* suggest that this V personifies a force analogous to the physical principle of entropy and that this force destines Western civilization to increasing decadence until it arrives at a terminal condition of inanimateness.

But all these manifestations of the elusive V are identified and connected only in retrospect, by a bumbling quest hero named Herbert Stencil, who is committed to reading history for signs of V in order to construct a reality that gives his own life some meaning. Stencil and the other protagonist, the self-proclaimed schlemiel Benny Profane, inhabit a postwar world in which people and inanimate objects have come to resemble each other so completely that Stencil suspects V has already achieved most of her aims. Yet the existence of V is increasingly in doubt as the quest proceeds, to the point where Stencil begins to wonder if she may amount to nothing more than "the recurrence of an initial and a few dead objects." His need to locate a force or conspiracy that will explain the contemporary world may have led him to interpret random phenomena as manifestations of that force or conspiracy. The dilemma is characteristically Pynchonesque; the ending of the novel refuses to resolve it.

*The Crying of Lot 49* (1966) is a shorter and generally more straightforward novel, in which actions occur in chronological sequence, so that readers are less involved with the problems of making connections within the story and more traditionally placed as observers of a hero who makes connections—which is to say, either discerns them in or projects them onto a satirically envisioned landscape of southern California at mid-century. The protagonist here has the quester's resonant name of Oedipa and the deflating surname of Maas—close to "more" in Spanish and "measure" in German—and is joined in her search by characters with names like Manny DiPresso, Stanley Koteks, and Genghis Cohen. The parodic names reinforce a theme of limits on human endeavor and especially on knowledge, most evocatively knowledge of "another mode of meaning behind the obvious." Like *V, The Crying of Lot 49* is concerned with the "plot" of history, conceived simultaneously as a threat to the quester and as a promise of "transcendent meaning."

The publication of *Gravity's Rainbow* in 1973 both secured the reputation of Thomas Pynchon and made him the most controversial figure in contemporary letters. On the strength of this 760-page encyclopedic work, Edward Mendelson declared, "Pynchon is, quite simply, the best living novelist in English," but the editorial board for the Pulitzer Prize, wary of the book's notorious difficulty and low-comic iconoclasm, overrode the unanimous opinion of the nominating jurors that this was the best American novel of the year. Both the acclaim and the hostility testify to the innovation of *Gravity's Rainbow*. In certain respects a sequel to or pre-text for *V* (its central symbol is the V-2 rocket), it develops narrative voices, themes, structural elements, and even characters introduced in the earlier novel while drawing even more extensively on literary, intellectual, economic, and social history and on the physical and biological sciences, as well as on theology and occultism, popular culture, folklore, social and linguistic theory, and mathematics. *Gravity's Rainbow* deals with the development during the Third Reich of the V-2 rocket, the prototype of all guided missiles, which would become the delivery system for the nuclear armaments being developed in the United States during the same period. The merging of the two technological "advances" culminates a "dream of annihilation" that according to Pynchon's visionary historicism has obsessed Western civilization for centuries. "Gravity's rainbow" symbolizes both the arc of the rocket and the possible trajectory of civilization itself, as it proceeds toward seemingly inevitable self-destruction.

Yet the question of inevitability is an ambiguous one in this novel, not only in terms of theme but also in terms of structure. The trajectory of the initially "main" plot, which concerns a GI named Tyrone Slothrop who appears to be erotically stimulated by being in London locations the V-2 will eventually hit, is complicated by so many subplots that it is difficult to ascertain what happens to this schlemiel-hero or what his denouement might mean. The clues that proliferate at first in apparent testimony to "the stone determinacy of everything, of every soul" continue to proliferate—and to lead in different directions. Moreover, characters (over 300 are developed in some detail), situations, and events burgeon wildly, and the narrative voice shifts without warning from slangy Americanism to the high-minded musings of German idealism to oddly private reflections and reminiscences to passages of rhymed verse. If this riotous multiplicity signals an absence of controls or limits, it also occurs in a context where controls or limits are rarely benign. Characters tend to be free to the extent that they evade outside attempts to define them. Inasmuch as the novel itself evades reduction to a single "authorized" reading, it suggests that no trajectory is ever wholly determined, and that perhaps the "course" of history allows for deviation and thus possibility.

*Vineland* (1989), Pynchon's first new fictional work in sixteen years, was the first of his novels to receive seriously mixed reviews, perhaps only an indication that *Gravity's Rainbow* was an impossible act to follow. *Vineland* continues the tradition of satirically named characters (Zoyd Wheeler, Isaiah Two Four, Weed Atman, and even Mucho Maas, carried over from *The Crying of Lot 49*) and deals with a conspiracy of indefinite proportions, in this case involving the FBI and its informers among the student radicals of the 1960s. But in this novel the emphasis is less on a corresponding tendency to "plot" connections in order to arrive at some sort of historical coherence than on character and the local relations between individuals, especially the relations of family. The central quest is that of a daughter for her absent mother, and while the process by which the two are united involves an impressive accumulation of information about international corporate practices and structures, the history of the Left in California, the effects of Reaganomics and the War on Drugs, and the popular culture of the 1980s, there are no epistemological impasses or withheld revelations. The "real story" is fully visible; in fact, *Vineland* is the closest Pynchon has yet come to a realist novel, its mode similar to the magical realism of such Latin American writers as Gabriel García Márquez (whom Pynchon has called the greatest living writer) in its easy accommodation of a group of latter-day Undead called the Thanatoids into the parodically heightened but recognizable California landscape.

Like Pynchon, Don DeLillo evolves complex narrative structures that mimic and develop his themes, which have to do both with contemporary political and social situations and with real and projected bodies of abstract knowledge. His great encyclopedic novel *Ratner's Star* (1976), which deals with the efforts of a fourteen-year-old mathematical genius to decode what seems to be a message from outer space, is an elaborate formal system that reflects and returns on itself like the meta-mathematics its protagonist is struggling to develop. Within the apparent self-containedness of this edifice, however, DeLillo's emphasis is on the ungrounded nature of knowledge, Goedelian uncertainty as the fundamental condition of contingent human being.

The uncertainty theme recurs in DeLillo's work, from the relatively early novels *End Zone* (1973) and *Great Jones Street* (1974), in which the systems explored for their coherence and explanatory capabilities are football and rock music respectively, to *The Names* (1982), which works with analogies between systems of language and economic and political systems: multinational capitalism and the oppositional communities and interests in the Third World. *White Noise* (1985) again focuses on language as a system, this time as an attempt to close off a contingency experienced as fear of death, and on the entropic waste produced by the various purportedly closed systems of American consumer culture. The brilliant and iconoclastic *Libra* (1988) uses the available information on the assassination of John F. Kennedy to construct a new and heavily conspiratorial explanation, like Coover's *The Public Burning* ventriloquizing a number of public figures, among them Lee Harvey Oswald.

DeLillo specializes in this sort of first-person account. His narrative voices assimilate a variety of influences—the stridency and hype of a saturating media, the specialized vocabularies of international business, the sciences, technology, and the information industry, and the anxious cadences of solitary individuals brooding over crime, cabals, terrorism, and their own inevitable deaths—into an intricate and nuanced prose that reflects and elaborates on his thematic preoccupation with language. The startling and sometimes shocking precision of this language makes him one of the foremost postmodern stylists.

Another groundbreaking stylist, Donald Barthelme, has been one of the leading figures in the current renaissance of the short story. His two novels, *Snow White* (1967) and *The Dead Father* (1977), share with the short fiction an intensely experimental quality deriving from a characteristic emphasis on visual effects and graphic play. Both, for instance, consist of short, apparently disjointed sections in a variety of typefaces, some of them first-person disquisitions, others brief scenes with patches of dialogue, still others made up of lists whose individual members seem arbitrarily related, both to each other and to the rest of the book.

But the novels also sustain a story line over a period of time, and for this reason constantly allude to, even as they do not realize, such traditional narrative effects as suspense, sympathy, and a sense of experiential depth. Far more than most of the stories, which attain a kind of immediacy from the way "unlike things are stuck together to make . . . a new reality," as Barthelme explained in a 1974 interview, the novels tend to be *about* fiction: about what narrative does or is supposed to do and about the problematic nature of the contract a text makes with its reader. "We like books that have a lot of *dreck* in them, matter which presents itself as not wholly relevant (or indeed, at all relevant) but which, carefully attended to, can supply a kind of 'sense' of what is going on," says one of the dwarfs in *Snow White,* and this explanation has bearing not only on the appeal of *Snow White* itself but on the use of detail for "reality effect" in the most meticulously realist novels. Both *Snow White* and the subsequent *The Dead Father* construct their situations around well-known, nearly archetypal stories, and both divest archetype of its seriousness, throwing the ideological implications into sharp relief. In a sense, Barthelme has decomposed cultural myths and recomposed them entirely of dreck: the result is at once deflating and curiously satisfying.

Like Pynchon, Coover in *The Public Burning,* and DeLillo in *Libra,* Ishmael Reed writes experimental novels that reinscribe United States history as a record of conspiracy. *The Free-Lance Pallbearers* (1967) sets up the terms of an opposition that recurs in *Yellow Back Radio Broke-Down* (1969), *Mumbo Jumbo* (1972), *The Last Days of Louisiana Red* (1974), and *Flight to Canada* (1976), in which a repressive white power structure attempts to put down a polytheistic and multicultural counter-society. Reed marshals impressive documentation in support of this vision of postindustrial America as the end product of a series of suppressions, managed by the dominant Western culture because of this culture's ascetic rationalism, commitment to the technologies of annihilation, and envy of people able to enjoy themselves. The presentation of evidence is ebullient in its frame-breaking: fiction and nonfiction mix promiscuously, as do past and present. For example, *Mumbo Jumbo,* set in the 1920s, is full of both period and anachronistic photographs (the Oakland Black Panthers and members of Nixon's cabinet cohabit in these pages with Louis Armstrong's band), footnotes (documenting, among other things, the African American lineage of President Warren G. Harding), and quotations from popular media and scholarly sources; the book concludes with a 104-item "Partial Bibliography." Reed sees his fictional technique as deriving from his commitment to a variety of media, and he locates his experimentation in the rich non-Western tradition it celebrates, in which artistic creation has always incorporated a variety of elements that in the West have been rigidly separated into genres.

Kurt Vonnegut, one of the most prolific of the postmodern novelists, arrived at his own brand of ontologically unsettling narrative experiment through popular science fiction. *Player Piano* (1952) and *The Sirens of Titan* (1959) are witty but generally conventional science fiction novels; *Mother Night* (1961) adds autobiographical elements that have become Vonnegut trademarks; *Cat's Cradle* (1963) turns the science fiction components to metafictional ends, making a *mise-en-abîme* of the Bokononist religion it describes, which like the novel itself refuses to cohere as a single vision of the world.

In *Slaughterhouse-Five* (1969), Vonnegut brings the autobiographical, the science fictional, and the metafictional together, using irreconcilable versions of a single story to show the impossibility of assimilating the horror of a World War II experience that is in significant respects Vonnegut's own experience. In making "Kurt Vonnegut" a character within the novel, Vonnegut dramatizes his own difficulty in dealing with the subject and makes the central narrative, about the experiences of the passive and uncomprehending Billy Pilgrim, a digression from or displacement of his own story. The science fiction component, provided by the intervention of extraterrestrials called Tralfamadorians, insists that the perception of human beings "stuck in time" is partial and distorted, but the Trafalmadorian viewpoint is unavailable to the human characters and the reader alike. The Tralfamadorians become part of the metafictional apparatus inasmuch as their simultaneous vision of all time rules out the suspense created by narrative teleology, and in particular rules out climax. *Slaughterhouse-Five* similarly evades coming to any satisfying or revelatory conclusion. Its quietistic maxim "So it goes" becomes the model of Vonnegut's revisionist history. Such subsequent novels as *Slapstick* (1976), *Deadeye Dick* (1982), and *Galapagos* (1985) also incorporate autobiographical elements and authorial personae, revise official history, and engage readers in dialogue by playing with the self-reflexive possibilities of fiction about fiction.

One of the most violent postmodernist assaults on narrative conventions and bourgeois norms of decorum comes from Kathy Acker, whose writing is a volatile mix of autobiography, plagiarism, pornography, parody, poststructuralist theorizing, and Marxist and feminist analysis. Her literary productions are in many respects aligned with contemporary work in the visual arts, in particular with the "image appropriation" of feminist painters and photographers that exactly reproduces a "masterpiece" of the dominant, masculine culture, but she is also repeating the colonizing and decentering gesture of French feminist theorist Luce Irigaray, who made one chapter of her book on the phallocentrism of the Western philosophical tradition a word-for-word transcription of part of Plotinus's *Enneads*. In a *mise-en-abîme* in *Don Quixote* (1986)—the title is a case in point— Acker associates her own work with the practice of "the Arabs," whom she presciently identifies as the "other" of Western civilization: "They write by cutting chunks out of all-ready written texts and in other ways defacing traditions: changing important names into silly ones, making dirty jokes out of matters that should be of the utmost importance to us, such as nuclear war." Such strategies are for her means of short-circuiting a society whose control extends into the most apparently personal and intimate areas of everyday life. Like her pornography, which starts "with the physical body, the place of shitting, eating, etc." in order "to break through our opinions and false education," this plagiarism aims to evade the tyranny imposed by habitual modes of representation.

For Acker, any such evasion can only be temporary, however, because there is nothing outside the already-existing symbolic order. Her strategies accordingly emphasize disruption: narratives are a pastiche of fragments in a variety of modes; characters change names, sexes, and sometimes species; in particular, the apparently autobiographizing "author" is also an effect of the writing and is represented as such in titles like *The Childlike Life of the Black Tarantula by the Black Tarantula* (1975), *The Adult Life of Henri Toulouse Lautrec by Henri Toulouse Lautrec* (1978), *Hello I'm Erica Jong* (1982), and *My Death My Life by Pier Paolo Pasolini* (1987). In a 1984 essay, Acker explains these destabilizing tactics in terms of an aesthetics of immediacy, which opposes art to description: "If art's to be more than craft, more than decorations for the people in power, it's this want, this existence. . . . Only the cry, art, rather than the description or criticism, is primary. The cry is stupid; it has no mirror; it communicates." The constant in her work is this "cry" of desire, but while the desire is always female it is never manifested as the expression of an essentialized woman-in-general, or even as the utterance of a unitary subject. Acker's work is relentlessly particular, another circumvention of a social control that imposes universals in order to regiment and commodify experience.

Like Vonnegut, Joanna Russ developed her structural innovations through manipulating the conventions of science fiction. Unlike Vonnegut (but like Samuel R. Delany), she has always used science fiction to explore alternative constructions of sexual difference, beginning with the relatively straightforward adventure novel *Picnic on Paradise* (1968), whose hero continues in the collections *Alyx* (1976) and *The Adventures of Alyx* (1986). *The Female Man* (1975) takes off from Russ's Nebula Award-winning short story "When It Changed" (1972), using that story's premise of an all-female planet called Whileaway to provide an origin for Janet, one of the four protagonists. The other protagonists, Jeannine, Jael, and Joanna, are, with Janet, clearly variants of a single person—who is clearly Joanna Russ—produced in "Garden of Forking Paths"-style parallel universes but brought together by the convention of time-travel—a situation that, according to the text, is also impossible. The narrative voice is distributed among the main characters; in addition, there is a third-person omniscient narrator who occasionally steps up a level and assumes the function of author (the women emerge "into a recreation center called The Trench or The Prick or The Crotch or The Knife. I haven't decided on a name yet") and occasionally literalizes the conventions of omniscient narration into another science fiction realm of fantastic being (having located the four J's in an elevator, this narrator advises, "Think of me in my usual portable form"). The parallel-universes arrangement allows various points of view on various possible sex-gender arrangements. The resulting confusions and observations are politically pointed and often uproariously funny. *The Two of Them* (1978) forgoes time-travel in presenting a meeting of two women from two radically different cultures but retains the frame-breaking narrator.

Samuel R. Delany uses the premises of science fiction to explore and unsettle a number of thematic and structural oppositions: freedom and slavery, inside and outside, familiar and alien, center and margin, fiction and criticism. His alternative universes are populous urban landscapes informed by myth, contemporary social theory, and poststructuralist literary and linguistic theory, where characters who are outsiders to the dominant culture work out their complicated relations to desire and power. Although all Delany's novels are set in the future, they are concerned with the recovery, or invention, of a submerged past, a narrative that can be called history but remains irreducibly multiple. *Dhalgren* (1975), probably the most radically experimental of Delany's works to date, plays with a present that is similarly plural, a "real story" that exists as a number of irreconcilable versions.

Like many of the postmoderns, Delany is fascinated with the possibilities of reinscription, to the point where many of his stories are revisions of his earlier stories or allude, often with frame-breaking effect, to his preceding writings, both fictional and nonfictional. His later novels have theoretical essays embedded in them or appended to them, but these essays in turn have fictional elements. For instance, the appendix to *Tales of Nevèrÿon* (1979) acknowledges that the stories are based on inscriptions of the famous Culhar' fragment, recently translated by the African American mathematician Leslie K. Steiner. Steiner is invoked repeatedly through the course of the Nevèrÿon tetralogy (1979–85) and has recently appeared in a volume that Delany edited, as author of several critical essays *on* Delany. She is, of course, a Delany character, although she never appears in avowedly fictional narratives. Similarly, the lecture on the Modular Calculus by Ashima Slade, which forms the appendix to *Triton* (1976), credits a real essay by Delany himself (a twentieth-century "writer of light, popular fictions") as the inspiration for one aspect of the scientific paradigm being developed. Delany thus becomes the historical antecedent for elements of his own fictions. The interpenetrations of text and commentary, fact and fiction, not only unsettle genre categories within the books but have recently redefined Delany as a public figure: he has been featured at several recent academic conferences as a poststructuralist theorist.

Molly Hite

# The Avant-Garde

The avant-garde has been much discussed and debated, its triumphs certified, its aporias cataloged. In the United States especially it has been relegated to the status of a historical phenomenon. The term of preference for "advanced" or "experimental" work produced since World War II is "postmodern." For reasons that will become apparent in what follows, I have thought to write of a contemporary avant-garde and thereby to avoid much of the confusion and sterile theorizing that too often accompany academic discussions of postmodern literature. If my decision to proceed in this way is valid, it will have to be justified by the insights into a variety of American writers who enjoy something like vanguard status in the late years of the twentieth century.

One further note. For reasons having to do with space and predilection, I have avoided anything resembling a historical survey of American avant-garde writing. Gertrude Stein is but a passing reference here. I argue that there is an avant-garde presently operating in the United States, and that it is possible to understand and to evaluate what it has accomplished. Though some may think it naive, I proceed from the assumption that there is something for which to be grateful in a genuine avant-garde, though it is important to distinguish the real thing from the meretricious. Though this chapter treats a variety of writers, it does not purport to be exhaustive or even to take on every famous vanguard novelist. Probably the most controversial omission is Thomas Pynchon, whose work has been much praised and much studied. Does it make sense to speak at some length of an

American avant-garde without taking him on? I think it does, and I believe that his work is best understood outside the framework established in the pages that follow.

The avant-garde novel in the United States is as elusive and various as the creations of vanguard artists in other media and countries. Often it seems not much more than a species of provocation, a foolishness tricked out in the fancy dress of scandal or chic obscurantism. At other times it offers a plausible defiance of ordinary novelistic conventions while managing at the same time to be impeccably dull, polemical, and repetitious. More rarely, it embodies its resistance to convention while also refusing the easy rewards of polemic and phony candor, unreflective disassociation and undifferentiated irony. If there are few really satisfying American avant-garde novels, the fact obviously has much to do with limitations of talent and seriousness, but here the consideration of such limitations is complicated by one's sense that avant-garde novels are not supposed to satisfy. Though few novelists will wish to be driven from the auditorium by outraged spectators during the course of a public reading, many are clearly bent on denying precisely the satisfactions promised by more accommodating writers. To dismiss an avant-garde novel by convicting it of "meaninglessness" or "randomness" when its very substance depends upon those qualities is, shall we say, a difficult business. Here, as elsewhere, readers and critics are well advised to know what they are dealing with before they open their mouths or compose eulogistic treatises on the death of this form or that.

One way of avoiding difficult issues is to deny that they exist. So the avant-garde may not seem so elusive if it is defined, simply, as anything that attracts few adherents, or aims to offend middlebrow sensibilities. Not long ago, at least in some circles, such qualities were routinely thought to be the only essential characteristics of avant-garde works. A novel largely without anecdotal content and on that score alone without appeal for ordinary readers was taken to be an advanced work. A novel—say, by Gertrude Stein—offensive by virtue of its stubborn commitment to abstractness, repetition, and prolixity, would also seem impressive for its stubborn refusal to be ingratiating or interesting. In such terms it is possible to know more or less securely what does and does not constitute "advanced" fiction. Other kinds of demanding fiction might then be categorized as "academic" or "formalistic" or "fabulistic," the special merit associated with a really bracing vanguardism reserved for a relative handful of writers.

The critic Leslie Fiedler, in his introduction to John Hawkes's novel *The Lime Twig* (1961), makes much of his man's "lonely" eccentricity, his distinction as "the least read novelist of substantial merit in the United States," his brave "experimentalism" and addiction to material that seems unpromising for the purposes of serious fiction. He also locates Hawkes's avant-gardism in his refusal to subscribe to "yesterday's avant garde," or to echo "other men's revolts." Hawkes may be an unpopular novelist, and proud of it, but he is not the sort of "esoteric" writer we associate with an earlier avant-garde. A downright original who refuses the "treacherous lucidity" of realist fiction, Hawkes denies us the narrative continuity and specious thematic coherence other novels condition us to anticipate. In sum, Fiedler's Hawkes is an avant-garde writer not because he offends, or refuses to be interesting, or confuses us, but because he belongs to no school and stands resolutely apart from the "ordinary" and "traditional." There may be in Hawkes a discernible "aspiration toward popular narrative," but that aspiration exists in tension with his dedication to "austerities" that certify his vanguard status.

Hawkes is an important test case for anyone interested in these matters. If in some way Gertrude Stein embodies the spirit of an originary modernist avant-garde, then Hawkes may be said not to fit the pattern. Leslie Fiedler can speak as emphatically as he likes about Hawkes's unpopular merits, but he cannot make of Hawkes even a wayward son of Stein. For Hawkes exhibits neither the single-mindedness nor the aestheticism of that hermetic precursor. Whatever the austerities of his fiction, he composes narratives with more or less developing characters and something like a subject or a content. The atmosphere of dream that so pervades much of his work is pointedly purposeful, bespeaking psychic dislocation or evoking a sense of entrapment that has some discernible relation to circumstance. When he fails, one is aware of a gap between intention and execution, aura and substance, of the disparity, say, between the intensity of nightmarish dread and the causes that might account for it. Hawkes's novels demand to be read and considered in such terms. Absurdity figures prominently in the novels, but Hawkes nowhere relies on it as an ostensibly adequate "explanation" for anything. Though he demands a responsively attentive reader, he does not expect what William Gass calls "a jaded eye," which is to say, a reader "for whom all the action, the incidents, the tension and suspense, are well-known and over and dead and gone," the reader, as Gass has it, of "Joyce and Beckett and Barth and Borges." Hawkes's reader is eager to be moved, willing to be wracked by suspense. If the action is limited, the incident thin, it is nonetheless evoked as a something happening, and one suffers it as a cresting momentum that carries within it significant if sometimes unnameable consequences. One is not only intrigued, but drawn in.

Hawkes is an avant-garde writer principally in his handling of surfaces, in his refusal to provide the kinds of continuity and closure that ordinarily distract readers from the rewards of surface. Character in Hawkes is not a random collocation of traits and activities, but neither is it anything like a stable entity. It is a shape and a word-surface suggesting but never quite embodying or delineating depths. In *The Lime Twig* a woman suffers and one is moved not by the meaning of her suffering or the depth of her reverie but by the austere evocation of her pain and bewilderment. In *Second Skin* (1963) a father kills himself, and one is moved not by his story—which we are never given—or by the impact of this deed on a young son: one is moved by the feverish accents and impeccably juxtaposed details of the telling—brief, resonant, almost tritely heartbreaking, but finally artifactual, a little arch, decidedly literary. In *Travesty* (1976) one is held not by the stale and tediously wicked ideas of the obsessed monologuist but by the sudden irruptions in the surface of his discourse, his linguistic instinct for "elbows of hot metal," "fields of oxygen," and the "grievous tabloidal gesture." It is not that the ideas in such a novel do not exist for us, but that they are not as important as they would be in another sort of work, and that the characters associated with those ideas are frankly an occasion for the performance of certain imaginative resources. Hawkes is an avant-garde writer in the degree that he resists a full commitment to an expansive novelistic or illusionistic treatment of evolving characters and ideas. In the end, his primary interest in language and in the formal management of narrative surfaces ensures that he remain at once a serious artist and a minority writer whose effectiveness is at best intermittent.

Though, in contrast to Hawkes, John Barth might aptly be described as the best-known little-read American novelist, he is unquestionably an avant-garde writer. Author of a famous essay on "The Literature of Exhaustion" (1967), Barth is dismayed that so many of his contemporaries continue to write in the manner of the nineteenth-century realists, and asserts that "to be technically out of date is likely to be a genuine defect." Though sharply critical of phony experimentalism, he is frankly committed to an art "that not many people can *do*: the kind that requires expertise and artistry as well as bright aesthetic ideas." Sometimes dismissed as a merely academic writer performing outlandish feats for professors easily impressed by dexterous prestidigitations, he is nonetheless a writer of great earnestness and intellectual range whose fiction poses basic questions about the avant-garde in the United States. Is it true, as he contends, that the prodigious virtuosity of the writing he admires is compatible with a capacity to "speak eloquently and memorably to our still-human hearts and conditions, as the great artists have always done"? Or is it the case that such ambitions can only distract the avant-garde writer from his true business, which is to astonish, delight, and impress? Barth is not alone in wishing it were possible to avoid stark dichotomies, but his work encourages them more than he will allow. Pages of Barth's novels and stories may be fun to read, but not many will accept that his extravagant fictions "speak eloquently and memorably to our still-human hearts."

Barth is chiefly celebrated as the author of the novels *The Sot-Weed Factor* (1960) and *Giles Goat-Boy* (1966), two of the most fantastic and relentless works in American literature. They are, moreover, works that seem to have been written not so much to be read as contended with. They are quintessential university novels, directed at readers for whom books are at the center of experience and language itself defines what is most important about us. Drawing upon, parodying, imitating, and echoing the literature of the past, Barth's novels are at once boisterous and long-winded, exuberant and earnest, unbuttoned and self-conscious. Embodying what one critic nicely calls a "visionary pedantry," the novels are also apt at times to seem silly, self-indulgent, mythomaniacal, excessive. Brilliantly comic and endlessly inventive, they are by turns playful and obsessive, as one might expect from a writer for whom language games, paradoxes, and philosophical conundrums are never-ending sources of wonder. Barth is in fact largely if not exclusively preoccupied with the issue of fictiveness and the way that language continues to embody and embolden the fictions by which we live. In no sense a philosophical novelist, Barth is nonetheless deeply aware of philosophical issues and clearly aspires to ask questions about the relationship between fiction and authenticity, unwitting imitation and deliberate emulation. That he poses these questions with no prospect of arriving at an orderly exposition of the crucial issues, let alone an answer, attests only to the fact that he is a novelist, not a philosopher. That he is shamelessly prolix and self-contradictory attests to his appetite for the performative and exasperating.

Indeed, that appetite says more about Barth's avant-garde credentials than anything else. One does not read Barth to be uplifted or edified or instructed in the ways of the world. A novel that imagines all of Western history as a gigantic university in which persons are routinely obsessed with passing exams is, to be sure, an allegorical fiction, but it is hardly an attempt to make sense of the world beyond the confines of its own created universe. That there are obvious references to the "real world" no one will doubt, but *Giles Goat-Boy* is more certainly an emblem of creation going about its not-so-usual business than a representation or a disquisition. The English critic Tony Tanner asks repeatedly for less "emphasis" on "the struggle or opposition between referentiality and reflexivity," but it is the intention of the avant-garde writer to fuel that opposition. Of course the important question is not which work is more referential than another, but what qualities of mind and spirit are embodied in a particular book and what purposes—literary or human—they serve. Barth's *Sot-Weed Factor* interests us in its own peculiar ways, ways that have little to do with the interest we take in a novel by Saul Bellow. But its uniqueness and its interest are in part a function of the implicit challenge it poses to our interest in Bellow. If we conclude that a fiction about storytelling and mythmaking is finally tedious, intolerably self-absorbed, and only intermittently a vital expression of the thing it clearly wishes to be, we do not thereby admit to a preference for referential fiction but simply respond to particular failures or limitations in a Barth.

One cannot get away from the fact that failure, boredom, emotional limitation, and linguistic excess are often inherent in the very enterprise and intention of avant-garde fiction. As one almost-official spokesman for the American avant-garde, Ronald Sukenick, asserts, for his kind of contemporary writer, "reality doesn't exist, time doesn't exist, personality doesn't exist." Literature, he maintains, is dead; reading and writing constitute at most a "considered boredom." Another spokesman, Jerome Klinkowitz, celebrates fiction that refuses to delight in anything but "the process" of composition itself, and has especial fondness for works that are insistently opaque, resist "ulterior meanings," and follow out their self-created patterns to "illogical conclusions." Like many other programmatic boosters and fellow travelers, such spokesmen are exclusively turned on by what they take to be the essentially oppositional posture of avant-garde fiction. John Barth's *Letters* (1979) is admired *because* it is longer than it needs or ought to be. William Gaddis's *JR* (1975) is touted for the very trivialization, arbitrariness, and repetitiveness that make it all but unreadable. Gilbert Sorrentino's *Mulligan Stew* (1979) is praised for its steady undermining of any interest a reader might take in its story, its characters, its topical references. That such works, in all their exasperating inconsequentiality, are created by gifted writers is a fact that one registers without quite knowing what to do with it. It's easy enough to answer the programmatic effusions of a Sukenick or a Klinkowitz, but it's something else again to dismiss utterly the brave if often misguided ambitions of a John Barth.

Robert Coover has worked the terrain ploughed by others, "stirring things up," as he has said, creating, fracturing, mythologizing, ironizing, entertaining, and confounding. Early a favorite of like-minded writers with a taste for "brightly painted paragraphs," compulsive stylization, "pseudo-dramas," and "virtuoso exercises," Coover has grown into something more. Though he remains in every sense a vanguard writer, he has demonstrated that advanced fiction can address important public issues without compromising its commitment to excess, risk, myth, and carnivalesque revelry. As much a satirist as Hawkes, and with as great an interest in the tendency of language to decline into self-parody, he nonetheless uses words to convey essential insights about the way human beings think and feel. To say of him, as one infatuate celebrant has written, that his "fictions defeat attempts to comment upon or clarify them," that in effect they deny "aboutness," is to take him for the predictably vanguard writer he has largely ceased to be. Like John Barth committed utterly to freedom of invention and the autonomous "reality" of his own fictions, he is at the same time more responsive to the claims of a "reality" not of his making and rather less willing to trust exclusively the arbitrary and reflexive. The author of the fiendishly clever *jeux* of *Pricksongs and Descants* (1969) has grown into the author of more substantial and troubling if still clever and outrageous works. The novels are, all of them, at one level exercises of a willfully unfettered imagination, the calculated exacerbations of a show-off with an inexhaustible repertoire of inventions to display. *The Origin of the Brunists* (1966) revolves around numerological puzzles and the antics of mystic sectarians. *The Universal Baseball Association, Inc.* (1968) is a wildly intricate work built around a baseball "game" — played with dice, charts, and statistics — which progressively devours every person and relationship tangled in the novel's complex weave. *The Public Burning* (1977) is a fantasist's version of a political novel conceived as a mix of the grotesque and the pathetic, the outré and the sober, the plausible and the impossible, the novelistic and the theatrical. *Gerald's Party* (1986) is a takeoff on detective stories and an intricately layered romance built around dreams, false leads, and memory. Together these novels constitute an ambitious project driven by irreverence, pride, and sheer joy in the power of language.

Such fiction as Coover writes typically features not only elements of pastiche and improvisation but what Robert Alter calls "a cavalier attitude toward consistency" and an "exhilaration of hysteria." Violating formal principles and ordinary (or "bourgeois") decorums, it is by turns arch and slapdash, innovative and innocent. Coover's novels presume the existence of a reader willing to work and to take his entertainments seriously, however riotous the idiom in which he is addressed. If in the end nothing can seem to such a reader *really* offensive or silly or significantly contradictory — if, in other words, Coover's most extravagant and novel gestures finally seem at best brilliant and amusing — the reader has at least been put through his intellectual paces and made to hang on the words of a continuously peremptory venturer.

Of course, for all of Coover's wayward brilliance, it may be that he does not deserve to be described as an avant-garde writer. By far his best work is the novel *The Public Burning,* a work that compels at least brief consideration in terms recommended by critics of the avant-garde like Renato Poggioli and Charles Newman. Poggioli describes a situation in which liberal democratic societies cannot but tolerate and finally welcome *all* "displays of eccentricity and nonconformity." Transgression—in a pluralistic culture that forbids nothing—thus becomes not only an acceptable but also an attractive and finally dominant style. The disorienting antics and studiously "offensive" violations of a Coover would then come to seem not only typical but also *de rigueur* for anyone making claims to a sophisticated readership. Understanding the terms under which he serves such a readership, a Coover will be hard put to stay ahead of their expectations. Offering the indiscriminate satire and subversive demythologizing that is the advanced novelist's stock-in-trade, Coover also slyly offers a psychological depth and compassionate tenderness that actually violate the "contract" that implicitly underwrites his relation to sophisticated readers (who are supposed to know better than to fall for character, depth, psychology, and so on). Overstepping plausibility at every turn, he grounds his novel in a conceptualization so rigorous and persuasive that the most bizarre and ridiculous gestures are made to seem purposeful and coherent and thereby to succumb to requirements associated with older, ostensibly "repressive" discursive regimes. In short, Coover does what he can to exempt his fiction from Poggioli's charge that the avant-garde can no longer be avant, that it is finally another conformist enterprise.

In *The Post-Modern Aura* (1985) Charles Newman ridicules the pretensions of the contemporary avant-garde and argues that in the United States there is none. If, as Newman has it, "the avant-garde defines itself historically by the rigidity of the official culture to which it opposes itself," then there can be no avant-garde that presumes upon the good-natured tolerance, affection, and support of a broad readership. Though, as Newman concedes, rigidity can be "hypothesized" when it does not in fact exist, a writer like Coover goes about his business in more or less blithe disregard of any constraint. The unquestioned assumption underlying such a procedure is that only cultural neanderthals and political reactionaries can *seriously* object to the effusions of clearly gifted writers. Since such persons are not to be taken seriously, and the traditional apparatus for judging works of art is no longer reliable or much in evidence, the literary virtuoso had best follow his instinct if he is to come up with genuinely adventurous and consequently admirable fictions. Though Newman does not train his sights on Coover, it is clear that even a novel with the obvious power of *The Public Burning* has more the character of a high-stepping entertainment than an insidiously subversive gesture. The peremptory "violations" practiced by a Coover look more and more like mainstream appeals to readers for whom the avant-garde is simply—as Newman says—"what's happening now."

*The Public Burning* attempts to combine political radicalism and a fully liberated aesthetics—an aesthetics in which everything goes and nothing is forbidden—with the intention of producing what is at once a critique and an expression of "America." By now probably the most widely read would-be avant-garde novel of its time, its success has as much to do with its "conventional" virtues as with its pyrotechnic dazzle. More various and affecting than anything by Hawkes, it is also as relentlessly inventive as anything by Barth. Many commentators stress the surprising humanity of its portrayals, however disfiguring the fantastic distortions and improbable scenarios to which characters are subjected. Others are equally, and rightly, impressed by the range and penetration of the political satire, noting that within the framework of a grotesque saturnalia Coover somehow provides a telling account of American politics in the 1950s. Coover's Richard Nixon is in many ways a great and complex character, the world in which he is made to move articulated with a shrewd command of political detail. Coover's decision to build so long a novel around the execution of Julius and Ethel Rosenberg is justified by his capacity to make of their story an emblem of American ideas of love, adversity, ambition, and justice. However much the novel is shaped, driven by Coover's determination to go too far, to handle ostensibly "real" characters and events with the brutally distorting contrivances of a cartoonist, the hyperbolic becomes in *The Public Burning* a necessary condition to which we object only if we are unable to appreciate all that we are given under its capacious auspices.

To emerge from rapt encounter with *The Public Burning* only to proclaim that it is no avant-garde creation, that it is too enjoyable, too accessible, too much a reflection of the quintessential energy and awfulness of "America" in its self-indulgence and imperial claim to anything it damn well pleases, is again to recall that "avant-garde" has typically signified a defiant exigency. It is possible, in other words, to regard such a novel as satisfying and successful and, at the same time, as demonstration that a postmodern avant-garde is rarely possible. The happy few, including Coover, who can preen triumphantly within—not the entrapping but the kindly—circumscriptions of language may be as much as postmodern fiction can offer. But it is a far cry from Coover's sense that all of experience is his for the taking, the eagerly complicitous reader his for the astonishing, and the remote high modernist sense of an ascetic vocation pursued without any prospect of general applause. For all of their extravagances and calculated indecencies, both Hawkes and Barth would seem better able than Coover to identify with Flaubert's assertions that "between the crowd and ourselves no bond exists" and that artists like himself must "climb into our ivory tower, and dwell there along with emptiness." One intends no disrespect to Coover when one concludes that *The Public Burning* is nowhere touched by any austere recognition of its own irrelevance.

More hermetic by far is the fiction of Walter Abish. From the moment his first novel, *Alphabetical Africa,* appeared in 1974, Abish was acclaimed as an avant-garde writer, his work typically described in the language of "defamiliarization," "surface," "parody," "fragmentation," and "artificiality." In most of his work he displays no wish to transform reality. He is content instead to build artificial structures evincing what the poet John Ashbery calls an "irrefutable logic." Readers with a limited appetite for "pure" fiction—the epithet comes from Abish—were not impressed. Neither did it help much to think of his work as proceeding from his self-confessed "distrust of the understanding that is intrinsic to any communication." Raised to a principle of composition and accepted as a given, Abish's "distrust" promised little in the way of fully engaging fictions. All too attractive to ideologues of postmodern metafiction, Abish's work and the terms he used to talk about it informed the cant employed by American critics like Jerome Klinkowitz who argued that everything is arbitrary and that there is no difference between fiction and reality. Though there is little but verbal life in works like *Alphabetical Africa,* they deserved better from academics like Klinkowitz, for whom the "fact" that we live in "post-structuralist times" (whatever that can mean) must necessarily prevent serious writers from acknowledging even perfectly obvious distinctions.

Abish's 1980 novel *How German Is It* is another matter entirely, a work of extraordinary precision that explores rather than simply buys into ideas of fictiveness and the unknowable. A quietly inexorable if also discontinuous meditation on the relationship of the "new" Germany to its Nazi past, Abish's novel on one hand invites the characterization routinely applied to his other fiction: it is fragmentary, parodic, inconclusive, and permeated by artifice. But one would not think to describe it as merely a linguistic tour de force, or as revolving about an arbitrarily chosen or merely "imaginary" landscape. Abish's focus is the Germany of the Federal Republic, the background for his concern the Nazi era and all it says, or might say, about Germany and even German-ness. The characters in the novel speak to one another in the accents of persons who might really exist. Particulars are marshaled with no sense that they are irrelevant. Enigma and obliquity are ever-present, not as manifests of an ostentatiously peremptory imagination but as reflections of pressing questions with which the novel is obsessed, as readers must be. While a critic like Klinkowitz can cheerfully insist that "the signifiers of language have no inherent relationship to the things they describe," Abish's novel treats failures of language as specific failures growing out of particular conditions. Though for Abish the unreliability of language is a problem with which human beings always contend, *How German Is It* also conveys an abiding concern about the degree to which particular discourses, institutions, cultures can be held responsible for their effort to obscure reality and obstruct memory. If in Abish's novel we are given to understand that the Nazi past is deliberately obscured in postwar Germany, that does not translate automatically into an abstract statement about the irrecoverability of the past. The reader who believes that for Abish one setting or culture is equivalent to another, a particular linguistic pattern a paradigm for all others, does not understand the tenor and design of Abish's novel. There the inaccessible, obscure, or forgotten is evoked not as a function of "the failures of language" but as a consequence of determinate intentions the novelist wishes to anatomize and understand. Whatever its reticence and indirection, the novel is a work of intensely focused moral urgency. When in the novel an architect says that "morality is not an over-riding issue in architecture," the context makes it clear that he is resorting to a sophisticated formula to evade what he ought to address. This is an instance not of the "failure of communication" but of the way that some human beings subvert the truth and violate their responsibility to speak truthfully or acknowledge what they know. The insight is not "general." It is a criticism of a kind of human failure, and it emerges from a conviction that it ought to be, and may be, possible for persons to do better.

What makes Abish's work an avant-garde novel is important. It is in no way an attempt to amuse, hector, or uplift a large audience. In an entertainment culture drawn to highly charged subjects and sensational treatments it takes on an explosive subject with a dryness and detachment that together bespeak an enormous aesthetic and moral scruple. At the same time, one never feels here that for Abish indirection is a stylistic fetish, opacity a standard postmodern decorum. Abish's commitment to the formal and philosophical premises of the work ensures that he refuse to provide the decisive answers, compellingly colorful characterizations, and dramatic actions favored by more "popular" writers. Even a symbolically charged incident, like the discovery of a mass grave beneath the streets of the town of Brumholdstein, is presented in such a way as to "resist any type of easy assimilation" or climactic resonance. So argues Abish's best critic, Maarten van Delden, who also notes that the extreme precision of the novel, drawing our attention to matters both large and small, ceaselessly "defamiliarizes" everything, compounding an aura established by the "narrator's habit of posing endless questions, even about the most trivial matters." Deconstructing the world of the new Germany, van Delden goes on, Abish depicts it "as a place of evasion and deception, of discontinuities between past and present . . . where the past is continually being evoked and then side-stepped." Relentlessly involving us in questions and plots we cannot but find interesting, Abish refuses "to tie together the various strands of his narrative" or to permit the creation of an unmistakable "moral center." Though nothing in these refusals seems at all perverse, it is clear that the avant-garde (or subversive) element in *How German Is It* proceeds from a radical skepticism, however much Abish here resists the claims of the arbitrary and meaningless. Unmoved by the usual forms of indeterminacy and iconoclasm, Abish here demonstrates that for a serious avant-garde writer—quite as Charles Newman demanded—there can be "more to fiction than fiction" and more than "the fatuity of form as final consolation."

William Gass has made himself an unapologetic spokesman for fiction and the consolations of form, assuming in one resounding essay after another an oppositional posture that has made him the foremost exemplar of the avant-garde in his generation. Though his fiction has not quite commanded the attention routinely devoted to his aesthetic tracts and polemics, he is surely one of the most accomplished and original writers around. From the first having inspired readers to speak of his essays and stories as "works of beauty" by a man "who loves words" more than anything else, he has insisted upon the autonomy, the purity of art while struggling to avoid the pallor and empty formalism of a bloodless aestheticism. To those turned off by the idiot ejaculations and glib spontaneities of would-be vanguardists like Jack Kerouac, Gass has seemed a model of pride, wit, cunning, and audacious verbal brilliance. He has been willing to make judgments and take risks, to make art as if it were possible actually to fail and to succeed. Though many younger writers out for the main chance show little interest in his work, they have read him; they know that he is out there, his best work an implicit challenge to their every indifferent sentence and self-indulgent yawp.

Gass's fiction includes an enormous novel-perpetually-in-progress entitled *The Tunnel*, the 1966 novel *Omensetter's Luck,* the 1968 story collection *In the Heart of the Heart of the Country,* and a bravura mixed-media fiction called *Willie Masters' Lonesome Wife* (1971). No one of these can quite indicate what the others are like. The stories are mostly without those teeming "barrages of verbiage"—John Gardner's description—that one finds in the other works. *Omensetter* is without the typographic puns and lunacies of *Willie. The Tunnel*—so far as one can tell from the extended sections published in periodicals—refuses the linear narrative continuity of *Omensetter.*

At the same time, one need only utter the words "William Gass" to call to mind certain tendencies that together help to place him. Ihab Hassan calls him "logophiliac, perhaps logopath, certainly myth-omane." Alvin Rosenfeld speaks of Gass's feeling for "the musical as well as the semantic character" of words, of a verbal "opulence" that can become "self-consciously flamboyant," "strutting," even "dandified." Tony Tanner finds in Gass a constant reminder that "it is precisely in the flamboyance and poetry—the whole 'aside' of style and language finely used—that we find our fun, our dignity." Gass's own essays also steer us in the inevitable direction, nowhere more pointedly than in "The Concept of Character in Fiction," where he announces his ambition "to carry the reader to the edge of every word so that it seems he must be compelled to react as though to truth as told in life, and then to return him, like a philosopher liberated from the cave, to the clear and brilliant world of concept, to the realm of order, proportion, and dazzling construction . . . to fiction, where characters, unlike ourselves, freed from existence, can shine like essence, and purely Be."

Though this is not the place for a full-scale analysis of such a formulation, it is clear that there is even more to Gass than his own statements reveal. Gass may want characters "unlike ourselves," but his figures sufficiently resemble us to make readers interested in them as if they were or might have been drawn from actual human beings. He may chiefly prize "concept," "order," and "proportion," but his fictions also provide elements of narrative development and recognizable setting. However strenuous his insistence upon consciousness and the internal, he situates his fictions in such a way as to anatomize and explain the instinct to turn inward: no inside without outside in Gass, no self without others, no sufficiency of language without the suggestion of an insufficiency, no shining like essence without traces of desolating everydayness. One thinks words, sentences, music as one reads Gass, but one thinks also of "life" and "experience" in ways that Gass is ever reluctant to allow. Some, like the critic Richard Gilman, deplore "the confusion of realms." Others dismiss the familiar trappings—characters, settings, themes, allegorical options—as so many opportunities for linguistic invention, for the surface play of ostensive signifiers. Gass tells them all what to believe, but no one is quite ready to take as gospel the word of so boisterous a "lie-minded man."

People who write of Gass typically describe the narrator as a "dominant consciousness" or a voice, and in fact there are grounds for doing so, as also for reverting now and again to talk of characters with backgrounds and features and reasons. *Omensetter*'s Jethro Furber is a kind of "verbal architecture," as Arthur M. Salzman suggests, but he also resembles a man. The landscape in Gass is a kind of metaphor for, rather than a straight depiction of, an actual physical environment, but for all the reverie and innerness and linguistic aura, we also feel and carry within us the powerful presence of what we take to be actual landscapes. We know that every feature of each such landscape has been created, dreamt, shaped, that it is a fabric of words to which we attend, but we give ourselves over to the half-illusion of place quite as we do in fictions with more palpably illusionistic designs upon us.

In short, one is tempted to say that in his fiction Gass knows things he cannot permit himself to know elsewhere. He knows, that is, how entirely his deep and joyous absorption in language exists in tension with, or in response to, another kind of absorption, more troubled, more diffuse. Characters in his fiction are hurt into language in a way that the confident master who speaks in the essays need not consider. In the fiction language is a refuge and a trap, in the essays it is all adventure, blessed method, consciousness electrified by beauty. Deeply alert to all that language cannot accomplish, Gass in his fiction tracks the vicissitudes of the language animal confronting inertia, grayness, confusion, even history. The power of the fiction comes from its capacity to evoke in language much that language is helpless to alter or register adequately. There is a pathos and a tension in the best of the fiction that is largely absent even from the already classic philosophical essays on representation, stylization, and the ontology of the sentence.

Is Gass an avant-garde writer? He has so wished to be that it would seem at least ungenerous to deny it. His least sustaining fiction, *Willie Masters,* has all the qualities of a willfully outrageous, incorrigibly digressive work, and if it isn't an all too typical avant-garde fiction, I don't know what is. The other fictions, including fragments of *The Tunnel,* are so complex, so full of every kind of aesthetic scruple that they feel like something else. In their overt attention to language and the obstacles they erect to comfortable appropriation, they are avant-garde works. In the range of palpable pleasures they afford, including the fellow feelings they sometimes enable, they are satisfying in a way that is not often associated with the avant-garde. Charles Newman asks "whether an aesthetic [like Gass's] so fully and systematically engaged against Pseudo-art allows itself the amplitude to authenticate itself." Gass is neither a Joyce nor a Tolstoy, but by pushing past the sometimes straitening requirements of his own aesthetic he has created fully convincing and ravishing fictions. These works almost confirm the irrelevance of discussions bearing on what is or is not avant-garde—discussions in which Gass himself has been an influential participant.

Gass early wrote on Donald Barthelme, celebrating his absorption in the trash of common experience and his success in placing himself "in the center of modern consciousness." Others, equally persuaded by Barthelme's skills and devices, have likened his work to light entertainment, "like the blowing of dandelion fluff: an inconsequential but not unpleasant way of passing the time." For Gass, Barthelme is an intrepid explorer gaily picking through the dreck left around us by television, books, political speeches, ordinary talk: "The aim of every media, we are nothing but the little darkening hatch they trace when, narrowly, they cross." For Barthelme's severest critics, his flattening of distinctions, his reduction of everything—as Gass puts it—to a "flatland junk yard," is a denial of meaning and a shallow toying with serious questions. Even readers deeply impressed by the variety of narrative modes in Barthelme, by his deft movement from parodies of narrative structure to playful lampoons of cultural institutions, are often in doubt as to what this sort of wit and intelligence can amount to. Gass would seem to claim enough by refusing to claim too much: he asserts that, in addition to the dreck and the play, "there is war and suffering, love and hope and cruelty" in Barthelme, but he doesn't tell us what these count for in Barthelme, how heavily they weigh upon us as we read, how much they are trivialized by the pervasive irony. From what point of view does Barthelme expose consciousness as "a shitty run of category errors and non sequiturs"? If, as Gass says, he "has the art to make a treasure out of trash," what precisely differentiates the treasure from the clever joke, and what in Barthelme authorizes the serious employment of so devalued a term as "treasure"? Gass nicely tells us what a Barthelme fiction is most apt to look like, but questions of force and significance are not much considered.

Barthelme is a kind of avant-garde writer in one sense at least: he writes for an audience that knows something about narrative devices and is sophisticated enough to appreciate parody. The problem, if there is one, is that Barthelme makes things very easy for this audience and may succeed as well as he does mainly by creating a community of sophisticates whose main credential is its willingness to be amused by the likes of Barthelme. It isn't hard, after all, to be sophisticated in the way that Barthelme requires. All that's asked, really, is that you be alert to the irony that undercuts everything, that you be too smart to be taken in, that you recognize the joke even if you don't quite get it. Never before has an avant-garde writer seemed so clubbable, so much intelligent fun, so wicked without wanting to hurt, so scathing without wanting any one party to feel singled out for abuse more than another. If serious conventional writing evokes emotion, then perhaps it is fair to say that Barthelme's depersonalization, his refusal to make us feel anything but superior, is a way of defying convention. But again, for all the wit and brilliance of Barthelme's contrivances, they cost us nothing; we accede to them with no reluctance. Critics like Charles Molesworth stress the "ironic resonance" established when Barthelme's characters come up with solemn value-judgments and straightforward "home truths": there is poignance, says Molesworth, in the need of characters to fall back "on ethical, normative measures that will allow them to comprehend their experience." But of course there is no real conflict in these passages. Readers know at once what is to be made of nostalgias and wisdom-statements in Barthelme. Where the context ensures that nothing be anything but silly or hopeless, where the voice is so perfectly—if narrowly—pitched, where the authorial control is consummate, there can be no genuine tension, no experience of menace or breakdown. It's not alone the artfulness, formal severity, or fantastic distortion that certifies the presence of an avant-garde work. Barthelme's fictional voice, "both coy and disaffected," as Molesworth says, is strangely status-affirming and comfortable in the postmodern age, and as such it lacks the final accent of fully affecting avant-garde fiction.

This is not to say that the best of the work is anything less than wonderful. If the novels *Snow White* (1967) and *The Dead Father* (1977) seem not much more than elaborate conceits, they do nonetheless embody qualities found in the more satisfying stories. Each contains passages that just about any contemporary writer would be pleased to have written. Each raises important questions that it refuses to address, however intent it is upon wringing from those questions what it can by way of aura and amusement. What makes the stories so much better than the novels is that in the shorter works we are not made to expect development or deepening of insights. In the novels Barthelme's refusal to press for development may itself be taken as a token of avant-garde defiance, but mostly it seems a matter of incapacity. Barthelme knows what he wants to do, and has a sly contempt for those who are inclined to go too far, to say more than they mean. In *The Dead Father* he writes a hilarious passage on the "true task" of the modern son, which is to reproduce the father, "but a paler, weaker version of him," and thereby to move "toward a golden age of decency, quiet and calmed fevers." It is possible to hear in this passage not the accent of angry rebuke but the mostly wistful accent of one who knows himself and his time too well to demand too much. As we interpret such words—hearing in them mostly biting satire or ironic self-acceptance—so will we be inclined to regard Donald Barthelme's relationship to the avant-garde.

Less problematic by far is Guy Davenport's posture. An inheritor of the high modernist tradition, drawn by training and disposition to what Hugh Kenner calls "the austere and astringent," Davenport is allusive, learned, precise, languorous, backward- and forward-looking all at once. Infatuated by things past, dreaming always of new collocations and conjunctions, he offers a combination of intellectual rigor and lyric sensuality, prudent attention to detail, and eccentric foraging (his word). Though characterizing himself as a maker of assemblages, a builder, Davenport uses an essentially collagist technique to create narratives with a strange and enchanting momentum. One is carried through a Davenport fiction not by a structured succession of events or by the promise of discoverable thematic coherence but by the steady unfolding of images and thoughts, the playful but never forced alternation of affinities and digressions. Working often with named historical or artistic figures—Charles Fourier, Ezra Pound, Franz Kafka—Davenport imagines and excavates, borrows and invents, states and evokes, ever intent—as he says—on making contact with "pioneers of the spirit," the better to grasp what is meant when we say that "man was created to understand the world."

Though such an enterprise is not by its nature inevitably an avant-garde project, in Davenport's hands it is altogether exigent, stimulating, and original. One would not think to place Davenport at the head of an aggressive formation, moving inexorably forward and spearheading an opening for others—the German writer Hans Magnus Enzensberger's view of the historic avant-garde. But then such a view little applies to most other plausible participants in an American vanguard. Davenport not only has no wish to lead but also manifestly refuses to write out of a sense of impatience with what is past. His works are created out of an abiding absorption in things loved, found, collected, retrieved, used, studied, assimilated, and shared. The continual surprise and pleasure afforded by the work has much to do with the delight it takes in handling its own materials, in fingering a skein of thought, a line, a physical detail, an almost forgotten fact of history, an image. Exchanges of words, confidences, emotions, couplings: these too are facts, materials, partially or barely recoverable presences like all the others in Davenport. His works are perpetually in advance of us and of most everyone else's work by virtue of what one critic calls its "almost archaic naivete," its warm yet simultaneously dispassionate embrace of the "literal" and the "encyclopedic," the "inconclusive" and the "visionary."

Davenport's several collections of short fiction contain a few novella-length works, including the lascivious rhapsody on the life of the Dutch Fourierist philosopher Adriaan van Hovendaal entitled "The Dawn in Erewhon." Though he has produced no full-scale novel, his writing is central to the achievement of avant-garde fiction in the United States, and aspects of his work are strangely novelistic. There is an expansiveness of vision, a leisureliness of pacing in Davenport that have nothing to do with the usual concision and implicitness of the short story. Indeed, such qualities distinguish most of the shorter stories as much as they do the longer. "A Field of Snow on a Slope of the Rosenberg," however elegant its organization around a single character and a single unifying experience, can accommodate all sorts of ideas and vagrant references, and one's quiet exhilaration at the end is mixed with disappointment that there is to be no more within a structure flexible enough to accommodate more. Just so, in the title story of his first collection, *Tatlin!* (1974), much of the richest material is not strictly entailed in the premise from which the fiction unfolds. There is nothing arbitrary or willful about these inclusions. The method is such as to justify itself, continuously, by finding what will serve, extend, illuminate, delight. Development is in the expansion of the evolving consciousness that is the fiction itself. Selection is, as in few other writers, inevitably a matter of addition, discovery leading—not inevitably, but plausibly—to discovery. In no other writer is there such variety of reference with so little ostentation; in no other so assured a combination of what the character Adriaan calls "meticulous draughtsmanship" and "voluptuous" or "generous" command. In Davenport the American avant-garde demonstrates a maturity, a poise and comeliness and elevation, that has not been much in evidence before.

Initially one is more apt to speak of enchantment and sorcery than of maturity in connection with the writing of Steven Millhauser. The author of several novels and collections of stories, he has frankly invited comparison with a wide range of precursors—from the Italo Calvino of *Invisible Cities* to the Vladimir Nabokov of *Pale Fire* and the Jorge Luis Borges of "Pierre Menard"—only to astonish readers with the extraordinary singularity of his work. Millhauser's aesthetic control and meticulous intelligence have been often remarked, but there are better reasons to think of him as the most mature of vanguard writers. A fantasist with a taste for the whimsical and farcical, Millhauser is also a strangely sober, sometimes melancholic writer. Though in every sense of the word an artificer, he can move within a sentence from inspired prestidigitation to disillusionment. For all of his commitment to creating "an air of legend," the better to set off creatures "perfect and complete in themselves," he is ever alert to the fact that "today's novelty is tomorrow's ennui," the marvelous "a revelation that never comes." If maturity is reflected in the achievement of a perfect balance between abandon and constraint, lightness and weight, innocence and irony, exhilaration and defeat, then Millhauser is the most mature of writers. What appears in his work as a reluctance to let go of childhood and its prerogatives seems upon reflection a persistent intimation of all that childhood, like art, cannot sustain. If, often, he trades in the eccentric or bizarre—one thinks of the erotic miniatures sometimes painted upon the sides and tips of the nipples of court ladies in "Cathay"—he never seems far from evoking what Goethe called "the spirit of eternal negation."

That the mood of a Millhauser fiction is quite different from anything to be found in other contemporary vanguard works is obvious. Nowhere else is there so haunting a combination of enchantment and disenchantment. A character speaks of "the obscenity of maturity" only to end by impressing upon us the frailty and bad faith of an undifferentiated commitment to play. Poetic activity is extolled only to issue in puerility or terminal self-absorption. Parody is systematically employed as a critique of particular conventions only to conclude by undercutting the validity of everything, including its own playful subversions. From delight in fluency and metamorphosis we move to an equally vivid "skepticism" and "the knowledge that we can never be satisfied" or fully taken in. The language itself embodies these alternations and ambivalences. Pregnant, even lugubrious passages suffused by the "secretive, dark and wayward" are also—simultaneously, deliberately—undercut, brushed by the academic, the finicky, the fanatically observant. From "abysmal promises," "the disillusionment of the body," and "I will teach you the death of roses, the emptiness of orgasms in sun-flooded loveless rooms" we move to or from the likes of "He thinks of Pope's tunnel at Twickenham, of the emergence of eighteenth century English gardens from the rigidity of French and Italian forms." At its best the language is so entirely a blend of the two dimensions, of the precise and the mysterious, light and dark, that one must speak not of shifts but of interanimating textures and tonalities: wish and recoil, dream and disinfatuation are one.

Millhauser made his reputation with the 1972 novel *Edwin Mullhouse,* a mock-biography of a "great" novelist, dead at eleven, and a wickedly suggestive portrayal of his "biographer," also his confidant and closest friend, Jeffrey Cartwright. For all its verbal high jinks and its intense remembrance of childish pleasure, it is a book of enormous sadness. In satirizing the romantic religion of art, including the nostalgias that often inform poetic reverie, the novel strikes at its own deepest affinities, at its own sense that in art alone there is the possibility of seeing and feeling truly. Like the character Edwin in his ostensive novel *Cartoons,* Millhauser "approaches a serious subject by means of comic and even ridiculous images." Like Jeffrey, ostensive narrator-author, Millhauser exalts and demeans, gives and takes back. Everywhere, even as it cavorts and puns and burlesques, the novel secretes a poisonous, anathematical will to put an end to its own high spirits. At its most self-canceling indulging a language of transparent excess, hyperbole, cliché, it turns its own generous extravagance to ridicule. With its every "woe to the writer, most wretched of the damned" and "who can fathom the soul of man? Friendship is a mystery. Curiosity killed the cat," the novel irrevocably undermines its troubled commitment to "literature," sincerity, and wisdom. Unable quite to renounce its visceral involvement in soul and seriousness, the novel is prey to the "peculiar vanity" of Edwin Mullhouse in wishing "to seem not quite serious." But for all its occasional playfulness, the novel does not really wish to sustain "the cute grin of a cartoon cherub," and where it does appear, as Jeffrey remarks, "that grin is itself the mask, beneath which lies a grimace of earnestness." Though one is necessarily reluctant to adopt the self-conscious observations of such a novel as if they were a reliable guide to its intentions, the reader may be certain that Millhauser knows exactly what is at stake and has installed within the novel as much as we need to discern its terrible urge to ironic self-disenchantment.

Millhauser's subsequent books emerge from the same vision and rely for their effects upon similar procedures. The most brilliant of these later works—including the novella "August Eschenburg" from *In the Penny Arcade* (1986) and the title story of *The Barnum Museum* (1990)—however singular, have all to do with inauthenticity and the diminishing prospects for creating serious art. In "August Eschenburg," these issues are the subject of the work; in other stories they flit in and out of focus as the discourse turns on one, then another related image or reflection. It is simple enough to mark out the dominant counters in "August," with its references to "world-irony," "love of truth," and the relation between art and "soul." Here, in a work whose resonance reminds us not of Borges but of Thomas Mann and *Confessions of Felix Krull*, we have a focused reflection on the capacity of art to "express spiritual states." Other works, in spite of their obvious interest in such questions, intermittently take up a variety of concerns, and with nothing like an urging toward substantive closure. Single images carry enormous weight in such fictions, sometimes reversing the primary thrust of the work in which they appear. But again, for all the paradox, invention, and irony, we cannot but discern the principal business of Millhauser's fiction.

The key to Millhauser's art, and to the avant-garde element in his outlook and practice, has much to do with irony. Millhauser is the most ironic of writers. He writes, that is to say, in a style at once extravagant and self-conscious, confident and guilty. What looks to be the smile of imagination eager to take everything for its province is also the self-mocking smile of one who knows too well that imagination can be neither innocent nor robust, effectual nor free. Irony in Millhauser is the sign of imagination disabused, slyly giving itself over to procedures by which it will exercise its powers only to confront the ultimate failure of those very powers. In the expression of this irony there is joy, but it is the harsh, pyrrhic joy of consciousness triumphant over its own creative powers and illusions. Millhauser creates in the Barnum Museum what he calls "a realm of wonder," but as he leads us through its "gaudy halls" and "brash abundance" he cannot but note "a certain coarseness," and worse, a capacity even in the most stirring exhibits to inspire "boredom and nausea," stupefaction, desolation. This is in itself only modestly disturbing, reflecting as it may what are merely changing moods. More insidious by far is the suggestion that the oppositions presented in such a work are themselves not to be seriously entertained, that the very language of wonder is itself so tainted by excess and cliché that it ought not to convey what it ostensibly intends. Even the disillusion so steadily interposed between the poet and his reverie is compromised, literary, inauthentic—not always farcical or ridiculous, but at least slightly exaggerated so as to seem a parody of an earlier mode of austere disillusion.

In fact, parody is so bound up with irony in Millhauser as almost to seem an integral component of his stance. This is not parody as we find it in other postmodern writers, in Barth or in Barthelme, to take two illustrious examples. In novels like *The Sot-Weed Factor* and *Giles Goat-Boy,* parody—say, of seventeenth-century English and American prose, or the language of savior myths—is employed to revivify our relation to the past and thereby to empower Barth's claim to a mythmaking novel of the future. In Barthelme, as Charles Molesworth has written, we have "a field of free-floating parody, where no anchoring content or style serves as the central vehicle of intention against which the other structures are judged or interpreted." This yields, in Barthelme, not only an indiscriminateness in the targeting of objectives but also "a feeling of the author's lack of responsibility," which enthusiasts rather celebrate as "decentering" or "undecidability." Millhauser's parody is neither future-oriented nor irresponsibly nihilistic, neither voraciously imperialistic nor indiscriminate. Neither can parody in Millhauser be reduced to an anxious competition with models or a desire to recuperate energies associated with earlier literary cultures. If he would surely agree with the painter Robert Motherwell that every intelligent artist carries the whole culture of modern art in his head, and that "his real subject" is likely to be that whole culture, he would no doubt find it harder to accept that "everything" he creates "is both an homage and a critique." Such a formulation too emphatically suggests that the writer proceeds with targets before him, that in parodying literary biography he is criticizing literary biography, that in simultaneously parodying and investing in romantic archetypes his primary goal is to say something about romanticism.

But Millhauser parodies in the more radical spirit of the Thomas Mann who in 1944 noted in his diary that "I myself know only one style: parody." This was not in Mann a boastful statement, and of course there is nothing boastful even in the most riotous of Millhauser's fictions. If, like Mann, Millhauser knows only parody, this must be understood as reflecting a disciplined refusal to escape from self-consciousness, from a sense of the potential or actual hollowness, conventionality, ludicrousness of his own best language and ideas. Erich Heller, in his 1958 book *Thomas Mann: The Ironic German*, develops this view of the radical artist with surpassing lucidity, and nowhere more powerfully than in a passage he quotes from Nietzsche: the artist, Nietzsche writes, "reaches the ultimate point of his greatness only when he has learned how to see himself and his art *beneath* himself—when he knows how to *laugh* at himself." Millhauser consistently sees himself and his art beneath himself: so one believes in reading his novels and stories. What he parodies, more than any genre-convention or empty discourse, is his own steadfast effort to rise above the conventional, the trivial, the shoddy. In parodying even the most lucid and earnest of literary employments, including the helplessly familiar language of affection and admiration,

Millhauser takes on what Heller terms "the misgiving that the pursuit of art may have become incompatible with authenticity." For Millhauser, the essential thrust of parody is not critique—however much he may criticize moribund forms and corruptions of spirit—but autocritique. The irony and pervasive melancholy of his art consist in its steady acknowledgment that the exercise of creative freedom can only authentically issue in the truth of its inadequacy.

Though other writers have adopted some such dark view of art and of the condition of language, few have expressed it with such seriousness and grave amusement. However obvious the differences between Millhauser and modernist masters like Mann and Kafka, he reminds us of their severe gaiety, their powers of detachment and melancholy serenity. The avant-garde element in Millhauser is clear not in his power to enrage or to shock but in his sense—expressed in a prose vigorous and precise—that to explore the boundaries of consciousness and invention is to discover not inexhaustibility but limit. The greatest of avant-garde writers have understood that an oppressive sense of limitation was inherent in the energetic, sometimes furious attempt to overcome expressive constraints. If the self-proclaimed avant-garde in the United States has often seemed unduly, not to say preposterously, overconfident, that has usually reflected a lack of seriousness associated with the view that limits exist only to be ignored or wished away. The German writer Hans Magnus Enzensberger writes of "the historic avant-garde" that "never did it try to play it safe with the excuse that what it was doing was nothing more than an 'experiment.' " The contemporary avant-garde, lacking the seriousness of its predecessors, too often adopts the guise of breakthrough and irresponsibility as "trademark and as camouflage." The fiction of Millhauser, in its exigence, reminds us of all that the imagination wishes it were free to accomplish, and impresses upon us the infinite longing for culminations we are increasingly without the resources to believe in. In so doing, Millhauser helps restore to the avant-garde project a scruple and seriousness largely abandoned by ambitious American writers in the late years of this century.

Robert Boyers

# Biographies of American Authors

Edward Abbey (1927–89)

Though Abbey was born in Pennsylvania, a preoccupation with the desert landscape of the Southwest—predominantly Arizona and New Mexico—and issues of the environment inform all of his fiction, as well as his life. His experience as a Park Ranger and firefighter finds resonance in his famous work *The Monkey Wrench Gang* (1975). His other works include *Desert Solitaire* (1968) and *The Fool's Progress* (1988). His final novel, *Hayduke Lives!* (1990), is a sequel to the popular *Monkey Wrench Gang*.

Walter Abish (1931–  )

Born in Vienna, Abish fled Austria with his family and arrived in Shanghai in 1940. In 1960 Abish came to the United States, where he worked as an urban planner. In his challenging, experimental fiction, Abish deconstructs the continuity of ordinary events. *Alphabetical Africa* (1974), *In the Future Perfect* (1977), and *How German Is It* (1980) have established Abish's reputation as a central voice among avant-garde novelists.

Kathy Acker (1947–  )

Raised in New York, Acker has lived in San Francisco, Seattle, and San Diego, where she has avowedly pursued a lifestyle corresponding to the stark merge of sexuality, feminism, and "punk" aesthetics inhabiting her fiction. Her novels include *Blood and Guts in High School* (1978), *Great Expectations* (1982), and, most recently, *Seven Cardinal Sins* (1990) and *In Memoriam to Identity* (1990).

## Louisa May Alcott (1832–88)

Alcott, daughter of Amos Bronson Alcott, was born in Germantown, Pennsylvania, and grew up in the transcendentalist circle of Emerson and Thoreau. At sixteen she published her first book, *Flower Fables*, and from an early age she worked to help support her family. Her first novel was *Moods* (1864). *Little Women* (1868–69) was an immediate success, and the family was at last economically secure. Her other novels include *An Old-Fashioned Girl* (1870), *Little Men* (1871), and *Under the Lilacs* (1878). Her last novel was *Jo's Boys* (1886), a sequel to *Little Women*. She died in Boston in 1888, only two days after her father.

## Horatio Alger, Jr. (1834–99)

He was born in Revere, Massachusetts, the son of a Unitarian minister, and was raised under a strict regimen of study and prayer in preparation for the ministry. He graduated from Harvard in 1852, entered Harvard Divinity School in 1855, but ran away to Paris before graduation exercises. He did enter the pulpit in 1864, but two years later fled again, to New York. There he became a close friend of Charles O'Connor of the Newsboys Lodging House, and began writing the boys' stories (of Ragged Dick, Tattered Tom, etc.) for which he is still remembered.

## Rudolfo Anaya (1937– )

Born in Pastura, New Mexico, Anaya has remained in the state of his birth. He is concerned with the life and image of Latinos in the Southwest and these concerns find articulation in his work. Anaya's most famous fiction is a trilogy about growing up in New Mexico: *Bless Me Ultima* (1972), *The Heart of Aztlan* (1976), and *Tortuga* (1979).

# Sherwood Anderson (1876–1941)

Born in southern Ohio to a poor and vagabond family, Anderson is best known for his collection of short stories, *Winesburg, Ohio* (1919), and for the influence his unadorned but poetic prose style and his "grotesque" characters had on other writers of his generation, notably Ernest Hemingway, Nathanael West, and William Faulkner. In 1912, after abruptly abandoning the mental pressures of a successful business career in Ohio, he moved to Chicago, where he became acquainted with and received encouragement from Carl Sandburg, Theodore Dreiser, and Floyd Dell, to pursue the creative life that he yearned for. A writer of naturalistic stories and novels (*Windy McPherson's Son* [1916], *Marching Men* [1917], *Poor White* [1920], *Many Marriages* [1923], *Tar* [1926], *Beyond Desire* [1932], *Kit Brandon* [1936]) set usually in the Midwest, he depicted the demoralizing effect of an increasingly industrialized and corporate-minded America upon the imagination and spirit of the common people, a theme that extended to his nonfiction writing (*Perhaps Women* [1931]; *Puzzled America* [1935]).

# Timothy Shay Arthur (1809–85)

Born in rural New York state, Arthur trained to be a watchmaker and worked for several years as a clerk before he became editor of the *Baltimore Athenaeum*. A regular contributor to *Godey's Lady's Book*, he eventually founded several magazines of his own, the most successful of which was *Arthur's Home Magazine*. He was a prolific writer of cautionary tales and moral tracts, most notably the sensational and melodramatic *Ten Nights in a Bar-Room, and What I Saw There* (1854), dramatized in 1858 by William Pratt.

# Isaac Asimov (1920– )

Asimov was born in Russia and was brought to New York City as a small child. He graduated at nineteen from Columbia University, received his Ph.D. from Columbia in 1948, and joined the faculty of Boston University in 1955. At eighteen he sold his first science fiction story. His first novel, *Pebble in the Sky*, was published in 1950, and Asimov embarked on an extremely prolific and eclectic writing career, sometimes under the pseudonym Paul French. His best-known work is the Foundation trilogy (*Foundation* [1951]; *Foundation and Empire* [1952]; and *Second Foundation* [1953]), to which he continues to add (*Foundation's Edge* [1982]; *Foundation and Earth* [1986]).

## Gertrude Atherton (1857–1948)

Born Gertrude Franklin in California, Atherton wrote several novels depicting California history, going back to its days as a Spanish colony: *Before the Gringo Came* (1894; revised in 1902 as *The Splendid Idle Forties*); *The Californians* (1898; revised 1935); *The Horn of Life* (1942). In addition she wrote short stories, essays, and a history of California (*Golden Gate Country* [1945]). *The Conqueror* (1902) is a fictionalized biography of Alexander Hamilton; her society novels include *Julia France and Her Times* (1912) and *Black Oxen* (1923).

## Margaret Atwood (1939–   )

Atwood was born in Ottawa, grew up in Toronto, attended the University of Toronto, and took a graduate degree from Radcliffe. She has published many collections of poetry and has taught at several Canadian universities. Her second volume of poetry (*The Circle Game* [1966]) won a Governor General's Award, and her study *Survival: A Thematic Guide to Canadian Literature* (1972) established her reputation as a critic. Her popular successes include *The Edible Woman* (1969), *Surfacing* (1972), *Lady Oracle* (1976), *Life Before Man* (1980), and *The Handmaid's Tale* (1985), for which she received a second Governor General's Award.

## Mary Austin (1868–1934)

Mary (Hunter) Austin was born in Illinois but moved to California at eighteen, where she made a study of Native American life and was involved with the artists' colony at Carmel before moving to Santa Fe, New Mexico, where she taught and continued her own research. Her fictional themes include the West and Native American culture, the life of Jesus, women, radical politics, and social reform. Her best-known works are *Land of Little Rain* (1903) and *The Ford* (1917).

## James Baldwin (1924–87)

Born in Harlem, New York City, Baldwin spent much of his spare time in the city library enthusiastically reading such authors as Harriet Beecher Stowe, Charles Dickens, and Horatio Alger. Throughout his difficult growing-up years, Baldwin endured much hostility from his fanatically religious stepfather, an experience that forms the theme of many of Baldwin's works, including his collection of stories, *Going to Meet the Man* (1965). At age fourteen, Baldwin underwent a religious conversion, which led to an evangelical calling until he was seventeen. Disenchanted with America's treatment of its African American population, in 1948 Baldwin purchased a one-way ticket to France. Although he returned sporadically to the United States, and was active in the Civil Rights movement, he remained an expatriate until his death. In such powerful and elegant novels as *Go Tell It on the Mountain* (1953) and *Giovanni's Room* (1955), and in such non-fiction as *Notes of a Native Son* (1955), *Nobody Knows My Name* (1961), and *The Fire Next Time* (1963), Baldwin explores life at the margins of society and what it means to be black in America. Other works include *If Beale Street Could Talk* (1974), *The Devil Finds Work* (1976), and *Just Above My Head* (1979).

## Amiri Baraka (1934–  )

Born LeRoi Jones, he grew up in Newark, New Jersey. Baraka attended a predominantly white private school and then Harvard University. Dismissed from school in 1954, he joined the United States Air Force. However, in the wake of the Red scare and the prevalent fear of communist insurgency, Baraka was dishonorably discharged in 1957 because of his "suspicious" activities. Baraka moved to New York's Greenwich Village, and became acquainted with the literati there. With his then wife, Hettie Cohn, Baraka edited a Beat journal, *Yugen,* publishing the work of Allen Ginsberg and Jack Kerouac. In 1960 Baraka visited Cuba. Tremendously affected by this trip, and later by the assassination of Malcolm X, Baraka left the Village for Harlem. During this same period, Baraka changed his name, combining Islamic and Bantu references. In 1979 Baraka joined the African Studies Department at SUNY/Stony Brook. His works detail his shifting and maturing political consciousness. They include *Preface to a Twenty Volume Suicide Note* (1961), *Dutchman* and *The Slave* (1964), *The Dead Lecturer* (1964), *Black Magic* (1969), *In Our Terribleness* (1970), *Jello* (1970), *Spirit Reach* (1972), and *The Autobiography of LeRoi Jones/Amiri Baraka* (1984).

## Djuna Barnes (1892–1982)

Barnes was born in New York state and joined the colony of American expatriates in Europe during the 1920s and 1930s. She was associated with the avant-garde and the bohemian, in terms of both her life and her art. Barnes's fiction gives free expression to her family traumas, her bisexuality, and her feminism. Sometimes published under the pseudonym Lydia Steptoes, Barnes's ironic, frequently grotesque works include *The Book of Repulsive Women* (1915), *Ryder* (1928), and *Nightwood* (1936).

## John Barth (1930–   )

Born in Maryland, Barth originally studied at the Juilliard School of Music. This early affinity for music is reflected in his first novel, *The Floating Opera* (1956). He was associated, by his own admission, with existentialism, and later with the postmodernist movement. Barth's challenging work rejects conventional conceptions of both narrative structure and truth. His novels include *The Sot-Weed Factor* (1960), *Giles Goat-Boy* (1966), *Lost in the Funhouse* (1968), *Chimera* (1972), *The Friday Book* (1984), and *The Tidewater Tales* (1987).

## Donald Barthelme (1931–89)

Born in Philadelphia, Barthelme and his family moved to Houston where his father practiced architecture, a subject later important to Barthelme's fiction. After serving two years in Korea, Barthelme relocated to New York where he soon achieved notoriety for his innovative minimalist stories that appeared in *The New Yorker*. A prominent postmodernist, Barthelme published his first collection of metafictional stories, *Come Back, Dr. Caligari,* in 1964, followed by *Unspeakable Practices, Unnatural Acts* (1968), *City Life* (1970), *Sadness* (1972), *Amateurs* (1976), *Great Days* (1979), and *Sixty Stories* (1981). His novels are *Snow White* (1967) and *The Dead Father* (1976).

## Saul Bellow (1915–  )

The son of a Russian Jewish émigré, and a Canadian by birth, Bellow came to Chicago when he was nine and grew up in the Midwest. He attended the University of Chicago and graduated from Northwestern University. A student of anthropology, Bellow began graduate work at the University of Wisconsin, but as his thesis persisted in "turning out to be a story," Bellow considered a career in literature. He worked on the WPA Federal Writers' Project where he became acquainted with a number of New York writers, notably Delmore Schwartz, and began teaching. Today regarded as a prominent American writer, Bellow received the Nobel Prize for literature in 1976, following the publication of *Humbolt's Gift* (1975). His works include *Dangling Man* (1944), *The Victim* (1947), *The Adventures of Augie March* (1953), *Seize the Day* (1956), *Henderson the Rain King* (1959), *Herzog* (1964), *The Dean's December* (1982), and *Some Die of Heartbreak* (1987).

## Thomas Berger (1924–  )

Presently a recluse and reluctant to reveal biographical details, Berger has lived in London and Manhattan. Frequently associated with the contemporary Western, Berger has written wide-ranging satiric fiction that often parodies iconographic images of American city and rural life. His novels include *Little Big Man* (1964), *Neighbors* (1980), and *Changing the Past* (1989).

## Marie-Claire Blais (1939–  )

Blais was born in Quebec City, the eldest child of a working-class family. At her parents' urging she left a convent school to train for secretarial work (which she hated—she held nine clerical jobs in three years). However, her first novel, *La belle bête* (1959), was an immediate success, and she received a Canada Council grant that allowed her to spend a year in Paris, where she immersed herself in French cinema and literature. In the early 1960s, Blais lived and worked on artist Mary Meigs's farm at Wellfleet, Massachusetts, and in 1971 she and Meigs moved to Brittany, where they spent four years. Blais's award-winning Francophone work includes *Une saison dans la vie d'Emmanuel* (1966), *Les manuscripts de Pauline Archange* (1968), and *Le sourd dans la ville* (1979; translated in 1980 as *Deaf to the City*).

## Jorge Luis Borges (1899–1986)

Born in Argentina, Borges was educated in Geneva, Switzerland. Upon completing his schooling, Borges returned to Buenos Aires in 1921. From 1939 to 1945 Borges worked as a librarian; and from 1955 to 1973 he worked as director of Biblioteca Nacional. From 1967 to 1968 Borges was the Elliot Norton Professor of Poetry at Harvard. Primarily on the reputation of one book of stories— *Labyrinths* (1962)—Borges established his reputation as a masterful, highly original, and important writer. Borges's influential stories are unique in their erudition—Borges was a notorious bookworm who possessed an encyclopedic range of knowledge—and their challenging metafictional themes. His works include *A Fever in Buenos Aires* (1923), *A Universal History of Infamy* (1935), *The Gardens of Forking Paths* (1941), *Doctor Brodie's Report* (1970), *The Book of Sand* (1970), and *A Borges Reader* (1981).

## Paul Bowles (1910–   )

Bowles was born in New York City. Acutely interested in music, he studied with composers Aaron Copland and Virgil Thomson. While traveling in Paris, Bowles became acquainted with Gertrude Stein and her circle of expatriates, who encouraged him to write. His works include *The Sheltering Sky* (1949), *Next to Nothing* (1976), *Points in Time* (1984), and *A Distant Episode* (1988).

# Richard Brautigan (1935–84)

Born in Tacoma, Washington, Brautigan moved to San Francisco, where he became involved in the burgeoning Beat movement, before living in various locations in the Western states and Japan. Textual playfulness and whimsy characterize his extensive body of fiction. *Trout Fishing in America* created an international sensation when it appeared in 1967. Brautigan committed suicide in 1984. His novels include *The Abortion: An Historical Romance* (1966) and *The Tokyo-Montana Express* (1980).

# Charles Brockden Brown (1771–1810)

Born in Philadelphia of a Quaker background, Brown was one of the first American professional authors. His writing career was brief, however, as economic pressures soon forced him to look elsewhere for his livelihood. Even so, he continued as editor and chief contributor to the *Literary Magazine and American Review* (1803–7) and to the *American Register* (1807–10). Brown was heavily influenced by the political and philosophical ideas of Thomas Jefferson and William Godwin, as demonstrated in his novels and in his treatise on the rights of women, *Alcuin: A Dialogue* (1798). His novels—*Wieland* (1798), *Ormond* (1799), *Arthur Mervyn* (1799, 1800), *Edgar Huntly* (1799), *Clara Howard* (1801), and *Jane Talbot* (1801)—were the first to incorporate authentically American characters, settings, and concerns. Just as important, his works transform the supernatural conventions of the Gothic novel into close studies of psychological aberration.

# William Wells Brown (ca. 1816–1884)

A pioneering historian of African American history (*The Black Man* [1863]; *The Rising Son* [1874]), Brown was born in Lexington, Kentucky, and was perhaps the son of George Higgins, a white slaveholder. Raised in St. Louis, he was hired out for a time to the print-shop of the *St. Louis Times*. In 1834 he escaped and, taking a job on a Lake Erie steamer, helped other fugitive slaves to freedom. Lacking formal schooling, he educated himself and in 1847 published his autobiographical *Narrative of William Wells Brown, a Fugitive Slave.*

His novel *Clotel; or, The President's Daughter* (London, 1853) was released in the United States in an expurgated form as *Clotelle: A Tale of the Southern States* (1864).

## Orestes Brownson (1803–76)

Brownson was born in Stockbridge, Vermont. He was six years old when his father died, and he was raised by strictly Puritan relatives. He had almost no formal education, but he became a well-known liberal editor and helped to found the Workingmen's Party. His religious affiliations shifted from Presbyterianism to Universalism; he was for a time an itinerant preacher, then a Unitarian minister. His eventual conversion to Catholicism is recounted in *The Convert* (1857). His two novels are *Charles Elwood; or, The Infidel Converted* (1840) and *The Spirit-Rapper* (1854).

## Charles Bukowski (1920–   )

Born in Germany, Bukowski immigrated to the United States at the age of two. He was raised in Los Angeles and still lives in southern California. Largely influenced by the irreverent rhythms and patterns of free association used by the Beat generation, Bukowski is an extraordinarily prolific writer of prose and poetry, authoring more than forty titles. These include *Flower, Fist and Bestial Wail* (1960), *Fire Station* (1970), *Post Office* (1971), *Factotum* (1975), *Ham on Rye* (1982), and *Barfly* (1984).

## Edgar Rice Burroughs (1875–1950)

Burroughs was born in Chicago, graduated from the Michigan Military Academy, and served briefly with the Seventh Cavalry in Arizona. He held a variety of jobs, and even tried dredging for gold before the publication of his first science fiction story, *Under the Moons of Mars* (1912). Though Burroughs is best known as the creator of Tarzan, whose adventures he chronicled in twenty-four volumes, his many sci-fi novels include such familiar titles as *The Warlord of Mars* (1919) and *At the Earth's Core* (1922).

## William Burroughs (1914–    )

Born in St. Louis, Missouri, Burroughs attended Los Alamos Ranch School in New Mexico and began what was to be an extensive and diverse educational experience. From 1932 to 1936, Burroughs attended Harvard and majored in English; from 1936 to 1937 he attended medical school at the University of Vienna; and in 1938 he attended graduate school in anthropology at Harvard. In 1944 Burroughs settled in New York City and began a long association with various countercultural figures, including Beats Jack Kerouac and Allen Ginsberg. Highly experimental, satiric, and demanding, Burroughs's fiction often draws upon his own experiences at the fringes of society. Burroughs's subjects include heroin addiction, homosexuality, and subversive politics. In 1962 he published *Naked Lunch* and in 1966 the Massachusetts Supreme Court ruled the book not obscene, following a long and controversial trial. His works include *Nova Express* (1964), *The Ticket That Exploded* (1967), *The Wild Boys* (1971), *Exterminator!* (1973), and *The Place of Dead Roads* (1983).

## George Washington Cable (1844–1925)

Cable was born in New Orleans, served in the Confederate Army, and was wounded twice. With little formal schooling, Cable set about a program of disciplined self-education, rising before daylight to study French. In 1873 his story " 'Sieur George" was published in *Scribner's Monthly*. Between 1873 and 1879 other stories appeared in *Scribner's* and *Appleton's*, and in 1879 a collection of his French-dialect stories, *Old Creole Days*, was published. His first novel, *The Grandissimes*, appeared the next year, to be followed by several more novels of the South and of Creole life. In 1885 Cable moved to Northampton, Massachusetts, where he lived for the rest of his life. Remembered today as a prominent figure of the local color movement, he was also a social and religious writer. His nonfiction work includes *The Silent South* (1885) and *The Busy Man's Bible* (1891).

## Truman Capote (1924–84)

Capote was born in New Orleans. He attended the prestigious academies of the Trinity School and St. John's, but left school at the age of seventeen. Fascinated by New York theater, Capote worked at a number of locales before being employed by *The New Yorker*. As he grew older, and more self-parodic, Capote became the friend of celebrities and often received more attention as a personality than as an author. Capote's prose is both sensitive and nostalgic. His works include *Other Voices, Other Rooms* (1948), *Local Color* (1950), *The Grass Harp* (1951), *Breakfast at Tiffany's* (1958), *In Cold Blood* (1966), and *Answered Prayers* (unfinished and posthumous, 1985).

## Alejo Carpentier (1904–80)

Born in Havana, Cuba, to a Russian mother and a French father, Carpentier was a Cuban political prisoner in the early 1930s. Though he lived for many years outside his native country, mostly in Paris and in Caracas, Venezuela, Carpentier returned to Cuba in 1959, where he became a member of the Cuban Communist Party and the National Assembly. His novels *¡Ēcue-Yamba-Ō!* (God Be Praised, begun in 1933 during his imprisonment and published in 1979), *El acoso* (1958; *The Chase*, 1989), *El siglo de las luces* (Explosion in a Cathedral, 1963), and *El recurso del método* (Reasons of State, 1976), combine "magic realism" with strong critiques of political oppression. Carpentier died in 1980 in Paris.

## Raymond Carver (1938–88)

Born in Clatskanie, Oregon, Carver attended California State University at Humbolt and later the University of Iowa. Despite his extensive teaching experience—at the universities of Iowa, Texas, California (Berkeley and Santa Cruz), and Syracuse—he persistently returned to the Pacific Northwest. Carver died in Port Angeles, Washington. Primarily a writer of short stories, Carver was also a poet of considerable talent. A self-avowed, recovered alcoholic, Carver explored the hidden vulnerabilities of character and exposed the revelatory aspects of ordinary experience. His works include *Will You Please Be Quiet, Please* (1977), *What We Talk About When We*

*Talk About Love* (1981), *Cathedral* (1984), *Fires, Essays, Poems and Stories* (1984), and *Where I'm Calling From* (1986).

## Raymond Chandler (1888–1959)

Chandler, who gained fame as a writer of "hard-boiled" detective fiction, was born in Chicago, educated in England, and moved to southern California in 1912. He began writing mystery stories when in his forties, and his first novel was *The Big Sleep* (1939), which introduced his famous detective, Philip Marlowe. It was an enormous success both as a novel and as a motion picture, as were *Farewell, My Lovely* (1940), *The Lady in the Lake* (1943), and *The Long Goodbye* (1954). Chandler himself was a cultured man, yet he (like Dashiell Hammett, for whom he had the greatest respect) depicted the underside of life in the great metropolises. His essay on the writing of crime fiction is included in *The Simple Art of Murder* (1950).

## Denise Chavez (1954–  )

Chavez is a native of New Mexico. *The Last of the Menu Girls* (1985) reflects her familiarity with the rhythms, language, and mythologies of the border regions, as well as Chavez's concern for the women of the Southwest.

## John Cheever (1912–82)

Born in Quincy, Massachusetts, Cheever was educated in New England. He attended the well-known Thayer Academy, but was expelled at the age of seventeen. This expulsion formed the basis of Cheever's first story, "Expelled," which was published by the *New Republic* in 1930. Committed to a literary career, Cheever moved to New York City where he wrote book synopses for MGM. During World War II, Cheever served in the United States Army and then returned to what would become a successful literary career. Living in New England suburbia, Cheever exposed the painful and sometimes humorous truths that haunt upper-middle-class existence. The biographies that have appeared since Cheever's death suggest that his life, too, had hidden aspects. Alcoholism, familial strife, and sexual guilt were aspects of Cheever's own life, as well as themes in his fiction. His works include *The Way Some People Live* (1943), *The Enormous Radio and Other Stories* (1953), *The Wapshot Scandal* (1964), *The Brigadier and the Golf Widow* (1964), *Bullet Park* (1969), and *Falconer* (1978).

## Charles Waddell Chesnutt (1858–1932)

Chesnutt was born in Cleveland to free African American parents from North Carolina. Though largely self-taught, he worked variously as an educator, reporter, accountant, and attorney before embarking on a literary career. Though best known for his collections of short stories (*The Conjure Woman* and *The Wife of His Youth*, both 1899), and for his use of regional dialect in the manner of Joel Chandler Harris, Chesnutt also produced a biography of Frederick Douglass (1899) and published three novels during his lifetime. *The House Behind the Cedars* (1900) and *The Marrow of Tradition* (1901) confront issues of racial identification and betrayal; *The Colonel's Dream* (1905) and another novel left unpublished at his death also center on the theme of racial injustice.

## Lydia Maria Child (1802–80)

Born in Medford, Massachusetts, she was the sister of Unitarian minister Convers Francis. From 1825 to 1828 she taught school at Watertown, Massachusetts, where she established the *Juvenile Miscellany* (1826). In 1828 she married attorney David Lee Child. Both she and her husband were dedicated abolitionists, and in 1833 she published *An Appeal in Favor of That Class of Americans Called Africans;* from 1840 to 1844 she was editor of *The National Anti-Slavery Standard.* In addition to her abolitionist activities, she was active in the causes of sex education and female suffrage. Though best known as an essayist, Child also wrote fictional works, including three historical romances: *Hobomok* (1824), *The Rebels* (1825), and *Philothea* (1836).

## Kate Chopin (1851–1904)

Born Katherine O'Flaherty, Chopin grew up in St. Louis, Missouri, in an affluent Catholic family. She married Oscar Chopin at the age of twenty and moved with him to Louisiana. When Chopin was thirty-four her husband died, and she raised their children alone. During this period, Chopin began to write professionally, though her efforts at composition were always combined with child care duties. Chopin's work explores the contrasts between Northern and Southern sensibilities, as well as the continuous tension between creativity and domesticity that Chopin believed must necessarily mark the work of a woman artist. Chopin's first novel, *At Fault* (1860), was followed by a collection of short stories entitled *Bayou Folk* (1894). A second collection of short pieces of fiction, *A Night in Acadie* (1897), established Chopin's reputation as a representative of the local color movement. Creole culture and language and the visual landscape of Louisiana found expression in Chopin's fiction. While *The Awakening* (1899) is largely viewed today as Chopin's literary masterpiece, the book was widely condemned at the time of its publication. The morbid sensuality of Edna Pontellier and the novel's exploration of a new and more independent kind of woman led to its critical rejection. Both the fictional Edna Pontellier and Chopin herself languished in literary obscurity until the 1960s. An increasing sensitivity to the particular problems of the female artist and a renewed interest on the part of publishers in women writers led to a reexamination and reappraisal of Chopin's work. Frequently anthologized today, Chopin now appears to hold a secure place within American literary history.

## Louis Chu (1915–70)

Chu was born in a village just outside Canton, China. He moved to Newark, New Jersey, at the age of nine. He received his degree in English from New York University, and later served in the United States Army. Ironically, perhaps, Chu was stationed in Kunming in southeastern China. After the conclusion of World War II, Chu lived in New York City, operating a Chinatown record shop and working as the city's only Chinese disc jockey. *Eat a Bowl of Tea* (1961) reflects Chu's concerns about the Asian American experience.

## Sandra Cisneros (1954–   )

Born in Chicago, Cisneros is a graduate of the University of Iowa Writers' Workshop. Interested in the manner in which race and gender structure her own life, Cisneros explores these themes in poetry and stories that have been described as "international graffiti." Her books include *Bad Boys* (1980), *The House on Mango Street* (1985), and *My Wicked, Wicked Ways* (1987).

## James Fenimore Cooper (1789–1851)

The eleventh child of William and Elizabeth (Fenimore) Cooper, James Kent Cooper (he added Fenimore after his father's death) was born in Burlington, New Jersey, and spent his youth in the still wild country around Cooperstown, on Otsego Lake in New York, where he gained firsthand acquaintance with the Native Americans and the landscape that would be featured in his Leatherstocking tales. He attended Yale for two years, but a youthful prank resulted in his dismissal in 1806. A stint in the Navy proved dull; in 1811 he resigned and married Susan De Lancey, who bore him six children. A famous anecdote recounts the beginning of Cooper's literary career: dissatisfied with a novel he was reading, he declared that he could do better himself; his wife's challenge to do so resulted in his first book, *Precaution* (1820). Writing fired Cooper's imagination and sense of adventure, and his second novel (*The Spy* [1821]) was a success. In addition to the Leatherstocking tales, the best known of which are *The Last of the Mohicans* (1826) and *The Deerslayer* (1841), he was a prolific writer in a variety of modes, from historical romance to social satire, producing scholarly naval histories, a utopian allegory, and even a precursor of the mystery novel. He died on the eve of his sixty-second birthday, September 14, 1851.

## Robert Lowell Coover (1932–   )

Born in Iowa, Coover served in the United States Navy and later studied literature at the University of Chicago. Innovative and experimental, his postmodern fiction often collapses traditional narrative structure to help explore the breakdown of social conventions and values in American society. His novels include *The Origin of the Brunists* (1966), *The Universal Baseball Association* (1968), *Spanking the Maid* (1981), and *Gerald's Party* (1986).

## Stephen Crane (1871–1900)

Crane, a native of Newark, New Jersey, attended Lafayette College and Syracuse University (a year each) before moving to New York City, where he earned a meager living as a free-lance reporter. His first novel, *Maggie: A Girl of the Streets* (1893), was published with money borrowed from his brother, and was a financial failure, but it did impress Hamlin Garland, who brought it to the attention of William Dean Howells. Crane's masterpiece, *The Red Badge of Courage,* was published in 1895. Because of its brilliant depiction of war, Crane found himself in demand as a war correspondent. Returning from an assignment in Cuba, Crane was shipwrecked, an experience that resulted in "The Open Boat" (1897), but his health was broken, and he died before his twenty-ninth birthday.

## Maria Cummins (1827–66)

Maria Susanna Cummins was born in Salem, Massachusetts, and was educated mainly at home by her father, a local judge. Her early stories appeared in various periodicals, most notably the *Atlantic Monthly.* In 1854 she published her first (and most popular) novel, *The Lamplighter,* the story of an orphan girl's struggle to independence. Cummins never married, and lived a quiet, domestic life with her family in Dorchester, Massachusetts. Her other novels include *Mabel Vaughan* (1857), *El Fureidis* (1860), and *Haunted Hearts* (1864).

## Richard Henry Dana, Jr. (1815–82)

Dana was born in Cambridge, Massachusetts, graduated from Harvard Law School, and was a founder of the Free Soil Party. In his junior year at Harvard, his studies were interrupted when he contracted a case of measles that affected his eyesight. In an attempt to recoup his health, he signed onto the brig *Pilgrim,* bound for California, as an ordinary seaman. His narrative of the voyage, describing the hardships and discipline aboard ship, was published anonymously in 1840 as *Two Years Before the Mast;* in 1841 he published *The Seaman's Friend,* a manual of admiralty law.

## Guy Davenport (1927–   )

Born in Anderson, South Carolina, Davenport was educated at Duke, Oxford, and finally Harvard universities; he received his Ph.D. from the last in 1961. Presently a professor at the University of Kentucky, Davenport continues to write essays, reviews, poems, libretti, and what have been called "assemblages"—finely crafted short stories that merge history, myth, and sociopolitical themes along with Davenport's poetic and innovative voice. His works include *Tatlin!* (1974), *Eclogues* (1981), and *Apples and Peas & Other Stories* (1984).

## Robertson Davies (1913–   )

Davies was born in Thamesville, Ontario, the son of a local newspaper publisher. He was educated at Upper Canada College, Toronto, in Kingston at Queen's University, and at Balliol College, Oxford, and has been variously an editor, educator, and dramatist as well as novelist. His novels include the Salterton trilogy, *Tempest-tost* (1951), *Leaven of Malice* (1954), and *A Mixture of Frailties* (1958), and the Deptford trilogy, *Fifth Business* (1970), *The Manticore* (1972), and *World of Wonders* (1975).

## Rebecca Harding Davis (1831–1910)

Born Rebecca Blaine Harding in Washington, Pennsylvania, she was largely self-educated, and began writing fiction while quite young. In 1861 her stories began to appear in the *Atlantic Monthly,* and in 1862 her first and most popular novel, *Margret Howth,* was published. In 1863 she married journalist L. Clarke Davis and moved to Philadelphia; she was herself an associate editor of the *New York Tribune* for several years. She was an early pioneer of the naturalistic style, exemplified in her famous short novel *Life in the Iron Mills* (1861). She was the mother of novelist Richard Harding Davis.

## Richard Harding Davis (1864–1916)

Davis's mother was writer Rebecca Harding Davis. He was born in Philadelphia, and achieved fame as a journalist, war correspondent, and editor of *Harper's Weekly*. His travels as a reporter provided material for many collections of stories; in addition he wrote twenty-five plays and several novels, the best known of which is *Soldiers of Fortune* (1897), a love story set against the backdrop of a South American revolution.

## Martin Robison Delany (1812–85)

Born a free African American in Charles Town, West Virginia, Delany was educated first by itinerant booksellers, briefly attended Harvard Medical School, and during the Civil War became the first African American major in the United States Army. In 1843 he established a newspaper, the *Mystery;* in 1852 he published *The Condition, Elevation, Emigration, and Destiny of the Colored People of the United States,* advocating the creation of a free black state. His novel, *Blake; or, The Huts of America,* was serialized between 1859 and 1862, but was not published in book form until 1970.

## Samuel Delany (1942–   )

Born in Harlem, New York, and educated in the Bronx, Delany has used metaphors of the city and ethnicity to shape his postmodern science fiction. Delany attended New York City College for two years. Highly influenced by the cultural dynamism of the 1960s, he dropped out of college to pursue a career as a writer. His first novel was finished in the same year (1962). Extraordinarily prolific, Delany numbers among his works *The Jewels of Aptor* (1962), *Captives of the Flame* (1963), *The Towers of Toron* (1964), *The Einstein Intersection* (1967), *Dhalgren* (1975), *Triton* (1976), and *Stars in My Pocket Like Grains of Sand* (1984).

## Joan Didion (1934–   )

Didion has the unusual distinction of being from a family that has resided in California for several generations. Born outside Stockton in 1934, Didion inherited a Western sensibility that marks all of her prose. Didion is a stylist who attempts to construct narratives but is always aware that she works in a literary terrain wherein narration is necessarily a deconstructive act. Her fictional works include *Run River* (1963), *Play It As It Lays* (1970), *A Book of Common Prayer*

(1977), and *Democracy* (1984). Didion's essays have also received critical acclaim. Her nonfiction works include *Slouching Towards Bethlehem* (1968), *The White Album* (1979), and *Salvador* (1983). Didion now lives in New York City and has merged her postmodern perspective with her concern for global politics. She remains one of the strongest voices in contemporary literature.

## Thomas Dixon (1864–1946)

Dixon was born in North Carolina, and was a Baptist minister before becoming a novelist. His novel *The Clansman* (1905) was part of a trilogy that included *The Leopard's Spots* (1902) and *The Traitor* (1907), and was adapted for the silent screen by D. W. Griffith as *The Birth of a Nation* (1915).

## Ivan Doig (1939–   )

Doig grew up in Montana where he later worked as a ranch-hand. His work chronicles in detail the development of the Montana highlands and places him in the arena of serious, contemporary Western writers. Doig's works include *This House of Sky* (1978), *Winter Brothers* (1980), *The Sea Runners* (1982), and a trilogy composed of *English Creek* (1984), *Dancing at the Rascal Fair* (1987), and *Ride with Me, Mariah Montana* (1990).

## John Dos Passos (1896–1970)

Dos Passos's life was politically focused from its beginning. The son of a prominent Wall Street lawyer, Dos Passos attended Choate School, explored Europe, and went on to Harvard University, where he became committed to leftist politics. In 1917 Dos Passos went to France and volunteered as an ambulance driver. Deeply affected by the brutality and violence that he witnessed during World War I, Dos Passos increased his devotion to left-wing politics and socially committed fiction. His works include *Three Soldiers* (1920), *Manhattan Transfer* (1925), *The 42nd Parallel* (1930), *1919* (1932), *The Big Money* (1936), *District of Columbia* (1952), and *Midcentury* (1961).

## Frederick Douglass (1817–95)

Douglass is best known for his autobiographical account of his enslaved youth and his subsequent escape from slavery. His *Narrative of the Life of Frederick Douglass* (1845) details Douglass's early life of bondage and his liberating discovery of his authorial voice. Douglass's work shows familiarity with previous texts concerning slavery and emancipation, but his book became the classic slave narrative, archetypal of its genre. The dates regarding Douglass's life are, by his own admission, unreliable, as slaves were not routinely provided with birth records. However, Douglass was born in Maryland, the son of a black slave woman and a free white male. After witnessing the dissolution of his family, the sexual abuse of his aunt, and beatings from his owners, Douglass escaped and made his way to New York in 1838. In 1841 Douglass attended an antislavery convention in Nantucket where he was "moved to speak," and he subsequently became involved in the abolitionist movement.

## Paul Laurence Dunbar (1872–1906)

The son of former slaves, Dunbar was born and grew up in Dayton, Ohio. Both his parents had taught themselves to read, and his mother especially shared and nurtured her son's early love of poetry and literature. Dunbar attended public school in Dayton and graduated in 1891. He began to receive public attention in 1892, but not until 1896, when William Dean Howells gave his poetry a substantial and favorable review in *Harper's Weekly*, did he get the boost needed to establish his reputation. Dunbar produced four novels, *The Uncalled* (1896), *The Love of Landry* (1900), *The Fanatics* (1901), and finally, in 1902, *The Sport of the Gods*. While the first three books featured white protagonists, *The Sport of the Gods*, one of the first works of African American social protest, chronicled the aspirations, disillusionment, and ultimate disintegration of family life for newly freed slaves in the North as well as in the South.

## William Eastlake (1917–   )

Born in Brooklyn, Eastlake worked his way west following World War II. While exploring the rugged Jemez Mountains of New Mexico, Eastlake developed a strong sense of the Western landscape, which pervades such novels as *Go in Beauty* (1956), *The Bronc People* (1958), and *Portrait of an Artist with Twenty-Six Horses* (1963). During the 1960s Eastlake served as a correspondent in Vietnam and wrote *The Bamboo Bed* (1969) based on his experiences.

## Ralph Ellison (1914–  )

Born in Oklahoma and named for Ralph Waldo Emerson as testimony to his parents' hope that their son would possess a literary sensibility, Ellison was reared to have both aesthetic and social concerns. At an early age Ellison accompanied his mother when she worked on civil rights projects. By the time of his adolescence Ellison was a skilled cornet player, and he studied music at the Tuskegee Institute. Ellison later moved to New York City where he was befriended by Richard Wright, and, under his tutelage, became active in the Federal Writers' Project. *Invisible Man* (1952), *Shadow and Act* (1964), and *Going to the Territory* (1986) all reflect Ellison's concerns with African American consciousness, aesthetics, and music.

## Louise Erdrich (1954–  )

Born in North Dakota, and an enrolled member of the Turtle Mountain Chippewa tribe, Erdrich witnessed at an early age both the imperiled condition of the American West and the problematic state of the reservation Native American. Erdrich served briefly as editor of *The Circle,* a Native American news journal. She now lives in New Hampshire, but her works reflect a continuing interest in Native American culture and the development of the West. Her works include *Jacklight* (1984), *Love Medicine* (1984), and *The Beet Queen* (1986).

## Augusta Jane Evans (1835–1909)

Evans was born near Columbus, Georgia, and was educated almost entirely at home by her mother. Upon the failure of her father's business, the family moved to Texas and then, in 1949, to Mobile, Alabama. In 1868 she married Lorenzo Madison Wilson, a rich Mobile businessman. Evans's novels—pious, sentimental, and erudite—have been frequently, and at times unfairly, ridiculed. She is chiefly re-membered for her phenomenally popular *St. Elmo* (1866), which sold over a million copies. Her other novels include *Inez: A Tale of the Alamo* (1855), *Beulah* (1859), *Macaria* (1863), *Vashti* (1869), *Infelice* (1875), and *At the Mercy of Tiberius* (1887).

## William Faulkner (1897–1962)

Faulkner was born in New Albany, Mississippi, but moved to Oxford early in his youth. He would maintain a home there for most of his adult life. After serving in the Royal British Air Force during World War I, attending the University of Mississippi, and taking a tour of Europe, Faulkner turned his attention to literature. His early novels brought him critical recognition, but it was the self-consciously pro-vocative *Sanctuary* (1931) that brought Faulkner fame. In 1950 Faulkner was awarded the Nobel Prize for literature. Plagued by al-coholism and marital discord, Faulkner continued to be a highly pro-lific author. He also worked briefly—and unhappily—as a Holly-wood screenwriter. Returning to the South, Faulkner taught at the University of Virginia. Acclaimed as one of the greatest of twentieth-century American writers, Faulkner explores the corrupt and some-times sinister structure of familial and Southern life in his fiction, as well as the way race and social class operate within that structure. Much of his work details the intrigues and dramas of his fictional Yoknapatawpha County and the antics of the nearly mythical Snopes family. Faulkner's numerous works include *The Marble Faun* (1924), *Soldier's Pay* (1926), *Sartoris* (1929), *The Sound and the Fury* (1929), *As I Lay Dying* (1930), *Light in August* (1933), *Absalom, Absalom!* (1936), *The Hamlet* (1940), *Requiem for a Nun* (1951), and *The Reivers* (1962).

## Frederick Faust (1892–1944)

Faust was born in Seattle, Washington, and died in Italy while work-ing as a war correspondent for *Harper's*. His Western novels (*Destry Rides Again* [1930]; *Singing Guns* [1938]; *Danger Trail* [1940]) were written under the pseudonym Max Brand. As Walter C. Butler he wrote crime fiction, and under his own name he published spy novels.

Other works of his include a volume of poetry (*The Village Street and Other Poems* [1922]) and *Calling Dr. Kildare* (1940).

## Fanny Fern (Sara Payson Willis) (1811–72)

Willis, best known under her pen name of Fanny Fern, was born in Portland, Maine, but was raised in the Boston area and attended Catharine Beecher's school in Hartford, Connecticut. Her first marriage, to Charles H. Eldredge (1837), appears to have been a happy one, but his death in 1846 left her with two children to support, which she attempted to do first through teaching and needlework, and then through the satirical essays (collected in *Fern Leaves from Fanny's Portfolio* [1853, 1854]) that eventually brought her fame and fortune as a newspaper columnist. In 1849 she married Samuel P. Farrington, from whom she was divorced three years later; in 1856 she married James Parton. Her first novel, *Ruth Hall* (1855), contains an unflattering portrait of her brother, Nathaniel Parker Willis; the second (*Rose Clark* [1856]) features two heroines, one an abandoned wife, the other a divorcée.

## Martha Finley (1828–1909)

Born in Chillicothe, Ohio, and educated in South Bend, Indiana, and in Philadelphia, Pennsylvania, Martha Finley (under the pseudonym Martha Farquharson) produced approximately one hundred children's novels, and is chiefly remembered today as the creator of Elsie Dinsmore, a heroine whose life is chronicled in twenty-eight volumes of the Elsie books, 1868–1905. Finley never married, and lived a quiet, domestic existence in Elkton, Maryland, from 1876 until her death at the age of eighty.

## F. Scott Fitzgerald (1896–1940)

Francis Scott Fitzgerald was born in St. Paul, Minnesota, into a moderately wealthy family. He entered Princeton University in 1913, but left in his senior year and entered the United States Army. In 1920 he married Zelda Sayre, and his first novel, *This Side of Paradise* (set at Princeton), was published. It caught the restless spirit of the times, and for several years Scott and Zelda Fitzgerald were the darlings of the "Jazz Age"—the name that he gave to the 1920s. During the twenties, his stories appeared in the *Saturday Evening Post* and *Scribner's,* and were collected in *Flappers and Philosophers* (1920), *Tales of the Jazz Age* (1922), and *All the Sad Young Men* (1926). Fitzgerald's masterpiece, *The Great Gatsby,* was published in 1925, but from that point on his life and career became increasingly troubled. *Tender Is the Night* (1934) reflects the tragedy of Zelda's breakdown, but Fitzgerald also suffered from physical and emotional problems. His experiences as a Hollywood screenwriter were the source materials for *The Last Tycoon,* which, though unfinished at Fitzgerald's death, was published posthumously in 1941.

## Mary Hallock Foote (1847–1938)

Born in Milton, New York, Foote was schooled as an artist and illustrator. In 1876 Foote married and moved west with her husband to California. As the wife of a miner and engineer, Foote traveled through much of the Western territory; she became particularly conversant with the terrain of California, Nevada, and Colorado. Her experiences are documented in her own Westerns—novels about the West but constructed from a female sensibility. Her works include *The Chosen Valley* (1892), *The Led-Horse Claim* (1895), and *Coeur D'Alene* (1895).

## Richard Ford (1944–  )

Ford was born in Jackson, Mississippi, and currently lives in New Orleans and in western Montana. Ford's neorealistic novels and stories reflect the rural topology of these regions—as well as the terrain of other Western states. Ford's novels include *A Piece of My Heart* (1976) and, most recently, *Wildlife* (1990).

## Hannah Foster (1759–1840)

Hannah (Webster) Foster was the daughter of a successful Boston merchant. In 1785 she married the Reverend John Foster of Brighton, Massachusetts, and bore him two daughters. Her novel, *The Coquette,* was published in 1797. This story of seduction was immediately popular, perhaps partly because of its basis in factual events.

She died in Montreal, where she had lived with her daughters following her husband's death.

## Mary E. Wilkins Freeman (1852–1930)

Freeman was born in Randolph, Massachusetts, and lived there until 1902, when she married and moved to New Jersey. She is best known for her local color stories, collected in *A Humble Romance* (1887), *A New England Nun* (1891), and *Edgewater People* (1918). Her novels include *Jane Field* (1893); a historical novel, *The Heart's Highway* (1900); and *The Portion of Labor* (1901). In addition, she wrote a play dealing with the Salem witchcraft trials, *Giles Corey* (1893), and a collection of supernatural tales, *The Wind in the Rosebush* (1903).

## Carlos Fuentes (1928–  )

Mexican author Carlos Fuentes was born in Panama City, Panama, the son of a career diplomat. As a result, his youth was exceptionally cosmopolitan. He attended the Colegio de Mexico and received a law degree from the National University of Mexico before studying economics at the Institute of Higher International Studies at Geneva, Switzerland. Fuentes's first novel was the experimental *La región más transparente* (1958; *Where the Air Is Clear,* 1960). Other major works include *La muerte de Artemio Cruz* (1962; *The Death of Artemio Cruz,* 1964); *Cambio de piel* (1967; *A Change of Skin,* 1968); and *Terra Nostra* (1975; English translation, 1976). In addition to his career as a novelist, short-story writer, and dramatist, Fuentes has held a number of governmental appointments, including that of Mexican Ambassador to France (1974–77), and he continues to be active as critic, lecturer, and political essayist.

## Gabriel García Márquez (1928–  )

García Márquez, Colombian-born novelist, short-story writer, and journalist, studied journalism and law at the University of Bogota and worked as reporter and foreign correspondent in Colombia, Europe, Venezuela, and the United States from 1950 to 1965. During the 1960s he lived in Mexico, where he wrote *Cien años de soledad* (1967; *One Hundred Years of Solitude,* 1970), a masterpiece of the peculiarly Latin American style known as "magic realism." In 1975 he published *El otoña del patriarca* (*The Autumn of the Patriarch,* 1976), also highly acclaimed, and in 1982 he was awarded the Nobel Prize for literature. From 1967 to 1975, García Márquez made his home in Barcelona, Spain; more recently he divides his time between his native Colombia and his residence in Mexico City. A recent novel is *El amor en los tiempos de cólera* (1985; *Love in the Time of Cholera,* 1988), and he continues to be an influential voice in the leftist press.

## Erle Stanley Gardner (1889–1970)

Gardner was a practicing California attorney who, though he wrote many novels under several pseudonyms, is most famous as the creator of defense attorney and sleuth Perry Mason, whose long life in print began with *The Case of the Velvet Claws* in 1933. Gardner also produced a series of crime-detection novels centered on the figure of district attorney Douglas Selby, who first appears in *The D. A. Calls It Murder* (1937).

## John Gardner (1933–82)

Born in Batavia, New York, Gardner grew up on a small farm and enjoyed the rhythms of a bucolic existence that would later flavor some of his fiction. Gardner attended DePauw University and Washington University in St. Louis, graduating in 1955. Increasingly intrigued by medieval literature, Gardner completed his graduate work at Iowa State University, receiving his doctorate degree in 1958. Despite his traditional academic direction, Gardner submitted a novel (*The Old Men*) as his dissertation. While teaching, Gardner not only engaged in writing criticism but also produced fiction and poetry. In 1966 he published *The Resurrection;* this novel was followed by a series of works that probed the past—Gardner's personal past and the world's more mythic history. Gardner continued to teach medieval literature at a number of institutions, including Oberlin College, California State University at San Francisco, and Bennington College. He also chaired the creative writing program at SUNY/Binghamton. Gardner died in a motorcycle accident at the age of forty-nine. His works include *The Wreckage of Agathon* (1970), *Grendel* (1971),

*The Sunlight Dialogues* (1972), *Nickel Mountain* (1973), *Jason and Medeia* (1973), *The King's Indian* (1974), *October Light* (1978), *On Moral Fiction* (1978), *Mickelsson's Ghosts* (1982), and *On Becoming a Novelist* (1983).

## Hamlin Garland (1860–1940)

Garland was born on a Wisconsin farm and grew up under the hardships of life on the prairies; his parents moved to Iowa and then the Dakota Territory trying to earn a living. He went to Boston in 1884, worked, and educated himself in the public library. In 1892 he published *Main-Travelled Roads,* bitter stories of life in the Middle West. This work and the many novels, stories, and autobiographies that followed brought financial success and critical acclaim.

## William Gass (1924–    )

Born in Fargo, North Dakota, and later trained in philosophy at Cornell University, Gass writes highly idiosyncratic, stylized fiction that merges experimentalism with familiar rural images of traditional American literature. Gass has lived in St. Louis since 1929 and teaches at Washington University. His works include *Omensetter's Luck* (1966), *In the Heart of the Heart of the Country* (1968), *The World Within the Word* (1978), *The First Winter of My Married Life* (1979), and *Habitations of the Word* (1985).

## Charlotte Perkins Gilman (1860–1935)

Gilman was raised by her mother in Hartford, Connecticut. Trained as an art teacher, Gilman married a fellow artist, Charles Stetson. Following the birth of her daughter, Gilman suffered a bout with depression that forms the basis for her story "The Yellow Wallpaper" (1892). Gilman subsequently divorced her first husband and married George Gilman, a cousin who shared her developing feminist perspective. Gilman's essays and speeches made her a significant member in the suffrage movement; she addressed the International Suffrage Convention in 1913 and the Woman's Peace Party in 1915. Her works, once out of print, have found renewed critical attention. They include

*Women and Economics* (1898), *Human Work* (1904), *Man-Made World* (1911), and the utopian *Herland* (1915).

## Zane Grey (1827–1939)

Born in Zanesville, Ohio, Grey had a successful dental practice, but by 1904 he found this vocation tedious. He began to write Westerns and in 1908 he published *The Last of the Plainsmen. Riders of the Purple Sage* (1912) established Grey as a popular success. Authoring more than sixty books, Grey traveled back and forth across the desert. He died at his home in Altadena, California. His works include *The Border Region* (1916), *The Man of the Forest* (1920), *The Call of the Canyons* (1924), *The Thundering Herd* (1925), *Arizona* (1934), *The Code of the West* (1934), *An American Angler in Australia* (1937), and *Black Mesa* (1955).

## Sutton Griggs (1872–1930)

Griggs was born in Texas, where he attended Bishop College before entering the Richmond Theological Seminary, from which he graduated in 1893. His career as a Baptist minister spanned three decades. Griggs's novels include *Imperium in Imperio* (1899), about an independent African American state within the United States; *Unfettered* (1902); and *The Hindered Hand; or, The Reign of the Repressionist* (1905). Griggs's racial and political views are detailed in *Wisdom's Call* (1911) and *Guide to Racial Greatness* (1923).

## A. B. Guthrie (1901–  )

Alfred Bertram Guthrie, Jr. was born in Indiana, grew up in Montana, and graduated from Montana State University (1923) before moving to Kentucky, where he was a journalist for twenty years. His first novel was *The Big Sky* (1947); he won the Pulitzer Prize for fiction in 1950 for *The Way West* (1949). The story of westward migration is continued in *These Thousand Hills* (1956).

## Dashiell Hammett (1894–1961)

Samuel Dashiell Hammett was born in Connecticut. His experiences as a Pinkerton detective in San Francisco provided background material for a new kind of crime writing, the "hard-boiled" school of detective fiction, exemplified in *The Maltese Falcon* (1930), which featured the tough, cynical Sam Spade. In 1932 Hammett published *The Thin Man,* introducing the witty, urbane Nick Charles to the canon of famous fictional detectives. Other major works include *Red Harvest* and *The Dain Curse* (both 1929) and *The Glass Key* (1931). While working as a scriptwriter during the era of the Hollywood "blacklist," Hammett was called before the House Committee on Un-American Activities; his refusal to testify resulted in a prison sentence.

## John Hawkes (1925–  )

Born in Stamford, Connecticut, Hawkes was reared and educated in New England, graduating from Harvard University in 1949. Hawkes has taught at a number of prestigious institutions, including Harvard, MIT, and Brown. Hawkes's fiction explores phenomena that seem at odds with his well-bred background. He is always aware of the horror that hovers beneath conventional life. His works include *The Cannibal* (1949), *The Beetle Leg* (1951), *The Goose on the Grave* and *The Owl* (1954), *The Lime Twig* (1961), *Second Skin* (1964), *The Personal Voice* (1964), *Innocence in Extremis* (1984), and *Whistlejacket* (1988).

## Nathaniel Hawthorne (1804–64)

Descended from Major William Hathorne, one of the original Puritan settlers of Massachusetts Bay Colony, Nathaniel Hawthorne was born in Salem, Massachusetts, where another of his ancestors, Major Hathorne's son John, had been one of the judges during the Salem witchcraft trials. At Bowdoin College, Hawthorne was a classmate of Franklin Pierce, Henry Wadsworth Longfellow, and Horatio Bridge. In 1841 he participated briefly in an experimental utopian community, Brook Farm, which provided material for *The Blithedale Romance* (1852). In 1842 he married Sophia Peabody, with whom he had three children, and in 1846 he was appointed surveyor at the Salem Custom House, which figures in his introductory essay to *The Scarlet Letter.* He lost this position in 1849 owing to a change of administrations. However, with the publication of *The Scarlet Letter* in 1850, his literary reputation was firmly established. Hawthorne was a reclusive man, but his work and his character drew many admirers, among them Herman Melville, who was a regular visitor while Hawthorne was working on *The House of the Seven Gables* (1851), and who dedicated *Moby-Dick* to him. His campaign biography of Pierce (1852) won him the consulship at Liverpool. He resigned in 1857, and traveled through France to Rome. *The Marble Faun* (1860) was the last novel completed before his death on May 19, 1864. Hawthorne's allegorical characters and symbolic mode were tools in an ongoing exploration of the human conscience; his short stories helped to establish the genre and, with his novels, are among the classics of American literature.

## Lafcadio Hearn (1850–1904)

Hearn was born in Greece, attended school in France and England, and came to the United States in 1869. He worked as a reporter in Cincinnati, New Orleans, and New York. In 1884 he published his first book, *Stray Leaves from Strange Literature,* translations from Théophile Gautier. His fascination with Oriental literature and the exotic led to *Some Chinese Ghosts* (1887), and his travels for *Harper's* resulted in *Two Years in the French West Indies* (1890). In 1890 he sailed for Japan, never to return. There he obtained a teaching job, married, and, under the name Koizumi Yakumo, became a Japanese citizen. During the remainder of his life he wrote extensively about his adopted home.

## Joseph Heller (1923–   )

Heller was born and educated in Brooklyn, New York. He later attended Columbia University and then worked in the theater and television. During World War II, Heller served in the United States Army Air Force and later satirized his experiences in *Catch-22* (1961). A writer of plays and fiction, Heller turned to teaching. Heller has emerged as a major parodic force in American literature. His works include *Something Happened* (1974), *Good as Gold* (1979), *God Knows* (1984), *No Laughing Matter* (1986), and *Picture This* (1988).

## Ernest Hemingway (1898–1961)

Born in Oak Park, Illinois, the son of a doctor with a fondness for fishing and camping, Hemingway worked briefly as a journalist and then volunteered as an ambulance driver for the Italian front in World War I. Hemingway was severely wounded, an experience that informed much of his subsequent fiction. Befriended by Gertrude Stein in postwar Paris, Hemingway became a part of the literary group that would later be characterized as the "Lost Generation." He gave voice to this generation in his first novel, *The Sun Also Rises* (1926). Structured around the masculine pursuits of bullfighting, hunting, fishing, boxing, and war, Hemingway's novels often project the sometimes ironic image of the warrior-writer. Hemingway's life resembled his fiction; sojourns in Paris, Spain, Africa, Cuba, and finally Idaho are reflected in his books. Suffering from depression, alcoholism, and suspected mental illness, Hemingway shot himself through the head, using the same shotgun that his father had used to commit suicide years before. Hemingway's many works include *A Farewell to Arms* (1929), *For Whom the Bell Tolls* (1940), *The Old Man and the Sea* (1953), and the posthumously published *Garden of Eden* (1985).

## Pauline Elizabeth Hopkins (1859–1930)

Hopkins was born in Portland, Maine, but grew up in Boston, where she attended public school. She was an actress, singer, and playwright as well as a novelist and short-story writer, editor, and essayist. Her first novel was *Contending Forces: A Romance Illustrative of Negro Life North and South* (1900). Three other novels (*Hagar's Daughter* [1901–2]; *Winona* [1902]; *Of One Blood* [1902–3]) were serialized in *The Colored American Magazine*.

## Paul Horgan (1903–   )

Born in Buffalo, New York, Horgan grew up there and in New Mexico, and much of his fiction is set in the Southwest. His devout Catholicism sets the tone for many of his works, including the trilogy composed of *Things as They Are* (1964), *Everything to Live For* (1968), and *The Thin Mountain Air* (1977). He won a Pulitzer Prize for his history of the Rio Grande (*Great River* [1954]) and for his biography of a pioneer bishop, *Lamy of Santa Fe* (1975).

## William Dean Howells (1837–1920)

Howells was born in Martin's Ferry, Ohio, and as a boy worked in his father's printing office. What Howells lacked in formal education (he had very little) he made up in diligent self-application both in and out of the printing office. His campaign biography of Abraham Lincoln (1860) won him an appointment as United States consul at Venice (1861-65). In Paris in 1862 he married Elinor Meade; they returned to the United States in 1865, where Howells associated himself first with the *New York Times* and *The Nation,* then in 1866 with the *Atlantic Monthly,* where he was editor in chief from 1872 until 1881. During this time and afterward, in his long association with *Harper's Monthly,* Howells exerted a strong and beneficent influence on American letters, promoting the work of many promising young artists, including Stephen Crane, Hamlin Garland, Frank Norris, Paul Laurence Dunbar, and Robert Herrick, as well as Samuel Clemens and Henry James. A prolific essayist, reviewer, critic, and novelist, Howells best expressed his own realistic style in such works as *A Modern Instance* (1882), *The Rise of Silas Lapham* (1885), *Indian Summer* (1886), and *A Hazard of New Fortunes* (1890). In his later years Howells received honorary degrees from Harvard, Yale, Columbia, and Oxford universities, and he was the first president of the American Academy of Arts and Letters, a post he held until his death.

## Zora Neale Hurston (1891–1960)

Born in Florida, Hurston graduated from Howard University and studied anthropology at Barnard College and Columbia University. In New York City in the midst of the Harlem Renaissance of the 1920s, she began publishing stories. Her first novel, *Jonah's Gourd Vine,* was published in 1934, followed by her best-known work, *Their Eyes Were Watching God,* in 1937. Despite her fine early writings, Hurston fell into obscurity and poverty; she suffered a stroke in October 1959 and died in January 1960, to be buried in an unmarked grave at Fort Pierce, Florida.

## Washington Irving (1783–1859)

Irving was born in New York City, youngest of eleven children. His health was delicate and he did not attend university; he did, however, gain fame as essayist, historian, biographer, and humorist, producing such works as the satirical *A History of New York* (by "Diedrich Knickerbocker," 1809) and *The Sketch Book of Geoffrey Crayon, Gent.* (1820), containing such classics as "Rip Van Winkle" and "The Legend of Sleepy Hollow." He served as secretary of the United States legation in London (1829–32), as minister to Spain (1842-45), but declined opportunities to become mayor of New York, a United States Congressman, or Secretary of the Navy.

## Helen Hunt Jackson (1830–85)

Born Helen Maria Hunt, in Amherst, Massachussets, Jackson was a poet and a friend of Emily Dickinson, who may be the subject of her novel *Mercy Philbrick's Choice* (1876). Her indictment of the United States government's policy toward Native Americans is conveyed in *A Century of Dishonor* (1881) and in her historical romance *Ramona* (1884), her most popular work, and the direct result of her participation in a governmental investigation of the plight of the California Mission Indians. The "Ramona Pageant" is still acted annually out-of-doors in its historical locale, near Hemet, California.

## Harriet Jacobs (1818–96)

Jacobs escaped from slavery, but freedom proved illusory. Jacobs was hidden in a small, windowless shed located off her grandmother's cabin. Incredibly, she remained concealed for seven years, before finally making her way to New York. Jacobs's autobiographical *Incidents in the Life of a Slave Girl* (1861) describes her experiences. Originally published under the pseudonym Linda Brent, Jacobs's narrative was for many years attributed to her editor, Lydia Maria Child. Recent scholarship has discounted these claims, and Jacobs's account is today considered to be a major work in the canon of slave narratives.

## Henry James (1843–1916)

Henry James, Jr., was born in New York City, the second son of Henry James, Sr., noted American religious philosopher, and younger brother of William James, pioneering psychological researcher. The James children received a various and dauntlessly experimental education on both sides of the Atlantic. Early immersion in European culture resulted in Henry's lifelong ambivalence toward his own American origins, and many of his best-known works—*The American* (1877), *The Europeans* (1878), *Daisy Miller* (1879), *The Portrait of a Lady* (1881)—deal with the conflicts between American and European values, customs, and character. A partial list of his novels includes such famous titles as *Washington Square* (1881), *The Bostonians* (1886), *The Spoils of Poynton* (1897), *What Maisie Knew* (1897), *The Awkward Age* (1899), *The Sacred Fount* (1901), *The Wings of the Dove* (1902), and *The Golden Bowl* (1904). He was a prolific writer of short stories ("The Beast in the Jungle"; "The Figure in the Carpet"), criticism ("The Art of Fiction"), biography (Nathaniel Hawthorne; W. W. Story), and cultural essays (*The American Scene* [1907]) as well. James lived in England from 1876 until his death; in sympathy with the British cause during World War I, he became a British citizen in 1915. During his lifetime his reputation prospered and declined, but today he is highly respected as an early master of psychological realism, formal structure, and narrative ambiguity, as well as for his ability to convey the nuances of human emotion and human consciousness.

## Sarah Orne Jewett (1849–1909)

Raised in the village of South Berwick, Maine, Jewett wrote fiction that frequently drew upon her rural experiences. A lifelong New Englander, Jewett died in the same house in which she was born. In the 1880s Jewett began a lifelong relationship with Annie Fields and together they established a literary center in Boston. Influenced by Harriet Beecher Stowe and the previous generation of women writers, Jewett's work combined a sensitivity to the rural environment with an interest in a female community and sensibility. Jewett's books include *Deephaven* (1877), *A Country Doctor* (1884), *A White*

*Heron and Other Stories* (1886), and the celebrated *The Country of the Pointed Firs* (1896).

## James Jones (1921–77)

Raised in Robinson, Illinois, Jones was educated at the University of Hawaii and was then stationed in Hawaii during World War II. A boxer, Jones participated in Golden Glove tournaments. He received a National Book Award for *From Here to Eternity* (1951), a work that was made into a successful film. Other works include *Some Came Running* (1958), *The Pistol* (1959), *The Thin Red Line* (1962), and *Go to the Widow-Maker* (1967).

## Maxine Hong Kingston (1940– )

Kingston was born in New York City, the child of first-generation Chinese immigrants. She grew up in Stockton, California, where she witnessed the restricted life of the Asian American woman. In her autobiographical *The Woman Warrior: Memoirs of a Girlhood Among Ghosts* (1976) and *China Men* (1980), Kingston incorporated Chinese myth, family history, and personal experience, exploring and articulating the previously repressed voices of Stockton's Chinatown. Her most recent work is *Tripmaster Monkey* (1989).

## Caroline Kirkland (1801–64)

Caroline (Stansbury) Kirkland was born in New York City, but with her husband, Samuel Kirkland, moved in the 1830s to the frontier town of Detroit. Their experiences as early settlers of Pinckney, Michigan, supplied material for *A New Home—Who'll Follow?* (1839, published under the pseudonym Mrs. Mary Clavers, reissued in 1874 as *Our New Home in the West*), a humorous exposé of pioneer life. In 1843 the family returned to New York, where she continued to write and was active in various social reform movements. She was the mother of novelist Joseph Kirkland.

## Joy Kogawa (1935– )

Kogawa was born in Vancouver, British Columbia. During World War II the family was moved, along with other Canadians of Japanese descent, to the interior, an experience that provided the material for her novel *Obasan* (1981). Her volumes of poetry include *The Splintered Moon* (1968), *A Choice of Dreams* (1974), and *Jericho Road* (1978).

## Margaret Laurence (1926–87)

Laurence was born Jean Margaret Wemys in Neepawa, Manitoba. She was educated at the University of Manitoba and in 1950 married Jack Laurence, whose work as an engineer took them to Africa, the setting of her novel *This Side Jordan* (1960). Her best-known work is a series of novels set in the fictional town of Manawaka, including *A Jest of God* (1966), winner of a Governor General's Award and adapted for the screen as *Rachel, Rachel*.

## Ursula Le Guin (1929–   )

Le Guin was born in California, daughter of anthropologist Alfred Kroeber and writer Theodora Kroeber (author of *Ishi of Two Worlds*). In the 1960s Le Guin began her professional writing career, publishing her first stories primarily in science fiction magazines. Le Guin's fiction predominantly engages feminist issues and themes, and often combines images from fantasy and science fiction in highly original ways. Her works include *A Wizard of Earthsea* (1968), *The Left Hand of Darkness* (1969), *The Lathe of Heaven* (1971), *The Language of the Night* (1979), and *The Compass Rose* (1982).

## George Lippard (1822–54)

Lippard was born in Chester County, Pennsylvania, and grew up in Philadelphia. He prepared for and rejected careers in both the Methodist ministry and the law; he was more successful as a journalist, but had to give up that profession owing to poor health. His fiction falls into the disparate categories of historical romance and urban exposé; the best known of his books is *The Monks of Monk Hall* (1844), later entitled *The Quaker City*, a sensational novel exposing vice in Philadelphia. His reputation was that of a radical and an eccentric; he was a friend of Edgar Allan Poe and may possibly have had some influence on Poe's writing.

## Clarice Lispector (1925–77)

Born in the Ukraine to Russian parents, Lispector was only two months old when her family arrived in Brazil. She began composing stories at the age of six; she worked as an editor at the Agencia Nacional while attending the National Faculty of Law in Rio de Janeiro, from which she graduated in 1943 at the age of eighteen. That year she finished her first novel, *Perto do coração selvagem* (1944; *Near to the Wild Heart,* 1990), and married. Her husband was a career diplomat, whose work took them abroad for a number of years, but in 1959 the couple separated and Lispector, with her two children, returned to Rio to settle permanently. Her literary reputation was established in 1961 with the publication of her second novel, *A macã no escuro* (*The Apple in the Dark,* 1986).

## Jack London (1876–1916)

John Griffith (Jack) London was born in San Francisco, grew up on the Oakland waterfront, and quit school at the age of fourteen. After a youthful career as an oyster-poacher, he joined a sealing expedition, roamed throughout the United States and Canada, studied briefly at the University of California, and in 1897 joined the rush for Klondike gold. He did not strike it rich in the gold fields, but his collection of Yukon stories, *Son of the Wolf,* appeared in 1900, establishing his reputation as a skillful and energetic storyteller. His novels reflect his interest in both the individual's struggle against civilized society (*The Call of the Wild* [1903]; *The Sea Wolf* [1904]) and the struggle of the lower classes against oppression (*The Iron Heel* [1908]; *The Valley of the Moon* [1913]). These concerns are also echoed in his autobiographical novel, *Martin Eden* (1909).

## Alison Lurie (1926–   )

Born in Chicago, Lurie was educated in the East, where she continues to live. After graduating from Radcliffe in 1947, Lurie was employed as a ghostwriter and also wrote a variety of critical pieces. A parent, Lurie combines an interest in children's literature with a keen awareness of language and critical issues. Her works include *The Nowhere*

*City* (1965), *Imaginary Friends* (1967), *The Language of Clothes* (1981), and *Foreign Affairs* (1984).

## Norman Mailer (1923– )

Mailer was born in Long Branch, New Jersey, and grew up in Brooklyn, New York. At sixteen Mailer graduated from Boys High School and entered Harvard University. He majored in aeronautical engineering, but was increasingly drawn to literary discourse. Mailer graduated in 1943 and was drafted into the United States Army in 1944. He served for eighteen months in the Philippines and in Japan. Controversy and charges of blatant sexism have surrounded Mailer. His penchant for the outrageous statement, his frequent fistfights, as well as the nonfatal stabbing of his second wife, Adele Morales (he has been married six times), have all contributed to his provocateur status. In 1967 Mailer was arrested for civil disobedience during a march on the Pentagon, and in 1969 he ran (unsuccessfully) for mayor of New York City. The themes that mark Mailer's life can also be clearly discerned in his fiction. His numerous works include *The Naked and the Dead* (1948), *Barbary Shore* (1951), *The Deer Park* (1955), *The White Negro* (1958), *Why Are We in Vietnam?* (1967), *The Armies of the Night* (1968), *The Prisoner of Sex* (1971), *Marilyn* (1973), *The Executioner's Song* (1979), *Ancient Evenings* (1983), and *Tough Guys Don't Dance* (1984).

## Antonine Maillet (1929– )

Maillet was born and grew up in the Acadian or Cajun community of Bouctouche, New Brunswick. Both her parents were teachers, and Maillet worked her way through university, alternately teaching and studying. She received an M.A. from the College Saint-Joseph de Memramcook in 1959, after which she studied at the University of Montreal, and in 1970 received a doctorate from Laval University, where she studied folklore. While her best-known work to date is the novel *Pelagie-la-Charrette* (1979; translated in 1982 as *Pelagie: The Return to a Homeland*), she has authored more than a dozen plays in addition to her fiction and scholarly works.

## Bernard Malamud (1914–86)

Born in Brooklyn, New York, Malamud graduated from Erasmus High School and the City College of New York, and eventually received a Master's degree at Columbia University. During the 1940s Malamud taught evening classes at Erasmus High and Harlem Evening High School, while working at the craft of writing. Malamud's artful and comic fiction often draws upon his urban experience, particularly in its evocation of the speech and mannerisms of working-class, recently immigrated Jews. His works include *The Natural* (1952), *The Assistant* (1957), *A New Life* (1961), and *The Stories of Bernard Malamud* (1983).

## Frederick Manfred (1912–   )

Originally christened Feike Feikema, Manfred was born in Rock Township, Doon, Iowa. A former roustabout, factory hand, and gas station attendant, Manfred transforms his experiences into lyrical evocations of Midwestern life. Manfred avoids the literary arenas of New York City and Los Angeles, and continues to live in the Midwest. Among his books are *Lord Grizzly* (1954), *Wanderlust* (1962), and *Green Earth* (1977).

## Paule Marshall (1929–   )

Born and largely reared in Brooklyn, New York, Marshall is the child of black immigrants from Barbados, West Indies. Marshall herself traveled to Barbados at the age of nine, and this trip proved to be highly influential in the shaping of her identity and aesthetics. Shortly after this expedition, Marshall's father left home to follow Father Divine in Harlem. Alone with her mother and other West Indian women, Marshall was constantly exposed to dialect and to African legend. Marshall graduated from Brooklyn College and later worked as a journalist. Intent on creating a pan-African sensibility, Marshall based her politics and literature on a revival of black cultural history. Her works include *Brown Girl, Brownstones* (1959), *Soul Clap Hands and Sing* (1961), *The Chosen Place, the Timeless People* (1979), *Praisesong for the Widow* (1983), and *Merle* (1985).

# John Joseph Mathews (1894–1978)

Listed on the Osage tribal roll, Mathews was reared in Oklahoma. After serving as a flight instructor during World War I, Mathews returned to Pawhusks, Oklahoma, where he watched the exploitation and corruption of Native Americans and the fading away of traditional tribal life. Mathews's works reflect the Native American experience and include *Wah' Kon-tah: The Osage and the White Man's Road* (1929) and *Sundown* (1934).

# Mary McCarthy (1912–89)

Born in Seattle, Washington, McCarthy worked as a book reviewer in New York, after attending Forest Ridge Convent in Seattle, Annie Wright Seminary in Tacoma, and Vassar College. McCarthy's work as a critic and fiction writer reflects her shrewd wit, a willingness to surprise her reader, and an acute political consciousness. Her works include *Venice Observed* (1950), *Theater Chronicles, 1937–1962* (1963), *The Group* (1963), and *Hanoi* (1968).

# Carson McCullers (1917–67)

McCullers was born in Columbus, Georgia, and was educated at Columbia University. Her original intent had been to study music at the Juilliard School of Music, but a financial accident prevented her enrollment. McCullers married, divorced, and remarried Reeves McCullers, a man who suffered from severe alcoholism and who committed suicide in 1953. McCullers herself was chronically ill from what is now believed to have been rheumatic fever. The distress and the loneliness suggested by McCullers's biography are mirrored in her works, which include *The Heart Is a Lonely Hunter* (1940), *Reflections in a Golden Eye* (1941), *The Member of the Wedding* (1946), *The Ballad of the Sad Café* (1951), *The Square Root of Wonderful* (1958), and *Clock Without Hands* (1961).

# Thomas McGuane (1939–   )

A dedicated sportsman and Westerner, McGuane writes fiction that recalls earlier male modernist writers, in particular Ernest Hemingway. McGuane, however, employs Western themes and tropes to achieve an ironic and highly individual vision of the West. Having exorcised the excesses of his earlier life, McGuane presently lives in Montana and raises cutting horses. Elegant, poetic, and funny, McGuane's fiction often powerfully evokes a sense of place. His works include *The Sporting Club* (1969), *The Bushwacked Piano* (1971), *Ninety-Two in the Shade* (1973), *Panama* (1978), *An Outside Chance* (1980), *Nobody's Angel* (1982), *Something to Be Desired* (1984), *To Skin a Cat* (1986), and *Keep the Change* (1989).

## Claude McKay (1889–1948)

Born in Clarendon Hills, Jamaica, McKay immigrated to the United States as a college student. He was awarded, by the Jamaican Institute of Arts and Sciences, a scholarship to study agriculture at Tuskegee Institute. McKay left college for New York City where he worked for such political journals as *The Liberator*. Poet and novelist, McKay became closely associated with the burgeoning Harlem Renaissance. Like many of his generation, McKay wandered through Europe as an expatriate during the years between the world wars. He returned to the United States and died in Chicago. His works include *Songs of Jamaica* (1912), *Harlem Shadows* (1922), *Home to Harlem* (1928), *Banjo* (1929), *Gingertown* (1932), *Banana Bottom* (1933), and *Harlem: Negro Metropolis* (1940).

## Herman Melville (1819–91)

Melville was born into a well-established family in New York City, where his father was a successful merchant. However, the business had failed and the family was heavily in debt when the father died in 1832. Melville, third oldest of eight children, left school to help support the family, and in 1837 he went to sea. His first novels, *Typee* (1846) and *Omoo* (1847), were based upon his sea adventures, and were popular and acclaimed. His next book, *Mardi* (1849), was more philosophical and less successful. Next came *Redburn* (1849) and *White-Jacket* (1840), works that appealed to a wider audience. Melville's masterpiece, *Moby-Dick* (1851), proved too challenging for most readers; he followed it with the highly complex *Pierre; or, The Ambiguities* (1852) and *The Confidence-Man* (1857), both financial failures. To earn money, he published more accessible short fiction in *Harper's Monthly* and *Putnam's Monthly Magazine,* some of which (including "Bartleby, the Scrivener" and "Benito Cereno") was collected in *The Piazza Tales* (1856), and a serialized historical novel, *Israel Potter* (1855). He published no further novels after 1857, and worked for the rest of his life as an officer in the New York Custom House. He did publish poetry, most notably *Battle-Pieces* (1866) and *Clarel* (1876), and in his last years returned to fiction with *Billy Budd, Sailor,* which was left unfinished at his death in 1891 and first published in 1924.

## Steven Millhauser (1943–   )

Millhauser was born in New York City and grew up in Connecticut. After working as a copywriter in New York, Millhauser studied medieval and Renaissance literature at Brown University from 1968 to 1971. These disparate influences find their way into Millhauser's satiric, demanding, and often parodic fiction, which often focuses on the banality, strangeness, and violence of ordinary life. Millhauser's most famous novel, *Edwin Mullhouse: The Life and Death of an American Writer, 1943–1954, by Jeffrey Cartwright* (1972), has been favorably compared to Vladimir Nabokov's *Pale Fire.* Other works include *Portrait of a Romantic* (1977).

## Margaret Mitchell (1900–1949)

Mitchell was a native of Georgia, the setting of her only novel, *Gone with the Wind,* the best-selling romantic saga of the Civil War and Reconstruction. A former feature writer, she spent a decade (much of it bedridden) writing *Gone with the Wind,* which won a Pulitzer Prize in 1936, and which was adapted for the screen in 1939 (the screen rights were sold for $50,000 only one month after publication). Mitchell was struck by an automobile on an Atlanta street and died in that city in 1949.

## N. Scott Momaday (1934–   )

Born in Lawton, Oklahoma, an heir to both Cherokee and Kiowa Indian culture, Momaday attended both reservation parochial and public schools, and eventually attended the University of New Mexico. He later received a Ph.D. from Stanford University and commenced his teaching career. Like his life, Momaday's work seeks to bridge the Native American and non-Native American worlds. His *House Made of Dawn* (1968) was awarded a Pulitzer Prize. His works include *The Journey of Tai-Me—Retold Kiowa Indian Folktales* (1968), *The Way to Rainy Mountain* (1969), *The Gourd Dancer* (1976), and *The Names: A Memoir* (1976).

## Toshio Mori (1910–   )

Born in San Francisco, Mori has spent his entire life in the California Bay area, except for the three years he spent in the Japanese relocation camp in Topaz Center, Utah. During this period, Mori wrote for and edited the camp magazine *Trek*. Mori had a brief career as a professional baseball player with the Chicago Cubs. He quit baseball in order to assist his parents, and began to write about the people in Chinatown, Oakland, and San Leandro. *Yokohama, California* (1949) details the experience of the Japanese Americans in California. Frequently anthologized, Mori has authored numerous short stories and has a number of manuscripts for novels that are, as yet, unpublished. His works include *Woman from Hiroshima* (1978) and *The Chauvinist and Other Stories* (1979).

## Wright Morris (1910–   )

Morris was born in Nebraska, and though he moved to California in 1961, the Midwest is the setting for many of his novels. These include *The Inhabitants* (1946), *The Works of Love* (1952), *Love Among the Cannibals* (1957), *A Life* (1973), and *Plains Song* (1980), which won an American Book Award. Morris's excellent photography appears in some of his books: *The Inhabitants, The Home Place* (1948), *God's Country and My People* (1968).

## Toni Morrison (1931–   )

Born in the industrial town of Lorain, Ohio, Morrison claims to have grown up in an environment relatively free of discrimination. In 1953 she graduated from Howard University in Washington, D.C., and went on to earn a Master's degree from Cornell University. She is presently a New Yorker. Morrison's innovative and lyrical fiction often integrates images from her rural upbringing with the sometimes disturbing realities of the minority urban experience. Her novels include *Sula* (1973), *Song of Solomon* (1977), and *Tar Baby* (1981).

## Vladimir Nabokov (1899–1977)

Born in the Czarist Russian city of St. Petersburg, Nabokov immigrated with his family after the Russian Revolution to London and Berlin. During his long, cosmopolitan life, Nabokov lived variously in Germany, Britain, France, and the United States. Educated at Trinity College, Cambridge, Nabokov taught at Wellesley College and Cornell University while in the United States during the 1940s and 1950s. Widely considered a literary genius—many consider Nabokov to be the most influential postmodern writer—he created difficult, metafictional books, characterized by a combination of erudition and humor. Incorporating aspects of the author's personal history, passions, and aesthetic prejudices—for example, Russian history, butterflies, chess, and word games—Nabokov's books include *Lolita* (1955), *Pale Fire* (1962), and *Ada* (1969). In 1960 Nabokov returned to Europe and lived in the top floor of the Palace Hotel in Montreux, Switzerland, until his death.

## Frank Norris (1870–1902)

He was born Benjamin Franklin Norris in Chicago. In 1884 the family moved to San Francisco, and when he was seventeen his father took him to Paris to study painting. From 1890 to 1894 he attended the University of California, then Harvard for one year, after which he worked as correspondent for *Collier's* and the *San Francisco Chronicle,* covering the Boer War. Upon his return from South Africa he worked for a San Francisco magazine, *The Wave,* which serialized his first novel, *Moran of the Lady Letty,* in 1898. That same year he went to Cuba to cover the Spanish-American War. When he returned the following year he took a position with Doubleday, which in 1899 published two of Norris's novels, *McTeague,* set in San Francisco, and *Blix. The Octopus* (1901) and *The Pit* (1903) were the first two volumes in a planned trilogy following the growing, selling, and distribution of California wheat. The final volume, *The Wolf*, was incomplete at Norris's death from a ruptured appendix in 1902.

## Joyce Carol Oates (1938–   )

Born in upstate New York, Oates studied at Syracuse University and at the University of Wisconsin. Her numerous teaching assignments include her present position as a professor at Princeton University. Oates often translates her personal experiences into fiction. Her small-town youth and suburban adolescence are explored and frequently parodied in her novels, and she provides the same self-mocking insight into the worlds of academia and art. A teacher and critic, and an exceedingly prolific and accomplished writer, Oates is on the board of the *Kenyon Review*. Her works include *By the North Gate* (1963), *With Shuddering Fall* (1964), *A Garden of Earthly Delights* (1967), *Expensive People* (1968), *them* (1969), *Wonderland* (1971), *New Heaven, New Earth* (1974), *Childwold* (1976), *Unholy Loves* (1979), *Bellefleur* (1980), *A Bloodsmore Romance* (1982), *Solstice* (1985), *Marya: A Life* (1986), and *You Must Remember This* (1987).

## Tim O'Brien (1946–   )

Born and educated in Minnesota, O'Brien was drafted into the United States Army following his graduation from college in 1968. Returning from Vietnam in 1970, O'Brien went to work for the *Washington Post*. Often surreal, O'Brien's fiction chronicles the experience of the Vietnam War. His novels include *If I Die in the Combat Zone* (1973), *Northern Lights* (1974), and *Going after Cacciato* (1978).

## Howard O'Hagan (1902–82)

O'Hagan was born in Lethbridge, Alberta, the son of a doctor whose practice took the family to Calgary, to Vancouver, and to a series of small railroad and mining towns in the Canadian Rockies. O'Hagan's major novel, *Tay John* (London, 1939), received little attention in Canada until its republication there in 1974. O'Hagan and his wife (painter Margaret Peterson) lived in Sicily from 1963 to 1974, when they returned to settle in Victoria, British Columbia.

## John Okada (1923–71)

Raised in Seattle, Washington, Okada was exposed at an early age to the language of the urban streets. He received two bachelor's degrees from the University of Washington, one in English and one in library science. He later received an M.A. in literature from Columbia University, where he met his wife Dorothy. Okada was a sergeant in the United States Air Force during World War II; he became embittered by the government's treatment of its Nisei population. Okada lived for some time in West Los Angeles. When Okada's *No-No Boy* (1957) was published, it was dismissed as "too coarse" and too Asian. After Okada's death, his widow offered his papers and manuscripts to the University of California at Los Angeles. The university rejected the papers as being unimportant and, in consequence, Dorothy Okada burned the manuscripts. It is only recently that Okada has received positive critical acclaim as a sensitive chronicler of the Japanese American experience.

## Tillie Lerner Olsen (1912–   )

Olsen's parents fled to the United States in 1905, following the failure of the 1905 Revolution in Russia. They eventually settled in Nebraska, where Olsen was reared. Very much a child of the working class, Olsen was forced by economic circumstances to leave school before graduating from high school. Before she reached the age of eighteen, Olsen had worked in the infamous meat-packing industry, as well as serving as a waitress and a domestic. Still in her adolescence, Olsen became an active member of the Young Communist League and was jailed at eighteen for her attempts to organize packing-house workers. When Olsen was nineteen she began working on a novel that she eventually published as *Yonnondio: From the Thirties* (1974). Throughout her life, Olsen remained concerned with issues of class and gender. During the 1950s she was harassed by the FBI. In recent years Olsen has received serious critical attention. Some of her work has found publication only in the last few decades. Despite her abbreviated formal education, Olsen has received numerous honorary degrees. Her works include *Tell Me a Riddle* (1961), *Silences* (1978), *Mother to Daughter, Daughter to Mother: A Day Book and Reader* (1984), and *Dream-Vision* (1984).

## Michael Ondaatje (1943–   )

Born in Colombo, Ceylon (now Sri Lanka), where the family owned a tea plantation, Ondaatje immigrated in 1952 to England, and at the age of nineteen to Montreal. His novels include *Coming Through Slaughter* (1976) and *In the Skin of a Lion* (1987); he has also edited a number of anthologies in addition to writing poetry, fiction, criticism, and screenplays. He has taught at the University of Western Ontario and, more recently, at Glendon College. He is the holder of two Governor General's Awards for poetry.

## Walker Percy (1916–90)

A Southerner, Percy was born in Birmingham, Alabama. He was educated at the University of North Carolina. Percy went North to attend medical school at Columbia University, obtaining his M.D. in 1941. While practicing at New York's Bellevue Hospital, Percy contracted tuberculosis. He retired from medicine and turned to literature. Percy's works include *The Moviegoer* (1961), *The Last Gentleman* (1966), *The Message in the Bottle: How Queer Man Is, How Queer Language Is, and What One Has to Do with the Other* (1975), and *The Second Coming* (1980).

## Elizabeth Stuart Phelps (1844–1911)

Baptized as Mary Gray, Phelps was born in Boston, the daughter of Elizabeth (Stuart) Phelps, a popular religious writer. She assumed her mother's name upon her mother's death. During a long period of reclusiveness following the death of her suitor in the Civil War, Phelps produced *The Gates Ajar* (1868), the first of her novels concerning the afterlife. In 1888 she married Herbert Dickinson Ward, who became an occasional co-author. Several of her novels (*Hedged In* [1870]; *The Silent Partner* [1871]; *The Story of Avis* [1877]; *Dr. Zay* [1882]) are strong indictments of the social restrictions applied to women.

## Edgar Allan Poe (1809–49)

Poe was born in Boston to itinerant actors, both of whom died while he was very young. Unofficially adopted by John Allen, of Richmond,

Virginia, he entered the University of Virginia in 1826, but left after only one year, following a bitter quarrel with Allen over debts. After brief stints in the United States Army and at West Point, Poe, destitute and wholly estranged from his one-time benefactor, located an aunt, Maria Clemm, and her daughter Virginia, whom he married in 1836. The remainder of his life is a chronicle of increasing desperation, as Poe tried to support his dependents on the unreliable income of his journalistic endeavors. Virginia died in 1847; Poe's depression deepened as his health and sanity deteriorated. In October 1849 he was found unconscious on a Baltimore street, and died four days later. Today, his literary legacy marks him as one of the most original creative minds of his time. His single novel, *The Narrative of Arthur Gordon Pym* (1838), is difficult to classify, but recounts the horrific adventures of a young stowaway on his voyage into a moral, as well as an Antarctic, abyss.

## Elizabeth Payson Prentiss (1818–78)

Though Elizabeth Prentiss was born in Maine, she lived most of her life in New York. She wrote religious and juvenile fiction, the best known of which is *Stepping Heavenward* (1869), the fictional "diary" of a religious woman.

## Manuel Puig (1932–  )

Puig was born in General Villegas, a small town in the province of Buenos Aires, Argentina. He attended the University of Buenos Aires before traveling in 1957 to Rome, where he studied at the Experimental Film Center. His best-known works are the novels *La traición de Rita Hayworth* (1968; *Betrayed by Rita Hayworth*, 1971) and *El beso de la mujer araña* (1976; *Kiss of the Spider Woman*, 1979). Apart from a short visit to Buenos Aires in 1967, Puig has made his home abroad, primarily in New York and Rome.

## Thomas Pynchon (1937–  )

Apart from the broad outlines of Pynchon's personal history, much about his life remains mysterious as a result of his legendary obsession with privacy. Born in Glen Cove, New York, Pynchon attended

Cornell University from 1953 to 1955, first studying physics, then English, dropped out to join the Signal Corps, and returned to school in 1957. While working as a technical writer for Boeing in Seattle, Pynchon achieved success writing stories. In 1963 he won the Faulkner Award for his first novel, *V*. A strange amalgam of spy thriller, quest mythology, alternate history, physics theory, puns, and self-reflexive literary games, the book draws on Pynchon's diverse education and interests, and immediately established him as a prodigious literary talent. Equally complex and challenging, *The Crying of Lot 49* (1966) and *Gravity's Rainbow* (1973) further established Pynchon's reputation as one of the most important writers of the last half of the century. His most recent novel is *Vineland* (1989).

## Ellery Queen

"Ellery Queen" was the name of a fictional detective and also the pseudonym under which two cousins, Manfred Lee (1905–71) and Frederic Dannay (1905–82), wrote numerous detective stories and novels, the first of which was *The Roman Hat Mystery* (1929). Their last collaboration was *A Fine and Private Place* (1971). In addition, they were joint editors of *Ellery Queen's Mystery Magazine*, established in 1941. They also wrote under the name of Barnaby Ross.

## John Rechy (1934–   )

Born in El Paso, Texas, and a graduate of Texas Western College, Rechy also attended the New School for Social Research in New York City. At home in both the Southwest and New York, Rechy produces works that examine the forbidden, dark aspects of urban existence and homosexuality. Now a relocated Californian, Rechy currently teaches at the University of Southern California. His works include *City of Night* (1963), *This Day's Death* (1969), *Numbers* (1976), *The Sexual Outlaw* (1977), *Rushes* (1979), *Body and Souls* (1983), and *Marilyn's Daughter* (1988).

## Ishmael Reed (1938–   )

Born in Chattanooga, Tennessee, Reed moved with his mother to New York state at the age of four. He grew up in Buffalo and later attended the university there. After graduation, Reed moved to New York City, where he worked with a number of journals and publishing firms. He cofounded the *East Village Other* and *Advance*. Relocating in California, Reed was president of Yardbird Publishing Company and director of Reed Cannon and Johnson Communications, becoming increasingly intrigued by the possibilities presented in video technology. During this period, Reed also taught at a number of universities, receiving appointments from the University of California at Berkeley, the University of Washington, and Yale University. Reed's fiction seeks to break away from the narrative-inspired autobiographical style associated with such African American writers as Richard Wright, Ralph Ellison, and James Baldwin, seeking instead to reinstate an African mythology and to parody traditional Western aesthetic forms. His works include *The Free-Lance Pallbearers* (1967), *Yellow Back Radio Broke-Down* (1971), *Catechism of D NeoAmerican Hoodoo Church* (1970), *Conjure* (1972), *Mumbo Jumbo* (1972), *The Last Days of Louisiana Red* (1974), *The Terrible Twos* (1982), and *Reckless Eyeballing* (1986).

## Jean Rhys (1895–1979)

Rhys was born in Dominica, an island in the British West Indies. As her Welsh surname suggests, Rhys's father was born in Wales and moved to the Indies in adulthood. But Rhys's mother was born in the British Indies and Rhys's life and fiction reflect the cultural diversity of her family life. Educated at convent schools and in London, Rhys later toured England as a chorus girl. Married for a time to poet Max Hamer, Rhys spent much of her life on the Continent. Her works include *The Left Bank* (1927), *After Leaving Mr. MacKenzie* (1930), the celebrated *Wide Sargasso Sea* (1966), *Tigers Are Better Looking* (1968), and *Smile Please: An Unfinished Biography* (1979).

## Mary Roberts Rinehart (1876–1958)

Rinehart was born in Pittsburgh, Pennsylvania, and was the author of popular mystery novels, including *The Circular Staircase* (1908; dramatized as *The Bat* in 1920), *The Man in Lower Ten* (1909), *The Door* (1930), *The Yellow Room* (1945), and *The Swimming Pool* (1952). In addition to horror stories and detective fiction, she wrote several plays and a series of humorous novels featuring "Tish," an eccentric spinster (*The Amazing Adventures of Letitia Carberry* [1911]; *Tish* [1916]; *The Best of Tish* [1955]).

## Marilynne Robinson (1944–  )

An alumna of Brown University, Robinson did her graduate work at the University of Washington in Seattle, and currently lives in Northampton, Massachusetts. Her first novel, *Housekeeping* (1981), makes reference to Robinson's own experiences in the Northwest. The problematic appearance of the past in contemporary life and the illusory nature of any attempt at permanence mark Robinson's work. Her second novel, *Mother Country* (1988), explores this familiar terrain.

## O. E. Rölvaag (1876–1931)

Ole Edvart Rölvaag was born in Norway, immigrated to the United States in 1896, and graduated from St. Olaf College in Minnesota, where he was for many years a professor of Norwegian (all of his fiction was first written in Norwegian). His best-known work is the trilogy composed of *Giants in the Earth* (1927), *Peder Victorious* (1929), and *Their Fathers' God* (1931), about the struggles of Norwegian immigrants in the Dakotas.

## Renato Ignacio Rosaldo (1912–  )

Born in Minatatlan, in the state of Veracruz, Mexico, Rosaldo came to the United States in 1930. He attended high school in Chicago and in 1942 he received a Ph.D. in Spanish from the University of Illinois. A committed advocate of Chicano concerns and a promoter of the Spanish language, Rosaldo is active in the MLA and in the American Association of Teachers. He co-authored *Six Faces of Mexico* (1966) and edited *Chicano: The Evolution of a People* (1973).

## Sinclair Ross (1908–  )

James Sinclair Ross was born in northern Saskatchewan, in a prairie setting that figures largely in his fiction, including his first novel, *As For Me and My House* (1941). Between 1942 and 1946 he served in the Canadian army in London, after which he returned to his prewar bank job, but continued writing, publishing his second novel, *The Well,* in 1958. Upon his retirement in 1968, he moved to Athens, Greece, where he finished *Whir of Gold* (1970), and then to Spain, returning to Canada in 1980.

## Philip Roth (1933– )

Born in Newark, New Jersey, Roth graduated from Bucknell University in 1954 and received his M.A. from the University of Chicago in 1955. Profoundly influenced by his own Jewish upbringing, Roth explores and satirizes the American Jewish experience, as well as American culture in general. His works include *Goodbye Columbus* (1959), *Letting Go* (1962), *And When She Was Good* (1967), *Portnoy's Complaint* (1969), *The Ghost Writer* (1979), *The Anatomy Lesson* (1983), *The Counterlife* (1986), and *Deception* (1990).

## Susanna Rowson (1762–1824)

Susanna (Haswell) Rowson was born in Portsmouth, England. Her father was a British naval lieutenant who was working as a customs collector in Massachusetts at the outbreak of the American Revolution. During the war, the family was interned and their property was confiscated; in 1778 Haswell and his family were returned to England, where Susanna worked as a governess for the Duchess of Devonshire. Her first novel, *Victoria,* was published there in 1786, and that same year she married William Rowson. In 1791 *Charlotte; or, A Tale of Truth,* a cautionary tale of seduction set in America, appeared. The following year Rowson's business failed, and the couple turned to the stage for their living. In America after 1793, Susanna wrote and acted in several social comedies and comic operas. In 1797 she gave up the theater to open a school for girls in Boston, but continued writing: dramas, novels, essays, and textbooks. *Lucy Temple,* a sequel to *Charlotte,* was published posthumously in 1828.

## Gabrielle Roy (1909–83)

Roy was born in what was, at the time, the village of Saint-Boniface, outside Winnipeg, Manitoba. The youngest of eleven children, she was unable to attend university, and instead obtained a teaching diploma from the Winnipeg Normal Institute. After several years as a schoolteacher, she traveled to London, where she studied acting briefly before embarking on a literary and journalistic career. Her first novel, *Bonheur d'occasion* (1945; translated in 1947 as *The Tin Flute*), garnered a Governor General's Award (her first of three) and the prestigious Lorne Pierce Medal; Roy won the French Prix Femina (the first Canadian to do so); and in 1947 she became the first woman fellow of the Royal Society of Canada.

## Joanna Russ (1937–   )

A native of New York City, Russ received her B.A. from Cornell University in 1957 and her M.F.A. from Yale University in 1960. Her subsequent teaching career has included appointments at Cornell, SUNY/Binghamton, and the University of Colorado. An avowed feminist, Russ writes science fiction that explores issues of gender, politics, and utopian ethics. Her works include *Picnic in Paradise* (1968), *And Chaos Died* (1970), *The Female Man* (1975), *The Adventures of Alyx* (1983), *Extra(ordinary) People* (1984), and *How to Suppress Women's Writing* (1983).

## J(erome) D(avid) Salinger (1919–   )

Born and bred in New York City, Salinger began writing stories at the age of fifteen. He published his first piece when he was twenty, while serving in the United States Army. During World War II, Salinger published a number of stories concerning GI life in *Collier's Magazine*. Little is known about Salinger's personal life; an extraordinarily private man, he lives in New England as a virtual recluse, refusing all interviews. His works include *The Catcher in the Rye* (1951), *Nine Stories* (1953), *Franny and Zooey* (1961), and *Raise High the Roof Beam, Carpenters* (1963).

## Catharine Maria Sedgwick (1789–1867)

Born in Stockbridge, Massachusetts, to a wealthy Berkshire family, Sedgwick received a first-rate education at Boston and Albany, and though she traveled little and never married, she was active in philanthropic concerns, in the Unitarian Church, and in literary and social circles. Her novels—domestic stories in an intentionally moral vein—include two historical romances, *Hope Leslie* (1827) and *The Linwoods* (1835), but all of her novels—*A New England Tale* (1822), *Redwood* (1824), *Clarence* (1830), and *Married or Single?* (1857)—present realistic depictions of New England home life and social customs. Sedgwick died at West Roxbury, Massachusetts, at the age of seventy-seven.

## Lydia Huntley Sigourney (1791–1865)

Born in Norwich, Connecticut, educated there and at Hartford, Sigourney began writing poetry at the age of eight. She taught school in Norwich, later opening her own school in Hartford. Her first book was *Moral Pieces in Prose and Verse* (1815), but her marriage in 1819 to Charles Sigourney ended her literary career for a time. She resumed writing for money—anonymously—when Mr. Sigourney's business declined; eventually she resumed the use of her name, publishing nearly seventy volumes of poetry and miscellaneous writings.

## Leslie Marmon Silko (1948– )

Raised in New Mexico and currently residing in Tucson, Arizona, Silko writes fiction rooted in her own tribal experience and in Navajo and Hopi history. Deeply concerned with the predicament of the Native American and the bifurcation of her own cultural life, Silko uses Indian legend, communal custom, and social injustice to structure her work. The troubled identity of the Native American— particularly the Indian woman—is a consistent theme. Silko first received critical attention for the poetry in *Laguna Woman* (1974) and for the fictional *Ceremony* (1977). These works were followed by *Storyteller* (1981), *The Delicacy and Strength of Lace* (1985), and a number of frequently anthologized stories, notably "Yellow Woman" and "Lullaby."

## William Gilmore Simms (1806–70)

A native of Charleston, South Carolina, Simms was the son of a shopkeeper who went bankrupt. With little formal education, he wrote poetry at an early age, read law, and was part owner and editor of the *City Gazette* before moving to New York in pursuit of a literary career. By 1835, when he returned to South Carolina, Simms had begun writing the romances of the Revolution and of Southern frontier history that would make him famous (his early works, *Guy Rivers* [1834], *The Yemassee* [1835], and *The Partisan* [1835], are the best known today). In the North, he was compared to Cooper, though his work is more realistic. In the South, he became a popular political figure, serving in the state legislature (1844–46) where he was an ardent Secessionist; he lost the lieutenant-governorship by only one vote. Simms wrote no novels after the outbreak of the Civil War, which cost him his Northern readership as well as his home and property. He died in Charleston on June 11, 1870.

## Upton Sinclair (1878–1968)

Born in Baltimore, Maryland, Sinclair grew up in New York City and attended Columbia University. While still an adolescent, he sold "juvenile" literature to a variety of popular magazines. In 1900 Sinclair left college to devote himself to his writing. His early novels were largely dismissed as sentimental fiction, but in 1904 Sinclair joined the Socialist Party of America and began to incorporate his social outrage into his fiction. He investigated the stockyards and oil fields and probed the lifestyles of the factory worker and piece-work laborer. In 1906 Sinclair founded Helicon Hall, an effort in cooperative living, and in 1934 he ran for governor of California on the EPIC (End Poverty in California) Democratic platform. His works include *The Jungle* (1906), *King Coal* (1917), *Oil* (1927), *Boston* (1928), and *The Profits of Religion* (1918).

## Isaac Bashevis Singer (1904–    )

The son of a rabbi, Singer was born in Radzymn, Poland. In 1935 Singer came to America and eventually attended Tachenioni Rabbinical Seminary. Presently a New Yorker, Singer writes lyrical and visionary fiction that often explores spiritual and religious themes. His works include *Gimpel the Fool and Other Stories* (1957), *The Slave* (1962), and *Short Friday* (1964).

## Elizabeth Oakes Smith (1806–93)

Born in North Yarmouth, Maine, Elizabeth Oakes Prince was married in 1823 to journalist and political humorist Seba Smith. After the Panic of 1837, she began contributing to periodicals in an attempt to bolster her family's income, and her poem "The Sinless Child" (1843) was favorably reviewed by Edgar Allan Poe. She produced several novels, including *The Western Captive* (1842), *Black Hollow* (1864), and *Bald Eagle* (1867). She was also active in the cause of women's suffrage (*Woman and Her Needs* [1851]).

## Susan Sontag (1933– )

Born in New York City, Sontag remains steadfastly an Eastern urbanite. As an undergraduate Sontag attended the University of California at Berkeley and the University of Chicago. She received her M.A. from Harvard University. Trained as a photographer, and maintaining an abiding interest in musical forms, Sontag combines a literary sensibility with extreme visual acuity. Novelist, critic, playwright, screenwriter, and essayist, Sontag is commonly credited with popularizing the sometimes arcane work of Roland Barthes and Walter Benjamin. Her iconoclastic interpretations have occasionally placed her outside of the Academy. Sontag's personal experiences are frequently reflected in her work. Her controversial visit to Vietnam finds expression in *Trip to Hanoi* (1968), and her painful encounter with cancer engendered *Illness as Metaphor* (1978). Other works include *Against Interpretation* (1966), *Styles of Radical Will* (1969), *Death Kit* (1967), *The Benefactor* (1967), *I, Etcetera* (1978), *Under the Sign of Saturn* (1981), and *AIDS and Its Metaphors* (1989).

## E. D. E. N. Southworth (1819–99)

Emma Dorothy Eliza Nevitte was born in Washington, D.C. In 1840 she married Frederick H. Southworth and moved to a Wisconsin farm, but soon Mrs. Southworth, pregnant and with a young son, returned to Washington. There she taught school and in 1847 published *Retribution*, the first in a long series of popular "potboilers" including *The Curse of Clifton* (1852), *The Hidden Hand* (1859), and

*The Fatal Marriage* (1869). During the 1860s her Georgetown home was a popular literary meeting place.

## Harriet Prescott Spofford (1835–1921)

A New Englander by birth, Spofford turned to journalism as a means of financial support. After her marriage she lived briefly in Washington, D.C. Her works detail New England life, most particularly the lives of women; her tone is realistic rather than nostalgic. Her books include *The Amber Gods and Other Stories* (1863), *A Scarlet Poppy and Other Stories* (1894), *Old Washington* (1906), and *The Elder's People* (1920).

## Wallace Stegner (1909–   )

Born in Lake Mills, Iowa, Stegner graduated from the University of Utah in 1930. Engrossed with the West since his youth, and interested in the patterns of expansion and the Mormon frontier experience, Stegner produces novels that deal with the problems of exploration. Since the publication of his first novel, *The Potter's House* (1938), Stegner's historical fiction has received critical acclaim. Deeply influenced by earlier Western writers, Stegner often celebrates his generic predecessors in his work. *The Angle of Repose* (1971) creates a fictional biography of Mary Hallock Foote. Stegner's numerous works include *Remembering Laughter* (1937), *Mormon Country* (1942), *Big Rock Candy Mountain* (1948), *The Preacher and the Slave* (1950), *All the Live Things* (1967), *The Spectator Bird* (1976), and *Recapitulation* (1979).

## Gertrude Stein (1874–1946)

Though Stein was born in Allegheny, Pennsylvania, she lived in Vienna and Australia; Passy, France; Baltimore, Maryland; Oakland and San Francisco, California; Cambridge, Massachusetts; and London, England, before settling in Paris in 1903. A charismatic expatriate during the heady days surrounding World Wars I and II, Stein and lifelong companion Alice B. Toklas drove for the American Fund for French Wounded during World War I but retired to the quietude of the French countryside during the German occupation of France during World War II. A prodigious author—Stein produced some 571 works during a career spanning forty-three years—Stein was extraordinarily influential as an experimental writer. Among those who frequented her Paris flat for advice and company were such writers as Ernest Hemingway, Djuna Barnes, and Hilda Doolittle. In the mid-1930s, after achieving fame with *The Autobiography of Alice B. Toklas* (1932), Stein returned to the United States to much acclaim. Stein died in Paris, with Toklas at her side. Her works include *Tender Buttons* (1914), *The Geographical History of America* (1936), *The Mother of Us All* (1949), and *Patriarchal Poetry* (1953).

## John Steinbeck (1902–68)

John Ernst Steinbeck was born in Salinas, California, and intermittently attended Stanford University, where he majored in marine biology. His first book was a romantic depiction of the career of buccaneer Henry Morgan (*Cup of Gold* [1929]), but *Tortilla Flat* (1935), set in Monterey, California, was his first popular success. This was followed by *In Dubious Battle* (1936), about striking migrant workers, *Of Mice and Men* (1937), and a collection, *The Long Valley* (1938). The struggle of migrant workers for survival and dignity is again the theme of *The Grapes of Wrath* (1939), which won a Pulitzer Prize. *Cannery Row* (1945) and *Sweet Thursday* (1954), set on the Monterey waterfront, are more lighthearted, but Steinbeck's serious moral and social concerns are foremost in *East of Eden* (1952) and *The Winter of Our Discontent* (1961). *Travels with Charley* was published in 1962, the same year that Steinbeck won the Nobel Prize in literature.

## Elizabeth Drew Stoddard (1823–1901)

Christened Elizabeth Barstow, Stoddard was born in Mattapoisett, Massachusetts, and was educated at the prestigious Wheaton Female Seminary. She married poet Richard Henry Stoddard. A fiction writer, Elizabeth Stoddard received widespread criticism for the supposed "immorality" of her work; she sought to reproduce the familiar terrain of New England but the region she perceived was marked by sexual desire and frequent violence. Praised by William Dean Howells, who reprinted some of her works, Stoddard received acclaim late in her life. Her most famous novel is *The Morgesons* (1862).

## Robert Stone (1937–   )

Stone was born in New York City, where he attended a Catholic high school and was briefly enrolled at New York University. Stone worked as a reporter during the Vietnam conflict, and his war experiences provide the basis for his award-winning *Dog Soldiers* (1974). Other works include *A Hall of Mirrors* (1967) and *A Flag for Sunrise* (1981).

## Harriet Beecher Stowe (1811–96)

Daughter of clergyman Lyman Beecher and sister of Henry Ward Beecher, Harriet Elizabeth Beecher was born in Litchfield, Connecticut. In 1832 her father was appointed president of Lane Theological Seminary, and Harriet accompanied him to Cincinnati, Ohio, where in 1836 she married Calvin E. Stowe, a professor of biblical literature at the seminary. On a visit to a Kentucky plantation she witnessed the conditions and effects of slavery, but it was not until 1850 (after the Stowes had returned to New England) and the passage of the Fugitive Slave Act that she wrote *Uncle Tom's Cabin* (1852), an immediate and controversial success. Her second novel, *Dred* (1856), again on the subject of slavery, was less successful. Next came *The Minister's Wooing* (1859), loosely based on her sister Catharine's life, followed by *The Pearl of Orr's Island* (1862) and *Agnes of Sorrento* (1862), a historical romance. *Oldtown Folks* (1869) is a romantic depiction of life in a post-Revolutionary Massachusetts village. In 1871 Stowe produced a social satire, *Pink and White Tyranny*, and *My Wife and I*, espousing the idea of careers for women. In 1875 the sequel to the latter, *We and Our Neighbors*, appeared, and in 1878 an autobiographical novel, *Poganuc People*. She lived mainly in Florida after the Civil War, but died at Hartford, Connecticut, on July 1, 1896.

## Ronald Sukenick (1932–   )

A devout Brooklynite for much of his life, Sukenick received a Ph.D. in 1962 from Brandeis University and today works as the Director of

Creative Writing at the University of Colorado at Boulder. Frustrated by the restrictions of commercial publishing, Sukenick helped establish the Fiction Collective in 1970, a writers' co-op devoted to publishing experimental fiction. Sukenick's commitment to the avant-garde is reflected in his innovative novels, which include *Out* (1973), *98.6* (1975), and *Long Talking Bad Conditions Blues* (1979).

## Tabitha Tenney (1762–1837)

Tabitha Tenney was a daughter of the prominent Gilman family of New Hampshire, and was married to Congressman Samuel Tenney. She wrote only one novel, the satirical *Female Quixotism: Exhibited in the Romantic Opinions and Extravagant Adventures of Dorcasina Sheldon* (1801), but this single work has secured her a place in the history of women's writing in America.

## Albion Tourgée (1838–1905)

Tourgée was born in Williamsfield, Ohio, and attended the University of Rochester (1859-61). He served as an officer in the Union Army during the Civil War, was twice wounded, and spent four months as a Confederate prisoner. During the Reconstruction he enjoyed a profitable career as a carpetbag politician. His novels, including *A Fool's Errand* (1879) and *Hot Plowshares* (1883), deal with the turbulent politics and race relations of the Civil War and the Reconstruction period. In 1897 he was appointed consul to Bordeaux, where he died.

## Mark Twain (Samuel Langhorne Clemens) (1835–1910)

Born in Missouri, and reared in the small town of Hannibal on the shores of the Mississippi River, Twain is often regarded as the quintessential American author. A complex figure, Twain combined social success and aspiration with a critical skepticism, and merged his humor with a sometimes bleak vision of the human condition. Twain's literature reflects his extensive and varied experience—he piloted a ship down the Mississippi, served briefly in a Confederate troop, and searched for gold in the Mother Lode district of California. Frustrated by his lack of financial remuneration in these fields, Twain turned to writing as a career. In 1870, following his marriage to the wealthy and well-connected Olivia Langdon, Twain established his household in Hartford, Connecticut. He also became a frequenter of European capitals. His numerous works include *The Innocents Abroad* (1869), *Roughing It* (1872), *The Adventures of Tom Sawyer* (1876), *A Tramp Abroad* (1880), *The Prince and the Pauper* (1882), *Life on the Mississippi* (1883), *The Adventures of Huckleberry Finn* (1885), *A Connecticut Yankee in King Arthur's Court* (1889), *The Tragedy of Pudd'nhead Wilson* (1894), and "The Mysterious Stranger" (published posthumously).

## John Updike (1932– )

The son of a writer (his mother) and a mathematics teacher (his father), Updike was born in Shillington, Pennsylvania. A highly motivated and successful student, Updike won a scholarship to Harvard University, where he was elected president of the humorous *Harvard Lampoon*. Upon his graduation in 1954, Updike went to England to study art at the Ruskin School of Drawing and Fine Arts. In 1955 Updike began to contribute to *The New Yorker,* and since that time he has published more than thirty books. A winner of numerous awards, including the National Book Award and the Pulitzer Prize, Updike has achieved a kind of celebrity status. Updike is a versatile author; he has written novels, short stories, poetry, plays, criticism, and children's books. His works include *The Same Door* (1959), *The Poorhouse Fair* (1959), *Rabbit Run* (1960), *Pigeon Feathers* (1962), *The Magic Flute* (1962), *Telephone Poles* (1963), *The Centaur* (1963), *Couples* (1968), *Bech: A Book* (1970), *Rabbit Redux* (1971), *Marry Me* (1976), *The Coup* (1978), *Rabbit Is Rich* (1980), *Bech Is Back* (1982), *Hugging the Shore* (1983), *The Witches of Eastwick* (1984), and *Roger's Version* (1986).

## Luisa Valenzuela (1938– )

Valenzuela is a native of Buenos Aires, Argentina. There she wrote for radio and worked as a reporter for the newspapers *La Nación* and *El Mundo.* She has lived in Mexico, Paris, and New York, where she settled in 1972. Her novels include *El gato eficaz* (Cat-o-Nine-Deaths, 1972); *Como en la guerra* (1977; *He Who Searches,* 1987), and *Cola de lagartija* (1983; *The Lizard's Tail,* 1983). She has been honored as a Fellow of the Institute for the Humanities (1981), was awarded a Guggenheim Fellowship in 1982, and was named Distinguished Writer in Residence, New York University (1985).

## Mario Vargos Llosa (1936–   )

Vargas Llosa was born in Arequipa, Peru. He graduated from the University of San Marcos in Lima in 1957 and attended the University of Madrid from 1957 to 1959. After a lengthy residence abroad, in Paris (where he helped to found the leftist journal *Libre*) and Barcelona, he returned to Peru in 1974. His first novel, *La ciudad y los perros* (1962; *The Time of the Hero*, 1966), created a sensation, and was followed in 1966 by his masterpiece, *La casa verde* (*The Green House*, 1968). He has been the recipient of many literary awards, and is recognized as a leading Latin American novelist, short-story writer, essayist, and critic.

## Gore Vidal (1925–   )

Vidal was born in the military establishment at West Point, New York. Vidal's life might best be described as cosmopolitan—he has traveled and lived in Europe, North Africa, and the Aleutian Islands. In 1960, Vidal was the Democratic candidate for the U.S. House of Representatives from New York's 29th Congressional District. His works include *Williwaw* (1946), *A Search for the King* (1950), *Washington, D.C.* (1967), *Myra Breckinridge* (1968), *Burr* (1973), and *Duluth* (1983).

## José Antonio Villarreal (1924–   )

A native of Los Angeles, Villarreal moved to Santa Clara when he was six. Here he was exposed to the economic plight of migrant workers and also learned Mexican folk tales. Villarreal's father, who reputedly lived for well over a hundred years, fought with Pancho Villa and greatly influenced his son's sense of history. After the United States entered World War II, Villareal enlisted in the Navy. Following the cessation of hostilities, Villarreal attended the University of California where he majored in English. Since then Villarreal has emerged as a leading force in Chicano literature. His works include *Poncho* (1959), *The Fifth Horseman* (1974), and *Clemente Chacon* (1984).

## Kurt Vonnegut (1922–  )

Born in Indianapolis, Indiana, the child of an architect, Vonnegut grew up in an atmosphere that encouraged his interest in technology and art. Vonnegut attended the Carnegie Institute of Technology (now Carnegie-Mellon University). As a young man Vonnegut worked at a variety of vocations, including a stint as a teacher at Massachusetts Hopefield School, work as a freelance writer, and employment as a police reporter for the Chicago City News Bureau. During World War II, Vonnegut served in the United States Army. He was captured and held as a POW, and received the Purple Heart in recognition of his valor. After his emergence as a novelist, Vonnegut received teaching appointments at a variety of prestigious institutions, including Harvard University and the University of Iowa's famed Writers' Workshop. Always interested in painting, Vonnegut exhibited his own art in 1980. Vonnegut's interests are multidisciplinary, embracing science, technology, art, and politics. His novels incorporate these themes and frequently blur the boundaries between fiction and science fiction. Vonnegut's numerous works include *Player Piano* (1952), *The Sirens of Titan* (1959), *Mother Night* (1962), *Cat's Cradle* (1963), *God Bless You, Mr. Rosewater; or, Pearls Before Swine* (1965), *Slaughterhouse-Five; or, The Children's Crusade* (1969), *Breakfast of Champions; or, Goodbye Blue Monday!* (1973), *Slapstick; or, Lonesome No More!* (1975), *Deadeye Dick* (1982), *Galapagos* (1985), and *Bluebeard* (1987).

## Lew Wallace (1827–1905)

Lewis Wallace was the son of David Wallace, governor of Indiana. His formal education ended at sixteen; though he was an avid reader, he disliked the confinement of the classroom. He served in the Mexican War and the Civil War, rising to the rank of major general. He was admitted to the bar in 1849, was elected to the Senate in 1856, became territorial governor of New Mexico in 1878, and was appointed minister to Turkey in 1881. His novels include *The Fair God*

(1873), about the Spanish conquest of Mexico, and *The Prince of India* (1893), as well as the best-selling *Ben-Hur* (1880).

## Susan B. Warner (1819–85)

Born in New York City, Warner lived most of her life in a dilapidated farmhouse on Constitution Island, in the Hudson River near West Point, where she and her sister Anna (under the pseudonyms Elizabeth Wetherell and Amy Lothrop) attempted to generate enough money from their writing to keep pace with their father's improvident investments and litigations. Warner's first novel, *The Wide, Wide World* (1850), which was (after several rejections) published on the recommendation of George P. Putnam's mother, quickly became one of the sentimental best-sellers of the nineteenth century, and was soon followed by *Queechy* (1852), launching Warner's career as a prolific novelist and author of children's stories.

## Frank J. Webb

There are no birth and death dates available for Webb. It is possible that he lived in England at some point before the publication of his novel, *The Garies and Their Friends*, in London in 1857. *The Garies* is among the earliest novels by an African American; it is a chronicle depicting the themes of interracial marriage, greed, and "passing" for white in the intermingled histories of three families: one white, one black, one mixed.

## James Welch (1940–   )

Welch was born in Browning, Montana, graduated from the University of Montana, and attended Northern Montana College. His novel *Winter in the Blood* (1974) is the story of a young man growing up on a Montana reservation, and is narrated by a character who is, like Welch, part Gros Ventre and part Blackfoot Indian. Welch's early poems are collected in *Riding the Earthboy 40* (1971).

## Eudora Welty (1909–   )

Welty was born and raised in Jackson, Mississippi. In her richly poetic, stylized fiction, Welty admittedly attempts to capture the rhythms and spirit of her Southern heritage. Welty attended Mississippi State College for Women, then graduated from the University of Wisconsin in 1929. In 1931 Welty returned to Mississippi and five years later published her first story, "The Death of a Traveling Salesman." Her works include *Losing Battles* (1970), *The Optimist's Daughter* (1972), *Collected Stories* (1980), and *One Writer's Beginnings* (1984), a memoir.

## Nathanael West (1903–40)

Born Nathan Wallenstein Weinstein, to Jewish immigrants in New York City, West made his way to the Pacific coast where he became obsessed with Hollywood and its lonely grotesques. *The Day of the Locust* (1939)—shocking in its exploration of the pathetic and perverse—remains West's most distinguished work. It was preceded by *The Dream Life of Balso Snell* (1931), *Miss Lonelyhearts* (1933), and *A Cool Million* (1934), as well as by a number of short stories and essays. West died in a car crash as he and his wife rushed northward from Mexico to attend the Hollywood funeral of F. Scott Fitzgerald.

## Edith Wharton (1862–1937)

The first woman to win a Pulitzer Prize, Wharton was born into the patrician world of New York society. She spent her formative years traveling between New York, Newport, and Europe, always accompanied by governesses and tutors. In 1885, at the age of twenty-three, Edith Jones married Edward Wharton, a wealthy Bostonian who was thirteen years her senior. Although the marriage would last twenty-eight years, the relationship was marked by long separations, mutual unhappiness, nervous illnesses, and finally divorce in 1913. A highly prolific writer, Wharton published fifty texts in the course of her life, and also left numerous unpublished volumes. *The Decoration of Houses* (1897), Wharton's first book, dealt with her ideas concerning interior design. Her first short stories appeared in *Scribner's Magazine,* and these short pieces were quickly followed by longer volumes, including *The Greater Inclination* (1899), *The Touchstone* (1900), *Crucial Instances* (1901), *The Valley of Decision* (1902), *Sanctuary* (1903), and *The Descent of Man and Other Stories* (1904). None of these works received a great deal of recognition until Wharton published *The House of Mirth* (1905). This was followed by *Madame de Treymes* (1907), *Ethan Frome* (1911), *The Reef* (1912), *The Age of Innocence* (1920), and *Old New York* (1924). Wharton's work also includes two war novels—*The Marne* (1918) and *A Son at the Front* (1923)—as well as the autobiographical *The Writing of Fiction* (1925) and *A Backward Glance* (1934). Wharton's indictment of the Gilded Age, her exploration of the conflict between tradition and social change, and her acknowledgment that the individual is essentially trapped by stronger exterior forces made hers a significant voice in the troubled canon of early modernism.

## Harriet E. Adams Wilson (1828?–1863?)

Wilson was probably born in Milford, New Hampshire, around 1827 or 1828, although there is other evidence that posits her birth in Fredericksburg, Virginia, in 1807 or 1808. Her only novel, *Our Nig,* was published in 1859. It is the story of a white orphan's marriage to an African American man, and the trials of their mulatto daughter, Frado, as she struggles for love and autonomy, against racism, poverty, and abandonment.

## Owen Wister (1860–1938)

Wister was born in Philadelphia, attended an Eastern preparatory school, graduated from Harvard University, and later matriculated at Harvard Law School. Suffering from poor health, Wister traveled to Wyoming in 1885 and was greatly impressed by the Western landscape. At the urging of his friend and former classmate, Theodore Roosevelt, Wister began to write about his Western experience, producing several biographies and a number of short stories that were published in *Harper's Magazine*. Wister's most famous work, *The Virginian* (1902), is dedicated to Roosevelt and translates the "rugged individualism" of the era into fiction.

## Herman Wouk (1915–   )

Born in New York City, Wouk grew up in a predominantly Jewish community. He was educated in New York City and graduated from

Columbia University. Interested in writing at an early age, Wouk did commercial writing and then produced radio plays. He entered the Navy in 1942 and was employed as an officer in the Pacific. This experience he would later describe in *The Caine Mutiny* (1951). Wouk has enjoyed great commercial success, and has also been the recipient of various awards, notably a Pulitzer Prize. His works include *Aurora Dawn* (1946), *The City Boy* (1948), *Marjorie Morningstar* (1955), *The Winds of War* (1971), and *War and Remembrance* (1980).

## Frances Wright (1795–1852)

Scottish-born radical and freethinker Frances Wright was the daughter of wealthy Scottish reformer James Wright. Wright is best known as the founder of the Nashoba Community in Tennessee (a model community where slaves were allowed to earn their freedom), for her volume *Views of Society and Manners in America* (London, 1821), and for her association with the radical New York journal, the *Free Enquirer*. She also produced a play (*Altorf* [1819]), the fictional tale *A Few Days in Athens* (1822), and was a popular—or notorious—public speaker (*Course of Popular Lectures* [1829]).

## Richard Wright (1908–60)

Born near Natchez, Mississippi, Wright created fiction that reflected the problems of growing up black in a highly prejudiced community. His character Bigger Thomas is an expression of the African American experience. Wright's most famous book, *Native Son* (1940), was followed by numerous other works, notably the autobiographical *Black Boy* (1945), as well as *Uncle Tom's Children* (1938), *The Outsider* (1953), *Savage Holiday* (1954), *The Long Dream* (1958), and *Eight Men* (1961).

# Selected Bibliography
## of Critical Works

Aaron, Daniel. "The Hyphenate Writer in American Letters." *Smith Alumnae Quarterly* (July 1964): 213–17.

Abzug, Robert H., and Stephen E. Maizlish, eds. *New Perspectives on Race and Slavery in America: Essays in Honor of Kenneth M. Stamp.* Lexington: University of Kentucky Press, 1986.

Achebe, Chinua. *Hopes and Impediments: Selected Essays.* New York: Doubleday, 1988.

Aldiss, Brian. *Billion Year Spree: The True History of Science Fiction.* Garden City, N.Y.: Doubleday, 1973.

Alegría, Fernando. *Nueva historia de la novela hispanomericana.* Hanover, N.H.: Ediciones del norte, 1986.

Allis, Jeanette B. *West Indian Literature: An Index to Criticism, 1930–1975.* Boston: G. K. Hall, 1981.

Alter, Robert. *Partial Magic: The Novel as a Self-Conscious Genre.* Berkeley: University of California Press, 1975.

Althusser, Louis. "Ideology and Ideological State Apparatuses: Notes Towards an Investigation." 1969; rpt. in *Lenin and Philosophy.* New York: Monthly Review Press, 1971.

*American Quarterly* 39.1 (Spring 1987). [Special Issue: Modernist Culture in America. Ed. Daniel Joseph Singal.]

Ammons, Elizabeth. *Conflicting Stories: American Women Writers at the Turn into the Twentieth Century.* New York: Oxford University Press, 1991.

Andrews, William L. *To Tell a Free Story: The First Century of Afro-American Autobiography, 1760–1865.* Urbana: University of Illinois Press, 1986.

Ash, Roberta. *Social Movements in America*. Chicago: Markham Publishing Company, 1972.

Ashcroft, Bill, Gareth Griffith, and Helen Tiffin. *The Empire Writes Back: Theory and Practice in Post-Colonial Literature*. New York and London: Routledge, 1989.

Atwood, Margaret. *Survival: A Thematic Guide to Canadian Literature*. Toronto: Anansi, 1972.

Baker, Houston A., Jr. *Blues, Ideology, and Afro-American Literature: A Vernacular Theory*. Chicago: University of Chicago Press, 1984.

——— "Handling Crisis: Great Books, Rap Music, and the End of Western Homogeneity." *Callalo* 13.2 (1989): 173–94.

——— *Modernism and the Harlem Renaissance*. Chicago: University of Chicago Press, 1987.

Baker, Houston A., Jr., ed. *Three American Literatures: Essays in Chicano, Native American, and Asian-American Literature for Teachers of American Literature*. New York: Modern Language Association of America, 1982.

Bakhtin, Mikhail. *The Dialogic Imagination*. Ed. Michael Holquist; trans. Caryl Emerson and Michael Holquist. Austin: University of Texas Press, 1981.

——— *Problems of Dostoevsky's Poetics*. Ed. and trans. Caryl Emerson. Theory and History of Literature Series, vol. 8. Minneapolis: University of Minnesota Press, 1984.

Barbrook, Alec, and Christine Bolt. *Power and Protest in American Life*. New York: St. Martin's Press, 1980.

Bardes, Barbara, and Suzanne Gossett. *Declarations of Independence: Women and Political Power in Nineteenth-Century American Fiction*. New Brunswick, N.J.: Rutgers University Press, 1990.

Barth, John. "The Literature of Exhaustion" and "The Literature of Replenishment." In *The Friday Book: Essays and Other Nonfiction*, pp. 62–78, 193–206. New York: G. P. Putnam's Son's, 1984.

Baudrillard, Jean. *Selected Writings*. Ed. Mark Poster. Stanford: Stanford University Press, 1988.

Baugh, Edward, ed. *Critics on Caribbean Literature*. London: Allen & Unwin, 1978.

Baym, Nina. "Melodramas of Beset Manhood: How Theories of American Fiction Exclude Women Authors." *American Quarterly* 33 (Summer 1981): 123–39.

——— *Novels, Readers, and Reviewers: Responses to Fiction in Antebellum America*. Ithaca, N.Y.: Cornell University Press, 1984.

——— *The Shape of Hawthorne's Career*. Ithaca, N.Y.: Cornell University Press, 1976.

——— *Woman's Fiction: A Guide to Novels by and about Women in America, 1820–1870*. Ithaca, N.Y.: Cornell University Press, 1978.

Behr, Edward. "The Muckraker's Contribution to Naturalistic Story-Telling." In *Seminaires 1978,* pp. 83–92. Ed. Jean Beranger, Jean Cazemajou, Pierre Spriet. Talence, France: Centre de Recherches sur l'Amérique Anglophone, Université de Bordeaux III, 1979.

Bell, Bernard W. *The Afro-American Novel and Its Tradition.* Amherst: University of Massachusetts Press, 1987.

Bell, Michael Davitt. *The Development of American Romance: The Sacrifice of Relation.* Chicago: University of Chicago Press, 1980.

Bennett, Tony, ed. *Popular Fiction: Technology, Ideology, Production, Reading.* New York and London: Routledge, 1990.

Benstock, Shari. *Women of the Left Bank: Paris: 1900–1940.* Austin: University of Texas Press, 1986.

Benstock, Shari, ed. *The Private Self: Theory and Practice in Women's Autobiographical Writings.* Chapel Hill: University of North Carolina Press, 1988.

Bercovitch, Sacvan, ed. *Reconstructing American Literary History.* Cambridge, Mass.: Harvard University Press, 1986.

Berg, Barbara J. *The Remembered Gate: Origins of American Feminism: The Woman and the City, 1800–1860.* New York: Oxford University Press, 1978.

Bhabha, Homi. "Of Mimicry and Man: The Ambivalence of Colonial Discourse." *October* 28 (1984): 125–34.

Billington, Ray. *The Protestant Crusade, 1800–1860: A Study of the Origins of American Nativism.* 1938; rpt. New York: Quadrangle Books, 1964.

Bingham, Edwin R., and Glen A. Love, eds. *Northwest Perspectives: Essays on the Culture of the Pacific Northwest.* Seattle: University of Washington Press, 1979.

Blanco, José Joaquín. *Función de medianoche: Ensayos de literatura cotidiana.* Mexico: Ediciones Era, 1981.

Bloom, Harold, ed. *American Fiction 1914–1945.* New York: Chelsea House, 1986.

Boase, Paul H., ed. *The Rhetoric of Protest and Reform, 1878–1898.* Athens: Ohio University Press, 1980.

Boelhower, William. *Through a Glass Darkly: Ethnic Semiosis in American Literature.* New York: Oxford University Press, 1987.

Boelhower, William, ed. *The Future of American Modernism: Ethnic Writing Between the Wars.* Amsterdam: Free University Press, 1990.

Bold, Christine. "Secret Negotiations: The Spy Figure in Nineteenth-Century American Popular Fiction." In Wesley K. Wark, ed., *Spy Fiction, Spy Films, and Real Intelligence.* London: Frank Cass, 1991.

——— *Selling the Wild West: Popular Western Fiction, 1860 to 1960.* Bloomington: Indiana University Press, 1987.

Boone, Joseph, and Michael Cadden. *Engendering Men.* New York: Routledge, 1990.

Bordwell, David, Janet Staiger, and Kristin Thompson. *The Classical Hollywood Cinema: Film Style and the Mode of Production to 1960.* New York: Columbia University Press, 1985.

Borus, Daniel H. *Writing Realism: Howells, James, and Norris in the Mass Market.* Chapel Hill: University of North Carolina Press, 1989.

Bottomore, Tom, and Robert Nisbet, eds. *A History of Sociological Analysis.* New York: Basic Books, 1978.

Bradbury, Malcolm, and David Palmer, eds. *The American Novel and the Nineteen Twenties.* London: Edward Arnold, 1971.

Bredahl, A. Carl, Jr. *New Ground: Western American Narrative and the Literary Canon.* Chapel Hill: University of North Carolina Press, 1989.

Brennan, Tim. "Cosmopolitans and Celebrities." *Race and Class* 31.1 (July/September 1989): 1–20.

Brodhead, Richard H. *Hawthorne, Melville, and the Novel.* Chicago: University of Chicago Press, 1976.

——— *The School of Hawthorne.* New York: Oxford University Press, 1986.

——— "Veiled Ladies: Toward a History of Antebellum Entertainment." *American Literary History* 1.2 (Summer 1989): 273–94.

Brodsky, Joseph. "The Condition of Exile." *The New York Review of Books,* January 21, 1988.

Brown, Gillian. "Getting in the Kitchen with Dinah: Domestic Politics in *Uncle Tom's Cabin.*" *American Literature Quarterly* 36.4 (Fall 1984): 503–23.

Brown, Herbert Ross. *The Sentimental Novel in America, 1789–1860.* Durham, N.C.: Duke University Press, 1940.

Bruce, Dickson D., Jr. *Black American Writing from the Nadir: The Evolution of a Literary Tradition, 1877–1915.* Baton Rouge: Louisiana State University Press, 1989.

Bryer, Jackson R., ed. *Sixteen Modern American Authors.* Vol. 2: *A Survey of Research and Criticism Since 1972.* Durham, N.C.: Duke University Press, 1990.

Buckley, Peter G. "The Case Against Ned Buntline: The 'Words, Signs, and Gestures' of Popular Authorship." *Prospects: An Annual of American Cultural Studies* 13: 249–72. New York: Cambridge University Press, 1988.

Budd, Louis. *Our Mark Twain: The Making of His Public Personality.* Philadelphia: University of Pennsylvania Press, 1983.

Buell, Lawrence. *New England Literary Culture: From Revolution Through Renaissance.* Cambridge: Cambridge University Press, 1986.

Burger, Peter. *Theory of the Avant-Garde.* Trans. Michael Shaw. Theory and History of Literature Series, vol. 4. Minneapolis: University of Minnesota Press, 1984.

Buters, R., J. Clem, and M. Moon. *Displacing Homophobia: Gay Perspective in Literature and Culture.* Durham, N.C.: Duke University Press, 1989.

Butler, Judith. "The Force of Fantasy: Feminism, Mapplethorpe, and Discursive Excess." *Differences: A Journal of Feminist Cultural Studies* 2:2 (1990): 105–25.

Cady, Edwin H. *The Light of Common Day: Realism in American Fiction.* Bloomington: Indiana University Press, 1971.

Cagnon, Maurice. *The French Novel of Quebec.* Boston: Twayne, 1986.

Calderón, Héctor, and José David Saldívar, eds. *Criticism in the Borderlands: Studies in Chicano Literature, Culture, and Ideology.* Durham, N.C.: Duke University Press, 1991.

Calinescu, Matei. *Five Faces of Modernity: Modernism, Avant-Garde, Decadence, Kitsch, Postmodernism.* Durham, N.C.: Duke University Press, 1987.

Campos, Julieta. *Función de la novela.* Mexico: Joaquín Mortiz, 1973.

Canclini, Néstor García. *Culturas Híbridas.* Mexico: forthcoming.

Carby, Hazel V. *Reconstructing Womanhood: The Emergence of the Afro-American Woman Novelist.* New York: Oxford University Press, 1987.

Carpentier, Alejo. *Tientos y diferencias.* Buenos Aires: Calicanto, 1967.

Carter, Everett. *Howells and the Age of Realism.* Hamden, Conn.: Archon Books, 1966.

Carton, Evan. *The Rhetoric of American Romance: Dialectic and Identity in Emerson, Dickinson, Poe and Hawthorne.* Baltimore: Johns Hopkins University Press, 1985.

Casey, Daniel J., and Robert F. Rhodes. *Irish-American Fiction.* New York: AMS Press, 1979.

Cash, W. J. *The Mind of the South.* New York: Alfred A. Knopf, 1941.

Castellanos, Rosario. *Mujer que sabe latín. . . .* 1973; Mexico: Fondo de cultura económica, 1984.

Cawelti, John G. *Adventure, Mystery, and Romance: Formula Stories as Art and Popular Culture.* Chicago: University of Chicago Press, 1976.

——— *The Six-Gun Mystique.* Bowling Green: Bowling Green State University Popular Press, 1971.

Centre for Contemporary Cultural Studies, University of Birmingham. *The Empire Strikes Back: Race and Racism in 70s Britain.* London: Hutchinson, 1982.

Certeau, Michel de. *The Practice of Everyday Life.* Trans. Steven Rendall. Berkeley: University of California Press, 1984.

Césaire, Aimé. *Discourse on Colonialism.* Trans. Joan Pinkham. New York: MR, 1972.

Chametzky, Jules. *Our Decentralized Literature: Cultural Mediations in Selected Jewish and Southern Writers.* Amherst: University of Massachusetts Press, 1986.

Charvat, William. *The Profession of Authorship in America, 1800–1870: The Papers of William Charvat.* Ed. Matthew J. Bruccoli. Columbus: Ohio State University Press, 1968.

Chase, Richard. *The American Novel and Its Tradition.* New York: Doubleday, 1957.

Cheyfitz, Eric. "*A Hazard of New Fortunes:* The Romance of Self-Realization." In *American Realism: New Essays,* pp. 42–65. Ed. Eric J. Sundquist. Baltimore: Johns Hopkins University Press, 1982.

Chin, Frank, et al. Introductions to *The Big Aiiieeeee! An Anthology of Asian American Writers,* pp. vi-lxiv. Washington, D.C.: Howard University Press, 1983.

Christian, Barbara. *Black Women Novelists: The Development of a Tradition, 1892–1976.* New York: Greenwood Press, 1980.

Clark, Robert. *History, Ideology and Myth in American Fiction, 1823–52.* London: Macmillan, 1984.

Clifford, James. "Traveling Cultures." In *Cultural Studies.* Eds. Larry Grossberg, Cary Nelson, Paula Treicher. New York: Routledge, forthcoming.

Coser, Lewis A. *Men of Ideas.* New York: Free Press, 1965.

Cott, Nancy F. *The Bonds of Womanhood: "Woman's Sphere" in New England, 1780–1835.* New Haven: Yale University Press, 1977.

Coultrap-McQuin, Susan. *Doing Literary Business: American Women Writers in the Nineteenth Century.* Chapel Hill: University of North Carolina Press, 1990.

Couser, G. Thomas. *Altered Egos: Authority in American Autobiography.* New York: Oxford University Press, 1989.

Cowley, Malcolm. *The Literary Situation.* New York: Viking Press, 1955.

Crane, Diana. *Invisible Colleges: Diffusion of Knowledge in Scientific Communities.* Chicago: University of Chicago Press, 1972.

Cross, Whitney. *The Burned-Over District: The Social and Intellectual History of Enthusiastic Religion in Western New York, 1800–1850.* 1950; rpt. New York: Harper Torchbooks, 1965.

Crowther, Duane S. "Quantifying the Sales Push." *Publishers Weekly* (April 8, 1988): 15–18.

Crump, G. B. *The Novels of Wright Morris: A Critical Interpretation.* Lincoln: University of Nebraska Press, 1978.

Cudjoe, Selwyn R. *Resistance and Caribbean Literature.* Athens: Ohio University Press, 1980.

Cudjoe, Selwyn R., ed. *Caribbean Women Writers: Essays from the First National Conference.* Wellesley, Mass.: Calaloux, 1990.

Cunliffe, Marcus, ed. *American Literature Since 1900.* New York: Peter Bedrick Books, 1987.

Dance, Daryl Cumber, ed. *Fifty Caribbean Writers: A Bio-Bibliographical Critical Sourcebook.* New York: Greenwood Press, 1986.

Darby, William. *Necessary American Fictions: Popular Literature of the 1950s.* Bowling Green: Bowling Green State University Popular Press, 1987.

Daugherty, Sarah B. "Howells, Tolstoy, and the Limits of Realism: The Case of *Annie Kilburn.*" *American Literary Realism, 1870–1910* 19.1 (Fall 1986): 21–41.

Davidson, Carter. "The Immigrant Strain in Contemporary American Literature." *English Journal* 25 (December 1936): 862–68.

Davidson, Cathy N. *Revolution and the Word: The Rise of the Novel in America.* New York: Oxford University Press, 1986.

Davidson, Edward H. *Poe: A Critical Study.* Cambridge, Mass.: Harvard University Press, 1957.

Davies, Carole Boyce, and Elaine Savory Fido, eds. *Out of the Kumbla: Caribbean Women and Literature.* Trenton, N.J.: Africa World Press, 1990.

Davis, David Brion, ed. *Ante-Bellum Reform.* New York: Harper & Row, 1967.

Davis, Mike. *City of Quartz: Excavating the Future in Los Angeles.* London: Verso, 1990.

Davis, Thadious M. *Faulkner's "Negro": Art and the Southern Context.* Baton Rouge: Louisiana State University Press, 1983.

Dayan, Joan. *Fables of Mind: An Inquiry into Poe's Fiction.* New York: Oxford University Press, 1987.

Dearborn, Mary V. *Pocahontas's Daughters: Gender and Ethnicity in American Culture.* New York: Oxford University Press, 1986.

Dekker, George. *The American Historical Romance.* Cambridge: Cambridge University Press, 1987.

Denning, Michael. *Mechanic Accents: Dime Novels and Working-Class Culture in America.* London: Verso, 1987.

Desan, Philippe, Priscilla Ferguson, and Wendy Griswold, eds. *Literature and Social Practice.* Chicago: University of Chicago Press, 1989.

Dixon, Melvin. *Ride Out the Wilderness: Geography and Identity in Afro-American Literature.* Urbana: University of Illinois Press, 1987.

Douglas, Ann. *The Feminization of American Culture.* New York: Alfred A. Knopf, 1977.

Dryden, Edgar. *The Form of American Romance.* Baltimore: Johns Hopkins University Press, 1988.

Dumont, Louis. *From Mandeville to Marx: The Genesis and Triumph of Economic Ideology.* Chicago: University of Chicago Press, 1977.

Eakin, Paul John. *American Autobiography: Retrospect and Prospect.* Madison: University of Wisconsin Press, 1991.

—— *Fictions in Autobiography: Studies in the Art of Self-Invention.* Princeton: Princeton University Press, 1985.

Easton, Robert. *Max Brand: The Big Westerner.* Norman: University of Oklahoma Press, 1970.

Eble, Kenneth E. *William Dean Howells.* 2d ed. Boston: Twayne, 1982.

Eco, Umberto. *Travels in Hyperreality.* San Diego: Harcourt Brace Jovanovich, 1983.

Eliot, T. S. "Professional, Or . . ." *The Egoist* 5 (April 1918).

Elliott, Emory. *Revolutionary Writers: Literature and Authority in the New Republic, 1725–1810.* New York: Oxford University Press, 1982.

Enzensberger, Hans Magnus. *The Consciousness Industry: On Literature, Politics and the Media.* New York: Seabury Press, 1974.

Epstein, Barbara Leslie. *The Politics of Domesticity: Women, Evangelism, and Temperance in Nineteenth-Century America.* Middletown, Conn.: Wesleyan University Press, 1981.

Erisman, Fred, and Richard W. Etulain, eds. *Fifty Western Writers: A Bio-Bibliographical Sourcebook.* Westport, Conn.: Greenwood Press, 1982.

Etulain, Richard W. *A Bibliographical Guide to the Study of Western American Literature.* Lincoln: University of Nebraska Press, 1982.

Etulain, Richard W., and Michael T. Marsden, eds. *The Popular Western: Essays Toward a Definition.* Bowling Green: Bowling Green State University Popular Press, 1974.

Everson, William. *Archetype West: The Pacific Coast as a Literary Region.* Berkeley: Oyez, 1976.

Fabre, Michel. *The World of Richard Wright.* Jackson: University Press of Mississippi, 1985.

Fairbanks, Carol. *Prairie Women: Images in American and Canadian Fiction.* New Haven: Yale University Press, 1986.

Falardeau, Jean-Charles. *Notre société et notre roman.* Montreal: Hurtubise HMH, 1967.

Feal, Rosemary Geisdorfer. "Spanish American Ethnobiography and the Slave Narrative Tradition: *Biografía de un cimarrón* and *Me llamo Rigoberta Menchú.*" *Modern Language Studies* 20 (1990): 100–111.

Ferguson, Robert A. *Law and Letters in American Culture.* Cambridge, Mass.: Harvard University Press, 1984.

Fernández Retamar, Roberto. *Calibán: Apuntes sobre la cultura en nuestra América.* Mexico: Editorial Diógenes, 1971. Trans. Edward Baker as *Caliban and Other Essays.* Minneapolis: University of Minnesota Press, 1989.

Fetterley, Judith. " 'Checkmate': Elizabeth Stuart Phelps's *The Silent Partner.*" *Legacy: A Journal of Nineteenth-Century American Women Writers* 3.2 (Fall 1986): 17–29.

Fiedler, Leslie A. *The Jew in the American Novel.* New York: Herzl Press, 1959.

——— *The Return of the Vanishing American.* New York: Stein, 1968.

—— *Waiting for the End*. New York: Delta, 1965.

Fields, Annie. *Life and Letters of Harriet Beecher Stowe*. Boston: Houghton Mifflin Co., 1898.

Fine, David, ed. *Los Angeles in Fiction: A Collection of Original Essays*. Albuquerque: University of New Mexico Press, 1984.

Fisher, Philip. *Hard Facts: Setting and Form in the American Novel*. New York: Oxford University Press, 1985.

—— "Partings and Ruins: Radical Sentimentality in *Uncle Tom's Cabin*." *Amerikastudien/American Studies* 28.3 (1983): 279–93.

Flaubert, Gustave. Letter to Louise Colet, p. 133. In *Selected Letters*. Trans. Francis Steegmuller. New York: Farrar, Strauss, 1954.

Fliegelman, Jay. *Prodigals and Pilgrims: The American Revolution Against Patriarchal Authority, 1750–1800*. New York: Cambridge University Press, 1982.

Flora, Joseph M., and Robert Bain, eds. *Fifty Southern Writers After 1900: A Bio-Bibliographical Sourcebook*. New York: Greenwood Press, 1987.

Foley, Barbara. "Women and the Left in the 1930s." *American Literary History* 2 (Spring 1990): 150–69.

Folsom, James K. *The American Western Novel*. New Haven: College and University Press, 1966.

Folsom, James K., ed. *The Western: A Collection of Critical Essays*. Englewood Cliffs, N.J.: Prentice-Hall, 1979.

Foner, Eric. *Free Soil, Free Labor, Free Men: The Ideology of the Republican Party Before the Civil War*. New York: Oxford University Press, 1970.

Ford-Smith, Honor. *Ring Ding in a Tight Corner: Funding and Organizational Democracy in Sistren, 1977–1988*. Toronto: ICAE, 1989.

Foster, David William. "The Demythification of Buenos Aires in Selected Argentine Novels of the Seventies." *Chasqui* 10.1 (1980): 3–25.

Fox, Richard W., and T. Jackson Lears, eds. *The Culture of Consumption: Critical Essays in American History, 1880–1980*. New York: Pantheon, 1983.

Fox, Robert Elliot. *Conscientious Sorcerers: The Black Postmodernist Fiction of Leroi Jones/Amiri Baraka, Ishmael Reed, and Samuel R. Delany*. New York, Westport, Conn., and London: Greenwood Press, 1987.

Fowler, Doreen, and Ann J. Abadie, eds. *Faulkner and Race: Faulkner and Yoknapatawpha 1986*. Jackson: University Press of Mississippi, 1987.

Franklin, H. Bruce. *War Stars: The Superweapon and the American Imagination*. New York: Oxford University Press, 1988.

Fredrickson, George M. *The Arrogance of Race: Historical Perspectives on Slavery, Racism, and Social Inequality*. Middletown, Conn.: Wesleyan University Press, 1988.

—— *The Black Image in the White Mind: The Debate on Afro-American Character, 1817–1914*. New York: Harper & Row, 1971.

Fribert, Lucy M., and Barbara A. White, eds. *Hidden Hands: An Anthology of American Women Writers, 1790–1870.* New Brunswick, N.J.: Rutgers University Press, 1988.

Friedman, Ellen G., and Miriam Fuchs, eds. *The Review of Contemporary Fiction: Kathy Acker, Christine Brook-Rose, Marguerite Young Number* 9.3 (Fall 1989).

Fussell, Paul. *The Great War and Modern Memory.* London: Oxford University Press, 1975.

Gardiner, Jane. "Form and Reform in *Looking Backward.*" *American Transcendental Quarterly* 2.1 (March 1988): 69–82.

Gass, William H. "A Fiesta for the Form." *The New Republic* (October 25, 1980): 33–39.

Gaston, Edwin W., Jr. *The Early Novel of the Southwest.* Albuquerque: University of New Mexico Press, 1961.

Gaston, Paul M. *The New South Creed: A Study in Southern Mythmaking.* Baton Rouge: Louisiana State University Press, 1970.

Gates, Henry Louis, Jr. *Figures in Black: Words, Signs, and the "Racial" Self.* New York: Oxford University Press, 1987.

———— *The Signifying Monkey: A Theory of Afro-American Literary Criticism.* New York: Oxford University Press, 1988.

Gates, Henry Louis, Jr., ed. *"Race," Writing, and Difference.* Chicago: University of Chicago Press, 1986.

Gayle, Addison. *The Way of the New World: The Black Novel in America.* Garden City, N.Y.: Doubleday, 1975.

Geary, Susan. "The Domestic Novel as a Commercial Commodity: Making a Best Seller in the 1850s." *The Papers of the Bibliographical Society of America* 70 (1976): 365–93.

Gedin, Per. *Literature in the Marketplace.* Trans. George Bisset. London: Faber & Faber, 1977.

Gibson, Donald B. *The Politics of Literary Expression: A Study of the Major Black Writers.* Westport, Conn.: Greenwood Press, 1981.

Gilkes, Michael. *The West Indian Novel.* Boston: Twayne, 1981.

Gillman, Susan. *Dark Twins: Imposture and Identity in Mark Twain's America.* Chicago: University of Chicago Press, 1989.

Gilman, Sander L. *Jewish Self-Hatred: Anti-Semitism and the Hidden Language of the Jews.* Baltimore: Johns Hopkins University Press, 1986.

Gilmore, Michael T. *American Romanticism and the Marketplace.* Chicago: University of Chicago Press, 1985.

Gilmore, William J. *Reading Becomes a Necessity of Life: Material and Cultural Life in Rural New England, 1780–1835.* Knoxville: University of Tennessee Press, 1989.

Glenn, Myra C. *Campaigns Against Corporal Punishment: Prisoners, Sailors, Women, and Children.* Albany: State University of New York Press, 1984.

Godard, Barbara, ed. *Gynocritics: Feminist Approaches to Canadian and Quebec Women's Writing.* Toronto: ECW, 1987.

González Echevarría, Roberto. *Alejo Carpentier: The Pilgrim at Home.* Ithaca, N.Y.: Cornell University Press, 1977.

—— *Myth and Archive: A Theory of Latin American Narrative.* Cambridge: Cambridge University Press, 1990.

—— *The Voice of the Masters: Writing and Authority in Modern Latin American Literature.* Austin: University of Texas Press, 1985.

Gougeon, Len. *Virtue's Hero: Emerson, Antislavery, and Reform.* Athens: University of Georgia Press, 1990.

Goulart, Ron. *Cheap Thrills: An Informal History of the Pulp Magazines.* New Rochelle, N.Y.: Arlington House, 1972.

Gould, Karen. *Writing in the Feminine: Feminism and Experimental Writing in Quebec.* Carbondale: Southern Illinois University Press, 1990.

Graff, Gerald. *Literature Against Itself: Literary Ideas in Modern Society.* Chicago: University of Chicago Press, 1979.

—— *Professing Literature: An Institutional History.* Chicago: University of Chicago Press, 1987.

Gramsci, Antonio. *Selections from Cultural Writings.* Ed. David Forgacs and Geoffrey Nowell-Smith. Cambridge, Mass.: Harvard University Press, 1985.

Grant, Barry Keith, ed. *Film Genre Reader.* Austin: University of Texas Press, 1986.

Gray, Richard. *Writing the South: Ideas of an American Region.* Cambridge: Cambridge University Press, 1986.

Green, Rose Basile. *The Italian-American Novel: A Document of the Interaction of Two Cultures.* Rutherford, N.J.: Fairleigh Dickinson University Press, 1974.

Gruber, Frank. *The Pulp Jungle.* Los Angeles: Sherbourne Press, 1967.

Gurr, Andrew. *Writers in Exile: The Identity of Home in Modern Literature.* Atlantic Highlands, N.J.: Humanities Press, 1981.

Guttmann, Allen. *The Jewish Writer in America: Assimilation and the Crisis of Identity.* New York: Oxford University Press, 1971.

Gwin, Minrose C. *The Feminine and Faulkner: Reading (Beyond) Sexual Difference.* Knoxville: University of Tennessee Press, 1990.

Habegger, Alfred. *Gender, Fantasy, and Realism in American Literature.* New York: Columbia University Press, 1982.

Halper, Albert. "Notes on Jewish-American Fiction." *The Menorah Journal* 20 (April 1932): 61–69.

Hamilton, Cynthia S. *Western and Hard-Boiled Detective Fiction in America: From High Noon to Midnight.* Iowa City: University of Iowa Press, 1987.

Hamilton, Roberta, and Michelle Barrett, eds. *The Politics of Diversity: Feminism, Marxism, and Nationalism.* London: Verso, 1986.

Harap, Louis. *In the Mainstream: The Jewish Presence in Twentieth-Century American Literature, 1950s–1980s.* New York: Greenwood Press, 1987.

Harlow, Barbara. *Resistance Literature.* New York and London: Methuen, 1987.

Harootunian, H. D., and Masao Miyoshi, eds. *Postmodernism and Japan.* Durham, N.C.: Duke University Press, 1989.

Harris, Sharon M. "Rebecca Harding Davis: From Romanticism to Realism." *American Literary Realism, 1870–1910* 21.2 (Winter 1989): 4–20.

Harris, Susan K. *Nineteenth-Century American Women's Novels: Interpretive Strategies.* Cambridge: Cambridge University Press, 1990.

Harris, Wilson. *Tradition, the Writer and Society: Critical Essays.* 1967; London: New Beacon, 1973.

Harrison, Dick. *Unnamed Country: The Struggle for a Canadian Prairie Fiction.* Edmonton: University of Alberta Press, 1977.

Hart, James D. *The Popular Book: A History of America's Literary Taste.* New York: Oxford University Press, 1950; Berkeley and Los Angeles: University of California Press, 1961.

Harter, Carol C., and James R. Thompson. *E. L. Doctorow.* Boston: Twayne, 1990.

Haskell, Thomas. *The Emergence of Professional Social Science: The American Social Science Association and the Nineteenth Century Crisis of Authority.* Urbana: University of Illinois Press, 1977.

Haslam, Gerald W., ed. *Western Writing.* Albuquerque: University of New Mexico Press, 1974.

Hassan, Ihab. *The Postmodern Turn.* Columbus: Ohio State University Press, 1987.

—— *Radical Innocence: Studies in the Contemporary American Novel.* Princeton: Princeton University Press, 1961.

—— *The Right Promethean Fire: Imagination, Science, and Cultural Change.* Urbana: University of Illinois Press, 1980.

Hedges, Elaine. "Introduction" to Meridel Le Sueur, *Ripening: Selected Work, 1927–1980,* pp. 1–28. Old Westbury, N.Y.: Feminist Press, 1982.

Heller, Erich. *The Ironic German: A Study of Thomas Mann.* Chicago: Regnery, 1958.

Heller, Thomas, et al., eds. *Reconstructing Individualism: Autonomy, Individuality, and the Self in Western Thought.* Stanford: Stanford University Press, 1986.

Hersh, Blanch Glassman. *The Slavery of Sex: Feminist-Abolitionists in America.* Urbana: University of Illinois Press, 1978.

Hirsch, David H. *Reality and Idea in the Early American Novel.* The Hague: Mouton, 1971.

Hite, Molly. *Ideas of Order in the Novels of Thomas Pynchon.* Columbus: Ohio State University Press, 1983.

Hobson, Fred. *Tell About the South: The Southern Rage to Explain.* Baton Rouge: Louisiana State University Press, 1983.

Holland, Laurence. *The Expense of Vision: Essays on the Craft of Henry James.* Princeton: Princeton University Press, 1964.

Homberger, Eric. *American Writers and Radical Politics, 1900–39— Equivocal Commitments.* New York: St. Martin's Press, 1986.

hooks, bell. "Postmodern Blackness." *Postmodern Culture* 1.1 (September 1990). PMC@NCSUVM.BITNET

Horkheimer, Max, and Theodor Adorno. *Dialectic of Enlightenment.* Trans. John Cumming. New York: Continuum, 1982.

Howard, June. *Form and History in American Literary Naturalism.* Chapel Hill: University of North Carolina Press, 1985.

Howe, Daniel Walker. *The Political Culture of the American Whigs.* Chicago: University of Chicago Press, 1979.

Howe, Irving. *World of Our Fathers.* New York: Simon and Schuster, 1976.

Hutcheon, Linda. *The Canadian Postmodern: A Study of Contemporary English-Canadian Fiction.* Toronto: Oxford University Press, 1988.

——— *Narcissistic Narrative: The Metafictional Paradox.* New York and London: Methuen, 1980.

——— *A Poetics of Postmodernism: History, Theory, Fiction.* New York and London: Routledge, 1988.

Huyssen, Andreas. *After the Great Divide: Modernism, Mass Culture, Postmodernism.* Bloomington: Indiana University Press, 1986.

Irvine, Lorna. *Sub/Version: Canadian Fictions by Women.* Toronto: ECW, 1986.

Jackson, Blyden. *A History of Afro-American Literature.* Baton Rouge: Louisiana State University Press, 1989–. 1 vol. to date.

Jameson, Fredric. *Postmodernism: or, The Cultural Logic of Late Capitalism.* Durham, N.C.: Duke University Press, 1991.

——— *Signatures of the Visible.* New York: Routledge, 1990.

Jay, Karla, and Joanne Glasgow. *Lesbian Texts and Contexts: Radical Revisions.* New York: New York University Press, 1990.

Jehlen, Myra. "The Family Militant: Domesticity versus Slavery in *Uncle Tom's Cabin.*" *Criticism: A Quarterly for Literature and the Arts* 31.4 (Fall 1989): 383–400.

Johannsen, Albert. *The House of Beadle and Adams and Its Dime and Nickel Novels: The Story of a Vanished Literature.* 2 vols. Norman: University of Oklahoma Press, 1950; supplement, 1962.

Johnson, Charles R. *Being & Race: Black Writing Since 1970.* Bloomington: Indiana University Press, 1988; Midland Book, 1990.

Johnson, Ira D., and Christiane Johnson, eds. *Les Américanistes: New French Criticism on Modern American Fiction.* Port Washington, N.Y.: Kennikat, 1978.

Jones, Anne Goodwyn. *Tomorrow Is Another Day: The Woman Writer in the South, 1859–1936.* Baton Rouge: Louisiana State University Press, 1981.

Jones, Daryl. *The Dime Novel Western.* Bowling Green: Bowling Green State University Popular Press, 1978.

Jordan, Winthrop D. *White Over Black: American Attitudes Toward the Negro, 1550–1812.* New York and London: Norton, 1977.

Joswick, Thomas P. " 'The crown without the conflict': Religious Values and Moral Reasoning in *Uncle Tom's Cabin.*" *Nineteenth-Century Literature* 39.3 (December 1984): 253–74.

Jozef, Bella. "Clarice Lispector: La recuperacíon de la palabra poética." *Revista iberoamericana* 50 (1984): 239–57.

Justus, James. *The Achievement of Robert Penn Warren.* Baton Rouge: Louisiana State University Press, 1981.

Kadushin, Arthur, Lewis A. Coser, and William W. Powell. *Books: The Culture and Commerce of Publishing.* New York: Basic Books, 1982.

Kampf, Louis. "Art for Politics Sake." *Working Papers* (Spring 1974): 84–89.

Kaplan, Amy. *The Social Construction of American Realism.* Chicago: University of Chicago Press, 1988.

Karcher, Carolyn L. *Shadow over the Promised Land.* Baton Rouge: Louisiana State University Press, 1980.

Karl, Frederick Robert. *American Fictions 1940–1980: A Comprehensive History and Critical Evaluation.* New York: Harper & Row, 1983.

Kasson, John. *Civilizing the Machine: Technology and Republican Values in America, 1776–1900.* 1976; rpt. New York: Penguin, 1977.

Katrak, Ketu H., and R. Radhakrishnan, guest editors. "Desh-Videsh: South Asian Expatriate Writing and Art." *The Massachusetts Review* 24.4 (Winter 1988–89).

Kazin, Alfred. *Bright Book of Life: American Novelists and Storytellers from Hemingway to Mailer.* Boston: Little, Brown and Company, 1973.

Keefer, Janice Kulyk. *Under Eastern Eyes: A Critical Reading of Maritime Fiction.* Toronto: University of Toronto Press, 1987.

Keith, W. J. *A Sense of Style: Studies in the Art of Fiction in English-Speaking Canada.* Toronto: ECW, 1989.

Kelley, Mary. *Private Women, Public Stage: Literary Domesticity in Nineteenth-Century America.* New York: Oxford University Press, 1984.

Kenner, Hugh. *A Homemade World: The American Modernist Writers.* New York: William Morrow and Company, 1975.

Kent, George. *Blackness and the Adventure of Western Culture.* Chicago: Third World Press, 1972.

Kerber, Linda K. *Women of the Republic: Intellect and Ideology in Revolutionary America.* Chapel Hill: University of North Carolina Press, 1980.

Kern, Stephen. *The Culture of Time and Space 1880–1918*. Cambridge, Mass.: Harvard University Press, 1983.

Kerr, Howard. *Mediums, and Spirit-Rappers, and Roaring Radicals: Spiritualism in American Literature, 1850–1890*. Urbana: University of Illinois Press, 1972.

Kessler-Harris, Alice, and Paul Lauter. "Introduction" to Feminist Press series of novels by women of the thirties. 4 vols. Old Westbury, N.Y.: Feminist Press, 1983–87.

Killam, G. D. *African Writers on African Writing*. London: Heinemann, 1973.

Kim, Elaine H. *Asian American Literature: An Introduction to the Writings and Their Social Context*. Philadelphia: Temple University Press, 1982.

King, Bruce, ed. *West Indian Literature*. London: Macmillan, 1979.

King, Richard. *A Southern Renaissance: The Cultural Awakening of the American South, 1930–1955*. Oxford: Oxford University Press, 1980.

Kingston, Paul William, and Jonathan R. Cole. *The Wages of Writing: Per Word, Per Piece, or Perhaps*. New York: Columbia University Press, 1986.

Kirby, Jack Temple. *Rural Worlds Lost: The American South, 1920–1960*. Baton Rouge: Louisiana State University Press, 1987.

Klein, Marcus. *Foreigners: The Making of American Literature, 1910–1940*. Chicago: University of Chicago Press, 1981.

Knapp, Bettina. *Gertrude Stein*. New York: Continuum, 1990.

Knoll, Robert E., ed. *Conversations with Wright Morris: Critical Views and Responses*. Lincoln: University of Nebraska Press, 1977.

Koestenbaum, Wayne. *Double Talk: The Erotics of Male Literary Collaboration*. New York: Routledge, 1989.

Kolodny, Annette. *The Land Before Her: Fantasy and Experience of the American Frontiers, 1630–1860*. Chapel Hill: University of North Carolina Press, 1984.

—— *The Lay of the Land: Metaphor as Experience and History in American Life and Letters*. Chapel Hill: University of North Carolina Press, 1975.

Kostelanetz, Richard. *The End of Intelligent Writing: Literary Politics in America*. New York: Sheed and Ward, 1974.

Kristeva, Julia. "Revolution in Poetic Language." In *The Kristeva Reader*, pp. 89–136. Ed. Toril Moi. New York and London: Basil Blackwell, 1986.

Krupat, Arnold. *For Those Who Come After: A Study of Native American Autobiography*. Berkeley: University of California Press, 1985.

Kuklick, Bruce. *The Rise of American Philosophy, Cambridge, Massachusetts, 1860–1930*. New Haven: Yale University Press, 1977.

Lamming, George. *The Pleasures of Exile*. London: Michael Joseph, 1960.

Landon, Brooks. *Thomas Berger*. Boston: Twayne, 1989.

Lang, Amy Schrager. "Slavery and Sentimentalism: The Strange Career of Augustine St. Clare." *Women's Studies: An Interdisciplinary Journal* 12.1 (1986): 31–54.

Larson, Magalia Sarfati. *The Rise of Professionalism: A Sociological Analysis.* Berkeley: University of California Press, 1977.

Laughlin, James. "New Directions: An Interview with James Laughlin." With Susan Howe and Charles Ruas. In *The Art of Literary Publishing: Editors on Their Craft*, pp. 13–48. Ed. Bill Henderson. Wainscott, N.Y.: Pushcart Press, 1980.

Lears, Jackson. *No Place of Grace: Antimodernism and the Transformation of American Culture, 1800–1920.* New York: Pantheon, 1981.

LeClair, Tom. *Into the Loop: Don DeLillo and the Systems Novel.* Urbana: University of Illinois Press, 1987.

Lee, L. L., and Merrill Lewis, eds. *Women, Women Writers, and the West.* Troy, N.Y.: Whitston, 1980.

Lee, Robert Edson. *From East to West: Studies in the Literature of the American West.* Urbana: University of Illinois Press, 1966.

Le Sueur, Meridel. *Harvest Song: Collected Essays and Stories.* Albuquerque: West End Press, 1990.

Leverenz, David. *Manhood and the American Renaissance.* Ithaca, N.Y.: Cornell University Press, 1989.

Levine, Robert S. *Conspiracy and Romance: Studies in Brockden Brown, Cooper, Hawthorne, and Melville.* New York: Cambridge University Press, 1989.

Liebowitz, Herbert. *Fabricating Lives: Explorations in American Autobiography.* New York: Alfred A. Knopf, 1989.

Ling, Amy. *Between Worlds: Women Writers of Chinese Ancestry.* New York: Pergamon Press, 1990.

Lodge, David. *The Modes of Modern Writing: Metaphor, Metonymy, and the Typology of Modern Literature.* Ithaca, N.Y.: Cornell University Press, 1977.

Love, Glen A. *New Americans: The Westerner and the Modern Experience in the American Novel.* Lewisburg, Pa.: Bucknell University Press, 1982.

Lyotard, Jean-François. *The Postmodern Condition: A Report on Knowledge.* Trans. Geoff Bennington and Brian Massumi. Minneapolis: University of Minnesota Press, 1984.

McCaffery, Larry, ed. *Postmodern Fiction: A Bio-Bibliographical Guide.* New York, Westport, Conn., and London: Greenwood Press, 1986.

McDowell, Deborah E., and Arnold Rampersad, eds. *Slavery and the Literary Imagination.* Baltimore: Johns Hopkins University Press, 1989.

McGregor, Gaile. *The Wacousta Syndrome: Explorations in the Canadian Langscape.* Toronto: University of Toronto Press, 1985.

McHale, Brian. *Postmodernist Fiction.* New York and London: Methuen, 1987.

Macherey, Pierre. *A Theory of Literary Production.* Trans. Geoffrey Wall. London: Routledge & Kegan Paul, 1978.

McLoughlin, William G. *Revivals, Awakenings, and Reform: An Essay on Religion and Social Change in America, 1607–1977.* Chicago: University of Chicago Press, 1978.

Madden, David, ed. *Proletarian Writers of the Thirties.* Carbondale, Ill.: Southern Illinois University Press, 1968.

Madison, Charles A. *Book Publishing in America.* New York: McGraw-Hill, 1966.

Malpezzi, Frances. "*The Silent Partner:* A Feminist Sermon on the Social Gospel." *Studies in the Humanities* 13.2 (December 1986): 103–10.

Marcus, Alan I., and Howard P. Segal. *Technology in America: A Brief History.* San Diego: Harcourt Brace Jovanovich, 1989.

Marinello, Juan. "Americanismo y cubanismo literarios." Prologue to Luis Felipe Rodríguez's *Marcos Antillo, Cuentos de Cañaveral.* Havana: n.d.

Martin, Wendy, ed. *New Essays on The Awakening.* Cambridge: Cambridge University Press, 1988.

Marx, Leo. *The Machine in the Garden: Technology and the Pastoral Ideal in America.* New York: Oxford University Press, 1964.

Masiello, Francine. "Discurso de mujeres, lenguaje de poder: Reflexiones sobre la critica feminista a mediados de la decada del 80." *Hispámerica* 15.45 (1986): 53–60.

Mayz Valenilla, E. *El problema de América.* Caracas: Universidad Central de Venezuela, 1969.

Meldrum, Barbara Howard, ed. *Under the Sun: Myth and Realism in Western American Literature.* Troy, N.Y.: Whitston, 1985.

Menand, Louis. *Discovering Modernism.* New York: Oxford University Press, 1987.

Meyer, Roy W. *The Middle Western Farm Novel in the Twentieth Century.* Lincoln: University of Nebraska Press, 1980.

Michaels, Walter Benn. *The Gold Standard and the Logic of Naturalism: American Literature at the Turn of the Century.* Berkeley: University of California Press, 1987.

Michaels, Walter Benn, and Donald E. Pease, eds. *The American Renaissance Reconsidered.* Baltimore: Johns Hopkins University Press, 1985.

Mills, Nicolaus. *American and English Fiction in the Nineteenth Century.* Bloomington: Indiana University Press, 1973.

Milton, John R. *The Novel of the American West.* Lincoln: University of Nebraska Press, 1980.

Modleski, Tania. *Loving with a Vengeance: Mass-Produced Fantasies for Women.* Hamden, Conn.: Archon Books, 1982.

Mogen, David, Mark Busby, and Paul Bryant, eds. *The Frontier Experience and the American Dream: Essays on American Literature.* College Station: A&M University Press, 1989.

Moss, John. *A Reader's Guide to the Canadian Novel.* 2d ed. Toronto: McClelland & Stewart, 1987.

——— *Sex and Violence in the Canadian Novel: The Ancestral Present.* Toronto: McClelland & Stewart, 1977.

Mott, Frank Luther. *Golden Multitudes: The Story of Best Sellers in the United States.* 1947; rpt. New York: R. R. Bowker, [1960].

Mulvey, Laura. *Visual and Other Pleasures.* Bloomington: Indiana University Press, 1989.

Mumford, Lewis. *The Myth of the Machine: The Pentagon of Power.* New York: Harcourt Brace Jovanovich, 1970.

Murch, A. E. *The Development of the Detective Novel.* New York: Philosophical Library, 1958.

Nelson, Cary. *Repression and Recovery: Modern American Poetry and the Politics of Cultural Memory, 1910–1945.* Madison: University of Wisconsin Press, 1989.

Neuman, Shirley, and Smaro Kamboureli, eds. *A Mazing Space: Writing Canadian Women Writing.* Edmonton: Longspoon/NeWest, 1986.

New, W. H. *A History of Canadian Literature.* London: Macmillan, 1989.

New, W. H., ed. *Native Writers and Canadian Literature.* Vancouver: University of British Columbia Press, 1990.

Newman, Charles. *The Post-Modern Aura: Fiction in an Age of Inflation.* Evanston, Ill.: Northwestern University Press, 1985.

Noel, Mary. *Villains Galore: The Heyday of the Popular Story Weekly.* New York: Macmillan, 1954.

Northey, Margot. *The Haunted Wilderness: The Gothic and the Grotesque in Canadian Fiction.* Toronto: University of Toronto Press, 1976.

Norwood, Vera, and Janice Monk, eds. *The Desert Is No Lady: Southwestern Landscapes in Women's Writing and Art.* New Haven: Yale University Press, 1987.

Nye, Russel B. *The Unembarrassed Muse: The Popular Arts in America.* New York: Dial Press, 1970.

O'Gorman, Edmundo. *La invención de America.* Mexico: Fondo de cultura económica, 1958.

Ohmann, Richard. *Politics of Letters.* Middletown, Conn.: Wesleyan University Press, 1987.

Oleson, Alexandra, and John Voss, eds. *The Organization of Knowledge in Modern America, 1860–1920.* Baltimore: Johns Hopkins University Press, 1979.

Olney, James, ed. *Autobiography, Essays Theoretical and Critical.* Princeton: Princeton University Press, 1980.

——— *Studies in Autobiography.* New York: Oxford University Press, 1988.

Olster, Stacey Michele. *Reminiscence and Re-Creation in Contemporary American Fiction.* Cambridge: Cambridge University Press, 1989.

Paradis, Suzanne. *Femme fictive, femme réelle: Le personnage féminin dans la roman féminin canadian-français, 1884–1966.* Quebec: Garneau, 1966.

Patai, Daphne, ed. *Looking Backward, 1988–1888: Essays on Edward Bellamy.* Amherst: University of Massachusetts Press, 1988.

Paterson, Janet. *Moments postmodernes dans le roman québécois.* Ottawa: PU d'Ottawa, 1990.

Pattee, Fred Lewis. *The Feminine Fifties.* New York: D. Appleton-Century Co., 1940.

Paz, Octavio. "Better to Be Ignored Than Illustrious" (interview). *Encounter* 1 (Winter 1989): 7–10.

Pease, Donald E. *Visionary Compacts: American Renaissance Writings in Cultural Context.* Madison: University of Wisconsin Press, 1987.

Pefanis, Julian. *Heterology and the Postmodern: Bataille, Baudrillard, and Lyotard.* Durham, N.C.: Duke University Press, 1990.

Pérez Firmat, Gustavo, ed. *Do the Americas Have a Common Literature?* Durham, N.C.: Duke University Press, 1990.

Peterson, Joyce Shaw. "Working Girls and Millionaires: The Melodramatic Romances of Laura Jean Libbey." *American Studies* 24 (Spring 1983): 19–35.

Petrone, Penny. *Native Literature in Canada: From the Oral Tradition to the Present.* Toronto: Oxford University Press, 1990.

Petter, Henri. *The Early American Novel.* Columbus: Ohio State University Press, 1971.

Pfaelzer, Jean. "Rebecca Harding Davis: Domesticity, Social Order, and the Industrial Novel." *International Journal of Women's Studies* 4.3 (May/June 1981): 234–44.

Pfeil, Fred. *Another Tale to Tell: Politics and Narrative in Postmodern Culture.* New York: Verso, 1990.

Philbrick, Thomas. *James Fenimore Cooper and the Development of American Sea Fiction.* Cambridge, Mass.: Harvard University Press, 1961.

Pilkington, William T., ed. *Critical Essays on the Western Novel.* Boston: G. K. Hall, 1980.

Pizer, Donald. *Hamlin Garland's Early Work and Career.* 1960. New York: Russell & Russell, 1969.

——— *Realism and Naturalism in Nineteenth-Century American Literature.* Rev. ed. Carbondale: Southern Illinois University Press, 1984.

Poggioli, Renato. *The Theory of the Avant-Garde.* Trans. Gerald Fitzgerald. Cambridge, Mass.: Harvard University Press, 1968.

Poniatowska, Elena. "La literatura de las mujeres es parte de la literatura de los oprimidos." *Fem* 6.21 (1982): 23–27.

Porte, Joel. *The Romance in America: Studies in Cooper, Poe, Hawthorne, Melville, and James.* Middletown, Conn.: Wesleyan University Press, 1969.

Porter, Dennis. *The Pursuit of Crime: Art and Ideology in Detective Fiction.* New Haven: Yale University Press, 1981.

Porter, Katherine Anne. *The Collected Essays and Occasional Writings of Katherine Anne Porter.* Boston: Houghton Mifflin/Seymour Lawrence, 1970.

Porter, M. Gilbert. *One Flew Over the Cuckoo's Nest: Rising to Heroism.* Boston: Twayne, 1989.

Porush, David. *The Soft Machine: Cybernetic Fiction.* New York and London: Methuen, 1985.

Pound, Ezra. Letter to Harriet Monroe, p. 13. In *The Letters of Ezra Pound, 1907–1941.* Ed. D. D. Paige. New York: Harcourt Brace & World, 1950.

Pratt, Linda Ray. "Afterword" to Meridel Le Sueur, *I Hear Men Talking and Other Stories,* pp. 225–36. Minneapolis: West End Press, 1984.

Pratt, Mary Louise. "The Short Story: The Long and Short of It." *Poetics* 10 (1981): 175–94.

Radway, Janice A. *Reading the Romance: Women, Patriarchy, and Popular Literature.* Chapel Hill: University of North Carolina Press, 1984.

Railton, Stephen. "Mothers, Husbands, and Uncle Tom." *The Georgia Review* 38.1 (Spring 1984): 129–44.

Ramchand, Kenneth. *The West Indian Novel and Its Background.* London: Faber & Faber, 1970.

Reddock, Rhoda. "Women Labour and Struggle in 20th Century Trinidad and Tobago: 1898–1960" (unpublished dissertation).

Reynolds, Clay, ed. *Taking Stock: A Larry McMurtry Casebook.* Dallas: Southern Methodist University Press, 1989.

Reynolds, David S. *Beneath the American Renaissance: The Subversive Imagination in the Age of Emerson and Melville.* New York: Alfred A. Knopf, 1988.

——— *Faith in Fiction: The Emergence of Religious Literature in America.* Cambridge, Mass.: Harvard University Press, 1981.

Reynolds, Larry J. *European Revolutions and the American Literary Renaissance.* New Haven: Yale University Press, 1988.

Rideout, Walter. *The Radical Novel in the United States, 1900–1954.* Cambridge, Mass.: Harvard University Press, 1956; New York: Hill and Wang, 1966.

Ridgely, J. V. *Nineteenth-Century Southern Literature.* Lexington: University Press of Kentucky, 1980.

Robinson, Forrest G., and Margaret G. Robinson. *Wallace Stegner.* Boston: Twayne, 1977.

Robles, Martha. *Escritoras en la cultura nacional.* 2 vols. 1985; Mexico: Diana, 1989.

Rocard, Marcienne. *The Children of the Sun: Mexican-Americans in the Literature of the United States.* Trans. Edward G. Brown, Jr. Tucson: University of Arizona Press, 1989.

Rodríguez Monegal, Emir. "Clarice Lispector en sus libros y en mi recuerdo." *Revista iberoamericana* 50 (1984): 231–38.

Roemer, Kenneth M. "The Literary Domestication of Utopia: There's No Looking Backward without Uncle Tom and Uncle True." *American Transcendental Quarterly* 3.1 (March 1989): 101–22.

Rogin, Michael Paul. *Subversive Genealogy: The Politics and Art of Herman Melville*. New York: Alfred A. Knopf, 1983.

Romero, Lora. "Bio-Political Resistance in Domestic Ideology and *Uncle Tom's Cabin*." *American Literary History* 1.4 (Winter 1989): 715–34.

Ronald, Ann. *The New West of Edward Abbey*. Albuquerque: University of New Mexico Press, 1982.

Rorabaugh, W. J. *The Alcoholic Republic: An American Tradition*. New York: Oxford University Press, 1979.

Rosaldo, Renato. *Culture and Truth: The Remaking of Social Analysis*. Boston: Beacon Press, 1989.

Rose, Willie Lee. *Race and Region in American Historical Fiction*. Oxford: Oxford University Press, 1979.

Rosenberg, Harold. *The Tradition of the New*. Chicago: University of Chicago Press, 1960; Phoenix Books, 1982.

Rosenfelt, Deborah. "From the Thirties: Tillie Olsen and the Radical Tradition." *Feminist Studies* 7 (Fall 1981): 371–406.

Ross, Andrew, ed. *Universal Abandon? The Politics of Postmodernism*. Minneapolis: University of Minnesota Press, 1988.

Rothman, David. *The Discovery of the Asylum: Social Order and Disorder in the New Republic*. Boston: Little, Brown and Company, 1971.

Rubin, Louis D., Jr. *The American South: Portrait of a Culture*. Baton Rouge: Louisiana State University Press, 1980.

Rubin, Louis D., Jr., et al., eds. *The History of Southern Literature*. Baton Rouge: Louisiana State University Press, 1985.

Ruddick, Lisa. *Reading Gertrude Stein: Body, Text, Gnosis*. Ithaca, N.Y.: Cornell University Press, 1990.

Ruffinelli, Jorge. "Los 80: Ingreso a la posmodernidad?" *Nuevo Texto Crítico* 3.6 (1990): 31–42.

Ruta, Suzanne. "Nine Months That Shook the World." *The New York Times Book Review* (August 20, 1989): 1, 30.

Said, Edward. *Orientalism*. New York: Vintage, 1978.

——— "Third World Intellectuals and Metropolitan Culture." *Raritan* 9.3 (Winter 1990): 27–50.

Saldívar, José David. *The Dialectics of Our America: Genealogy, Cultural Critique, and Literary History*. Durham, N.C.: Duke University Press, 1991.

Saldívar, Ramón. *Chicano Narrative: The Dialectics of Difference*. Madison: University of Wisconsin Press, 1990.

Sánchez, Rosaura. "Postmodernism and Chicano Literature." *Aztlán* 18:2 (1989): 1–14.

Sánchez Vasquez, Adolfo. "Radiografía del posmodernismo." *Nuevo Texto Critico* 3.6 (1990): 5–15.

Sangari, Kumkum. "The Politics of the Possible." *Cultural Critique* 7 (1987): 157–86.

Sangari, Kumkum, and Sudesh Vaid, eds. *Recasting Women: Essays in Colonial History*. New Delhi: Kali for Women, 1989.

Scheer, Steven C. *Pious Impostures and Unproven Words: The Romance of Deconstruction in Nineteenth-Century America*. Lanham, Md.: University Press of America, 1990.

Schivelbusch, Wolfgang. *The Railway Journey: The Industrialization of Time and Space in the Nineteenth Century*. 1977; rpt. Berkeley and Los Angeles: University of California Press, 1986.

Scholes, Robert, and Eric S. Rabkin. *Science Fiction: History, Science, Vision*. New York: Oxford University Press, 1977.

Schubnell, Matthias. *N. Scott Momaday: The Cultural and Literary Background*. Norman: University of Oklahoma Press, 1985.

Schwartz, Lawrence. *Creating Faulkner's Reputation: The Politics of Modern Literary Criticism*. Knoxville: University of Tennessee Press, 1988.

Sedgwick, Eve Kosofsky. *Between Men: English Literature and Male Homosocial Desire*. New York: Columbia University Press, 1986.

Sefchovich, Sara. *Mujeres en espejo*. Mexico: Folios Ediciones, 1983.

Segal, Howard P. *Technological Utopianism in American Culture*. Chicago: University of Chicago Press, 1985.

Sekora, John, and Darwin Turner, eds. *The Art of the Slave Narrative: Original Essays in Criticism and Theory*. Macomb: Western Illinois University Press, 1982.

Shek, Ben-Zion. *Social Realism in the French Canadian Novel*. Montreal: Harvest House, 1977.

Shulman, Robert. *Social Criticism and Nineteenth Century American Fictions*. Columbia: University of Missouri Press, 1987.

Simonson, Harold P. *Beyond the Frontier: Writers, Western Regionalism and a Sense of Place*. Fort Worth: Texas Christian University Press, 1989.

Simonson, Rick, and Scott Walker, eds. *Multi-Cultural Literacy: Opening the American Mind*. Minnesota: Graywolf Press, 1988.

Singal, Daniel Joseph. *The War Within: From Victorian to Modernist Thought, 1919–1945*. Chapel Hill: University of North Carolina Press, 1982.

Skårdal, Dorothy Burton. *The Divided Heart: Scandinavian Immigrant Experience Through Literary Sources*. Lincoln: University of Nebraska Press, 1974.

Slotkin, Richard. *The Fatal Environment: The Myth of the Frontier in the Age of Industrialization, 1800–1890*. New York: Atheneum, 1985.

—— *Regeneration Through Violence: The Mythology of the American Frontier, 1600–1860.* Middletown, Conn.: Wesleyan University Press, 1973.

Smart, Patricia. *Ecrire dans la maison du père.* Montreal: Editions Québec/ Amérique, 1988.

Smith, Henry Nash. *Democracy and the Novel: Popular Resistance to Classic Writers.* New York: Oxford University Press, 1978.

—— *Virgin Land: The American West as Symbol and Myth.* Cambridge, Mass.: Harvard University Press, 1950.

Smith, Lillian. *Killers of the Dream.* 1949; rev. ed. New York: Norton Library, 1978.

Smith, Sidonie. *A Poetics of Women's Autobiography: Marginality and the Fictions of Self-Representations.* Bloomington: Indiana University Press, 1987.

Smith, Valerie. *Self-Discovery and Authority in Afro-American Narrative.* Cambridge, Mass.: Harvard University Press, 1987.

Smith-Rosenberg, Carroll. *Disorderly Conduct: Visions of Gender in Victorian America.* New York: Oxford University Press, 1986.

Sollers, Philippe. "The Novel and the Experience of Limits." In *Surfiction: Fiction Now . . . and Tomorrow*, pp. 59–74. Ed. Raymond Federman. Chicago: Swallow Press, 1981.

Sollors, Werner. *Beyond Ethnicity: Consent and Descent in American Culture.* New York: Oxford University Press, 1986.

Sollors, Werner, ed. *The Invention of Ethnicity.* New York: Oxford University Press, 1989.

Solotaroff, Ted. "The Publishing Culture and the Literary Culture." *Library Quarterly* 54.1 (1984): 72–80.

Sommer, Doris. " 'Not Just a Personal Story': Women's *Testimonios* and the Plural Self." In Bella Brodzki and Celeste Schenck, *Life/Lines*, pp. 107–30. Ithaca, N.Y.: Cornell University Press, 1988.

Sonnichsen, C. L. *From Hopalong to Hud: Thoughts on Western Fiction.* College Station: Texas A&M University Press, 1978.

Soyinka, Wole. *Art, Dialogue and Outrage: Essays on Literature and Culture.* Ibadan: New Horn Press, 1988.

—— "Twice-Bitten: The Fate of Africa's Culture Producers." *PMLA* (January 1990): 110–20.

Spengemann, William C. *The Adventurous Muse: The Poetics of American Fiction, 1789–1900.* New Haven: Yale University Press, 1977.

—— *A Mirror for Americanists: Reflections on the Idea of American Literature.* Hanover, N.H.: University Press of New England, 1989.

Spivak, Gayatri. *The Postcolonial Critic: Interviews, Strategies, Dialogues.* Ed. Sarah Harasym. New York and London: Routledge, 1990.

Starr, Kevin. *Americans and the California Dream, 1850–1915.* New York: Oxford University Press, 1973.

———— *Inventing the Dream: California Through the Progressive Era.* New York: Oxford University Press, 1985.

Stauffer, Helen, and Susan J. Rosowski, eds. *Women and Western American Literature.* Troy, N.Y.: Whitston, 1982.

Stegner, Wallace. *One Way to Spell Man: Essays with a Western Bias.* Garden City, N.Y.: Doubleday, 1982.

———— *The Sound of Mountain Water.* Garden City, N.Y.: Doubleday, 1969.

Stegner, Wallace, and Richard W. Etulain. *Conversations with Wallace Stegner on Western History and Literature.* Salt Lake City: University of Utah Press, 1983.

Steiner, George. *On Difficulty, and Other Essays.* Oxford: Oxford University Press, 1978.

Stepto, Robert. *From Behind the Veil: A Study of Afro-American Narrative.* Urbana: University of Illinois Press, 1979.

Stern, Madeleine B., ed. *Publishers for Mass Entertainment in Nineteenth Century America.* Boston: G. K. Hall, 1980.

Stoehr, Taylor. *Hawthorne's Mad Scientists: Pseudoscience and Social Science in Nineteenth-Century Life and Letters.* Hamden, Conn.: Archon Press, 1978.

Stone, Albert E. *Autobiographical Occasions and Original Acts: Versions of American Identity from Henry Adams to Nate Shaw.* Philadelphia: University of Pennsylvania Press, 1982.

Stratford, Philip. *All the Polarities: Comparative Studies in Contemporary Canadian Novels in French and English.* Toronto: ECW, 1986.

Suggs, Christian. "Introduction" to Clara Weatherwax, *Marching! Marching!* Detroit: Omnigraphics, 1990.

Sundquist, Eric J., ed. *American Realism: New Essays.* Baltimore: Johns Hopkins University Press, 1982.

———— *New Essays on Uncle Tom's Cabin.* New York and Cambridge: Cambridge University Press, 1986.

Susman, Warren I. *Culture as History: The Transformation of American Society in the Twentieth Century.* New York: Pantheon, 1984.

Symons, Julian. *Makers of the New: The Revolution in Literature, 1912–1939.* London: Andre Deutsche Limited, 1987.

Tamburri, Anthony Julian, et al. *From the Margins: Writings in Italian Americana.* West Lafayette, Indiana: Purdue University Press, 1990.

Tanner, Tony. *City of Words: American Fiction, 1950–1970.* New York: Harper & Row, 1971.

Taylor, J. Golden, editor in chief; Thomas J. Lyon, senior editor. *A Literary History of the American West.* Fort Worth: Texas Christian University Press, 1987.

Taylor, Walter Fuller. *The Economic Novel in America.* New York: Octagon Books, 1964.

Tebbel, John. *A History of Book Publishing in the United States.* 4 vols. New York: R. R. Bowker, 1975.

Thacker, Robert. *The Great Prairie Fact and Literary Imagination.* Albuquerque: University of New Mexico Press, 1989.

Thurston, Jarvis. "Little Magazines: An Imaginary Interview with Jarvis Thurston." *The Missouri Review* 7.1 (Fall 1983): 232–35.

Tichi, Cecelia. *Electronic Hearth: The Acculturation of Television in the United States.* New York: Oxford University Press, 1991.

—— *Shifting Gears: Technology, Literature, Culture in Modernist America.* Chapel Hill: University of North Carolina Press, 1987.

—— "Television and Recent American Fiction." *American Literary History* 1.1 (Spring 1989): 110–30.

Toker, Leona. *Nabokov: The Mystery of Literary Structures.* Ithaca, N.Y.: Cornell University Press, 1989.

Tompkins, Jane P. *Sensational Designs: The Cultural Work of American Fiction, 1790–1860.* New York: Oxford University Press, 1985.

—— "Sentimental Power: *Uncle Tom's Cabin* and the Politics of Literary History." *Glyph* 8 (1981): 79–102.

Toye, William, ed. *The Oxford Companion to Canadian Literature.* Toronto: Oxford University Press, 1983.

Trachtenberg, Alan. *The Incorporation of America: Culture and Society in the Gilded Age.* New York: Hill and Wang, 1982.

Trilling, Lionel. *The Liberal Imagination.* New York: Charles Scribner's Sons, 1976.

Trinh T. Minh-ha. *Woman, Native, Other: Writing Postcoloniality and Feminism.* Bloomington: Indiana University Press, 1989.

Tyrell, Ian R. *Sobering Up: From Temperance to Prohibition in Antebellum America, 1800–1860.* Westport, Conn.: Greenwood Press, 1979.

Updike, John. "The Author as Librarian." *The New Yorker* 41 (October 30, 1965): 245.

VanDerBeets, Richard. *The Indian Captivity Narrative: An American Genre.* New York: University Press of America, 1984.

Veblen, Thorstein. *The Theory of Business Enterprise.* New York: Charles Scribner's Sons, 1904.

Vinson, James, ed. *Twentieth-Century Western Writers.* Detroit: Gale, 1982.

Wagner-Martin, Linda. *The Modern American Novel 1914–1945: A Critical History.* Boston: Twayne, 1990.

Wald, Alan M. *James T. Farrell: The Revolutionary Socialist Years.* New York: New York University Press, 1978.

Walker, Don D. *The Adventures of Barney Tullus.* Albuquerque: University of New Mexico Press, 1988.

Wallace, James D. *Early Cooper and His Audience.* New York: Columbia University Press, 1986.

Walters, Ronald G. *American Reformers, 1815–1860.* New York: Hill and Wang, 1978.

Warner, Michael. *The Letters of the Republic: Publication and the Public Sphere in Eighteenth-Century America.* Cambridge, Mass.: Harvard University Press, 1990.

Warshow, Robert. *The Immediate Experience: Movies, Comics, Theatre, and Other Aspects of Popular Culture.* Garden City, N.Y.: Doubleday, 1962.

Washington, Mary Helen. *Invented Lives: Narratives of Black Women, 1860–1960.* Garden City, N.Y.: Doubleday, 1987.

Watson, Carole McAlpine. *Prologue: The Novels of Black American Women, 1891–1965.* New York: Greenwood Press, 1985.

Watt, Ian. *The Rise of the Novel.* Berkeley: University of California Press, 1957.

Waugh, Patricia. *Metafiction: The Theory and Practice of Self-Conscious Fiction.* New York and London: Methuen, 1984.

West, James L. W. *American Authors and the Literary Marketplace Since 1900.* Philadelphia: University of Pennsylvania Press, 1988.

Westbrook, Max. *Walter Van Tilburg Clark.* Boston: Twayne, 1969.

*Western American Literature,* 1966–. [Quarterly journal of the Western Literature Association; published at Utah State University.]

Whiteside, Thomas. *The Blockbuster Complex.* Middletown, Conn.: Wesleyan University Press, 1981.

Wiebe, Robert. *Search for Order, 1877–1920.* New York: Hill and Wang, 1967.

Wilde, Alan. *Middle Grounds: Studies in Contemporary American Fiction.* Philadelphia: University of Pennsylvania Press, 1987.

Williams, Raymond. *Television: Technology and Cultural Form.* 1974; rpt. New York: Schocken, 1975.

Winchell, Mark Royden. *Joan Didion.* Rev. ed. Boston: Twayne, 1989.

Wyatt, David. *The Fall into Eden: Landscape and Imagination in California.* Cambridge: Cambridge University Press, 1986.

Yellin, Jean Fagan. *The Intricate Knot: Black Figures in American Literature, 1776–1863.* New York: New York University Press, 1972.

——— *Women and Sisters: The Antislavery Feminists in American Culture.* New Haven: Yale University Press, 1989.

Zaretsky, Eli. *Capitalism, the Family, and Personal Life.* New York: Harper & Row, 1976.

Ziegler, Heide, ed. *Facing Texts: Encounters Between Contemporary Writers and Critics.* Durham, N.C.: Duke University Press, 1988.

Ziff, Larzer. *Literary Democracy: The Declaration of Cultural Independence in America.* New York: Viking Press, 1981.

Zimmerman, Bonnie. *The Safe Sea of Women: Lesbian Fiction, 1969–1989.* Boston: Beacon Press, 1990.

# Notes on Contributors

Elizabeth Ammons is Professor of English and of American Studies at Tufts University. She is the author of *Edith Wharton's Argument with America* and *Conflicting Stories: American Women Writers at the Turn into the Twentieth Century.* She is also the editor of *Critical Essays on Harriet Beecher Stowe, How Celia Changed Her Mind and Selected Stories by Rose Terry Cooke,* and *Short Fiction by Black Women, 1900–1920.*

Christine Bold is Assistant Professor of English at the University of Guelph, Canada. She is author of *Selling the Wild West: Popular Western Fiction, 1860 to 1960,* as well as several essays on United States popular culture and 1930s writing.

Robert Boyers founded the American intellectual journal *Salmagundi* in 1965, and continues to edit it at Skidmore College in Saratoga Springs, New York, where he is also Professor of English and Director of the New York State Summer Writers Institute. He writes frequently for such publications as *The New Republic, TLS, Dissent, The American Scholar, Partisan Review,* and the *New York Times Book Review.* The most recent of his six books are *Atrocity and Amnesia: The Political Novel Since 1945* and *After the Avant-Garde.*

Bill Brown, who teaches at the University of Chicago, has published work in *Arizona Quarterly, Cultural Critique,* and *Critical Inquiry,* among other journals; he is the author of *Recreation and Representation in America, 1880–1910* (forthcoming).

Debra A. Castillo is Associate Professor of Romance Studies and Comparative Literature at Cornell University. She is author of *The Translated World: A Postmodern Tour of Libraries in Literature* and *Talking Back: Strategies for a Latin American Feminist Literary Criticism* (forthcoming). She has published numerous essays on contemporary Latin American, Spanish, United States Hispanic, and British commonwealth fiction. She is editor of *Diacritics*, as well as book review editor of *Letras femeninas*.

Ed Cohen is the author of *Talk on the Wilde Side: Towards a Genealogy of the Discourse on Male (Homo)Sexuality* (forthcoming), as well as a number of articles on gender and cultural studies. He currently teaches in the English Department at Rutgers University and works as a counselor for people with life-threatening illnesses at the Manhattan Center for Living.

Arnold E. Davidson is Professor of Canadian Studies at Duke University. He has written *Mordecai Richler,* coedited *The Art of Margaret Atwood,* edited the MLA volume *Studies on Canadian Literature: Introductory and Critical Essays,* and published many essays on Canadian fiction.

Cathy N. Davidson is Professor of English at Duke University and editor of *American Literature.* Her most recent books are *Revolution and the Word: The Rise of the Novel in America* and *Reading in America: Literature and Social History.* She is general editor for Oxford University Press's Early American Women Writers series and is currently coediting the *Oxford Companion to Women's Writing in the United States.*

Thadious M. Davis is Professor of English at Brown University. She is the author of *Faulkner's "Negro": Art and the Southern Context,* and a biography of Nella Larsen, *Engendering Self in the Harlem Renaissance.* Coeditor of three volumes on African American authors for *The Dictionary of Literary Biography,* she has published essays on Southern and African American literature.

Joan Dayan's *Fables of Mind: An Inquiry into Poe's Fiction,* was published in 1987. She is currently a fellow at the Shelby Cullom Davis Center for Historical Studies at Princeton University, where she is completing a book called "Haiti, History, and the Gods."

Emory Elliott is Presidential Chair of English at the University of California, Riverside. He is the author of *Power and the Pulpit in Puritan New England* and *Revolutionary Writers: Literature and Authority in the New Republic,* as well as the editor of several books in American literature including the *Columbia Literary History of the United States.* He is also series editor for *The American Novel* for Cambridge University Press and for *Penn Studies in Contemporary American Fiction.*

Thomas J. Ferraro is Assistant Professor of English at Duke University. He has published several essays on twentieth-century ethnic literature and film.

Michael T. Gilmore is Professor of English at Brandeis University. He is the author of *American Romanticism and the Marketplace* and a contributor to the forthcoming *Cambridge History of American Literature*.

Phillip Brian Harper is Assistant Professor of English and Afro-American Studies at Harvard University, where he teaches courses in English literary modernism, nineteenth- and twentieth-century United States literature, Afro-American culture, and contemporary cultural studies. His current scholarship, on social marginality and postmodern fiction, and on social division in African American culture, has been supported by grants from the Mellon Foundation, the Ford Foundation, and the National Endowment for the Humanities.

Molly Hite is Associate Professor of English at Cornell University. She is the author of *Ideas of Order in the Novels of Thomas Pynchon, The Other Side of the Story: Structures and Strategies of Contemporary Feminist Narrative,* the academic novel *Class Porn,* and articles on contemporary literature, feminist theory, and the discipline of literary studies.

Amy Kaplan is Associate Professor of English at Mount Holyoke College. She is the author of *Social Construction of American Realism,* and has authored several essays on American realists and American imperialism in journals such as *PLMA, ELH,* and *American Literary History.* She is currently at work on a book about American imperialism.

Ketu H. Katrak, who grew up in Bombay, India, is currently Associate Professor of English at the University of Massachusetts, Amherst. She is the author of *Wole Soyinka and Modern Tragedy: A Study of Dramatic Theory and Practice* and coeditor with H. L. Gates, Jr., and James Gibbs of *Wole Soyinka: A Bibliography of Primary and Secondary Sources.* She has published essays on African, Indian, and Caribbean literatures in journals such as *Modern Fiction Studies, Third World Affairs, Black American Literature Forum,* and *Journal of Commonwealth Literature,* among others.

Paul Lauter is A. K. and G. M. Smith Professor of Literature at Trinity College. He is coordinating editor of the groundbreaking *Heath Anthology of American Literature.* His most recent book is *Canons and Contexts.* He is a member of the editorial board of *Radical Teacher,* the board of Resist, has served as editor and treasurer of The Feminist Press, and has worked both as activist and academic through much of his life.

Robert S. Levine is Associate Professor of English at the University of Maryland, College Park. He is the author of *Conspiracy and Romance: Studies in Brockden Brown, Cooper, Hawthorne, and Melville.*

James H. Maguire, Professor of English at Boise State University, has served as coeditor of BSU's Western Writers Series since its founding in 1972. He is the author of *Mary Hallock Foote* and the editor of *The Literature of Idaho: An Anthology.*

Terence Martin is Distinguished Professor of English at Indiana University. He has published numerous studies and editions of nineteenth-century American writers, among them *The Instructed Vision: Scottish Common Sense Philosophy and the Origins of American Fiction* and *Nathaniel Hawthorne.* He is an associate editor of *American National Biography.*

Nellie McKay is Professor of American and Afro-American Literature at the University of Wisconsin, Madison. She is the author of *Jean Toomer, Artist: A Study of His Literary Life and Work, 1894–1936,* editor of *Critical Essays on Toni Morrison,* and associate general editor of the forthcoming *Norton Anthology of Afro-American Literature.* She is currently working on a study of autobiographical narratives of African American women.

Susan Mizruchi is Assistant Professor of English at Boston University. She is the author of *The Power of Historical Knowledge: Narrating the Past in Hawthorne, James, and Dreiser,* as well as articles on James and Melville.

Margot Norris is Professor of English and Comparative Literature at the University of California, Irvine. Her essays have appeared in *PMLA, ELH,* and *MLN* and in various collections of books, including work on Joyce, Kafka, Ibsen, and Puig. She is the author of *The Decentered Universe of "Finnegans Wake"* and *Beasts of the Modern Imagination: Darwin, Nietzsche, Kafka, Ernst, and Lawrence.* Her new book on James Joyce's critique of modernism will be published by the University of Texas Press in 1992.

Patrick O'Donnell is the Eberly Professor of American Literature at West Virginia University. He is the author of *John Hawkes; Passionate Doubts: Designs of Interpretation in Contemporary American Fiction;* and *Echo Chambers: Figuring Voice in Modern Narrative* (forthcoming). He is the coeditor of *Intertextuality and Contemporary American Fiction,* and the editor of *New Essays on The Crying of Lot 49.* Presently he is working on a book about paranoia and contemporary American fiction.

Sandra Pouchet Paquet is Assistant Professor of English at the University of Pennsylvania, where she teaches Caribbean Literature and African American

Literature. She is the author of *The Novels of George Lamming* and is writing a book on West Indian autobiography.

Lora Romero is Assistant Professor of English at the University of Texas, Austin. She has written articles on Cooper and Stowe, as well as on minority discourse. She is currently completing a book entitled *Domestic Fictions: A New Historicist Reading of the American Renaissance.*

Jeffrey Rubin-Dorsky is Associate Professor of English and American Studies at the University of Colorado at Colorado Springs. He has published essays in nineteenth-century American literature and culture and in Jewish American literature, and he is the author of *Adrift in the Old World: The Psychological Pilgrimage of Washington Irving.* He is currently writing a book on masculinity and heroism in American literature and culture.

José David Saldívar is Associate Professor of American Literature and Cultural Studies at the University of California, Santa Cruz. He is the editor of *The Rolando Hinojosa Reader: Essays Historical and Critical,* coeditor of *Criticism in the Borderlands: Studies in Chicano Literature, Culture, and Ideology,* and author of *The Dialectics of Our America: Genealogy, Cultural Critique, and Literary History* and articles on cultural studies, Chicano literary criticism, and the institution of literary studies.

Robert Shulman has written *Social Criticism and Nineteenth-Century American Fictions* and numerous essays on nineteenth- and twentieth-century American literature, culture, and politics for such journals as *PMLA, American Literature, ELH,* and *Massachusetts Review.* He is Professor of English at the University of Washington and was a visiting professor of American Studies and English at the University of Minnesota. He is currently writing a book on *Political Art and the Politics of the Literary Canon: The 1930s Left Reconsidered.*

Valerie Smith is Associate Professor of English at the University of California, Los Angeles. The author of *Self-Discovery and Authority in Afro-American Narrative,* she has published essays on African American feminist literature and theory. She is currently completing a book of essays on race, gender, and culture.

Cecelia Tichi is the William R. Kenan Jr. Professor of English at Vanderbilt University. She is interested in literary-cultural relations, and her work spans Puritan New England through the television age. Her books include *New World, New Earth: Environmental Reform in American Literature from the Puritans through Whitman; Shifting Gears: Technology, Literature, Culture in Modernist America;* and *Electronic Hearth: The Acculturation of Television in the United States.*

John M. Unsworth is Assistant Professor in the Department of English at North Carolina State University. He is coeditor of *Postmodern Culture,* an electronic journal available on Bitnet and Internet. He has published articles on John Hawkes, Gilbert Sorrentino, Carlos Baker, Wallace Stevens, Henry Fielding, and electronic publishing.

David Van Leer is Associate Professor of English and American Literature at the University of California, Davis. Author of *Emerson's Epistemology,* a study of Emerson and Kant, he is currently at work on a companion volume treating Poe's relation to Newtonian physics. His essays on contemporary culture for *The New Republic* and elsewhere are collected in *The Queening of America: Gay Culture in Straight Society.*

Cornel West is Professor of Religion and Director of African American Studies at Princeton University. His publications include *Prophesy Deliverance! An Afro-American Revolutionary Christianity; Prophetic Fragments; Post-Analytic Philosophy* (coedited with John Rajchman); and *The American Evasion of Philosophy: A Genealogy of Pragmatism.*

Christopher P. Wilson is Associate Professor of English and Director of American Studies at Boston College. He is the author of *The Labor of Words: Literary Professionalism in the Progressive Era* and *White Collar Fictions* (forthcoming).

# Index

Aaron, Daniel, 383

Abbey, Edward, 753; *The Brave Cowboy*, 459; *Desert Solitaire*, 459; *Hayduke Lives*, 459; *Jonathan Troy*, 459; *The Monkey Wrench Gang*, 459

Abish, Walter, 753; *Alphabetical Africa*, 736; *How German Is It*, 737–39

Abolition, 140–43, 218–22; Emerson and, 130–31; Melville and, 150–51; slave narratives and, 39–41; *Uncle Tom's Cabin* and, 144–46

Abolitionists: Poe's view, 97–98; women, views of, 101

Abortion, fictional account, 354

Abrams, M. H., 10

Academia: and literary success, 692–94; male novelists and, 46; and postmodernism, 516–17; post–World War II, 488–89

Acculturation: Native American, in Canada, 576; novels of, 532–34

Achebe, Chinua, *Anthills of the Savannah*, 665

Acker, Kathy, 698, 699, 706, 723–24, 753–54; *The Adult Life of Henri Toulouse Lautrec by Henri Toulouse Lautrec*, 723; *The Childlike Life of the Black Tarantula by the Black Tarantula*, 723; *Don Quixote*, 699, 723; *Hello I'm Erica Jong*, 723; *Kathy Goes to Haiti*, 699; *My Death My Life by Pier Paolo Pasolini*, 723

Adamic, Louis, 400

Adams, Andy, *The Log of a Cowboy*, 439

Adams, Brooks, 250

Adams, Henry, *Democracy*, 157

Adams, John, 13

Addams, Jane, 125, 269; *Twenty Years at Hull House*, 381

Adisa, Opal Palmer, 653

Adorno, Theodor, 210, 679

Adultery novels, Fitzgerald and, 324

Adventure fiction, 289, 359–60, 378–79; antebellum novels, 51; detective novels, 372–78; frontier novels, 438; late nineteenth century, 257–58; of Melville, 80; Westerns, 366–71; by women, 52

Advertising of books, 53

Aesthetics: liberated, Coover and, 735; male definition, 46

Aesthetic standards, American literary canon and, 128

Affectionate appropriation, slavery and, 99–100

Africa, Canadian novels set in, 584

African Americans, 98–100, 409–13; antebellum, 55; Du Bois and, 206–10; Faulkner and, 427–30; Mailer

African Americans *(Continued)*
and, 493; migration of, 408; and
post–Civil War reconciliation, 247–
48; writings about, 417–20
—women, 268, 269; and domesticity,
127–28; Hurston and, 423–24; as
writers, 270, 273, 283, 496
—writers, 421–25; antislavery, 150–
53; autobiographical writings, 37–
41; late nineteenth-century realist,
178–81; late twentieth century,
495–97; postmodern, 522–23, 529–
30, 699; proletarian fiction by, 346–
50; and reform movements, 154;
regional fiction, 430–36; and romance, 105; and temperance movement, 142; and women's issues,
152–53
African peoples: and English language,
656; importation of, 92; postcolonial societies, 668
Age of Protest and Reform, 216, 228
Agrarian movement, 408, 414
Agrarian revolt, fiction of, 235–36
Agustin, José: *Ciudades desiertas*, 631;
"Cuál es la onda," 631; *De perfil*,
631; *Se está hacienco tarde*, 631
Aidoo, Ama Ata, 667
Alcohol consumption, nineteenth cen-
tury, 136
Alcott, Louisa May, 126, 754; *Behind a
Mask*, 120; *Little Women*, 113,
121; *Work*, 125
Alcott, William, 137
Alegría, Claribel, *No me agarran viva:
La mujer salvadoreña en la lucha
(They'll Never Take Me Alive)*, 647
Alegría, Fernando, 523
Alexander, Meena, 653
Alger, Horatio, 298, 357, 754; *Ragged
Dick; or, Street Life in New York*,
357; *Struggling Upward*, 358
Algren, Nelson: *The Man with the
Golden Arm*, 341; *Somebody in
Boots*, 341; *A Walk on the Wild
Side*, 341
Alien and Sedition Acts (1798), 13
Alienation, post–World War II, 487,
492

Allegory, *A Connecticut Yankee in King
Arthur's Court* as, 256
Allen, Garland, 211
Allen, Paula Gunn, *The Woman Who
Owned the Shadows*, 457
Allende, Isabel, 522, 615
Allfrey, Phyllis Shand, 594; *The Orchid
House*, 603
"The All Jamaica Library," 590
Allusions, in postmodern fiction, 704–6,
710, 716
Alter, Judy, *Mattie*, 440
Alter, Robert, 733
Alternative publishing, 681
Althusser, Louis, 522
America, early idea of, 9
American artists, and European culture,
311–12
American autobiography, 27, 29; and
slave narratives, 37–39
American Colonization Society, 140
American culture, 515; James and,
163–64
American imperialism, 654
*The American Journal of Sociology*,
192, 201
American literature: postmodern views,
517–18; mid-twentieth-century
views, 488–89
American novelists, late nineteenth cen-
tury, and sociology, 190–215
American novels: early, 6–25; publish-
ers and, 53–54
American proletarianism, 331–56
American reform, origins of, 131–32
American Renaissance, 128; and male
novelists, 118; and women, 113–15;
and women novelists, 112–13; wom-
en's novels and, 128–29
American Revolution: historical fiction,
259; story paper tales, 291
American Social Science Association,
192
American society, story papers and, 291
American Studies, 489
American Temperance Union, 137–38
American Tract Society, 137, 147
American writers, and World War I,
318

American writings, European publication, 7

Amoroso Lima, Alceu, 624

Anaya, Rudolfo, 406, 754; *Bless Me, Ultima*, 453

Anderson, Benedict, 241, 531

Anderson, Laurie, 228, 516

Anderson, Margaret, 312

Anderson, Sherwood, 315, 327, 408, 755; and race, 409–10; *Dark Laughter*, 410; "Notes Out of a Man's Life," 410; *Winesburg, Ohio*, 327

Andrews, William L., 91; *To Tell a Free Story: The First Century of Afro-American Autobiography, 1760–1865*, 37, 40

Angers, Marie-Louise-Félicité. *See* Conan, Laure

*Anglo-African Magazine*, 151

Anglo-Saxon immigrants, 383

Anglo-Saxon masculinity, American identity and, 263–64

Anomie, Durkheim's idea, 198

Antebellum novels: by African Americans, 55–56; marketplace, 47–71; reform issues, 131; temperance, 139–40

Anthony, Michael, 600, 602–3; *The Games Were Coming*, 603; *Green Days by the River*, 603; *The Year in San Fernando*, 595, 603

Anthony, Susan B., 142

Anti-Catholicism, 147

Anti-clericalism, Canadian, 570

Anti-communist movement, 486

Antimodernism of Western fiction, 369–71

Antin, Mary, *The Promised Land*, 385, 387

Antipatriarchal aspects of domesticity cult, 118–26

Anti-Semitism, 490; of Hemingway, 321

Antislavery movement, 218–22. *See also* Abolition

Antitechnological fiction, 467, 479

*The Anvil*, 343

Anzaldúa, Gloria, 539; *Borderlands/La Frontera*, 532

Apollinaire, Guillaume, 318

Apprenticeship system, printed literature and, 51

Appropriation of language, Valenzuela and, 641–42

Apthorp, Fanny, 15–16

Aquin, Hubert: *Neige noire* (*Hamlet's Twin*), 580, 582; *Prochain épisode*, 571

Architecture, postmodern, 516

Argentina, fiction of, 632–41

*Argosy*, 359

Armstrong, Jeannette C., 577; *Slash*, 576

Arnold, Matthew, *Culture and Anarchy*, 317

Arrighi, Antonio A., *The Story of Antonio, the Galley Slave*, 398

Art: Acker's views, 723–24; commercialization of, 517, 518; fiction as, 272–73; industrial, 173–74; modernist views, 317; nineteenth-century America and, 48; nineteenth-century novel as, 66; proletarian, 331–32; and social values, 334–35

Arthur, Timothy Shay, 114, 139, 755; *Six Nights with the Washingtonians*, 139; *Ten Nights in a Bar-Room, and What I Saw There*, 139–40

Artists: American, and European culture, 311–12

—women as, 271, 272–73; Cather and, 278–80; novels about, 275; Wharton and, 276–77

Ashbery, John, 736

Ashbridge, Elizabeth, 31

Asian American writers, 405, 406, 499–500; Western fiction, 462–63

Asian immigrants, 406

Asimov, Isaac, 755–56; *I, Robot*, 361

Assimilation: minority fiction and, 502; Native American, in Canada, 576

Associationism, Hawthorne and, 134–35

As-told-to narratives, 4; Native American autobiography, 44; slave autobiographies, 37

Astor Place Riot (1849), 290

*Astounding*, 364

Asturias, Miguel Angel, 524
Atherton, Gertrude, 283, 457, 756
Attaway, William, 332; *Blood on the Forge*, 348–49
Attenborough, Richard, *Gandhi* (film), 658
Atwood, Margaret, 756; *Bodily Harm*, 584; *Cat's Eye*, 567; *The Handmaid's Tale*, 567, 582; *The Journals of Susanna Moodie*, 574; *Lady Oracle*, 579; *Surfacing*, 567, 583; *Survival: A Thematic Guide to Canadian Literature*, 565, 566
Auden, W. H., 389
Audience, literary, 679, 685, 688–90; for dime novels, 293–94, 297, 300–301; nineteenth century, 114; postmodern fiction and, 701
Augustine, St., *Confessions*, 26
Austen, Jane, *Pride and Prejudice*, 17
Austin, Mary, 273, 283, 756–57
Authenticity: female, nineteenth-century views, 120, 123; in Western fiction, 461–62
Authorial voices, 703; in dime novels, 299–300; in story-paper fiction, 290
Authority, 4–5, 13–14; in autobiography, 27; Cooper and, 24; gothic novels and, 22–23
Authors: income of, 681–82; publishers and, 680–81
Authorship, 4–5, 679, 689; of dime novels, 292–93; in early America, 12; nineteenth-century women and, 64–65; novels about, 52; postmodern capitalism and, 680; professionalism of, nineteenth century, 67–70
Autobiography: Asian American, 499; ethnic, 385; expatriation and, 650; and fiction, 4–5, 9, 26–45; immigrant experience, 382, 384, 398; proletarian, 333, 334–44
Automatic writing, 313, 525
Autonomy: of artist, 691; literary, 59–60, 67; personal, Native Americans and, 43
Avant-garde, 691, 726–51; Joyce and, 327; postmodernism and, 697–98; Stein and, 314

Averill, Charles, *The Secret Service Ship; or, The Fall of San Juan D'Ulloa*, 289

B. Dalton, 687
Baker, Houston, 540
Bakhtin, Mikhail, 358, 705
Baldwin, James, 348, 496, 662, 757; *Another Country*, 496; *Giovanni's Room*, 502, 547–48; *Go Tell It on the Mountain*, 496; *Just Above My Head*, 496
Balloon of experience, James's idea, 74
Ballou, Adam, 133
Ballou, Maturin Murray, 290; *Fanny Campbell, the Female Pirate Captain*, 290; *Red Rupert, the American Bucanier*, 290
Balmer, Edwin, *When Worlds Collide*, 365
Balzac, Honoré: Fuentes and, 620
Banks, Russell, 520
Bannon, Ann, 501
Bantam Books, 686; lesbian paperbacks, 501
Baraka, Amiri, 757–58
Barbados, 89; writers from, 594–96
Barlow, Joel, 468
Barnes, Djuna, 328–29, 330, 408, 756; *Ladies Almanack*, 328; *Nightwood*, 501
Barnet, Miguel, 609, 646
Barney, Natalie, 312
Baroque quality of Latin American fiction, 611–13
Barrack-yard novels, 592, 599
Barrett, Elizabeth, *The Drama of Exile and Other Poems*, Poe's review, 101
Barrio, Raymond, *The Plum Plum Pickers*, 453
Barrios de Chungara, Domitila, 647; *Si me permiten hablar . . .*, 646–47
Barth, John, 516, 699, 730–32, 733, 736, 756; *Chimera*, 703, 712; *The End of the Road*, 711; "A Few Words About Minimalism," 535–36; *The Floating Opera*, 711; *Giles Goat-Boy*, 699, 711, 730, 731, 749; *Letters*, 711, 732; "The Literature

of Exhaustion," 610, 702, 710–11, 730; "The Literature of Replenishment," 610, 698–99; *Lost in the Funhouse*, 711–12; and parody, 749; *Sabbatical: A Romance*, 699, 711; *The Sot-Weed Factor*, 711, 730, 731, 749; *Tidewater Tales*, 712

Barthelme, Donald, 516, 698, 699, 706, 720–21, 742–44, 756–57; *The Dead Father*, 699, 720–21, 743–44; Gass and, 742; and parody, 749–50; *Snow White*, 699, 704, 705, 720–21, 743–44

Barton, Rebecca Chalmers, *Witnesses for Freedom: Negro Americans in Autobiography*, 28

Baseball novels, 358

Baudelaire, Charles: Poe and, 60, 66

Baudrillard, Jean, 483, 516

Baym, Nina, 64, 73, 85, 289, 295

Beach, Rex, *The Iron Trail: An Alaskan Romance*, 477

Beach, Sylvia, 312, 321

*The Beacon* (Trinidad review), 592, 593

Beadle, Irwin, 295

Beadle and Adams, publishers, 291–97, 299, 438

*Beadle's Half-Dime Library*, 296

*Beadle's Monthly*, 297

*The Beast from 20,000 Fathoms* (film), 362

Beat movement, 446, 492–93

Beattie, Ann, 482

Beattie, James, *Dissertations Moral and Critical*, 76–77

Beauchemin, Yves, 572

Beaulieu, Victor-Lévy, *Monsieur Melville*, 582

Beauty, language of, realism and, 172, 173

Beckett, Samuel, 327, 654

Beecher, Catharine, 120–21, 142; *The American Woman's Home*, 121; *A Treatise on Domestic Economy*, 120–21

Beecher, Lyman, 145; *Plea for the West*, 147; *Six Sermons on Intemperance*, 136

Behn, Aphra, *Oroonoko*, 8

Belgrave, Valerie, 605

Bell, Michael Davitt, 72

Bell, Thomas, *Out of This Furnace*, 349, 383

Bellamy, Edward, *Looking Backward, 2000–1887*, 228–30, 470, 475–76

Belli, Giaconda, 610

Bellow, Saul, 402, 759; *The Adventures of Augie March*, 497; *Herzog*, 498; *Henderson the Rain King*, 498; *Humboldt's Gift*, 497; *Mr. Sammler's Planet*, 498; *Seize the Day*, 497–98; *The Victim*, 403

Benezet, Anthony, 140

Benjamin, Park, 287

Benoit, Jacques, 572

Bercovici, Konrad, 386

Berger, Thomas, 759; *Little Big Man*, 448–49

Bergon, Frank, *Shoshone Mike*, 461

Bergson, Henri, 314

Berry, Don: *Moontrap*, 447; *To Build a Ship*, 447; *Trask*, 447

Bersianik, Louky: *L'Euguelionne*, 582; *Le Piquenique sur l'Acropole: Cahiers d'Ancyl*, 581

"Bertha M. Clay" stories, 297

Bessette, Gerard, *Le Libraire* (*Not for Every Eye*), 570

Best-sellers, 504–5, 688; canonization and, 70; early American, 5; Russian Jewish, 385

—nineteenth century, 114, 139, 258, 271, 294; anti-Catholic, 147; early, 47, 54; late, 303, 304

Beti, Mongo, 668

Bicultural texts, Native American autobiography as, 44–45

*Bildungsroman*: female, 110; gay, 551; West Indian, 600

*Bim* (literary review), 593

Binding of books, 49

Biracial society: Faulkner and, 426–27; Wright and, 431

Bird, Robert Montgomery, *Nick of the Woods; or, The Jibbenainosay*, 51, 87, 294, 437

Bird, William, 92

Birth rate, 268; Canadian, 570; and literary market, 49
Bishop, W. H., 292
Bissoondath, Neil, *A Casual Brutality*, 575, 584
Black Britishers, 653, 659, 661–62
*Black Mask*, 373
Black nationalism, Griggs and, 248
Blackness, power of, 106–8
Blacks. *See* African Americans
Blackwell, Elizabeth, 126
Blais, Marie-Claire, 569, 759–60; *Un Joualonais, sa Joualonie (St. Lawrence Blues)*, 571; *Une saison dans la vie d'Emmanuel (A Season in the Life of Emmanuel)*, 569
Blaise, Clark, *A North American Education*, 561
*Blast: The Review of the Great English Vortex*, 317–18
Blockbuster publishing, 680, 686
Blodgett, E. D., 573
Bloomer, Amelia, 137
Board of Aliens Commission, Massachusetts, 192
Boas, Franz, 421
Bojer, Johan, 389
Bok, Edward, *The Americanization of Edward Bok*, 385
Bolívar, Simón: García Márquez and, 527–28
Bombal, María Luisa, 623
Bondage, Poe and, 93–94
Bonner, Robert, 287
Bonnin, Gertrude. *See* Zitkala-Ša
Bontemps, Arna: *Black Thunder*, 349–50, 421; *God Sends Sunday*, 421
Book clubs, 359, 685
*The Bookman*, 297
Book-of-the-Month Club, 400, 530, 685, 698
Book retailers, mass-market, 687–88
Books, production economics, 678–83: early American, 48
Book Union, 339
Boom, Latin American literature, 613, 615, 616, 625
Booth, Wayne C., 445

Borderland theorists, 539
Borders, nationhood and, 242–43
Borges, Jorge Luis, 327, 609, 610–11, 616–18, 760; "The Circular Ruins," 617; *Ficciones*, 616, 617; "The Garden of Forking Paths," 704; "Tlön, Uqbar, Orbis Tertius," 617
Bosco, Monique, 572
Boston Female Anti-Slavery Society, 142
Bourdieu, Pierre, *Distinction: A Social Critique of the Judgement of Taste*, 694
Bourgeois classes, and individualism, 333
Bourne, Randolph, 381
Bower, B. M. (Bertha Muzzy Sinclair), 443; *Points West*, 367–68
Bowering, George: *Burning Water*, 563, 565; *Caprice*, 563
Bowles, Paul, 760; *The Sheltering Sky*, 491–92
Boyesen, Hjalmar Hjorth, *Gunnar*, 389
Boyhood, idealization of, 255–56
Brace, Charles Loring, *The Dangerous Classes of New York*, 381
Brackenridge, Hugh Henry, *Modern Chivalry*, 20–21
Bradbury, Malcolm, 535
Bradbury, Ray, *Fahrenheit 451*, 480
Bradford, William, *History of Plimmoth Plantation*, 7, 31
Bradstreet, Anne, 31
Braeme, Charlotte M., 297
Brand, Max. *See* Faust, Frederick
Brathwaite, Edward Kamau, 587–88, 655
Braun, Matt, *Mattie Silks*, 440
Brautigan, Richard, 450, 761; *The Hawkline Monster*, 450; *So the Wind Won't Blow It All Away*, 450; *The Tokyo-Montana Express*, 450; *Trout Fishing in America*, 450
Breton, André, 523
Bridgman, Richard, *The Colloquial Style in America*, 11
Briggs, Charles, *The Adventures of Harry Franco: A Tale of the Great Panic*, 149

Brink, Carol Ryrie, 457
Brinsmade, Herman, *Utopia Achieved: A Novel of the Future*, 475
Brisbane, Albert, *Social Destiny of Man*, 133
Briscoe, Mary, *American Autobiography, 1945–1980*, 28
British West Indian Federation, 589
Broadcast programming, 481–82
Brodber, Erna: *Jane and Louisa Will Soon Come Home*, 595, 604–5; *Myal*, 604–5
Brodhead, Richard, 72
Brodsky, Joseph, "Condition of Exile," 651–52
Brody, Alter, 388
Brooke, Frances, *The History of Emily Montague*, 558
Brooke, Rupert, 318
Brook Farm, 133; Hawthorne and, 134
Brooks, Cleanth, 488
Brooks, Gwendolyn, *Maud Martha*, 497
Brossard, Nicole: *L'Amèr, ou le chapitre effrité (These Our Mothers; or, The Disintegrating Chapter)*, 579; *Le Désert Mauve (Mauve Desert)*, 581
*Brother Jonathan* (story paper), 287
Brown, Alanna Kathleen, 281
Brown, Charles Brockden, 22–23, 47–49, 72, 465, 761; *Arthur Mervyn*, 22; *Edgar Huntly*, 22; *Ormond*, 22; *Wieland*, 22–23, 53, 437
Brown, Charlotte Hawkins, 269
Brown, Dee: *Bury My Heart at Wounded Knee*, 455; *Creek Mary's Blood*, 455
Brown, Gillian, 91
Brown, William Hill, *The Power of Sympathy*, 6–9, 15–16
Brown, William Wells, 142, 761–62; *Clotel; or, The President's Daughter*, 55–56, 151–52, 228
Brownson, Orestes, 762; "The Laboring Classes," 148; *The Spirit-Rapper*, 135
Bruss, Elizabeth, 27
Brutus, Dennis, 651, 668

Bryant, Louise, 337
Buckler, Ernest, *The Mountain and the Valley*, 565–66, 578
Buckley, Peter, 290–91
Buckley, William, 518
Buffalo Bill (William F. Cody), 296, 438
Bukowski, Charles, 762; *Ham on Rye*, 451
Bulosan, Carlos, 405; *America Is in the Heart*, 462
Bunkley, Josephine, *Miss Bunkley's Book: The Testimony of an Escaped Novice from the Sisterhood of Charity*, 147
Buntline, Ned (E. Z. C. Judson), 288, 290–91, 296, 299, 438; *Mysteries and Miseries of New York*, 147; *Saul Sabberday, the Idiot Spy; or, Luliona, the Seminole*, 291
Burdick, Eugene, *The Ugly American*, 490
Burger, Peter, 691
Burgos, Elizabeth, 646
Burke, Edmund, 97; *Reflections on the Revolution in France*, 92
Burke, Fielding (Olive Tilford Dargan), 350; *Call Home the Heart*, 338, 351–52; *A Stone Came Rolling*, 339, 352
Burned-over district, 132
Burroughs, Edgar Rice, 362–63, 762; *At the Earth's Core*, 362; *The Princess of Mars*, 362; *Tarzan of the Apes*, 362
Burroughs, William, 502, 763; *Naked Lunch*, 493
Bushnell, Horace, *Christian Nurture*, 121
Business, writing as, 48–49
Butler, Judith, 522

Cable, George Washington, 246, 763; *The Grandissimes*, 243–44
Cady, Edwin H., 439
Cage, John, 516
Cahan, Abraham, 159; *The Rise of David Levinsky*, 386; *Yekl: A*

Cahan, Abraham (*Continued*)
Tale of the New York Ghetto, 385–86
Cain, James M.: *Double Indemnity*, 377, 378; *The Postman Always Rings Twice*, 377, 450
Callenbach, Ernest, *Ecotopia*, 459–60
Calvino, Italo, 610
Cambridge, Joan, 653
Campbell, John W., *Islands of Space*, 364
Campbell, Maria: *Halfbreed*, 576; *The Book of Jessica*, 576–77
Campos, Julieta, 642–45; *Función de la novela*, 642; *Tiene los cabellos rojizos y se llama Sabina*, 643–45
Camus, Renaud, *Tricks*, 550–51
Canada: fiction of, 558–85; Mukherjee's views, 672–73, 677
Canadian Renaissance, 577
Canfield, Dorothy, *The Home-Maker*, 388
Cantwell, Robert, *The Land of Plenty*, 344, 345
Capitalism, 50, 168; and culture, 285, 518; Dos Passos and, 479; Du Bois and, 210; Howells and, 184–85; and literary marketplace, 679; and naturalist fiction, 203–4; nineteenth-century writers and, 67; Norris and, 261–62; novel form and, 344; regionalism and, 256; slavery and, 221
Capote, Truman, 764; *Answered Prayers*, 502; *Breakfast at Tiffany's*, 502; *In Cold Blood*, 449
Capps, Benjamin, *A Woman of the People*, 440
Captivity narratives, 31–33; anti-Catholic, 147; Native Americans and, 45
Cárdenal, Ernesto, 610
Careers for women, nineteenth century, 126
Carew, Jan, 594, 597, 598; *Black Midas*, 598; *The Wild Coast*, 598
Caribbean fiction, 586–606
Caribbean Rim immigrants, 406

"Caribbean Voices" (literary review), 593
Caribbean writers, 656, 668–69, 671
Caricature, in nineteenth-century romance, 81, 83–84
Carlyle, Thomas, and slavery, 93
Carpentier, Alejo, 521, 522, 524–26, 609, 611–12, 764; *Explosion in a Cathedral*, 525; *The Kingdom of This World*, 524–26; "Prologue," 523, 526
Carrier, Roch, *La Guerre, Yes Sir!*, 571
Carroll and Graf, publishers, 393
Carver, Raymond, 521, 535, 764–65; *What We Talk About When We Talk About Love*, 535
Cash, W. J., *The Mind of the South*, 416–17
Caspary, Vera, *Thicker Than Water*, 393
Cassatt, Mary, 268
Castellanos, Rosario, 610, 633–34, 636; *Balún Canán* (*The Nine Guardians*), 633; *Oficio de Tinieblas*, 633
Catalog, in postmodern fiction, 705
Categories, literary, 701
Cather, Willa, 268, 270, 273, 278–80, 282, 283, 441; *Death Comes for the Archbishop*, 280, 441; *A Lost Lady*, 441; *My Ántonia*, 280, 441; *O Pioneers!*, 441; *The Professor's House*, 280, 441; *The Song of the Lark*, 279–80, 441
Catholic communities, novels of, 403
Catholic immigration, fear of, 146–47
Cautela, Giuseppe, 398
Censorship, 668
*The Century* (magazine), 303
Césaire, Aimé, 92: *Discourse on Colonialism*, 654
Cezanne, Paul: Stein and, 313
Chain bookstores, 687–88
Chametzky, Jules, 340, 384
Chanady, Amaryll Beatrice, 523
Chandler, Raymond, 371, 375, 765; *The Big Sleep*, 374, 376–77, 450; *Farewell, My Lovely*, 376, 377; *The Simple Act of Murder*, 374

Chang, Diana, 405

Change, Quebec and, 568–69

Channing, William Ellery, 132

Character: conduct and, 123; in early American novels, 10; in Gass's fiction, 740–41; in Hawkes's fiction, 729; in postmodern fiction, 705–6, 716, 718

Charles Scribner's Sons, 389

Charvat, William, 58, 689

Chase, Richard, 72

Chauveau, Pierre-Joseph-Olivier, 573

Chavez, Denise, 765; *The Last of the Menu Girls*, 536

Cheap fiction, nineteenth century, 287

Cheever, George B., *Deacon Giles' Distillery*, 138

Cheever, John, 508, 765–66; *Falconer*, 508; *The Wapshot Chronicle*, 508; *The Wapshot Scandal*, 508

Cheney, Harriet Vaughan, *A Peep at the Pilgrims*, 123–24

Chesebro, Caroline, *Isa: A Pilgrimage*, 111, 139

Chesnutt, Charles, 161, 178–81, 187, 188, 241, 766; *The Conjure Woman*, 244–45; "The Goophered Grapevine," 245; *The House Behind the Cedars*, 178, 181–82, 187; *The Marrow of Tradition*, 178–81, "Po' Sandy," 245

Chicago, literary activity, 311–12, 407

Chicago World's Columbian Exposition (1893), 189, 242, 251–52

Chicano novels, 453, 501; *fotonovela* realist, 539–40

Chicanos. *See* Mexican American writers

Child, Lydia Maria, 42, 105, 766, 786; *The American Frugal Housewife*, 116; *An Appeal for the Indians*, 122; *An Appeal in Favor of That Class of Americans Called Africans*, 91, 142; *Hobomok*, 112, 122; and influence of women, 116; *The Mother's Book*, 116, 122; *Philothea*, 119; Poe's reviews, 102; *A Romance of the Republic*, 119

Childhood, idealization of, 255–56

Childhood illness, African American writers and, 434

Chin, Frank, 406

Chinese American fiction, 499

Chinese immigrants, first women novelists, 277

Chopin, Kate, xii, 267–68, 270, 273, 283, 766–67; *The Awakening*, 176, 225, 230–31, 254

Christian, Barbara, 670

Christianity: domestic ideology and, 127–28; sociology and, 192

Christian Millennium, technology and, 468

Christie, Agatha, 373

Christmas Rebellion, 97

Chu, Louis, 405, 767; *Eat a Bowl of Tea*, 499

Church, and novels, 12–13

Churchill, Winston, 283; *Richard Carvel*, 259

Ciambelli, Bernardino, 398

Cinema: *film noir*, 377–78; Westerns, 367, 370–71, 440–41

Cisneros, Sandra, 767–68; *The House on Mango Street*, 536

Civil disobedience, Emerson and, 130

Civilizing influence of women, nineteenth-century idea, 115–17, 126

Civil Rights movement, Warren and, 416

Civil War, 157, 240; Crane and, 249; and dime novel readership, 293; domesticity cult and, 121–22; reinterpretations, 243

Clark, Walter Van Tilburg, 442–43; *The City of Trembling Leaves*, 443; *The Ox-Bow Incident*, 442–43; *The Track of the Cat*, 443

Clarke, Austin: *The Bigger Light*, 596; *The Meeting Point*, 596; *The Prime Minister*, 575; *Storm of Fortune*, 575

Class, social, 217; gender and, 283–84; postmodern, 520; rebellion against, 276

Class conflict: late nineteenth century, 158; Norris and, 262–63; women's views, 338

Class distinctions: Davis and, 174–77; eighteenth century, 34; proletarianism and, 337–38

Classics, literary: Canadian, 577–78; nineteenth century, 70–71

Classic tradition, definition of, 111–12

Class relations, Chesnutt and, 179–80

Clemens, Samuel Langhorne. *See* Twain, Mark

Clemm, Maria, 94

Cliff, Michelle, 653, 670; *Abeng*, 605; *Claiming an Identity They Taught Me to Despise*, 605; *The Land of Look Behind*, 605; *No Telephone to Heaven*, 605

Clubs, and social change, 268

Cody, William F. *See* Buffalo Bill

Cohen, Matt, *The Disinherited*, 561

Colcord, Lincoln, 390

Cold War, 486; and postmodernism, 516; and proletarian art, 331–33

Cole, Jonathan R., *The Wages of Writing*, 681–82

Collage: Davenport and, 744; Stein's writing as, 314

Collective identification, 200

Collins, Merle, 653

Colloquial language, Twain's realism, 172

Colonialism, 254; American, 258; Euro-American, 30; fiction of, 257

Colonial period, historical fiction, 259

Colonization, fiction and, 650

*The Colored American Magazine*, 273–74

Coltelli, Laura, 456

Coming-of-age stories, gay, 551–52

"Coming out" stories, 551–52

*Commentary*, symposium on Jewish writers, 402, 403

Commercialism, women writers and, 64–65

Commercialization of arts, 517, 518

Commercial novels, 294, 504–5

Commercial realism, 691

Committed writers, Latin American, 614

Commodification: of arts, 669; of culture, 285, 517, 518; of marginality, 666–67; of women, 118–19, 201

Communalism, decline of, 50

Communism, 327, 334–37, 485–86; art and, 331–32; artists and, 353; novels of, 393

Communist Party, 343–44; and women, 338–39

Communitarian reform groups, 133–35

Community, sense of, and racism, 205

Community biographies, early American, 31

Competition from women, male writers and, 62–63

Complex marriage, Oneida community, 134

Compromise of 1850, 218

Conan, Laure (Marie-Louise-Félicité Angers), *Angéline de Montbrun*, 580, 581

Conduct, character and, 123

Conflicts, unresolved, in African American novels, 349

Conformity of avant-garde, 734–35

Conglomerate ownership of publishers, 686–87

Congreve, William, *Incognita*, 73

Connors, Ralph, *The Sky Pilot: A Tale of the Foothills*, 562

Conrad, Joseph: Fitzgerald and, 324–25

Conroy, Jack, 334, 344, 346; *The Disinherited*, 342–43

Conscience, Howells and, 184

Consciousness, national, West Indian, 590

Consciousness of kind concept, 205

Conservation movement, Western novelists and, 446–47

Conservatism: of environment novels, 503; and postmodernism, 518; post–World War II, 485–88

Construction of gender, 542–57

Consumer capitalism, views of, 168

Consumption, postmodern capitalism and, 679
Control, desire for, social reform and, 136
Convent captivity novels, 147
Conventions, literary, 162; nineteenth century, 112–13; postmodern fiction and, 699–701, 704–5; realist, 170, 172
Conversion narratives, 31–33; Native Americans and, 45
Cook, William Wallace, 293, 297
Cooper, James Fenimore, 8, 23–25, 51, 57–59, 72, 438, 465, 766; *Afloat and Ashore*, 149; *The Chainbearer*, 143, 466; classic tradition and, 112; *Home as Found*, 471; *The Last of the Mohicans*, 51, 54, 87, 112; Leatherstocking tales, 294, 437; *The Pioneers*, 58, 59; *Precaution*, 58, 113; *The Redskins*, 143; revenge theme, 87; *Satanstoe*, 143; sea fiction, 149; *The Spy*, 23, 58, 59, 113; and technology, 466, 471; Twain and, 161; *The Ways of the Hour*, 58, 143; and women, 113; and women's rights, 143
Cooptation, minority fiction and, 502
Coover, Robert, 524–25, 706, 712–16, 732–36, 768; *Gerald's Party*, 733; *The Origin of the Brunists*, 713, 733; *Pricksongs and Descants*, 713, 733; *The Public Burning*, 699, 704, 714–16, 733–36; *The Universal Baseball Association*, 702, 704–6, 713–14, 733
Copyright laws, 12, 48
Corpi, Lucha, *Delia's Song*, 453
Cortázar, Julio, *62: Modelo para armar*, 639
Cortina, Leonor, *Lucia*, 647
Coser, Lewis A., *Books: The Culture and Commerce of Publishing*, 683–86
Cosmopolitan novels, 653
Cott, Nancy, 506
Council on Books in Wartime, 686
Counterculture movement, 492

Couser, G. Thomas, 26, 36; *Altered Egos*, 29
Coverdale, Henry Standish (pseud.), *The Fall of the Great Republic*, 471–72
Cowley, Malcolm, 336, 383
Crane, Diana, 692
Crane, Stephen, 196, 769; *Maggie: A Girl of the Streets*, 225, 385; "The Open Boat," 199; *The Red Badge of Courage*, 225, 226, 249–50, 304; typecasting, 200
Crates, Joan, *Breathing Water*, 576
Creolization, 89–90; novels of, 600, 602
Crèvecoeur, St. John de, *Letters from an American Farmer*, 91
Crisis, contemporary, 540
Critical social theory, Du Bois and, 210
Criticism, literary: of autobiography, 28–29; Caribbean, 597; and ethnic novels, 386–87, 494; late nineteenth century, 161; mid-twentieth century, 485, 488; and popular literature, 286; and postmodern fiction, 701; and proletarianism, 332; Russian Jewish establishment, 388; of Western fiction, 442–43
Crumley, James, 456
Cubism, 313–14
Cudjoe, Selwin R., *Caribbean Women Writers: Essays from the First International Conference*, 604
Cullerton, Beatrice, *In Search of April Raintree*, 576
Cultural clashes: frontier novels, 438; magic realism and, 525
Cultural imperialism, 613, 655; Puig and, 628
Cultural influences in Native American autobiography, 45
Cultural mediation, literature of, 384, 406
Cultural relativism: Chicano novels and, 453; nineteenth century, 122–23
Cultural values in Western fiction, 464
Cultural voice, in novels, 10–11, 14
Culture: literary, economy and, 49; popular, 285–86; postmodern, 515–

Culture (*Continued*)
20; proletarian, Communist Party
and, 343–44
—American, 12; influence of women,
113–17, 124–25
Cummins, Maria Susanna, 114, 271,
769; *The Lamplighter*, 54, 116, 117,
123, 127
Curran, Mary Doyle, 397–98; *The Parish and the Hill*, 404
Custodial mission of women, domestic
ideology, 126–27
Cyberpunk fiction, 484

D'Agostino, Guido, 398
Dahlberg, Edward: *Bottom Dogs*, 339–
40; *From Flushing to Calvary*, 339–
40; *Those Who Perish*, 339–40
Daly, Carroll John, *The Snarl of the
Beast*, 373
Dana, Richard Henry, 769; *Two Years
Before the Mast*, 149–50
Dangarembga, Tsitsi, *Nervous Conditions*, 657–68
D'Angelo, Pascal, *Son of Italy*, 398
Dannay, Frederic (Ellery Queen), 802
Dargan, Olive Tilford. *See* Burke, Fielding
Dartmouth College, 43
Davenport, Guy, 744–46, 770; "The
Dawn in Erewhon," 745; "A Field
of Snow on a Slope of the Rosenberg," 745; *Tatlin!*, 745–46
Davidson, Carter, 386; "The Immigrant
Strain in American Literature," 391
Davidson, Cathy N., 9, 19; *Revolution
and the Word*, 14
Davidson, Donald, 416
Davidson, Edward, 82
Davies, Carole Boyce, *Out of the Kumbla: Caribbean Women and Literature*, 604
Davies, Robertson, 567, 579, 770; *Fifth
Business*, 578
Davis, H. L.: *Honey in the Horn*, 443;
*Winds of Morning*, 443
Davis, Rebecca Harding, 188, 238, 335,
770; "At the Station," 160; and exploitation of women, 152; James's

view, 162; *Life in the Iron Mills*,
152, 157, 160, 172–78, 222–26;
*Margret Howth*, 152, 178; realism
of, 160–61; *Waiting for the Verdict*,
178, 187
Davis, Richard Harding, 283, 770–71;
*Soldiers of Fortune*, 259, 477
Dearborn, Mary, 392
Death: of loved one, nineteenth-century
view, 127; of young person, moral
value of, 125
de Boissiere, Ralph, 592, 593; *Crown
Jewel*, 593; *Rum and Coca Cola*,
593
de Burgos, Julia, 610
de Camp, L. Sprague, *Lest Darkness
Fall*, 361
DeCapite, Michael, 398; *Maria*, 399
Decentralization of literature, 250–51
Declaration of Independence, 91
Deconstruction of gender, 542–43
De Forest, John William, *Miss Ravenel's
Conversion from Secession to Loyalty*, 240–41
de Graff, Robert, 359
Delany, Martin Robison, 151, 771;
*Blake; or, The Huts of America*,
55–56, 151
Delany, Samuel R., 699, 704, 724–25,
771; *Dhalgren*, 725; *The Motion of
Light in Water*, 556; Nevèrÿon series, 705, 725; *Stars in My Pocket
Like Grains of Sand*, 554–57; *Tales
of Nevèrÿon*, 725; *Triton*, 725
Deleuze, Giles, 513
DeLillo, Don, 403, 698, 706, 707, 719–
20; *End Zone*, 720; *Great Jones
Street*, 720; *Libra*, 699; *The Names*,
720; *Ratner's Star*, 705; *White
Noise*, 706
De Lima, Clara Rosa, 605; *Tomorrow
Will Always Come*, 603–4
de Lisser, Herbert G., 590–91; *Jane's
Career*, 591; *Susan Proudleigh*, 591;
*The White Witch of Rosehall*,
590–91
Dell, Floyd, 337
Democracy: autobiography and, 27;
Brackenridge and, 21; novels and,

14; story papers and, 288, 289; Western novels and, 369

Democratic societies, avant-garde and, 734

Demythologizing, 10–11; avant-garde and, 734

Denning, Michael, 286, 293, 300

Dennis, Patrick (Edward Everett Tanner), *Auntie Mame*, 502

Depression, economic, 326; African Americans and, 348; in Canada, 570; ethnic novels, 392; and proletarian art, 331–32, 334–46; pulp magazines, 359

Derrida, Jacques, 516

Desktop publishing, 681

Detective fiction: African American, 496; dime novels, 294, 297; Native American, 455–56; twentieth century, 371–78

*Detective Story Magazine*, 359

*Detective Tales*, 373

Determinism: of Davis's work, 225–26; and individualism, 193

Development, female, novels of, 110

Dew, Thomas R., 96

Dexter, Pete, *Deadwood*, 461

Dialects, 251; Québécois, 571

Dialect tales, post–Civil War, 244–45

Díaz del Castillo, Bernal, *True History of the Conquest of New Spain*, 525

Dickens, Charles, *Martin Chuzzlewit*, 8

Dickinson, Anna, 236

Dickstein, Morris, 393

Diction, concreteness of, 11

Didion, Joan, 771–72; *Play It as It Lays*, 451

DiDonato, Pietro, 398, 399–400; *Christ in Concrete*, 399–400

Difference: identity and, 202–3; racial, social evolution and, 206; social, regionalism and, 251

"Difficult fiction," 695, 700

Dime novels, 52, 285, 286, 291–302, 304, 438; science fiction, 361

Dirkin, Douglas Leader, 391

Disappearances, Latin America, 627

Disencumbered experience, romance and, 76

Distribution of books, 685; nineteenth century, 49

Divorce, nineteenth century, 143–44

Dix, Dorothea, 149

Dixon, Thomas, 241, 247–48, 772; *The Clansman*, 363; *The Leopard's Spots*, 247

Doctorow, E. L., 521, 538–39; *Billy Bathgate*, 538; *The Book of Daniel*, 11; *Loon Lake*, 538; *Ragtime*, 538; *Welcome to Hard Times*, 448; *World's Fair*, 538

Doig, Ivan, 462, 772; *Dancing at the Rascal Fair*, 462; *English Creek*, 462; *Ride with Me, Mariah Montana*, 462; *This House of Sky*, 462

Domesticity, 115–29, 688–89; antebellum novels, 51; industrial world and, 223–24; post–World War II, 486, 506–7; reform fiction and, 230–31, 238–39; reform movements and, 225; slavery and, 220–22; technology and, 473–74

Domestic novels, 110–11, 271–72; nineteenth century, 56, 60, 65–66, 69–70; story papers, 289–90

Domination, desire for, social reform and, 136

Donleavy, J. P., 403

Donnelly, Ignatius, *Caesar's Column*, 472

Donoso, José, *The Obscene Bird of Night*, 615–16

Doolittle, Hilda ("H.D."), 312

Dooner, P. W., *Last Days of the Republic*, 471

Dorris, Michael, *A Yellow Raft in Blue Water*, 457

Dos Passos, John, 322–23, 326, 477, 489, 772; *The Big Money*, 467; influence of, 345; *Manhattan Transfer*, 322; and technology, 478–79; *Three Soldiers*, 465; *U.S.A.*, 322, 345, 354, 477

Dostoevsky, Feodor: Hemingway and, 321

Double-consciousness of African Americans, 209–10
Doubleday, publishers, 683
Doubles, as literary device, 179–80
Douglas, Ann, *The Feminization of American Culture*, 91
Douglas, John, 610
Douglass, Frederick, 142, 773; and Chicago world's fair, 189; *The Heroic Slave*, 150–51; *The Life and Times of Frederick Douglass*, 40; *My Bondage and My Freedom*, 40; *The Narrative of the Life of Frederick Douglass, an American Slave, Written by Himself*, 39–40, 220
Doval, Jorge, 527
*Dragnet Magazine*, 373
Dreams, Native American accounts, 43–44
Dream tales, Twain and, 169
Dreiser, Theodore, 283, 271; *An American Tragedy*, 191, 204; Fitzgerald and, 324; *Jennie Gerhardt*, 283; naturalist fiction, 203–4; *Sister Carrie*, 204, 225, 226, 283
Drury, Allen, *Advise and Consent*, 490
Dryden, Edgar A., 72
Du Bois, W. E. B., 193, 204–10, 333; *The Philadelphia Negro*, 191, 206–8; *The Quest of the Silver Fleece*, 210; *The Souls of Black Folk*, 204, 208–10, 249, 413; *The Suppression of the African Slave-Trade*, 206
Duchamp, Marcel, *Nude Descending a Staircase*, 311
Ducharme, Réjean, 572
Dunbar, Paul Laurence, 773
Dunbar-Nelson, Alice, 270, 273
Dunne, Finley Peter, 395
Dunne, John Gregory: *Dutch Shea, Jr.*, 451; *True Confessions*, 451
Dupee, F. W., *Henry James*, 271–72
Duplechan, Larry, *Blackbird*, 551
Durkheim, Emile, 206; *L'Année Sociologique*, 201; *Suicide*, 198
Duty, domesticity and, 123
Dystopia, nineteenth-century novels of, 471–74

Eagleton, Terry, 655
Eakin, Paul John, *Fictions in Autobiography: Studies in the Art of Self-Invention*, 29
Eakins, Thomas, 196; *The Gross Clinic*, 197
Early American novels, 6–25
Early twentieth century, 309; fiction, 335; immigration, 380–81
Earth First! movement, 459
Eastern European immigrants, 373
Eastlake, William, 445–46, 773–74; *The Bronc People*, 445, 446; *Go in Beauty*, 445; *Portrait of an Artist with Twenty-Six Horses*, 445
Eastman, Max and Crystal, 337
East Side novelists, 386–89, 394
Eaton, Edith. *See* Sui Sin Far
Eaton, Winnifred. *See* Onoto Watanna
Eclecticism, 691
Eco, Umberto, 483
Economic factors in growth of novel, 48–50
Economic novels, Westerns as, 369
Economic power, fiction and, 5
Economic status of writers, nineteenth century, 47–48, 58
Economy: and literary development, 49, 54–55; and popular fiction, 287; of publishing, 680–90, 695
Edgell, Zee, 605
Editors, 683–84
Education: colonialist, 650, 655, 657–68
—of women, 269; early American ideas, 15–16, 115; patriarchal view, 118–19
Educators, eighteenth century, 115
Edwards, Jonathan, 13; *Personal Narrative*, 31
Effectism of Western novels, 439, 440
Efficiency movement, 476; and prose style, 477–78
Eggleston, Edward, *The Hoosier Schoolmaster*, 255
Ehrlich, Gretel, *Heart Mountain*, 462
Eighteenth century: publishing, 52–53; reading of novels, 13

—writings, 3–5, 59; autobiographical, 31–34

Einstein, Albert, 314

Eisenhower, Dwight D., 485

Electronic technology, 681; fiction and, 480–84; symbolism of, 466–67

Eliot, George: Hawthorne and, 60

Eliot, T. S., 312, 316, 691; American society viewed by, 519; and Barnes, 328; essay on Joyce's *Ulysses*, 317; and Hemingway, 319; *The Waste Land*, 320; and World War I, 318

Elite groups: academic, literacy of, 693; invisibility of, 197; nineteenth century, and reform movements, 133; and social reform, 146–48; sociology and, 201–2; women, and social reform, 269

Elitism: of Stowe, 146; of Wister's *The Virginian*, 439

Elizondo, Salvador, *Farabeuf*, 631

Elkin, Stanley, 402; *The Dick Gibson Show*, 480

Ellis, Edward, 299; *Seth Jones; or, The Captives of the Frontier*, 295–96; *Steam-Man of the Plains*, 361

Ellis, Trey, *Platitudes*, 482

Ellison, Ralph, 285, 430, 496, 774; *Invisible Man*, 435–36, 495

Eltis, David, "Free and Coerced Transatlantic Migration: Some Comparisons," 92

Emerson, Ralph Waldo, 123, 163; and alcohol, 136; "The American Scholar," 132; "Emancipation in the British West Indies," 130; "Man the Reformer," 130; "New England Reformers," 130; and realism, 162; and reform, 130–33; "Self-Reliance," 468–69; and technology, 468–71; Yezierska and, 387–88; "The Young American," 169

Empire, American, 258

Empirical first-person authority, 27

Encyclopedic postmodern fiction, 705

Enfranchisement of women, domestic ideology and, 126–27

Engineers, as popular heroes, 476–77

England, George Allen: *The Afterglow*, 363; *Darkness at Dawn*, 363; "The Lunar Advertising Co.," 363

English language: British colonialism and, 655–56; early American writers and, 11. See also Language

English-language fiction, postmodern, 699

English-language writers: colonialism and, 650; postcolonial, 652

English poets, World War I, 318

English-speaking Caribbean, novel development, 586–606

Enlightenment: and abolitionist movement, 140; and social reform, 132; and sociology, 192; youth viewed by, 115

En'Owkin Writing Center, 577

Entrée, cultural, 519–20

Environment, literature of, 459–60, 503–9

Enzensberger, Hans Magnus, 745, 751

Epic poems, technological themes, 468

Erasure, works written under, 566

Erdrich, Louise, 457, 774; *The Beet Queen*, 457; *Love Medicine*, 457; *Tracks*, 457

Erisman, Fred, 455–56

Erotic power of women, nineteenth-century idea, 124–25

Escape narratives, nineteenth century, 257–58; sea fiction, 148–51

Escapism: of science fiction, 365; Westerns and, 368

Essentialist view of social change, 207

Ethnic identity: gender and, 283–84; Mukherjee and, 673; novels of, 494–95

Ethnic literature, 44, 382–406, 494–95; autobiography, 27; Canada, 573–77; late twentieth century, 499–501; early American, 9

Etzler, Johann A., *The Paradise within the Reach of All Men, without Labour, by the Powers of Nature and Machinery*, 469

European Americans, World War II, 402

European immigration, 92; autobiographical writings, 31. *See also* Immigration

European modernism, magic realism and, 524

European poetry, World War I, 318

Evangelicalism: and Catholic immigration, 147; and social reform, 131–32; in *Uncle Tom's Cabin*, 145

Evans, Augusta Jane, 774–75; *St. Elmo*, 110, 298

Evans, Max, *The Rounders*, 440

Evans, May Garrettson, 94

Evil, socially constructed, James and, 167–68

Evolution, social: contradictory groups, 202; Du Bois and, 206; James and, 200

Evolutionary analysis of society, 192–93

Excesses, in avant-garde fiction, 732

Exclusivity, autonomy and, 691

Exile, 649, 650–52; education and, 655; literature of, 654; political, 668

Existentialism, 487, 489, 491–92, 494; Mailer and, 493

Expansionism, late nineteenth century, 158

Expatriate movement, 312

Expatriate writers: Nabokov, 707; West Indian, 593, 596, 600

Expatriation, 649–51; education and, 657; in Canada, Mukherjee and, 672–73

Experience, modes of, in early American novels, 10

Experimental writing: Canadian, 571, 579, 581; early twentieth century, 335; postmodern, 699; proletarian, 344–46; Stein and, 215; by women, 695, 699

Exploitation: Western novels and, 437; of women, nineteenth century, 152–53

Explorers, autobiographical writings, 29–30

Expression, means of, in early American writings, 11

Expressionism, Fitzgerald and, 326

Fable: Melville and, 87; Twain and, 169

Fact, early American fiction based on, 14–18

Factory workers, dime novels and, 294

FactSheet Five, 681

Failure, avant-garde fiction and, 731–32

Fairchild, Henry Pratt, *The Melting-Pot Mistake*, 381

Falardeau, Jean-Charles, *Notre société et son roman*, 572

Family: public supervision, 50; rebellion against, 278

*Family Story Paper*, 297

Fanon, Frantz, 657; *Black Skin, White Masks*, 106

Fantasy, 302; Butler's views, 522

Fante, John, *Wait Until Spring, Bandini*, 398–99

Farah, Nurrudin, 668

Farm conditions, reform of, 235–36

Farnsworth, Robert M., Chesnutt viewed by, 181

Farrell, James T., 326, 395–97; *Judgment Day*, 396; *Studs Lonigan*, 354, 396–97; *Young Lonigan*, 396; *The Young Manhood of Studs Lonigan*, 396, 397

*Far West* (magazine), 302–3

Far West, political rhetoric, 294–95

Fascism, 317

Fashionable life, femininity and, nineteenth-century views, 120

Fathers, immigrant, 676

Faulkner, William, 315, 322, 426–30, 432, 775; *Absalom! Absalom!*, 428, 703; Anderson and, 327; *As I Lay Dying*, 444; *Flags in the Dust*, 427; *Go Down, Moses*, 428, 432; *Intruder in the Dust*, 428, 432; *Light in August*, 428, 434; *Sartoris*, 427; *Soldier's Pay*, 427; *The Sound and the Fury*, 326, 427, 432

Fauset, Jessie, 411, 420–21; *There Is Confusion*, 420–21

Faust, Frederick (Max Brand), 366, 379, 775–76; *Hired Guns*, 366, 367; Montana Kid series, 440; *The Untamed*, 366

Feal, Rosemary Geisdorfer, 646–47
Fee, Margery, 576
Fees for story-paper writings, 288
Female experience, proletarian, 350. *See also* Women
Feminine mystique, 486
Femininity, nineteenth-century ideas, 111, 272
Feminism: and abolitionism, 142–43, 218; in Alcott's *Work*, 125–26; Bellamy's *Looking Backward* and, 230; Butler and, 522; communism and, 339; domesticity and, 118–26; early American, 18–19, 126–27; and experimental fiction, 699; Garland and, 235–36; in Hurston's novels, 424; late nineteenth century, 269; and lesbian fiction, 501–2; in nineteenth-century domestic novels, 113; post–World War II, 505–7; and slave autobiography, 41–42; of Stein, 316; in *Uncle Tom's Cabin*, 144–45; and Western fiction, 457–58; of Yezierska, 387–88
Feminist writing: Canadian, 567, 581; Caribbean, 604–5; Latin American, 614–15, 629, 633–47; nineteenth century, 111; postmodern, 532, 698, 723–24
Feminization of American culture, 114–17
Ferguson, Adam, *Essay on the History of Civil Society*, 191–92
Fergusson, Harvey: *The Conquest of Don Pedro*, 443; *Grant of Kingdom*, 443
Fern, Fanny (Sara Payson Willis), 65, 776; and marriage, 143–44; *Rose Clark*, 143–44; *Ruth Hall*, 54, 63–64, 69, 87, 111, 143, 152
Fernández Retamar, Roberto, 613–14; *Calibán*, 613
Ferré, Rosario, 623, 635–36; *Maldito amor* (*Sweet Diamond Dust*), 635; *Papeles de Pandora*, 635
Ferro, Robert, *The Family of Max Desir*, 551
Ferron, Jacques, *La Nuit* (*Quince Jam*), 570

Fiction, 5; autobiography and, 4–5, 29, 45; avant-garde, 727–51; domesticity and, 110–29; early American views, 9–10; early twentieth century, 309–10; economy and, 49–50; gender and, 267–84; immigrant experience, 382; late nineteenth century, 157–58; republican ideology and, 48; and social reform, 131–54, 217–39; and technology, 465–84
Fiction Collective, 813
Fido, Elaine Savory, *Out of the Kumbla: Caribbean Women and Literature*, 604
Fiedler, Leslie, 285–86, 383, 395, 403, 728
Fielding, Henry, *Joseph Andrews*, 4
Fields, James T., 61
Fifth House Publishing, 577
Fillmore, Millard, 218
*Film noir*, 377–78
Films. *See* Cinema
Financial affairs, nineteenth-century women and, 65
Financial status of writing profession, 47–48; nineteenth century, 58
Findley, Timothy: *Famous Last Words*, 582; *Not Wanted on the Voyage*, 566, 582
Fine, David, *Los Angeles in Fiction*, 451
Finley, Martha, 776; *Elsie Dinsmore*, 110, 123
Finney, Charles Grandison, 132, 133, 136; and novel reading, 137–38; and slavery, 140–41
*Fireside Companion*, 297
First-person narratives, Native American, 43
First-person pronoun: and authority, 26–27; autobiography and, 28–29
Fisher, Dexter, 281
Fisher, Philip, 197; *Hard Facts*, 98
Fisher, Rudolph, 422
Fisher, Vardis: *Dark Bridwell*, 443; *In Tragic Life*, 443
Fitzgerald, F. Scott, 312, 315, 322, 323–26, 395, 408, 428–29, 451, 776–77; *Flappers and Philosophers*,

Fitzgerald, F. Scott (*Continued*)
323; *The Great Gatsby*, 323, 324–
26; *The Last Tycoon*, 323; *Tales of
the Jazz Age*, 323; *Tender Is the
Night*, 326; *This Side of Paradise*,
323
Fitzgerald, Zelda Sayre, 323, 428,
776–77
Flack, Richard, 338
*The Flag of Our Union* (story paper),
289, 290
Flaubert, Gustave, 691, 736; Fitzgerald
and, 324; *Madame Bovary*, 74;
Stein and, 312
Fliegelman, Jay, 22
Flight from society, male novels of,
117–18
Flint, Timothy, *The Shoshonee Valley*,
437
Flores, Angel, "Magic Realism in Span-
ish American Fiction," 523–24
Flow, in broadcast programming,
481–82
Flynn, Robert, *North to Yesterday*,
461
*Flynn's Clues*, 373
*Focus* (literary review), 593
Foerster, Norman, 397
Foley, Barbara, 338
Folio, Fred, *Lucy Boston; or, Women's
Rights and Spiritualism*, 143
Folk culture: Hurston and, 421–22;
mass literature and, 286; Toomer
and, 418–19
Foote, Arthur, 452
Foote, Mary Hallock, 438, 452, 777;
*The Led-Horse Claim*, 438
Forbes, Kathryn (Kathryn Anderson
McLean), *Mama's Bank Account*,
504–5
Ford, John: *Stagecoach* (film), 367;
*Straight Shooting* (film), 370
Ford, Paul Leicester, *Janice Meredith*,
259
Ford, Richard, 449–50, 777; *The
Sportswriter*, 484; *Wildfire*, 450
Ford-Smith, Honor, 655, 668
Foreign novels, pirated, 48
Forgione, Louis, *Men of Silence*, 398

Formula fiction, 305; adventure stories,
360; and American ideology, 358–
59; detective novels, 371–78; dime
novels, 294–97, 298; frontier narra-
tives, 438; pulp magazines, 302,
359; story papers, 288–89; West-
erns, 366–71, 437, 439–40
Foster, David William, 629–30
Foster, Hannah, 777; *The Coquette*, 5,
9, 16–18, 52
*Fotonovela* realism, 539–41
Foucault, Michel, 202, 516
Fourier, Charles, 133
Fowler, Orson, 137
Fox, John, *The Boys on the Rock*, 551
Fox, Mary, *The Ruined Deacon*, 138
Fragmentation of self, gothic novels
and, 22
France, Americans in, 312
Frank, Andre Gunder, 528
Frank, Waldo, *Holiday*, 418
Frankfurt School, and popular culture,
285
Franklin, Benjamin: and abolition, 140;
*Autobiography*, 27, 35–37
Franklin, Temple, 36
Free African Americans, 55
Freeman, Mary E. Wilkins, 250, 254–
55, 778; "A Church Mouse," 255;
"A New England Nun," 255; *Pem-
broke*, 254–55; "The Revolt of
'Mother,' "255
French, Paul. *See* Asimov, Isaac
French Canada, 567–73
French feminism, influence in Canada,
581
French intellectuals, and postmodern-
ism, 516–17
French Revolution, Poe and, 97
Freud, Sigmund, 487; *Interpretation of
Dreams*, 313
Freudianism, 489
Friedan, Betty, 486; *Feminine Mystique*,
505
Friedman, Bruce Jay, 402
Frontiers, nationhood and, 242–43
Frontier stories, 437–38; dime novels,
294–97; romances, 260–61, 294–97
Frost, Robert, 311

Frothingham, Charles, *The Convent's Doom*, 147
Frye, Northrop, 577
Fuchs, Daniel, Williamsburg trilogy, 393
Fuentes, Carlos, 522, 613, 620–21, 778; *Christopher Unborn*, 620–22; *The Death of Artemio Cruz*, 620; *Terra Nostra*, 620–21
*The Fugitive* (magazine), 414
Fugitives, 408, 414
Fugitive Slave Act, 217–18
Fuller, Margaret, *Woman in the Nineteenth Century*, 101–2, 134, 142–43
Fulton, Robert, 468
Fundamentalism, 660
Fussell, Paul, *The Great War and Modern Memory*, 318
Futurology, 539

Gaddis, William, *JR*, 732
Gaer, Yosef, 388
Gaines, Ernest, *A Gathering of Old Men*, 432; "The Sky Is Gray," 434
Gale, Zona, 283
Gallant, Mavis, 567
Gallegos, Rómulo, *Doña Barbara*, 611
Galsworthy, John, *The Forsyte Saga*, 314
García Canclini, Néstor, 539
García Márquez, Gabriel, 521, 522, 526–28, 610, 616, 618–20, 719, 778–79; *The Autumn of the Patriarch*, 526, 619; "Big Mama's Funeral," 526; *The General in His Labyrinth*, 523, 527–28, 619; *Leafstorm*, 526; *No One Writes to the Colonel*, 619; *One Hundred Years of Solitude*, 526–28, 529, 615–16, 618–19
Gardner, Erle Stanley, 371–72, 779; *The Case of the Velvet Claws*, 371
Gardner, John, 699, 739, 779–80; *October Light*, 480
Garfield, James, and Wallace, 258
Garland, Hamlin, 250, 780; *Boy Life on the Prairie*, 255; "God's Ravens," 253; and Howells, 234;

"The Land of the Straddle-Bug," 236; "The Lion's Paw," 255; "Local Color in Fiction," 251–52; *Main-Travelled Roads*, 252; and regionalism, 251–52, 253; *Rose of Dutcher's Coolly*, 236; *A Spoil of Office*, 226, 235–36
Garrison, William Lloyd, 39, 140–41, 142
Garro, Elena, 623
Gaspé, Philippe-Ignace-François Aubert de, *L'Influence d'un livre*, 567
Gaspé, Philippe-Joseph Aubert de, *Les Anciens Canadiens*, 567
Gass, William, 609, 729, 739–42, 780; "The Concept of Character in Fiction," 740; *In the Heart of the Heart of the Country*, 739; *Omensetter's Luck*, 739, 741; *The Tunnel*, 739, 741; *Willie Masters' Lonesome Wife*, 739
Gates, Henry Louis, Jr., 413
Gaudier-Brzeska, Henri, 317, 318
Gay community, postwar period, 501–2; fiction, 502, 549–57
Gaze, male, domesticity and, 123–26
Gedin, Per, 679, 680, 692
Geertz, Clifford, 531
Gender: construction of, 542–57; and income from writing, 682; modernism and, 316; proletarianism and, 333, 351–52; as social category, 217; taste and, 694–96; technology and, 475
—and fiction, 267–84; Latin America, 629–31; nineteenth century, 51, 111–12; science fiction, 360–61
—stereotyping: post–World War II, 486; women writers and, 505–7
General welfare, and private interest, 50
Genre fiction, 465, 682
German Jewish merchants, immigrant novels, 384–85
Gernsback, Hugo, *Ralph 124C 41+*, 360
Ghetto narratives, 382
Gibbons, Kaye, *Ellen Foster*, 430
Giddings, F. H., 205
Gilded Age, 158

Gillette, King Camp, *The Human Drift*, 474
Gilman, Charlotte Perkins, 333, 780–81; *Herland*, 475; *The Man-Made World*, 272–73; "Men and Art," 272–73; "The Yellow Wallpaper," 176, 230–31
Gilman, Richard, 740
Gilroy, Beryl, 653
Giquère, Diane, 572
Glantz, Margo, 623
Glasgow, Ellen, 267, 273, 283
Glass, Montague, 389
Glass, Philip, 516
Gloss, Molly, *The Jump-Off Creek*, 462
Godard, Barbara, "The Discourse of the Other: Canadian Literature and the Question of Ethnicity," 573
Godbout, Jacques: *Le Couteau sur la table (The Knife on the Table)*, 570; *Salut Galarneau! (Hail Galarneau!)*, 571
*Godey's Lady's Book*, 91, 121–22, 303
Godfrey, Dave, *The New Ancestors*, 584
*The God That Failed*, 486
Gold, Michael, 343–44; "Go Left, Young Writers," 337; *Jews Without Money*, 334–39, 393–94
Goldman, Emma, 268–69, 323
Goldwyn, Samuel: *The Border of the Legion* (film), 370; and Yezierska, 388–89
Gonzales, Ambrose, *Black Border*, 420
González Echevarría, Roberto, 523–24, 525, 611, 625–26; *Myth and Archive*, 626; *The Voice of the Masters*, 625–26
Goodison, Lorna, 667
Goodman, Paul, *Growing Up Absurd*, 485
Gordon, Mary, 404
Gothic novels: early American, 21–23; nineteenth century, 47, 87
Goyen, William, 461
Graff, Gerald, 692–93
Graham, Sylvester, 137
Granich, Itzok. See Gold, Michael
Grass, Günter, 678

Grau, Shirley Ann: *The Black Prince and Other Stories*, 414; *The Keepers of the House*, 414
Graves, Michael, 516
Great American Novel, search for, 241
Great Britain: colonialism, 655; ex-colonial immigrants, 652–53; literary culture, 47
Great Depression, 326; African Americans and, 348; in Canada, 570; ethnic novels, 392; and proletarian art, 331–32; proletarian fiction and, 334–46; pulp magazines, 359
Greenberg, Robert M., 347
Greene, Anna Katherine, *That Affair Next Door*, 373
Greenwich Village Bohemia, 337
Gregory, Horace, 353
Grenfell, Julian, 318
Grey, Francis, *The Curé of St. Philippe*, 562
Grey, Zane, 370–71, 439–40, 443, 781; *The Call of the Canyon*, 370, 371; *The Last of the Plainsmen*, 371; *Riders of the Purple Sage*, 368; *The Shepard of Guadeloupe*, 370; *30,000 on the Hoof*, 370
Griffith, D. W.: *The Birth of a Nation* (film), 274, 363, 772; *Ramona* (film), 370
Griffiths, Linda, *The Book of Jessica*, 576–77
Griggs, Sutton, 241, 781; *Imperium in Imperio*, 248
Grimké, Angelina, *Letters to Catharine E. Beecher*, 142
Grimké, Sarah, 142, 143
Griswold, Rufus, 287
Group culture, Native Americans and, 43–44
Group identity: late twentieth century, 494–95; minority fiction and, 503–5
Groups, social reform, 133
Grove, Frederick Philip, *Settlers of the Marsh*, 564
Guattari, Félix, 513
Guest, Judith, *Ordinary People*, 682–83
Guillén, Nicolás, 524, 609
Guilt, Latin American writing and, 614

Gulf and Western, 687

Gurr, Andrew, 650–51

Guthrie, A. B., 781; *The Big Sky*, 443; *The Way West*, 443

Gutman, Herbert, 177

Guy, Rosa, 605; *Bird at My Window*, 603–4

Guyana, fiction from, 596–98

Habegger, Alfred, 271–72

Habermas, Jürgen, 521

Habit, psychology of, 211

Hacker, Marilyn, 556

Hacking, Ian, "Making Up People," 191, 215

Hale, Sarah, 65, 91, 122; *The Lecturess*, 122; *Northwood*, 122

Haliburton, Thomas C., *The Clockmaker; or, The Sayings and Doings of Samuel Slick of Slickville*, 560, 561

Hall, G. Stanley, 255

Hall, Oakley, 455

Halper, Albert, 386; *Union Square*, 345

Hammett, Dashiell, 373, 781–82; *The Maltese Falcon*, 374, 376, 450; *Red Harvest*, 373, 374–76

Hansen, Marcus, 389

Hapgood, Hutchins, *The Spirit of the Ghetto*, 381

Hard-boiled detective fiction, 372–78

Haring, Keith, 552

Harland, Henry (Sidney Luska): *Mrs. Prexiada*, 384; *The Yoke of the Thorah*, 384

Harlem Renaissance, 322, 421; Hurston and, 422

Harlequin Romances, 301, 378

Harlow, Robert, *Scann*, 565

Harmony Society, 133

Harper, Frances Ellen, 142, 273, 283; *Iola Leroy*, 228

Harper Bros., publishers, 53

*Harper's Monthly Magazine*, 27, 303

*Harper's Weekly*, 303

Harrigan, Edward, 395

Harris, Joel Chandler, Uncle Remus stories, 244

Harris, Mark: *Bang the Drum Slowly*, 492; *The Southpaw*, 492

Harris, Wilson, 587, 589, 593, 594, 596–97

Harrison, Dick, *Unnamed Country: The Struggle for a Prairie Fiction*, 562

Harrison, James, 96

Harte, Bret, 438

Haslam, Gerald, 446

Hassan, Ihab, 319, 521, 739

Hawkes, John, 701–2, 707, 709–10, 728–29, 736, 782; *The Lime Twig*, 728, 729; *Second Skin*, 706, 709–10, 729; *Travesty*, 729

Hawley, Cameron, *Executive Suite*, 507

Hawthorne, Nathaniel, 5, 8, 52, 60–62, 66–69, 72, 465, 782–83; "The Artist of the Beautiful," 75; "The Birthmark," 83–84; *The Blithedale Romance*, 63, 66, 75, 134–36; and caricature, 83–84; "The Custom-House," 75, 92; and domestic novels, 112; "Ethan Brand," 83–84; "The Haunted Mind," 76–77; *The House of the Seven Gables*, 52, 59, 66, 73, 75, 87, 112, 135–36; and imagination, 75–77; "The Man of Adamant," 83; *The Marble Faun*, 75, 87; and mesmerism, 135–36; "The Minister's Black Veil," 84; *Mosses from an Old Manse*, 53; "My Kinsman, Major Molineux," 84; "A Parable," 84; and realism, 162; and reform, 134–36; and romance, 73, 105; *The Scarlet Letter*, 50, 61, 63, 83–86, 112, 117; "The Snow-Image," 75; *Twice-Told Tales*, Poe's review, 105; and women writers, 62–63, 110, 117, 271

Haycox, Ernest, 367

Haymarket Riot, 158

Head, Bessie, 651; *A Question of Power*, 671–72

Health reforms, nineteenth century, 137

Heap, Jane, 312

Hearn, Lafcadio, 783; *Chita*, 254

Hearne, John, 593, 594, 598; *Autumn Equinox*, 599; *The Faces of Love*, 599; *Land of the Living*, 599–600;

Hearne, John (*Continued*)
Stranger at the Gate, 599; *The Sure
Salvation*, 600; *Voices under the
Window*, 599
Heath, Stephen, 644
Hébert, Anne, *Kamouraska*, 580
Hegel, Georg Wilhelm Friedrich, *Phe-
nomenology of Mind*, 104
Heidegger, Martin, *Being and Time*,
487
Heller, Erich, *Thomas Mann: The
Ironic German*, 750–51
Heller, Joseph, 783–84; *Catch-22*, 491
Helper, Hinton, 54–55
Hemingway, Ernest, 249, 312, 314,
315, 318–22, 408, 477–78, 479,
784; *Death in the Afternoon*, 321;
*A Farewell to Arms*, 319; *For
Whom the Bell Tolls*, 321; *Green
Hills of Africa*, 321; influences on,
324; *In Our Time*, 477; *A Move-
able Feast*, 322; *The Old Man and
the Sea*, 321; *The Sun Also Rises*,
319–20, 477–78
Hémon, Louis, *Maria Chapdelaine*, 568
Henry, Will, *From Where the Sun Now
Stands*, 440
Hentz, Caroline Lee, 64; *Linda*, 64,
110; *The Planter's Northern Bride*,
145
Herberg, Will, 402
Herbst, Josephine, 332, 339, 345, 353,
354–55; *The Executioner Waits*,
354; *Pity Is Not Enough*, 354; *Rope
of Gold*, 354–55
Hernández, Jaime and Gilbert, 539–41;
*Chelo's Burden*, 540; *Heartbreak
Soup*, 540; *House of Raging
Women*, 540; *Locas*, 540; *Love and
Rockets*, 539–40; *Las Mujeres Peri-
das*, 540; *Music for Mechanics*, 540;
*The Reticent Heart*, 540
Heroes: in adventure fiction, 378–79; in
formula Westerns, 366; in frontier
novels, 438
Heroic tales, dime novels, 294
Heroine, democratic, working girl as,
298
*Hester Street* (film), 385

Heyward, DuBose, 417, 418; *Mamba's
Daughters*, 418; *Porgy*, 418
Higginson, Thomas Wentworth, 132
High modernism, 318–19, 326–27; con-
servatism of, 316–17; Davenport
and, 744; lesbian fiction, 501; post-
modernism and, 521
Highsmith, Patricia, *The Price of Salt*,
501–2
Hijuelos, Oscar, 406
Hildreth, Richard, *The Slave; or, Memoirs of Archy Moore*, 141
Hillerman, Tony, 455–56; *The Blessing
Way*, 455; *Coyote Waits*, 455; *Talking God*, 455; *A Thief of Time*, 455
Himes, Chester, 495–96; *Cotton Comes
to Harlem*, 495; *The Heat's On*,
495; *If He Hollers Let Him Go*,
495; *The Real Cool Killers*, 495
Hirsch, David H., 72
Hirsch, E. D., Jr., *Cultural Literacy*,
666
Historical narrative: García Márquez
and, 618; postmodern, 533
Historical novels, 15–18, 252; Twain
and, 256; West Indies, 598–99
—romances: Cooper and, 58; Jamaican, 590–91; nineteenth century,
112, 158, 257–63; by women, 119–
20, 123–24
Historiographic metafiction: Canadian,
565; postmodernism and, 522, 705
History, xiii; collective sense, 514; Latin
American, reevaluation of, 607–9;
postbellum fiction and, 157; post-
modernism and, 538–39, 714–16,
718–19, 721
Hobsbawm, Eric, 197
Hobson, Laura Z., *Gentleman's Agreement*, 490
Hodge, Merle, 605; *Crick Crack Monkey*, 595
Hodgin, Jack, *Invention of the World*,
565
Hofstadter, Richard, 488
Holleran, Andrew, *Dancer from the
Dance*, 549
Holmes, John Clellon, *Go*, 492
Holocaust novels, 403

Holt, Hamilton, editor, *The Life Stories of Undistinguished Americans as Told by Themselves*, 384
Home: expatriate, 654; and identity, 651–52; social reform and, 238–39; work in, nineteenth century, 52
Homestead strike, 158
Homophobia, of Hemingway, 321
Homosexuality: Baldwin and, 496; Cather and, 279–80; Latin America, 627, 629–31; literature of, 544–57; post–World War II, 501–2
Hood, Hugh, *The New Age*, 566
Hooks, Bell, 695
Hopedale Community, 133
Hopkins, Pauline, 159, 267, 273–75, 282, 283, 784; *Contending Forces*, 273–75; *Hagar's Daughter*, 274; *Of One Blood*, 274–75; *Winona*, 274
Horgan, Paul, 784–85; *Far from Cibola*, 443; *Whitewater*, 443
Horkheimer, Max, 210
Hospital, Janette Turner, 567
Hostility, in naturalist fiction, 202
Hough, Emerson, *The Covered Wagon*, 446
House Un-American Activities Committee (HUAC), 486
Housewives, post–World War II novels of, 506–7
Howe, E. W., 438; *The Story of a Country Town*, 255
Howe, Irving, 395
Howells, William Dean, 27, 158, 188, 196, 385, 785; *Annie Kilburn*, 232–33; *A Hazard of New Fortunes*, 168, 183–84, 233–34, 466; influences on, 271–72; "Mr. James's Later Work," 271; and realism, 161, 168, 181–82; and regional fiction, 250; *The Rise of Silas Lapham*, 157, 182–87; *Through the Eye of the Needle*, 168; *A Traveler from Altruria*, 168
How-to manuals, novels as, 51, 69
Hughes, Langston, 322, 422; *Not Without Laughter*, 421
Hugo, Richard, 462
Hulme, T. E., 317, 318

Human body, detective fiction and, 375–76
Human reciprocity, sociological view, 190
Hum-ishu-ma (Mourning Dove), 270–71, 273, 280–82, 283, 455; *Cogewea, the Half-Blood*, 280–82; *Coyote Stories*, 282
Humor: Canadian, 560–61; Caribbean, 601–2; Southwestern, 55
Humphrey, William, 461
Hurst, Fannie, 386
Hurston, Zora Neale, 268, 322, 421–25, 785; "The Eatonville Anthology," 422; *Jonah's Gourd Vine*, 422, 423; *Moses, Man of the Mountain*, 423; *Mules and Men*, 421–22; *Their Eyes Were Watching God*, 348, 422, 423–24
Hutcheon, Linda, 522, 565, 585; *Study of Contemporary English-Canadian Fiction*, 583
Huxley, Aldous, 451
Hyperreality, 483–84

Idealization: of negroes, 91; Poe and, 94–95; of women, slavery and, 102
Ideas, avant-garde, 729
Identity, 29, 202–3; Cable and, 243–44; cultural, minority fiction and, 503–5; hiding of, 278; home and, 651–52; homosexual, 551–55; Jewish, 403; literature of, post–World War II, 509; of Mukherjee, 673–74; naming and, 675; negotiation of, 652–53; novels of, 494; postcolonial, 649, 659–61; primitive, views of, 264; racism and, 187; society and, 485–509; Stein and, 212; Twain and, 246
— national, 242; African American, 248; American, 27, 408–9; Canadian, 565; Caribbean, 588–90, 603, 604–5; *Connecticut Yankee* and, 257; Latin American, 608, 613; Native American, 43; racism and, 263; regionalism and, 251
— racial, 106, 409, 435–36; Hurston and, 423; in slave narratives, 38

Ideology: American, formula fiction and, 358–59; Caribbean, 589; of domesticity, 115–17, 118; and fiction, 50; realism and, 522; science fiction and, 363–64; of slavery, Poe and, 102; Stein and, 213–15; of technology, 467; of Western fiction, 369

*I'll Take My Stand: The South and the Agrarian Tradition by Twelve Southerners*, 415

Imagery: in Chesnutt's realism, 180; sexual, James and, 165

Imagination: African Americans and, 105; in autobiography, 45; Hawthorne and, 75–77; James and, 163, 166–67; in Native American autobiography, 44; Poe and, 77–80; reading and, 543–45; realist fiction and, 187, 199

Imagism, 317

Immigrant women, 269; suffragists and, 126; as writers, 273

Immigration, 380–81; Britain and, 653; Catholic, fear of, 146–47; democratization of laws, 406; and literary market, 49; Mukherjee and, 672–73; nineteenth century, 158, 268; race and, 92; and regionalism, 251; sociology and, 192; twentieth century, 408, 409. *See also* Migrations
—novels of, 382–406, 403–4, 653, 660–65, 674–77; Canadian, 574–75; reform novels, 236–38; Scandinavian, 389; Westerns, 441; West Indian, 595, 600–602

Imperialism: American, 259–60, 654; literature of, 650, 658; Norris and, 263; post–Civil War, 248–49; technology and, 469–70

Inclusion, cultural, 519–20

Income from writing, 681–82, 689

Indian captivity narratives, 31–33

Indians. *See* Native Americans

*Indigenista* novels, 611

Individual experience, realist fiction, 199

Individualism: American, 359; autobiography and, 27; Bellow and, 497;

capitalism and, 344; communism and, 353; in detective fiction, 374; Du Bois and, 208; Hemingway and, 321; mid-twentieth century, 485, 489–94; Native Americans and, 43; post–World War II, 486–87; and social control, 195–96; sociology and, 193; and technology, 469; type categories and, 191; working class and, 333

Individuality, Stein and, 212–13

Industrialism, 285, 465–66

Industrialization of Canada, 570

Industrial reform, 227–28, 232–33; Sinclair's *The Jungle* and, 237–38

Industry, realist novels of, 223–26

Inés de la Cruz, Sor Juana, 624

Inflation: postmodern capitalism and, 679; in publishing prices, 686

Influence of women, nineteenth century, 115–17; erotic nature of, 124–25

Ingraham, Prentiss, 296, 299, 438

Initiation journey, captivity narrative as, 32–33

Innocence, nostalgia for, 255–56

Instability of early American novels, 6

Institutional authority, reform and, 149–50

Institutions of social reform, 148–49

Insurrection of lower class, fears of, 147

Intellectualism, and Marxism, 485–86

Intellectuals, immigrant, 381

Intellectual women, nineteenth century, 63; African American, 127; and Civil War, 122; and social work, 126

Interconnectedness, Caribbean, 587–88

Interdependence, realist fiction and, 200

Internal colonization, 650, 654–55

Internalization, in realist fiction, 199

International aid agencies, 668–69

International copyright, lack of, 12

Interracial community, post–Civil War views, 246–48, 261

Interracial marriage, as theme, 122

Interrelation of social categories, 217

Intimacy, forced, of slavery, 90–91

Invisibility, social, 545–46; privileged, of rich people, 197

Irigaray, Luce, 723

Irish ethnic novels, 384, 395–98, 403, 404

Irony: Fitzgerald and, 324; Millhauser and, 749, 751; in Western fiction, 445

Irving, Washington, 7, 11, 12, 57–59, 72, 786; *The Alhambra*, 58; *Bracebridge Hall*, 58; and fiction, 9–10; *History of New York*, 58–59; *The Sketch Book of Geoffrey Crayon, Gent.*, 58–59

Isherwood, Christopher, 451

Islas, Arturo, 521, 522, 524, 528–29, 530; *Migrant Souls*, 522, 530, 531–32; *The Rain God*, 453, 522, 530–31

Italian ethnic novels, 384–85, 398–401, 404–5

Jackson, Helen Hunt, 241, 438, 786; *Ramona*, 260–61, 438; movie of, 370

Jackson, Shirley: *Life Among the Savages*, 507; "The Lottery," 507; *We Have Always Lived in the Castle*, 507

Jackson, William Henry, 370

Jacobs, Barbara, 623

Jacobs, Harriet, 127, 786; *Incidents in the Life of a Slave Girl, Written by Herself*, 39, 40–43, 105, 153

Jaffe, Rona, *The Best of Everything*, 506

Jamaica: novels from, 590, 598–600; slave revolt, 97

James, C. L. R., 592–93; *The Black Jacobins*, 593; *The Case for West Indian Self-Goverment*, 593; *Minty Alley*, 592, 593; "Triumph," 592

James, Henry, 188, 196, 787; *The American*, preface to, 74; "American Heiress," 191; *The Art of Fiction*, 161; *The Awkward Age*, 200–201, 203; bosses viewed by, 197; and Civil War, 240; and Davis, 162; Fitzgerald and, 324; *The Golden Bowl*, 168; Howells and, 182; influences on, 271–72; *In the Cage*, 197–99; "The Jolly Corner," 168; *The Portrait of a Lady*, 162–68; realism of, 168; and romance, 74; typecasting, 200; *The Wings of the Dove*, 168

James, William, 312, 313; Stein and, 211; *The Varieties of Religious Experience*, 195

Jameson, Fredric, 378, 517, 518, 521, 568, 699; "Postmodernism; or, The Cultural Logic of Late Capitalism," 538–39

Janklow, Morton, 684

Japanese Americans, 499–500

Japanese culture, Hearn and, 254

Jasmin, Claude, *Pleure pas, Germaine*, 571

Jazz, 409

Jazz Age, Fitzgerald and, 323

Jefferson, Thomas, 13, 53, 54, 56; *Notes on the State of Virginia*, 93, 102; and reform, 132; and slavery, 93, 102

Jewett, Sarah Orne, 159, 273, 282, 787–88; Cather and, 279; *The Country of the Pointed Firs*, 250–51, 253–54, 255; regionalism of, 252–54, 255

Jewish Americans, novels by, 495, 497–99

Jewish ethnic novels, 384–87, 402; depression years, 393

Jim Crow laws, 411, 430

Joaquín Blanco, Jose, 628

*Joaul* (Québécois dialect), 571

John Reed Clubs, 343–44

Johns Hopkins Medical School, 211–12

Johnson, Amelia, 283

Johnson, Diane, *The Shadow Knows*, 461

Johnson, Dorothy, 457

Johnson, Edward, *The Wonder-Working Providence of Sions Saviour in New-England*, 31, 468

Johnson, James Weldon, *The Autobiography of an Ex-Coloured Man*, 278, 416
Johnson, Philip, 516
Johnston, Mary, *To Have and to Hold*, 259
Jolas, Eugene, 327
Jonas, George, *Final Decree*, 574
Jones, "Buffalo," 370
Jones, Douglas C., 455
Jones, James, 788; *From Here to Eternity*, 491
Jones, LeRoi. *See* Baraka, Amiri
Jones, Marion Patrick: *Jouvert Morning*, 605; *Pan Beat*, 605
Jordan, Winthrop, 91
Journalism: late nineteenth century, 250; sociological, 381
Joyce, James, 314, 327, 654; and Barnes, 328; *Dubliners*, 313; *Finnegans Wake*, 327; *A Portrait of the Artist as a Young Man*, 313, 327; Pound and, 313; *Ulysses*, 326
Judicial system, mid-twentieth-century novels and, 490
Judson, E. Z. C. *See* Buntline, Ned
Justice, in Western fiction, 368
Juvenile fiction: dime novels, 294; early twentieth century, 357–58; nickel series, 300

Kadushin, Arthur, *Books: The Culture and Commerce of Publishing*, 683–86
Kafka, Franz, 524
Kang, Younghill, 383; *East Goes West*, 405
Kaplan, Louis, *Bibliography of American Autobiographies*, 28
Kattan, Naim, 574
Kazan, Elia, *America! America!*, 404
Kazin, Alfred, 395; *A Walker in the City*, 404
Keckley, Elizabeth, 127
Keeble, John, *Yellowfish*, 461
Kelley, Emma Dunham, 283
Kennedy, John F., 490
Kennedy, Louise, 671

Kenner, Hugh, 744; *A Homemade World*, 313
Kerouac, Jack, 739; *The Dharma Bums*, 447; *On the Road*, 446, 493
Kerr, Jean: *Please Don't Eat the Daisies*, 507; *The Snake Has All the Lines*, 507
Kerslake, Susan, *Penumbra*, 566
Kesey, Ken, *One Flew Over the Cuckoo's Nest*, 447–48, 493
Kessler-Harris, Alice, 389
Khan, Ismith, 600; *The Jumbie Bird*, 602; *The Obeah Man*, 602
Kincaid, Jamaica, 604–5, 653, 669–70, 670–72; *Annie John*, 595, 605, 671; *At the Bottom of the River*, 671; *Lucy*, 605, 671, 672; *A Small Place*, 672
King, Stephen, *Misery*, 87
King, Thomas, *Medicine River*, 576
Kingston, Maxine Hong, 406, 462, 463, 521, 522, 524, 528–29, 533, 653, 669, 788; *China Men*, 463, 522, 533–34; *Tripmaster Monkey*, 463, 522; *The Woman Warrior*, 463, 522, 533
Kingston, Paul W., *The Wages of Writing*, 681–82
Kinsella, Thomas, *Shoeless Joe*, 581–82
Kinsey, Alfred C., *Sexual Behavior in the Human Male*, 546
Kipling, Rudyard, 658; influence of, 263; "A White Man's Burden," 249
Kirby, William, *The Golden Dog*, 562
Kirkland, Caroline, 788
Kirkland, Joseph, *Zury*, 255
Kitsch, postmodern fiction as, 690–91
Klein, Marcus, 345, 393
Klinkowitz, Jerome, 448, 732, 736–37
Knight, Sarah Kemble, *The Journal of Madam Knight*, 33–34
Kogawa, Joy, 406, 567, 573–74, 653, 788–89; *Obasan*, 574, 575
Kollwitz, Käthe, 178
Kostelanetz, Richard, 686
Kramer, Hilton, 517, 518
Kramer, Larry, *Faggots*, 549
Krause, Herbert, *Wind Without Rain*, 441

Krauze, Ethel, 628–29
Kreiner, Philip: *Contact Prints*, 564; *Heartlands*, 584
Kristeva, Julia, 700
Kroetsch, Robert, 564, 565, 566, 585; *Badlands*, 580, 582; *Gone Indian*, 563
Kromer, Tom, *Waiting for Nothing*, 340–41
Kruger, Barbara, 516
Krupat, Arnold, 43, 44
*Künstlerroman*, Canadian, 580
Kureishi, Hanif, 653, 659, 661–65; *The Buddha of Suburbia*, 663–65; "The Rainbow Sign," 661–62
*Kyk-over-al* (literary review), 593

Laberge, Albert, *La Scouine* (*Bitter Bread*), 569
Labor movement, 148, 322
Labor unrest, 158, 327
Lacombe, Patrice, *La terre paternelle*, 568
*Ladies' Home Journal*, 371
Ladoo, Harold Sonny, *Yesterdays*, 575
La Farge, Oliver, *Laughing Boy*, 409
Lamming, George, 587, 589, 594–96, 600; *The Emigrants*, 594, 595; *In the Castle of My Skin*, 589, 594, 595; *Natives of My Person*, 594, 595; *Of Age and Innocence*, 594; *The Pleasures of Exile*, 595–96; *Season of Adventure*, 594, 595; *Water with Berries*, 595, 595
L'Amour, Louis, 440
Land, importance of: in frontier novels, 438; in Western fiction, 441, 446–47, 459–60
Landon, Brooks, 449
Langer, Elinor, 355
Language: Abish and, 737; Barth and, 730–31; class differences and, 174–75; colonialism and, 655–56; dialects, 251, 571; of early American novels, 11; experimental, Stein and, 215; Gass and, 741; Millhauser and, 747; New Critics and, 488; postcolonial, 661; postmodernism and,

700; of realism, 172; and reality, 448, 620–21; of social types, 191; women's appropriation of, 641–42
Lapolla, Garibaldi Marto, 398
Larsen, Nella, 411, 420; *Quicksand*, 421
Larson, Magalia, 568, 691
Late nineteenth century: realism, 160–88; women's status, 269
Late twentieth century: literary marketplace, 679–96; postmodern fiction, 697–725
Latin American fiction, 607–48
Latin American immigrant writers, 406
Laughlin, James, 693
Laurence, Margaret, 584, 789; *A Bird in the House*, 580; *The Diviners*, 578; *The Stone Angel*, 564, 578
Law: of immigration, 381, 406; status of, in Western fiction, 368
Lawrence, D. H.: influence on Le Sueur, 350–51; *The Rainbow*, 314; *Studies in Classic American Literature*, 51
Lea, Tom, 461
Leacock, Stephen, *Sunshine Sketches of a Little Town*, 560, 561
League of American Writers, 344
Leal, Luis, 524
Lean, David, *A Passage to India* (film), 658
Leatherstocking tales, Cooper, 294, 437
Leavis, F. R., *The Great Tradition*, 488
Leavitt, David, *The Lost Language of Cranes*, 551
Lecker, Robert, 578
Lederer, William J., *The Ugly American*, 490
Lee, Ann, 133
Lee, C. Y., *The Flower Drum Song*, 500
Lee, Dennis, 579
Lee, Eliza Buckminster, *Parthenia*, 119–20
Lee, Harper, *To Kill a Mockingbird*, 490
Lee, Manfred (Ellery Queen), 802

Lee, Sky, *Disappearing Moon Cafe*, 574

Left, political, and sexuality of women, 351. *See also* Communism; Communist Party

Legal status of women, nineteenth century, 65, 142–43

Le Guin, Ursula, 789; *Always Coming Home*, 460

Leiber, Fritz, *Gather Darkness*, 365

Lemelin, Roger, *Au pied de la pente douce (The Town Below)*, 569

Leonard, John, 661

Leprohon, Rosanna, *Antoinette de Mirecourt; or, Secret Marrying and Secret Sorrowing, a Canadian Tale*, 562

Lesbianism, 279, 545; Barnes and, 328
—literature of, 501, 551–52; Latin American, 629–30; postwar, 505

Lesley, Craig, *Winterkill*, 461

Le Sueur, Meridel, 326, 332, 339, 350–53, 457; "Annunciation," 351; *The Girl*, 332, 350–51; *Harvest Song*, 352; *I Hear Men Talking*, 332, 351, 352–53; "I Was Marching," 353; "Spring Story," 351; "What Happens in a Strike," 352; "Women on the Breadlines," 352

Levin, Meyer, *The Old Bunch*, 393

Levine, Robert, 72

Lewis, H. H., 344

Lewis, R. W. B., 395; *The American Adam*, 489

Lewis, Sinclair, 271, 335; *Main Street*, 283

Lewis, Wyndham, 317

Lewisohn, Ludwig, *The Island Within*, 387

Leyner, Mark, *My Cousin, My Gastroenterologist*, 484

Libbey, Laura Jean, 159, 293, 297–300; *Leonie Locke; or, The Romance of a Beautiful New York Working-Girl*, 299

Liberalism, 50

Liberal sociology, 197

Liberation, rhetoric of, 647

*The Liberator*, 141, 346

Liberty, gothic novels and, 22–23

"Libraries," publishers' series, 53

Liebowitz, Herbert, *Fabricating Lives: Explorations in American Autobiography*, 29

Limitations, avant-garde and, 732, 751

Lincoln, Abraham, and *Uncle Tom's Cabin*, 144

Ling, Amy, 277

Linguistic alienation, Latin American, 613

Linguistic excess, in avant-garde fiction, 732

Linn, James Weber, 396

Lippard, George, 48, 51, 148, 288, 789; *New York: Its Upper Ten and Lower Million*, 148; *The Quaker City; or, The Monks of Monk Hall*, 47, 54, 138, 148

Lispector, Clarice, 624–25, 636–37, 790; *Água viva*, 625, 636–37; *Family Ties*, 625; "The Fifth Story," 637; *The Passion According to G.H.*, 625

Literacy, 49, 693

Literary canon, 56, 128–29, 178; and financial success, 70

Literary criticism. *See* Criticism, literary

Literary culture: antebellum, 51; economy and, 49; regional, 407–8

Literary fiction, publication of, 683–84

Literary Guild, 685

Literary historians, and nineteenth-century women, 111–15

Literary reviews, West Indies, 592, 593

Literary Western novels, 437–64

Literature: American, 6–7; early American views, 12; mass marketing, nineteenth century, 53; mid-twentieth-century views, 488; postmodern, 516; television and, 480–84; Vargas Llosa's views, 623

Little magazines, 407, 414

Littlepage trilogy, Cooper, 143

*Little Review*, 312

Liveright, Horace, 393; and Yezierska, 388

Living gospel, women as, 124

Loaeza, Guadalupe, 632

Local color, 250–56; Cable and, 244; economic depression and, 392; Western, 438

Locke, Alain, 28; *The New Negro*, 421

Locklin, Gerald, *The Case of the Missing Blue Volkswagen*, 450

Lockwood, John, *An Essay on Flogging*, 149

Loeb, Harold, 320

London, Jack, 263, 335, 790; *The Call of the Wild*, 264–65; *The Iron Heel*, 236–37, 341; *Martin Eden*, 439; *People of the Abyss*, 236; and primordial violence, 264–65; *The Sea-Wolf*, 264, 439; *White Fang*, 264, 265–66

Long, Edward, *History of Jamaica*, 89, 103

Long, Huey P., 415

Longfellow, Henry Wadsworth, *Poems on Slavery*, Poe's comments, 96

Lorde, Audre, 670

Los Angeles, novels of, 451, 454

Loss of control, fear of, Hawthorne and, 136

Lost generation novelists, 314–15

Love, Glen A., 447

Love: between women, Cather and, 279–80; possession and, 95; romantic, nineteenth-century ideas, 124–25; slavery and, Poe's views, 99–100; in Western fiction, 368–69

Lovelace, Earl, 592, 600, 602–3, 653; *The Dragon Can't Dance*, 603; *The Wine of Astonishment*, 603

Lovett, Robert Morss, 396

Lower classes: naturalist fiction, 202–4; observation of, 197–98; realist fiction, 197–99

—white: social reformers and, 147–49; Stowe and, 146

Loyalty, individualism and, 195

Lugones, Leopoldo, 610–11

Luhan, Mabel Dodge, 409

Lukács, Georg, 157–58

Lurie, Alison, 451, 505, 790–91

Luska, Sidney. *See* Harland, Henry

Lyotard, Jean-François, 366, 516, 521, 691, 714

Lytle, Andrew, 416

Mabbott, Thomas O., 104

McCarthy, Joseph, 486

McCarthy, Mary, 793; *The Group*, 505

*McClure's* magazine, 386

McCorkle, Jill, *The Cheer Leader*, 481

McCoy, Horace, *They Shoot Horses, Don't They?*, 450

McCullers, Carson, 429–30, 505, 793; *The Ballad of the Sad Café*, 505; *The Heart Is a Lonely Hunter*, 505; *The Member of the Wedding*, 429, 505

McCutcheon, George Barr, *Graustark*, 259

MacDermott, Thomas (Tom Redcam): *Becka's Buckra Baby*, 590; *One Brown Girl and — : A Jamaican Story*, 590

McDonald, Ian, *The Hummingbird Tree*, 595

McGregor, Gaile, *The Wacousta Syndrome*, 559

McGuane, Thomas, 449–50, 793–94; *Keep the Change*, 450

McHale, Brian, 703

Machine: symbolism of, 466–67; technology, 465–66

McKay, Claude, 332, 346, 383, 422, 591–92, 794; *Banana Bottom*, 348, 591–92, 600; *Banjo*, 347–48, 591; *Home to Harlem*, 346–47, 591; *The Negroes in America*, 346; *Trial by Lynching*, 346

McLean, Kathryn Anderson. *See* Forbes, Kathryn

McLennan, Hugh: "Boy Meets Girl in Winnipeg: Who Cares?," 560; *The Watch That Ends the Night*, 578

McLennan, J. F., *Primitive Marriage*, 200

McLuhan, Marshall, *The Gutenberg Galaxy*, 485

McMurtry, Larry: *All My Friends Are Going to Be Strangers*, 460; *Cadillac Jack*, 460; *The Desert Rose*, 460; *Horseman, Pass By*, 460; *The Last Picture Show*, 460; *Leaving Chey-*

McMurtry, Larry (*Continued*)
enne, 460; *Lonesome Dove*, 460–
61; *Moving On*, 460; *Somebody's
Darling*, 460; *Terms of Endearment*,
460
McNally, William, *Evils and Abuses
in the Naval Merchant Service*,
149
McNickle, D'Arcy, 455
McPartland, John, *No Down Payment*,
507
McWhorter, Lucullus Virgil, 280–82
Madison, Charles, 359
Magazines: communist, 343–44; late
nineteenth century, 158; limited-
circulation, 681; literary, 407;
middle-brow, 303
Magdalene Societies, 137
Magic realism, 457, 522–28; Canadian,
565; García Márquez and, 618
Mahan, A. T., 258
Mailer, Norman, 403, 791; *Advertise-
ments for Myself*, 493; *An American
Dream*, 493; *The Armies of the
Night*, 493; *The Executioner's Song*,
449; *The Naked and the Dead*, 493;
"The White Negro," 493; *Why Are
We in Vietnam?*, 449
Maillet, Antonine, 791; *Pélagie-La-
Charrett*, 572
Mail-order book clubs, 359
Mais, Roger, 592, 593, 594, 598; *Black
Lightning*, 599; *Brother Man*, 599,
600; *The Hills Were Joyful To-
gether*, 599
Major, André, 579
Majors, Charles, *When Knighthood
Was in Flower*, 259
Makhoere, Caeserina Kona, 651
Malamud, Bernard, 498, 674, 792; *The
Assistant*, 403; "Fidelman" stories,
403; *The Fixer*, 498; *The Natural*,
492; *A New Life*, 449; *The Tenants*,
498
Male novels: antebellum, 51; environ-
ment literature, 507–9
Male writers, 689–90, 694, 695, 696;
Canadian, 580; domestic fiction by,
52; postmodern, 698; and women,

277, 283; working-class, fiction by,
336
—nineteenth century, 46, 56–59,
114, 117–18; motivation for writ-
ing, 66–67; quality of work, 128;
and women, 69–70, 113–15
Manfred, Frederick, 792; *The Golden
Bowl*, 443, 458; *The Manly-Hearted
Woman*, 455; *Riders of Judgment*,
443
Mangione, Jerre, 398–401; *Mount Alle-
gro*, 400–401, 404
Manhood in battle, views of, 249–50
Manifest Destiny doctrine, 288
Mann, Horace, 148
Mann, Thomas, 750; *Buddenbrooks*,
314
Marchessault, Jovette, *La Mère des herbes (Mother of the Grass)*, 581
Marginality, 666–67
Marginalization of postcolonial writers,
651
Marinello, Juan, 613
Marinetti, Filippo, 317
Marketplace, literary, 685; early Ameri-
can, 46–71; and environment litera-
ture, 507; ethnicity and, 381–406;
late twentieth century, 679–96; and
marginality, 666
Market society, 50; literature in, 48–49;
postmodern, 518–20; and realist
writing, 161; self defined by,
166–67
Markoosie, *Harpoon of the Hunter*,
576
Marks, Elaine, 641
Marlatt, Daphne, *Ana Historic*, 565
Marlyn, John, 574
Marovitz, Sanford E., 455
Marriage, 143; late nineteenth century,
200–201; in Oneida community,
134; in Western fiction, 367–68
Married Women's Property Act (1848),
143
Marshall, Paule, 406, 653, 669, 792;
*Brown Girl, Brownstones*, 497, 670;
*The Chosen Place, the Timeless Peo-
ple*, 670; *Praisesong for the Widow*,
670; "Shaping the World of My

Art," 670; *Soul Clap Hands and Sing,* 670

Martian novels, Burroughs, 362–63

Martin, Helen Reimensnyder, *Tillie, a Mennonite Maid,* 383

Marx, Leo, *The Machine in the Garden,* 489

Marxism, 485–86; and postmodernism, 516–17, 522

Masculinity: nineteenth-century ideas, 111–12, 115–16; Norris's view, 263

Masiello, Francine, 642

Mason, Bobbie Ann, 482

Massachusetts, Board of Aliens Commission, 192

Massachusetts Society for the Suppression of Intemperance, 137

Mass culture: multicultural, 517–18; realism, 535–37

*The Masses,* 337

Mass market, 53, 359; lesbian paperbacks, 501; nineteenth century, 285–305; postmodern fiction and, 690–91

Mass media: and popular culture, 286; publishing and, 686

Master-slave relationship, Poe's view, 98

Mastery: abuses of, in antislavery fiction, 141, 145; sexual, 153

Mather, Cotton: *Diary,* 31; *Magnalia Christi Americana,* 31; *Paterna,* 31

Mather, Increase, 468; *Wo to Drunkards,* 136

Mathews, John Joseph, 455, 793

Matisse, Henri, 316; *La Femme au Chapeau,* 314

Matthiessen, F. O., *American Renaissance,* 128

Matto de Turner, Clorinda, *Aves sin nido,* 611

Mayz Valenilla, E., 608

MCA, 687

Meatpacking industry, reform of, 238

Medina, Enrique: *Strip-Tease,* 632–33; *Las tumbas,* 632

Meditative realism, postmodern, 537

Meigs, Mary, 760

Meller, Sidney, *Roots in the Sky,* 393

Melodramas: dime novels, 294–97; story paper, 288–90

Melville, Herman, 7, 8, 60–62, 66–70, 72, 84, 149, 335, 783, 794–95; and American writers, 128; "Bartleby, the Scrivener," 51, 84, 91, 176, 179; "Benito Cereno," 87, 90–91, 99, 150–51; *Billy Budd, Sailor,* 87, 193–95; *The Confidence-Man,* 74, 88, 106, 138; and domestic novels, 112–13; and fiction, 73–74; "Hawthorne and His Mosses," 112, 128; *Israel Potter,* 465; *Mardi,* 73, 80–81; *Moby-Dick,* 8, 51, 68, 84, 86–87, 90, 106–7, 138, 467, 479–80; *Omoo,* 80; "The Paradise of Bachelors and the Tartarus of Maids," 138; *Pierre; or, The Ambiguities,* 62–64, 67–70, 98, 106, 112–13; and race, 90–91; *Redburn,* 51, 61, 138, 149, 162; and reform, 149–50; and romance, 80–81; and slavery, 99, 106; and technology, 479–80; temperance themes, 138; *Typee,* 61, 80; *White-Jacket,* 51, 61, 138, 149–50; work novels, 51

Memoirs, autobiographical, Native Americans and, 45

Memory, and autobiography, 29

Men, readers of popular fiction, 359. *See also* Male writers; Masculinity

Mena, María Cristina, 271

Menand, Louis, 691

Menchú, Rioberta, *Me llamo Rigoberta Menchú y así me nació la conciencia,* 646

Mencken, H. L., 342, 420–21; "The Sahara of the Bozarts," 417; and South, 417–18

Mendelson, Edward, 717

Mendes, Alfred H., 592, 593; *Black Fauns,* 592; *Pitch Lake,* 592

Menippean satire, 450, 705

Mental colonization, 650, 654, 655

Mesmerism, Hawthorne and, 135–36

Metafictional strategies, 700–703; in Barth's fiction, 711–12; in Nabo-

Metafictional strategies (*Continued*)
kov's fiction, 708–10; of Vonnegut,
722
Metalious, Grace, *Peyton Place*, 506
Mexican American writers, 453, 500–
501; postmodern realist, 530
Mexican women, first novel in English
by, 271
Mexico: fiction in, 628–32; Spanish
conquest, 258
Middle class: African American, 411,
420–41; book market, 46; ethnic
writers, 402–6; and fiction, 50; and
industrial working conditions, 223–
24; and novel reading, 688–89; realist literature and, 158, 197
—intellectuals: 1920s, 337; leftist,
353–54
—women: Howells and, 183–84;
moral reform societies, 137; nineteenth century, 114; and workers,
173, 177
Migrations: African American, 408;
contemporary, 649–51; postcolonial,
659, 678
Millenialists, 133
Millhauser, Steven, 746–51, 795; *The
Barnum Museum*, 748–49; *Cartoons*, 747; *Edwin Mullhouse*, 747–
48; *In the Penny Arcade*, 748
Mills, C. Wright, *The Power Elite*,
485
Mills, Nicolaus, 72
Minimalism, postmodern, 535–36
Minister, Edith May Dowe, *Our Natupski Neighbors*, 383
Minority groups, 652–53, 669; and au-
tobiography, 27; early American, 9;
internal colonization, 655; novels of
identity, 494–95
Minority writers, proletarian fiction,
333
*Mise en abîme*, 702; Acker, 723; Von-
negut, 722
Missionary Westerns, Canadian, 562
Mistral, Gabriela, 609
Mitchell, Donald, 114
Mitchell, Margaret, 795; *Gone With
the Wind*, 389

Mitchell, S. Weir, 231; *Hugh Wynne,
Free Quaker*, 259
Mitchell, W. O.: *The Vanishing Point*,
563; *Who Has Seen the Wind*, 578
Mittelholzer, Edgar, 593, 594, 597–98;
*Children of Kaywana*, 598; *Coren-
tyne Thunder*, 598; *The Harrowing
of Hubertus*, 598; *Kaywana Blood*,
598; *A Morning at the Office*, 598;
*Shadows Move Among Them*, 598
Modern art movement, 311
*Modern Electrics* (magazine), 360
Modernism, 311–30, 476, 516, 697;
Emerson and, 470; of Faulkner,
427; immigrant novels, 394–95;
metafictional situations, 702; Pound
and, 465–66; in proletarian fiction,
345–46; Stegner and, 452
Modernization, Western novels and,
369–71
Modleski, Tania, 378
Molesworth, Charles, 743, 749
Molloy, Sylvia, 629
Momaday, N. Scott, 453–55, 457, 795–
96; *The Ancient Child*, 457; *House
Made of Dawn*, 453–55, 456; *The
Way to Rainy Mountain*, 454
Money: Davis and, 176; early realists
and, 188; evil and, in James's view,
167; Twain and, 171–72
Monk, Maria, *Awful Disclosures of the
Hotel Dieu Nunnery*, 147
Monomania: and caricature, 83–84;
and revenge, 86–87
Monroe, Harriet, 312
Montaigne, Michel de, *Essays*, 26
Montana Kid series, Brand, 440
Montejo, Esteban, autobiography, 646
Montgomery, Lucy Maud, *Anne of
Green Gables*, 561
Monthly magazines, 303
Moore, Brian, *The Luck of Ginger Cof-
fey*, 574–75
Moral difference between sexes, domes-
ticity and, 124–26
Moral improvement, novels of, 219
Moral realism, 488
Moral reform societies, 137
Moral standards, women and, 126, 219

Moral value: nineteenth century, 65–67; post–World War II, 491–92

Moral vision, 10–11; in Cooper's novels, 23–25

More, Hannah, *Strictures on the Modern System of Female Education*, 118–19, 120

Morejón, Nancy, 610

Mori, Toshio, 796; *The Woman from Hiroshima*, 462–63; *Yokohama, California*, 500

Mormons, 133

Moroso, John Antonio, 398

Morrell, Benjamin, *Narrative of Four Voyages*, 107

Morris, Wright, 443, 445, 796; *Ceremony in Lone Tree*, 445; *The Field of Vision*, 444–45; *Love Among the Cannibals*, 445; *Plains Song*, 445

Morrison, Toni, 505, 520–22, 524, 528–29, 796–97; *Beloved*, 87, 105; *The Bluest Eye*, 670; *Song of Solomon*, 522, 529, 530; *Sula*, 522, 529–30; *Tar Baby*, 529

Morton, Perez, 15–16

Mother figures, African American writers and, 434–35

Motherhood: nineteenth-century ideas, 116; Revolutionary-era idea, 115

Motherwell, Robert, 750

Motivation for writing, nineteenth century, 65–67

Mott, Frank Luther, 303

Mott, Lucretia, 142

Mountain men, novels about, 447

Mourning Dove. *See* Hum-ishu-ma

Movements, reform, 132–33

Movies. *See* Cinema

Muckraking journalism, 236

Mugwump reform, 157

Mukherjee, Bharati, 653, 669–70, 672–78; *Darkness*, 672–74, 676; *Jasmine*, 671, 674, 675, 677–78; *The Middleman and Other Stories*, 676–77; *The Tiger's Daughter*, 674–75; *Wife*, 674, 675

Muller, Arnold, *Bram of the Five Corners*, 383

Multicultural mass culture, 517–18

Multinational culture, postmodern, 699

Mumford, Lewis, 360

Munro, Alice: *The Beggar Maid*, 560; *Lives of Girls and Women*, 561, 580; *Who Do You Think You Are?*, 560

Munro, George, 291

Munro, Norman, 291

Munsey, Frank, 359

Murder mysteries. *See* Detective fiction

Murfree, Mary, *In the "Stranger People's" Country*, 252

Murray, Anna, 39

Murray, John, 80

Murray, Judith Sargent, 115

Music: popular, mass culture, 517; postmodern, 516

Mystic experiences, Native American accounts, 43–44

Nabokov, Vladimir, 327, 699, 704–7, 797; *Ada*, 699, 708; *Lolita*, 699, 707, 710; *Pale Fire*, 699, 702, 707–9, 710

Naipaul, Shiva, 600, 602; *The Chip-Chip Gatherers*, 602; *The Fireflies*, 602

Naipaul, V. S., 587–89, 594, 600, 601–2; *A Bend in the River*, 602; *The Enigma of Arrival*, 595, 601, 602; *Guerrillas*, 601, 602; *A House for Mr. Biswas*, 601–2; *The Middle Passage*, 601; *Miguel Street*, 601; *The Mimic Men*, 595, 601, 602; *The Mystic Masseur*, 601–2; *The Suffrage of Elvira*, 601–2

Narrative, x–xi; autobiographical, 26–28; Latin American, 611, 625–26; marketplace for, 695; postmodern voices, 704

Narrative frames, breaking of, 703

Nashoba Community, 820

Nashville Fugitives, 408, 414

Nation, Carry, 236

National Coming Out Day, 552

National consciousness, West Indian, 590

National identity, 243–44; African Americans and, 248; *Connecticut Yankee* and, 257; racism and, 263; regionalism and, 251

Nationalism: Canadian, 566; cultural, West Indian, 592; in dime novels, 294; postmodern, 519; story papers and, 288, 289

National literature, post–Civil War, 241

National mind, Stein's idea, 213

National narrative, technology and, 468

National reconciliation, post–Civil War: *Connecticut Yankee* and, 257; as fiction theme, 240–41, 243–49, 439; regionalism and, 251; Twain and, 245–46

National traditions, 259

National unity, symbols of, 262

Nationhood, 241–42

Native American Renaissance, 456–57

Native Americans, 260–61, 409; autobiographical writings, early, 43–44; Canadian, 575–77; Canadian fiction and, 563; captivity narratives and, 31–32; colonialization and, 30; Eastlake's view, 445; Faulkner and, 427; fiction of, 453–57; nineteenth century, 268; in Southern states, 412; women authors, 270–71, 280–82

Nativism, nineteenth century, 146–47

Naturalism, 697; economic depression and, 392; historical context, 263; immigrant novels, 394; James and, 200, 202; late nineteenth century, 157–59, 202–4; and national identity, 263; in Phelps's work, 226–27; in proletarian fiction, 345; and reform fiction, 225; Western, 438

Nature writers, environmentalists, 459

Naval reform, 149

Negroes. *See* African Americans

Nelson, Cary, 333

Nelson, Jane, 460

Neobaroque style, Latin American, 612–13

Neogothic fiction, 327

Neorealism: African American writers, 496; Mailer and, 493; war novels, 491; in Western fiction, 461, 462

Neruda, Pablo, 609

Nettleford, Rex, 656

Neutral territory, for romance, Hawthorne's idea, 75–76

Nevèrÿon series, Delany, 705

New, W. H., 584

*The New Criterion*, 517

New Criticism, 330, 488

"New ethnics," 405–6

New Harmony Society, 133

Newman, Charles, 690, 699, 734, 739, 742; *The Post–Modern Aura*, 687, 734–35

*The New Masses*, 344, 353

"New Negroes," 409, 421; Hurston and, 422

Newspapers, and fiction, 50, 203–4

New-wave literature, Mexican, 631–32

*New World* (story paper), 287

New York City: black population, 411; as literary center, 407

*The New Yorker*, 508

*New York Ledger* (story paper), 287, 289

New York State, Married Women's Property Act, 143

New York State Temperance Society, 137

*New York Times*, and Kerouac's *On the Road*, 446

*New York Times Book Review*: and Puzo's *The Fortunate Pilgrim*, 405; and Roth's *Call It Sleep*, 395

*New York Tribune*, dime novel advertisements, 293

*New York Weekly* (story paper), 287, 294, 297

New York Workingman's Party, 148

*New York World*, 250

Ngugi wa Thiong'o, 656, 668

Nichols, John, 449; *American Blood*, 450

Nichols, Mary Gove, 137

Nichols, Mary Sargeant, *Mary Lyndon*, 144

Nickel series, 287, 300, 301–2

Nietzsche, Friedrich Wilhelm, 750
Niggli, Josephina, *Mexican Village*, 501
Nineteenth Amendment, 269
Nineteenth century, 4–5; book market, 46–71; captivity narratives, 32; domestic novels, 110–29; immigration, 380; influence of women, 113–17, 124–25; Native American autobiography, 44; publishing, 52–54; science fiction, 361; sentimental novels, 52; social reform movements, 216; symbolism of machinery, 471
Non-European immigrants, 383
Nonfictional texts, in postmodern fiction, 704
Nonfiction novels, 449
Nonfiction writing, income from, 682
Nonnarratable state, science fiction, 364
Nonverbal forms, cultural memory and, 656
Non-Western cultures, domesticity and, 122
Norris, Frank, 263, 271, 283, 797–98; "The Frontier Gone at Last," 263; *McTeague*, 203, 225, 226, 263, 439; naturalist fiction, 203, 204; *The Octopus*, 261–63, 439, 471; *The Pit*, 225; *Responsibilities of the Novelist*, 267; *Vandover and the Brute*, 203, 264
Norris, Kathleen, *Mother*, 373
*North American Review*, dime novel reviews, 293
Northern states, nineteenth-century racism, 153
*Norton Anthology of American Literature*, 177
Norwegian-American novels, 389
Nourbese Philip, Marlene, 653, 670; *She Tries Her Tongue: her silence softly breaks*, 656–57
Nova Scotia, 572
*Novela de la tierra*, 611
*Novela de la transa*, 628, 631, 632–33, 641
Novelistic techniques in autobiography, 42–43, 45

Novelists: early American, 14; late nineteenth century, and sociology, 190–215; women as, Norris's view, 267–68. *See also* Women, as writers; Writers
Novels, x–xi, 9, 665; abolitionist, 141–43, 150–54; audience for, 688–90; avant-garde, 727–51; capitalism and, 344; early American, 6–25; eighteenth century, 3–5; Hawthorne's idea, 73; nineteenth century, 57, 157–58; and social reform, 131–54; writing of, nineteenth-century views, 116–17
Nowlan, Alden, *Various Persons Named Kevin O'Brien*, 561
Noyes, John Humphrey, 134
Nugent, Lady Maria, Jamaica journal, 89
Nunez-Harrell, Elizabeth, 605

Oates, Joyce Carol, 505, 520, 521, 535, 536–37, 798; "Where Are You Going, Where Have You Been?," 537
O'Brien, Edward J., 387, 399
O'Brien, Fitz-James, 395
O'Brien, Sharon, 278
O'Brien, Tim, 798
Ocampo, Silvina, 623
Ocampo, Victoria, 623
Occom, Samson, *Sermon Preached at the Execution of Moses Paul*, 43
Occupational ideals of nineteenth-century writers, 67–68
O'Connor, Edwin, 403
O'Connor, Flannery, 430, 491; *Everything That Rises Must Converge*, 414; *The Violent Bear It Away*, 414; *Wise Blood*, 414, 491
*October*, 517
Odets, Clifford, *Waiting for Lefty*, 341
Odum, Howard, 412
Offensiveness, avant-garde and, 727–28
O'Gorman, Edmundo, *The Invention of America*, 607
O'Hagan, Howard, 798; *Tay John*, 562–63
O'Hara, John, 395, 451

Ohmann, Richard, "The Shaping of a Canon: U.S. Fiction, 1960–1975," 692, 694

Okada, John, 405, 799; *No-No Boy*, 463, 500

Olerich, Henry, *A Cityless and Countryless World: An Outline of Practical Co-operative Individualism*, 474–75

Oliva, Gladstone, 527

Olsen, Tillie, 344, 346, 350, 799; "The Iron Throat," 355; *Silences*, 458; *Tell Me a Riddle*, 404; *Yonnondio: From the Thirties*, 332, 338, 355–56, 393, 458

Ondaatje, Michael, 567, 800; *The Collected Works of Billy the Kid*, 579; *Running in the Family*, 579

Oneida community, 134

O'Neill, Eugene, 395

Onoto Watanna (Winnifred Eaton), 270, 277–78, 282, 283; *A Japanese Nightingale*, 278; *Me*, 278

Oppositionalism in avant-garde fiction, 732

Oral forms, 667, 669; Native American autobiography, 44

Ordonez, Cayetano, 320

Orphans, in women's novels, 123, 127

Orphée, Elvira, 623

Orrego, Claudio, *Detenidos-desaparecidos: Una herida abierta*, 647

Ostenso, Martha, 389, 391–92; *Wild Geese*, 391, 392

Otherness, race and, 409–11

Outlaws, dime novels and, 294, 296

Owen, Robert, 133

Owen, Wilfred, 318

Pagano, Jo, 398

Page, Myra, 350; *Gathering Storm: A Story of the Black Belt*, 338, 352

Page, Thomas Nelson, *In Ole Virginia*, 244

Palfrey, Gorham: Emerson and, 130

Panetta, George, 398

Panneton, Philippe. *See* Ringuet

Panunzio, Constantine, *The Soul of an Immigrant*, 398

Paperback books, 359, 504, 685–86

Papermaking improvements, 49

Paradis, Suzanne, 572

Paralyzed artist theme, 565–66

Paris: Americans in, 312; Hemingway and, 322

Parizeau (Poznanska), Alice, 574

Parker, Cynthia Ann, 440

Parker, Theodore, 91; "A Sermon on Merchants," 148

Parochial nature of American culture, 12

Parody: in Millhauser's works, 747, 749–51; in Poe's works, 78

Parrington, Vernon L., 390

*Partisan Review*, 326–27, 345; and Roth's *Call It Sleep*, 395

Partnoy, Alicia, 635

Parton, Sarah Payson Willis. *See* Fern, Fanny

Past, post–Civil War writers and, 241–43

Pastor, Rose, 387

Paternalistic society, reform novels, 230–32

Patri, Angelo, *The Spirit of America*, 385

Patriarchal character, Poe's view, 98

Patriarchal society: colonial, and education of women, 657; domesticity and, 118–26; sexual mastery, 153; slave narrative and, 42; Stein and, 213–14; Stowe and, 144–45; temperance novels and, 138–40

Patten, Gilbert (Burt L. Standish), 357; *Frank Merriwell at Yale*, 357–58; *Frank Merriwell in Wall Street*, 358

Patten, Simon, *The New Basis of Civilization*, 358

Patterson, Orlando, 592, 594, 598; *The Children of Sisyphus*, 599; *Die the Long Day*, 599

Paulding, James Kirke: *The Dutchman's Fireside*, 437; *Slavery in the United States*, 101; Poe's review, 90, 96–101, 104

Paz, Octavio, 609, 622

Pearson, Ridley, 456
Peckham, Morse, 618
Pells, Richard, 341
Pellucidar series, Burroughs, 362–63
Peoples of color, 652–53; Faulkner and, 427; literature of, 406; migrations of, 650; postmodern writers, 522; status in U.S., 655. *See also* African Americans; Native Americans
Percy, Walker, 800; *The Last Gentleman*, 491; *Love in the Ruins*, 491; *The Moviegoer*, 491; *The Second Coming*, 491
Perera, Padma, 653
Perfectionism, nineteenth century, 140
Perfectionist theology, 132
Periodicals, and works of fiction, 50
Personal life, public affairs and, 50
Personal property, slaves as, 221–22
*Perspective* (magazine), 692
Perversity, Poe and, 82
Peterkin, Julia, 417–18; *Black April*, 417; *Bright Skin*, 418; *Green Thursday*, 417; *Scarlet Sister Mary*, 417–18
Peters, Fritz (Arthur Anderson Peters), *Finistere*, 502
Peterson, Joyce Shaw, 301
Peterson, Levi, *The Backslider*, 461–62
*Peterson's Magazine*, 303
Petry, Ann, *The Street*, 496–97
Phelps, Elizabeth Stuart, 238, 282, 335, 800; *The Gates Ajar*, 127; *The Silent Partner*, 226–28, 232
Philosophical novels, postmodern, 711
Philosophy, post–World War II, 486–87
Photography, postmodern, 516
Picaresque novels: early American, 19–21; female, 110
Pierce, Franklin, 62
Pioneer-prairie novels, 441. *See also* Frontier stories
Pirated works, 48; early American publication, 7; in story papers, 288
Pita Rodríguez, Felix, 524
Place: Canadian novels of, 561–65; individual and, 469
Plantation tradition, 244
Plante, David, *The Family*, 404

Plath, Sylvia, *The Bell Jar*, 505
Plots: early American, 10; postmodern, 705, 716
Pocahontas, 30
Pocket Books, 359, 685–86
Poe, Edgar Allan, 51, 55, 60–62, 66–70, 72, 90, 800–801; "Balloon Hoax," 361; "Berenice," 77–78, 95; "The Black Cat," 82, 98; "The Cask of Amontillado," 82; detective fiction, 375; *Eureka*, 61, 91, 102, 107; "The Facts in the Case of M. Valdemar," 81; "The Fall of the House of Usher," 66; "For Annie," 95; "The Gold Bug," 96; "Hans Pfaal," 361; "Hop-Frog," 81–82, 103–4; "How to Write a Blackwood Article," 70, 78–79; and imagination, 77–80; and intellectual women, 63; "King Pest," 81; "Landor's Cottage," 95; "Ligeia," 95; "Lionizing," 82; "The Literati of New York City," 101–2; "Loss of Breath," 78; "The Man of the Crowd," 375; "Marginalia," 78, 79; Matthiessen and, 128; "Morella," 95; "The Murders in the Rue Morge," 96, 103; *The Narrative of Arthur Gordon Pym*, 51, 82–83, 107–9; "Paulding-Drayton Review," 96–101, 104; "The Philosophy of Composition," 69; "The Power of Words," 79; "A Predicament," 78–79; "The Raven," 69; and revenge, 81–83; review of Hawthorne's *Twice-Told Tales*, 105; science fiction, 361; and slavery, 93–94, 96–104; "The System of Doctor Tarr and Professor Fether," 103; "A Tale of Jerusalem," 82; *Tales*, 53; "The Tell-Tale Heart," 82; "To Helen," 95; "To Marie Louise Shew," 95; and women, 94–95
*The Poe Log: A Documentary Life of Edgar Allan Poe*, 94
Poetry: proletarian, 344; Puritan, 31
*Poetry* (magazine), 312, 314
Poets, Latin American, 609
Poggioli, Renato, 734

Poirier, Richard, 488
Political exile, 651, 668
Political fantasies, post–Civil War, 247–48
Politicalization of American fiction, early twentieth century, 326–27
Politics, fiction and, 14, 128–29; American novel, 25; avant-garde, 735; gothic novels, 22; Irish American novels, 403; picaresque novels, 19–20; postmodern, 700; science fiction, 365; story papers, 288, 290–91
Pollack, Simon, *The Autobiography of Simon Pollack*, 383
Poniatowska, Elena, 623; *Hasta no verte Jesús mío*, 647
Poole, Ernest, *The Voice of the Street*, 384–85
Poovey, Mary, 543
Popular culture, 285–86
Popular fiction, 378–79, 504–5; late nineteenth century, 285–305; twentieth century, 357–79
Popularity: Melville's views, 68; Poe's views, 69
Popular press, rise of, 13
Popular taste, 694–95
Population growth, and literary market, 49
Populism, 235; early twentieth century, 322
Porte, Joel, 72
Porter, Cole, 542
Porter, Edwin S., *The Great Train Robbery* (film), 440
Porter, Katherine Anne, 425–26, 430; *The Leaning Tower and Other Stories*, 425–26; *Old Mortality*, 426; "The Old Order," 425–26; *Pale Horse, Pale Rider*, 426
Porter, William T., 55
Portis, Charles, *True Grit*, 461
Possession: love and, 95; politics of, James and, 165–66
Possessions, material, realists and, 187
Postbellum novels, 157–58
Postcoloniality, 649, 651–53; and marginality, 667
Post-Holocaust novels, 403

Postimpressionism, 313
Postindustrial culture, 485
Postmodern fiction, 690, 697–725
Postmodernism, 327–29, 515–22, 679, 697; avant-garde and, 726; Roth and, 498; Western, 450
Postmodern realism, 521–41
Poststructuralist theories, 700
Post–World War II era, 485; immigrant novels, 404–6
Potok, Chaim: *The Chosen*, 404, 504; *My Name Is Asher Lev*, 504
Potter, Alicia Rivero, 643
Poulin, Jacques, 572
Pound, Ezra, 312–14, 316, 317, 329–30, 465–66, 476, 691; Hemingway and, 321; *Hugh Selwyn Mauberley*, 318, 329; "Why Books?," 317; and World War I, 318
Powell, William W., *Books: The Culture and Commerce of Publishing*, 683–86
Power: sexual, James and, 164–65; of women, nineteenth-century ideas, 116, 124–25; of words, views of, 79–80
Power relations: early American, 14; in *Uncle Tom's Cabin*, 144–45
Powers, J. F., 403, 490–91; *Morte d'Urban*, 491; *Wheat That Springeth Green*, 491
Powhatan, 30
Pratt, Linda Ray, 352
Pratt, Mary Louise, "The Short Story: The Long and Short of It," 536
Pratt, William, 755
Prentiss, Elizabeth Payson, 801
Presentational realism, 162
Prestige of authors, 684–85, 689
Preston, Dickson J., *Young Frederick Douglass: The Maryland Years*, 40
Primitive identity, views of, 264
Primitive peoples, sociological study, 202
Primordial power, views of, 264
Principle, and authenticity of self, 123
Printed literature, and economic structures, 51
Printing technology, 49

Prison, symbolism of, 176
Private interest, and general welfare, 50
Problem novels, mid-twentieth century, 490
Production-line techniques of authorship, 292–93
Profession, writing as, 48–49; Cooper and, 58; nineteenth century, 47, 67–70
Professionalism: in intellectual life, 679; literary, 70, 691–94; neutrality of, 196; of women novelists, nineteenth century, 64–65
Profits, in publishing, 680–81, 683–84, 686
Progressive Era, women's status, 269
Proletarianism: early twentieth century, 331–56; in fiction, 327, 393, 400
Promotional campaigns, nineteenth century, 53
Property laws, and women, 143
Prose style, efficiency movement and, 477–78
Prostitutes, reform societies, 137
Protestant elite, and social reform, 133, 146–48
Protestant Reformation, 132
Protestant revivals, nineteenth century, 132
Protest fiction, 335; early twentieth century, 326–27; environmentalist, 459–60; and regionalism, 254–55; Steinbeck's writing as, 442
Pseudo literacy, 693
Pseudonym, slave autobiography and, 42–43
Psychoanalytic movement, 487
Psychological realism, James and, 167–68
Psychology, Stein's studies, 211
Publication of postcolonial novels, 665–66
Public issues, avant-garde fiction and, 732
Public sphere, personal life and, 50
Publishers, 52–54, 287, 305, 679; of Canadian authors, 560; of dime novels, 292; Native Canadian, 577; nineteenth century, 48–49, 114–15,

158; postmodern, 680; and regionalism, 251
*Publishers Weekly*, 287, 680; and Max Brand, 366
Puig, Manuel, 522, 626–28, 642, 801; *Betrayed by Rita Hayworth*, 626; *Heartbreak Tango*, 626; *Kiss of the Spider Woman*, 627; *Pubis Angelical*, 626
Pulp magazines, 302, 359; detective fiction, 373
Pupin, Michael, *From Immigrant to Inventor*, 385
Pure Food Bill (1907), 238
Puritan autobiographies, 31–33
Puritanism, domesticity and, 123
Puritans: and Native Americans, 32; and technology, 468
Putnam, Emily, 268
Putnam's, publishers, 53
Puzo, Mario, *The Fortunate Pilgrim*, 404–5; *The Godfather*, 405
Pynchon, Thomas, 451, 520, 702–3, 706, 716–19, 726–27, 801–2; *Gravity's Rainbow*, 698, 704–7, 717–19; *The Crying of Lot 49*, 704, 717; *V*, 716–17; *Vineland*, 464, 719

Quakers, autobiographical writings, 31
Quasi journalists, 56–57
Quebec: literature of, 562, 567–73; women writers, 580–81
Queen, Ellery, pseud., 802
Quick, Herbert, *Vandermark's Folly*, 441
Quiet Revolution, Canada, 570
Quinto Sol publishing house, 500–501

Raban, Jonathan, 676–77
Race, 409–11; American society and, 217, 411–14; gender and, 283–84; proletarianism and, 346–50; regionalism and, 420–36; romance and, 89–109; science fiction and, 361; sociology and, 190, 205; Southerners and, 416–20; Warren and, 415–16

Race (*Continued*)
—and identity, 106, 243–44, 409;
    novels of, 421–25, 494–95; Twain
    and, 246
Race relations, realist novels of, 178–
    81, 187–88
Racial violence, 412; fear of, 145–46
Racism, 91–92, 263, 655; of Cather,
    280; of Hemingway, 321–22; in
    Jamaican novels, 591; of Mailer,
    493; mid-twentieth century, 490;
    migrations and, 659; Mukherjee
    and, 677; nineteenth century, 153–
    54; post–Civil War, 248–49; prole-
    tarianism and, 333, 351; science
    fiction and, 362–63; Twain and,
    245–46; women and, 269, 273–
    75
Radway, Janice, 301
Rage, Wright and, 431
Railroad: strikes, nineteenth century,
    158; symbolism of, 262–63
Ramchand, Kenneth, *The West Indian
    Novel and Its Background*, 593–94
Ransom, John Crowe, 416, 488
Rap performances, 540
Ravage, M. E., *An American in the
    Making*, 385
Ravenscroft, Arthur, 671
Ravits, Martha, 458
Reading, 543–45, 693; postmodernism
    and, 702–3
Reading habits, early American, 13
Reading public, 679, 685, 688–90, 729;
    of avant-garde novels, 733; contri-
    butions to pulp magazines, 302–3;
    of dime novels, 293–94, 297, 300–
    301; nineteenth century, 113–14,
    147; post–Civil War, 251; women,
    271, 283, 695
Realism, 10, 697; Althusser's views,
    522; Civil War and, 240–41; ethnic,
    382; Howells and, 181–87; late
    nineteenth century, 157–88, 197–
    200; in Latin American fiction, 611;
    magic realism and, 524; moral, mid-
    twentieth-century idea, 488; post-
    modern, 521–41; reform fiction and,
    225–26; Western, 438

Reality: Coover and, 733; postmodern
    views, 700, 702–3
Rebellion: Canadian fiction of, 571;
    male, novels of, 117–18; mid-
    twentieth-century models, 492–93
Rechy, John, 406, 502, 802; *City of
    Night*, 450, 492
Reciprocity: human, sociological view,
    190; in slavery, 99–100
Reconciliation, post–Civil War, 243–49
Redcam, Tom. *See* MacDermott,
    Thomas
Reed, Ishmael, 516, 699, 701–2, 721–
    22, 802–3; *Flight to Canada*, 721;
    *The Free-Lance Pallbearers*, 721;
    *The Last Days of Louisiana Red*,
    721; *Mumbo Jumbo*, 704, 721; *Yel-
    low Back Radio Broke-Down*, 450,
    721
Reed, John, 337
Reed, Rebecca Theresa, *Six Months in a
    Convent*, 147
Reeve, Clara, *The Progress of Romance*,
    73
Reform, 216–17; individualism and,
    493–94; nineteenth century, 130–54,
    217–39; social, slave narratives and,
    39–41
Reformatory institutions, 148–49
Reform movements, 132–33, 216
Reform organizations, and sociology,
    192
Regionalism, 250–56, 407; Canadian,
    561–65, 567–73; and national iden-
    tity, 263; race and, 412, 420–36;
    Southern, 412–21; Western, 463–64
Regional recovery projects, 158
Reid, Vic, 593, 594; *The Leopard*, 598;
    *New Day*, 598–99
Religion: in Canada, 568; captivity nar-
    ratives and, 32–33; mid-twentieth-
    century novels and, 491; and re-
    form, 132
Religious revivals, nineteenth century,
    132–33; domestic fiction and, 289
Remarque, Erich Maria, *All Quiet on
    the Western Front*, 319
Remington, Frederic, 304
Renan, Ernest, 241–42

Renaud, Jacques, *Le cassé*, 571

Renfroe, Martha Kay. *See* Wren, M. K.

Republicanism, 48, 50; Howells and, 184–86; picaresque novels and, 19–20; and working classes, 148

Republican motherhood, Revolutionary-era idea, 115

Republican Party, 147

Reunions, post–Civil War, 250

Revenge, romance and, 74, 81–88

Revivalism, nineteenth century, 132–33; domestic fiction and, 289

Revolutionary change, 14–15; Davis and, 176; reform and, 217

Revolutionary fervor, Hawthorne and, 84

Reynolds, Clay, 461

Reznikoff, Charles, *By the Waters of Manhattan*, 387

Rhodes, Eugene Manlove, *Barnsford in Arcadia*, 368

Rhys, Jean, 594, 803; *Voyage in the Dark*, 604; *Wide Sargasso Sea*, 89, 603, 604

Ribalow, Harold, 383

Rich, Adrienne, 545, 547

Richards, David Adams: *Blood Ties*, 561; *Road to the Stilt House*, 561

Richardson, Dorothy, *The Long Day: The Story of a New York Working Girl*, 301

Richardson, John, *Wacousta; or, The Prophecy: A Tale of the Canadas*, 559

Richardson, Samuel, 12, 110; *Pamela*, 7

Richler, Mordecai, 402; *The Apprenticeship of Duddy Kravitz*, 575, 578

Richter, Conrad, *The Sea of Grass*, 443

Rideout, Walter, *The Radical Novel in the United States, 1900–1954*, 331

Ridgway, Henry, 94

Riesman, David, *The Lonely Crowd*, 485

Riis, Jacob, *How the Other Half Lives*, 225, 381; *The Making of an American*, 385

Riley, Joan, 653

Rinehart, Mary Roberts, 283, 803–4; *The Circular Staircase*, 373; *The Man in Lower Ten*, 373; *The Window at the White Cat*, 373

Ringuet (Philippe Panneton), *Trente arpents (Thirty Acres)*, 569

Ríos, Alberto, *The Iguana Killer*, 522, 536

Rivera, Edward, 406

Rivera, Tomás, ". . . *y no se lo tragó la tierra*," 453

Robbins, Tom, *Even Cowgirls Get the Blues*, 450

Robinson, Forrest, 452–53

Robinson, Marilynne, 804; *Housekeeping*, 458–59

Rodríguez, Richard, 406

Rodríguez Monegal, Emir, 624

Roffé, Reina, 642; *Monte de Venus*, 629–30

Roh, Franz, *Nach-Expressionismus: Magischer Realismus*, 523

Rolfe, Edwin, 344

Rollins, William, *The Shadow Before*, 344–45

Rölvaag, Ole Edvart, 389–91, 804; *Amerika-Breve*, 390; *Giants in the Earth*, 390, 441; *I de Dage*, 390; *Peder Victorious*, 391; *Their Fathers' God*, 391

Romains, Jules, 345

Romances, literary, 5, 10, 51, 72–88; domestic novels and, 112; Hawthorne and, 66, 69; historical, 257–63; race and, 89–109

*Le roman de la terre*, 568–69

Romantic temperament, and romance form, 74

Ronald, Ann, 459

Rooke, Leon, 567; *Shakespeare's Dog*, 582

Roosevelt, Franklin Delano, 402

Roosevelt, Theodore, 304, 358; *The Strenuous Life*, 249; *The Winning of the West*, 363–64; and women's rights, 270

Rosaldo, Renato Ignacio, 539, 804; "Fables of the Fallen Guy," 536

Rosenberg, Ann, *The Bee Book*, 579

Rosenberg, Harold, *The Tradition of the New*, 693

Rosenberg, Isaac, 318
Rosenfeld, Alvin, 739–40
Rosenfeld, Isaac, 383, 401; *Passage from Home*, 404
Rosenfeld, Paul, *A Boy in the Sun*, 387
Rosenfelt, Deborah, 352
Rosenthal, Bernard, "Poe, Slavery, and the *Southern Literary Messenger*: A Reexamination," 96
Rosler, Martha, 516
Ross, E. A., *Social Control*, 195
Ross, Leonard Q. (Leo Rosten), *The Education of H\*Y\*M\*A\*N\* K\*A\*P\*L\*A\*N*, 504–5
Ross, Sinclair, 804–5; *As for Me and My House*, 565, 578
Rossiter, Clinton, 488
Rosten, Leo. *See* Ross, Leonard Q.
Roth, Henry, 393; *Call It Sleep*, 394–95
Roth, Philip, 402, 498–99, 805; *The Anatomy Lesson*, 499; *The Ghost Writer*, 499; *Goodbye, Columbus*, 498; *Portnoy's Complaint*, 498; *The Prague Orgy*, 499; *Zuckerman Bound*, 499; *Zuckerman Unbound*, 499
*Rough Rider Weekly*, 300
Rousseau, Jean-Jacques, *Confessions*, 26; *Emile*, 118; view of women, 118–19
Rowlandson, Joseph, 32
Rowlandson, Mary, *A True History of the Captivity and Restoration of Mrs. Mary Rowlandson*, 31, 32–33
Rowson, Susanna, 47–48, 805; *Charlotte Temple*, 5, 7–8, 9, 18–19, 52
Roy, Gabrielle, 572, 805–6; *Alexandre Chenevert (The Cashier)*, 569–70; *Bonheur d'occasion (The Tin Flute)*, 569, 578; *La Petite Poule d'eau (Where Nests the Water Hen)*, 572
Royce, Josiah, 381; *The Philosophy of Loyalty*, 195
Royot, Daniel, 449
Rubin, Gayle, "The Traffic in Women," 200–201
Rule, Jane, *Desert of the Heart*, 502
Rulfo, Juan, 524

Rural families, problems of, 235–36
Rural life, views of, 253
Rush, Benjamin, 115, 136
Rushdie, Salman, 653–54, 658, 659–60, 678; *Haroun and the Sea of Stories*, 661; *Midnight's Children*, 660; *The Satanic Verses*, 660–61; *Shame*, 660
Russ, Joanna, 505, 579, 698, 699, 702, 806; *The Adventures of Alyx*, 724; *Alyx*, 724; *The Female Man*, 699, 704, 706, 724; *Picnic on Paradise*, 724; *The Two of Them*, 724; "When It Changed," 724
Russian Jews, ethnic novels, 383, 404
Russian Revolution, 322
Ruta, Suzanne, 621

Sacco and Vanzetti case, 323
Sacrifice, and social control, 194–95
Sadism, of Hemingway, 322
Saint-Domingue revolution, 92
St. Omer, Garth, 594
Sainz, Gustavo: *Corazón de palabras*, 631; *Gazapo*, 631; *Obsesivos días circulares*, 631
Salas, Floyd, *Tattoo the Wicked Cross*, 453
Saldívar, José David, *The Dialectics of Our America*, 526
Salinger, J. D., 806; *The Catcher in the Rye*, 492; *Franny and Zooey*, 492; *Raise High the Roof Beam, Carpenters*, 492; *Seymour: An Introduction*, 492
Salkey, Andrew, 594, 598; *A Quality of Violence*, 600
Salvation, male: women and, 124–25
Salzman, Arthur M., 741
Same-sex relationships, Cather and, 279–80
Sam Sharpe Insurrection, 97
Sanchez, Thomas, *Rabbit Boss*, 455
Sandburg, Carl, 311
Sandoz, Mari, 457
San Francisco, as literary center, 407
Santos, Bienvenido, 653
Sarduy, Severo, 626; *Cobra*, 628
Saroyan, William, 383
Sarraute, Nathalie, 699

Sartre, Jean-Paul, *Being and Nothingness*, 487
Satie, Erik, 314
Satire: avant-garde, 734; in postmodern fiction, 705; of the West, 450
Savard, Felix-Antoine, *Menaud, maîtredraveur (Master of the River)*, 568
Sayre, Robert F.: *The Examined Self: Benjamin Franklin, Henry Adams, Henry James*, 28l; and Franklin, 36
Sayre, Zelda. *See* Fitzgerald, Zelda Sayre
Scandinavian ethnic novels, 384, 389–92
Scarborough, Dorothy, 457
Scholarship, postcolonial, 656
Schools: Canadian, literature in, 578; and literary market, 49
Schulberg, Budd, 451; *What Makes Sammy Run?*, 402–3
Schwartzwald, Robert, 574
Science fiction, 360–66, 371; Acker and, 724; Delany and, 724–25; gay, 554–56; postmodern, 699; Vonnegut and, 722
Scientific method, sociology and, 192, 215
*Scribner's Monthly*, 303
Sea fiction, nineteenth century, 148–51
Seaforth, Sybil, 605
Sedgwick, Catharine Maria, 64–65, 806–7; *Clarence*, 120; *Home*, 110; *Hope Leslie*, 122–23; *A New-England Tale*, 122; *The Poor Rich Man and the Rich Poor Man*, 120
Sedgwick, Eve, 637
Sedition Act (1918), 323
Seduction novels, 7, 12, 219; early American, 15–19; nineteenth century, 110
Seeger, Alan, 318
Segregation, racial, 411–12, 430
Selby, Hubert, *Last Exit to Brooklyn*, 492
Self: American, early creation, 30; caricature of, 81; construction of, 29; creation of, by Franklin, 36; destruction of, Poe and, 82; female, domesticity and, 121–23; gothic novels

and, 22–23; James's view, 164–67; reform of, Emerson's views, 130–31
Self-control, slavery and, abolitionist views, 141
Self-exploitation, 682
Self-reliance, nineteenth-century views, 123
Self-sacrifice, female: Canadian theme, 568; Howells and, 182–83, 186
Selvon, Sam, 587, 589, 594, 596, 600–601; *A Brighter Sun*, 600; *The Lonely Londoners*, 596, 601; *Moses Ascending*, 596, 601; *Moses Migrating*, 596, 601; *Turn Again Tiger*, 600
Seneca Falls, women's rights convention, 143, 218
Sensational novels, nineteenth century, 57
Sensation fiction, female, 110
Sentimental novels: early American, 15–19; dime novels and, 295; nineteenth century, 52, 56, 60, 110, 219; reform movements and, 222; story papers, 289–90
Serialized fiction: in magazines, 303; in story papers, 291
"Serious" fiction, 696
Setting, in Gass's fiction, 740–41
Settlement, Western, novels of, 437–38
Seventeenth-century writings: autobiographical, 29–31; captivity narratives, 32–33
Sewall, Samuel, *Diary*, 31
Sex, in Western novels, 440
Sexes, moral difference between, domestic ideology and, 124–26
Sexism, in postmodern fiction, 698
Sexuality, 542–43; early realists and, 188; gay, and gender, 551; James and, 163; literary treatments, post–World War II, 501–2
—female: Lesbianism and, 279; Le Sueur and, 351; post–World War II, 506
Sexual power, James and, 164–65
Sexual tyranny, slave narrative and, 41–42

Shakers, 133

Shakespeare and Company (bookstore), 312, 321

Shame, Wright and, 432

Shand, Hubert, *White and Black*, 420

Sheer, Steven C., 72

Shelley, Mary, 361

Sheperd, Thomas, autobiography, 26

Shinebourne, Janice, 605

Shipboard life, reform of, 149

Short, Luke, *Rimrock*, 440

Short stories: avant-garde, 720–21, 744, 745–46; postmodern, 535–36

*Shuffle Along* (musical revue), 411

Shulman, Max, *Rally Round the Flag, Boys!*, 507

Sigourney, Lydia Huntley, 807; *Letters to Mothers*, 126

Silko, Leslie Marmon, 457, 807; *Ceremony*, 456; *Storyteller*, 457

Simmel, Georg: "How Is Society Possible?" 199; *The Philosophy of Money*, 212

Simms, William Gilmore, 51, 55, 73, 807–8; *Woodcraft*, 145–46; *The Yemassee*, preface to, 73

Simpson, Mona, *Anywhere but Here*, 466

Simulation, 483–84

Sinclair, Bertha Muzzy. *See* Bower, B. M.

Sinclair, Upton, 335, 808; *The Jungle*, 226, 236–38, 471

Singer, Isaac Bashevis, 808; *Enemies: A Love Story*, 498; *The Family Moskat*, 498

Sisterhood of Reforms, 132

Sisterhood of women, and slavery, 153

Škvorecký, Josef, 574

Sky, Gino, *Appaloosa Rising*, 450

Slave narratives, 55–56; autobiographical, 37–41; Native Americans and, 45

Slave revolts, fictional accounts, 151

Slavery: African American writers and, 150–53; domesticity and, 119; Du Bois and, 206; Emerson and, 130–31; Melville and, 150; post–Civil War views, 243–46; reform movement, 218–22; romanticization of, 244, 89–109; Stowe's depiction, 144–45; Warren and, 415–16; women and, 142–43

Slave women, status of, 153

Slesinger, Tess, 353–54; "Missis Flinders," 354; *Time: The Present*, 353; *The Unpossessed*, 353–54

Small, Albion, 190, 193, 196, 201

Smedley, Agnes, 339; *Daughter of Earth*, 334–39, 350

Smertenko, Johan, 388

Smith, Adam, 48–49, 50, 70; *Wealth of Nations*, 47

Smith, Betty, *A Tree Grows in Brooklyn*, 504

Smith, E. E., Skylark series, 361; *The Skylark of Space*, 361

Smith, Elizabeth Oakes, 809; *Riches Without Wings*, 120

Smith, Francis, *Bertha Bascomb, the Sewing Machine Girl*, 294

Smith, Gerrit, 142

Smith, Henry Nash, *Virgin Land*, 489

Smith, John, 30

Smith, Lillian, 411–12, 426; *Killers of the Dream*, 424; *Strange Fruit*, 424

Smith, Ormond, 292, 357

Smith, Ray, *Lord Nelson Tavern*, 561

Snyder, Gary, 447

Snyder, Richard E., 686, 688

Social categories, 217

Social change, 509; Davis's views, 176; Du Bois and, 208–10; formula fiction and, 378; and literature of environment, 505; Melville and, 193; mid-twentieth-century novel and, 489–90; national literature and, 241; nineteenth century, 268–69, 190; nineteenth-century realism and, 161; post–World War II, 494; proletarian fiction and, 333–34, 336–39; sentimental novels and, 219; story papers and, 291; Western fiction and, 366–67; women writers and, 283. *See also* Social reform

Social class: Davis and, 174–77; eighteenth-century views, 34; gender and, 283–84; psychoanalysis and, 487

Social control: and vigilance, 197–99; typecasting and, 194–96

Social Darwinism, science fiction and, 362

Social determinism, and individualism, 193

Social evolution: contradictions, 202; Du Bois and, 206; James and, 200

Social injustice, Melville and, 67

Socialism, 333, 336–37, 485–86; Bellamy and, 229–30; literary criticism and, 332

Socialist literature, 489

Socialist realism, Du Bois and, 210

Socialization of women, Hindu, 675

Social realism, late nineteenth century, 157–59, 197–200

Social reform, 130–54, 216; Emerson and, 130–31; slave narratives and, 39–41; women and, 236. *See also* Social change

Social reformers, observation of lower classes, 197

Social science: fiction and, 189–215; immigrant experience, 382

Social scientific method, Stein and, 215

Social types, language of, 191

Social value: art and, 334–35; in autobiography, 26; in Western fiction, 464

Social work for women, domestic ideology and, 125–26

Society: and identity, 485–509; knowledge of, to sociologists, 191–92; nineteenth century, influence of women, 115–17, 124–25; Western fiction and, 367–68

—early American, 3–5, 12–14; Cooper and, 23–25; gothic novels and, 22; women's status, 16–19

Sociological journalism, 381

Sociology, 189–91

Solecki, Sam, 565

Sollers, Philippe, 700

Sollors, Werner, 380

Solotaroff, Ted, 686, 693; "The Publishing Culture and the Literary Culture," 694–95

Sommer, Doris, 641

Sone, Monica, *Nisei Daughter*, 500

Sontag, Susan, 809

Sophistication, Barthelme and, 743

Sorensen, Virginia, 457–58

Sorrentino, Gilbert, *Mulligan Stew*, 732

*Southern Literary Messenger*, 96

Southern states: literary culture, 54–55, 407; Poe and, 93; racial issues, 412–14; regional writing, 414–21; Twain and, 245–46

Southern writers: African American, 430–36; and race, 425–31

Southey, Robert, 26

Southworth, E. D. E. N., 271, 282, 289–90, 809–10; *The Hidden Hand*, 110

Soviet Union, 343; influences on American writers, 333, 334–35

Soyinka, Wole, 667; "Twice-Bitten: The Fate of Africa's Culture Producers," 668

Space travel, 361, 364–65

Spanbauer, Tom, 461

Spanish-American War, 158, 248–49

Spanish conquest, 622

Spector, Herman, 344

Spencer, Herbert, 206

Spengemann, William, 8

Spengler, Oswald, *Decline of the West*, 525

Spicer, Jack, 450

Spillane, Mickey: *I, the Jury*, 372; *Vengeance Is Mine*, 378

*The Spirit of the Times*, 55

Spiritual autobiography, 31–33; African American, 38–39; early American, 31–33

Spiritualism, Hawthorne and, 134–35

Spivak, Gayatri, 648

Spofford, Harriet Prescott, 810

Sports novels, 357–58

Stadler, Ernst, 318

Stafford, Jean, 458

Standardization, of domestic novels, 113

Standish, Burt L. *See* Patten, Gilbert
Stanton, Elizabeth Cady, 126, 142, 143, 218
Static analysis of society, 192–93
Status, alternative publishing and, 681
—of women: early American, 15–19; late nineteenth century, 269
Stearns, J. F., 116
Steffens, Lincoln, 237
Stegner, Wallace, 439, 443–44, 446, 810; *Angle of Repose*, 451–53; *The Big Rock Candy Mountain*, 443–44
Stein, Gertrude, 193, 204–5, 312–16, 330, 408, 727, 728, 810–11; *The Autobiography of Alice B. Toklas*, 311, 316; Hemingway and, 321; *The Making of Americans*, 204, 210–15, 314–15; "Melanctha," 409; *Q.E.D.; or, Things as They Are*, 316; *Tender Buttons*, 314; *Three Lives*, 312, 313, 316, 409, 501
Steinbeck, John, 326, 441–42, 489, 811; *East of Eden*, 442; *The Grapes of Wrath*, 342–43, 400, 442, 446, 458; *In Dubious Battle*, 441–42; *Of Mice and Men*, 442
Steiner, Edward, *From Alien to Citizen*, 385
Steiner, George, *On Difficulty, and Other Essays*, 693
Steinmetz, S. R., 201
Stella, Joseph, 384–85
Stephens, Ann S., 52, 296; *Fashion and Famine*, 120, 147; *Malaeska: The Indian Wife of the White Hunter*, 122, 295, 438; *The Old Homestead*, 152
Steptoes, Lydia. *See* Barnes, Djuna
Stereotypes, homosexual, 502
Sterling, J., 657
Stern, Robert A. M., 516
Sterne, Laurence: Fuentes and, 620–21; *A Sentimental Journey*, 7
Stoddard, Elizabeth Drew, 282, 811–12; *The Morgesons*, 110, 139
Stokes, James Phelps Graham, 387
Stone, Albert E., *Autobiographical Occasions and Original Acts*, 28–29

Stone, Monica, 405
Stone, Robert, 451, 521, 535, 537, 812; *Dog Soldiers*, 493; *A Flag for Sunrise*, 537–38
Stories, proletarian, 344
Story papers, 286–91, 304
Storytelling, postmodern return to, 528–29
Stout, Rex, *Over My Dead Body*, 377
Stowe, Calvin, 65
Stowe, Harriet Beecher, 64, 114, 812; *Dred: A Tale of the Great Dismal Swamp*, 146; *A Key to Uncle Tom's Cabin*, 146; *The Minister's Wooing*, 124; *Oldtown Folks*, 124; *Pearl of Orr's Island*, 117, 125; and reform fiction, 238; *Uncle Tom's Cabin*, 50, 52, 54, 55, 65–66, 119, 124, 125, 144–46, 217–22, 226, 241
Stramm, August, 318
Stratford, Philip, *All the Polarities*, 572–73
Straus, Roger, III, 684
Stream of consciousness: immigrant novels, 394–95; Stein and, 314
Street and Smith (publishers), 291, 292–94, 296–97, 300, 357; pulp magazines, 302, 359
Street theater, 667
Stribling, T. S., 417; *Birthright*, 420
Strikes, late nineteenth century, 158
Strong, Josiah, 258
Strunk, William, Jr., *The Elements of Style*, 478
Style of writing: efficiency movement and, 478; of James, 168; postmodern, 516, 706–7
Subsidiary rights, 686
Suburban novels, 507
Success: novels of, 357–59; immigrant experience, 385
Such, Peter, *Riverrun*, 563
Suckow, Ruth, 458
Sue, Eugène, 288
Suffragists, and domestic ideology, 126
Suggs, Christian, 344
Suicide, realist symbolism, 176
Sui Sin Far (Edith Eaton), 270, 273, 277

Sukenick, Ronald, 732, 812–13
Sully-Prudhomme, René-François-
Armand, 578
Sundquist, Eric, 91
Surface, in Hawkes's fiction, 729
Surrealism, 327; Carpentier and,
524–25
Survival manuals, nineteenth century,
51
Susman, Warren, 343
Sutherland, Ronald, *Second Image*,
572
Swan, Susan, *Biggest Modern Woman
of the World*, 580, 583–84
Symbolism: in captivity narrative, 33; in
Chesnutt's writing, 180; in Cooper's
novels, 23–25; in Eastlake's work,
445; in Howells's writing, 184; in
naturalist novels, 226–27
Syntax, simplicity in, 11

*Taking Stock: The Calgary Conference
on the Canadian Novel*, 577–79
Talk story: Chinese, 533; postmodern,
534
Tan, Amy, 406, 462; *The Joy Luck
Club*, 463
Tanner, Edward Everett. *See* Dennis,
Patrick
Tanner, Tony, 731, 740
Tarbell, Ida, 236–37
Taste, literary, 694–95
Tate, Allen, 416
Tatum, Stephen, 456
Taylor, Edward, 31
Taylor, Frederick Winslow, 476, 479
Technique, literary, nineteenth-century
writers and, 69
Technocracy: postmodern capitalism as,
679; science fiction of, 365–66
Technocratic utopians, 469
Technological changes in publishing,
681; and literary market, 49
Technologic analysis of society, 193
Technology, fiction and, 51, 465–84;
science fiction, 361–66
Television, fiction and, 480–84; symbol-
ism of, 466–67; Westerns, 441

Temperance movement, 136–40, 236;
abolitionists and, 142; *Uncle Tom's
Cabin* and, 144
Tenney, Tabitha, 813
Testimonios, 645–48
Theater of Cruelty, 450, 448
*Them!* (film), 362
Theory of slavery, Poe, 98–99
Theriault, Yves, *Agaguk*, 576
Theytus Books, 577
Third world nations, 650
Third world writers, 665
Thomas, Audrey, 567, 579; *Blown Fig-
ures*, 584; *Munchmeyer and Pros-
pero on the Island*, 580
Thomas, Lewis, 464
Thomas, Piri, 406
Thomas, W. I., "The Psychology of
Race-Prejudice," 205
Thompson, G. R., *Poe's Fiction: Ro-
mantic Irony in the Gothic Tales*,
109
Thompson, George, *New-York Life*, 51
Thoreau, Henry David, 469; Emerson
and, 470
Thurman, Wallace, *Infants of the
Spring*, 422
Ticknor, Caroline, 229; *Poe's Helen*,
Woolf's review, 95
Time travel, 361
"Tip Top Weekly," 357
Tobenkin, Elias, 386; *Witte Arrives*,
385
Toklas, Alice B., 311
Tolstoy, Leo Nikolaevich, Hemingway
and, 321
Tomasi, Mari, 398, 399; *Like Lesser
Gods*, 399
Tompkins, Jane, 289
Tom Swift series, 477
Toomer, Jean, 418–20, 422; *Cane*, 421
Tourgée, Albion, 813
Tourism, regionalism and, 252–53
Tousey, Frank, 206, 291
Trachtenberg, Alan, *The Incorporation
of America*, 189
Traditions, national, 259
Trakl, Georg, 318
Transcendentalists, 133

Transnational novels, 660
Transportation, and literary market, 49
Travel narratives, 34
Travers, Robert (John D. Voelker), *Anatomy of a Murder*, 490
Tremblay, Michel, 572
Trilling, Diana, 401
Trilling, Lionel, 72, 386, 492; *The Liberal Imagination*, 488
Trinh Minh-ha, *Woman, Native, Other*, 614
*Trinidad* (magazine), 592
Trinidad, writing in, 592, 600–603
Trollope, Anthony, *North America*, 8
Trollope, Frances, 8
Trotsky, Leon, *Literature and Revolution*, 343
Truth, Sojourner, 127, 142
Truth: autobiography and, 45; Melville and, 67; mid-twentieth-century views, 488
Truth-value, in autobiography, 28–29
Tucker, Nathaniel Beverley, 96
Tully, Jim, *Shanty Irish*, 395
Turgenev, Ivan Sergeyevich, Hemingway and, 321
Turner, Frederick Jackson, "The Significance of the Frontier in American History," 242
Twain, Mark (Samuel Langhorne Clemens), 8, 162, 168–72, 188, 196, 813–14; *The Adventures of Huckleberry Finn*, 20, 117–18, 168, 172, 187, 245–46, 304, 324; *The Adventures of Tom Sawyer*, 168, 255–56, 304; *A Connecticut Yankee in King Arthur's Court*, 168, 256–57, 361, 466–67, 470, 472–74; and Cooper, 161; "Fenimore Cooper's Literary Offenses," 161; *The Gilded Age*, 168; Howells and, 182; *The Innocents Abroad*, 252; *Life on the Mississippi*, 168, 245; "The Man That Corrupted Hadleyburg," 169; "The Mysterious Stranger," 169; "Old Times on the Mississippi," 168, 169–72; *Personal Recollections of Joan of Arc*, 256; and picaresque novels, 20; *Pudd'nhead Wilson*, 157,
169, 187, 245–46; and racism, 187–88; regionalism of, 252–54; *Roughing It*, 253–54; and Southern society, 245–46; "The United States of Lyncherdom," 187–88
Twentieth century. *See* Early twentieth century; Late twentieth century; Post–World War II era
Twysden, Duff, 320
Type categories, 205; Du Bois and, 209; late nineteenth century, 191; realist fiction and, 199–200; and social control, 194–96; sociology and, 201; Stein and, 210–15

Undesirable characters, naturalist fiction, 203
Unger, Douglas, 461
Union activity, 322
United States: Canada and, 583–84; immigrants, 653; internal colonization, 654–55; literary culture, 47; Mukherjee's views, 677; nineteenth century, cultural influences, 48; and postmodern fiction, 699; twentieth century, 408
Universality of truth, 488
University of Chicago, 189
Unmarketable fiction, 690
Unsettled nature of early American society, 13, 14
Unsolicited novels, publication of, 683
Updike, John, 508–9, 814; Borges viewed by, 616; *The Centaur*, 508; *Couples*, 508–9; *A Month of Sundays*, 449; *Rabbit at Rest*, 509; *Rabbit Is Rich*, 509; *Rabbit Redux*, 509; *Rabbit Run*, 509; *S.*, 449
Upfield, Arthur W., Hillerman and, 455
Uplifting fiction, 116
Upward mobility, fiction of, 382
Urban fiction: dime novels, 297; story papers, 288; Western, 450–51, 460
Urbanization: Canadian, 570; twentieth century, 407–8
Urban literary centers, 407
Urban reform movement, 147–49
Urban Westerns, 450–51, 460
Uslar Pietri, Arturo, 523, 524

Utopianism: Emerson and, 469; nineteenth century, 471; reform novels and, 227–30; technological novels, 474–76
Utopian novels, Howells, 168

Valdez, Luís, 406
Valenzuela, Luisa, 637–42, 814–15; *Other Weapons*, 637–41
Valgardson, W. D., 574
Values: American, James and, 164; literary, determination of, 696
van Delden, Maarten, 738
VanDerBeets, Richard, *The Indian Captivity Narrative: An American Genre*, 32
Van Dine, S. S. (Willard Huntington Wright), 374
Van Doren, Carl, 386
van Herk, Aritha, *Places Far from Ellesmere*, 567, 582
Van Vechten, Carl, 410–11; *Nigger Heaven*, 411
Vargas Llosa, Mario, 622–23, 815; *Captain Pantoja and the Special Service*, 622; *Conversation in the Cathedral*, 622; *The Green House*, 622–23; *Who Killed Palomino Molero?*, 622
Vasquez, Richard, *Chicano*, 453
Vassière, Pierre de, 90
Veblen, Thorstein, 360; *The Theory of the Leisure Class*, 200; workmanship principle, 68
Vecki, Victor, *Threatening Shadows*, 383
Vega, Ana Lydia, 623
Ventura, Luigi Donato, *Peppino*, 385
Venturi, Robert, 516
Verdugo, Patricia, *Detenidos-desaparecidos: Una herida abierta*, 647
Vernacular realism of Twain, 168, 172
Verne, Jules, 361
Vespucci, Amerigo, 6
Victor, Metta Victoria, 139, 297; *The Dead Letter*, 297; *Fashionable Dissipation*, 139; *Maum Guinea and Her Plantation "Children,"* 297; *The Senator's Son*, 139
Victorian era, ideal women, 279
Vidal, Gore, 815; *The City and the Pillar*, 502
Vietnam War, 453
Viezzer, Moema, 647
Vigilance, social control and, 197–99
Viking Press, 682–83
Villa, Silvio, 398
Villarreal, José Antonio, 406, 815–16; *Pocho*, 453, 501
Vinciguerra, Francesca (Frances Winwar), 398
Violence: effectism and, 439; late twentieth century, 451; male, Oates and, 537; in postmodern culture, 520; in postmodern fiction, 698; in Western novels, 440
Viramontes, Helena María, 521, 535; *The Moths and Other Stories*, 522, 536
Virtual reality, 483–84
Virtue, social, nineteenth-century ideas, 115–17
Virtuous behavior, Cooper and, 23–25
Vizenor, Gerald, *Darkness in Saint Louis Bearheart*, 457
Voelker, John D. *See* Travers, Robert
Voice, cultural, novelists and, 10–11, 14
Vonnegut, Kurt, 816; *Cat's Cradle*, 722; *Deadeye Dick*, 722; *Galapagos*, 722; *Mother Night*, 722; *Player Piano*, 722; *The Sirens of Titan*, 722; *Slapstick*, 722; *Slaughterhouse-Five*, 699, 703, 704, 722
Vorticism, 317
Voting rights for women, 269; domestic ideology and, 126–27; Emerson and, 131; nineteenth century ideas, 116; T. Roosevelt and, 270

Wage slavery, 148, 157; women and, 152
Walcott, Derek, 587, 653
Waldenbooks, 687
Waldseemüller, Martin, 6

Walker, Alice, *The Third Life of Grange Copeland*, 432
Walker, Maggie, 268
Wallace, Lew, 816–17; *Ben-Hur*, 258–59; *The Fair God*, 258
Wallant, Edward Lewis, *The Pawnbroker*, 403
Walton, Eda Lou, 394
War, glorification of, 317
Ware, William, 114
Warner, Charles Dudley, 272
Warner, Marian, *The Vanishing American*, 370
Warner, Susan B., 64, 65, 114, 271, 282, 817; *The Wide, Wide World*, 52, 110, 123
Warner, William, 481
Warner Communications, 687
War of 1812, 49
War poetry, World War I, 318
Warren, Austin, 397
Warren, Robert Penn, 414–16, 488; *All the King's Men*, 415; *At Heaven's Gate*, 415; *Band of Angels*, 415; "The Briar Patch," 415; *Brother to Dragons*, 415–16; *The Cave*, 415; *Chief Joseph of the Nez Percé*, 416; *John Brown: The Making of a Martyr*, 415; *Night Rider*, 415; *A Place to Come To*, 415; "Prime Leaf," 415; *Segregation: The Inner Conflict in the South*, 416; *Who Speaks for the Negro?*, 416; *World Enough and Time*, 415
Warshow, Robert, 301
War stories, 249–50; dime novels, 294; Native American, 43–44; story papers, 289
Washington, Booker T., 274, 435; *Up From Slavery*, 435
Washington, George: Cooper and, 24
Washington, Mary Helen, 497
Washingtonian Societies, 137
Waters, Frank: *The Man Who Killed the Deer*, 443; *The Woman at Otowi Crossing*, 443
Watson, Sheila, *The Double Hook*, 565, 578, 579
Waugh, Evelyn, 451

Waugh, Patricia, 673
Wayne, John, 367
Weatherwax, Clara, 332; *Marching! Marching!*, 339, 345
Webb, Frank J., 817; *The Garies and Their Friends*, 55–56
Weber, Max, "Protestant Ethic," 191
Webster, Daniel, 218
*The Weekly Anglo-African*, 151
Weems, Mason, *The Drunkard's Looking Glass*, 138
Weininger, Otto, *Sex and Character*, 212
Welch, James, 457, 817; *Fools Crow*, 457; *Winter in the Blood*, 456
Weld, Theodore, 142; *Slavery As It Is*, 141
Wellek, René, 397, 488
Wells, H. G., 249, 361; *The War of the Worlds*, 362
Wells, Ida B., 236, 269
Welty, Eudora, 817–18
West, Cornel, 521, 699
West, James L. W., *American Authors and the Literary Marketplace Since 1900*, 685
West, Nathanael, 451, 818; Anderson and, 327; *The Day of the Locust*, 327; *Miss Lonelyhearts*, 327
West: deromanticization of, 261–63; idealization of, 255, 259–61
Westbrook, Max, 442, 443
Western fiction: Canadian, 562–65; dime novels, 294–97; formulaic, 366–71; gentrification of, 304; late twentieth century, 437–64
*Western Story Magazine*, 302
West Indies, 586; Canadian novels set in, 584. *See also under* Caribbean
Wharton, Edith, 267, 270, 273, 275–77, 282, 283, 283, 818–19; *The Age of Innocence*, 276; *The House of Mirth*, 225; *The Touchstone*, 276
Wheat, symbolism of, 262–63
Wheeler, Edward L., 296, 299, 438; *Deadwood Dick, the Prince of the Road; or, The Black Rider of the Black Hills*, 301

Whistler, Henry, 89

White, E. B., *The Elements of Style*, 478

White, Edmund: *The Beautiful Room Is Empty*, 553; *A Boy's Own Story*, 551, 552–53

White, Walter, 411, 420; *The Fire in the Flint*, 420

White City, 189–91

Whitehead, Alfred North, 314

Whiteness, symbolism of, 106, 108–9, 189–91

Whiteside, Thomas, 680, 686, 687

White Southern writers, and blacks, 417–20

Whitman, Elizabeth, 16

Whitman, Sarah Helen, 104

Whitman, Walt, 8, 104; and Civil War, 157; *Franklin Evans*, 138; *Leaves of Grass*, preface to, 104; *Specimen Days*, 157

Whittaker, Frederick, 285, 293; *Larry Locke, the Man of Iron; or, A Fight for Fortune. A Story of Labor and Capital*, 301

Whyte, William H., *The Organization Man*, 485

Wiebe, Rudy, *The Temptations of Big Bear*, 563

Wilder, Billy, *Double Indemnity* (film), 378

Wilderness, importance of, in Western fiction, 459

*Wild West Weekly*, 296

Willard, Frances, 236

Williams, Denis, 597; *Other Leopards*, 598

Williams, Jeanne, 440

Williams, Raymond, 304, 526; *Keywords*, 286; *Television: Technology and Cultural Form*, 481–82

Williams, Tennessee, 430

Williams, William Carlos, 311

Williamsburg trilogy, Fuchs, 393

Williamson, Jack, *The Humanoids*, 365–66

Willis, N. P., 63

Willis, Sara Payson. See Fern, Fanny

Wilmington, North Carolina, Riot (1898), 179

Wilson, Amrit, *Finding a Voice*, 676

Wilson, Augusta Evans, *St. Elmo*, 110

Wilson, Edmund, 323

Wilson, Ethel, *Swamp Angel*, 564

Wilson, Harriet E. Adams, 282, 819; *Our Nig; or, Sketches from the Life of a Free Black*, 55–56, 127–28, 152–53

Wilson, Sloan, *The Man in the Gray Flannel Suit*, 507–8

Wilson, Woodrow, 411

Winchell, Mark Royden, 451

Winther, Sophus K., *Take All to Nebraska*, 441

Winwar, Frances. See Vinciguerra, Francesca

Wiseman, Adele, 574

Wister, Owen, 304, 819; *The Virginian*, 259–60, 304, 368–70, 439

Woiwode, Larry, *Beyond the Bedroom Wall*, 461

Wolfe, Thomas, 575

Wolitzer, Meg, *This Is Your Life*, 466–67

Wolman, John, 31

Womanhood: nineteenth-century ideal, 57, 60, 65, 118–19; Victorian stereotype, 219

Woman Movement, 270

Women: abolitionists, 142–43; and art, 272–73; change in status, 298; colonial, education of, 657; early American views, 15–19; exploitation of, nineteenth century, 152; idealization of, slavery and, 102; metaphoric exile, 651; moral superiority of, 124–26; nineteenth century, 50, 114, 142–43, 276; and social change, 268–70; and social reform, 236; Southern, 424–25; and temperance movement, 137; Victorian ideal, 279; West Indian, 594; Wright and, 433–34

——African American, 268, 269; and domesticity, 127–28; Hurston and, 423–24

Women (*Continued*)
—as audience, 688–89; for dime novels, 297, 301
—fictional representations: in adventure fiction, 378; in detective novels, 371–73, 376–78; in frontier novels, 438; by Hemingway, 322; in Latin American fiction, 615; by Poe, 94–95, 97, 101–2; in realist fiction, 187, 200–201; in Western fiction, 367–68, 371
—immigrant, 269; suffragists and, 126; as writers, 273
—status of: nineteenth century, 142–43; post–World War II, 486; reform novels and, 230–32, 235–36; in slavery, 153
—work of, 268, 269; antebellum novels and, 51; domestic ideology and, 125–26; 1930s, 338
—as writers, 5, 270–84, 338, 694–95, 695; of adventure narratives, 52; African American, 270, 273, 283, 421–25, 496; Canadian, 561; Cather and, 278–79; of detective stories, 297, 373; of dime novels, 297; and divorce, 143–44; of experimental fiction, 699; Hawthorne and, 69; immigrant, 273; Irish American, 397–98; Italian American, 398, 399; Latin American, 623–25, 629, 633–47; male writers and, 62–63; Native American, autobiographical writings, 45; nineteenth century, 46, 56–57, 59–60, 110, 114, 282–83; Norris's view, 267–68; Poe and, 70; postmodern, 698, 723; professionalism of, 64–65; of proletarian fiction, 333; Southern, 425–26; of technological utopias, 475; of Western fiction, 367–68, 457–58, 462; working class, 350–56
Women's clubs, 268
Women's magazines, 303
Women's movement, abolitionism and, 142–43
Women's narratives, in story papers, 289–90
Women's novels: Canadian, 579–81;

Caribbean, 603–4; detective novels and, 373; nineteenth century, 110–11; post–World War II, 505–7; temperance themes, 138–40
Women's suffrage: domestic ideology and, 126–27; Emerson and, 131
Wong, Jade Snow, *Fifth Chinese Daughter*, 500
Wong, Shawn, 406
Wood, Thelma, 328
Woods, Clement, *Nigger*, 420
Woodward, C. Vann, 411
Woolf, Virginia, 95, 314
Woolson, Constance Fenimore, 282
Workers, expatriate, 653
*Worker's Dreadnaught*, 346
Working class, 331–56; and cheap fiction, 293–94; and dime novels, 300–301; ethnic novels, 384, 385; migrants, 659; nineteenth century, 177; temperance movement and, 137; white, social reformers and, 146, 147
—writers, 343–44; women, 1930s, 350–56
Working conditions, reform fiction, 232–33, 227–28
Working-girl romances, 297
Workplace novels, post–World War II, 506
World's Anti-Slavery Convention (1840), 142, 218
World's Columbian Exposition (1893), 189, 242, 251–52
World War I, 318; Hemingway and, 319
World War II, 491; Canada and, 570; and ethnic literature, 401–2; paperback books, 359, 686
Worship, domesticity and, 121
Wouk, Herman, 819–20; *The Caine Mutiny*, 490; *Marjorie Morningstar*, 504
Wren, M. K. (Martha Kay Renfroe), 456
Wright, Frances, 133, 148, 820
Wright, Frank Lloyd, 197
Wright, Harold Bell, 283; *The Winning of Barbara Worth*, 477

Wright, Richard, 326, 344, 413, 430–31, 489, 820; *Black Boy*, 433, 434; "Bright and Morning Star," 348–49; *Eight Men*, 433; "The Ethics of Living Jim Crow," 433; *Lawd Today*, 433; *The Long Dream*, 433, 434; "The Man Who Killed a Shadow," 431; *Native Son*, 87, 348, 432–33, 495; *The Outsider*, 433; *Savage Holiday*, 434; *Uncle Tom's Children*, 348, 433; *White Man, Listen!*, 431
Wright, Robert C., 455
Wright, Willard Huntington. *See* Van Dine, S. S.
Writers, 694–95; identities of, 652–53; Stein's view, 213–14. *See also* Male writers; Women, as writers
Wylder, Delbert, 446
Wylie, Philip, *When Worlds Collide*, 365

Wynter, Sylvia, 594; *The Hills of Hebron*, 603

Yarborough, Richard, 349
Yezierska, Anzia, 273, 387–89; *Bread Givers*, 388, 389; "Fat of the Land," 387; *Hungry Hearts*, 387, 388–89; *Red Ribbon on a White Horse*, 389; *Salome of the Tenements*, 387, 388
*Young Rough Rider Weekly*, 296–97
Youth, Enlightenment concept, 115

Zalaquett, José, 618
Zapata, Luis, *En jirones*, 630–31
Zitkala-Ša (Gertrude Bonnin), 270–71
Zollinger, Norman, 461
Zugsmith, Leane, *A Time to Remember*, 339, 345